CLIMATE CHANGE IMPACTS ON OCEAN AND COASTAL LAW

Climate Change Impacts on Ocean and Coastal Law

U.S. AND INTERNATIONAL PERSPECTIVES

Edited by Randall S. Abate

OXFORD
UNIVERSITY PRESS

Oxford University Press is a department of the University of Oxford. It furthers the University's objective of excellence in research, scholarship, and education by publishing worldwide.

Oxford   New York

Auckland   Cape Town   Dar es Salaam   Hong Kong   Karachi   Kuala Lumpur   Madrid
Melbourne   Mexico City   Nairobi   New Delhi   Shanghai   Taipei   Toronto

With offices in

Argentina   Austria   Brazil   Chile   Czech Republic   France   Greece   Guatemala   Hungary
Italy   Japan   Poland   Portugal   Singapore   South Korea   Switzerland   Thailand
Turkey   Ukraine   Vietnam

Oxford is a registered trademark of Oxford University Press in the UK and certain other countries.

Published in the United States of America by
Oxford University Press
198 Madison Avenue, New York, NY 10016

Library of Congress Cataloging-in-Publication Data
Climate change impacts on ocean and coastal law : U.S. and international perspectives / edited by
Randall S. Abate.
    pages cm
    Includes bibliographical references and index.
    ISBN 978-0-19-936874-7 ((hardback) : alk. paper)
1. Climatic changes—Law and legislation. 2. Environmental law, International. 3. Coastal zone management—
Law and legislation. 4. Marine resources conservation—Law and legislation. 5. Coastal zone management—
Law and legislation—United States. I. Abate, Randall, editor.
    K3585.5.C554 2015
    341.4'5—dc23
                                                                                                            2014022834

9 8 7 6 5 4 3 2

Printed in the United States of America on acid-free paper

Note to Readers
This publication is designed to provide accurate and authoritative information in regard to the subject matter covered. It is based upon sources believed to be accurate and reliable and is intended to be current as of the time it was written. It is sold with the understanding that the publisher is not engaged in rendering legal, accounting, or other professional services. If legal advice or other expert assistance is required, the services of a competent professional person should be sought. Also, to confirm that the information has not been affected or changed by recent developments, traditional legal research techniques should be used, including checking primary sources where appropriate.

(Based on the Declaration of Principles jointly adopted by a Committee of the American Bar Association and a Committee of Publishers and Associations.)

For Nigara, the "Princess of Tides,"
whose passion for the majesty and serenity of the ocean and coastal environment
helped inspire my commitment to undertake this book project.

Contents

Editor and Contributor Biographies

Randall S. Abate is a Professor of Law, Director of the Center for International Law and Justice, and Project Director of the Environment, Development & Justice Program at Florida A&M University College of Law in Orlando, Florida. At Florida A&M, Professor Abate teaches Environmental Law, International Environmental Law, Environmental Justice, Human Rights and the Environment Seminar, Advanced Topics in Environmental Law Seminar, Ocean and Coastal Law Seminar, Public International Law, Animal Law, Climate Change Law and Indigenous Peoples Seminar, and Constitutional Law I and II. Professor Abate joined the Florida A&M College of Law faculty in 2009 with fifteen years of full-time law teaching experience at five law schools. He has taught international and comparative environmental law courses in summer study abroad programs in Nairobi, Vancouver, Buenos Aires, and Northern India, and taught International Ocean Law in Stetson University College of Law's Winter Intersession program in the Cayman Islands in 2008. Prior to joining the Florida A&M College of Law faculty, he taught Ocean and Coastal Law courses at Rutgers School of Law-Camden and Florida Coastal School of Law. Professor Abate supervises a group of NOAA fellows at Florida A&M College of Law who conduct research on ocean and coastal law and policy issues in the Gulf of Mexico as part of a multi-year NOAA grant to a consortium of universities.

Professor Abate has published and presented widely on environmental law topics, with a recent emphasis on climate change law and justice, and ocean law and policy. His articles on climate change law and justice have appeared in several law journals, including the *Stanford Environmental Law Journal, Cornell Journal of Law and Public Policy, Connecticut Law Review, Duke Environmental Law and Policy Forum, Washington Law Review, William & Mary Environmental Law and Policy Review, Ottawa Law Review, and Fordham Environmental Law Review.* His articles on ocean law and policy have appeared in the *Journal of International Wildlife Law and Policy,* the *Oregon Law Review,* and the *Pace Environmental Law Review.* He also contributed a chapter on ocean iron fertilization in CLIMATE CHANGE GEOENGINEERING: PHILOSOPHICAL PERSPECTIVES, LEGAL ISSUES, AND GOVERNANCE FRAMEWORKS (Wil Burns & Andrew Strauss eds. Cambridge University Press, 2013). Professor Abate is the co-editor (with Professor Elizabeth Kronk Warner of the University of Kansas School of Law) of CLIMATE CHANGE AND INDIGENOUS PEOPLES: THE SEARCH FOR LEGAL REMEDIES (Edward Elgar 2013). He delivered a climate change law and justice lecture series in three cities in Brazil in 2010, and also delivered climate change law and justice lectures in Nairobi and Buenos Aires in 2012. Professor Abate taught a *Climate Change Law and Justice* course at the National Law Academy in Odessa, Ukraine, in 2013 on a Fulbright Specialists grant, and taught *Climate Change Adaptation Law and Justice* in the inaugural Summer Environmental Law Program at China University of Political Science and Law in Beijing in 2014. Early in his career, Professor Abate handled environmental law matters at two law firms in Manhattan. He holds a BA from the University of Rochester and a JD and MSEL (Environmental Law and Policy) from Vermont Law School.

CONTRIBUTING AUTHORS

Sara C. Aminzadeh is the Executive Director of California Coastkeeper Alliance (CCKA), a fifteen-year old network of Waterkeeper organizations fighting for clean water for California's diverse communities and ecosystems. Ms. Aminzadeh directs CCKA initiatives to protect and defend California's ocean, bays, and rivers, including CCKA's climate change adaptation program to help California communities prepare for sea-level rise and ocean acidification. In 2010, she helped launch the California King Tides Initiative to allow people to visualize sea-level rise impacts to communities and ecosystems by creating an archive of photographs depicting ultra-high tides. Her student note, "A Moral Imperative: The Human Rights Impacts of Climate Change," was one of the first publications to explore human rights impacts of climate change. Ms. Aminzadeh has been researching and writing about the subjects of climate change, human rights, and sea-level rise for more than ten years, including work at the Center for International Environmental Law and the International Criminal Tribunal for the former Yugoslavia. She received her J.D. from the University of California, Hastings College of the Law, where she served as Co-Editor-in-Chief of the *Hastings International and Comparative Law Review,* and was a member of Hastings' inaugural Stetson International Environmental Law Moot Court team. She also holds a BA in Environmental Studies and Political Science from the University of California, Santa Barbara.

Dr. Lowell Bautista is a Lecturer at the School of Law and a Staff Member at the Australian National Centre for Ocean Resources and Security (ANCORS), Faculty of Law, Humanities and the Arts, University of Wollongong. He is a lawyer with more than a decade of experience in legal and policy research, litigation, and consultancy. He holds a Bachelor of Arts in Political Science, *cum laude*, and a Bachelor of Laws (LL.B) degrees from the University of the Philippines, a Master of Laws (Marine and Environmental Law) degree from Dalhousie University in Canada, and a Doctor of Philosophy (PhD) in law from the University of Wollongong. His areas of research include territorial and maritime boundary issues in the Asia-Pacific, the South China Sea, Philippine maritime and territorial issues, maritime piracy and terrorism, international humanitarian law, underwater cultural heritage, and international environmental law, topics on which he has also published. Dr. Bautista has participated in numerous research and consultancies, as well as in the preparation of submissions, opinions, and reports for government department and agencies in Australia and in the Philippines, as well as for regional and international organizations. On numerous occasions, Dr. Bautista has provided confidential advice and opinions on matters pertaining to offshore oil and gas resources, the law of the sea, the South China Sea, maritime boundary delimitation, and public international law to the Philippine government, and to private companies in the Philippines and Australia.

Bettina Boschen is a PhD Research Associate at the Netherlands Institute for the Law of the Sea (NILOS) at Utrecht University. She received her LL.M. in Public International Law from Reading University in the United Kingdom before specializing in the law of the sea, and is an alumna of the Rhodes Academy of Ocean Law and Policy. A member of the Law of the Sea Interest Group of the European Society of International Law, her research interests cover the theme of ocean governance and sustainable development in the age of globalization. This broad research interest is driven by her PhD research, which focuses on the content of the legal principles of the "freedom of the high seas" and the "common heritage of mankind," and their influence on the elaboration of the regime governing areas beyond national jurisdiction since the adoption of the UN Convention on the Law of the Sea. Ms. Boschen has attended numerous expert meetings and academic symposia on high seas governance and closely follows the developments at the United Nations concerning the development of a potential new implementation agreement on areas beyond national jurisdiction.

Elizabeth Burleson received her LL.M. in International Law from the London School of Economics. As an energy law consultant (BurlesonInstitute), law professor, and Fulbright Senior Specialist, Burleson has taught Energy Law, Human Rights and Environment, International Environmental Law, Public International Law, UN Law, International Law and China, Land Use, Property Law, International Economic Law, Trade, and the Environment, Water Law, and Environmental Law. Focusing on emerging international law, she has been an advisor to UNICEF's Senior Advisor for the Environment and to the New York Director of UNEP. She has also written reports for UNESCO and UNDP. She has presented on treaty making for the UN Office of Legal Affairs and UNITAR, having participated in the drafting process for the United Nations Framework Convention on Climate Change (UNFCCC), Agenda 21, and the Rio Declaration. She is an expert contributor to the Intergovernmental Panel on Climate Change (IPCC). Professor Burleson was a member of the UNICEF delegation to the Bali Climate Conference; the NWF and UNEP delegations to the Copenhagen Climate Conference; and the IUCN and ASIL delegations to the Cancun, Durban and Doha Climate Conferences. She is on the International Law Association's Committees on Sea-Level Rise and on the Principles Relating to Climate Change, IUCN's Climate Change Core Group, and the National Wildlife Federation President's Advisory Council. She has also conducted legal research for Amnesty International's London-based International Secretariat and New York-based research division and has provided climate-energy expertise to the Japanese, Uruguayan, and French governments. She has also provided legal advice to small island states and least developed countries through the Legal Response Initiative.

Jason Busch is Executive Director of Oregon Wave Energy Trust (OWET), a nonprofit public-private partnership funded by the Oregon Innovation Council to support the responsible development of ocean energy in Oregon and the jobs this new industry will create. Mr. Busch has been closely involved in the Oregon Territorial Sea Planning (TSP) process and the development of a grid-connected test site in Oregon. He serves as a liaison among the state, stakeholders, and ocean energy developers to ensure the TSP is balanced between current and future ocean users. Prior to joining Oregon Wave Energy Trust, Mr. Busch was Principal at Sustainable Legal Solutions LLC, where he provided legal services specializing in renewable energy company start-ups and project development. Previously, he was an attorney for Ater Wynne and Stoel Rives in Portland, Oregon. Mr. Busch holds a BA in Political Science from Texas A&M University, an MA in Philosophy from the University of Southern Mississippi, and a JD from the University of Oregon School of Law, graduating with honors and admitted to the Order of the Coif. In 2012, Mr. Busch received the Portland Daily Journal of Commerce (DJC) Up & Coming Lawyer Award.

Robin Kundis Craig is the William H. Leary Professor of Law at the University of Utah S.J. Quinney College of Law in Salt Lake City, Utah, where she is also affiliated with the Wallace Stegner Center for Land, Resources, and the Environment. Professor Craig specializes in all things water, including the relationships between climate change and water, water and energy, the Clean Water Act, the intersection of water issues and land issues, marine biodiversity and marine protected areas, water law, and the relationships between environmental law and public health. She is the author or coauthor of five books: THE CLEAN WATER ACT AND THE CONSTITUTION (ELI 2d ed. 2009), ENVIRONMENTAL LAW IN CONTEXT (Thomson/West 3d ed. 2012), TOXIC AND ENVIRONMENTAL TORTS (Thomson/West 2010), COMPARATIVE OCEAN GOVERNANCE: PLACE-BASED

PROTECTIONS IN AN ERA OF CLIMATE CHANGE (Edward Elgar 2012), and MODERN WATER LAW (Foundation Press 2013). She has also written more than fifty law review articles and book chapters. She has been appointed to the 2014 National Research Council Committee to Review the Edwards Aquifer Habitat Conservation Program; has served on three successive National Research Council committees on the Clean Water Act and the Mississippi River; has consulted on water quality issues with the government of Victoria, Australia, and the Council on Environmental Cooperation in Montreal, Quebec, Canada; and was one of twelve marine educators chosen to participate in a 2010 program in the Papahanamokuakea Marine National Monument, spending a week on Midway Atoll. Professor Craig serves as Co-Chair of the ABA Section on Environment, Energy, and Resources' (ABA SEER's) Water Resources Committee and as a consultant to the Environmental Defense Fund; she will also serve as the Chair of the 2015 ABA SEER Water Law Conference. At the University of Utah, she teaches Environmental Law, Water Law, Ocean and Coastal Law, Toxic Torts, and Property.

Melissa Trosclair Daigle is a Research Associate for the Louisiana Sea Grant Law and Policy Program, where she has been employed since 2008. Mrs. Daigle is heavily involved in research and outreach activities with local coastal communities in the areas of resiliency, hazard mitigation, sea-level rise, and climate change. She works with local governments to keep them informed of recent legal developments in those areas, and also provides legal information on a range of topics related to coastal law to constituents across the Louisiana coast. She currently oversees six legal interns employed by the program. Mrs. Daigle received her BA in English from Nicholls State University in 2003, her MA in English from Louisiana State University in 2005, and her JD and BCL from the Paul M. Hebert Law School at Louisiana State University in 2008.

Jordan Diamond is a Staff Attorney and Co-Director of the Ocean Program at the Environmental Law Institute (ELI). Since joining ELI in 2008, she has focused on identifying ways to improve domestic and international ocean and coastal law and policy, with an emphasis on integrated and comprehensive approaches to marine management. Recent initiatives have focused on the Arctic and the Gulf of Mexico, including efforts to strengthen Alaska Native engagement in marine resource management processes in the U.S. Arctic and supporting community engagement in Gulf of Mexico restoration and recovery following the *Deepwater Horizon* oil disaster. In addition to her work at ELI, Ms. Diamond is also the Academic Coordinator for the Law of the Sea Institute at the University of California, Berkeley School of Law (Berkeley Law). She holds a JD with a Certificate of Specialization in Environmental Law from Berkeley Law and a BA in Earth and Environmental Sciences with a Certificate in Environmental Studies from Wesleyan University.

Dr. Meinhard Doelle is a Professor of Law, and Associate Dean of Research, at Dalhousie University, Schulich School of Law, where he also serves as the Director of the Marine & Environmental Law Institute. From 1996 to 2001, he was the Executive Director of Clean Nova Scotia. He has been involved in the practice of environmental law in Nova Scotia since 1990, and in that capacity drafted the Nova Scotia Environment Act in 1992. He is environmental counsel to the Atlantic Canada law firm of Stewart McKelvey. From 2000 to 2006, Professor Doelle was a nongovernmental member of the Canadian delegation to the UN climate change negotiations. From January to May 2008, he was a visiting scholar at the Environmental Law Center of the IUCN in Bonn, Germany. Dr. Doelle has written on a variety of environmental law topics, including climate change, energy, invasive species, environmental assessments, and public participation in environmental decision-making. He holds a B.Sc., LL.B., and JSD from Dalhousie University and an LL.M. from Osgoode Hall Law School, York University.

Susan E. Farady is an Assistant Professor of Ocean Studies and Marine Affairs at the University of New England in Biddeford, Maine. She teaches courses in interdisciplinary marine law and policy, oversees curriculum offerings, and researches ocean governance and marine spatial planning issues. Previously, she was the Director of the Marine Affairs Institute and the Rhode Island Sea Grant Legal Program, and adjunct faculty at the Roger Williams University School of Law. In that capacity, she was responsible for the education, outreach, and research programs of the Institute, including the joint degree program with the University of Rhode Island Department of Marine Affairs, activities with Rhode Island Sea Grant, and marine affairs curriculum and outreach activities at the School of Law. Professor Farady has published and presented on marine protected areas, the National Marine Sanctuary Act, and marine governance reform; regularly presents on marine policy and law topics; and is coauthor of a textbook, MARINE AND COASTAL LAW (2d ed. 2010). Prior to joining Roger Williams University, she opened and directed the New England office of The Ocean Conservancy, where she worked on marine ecosystem conservation initiatives and ocean governance reform. Her other experience includes five years as a practicing attorney, positions in marine biology research, and four years as professional crew aboard sail training vessels and yachts. Professor Farady serves as an advisor to several government, nonprofit, and academic bodies engaged in marine and environmental issues. She holds a bachelor's degree in biology from the University of Colorado, participated in the SEA (Sea Education Association) program, and received her JD from Vermont Law School.

Ivy Newman Fredrickson is a Staff Attorney for Conservation Programs at Ocean Conservancy. She has a background in advocacy campaigns focused on fisheries management, climate change, forest conservation, and hardrock mining. Ms. Fredrickson first became involved in marine policy issues during the successful efforts to reauthorize the Magnuson-Stevens Fishery Conservation and Management Act. As a Field Manager for the National Environmental Trust, and later, the Pew Environment Group, she supervised and directed a team of organizers and consultants in various states, and engaged in lobbying efforts on Capitol Hill. She also worked as a law clerk in the General Counsel's office at the Bonneville Power Administration, and with the International Environmental Law Project on topics such as legal tools for the protection of coral reefs, and catch limits for bluefin tuna. She coauthored a chapter on the National Environmental Policy Act in OCEAN AND COASTAL LAW AND POLICY. She holds a BS in Environmental Studies from the University of Oregon, and a JD and a Certificate in Environmental and Natural Resources Law from Lewis & Clark Law School.

Megan M. Herzog is the Emmett/Frankel Fellow in Environmental Law and Policy at UCLA School of Law, where she teaches Ocean and Coastal Law and Policy and conducts research on environmental issues for the Emmett Institute on Climate Change and the Environment. She also works closely with UCLA's Wells Environmental Law Clinic. Prior to joining the UCLA Law faculty, she was a Fellow and member of the Ocean Program at the Environmental Law Institute in Washington, DC. She worked with the Institute's Ocean Program on restoration, litigation, and penalties following the BP *Deepwater Horizon* oil spill; ocean ecosystem-based management; and other domestic and international environmental law issues. She has worked as a law clerk domestically at the Center for Biological Diversity, California Coastal Commission, and Center for Ocean Solutions, as well as internationally at the Water & Energy Users' Federation of Nepal and the Centre for Law and Society in South Africa. She has published on a range of environmental law topics, including coastal climate change adaptation and takings, plastic marine debris control, and greenhouse gas regulation. She received her JD from Stanford Law School, where she served as Co-Editor-in-Chief of the *Stanford Journal of Law, Science & Policy* and Team Leader of the Bhutan Law and Policy Project. She also holds an MS in Environment & Resources from Stanford University, and a BA, *magna cum laude*, from Mount Holyoke College.

Megan E. Higgins is a Senior Environmental Scientist with the international consulting company, Tetra Tech, Inc. As a project manager, Ms. Higgins's focus is on the development of project permitting strategies and environmental evaluation associated with energy projects, specifically offshore renewable energy ones. She provides her clients with expertise in bridging legal permitting requirements with science-based technical information. Prior to her current position, Ms. Higgins held positions as Senior Environmental Scientist at Ecology and Environment, Inc.; Research Counsel at Roger Williams University School of Law's Marine Affairs Institute and the Rhode Island Sea Grant Legal Program; and Coastal Policy Analyst at the Rhode Island Coastal Resources Management Council, where she researched and drafted policy for the Rhode Island Coastal Resources Management Program. As an Adjunct Professor, Ms. Higgins has taught at RWU School of Law and Lewis & Clark Law School, offering courses on climate change, energy policy, and the legal development of siting and permitting offshore renewable energy projects. She has published on a range of coastal zone management issues, primarily those involving climate change, offshore energy, and integrated approaches to ocean governance. Ms. Higgins holds a BS from the University of Vermont, a JD from Roger Williams University School of Law, and a Master of Marine Affairs from the University of Rhode Island.

Dr. Kamrul Hossain is an Adjunct Professor of International Law at the University of Lapland. He is currently working as a senior researcher at the Northern Institute for Environmental and Minority Law (NIEM) of the Arctic Centre in the University of Lapland. He led the NIEM as the Director (*ad-interim*) for four months in 2011. He has been actively involved in almost all of the research projects that the Institute has undertaken since 2006. Dr. Hossain has played key roles in the preparation of a number of research projects and funding applications, and has coordinated a number of research projects, including the EU-funded project, "Understanding and Strengthening European Union-Canada Relations in Law of the Sea and Ocean Governance." Dr. Hossain has published several scholarly articles in high quality international journals. He served as the Special Editor for Volume 3 of the YEARBOOK OF POLAR LAW published in 2011. He regularly teaches at the University of Lapland, and periodically at other foreign universities. He completed visiting fellowships at a number of foreign universities, including the University of Toronto in Canada, Scott Polar Research Institute of the University of Cambridge in the United Kingdom, and Muroran Institute of Technology in Japan. He has received a number of prestigious awards, including the SYLFF Fellowship at the University of Helsinki. In 2012, Dr. Hossain was awarded a Faculty Research Fellowship by the Canadian Department of Foreign Affairs and International Trade (DFAIT).

Jennifer Huang is an International Fellow at the Center for Climate and Energy Solutions (C2ES). Ms. Huang tracks and researches international climate policy, focusing on key issues in the UN Framework Convention on Climate Change (UNFCCC) negotiations, and helps facilitate dialogue among international policymakers and stakeholders. Prior to joining C2ES, she worked as a Law Clerk at the White House Council on Environmental Quality and as a Legal Intern in the Ad Hoc Working Group on the Durban Platform for Enhanced Action (ADP) Implementation Strategy Unit at the UNFCCC secretariat in Bonn, Germany. Ms. Huang also has a background in international criminal law and international human rights, with a special interest in human rights and climate change. She has authored articles on renewable energy and the U.S. military as well as on Darfur genocide reparations before the International Criminal Court. She is also a member of the New York City Bar Association's International Environmental Law Committee. Ms. Huang is completing an LL.M degree in Environmental Law with a focus on climate change at Pace Law School. She holds a JD with Certificates in International and Environmental Law from Pace Law School and an interdisciplinary BA in War and Military Studies from New York University.

Eric V. Hull is an Associate Professor of Law at Florida Coastal School of Law. Professor Hull has published on environmental and maritime law topics, with an emphasis on the impact of pollution on ocean and coastal systems, human health, and the environment. Most recently, his scholarship has addressed legal issues arising from climate change, coastal development, ocean acidification, marine invasive species, and vessel emissions. His work has been published in the *NYU Environmental Law Journal, Georgetown*

International Environmental Law Review, Duke Environmental Law and Policy Forum, UCLA Journal of Environmental Law and Policy, Temple Law Review, University of San Francisco Maritime Law Journal, and others. His work on the management of marine resources in U.S. waters has been included in an international text on ocean and coastal governance. Professor Hull coordinates Florida Coastal's environmental law program and teaches courses in Administrative Law, Environmental Law, Environmental and Toxic Torts, Climate Change Law and Policy, Ocean and Coastal Law, Property Law, and Zoning and Land Use Law. He holds an LL.M. in Environmental and Land Use Law from the University of Florida, where he graduated first in his class and received the book award in Environmental Justice; a JD from Barry University, where he graduated with honors and served as the Editor-in-Chief of the *Barry Law Review*; an MS in Coastal Zone Management and an MS in Marine Biology from Nova Southeastern University's Oceanographic Center; and a BS in Biology from Providence College.

Janis Searles Jones is the Chief Operating Officer at Ocean Conservancy. She leads Ocean Conservancy's teams of scientists, attorneys, and advocates as they focus on key ecosystems from the Arctic to the Gulf of Mexico, and on systemic marine conservation issues, from climate change and ocean acidification to plastics and governance. A respected expert in the marine conservation field, Ms. Jones is a frequent speaker and lecturer on ocean and coastal law and the interface of science, law, and policy in advancing conservation. She also authored chapters on sustainable use of ocean resources in OCEAN AND COASTAL LAW AND POLICY and ECOSYSTEM-BASED MANAGEMENT FOR THE OCEANS. Prior to joining Ocean Conservancy, Ms. Jones was Senior Regional Counsel and Policy Adviser for Oceana, covering the Pacific region from Alaska to California. She also worked as a staff attorney for the Alaska office of Earthjustice where her docket was dominated by marine issues. Ms. Jones graduated from Reed College with a degree in history, and holds a JD and a Certificate in Environmental and Natural Resources Law from Lewis & Clark Law School, where she is a Distinguished Environmental Law Alumnus and an adjunct faculty member.

Patrick W. Krechowski is a Florida attorney with sixteen years of practice experience in governmental, environmental, land use, and title insurance law, and six years of law school teaching experience. Mr. Krechowski has previously served as an Assistant Attorney General with Florida's Office of the Attorney General and as an Assistant General Counsel with both the Florida Department of Environmental Protection and the St. Johns River Water Management District. During his time with FDEP, he served as the program attorney for the Office of Beaches and Coastal Systems dealing with permitting, rulemaking, enforcement, and administrative litigation in matters situated exclusively on the "sandy beaches" of the state of Florida. He also practiced as an associate at an environmental and administrative law firm, and operated his own small practice dealing almost exclusively with coastal matters. For over five years, he served as a senior in-house counsel at a Fortune 500 company headquartered in Jacksonville,

Florida. Currently, he is Of Counsel with GrayRobinson, a full-service Florida law firm, and serves as City Attorney for Neptune Beach, Florida. Since 2008, Mr. Krechowski has taught courses in Ocean and Coastal Law and Environmental Law as an adjunct professor at Florida Coastal School of Law, including environmental and marine-based courses as part of the law school's Logistics and Transportation Law LL.M. and certification program. He regularly speaks on environmental and coastal issues at both the Florida Chambers Environmental Permitting Summer School and as a member of the Florida Bar's Environmental and Land Use Law Section. He holds a BS in criminal justice from Florida State University and a JD from Nova Southeastern University.

Dr. Sarah Krejci received her PhD in Oceanography from Florida Institute of Technology. She also holds an MS in Marine Biology from Florida Institute of Technology and a BS in Marine Biology from Roger Williams University. She is currently a postdoctoral researcher and adjunct professor at Bethune-Cookman University. Her research focuses on seagrass ecosystems and how anthropogenic impacts on coastal systems impact seahorse and pipefish populations. She also has extensive experience in marine ornamental aquaculture as a tool for fisheries conservation. She has taught a variety of marine-related courses, including Mitigation and Restoration of Coastal Ecosystems. Currently, she is constructing a website, IRLSCIENCE.ORG, which will outline events and volunteer opportunities for the public to become more involved in conservation of the Indian River Lagoon, a coastal estuary on Florida's east coast. Additionally, it will summarize research occurring within the lagoon and conservation needs.

Adena Leibman is a Staff Attorney at Ocean Conservancy. She is a graduate of Lewis & Clark Law School where she received a Certificate in Environmental and Natural Resources Law. During law school, she clerked for the Bonneville Power Administration and U.S. Department of Justice Environmental Enforcement Section. Prior to moving to the West Coast, she served as a NOAA Sea Grant Knauss Fellow with U.S. Senator Sheldon Whitehouse (RI). Ms. Leibman also holds a BS and MS in Marine Science from the University of South Carolina, with a focus on loggerhead sea turtle population genetics.

Jaclyn Lopez is a staff attorney with the Center for Biological Diversity. The Center is a national environmental nonprofit whose mission is to protect and conserve endangered species through science, media, and litigation. Ms. Lopez is admitted to practice in Florida and California and practices public interest environmental law at the Center. Her efforts focus on the conservation of imperiled species in the southeast and Caribbean. She was involved in litigation regarding the *Deepwater Horizon* oil spill and cleanup, as well as the subsequent efforts to reform the regulation of oil and gas development in the Outer Continental Shelf. She has litigated to protect imperiled sea turtles from shrimp fisheries and manages the Center's southeast advocacy work with respect to species protections against the threats of climate change, specifically ocean acidification and sea-level rise. She has published and presented on a variety of coastal and ocean threats, including the use of dispersants, oil and gas exploration and development activities, and sea-level rise and fisheries impacts to imperiled species. Ms. Lopez earned her MS in urban planning from the University of Arizona, her JD from the University of Denver, and her LL.M. from the University of Florida. She is an adjunct professor at Stetson College of Law, co-teaching the environmental law section of the Interviewing and Counseling course and Topics in Biodiversity.

Jan McDonald is New Star Professor of Environmental Law and Associate Dean (Research) at University of Tasmania's Faculty of Law, and a leading expert in the legal and policy dimensions of climate change adaptation. She was previously Director of the Climate Change Response Program and Professor of Environmental Law and Policy in the Griffith School of Environment, and in 2007, she established the National Climate Change Adaptation Research Facility, a Commonwealth-funded interdisciplinary effort to generate the information needed by decision-makers in government and in vulnerable sectors and communities to manage the risks of climate change impacts. Professor McDonald is a member of the Tasmanian Climate Action Council and consults with local and state governments in Australia about the legal implications of coastal climate risks, and has recently completed a major research project examining the planning law framework for adaptation in Australia. She is a Contributing Author to the "Australasia" chapter of the IPCC WGII's Fifth Assessment Report.

Chad J. McGuire is Associate Professor of Environmental Policy and Chair, Department of Public Policy at the University of Massachusetts—Dartmouth, where he directs the graduate programs in environmental policy for the Department of Public Policy. He is also an attorney licensed to practice law in California, Nevada, and Massachusetts. His background is in environmental law and environmental science. Professor McGuire teaches, writes, and practices in the fields of environmental law, policy, sustainability, and dispute resolution; he has published more than twenty scholarly articles and two academic texts on these topics over the last ten years. He has worked on policy issues related to climate change, coastal management, fisheries, and land use patterns. His expertise has been sought in both private and public forums, and he has served on committees for both nonprofit and government entities. He has more than fifteen years of experience in the environmental management field. Professor McGuire holds a B.Sc. and M.Sc. in Environmental Science from the University of Massachusetts, a JD from Thomas Jefferson School of Law, and an LL.M. from the University of San Diego School of Law with specialization in Environmental Law.

Dr. Richard J. McLaughlin is Endowed Chair for Marine Policy and Law at the Harte Research Institute for Gulf of Mexico Studies (HRI) at Texas A&M University—Corpus Christi. Prior to joining HRI, Dr. McLaughlin was Professor of Law and Ray and Louise Stewart Lecturer at the University of Mississippi School of Law where he regularly taught International Law, Property Law, Admiralty Law, Ocean and Coastal Law, International Environmental Law, and other courses. Dr. McLaughlin has research interests in a broad range of marine and coastal policy and legal issues, including the international law of the sea, ocean energy policies, ocean and coastal governance, and marine ecosystem-based management. He has been actively involved in a variety of leadership positions in the marine law and policy field, is a former Fulbright Scholar to Japan, and has published more than eighty articles and monographs on marine and coastal policy issues. He currently serves on the Outer Continental Shelf Scientific Advisory Committee, a group that advises the Bureau of Ocean Energy Management (BOEM) regarding development of Outer Continental Shelf energy and mineral resources. Dr. McLaughlin holds a BA from Humboldt State University, a JD from Tulane Law School, an LL.M. in Marine Law and Policy from the University of Washington School of Law, and a JSD from Boalt Hall School of Law, University of California at Berkeley.

Dr. Kathryn Mengerink is a Senior Attorney and Co-Director of the Ocean Program at the Environmental Law Institute (ELI). Under her leadership, the Ocean Program has launched law and policy projects related to regional ocean management, fisheries management and enforcement, and ocean and coastal restoration. In Alaska, Dr. Mengerink's work focuses on supporting the role and rights of Alaska Natives in managing ocean resources. She regularly convenes and facilitates working groups, panels, and meetings. In addition to her role at ELI, she is a Lecturer and Academic Coordinator at Scripps Institution of Oceanography (SIO), where she teaches ocean law and policy and runs a graduate summer course on marine biodiversity, conservation, and global change. She holds a PhD in Marine Biology from SIO, University of California, San Diego; a JD with a Certificate of Specialization in Environmental Law from the University of California, Berkeley School of Law; and a BS in Zoology from Texas A&M University.

Timothy M. Mulvaney joined the faculty of Texas A&M University School of Law in 2009. His scholarship explores the many conflicts at the intersection of property, land use, and environmental law, with a particular focus on constitutional takings jurisprudence. Professor Mulvaney has published articles on these topics in the primary, secondary, or online law journals of Yale University, U.C. Berkeley, U.C. Davis, George Mason University, Baylor University, Tulane University, Florida State University, and the University of Richmond. Among other affiliations, he is the current Chair of the American Association of Law Schools Section on Property and a contributor to the Environmental Law Prof Blog. Professor Mulvaney earned his JD from the Villanova University School of Law and his BA in Economics from Haverford College.

Dr. Marcos A. Orellana is Director of the Center for International Environmental Law's (CIEL's) Human Rights and Environment Program and Adjunct Professor at the American University Washington College of Law. At CIEL, Dr. Orellana has worked with NGOs and local communities worldwide to strengthen tools to protect the vital functions of the planet and secure global environmental justice, including with respect to chemicals and waste, oceans and biodiversity, and trade and investment. Prior to joining CIEL, Dr. Orellana was a Fellow to the Lauterpacht Research Centre for International Law of the University of Cambridge, United Kingdom. He also was a Visiting Scholar with the Environmental Law Institute in Washington DC, and Instructor Professor of international law at the Universidad de Talca, Chile. Dr. Orellana has acted as legal counsel to the Chilean Ministry of Foreign Affairs on international environmental issues. In that capacity, Dr. Orellana has worked on multilateral environmental agreements and the Rio+20 process. Dr. Orellana has also provided legal advice to several international institutions, including the UN Environment Programme and the Office of the High Commissioner for Human Rights. He holds an LL.M. and SJD from the American University Washington College of Law.

Stephanie Showalter Otts is the Director of the National Sea Grant Law Center and the Mississippi-Alabama Sea Grant Legal Program at the University of Mississippi School of Law. She received a BA in History from Pennsylvania State University and a JD and Masters of Studies in Environmental Law from Vermont Law School. She is licensed to practice law in Pennsylvania and Mississippi. As Director, she oversees a variety of legal education, research, and outreach activities, including providing legal research services to Sea Grant constituents on ocean and coastal law issues. Her duties also include the supervision of law student research and writing projects and providing assistance to organizations and governmental agencies with interpretation of statutes, regulations, and case law. Professor Otts also holds an adjunct position at the University of Mississippi School of Law where she teaches Ocean and Coastal Law, Natural Resources, and Wetlands Law and Regulation. Her research on natural resources, marine, and environmental law issues has been published in a variety of publications. She has conducted extensive research on marine and freshwater invasive species. Recent relevant publications include "U.S. Regulatory Framework for Genetic Biocontrol of Invasive Fish" in the journal *Biological Invasions* (September 2012) and "Legislative and Regulatory Efforts to Minimize Expansion of Invasive Mussels through Watercraft Movements" 3 *Arizona Journal of Environmental Law and Policy* 61 (2013).

Dr. Margaret E. Peloso is an attorney in the Washington, DC office of Vinson & Elkins LLP, where her practice focuses on climate change and environmental law. Prior to joining V&E, Dr. Peloso received her Ph.D. from the Nicholas School of the Environment at Duke University, where her dissertation focused on legal and policy issues related to adaptation to sea-level rise in the United States. Dr. Peloso also holds a JD from Stanford and a Masters of Environmental Management and BS in Biology from Duke University. She recently completed a two-year term as a co-chair of the American Bar Association Section of Environment Energy and Resources committee on Climate Change, Sustainable Development, and Ecosystems, and publishes regularly on both climate change regulation and adaptation. Her current book project, *Adapting to Rising Sea Levels: Legal Challenges and Opportunities*, will be released by Carolina Academic Press in 2015.

Keith W. Rizzardi is an Assistant Professor of Law at St. Thomas University School of Law where he teaches administrative law, environmental law, legal ethics and negotiation, and directs a summer water law program in the Netherlands. An experienced government lawyer, he has chaired the Marine Fisheries Advisory Committee for the U.S. Department of Commerce, represented the South Florida Water Management District on the Everglades restoration, served as an attorney for the U.S. Department of Justice working on wildlife and marine resources matters, and mediated human resources disputes for the U.S. Department of Defense. In addition to being a member of the Florida Bar, he is recognized as a Board Certified Specialist in State and Federal Administrative Practice, a Certified Compliance and Ethics Professional, and a Florida Master Naturalist. Professor Rizzardi holds a BA from the University of Virginia, a JD from the University of Florida, and an MPA from Florida Atlantic University.

David Roche is a Staff Attorney at the Environmental Law Institute (ELI). He works with ELI's Ocean Program on regional ocean and coastal governance issues, with an emphasis on supporting coastal community health and resilience in the U.S. Arctic and Gulf of Mexico. He holds a JD, *magna cum laude,* from Duke University School of Law, a master's degree in Environmental Science from Duke's Nicholas School of the Environment, and a BA in Environmental Science from Columbia University.

Miyoko Sakashita is the oceans director at the Center for Biological Diversity, a non-profit conservation organization that uses science and law to protect imperiled wildlife and native habitat. In recent years, her focus has been on using existing laws to address many of the threats to ocean ecosystems, ranging from ocean acidification and global warming to destructive fisheries and oil pollution. The Center has been the principal organization securing Endangered Species Act protections for marine mammals over the past decade, and for many other marine plants and animals as well. She has played a key role in developing legal approaches to ocean acidification, including efforts under the Clean Water Act aimed at compelling the U.S. government to take steps to curb ocean acidification. Ms. Sakashita holds a JD from UC Berkeley Law School with a Certificate in Environmental Law. She also earned a BS in Environmental Science and Policy Management from UC Berkeley.

Alexis K. Segal is the co-founder of Biscayne Bay Waterkeeper (BBWK), based in Miami Beach, Florida, and served as its Executive Director and Waterkeeper from its launch in January 2011 until December 2013. The mission of BBWK is to defend, protect, and conserve the aquatic integrity of Biscayne Bay and its surrounding waters through citizen involvement and community action. BBWK is a member of the international Waterkeeper Alliance, joining over 200 organizations worldwide to ensure swimmable, fishable, and drinkable water for everyone. In its most recent campaign, BBWK led a grassroots and legal initiative to raise awareness and incorporate sea-level rise and climate impact data into Miami-Dade County's sewage infrastructure repair and construction plans, earning recognition for the organization in publications such as the *Wall Street Journal* and *Rolling Stone* magazine. Ms. Segal holds a B.S. from Georgetown University and a JD from Emory University School of Law. Recently, she received a Southeast Climate Consortium fellowship to study the impacts of climate change in relation to the legal system at the University of Florida, Levin College of Law, while earning an LL.M. in Environmental and Land Use Law in August 2013. As an Everglades Foundation Fellow, Ms. Segal currently serves as Ecosystems Policy Advisor at the Council on Environmental Quality.

Ramona Sladic is a Canadian lawyer based in Yellowknife, Northwest Territories, located in Canada's central arctic region. She practices environmental, natural resource, and Aboriginal law, with a focus on arctic region environmental regulatory matters. She is currently a Fulbright Scholar at George Washington University where she is completing a specialized LL.M. in Environmental Law, and is a Visiting Attorney at the Environmental Law Institute (ELI). She holds an LL.B. with a Certificate of Specialization in Marine Law from Dalhousie University, Schulich School of Law, and a BA (Honours) from Carleton University. Her main academic interests include arctic environmental matters, the balancing of interests in natural resource development projects, and Aboriginal consultation and accommodation issues in the environmental and natural resource contexts.

Dr. Erika J. Techera is Professor and Dean of Law at The University of Western Australia, and member of the Oceans Insitute. Dr. Techera teaches and researches in a range of international and comparative environmental law areas including marine environmental governance, cultural heritage law, and indigenous peoples and natural resource management. She holds an LL.B. (Hons.) from the University of Technology, Sydney, a master's degree in Environmental Law (M. Env. Law), and an LL.M. in International Environmental Law from Macquarie University. Her PhD (Macquarie University) research explored the role of customary law in community-based marine management in the South Pacific. She has published more than fifty papers, and her books include MARINE ENVIRONMENTAL GOVERNANCE: FROM INTERNATIONAL LAW TO LOCAL PRACTICE (Routledge, 2012), THE ROUTLEDGE HANDBOOK OF INTERNATIONAL ENVIRONMENTAL LAW (co-edited with S. Alam, J.H. Bhuiyan, and T.M.R. Chowdhury) (Routledge, 2013), and SHARKS: CONSERVATION GOVERNANCE AND MANAGEMENT (edited with N. Klein) (Earthscan, 2014). She has been a Visiting Scholar at the University of Hawai'i, William S. Richardson School of Law, and regularly presents papers at international, regional, and national conferences. Her previous positions include Director of the Centre for International & Environmental Law and Co-Director of the Centre for Climate Futures at Macquarie University, Sydney. Dr. Techera practiced as a barrister in Sydney, Australia, for several years prior to becoming an academic. She is a member of the IUCN Commission on Environmental Law and World Commission on Protected Areas.

Dr. David L. VanderZwaag holds the Canada Research Chair (Tier 1) in Ocean Law and Governance at Dalhousie University, Halifax, Canada, where he teaches international environmental law. He is the past Co-director of Dalhousie's interdisciplinary Marine Affairs Program (1986–1991) and the past Director of the Marine &

Environmental Law Institute. Professor VanderZwaag is a member of the IUCN's World Commission on Environmental Law (WCEL) and Co-chair of the WCEL's Specialist Group on Oceans, Coasts & Coral Reefs. He is a co-founder of the Australian-Canadian Oceans Research Network (ACORN) and has had extensive research and lecturing experience in South and Southeast Asia, the South Pacific, Europe, and the Caribbean. He is an elected member of the International Council of Environmental Law. Dr. VanderZwaag has authored more than 150 papers in the marine and environmental law field. His most recent book publications are: POLAR OCEANS GOVERNANCE IN AN ERA OF ENVIRONMENTAL CHANGE (edited with Tim Stephens) (Edward Elgar, 2014) and RECASTING TRANSBOUNDARY FISHERIES MANAGEMENT ARRANGEMENTS IN LIGHT OF SUSTAINABILITY PRINCIPLES: CANADIAN AND INTERNATIONAL PERSPECTIVES (edited with D.A. Russell) (Martinus Nijhoff, 2010). He has written widely on polar law and policy issues including co-leading the writing of the Governance of the Arctic Shipping chapter of the Arctic Marine Shipping Assessment (Arctic Council 2009) and co-editing TRANSIT MANAGEMENT OF THE NORTHWEST PASSAGE: PROBLEMS AND PROSPECTS (Cambridge University Press, 1988, reprinted 2008). Professor VanderZwaag holds a PhD (1994, University of Wales, Cardiff); LL.M. (1982, Dalhousie Law School); JD (1980, University of Arkansas Law School); M.Div. (1974, Princeton Theological Seminary); and BA (1971, Calvin College).

Julia B. Wyman is an environmental attorney with national policy experience. Ms. Wyman is currently the Interim Director at the Marine Affairs Institute (MAI), a partnership of the Roger Williams University School of Law, Rhode Island Sea Grant Legal Program, and the University of Rhode Island. Ms. Wyman is also an adjunct faculty member at the Roger Williams University School of Law, where she teaches Climate Change Law and Policy. Before her appointment to Interim Director, Ms. Wyman was the Staff Attorney at the MAI. Prior to her work at the MAI, she served as the Policy Analyst at the Coastal States Organization (CSO) in Washington, DC. CSO represents the governors of the thirty-five coastal states, commonwealths, and territories on legislative and policy issues relating to the sound management of coastal, Great Lakes, and ocean resources. At CSO, Ms. Wyman managed the climate change portfolio, as well as the Legal Council. Ms. Wyman's work at CSO included producing several documents on climate change and climate change adaptation, including: *The Role of Coastal Zone Management Programs in Adaptation to Climate Change, Second Annual Report of the Coastal States Organization's Climate Change Work Group* (September 2008), and *The Faces of Climate Change Adaptation: The Need for Proactive Protection of the Nation's Coasts* (May 2010), examining current climate change adaptation examples in several states and proposing needs of other coastal states to adequately adapt to climate change. Ms. Wyman is an editor for the American Bar Association's Section of Environment, Energy, and Resources, *Year in Review* Marine Resources chapter, and in 2012 was the recipient of The Coastal Society's *Robert W. Knecht Award for Professional Promise*. Ms. Wyman holds a JD from the University of Maine School of Law and a BA from Trinity College in Connecticut.

Acknowledgments

MANY PEOPLE MADE valuable contributions to this book. The book would not have been possible without the exceptional chapters that were prepared for this book by leading climate change and ocean and coastal law, policy, and science scholars and practitioners throughout the world. The editor is especially grateful to the NOAA-ECSC Fellows in Ocean and Coastal Law and Policy (Kayann Chambers, Cindi McGee, Cameryn Rivera, Loren Vasquez) and the International Human Rights Fellows (Tia Crosby and Megan Reid) at Florida A&M University College of Law who provided outstanding research assistance for this project. Several volunteer research assistants also devoted valuable time and energy to this project. Volunteer assistants who provided indispensable assistance far above and beyond the call of duty were Danielle Murray, Esq., Lindsay Walton, Esq., and Julie Suen, J.D., LL.M. Several other volunteer attorney and student research assistants who also provided valuable research, citation checking, and editing and proofreading efforts were attorneys Crystal Anderson, Bette Collazo, Dina Elmusa, Mfon Etukeren, Jerry Leakey, Elizabeth Nakagoshi, Michael Nichola, and Jeffery Ray; and students Ava Azad, Kiah Barrette, Cindy Campbell, Sabrina Collins, Kate Marples, and Karina Valencia. Finally, the editor is grateful to his faculty assistant, Celia Westbrook, for her indispensable efforts in coordinating the assembly of the final manuscript of this book.

This book project was supported by the National Oceanic and Atmospheric Administration, Office of Education Educational Partnership Program award (NA11SEC4810001). Its contents are solely the responsibility of the editor and do not necessarily represent the official views of the U.S. Department of Commerce, National Oceanic and Atmospheric Administration.

Foreword

CLIMATE CHANGE IMPACTS on the ocean will—or at least should—affect a broad spectrum of law and policy. The three primary impacts of climate change on oceans—increasing ocean temperatures, changing ocean currents, and ocean acidification—have broad direct implications for world weather patterns, marine biodiversity, sea-level rise, and shipping. Less directly, these three impacts affect coastal management and development, international food security, international political security, global population movements, and, ultimately, the magnitude of climate change itself.

Relatively small changes in ocean temperature can have significant effects on both world weather and marine fisheries, with potentially devastating effects on dependent communities. For context, strong El Niño events in the Pacific Ocean are characterized by sea-surface temperature increases of about 1.5°C to 2.5°C.[1] This small change is sufficient to alter fish population distributions and weather patterns throughout a sizeable portion of the world. Moreover, archeologists in South America now attribute several historical collapses of communities along the western coast of what is now Peru to strong El Niño events.[2] Climate change, however, may make El Niño-like increases in sea surface temperatures a worldwide phenomenon, with unpredictable results both on

---

[1] National Oceanic and Atmospheric Administration, *El Niño FAQs: What Are Typical El Niño Characteristics?*, http://www.cpc.ncep.noaa.gov/products/analysis_monitoring/ensostuff/ensofaq.shtml#NINOCHAR (last modified Apr. 26, 2012).

[2] Hillary Mayell, "Fall of Ancient Peruvian Societies Linked With El Niño," *National Geographic News*, July 24, 2001, http://news.nationalgeographic.com/news/2001/07/0723_elninoperu.html.

land and in the ocean. According to the Intergovernmental Panel on Climate Change's ("IPCC's") 2013–2014 Fifth Assessment Report, "[a]bout 93 percent of the excess heat energy stored by the earth over the last 50 years is found in the ocean."[3] Sea surface temperatures have risen about 0.78°C above the averages experienced from 1850 to 1900,[4] a worldwide increase already halfway to levels that trigger El Niño conditions. Of course, any given year can be warmer than this global average, and "[a]ll ten of the warmest years [in the ocean] have occurred since 1997, with 2010 and 2005 effectively tied for warmest year on record."[5] Finally, it is also now likely that ocean warming has penetrated deeper than 3000 meters below the surface,[6] with unknown long-term consequences.

Warming ocean temperatures are melting ice, changing currents, and altering fish populations. NASA scientists stunned the world in May 2014 by declaring the melting of the western Antarctic ice sheet—and the consequent sea-level rise—"inevitable."[7] The five Arctic Ocean nations (the United States, Russia, Canada, Norway, and Denmark via Greenland) are already anticipating ice-free summers in the Arctic Ocean, with significant implications for global shipping, national and international security, fishing, and offshore oil and gas drilling. All of these nations except the United States have filed claims under the United Nations Convention on the Law of the Sea for extended continental shelf jurisdiction (the United States is not a party to the Convention), and all five anticipate increased oil and gas exploration and drilling (ironically, exacerbating the root causes of climate change), increased commercial shipping, and increased fishing in the Arctic Ocean. Indeed, in August 2009 the United States anticipatorily closed the federal waters off of Alaska to commercial fishing to prevent climate change–facilitated overfishing and ecosystem decimation in newly accessible waters.[8]

Changes in ocean temperature are also already changing fisheries around the world, with important potential consequences for both global food security and fisheries management. Ocean ecosystems respond to climate change impacts at varying rates,[9] so that impacts on marine species will also vary considerably. Nevertheless, rising ocean temperatures are both damaging coral reef ecosystems and causing fish stocks to shift away

---

[3] Working Group I, Intergovernmental Panel on Climate Change, Climate Change 2013: The Physical Science Basis 260 (2013), *available at* http://www.ipcc.ch/report/ar5/wg1/ [hereinafter 2013 IPCC Physical Science].

[4] *Id.* at 193.

[5] *Id.*

[6] *Id.* at 263.

[7] Justin Gillis & Kenneth Chang, "Scientists Warn of Rising Oceans from Polar Melt," N. Y. Times, May 12, 2014, http://www.nytimes.com/2014/05/13/science/earth/collapse-of-parts-of-west-antarctica-ice-sheet-has-begun-scientists-say.html?_r=0.

[8] Alaska Regional Office, NOAA Fisheries, *Arctic Fisheries*, https://alaskafisheries.noaa.gov/sustainable-fisheries/arctic/ (last viewed Sept. 6, 2014).

[9] Hans-O. Pörtner & David Karl, Coordinating Lead Authors, *Ocean Systems*, at 3, *in* Intergovernmental Panel on Climate Change, Climate Change 2014: Impacts, Adaptation, and Vulnerability (2014), *available at* http://ipcc-wg2.gov/AR5/images/uploads/WGIIAR5-Chap6_FGDall.pdf [hereinafter 2014 IPCC Ocean Systems].

from their traditional ranges.[10] Continuing increases in sea temperatures will almost certainly lead to localized extinctions of various marine species, especially in the polar and tropical regions[11] and especially if increasing temperatures continue to decrease the ocean's dissolved oxygen content.[12] Even if fisheries management laws in coastal nations had been completely effective before climate change—which they were not—these new continual changes in fish populations' ranges and status pose an ever-increasing challenge to the prevailing law of coastal fisheries management.

In addition, in 2014 the IPCC explicitly noted the threat to world food security deriving from climate change impacts on marine biodiversity.[13] The net result of climate change impacts on fish stocks could be reduced catches of fish overall.[14] Reduced fish catches would in turn exacerbate instabilities in global food supply just as demand for seafood is increasing,[15] potentially leading to mass starvations, huge numbers of human refugees, political unrest, and violence.

Sea-level rise is another potential source of global instability, although the most immediate challenges it poses are to coastal management policies and disaster preparedness. The IPCC Fifth Assessment Report concluded with very high confidence that coastal systems are "particularly sensitive" to sea level as well as to ocean temperature and ocean acidification.[16] The oceans expand in response to increased temperatures, and melting land-based glaciers also contribute to sea-level rise,[17] but these usually are slow processes. As a result, sea-level rise probably will pose a threat to coastal communities for centuries.[18] Globally, sea level rose an average of eight inches between 1880 and 2009, and the rate is accelerating.[19] Moreover, as the Union of Concerned Scientists has pointed out, "[e]ven if global warming emissions were to drop to zero by 2016, scientists project

---

[10] *Id.*

[11] *Id.*

[12] 2013 IPCC PHYSICAL SCIENCE, *supra* note 3, at 295.

[13] 2014 IPCC OCEAN SYSTEMS, *supra* note 9, at 3–5.

[14] *Id.* at 4. *See also* INTERGOVERNMENTAL PANEL ON CLIMATE CHANGE, CLIMATE CHANGE 2014: IMPACTS, ADAPTATION, AND VULNERABILITY: SUMMARY FOR POLICYMAKERS 17 (2014), *available at* http://ipcc-wg2.gov/AR5/images/uploads/WG2AR5_SPM_FINAL.pdf [hereinafter 2014 IPCC IMPACTS SPM].

[15] MATTHEW HUELSENBECK, OCEANA, OCEAN-BASED FOOD SECURITY THREATENED IN A HIGH CO₂ WORLD: A RANKING OF NATIONS' VULNERABILITY TO CLIMATE CHANGE AND OCEAN ACIDIFICATION 2, 5 (Sept. 2012), *available at* http://oceana.org/sites/default/files/reports/Ocean-Based_Food_Security_Threatened_in_a_High_CO2_World.pdf.

[16] Poh Poh Wong & Inigo J. Losada, *Coastal Systems and Low-Lying Areas*, at 2, *in* INTERGOVERNMENTAL PANEL ON CLIMATE CHANGE, CLIMATE CHANGE 2014: IMPACTS, ADAPTATION, AND VULNERABILITY (2014), *available at* http://ipcc-wg2.gov/AR5/images/uploads/WGIIAR5-Chap5_FGDall.pdf [hereinafter 2014 IPCC COASTAL SYSTEMS].

[17] Union of Concerned Scientists, *Causes of Sea-Level Rise: What the Science Tells Us* (2013), http://www.ucsusa.org/global_warming/science_and_impacts/impacts/causes-of-sea-level-rise.html (last modified Apr. 15, 2013).

[18] 2014 IPCC COASTAL SYSTEMS, *supra* note 16, at 2.

[19] Union of Concerned Scientists, *supra* note 17.

another 1.2 to 2.6 feet of global sea level rise by 2100 as oceans and land ice adjust to the changes we have already made to the atmosphere."[20] However, as the IPCC emphasizes, varying local factors such as subsidence or uplifting, sediment transport, and the extent of coastal development means that different coastal locations will experience potentially significantly greater or lesser sea-level rise than the global average.[21] As a result, "one size fits all" approaches to coastal law are unlikely to be appropriate or helpful—there are unlikely to be coastal climate change panaceas—but coastal retreat policies are likely to become increasingly necessary in many places as coastal armoring fails.

Sea-level rise can destabilize societies, and hence will demand other kinds of innovations in law and policy as well. Disasters such as Hurricane Katrina in New Orleans and Hurricane Sandy along the East Coast of the United States, or flooding and typhoons in places such as Bangladesh, will only become more destructive as sea-level rises and storm surges become more powerful.[22] As such, coastal communities need better disaster planning, ranging from coastal building codes to emergency supplies to better escape routes. In addition, sea-level rise is already causing or contributing to existential threats to many communities around the globe, from the Village of Kivalina in Alaska to Pacific island nations such as Kiribati. Like threats to global food security, the physical displacement of populations and destruction of sovereign territory demands innovation in refugee status and immigration laws, and perhaps even new definitions of sovereignty.

Another important aspect of climate change impacts on the ocean is that such impacts are synergistic—that is, they tend to combine with other human-induced stressors in the coastal environment, such as pollution, to exacerbate undesirable ecological and social effects. As the IPCC notes, "[f]or many other coastal changes, the impacts of climate change are difficult to tease out from human-related drivers (e.g., land use change, coastal development, pollution) (*high agreement, robust evidence*)."[23] Coral reefs provide perfect examples: most coral species are highly sensitive to increasing ocean temperatures and ocean acidification, but those climate-change impacts are often made worse by the fact that most coral reef ecosystems are already stressed from pollution and overfishing.[24] Synergistic impacts also pose a threat to fisheries: "The progressive expansion of oxygen minimum zones and anoxic 'dead zones'"—phenomena attributable to land-based nutrient pollution, changing upwelling patterns, and/or increasing ocean temperatures, depending on location—"is projected to further constrain fish habitat.... Climate change adds to the threats of over-fishing and other non-climatic stressors,

---

[20] *Id.*

[21] 2014 IPCC COASTAL SYSTEMS, *supra* note 16, at 3.

[22] Aslak Grimsted, John C. Moore & Svetlana Jevrejeva, *Projected Atlantic Hurricane Surge Threat from Rising Temperatures*, 110:14 PNAS: PROCEEDINGS OF THE NATIONAL ACADEMY OF SCIENCES 5369, 5372 (Apr. 2, 2013).

[23] 2014 IPCC COASTAL SYSTEMS, *supra* note 16, at 2.

[24] World Wildlife Fund Global, *Coral Reefs: Threats*, http://wwf.panda.org/about_our_earth/blue_planet/ coasts/coral_reefs/coral_threats/ (last visited Sept. 7, 2014).

thus complicating marine management regimes *(high confidence)*."[25] Such synergistic impacts underscore the need for coastal nations to address effectively the traditional and well-known stressors to coastal socioecological systems and their resilience—overdevelopment, destruction of coastal ecosystems, and pollution of all types. Climate change, in other words, should intensify rather than change the traditional focus of coastal law.

Ocean acidification creates a more insidious problem for ocean and coastal law. The oceans have buffered climate change impacts in the atmosphere by absorbing carbon dioxide. Indeed, according to the IPCC, "The ocean contains 50 times more carbon than the atmosphere . . . and is at present acting to slow the rate of climate change by absorbing about 30% of human carbon dioxide (CO_2) emissions from fossil fuel burning, cement production, deforestation, and other land use change."[26] However, this global protection comes at a marine price. Once in the ocean, carbon dioxide undergoes chemical reactions that lower seawater's naturally basic pH levels, a phenomenon known as ocean acidification.[27] Almost all life processes are exquisitely sensitive to pH levels. For example, human blood, like the oceans, is slightly basic, and changes of as little as 0.35 pH units or less away from normal can lead to coma, convulsions, and death. According to the IPCC, the *average* pH of the ocean's surface waters has already dropped 0.1 pH units, and "by the end of this century, the average surface ocean pH could be lower than it has been for 50 million years."[28] In the United States, a more acute ocean acidification problem in Puget Sound than the global average has already prompted the state legislature to enact ocean acidification legislation. In larger legal terms, ocean acidification provides one of the main arguments for why reduction in carbon dioxide emissions is the only long-term "fix" for climate change.

Paying attention to climate change impacts on the Earth's oceans and coasts thus suggests many foci for increased attention in ocean and coastal law. The increased threats that climate change poses to marine biodiversity—and the consequent threats that arise to international food security, community stability, public health, and national security—counsels that the nations of the world redouble their efforts to protect that resource. Specifically, nations should more effectively manage fisheries for long-term productivity; protect more of the ocean's critical habitat areas in marine protected areas and through marine spatial planning; develop cooperative management arrangements for shifting fisheries, akin to the legal structures already in place for highly migratory species; and develop policies for the use of oceans for mariculture (marine aquaculture). Cumulative and accumulating impacts to coastal communities from changing ocean temperature, changing ocean currents, sea-level rise, worsening storm surge impacts, ocean acidification, overfishing, and coastal development counsels coastal nations to

---

[25] 2014 IPCC IMPACTS SPM, *supra* note 14, at 17.

[26] 2013 IPCC PHYSICAL SCIENCE, *supra* note 2, at 260.

[27] *Id.* at 295, Box 3.2.

[28] *Id.*

invest significantly in adaptation planning and innovative coastal management, including coastal retreat policies. At the same time, these impacts also suggest that the international community needs to reconsider international refugee status, the legal status and rights of displaced island and coastal nations, international aid policies, and immigration law. All of these impacts counsel more serious international attention to climate change mitigation and laws to reduce greenhouse gas emissions. However, ocean acidification in particular demonstrates that any attempt to deal with climate change other than reducing the amount of carbon dioxide in the atmosphere condemns the world's oceans to an increasingly damaged state for generations to come.

It is time for the lawyers and policymakers to get down to some serious work on these issues, and the discussions that you are about to read provide a good start.

Robin Kundis Craig

William H. Leary Professor of Law

University of Utah, S.J. Quinney College of Law

Preface

OCEAN AND COASTAL law has grown rapidly in the past two decades as a specialty area within natural resources law and environmental law. Protection of oceans and coasts has received increased attention in the past decade because of sea-level rise, beach erosion, ocean acidification, the global overfishing crisis, widespread depletion of marine biodiversity such as marine mammals and coral reefs, and marine pollution. Dozens of law schools in the United States and abroad offer courses in ocean and coastal law, law of the sea, and variations thereof, and several law schools have developed specialty programs in these areas.

Paralleling the growth of ocean and coastal law, climate change regulation has emerged as a focus of international environmental diplomacy in the past three decades and has grown exponentially during this period. It has gained increased attention in the wake of disturbing and abrupt climate change impacts throughout the world ranging from the displacement of small, low-lying Pacific island nations and indigenous communities in the Arctic from coastal erosion, to widespread drought, flooding, and desertification in developing nations, to increased extreme storm events such as Hurricanes Katrina and Sandy. Arctic melting has opened up shipping lanes in the Arctic and a corresponding clash of sovereign interests in the region. All of these developments related to climate change have profound implications for ocean and coastal regulation.

The time has come for these two intersecting spheres of regulation—climate change and ocean and coastal management—to work together for mutual gain. This book integrates these two worlds into one comprehensive volume. It addresses whether and how ocean and coastal law will respond to the regulatory challenges that climate change presents to resources in the oceans and coasts of the United States and the world. The book is divided into two major units—one for oceans and the other for coasts—and addresses a range of regulatory challenges from the perspectives of U.S. law, foreign domestic law, and international law.

Introduction

THIS BOOK COVERS two vast and growing areas of the law—climate change law and ocean and coastal law—in one volume. This introduction seeks to facilitate the reader's understanding of the book's coverage and organization. First, it will explain the terminology used in this book and what topics are included within that coverage. Second, a chapter-by-chapter summary of the book's contents will provide a roadmap for what topics the book covers and how those topics are addressed. Third, the difficult editorial decisions to include some topics and exclude others will be explained.

For purposes of this book, "climate change law" includes U.S. domestic, foreign domestic, and international law addressing efforts to mitigate the causes and adapt to the effects of climate change. "Ocean and coastal law" includes U.S. and foreign domestic ocean law, international ocean law, and U.S. and foreign domestic laws that address management of coastal areas. It includes the marine law dimensions of the law of the sea, but does not cover maritime law (with the exception of Chapter 14's consideration of climate change impacts on Arctic shipping).

Chapter 1 sets the stage for the book by examining the scientific foundations of climate change impacts to ocean and coastal resources. It also considers how these impacts affect ocean and coastal law and policy and describes recent efforts to respond to these regulatory challenges. These legal responses are addressed in the ensuing chapters.

The book is divided into two units: one for oceans and the other for coasts. The oceans unit is addressed in Chapters 2–18. This unit begins with a subunit on ocean governance challenges in the United States. The first challenge addressed is ocean acidification, which is covered in Chapters 2 and 3. Chapter 2 examines how the federal Clean Water

Act and other domestic environmental laws may be used to regulate ocean acidification. It also provides a case study from the state of Washington, which is a leader on ocean acidification law and policy responses. Approaching ocean acidification from another legal angle, Chapter 3 addresses the federal Clean Air Act as a possible tool to combat this vexing problem.

The U.S. ocean governance challenges subunit then addresses impacts to fisheries and marine habitat. This cluster of chapters begins with a brief introduction to the Magnuson-Stevens Act, which is the foundation for the fisheries management regime in the United States and sets the context for the next three chapters. Chapters 4–6 address impacts to fisheries and marine habitat at the regional level, covering New England, the Gulf of Mexico, and the Pacific and the Arctic, respectively. Chapter 7 then addresses how the Endangered Species Act can be used to regulate climate change impacts to marine habitat, with a case study on coral reef protection.

The remaining chapters in the U.S. ocean governance unit address a wide range of topics that are vitally important in responding to climate change impacts. Chapter 8 addresses offshore wind and wave energy governance as a form of climate change mitigation. It first addresses the need to transition from fossil-fuel-based sources to these renewable sources of energy, and then addresses ocean governance challenges associated with these energy sources. Chapter 9 addresses climate change impacts to marine mammals' habitat and how these impacts pose regulatory challenges under the Marine Mammal Protection Act that jeopardize the continued viability of marine mammals that are especially vulnerable to such changes. Chapters 10 and 11 address the problem of marine invasive species. Chapter 10 provides an overview of the regulatory framework governing marine invasive species and explores case studies to illustrate the applicability of this regime in the climate change context. Chapter 11 revisits the Endangered Species Act's role, this time in the narrower context of how current responses to marine invasive species and climate change may affect application of the ESA to protect marine species.

The book then proceeds to address several international ocean governance challenges in Chapters 12–19. Chapter 12 provides an overview of international governance challenges that are addressed in greater depth in subsequent chapters. Chapters 13–15 comprise a subunit on ocean governance challenges in the polar regions, which is where climate change impacts on marine resources are most severe. Chapters 13 and 14 address the regulation of Arctic marine resources and Arctic shipping in response to climate change impacts, respectively, whereas Chapter 15 examines possible adjustments to several binding and non-binding international law regimes to improve governance of the fragile Antarctic marine environment in the climate change era.

The remaining chapters in the oceans unit address other important international ocean governance challenges. Chapter 16 considers how climate geoengineering methods that use the oceans to advance climate change mitigation objectives pose challenges for dispute resolution under the UNFCCC and UNCLOS. Chapter 17 addresses the regulation of ocean iron fertilization under the London Protocol as a potentially viable yet highly controversial method of climate change mitigation. Chapter 18 concludes the oceans unit by examining the marine environmental law frameworks in the Indian Ocean and how these regimes can respond to climate change impacts.

Unit II addresses challenges in protecting coasts from climate change impacts from the perspectives of U.S., foreign domestic, and international law. This unit begins with a subunit addressing national and regional perspectives in the United States in addressing coastal adaptation to climate change impacts. Chapter 19 addresses the role of federalism in coastal adaptation strategies under the Coastal Zone Management Act. Chapter 20 addresses coastal construction and beach nourishment in response to beach erosion from severe storms and sea-level rise. Chapter 21 considers how temporary takings issues arise in the context of coastal adaptation to climate change impacts. Chapter 22 concludes this subunit by considering climate change adaptation strategies in the New England region.

The unit on coasts then considers state case studies in coastal climate adaptation. Chapter 23 addresses climate change impacts on Alaska Natives' access to marine subsistence resources in coastal communities. Chapter 24 considers regulatory initiatives to adapt to sea-level rise in California. Chapters 25 and 26 shift the focus to case studies in the Southeast. Chapter 25 addresses sea-level rise and species impacts in Florida and how the Endangered Species Act can help in adaptation efforts, whereas Chapter 26 examines how coastal communities in Louisiana are adapting to climate change impacts.

The unit on coasts concludes with international and comparative law perspectives on coastal adaptation. Chapter 27 addresses international human rights law dimensions of coastal climate change adaptation. Chapters 28 and 29 shift the focus to case studies in Pacific Rim nations, where coastal climate change adaptation efforts are of utmost importance. Chapter 28 addresses coastal adaptation to climate change in Australia, whereas Chapter 29 addresses coastal climate adaptation measures in the Philippines at the national and local levels.

It is impossible for a single volume to address all potential dimensions of climate change impacts on ocean and coastal law throughout the world. Therefore, the editor had to make difficult decisions regarding the scope and coverage of this first edition. This edition focuses on many of the most pressing problems in ocean and coastal law governance (e.g., sea-level rise, ocean acidification, marine invasive species, beach erosion, protection of marine biodiversity, climate geoengineering of the oceans, offshore wind and wave energy, and human rights dimensions of coastal climate adaptation). It draws on compelling cases studies from several "hot spots" throughout the world that provide valuable illustrations of these impacts and regulatory challenges (e.g., the polar regions, the Indian Ocean region, the Pacific Rim region, and vulnerable coastal states in the United States). Subsequent editions of the book may include coverage of additional management challenges and other important regions of the world (e.g., Africa, Europe, and the Caribbean) to consider these regions' experiences in seeking to respond to these challenges.

1   Climate Change Impacts on Ocean and Coastal Law:
SCIENTIFIC REALITIES AND LEGAL RESPONSES
Randall S. Abate and Dr. Sarah Ellen Krejci

Introduction

> *Rising sea level will be the single most profound geologic change in recorded human history.*
> *It will transform our physical world beyond anything we can imagine, dwarfing continents*
> *and eliminating some nations. Coastlines will move inland by hundreds and, in some places,*
> *thousands of feet this century. The impacts will be far greater during the next century. Trillions of*
> *dollars of the most valuable real estate and infrastructure will vanish.*[1]

The oceans and coasts of the world are under siege from a broad spectrum of climate-change-related threats. The most significant of these threats is the challenge that sea-level rise poses to ocean and coastal resources. In addition, climate change presents a series of secondary challenges to the physical, chemical, and biological integrity of ocean and coastal resources such as ocean acidification, impacts to species and habitats, increased intensity of tropical cyclone activity, changes in ocean stratification and circulation, and saltwater intrusion.

In 2013, there have been many significant responses at the international and U.S. domestic levels to the impacts of climate change on the marine environment. Three of these responses deserve mention here. First, on September 30, 2013, the Intergovernmental Panel on Climate Change (IPCC) released Part 1 of its highly anticipated Fifth Assessment Report.[2] The report concluded that it is "extremely likely"[3] that human activity is the principal cause of climate change. The Fifth Assessment Report predicts a sea-level rise between twenty-six and eighty-one centimeters by the end of the century.[4]

Second, on April 16, 2013, the White House released the National Ocean Policy Implementation Plan.[5] The Plan seeks to coordinate the actions of various government

---

[1] JOHN ENGLANDER, HIGH TIDE ON MAIN STREET: RISING SEA LEVEL AND THE COMING COASTAL CRISIS 3 (2012).

[2] ULRICH CUBASCH ET AL., WORKING GROUP I CONTRIBUTION TO THE IPCC FIFTH ASSESSMENT REPORT CLIMATE CHANGE 2013: THE PHYSICAL SCIENCE BASIS (2014), *available at* http://www.climatechange2013.org/images/uploads/WGIAR5_WGI-12Doc2b_FinalDraft_All.pdf.

[3] The IPCC defines "extremely likely" as 95 to 100 percent certainty. *See id.* at TS-4. The IPCC Fourth Assessment Report in 2007 concluded that it was "very likely" that human activity was the main cause, defined as 65 to 90 percent certainty. CONTRIBUTION OF WORKING GROUP III TO THE FOURTH ASSESSMENT REPORT OF THE INTERGOVERNMENTAL PANEL ON CLIMATE CHANGE, 2007 (B. Metz et al. eds., 2007), *available at* http://www.ipcc.ch/publications_and_data/ar4/wg3/en/contents.html.

[4] LISA ALEXANDER ET AL., INTERGOVERNMENTAL PANEL ON CLIMATE CHANGE, TWELFTH SESSION OF WORKING GROUP I APPROVED SUMMARY FOR POLICYMAKERS 25 (2013), http://www.climatechange2013.org/images/uploads/WGIAR5-SPM_Approved27Sep2013.pdf.

[5] Nat'l Ocean Council, *National Ocean Policy Implementation Plan* (2013), *available at* http://www.whitehouse.gov//sites/default/files/national_ocean_policy_implementation_plan.pdf.

agencies to protect the nation's oceans and coasts and calls for the creation of an Ocean Council comprised of officials from twenty-seven federal agencies to implement the Plan.[6] Among many objectives, the Plan seeks to assess the vulnerability of oceans and coastal communities to climate change impacts and implement adaptation strategies to combat the effects of ocean acidification and sea-level rise.[7]

Third, a team of experts provided technical input for a report, *Ocean and Marine Resources in a Changing Climate: Technical Input to the 2013 National Climate Assessment,*[8] which was released in June 2013. The report provides a comprehensive assessment of climate change impacts to oceans and marine resources, divided into seven categories: (1) Introduction and Context; (2) Climate-Driven Physical Changes in Marine Ecosystems; (3) Impacts of Climate Change on Marine Organisms; (4) Impacts of Climate Change on Human Uses of the Ocean; (5) International Implications of Climate Change; (6) Management Challenges, Adaptations, Approaches, and Opportunities; and (7) Sustaining the Assessment of Climate Impacts on Oceans and Marine Resources.[9] The scope of coverage in the report reflects the breadth of climate change impacts on ocean and coastal law. Several of these topics will be covered in the chapters in this volume.

These three responses are but a few significant examples of the growing concern in the United States and throughout the world regarding the impacts of climate change on ocean and coastal resources and how law and policy can respond to these challenges. This chapter provides an overview of the physical, chemical, and biological underpinnings of the climate change impacts that currently plague ocean and coastal resources and briefly addresses some of the law and policy responses to these challenges at the international, national, and sub-national levels.

I. Background

A. EARTH'S CLIMATE

The primary source of energy for Earth's climate is radiation from the Sun. An energy balance exists between incoming and outgoing solar radiation, but slight imbalances can bring about global heating or cooling. "Forcing" is the term used to describe disruptions in the main elements that impact Earth's climate, including solar energy, atmospheric circulation, ocean currents, and even volcanic eruptions that lead to changes in climate.[10] Natural sources of forcing are behind geological shifts in climate from extreme glacial periods of extensive ice coverage to interglacial periods of ice retreat.

---

[6] *Id.*

[7] *See generally* Benjamin Sloan, *White House Releases National Oceans Plan,* 12(3) SANDBAR 10 (2013).

[8] OCEAN AND MARINE RESOURCES IN A CHANGING CLIMATE: TECHNICAL INPUT TO THE 2013 NATIONAL CLIMATE ASSESSMENT (Roger Griffis & Jennifer Howard eds., 2013).

[9] *Id.* at ii–iv.

[10] For an extensive review of forcing elements, see generally *supra* note 2 at 8-1; WALLACE S. BROECKER, THE GLACIAL WORLD ACCORDING TO WALLY 1 (1995).

The amount of solar radiation arriving on Earth is affected by astronomical phenomena that occur over varying time scales from millions to hundreds of years. These phenomena include changes in the luminosity of the sun,[11] solar sunspot activity,[12] and changes in Earth's orbit. Even small changes in solar radiation are associated with large regional changes in temperature on Earth.[13]

Thirty percent of incoming solar radiation is reflected from Earth by the air, clouds, land masses, and the ocean. This reflected energy is known as the Earth's albedo, and is what causes the illumination of Earth in space.[14] The remaining percentage is absorbed at the surface and eventually reradiated into space. Radiation leaving Earth is slowed down by the presence of water vapor and other gases in the atmosphere that trap radiation and warm the Earth's surface, a process known as the greenhouse effect.[15]

Trapped heat is moved around Earth through atmospheric and ocean circulation cells. Atmospheric circulation cells affect wind patterns, which are responsible for major oceanic currents and shallow ocean circulation.[16] Oceanic western boundary currents such as the Gulf Stream and the Kuroshio Current move heat from warm equatorial waters toward the poles, which produces mild winters in northern areas such as Europe and Japan.[17]

An example of an important coupling of atmospheric and oceanic conditions is El Niño Southern Oscillation (ENSO), which occurs in the Pacific Ocean. In ENSO conditions, dominant winds weaken, which lead to shifts in atmospheric pressure, relaxation of important ocean currents, and alterations in global precipitation.[18] Increased tropical moisture during ENSO events can expand across the globe to areas of India, Africa, Central America, and South America.[19] Under normal conditions, wind patterns and currents bring nutrient-rich water to the surface, resulting in immense biological production. The reduction of nutrient flow during ENSO events has reduced primary production, collapsed fisheries, and led to mass deaths of marine mammals.[20]

---

[11] *See generally* Michael J. Newman & Robert T. Rood, *Implications of Solar Evolution for the Earth's Early Atmosphere*, 198 SCI. 1035 (1977).

[12] *See generally* Richard C. Willson & Hugh S. Hudson, *Solar Luminosity Variations in Solar Cycle 21*, 332 NATURE 810 (1988); Richard C. Willson & Hugh S. Hudson, *The Sun's Luminosity over a Complete Solar Cycle*, 351 NATURE 42 (1991).

[13] *See generally id.*

[14] ELIZABETH KAY BERNER & ROBERT A. BERNER, GLOBAL ENVIRONMENT: WATER, AIR, AND GEOCHEMICAL CYCLES 9–12 (1995).

[15] *Id.* at 13.

[16] *Id.* at 18–19.

[17] *Id.* at 15.

[18] *See supra* note 3, at 235–40.

[19] Chester F. Ropelewski & Michael S. Halpert, *Global and Regional Scale Precipitation Patterns Associated with the El Niño/Southern Oscillation*, 115 MONTHLY WEATHER REV. 1606, 1625 (1987).

[20] Peter W. Glynn, *El Niño-Southern Oscillation 1982–1983: Nearshore Population, Community, and Ecosystem Responses*, 19 ANN. REV. ECOLOGY & SYSTEMATICS 309 (1988).

B. ANTHROPOGENIC CLIMATE CHANGE

Excess buildup of persistent greenhouse gases, primarily carbon dioxide (CO_2), in the atmosphere is the primary force driving current changes in Earth's climate.[21] Excess greenhouse gases would prevent radiation from leaving Earth and lead to warming of the surface. Greenhouse gases include CO_2, methane, chlorofluorocarbons (CFCs), and nitrous oxide. Carbon dioxide concentrations account for 80 percent of the total forcing caused by greenhouse gases[22] and exceed levels measured from the past 800,000 years.[23]

The effects of increased global temperature are already evident: ice sheet coverage is waning in polar regions, glaciers are shrinking, and spring snow cover is decreasing in the Northern Hemisphere.[24] In the last interglacial period, polar ice melt was a major contributor to sea-level rise.[25] Current estimates of sea-level rise of 2.8 mm per year balance out with estimates of glacier and sea ice melt, land water storage, and thermal expansion.[26] Ninety percent of the additional energy remaining on Earth has accumulated in the ocean, as evidenced by increased ocean temperatures.[27] The extra energy absorption leads to expansion of ocean water, which contributes to sea-level rise. The transport of warmer waters into the circumpolar deepwater current[28] is attributed to increasing rates of glacial retreat, thinning, flow, and ungrounding in Western Antarctica.[29] This faster addition of water is predicted to significantly contribute to sea-level rise and lead to the destabilization of other glaciers.

The emission of CO_2 is the major determinant in mean global surface warming. Even if current emissions stopped, the effects of the emissions will be felt for many centuries to millennia.[30] Extensive focus has been placed on the links between excess atmospheric CO_2 and changing climate; however, excess atmospheric CO_2 also causes physical and chemical changes to oceans and coasts.

---

[21] *See supra* note 2, at 8-1 to 8-139.

[22] *See supra* note 2, at 8–20.

[23] *See supra* note 4. Anthropogenic additions of ozone, atmospheric water vapor, and changes in Earth's albedo are forcings that also alter the energy balance of Earth. Many of these anthropogenic forcings are interactive, making predictions about the overall impacts of anthropogenic perturbations challenging. *See supra* note 3, at 503–05.

[24] *See supra* note 4, at 5.

[25] *See generally* NEEM Cmty. Members, *Eemian Interglacial Reconstructed from a Greenland Folded Ice Core*, 493 NATURE 489 (2013).

[26] *See supra* note 4, at 7.

[27] *See supra* note 2, at 4.

[28] *See generally* Stanley S. Jacobs, et al., *Stronger Ocean Circulation and Increased Melting under Pine Island Glacier Ice Shelf*, 4 NATURE GEOSCI. 519 (2011).

[29] *See generally* E. Rignot, et al., *Widespread, Rapid Grounding Line Retreat of Pine Island, Thwaites, Smith, and Kohler Glaciers, West Antarctica, from 1992 to 2011*, 41 GEOPHYSICAL RES. LETTERS 3502 (2014); Ian Joughin, Benjamin E. Smith & Brooke Medley, *Marine Ice Sheet collapse potentially under way for the Thwaites Glacier Basin, West Antarctica*, 344 SCI. 735 (2014).

[30] *See supra* note 4, at 19.

II. Physical and Chemical Changes to Oceans and Coasts

A. SCIENTIFIC UNDERPINNINGS

There are two principal consequences of increased CO_2 in the atmosphere and marine ecosystems: (1) ocean acidification, and (2) increasing ocean temperature.[31] The first subsection of this part of the chapter addresses the causes and consequences of ocean acidification, whereas the remaining four subsections examine important impacts to ocean and coastal resources, which flow from increasing ocean temperature.

1. Ocean Acidification

In the last five decades, 24 percent to 33 percent of anthropogenically produced CO_2 has been absorbed by the oceans.[32] Although this additional uptake of CO_2 mitigates the rate and severity of climate change felt on land, it is not without consequences on ocean water chemistry. The current chemical alterations are collectively termed "ocean acidification" due to the effect of reduced ocean pH. Altered pH is only one symptom of changing ocean chemistry.[33]

Once a molecule of CO_2 is absorbed into the ocean it undergoes a series of chemical reactions leading to the troublesome addition of a hydrogen ion (H^+) and the loss of a carbonate ion (CO_2^{3-}). As hydrogen ions are created, the pH of ocean water decreases and becomes more acidic. Carbonate ions bond with calcium to form calcium carbonate ($CaCO_3$), which is an essential building block for the skeletons of marine invertebrates including corals, snails, crabs, and certain plankton species, as well as plant species such as coralline algae.

Surface waters, especially shallow, warm tropical waters, are generally supersaturated with carbonate ions. This condition allows for the easy formation of carbonate skeletons in marine organisms, which accounts for the abundance of coral reefs in these areas. If the saturation of carbonate ions drops, it becomes energetically costly for organisms to build and maintain carbonate skeletons, resulting in reduced growth and reduced skeleton density.[34] In some cases, drops in carbonate ion availability can lead to "dissolution," which is the dissolving of carbonate skeletons. There are naturally occurring areas such as the deep ocean and cold, high-latitude waters where the quantity of carbonate ions in addition to other physical factors such as temperature, salinity, and pressure impact the ability of organisms to absorb carbonate, which leads to skeleton

---

[31] OCEAN AND MARINE RESOURCES IN A CHANGING CLIMATE, *supra* note 8, at 2.

[32] Jean-Pierre Gattuso et al., *Ocean Acidification and Its Impacts: An Expert Survey*, 117 CLIMATIC CHANGE 725, 726 (2013); Corinne Le Quéré et al., *Trends in the Sources and Sinks of Carbon Dioxide*, 2 NATURE GEOSCI. 831, 834 (2009).

[33] The current change in ocean pH is a drop of 0.1, which is a 26 percent increase in hydrogen ions. *See supra* note 2, at 3–5.

[34] Richard A. Feely et al., *Impact of Anthropogenic CO_2 on the $CaCO_3$ System in the Oceans*, 305 SCI. 362, 365, Table S1 (2004).

dissolution.[35] Dissolution and reduced saturation are becoming more prevalent in areas that were historically abundant in carbonate skeleton growth, such as coral reefs, which jeopardizes the future of these ecosystems.[36]

The ability of carbon to be stored in marine organisms allows for the oceans to absorb large quantities of atmospheric CO_2, which has buffered the Earth from more immediate impacts of excess CO_2 in the atmosphere. Reduction in carbonate skeleton formation in addition to skeleton loss means less atmospheric CO_2 can be stored in the ocean.[37]

In addition to the impact of CO_2 on ocean acidification, the burning of fossil fuels and fertilizer usage in agriculture also introduces strong acids (HNO_3 and H_2SO_4) as well as bases (NH_3) into ocean waters. Organisms nitrify NH_3 into nitrate NO_3, leading to additional acidification in ocean and coastal regions. The global impact of this acidification amounts to only about 3 percent. Nevertheless, inputs are estimated to increase in the next several decades and may account for 10–50% of acidification in coastal waters due to the proximity of source pollution from rivers and groundwater. Introduction of nitrate species into coastal systems has profound fertilizer effects on marine primary producers, phytoplankton, and submerged aquatic species, which lead to further changes in ocean chemistry.[38]

The multifaceted changes occurring in ocean chemistry during ocean acidification result in a variety of impacts on biological organisms. If we focus only on ocean acidification, organisms are faced with changes in ocean pH, changes in carbonate availability, changes in the depth of carbonate dissolution, and addition of fertilizers. These effects impact ocean biology on a variety of spatial scales from cellular, to organismal, to ecosystematic. This complexity of effects and impacts makes generalizations about the impacts of ocean acidification on ocean biology globally difficult as some species may be positively impacted while others are negatively impacted. Changes or shifts in species that rely on carbonate skeletons are anticipated to occur, and these changes are likely to have profound impacts on marine ecosystems, including non-carbonate-dependent species. Current conditions of climate change are mild in comparison to other geological conditions; however, the unprecedented rate of change occurring in modern times may outpace marine organisms' ability to adapt to changing ocean chemistry.

Ocean acidification has profound impacts on coral reef systems. Exposure to highly acidic water can lead to complete dissolution of coral skeletons, but some coral polyps can still survive and even regrow their skeletons if pH returns to an ideal level.[39] Despite this remarkable adaptability, the current climate change conditions present several

---

[35] *See generally id.*

[36] Scott C. Doney et al., *Ocean Acidification: The Other CO_2 Problem*, 1 MARINE SCI. 169, 173–74 (2009).

[37] Andy Ridgwell & Richard E. Zeebe, *The Role of the Global Carbonate Cycle in the Regulation and Evolution of the Earth System*, 234 EARTH & PLANETARY SCI. LETTERS 299, 300 (2005).

[38] *See generally* Scott C. Doney et al., *Impact of Anthropogenic Atmospheric Nitrogen and Sulfur Deposition on Ocean Acidification and the Inorganic Carbon System*, 104 PROC. NAT'L ACAD. SCI. 14580 (2007).

[39] *See generally* Maoz Fine & Dan Tchernov, *Scleractinian Coral Species Survive and Recover from Decalcification*, 315 SCI. 1811 (2007).

challenges for corals and coral communities. As oceans acidify, coral skeleton production will decrease and the rate of dissolution will increase.[40] In addition to changes in ocean chemistry, corals are also faced with perturbations from increased temperature, overfishing, and pollution that increase reef degradation. The multitude of coral reef stressors at play may suggest reefs are headed toward global-scale loss[41]; however, corals have survived through five mass extinction events in Earth's history, which suggests a capacity for coping with stress and a potential for adaptation.[42]

Reduction in calcification rates and increased dissolution also negatively impact ecologically important coralline algae species such as *Halimeda* and coralline red algae in the same ways as coral species.[43] Evidence suggests that other fleshier submerged aquatic vegetation (SAV), such as some species of seagrasses and macroalgae, may benefit from increased CO_2 concentrations in ocean water, which will enhance photosynthesis and growth rates.[44]

The increase of CO_2 into the ocean could also increase phytoplankton species growth, but studies show mixed results of positive and negative effects.[45] Some phytoplankton species have carbonate skeletons and would be negatively impacted by changes in ocean pH and carbonate dissolution depths, as seen in corals.[46] Effects of pH changes are also species specific, with some species growing well in a wide range of pH and others limited by a 1.0 pH range.[47] Predicting the effects of ocean acidification on phytoplankton abundance and diversity is complicated by simultaneous changes in temperature, nutrient availability, and light that occur related to climate change. Variations in any single factor can lead to large shifts in phytoplankton communities, which would reverberate through oceanic and coastal food webs.

The overall effect of ocean acidification on survival, calcification, growth, and reproduction of marine organisms is negative.[48] Research suggests that corals, echinoderms, fish, and mollusks have sustained the largest impacts, while crustaceans appear resistant to changes.[49]

---

[40] *See* Doney et al., *supra* note 36, at 177.

[41] *See generally* Ove Hoegh-Guldberg, *Climate Change, Coral Bleaching and the Future of the World's Coral Reefs*, 50 MARINE FRESHWATER RESOURCES 839 (1999).

[42] John M. Pandolfi et al., *Projecting Coral Reef Futures under Global Warming and Ocean Acidification*, 333 SCI. 418, 421 (2011).

[43] *See* Doney et al., *supra* note 36, at 176.

[44] *See generally* Marguerite Koch et al., *Climate Change and Ocean Acidification Effects on Seagrasses and Marine Macroalgae*, 19 GLOBAL CHANGE BIOLOGY 103 (2013). The benefit of CO_2 will not be uniform across all species of SAV, however. Shifts in carbon availability will likely lead to competitive interactions not only between seagrass species, but also between seagrass and their epiphytic communities. Increased shading from an overgrowth of epiphytes may lead to a rapid decline of seagrass meadows.

[45] John M. Guinotte & Victoria J. Fabry, *Ocean Acidification and Its Potential Effects on Marine Ecosystems*, 1134 ANNALS NEW YORK ACAD. SCI. 320, 333 (2008).

[46] *See* Doney et al., *supra* note 36, at 176.

[47] *See* Guinotte & Fabry, *supra* note 45, at 333.

[48] Kristy J. Kroeker et al., *Meta-analysis Reveals Negative Yet Variable Effects of Ocean Acidification on Marine Organisms*, 13 ECOLOGY LETTERS 1419, 1426–28 (2010).

[49] Astrid C. Wittmann & Hans-O. Pörtner, *Sensitivities of Extant Animal Taxa to Ocean Acidification*, NATURE CLIMATE CHANGE 1 (2013) (advance online publication at 4–5).

2. Ocean Stratification

Oceans can be divided into two parts. The surface layer is well mixed by winds and has an abundance of light that can support large stocks of phytoplankton. Carbon dioxide, nutrients, and light are required in specific quantities to support photosynthesis and associated food webs. Phytoplankton often exhausts nutrient supplies in the surface layer, and thus nutrient supply becomes a limiting agent in phytoplankton biomass.

Below the surface layer is the remaining deep layer of the ocean. This layer is characterized by dark, cold, less-mixed oxygen-rich water. Although the deep layer is rich in nutrients, the lack of light prohibits photosynthesis. The division between the surface layer and deep layer is known as the thermocline, which is characterized by a rapid decline in temperature. The thermocline is often associated with a pycnocline, which marks differences in water density between the surface and deep layers. Differences in water density increase the amount of energy required to mix layers of ocean water.

The upper surface layer of the oceans is currently absorbing the excess heat on Earth, which causes ocean stratification.[50] Increasing temperature is expected to reinforce the strength of the thermocline, which will make mixing of the water column more difficult and limit the flow of nutrients to phytoplankton at the surface.[51] Reduction in primary production and changes in phytoplankton species composition are likely to occur with increased ocean stratification.[52]

Areas of upwelling exist where wind and currents pull surface waters away from land-masses. Surface waters are then replaced by cold nutrient-rich water from the deep layer. Upwelling occurs along coasts and islands, and along the equator. The result of upwelling is an explosion of phytoplankton biomass, which supports extensive zooplankton communities that are the basis for major fisheries. Although upwelling areas are small in size, the supported biomass rivals primary production of rainforests.[53] The anticipated changes in wind patterns and ocean currents, such as increased frequency of ENSO events due to climate change, reduce upwelling and have catastrophic impacts to the higher trophic levels including fisheries, marine mammals, and seabirds.[54]

The large quantity of organic material produced in the upper surface layers as a result of primary production falls through the water column when organisms die. The digestion of organic material by bacteria strips oxygen from the water and releases CO_2. The pycnocline acts as a barrier that builds up oxygen-depleted water known as

---

[50] *See supra* note 4.

[51] *See generally* Michael J. Behrenfeld et al., *Climate-Driven Trends in Contemporary Ocean Productivity*, 444 Nature 752 (2006).

[52] *See generally* Philip W. Boyd & Scott C. Doney, *Modelling Regional Responses by Marine Pelagic Ecosystems to Global Climate Change*, 29 Geophysical Res. Letters 53–1 (2002).

[53] Keith A. Sverdrup & E. Virginia Armbrust, An Introduction to the World's Oceans 369 (10th ed. 2008).

[54] *See generally* Glynn, *supra* note 20.

the Oxygen Minimum Zone. Oxygen concentrations in this zone can reach hypoxic conditions, where organisms struggle to survive.[55] Hypoxic events are prevalent in coastal estuaries due to eutrophication, and these events are associated with extensive fish and invertebrate kills.[56] Evidence exists that the lack of water mixing due to ocean stratification is causing the Oxygen Minimum Zone to expand into surface waters and onto continental shelves, exposing marine communities to a greater frequency of hypoxic events.[57]

3. Tropical Cyclone Activity

Warming of the upper layer of the ocean increases ocean thermal energy, which may lead to increases in tropical cyclone activity and intensification. The amount of energy available in the water column between the ocean surface and where water drops below 26°C is known as Tropical Cyclone Heat Potential (TCHP).[58] The greater the TCHP, the more likely tropical cyclones that pass over the area will intensify through absorbing the heat stored in the ocean.[59]

Current theory and model simulations suggest that tropical cyclone duration, intensity, and frequency are expected to increase with ocean warming.[60] Tropical cyclone activities represent natural disturbances to coastal communities and play important roles in habitat complexity and biodiversity.[61] Increased tropical storm activity may negatively impact coral and seagrass habitats, which are already under stress from a multitude of anthropogenic disturbances.[62]

---

[55] *See generally* Lisa A. Levin, *Oxygen Minimum Zone Benthos: Adaptation and Community Response to Hypoxia, in* 41 OCEANOGRAPHY AND MARINE BIOLOGY: AN ANN. REV. 1 (R.N. Gibson & R.J.A. Atkinson eds., 2003).

[56] *See generally* J. Zhang et al., *Natural and Human-Induced Hypoxia and Consequences for Coastal Areas: Synthesis and Future Development*, 7 BIOGEOSCI. 1443 (2010).

[57] *See generally* William F. Gilly et al., *Oceanographic and Biological Effects of Shoaling of the Oxygen Minimum Zone*, 5 ANN. REV. MARINE SCI. 393 (2013).

[58] *See generally* G.J. Goni & J. Knaff, *Tropical Cyclone Heat Potential*, 89 BULL. AM. METEOROLOGICAL SOC'Y 43 (2007).

[59] *See generally* Lynn K. Shay et al., *Effects of a Warm Oceanic Feature on Hurricane Opal*, 128 MONTHLY WEATHER REV. 1366 (2000).

[60] *See generally* Thomas R. Knutson et al., *Tropical Cyclones and Climate Change*, 3 NATURE GEOSCI. 157 (2010).

[61] *See generally* Larry G. Harris et al., *Community Recovery after Storm Damage: A Case of Facilitation in Primary Succession*, 224 SCI. 1336 (1984); R.H. Karlson & L.E. Hurd, *Disturbance, Coral Reef Communities, and Changing Ecological Paradigms*, 12 CORAL REEFS 117 (1993).

[62] Shaun K. Wilson et al., *Multiple Disturbances and the Global Degradation of Coral Reefs: Are Reef Fishes at Risk or Resilient?*, 12 GLOBAL CHANGE BIOLOGY 2220 (2006); Carlos M. Duarte, *The Future of Seagrass Meadows*, 29 ENVTL. CONSERVATION 192 (2002); Frederick T. Short & Hilary A. Neckles, *The Effects of Global Climate Change on Seagrasses*, 63 AQUATIC BOTANY 169 (1999); Toby A Gardner et al., *Hurricanes and Caribbean Coral Reefs: Impacts, Recovery Patterns, and Role in Long-Term Decline*, 86 ECOLOGY 174 (2005).

4. Shifting Atmospheric and Ocean Circulation

The deep ocean layer is divided into water masses based on density. The density differences between layers make vertical movement of water difficult. Water masses slowly move horizontally across ocean basins in a pattern known as "thermohaline circulation."[63] The movement of deep ocean water masses begins at the surface in the North Atlantic and Antarctic where changes in water temperature, precipitation, addition of freshwater, and ice formation increase seawater density, causing it to sink into the deep layer.[64] Deep water flows south along the Atlantic Ocean into the Indian and Pacific Oceans, where some water is forced to the surface in upwelling zones and the rest eventually heats and rises to the surface.[65]

Thermohaline circulation is sensitive to changes in temperature and salinity[66] and is responsible for much of the ocean's ability to move heat from the tropics to the midlatitudes.[67] Shifts in the positions of oceanic gyres and associated atmospheric circulation cells are being observed. Due to the short data set, however, it is unclear if these are normal oscillations or evidence of climate change.[68] Decreasing sea ice coverage due to increasing surface water temperatures has increasingly been related to changes in atmospheric circulation in the Arctic and beyond.[69] Shifts in wind-driven circulation due to the changes in atmospheric circulation cells have been associated with increased ocean stratification, reduced nutrients, reduced phytoplankton biomass, shifts in phytoplankton species, and the collapse of sardine populations.[70]

5. Saltwater Intrusion

As sea level rises, water will inevitably flood onto coastlines and threaten coastal freshwater resources worldwide. Coastal estuaries exist where freshwater rivers meet the ocean, creating gradients of salinity and temperature that vary based on riverine output and tidal flow. Saltwater intrusion (SI) can occur indirectly from an increase in drought conditions, which would reduce freshwater input, or more directly through oceanic encroachment

---

[63] *See* BERNER & BERNER, *supra* note 14, at 21.

[64] *Id.*

[65] *Id.* at 23.

[66] *Id.* at 24.

[67] *See supra* note 2, at 26.

[68] *Id.* at 31.

[69] *See generally* Elizabeth N. Cassano et al., *Atmospheric Impacts of an Arctic Sea Ice Minimum as Seen in the Community Atmosphere Model*, 34 INT'L J. CLIMATOLOGY 766 (2014); Thomas J. Ballinger & Jeffrey C. Rogers, *Atmosphere and Ocean Impacts on Recent Western Arctic Summer Sea Ice Melt*, 7 GEOGRAPHY COMPASS 686 (2013).

[70] *See generally* Gordon T. Taylor et al., *Ecosystem Responses in the Southern Caribbean Sea to Global Climate Change*, 109 PROC. NAT'L ACAD. SCI. 19315 (2012).

due to sea-level rise.[71] Either scenario may lead to shifts in plant,[72] animal,[73] and microbial communities.[74]

A direct impact of SI on humans is the encroachment of saltwater into coastal aquifers. Groundwater flows under the surface of coastal areas in an aquifer and serves as a main source of freshwater. Ocean water penetrates into coastal aquifers below the freshwater. Differences in density between the water masses form a natural boundary that prevents contamination of oceanic minerals and salts into the freshwater layer.[75] Increased extraction of freshwater through pumping can drive ocean water farther into the aquifer rendering the freshwater unfit for consumption.[76] SI can also be exacerbated by climate change through rising sea levels, increased storm surges associated with tropical cyclone activity, increased utilization of groundwater sources associated with increased population, and reduced aquifer recharge due to changes in precipitation.[77]

B. LAW AND POLICY ASPECTS

This section addresses three areas in which law and policy responses have been most active in addressing the physical and chemical changes to ocean and coastal resources from climate change: (1) ocean acidification; (2) increased intensity of tropical cyclones; and (3) sea-level rise, coastal adaptation, and takings.

Existing treaties and federal statutes have been considered to help combat the ocean acidification crisis. For example, the United Nations Convention on the Law of the Sea (UNCLOS) could help address the problem at the international level.[78] The Clean Water Act[79] and the Endangered Species Act[80] provide potential starting points for regulating aspects of the ocean acidification problem in the United States.[81]

---

[71] Aat Barendregt & Christopher W. Swarth, *Tidal Freshwater Wetlands: Variation and Changes*, 36 ESTUARIES & COASTS 445, 451 (2013).

[72] *See generally* Caitlin Mullan Crain et al., *Physical and Biotic Drivers of Plant Distribution across Estuarine Salinity Gradients*, 85 ECOLOGY 2539 (2004).

[73] *See generally* S. Kupschus & D. Tremain, *Associations between Fish Assemblages and Environmental Factors in Nearshore Habitats of a Subtropical Estuary*, 58 J. FISH BIOLOGY 1383 (2001).

[74] *See generally* Nathaniel B. Weston et al., *Ramifications of Increased Salinity in Tidal Freshwater Sediments: Geochemistry and Microbial Pathways of Organic Matter Mineralization*, 111 J. GEOPHYSICAL RES.: BIOGEOSCI.1 (2005–2012) (2006).

[75] *See generally* JACOB BEAR, SEAWATER INTRUSION IN COASTAL AQUIFERS: CONCEPTS, METHODS AND PRACTICES (1999).

[76] *See generally* Adrian D. Werner et al., *Seawater Intrusion Processes, Investigation and Management: Recent Advances and Future Challenges*, 51 ADVANCES WATER RESOURCES 3 (2013).

[77] *See generally id.*

[78] *See generally* Verónica González, *An Alternative Approach for Addressing CO2-Driven Ocean Acidification*, 12 SUSTAINABLE DEV. L. & POL'Y 45 (2012) (discussing how UNCLOS can be used to combat ocean acidification).

[79] Clean Water Act, 33 U.S.C. §§ 1251–1387 (2012).

[80] Endangered Species Act, 16 U.S.C. §§ 1531–1544 (2012).

[81] *See generally* Kate Halloran, *Using the Clean Water Act to Protect Our Ocean's Biodiversity*, 10 SUSTAINABLE DEV. L. & POL'Y 23 (2010) (discussing EPA's review of comments on how to address ocean

Existing law may be insufficient to manage the new and vexing challenge of ocean acidification, however. At the international level, a new treaty focused exclusively on ocean acidification may be necessary.[82] Domestic responses also are underway. For example, in an effort to mitigate the crippling impacts to its shellfish industry, the state of Washington has enacted legislation to study and respond to ocean acidification.[83]

The increased intensity of tropical cyclones associated with warmer waters from climate change has caused impacts that have triggered legal responses. Two prominent examples of these law and policy responses are the public nuisance case filed by victims of Hurricane Katrina and the adaptation response in New Jersey in the wake of Hurricane Sandy.

In *Comer v. Murphy Oil USA*, the plaintiffs sued electric utilities, oil companies, coal companies, and chemical companies seeking damages for property damages from Hurricane Katrina. The plaintiffs filed a public nuisance claim based on federal common law, alleging that the impacts from Hurricane Katrina had been intensified by the defendants' contributions to global warming. The district court dismissed the case on standing and political question grounds,[84] but the United States Court of Appeals for the Fifth Circuit reversed.[85] The Fifth Circuit ultimately dismissed the case in a rehearing *en banc*.[86] By 2013, in addition to *Comer*, U.S federal courts had dismissed all climate change public nuisance claims based on federal common law in *American Electric Power v. Connecticut* and *Native Village of Kivalina v. ExxonMobil Corp.* Therefore, the courts have effectively closed the door for possible injunctive relief or damages for these

---

acidification through listing of impaired waters under section 303(d) of the Clean Water Act); Blake Armstrong, *Maintaining the World's Marine Biodiversity: Using the Endangered Species Act to Stop the Climate Change Induced Loss of Coral Reefs*, 18 HASTINGS W.-NW. J. ENVTL. L. & POL'Y 429 (2012) (noting that the Endangered Species Act is not particularly useful for combating effects of climate change). For further discussion of U.S. environmental law's efforts to regulate ocean acidification, see infra Chapters 2 and 3 addressing the Clean Water Act and the Clean Air Act, respectively.

[82] *See generally* Heidi R. Lamirande, *From Sea to Carbon Cesspool: Preventing the World's Marine Ecosystems from Falling Victim to Ocean Acidification*, 34 SUFFOLK TRANSNAT'L L. REV. 183 (2011) (analyzing the need for an ocean acidification treaty).

[83] *See* Diane Deitz, *Ocean of Change: Changing Chemistry of Seawater Poses Lethal Threat to Marine Life*, REGISTER-GUARD (OREGON), Sept. 22, 2013, http://www.registerguard.com/rg/news/local/30407375-75/ocean-waters-acidification-oyster-oregon.html.csp (based on recommendations from governor-appointed panel on ocean acidification, Washington legislature invested $1.82 million into an ocean acidification research center at the University of Washington to study the problem and assist the shellfish industry in Puget Sound and Willapa Bay); *see also* Juliet Eilperin, *Washington State Confronts Ocean Acidification*, WASH. POST, Nov. 27, 2012, http://articles.washingtonpost.com/2012-11-27/national/35512233_1_ocean-acidification-washington-state-human-generated-carbon-emissions (discussing Washington's new law requiring more funding for state agencies to fight ocean acidification). For further discussion, see infra Chapter 2 addressing the federal Clean Water Act and Washington State's ocean acidification program.

[84] *See* Comer v. Murphy Oil USA, 2007 WL 6942285 (S.D. Miss. 2007).

[85] *See generally* Comer v. Murphy Oil USA, 585 F.3d 855 (5th Cir. 2009).

[86] *See* Comer v. Murphy Oil USA, 607 F.3d 1049 (5th Cir. 2010) (*en banc*).

climate-change-related federal common law claims on the ground that such claims are displaced by the federal Clean Air Act.[87]

A more successful legal response to hurricane-related impacts purportedly intensified by climate change occurred in the wake of Hurricane Sandy in New Jersey. Established by an Executive Order issued on December 7, 2012, the Hurricane Sandy Rebuilding Task Force released a report, which included sixty-nine recommendations to help the region devastated by Hurricane Sandy recover and rebuild in the wake of the storm. The Task Force is comprised of representatives from more than twenty federal departments and agencies, with contributions from state and local governments.[88] In January 2013, Congress passed the Disaster Relief Appropriations Act, 2013, which provided approximately $50 billion to support rebuilding in the region.[89] Therefore, the legislative and executive branches have proved to be more productive avenues than the judiciary for relief for hurricane-related damages associated with climate-change-enhanced tropical cyclones.

Sea-level rise has prompted extensive coastal adaptation measures throughout the United States and abroad. In the United States, these adaptation measures have clashed with private property rights and have prompted litigation involving claims alleging government taking of private property without just compensation.[90] Similar to the response to tropical cyclone impacts, the most productive efforts to promote adaptation to sea-level rise have been at the state and local legislative levels. Retreat from the coast has emerged as the preferred adaptation response to sea-level rise.[91]

III. Biological Changes to Oceans and Coasts

A. SCIENTIFIC UNDERPINNINGS

The chemical and physical changes in the ocean that occur in periods of global climate change have profound impacts on marine organisms. Increased ocean temperatures impact species directly by influencing factors such as biochemical reactions, growth,

---

[87] *See* American Elec. Power Co. v. Connecticut., 131 S. Ct. 2527, 2537 (2011); Native Village of Kivalina v. ExxonMobil Corp., 696 F.3d 849, 856–58 (9th Cir. 2012).

[88] For the full report, see HURRICANE SANDY REBUILDING TASK FORCE, HURRICANE SANDY REBUILDING STRATEGY (2013), http://portal.hud.gov/hudportal/documents/huddoc?id=HSRebuildingStrategy.pdf.

[89] *See* Disaster Relief Appropriations Act, 2013, Pub. L. 113–2, https://www.govtrack.us/congress/bills/113/hr152/text. (last visited Aug. 2, 2014).

[90] *See generally* Donna Christie, *Sea Level Rise and Gulf Beaches: The Specter of Judicial Takings*, 26 J. LAND USE & ENVTL. L. 315 (2011) (discussing judicial takings analysis raised in the *Stop the Beach Renourishment* litigation in the Florida and U.S. Supreme Courts).

[91] *See, e.g.*, Peter Byrne, *The Cathedral Engulfed: Sea-Level Rise, Property Rights, and Time*, 73 LA. L. REV. 69 (2012) (arguing that regulators should encourage or mandate retreat as the preferred coastal adaptation strategy while seeking to minimize risk of and liability for regulatory takings); Robin Kundis Craig, *A Public Health Perspective on Sea-Level Rise: Starting Points for Climate Change Adaptation*, 15 WIDENER L. REV. 521 (2010) (proposing construction and siting regulations and a retreat strategy to address saltwater intrusion and other public health problems associated with sea-level rise).

and reproduction. Temperature-induced alterations in sea level, ocean stratification, sea ice coverage, ocean circulation, oxygen concentration, and freshwater input lead to additional species impacts.[92] Species are also impacted by the chemical effects of CO_2 addition through changes in primary production, carbonate saturation, and ocean acidity.[93] Changes in oceanic conditions are not uniform and vary geographically, seasonally, and diurnally, which complicates predictions about the impacts of climate change on marine biota.[94] The cumulative impacts of climate can alter physiology, behavior, and demographic traits, such as reproduction and size.[95] These alterations can lead to shifts in phenology, range and distribution, community composition and interactions, and ecosystem structure.[96]

1. Physiological Changes

Physiological changes occur at the organism level in response to environmental changes and are the principal determinant of a species' ability to tolerate environmental change.[97] Temperature can influence an individual's biochemical reactions, metabolic rates, feeding, growth, and reproduction, ultimately affecting population growth and size.[98] Organisms are capable of acclimating to an environmental change by adjusting their physiology to compensate via phenotypic plasticity, or the ability to change physiology without altering genetic makeup.

Phenotypic adjustments are often at the expense of fitness.[99] For example, acclimating to a temperature shift may cause changes in reproductive output or growth, or both.[100] If the environmental change is prolonged, natural selection can occur in which certain genetic traits are favored, thereby promoting a population's ability to adapt. Genetic adaptation is slow and irreversible. If an environmental disturbance is prolonged and outside the range of an organism's ability to adapt, the population may die or be forced to migrate to a more desirable location.[101] In some cases, environmental changes may benefit species by increasing food or nutrients, reducing physiological costs, or reducing competition; however, for some species, changes in environmental conditions are

---

[92] Scott C. Doney et al., *Climate Change Impacts on Marine Ecosystems*, 4 MARINE SCI. 11, 12 (2012).

[93] *See supra* Section II of this chapter.

[94] Brian Helmuth et al., *Biophysics, Physiological Ecology, and Climate Change: Does Mechanism Matter?*, 67 ANN. REV. PHYSIOLOGY 177, 178 (2005).

[95] Doney et al., *supra* note 90, at 12.

[96] *See generally* Gian-Reto Walther et al., *Ecological Responses to Recent Climate Change*, 416 NATURE 389 (2002).

[97] Doney et al., *supra* note 92, at 16.

[98] Rebecca L. Kordas et al., *Community Ecology in a Warming World: The Influence of Temperature on Interspecific Interactions in Marine Systems*, 400 J. EXPERIMENTAL MARINE BIOLOGY & ECOLOGY 218, 219–20 (2011).

[99] Helmuth et al., *supra* note 94, at 179.

[100] *Id.*

[101] *Id.*

stressful, leading to higher mortality, reduced growth, smaller size, and reduced reproduction.[102] Changes on an organism level are the mechanisms behind larger patterns observed in populations and shifts in ecosystems.[103]

2. Phenology

Phenology relates to the timing and seasonal activity of animals and plants.[104] Increases in global temperature have led to earlier timing of seasonal activities such as reproduction, migration, and food production in freshwater, marine, and terrestrial ecosystems.[105] Seasonal timing takes advantage of conditions that maximize growth and reproduction while minimizing sensitive life history stages' exposure to stress.[106] For example, fish reproduce at optimal prey densities and minimal predator densities to improve larval survivorship.[107]

Shifts in the pulse of primary production may lead to trophic mismatch, where optimal prey for key life history stages are misaligned, leading to poor recruitment of higher trophic levels and ecosystem changes.[108] Middle and high latitudes may have greater sensitively to trophic mismatch due to the presence of pulsed plankton production.[109] Phenological shifts are linked to reductions in fitness and population declines, which may increase population extinctions and reduce biodiversity and fisheries production.[110]

3. Range and Distribution

Warming oceans have altered the latitudinal and depth distributions of marine organisms.[111] Northward expansion of southern species from a variety of taxonomic groups has already been observed, while the range of coldwater species has contracted.[112] In

---

[102] Doney et al., *supra* note 92, at 16.

[103] *See generally* Helmuth et al., *supra* note 94.

[104] Walther et al., *supra* note 96, at 389.

[105] *See generally id.*; William J. Sydeman & Steven J. Bograd, *Marine Ecosystems, Climate and Phenology: Introduction*, 393 MARINE ECOLOGY PROGRESS SERIES 185 (2009); Stephen J. Thackeray et al., *Trophic Level Asynchrony in Rates of Phenological Change for Marine, Freshwater and Terrestrial Environments*, 16 GLOBAL CHANGE BIOLOGY 3304 (2010); Camille Parmesan & Gary Yohe, *A Globally Coherent Fingerprint of Climate Change Impacts across Natural Systems*, 421 NATURE 37 (2003).

[106] Rubao Ji et al., *Marine Plankton Phenology and Life History in a Changing Climate: Current Research and Future Directions*, 32 J. PLANKTON RES. 1355, 1356 (2010).

[107] *See generally* D.H. Cushing, *Plankton Production and Year-Class Strength in Fish Populations: An Update of the Match/Mismatch Hypothesis*, 26 ADVANCES MARINE BIOLOGY 249 (1990).

[108] *See generally* Martin Edwards & Anthony J. Richardson, *Impact of Climate Change on Marine Pelagic Phenology and Trophic Mismatch*, 430 NATURE 881 (2004).

[109] Ji et al., *supra* note 106, at 1359; *see generally* Edwards & Richardson, *supra* note 106.

[110] *See* Thackeray et al., *supra* note 105, at 3310.

[111] Doney et al., *supra* note 92, at 16.

[112] *See generally* Raphael D. Sagarin et al., *Climate-Related Change in an Intertidal Community over Short and Long Time Scales*, 69 ECOLOGICAL MONOGRAPHS 465 (1999); Sally J. Holbrook et al., *Changes in an*

the Gulf of Mexico, where landmasses prohibit northward expansion, species have been observed migrating to deeper, cooler depths.[113]

Range shifts are also being documented with invasive species related to changes in sea surface temperature.[114] Many invasive species are introduced via anthropogenic vectors, such as ballast water in ships, to distant locations that they would normally not be able to reach independently.[115] Nevertheless, shifting communities due to changes in ocean conditions have the same potential negative impacts on the recipient communities that invasive species do.[116] Shifts in species range and distribution contribute to changes in community composition and biodiversity, which can lead to alterations in ecosystems.[117]

4. Community Composition and Species Interactions

Phenology and range shifts of marine species lead to complex changes in community structure and interactions between species, particularly related to food webs and predator-prey relationships.[118] A change in phytoplankton composition from diatoms to dinoflagellates is associated with shifts in zooplankton composition and, ultimately, the loss of fish recruitment.[119] Range shifts lead to interspecific competition between species, which are important components in structuring marine ecosystems. As ranges shift, novel interactions between species are likely to occur, which will further influence ecosystem structure.[120] Interacting species will differ in their environmental tolerances, leading to one species outcompeting the other for resources.[121] If the competitive interactions related to temperature involve

---

Assemblage of Temperate Reef Fishes Associated with a Climate Shift, 7 ECOLOGICAL APPLICATIONS 1299 (1997); Sarah K. Berke et al., *Range Shifts and Species Diversity in Marine Ecosystem Engineers: Patterns and Predictions for European Sedimentary Habitats*, 19 GLOBAL ECOLOGY & BIOGEOGRAPHY 223 (2010); A.J. Southward et al., *Seventy Years' Observations of Changes in Distribution and Abundance of Zooplankton and Intertidal Organisms in the Western English Channel in Relation to Rising Sea Temperature*, 20 J. THERMAL BIOLOGY 127 (1995); Rachel Przeslawski et al., *Using Rigorous Selection Criteria to Investigate Marine Range Shifts*, 113 ESTUARINE, COASTAL & SHELF SCI. 205 (2012).

[113] Malin L. Pinsky et al., *Marine Taxa Track Local Climate Velocities*, 341 SCI. 1239, 1240 (2013).

[114] *See generally* Marc Ruis et al., *Range Expansions across Ecoregions: Interactions of Climate Change, Physiology and Genetic Diversity Physiology and Genetic Diversity*, 23 GLOBAL ECOLOGY & BIOGEOGRAPHY 76 (2014).

[115] Cascade J.B. Sorte et al., *Marine Range Shifts and Species Introductions: Comparative Spread Rates and Community Impacts*, 19 GLOBAL ECOLOGY & BIOGEOGRAPHY 303, 304 (2010).

[116] *Id.* at 310.

[117] Doney et al., *supra* note 92, at 18.

[118] Walther et al., *supra* note 96, at 393.

[119] *See generally* Jürgen Alheit, *Consequences of Regime Shifts for Marine Food Webs*, 98 INT'L J. EARTH SCI. 261 (2009).

[120] Marco Milazzo et al., *Climate Change Exacerbates Interspecific Interactions in Sympatric Coastal Fishes*, 82 J. ANIMAL ECOLOGY 468, 469 (2012).

[121] Kordas et al., *supra* note 98, at 220–21.

keystone species,[122] the changes in communities will be larger than the effects of temperature changes alone.[123]

Warmer water temperatures are also expected to increase disease in marine communities, as growth rates of bacteria, virus, and fungi show positive correlations with temperature.[124] Corals in particular may be influenced by opportunistic pathogens that occur during bleaching events or because pathogens may induce bleaching events.[125] Overall, changes in community structure and species interactions are complicated. Therefore, it is difficult to make predictions about how climate change influences ecosystems.[126]

5. Ecosystem Structure

How ecosystems are impacted by changing environmental conditions depends on how food webs are controlled. "Bottom-up" controls depend on sufficient resources being available at the previous trophic level; "top-down" control is exerted by predators that keep lower trophic levels in check; and "wasp-waste" controls are regulated by intermediate species that control both lower trophic levels and the presence of top predators.[127] Increased temperature, vertical stratification, and reduced nutrient availability negatively impact bottom-up controls on marine primary production.[128] Overfishing and invasive species introductions lead to alterations in top-down and wasp-waste systems.[129] The loss of even a single species can have important consequences for community and ecological structure.[130]

a. Effects on Habitats
One-quarter of marine species associate with coral reefs,[131] which are ecosystems that are highly sensitive to changes in temperature and pH.[132] A symptom of coral stress is

---

[122] "Keystone species" refers to a species that has a disproportionate impact on a marine ecosystem in relation to its abundance. *See generally* R.T. Paine, *A Conversation on Refining the Concept of Keystone Species*, 9 CONSERVATION BIOLOGY 962 (1995).

[123] *See generally* Eric Sanford, *Regulation of Keystone Predation by Small Changes in Ocean Temperature*, 283 SCI. 2095 (1999).

[124] *See generally* C. Drew Harvell et al., *Climate Warming and Disease Risks for Terrestrial and Marine Biota*, 296 SCI. 2158 (2002).

[125] *See id.* at 2161.

[126] Doney et al., *supra* note 92, at 19.

[127] Aleheit, *supra* note 119, at 266.

[128] *See supra* Section II of this chapter for physical details on these conditions.

[129] *See generally* Julia K. Baum & Boris Worm, *Cascading Top-Down Effects of Changing Oceanic Predator Abundances*, 78 J. ANIMAL ECOLOGY 699 (2009); Kenneth T. Frank et al., *The Ups and Downs of Trophic Control in Continental Shelf Ecosystems*, 22 TRENDS ECOLOGY & EVOLUTION 236 (2007).

[130] *See generally* Christopher D.G. Harley et al., *The Impacts of Climate Change in Coastal Marine Systems*, 9 ECOLOGY LETTERS 228 (2006).

[131] Doney et al., *supra* note 92, at 23.

[132] Hoegh-Guldberg, *supra* note 41, at 843.

mass bleaching events, where endosymbiotic dinoflagellates are expelled from coral tissue, making the white coral skeleton visible.[133] Bleaching events have been increasing in intensity and frequency worldwide.[134] Severe bleaching results in coral death whereas moderate bleaching results in reduced fitness,[135] including reduced growth, calcification, and fecundity.[136] Additionally, corals that survive bleaching events may be more susceptible to disease.[137] A shift of 1°C (1.8°F) for three to four weeks is enough of a stressor to trigger massive coral bleaching.[138] Ocean acidification and the reduction in carbonate saturation depth make secreting and maintaining coral skeletons more difficult, may lead to skeleton loss, and disrupts growth of new recruits.[139] Reduced coral growth may inhibit the ability of corals to keep up with rising sea levels, known as "drowned reefs."[140] Reduced skeleton density may leave corals fragile and more vulnerable to storm damage.[141] Even small declines in coral abundance have been attributed to a reduction in fish and fish diversity.[142]

The stressors that coral reefs face in addition to those associated with climate change, such as overfishing, sedimentation, and eutrophication, increase their vulnerability to future changes.[143] A reduction in coral habitat complexity and structure would have major impacts on socioeconomics around the world, from reduction in fishing, tourism, storm protection, and protection from coastal erosion.[144]

Important energy exchanges exist between coral reefs and coastal wetlands such as mangrove forests and seagrass beds, which are imperiled from climate change.[145] These nearshore ecosystems must keep pace with sea-level rise through accretion of sediments; however, the current rate of sea-level rise may surpass these ecosystems' ability to adapt.[146] Additionally, the presence of coastal infrastructure and armoring along coasts may impede the ability of nearshore ecosystems to expand landward in response to rising sea levels.[147] Migration of habitats may lead to displacement of ecosystems. For example,

---

[133] B.E. Brown, *Coral Bleaching: Causes and Consequences*, 16 CORAL REEFS S129, S135 (1997).

[134] Ove Hoegh-Guldberg et al., *Coral Reefs under Rapid Climate Change and Ocean Acidification*, 318 SCI. 1737, 1740 (2007).

[135] Doney et al. *supra* note 92, at 23.

[136] *See generally* Ove Hoegh-Guldberg, *Climate Change, Coral Bleaching and the Future of the World's Coral Reefs*, 50 MARINE FRESHWATER RESOURCES 839 (1999).

[137] Laura D. Mydlarz et al., *Innate Immunity, Environmental Drivers, and Disease Ecology of Marine and Freshwater Invertebrates*, 37 ANN. REV. ECOLOGY, EVOLUTION & SYSTEMATICS 251, 274–78 (2006).

[138] Hoegh-Guldberg, *supra* note 41, at 843.

[139] Doney et al., *supra* note 92, at 23.

[140] *See generally* R. Grigg et al., *Drowned Reefs and Antecedent Karst Topography, Au'au Channel, SE Hawaiian Islands*, 21 CORAL REEFS 73 (2002).

[141] Doney et al., *supra* note 92, at 23.

[142] *See generally* Wilson et al., *supra* note 60.

[143] Doney et al., *supra* note 92, at 24.

[144] Hoegh-Guldberg et al., *supra* note 134, at 1741–42.

[145] Doney et al., *supra* note 92, at 21.

[146] Barendregt & Swarth, *supra* note 71, at 451.

[147] *Id.*

migration of mangroves may displace salt marsh communities, which will influence ecosystem structure and biogeochemical cycling.[148] Coastal wetlands face multiple anthropogenic disturbances that impact their resiliency to climate change such as sedimentation, nutrient addition, physical disturbance, invasive species, disease, overfishing, aquaculture, overgrazing, and algal blooms.[149]

Seagrasses are important habitats for marine fish, marine mammals, and sea turtles; however, accelerating seagrass loss is being documented worldwide.[150] Mangrove forests are decreasing by 1–2 percent per year due to deforestation, and are predicted to decrease by 10–20 percent by 2100.[151] Loss of coastal wetlands would negatively impact the important ecosystem services that these habitats provide for humans, including serving as nursery grounds for commercially and recreationally important species, filtering sediment and pollutants, protecting against storms and coastal erosion, and storing carbon.[152]

b. Effects on Species

Marine mammals are faced with indirect and direct impacts of climate change. Ocean temperature can play a crucial role in determining ranges of mammal species, whether they are northern or southern limits.[153] Large migrating species have a greater tolerance to changing temperatures, but restricted species located in polar regions may be more susceptible to warming temperatures.[154] Abundance of prey species impacts distributions, abundance, migration, and reproductive success of marine mammals. Changing ocean conditions including temperature, ocean currents, and ocean chemistry can lead to dramatic changes in food webs that support marine mammals.[155] Changes in phenology of prey species could also lead to trophic mismatch with mammal species, and shifting distributions can lead to increased competition among mammal species.[156] Increased temperature and reduced fitness from changes in prey abundance can leave mammal species more susceptible to disease, contaminants, and death.[157]

---

[148] See generally Michael J. Osland et al., Winter Climate Change and Coastal Wetland Foundation Species: Salt Marshes vs. Mangrove Forests in the Southeastern United States, 19 GLOBAL CHANGE BIOLOGY 1482 (2013).

[149] See generally Robert J. Orth et al., A Global Crisis for Seagrass Ecosystems, 56 BIOSCI. 987 (2006).

[150] Id. at 990; see generally Michelle Waycott et al., Accelerating Loss of Seagrasses across the Globe Threatens Coastal Ecosystems, 106 PROC. NAT'L ACAD. SCI. 12377 (2009). Many recreationally and commercially important species, such as seahorses, are seagrass-dependent, and are threatened or in danger of overexploitation and extinction. See generally A. Randall Hughes et al., Associations of Concern: Declining Seagrasses and Threatened Dependent Species, 7 FRONTIERS ECOLOGY & ENV'T 242 (2009).

[151] See generally Daniel M. Alongi, Mangrove Forests: Resilience, Protection from Tsunamis, and Responses to Global Climate Change, 76 ESTUARINE, COASTAL & SHELF SCI. 1 (2008).

[152] Doney et al., supra note 92, at 21.

[153] J.A. Learmonth et al., Potential Effects of Climate Change on Marine Mammals, 44 OCEANOGRAPHY & MARINE BIOLOGY 431, 446 (2006).

[154] Id.

[155] See generally supra Sections II and III of this chapter.

[156] Learmonth et al., supra note 153, at 447–48.

[157] Id. at 449.

Changes in polar bear prey species due to reductions in sea ice coverage has led to increased contaminate concentrations in polar bear tissue, which can lead to endocrine, immune, and reproductive issues.[158] In polar regions, reduction in ice coverage negatively impacts the reproductive success of many mammal species as ice is used for breeding, birthing, and feeding of pups.[159] Polar bears in particular have shown negative correlations of survival and reproduction with sea ice coverage.[160]

Increased temperature is a major concern for sea turtle populations, which experience temperature-dependent sex determination. Increased temperatures may lead to single-sex populations of females within the next decade.[161] However, males in some populations have been shown to increase their frequency of breeding, which reduces the effects of a female-biased population.[162] Shading of nests has been successful in reducing female-biased hatchlings, but is not a realistic solution to preventing sex-biased populations in the long term.[163] Sea turtle nesting locations occupy specific temperature and precipitation niches that may be impacted by climate change, leading to shifts in the location of nesting areas.[164] Climate change also impacts sea turtle populations through loss of coastal wetlands used for feeding grounds.[165]

Fisheries distribution and abundance are tied to oceanographic features such as prey abundance, temperature, oxygen content, and acidity, all of which demonstrate shifts due to climate change.[166] Climate change has a variety of direct and indirect impacts on fishery species that reverberate throughout ecosystems and impact global food production.[167] The most vulnerable fisheries may be bottom-dwelling, benthic invertebrates, where habitat loss or shifts are occurring, in addition to top predators.[168] The combined

---

[158] *See generally* Melissa A. McKinney et al., *Sea Ice-Associated Diet Change Increases the Levels of Chlorinated and Brominated Contaminants in Polar Bears*, 43 ENVTL. SCI. & TECH. 4334 (2009).

[159] Learmonth et al., *supra* note 153, at 451.

[160] Andrew E. Derocher, *Climate Change: The Prospects for Polar Bears*, 468 NATURE 905, 905 (2010).

[161] *See generally* Juan Patino-Martinez et al., *A Potential Tool to Mitigate the Impacts of Climate Change to the Caribbean Leatherback Sea Turtle*, 18 GLOBAL CHANGE BIOLOGY 401 (2012).

[162] *See generally* Graeme C. Hays et al., *Breeding Periodicity for Male Sea Turtles, Operational Sex Ratios, and Implications in the Face of Climate Change*, 24 CONSERVATION BIOLOGY 1636 (2010).

[163] *See generally* Patino-Martinez et al., *supra* note 161.

[164] *See generally* David A. Pike, *Climate Influences the Global Distribution of Sea Turtle Nesting*, 22 GLOBAL ECOLOGY & BIOGEOGRAPHY 555 (2013).

[165] *See generally* MMPB Fuentes et al., *Management Strategies to Mitigate the Impacts of Climate Change on Sea Turtle's Terrestrial Reproductive Phase*, 17 MITIGATION & ADAPTATION STRATEGIES FOR GLOBAL CHANGE 51 (2012).

[166] *See generally* Georg H. Engelhard et al., *Nine Decades of North Sea Sole and Plaice Distribution*, 68 ICES J. MARINE SCI.: J. DU CONSEIL 1090 (2011); William WL Cheung et al., *Integrating Ecophysiology and Plankton Dynamics into Projected Maximum Fisheries Catch Potential under Climate Change in the Northeast Atlantic*, 68 ICES J. MARINE SCI.: J. DU CONSEIL 1008 (2011).

[167] *See generally* Anne B. Hollowed et al., *Projected Impacts of Climate Change on Marine Fish and Fisheries*, 70 ICES J. MARINE SCI.: J. DU CONSEIL 1023 (2013).

[168] E.A. Fulton, *Interesting Times: Winners, Losers, and System Shifts under Climate Change around Australia*, 68 ICES J. MARINE SCI.: J. DU CONSEIL 1329, 1334 (2011).

impacts of climate change and the long history of human exploitation of fisheries greatly impacts ecosystem function, biodiversity, and resilience to disturbance.[169] The future success of marine fisheries will depend on an integrated approach to managing the negative effects caused by climate change.[170]

B. LAW AND POLICY ASPECTS

Three federal statutes primarily govern the possible legal response to biological impacts from climate change: the Endangered Species Act (ESA), the Marine Mammal Protection Act (MMPA), and the Magnuson-Stevens Act (MSA). However, none of these statutes is well equipped to directly respond to climate change impacts.

The polar bear was the first species to be listed as threatened under the Endangered Species Act exclusively on the basis of climate change impacts. The listing first occurred in 2007, and has been the subject of controversy[171] and extensive litigation since that time. In March 2013, the D.C. Circuit upheld the polar bear's listing under the Endangered Species Act as a threatened species on the basis of the continued destruction of sea ice habitat caused by climate change.[172] The initial listing decision, and the D.C. Circuit's decision to uphold it, provides important confirmation that climate change imperils polar bears and other Arctic species.

Due to the threats from ocean acidification and other stressors, many coral species are being considered for protection or reclassification under the ESA as threatened or endangered species. Two coral species in the Caribbean, elkhorn and staghorn, have been listed as threatened species under the ESA since 2006.[173] In 2013, the National Marine Fisheries Service (NMFS) proposed to reclassify the protection of elkhorn and staghorn coral species from threatened to endangered status.[174] In addition, NMFS has proposed the listing of sixty-six coral species (fifty-nine in the Pacific and seven in the Caribbean) for threatened or endangered status. NMFS anticipates final decisions on these proposed listings in June 2014.[175]

---

[169] See generally Carl Folke et al., *Regime Shifts, Resilience, and Biodiversity in Ecosystem Management*, 35 ANN. REV. ECOLOGY, EVOLUTION & SYSTEMATICS 557 (2004).

[170] See generally R. Ian Perry et al., *Sensitivity of Marine Systems to Climate and Fishing: Concepts, Issues and Management Responses*, 79 J. MARINE SYS. 427 (2010).

[171] See, e.g., Peyton Knight & Amy Ridenour, *Listing the Polar Bear under the Endangered Species Act because of Projected Global Warming Could Harm Bears and Humans Alike*, 566 NAT'L POLICY ANALYSIS 1 (2008), http://www.nationalcenter.org/NPA566.html.

[172] See *In re* Polar Bear Endangered Species Act Listing and Section 4(d) Rule Litigation, 709 F. 3d 1, 9 (D.C. Cir. 2013).

[173] See NOAA Fisheries Service, Threatened Elkhorn and Staghorn Corals (Acropora sp.), http://sero.nmfs. noaa.gov/pr/esa/acropora.htm (last visited Oct. 21, 2013).

[174] See Office of Protected Resources, NOAA Fisheries Service, Corals Proposed for Listing under the ESA (Sept. 19, 2013), http://www.nmfs.noaa.gov/pr/species/invertebrates/corals.htm.

[175] Id.

The MMPA has not been nearly as effective as the ESA in addressing climate change impacts to marine species. Climate change has had an impact on seagrass beds, which in turn has had a negative impact on manatees, which rely on seagrass as a food source.[176] The MMPA focuses on specific human-caused harms to select groups of marine mammals, including the manatee. Habitat protection is not a specified harm included in the MMPA, however.[177]

Climate change has impacted fisheries throughout the United States and the world in many ways. The MSA is the federal statute that addresses fisheries management in the United States. The MSA has generally worked well in helping U.S. fisheries rebound from near collapse from overfishing.[178] Despite widespread awareness of the devastating impacts that climate change has on fisheries, the need to address these impacts at the domestic and international levels is only in the early stages of development. For example, merely half of the regional fisheries management organizations (RFMOs) in the world have incorporated climate change considerations into their regulations.[179] The principal challenge is to develop enhanced regional fisheries management domestically and internationally because climate-change-induced shifts in cells is causing species of fish to relocate to areas in which they have not traditionally been found.

Conclusion

Climate change is impacting marine and coastal resources globally. Ocean temperature has increased due to energy being trapped by excess CO_2 in the atmosphere. Increased temperatures can lead to physical changes in oceans including: thermal expansion, which increases saltwater intrusion into coastal aquifers; ocean stratification; tropical cyclone activity; and atmospheric and ocean circulation. Excess CO_2 and other anthropogenic acids have dissolved into oceans creating more-acidic water. Physical changes in the ocean related to excess CO_2 have complex impacts on marine organisms and ecology.

Biological impacts are not universal, due to geographical and temporal variation. Variations also occur among and within species as well as between individuals. Physical ocean changes affect physiology, phenology, range and distribution, community composition, and species interactions of marine organisms. Physical ocean changes have a combination of direct and indirect impacts on marine species, habitats, and ecosystems.

---

[176] *See* Dr. Katie Tripp, Manatees and the Changing Climate, http://www.savethemanatee.org/news_feature_global_warming.html (last visited Oct. 21, 2013).

[177] Michael Bhargava, *Of Otters and Orcas: Marine Mammals and Legal Regimes in the North Pacific*, 32 Ecology L.Q. 939, 971 (2005); Susan C. Alker, *The Marine Mammal Protection Act: Refocusing the Approach to Conservation*, 44 UCLA L. Rev. 527, 567 (1996).

[178] *See generally* Pew Charitable Trusts and Ocean Conservancy, The Law That's Saving American Fisheries: The Magnuson-Stevens Fishery Conservation and Management Act (2013), http://www.oceanconservancy.org/our-work/fisheries/msa-the-law-thats-saving.pdf.

[179] *See generally* Ocean and Marine Resources in a Changing Climate, *supra* note 8, section 5.

Positive and negative changes in marine resources are being observed throughout the globe. These changes will ultimately result in different compositions and quantities of marine resources for humans.

International and U.S. domestic law responses to the complex reality of climate change have just begun and face many challenges in the years ahead. All of these legal responses—treaties, statutes, and creative common law theories—rely heavily on the growing body of scientific literature addressing climate change impacts on ocean and coastal systems. This chapter has outlined some of the complexities of these scientific realities and how the law must find ways to regulate the impacts of climate change on these fragile and indispensable marine and coastal resources. The chapters that follow explore multiple dimensions of these regulatory challenges and offer some strategies and hope in our efforts to manage these impacts at the domestic and international levels.

I Oceans

2 Curbing CO$_2$ Pollution:

USING EXISTING LAWS TO ADDRESS OCEAN ACIDIFICATION
Miyoko Sakashita

Introduction

The ocean's uptake of carbon dioxide is dramatically changing seawater chemistry and causing the ocean to become more acidic. Ocean acidification poses a significant threat to marine species from plankton to coral reefs. Although the understanding of ocean acidification is growing through an emerging body of science, law and policy are lagging behind. To prevent the worst impacts of ocean acidification, carbon dioxide emissions must be rapidly reduced.

Although no state or federal law explicitly regulates ocean acidification, several existing laws are of sufficient regulatory scope to address ocean acidification. Chief among these is the Clean Water Act (CWA), the nation's strongest law protecting water quality.

The CWA aims to "restore and maintain the chemical, physical and biological integrity of the Nation's waters."[1]

This chapter explores the potential to use this water pollution law to regulate carbon dioxide for its contribution to ocean acidification. It discusses how the Act gives states and the Environmental Protection Agency (EPA) the authority and duty to regulate carbon dioxide emissions causing ocean acidification. Additionally, it will explore the benefits and limitations of using the CWA to protect marine species from the threat of ocean acidification.

I. Ocean Acidification Threatens Ocean Ecosystems

Ocean acidification has been called the evil twin of climate change.[2] It has the same root cause as climate change: carbon dioxide emissions from power plants, cars, and land use changes. The oceans absorb 22 million tons of carbon dioxide each day,[3] which has caused seawater acidity to increase by 30 percent since the beginning of industrial times.[4] If CO_2 continues unabated, the oceans may become 170 percent more acidic by the end of the century.[5]

Ocean chemistry is changing at a rate faster than it has in 300 million years—a period that includes four mass extinctions.[6] Ocean acidification is fundamentally altering our oceans, with profound impacts on marine diversity. Although the biological responses to ocean acidification are varied, an analysis of hundreds of studies found that the impacts on marine life are overwhelmingly negative—with ocean acidification impairing the survival, growth, reproduction, and other functions of species.[7]

Although the worst consequences of ocean acidification are predicted for the future, its impacts are already being observed around the world. For example, in the Great Barrier Reef, corals are growing more sluggishly and, since the 1990s, calcification of

---

[1] 33 U.S.C. § 1251(a) (2012).

[2] Associated Press, *Ocean Acidification Is Climate Change's "Equally Evil Twin"*, HUFFINGTON POST (July 9, 2012), http://www.huffingtonpost.com/2012/07/09/ocean-acidification-reefs-climate-change_n_1658081.html.

[3] Richard A. Feely et al., *Evidence for Upwelling of Corrosive "Acidified" Water onto the Continental Shelf*, 320 SCI. 1490, 1490 (2008).

[4] James C. Orr et al., *Anthropogenic Ocean Acidification over the Twenty-First Century and Its Impact on Calcifying Organisms*, 437 NATURE 681, 681 (2005).

[5] INT'L GEOSPHERE-BIOSPHERE PROGRAMME, INTERGOVERNMENTAL OCEANOGRAPHIC COMM'N & SCIENTIFIC COMM. ON OCEANIC RESEARCH, OCEAN ACIDIFICATION SUMMARY FOR POLICYMAKERS—THIRD SYMPOSIUM ON THE OCEAN IN A HIGH-CO_2 WORLD 5 (2013), *available at* http://www.igbp.net/download/18.30566fc6142425d6c91140a/1385975160621/OA_spm2-FULL-lorez.pdf.

[6] Bärbel Hönisch et al., *The Geological Record of Ocean Acidification*, 335 SCI. 1058, 1058 (2012).

[7] Kristy J. Kroeker et al., *Impacts of Ocean Acidification on Marine Organisms: Quantifying Sensitivities and Interaction with Warming*, 19 GLOBAL CHANGE BIOLOGY 1884, 1884–96 (2013).

massive porites has declined by 14 percent.[8] In the Pacific Northwest, shellfish hatcheries have witnessed massive die-offs of oyster larvae from ocean acidification that has caused losses of up to 80 percent of production.[9] In the Southern Ocean, plankton that are the base of the marine food web are also growing weaker, thinner shells due to acidification.[10] These are just the early warning signs that signal some of the major shifts that marine ecosystems will experience due to ocean acidification.

Ocean acidification impairs the ability of marine animals to build the shells and skeletons they need to survive. Carbon dioxide strips seawater of the chemicals that animals need for shellbuilding, or calcification. In studies, corals, coralline algae, plankton, mollusks, and other shellfish exposed to future levels of ocean acidification have all experienced problems.[11]

Even animals that do not have shells are at risk because ocean acidification disrupts other biological functions. Changes in the ocean's carbon dioxide concentration result in accumulation of carbon dioxide in the tissues and fluids of fish and other marine animals, called hypercapnia, and increased acidity in the body fluids, called acidosis.[12] These impacts can cause a variety of problems for marine animals, including difficulties with acid-base regulation, calcification, growth, respiration, energy turnover, predation response, and mode of metabolism. Studies have shown adverse impacts in squid and

---

[8] Glenn De'ath et al., *Declining Coral Calcification on the Great Barrier Reef,* 323 SCI. 116, 116 (2009).

[9] Alan Barton et al., *The Pacific Oyster, Crassostrea Gigas, Shows Negative Correlation to Naturally Elevated Carbon Dioxide Levels: Implications for Near-Term Ocean Acidification Effects,* 57 LIMNOLOGY & OCEANOGRAPHY 698, 698 (2012); WASH. STATE BLUE RIBBON PANEL ON OCEAN ACIDIFICATION, OCEAN ACIDIFICATION: FROM KNOWLEDGE TO ACTION, WASHINGTON STATE'S STRATEGIC RESPONSE 3–4 (2012); Craig Welch, *Sea Change,* SEATTLE TIMES (Sept. 12, 2013), http://apps.seattletimes.com/reports/sea-change/2013/sep/11/pacific-ocean-perilous-turn-overview/.

[10] Andrew D. Moy et al., *Reduced Calcification in Modern Southern Ocean Planktonic Foraminifera,* 2 NATURE GEOSCI. 276, 276 (2009).

[11] Barton et al., *supra* note 9; Orr et al., *supra* note 4; Ulf Riebesell et al., *Reduced Calcification of Marine Plankton in Response to Increased Atmospheric CO2,* 407 NATURE 364, 364 (2000); Stephanie C. Talmage & Christopher J. Gobler, *Effects of Elevated Temperature and Carbon Dioxide on the Growth and Survival of Larvae and Juveniles of Three Species of Northwest Atlantic Bivalves,* 6 PLoS ONE e26941, e26941 (2011); Stephanie C. Talmage & Christopher J. Gobler, *The Effects of Elevated Carbon Dioxide Concentrations on the Metamorphosis, Size, and Survival of Larval Hard Clams (Mercenaria Mercenaria), Bay Scallops (Argopecten Irradians), and Eastern Oysters (Crassostrea Virginica),* 54 LIMNOLOGY & OCEANOGRAPHY 2072, 2072 (2009); Ilsa B. Kuffner et al., *Decreased Abundance of Crustose Coralline Algae due to Ocean Acidification,* 1 NATURE GEOSCI. 114, 114 (2008). *See generally* Joan A. Kleypas & Kimberly K. Yates, *Coral Reefs and Ocean Acidification,* 22 OCEANOGRAPHY 108 (2009); Joan A. Kleypas et al., *Impacts of Ocean Acidification on Coral Reefs and Other Marine Calcifiers: A Guide for Future Research* (2006).

[12] Royal Society, OCEAN ACIDIFICATION DUE TO INCREASING ATMOSPHERIC CARBON DIOXIDE 19 (2005); Hans Pörtner, Martina Langenbuch & Anke Reipschlager, *Biological Impact of Elevated Ocean CO2 Concentrations: Lessons from Animal Physiology and Earth History,* J. OCEANOGRAPHY 705, 705 (2004); Atsushi Ishimatsu et al., *Effects of CO2 on Marine Fish: Larvae and Adults,* J. OCEANOGRAPHY 731, 738 (2004).

fish, among other animals.[13] For example, when exposed to acidification, orange clown-fish suffer a type of brain malfunction that interferes with their homing abilities and makes them five-to-nine times more likely to swim toward a predator.[14] Scientists are also learning about other impacts of acidification such as the decreasing noise absorption of seawater that may alter the acoustic environment for marine life,[15] and increasing toxicity of harmful algal blooms that may heighten the risk of fish kills, marine mammal illness, and even paralytic shellfish poisoning in humans.[16]

Ocean acidification has the potential to massively disrupt ecosystems and food chains. For example, predictions include shifts in species' ranges, changes in food availability, and population declines. Changes in ocean chemistry are fundamentally altering the ocean ecosystem, and ocean acidification is irreversible within a reasonable time frame. Although the impacts will be varied depending on the region and ecosystem, our marine waters are already changing and will be tremendously altered in the future.

II. Fitting Ocean Acidification into the Clean Water Act Framework

The Clean Water Act (CWA) has a broad mandate to protect water quality. Efforts are underway to use the framework of this water pollution law to address ocean acidification.

Congress enacted the CWA with the express purpose of "restor[ing] and maintain[ing] the chemical, physical, and biological integrity of the Nation's waters."[17] The goals of the CWA are to guarantee "water quality which provides for the protection and propagation of fish, shellfish, and wildlife and provides for recreation" and to promptly eliminate water pollution.[18]

Although best known for the regulatory scheme of requiring water pollution permits, there is another provision of the CWA that aims to address pollution that originates from various sources or when efforts to control pollution have proven inadequate.

---

[13] *See generally* Ishimatsu et al., *supra* note 12; Pörtner et al., *supra* note 12; Rui Rosa & Brad A. Seibel, *Synergistic Effects of Climate-Related Variables Suggest Future Physiological Impairment in a Top Oceanic Predator*, 105 Proc. Nat'l Acad. Sci. 20776, 20776 (2008).

[14] Maud C.O. Ferrari et al., *Intrageneric Variation in Antipredator Responses of Coral Reef Fishes Affected by Ocean Acidification: Implications for Climate Change Projections on Marine Communities*, 17 Global Change Biology 2980, 2985 (2011); Philip L. Munday et al., *Ocean Acidification Impairs Olfactory Discrimination and Homing Ability of a Marine Fish*, 106 Proc. Nat. Acad. Sci. 1848, 1850 (2009); Stephen D. Simpson et al., *Ocean Acidification Erodes Crucial Auditory Behaviour in a Marine Fish*, 7 Biology Letters 917, 917 (2011).

[15] Keith C. Hester et al., *Unanticipated Consequences of Ocean Acidification: A Noisier Ocean at Lower pH*, 35 Geophysical Res. Letters L19601, L19601 (2008).

[16] Avery O. Tatters et al., *High CO_2 and Silicate Limitation Synergistically Increase the Toxicity of Pseudo-Nitzschia Fraudulenta*, 7 PLoS One e32116, e32116 (2012).

[17] 33 U.S.C. § 1251(a) (2012).

[18] *Id.*

This provision has been used to combat atmospheric sources of water pollution such as mercury, polychlorinated biphenyls (PCBs), and acid rain—and now ocean acidification.

The CWA requires states to establish water quality standards that set out water quality goals for each water body; in turn, these standards serve as a basis for regulation of water pollution.[19] For example, all states have adopted standards for seawater acidity (pH) and standards to protect aquatic life. These standards and others are relevant to and can be used to gauge the extent that ocean acidification is impairing water quality. Moreover, in 2013, EPA convened a technical workgroup to examine whether additional standards should be adopted to measure ocean acidification.[20]

Based on these standards, section 303(d) of the CWA requires states to establish a list of impaired water bodies within their boundaries for which existing pollution controls "are not stringent enough to implement any water quality standard applicable to such waters."[21] Every two years states must assess water bodies and develop a list of waters not meeting water quality standards—also known as impaired waters.[22] This is a public process through which a state must solicit and examine all readily available data and information that could help in making a water quality determination.[23] Once a state develops its impaired waters list, EPA provides oversight and must either approve or disapprove the impaired waters list and add any waters that should be included.[24] For over a decade, EPA has guided states to "list all waters impaired either entirely or partially due to pollutants from atmospheric deposition."[25] EPA now explicitly recommends that states identify waters impaired by ocean acidification on its 303(d) lists and conduct water quality assessments on ocean acidification.

In 2010, EPA authorized the CWA section 303(d) as a mechanism to address ocean acidification. This outcome was the result of legal advocacy. In 2009, an environmental organization filed a lawsuit challenging EPA's approval of Washington State's impaired waters list for failing to identify waters impaired by ocean acidification.[26] Under a settlement agreement, EPA solicited public comment about ocean acidification and the 303(d) program and agreed to make a determination about how to proceed with its section 303(d) program in light of ocean acidification. In its decision

---

[19] 33 U.S.C. § 1313(a)–(c) (2000); 40 C.F.R. § 130.3 (2001).

[20] Letter from Nancy Stoner, Acting Adm'r, Envtl. Prot. Agency, to Miyoko Sakashita, Ctr. for Biological Diversity (May 17, 2013) (on file with author).

[21] 33 U.S.C. § 1313(d) (2012).

[22] 40 C.F.R. § 130.7(d) (2014).

[23] 40 C.F.R. § 130.7(b)(5) (2014). *See also* Sierra Club v. Leavitt, 488 F.3d 904 (11th Cir. 2007).

[24] 33 U.S.C. § 1313(d)(2) (2012); 40 C.F.R. § 130.7(d)(2) (2014).

[25] Envtl. Prot. Agency, Frequently Asked Questions about Atmospheric Deposition: A Handbook for Watershed Managers 65 (2001).

[26] *Center for Biological Diversity v. EPA*, Case no. 2:09-cv-00670-JCC (W.D. Wash. filed May 14, 2009).

memorandum, EPA confirmed that the CWA has the breadth to address ocean acidification:

> EPA has concluded that States should list waters not meeting water quality standards, including marine pH [water quality criteria], on their 2012 303(d) lists, and should also solicit existing and readily available information on [ocean acidification] using the current 303(d) listing program framework.[27]

Once a water body is listed as impaired pursuant to CWA section 303(d), the state and EPA have the authority and duty to control pollutants from all sources that are causing the impairment. Specifically, they must establish total maximum daily loads of pollutants that a water body can receive and still attain water quality standards.[28] States then implement the maximum loads by incorporating them into the state's water quality management plan and controlling pollution from point sources and nonpoint sources.[29] The goal of section 303(d) is to ensure that our nation's waters attain water quality standards whatever the source of pollution.

There is a viable path for using the 303(d) program to address ocean acidification: first by listing waters impaired by ocean acidification, and then by establishing total maximum daily loads for carbon dioxide that causes such impairment. These maximum loads can be created and implemented on a regional or national scale. Thus, there could be nationwide targets for carbon dioxide emissions that are allocated among all significant sources toward the goal of preventing harmful ocean acidification. Although the CWA provides a framework for addressing ocean acidification complete with EPA's approval, there has been little progress in using the law to tackle ocean acidification.

A. A CASE STUDY IN THE PACIFIC NORTHWEST

Even on the front lines of ocean acidification where visible impacts of it are already occurring, EPA has declined to identify any waters as impaired. Since 2005, oysters have failed to reproduce in Willapa Bay in the Pacific Northwest.[30] A few years later, shellfish hatcheries in Washington and Oregon witnessed massive die-offs of oyster larvae—nearly causing the industry to collapse and causing panic in the nation's top oyster-producing region.[31] At first, it was a mystery.

---

[27] Memorandum from Denise Keehner, Dir., Office of Wetlands, Oceans & Watersheds, Envtl. Prot. Agency, to Water Div. Dirs., Regions 1–10 (Nov. 15, 2010), http://water.epa.gov/lawsregs/lawsguidance/cwa/tmdl/upload/oa_memo_nov2010.pdf.

[28] 33 U.S.C. § 1313(d) (2012).

[29] 33 U.S.C. § 1313(e) (2012); 40 C.F.R. §§ 130.6, 130.7(d)(2) (2014).

[30] WASH. STATE BLUE RIBBON PANEL ON OCEAN ACIDIFICATION, *supra* note 9.

[31] *Id.*

Around the same time, scientists reported that waters affected by ocean acidification were upwelling along the entire West Coast of the United States, exposing marine life to corrosive conditions.[32] Tidepool monitoring on the northwestern tip of Washington documented remarkable changes in acidity with pH declining more than 0.4 units—a 60 percent increase in acidity—between 2000 and 2008.[33] This corresponded with ecosystem shifts in the tidepools: animals without shells replaced calcifying organisms during periods of increased acidity.[34] Meanwhile, surveys of Puget Sound recorded corrosive waters every year since 2008, and about 25 percent of the change could be attributed to anthropogenic carbon dioxide.[35] In 2012, the oyster die-offs were definitively linked to ocean acidification.[36]

The Pacific Northwest has found itself at the epicenter of the ocean acidification crisis. This crisis has revealed that this region is especially vulnerable to the impacts of ocean acidification. Adding carbon dioxide to the region's upwelling waters, in which carbon-dioxide-rich waters from the deep ocean are drawn up to the surface, results in a sort of hyper-acidification.[37] Surveys of coastal waters showed carbon dioxide levels that were not expected until the end of the century.[38] The area has become an early warning sign for changes that are coming to all oceans worldwide.

In response, Washington governor Christine Gregoire convened a top-notch Blue Ribbon Panel to document the latest scientific information on ocean acidification and to recommend policy and research actions to respond to acidification and its impact on the shellfish industry. The Panel's Report identified forty-two actions in the areas of (1) reducing carbon dioxide emissions, (2) reducing land-based contributions to acidification, (3) increasing adaptation and remediation abilities, (4) monitoring and research of the causes and effects of ocean acidification, and (5) educating the public and decision-makers about the problem.[39] Among the actions, the panel recommended some steps under the CWA, including evaluating ocean acidification water quality criteria. In 2012, Governor Gregoire issued an executive order advancing the Blue Ribbon Panel's policy recommendations on ocean acidification.[40] And in 2013, the state legislature passed a bill creating the Marine Resources Advisory Council to assist in implementing the Panel's recommendations.[41]

---

[32] Feely et al., *supra* note 3.

[33] J. Timothy Wootton et al., *Dynamic Patterns and Ecological Impacts of Declining Ocean pH in a High-Resolution Multi-Year Dataset*, 105 Proc. Nat'l Acad. Sci. 18848, 18849 (2008).

[34] *Id.*

[35] Stephanie Moore et al., Puget Sound Marine Waters: 2011 Overview 36–39 (2011); Richard A. Feely et al., *The Combined Effects of Ocean Acidification, Mixing, and Respiration on pH and Carbonate Saturation in an Urbanized Estuary*, 88 Estuarine, Coastal & Shelf Sci. 442, 442 (2010).

[36] Barton et al., *supra* note 9.

[37] *Id.*

[38] *Id.*

[39] Wash. State Blue Ribbon Panel, *supra* note 9.

[40] Wash. Exec. Order No. 12-07 (2012).

[41] S. 5603, 63rd Leg., Reg. Sess. § 4 (Wash. 2013).

Alongside Washington's leadership on ocean acidification, the region was also poised to test the CWA framework for regulating acidification. The CWA mandates that waters failing to attain water quality standards should be identified as impaired.[42] Washington's standards require that waters "[m]ust support extraordinary quality…clam, oyster, and mussel rearing and spawning," and marine pH must have less than 0.2 units of variation.[43] Oregon's standards require that waters "support aquatic species without detrimental changes in the resident biological communities" and "be free from dissolved gasses, such as carbon dioxide…, in sufficient quantities…to be deleterious to fish or other aquatic life."[44] Studies show that acidified seawater from ocean intakes has killed billons of oyster larvae in Washington and Oregon hatcheries.[45] Surveys further report that during certain seasons surface waters are corrosive to marine life along the entire Pacific Coast.[46] Finally, monitoring recorded that coastal pH declined in excess of 0.4 units at the northwestern tip of the Olympic Peninsula in Washington State.[47] Do these impacts violate water quality standards and therefore warrant identification as impaired waters?

This is the issue to be resolved in *Center for Biological Diversity v. EPA*.[48] In that case, an environmental organization challenged EPA's approval of Oregon and Washington's 2010 impaired waters lists that omitted any waters impaired by ocean acidification.

B. CONSTRAINTS TO CLEAN WATER ACT IMPLEMENTATION

There are, however, obstacles to implementing the CWA. Chief among them is the lack of political will to do anything to stop ocean acidification. While the technical barriers to using the CWA to address ocean acidification are readily overcome, removing the apathy that is preventing EPA and the states from responding will be the crux of the challenge.

The first constraint that water quality managers often raise is that there is a paucity of long-term monitoring data, which precludes regulators from making effective water quality determinations for ocean acidification. In its 2010 memo, EPA identified this regulatory challenge for states by emphasizing that in many places information may not be available for impaired waters listings: "EPA recognizes that information is absent or limited for [ocean acidification] parameters and impacts at this point in time, therefore, listings for [ocean acidification] may be absent or limited in many states."[49] Indeed,

---

[42] 33 U.S.C. § 1313(d) (2012).

[43] WASH. ADMIN. CODE §§ 173-201A-210(1)(a)(i), 210(1)(f) (2011).

[44] OR. ADMIN. R. 340-041-0011, -0031 (2003).

[45] Barton et al., *supra* note 9.

[46] Feely et al., *supra* note 3; Feely et al., *supra* note 35.

[47] Wootton et al., *supra* note 33.

[48] Ctr. for Biological Diversity v. Envtl. Prot. Agency, Case No. 13-1866 (W.D. Wash. filed Oct. 2013).

[49] Memorandum from Denise Keehner, *supra* note 27, at 4.

long-term monitoring of ocean acidification is available only in a few areas such as Washington State. However, the body of scientific information on ocean acidification is growing by leaps and bounds, and there are a number of monitoring stations coming online.[50] Ultimately, the data gaps will be closed and a full picture of how ocean acidification is impacting water quality will emerge.

Second, EPA and states lack clear methods for evaluating ocean acidification against water quality standards. States have been reluctant to evaluate ocean acidification data—and therefore identify impaired waters—without guidance from EPA. State water quality managers have not embraced their role in evaluating ocean acidification as part of their biennial water quality assessments. For example, in response to comments on their draft 2010 impaired waters lists, several states indicated that they anticipated EPA direction on the issue of ocean acidification. There are well-established methods for measuring ocean acidification and its impacts.[51] EPA can play a vital role in translating these methods for state water quality agencies to make determinations for their impaired waters lists. EPA committed to publishing such guidance in 2010:

> EPA will provide additional 303(d) guidance to the States...This future [ocean acidification] guidance may be in the form of stand-alone [ocean acidification integrated report] guidance, or as part of EPA's routine, biennial [integrated report] update.[52]

Yet, to date EPA has not issued the promised document. Until it does, states will likely continue to shun their duties to meaningfully examine ocean acidification.

Third, states lack the impetus to regulate this issue. For example, Washington State considers the 303(d) program the wrong tool to address ocean acidification.[53] This problem stems from a lack of political will. Until recently, ocean acidification was not even on the radar screen for water quality managers. Even though it is clearly a threat to water quality, there is continuing reluctance by policymakers and government officials to make

---

[50] Jean-Pierre Gattuso & Lina Hansson, *Ocean Acidification: Background and History*, in OCEAN ACIDIFICATION 1, 9–13 (2011); Juliet Eilperin, *Global Ocean Acidification Monitoring Network to Launch at Rio Summit*, WASH. POST, June 16, 2012, *available at* http://www.washingtonpost.com/national/health-science/global-ocean-acidification-monitoring-network-to-launch-at-rio-summit/2012/06/16/gJQAY9bFiV_story.html.

[51] *See, e.g.*, EUR. COMM'N, GUIDE TO BEST PRACTICES FOR OCEAN ACIDIFICATION RESEARCH AND DATA REPORTING (Ulf Riebesell et al. eds., 2010); NAT'L RESEARCH COUNCIL, OCEAN ACIDIFICATION: A NATIONAL STRATEGY TO MEET THE CHALLENGES OF A CHANGING OCEAN (2010); PICES SPECIAL PUBL'N 3, GUIDE TO BEST PRACTICES FOR OCEAN CO2 MEASUREMENTS (Andrew G. Dickson et al. eds., 2007).

[52] Memorandum from Denise Keehner, *supra* note 27.

[53] Sandy Howard, *Polluted Waters Listings Will Not Fix the Problem of Declining pH on Marine Waters*, ECOCONNECT (June 16, 2011), http://ecologywa.blogspot.com/2011/06/polluted-waters-listings-will-not-fix.html.

the deep cuts needed in carbon dioxide emissions. Admittedly, it is not easy to control all the types of pollution that are affecting water quality, from runoff that is causing dead zones to mercury emissions that result in fish consumption advisories across the country. Although incredibly successful, the CWA has fallen short of its drafters' ambitious goals to end water pollution because it has been plagued with delays and political constraints. Yet, rather than providing an excuse, the CWA's regulatory shortfalls should be a call to action: a call for robust use of this powerful water pollution law.

These three problems can be overcome to attain this goal. Section 303(d) of the CWA has a long history of being ignored. The courts, however, have played a major role in ensuring accountability. For example, courts have applied action-forcing mechanisms to section 303(d), thereby compelling EPA to act when states do not. In response to states' failure to submit any impaired waters lists and maximum loads for Lake Michigan, in *Scott v. City of Hammond,* the Seventh Circuit determined that the states' inaction should be interpreted as a constructive submission of no lists or maximum loads, thus triggering EPA's duty to approve or disapprove and establish them itself.[54] The Court of Appeals concluded that it was "unlikely that an important aspect of the federal scheme of water pollution control could be frustrated by the refusal of states to act."[55] The constructive submission doctrine has repeatedly compelled EPA action. For example, the Ninth Circuit upheld an injunction forcing EPA to develop maximum loads when Alaska had failed to submit them for over a decade.[56] But section 303(d) is not a silver bullet for water pollution control because EPA allows impaired waters to languish without total daily maximum loads for up to thirteen years.

Reluctance by states and EPA to embrace the CWA to address ocean acidification should not undermine the power of this water pollution law. There are many benefits to using the CWA, which has successfully fought water pollution for forty years. In passing the nation's strongest water protection law, Congress understood that new forms of water pollution would arise, and used broad and flexible language to enable the Act to respond to such future challenges. Not long ago, the same criticism was made of the Clean Air Act. Yet in *Massachusetts v. EPA,* the Supreme Court affirmed that greenhouse gases could be regulated under the Clean Air Act, leading to the only rules that the United States has adopted to curb greenhouse gases.[57]

It is not a question of if, but when the first waters will be listed as impaired due to ocean acidification. And when they are identified, a duty under the CWA will be triggered for states and EPA to take steps to reduce the pollution that is causing the impairment.

---

[54] Scott v. City of Hammond, 741 F.2d 992, 996 (7th Cir. 1984).

[55] *Id.* at 997.

[56] Alaska Ctr. for the Env't v. Browner, 20 F.3d 981 (9th Cir. 1994).

[57] Massachusetts v. EPA, 549 U.S. 497 (2007).

III. Benefits of Using the Clean Water Act to Address Ocean Acidification

Perhaps the biggest question is to what extent the CWA can do anything about ocean acidification or the carbon dioxide pollution that is causing it. There are many ways in which the Clean Water Act could be leveraged against ocean acidification. These regulatory responses range from simple to complex.

First, there are benefits from the listing process alone, including monitoring and raising awareness of ocean acidification. Second, identification of impaired waters triggers other tools in the CWA that can be brought to bear on the problem of ocean acidification. Listing will assist in controlling local stressors, such as runoff, that amplify acidification, and—most important—it can result in needed reductions in carbon dioxide emissions that cause acidification.

A. BENEFITS FROM THE IMPAIRED WATERS LISTING PROCESS

Although the Clean Water Act does not confer regulatory benefits on impaired waters until they are listed, the process itself confers significant non-regulatory benefits. The process of nominating waters for impaired listing for ocean acidification, efforts to adopt ocean acidification water quality standards, and accompanying litigation has helped raise awareness of ocean acidification. The process resulted in EPA action and significant media coverage, and mobilized public participation, which flooded states and EPA with tens of thousands of comments from the public urging action to prevent ocean acidification. Even Congress has taken an interest, urging in a letter to EPA signed by forty-four members of Congress that EPA boldly use the CWA to address ocean acidification and publish guidance.[58]

Listing also provides a mechanism for monitoring and assessment of ocean acidification, which will help identify hot spots as well as potential refuges. Managing areas for ocean acidification preparedness can flow from gaining a clear picture of how ocean acidification is affecting our coasts. States are now receiving and evaluating during their water quality assessments information on ocean acidification, and EPA has recommended that they specifically solicit data on ocean acidification.[59] This process can also serve as an impetus for new coastal monitoring programs and upgrading coastal pH monitoring to more accurately measure ocean acidification.

Use of the impaired water process elevates the issue of ocean acidification so that it will be a priority for water quality management for EPA and the coastal states. This can help direct resources and funding to address acidification. Now that pressure has been

---

[58] Letter from Lois Capps et al., Members of Congress, to Lisa Jackson, Adm'r, Envtl. Prot. Agency (May 21, 2010) (on file with author).

[59] Memorandum from Denise Keehner, *supra* note 27.

put on the EPA to use the CWA to address ocean acidification, the agency has become an important cooperating agency with states on this issue.

B. REGULATING OCEAN ACIDIFICATION

For waters that are impaired there are important regulatory consequences that can mitigate the effects and reduce carbon dioxide pollution that causes ocean acidification. First, there is a duty to establish a total maximum daily load—this is the amount of a pollutant that can be added to a water body each day without violating water quality standards.[60] Second, regulations prohibit new discharges that may contribute to water quality violations of impaired waters.[61] Importantly, the CWA is a science-based statute and, therefore, all controls must be based on science.[62] This mandate not only requires the government to evaluate the emerging science on ocean acidification, but it also provides a strong basis for regulation founded on science.

According to the United States Court of Appeals for the Ninth Circuit, "[a maximum load] defines the specified maximum amount of a pollutant which can be discharged or 'loaded' into the water at issue from all combined sources."[63] They act "as a link in an implementation chain" that seeks to attain water quality goals through all Clean Water Act Programs from permits to nonpoint-source pollution plans.[64] As a part of the process, the sources of pollution are identified, and then each source is allocated a proportion of the allowable load.[65] The goal of setting maximum load is for a state to incorporate it into an implementation plan.[66]

The implementation of maximum loads is flexible and can take a number of forms. Point sources are required to meet loads through discharge permits, and nonpoint sources can be controlled through a variety of state, regional, or national programs. Some of these are regulatory, volunteer, or incentive based. Moreover, grants and other assistance are available to reduce pollution and implement maximum loads.[67]

---

[60] 33 U.S.C. § 1313(d)(1) (2012).

[61] 40 C.F.R. § 122.4(i) (2014).

[62] *See, e.g.*, 33 U.S.C. § 1314(a)(1) (2012) (requiring the latest scientific knowledge in setting national water quality criteria); 33 U.S.C. § 1313(d)(1)(c) (2012) (establishing that total maximum daily loads (TMDLs) should be set at levels necessary to meet water quality standards with a margin of safety); Upper Blackstone Water Pollution Abatement Dist. v. EPA, 690 F.3d 9 (1st Cir. 2012), *cert. denied* (upholding effluent limitations in a sewage discharge permit because extensive scientific record established the limits were necessary to meet water quality standards).

[63] Dioxin/Organochlorine Ctr. v. Clarke, 57 F.3d 1517, 1520 (9th Cir. 1995).

[64] Pronsolino v. Nastri, 291 F.3d 1123, 1129 (9th Cir. 2002).

[65] 33 U.S.C. § 1313(d) (2012).

[66] 33 U.S.C. § 1313(d)(2), (e) (2012).

[67] 33 U.S.C. § 1329 (2012).

Commentators have noted that this approach can build resilience to ocean acidification in local ecosystems and buy time to cut carbon dioxide emissions.[68] Local seawater acidity can be exacerbated by nutrient runoff and other pollutants, so reducing or mitigating those land-based contributions to acidification can be effective. Section 303(d) and other programs under the CWA can reduce such pollution by mandating prevention of storm-water surges, coastal and riparian vegetation buffers, wetland restoration, and improved treatment of runoff.[69] Moreover, effluent limitations could assist in preparedness for or adaptation to ocean acidification; for example, "if a coral reef ecosystem experiencing ocean acidification is also receiving low-pH discharges from point sources, reducing those point source impacts could reduce the overall stresses to the reefs."[70]

The CWA has a role beyond mitigating local stressors that amplify the impacts of ocean acidification in that it can also assist in reducing carbon dioxide pollution. There are three central tenets for an ocean acidification total maximum daily load rule: (1) it should be national or regional, (2) it should complement existing regulation of carbon dioxide under the Clean Air Act and state laws, and (3) it should be consistent with reaching atmospheric carbon dioxide goals that are needed to prevent the worst impacts of ocean acidification.

First, a national problem requires a national solution; thus national or regional total maximum daily loads would be best for ocean acidification. The sources of ocean acidification are not confined to a single state, but this is not unique for water pollution. The CWA has already grappled with downstream and cross-border pollution.[71] Indeed, EPA has clear authority to require a discharge permit to comply with a downstream state's water quality standards.[72]

Mercury pollution illustrates how the CWA can address ocean acidification. Like carbon dioxide pollution, mercury pollution originates from global sources, such as air emissions from coal-fired power plants. Three-quarters of the mercury deposited in U.S. waters originates from international sources, excluding Canada; nonetheless there is a well-established program under the CWA for atmospheric mercury.[73] Several states have fish consumption advisories based on concerns about elevated mercury levels in

---

[68] *See, e.g.*, Ryan P. Kelly et al., *Mitigating Local Causes of Ocean Acidification with Existing Laws*, 332 Sci. 1036 (2011).

[69] *Id.*

[70] Robin K. Craig, *Climate Change Comes to the Clean Water Act: Now What?*, 1 Wash & Lee J. Energy, Climate & Env't 9, 31 (2010).

[71] *See, e.g.*, City of Milwaukee v. Illinois, 451 U.S. 304 (1981) (concerning Milwaukee's battle with Illinois over sewage discharges into Lake Michigan); Gulf Restoration Network v. Jackson, No. 12-677, 2013 U.S. Dist. LEXIS 134811 (E.D. La. Sept. 20, 2013) (concerning EPA authority to set water quality standards for multiple states whose runoff contributes to the Gulf of Mexico dead zone).

[72] *See* Arkansas v. Oklahoma, 503 U.S. 91 (1992).

[73] Memorandum from Craig Hooks, Dir., Office of Wetlands, Oceans & Watersheds, Envtl. Prot. Agency, to Regions 1–X Water Div. Dirs. 3 (Mar. 8, 2007), http://water.epa.gov/lawsregs/lawsguidance/cwa/tmdl/upload/2007_03_08_tmdl_mercury5m_Mercury5m.pdf.

fish, and about 8,500 waterbodies are impaired by mercury.[74] To address the obstacle of cross-border pollution, several states collaborated on a regional total maximum daily load program to address mercury pollution.[75]

EPA has authority to take the lead in establishing maximum loads for problems that involve impaired waters in more than one state.[76] And there can be cooperative total maximum daily loads among states when the sources are widespread. Even absent a national or regional approach, however, individual state programs could be an important step toward reducing a portion of carbon dioxide emissions. The annual carbon dioxide emissions from California and Texas both rank within the top twenty globally among top greenhouse gas emitting countries.

Second, carbon dioxide targets and allocations can complement targets and requirements under the Clean Air Act, and state or local programs for greenhouse gas reductions. Notably, the CWA section 303(d) is intended to step in where other sorts of pollution control programs have proven insufficient to address the water quality problem. Maximum loads for mercury and acid rain, for example, include monitoring and actions that boost efforts under the Clean Air Act.

Undoubtedly, newly developed rules to curb carbon dioxide emissions under the Clean Air Act will be important in preventing ocean acidification. Nevertheless, the proposed reductions are far from sufficient to stop the harmful impacts of ocean acidification. For example, to date EPA has proposed only one rule under new source pollution standards, which would reduce emissions from new power plants—but admittedly not enough because "the EPA projects that this proposed rule will result in negligible CO_2 emission changes."[77] Despite the great potential of Clean Air Act regulations to prevent ocean acidification, EPA has instead proposed weak rules. Therefore, the CWA and other environmental laws are essential to fill in the gaps. These flagship environmental laws can work together to create a comprehensive strategy to reduce carbon dioxide to levels that will protect our oceans' biological diversity from the harmful impacts of ocean acidification.

Third, a maximum load should be consistent with reaching atmospheric carbon dioxide levels that will prevent the worst impacts of ocean acidification. Scientists tell us that carbon dioxide emissions will need to be stabilized below current levels at 350 ppm to avoid perilous biological consequences of ocean acidification.[78] The best-available science

---

[74] *Id.*

[75] Northeast Regional Mercury TMDL, NEW ENGLAND INTERSTATE WATER POLLUTION CONTROL COMM'N, (2007), http://www.neiwpcc.org/mercury/MercuryTMDL.asp (describing regional cleanup plan among CT, ME, MA, NH, NY, RI, and VT to reduce mercury pollution in water).

[76] *See, e.g.,* Scott v. City of Hammond, 530 F. Supp. 288 (N.D. Ill. 1981), *aff'd in part, rev'd in part,* 741 F.2d 992 (7th Cir. 1984).

[77] Standards of Performance for Greenhouse Gas Emissions from New Stationary Sources: Electric Utility Generating Units, EPA-HQ-OAR-2013-0495, at 344 (proposed Sept. 20, 2013) (codified at 40 C.F.R. pt. 60).

[78] Long Cao & Ken Caldeira, *Atmospheric CO2 Stabilization and Ocean Acidification*, 35 GEOPHYSICAL RES. LETTERS 1, 1 (2008); James Hansen et al., *Target Atmospheric CO2: Where Should Humanity Aim?*, 2 OPEN ATMOSPHERIC SCI. J. 217, 217 (2008).

indicates that the atmospheric CO_2 concentration must be reduced to at most 350 ppm, and perhaps much lower (300–325 ppm CO_2), to protect corals from the synergistic threats of ocean warming, ocean acidification, and other impacts.[79]

Developing a total maximum daily load and implementing it for carbon dioxide pollution will be complex, and like other maximum loads, it will take many years. Nevertheless, the breadth of the law provides flexibility to develop a science-based, feasible approach. It is quite possible that as the science evolves and the economic impacts of ocean acidification are felt, EPA and states will find the motivation to fully implement this water pollution law and boldly use their authority to prevent acidification.

Conclusion

The benefits of using the Clean Water Act as an approach to addressing ocean acidification are threefold. Most important, the law is already on the books, so time-consuming new legislation to control ocean acidification will not need to be drafted. Second, federal and state agencies already have the expertise and structure in place to implement the law. The CWA has been successfully applied to traditional and emerging pollution problems for four decades. Third, the CWA provides a science-based framework for the regulation of carbon dioxide. Although carbon dioxide has only recently been recognized as a form of water pollution, the CWA, properly applied, is an essential tool in preventing ocean acidification.

---

[79] Cao & Caldeira, *supra* note 78; Hansen et al., *supra* note 78. *See also* Simon D. Donner, *Coping with Commitment: Projected Thermal Stress on Coral Reefs under Different Future Scenarios*, 4 PLoS ONE e5712 (2009); Katharina E. Fabricius et al., *Losers and Winners in Coral Reefs Acclimatized to Elevated Carbon Dioxide Concentration*, 1 NATURE CLIMATE CHANGE 165 (2011); Katja Frieler et al., *Limiting Global Warming to 2°C Is Unlikely to Save Most Coral Reefs*, 3 NATURE CLIMATE CHANGE 165 (2012); Ove Hoegh-Guldberg et al., *Coral Reefs under Rapid Climate Change and Ocean Acidification*, 318 SCI. 1737 (2007); U.N. ENV'T PROGRAMME, CLIMATE CHANGE SCI. COMPENDIUM 2009 (Catherine McMullen & Jason Jabbour eds., 2009); J.E.N. Veron et al., *The Coral Reef Crisis: The Critical Importance of <350ppm CO2*, 58 MARINE POLLUTION BULL. 1428 (2009).

3 Using the Clean Air Act to Address Ocean Acidification

Dr. Margaret E. Peloso*

---

* The author would like to thank Deborah Raichelson and Jordan Rodriguez for their assistance in preparing this chapter. The author is also grateful to Randy Abate and his research assistants for their thoughtful edits, which have improved the quality of this chapter.

Introduction

Ocean acidification (OA) is commonly referred to as "the other CO_2 problem."[1] Although there is broad scientific consensus that higher atmospheric concentrations of CO_2 are driving acidification of the oceans, OA has received less attention from the scientific and policy communities than large-scale climatic changes that are caused by increasing atmospheric CO_2 concentrations.[2] Ocean acidification presents a particularly significant policy challenge because its main driver is the deposition of CO_2 in the air into the ocean.

Although there are a number of local contributors to OA that can be addressed as a short-term mitigation strategy, any meaningful long-term action to reduce the impacts of OA will require concerted action to limit and ultimately reduce atmospheric concentrations of CO_2.[3] As a result, although acidifying oceans are a water problem, they have an air solution. Therefore, this chapter will focus on the use of the Clean Air Act as a tool to address OA.

This chapter proceeds in five sections. Sections I and II explain the problem of OA and the relationship between atmospheric CO_2 concentrations and acidification of the oceans. Section III sets forth the basic framework of the Clean Water Act and explains its limitations in addressing atmospheric CO_2 concentrations. Section IV examines the potential use of the Clean Air Act to regulate atmospheric CO_2 emissions to address OA, with a particular emphasis on the potential for a secondary national ambient air quality standard focused on OA. Finally, Section V notes the need for international action to reduce CO_2 emissions if the threats of OA are to be minimized.

I. The Problem of Ocean Acidification

"Ocean acidification" is a term used to describe declines in the pH of ocean waters. As waters become more acidic, they have the potential to cause a variety of physiological impacts in marine organisms.[4] These adverse impacts not only have the potential to threaten the survival of particular marine species, but also have the potential to disrupt larger marine food webs and the societies that depend upon them.[5]

---

[1] Scott C. Doney et al., *Ocean Acidification: The Other CO2 Problem*, 1 ANN. REV. MARINE SCI. 169 (2009).

[2] Jean-Pierre Gattuso, Katharine J. Mach & Granger Morgan, *Ocean Acidification and Its Impacts: An Expert Survey*, 117 CLIMATE CHANGE 725, 725 (2013).

[3] Ryan P. Kelly & Margaret R. Caldwell, *Ten Ways States Can Combat Ocean Acidification (and Why They Should)*, 37 HARV. ENVTL. L. REV. 57, 100–03 (2013).

[4] Doney et al., *supra* note 1; THE ROYAL SOCIETY, OCEAN ACIDIFICATION DUE TO INCREASING ATMOSPHERIC CARBON DIOXIDE (2005).

[5] Ocean Acidification and Marine pH Water Quality Criteria, 74 Fed. Reg. 17,484, 17,485 (Apr. 15, 2009).

In its 2009 Endangerment Finding, which concluded that atmospheric greenhouse gas concentrations threaten public health and welfare, the EPA concluded that one of the scientific justifications for its policy decision to regulate greenhouse gas emissions was the threat of OA. EPA noted that "[c]limate change and ocean acidification will likely impair a wide range of planktonic and other marine calcifiers such as corals."[6] EPA has also identified ocean acidity as a climate change indicator.[7] Since EPA issued the Endangerment Finding in 2009, there have been numerous studies and reports published calling attention to the need for additional research to better understand the potential threats and impacts of OA.[8]

In 2011, the IPCC issued a workshop report examining the impacts of OA on marine biology and ecosystems.[9] The Workshop Report concluded that "recent changes in ocean surface water chemistry can be unequivocally linked to atmospheric CO_2."[10] However, the Workshop Report noted that larger phenomena, such as ocean circulation, may impact acidification of the entire ocean water column over time. The Working Group report noted the range of potential threats that OA may pose to marine organisms and ecosystems, but recognized that the responses of individual species and whole ecosystems are likely to be highly complex and cannot be well characterized at this time.[11]

Individual studies have demonstrated that particular organisms exhibit a range of responses to OA. In many cases, studies demonstrate that marine calcifiers—organisms that use calcium carbonate from seawater to build hard structures in their bodies—are likely to be adversely impacted by OA.[12] For example, research on coral concludes that OA will slow the rate of coral calcification, meaning that corals will be smaller, have weaker skeletons, or have to invest more energy to build their skeletons.[13] Ocean

---

[6] Endangerment and Cause or Contribute Findings for Greenhouse Gases under Section 202(a) of the Clean Air Act, 74 Fed. Reg. 66,496, 66,534 (Dec. 15, 2009) (to be codified at 40 C.F.R. ch. 1).

[7] *Climate Change Indicators in the United States: Ocean Carbon Dioxide Levels and Acidity, 1983–2011*, United States Environmental Protection Agency (2012), http://www.epa.gov/climatechange/science/indicators/oceans/acidity.html.

[8] *See, e.g.*, Interagency Working Group on Ocean Acidicfication, Strategic Plan for Federal Research and Monitoring of Ocean Acidificaiton 6–7 (2014), *available at* http://www.whitehouse.gov/sites/default/files/microsites/ostp/NSTC/iwg-oa_strategic_plan_march_2014.pdf; Richard A. Feeley et al., Scientific Summary of Ocean Acidification in Washington State Marine Waters 101–03 (2012), *available at* https://fortress.wa.gov/ecy/publications/publications/1201016.pdf.

[9] Intergovernmental Panel on Climate Change, Workshop Report of the Intergovernmental Panel on Climate Change Workshop on Impacts of Ocean Acidification on Marine Biology and Ecosystems (Christopher B. Field et al. eds., Jan. 17–19, 2011), *available at* http://www.ipcc-wg2.gov/meetings/workshops/OceanAcidification_WorkshopReport.pdf.

[10] *Id.* at 5.

[11] *See, e.g., id.* at 12, 17, 26, 46, 111.

[12] *See generally* Kristy J. Kroeker et al., *Meta-analysis Reveals Negative Yet Variable Effects of Ocean Acidification on Marine Organisms*, 13 Ecology Letters 1419 (2010).

[13] O. Hoegh-Guldberg et al., *Coral Reefs under Rapid Climate Change and Ocean Acidification*, 318 Sci. 1737, 1738 (2007).

acidification has also been shown to have negative impacts on oyster populations in the Pacific Northwest, resulting in decreased larval settlement and slower growth rates.[14]

Despite these potential threats, OA has struggled to gain traction as a policy issue. This may be in part because most studies of OA that have been conducted to date have focused on individual organisms and therefore are limited in their ability to draw conclusions about broader impacts on marine ecosystems and the human societies that depend upon them.[15] Furthermore, although there is strong scientific consensus regarding the chemical processes that are driving OA and emerging consensus that OA will adversely impact biological and ecological processes, a survey of experts found that there was a lower degree of consensus regarding the broader socioeconomic impacts (such as impacts on food security) that are likely to result.[16] This is not to suggest that action on OA is not needed—actions to reduce OA will be necessary to avoid significant impacts to marine ecosystems—but rather to demonstrate the challenges in creating a message to drive concerted policy action on OA.[17]

II. Causes of Ocean Acidification

The primary cause of OA is increasing atmospheric concentrations of CO_2. In order to understand how increasing atmospheric CO_2 concentrations lead to more acidic ocean waters, the chemical relationships between the atmosphere and the surface of the ocean must be examined. CO_2 in the atmosphere dissolves in surface waters of the ocean, creating carbonic acid.[18] This carbonic acid can break down, releasing hydrogen ions and bicarbonate and carbonate ions.[19] The hydrogen ions are an acidic component that lowers the pH of seawater. Over time, this will impact the availability of carbonate in the water, which is a key building block in the skeletons of many marine animals, including plankton and shellfish.[20] The reactions between the atmosphere and the ocean that lead to acidification are equilibrium reactions.[21] This means that increasing the concentration of CO_2 in the atmosphere will increase OA. Conversely, if atmospheric CO_2 concentrations were to decline, the ocean would slowly become less acidic.

---

[14] Alan Barton et al., *The Pacific Oyster,* Crassostrea gigas, *Shows Negative Correlation to Naturally Elevated Carbon Dioxide Levels: Implications for Near Term Ocean Acidification Effects,* 57 Limnology & Oceanography 698, 706–07 (2012).

[15] Sam Dupont & Hans-O Pörtner, *A Snapshot of Ocean Acidification Research,* 160 Marine Biology 1765, 1769–90 (2013).

[16] Gattuso et al., *supra* note 2, at 726.

[17] A good example of work along these lines is seen in the efforts of the Center for Ocean Solutions to create comprehensive approaches to address the many causes of ocean acidification. *See* Center for Ocean Solutions Focal Areas, http://www.centerforoceansolutions.org/initiatives/climate-change-initiative (last visited May 2, 2014).

[18] Doney et al., *supra* note 1, at 172.

[19] *Id.*

[20] *Id.*

[21] *Id.* at 171.

The chemistry driving OA described above is applicable only to the surface layer of the ocean, where ocean waters are in direct contact with the air. However, the ocean operates like a giant conveyor belt with ocean circulation patterns causing surface waters to be transported to the deep ocean. Through this conveyor belt process, the oceans have been acting as a major carbon sink—removing carbon from the atmosphere and storing it in the deep ocean where it will not be rereleased until the deep ocean water returns to the surface. This ocean carbon cycling helps to explain why the amount of warming experienced to date is less than what would be expected based on the total amount of greenhouse gases that have been released to the atmosphere.[22] However, recent studies have shown that some of the acidic water from the deep ocean, which absorbed atmospheric carbon decades if not centuries ago, is coming back to the surface during upwelling events and adding to localized OA.[23]

In addition to atmospheric CO_2, there are a number of other causes of OA. These include sulfur dioxide precipitation, hypoxia, eutrophication, and emissions and runoff from the application of acidic fertilizers.[24] Like CO_2, sulfur dioxide in the atmosphere can react with the surface of the water and cause acidification.[25] Sulfur dioxide is considered a localized cause of OA because, unlike CO_2, elevated atmospheric sulfur dioxide concentrations are localized to areas where the sulfur dioxide is emitted. Hypoxia refers to a state where the oxygen in ocean waters is depleted. The decay of organic material during hypoxic events can increase the amount of dissolved CO_2 in coastal waters, magnifying the effects of OA.[26] Eutrophication refers to a condition where excess nutrients in the water column stimulate the growth of algae, which ultimately die off and decompose in the water.[27] Eutrophication worsens the impacts of OA because the decomposition consumes available oxygen in the water column and releases additional CO_2 into the water as a byproduct of bacterial respiration of the dead algae.[28] Emissions and runoff from the

---

[22] Monika Rhein et al., *Chapter 3 Observations: Ocean* 255, 260, *in* CLIMATE CHANGE 2013: THE PHYSICAL SCIENCE BASIS. CONTRIBUTION OF WORKING GROUP I TO THE FIFTH ASSESSMENT REPORT OF THE INTERGOVERNMENTAL PANEL ON CLIMATE CHANGE (T.F. Stocker et al., eds. 2013), *available at* http://www.climatechange2013.org/images/report/WG1AR5_Chapter03_FINAL.pdf.

[23] Richard A. Feely et al., *Evidence for Upwelling of Corrosive "Acidified" Water onto the Continental Shelf*, 320 SCI. 1490, 1492 (2008). Upwelling is the process by which deep ocean waters return to the surface. Upwelling happens when prevailing winds push the surface water of the ocean away from the shore and deeper ocean waters move in to replace it. National Oceanic and Atmospheric Administration, Ocean Facts: Upwelling, http://oceanservice.noaa.gov/facts/upwelling.html (last visited May 9, 2014).

[24] R.P. Kelly et al., *Mitigating Local Causes of Ocean Acidification with Existing Laws*, 332 SCI. 1036 (2011).

[25] Secondary National Ambient Air Quality Standards for Oxides of Nitrogen and Sulfur, 77 Fed. Reg. 20,217, 20, 224–25 (Apr. 3, 2012) (to be codified at 40 C.F.R. pt. 50).

[26] Frank Melzner et al., *Future Ocean Acidification Will Be Amplified by Hypoxia in Coastal Habitats*, 160 MARINE BIOLOGY 1875, 1877 (2013).

[27] *Environmental Health—Toxic Substances: Eutrophication*, USGS http://toxics.usgs.gov/definitions/eutrophication.html (last visited May 6, 2014).

[28] *Increasing Atmospheric CO2 and Eutrophication Combine to Acidify Coastal Bottom Waters*, THE NATIONAL CENTERS FOR COASTAL OCEAN SCIENCE, NOAA NATIONAL OCEAN SERVICE (Feb. 5, 2012), http://

application of acidic fertilizers are direct contributors of acidic inputs to receiving waters and thereby can increase localized acidification. Although each of these factors plays an important role in exacerbating the localized impacts of OA, their effects are dwarfed by the acidification caused by increasing atmospheric CO_2 concentrations. As a result, any policy approaches that minimize the potential threats of OA must include a mechanism to reduce CO_2 emissions in order to lower atmospheric CO_2 concentrations.

III. Limitations of the Clean Water Act to Regulate Ocean Acidification

The goal of the Clean Water Act (CWA) is "to restore and maintain the chemical, physical, and biological integrity of the Nation's waters."[29] The Act attempts to reach this goal by establishing "complementary technology-based and water-quality based approaches to water pollution control."[30] Congress created the technology-based component of the CWA—the National Pollutant Discharge Elimination System (NPDES) permitting program—in recognition of the fact that an approach based solely on water quality standards "was deemed insufficiently effective" because regulation of pollution at its source (point source) is necessary to protect water quality.[31] As a result, CWA permits are based on both technology-based limitations and limitations that are needed to meet the water quality standards for the receiving water body.[32]

A. THE NPDES PERMITTING PROGRAM AND ITS APPLICABILITY TO ACIDIFICATION

The NPDES permit program is the primary means by which the CWA protects water quality. NPDES permits are needed for each point source of water pollution.[33] All NPDES permits contain technology-based effluent limitations, relying on three different control technology standards. The applicable technology control standard depends on whether a pollutant is "conventional," "nonconventional," or toxic. Under the CWA, "conventional" pollutants are those that can be treated in municipal sewage treatment systems, and include fecal coliform, pH, and total suspended solids.[34]

All conventional pollutants (those that are neither unconventional nor toxic) must be controlled through the application of either the best practicable control technology currently available ("BPT") or the more stringent best conventional pollutant control

---

coastalscience.noaa.gov/news/climate/increasing-atmospheric-co2-and-eutrophication-combine-to-acidify-coastal-bottom-waters/.

[29] 33 U.S.C. § 1251(a) (2012).

[30] *Water Quality Standards History*, UNITED STATES ENVIRONMENTAL PROTECTION AGENCY, http://water.epa.gov/scitech/swguidance/standards/history.cfm (last visited July 28, 2014).

[31] *Id.*

[32] 40 C.F.R. § 122.22 (2014).

[33] 33 U.S.C. § 1342(a)(1) (2012).

[34] 33 U.S.C. § 1314(a)(4) (2012); 40 C.F.R. § 401.16 (2014).

technology ("BCT"). BPT limits are set by identifying the best-performing sources in a particular category and setting effluent limitations based on those sources.[35] BPT also requires that EPA conduct a limited cost-benefit analysis in setting effluent limitation standards.[36] BCT controls are more stringent than BPT controls, and rely on the best technology that is available (as compared to the "average of the best sources" approach used in setting BPT).[37] However, BCT can be required at a facility only if it is deemed cost-effective under two required tests.[38]

All pollutants that are not conventional fall into the categories of nonconventional or toxic pollutants.[39] These pollutants are subjected to the more stringent standard of best available technology economically achievable ("BAT").[40] EPA sets BAT limits based on the best performing sources in the industry; these limits are based on EPA's judgment of the outer limit of what is technically achievable.[41] As such, EPA may set BAT limits based on actual plant operations, pilot plant studies, or laboratory-scale studies.[42]

If the NPDES program could be applied to point sources to combat OA, one important issue in evaluating the extent to which NPDES permits can limit sources of ocean acidification is which control technology standards may apply to point sources that contribute to acidification. As discussed in more detail below, efforts to address OA have focused on encouraging EPA and the states to set water quality standards for pH. Under the CWA's definitions, pH would be a "conventional pollutant" subject to BPT or BCT standards. However, CO_2—the primary cause of pH decreases in the ocean—is a "nonconventional pollutant,"[43] and therefore would be subject to the more stringent BAT standards if it were subject to regulation under the NPDES program.

B. LIMITATIONS ON THE APPLICABILITY OF THE NPDES PERMITTING PROGRAM TO ATMOSPHERIC CARBON DIOXIDE

The technology-forcing standards of the NPDES program are applicable only to point sources of pollution. Under the NPDES program, point sources are defined as:

[A]ny discernible, confined and discrete conveyance, including but not limited to any pipe, ditch, channel, tunnel, conduit, well, discrete fissure, container, rolling

---

[35] 33 U.S.C. § 1311(b)(2)(E) (2012).

[36] 33 U.S.C. § 1314(b)(2)(B) (2012).

[37] SECTION OF ENVIRONMENT, ENERGY, AND RESOURCES, AMERICAN BAR ASSOCIATION, THE CLEAN WATER ACT HANDBOOK 35 (Mark A. Ryan ed., 3d ed. 2011).

[38] Best Conventional Pollutant Control Technology; Effluent Limitations Guidelines, 51 Fed. Reg. 24,974, 24,975 (July 9, 1986).

[39] 33 U.S.C. § 1314(a)(4) (2012) (listing conventional pollutants); 33 U.S.C. § 1317(a)(1) (2012) (listing toxic pollutants); 40 C.F.R. § 401.15 (2014) (listing toxic pollutants); 40 C.F.R. § 401.16 (2014) (listing conventional pollutants).

[40] 33 U.S.C. § 1314(b)(2)(B) (2012).

[41] *Id.*

[42] THE CLEAN WATER ACT HANDBOOK, *supra* note 37, at 37 and n.108.

[43] 40 C.F.R. § 401.16 (2014).

stock, concentrated animal feeding operation, or vessel or other floating craft, from which pollutants are or may be discharged. This term does not include agricultural stormwater discharges and return flows from irrigated agriculture.[44]

The Act further defines discharge of a pollutant to mean "(A) any addition of any pollutant to navigable waters from any point source, (B) any addition of any pollutant to the waters of the contiguous zone or the ocean from any point source other than a vessel or other floating craft."[45] Courts have interpreted these definitions to limit the application of the NPDES permitting program to only those discrete sources that discharge pollutants to water thorough a defined, discrete conveyance.[46] As a result, the NPDES permitting program does not reach any forms of non–point sources pollution, such as runoff. In addition, the NPDES permitting program cannot be used to regulate pollution produced by the atmospheric deposition of air pollutants.

In a recent decision, the District Court of Alaska considered whether loading activities at a coal transport facility were point sources subject to permitting under the NPDES program.[47] Among other alleged violations, the plaintiffs claimed that wind-blown coal dust from the facility that landed in the adjacent water body should be subject to NPDES permitting requirements. The court disagreed, concluding "coal blown into the Bay as airborne dust is not a point source discharge and is therefore exempt from NPDES permitting requirements."[48] The court explained that it was the aerosol nature of the coal dust that caused it to be a nonpoint source pollutant beyond the CWA's reach. To clarify its point, the court noted that the coal dust pile at issue could be subject to regulation under the NPDES program if pollutants traveled from the pile through a point source to the water.[49] The court further explained that "[t]he law is clear that a plaintiff seeking to establish a point source discharge, even in the context of airborne pollution, must prove more than that the pollutant originated from an identifiable source. Regardless of from where the pollution originates, a plaintiff must prove that 'the pollut[ant] reache[d] the water through a confined, discrete conveyance.'"[50]

In contrast, the Second and Ninth Circuits have both concluded that aerial spraying of pesticides is a form of point source pollution that requires a NPDES permit.[51] In

---

[44] 33 U.S.C. § 1362(14) (2012).

[45] 33 U.S.C. § 1362(12) (2012).

[46] *See infra* notes 47–50 and accompanying text.

[47] Alaska Cmty. Action on Toxics v. Aurora Energy Servs., LLC, 940 F. Supp. 2d 1005 (D. Alaska 2013).

[48] *Id.* at 1022.

[49] *Id.* at 1024.

[50] *Id.* at 1026 (quoting Trustees for Alaska v. EPA, 749 F.2d 549, 558 (1984)).

[51] Peconic Baykeeper, Inc. v. Suffolk Cnty., 600 F.3d 180, 188–89 (2d Cir. 2010) (holding that helicopters spraying pesticides for mosquito control were point sources under the Clean Water Act); League of Wilderness Defenders v. Forsgren, 309 F.3d 1181, 1185 (9th Cir. 2002) (finding that direct spraying of pesticides from an aircraft onto water met the statutory requirements to be point source pollution).

Peconic Baykeeper, the Second Circuit determined that helicopters conducting aerosol spraying of pesticides are point sources under the CWA because "[t]he pesticides were discharged 'from' the source, and not from the air."[52] Thus, while the District Court of Alaska's holding seems to clearly establish that wind-blown dust and similar sources would not be point source discharges, the Second and Ninth Circuits establish equipment used for aerosol application of pollutants could be a point source within the meaning of the NPDES permitting program.

There are important factual distinctions between the Second and Ninth Circuit cases that suggest that a reviewing court would decline to find that point sources of CO_2 into the air qualify as point sources subject to regulation under the CWA. The pesticide spraying equipment considered in these cases used was a discrete conveyance for pesticides that were intended to reach the water. In contrast, CO_2 that is emitted to the atmosphere is more equivalent to non–point source pollution, for example, pesticides applied to land that are conveyed to water via runoff. The remoteness in both time and space between the stack discharging CO_2 into the air and the waters that are ultimately acidified suggests that CO_2 cannot be treated as a point source pollutant under the CWA. This is particularly so because CO_2 emitted to the air becomes a water pollutant through the process of atmospheric deposition—a process that is specifically defined by EPA guidance as a type of non–point source pollution under the CWA.[53] A further distinction that is potentially significant is that those using the pesticide spraying equipment considered by the Second and Ninth Circuit did not require Clean Air Act permits to spray those pesticides into the air, which is in direct contrast to point sources of air pollution that are already subject to regulation under the Clean Air Act. CO_2 is an "air pollutant" under the Clean Air Act; therefore, point source emissions of CO_2 are potentially subject to regulation under the CAA.

As a result, the major technology-forcing provision of the CWA that is the focus of compliance and enforcement cannot be used as a tool to combat the major cause of OA—atmospheric deposition of CO_2 into ocean waters. Recognizing these limitations, parties that have sought to address OA through the CWA have relied on the Act's non–point source provisions. As explained in more detail below, these provisions can provide an important tool to combat localized causes of OA, but may only be marginally effective in combatting acidification caused by increasing atmospheric CO_2 concentrations.

---

[52] *Peconic Baykeeper*, 600 F.3d at 188.

[53] *See* UNITED STATES ENVIRONMENTAL PROTECTION AGENCY, FREQUENTLY ASKED QUESTIONS ABOUT ATMOSPHERIC DEPOSITION: A HANDBOOK FOR WATERSHED MANAGERS 2 (EPA-453/R-01-009, Sept. 2001), *available at* http://water.epa.gov/lawsregs/lawsguidance/cwa/tmdl/airdeposition_handbook.cfm.

C. NON−POINT SOURCE POLLUTION CONTROL AS A TOOL TO
COMBAT OCEAN ACIDIFICATION

Efforts to address OA under the CWA to date have focused on attempts to convince EPA and the states to establish water quality standards for OA in the form of pH standards.[54] Water quality standards are the backbone of the CWA's water-quality-based prong. The Act requires each state to promulgate and submit for EPA approval water quality standards that are consistent with the requirements of the CWA.[55] The EPA has promulgated regulations that set forth the requirements for state water quality standards.[56] States' water quality standards must designate uses for the water body (e.g., recreation, water supply, aquatic life, agriculture) and apply water quality criteria (numeric pollutant concentrations and narrative requirements) to protect the designated uses.[57] Each state must also establish an anti-degradation policy to maintain and protect existing uses and high quality waters.[58]

The CWA requires EPA to establish or develop water quality criteria, which are objective measures of ambient water quality designed to protect different designated uses.[59] Water quality criteria contain numeric criteria for specific parameters (e.g., temperature or pH), toxicity criteria to protect against aggregated effects of toxins, and narrative criteria that describe the desired condition of the water body.[60] In developing the water quality criteria, EPA must ensure that the criteria reflect the latest scientific knowledge on

> the kind and extent of all identifiable effects on health and welfare including, but not limited to, plankton, fish, shellfish, wildlife, plant life, shorelines, beaches, esthetics, and recreation which may be expected from the presence of pollutants in any body of water,…on the concentration and dispersal of pollutants, or their byproducts, through biological, physical, and chemical processes; and…on the effects of pollutants on biological community diversity, productivity, and stability,

---

[54] CENTER FOR BIOLOGICAL DIVERSITY, PETITION FOR ADDITIONAL WATER QUALITY CRITERIA AND GUIDANCE UNDER SECTION 304 OF THE CLEAN WATER ACT, 33 U.S.C. § 1314, TO ADDRESS OCEAN ACIDIFICATION, BEFORE THE ENVIRONMENTAL PROTECTION AGENCY (Apr. 17, 2013), *available at* http://www.biologicaldiversity.org/campaigns/ocean_acidification/pdfs/EPA_OA_petition_2013. pdf; Letter from Miyoko Sakashita, Center for Biological Diversity Ocean Program Attorney, and Anna Moritz, Ocean and Climate Program Law Clerk, to Susan Braley, Washington Department of Ecology, *Request to Add Washington Oceans to the 303(d) List of Impaired Waters due to Carbon Dioxide Pollution and Ocean Acidification and Revise Current Water Quality Standards for PH* (Aug. 15, 2007), *available at* http:// www.biologicaldiversity.org/campaigns/ocean_acidification/pdfs/WA_303d_letter_08-15-07.pdf.

[55] 33 U.S.C. § 1313(a) (2012).

[56] 40 C.F.R. § 131 (2014).

[57] 40 C.F.R. § 131.10 (2014); 40 C.F.R. § 131.11 (2014).

[58] 40 C.F.R. § 131.12 (2014).

[59] 33 U.S.C. § 1314(a) (2012).

[60] 33 U.S.C. § 1314(a)(1) (2012); 40 C.F.R. § 131.11 (2014).

including information on the factors affecting rates of eutrophication and rates of organic and inorganic sedimentation for varying types of receiving waters.[61]

When states promulgate their own water quality standards, they must either include water quality criteria that have been developed by EPA or draw upon other scientifically defensible methods to establish their own criteria.[62]

Once states establish water quality standards for water bodies under their jurisdiction, they must periodically determine whether they have met or failed to attain the established standards.[63] Section 303(d) of the CWA requires all states to submit a list of impaired and threatened waters—those that do not meet applicable water quality standards—for EPA approval every two years.[64] Waters included on the section 303(d) are referred to as "impaired waters."[65] Once a waterbody is included on the section 303(d) list, the CWA requires that the state develop a total maximum daily load (TMDL) to address the sources of impairment.[66]

A TMDL is the total amount of a particular pollutant that can be added to a waterbody from all sources without exceeding the water quality criteria.[67] Importantly, the TMDL must account for all sources of a pollutant, including point sources, non–point sources, and air deposition.[68] The TMDL has two main components: the waste load allocation ("WLA"), which is the portion of the TMDL that is allocated to point sources of pollution, and the load allocation ("LA"), which is the portion of the TMDL allocated to non-point and background sources.[69] Because they can include sources of air deposition as non-point or background sources, TMDLs represent a potentially important tool to address OA. However, to date the TMDL program has struggled to determine how to address non–point sources of water pollution,[70] and even greater challenges are in store for attempts to factor regulation of atmospheric deposition into TMDLs. This is particularly so because any attempt to address atmospheric sources of CO_2 under a TMDL would first have to explain why the classification of atmospheric CO_2 is a source of non-point source pollution rather than a result of background concentrations of CO_2.

In 2009, the Center for Biological Diversity (CBD) filed a lawsuit against EPA for approving Washington State's section 303(d) list, which did not include coastal waters as

[61] 33 U.S.C. § 1314(a)(1) (2012).
[62] 40 C.F.R. § 131.11(b) (2014).
[63] 33 U.S.C. § 1313(c) (2012); 40 C.F.R. § 130.7(d) (2014).
[64] 33 U.S.C. § 1313(d) (2012); 40 C.F.R. § 130.7(d) (2014).
[65] 40 C.F.R. § 130.7(d) (2014).
[66] 33 U.S.C. § 1313(d)(1)(C) (2012).
[67] *Id.*
[68] 40 C.F.R. § 130.7 (2014).
[69] *Id.*; 40 C.F.R. § 130.2(g) (2014) (explaining that load allocations include both nonpoint and background sources).
[70] THE CLEAN WATER ACT HANDBOOK, *supra* note 37, at 207–29.

impaired for marine pH due to acidification.[71] CBD argued that the existing water quality criterion for pH in marine waters, which EPA first issued in 1976, was not protective enough to address decreasing pH levels caused by rising CO_2 emissions. CBD hoped that if states adopted more stringent marine pH criteria in their water quality standards, more waters would be identified as impaired, and would therefore require TMDLs to reduce CO_2 emissions responsible for the violations of the standards.

EPA and CBD announced the settlement of the lawsuit in March 2010. As part of the settlement, EPA sought public comments on what it should consider when determining whether to list waters as threatened or impaired by OA under the CWA section 303(d) program and how to develop TMDLs for such listed waters.[72] EPA asked for comments on: (1) methods for states to monitor OA and its impacts on marine life and ecosystems, (2) how states should determine whether marine waters are impaired by acidification, and (3) recommendations for developing TMDLs for marine waters that are impaired by acidification.[73] In November 2010, EPA issued a memorandum advising coastal states to include "waters not meeting water quality standards, including marine pH [water quality criteria], on their 2012 303(d) lists" and to also "solicit existing and readily available information on [OA] using the current 303(d) listing program framework."[74] The memorandum urged states to focus on waters particularly vulnerable to OA, including coral reefs, marine fisheries, and shellfish resources.[75] The agency observed that all twenty-three coastal states and five territories had already established marine pH water quality criteria similar to EPA's CWA section 304(a)(1) recommended national criterion, and more than half of the states had implemented coastal monitoring programs.[76] Furthermore, it noted that several states provide water quality criteria for other OA parameters, such as dissolved oxygen, and a few had created narrative or numeric biocriteria that could reflect OA impacts for marine waters containing coral reefs.[77]

Even though EPA's 2010 memorandum contemplates using the CWA's section 303(d) program to address OA, EPA and the states would confront two major challenges if they further developed such a strategy. The first challenge that EPA will confront concerns the scope of its legal authority under the CWA. Although the EPA or a state could set a TMDL that includes a load allocation for CO_2 from atmospheric deposition, such a load allocation would have to be enforced using legal authorities other than the CWA.[78]

---

[71] Complaint, Center for Biological Diversity v. EPA, No. 2:09-cv-00670 (W.D. Wash. May 14, 2009).

[72] Clean Water Act Section 303(d): Notice of Call for Public Comment on 303(d) Program and Ocean Acidification, 75 Fed. Reg. 13,537, 13, 537–40 (Mar. 22, 2010).

[73] Id.

[74] Memorandum from Denise Keehner, Dir. of EPA Office of Wetlands, Oceans and Watersheds, Integrated Reporting and Listing Decisions Related to Ocean Acidification 4 (Nov. 15, 2010), available at http://water.epa.gov/lawsregs/lawsguidance/cwa/tmdl/upload/oa_memo_nov2010.pdf.

[75] Id.

[76] Id.

[77] Id.

[78] See, e.g., UNITED STATES ENVIRONMENTAL PROTECTION AGENCY, TMDLs WHERE MERCURY LOADINGS ARE PREDOMINANTLY FROM AIR DEPOSITION 21 (Sept. 2008), available at http://water.epa.

There is limited precedent for TMDL programs that reduce atmospheric deposition into marine waters. For example, EPA has developed guidance for regional TMDL programs that reduce atmospheric mercury pollution.[79] EPA's guidance specifically notes "the tools and approaches described here may be useful in other situations where the pollutant loadings are primarily from air deposition."[80] EPA's guidance explains that where possible load allocations should separate out natural background sources and non–point sources and states that "[i]n TMDLs where mercury loadings are predominantly from air deposition, the LA may consist entirely or largely of contributions from air deposition."[81] The guidance further suggests that states may wish to separate the air deposition load allocation into in-state and out-of-state components as well as allocations to particular categories of sources.[82] However, the guidance makes clear that the TMDL process itself does not provide a means by which air emissions can be regulated directly.[83] Thus, the scope of authority under the TMDL framework does not provide a direct means to demand reductions in air emissions from point sources, which could be used to address GHG emissions. However, TMDLs can be an important tool to reduce other sources of OA by establishing WLAs and LAs for those sources that account for the impacts of atmospheric deposition of background CO_2 concentrations.

The second challenge is practical. Although CO_2 is a source of atmospheric deposition that can be considered in the creation of a TMDL, carbon dioxide poses unique problems of traceability and redressability that would make controls exceedingly difficult to implement in practice. Carbon dioxide is a globally mixed pollutant that remains in the atmosphere for centuries, making it difficult, if not impossible, to determine which state or nation—let alone which specific emitter—is responsible for carbon dioxide that appeared in the waters under a particular state's jurisdiction. In theory, a state could attempt to simplify this challenge following EPA's suggestion in the mercury TMDL guidance and allocating to itself a CO_2 emissions reduction commitment that seeks

---

gov/lawsregs/lawsguidance/cwa/tmdl/mercury/upload/2008_10_01_tmdl_pdf_document_mercury_tmdl_elements.pdf (explaining that for in-state sources of air pollution, "implementation [of a TMDL] may include adopting appropriate emissions reductions using authorities other than the Clean Water Act.".

[79] UNITED STATES ENVIRONMENTAL PROTECTION AGENCY, NORTHEAST REGIONAL MERCURY TOTAL MAXIMUM DAILY LOAD (Oct. 24, 2007), *available at* http://www.epa.gov/region1/eco/tmdl/pdfs/ne/Northeast-Regional-Mercury-TMDL.pdf.

[80] UNITED STATES ENVIRONMENTAL PROTECTION AGENCY, TMDLs WHERE MERCURY LOADINGS ARE PREDOMINANTLY FROM AIR DEPOSITION (Sept. 2008), *available at* http://water.epa.gov/lawsregs/lawsguidance/cwa/tmdl/mercury/upload/2008_10_01_tmdl_pdf_document_mercury_tmdl_elements.pdf.

[81] *Id.* at 15.

[82] *Id.*

[83] This approach is also evident in the northeast regional TMDL for mercury, which expressly states that it relies on reductions in air emissions using authority under the Clean Air Act. In addition to noting the reductions that have been achieved in the participating Northeast states, the TMDL says that to meet state goals, the Northeast states recommend that the EPA exercise its authority under the Clean Air Act to establish performance standards for power plants. NORTHEAST REGIONAL MERCURY TOTAL MAXIMUM DAILY LOAD, *supra* note 77.

to limit the contribution of atmospheric deposition to OA. However, neither EPA nor the states has the authority to directly impose limitations on air emissions from point sources under the CWA. To accomplish this, they must turn to the Clean Air Act and equivalent state laws.

IV. The Clean Air Act as a Tool to Regulate Ocean Acidification

Because ocean acidification cannot be addressed in the long term without reducing atmospheric concentrations of CO_2, the Clean Air Act (CAA) is a potentially important tool for combatting OA in the U.S. domestic context. The CAA not only provides for the direct regulation of sources or air pollution but also provides a mechanism to set standards for ambient concentrations of air pollutants in order to protect ecosystem health. Thus, the CAA is a potentially powerful legal tool to address ocean acidification.

A. OVERVIEW OF REGULATION OF SOURCES UNDER THE CAA

Title I of the CAA addresses pollution from stationary sources (e.g., power plants, factories), while Title II regulates pollution from mobile sources (e.g., cars and trucks). Under the CAA, the EPA is granted authority to regulate "air pollutants," which are defined under the Act as "any air pollution agent or combination of such agents, including any physical, chemical, biological, radioactive . . . substance or matter which is emitted into or otherwise enters the ambient air."[84] The CAA creates explicit regulatory structures for two types of air pollutants: criteria pollutants and hazardous air pollutants.

Criteria pollutants are pollutants that EPA determines "cause or contribute to air pollution which may reasonably be anticipated to endanger public health or welfare."[85] Currently, the six criteria pollutants are ozone, particulate matter, carbon monoxide, nitrogen oxides, sulfur dioxide, and lead.[86] Once EPA lists a pollutant as a criteria pollutant under section 108, it is required to establish national ambient air quality standards (NAAQS).[87] There are two types of NAAQS that EPA can set. The primary NAAQS are intended to protect public health, while the secondary NAAQS are intended

---

[84] 42 U.S.C. § 7602(g) (2012).

[85] 42 U.S.C. § 7408(a)(1)(A) (2012).

[86] Review of National Ambient Air Quality Standards for Carbon Monoxide, 76 Fed. Reg. 54,293 (Aug. 31, 2011) (to be codified at 40 C.F.R. pts. 50, 53, and 58); National Ambient Air Quality Standards for Lead, 73 Fed. Reg. 66,964 (Nov. 12, 2008) (to be codified at 40 C.F.R. pts. 50, 51, 53, and 58); Primary National Ambient Air Quality Standards for Nitrogen Dioxide, 75 Fed. Reg. 6473 (Feb. 9, 2010) (to be codified at 40 C.F.R. pts. 50 and 58); National Ambient Air Quality Standards for Nitrogen Dioxide, 61 Fed. Reg. 52,852 (Oct. 8, 1996) (to be codified at 40 C.F.R. pt. 50); National Ambient Air Quality Standards for Ozone, 73 Fed. Reg. 16,436 (Mar. 27, 2008) (to be codified at 40 C.F.R. pts. 50 and 58); Primary National Ambient Air Quality Standard for Sulfur Dioxide, 75 Fed. Reg. 35,519 (June 22, 2010); Sulfur Oxides, 38 Fed. Reg. 25,678 (Sept. 14, 1973) (to be codified at 40 C.F.R. pt. 50).

[87] 42 U.S.C. § 7409(a)(1)(A) (2012).

to protect the environment.[88] EPA has established primary NAAQS for each of the six criteria pollutants.[89] EPA has also issued secondary NAAQS for each of the criteria pollutants with the exception of carbon monoxide.[90]

Once the EPA has established the NAAQS, the CAA directs the governor of each state to submit a list of areas that meet the NAAQS within the state and those that do not ("nonattainment areas").[91] The state is then charged with developing a state implementation plan (SIP) that describes how it will bring the nonattainment areas into compliance with the NAAQS and maintain air quality in areas that already meet the NAAQS.[92] The measures contained in the SIP can include both permitting requirements for new sources of air pollution as well as requirements for additional, more stringent pollution controls at existing sources in nonattainment areas.

The attainment status of a particular area determines which permitting program will apply to new sources of air pollution that will be constructed as well as to modifications of existing sources. In nonattainment areas, new sources must undergo nonattainment new source review and demonstrate that the new source will implement the lowest achievable emissions rate and offset any new emissions of any pollutants for which the area is in nonattainment.[93] In areas that are currently attaining the NAAQS, the relevant permitting program is the prevention of significant deterioration (PSD) program, which is intended to ensure that new sources of air pollution do not cause an area to fall out of attainment.[94] One of the primary requirements of the PSD permitting process is that the permit include emissions limitations that are equivalent to the installation of the best available control technology (BACT). EPA's regulations recommend, but do not require, that all best available control technology evaluations follow EPA's five-factor top-down analysis.[95] EPA's top-down BACT process requires the following five steps:

1) Identify all available control technologies;
2) Eliminate technically infeasible control options;
3) Rank remaining control options;
4) Evaluate site-specific factors that may limit the ability to use the highest ranked option; and
5) Select BACT.[96]

---

[88] 42 U.S.C. § 7409(b) (2012).

[89] 40 C.F.R. pt. 50 (2014).

[90] *Id.*

[91] 42 U.S.C. § 7410(a)(1) (2012).

[92] *Id.*

[93] 40 C.F.R. § 51.165 (2014).

[94] 40 C.F.R. § 51.166 (2014).

[95] United States Environmental Protection Agency, *New Source Review Workshop Manual: Prevention of Significant Deterioration and Nonattainment Area Permitting* (draft, Oct. 1990), *available at* http://www. epa.gov/ttn/nsr/gen/wkshpman.pdf.

[96] *Id.*

The CAA thus adopts a technology-forcing system to achieve ambient air quality goals. However, unlike the Clean Water Act, the CAA begins with the national ambient air quality standards and works backward to determine appropriate technological controls.

B. HISTORY OF GHG REGULATION UNDER THE CAA

In 2007, the Supreme Court issued its opinion in *Massachusetts v. EPA*, where it held that greenhouse gases (GHGs) are an "air pollutant" under the CAA.[97] Following the Supreme Court's decision, in 2009 EPA issued the Endangerment Finding—a regulatory finding that is a necessary prerequisite to regulation under the CAA.[98] In the Endangerment Finding, EPA concluded that increasing global concentrations of six greenhouse gases—carbon dioxide, methane, nitrous oxide, hydroflourocarbons, perflourocarbons, and sulfur hexaflouride—present threats to public health and the environment that are sufficiently serious to warrant regulation under the CAA.[99] While concluding that GHGs should be subject to regulation under the CAA, EPA did not set national ambient air quality standards for GHGs.[100]

EPA released several other rules following the Endangerment Finding. First, in response to the petition for rulemaking at issue in *Massachusetts v. EPA*, EPA issued the Tailpipe Rule, which regulates GHG emissions from passenger cars.[101] EPA concluded that once it issued the Tailpipe Rule under Title II of the CAA, GHGs became a pollutant "subject to regulation" under all parts of the CAA. Because the PSD program is applied to all pollutants that are "subject to regulation," EPA concluded that the PSD program automatically became applicable to new stationary sources of GHGs.[102] At the statutory thresholds of 100 tons per year (tpy) or 250 tpy, EPA estimated that 6 million sources—including hospitals and other large buildings—would be major sources of GHGs.[103] Concluding that this would be an "absurd result," EPA proposed the Tailoring Rule to raise the threshold amount of GHG emissions that would trigger a permitting requirement.[104] Under the Tailoring Rule, GHG PSD permits are required for sources

---

[97] Massachusetts v. EPA, 549 U.S. 497 (2007).

[98] Endangerment and Cause or Contribute Findings, *supra* note 6, 74 Fed. Reg. 66,496.

[99] *Id.*

[100] United States Environmental Protection Agency, *Regulating Greenhouse Gas Emissions under the Clean Air Act* (July 11, 2008), *available at* http://www.epa.gov/climatechange/Downloads/anpr/ANPRPreamble.pdf.

[101] Light-Duty Vehicle Greenhouse Gas Emission Standards and Corporate Average Fuel Economy Standards, 75 Fed. Reg. 25,323 (May 7, 2010) (to be codified at 40 C.F.R. pts. 85. 86, 531, 533, 536–38, and 600).

[102] *Id.*

[103] Prevention of Significant Deterioration and Title V Greenhouse Gas Tailoring Rule, 75 Fed. Reg. 31,513 (June 3, 2010) (to be codified at 40 C.F.R. pts. 51, 52, 70, and 71).

[104] *Id.*

that are otherwise subject to PSD permitting that emit more than a threshold level of GHGs (the "anyway sources").[105]

President Obama's Climate Action Plan and an Accompanying Presidential Memorandum to EPA set forth goals for the establishment of additional GHG regulations for the power sector in the coming years.[106] In order to meet the first deadline established in the Presidential Memorandum, EPA proposed new source performance standards (NSPS) for GHGs from power plants in September 2013.[107] These standards apply only to brand new power plants and new generation units at existing plants. Once promulgated, the NSPS become the floor for a BACT analysis, meaning that no new PSD permit can be issued for a power plant that contains GHG emissions limits less stringent than those specified in the NSPS.[108] EPA's proposed standards for existing plants will require that natural gas plants meet an emissions limitation that is equivalent to the use of natural gas combined cycle technology, while coal-fired power plants would be required to meet an emissions limitation that is equivalent to the partial implementation of carbon capture and sequestration technology.[109]

In June 2014, EPA proposed GHG standards for modified power plants as well as performance standards for existing power plants.[110] The proposed standards for existing power plants impose state-specific targets for CO_2 emissions from power generation and give states broad discretion in how to implement programs to meet these goals.[111] Although the final form of these standards may change, if finalized, they will represent a significant milestone in GHG regulations because they will mark the first federal-level regulations that could require existing emitters to curtail their GHG emissions.

Through these programs, the EPA has begun to regulate CO_2 emissions from cars and major stationary sources, which is a significant first step toward addressing increasing atmospheric CO_2 concentrations. Although all programs to reduce CO_2 emissions

---

[105] *Id.* at 31,516. Note that the Supreme Court's recent decision in Utility Air Regulatory Group v. EPA limited the EPA's jurisdiction over stationary sources under the tailoring rule to "anyway sources," meaning the second class of sources covered by the Tailoring Rule—sources not otherwise subject to PSD permitting that emit 100,000 tpy or more of GHGs—are no longer subject to permitting. Utility Air Resources Group v. EPA, No. 12-1146, slip op. at 27 (S. Ct. June 23, 2014). Note that the *UARG* did not specifically uphold EPA's 75,000 tpy of GHG threshold for the anyway sources but rather said EPA must have a [proper justification] for the threshold level of GHGs required to subject an "anyway source" to GHG PSD permitting.

[106] Executive Office of the President, The President's Climate Action Plan (June 2013), *available at* http://www.whitehouse.gov/sites/default/files/image/president27sclimateactionplan.pdf.

[107] United States Environmental Protection Agency, *Standards of Performance for Greenhouse Gas Emissions from New Stationary Sources: Electric Utility Generating Units* (Sept. 20, 2013), *available at* http://www2.epa.gov/sites/production/files/2013-09/documents/20130920proposal.pdf.

[108] Reconsideration of Interpretation of Regulations That Determine Pollutants Covered by Clean Air Act Permitting Programs, 75 Fed. Reg. 17,003 (Apr. 2, 2010).

[109] Standards of Performance for Greenhouse Gas Emissions from New Stationary Sources: Electric Utility Generating Units, 79 Fed. Reg. 1429 (Jan. 8, 2014).

[110] 79 Fed. Reg. 34,830 (June 18, 2014).

[111] *Id.*

will help address the problem of ocean acidification by decreasing additional future contributions of CO_2 to the atmosphere, it is possible they will not achieve significant reductions in global atmospheric GHG concentations and lack a focus on actual environmental conditions in the ocean. In contrast, secondary national ambient air quality standards, discussed in the next subsection, provide a way to address the United States' CO_2 emissions that focuses on preventing or reversing ocean acidification.

C. CAN SECONDARY NAAQS BE USED AS A TOOL TO PROTECT AGAINST OCEAN ACIDIFICATION?

When EPA issued the Endangerment Finding, it declined to establish national ambient air quality standards for GHGs.[112] However, EPA made a number of findings regarding the environmental impacts of increasing GHG concentrations.[113] Specifically addressing ocean acidification, the technical support document for EPA's Endangerment Finding states that ocean acidification will impact the health of marine calcifiers that "play important roles in marine ecosystems by serving as the base of food chains, providing substrate, and helping regulate biogeochemical cycles."[114] While noting that these impacts could have effects throughout the food chain, the technical support document found that "the response of marine biota to ocean acidification is not yet clear, both for the physiology of individual organisms and for ecosystem functioning as a whole."[115]

EPA has issued secondary NAAQS for all of the criteria pollutants except for carbon monoxide.[116] The secondary NAAQS for SO_2 and oxides of nitrogen ("NO_x") have both been established to address the potential impacts of acidifying deposition.[117] The NO_x standard is currently set at an annual mean of 53 ppb.[118] This level was selected based on the goal of protecting visibility, and at the time the EPA concluded that "there is not yet enough consistent scientific information to support a revision of the current secondary standard to protect these aquatic systems."[119] The current SO_2 secondary standard is a three-hour average of 0.5 ppm.[120] This level is retained from EPA's original 1973

---

[112] Endangerment and Cause or Contribute Findings, *supra* note 6, 74 Fed. Reg. at 66,497.

[113] *Id.* at 66,498.

[114] Climate Change Division, Office of Atmospheric Programs, United States Environmental Protection Agency, *Technical Support Document for Endangerment and Cause or Contribute Findings for Greenhouse Gases under Section 202(a) of the Clean Air Act* at 134 (Dec. 7, 2009).

[115] *Id.*

[116] United States Environmental Protection Agency, *National Air Quality Standards, available at* http://www.epa.gov/air/criteria.html (last visited July 28, 2014).

[117] United States Environmental Protection Agency, Office of Air Quality Planning Standards, *Draft Scope and Methods Plan for Risk/Exposure Assessment: Secondary NAAQS Review for Oxides of Nitrogen and Oxides of Sulfur* (Mar. 2008), *available at* http://www.epa.gov/ttn/naaqs/standards/no2so2sec/data/20080305_draft_scope.pdf.

[118] *National Air Quality Standards, supra* note 116.

[119] Effluent Guidelines Plan, 61 Fed. Reg. 52,582 (Oct. 7, 1996).

[120] *National Air Quality Standards, supra* note 116.

proposal,[121] even though the primary NAAQS for SO_2 was revised to become substantially more stringent in 2010.[122]

Of particular interest in considering whether a secondary NAAQS could be used to address ocean acidification is EPA's 2012 proposal for a combined secondary standard for SO_2 and NO_x, which was never finalized.[123] EPA first set secondary standards for NO_x and SO_2 in 1971. Yet the current secondary NO_x and SO_2 standards protect only land-based ecosystems, not water quality and aquatic ecosystems.[124] In 2011, EPA concluded that present levels of NO_x and SO_2 contribute to acidification of aquatic ecosystems through acid rain, and also determined that the existing secondary NAAQS for NO_x and SO_2 did not provide adequate protection for those waters.[125] Ultimately, however, the agency did not establish any additional secondary NAAQS to protect against these effects for ecosystems, reasoning that the available scientific data was not sufficient to set standards with the requisite degree of protection.[126]

In its assessment of the need for new secondary NAAQS for SO_2 and NO_x, EPA proposed to establish the NAAQS based on an aquatic acidification index (AAI) to protect against the adverse environmental impacts caused by acid deposition.[127] EPA noted that the AAI would reflect the use of an ecological indicator to protect against an ecological effect and "would necessarily be more complex than the NAAQS that have been set historically to address effects associated with ambient concentrations of a single pollutant."[128] Fundamentally EPA's approach would have taken an ecological indicator—aquatic acidification—and linked it to deposition and ultimately to allowable concentrations of SO_2 and NO_x in the air.[129] According to EPA's review of the secondary NAAQS, the AAI was designed to be an ecologically relevant standard to determine acceptable atmospheric concentrations of SO_2 and NO_x.[130] EPA's selected ecological indicator underlying the AAI was acid neutralizing capacity, a measure of the ability of a water body to neutralize acidifying deposition and thereby resist the adverse ecological consequences that would result.[131]

---

[121] United States Environmental Protection Agency, National Environmental Research Center Office of Research and Development, *Effects of Sulfur Oxide in the Atmosphere on Vegetation; Revised Chapter 5 for Air Quality Criteria for Sulfur Oxides* (Sept. 1973).

[122] Primary National Ambient Air Quality Standard for Sulfur Dioxide, *supra* note 86.

[123] Secondary National Ambient Air Quality Standards for Oxides of Nitrogen and Sulfur, 76 Fed. Reg. 46,083 (proposed Aug. 1, 2011) (to be codified at 40 C.F.R. pt. 50).

[124] *Id.*

[125] *Id.*

[126] Secondary National Ambient Air Quality Standards (2012), *supra* note 25.

[127] Secondary National Ambient Air Quality Standards for Oxides of Nitrogen and Sulfur, *supra* note 123, 76 Fed. Reg. at 46,118.

[128] Secondary National Ambient Air Quality Standards (2012), *supra* note 25, 77 Fed. Reg. at 20,242.

[129] *Id.* at 20,243–44.

[130] *Id.* at 20,244.

[131] *Id.*

EPA failed to set additional secondary NAAQS for NO_x and SO_2 for reasons related to the structure of the CAA and the lack of scientific data. The CAA requires NAAQS to be both national in scope and to provide the requisite degree of protection, meaning the standards must be neither more nor less stringent than necessary. Because geological conditions in many regions of the United States provide natural resistance to the effects of acid rain, EPA tried to establish secondary NAAQS that would apply nationwide yet also could account for these differences.[132] EPA identified eighty-four "ecoregions" based on factors relevant to acid rain in aquatic ecosystems. However, EPA ultimately concluded that it could not determine with an acceptable degree of scientific certainty that the secondary NAAQS developed under this approach would provide the requisite degree of protection for each ecoregion. EPA's reason for declining to set new secondary NAAQS was uncertainty about ecological and atmospheric models and limits to the available field data. EPA said that an important, but missing, piece of field data needed to determine the requisite degree of protection is a "critical load"—the amount of acid rain that an area can tolerate before ecological damage occurs. The number of critical load estimates for the eighty-four ecoregions ranged from about seven hundred estimates for one ecoregion to fewer than five estimates for several ecoregions.

To resolve the uncertainty related to modeling and field data, EPA launched a five-year pilot program to collect additional data for the next review of the NAAQS, which could then be used to create a multi-pollutant program to address acidification. EPA described this pilot program in its April 2012 final rule notice, stating that it would inform future reviews of NAAQS to address acid rain.[133] As recognized in the design of EPA's pilot program, the impacts of acidifying deposition from SO_2 and NO_x tend to vary at the ecoregion scale.[134] Further, EPA's final rule noted that there would be significant complexity in the implementation of a secondary NAAQS for SO_2 and NO_x based on aquatic acidification because of this regional variation. The final rule states:

> Consideration of an AAI-based secondary standard for oxides of nitrogen and sulfur would present significant implementation challenges because it involves multiple, regionally-dispersed pollutants and relatively complex compliance determinations based on regionally variable levels of NO_y and SO_x concentrations that would be necessary to achieve a national [Acid Neutralization Capacity] target.[135]

In addition to these challenges expressly identified by the EPA, there remains the more fundamental question of whether the CAA, which requires EPA to set a single national

---

[132] EPA described this approach for developing NAAQS for acid rain in its 2011 proposed rule. *See* Secondary National Ambient Air Quality Standards (proposed 2011), *supra* note 123, 76 Fed. Reg. at 46,084.

[133] Secondary National Ambient Air Quality Standards for Oxides of Nitrogen and Sulfur, *supra* note 25, 77 Fed. Reg. at 20,264.

[134] *Id.*

[135] *Id.* at 20,266.

ambient air quality standard, could legally accommodate the type of regional approach EPA contemplates with an AAI-based secondary NAAQS.

However, the AAI is a potentially important example of how EPA could use a secondary NAAQS to address ocean acidification. Unlike SO_2 and NO_x, which tend to drive acidification when present in locally acute concentrations, CO_2 is a globally mixed pollutant for which a single national ambient air quality standard could be technically justified. Given that the major driver of ocean acidification is the equilibrium reaction taking place between the atmosphere and the surface of the ocean, an ambient CO_2 standard could be established as a single national standard for atmospheric CO_2 concentrations and would not face the challenge of addressing regional variations, which has been an obstacle in addressing the effects of local acidification driven by SO_2 and NO_x under the CAA.

V. The Need for International Action

Although a secondary NAAQS for CO_2 could legally be established, such a NAAQS would not be achievable based on the actions of the United States alone. Because CO_2 is a long-lived globally mixed pollutant, even if aggressive actions are taken in the United States to reduce CO_2 emissions, these actions will do little to address the threat of ocean acidification without similar actions being taken by the entire international community. Actions to reduce local contributions to ocean acidification can serve as a meaningful tool to buy time, but the only way to address the major source of ocean acidification will be to reduce global atmospheric concentrations of CO_2.

Even if EPA were to establish a secondary NAAQS for CO_2, it would only facilitate the regulation of atmospheric CO_2 emissions in the United States. Because CO_2 persists in the atmosphere for hundreds of years and is a globally mixed pollutant, actions by only one country will not be sufficient to reduce global atmospheric concentrations of CO_2. Because it is these global concentrations that drive the acidification of the ocean, action by all major GHG emitters will be required to address the challenge of ocean acidification. Although beyond the scope of this chapter, international legal instruments exist that could be used to address ocean acidification; and most important, additional international commitments to reduce GHG emissions under the United Nations Framework Convention on Climate Change or another legal instrument will be necessary to reduce global CO_2 emissions.

Conclusion

Because ocean acidification is primarily driven by increasing atmospheric concentrations of CO_2, a comprehensive strategy to address ocean acidification must include tools to reduce emissions of CO_2 as an air pollutant. As such, the Clean Air Act is a potentially important tool to combat ocean acidification. Although the Clean Water Act can and should be used to address other causes of ocean acidification, addressing these causes alone will not be enough, and the Clean Water Act is limited in its ability to address ambient atmospheric concentrations. Consequently, action under the CAA is necessary.

Although current actions under the CAA to curb CO_2 emissions may slow the increase in atompsheric GHG concentrations and thereby limit some future acidifying deposition, the most protective tool available under the CAA would be for EPA to set a secondary NAAQS for CO_2 aimed at minimizing the threats posed by ocean acidification. However, given that EPA has to date declined to set NAAQS for GHGs, a secondary NAAQS to address ocean acidification is likely to be politically untenable. As with all climate challenges related to increasing atmospheric concentrations of CO_2, domestic action is necessary but alone will not be sufficient. Thus, coordinated international action to address global atmospheric CO_2 concentrations will be central to limiting the impacts of ocean acidification.

Introduction to the Magnuson-Stevens Act*

THE MAGNUSON-STEVENS ACT (MSA)[1] is the principal federal law governing marine fisheries in the United States. The Act regulates the conservation and management of fishery resources.[2] The MSA was first passed in 1976 as the Fishery Conservation and Management Act, and has been amended several times and reauthorized

---

* The editor gratefully acknowledges Lindsay Walton, Esq. for preparing this valuable introduction, which provides context for the discussion in chapters 4–6.

[1] 16 U.S.C. §§ 1801–1883 (2012).

[2] The Pew Charitable Trusts, *Managing Fish and Fishing in America's Oceans*, ENVTL. INITIATIVES (Aug. 8, 2011), http://www.pewenvironment.org/news-room/fact-sheets/managing-fish-and-fishing-in-americas-oceans-328450.

twice—first by the Sustainable Fisheries Act of 1996, and second by the Magnuson-Stevens Reauthorization Act of 2006.[3]

Congress declared the following purposes in the MSA: (1) to conserve and manage the United States fishery resources by establishing an exclusive economic zone off the coasts of the United States to prevent foreign fishing; (2) to support and encourage international fishery agreements for conservation and management of highly migratory species; (3) to promote domestic commercial and recreational fishing under conservation and management principles; (4) to provide requirements for preparation and implementation of fishery management plans to achieve and maintain, on a continuing basis, the optimum yield from each fishery; (5) to establish Regional Fishery Management Councils to manage fishery resources through the preparation, monitoring, and revision of Fishery Management Plans, which will enable stakeholder participation and will consider the state's social and economic needs; (6) to encourage development by the U.S. fishing industry of fisheries which are underutilized or not utilized by U.S. fishermen; and (7) to promote the protection of essential fish habitat.[4]

I. History of the Magnuson-Stevens Act

A. FISHERY CONSERVATION AND MANAGEMENT ACT OF 1976

Although the modern Magnuson-Stevens Act provides a powerful legal framework for fishery conservation and sustainability, the 1976 Fishery Conservation and Management Act was initially enacted in order to *promote* fishing in U.S. waters:[5] that is, to promote *domestic* fishing, as the original intent of the Act focused on cultivating the domestic fishing industry and managing foreign exploitation of U.S. fisheries.[6] To fulfill this objective, Congress established an Exclusive Economic Zone (EEZ), extending 200 miles and regulating ocean fishing within 3.4 million square miles of sea.[7] Foreign fleets were restrained from fishing, and sustainable management practices were mandated to rebuild fish populations for American fishermen's use.[8]

The Fishery Conservation and Management Act of 1976 was a success. Unfortunately, it was so successful that the expansion of the domestic fishing industry led to exploitation of many species, due to overfishing.[9]

---

[3] Act of Apr. 13, 1976, Pub. L. No. 94-265, 90 Stat. 331; Act of Oct. 11, 1996, Pub. L. No. 104-297, 110 Stat. 3559; Act of Jan. 12, 2007, Pub. L. No. 109-479, 120 Stat. 3575.

[4] 16 U.S.C. § 1801(b) (2012).

[5] *The Law That's Saving American Fisheries: The Magnuson-Stevens Fishery Conservation and Management Act*, THE OCEAN CONSERVANCY, http://www.oceanconservancy.org/our-work/fisheries/ff-msa-report-2013.pdf.

[6] Sarah M. Kutil, *Scientific Certainty Thresholds in Fisheries Management: A Response to Changing Climate*, 41 ENVTL. L. 233 (2011).

[7] THE OCEAN CONSERVANCY, *supra* note 5.

[8] Kutil, *supra* note 6.

[9] THE OCEAN CONSERVANCY, *supra* note 5.

Overfishing of a stock occurs when the rate or level of fishing mortality "jeopardizes the capacity of a fishery to produce the maximum sustainable yield on a continuing basis."[10] In fishery management, the maximum sustainable yield (MSY) is the amount of fish that can be taken from oceans over an indefinite period of time without depleting the resource.[11] American fishermen under the 1976 Act were surpassing MSY levels for many stocks, which led to overfishing. Stricter protection of ocean fisheries was needed, and several years later, the Sustainable Fisheries Act was conceived.

B. THE 1996 AMENDMENTS: THE SUSTAINABLE FISHERIES ACT

The 1996 Sustainable Fisheries Act recognized stock depletion and shifted focus of the Act to conservation of fish populations.[12] Although the original Act mandated sustainable management to prevent overfishing, it included no specific law or guidance to meet this requirement.[13] The 1996 amendments aimed to fill this gap by setting deadlines for rebuilding overfished populations, adding requirements to minimize harm to by-catch,[14] establishing MSY as the catch limit (but prohibiting overfishing for social or economic reasons), and identifying essential fish habitat.[15,16]

Despite the 1996 Amendments, the Magnuson-Stevens Act again failed to prevent overfishing in U.S. waters.[17] Though the congressional intent for conservation was reflected in the Act, it still lacked accountability measures necessary to prevent catches from exceeding limits.[18]

C. THE 2006 AMENDMENTS: THE MAGNUSON-STEVENS FISHERY CONSERVATION AND MANAGEMENT REAUTHORIZATION ACT OF 2006

The Magnuson-Stevens Fishery Conservation and Management Reauthorization Act of 2006 added some "teeth" to the MSA and strengthened the 1996 conservation goals by enacting strict legal mandates. The Amendments required science-based annual catch limits and accountability measures to meet objectives, and set a strict deadline to end overfishing.[19]

---

[10] 16 U.S.C. § 1802(34) (2007).

[11] Kutil, *supra* note 6.

[12] The Pew Charitable Trusts, *supra* note 2.

[13] THE OCEAN CONSERVANCY, *supra* note 5.

[14] By-catch is the unwanted fish and marine life caught during fishing for a specific species and discarded. 16 U.S.C. § 1802(2) (2012).

[15] Essential fish habitat is "the waters and substrate necessary to fish for spawning, breeding, feeding or growth." 16 U.S.C. § 1802(10) (2012).

[16] *See generally* Peter Shelley, *Have the Managers Finally Gotten It Right? Federal Groundfish Management in New England*, 17 ROGER WILLIAMS U.L. REV. 21 (2012).

[17] THE OCEAN CONSERVANCY, *supra* note 5.

[18] *Id.*

[19] *Id.*

Many consider annual catch limits (ACLs) the crux of the Magnuson-Stevens Act and a key mechanism to prevent overfishing. If ACLs are met or exceeded, accountability measures are triggered. Accountability measures are controls designed to prevent ACL overage and resolve overage if it occurs.[20] These measures may come in the form of seasonal closures, shortening of the fishing season, individual fishing quotas, and gear restrictions.[21] For example, in December 2013, accountability measures were triggered to close the fishery for Gulf of Maine shrimp after experts found the stock to be in the poorest condition they had ever seen.[22]

The 2006 Amendments set strict deadlines, requiring that ACLs and accountability measures be established by 2010 for overfished fisheries and 2011 for all other fisheries.[23] As of June 2013, overfishing had ended for twenty-two (58 percent) of the thirty-eight domestic U.S. stocks that were subject to overfishing in 2007 when the Magnuson-Stevens Act was reauthorized.[24]

II. Implementation of the Magnuson-Stevens Act

The Magnuson-Stevens Act is implemented by the Secretary of Commerce through the National Marine Fisheries Service (NMFS) of the National Ocean and Atmospheric Administration (NOAA).[25] It establishes eight regional fishery management councils, comprised of fishing stakeholders, that manage the fisheries within each council's geographical jurisdiction.[26] Under this unique design, the councils develop fishery management plans in accordance with ten national standards for fishery conservation and management that are contained within the MSA.[27]

---

[20] 50 C.F.R. § 600.310 (2014).

[21] *Id.*

[22] Tom Porter, *Fishery Closure Puts New England's Shrimp Season on Ice*, NPR (Feb. 7, 2013), http://www.npr.org/blogs/thesalt/2013/12/07/249275097/fishery-closure-puts-new-englands-shrimp-season-on-ice.

[23] Shelley, *supra* note 16.

[24] Written Testimony of Samuel D. Rauch III, Acting Assistant Administrator, National Marine Fisheries Service: Hearing on Magnuson-Stevens Fishery Conservation and Management Act Before the Comm. on Natural Res., U.S.H.R. (Sept. 11, 2013) (citing NMFS Office of Sustainable Fisheries, *2013 Quarterly Stock Status Reports, available at* http://www.nmfs.noaa.gov/sfa/statusoffisheries/SOSmain.htm).

[25] Jay Zitter, Annotation, *Validity, Construction, and Application of Magnuson Fishery Conservation and Management Act Provision Providing for National Standards for Fishery Conservation and Management (16 U.S.C.A. § 1851)*, 30 A.L.R. Fed. 2d 411 (2008).

[26] NOAA, Regional Fishery Management Councils, FISHERIES, http://www.nmfs.noaa.gov/sfa/management/councils/ (last visited Dec. 7, 2013).

[27] 16 U.S.C. § 1851(a) (2012).

A. REGIONAL FISHERY MANAGEMENT COUNCILS

In drafting the MSA, Congress recognized differences among U.S. fisheries and established a regional system for fishery management.[28] There are eight Fishery Management Councils (FMCs) in the United States, representing the New England, Mid-Atlantic, South Atlantic, Caribbean, Gulf of Mexico, Pacific, North Pacific, and Western Pacific regions.[29] Council members must be nominated by state governors and approved by the Secretary of Commerce.[30] Members represent diverse sectors, including commercial and recreational fishing, environmental, academic, and government interests, and others with expertise in fisheries management.[31] This distinctive arrangement allows the stakeholders in the fishery to actually make management decisions for the fishery.[32]

The councils are charged with developing Fishery Management Plans and amendments, developing rebuilding plans, assembling committees and advisory panels, developing research priorities in conjunction with Scientific and Statistical Committees, setting annual catch limits based on best available science, and conducting meetings for public participation in management.[33]

B. FISHERY MANAGEMENT PLANS

When it is determined by the Secretary of Commerce that a fishery is or is approaching overfished status, the regional council must develop and implement a Fishery Management Plan (FMP) and amend it as necessary.[34] FMPs include data to specify how a fishery will be managed in order to "achieve and maintain, on a continuing basis, the optimum yield from each fishery."[35] FMPs must comply with the ten national standards set forth in the Act.[36] The National Marine Fisheries Service determines whether an FMP complies with the Magnuson-Stevens Act and other applicable law, and the Secretary of Commerce may then approve, disapprove, or partially approve the plan.[37] If approved, federal regulations are promulgated and the plans are implemented.[38]

---

[28] The Pew Charitable Trusts, *supra* note 2.

[29] *Id.*

[30] THE OCEAN CONSERVANCY, *supra* note 5.

[31] NOAA, *supra* note 26.

[32] *Id.*

[33] *Id.*

[34] 16 U.S.C. § 1852(h)(1) (2012).

[35] *Id.* §§ 1801(b)(4), 1853 (2012).

[36] Kutil, *supra* note 6.

[37] Zitter, *supra* note 25.

[38] THE OCEAN CONSERVANCY, *supra* note 5.

C. NATIONAL STANDARDS

The Magnuson-Stevens Act includes ten national standards[39] that FMPs and amendments must follow to meet environmental and economic priorities[40] and ensure that sustainability goals are achieved.

These standards state: (1) Conservation and management measures shall prevent overfishing while achieving optimum yield; (2) Measures shall be based on the best scientific information available; (3) To the extent practicable, individual fish species shall be managed as a unit throughout its range and interrelated stocks of fish shall be managed as a unit or in close coordination; (4) Measures shall not discriminate between residents of different states and any allocation of privileges shall be fair and equitable; (5) Where practicable, conservation and management measures shall promote efficiency, but no measure shall have economic allocation as its sole purpose; (6) Measures shall allow for variations and contingencies in fisheries, fishery resources, and catches; (7) Where practicable, measures shall minimize costs and avoid duplications; (8) Consistent with conservation requirements of the Act, measures shall consider the importance of fishery resources to fishing communities to provide for the participation of and minimize adverse impacts to such communities; (9) Measures shall minimize by-catch or mortality from by-catch; (10) Measures shall promote safety to human life at sea.[41]

The national standards are often the subject of litigation, with courts considering whether a particular FMP complies.[42] Many council members, scholars, and others involved with fishery management note the challenge in meeting the standards because of their perceived competing objectives.[43] For example, National Standard 1 requires that conservation and management measures "shall prevent overfishing while achieving, on a continuing basis, the optimum yield from each fishery for the United States Fishing industry."[44] How do fishery managers reconcile requirements to both prevent overfishing *and* achieve optimum yield on a continuing basis?

III. The Magnuson-Stevens Act and Climate Change

While the Magnuson-Stevens Act has evolved to prevent overfishing, another threat to fisheries is emerging—climate change. Generally, fisheries are vulnerable to changes in environmental conditions, including the effects of climate change.[45] Rising ocean

---

[39] 16 U.S.C. § 1851(a) (2012).

[40] The Pew Charitable Trusts, *supra* note 2.

[41] 16 U.S.C. § 1851(a) (2012).

[42] Zitter, *supra* note 25.

[43] Shelley, *supra* note 16.

[44] 16 U.S.C. § 1851(a)(1) (2012).

[45] *Climate Impacts on Agriculture and Food*, EPA, http://www.epa.gov/climatechange/impacts-adaptation/agriculture.html (last updated Sept. 9, 2013).

temperatures and extreme weather are among some of the "new" dangers that impair fish reproduction, growth, migration patterns, and habitats.

As oceans warm, it is predicted that populations will become displaced as they move toward the poles and to deeper waters.[46] Water temperature changes can also influence development, reproduction, timing of spawning and migration, and growth of stock.[47] Extreme weather, including storms, heat waves, droughts, and floods may cause harm to fish populations and essential fish habitat.

The economic consequences from climate change on U.S. fisheries could be great. Fish movement may exacerbate catch uncertainty as the distribution of stock shifts.[48] Fishermen may find reductions in body size and changes in species composition.[49] These effects could cause a decrease in availability—or worse, end availability altogether— hurting the U.S. fishing industry and consumers.

The threats of climate change concern all stakeholders in fishery management, who appear to have at least one goal in common: continuing, sustainable fish populations. The Magnuson-Stevens Act has evolved to address overfishing and protect our fisheries. It must now continue to evolve and adapt to tackle the effects of climate change and ensure the sustainable management of fisheries.

---

[46] THE OCEAN CONSERVANCY, *supra* note 5.

[47] EPA, *supra* note 45.

[48] The Pew Charitable Trusts, *Climate Change Impacts on Global Fisheries*, ENVIRONMENTAL INITIATIVES (Nov. 20, 2011), http://www.pewenvironment.org/news-room/other-resources/climate-change-impacts-on-global-fisheries-85899366668.

[49] *Id.*

4 Moving Targets:
FISHERIES MANAGEMENT IN NEW ENGLAND IN THE MIDST OF CLIMATE CHANGE
Susan E. Farady

Introduction

> *The herring are not in the tides as they were of old;*
> *My sorrow! for many a creak gave the creel in the cart*
> *That carried the take to Sligo town to be sold,*
> *When I was a boy with never a crack in my heart.*

WILLIAM BUTLER YEATS, "The Meditation of the Old Fisherman"

It is well documented that climate change is directly impacting marine life.[1] Warmer, more acidic ocean waters affect species range, availability of food sources, and overall resilience. Along the East Coast of the United States, these impacts are being observed on species of commercial significance.[2] This chapter will examine the status of selected commercial fish species in New England, the management options available in response to the impacts of climate change, and considerations for future legal and management responses to impacts of climate change on fisheries.

I. Selected New England Fisheries

A. LOBSTER

American lobster (*Homarus americanus*) is an iconic New England fishery species. Recent fishery management issues illustrate how changes in lobster populations caused by climate change can impact a traditional fishery. Lobster in America has evolved from the early days of the United States, when the residents of Massachusetts Bay Colony found it washed up on beaches in two-foot-high piles. Governor William Bradford of Plymouth Plantation was embarrassed to admit to newly arrived colonists that lobster was the only food they could share with their friends. The Colony had to incorporate language in to contracts for indentured servants promising they would not be fed lobster more than three times a week.[3] The perception of lobster began to change as railways spread across the United States in the 1800s and railway managers realized they could serve lobster cheaply to passengers who might have no idea what it was and thought of it as something exotic; the price of lobster coincidentally began to rise.[4] Lobster was firmly established as a luxurious delicacy by the 1950s; an image of a lobster now adorns Maine license plates, where it is considered part and parcel of the New England tourist experience, and lobster is valued worldwide as a high-end food product.[5]

The stock has typically ranged from along the coasts and shores of the northern Canadian maritime provinces of Newfoundland and Nova Scotia, along the New England states from Maine to Connecticut, and down to North Carolina. The inshore U.S. fishery is most abundant from Maine to New Jersey, while the offshore U.S. fishery

---

[1] *See* Roger Griffis & Jennifer Howard, *Ocean and Marine Resources in a Changing Climate* (2013), *available at* http://cakex.org/virtual-library/oceans-and-marine-resources-changing-climate-technical-input-2013-national-climate-a.

[2] *Navigating Management and Governance Complexity in a Changing Environment* at 5, Discussion Document for East Coast Climate Change and Fisheries Governance Workshop, Mar. 19–21, 2014, http://static.squarespace.com/static/511cdc7fe4b00307a2628ac6/t/53220f84e4b0063da86ecd00/1394741124878/Discussion%20Document_Final.pdf (last visited Mar. 19, 2014).

[3] Daniel Luzer, *How Lobster Got Fancy*, Pacific Standard (June 7, 2013), http://www.psmag.com/navigation/business-economics/how-lobster-got-fancy-59440/.

[4] *Id.*

[5] *Id.*

occurs from Maine to North Carolina, with abundance declining from north to south.[6] Lobster is managed under a dual regulatory regime. States manage the fishery within their state waters from 0 to 3 miles out; the federal government via the Atlantic States Marine Fisheries Commission manages the resource in the EEZ from 3 to 200 miles offshore.[7] Lobster is fished by the deployment of fixed bottom-tending gear or "lobster pots." The pots are essentially crates encircled with mesh, with two places where lobster can enter and exit, attracted by a bag of bait inside. The pots are oftentimes connected by line and are dropped by a fishing vessel onto the bottom where they remain for up to several days before being retrieved by the vessel.[8]

Most U.S. lobster has historically been landed in northern New England waters in the Gulf of Maine, with Maine taking the lion's share, but a profitable fishery has also existed in southern New England, in the waters south of Cape Cod and off Rhode Island, and into Long Island Sound.[9] Trouble began for the southern New England (SNE) lobster fishery in the mid-1990s when a virulent version of epizootic lobster shell disease, previously observed only as occasional black spots in lobsters held in tanks, emerged in southern New England wild lobster stocks.[10] The disease, caused by a bacteria, produces black spots on the lobster's shell, which can then turn into holes that penetrate the shell. These openings can then allow the lobster's soft inner membranes to fuse with the hard outer shell, which in turn leaves the animal vulnerable to disease, interferes with molting and growth, and can ultimately cause death when the lobster's protective outer shell literally rots away.[11] Between 1998 and 2004, lobster landings in Buzzards Bay, Massachusetts, on the south side of Cape Cod, Massachusetts, were down 50 percent, in large part due to the impacts of lobsters with diseased shells.[12] Although the disease is not harmful to humans, and does not impact the lobster meat, diseased lobsters are unmarketable in the valuable live lobster market, which significantly impacts fishermen profits.

In the summer of 1999, an extensive outbreak of lobster shell disease dramatically impacted southern New England lobster, and landings plummeted as a result. For

---

[6] *Atlantic Lobster*, Atlantic States Marine Fisheries Commission, http://www.asmfc.org/species/american-lobster (last visited Mar. 18, 2014).

[7] *American Lobster, Management Information*, NOAA Fisheries Greater Atlantic Region, http://www.nero.noaa.gov/sustainable/species/lobster/ (last visited Mar. 19, 2014).

[8] See *FISHWATCH, U.S. Seafood Facts, American Lobster*, NOAA, http://www.fishwatch.gov/seafood_profiles/species/lobster/species_pages/american_lobster.htm (last visited Mar. 19, 2014) and Patrice McCarron & Heather Tetrault, *Lobster Pot Configurations in the Gulf of Maine*, Maine Lobstermen's Association (2012), http://www.mainelobstermen.org/pdf/Lobster_Gear_Report.pdf.

[9] *Atlantic Lobster, supra* note 6.

[10] See Sara E. Pratt, *A Mysterious Disease Afflicts Lobster Shells*, 46 WOODS HOLE OCEANOGRAPHIC INSTITUTION OCEANUS MAG. (2008), *available at* https://www.whoi.edu/oceanus/feature/a-mysterious-disease-afflicts-lobster-shells.

[11] *Id.*

[12] *Id.*

example, Long Island Sound landings of market-sized lobsters went from 11 million pounds in 1997 to 2.5 million pounds in 2002.[13] By 2007, landings were down 70–90 percent compared to 1998.[14] The 1999 outbreak has been attributed to both extensive use of pesticides ashore to control mosquitos in response to outbreaks of West Nile virus and to warming of ocean waters.[15] Subsequent research has confirmed the role of warming ocean waters on this southernmost range of the species, noting that the southern range of lobster has moved forty-three miles northward in the last decade.[16]

By May 2010, the ASFMC Lobster Technical Committee ("TC") announced that the SNE lobster stock was "experiencing recruitment failure caused by a combination of environmental drivers and continued fishing mortality."[17] The TC then recommended a five-year complete moratorium to spur stock rebuilding. Other management options were to do nothing, or to reduce harvest by 50–75 percent through measures affecting legal landing size, closed seasons, and elimination of an extra allotment of 10 percent of total trap tags to account for lost traps and/or tags.[18] The TC's recommendation for a total moratorium underwent extensive peer review and was verified.[19] In fact, there seemed to be little dispute among the managers about the situation they faced with irrefutable scientific information and a difficult management decision. As reported by *Commercial Fisheries News*, managers concluded that "the southern New England lobster stock was experiencing such profound environmental changes that all the stock rebuilding measures in the world might not matter anyway, so the most humane way to address the situation was to help the people who were left in the fishery transition to the next step."[20] The management plan ultimately adopted in August 2011 was to reduce landings "by 10% in each area managed by local management teams."

[13] *See* Nancy C. Balcom, *Lobster Resource Shows No Sign of Recovery as Research Progresses*, 3 CONN. SEA GRANT WRACK LINES (2002), *available at* http://seagrant.uconn.edu/publications/magazines/wracklines/springsummer03/lobstawl.pdf.

[14] *See* Anthony Faiola, *What's Killing the Lobsters of Long Island Sound?*, WASH. POST, Oct. 7, 2007, *available at* http://www.washingtonpost.com/wp-dyn/content/article/2007/10/06/AR2007100600874.html.

[15] *See id.*

[16] *See* Derrick Z. Jackson, *New England's Threatened Lobster*, BOS. GLOBE, Oct. 12, 2013, *available at* http://www.bostonglobe.com/opinion/columns/2013/10/11/lobster-now-pot-climate-change/Swxs8MtVUSoh84YgKwSC5O/story.html.

[17] American Lobster Technical Committee, *Recruitment Failure in the Southern New England Lobster Stock*, 1 (Apr. 17, 2010), *available at* http://www.asmfc.org/uploads/file/april2010_SNE_Recruitment_Failure_TCmemoB.pdf.

[18] Janice Plante, *ASMFC Lobster Board Backs Off 50%–75% Reduction; SNE Landings Cut to Ttart at 10%*, COMMERCIAL FISHERIES NEWS, Sept. 2011, at 1.

[19] *Id.; see also* Center for Independent Experts, External Independent Peer Review, *Recruitment Failure in the Southern New England Lobster Stock* (Oct. 11, 2010), *available at* http://www.asmfc.org/uploads/file/amLobster_CIE_Reports_2010.pdf.

[20] Plante, *supra* note 18, at 8.

By 2012, new management measures were in place to "reduce fishing exploitation," including size restrictions and various closures.[21] In 2013, a series of management measures were put in place, and others put out for public comment, to reduce the number of licensed lobster traps, which were "intended to enhance the ability of lobster business owners to plan for their future fishing operations as trap reductions are initiated."[22] Additionally, a closed season in Long Island Sound occurred in the fall of 2013 to help meet the ASMFC 10 percent reduction target.[23] The ASMFC reported in fall 2013 that "Members of the Board and TC believe that environmental and ecosystem changes have reduced the resource's ability to rebuild to historical levels," yet allowed fishing to continue amidst a series of complex measures to reduce traps and total fishing effort. [24]

The impacts of climate change on lobster have already had devastating effects in southern New England. The changes in New England's lobster stocks as a result of climate change are most likely not going to be limited to the SNE stock, and the difficult choices that the ASFMC managers addressed may also challenge other managers in the future regarding the fate of stocks off Massachusetts, New Hampshire, and Rhode Island. Annual lobster landings in Buzzards Bay, Massachusetts, in 2012 were 72,000 pounds, compared to 400,000 pounds per year in the 1990s and just under 1 million pounds in the 1980s.[25] Stocks within the Gulf of Maine appear to be shifting northward, and some cases of shell disease have been detected, although there is not enough data to know to what extent.[26] The coastal communities of Maine are not only currently landing the highest volume of lobster, but are nearly 100 percent dependent on lobster, as an outcome of complex fishery management and ecosystem factors. A dramatic downturn in lobster populations could have devastating effects on these communities.[27] Climate change impacts are most likely going to become a key part of management conversations regarding lobster stocks in the Gulf of Maine, including how to deal with fishermen dependent on stocks that will most likely decline.

[21] *See* ASMFC, *ASMFC Lobster Board Approves Area-Specific Measures to Reduce Fishing Exploitation on Southern New England Stock by 10%,* (Feb. 8, 2012), http://www.asmfc.org/uploads/PDF/pro4LobsterAddendumXVIIApproval.pdf.

[22] ASMFC, *ASMFC American Lobster Board Approves Addendum XXII and Releases Draft Addendum XXIII for Public Comment* (Oct. 30, 2013), http://www.asmfc.org/uploads/file/pr47AmLobsters_AddXXII_XXIII.pdf.

[23] Mark Harrington, *Lobstermen Brace after LI Sound Closed to Fishing,* NEWSDAY (Sept. 4, 2013), http://www.newsday.com/long-island/lobstermen-brace-after-li-sound-closed-to-fishing-1.6013464.

[24] ASMFC, *supra* note 22.

[25] *See* Jackson, *supra* note 16.

[26] Beth Staples, *The Gulf: Will Warming Waters Change Marine Life as We Know It?,* UMAINE TODAY (Fall 2013), *available at* https://umainetoday.umaine.edu/archives/fall-2013/the-gulf/.

[27] *Id.*

B. LONGFIN OR "LOLIGO" SQUID

Longfin squid (*Loligo pealeii*), typically called "loligo squid," is a species whose full range in the northwest Atlantic has extended from Maine to Florida, with greatest abundance from Georges Bank to Cape Hatteras. The U.S. fishery began in the late 1800s when the squid were harvested for bait.[28] Foreign vessels heavily fished longfin squid in U.S. waters from the 1960s to the 1980s. A domestic fleet developed after the passage of the Magnuson-Stevens Act, and since then a domestic fleet operates primarily in mid-Atlantic and southern New England waters.[29] Known for their mild, sweet flesh, longfin squid were recently the subject of legislation introduced at the Rhode Island General Assembly in 2013, and reintroduced in 2014, to declare "Rhode Island-style" calamari—fried squid rings tossed with pickled hot peppers—as the official state appetizer.[30]

In fact, the proposed legislation notes the crux of the issue with longfin squid management related to the effects of climate change. The bill notes that Rhode Island is the "east coast capital of squid," with the largest squid-fishing fleet on the Eastern Seaboard accounting for nearly 50 percent of all loligo squid landings, in turn making the fishery the state's most valuable commercial one.[31] The center of the loligo squid population (along with butterfish, summer flounder, and black sea bass) has moved steadily northward since the 1990s from waters off the coasts of New York and New Jersey to those off Rhode Island and Massachusetts shores.[32] Yet loligo squid is managed under the jurisdiction of the Mid-Atlantic Fishery Management Council (MAFMC). Rhode Island is not a member of the MAFMC, and thus lacks a vote on squid fishery management decisions. This situation has been noted by the Rhode Island congressional delegation since 2006. As recently as 2013, Senator Jack Reed has repeatedly introduced legislation to add Rhode Island representatives to the MAFMC.[33] As fish stocks move in response to changing ocean temperatures, acidity, and predator and prey species availability, this type of jurisdictional dilemma is likely to occur more often.

---

[28] Lisa Hendrickson & Larry Jacobsen, *NEFSC Status: Longfin Inshore Squid* (revised Dec. 2006), *available at* http://www.nefsc.noaa.gov/sos/spsyn/iv/lfsquid/.

[29] *Id.*

[30] H. 7446, *An Act Relating to State Affairs and Government—State Emblems,* Jan. session (2014), http://webserver.rilin.state.ri.us/BillText/BillText14/HouseText14/H7446.pdf; Reid Wilson, *Rhode Island Officials Push to Designate Official State Appetizer,* WASH. POST, Feb. 13, 2014, *available at* http://www.washingtonpost.com/blogs/govbeat/wp/2014/02/13/rhode-island-lawmakers-push-to-designate-official-state-appetizer/.

[31] *See* H. 7446, *supra* note 30.

[32] Mary Hudson & Jonathan Peros, *Preparing for Emerging Fisheries: Mid-Atlantic Stocks on the Move,* Gulf of Maine Research Institute (Sept. 2013), *available at* http://gmri.org/upload/files/Preparing%20for%20Emerging%20Fisheries%209-25-13%20copy.pdf.

[33] Press Release, Reed and Langevin Seek to Give RI Fishermen a Say on Squid Management (Apr. 4, 2013), *available at* http://www.reed.senate.gov/news/release/reed-langevin-seek-to-give-ri-fishermen-a-say-on-squid-management.

C. ATLANTIC COD

The Atlantic codfish (*Gadus morhua*) is found on both sides of the North Atlantic Ocean. The northwest Atlantic codfish stock occurs as far north as Greenland and as far south as North Carolina. United States' stocks are managed by the New England Fishery Management Council as two different stocks, Georges Bank and Gulf of Maine.[34] The cod is a fish that has been of great historical and economic importance for centuries to not only the United States, but also to Canada, Europe, and Native Americans.[35] Codfish otoliths (ear bones) are a common find in Native American middens, while Viking and Basque fishermen were among the first Europeans to travel to the rich waters off North America in pursuit of cod, which was dried and cured for long-term storage.[36] Descriptions of the "New World" discovered by Christopher Columbus and John Cabot included codfish as big as men, and plentiful enough to be scooped out of the ocean using a basket.[37] The impact of climate change on these fish as waters warm has exacerbated the already-harmful effects of modern fishing practices that have decimated these once-plentiful stocks.

Cod was an integral part of America's founding. The Pilgrims were attracted by the label "Cape Cod" on John Smith's map from his early explorations in the 1600s and were interested in profiting from codfish though they knew little about fishing.[38] During the brutal winter of 1621, as the Pilgrims were starving, British ships were off the New England coast filling their holds with codfish.[39] The Native Americans took pity on the starving Pilgrims and showed them how to catch cod among other fish and shellfish species, and the Pilgrims established fishing stations along the coastline of Massachusetts and Maine.[40]

Codfish continued to play a vital role in the young U.S. economy and identity. It was part of the "triangle trade" of slaves, rum, and salt fish that contributed to the young nation's wealth.[41] It was such a key component of Massachusetts's identity that a carved wooden codfish known as "the sacred cod" has hung inside the seat of Massachusetts government since the 1700s, well before the founding of the United States; it currently resides inside the chambers of the Massachusetts House of Representatives.[42] The fishery

---

[34] Ralph Mayo & Loretta O'Brien, *NEFSC Status: Atlantic Cod* (revised Dec. 2006), *available at* http://www. nefsc.noaa.gov/sos/spsyn/pg/cod/.

[35] Jennifer Kennedy, *Brief History of Cod Fishing,* ABOUT.COM, Marine Life, Education, http://marinelife. about.com/od/conservation/p/historyofcodfishing.htm (last visited Mar. 19, 2014).

[36] *Id.*

[37] Steven A. Murawski, *Brief History of the Groundfishing Industry of New England,* http://www.nefsc.noaa. gov/history/stories/groundfish/grndfsh1.html and http://www.nefsc.noaa.gov/history/stories/groundfish/ grndfsh2.html (last visited Mar. 19, 2014).

[38] Kennedy, *supra* note 35.

[39] *Id.*

[40] *Id.*

[41] Murawski, *supra* note 37.

[42] *History of the Sacred Cod*, Boston Univ. Ecological and Evolutionary Ethology of Fishes, https://www. bu.edu/eeef/sacredcodhistory.html (last visited Mar. 19, 2014).

was conducted for the next 150 years by sailing vessels going out to the fishing grounds on Georges Bank and the Grand Banks off Newfoundland; smaller vessels, dories, were launched from the large "mother" vessel, and fishermen would row out and fish out of the dory using hand lines.[43] The efficiency of the fishery began to increase in the 1920s as sailboats were phased out and replaced by vessels driven by engines, which were able to go farther and more reliably than vessels solely dependent on the wind.[44]

A dramatic increase in catches occurred after World War II, as navigation and engineering technology developed to serve wartime purposes was applied to bigger, faster fishing boats that could go far offshore away from their homeports, catch more fish with the use of large trawling gear that dragged behind the vessels, and store and freeze it aboard.[45] Likewise, there was a dramatic increase in foreign vessels from the Soviet Union and other countries fishing off the coast of the United States on the rich codfish and other groundfish stocks. This development contributed in no small part to the passage of the Magnuson-Stevens Act (MSA) in 1976, and the United States declaring its Exclusive Economic Zone (EEZ) out to two hundred miles, in order to protect the stocks from foreign factory trawlers.[46]

Once the codfish in U.S. waters were available exclusively for the U.S. fleet, the fishery was aggressively conducted; the U.S. government encouraged growth in the fishery through tax subsidies for vessel owners to build bigger, more powerful boats.[47] Although landings increased for a few years, it did not take long for the stock to demonstrate signs of depletion. By the late 1980s and early 1990s, the codfish off New England were at low levels and the subject of much litigation by conservation groups advocating for more conservative management.[48] Ultimately, more restrictions were imposed on fishing as a result of both litigation and amendments to the law in 1996 and 2006, including designating different types of closed areas, restrictions on gear type, and limitations on catch and time spent fishing under a "days at sea" calculation.[49] Despite much litigation and regulation, overfishing of cod stocks continued, and continues. Gulf of Maine cod has been overfished for fifteen of the past seventeen years, and Georges Bank cod has been overfished for thirteen of the last seventeen years.[50]

---

[43] Murawski, *supra* note 37.

[44] *Id.*

[45] *Id.*

[46] *Id.*

[47] *Id.*

[48] *See* Peter Shelley, *Have the Managers Finally Gotten It Right? Federal Groundfish Management in New England*, 17 ROGER WILLIAMS U. L. REV. 21 (2012).

[49] *Id.*

[50] *Strengthening Fishing Communities and Increasing Flexibility in Fisheries Management: Hearing on a Bill to Improve and Strengthen Many Provisions of the Current Magnuson-Stevens Fishery Conservation and Management Act Before the H. Comm. on Natural Resources,* 113th Cong. 2 (2014) (statement of Peter Shelley, Esq., Vice President Conservation Law Foundation), *available at* http://naturalresources.house. gov/calendar/eventsingle.aspx?EventID=367382.

Managing to protect cod as a single species is further confounded by its habits and the ecosystem in which it functions. Cod are considered one of several species of "groundfish" managed by the New England Fishery Management Council under one plan.[51] The fish are often found and caught together, so it is difficult to develop effective regulations that specifically address catches of just one of these species.[52] The fishery changed after the 2006 MSA amendments from being managed using primarily "input controls," (i.e., measures that control the amount of effort put into the fishery, such as number of days fished, mesh size, and closed areas) especially "days-at-sea," to an "output control" method that allocates a portion of the total harvest to eligible fishermen, primarily to provide managers a better means of reaching the law's accountability measures.[53]

The fishery's most recent management crisis began in 2011, when managers learned that recent assessments indicated codfish stocks were in much worse shape than previous assessments had indicated. For example, fishing mortality on Gulf of Maine cod was five times higher than it should be, spawning stock biomass was only one-fifth of what it should be, and even if no fishing occurred in the future, there was no chance the stock would be rebuilt by the 2014 deadline.[54] As a result, managers reduced 2013 quotas of Gulf of Maine cod by 80 percent and Georges Bank cod by 61 percent.[55] Amidst the dire scientific news was more litigation. Massachusetts municipalities and fishing ports of New Bedford and Gloucester filed a lawsuit challenging the groundfish management plan in place since 2010. Ultimately, the First Circuit Court of Appeals upheld a lower court decision in favor of the government and an intervening conservation organization after two years of litigation. The court determined that some of the town of New Bedford's claims were "misguided" or "inaccurate," and that they had "no textual basis for the argument."[56]

Regardless of how one characterizes the past thirty years of the New England groundfish fishery, the results to date are clear: there is significantly less fishing effort and fewer fishermen, and codfish stocks remain in dire straits. The impacts of climate change and fishing practices have played, and will continue to play, a significant role in the status

---

[51] Fifteen species of fish are managed under the Northeast Multispecies Large Mesh/Groundfish Plan. These fish all live near the bottom and feed on benthic organisms. *See* New England Fishery Management Council, *Northeast Multispecies Fishery Management Plan,* http://nefmc.org/nemulti/summary/large_mesh_multi.pdf (last visited Mar. 19, 2014).

[52] *See id.*

[53] Jonathan M. Labaree, *Sector Management in New England's Groundfish Fishery: Dramatic Change Spurs Innovation,* Gulf of Maine Research Institute (Aug. 2012), *available at* http://gmri.org/upload/files/Sector%20Review%20Report.pdf.

[54] Janice M. Plante, *2012 Priorities: GOM Cod, Other Crises Trump Accumulation Limits,* COMMERCIAL FISHERIES NEWS, Jan. 2012, at 10.

[55] *Atlantic Cod,* NOAA Fishwatch, http://www.fishwatch.gov/seafood_profiles/species/cod/species_pages/atlantic_cod.htm (last updated Feb. 10, 2014).

[56] Peter Shelley, *Court Upholds New England's Landmark Fishing Law,* CONSERVATION LAW FOUNDATION BLOG (Nov. 30, 2012), http://www.clf.org/blog/tag/new-bedford-v-locke/.

of this stock, and the likelihood that codfish stocks can rebuild.[57] There is strong evidence that as waters warm, these codfish stocks (as well as others) are shifting north, that stocks already diminished by fishing effort contract into smaller areas, and that key zooplankton that codfish prey upon are declining in response to warmer, more acidic waters.[58] These changes are not limited to codfish and have had biological consequences on multiple levels in the food chain.[59] As oceanographic conditions continue to shift as a result of climate change, it is likely that the state of codfish stocks will change, and fishery management questions will become more complex.

II. Key Components of Existing Fishery Management

The primary law governing domestic fishery management is the Magnuson-Stevens Fishery Management and Conservation Act (MSA), initially passed in 1976 with significant amendments in 1996 and 2006.[60] Fisheries are governed by Regional Councils. The Councils act as a unique stakeholder-dominated management interface between the federal government and citizens. The Councils are made up of state government representatives as well as stakeholder representatives. Councils have the responsibility for developing fishery management plans based on scientific advice, with the National Oceanic and Atmospheric Association (NOAA) retaining the authority for approving or rejecting a Council's recommendations for consistency with the law. Fishery management under the MSA via the Council system has a few key components that are relevant for this analysis of the challenges illustrated by the selected New England species in this chapter. Specifically:

1. **Definition of geographic range.** The management of any given fishery is based on where it is defined to occur, and hence responsibility for management must be designated to the appropriate regional fishery management council.
2. **Parameters of appropriate catches.** Councils decide how much of a stock can be landed based on input from their Scientific and Statistics Committees (SSCs) based on legal and scientific standards that in effect intend to allow enough harvest to keep fishermen in business and consumers fed while allowing enough stock to remain to be able to propagate future generations of fish.

---

[57] Heather Goldstone, *Climate Change Forces Re-evaluation of Fishery Management,* WCAI (July 17, 2013), http://capeandislands.org/post/climate-change-forces-reevaluation-fishery-management.

[58] Kevin D. Friedland et al., *Thermal Habitat Constraints on Zooplankton Species Associated with Atlantic Cod* (Gadus morhua) *on the U.S. Northeast Continental Shelf,* PROGRESS OCEANOGRAPHY (2013), *available at* http://dx.doi.org/10.1016/j.pocean.2013.05.011.

[59] *Id.*

[60] For a helpful background discussion of the Magnuson-Stevens Act, *see supra* "Introduction to the Magnuson Stevens Act," immediately prior to Chapter 4 in this volume.

This determination is calculated using information from past assessments and catches, and attempts to forecast stock conditions in the future.

3. **Who can participate in the fishery.** Decisions are also made regarding *who* is eligible to participate in a given fishery. This determination can be based on an individual's fishing history and, depending on the management system used, may be allocated as a tradable quota either to an individual or a group of fishermen, or as an individual limit.

Fishery management decisions under the MSA have been the subject of controversy among regulators and stakeholders to date, even in relatively stable climatic conditions. These decisions will not get any easier, and the MSA in its current state will become less useful as the climate changes. Climate change is impacting where fish occur, and hence where management jurisdiction is currently defined will not be true in the future. Similarly, predicting how many fish can be caught using past stock assessments will become less and less reliable as those stocks move, contract, or decline in response to warmer, more acidic oceans. Finally, deciding who can participate in a fishery based on past fishing activity will become more difficult, as fishermen can no longer catch the species they used to catch in a particular area, and may not have licenses to catch new species moving into their fishing grounds.

Another important regulatory regime for U.S. fisheries is the Atlantic States Marine Fisheries Commission (ASMFC). Since the 1940s, the ASMFC coordinates fishery management in state waters for all of the states along the Atlantic coast. The ASMFC started off as a voluntary compact among the states, and was formalized in 1993 when Congress passed the Atlantic Coastal Fisheries Cooperative Management Act (ACFCMA).[61] ACFCMA provides ASMFC the authority to create coastal fishery management plans (CFMPs) for stocks that move among different state waters, but generally do not enter the EEZ. If a state does not adopt the measures prescribed in a CFMP, the Secretary of Commerce can impose a moratorium on that fishery in that state. ASMFC can also manage in federal waters when a fishery management plan (FMP) has not been already adopted for a stock that moves between state and federal waters. ASMFC is required to consult with the appropriate Regional Fishery Management Councils when developing a CFMP and accompanying regulations in this situation.[62] The cross-jurisdictional nature of the ASMFC regime may provide a useful model for future fisheries management that can respond to changes in fish stocks and fishing effort beyond traditional jurisdictional boundaries as a result of climate change.

---

[61] Atlantic Coastal Fisheries Cooperative Management Act, 16 U.S.C. §§ 5101–5108 (2012).

[62] *See also About Us,* Atlantic States Marine Fisheries Commission, http://www.asmfc.org/about-us/program-overview (last visited Mar. 19, 2014).

III. Responding to Climate Change Impacts in New England Fisheries

Each New England fishery in this chapter provides a unique context for examining the impacts of climate change on fisheries management, the challenges posed to existing fishery law and management regimes by climate change, and areas where existing law and management may need to be adjusted. This section will examine each fishery for the lessons that can be gathered in seeking to respond to climate change impacts.

A. SNE LOBSTER

The case of the SNE lobster stock presents the question of what should be done when it is clear a stock can no longer support a viable commercial fishery. In this situation, managers had warning signs that the stock was in decline well before the recommendation to shut down the fishery completely. It took almost two years for managers to act, and when they acted, the management decision was an incremental 10 percent reduction in effort.

So how did management go from a recommendation to stop *all* fishing immediately, to long-term incremental reductions? Managers were well aware of the dire nature of the stock status. Similarly, they were fully aware that anything less than a full moratorium would do little, if anything, to help the stock recover, or at the very least, not get any worse. They deliberately chose to give up on the stock and slowly transition fishermen off of dependence on that fishery, at the expense of the remaining lobsters and the impact on the rest of the ecosystem of continued lobster fishing. The dilemma that the ASMFC Lobster Board faced is one that managers may face again regarding stocks under significant stress, namely, how to weigh the benefits of not inflicting further fishery pressure on a stressed stock against the benefits of gradually phasing out the economic interests dependent on that fishery.

What can be learned from the SNE lobster stock experience? Here are a few considerations, with perhaps more questions than answers:

1. **Timeliness.** It took nearly a year and a half after the 2010 assessment, recommending a complete moratorium, for managers to act. Furthermore, there were signals for at least the preceding decade before that assessment that the stock was in decline. Would it have made a difference for the stock status, and ultimately on those who fish that stock, if all fishing had stopped within a few months after the assessment recommendations?

2. **Realistic assessment of a stressed fishery.** Despite years of scientific research, management actions, and public process, and extensive publicity about the state of the SNE lobster and the accompanying management dilemma, there appears to still be at least some level of denial among fishermen. In a story from September 2013 regarding the three-month closure of lobstering in Long Island

Sound, the head of the Long Island Sound Lobstermen Association was quoted as saying "In the end it [the closure] is about market share," and that he believed that "powerful interests" on the ASMFC, such as representatives from Maine and New Hampshire, pushed for closure of the Sound to increase their reach into Long Island, that the closure was a "feel-good" gesture by the regulators whom he wished "would go away and leave us alone."[63] The same article included quotes from another fisherman as saying "it's good they're giving it [the stock] a rest," and other information that clearly demonstrated it was essentially impossible to make a living lobstering in this area.[64] Perhaps there is little that can be done to impact stakeholder perception about manager motivation, as well as media coverage that emphasizes the controversy and the superficial, yet easily understood, story of fishing shutdowns and related human impacts. However, this example illustrates a need to consider different stakeholder engagement and communication about the nature of the problem and available solutions, as the perception of industry leaders and media coverage can certainly feed into the management outcome.

3. **Trade-off analysis**. What has been remarkable about the SNE lobster example is how overtly the nature of the decision was recognized early on. There was little real debate since 2010 about the state of the stock, and the ultimate future of the fishery, in contrast to other fisheries such as New England groundfish and countless others where rancorous debate about the validity of the science and the future of the fishery dominates management discussions. Here, it was stated repeatedly that there was little chance the stock could ever recover enough to support a sustainable fishery; the fishery was going to end, and the question was how and when to do it. The ultimate decision was made to err on the side of "phasing out" fishing effort incrementally over many years, the intent being to gradually provide fishermen time to find other means of making a living.

This "phasing-out" decision was perfectly rational and one that was well-debated in a democratic process, but was it made with a true calculation of the costs and benefits? It may have been less costly, and arguably more "culturally sensitive," to provide direct economic relief to fishermen during severe fishery cutbacks as opposed to a longer period of attrition and financial loss and incremental cutbacks. It is doubtful whether an immediate moratorium could have provided any chance for the stock to recover and adapt, but there is at least a question of whether that action could have eventually provided a sustainable SNE fishery, even if greatly reduced. Managers may also need to consider the impacts of gradually allowing fishermen to shift fishing pressure on other stocks to avoid the unintended consequence of triggering another fishery collapse.

---

[63] *See* Harrington, *supra* note 23.
[64] *Id.*

Ecological impacts may also need to be considered in the context of the appropriate management action to take when a stock is in collapse. Managers may also need to consider the ecological consequences of continued fishing pressure on a collapsed stock, as there may be impacts on other parts of the ecosystem caused by removal of the SNE lobster stock. Even if there was no chance at all for any SNE lobster to recover and there are no ecological impacts caused by the species' absence, it may be desirable to remove all fishing pressure and give any remaining species, presumably those at this point that are apparently survivors of shell disease and somewhat adapted to changing conditions, the chance to move north and perhaps genetically influence the resilience of remaining stocks.

B. LOLIGO SQUID

The situation with loligo squid illustrates what can be anticipated to become a common dilemma in fishery management in the climate change era: a stock shifts to a location and a significant fishery develops outside the defined boundaries of the assigned Regional Fishery Management Council. This is well documented over several years with the loligo squid fishery in Rhode Island, and has been recognized by Senator Jack Reed in his efforts to get a singular law passed to address the situation, and even by the state legislature in the effort to name a loligo squid dish the official state appetizer. Yet management remains at the MAFMC where Rhode Island is not a participant. This raises some key questions about how fishery management can respond to such a situation:

1. **Trigger.** What is the appropriate trigger to declare that a fishery is no longer where it used to be? The law contains definitions, targets, and triggers for many management actions, when a stock is "overfished," what the ACL is, and what the rebuilding target and the rebuilding time frame is, yet no legal guidance on how to consider a shifting stock. Perhaps it is when a certain percentage of landings and/or the fleet is now coming from a different state outside of the MAFMC's jurisdiction, such as nearly 50 percent of loligo squid being landed in Rhode Island, and the largest loligo squid fleet homeported in Rhode Island. It is also worth considering how long any such shift should be observed to confirm that it is indeed a true shift and not just a one- or two-season anomaly.

2. **Geographic scale.** As a stock such as loligo squid moves to waters under the jurisdiction of another Council, is it worthwhile to consider whether the current geographic scale and definitions of Council jurisdiction will continue to make sense. For example, if species continue to shift farther northward, perhaps the boundaries between the current Mid-Atlantic and New England Councils' jurisdiction should be re-evaluated. There may also need to be some sort of an ad hoc "transition zone" body that can include members from adjacent existing Councils to address management of stocks that appear to be a in a state of

geographic flux. As the conditions of warmer, more acidic waters redefine ecological zones, fixed bottom topography and character may become more important as features around which to draw jurisdictional lines.

3. **Management options**. The situation with loligo squid illustrates a much more dynamic fishery management situation than either managers or fishermen are accustomed to, and suggests a need to re-examine the way fishing efforts are managed and defined. For example, it may no longer make sense to have single species FMPs and licenses, when it appears stocks are moving, and in some cases moving rapidly. Furthermore, it may be an illogical expenditure of management effort, research dollars, and stakeholder engagement for management and fishermen to continue to focus on a species that is moving out of their jurisdiction, at the cost of not being able to pursue a species moving into their jurisdiction because they have not prepared the necessary assessment, plan, and permitting structure. As species move into places where they have not been fished before, managers will need to determine how to allocate access to new entrants who do not have any history of landings, transition out previous entrants from an obsolete fishery, and provide access and incentives for fishermen to target new stocks that are moving in. Perhaps what is needed is a more flexible regional "ecosystem" permit structure that gives fishermen access to more than one stock within a region, as the presence and absence of stocks ebbs and flows over a season and over years, if the science that supports fishery management decisions can be redesigned to inform such decisions, assessing stocks in an ecosystem range parameter rather than a single-species format.

C. ATLANTIC COD

Atlantic cod may already be a cautionary tale, yet may also present some valuable insight into the future of climate-impacted fishery management. The latest research information about how codfish are reacting to changing ocean conditions is more complex than overfishing pressures or moving to colder waters. Rather, the research suggests deficiencies in plankton at the bottom of the food web are also contributing to the dire situation of Atlantic cod.[65] This plankton also supports many other parts of the food chain, such as whales. This situation reveals the complexity of striving to selectively manage species of commercial interest while they are most likely being impacted by the impacts of climate change that also impact many other species. Issues to be considered are:

1. **Accurately assessing stock status**. Given that the current method of forecasting future available stocks based on past historical status is rapidly becoming irrelevant as fish behavior changes, it might be more accurate to assess the true

---

[65] *See* Friedland et al., *supra* note 58.

status of a climate-stressed stock by also including key ecosystem indicators in addition to the numbers of fish relative to past assessments. In this situation, the availability, or the lack thereof, of a key zooplankton prey species may be an important signal regarding the ability of the stock to produce spawning stock biomass, recover from and withstand fishing pressure, and be a thriving fishery, whereas numbers of fish may not fully indicate the true status of the stock.

2. **Accurate characterization of the fishery's future**. Similar to both SNE lobster and loligo squid, it is clear that the Atlantic codfish fishery is not currently, and most likely will not ever be, what it was. Because of the cod's position in the food chain as a predator, unlike the lobster as a scavenger, there may be more significant ecological trade-offs to continuing to fish the species, when making the cost-benefit analysis of allowing a continued, albeit greatly reduced, fishery, versus stopping all fishing pressure and inflicting economic harm. If a moratorium were to occur, other management measures should be considered, above and beyond the declaration of a fishery crisis and availability of federal funds, to lessen economic distress on the remaining fishermen and shift effort to new stocks becoming more available in that ecoregion.

IV. Future Fishery Management Responses

These selected examples of New England fisheries impacted by climate change demonstrate a need to reconsider how fishery management and law should be structured in the future. It is clear that how scientific information is used and how it is currently applied in making management decisions does not operate well when fish stocks and fishing efforts are reacting in very different ways now than they have in the past, as a result of changing ocean conditions. Conditions are only going to continue to change, and, ideally, the fishery management structure needs to change as well.

Professor Robin Kundis Craig has provided some valuable guiding principles for reforming fishery management in the climate change era:

1. Vigilant monitoring and assessment;
2. Promote resilience, including eliminating or reducing non–climate related stressors, such as fishing effort;
3. Utilize much more long-term, interdisciplinary, and coordinated planning;
4. Use a more flexible, principled flexible regulatory regime; and
5. Overtly accept climate change adaptation in management decisions.[66]

---

[66] *See* Robin Kundis Craig, *Stationarity Is Dead—Long Live Transformation: Five Principles for Climate Change Adaptation Law*, 34 HARV. ENVTL. L. REV. 9 (2010).

In addition to the principles that Professor Craig proposed to guide development of a new fishery management system, the following should also be considered:

1. *Make fishing access more geographically based as opposed to species based.* Providing fishermen with a regional permit as opposed to a groundfish permit or a squid permit could provide fishermen and managers the flexibility to fish for stocks as they move in and out of geographic areas.

2. *Establish a system that provides fishermen who have never fished a species access to that species if it moves into their area, putting less of a premium on "fishing history" as the currency to allocate future access.* This could be accomplished via the use of permit banks, or by treating fishing access as a kind of commodity or future to be traded.

3. *Establish triggers that more accurately reflect the status of a stock or fishery in response to climate change, instead of simply "overfished" or "overfishing is occurring."* Both managers and fishermen need to more specifically focus on what is at stake in order to have honest discussions about what to do. Is it worth chasing the last cod or lobster? What are the environmental consequences of extirpating a particular stock from a particular area? Can fishing efforts be diverted to other species?

4. *Establish a more flexible way for management to move between regional councils.* There could be ad hoc "transition zone" committees made up of members that ensure that management of a stock such as squid follows it as it moves, so as to more accurately reflect the representation and geographic range of the fishery and the species.

5. *Shift assessment and monitoring of fish stocks to more closely adhere to topographic features.* Water conditions are changing, as are the systems of animals and plants functioning within them; topographic features are not. It might make more sense for the New England Regional FMC to devise FMPs for the Georges Bank Fishery Area, or the Stellwagen Bank/Jefferys Ledge Fishing Area, instead of for specific species. Additionally, it is imperative to establish some sentinel control sites to be able to assess how conditions are changing outside of fishing effort.

Although not intended to specifically address the impacts of climate change, current suggestions for reauthorization of the MSA could also be utilized to make fishery management more responsive to climate change. For example, language intended to make rebuilding under the MSA more flexible contains language regarding considering the depleted condition of a stock when it may be "outside the jurisdiction of the Council or the rebuilding program cannot be effective only by limiting fishing activities," and "evaluating environmental impacts on rebuilding progress."[67] Similarly, the draft legislation

---

[67] Strengthening Fishing Communities and Increasing Flexibility in Fisheries Management Act, H.R. 4742, § 3, (a)(2)(B)(II), (a)(2)(E), 113th Congress (2013).

touches on a climate change consideration regarding the ACL requirement: "In establishing annual catch limits a Council *may* consider changes in an ecosystem...."[68] These suggested changes are contemplating some consideration of climate change, but they do not adequately address the changed regime that fisheries are going to continue to operate in, and do not sufficiently overhaul the management system.

The challenge of making MSA more responsive to the impacts of climate change involves changing a key assumption from one that the ecosystem and fisheries are operating in a stable state as informed by past data, to one that the ecosystem and fish stocks are changing.[69] Additionally, a shift in management note to "ecosystem-based fishery management" (EBFM) that can incorporate triggers for management actions based on the changes to the ecosystem caused by climate change will require a better understanding of all impacts on the system, not just the number of fish in a stock and the amount caught by fishermen. An EBFM approach that can better inform fishery management decisions in a changing system will need to include information on how environmental changes and fishing efforts are influencing ecological indicators, as well as information on what specific pressure causes significant changes to ecosystem function.[70]

Conclusion

Our current fishery management regime is inadequate to respond to changes in fish stocks and the ecosystem caused by climate change. The impacts of climate change have already had significant impacts on New England fisheries, and the communities that have depended on them for generations, and the evidence is clear that these impacts will continue. Current fishery management needs to be revised to take into account how fish stocks are reacting to climate change, and to develop a regime that can manage fishing efforts more responsively to changes in where fish are found, how many of them there are, and who is catching them.

Law can be notoriously slow to catch up to the realities of changing environmental conditions, and to be creative in responding to issues. Fishery management needs to be overhauled quickly, and with a radical re-evaluation of what the legal principles are, how scientific information is applied, and what economic incentives can be used to ensure there is a future for sustainable fisheries in New England.

---

[68] *Id.* § 4, (a)(m)(1) (emphasis added).

[69] *Navigating Management and Governance Complexity, supra* note 2, at 7.

[70] *See* Scott Large et al., *Defining Trends and Thresholds in Response of Ecological Indicators to Fishing and Environmental Pressure,* 70 ICEA J. MARINE SCI. 755 (2013).

5 Responding to Climate Change Impacts to Fisheries and Marine Habitat in the Gulf of Mexico
Dr. Richard J. McLaughlin*

Introduction

The Gulf of Mexico (GOM) is globally important as a center of marine biodiversity, fisheries, hydrocarbon development, maritime transport, and recreation, making it one of the most productive ecosystems in the world.[1] The GOM accounts for an average of 1.3 billion pounds of commercial fishery landings per year, yielding a value of $662 million.[2]

---

* The author would like to acknowledge the help of Ph.D. student Heather Wade for her research assistance on the chapter.

[1] *See generally* Ivonne Cruz & Richard J. McLaughlin, *Contrasting Marine Policies in the United States, Mexico, and Cuba and the European Union: Searching for an Integrated Strategy for the Gulf of Mexico Region*, 51 OCEAN & COASTAL MGMT. 51 (2008).

[2] National Ocean Service, *Gulf of Mexico at a Glance*. Washington DC: U.S. Department of Commerce, National Oceanic and Atmospheric Administration 10 (2008).

About 25 million marine recreational fishing trips are also taken in the GOM each year, accounting for 28 percent of the total U.S. marine recreational fishing trips.[3] Climate change could have a significant effect on all aspects of fisheries resources in the region, including the spatial distribution of fish, recruitment and growth, quality and quantity of commercial and recreational catches, and the resulting economic consequences to those who depend on fisheries-related activities for their living.

More broadly, climate change will have a number of important impacts on coastal and marine ecosystem health in the GOM. These include shifts in water temperature and currents, destruction of coastal wetlands due to accelerated sea-level rise, changes in freshwater inflows, introduction of invasive species, ocean acidification, and little understood mixing of waters between the continental shelf and shallower areas that will affect the availability of nutrients and disposition of larval and juvenile organisms.[4]

Changing environmental conditions require modifications of existing fisheries resources management strategies and policies, coupled with adequate enforcement. This chapter will describe the unique natural and anthropogenic characteristics of the GOM and how global climate change may impact fisheries resources in the region. It will also examine the current fisheries management regimes of the three nations that surround the GOM and recommend actions that may more adequately address the challenges that are likely to emerge due to climate change.

I. Gulf of Mexico Physical Environment

The physical environment of the GOM is one of great diversity, both in terms of land and water. The Gulf is 1,600 kilometers east to west, 900 kilometers north to south, and has 1.5 million square kilometers of surface area, making it the ninth largest body of water in the world. When all bays and estuaries are included, the total shoreline for the GOM is over 27,000 kilometers in the United States alone.[5]

Much of the built environment in the GOM Region is found in what is called the Coastal Belt. The Coastal Belt includes U.S. counties that are entirely contained within or intersect the boundaries of Coastal and Estuarine Drainage Areas in the United States, *municipios* (equivalent to U.S. counties) that are entirely contained within or intersect coastal watershed boundaries in Mexico, and *municipios* of the five provinces that front the GOM in Cuba.[6] Coastal areas of the GOM are growing quickly in population, and a

---

[3] *Id.* at 9.

[4] John W. Day et al., *Global Climate Change Impacts on Coastal Ecosystems in the Gulf of Mexico: Considerations for Integrated Coastal Management, in* GULF OF MEXICO: ORIGIN, WATERS, AND BIOTA, 4 ECOSYSTEM MANAGEMENT 262–64 (John W. Day & Alejandro Yanez-Arancibia eds., 2013).

[5] F. Moretzsohn et al., General Facts about the Gulf (2014), *available at* http://www.gulfbase.org/facts.php.

[6] D. Yoskowitz et al., Gulf 360: State of the Gulf of Mexico. Texas A&M University-Corpus Christi, Texas: Harte Research Institute for Gulf of Mexico Studies (2013).

number of key sectors of the region's economy, including offshore energy, vessel construction, fishing, marine transportation, and tourism, are concentrated there. Population of the five U.S. GOM states is projected to increase about 40 percent, from 44.2 million in 1995 to 61.4 million in 2025.[7] GOM coastal populations are also growing in Cuba and Mexico. In the Mexican states of Tabasco, Campeche, and Quintana Roo, almost the entire state populations live in coastal *municipos*.[8] Land cover along the Coastal Belt includes land uses such as cropland, forests, grasslands, wetlands, and urban areas. The pressure exerted by population growth and economic development has changed the natural function of many GOM coastal lowland areas where natural resources are being degraded by inappropriate land use decisions.[9] These issues become aggravated by global climate change, which will accelerate sea-level rise and other environment-related factors.

Ocean currents are an important physical component of the GOM because they allow for the transportation of life, nutrients, and pollutants across the entire Gulf. These currents are complex and can have major implications for various environmental conditions. Water enters the Gulf of Mexico through the Yucatan Strait and exits through the Florida Strait. This specific current circulates as the Loop Current, which eventually turns into the Gulf Stream of the Atlantic Ocean. Separation from the Loop Current takes place, creating eddies that affect regional current patterns.[10] These isolated eddies are an important part of the ocean currents in the Gulf because they can "incubate red tides, affect intensity of hurricanes, and transport invasive species."[11] The interchange between ocean currents and these natural and physical processes are important to the overall health of the GOM, and they all may be exacerbated by climate change.

A large variety of wildlife depends on the ecosystems in the Gulf of Mexico. Examples of some of the more charismatic animals include sea turtles, waterfowl, wading birds, shorebirds, songbirds, and whale sharks. Five of the world's seven sea turtles make their home in the Gulf of Mexico. These are the Kemp's Ridley, Loggerhead, Leatherback, Hawksbill, and Green turtles. These five species are considered endangered, and their decline can be attributed to incidental catching by the fishing industry, habitat destruction, capture for food or consumer products, and the harvesting of eggs.[12] Approximately

---

[7] *Id.* at 28.

[8] David Zarate Lomeli at al., *Toward a Regional Program for ICZM in the Mexican Area of the Gulf of Mexico and the Caribbean: An Analysis Revisiting Two Decades of Publications, in* GULF OF MEXICO: ORIGIN, WATERS, AND BIOTA, 4 ECOSYSTEM MANAGEMENT 417, 421 (John W. Day & Alejandro Yanez-Arancibia eds., 2013).

[9] Alejandro Yanez-Arancibia & John W. Day, *Systems Approach for Coastal Ecosystem-Based Management in the Gulf of Mexico: Ecological Pulsing, the Basis for Sustainable Management, in* GULF OF MEXICO: ORIGIN, WATERS, AND BIOTA, 4 ECOSYSTEM MANAGEMENT 371–92 (John W. Day & Alejandro Yanez-Arancibia eds., 2013).

[10] Harriet L. Nash & Richard J. McLaughlin, *Opportunities for Trinational Governance of Ecologically Connected Habitat Sites in the Gulf of Mexico,* 4 KOREAN MAR. INST. INT'L J. MAR. AFF. & FISHERIES 1, 7–8 (2012).

[11] Yoskowitz et al., *supra* note 6.

[12] *See* NOAA Fisheries Office of Protected Resources, Sea Turtles Overview (2014), *available at* http://www. nmfs.noaa.gov/pr/species/turtles/.

one billion neotropical migratory birds depend on the GOM at some point in their annual cycles. Whale sharks are also highly migratory and depend on both offshore and inshore Gulf waters for migration.[13]

Important marine habitat features such as hard and soft banks, coral reefs, and even man-made structures such as oil platforms create biological connectivity within the GOM and Wider-Caribbean Region.[14] Connectivity occurs in the marine environment through pelagic larval dispersal as well as juvenile recruitment and post-settlement adult movement patterns.[15] Perturbations of existing weather, ocean temperature, or marine current patterns caused by climate change may disrupt ecological connectivity and bio-diversity in the GOM.

II. Effects of Climate Change on Gulf of Mexico Fisheries

Many studies have confirmed the relationships between fisheries yields and the physi-cal characteristics of estuarine and other shallow-water systems.[16] These shallow-water areas are especially vulnerable to physical changes in temperature, salinity, sea-level rise, and other environmental characteristics caused by climate change. The high pri-mary productivities of these areas are brought about by high nutrient loads, freshwa-ter inputs, shallow depths, large amounts of tidal mixing, and vegetated sea bottoms.[17] Moreover, estuaries serve as nursery areas for many fishes that spawn offshore, move into estuaries for part of their life cycles, and then return to sea for the remainder of their lives. About 50 percent of U.S. fishery yields have historically been harvested from estuarine or estuarine-dependent species. This figure is even higher in the GOM.[18] Estuarine-dependent species dominate commercial and recreational catches including menhaden, shrimp, and others.[19]

Studies also support the theory that the large abundance of fisheries in the Gulf may be due not just to the availability of traditionally defined and geographically limited estuarine-systems, but also to the estuarine-like conditions that cover large portions

---

[13] Yoskowitz, *supra* note 6.

[14] Nash & McLaughlin, *supra* note 10, at 8–9. This connectivity can occur as genetic connectivity based on temporal "stepping stones" in the context of a large spatial scale or demographic connectivity, which occurs from the effects of geographic "stepping stones" over a long temporal scale. *See also* R.K. Cowen, *Oceanographic Influences on Larval Dispersion and Retention and Their Consequences for Population Connectivity, in* CORAL REEF FISHES: DYNAMICS AND DIVERSITY IN A COMPLEX ECOSYSTEM 149–70 (P.F. Sale ed., 2002).

[15] Nash & McLaughlin, *Id.*

[16] Day & Yanez-Arancibia, *supra* note 4, at 262–64.

[17] *Id.*

[18] E.D. Houde & E.S. Rutherford, *Recent Trends in Estuarine Fisheries: Predictions of Fish Production and Yields*, 16 ESTUARIES 161–76 (1993).

[19] Day & Yanez-Arancibia, *supra* note 4.

of the inner continental shelf during high river discharge periods.[20] Determining the relative contributions to fisheries production of traditional estuaries versus the larger estuarine-like continental shelf areas may be key in effectively managing commercial and recreational fisheries in the Gulf over a long time frame.[21] Uncertainty over the long-term effects of climate change and resulting habitat alteration in the Gulf significantly complicate the task of making informed management choices.

Coastal wetlands and estuaries, as well as the estuarine-like continental shelf areas of the GOM, are profoundly affected by the amount of freshwater discharge they receive. These freshwater inputs deliver important nutrients and suspended sediments, which increase biological production and provide materials for accretion of wetland soils and vegetation. In addition, the mixing of freshwater and seawater in estuaries and the pulsed additions of river discharge onto the inner continental shelf is essential for high coastal ecosystem and fisheries productivity.[22] Global climate change may affect the amounts and distribution of freshwater inflows into the GOM. According to ecologist, Dr. Paul Montagna:

> Climate change threatens to change precipitation and temperature patterns in vast regions of the globe. Even with no change in precipitation, increased temperature will increase evapotranspiration, thus creating water deficits in many regions. Although dewatering of estuaries at the current time is driven largely by coastal development and human demand for freshwater, current water management practices may not be adequate to cope with the impacts of climate change.[23]

In the coming decades, damages to coastal ecosystems caused by human alteration of freshwater inflows will be aggravated when added to the effects derived from climate change.[24] The manner and location of these changes are unpredictable, but will undoubtedly place additional stress on the ecological integrity of many coastal areas in the GOM as well as challenge existing water resource management approaches.[25]

Ocean acidification is another issue of concern to fisheries in the GOM. Higher levels of carbon dioxide in the atmosphere are absorbed in the oceans and directly affect organisms' ability to form skeletal structures.[26] Carbon dioxide dissolves in ocean water,

---

[20] *Id.*

[21] *Id.*

[22] *Id.* at 256–60.

[23] PAUL A. MONTAGNA, TERENCE A. PALMER & JENNIFER BESERES POLLACK, HYDROLOGICAL CHANGES AND ESTUARINE DYNAMICS 3 (2012).

[24] Day & Yanez-Arancibia, *supra* note 4, at 259–60 (describing several general circulation models that attempt to predict freshwater inflow to estuaries in the Gulf Region).

[25] MONTAGNA ET AL., *supra* note 23, at 23–77 (providing a variety of case studies of how freshwater inflow is managed in the United States and globally).

[26] NOAA, PMEL Carbon Program, *Ocean Acidification: The Other Carbon Dioxide Problem, available at* http://www.pmel.noaa.gov/co2/story/Ocean+Acidification (last visited Feb. 18, 2014).

causing a lowering of the pH level and acidification of the water. Studies have shown that acidification interferes with the ability of marine organisms to build their shells and skeletons from calcium carbonate. This affects important organisms such as corals, oysters, clams, mussels, snails, phytoplankton, and zooplankton.[27] Although ocean acidification may not directly affect fish stocks, it could have far-reaching implications on the marine food web and the availability of important food sources for commercially and recreationally important fish species.

Increases in global temperatures have also created a poleward shift in the range and distribution of fish species in the Gulf of Mexico to other parts of the global ocean.[28] Small increases in water temperature may significantly affect species interactions, habitat, and recruitment. A recent study that compared fish assemblages within seagrass meadows of the northern Gulf of Mexico between the 1970s and 2006–2007 revealed numerous additions of warm-water fish that were completely absent during the 1970s.[29] These range expansions may increase local biodiversity in the short-term by extending the range of tropical or subtropical species northward into historically cooler waters. However, over longer timescales, these poleward expansions may trigger consequences similar to those that occur when non-indigenous species invade new areas, which include changes in the local dynamics of competition, predation, herbivory, and parasitism.[30]

There is still much uncertainty as to the impacts climate change will have on invasive species, and specifically aquatic invasive species (AIS). Some predicted impacts include a decline in native species, the presence of food web disturbances, degraded habitats, and impacts to recreation, aesthetics, and infrastructure.[31] When climate-induced changes are coupled with existing anthropogenic stressors such as overfishing, chemical pollution, hypoxic zones, and habitat destruction, the impacts of biological invasions will likely be much worse.[32] Two notable examples of AIS introduced into the GOM are the black tiger shrimp and the lionfish. Black tiger shrimp began showing up in the GOM in 2006 and have steadily increased every year since, with significant increases in 2011. The black tiger shrimp is the largest species of shrimp in the world. These shrimp can grow to be a foot in length, are predatory and believed to be carnivorous, and could potentially

---

[27] Woods Hole Oceanographic Institution, *Ocean Acidification, available at* http://www.whoi.edu/main/topic/ocean-acidification (last visited Feb. 18, 2014).

[28] *See* William W.L. Cheung et al., *Large-Scale Redistribution of Maximum Fisheries Catch Potential in the Global Ocean under Climate Change*, 16 GLOBAL CHANGE BIO. 24 (2010).

[29] *See* F. Joel Fodrie et al., *Climate-Related, Decadal-Scale Assemblage Changes of Seagrass-Associated Fishes in the Northern Gulf of Mexico*, 16 GLOBAL CHANGE BIO. 48 (2010).

[30] *Id.*

[31] *See* F.J. Rahel & J.D. Olden, *Assessing the Effects of Climate Change on Aquatic Invasive Species*, 22 CONSERVATION BIO. 521 (2008).

[32] Eric V. Hull, *Climate Change and Aquatic Invasive Species: Building Coastal Resilience through Integrated Ecosystem Management*, 25 GEO. INT'L ENVTL. L. REV. 51, 77 (2012).

deplete the stock of native shrimp species.[33] Lionfish are venomous fish that can populate habitat in a short amount of time. These invasive fish reduce native fish populations by eating them or chasing them out of their habitat. For the past decade they have been found in the South Atlantic and Caribbean regions, but have recently made their way into the GOM.[34] Although significant uncertainty exists as to how AIS will react to climate change, it can be assumed that changes to AIS will take place in terms of distribution, spread, and abundance, and their associated impacts.[35]

III. International Fisheries Management in the Gulf of Mexico

The GOM is a large international sea surrounded by three sovereign nations: the United States, Mexico, and Cuba. It provides important habitat for many transboundary living marine resources, ranging from highly migratory species and straddling stocks of pelagic and demersal fishes to sessile invertebrates.[36] Most transboundary species exhibit characteristics indicating connectivity with the existing ecological network within the Wider-GOM/Caribbean Region. These species may rely for all or part of their life histories on natural hard and soft banks, hard-substrate reefs, coastal wetlands, or man-made structures, such as offshore oil platforms, as important habitat features. Protecting these habitat types and providing for a healthy marine ecosystem, including the stability of fisheries, is essential to the overall health of the GOM marine ecosystem and to the coastal communities that depend on them.

Fisheries resources in the GOM are managed through a combination of international and domestic laws and policies. At the international level, the most important source of legal authority is the United Nations Convention on the Law of the Sea (UNCLOS).[37] Mexico and Cuba are parties to UNCLOS.[38] The United States has not formally acceded to the Convention, but it has joined the rest of the international community in recognizing nearly all of the substantive provisions of UNCLOS (including all of the fisheries

---

[33] Charley Cameron, *Giant Invasive Predator Tiger Shrimp Settle in the Gulf of Mexico*, WALL ST. J., Sept. 16, 2013, *available at* http://inhabitat.com/invasive-predator-tiger-shrimp-settle-in-the-gulf-of-mexico/.

[34] Melissa Gaskill, *As Lionfish Invade the Caribbean and Gulf of Mexico, Conservationists Say Eat Up*, SCI. AMER., Dec. 11, 2013, *available at* http://www.scientificamerican.com/article/does-eating-lionfish-work/.

[35] Sara Grise, *Predicting Climate Change Impacts on Invasive Species in Pennsylvania*, Pennsylvania Sea Grant, *available at* http://www.srbc.net/programs/docs/wqacaisclimatechange052510.PDF (last visited July 16, 2014). For a more detailed discussion of the impacts of climate change on aquatic invasive species management, see *infra* Chapters 10 and 11.

[36] Nash & McLaughlin, *supra* note 10. Pelagic fishes live or grow near the surface of the open ocean; demersal fishes live close to the seabed of the ocean, and sessile organisms spend their lives attached to a solid substrate such as rocks, coral, or offshore structures.

[37] United Nations Conference on the Law of the Sea, opened for signature Dec. 10, 1982, U.N. Doc. A/CONF.62/122 (1982), 1833 U.N.T.S. 397 (entered into force Nov. 16, 1994).

[38] As of this writing, 166 nations have ratified/acceded to UNCLOS. A list of State Parties is available at http://www.un.org/depts/los/reference_files/status2010.pdf.

provisions) as reflecting customary international law, which is binding even on those nations that do not become parties to the Convention.[39]

In the GOM, the vast majority of the living marine resources fall within one of the three surrounding nations' national jurisdictions. Articles 56 and 57 of UNCLOS provide each coastal state with the exclusive authority to explore, exploit, conserve, and manage its living and nonliving resources extending to two hundred nautical miles from its shoreline. Within each nation's two-hundred-mile Exclusive Economic Zone (EEZ), UNCLOS provides almost unlimited authority to coastal states to manage living resources as they see fit. The extent of this discretion has led one knowledgeable observer to quip: "This treaty delegates virtually complete authority for managing fisheries, including conservation, utilization, and allocation, to the coastal states of the world."[40] Consequently, the United States has fisheries management authority over most of the northern GOM, Mexico the southern and southwestern GOM, and Cuba the Southeastern. Two areas, each about the size of the U.S. state of New Jersey and known as the Western and Eastern Gaps, are located in areas beyond the two-hundred-mile EEZ of any of the three nations. These two areas remain part of the high seas and are open to fisheries exploitation by vessels from any member of the international community, although little commercial or recreational fishing is currently occurring in either area. For a map of the Gulf showing these jurisdictional zones, see Figure 5.1.

UNCLOS defines the GOM as a semi-enclosed sea and encourages nations to engage in international cooperation regarding living marine resources and protection and preservation of the marine environment in such areas.[41] Historically, the three nations have not made significant efforts to coordinate fisheries management activities on an international scale.[42] More cooperation has occurred in regard to international efforts to protect and conserve marine and coastal habitat and specific GOM species such as sea turtles, sharks, and marine mammals.[43] A significant number of less formal and non-binding international agreements, memoranda of understanding, and professional

---

[39] This policy was originally set forth in President Reagan's Proclamation, which established a U.S. two-hundred-mile exclusive economic zone. Proclamation No. 5030, 48 Fed. Reg. 10,605 (1983). The accompanying policy statement is found in President's Statement on United States Oceans Policy, 1983 PUB. PAPERS 378 (Mar. 10, 1983).

[40] William T. Burke, *Fishing in the Bering Sea Donut: Straddling Stocks and the New International Law of Fisheries*, 16 ECOLOGY L.Q. 285, 316 (1989).

[41] UNCLOS, arts. 123, 197.

[42] Cruz & McLaughlin, *supra* note 1. The United States and Mexico, but not Cuba, are parties to the International Convention for the Conservation of Atlantic Tunas. All three are parties to the Western Central Atlantic Fishery Commission, which encourages conservation and rational, sustainable management of transboundary resources, under the auspices of the United Nations Food and Agricultural Organization.

[43] *See* Harriet L. Nash & Richard J. McLaughlin, *A Policy Approach to Establish an International Network of Marine Protected Areas in the Gulf of Mexico Region*, 6 AUSTRALIAN J. MAR. & OCEAN AFF. 1 (2014) (providing chronological list of all international conventions concerning GOM species and habitat conservation and management).

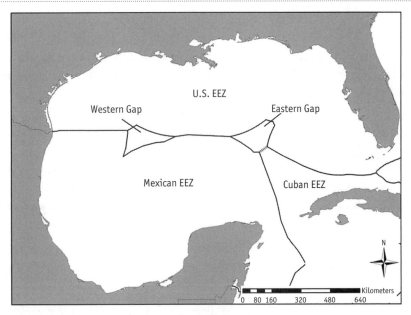

FIGURE 5.1 Exclusive Economic Zones in the Gulf of Mexico.
Note: The boundary between Cuba's EEZ and the Eastern Gap has not yet been agreed upon formally. Map adapted from Harriet L. Nash and Richard J. McLaughlin, *A Policy Approach to Establish an International Network of Marine Protected Areas in the Gulf of Mexico Region*, 6 AUSTRALIAN J. MAR. & OCEAN AFF. 1 (2014).

workshops relating to living marine resources in the GOM have occurred during the past decade, but relatively few involve Cuba.[44] Although these informal collaborative efforts are extremely important in laying a foundation for the future management of shared living marine resources, none of the formal or informal international agreements deals directly with the impact of climate change on these resources. Sustained efforts to create a network of biologically connected marine-protected areas in the GOM are very important and provide additional resilience to climate-impacted marine ecosystems, but these efforts should not be viewed as a substitute to dealing with direct impacts of climate change on fisheries resources.[45]

Within their respective two-hundred-mile EEZs, each of the three nations bordering the GOM has its own set of fisheries management policies, laws, and regulations. As a general proposition, the United States, Mexico, and Cuba employ a bifurcated approach toward the management of living marine resources and their habitats. Regulatory measures are focused on (1) sustainable management of species and/or populations targeted

---

[44] *Id.*

[45] *Id.* (noting that the design and implementation of an international network of marine protected areas to conserve shared transboundary living marine resources in the GOM provides an opportunity for innovative marine policy at a regional scale). *See* discussion *infra* notes 73–77 and accompanying text. *See also* Robin Kundis Craig, *Ocean Governance for the 21st Century: Making Marine Zoning Climate Change Adaptable*, 36 HARV. ENVTL. L. REV. 305 (2012) (arguing that increased use of marine protected areas should be promoted as a climate change adaptation strategy in threatened marine ecosystems).

by a fishery, or (2) species and/or populations in need of conservation protection, based on their rarity or rapidly declining abundance.[46] Although ecosystem-based management is recognized and employed to some degree in all three nations, ecological complexities present practical hurdles to resource managers, particularly while management authority remains sectoral.[47] For example, ecosystem-based models, in addition to traditional measures such as stock assessments and past fishing efforts, should integrate many anthropogenic influences on ocean ecosystems, including eutrophication and induction of nuisance algal blooms; habitat destruction, fragmentation, and degradation; species introductions, extinctions, and endangerments; chemical pollution; and finally anthropogenic and natural global climate change.[48] Given the extraordinary complexity of modeling multiple processes of this kind, it is not surprising that climate change has not played a prominent role in how fisheries are currently managed in the GOM.

IV. U.S. Fisheries Management

Managing fisheries resources in U.S. waters poses a degree of jurisdictional complexity that Mexico and Cuba do not face. Within U.S. ocean waters, jurisdiction is divided between federal and state government authorities.[49] In federal waters, fisheries management authority depends primarily on the Magnuson-Stevens Fishery Conservation and Management Act (MSA), originally enacted in 1976, and the formal and informal actions delegated to federal natural resource regulatory agencies, such as the National Oceanic and Atmospheric Administration (NOAA).[50]

Amendments to the MSA in 1996 and 2006[51] have increased its conservation focus and strengthened the role that science should play in decision-making. However, no explicit mention of climate change or particular level of scientific certainty is required

---

[46] Nash & McLaughlin, *supra* note 43, at 3.

[47] *Id.*

[48] Louis W. Botsford et al., *The Management of Fisheries and Marine Ecosystems*, 277 SCI. 509, 514 (1997).

[49] Congress enacted the 1953 Submerged Lands Act, 43 U.S.C. §§ 1301–1315 (2012), granting to the coastal states all federal proprietary rights out to three nautical miles. Texas and the Gulf Coast of Florida received nine nautical miles based on historic claims. The federal government claims rights in the natural resources seaward of these state waters. *See* DONNA R. CHRISTIE & RICHARD G. HILDRETH, COASTAL AND OCEAN MANAGEMENT LAW IN A NUTSHELL 131, 133 (3d ed. 2007).

[50] *See supra* introduction to the Magnuson-Stevens Act for a comprehensive discussion of the Act and its frequent reauthorizations.

[51] Magnuson-Stevens Fishery Conservation and Management Reauthorization Act of 2006, Pub. L. No. 109-479, 120 Stat. 3575 (2007). The 1996 reauthorization shifted the focus from building up the American fishing fleet to the conservation and rebuilding of overfished stocks. The 2006 reauthorization "addresses the timeline for rebuilding stocks; establishes a regional cooperative research and monitoring program and a regional ecosystem study; strengthens the role of science in decision-making; develops new measures for fish habitat; and authorizes limited access privilege programs (LAPPS)." Niki L. Pace, *Ecosystem-Based Management under the Magnuson-Stevens Act: Managing the Competing Interests of the Gulf of Mexico Red Snapper and Shrimp Fisheries*, 2 SEA GRANT L. & POL'Y J. 1, 4 (2010).

by the legislation. All regional fishery management plans must comply with the Act's ten National Standards for Conservation and Management.[52] According to one commentator, the application of the ten Standards "prioritizes conservation goals by requiring economic concerns be consistent with conservation measures. However, it also uses phrases such as 'to the extent practicable' to reserve discretion for the Councils [the eight Regional Federal Fishery Management Councils] and NMFS [National Marine Fisheries Service] in determining the practicability of conservation."[53] The MSA also places a heavy emphasis on overfished stocks. The Act treats federal fisheries as open access and does not require regulation until a stock is subject to overfishing.[54] Unless a stock is subject to overfishing, any conservation measures adopted must justify any economic impacts of conservation by establishing specific goals and providing criteria by which achieving those goals may be measured.[55] Concern has also been raised in some quarters that enforcement of the MSA has shifted to a preoccupation with just one major concern, "overfishing," to the detriment of other biological and socioeconomic concerns.[56]

There is a wide range of scholarly commentary on why the Regional Councils continue to implement the MSA using substantial discretion to further the economic interests of recreational and commercial fishing interests to the detriment of conservation.[57] Some of the commercially centered discretion in the MSA is structural and an intended feature of the legislation. However, scientific uncertainty inherent in fisheries management also plays an important role in Councils and regulators erring on the side of exploitation when the science is unclear.[58] Scientific uncertainty does not warrant precautionary closures under the MSA "unless they can be justified by scientific information, assessed according to scientific criteria, are temporarily limited, and not overly detrimental to commercial interests without sufficient, measurable environmental goals."[59] Given this extraordinarily difficult standard to meet, only one Regional Council, the North Pacific Fishery Management Council (NPFMC), has closed sections of the ocean to

---

[52] 16 U.S.C. § 1851 (2012).

[53] Sarah M. Kutil, *Scientific Certainty Thresholds in Fisheries Management: A Response to a Changing Climate*, 41 ENVTL. L. 233, 241 (2011).

[54] Marian Macpherson & Miriam McCall, *Judicial Remedies in Fisheries Litigation: Pros, Cons, and Prestidigitation?*, 9 OCEAN & COASTAL L.J. 1, 6 (2003).

[55] *Id.* at 248–49.

[56] Brian Rothchild, *Rewriting the Magnuson-Stevens Act*, Keynote address delivered at the 2013 Pacific Marine Expo, Nov. 20, 2013, *available at* http://www.aifrb.org/2013/12/brian-rothchilds-keynote-address-rewriting-the-magnuson-stevens-act/.

[57] *See, e.g.*, Thomas A. Okey, *Membership of the Eight Regional Fishery Management Councils in the United States: Are Special Interests Over-Represented?*, 27 MARINE POL'Y 193 (2003); JOSH EAGLE ET AL., TAKING STOCK OF THE REGIONAL FISHERY MANAGEMENT COUNCILS, 4 (2003); Roger Fleming & John D. Crawford, *Habitat Protection under the Magnuson-Stevens Act: Can It Really Contribute to Ecosystem Health in the Northwest Atlantic?*, 12 OCEAN & COASTAL L.J. 43, 47–48 (2006).

[58] Kutil, *supra* note 53, at 242–43.

[59] *Id.* at 249.

fishing because of the scientific uncertainty of data due to climate change.[60] Because of the historic absence of commercial fisheries data coupled with the lack of scientific certainty regarding the impacts of present climate change, the NPFMC has prohibited exploitation until more data becomes available. The NPFMC moratorium in the Arctic is ground-breaking given the legal constraints imposed under the MSA limiting regulation to instances of "overfishing" except under exceptional circumstances.[61] It is viewed as the first step in negotiating a multilateral moratorium in waters of the Arctic, which has been attracting increased international commercial fishing attention as important species migrate north into warming waters.[62]

The NPFMC moratorium will serve as an important case study, but a similar decision to implement a precautionary closure to some fisheries in the GOM due to scientific uncertainty of climate change is nearly impossible for a variety of reasons. First, the Arctic closure occurred in an environmentally pristine area where little commercial fishing currently exists. Second, unlike many other areas of the world, including the GOM, where basic biological information is to some degree understood, very little is known about the functioning of the Arctic marine ecosystem. Finally, there is no recreational fishing taking place in the Arctic, and the moratorium drew the almost unprecedented support of both the conservation community and the commercial fishing industry.[63] This unusual alignment of interests is not likely to exist in other parts of the ocean, including the GOM. In light of legal restrictions under the MSA and political realities in the GOM region, less ambitious fisheries management strategies are appropriate to deal with global climate change in the GOM.

V. Cooperation with Mexico and Cuba

This chapter does not seek to provide a detailed discussion of Mexico's and Cuba's fisheries management programs. Instead, a few general observations may be helpful in understanding whether regional approaches to dealing with climate change in the GOM are possible. The Mexican and Cuban federal governments are much more centralized than that of the United States. This centralization generally means that the design and implementation of a single effective approach to management,

---

[60] Nat'l Oceanic and Atmospheric Admin. Fisheries, Amendments to Bering Sea and Gulf of Alaska Fishery Management Plans, 2, *available at* http://www.fakr.noaa.gov/sustainablefisheries/amds/ (last visited Feb. 17, 2014). ("The Arctic Management Area is closed to commercial fishing until such time in the future that sufficient information is available with which to initiate a planning process for commercial fishery development.").

[61] Kim Murphy, *U.S. Bans Expanded Commercial Fishing in the Arctic*, L.A. TIMES, Aug. 20, 2009, *available at* http://latimesblogs.latimes.com/greenspace/2009/08/us-bans-expanded-commercial-fishing-in-the-arctic.html.

[62] *Id.*

[63] *Id.*

regulation, and enforcement should be somewhat easier for these countries. Despite this perceived advantage, Mexico's legislative and administrative framework dealing with coastal and marine issues is highly fragmented and fraught with conflict.[64] Interagency cooperation is very weak and undefined. For example, *Secretaria de Medio Ambiente y Recusos Naturales* (SEMARNAT) is the primary federal environmental agency, but the *Comision Nacional de Aquacultura y Pesca* (CONAPESCA), which is located in a different ministry, has sole authority over fishing restrictions. The federal statute that focuses on resource extraction trumps the statute requiring environmental protection; as a result, fisheries are managed by CONAPESCA for the purpose of maximizing production, with little regard for environmental protection or conservation of living marine resources.[65] Cooperation between the agencies is very weak, if it occurs at all.[66] Serious ocean planning efforts, including impacts from global climate change, have been undertaken in recent years under the leadership of SEMARNAT.[67] However, how successful these efforts will become and whether they will effectively deal with international and regional climate change issues in the GOM remains to be seen.

Cuba may be the GOM region's leader regarding integrated coastal management plans and organizations. This is likely due in part to Cuba's socialist political system, which provides fewer bureaucratic hurdles and a more centralized regulatory structure.[68] Its national environmental strategy emphasizes Cuba's respect for the importance of international environmental norms and policies, while stressing the importance of retaining sovereign control over Cuba's natural resources.[69] The model continues to be based predominantly on a socialist platform, which incorporates sustainable development as an intrinsic value of Cuba's revolutionary foundation.[70] Because government planning is a top priority of socialist regimes, Cuba may, in theory, be the best positioned of the three GOM nations to respond to global climate change. However, a number of barriers limit the nation's ability to address environmental protection and fisheries management efforts. At an institutional level, the lack of personnel, transportation, financial resources, and monitoring systems prevent government agencies from effectively doing their jobs. Even more serious obstacles are presented as a result of the decades-long political animosity between Cuba and the United States. Poor political relations have made collaborative marine policy initiatives exceedingly difficult. Although there have been

---

[64] Lomeli et al., *supra* note 8, at 428.

[65] Nash & McLaughlin, *supra* note 43, at 16.

[66] J. Fragas & A. Jesus, *Coastal and Marine Protected Areas in Mexico, in* INTERNATIONAL COLLECTIVE IN SUPPORT OF FISHWORKERS 4–9 (2008).

[67] Cruz & McLaughlin, *supra* note 1, at 830–31.

[68] Nash & McLaughlin, *supra* note 43, at 27.

[69] Cruz & McLaughlin, *supra* note 1, at 831–32.

[70] *Id.*

some joint marine conservation achievements, most are of limited scale and primarily involve scientist-to-scientist cooperation.[71]

Increased international cooperation among the United States, Mexico, and Cuba to address global climate change in the GOM should be encouraged. Recently, scientists from the three nations have collaborated more frequently to address environmental concerns regarding shared living marine resources. This trend should continue and may provide scientific information relating to biological connectivity, species aggregations, ecological functions, and other data useful to addressing climate change impacts in the GOM. It is much less likely, at least in the near term, that cooperative policy or shared governance mechanisms toward climate change will develop.

VI. Future Steps

The MSA is up for reauthorization in 2014. However, due to the heavily politicized atmosphere associated with climate change generally and with the MSA amendment process itself, there is little likelihood that any provision relating to climate change will find its way into the amended fisheries-related legislation.[72] Rather than addressing the issue through legislative or regulatory actions, the most effective approach to dealing with the impact of climate change on fisheries resources in the GOM may be to support and enhance existing science and policy initiatives.

Three existing programs address aspects of the impacts of climate change on the environmental and economic health of the GOM. The first is the ongoing effort to create an international network of marine protected areas to conserve shared transboundary living marine resources in the GOM. For nearly a decade, scientists, resource managers, and policy analysts from the United States, Mexico, and Cuba have been collaborating on efforts to identify and protect habitat nodes with high biological connectivity, species abundance, and/or species richness.[73] A protected network of this kind would serve as an ecological insurance policy in the face of natural and anthropogenic threats. Protecting ecological connectivity through a network of protected habitats would help secure resiliency in response to climate change while also recognizing shifting species distributions and other structural and functional transitions.

---

[71] For a discussion of some of these efforts, see Nash & McLaughlin, *supra* note 43, at 27–28; and Trinational Initiative, Fifth Annual Trinational Initiative Meeting, *available at* http://www.trinationalinitiative.org/ (last visited Feb. 20, 2014).

[72] For a flavor of how politics may impact this reauthorization process, compare two opposing views of the Strengthening Fishing Communities and Increasing Flexibility in Fisheries Management Act, a bill proposed by Doc Hastings, Chairman of the House of Representatives Natural Resources Committee. *Compare* http://fishery.about.com/od/FishingRegulations/fl/Draft-Magnuson-Stevens-Fishery-Act.htm *with* http://www.pewenvironment.org/news-room/other-resources/reversing-course-hastings-empty-oceans-act-would-repeat-failed-fishery-policies-of-the-past-85899535977.

[73] Nash & McLaughlin, *supra* note 10, at 3.

A series of well-attended international forums have been held since 2008 with the intention of "creating a network of special ocean places to strengthen the ecology, economy, and culture of the Gulf of Mexico."[74] To advance this effort, Dr. Harriet Nash proposes the creation of an International Gulf of Mexico Marine Protected Area Network (IGOMMPAN), which would use a stepping stone approach to protect biological connectivity, biodiversity, rare and sensitive habitats, and ecological functions.[75] Establishing and implementing IGOMMPAN will ensure ecosystem resiliency if climate change or other anthropogenic or natural disasters reduce or eliminate any ecosystem functions in a particular location.[76] The ecosystem resiliency provided by IGOMMPAN would diminish chronic threats such as pollution, invasive species, or climate change, and distribute and thereby reduce and mitigate ecological risk in the GOM.[77]

A second initiative that would provide some benefit to future climate change would be to continue ongoing research on the ecological benefits of Rigs-to-Reef and other artificial reef programs in the GOM.[78] Use of obsolete offshore structures for artificial reefs, known as Rigs-to-Reefs, has been occurring in the GOM for over two decades, and California has also recently enacted legislation authorizing the practice in that state's waters.[79] All five states that border the Gulf have active artificial reef programs. Due to the proximity of offshore platforms, however, only Louisiana and Texas rely heavily on oil and gas structures for reef material.[80]

---

[74] Beyond the Horizon (2011), *available at* http://www.mote.org/clientuploads/4nadine/beyondhorizon/BeyondtheHorizon_4web.pdf (last visited Feb. 20, 2014). *See also A Scientific Forum on the Gulf of Mexico: The Islands in the Stream Concept. Marine Sanctuaries Conservation Series NMSP-08-04. Silver Spring, MD: U.S. Dept. of Commerce, NOAA, National Marine Sanctuary Program* (K.B. Richie & B.D. Keller, eds., 2008); *Summer Workshop on Governance for the Gulf of Mexico: Overcoming International Obstacles to Create Marine Protected Areas in the Gulf of Mexico, Extended Report.* Corpus Christi, TX: Harte Research Institute for Gulf of Mexico Studies, TAMUCC in collaboration with Gulf of Mexico, LME Project and Universidad Veracruzana (Ivonne Cruz & Richard McLaughlin, eds. 2010), *available at* http://harteresearchinstitute.org/images/research/marinepolicy/governance/extended_report.pdf; and Trinational Initiative, *supra* note 71.

[75] Harriet L. Nash, Trinational Governance to Protect Ecological Connectivity: Support for Establishing an International Gulf of Mexico Marine Protected Area Network (2013) (unpublished PhD dissertation, Texas A&M University–Corpus Christi) (on file with author). *See also* Nash & McLaughlin, *supra* note 43, at 24–29.

[76] *Id.* at 93–94.

[77] L. Pendleton et al., *Marine Protection in the Gulf of Mexico: Current Policy, Future Options, and Ecosystem Outcomes,* Nicholas Institute of Environmental Policy Solutions, Duke University (2010), *available at* http://nicholasinstitute.duke.edu/oceans/management/marine-protection-in-the-gulf-of-mexico-current-policy-future-options-and-ecosystem-outcomes#.UwZ_S6PnbIU (last visited Feb. 20, 2014).

[78] The following discussion of Rigs-to-Reefs is adapted from Richard McLaughlin, *"Idle Iron" versus "Rigs to Reefs": Surviving Conflicting Policy Mandates in the Gulf of Mexico,* Proceedings of the Law of the Sea Institute Conference on Science, Technology, and New Challenges to Ocean Law, Berkeley, CA (Oct. 2013) (publication pending).

[79] California Marine Resources Act, Cal. Fish & Game Code § 6601 (West 2010).

[80] Mark J. Kaiser, *The Louisiana Artificial Reef Program*, 30 MARINE POL'Y 605, 605 (2006).

Extensive research has shown that using the structures as artificial reefs may create significant benefits by providing habitat for fish and other marine life. For example, researchers report fish densities to be twenty to fifty times higher at artificial reefs created by oil and gas platforms than in nearby open water areas.[81] Despite this general understanding that reefed platforms create rich marine habitats, no definitive answer has yet to be provided for the essential ecological question of whether artificial reefs facilitate actual increases in fish biomass or merely cause fish to aggregate near the reef with no net increase in reproduction or survival.[82] Researchers are actively pursuing studies to address the production versus attraction hypotheses.[83] Nevertheless, it is recognized that the use of Rigs-to-Reefs in deeper waters and in situations where reef degradation is extreme will likely be useful in rejuvenating reef communities to some degree.[84]

Research evaluating the ecological benefits of Rigs-to-Reefs and other artificial reef programs that are intended to provide additional hard substrate in substrate-poor environments such as the GOM should be enhanced. Just as a biologically connected network of strategically placed marine connected areas could provide resilience to respond to ecological disturbances such as climate change, so could a network of artificial reef structures.

A final set of measures that could aid in reducing the threat of climate change to GOM fisheries would be to adopt a Gulf-wide program to establish environmental flow standards that provide for more ecological integrity in the region's bays and estuaries. The significant ecological value of fresh-water inflows to the environmental health of shallow-water systems has been described in previous portions of this chapter.[85] These values will be severely strained as climate change shifts weather patterns and makes water resource management predictions even more difficult. At present, in the GOM Region, only Texas and Florida have established policies that attempt to regulate environmental flows into coastal bays and estuaries.[86]

Texas has the most well-developed regulatory program in the GOM Region to deal with instream and freshwater flows.[87] For nearly four decades, Texas has had legislatively

---

[81] Les Dauterive, *Rigs-to-Reefs Policy, Progress, and Perspective*, OCS Report, MMS 2000-073, at 2 (Oct. 2000).

[82] Kara K. McQueen-Borden, *Will the Rigs-to-Reefs Experiment Be Based on the "Best Scientific Information Available"?*, 87 TUL. L. REV. 1281, 1286 (2013) (discussing the existing knowledge gap concerning the effectiveness of rigs as artificial reefs).

[83] *Id.* at 1286–90 (summarizing many of these studies).

[84] P.I. Macreadie, A.M. Fowler & D.J. Booth, *Rigs to Reefs: Will the Deep Sea Benefit from Artificial Habitat?*, 9 FRONTIERS ECOLOGY & ENV'T 455–61 (2011).

[85] *See supra* notes 16–25 and accompanying text.

[86] MONTAGNA ET AL., *supra* note 23, at 23–53.

[87] "Instream flows" deals with freshwater flowing in rivers and streams. "Freshwater inflow" refers to freshwater that flows into estuaries and bays from rivers and streams. *See* Texas Water Development Board, *Water for Texas 2012 State Water Plan, available at* http://www.twdb.state.tx.us/surfacewater/flows/index.asp (last visited Feb. 23, 2014).

adopted programs to evaluate the environmental needs for bays and estuaries.[88] However, it has only been since 2007, with the enactment of Senate Bill 3, that the state has adopted a legislative procedure to receive input from stakeholders, scientists, and government agencies to prioritize and establish appropriate environmental flow standards for all river basin and bay systems of the state.[89] The legislation amends the Texas Water Code by inaugurating a process that takes a consensus-based approach using scientific advisory committees to provide technical expertise to a group of stakeholders from each river basin and bay system. The stakeholders' group consists of at least seventeen members that should include agricultural water users, agricultural irrigation users, free-range livestock farmers, commercial fishermen, and environmentally concerned individuals.[90] Recommendations are submitted to the Texas Commission on Environmental Quality (TCEQ), which then sets a recommended flow standard for that particular river basin and bay system. However, Texas' environmental flows allocation process has yet to achieve its stated goal of establishing environmental flow standards that provide for a sound ecological environment. Among the issues cited as potential weaknesses include: (1) the centralized nature of the recommendation process, which places too much discretion in the hands of TCEQ as the final recommending authority; (2) a failure to provide consistent long-term funding; (3) a failure to provide for appropriate performance review; (4) TCEQ's ability to make water temporarily available for other uses besides environmental allocation; (5) the statutory limit that prevents any adjustment to existing water right permits in excess of 12.5 percent; and (6) the ability of TCEQ to modify environmental flow standards to the maximum extent reasonable when considering human water needs.[91]

Despite these concerns regarding funding and the possibility that environmental flow standards may be disregarded under certain conditions and do not entirely assure a constant protection of bay and estuary environmental health, Texas has created a comprehensive management system to respond to climate change that no other state in the nation has contemplated. Texas' environmental flows legislation contains adaptive management components that will allow it to examine future outcomes and modify methodologies accordingly. Given the extraordinary environmental importance of GOM shallow-water areas as nursery grounds and habitat for commercial and recreational species and the vulnerability of these areas to damaging changes brought about by climate change, all of the states in the GOM Region should examine new and innovative methods of managing freshwater inflows. Texas' approach may be useful as a model,

---

[88] *Id.*

[89] MONTAGNA ET AL., *supra* note 23, at 23–39. *See also* Lucy M. Flores, An Analysis of Texas Senate Bill 3 by Means of the Integrated Water Resources Management Spiral Model (2013) (unpublished Master's Thesis, Texas A&M University–Corpus Christi) (on file with author).

[90] Flores, *supra* note 89, at 6.

[91] *Id.* at 32–40.

but each state needs to examine its own unique environmental, political, and economic conditions to properly address environmental flow allocation.

Conclusion

Climate change will modify existing weather, water temperature, marine current patterns, and fresh water inflows in the GOM. It will also cause shifts in locations and numbers of invasive species and accelerate the phenomenon of ocean acidification. These perturbations will disrupt ecological connectivity and biodiversity and significantly impact fisheries resources in the region. It is unlikely that policy responses to climate change will be incorporated into federal legislation such as the MSA in the near-term. Instead, the most effective fisheries management strategies to address climate change will involve three strategies. First, pursue cooperative engagement with Mexico and Cuba on understanding the key elements that maintain biological connectivity and biodiversity and work toward creating a network of marine protected areas to sustainably manage transboundary living marine resources. Second, continue ongoing research to determine the ecological benefits of Rigs-to-Reef and other artificial reef programs in the GOM. Unlike many ocean environments, the GOM contains very little hard substrate on its sea bottom. Providing structures such as artificial reefs may improve the resiliency of some fisheries to climate change. Finally, promote better understanding of the ways that shallow-water areas such as estuaries and estuarine-like inner continental shelf areas contribute to the health of fisheries resources in the GOM. For example, determining the role that pulses play during high river discharge periods and identifying appropriate levels of freshwater inflow during other periods is necessary to effectively adapt to climate change.

Given the political controversy associated with climate change in the United States, there will be significant hurdles to overcome in addressing the challenges posed in this chapter. Nevertheless, innovative actions in both the scientific and policy realms need to be developed so that important fisheries resources can be sustainably managed in the face of long-term environmental change. The challenge will be in finding the right balance so that fisheries can be successfully managed without compromising important ecosystem services or the human well-being of those who depend on the Gulf.

6 Climate Change Impacts to Fisheries and Habitat in the Pacific and the Arctic

Janis Searles Jones, Ivy Fredrickson and Adena Leibman*

---

* The authors would like to acknowledge Claudia Friess and Dr. Sarah Cooley for their contributions to the chapter.

Introduction

In the last two decades or more, much of the discussion regarding management and conservation of ocean resources has focused on fisheries management, and much of the fisheries management focus has been on those regions where overfishing has driven targeted fish stocks to unsustainable levels. With that focus, our nation has made unprecedented progress in ending overfishing and restoring depleted fish populations in those regions. Much of this success is rooted in the sustainable fishing mandate and science-based management provisions of the Magnuson-Stevens Act.[1]

In many regions, including the Pacific, these successes have helped build more abundant and healthier fish populations and created economic benefits for the fishing industry and coastal communities. In other regions, such as the North Pacific, fisheries managers have distinguished themselves over time by applying science-based tools and making judicious and conservative management decisions to generally avoid overfishing. Where there was overfishing, the Magnuson-Stevens Act now has our nation on track to ensure that overfishing is indeed ended and overfished species are rebuilt, benefitting our oceans and those dependent on them. Where overfishing was not occurring, the Magnuson-Stevens Act has provided some tools for progressive fisheries management. Much of the management and conservation attention has been focused on the impact of fisheries on the marine environment.

At the same time, however, the very medium that fish inhabit—the ocean—is changing in fundamental ways, and turning on its head the classic management question about the impact of fisheries on the environment. We now need to be asking the additional question: What is the impact of the environment on fisheries?

This chapter explores climate change impacts to marine habitats and fisheries in the Pacific and Arctic regions and discusses some currently used legal and regulatory tools for adapting ocean management to the effects of climate change off the West Coast of the United States. Section I describes the marine habitat and fisheries in these two regions. Section II outlines two major oceanographic phenomena that affect both regions. Section III discusses the impact of climate change and ocean acidification on habitat and fish in the Pacific and Arctic regions. Finally, Section IV examines some of the fishery management responses in both areas.

I. The Habitats and Fisheries of the Pacific and North Pacific/Arctic

The Pacific and North Pacific/Arctic regions span: (1) the California Current Ecosystem in the Pacific Ocean; (2) the waters off Alaska, including the Gulf of Alaska; (3) the

---

[1] 16 U.S.C. §§ 1801–1891 (2012). For a general overview of the Magnuson-Stevens Act, *see supra* "Introduction to the Magnuson-Stevens Act," immediately preceding Chapter 4.

Aleutian Islands region; (4) the Eastern Bering Sea and Arctic waters off Alaska, including the Bering Strait; and (5) the Beaufort and Chukchi Seas.

A. PACIFIC

The Pacific Ocean's California Current Ecosystem is a highly productive ecosystem fueled by seasonal upwelling of cold, nutrient-rich water. The Pacific's seasonal cycles support a wide variety of fish, including small forage species such as sardines, anchovies, and herring, which serve as food for larger fish species such as salmon and tuna, as well as for other marine mammals and seabirds.

The Pacific Fishery Management Council ("Pacific Council") is one of the eight regional fishery management councils established by Congress in the Magnuson-Stevens Act, and is responsible for the conservation and management of fisheries in the exclusive economic zone off the coasts of Washington, Oregon, and California. The Pacific Council exercises its jurisdiction over more than one hundred species, grouped into five fishery management plans (FMPs): Groundfish, Coastal Pelagic Species (sardines, anchovies, mackerel), Highly Migratory Species (tunas, sharks, swordfish), Salmon, and Pacific Halibut.[2] The ranges for several of these species span multiple jurisdictions, with associated international fishery management organizations: the International Pacific Halibut Commission (for Pacific halibut),[3] the Western and Central Pacific Fisheries Commission (for albacore tuna and other highly migratory species),[4] and the Inter-American Tropical Tuna Commission (for yellowfin tuna and other highly migratory species).[5] In addition to federal fisheries in the California Current Ecosystem, there are active commercial and recreational fisheries in state waters.[6]

According to the National Marine Fisheries Service (NMFS), commercial fishing in the Pacific Region resulted in landings of approximately 1.2 billion pounds of finfish and shellfish, earning $710 million in landings revenue in 2011.[7] Over 1.5 million recreational saltwater anglers took 6.1 million fishing trips in the Pacific Region in 2011.[8]

---

[2] Pac. Fishery Mgmt. Council, Who We Are and What We Do, www.pcouncil.org (last visited Feb. 28, 2014).

[3] Int'l Pac. Halibut Comm'n, Welcome to the IPHC, http://www.iphc.int/ (last visited Feb. 28, 2014).

[4] Western & Central Pacific Fisheries Comm'n, http://www.wcpfc.int/ (last visited Feb. 28, 2014).

[5] Inter-American Tropical Tuna Comm'n, http://www.iattc.org/HomeENG.htm (last visited Feb. 28, 2014).

[6] *See, e.g.*, OREGON DEPT. OF FISH & WILDLIFE, POUNDS AND VALUES OF COMMERCIALLY CAUGHT FISH AND SHELLFISH LANDED IN OREGON, 2004–2013 (2014), http://www.dfw.state.or.us/fish/commercial/landing_stats/2013/10_Yr_lbs_$_by_year.pdf.

[7] NAT'L MARINE FISHERIES SERV. (NMFS), NOAA TECHNICAL MEMO. NMFS-F/SPO-128, FISHERIES ECONOMICS OF THE UNITED STATES 25 (2012), https://www.st.nmfs.noaa.gov/Assets/economics/documents/feus/2011/FEUS%202011-Revised.pdf.

[8] *Id.* at 27.

United States' waters off Alaska are comprised of numerous productive ecosystems. Cold, nutrient-rich waters, moderately high productivity, and high biological diversity define the Gulf of Alaska.[9] The Gulf of Alaska supports numerous commercially important fisheries, including crab, shrimp, rockfish, salmon, and halibut. The Aleutian Islands and Bering Sea are also moderately high productivity regions with commercially important fisheries, including crab, Atka mackerel, cod, salmon, herring, rockfish, skate, sole, pollock, and others. Habitats range from deep-sea basins to sloping shelves and islands, which are the steep peaked tips of submarine volcanos in the Aleutian archipelago.[10]

The Beaufort and Chukchi seas are high-latitude, low productivity regions with Arctic climates highly influenced by seasonal conditions and sea ice. Ice typically forms in the region in October and November and remains until May, June, or July.[11] Ice floes are driven by wind and currents. As sea ice melts, it affects the salinity and density of ocean water, which changes ocean circulation patterns and impacts biological productivity.[12]

The fisheries of the North Pacific region—the exclusive economic zone off of the state of Alaska—are some of the most productive ones in the world.[13] According to economic data collected by NMFS, North Pacific commercial fishermen harvested approximately 5.3 billion pounds in 2011, earning over $1.9 billion.[14] Landings revenue for salmon was highest at $565 million, walleye pollock earned $363 million, crab earned $249 million, and Pacific cod earned $210 million.[15] More than 286,000 recreational saltwater anglers went fishing in Alaska in 2011, 56 percent of whom were nonresidents.[16]

II. Major Oceanographic Phenomena: Upwelling and the El Niño Southern Oscillation Cycle

Upwelling is a major oceanographic phenomenon in the deep ocean and along coastlines by which deeper waters are transported toward the surface.[17] Upwelling is important

---

[9] *See* NOAA Integrated Ecosystem Assessment, About the Alaska Complex, http://www.noaa.gov/iea/regions/alaska-complex/about.html (last visited Feb. 28, 2014).

[10] *Id.*

[11] Andrew E. Hartsig et al., *Arctic Bottleneck: Protecting the Bering Strait Region from Increased Vessel Traffic*, 18 OCEAN & COASTAL L.J. 35, 38 (2012) (citing ARCTIC COUNCIL, ARCTIC MARINE SHIPPING ASSESSMENT 2009 REPORT 106 (2009), http://www.pame.is/images/stories/AMSA_2009_Report/AMSA_2009_Report_2nd_print.pdf).

[12] *Id.* at 39 (citing Dagmar Budikova, *Role of Arctic Sea Ice in Global Atmospheric Circulation: A Review*, 68 GLOBAL & PLANETARY CHANGE 149, 153 (2009)).

[13] Alaska Dep't of Fish & Game, Commercial Fisheries Information, http://www.adfg.alaska.gov/index.cfm?adfg=fishingCommercialByFishery.main (last visited Feb. 28, 2014).

[14] NMFS, *supra* note 7, at 17.

[15] *Id.*

[16] *Id.* at 18.

[17] Nat'l Ocean Serv., NOAA, Ocean Facts: Upwelling, http://oceanservice.noaa.gov/facts/upwelling.html (last visited Feb. 28, 2014).

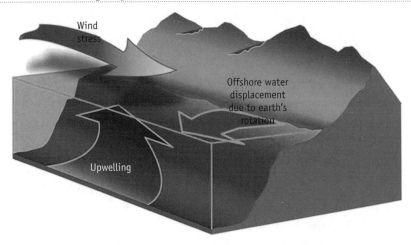

UPWELLING DIAGRAM, FIGURE 6.1 Displaced surface water is replaced by cold, nutrient-rich water that "wells up" from below.

Photo credit: NOAA Fisheries, Northwest Fisheries Science Center.

because deeper, cooler waters tend to be nutrient rich. Driven by wind, that upwelled water replaces warmer surface water, which is often nutrient-depleted (See Figure 6.1.). The nutrients in the upwelled water support the growth of phytoplankton (microscopic marine plants), often making these areas have high biological productivity. In other words, where there is upwelling, there will often be good fishing.[18] Variability in the timing and strength of seasonal upwelling has far-reaching impacts on fisheries in the waters off the West Coast. Years with weak upwelling can result in fisheries collapse. Conversely, large populations of small fish such as anchovies boom when upwelling is strong.[19]

Upwelling in the Pacific Ocean and Bering Sea are influenced by the two phases of the El Niño Southern Oscillation (ENSO) cycle, which causes variations in upwelling intensity from year to year.[20] Climate change is expected to intensify the ENSO cycle. Models show that increased greenhouse gas concentrations will result in more frequent El Niño-like conditions.[21] ENSO has the potential to affect fisheries in at least three ways. First, ENSO can impact the abundance and distribution of various fish species because changes in ocean conditions affect primary productivity, which impacts the rest of the food web. Second, ENSO-influenced changes in temperature can affect rates of population growth, survival, and distribution. During an El Niño event, species that prefer warm water tend to become more prevalent in normally colder water regions of

[18] *Id.*

[19] Felicia C. Coleman & Laura E. Petes, *Getting Into Hot Water: Ecological Effects of Climate Change in Marine Environments*, 17 SOUTHEASTERN ENVTL. L.J. 337, 351–52 (2009) (citing Patrick Lehodey et al., *Climate Variability, Fish, and Fisheries*, 19 J. CLIMATE 5009, 5021 (2006)).

[20] Nat'l Ocean Serv., NOAA, Ocean Facts: El Niño and La Niña, http://oceanservice.noaa.gov/facts/nino-nina.html (last visited Feb. 28, 2014).

[21] Axel Timmermann et al., *Increased El Niño Frequency in a Climate Model Forced by Future Greenhouse Warming*, 398 NATURE 694, 696 (1999).

North (and South) America's Pacific coast. Third, ENSO can also affect recruitment of young fish to adult populations.[22]

For example, the timing of the spring transition in the Pacific—a switch from predominantly northward currents to southward currents—and the strength of upwelling affect recruitment success for a variety of marine species such as sablefish, rockfish, barnacles, and seabirds.[23] Along central and northern California, recruitment for two rockfish complexes was found to respond quite differently to ENSO events.[24] Recruitment of midwater aggregating rockfishes such as widow, yellowtail, olive, and blue rockfish was highest during La Niña periods whereas recruitment for sedentary benthic species such as kelp, gopher, yellow, copper, China, and quillbar rockfish was highest during El Niño events.[25] Studies have also found that El Niño events cause "declines in sardine, anchovy, skipjack tuna, and other pelagic fish populations."[26]

These major oceanographic phenomena have significant impacts on the marine environment, and correspondingly significant impacts on fisheries and habitats of the Pacific, North Pacific, and Arctic. Against this backdrop, we will now shift to outlining the additional impacts of climate change.

III. Global Climate Change and Ocean Acidification

The increase of carbon in the atmosphere is having numerous and significant impacts on the ocean. It is estimated that the oceans have absorbed over 90 percent of the heat added to the global climate system through increased atmospheric CO_2 concentrations over the past fifty years.[27] As a consequence, ocean temperatures are rising, particularly in surface waters.[28] This is resulting in significant impacts to marine habitats. Global climate models project changes in wind patterns and ocean currents, and loss of sea ice

---

[22] Recruitment is the abundance of age-o fish, or the number of surviving fish that enter the fishery each year.

[23] *See, e.g.,* Carrie A. Holt & André E. Punt, *Incorporating Climate Information into Rebuilding Plans for Overfished Groundfish Species of the U.S. West Coast,* 100 FISHERIES RES. 57 (2009); Michael J. Schirripa & J.J. Colbert, *Interannual Changes in Sablefish* (Anoplopoma fimbria) *Recruitment in Relation to Oceanographic Conditions within the California Current System,* 15 FISHERIES OCEANOGRAPHY 25 (2006).

[24] THE ECOLOGY OF MARINE FISHES: CALIFORNIA AND ADJACENT WATERS 417 (Larry G. Allen, Daniel J. Pondella II & Michael H. Horn eds., 2006).

[25] *Id.*

[26] Coleman & Petes, *supra* note 19, at 352 (citing Stephen A. Arnott & Graeme D. Ruxton, *Sandeel Recruitment in the North Sea: Demographic, Climatic, and Trophic Effects,* 238 MARINE ECOLOGY PROGRESS SERIES 199, 201 (2002); Martin J. Attrill & Michael Power, *Climatic Influence on a Marine Fish Assemblage,* 417 NATURE 275, 275 (2002)).

[27] Magdalena A. Balmaseda, Kevin E. Trenberth & Erland Källén, *Distinctive Climate Signals in Reanalysis of Global Ocean Heat Content,* 60 GEOPHYSICAL RES. LETTERS 1754, 1754 (2013).

[28] Sydney Levitus et al., *World Ocean Heat Content and Thermosteric Sea Level Change (0–2000 m), 1955–2010,* 39 GEOPHYSICAL RESEARCH LETTERS L. 10603, at 4 (2012) ("One important result presented here is that each major ocean basin has warmed at nearly all latitudes.").

in polar regions.[29] Abiotic conditions such as temperature, salinity, oxygen, and pH levels of the ocean are changing. Biotic conditions such as shifts in predator and prey relationships, population productivity, distribution,[30] phenology,[31] and key characteristics of fish populations such as growth[32] are also changing. In addition, CO_2 uptake by the oceans is altering seawater carbonate chemistry in the form of ocean acidification. These changes affect the distribution, phenology, abundance, community structure, and demography of marine organisms.[33] These effects of global climate change layer on top of existing seasonal, interannual, and decadal natural cycles.

There is emerging general consensus that climate change and ocean acidification, both driven by emissions of CO_2 and other greenhouse gases, have become the main threat to the ocean. The following discussion will address three aspects of that threat as it relates to the Pacific and North Pacific/Arctic marine environments: (1) the impacts of ocean acidification, (2) the loss of sea ice habitat, and (3) the corresponding impacts on fish in both regions as a result of climate change.

A. OCEAN ACIDIFICATION AS HABITAT CHANGE

Over millennia, the ocean is responsible for maintaining the balance of carbon dioxide in the atmosphere. In response to the massive release of carbon dioxide (CO_2) into the atmosphere from human deforestation and industrial activities, the ocean has absorbed approximately 25 percent of this total excess carbon dioxide.[34] In a decadal study spanning 2002 to 2011, the oceans took up about 27 percent of the annual global carbon dioxide emissions.[35] When atmospheric CO_2 levels rise so quickly, the ocean's response acts to decrease seawater pH (increasing its acidity) in a process called ocean acidification.

---

[29] Intergovernmental Panel on Climate Change, Working Group I Contribution to the Fifth Assessment Report of the IPCC: Climate Change 2013—The Physical Science Basis 39–46 (2013), http://www.climatechange2013.org/report/.

[30] *See, e.g.,* William W.L. Cheung et al., *Projecting Global Marine Biodiversity Impacts under Climate Change Scenarios,* 10 Fish & Fisheries 235 (2009); Allison L. Perry et al., *Climate Change and Distribution Shifts in Marine Fishes,* 308 Sci. 1912 (2005).

[31] *See, e.g.,* Martin Edwards & Anthony J. Richardson, *Impact of Climate Change on Marine Pelagic Phenology and Trophic Mismatch,* 430 Nature 881 (2004); Martin J. Genner et al., *Temperature-driven Phenological Changes within a Marine Larval Fish Assemblage,* 32 J. Plankton Res. 699 (2010).

[32] *See, e.g.,* William W.L. Cheung et al., *Shrinking of Fishes Exacerbates Impacts of Global Ocean Changes on Marine Ecosystems,* 3 Nature Climate Change 254 (2013), *available at* http://www.nature.com/nclimate/journal/v3/n3/full/nclimate1691.html.

[33] Elvira S. Poloczanska et al., *Global Imprint of Climate Change on Marine Life,* 3 Nature Climate Change 919, 919 (2013).

[34] Scott C. Doney, Laurent Bopp & Matthew C. Long, *Historical and Future Trends in Ocean Climate and Biogeochemistry,* 27 Oceanography 108, 113 (2014) (citing Christopher L. Sabine & Toste Tanhua, *Estimation of Anthropogenic CO2 Inventories in the Ocean,* 2 Ann. Rev. Marine Sci. 269 (2010)).

[35] *Id.* at 114 (citing Corinne Le Quéré et al., *Trends in the Sources and Sinks of Carbon Dioxide,* 2 Nature Geosci. 831 (2009)).

As a result of increasing emissions, acidification is occurring at a rate faster than at any other time in geological history.[36]

In addition to increasing seawater's acidity, ocean acidification decreases the amount of carbonate ions in seawater. The shells and skeletons of many marine organisms are made from calcium carbonate (calcite or aragonite).[37] Low-carbonate waters tend to slow shell and skeleton growth of many marine organisms, or even corrode existing shells.[38] Corals and shellfish, for example, grow more slowly and die more often under acidified conditions.[39] Emerging research suggests that even non-calcified organisms, such as clownfish, may experience harm related to the change in acidity, such as decreases in neurotransmitter levels, immune system responses, and respiratory efficiency.[40] In short, ocean acidification is fundamentally altering the chemistry of the ocean, the very medium in which marine life exists, with likely corresponding existential effects for some species, and cascading effects for others.

High latitude regions such as the sub-Arctic North Pacific are expected to be strongly affected by the combination of ocean acidification and increasing temperatures. Generally speaking, Arctic ecosystems are characterized by simple food webs and relatively low biodiversity.[41] Together with other factors, such as colder temperatures and decreased salinity due to river inflows and melting sea ice, the Arctic Ocean is particularly sensitive to acidification.[42] The Arctic Ocean is projected to experience pH declines of up to 0.45 units over the next century,[43] and researchers conclude "it is highly likely that a significant change will occur in Arctic marine ecosystems due to ocean

---

[36] Bärbel Hönisch et al., *The Geological Record of Ocean Acidification*, 335 SCI. 1058, 1062 (2012).

[37] INT'L GEOSPHERE-BIOSPHERE PROGRAMME (IGBP), INTERGOVERNMENTAL OCEANOGRAPHIC COMM'N, SCIENTIFIC COMM. ON OCEANIC RESEARCH, OCEAN ACIDIFICATION SUMMARY FOR POLICYMAKERS: THIRD SYMPOSIUM ON THE OCEAN IN A HIGH-CO2 WORLD 7 (2013), http://www. igbp.net/download/18.30566fc6142425d6c91140a/1385975160621/OA_spm2-FULL-lorez.pdf.

[38] *See, e.g.*, Kristy J. Kroeker, *Impacts of Ocean Acidification on Marine Organisms: Quantifying Sensitivities and Interaction with Warming*, 19 GLOBAL CHANGE BIOLOGY 1884, 1888–94 (2013); James C. Orr et al., *Anthropogenic Ocean Acidification over the Twenty-First Century and Its Impact on Marine Organisms*, 437 NATURE 681, 685 (2005).

[39] IGBP, *supra* note 37, at 16–18. A few organisms, such as seagrasses and some phytoplankton, thrive under acidified conditions.

[40] *See generally* Göran E. Nilsson et al., *Near-Future Carbon Dioxide Levels Alter Fish Behaviour by Interfering with Neurotransmitter Function*, 2 NATURE CLIMATE CHANGE 201 (2012). *See also* OCEAN ACIDIFICATION (Jean-Pierre Gattuso & Lina Hansson eds., 2011).

[41] ARCTIC MONITORING & ASSESSMENT PROGRAMME (AMAP), AMAP ASSESSMENT 2013: ARCTIC OCEAN ACIDIFICATION 4 (2013), http://www.amap.no/documents/download/1577.

[42] *Id.* at 3–4.

[43] Thomas P. Hurst, Elena R. Fernandez & Jeremy T. Mathis, *Effects of Ocean Acidification on Hatch Size and Larval Growth of Walleye Pollock* (Theragra chalcogramma), 70 ICES J. MARINE SCI. 812, 812 (2013) (citing Marco Steinacher et al., *Imminent Ocean Acidification Projected with the NCAR Global Coupled Carbon Cycle-Climate Model*, 6 BIOGEOSCI. 515 (2009); Michiyo Yamamoto-Kawai et al., *Aragonite Undersaturation in the Arctic Ocean: Effects of Ocean Acidification and Sea Ica Melt*, 236 SCI. 1098, 1099 (2009)).

acidification."[44] Clams and crabs, for example, are important for both traditional subsistence and modern commercial harvests, and are at risk from ocean acidification,[45] with numerous possible socioeconomic effects that have yet to be fully evaluated. More work needs to be done to understand fully the impact of ocean acidification on Arctic systems and peoples.

In the Pacific Northwest, biological and economic impacts from ocean acidification have been clearly documented. Multiple years of oyster larvae failure in Pacific Northwest hatcheries have been traced to ocean acidification,[46] which has jeopardized a $100-million-a-year industry.[47]

B. LOSS OF SEA ICE HABITAT

The seasonal advance and retreat of sea ice plays a critical role in the Bering Strait, Chukchi and Beaufort Seas, and Arctic Ocean.[48] Sea ice typically forms in the region in October and November, and then retreats northward in May, June, and July.[49] Ice movement is dynamic, and has been observed at speeds as high as twenty-seven nautical miles per day.[50] According to the 2009 Arctic Marine Shipping Assessment, "[t]he future sea ice extent in the vicinity of the Bering Strait is projected to change only slightly in spring (April and May); however, a significant reduction (later freeze-up) is projected for the future in November and December."[51] The average extent of sea-ice cover in summer has

---

[44] AMAP, *supra* note 41, at 54.

[45] Kroeker, *supra* note 38, at 1888. *See also* William C. Long et al., *Effects of Ocean Acidification on Juvenile Red King Crab* (Paralithodes camtschaticus) *and Tanner Crab* (Chionoecetes bairdi) *Growth, Condition, Calcification, and Survival*, 8 PLOS ONE E60959, at 4–8 (2013), http://www.plosone.org/article/fetchObject.action?uri=info%3Adoi%2F10.1371%2Fjournal.pone.0060959&representation=PDF.

[46] IGBP, *supra* note 37, at 10 (citing Alan Barton et al., *The Pacific Oyster,* Crassostra gigas, *Shows Negative Correlation to Naturally Elevated Carbon Dioxide Levels: Implications for Near-Term Ocean Acidification Effects*, 57 LIMNOLOGY & OCEANOGRAPHY 698 (2012); George G. Waldbusser et al., *A Developmental and Energetic Basis Linking Larval Oyster Shell Formation to Acidification Sensitivity*, 40 GEOPHYSICAL RES. LETTERS 2171 (2013)).

[47] NOAA, OCEAN AND GREAT LAKES ACIDIFICATION RESEARCH PLAN 42 (2010), http://www.pmel. noaa.gov/co2/files/feel3500_without_budget_rfs.pdf. Broader estimates of the economic consequences of ocean acidification are few in number. General agreement exists that declines in shellfisheries will lead to economic losses, but the extent of the losses is uncertain. One study has estimated up to nearly a 13 percent reduction in revenue from U.S. mollusk harvests by 2060 due to acidification in a business-as-usual CO2 emissions scenario, or the IOCC A1FI scenario. *See* Sarah R. Cooley & Scott C. Doney, *Anticipating Ocean Acidification's Economic Consequences for Commercial Fisheries*, 4 ENVTL. RES. LETTERS 024007, at 5 tbl. 3 (2009). *See also* Jean-Pierre Gattuso, Katharine J. Mach & Granger Morgan, *Ocean Acidification and Its Impacts: An Expert Survey*, 117 CLIMATIC CHANGE 725, 731–37 (2013).

[48] Hartsig et al., *supra* note 11, at 38.

[49] *Id.* (citing ARCTIC COUNCIL, ARCTIC MARINE SHIPPING ASSESSMENT 2009 REPORT 106 (2009), http://www.pame.is/images/stories/AMSA_2009_Report/AMSA_2009_Report_2nd_print.pdf).

[50] *Id.* at 39.

[51] ARCTIC COUNCIL, ARCTIC MARINE SHIPPING ASSESSMENT 2009 REPORT 106 (2009), http://www. pame.is/images/stories/AMSA_2009_Report/AMSA_2009_Report_2nd_print.pdf.

declined by 15–20 percent over the past thirty years and is expected to accelerate, with the near total loss of sea ice in summer projected by 2100.[52] As sea ice melts, it changes the salinity and density of ocean water, affecting ocean circulation patterns across hundreds of square miles.[53] Please refer to Figure 6.2 which is located between pages 118 and 119.

The loss of sea ice is significant for two reasons. First, sea ice acts as a form of habitat as well as a driver of ecological processes. It provides a habitat for photosynthetic algae, which are critical for biological productivity.[54] The algae eventually sink to the sea floor, enhancing benthic production and resulting in some of the highest levels of soft-bottom benthic faunal biomass in the world.[55] In addition, sea ice is a nursery ground for fish and invertebrates.[56] For example, sea ice is used as a nursery ground for Arctic cod, a key species in the Arctic and an important food source for many marine mammals and birds.[57]

Second, the absence of sea ice will allow for an increase in commercial and industrial activities in previously ice-covered areas, including fishing, shipping, and oil and gas production.[58] The Arctic and Bering Strait region currently experiences a very low volume of commercial vessel traffic.[59] This is expected to change, however, as sea ice becomes more and more sparse, clearing the way for increased vessel traffic from trans-Arctic shipping routes and transport related to increased oil and gas exploration in the Arctic region. A report by the Alaska state legislature found an increase in Arctic maritime traffic between 2006 and 2012.[60] Further, the Arctic Marine Shipping Assessment observed that transportation of oil and gas using the Northern Sea Route is "technically and economically feasible," and anticipated that by 2020, the volume of oil and gas transported via the Northern Sea Route could be as high as 40 million tons per year.[61] The

---

[52] Arctic Climate Impact Assessment, Impacts of a Warming Arctic: Arctic Climate Impact Assessment 13 (2004), http://www.amap.no/documents/download/1058. *See also* Anne B. Hollowed et al., *Projected Impacts of Climate Change on Marine Fish and Fisheries*, 70 ICES J. Marine Sci. 1023 (2013).

[53] Hartsig et al., *supra* note 11, at 39 (citing Budikova, *supra* note 12, at 153).

[54] *Id.* at 41 (citing Christopher Krembs & Jody Deming, Sea Ice: A Refuge for Life in Polar Seas?, http://www.arctic.noaa.gov/essay_krembsdeming.html (last visited Jan. 15, 2014)).

[55] *Id.* at 42 (citing Jacqueline M. Grebmeier et al., *Ecosystem Dynamics of the Pacific-Influenced Northern Bering and Chukchi Seas in the Amerasian Arctic*, 71 Progress Oceanography 331, 331–32 (2006)).

[56] *Id.* at 41.

[57] *Id.* (citing Krembs & Deming, *supra* note 54).

[58] Final Rule to Implement the Arctic Fishery Management Plan, 74 Fed. Reg. 56,734, 56,734, 56,738 (Nov. 3, 2009) (to be codified at 50 C.F.R. pt. 679).

[59] Hartsig et al., *supra* note 11, at 46. *See, e.g.*, Arctic Council, *supra* note 51, at 85 (maps showing relatively low maritime traffic in the Bering Strait region); *id.* at 89 (noting that in 2004, the total number of vessels operating in the entire circumpolar Arctic amounted to "less than 2 percent of the world's registered fleet of oceangoing vessels over 100 gross tonnage").

[60] Alaska State Legislature, Findings & Recommendations of the Alaska Northern Waters Task Force 14 (2012), http://housemajority.org/coms/anw/pdfs/27/NWTF_Full_Report_Color.pdf.

[61] Hartsig et al., *supra* note 11, at 50 (citing Arctic Council, *supra* note 51, at 5).

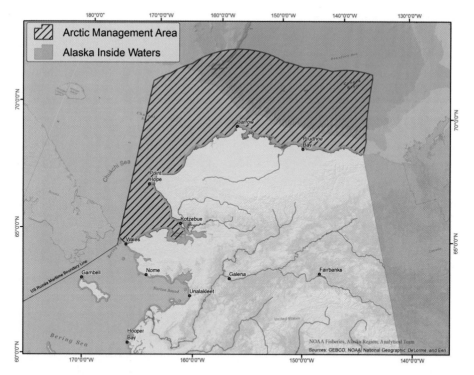

ARCTIC MANAGEMENT AREA MAP, FIGURE 6.3 The Arctic Management Area spans the Chukci and Beaufort Seas north of Alaska.

Photo credit: NOAA Fisheries, Alaska Region, Analytical Team. GEBCO, NOAA, National Geographic, DeLorme, and Esri.

September 16, 2012 (summer minimum)

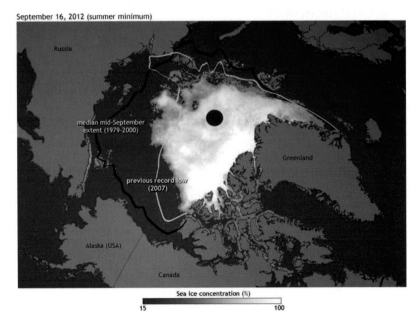

ARCTIC SEA ICE MAP, FIGURE 6.2 The amount of sea ice covering the Arctic Ocean at the end of summer is now considerably lower than the average from 1979 to 2000.

Photo credit: NOAA Climate.gov, based on data provided by the National Snow & Ice Data Center.

U.S. Coast Guard reports that vessels traveling through the Bering Strait in the summer nearly doubled over a four-year period, from 130 in 2009 to 250 in 2012.[62] In early 2014, the Canadian government announced that it would invest in mapping shipping lanes through the Arctic to lay the foundation for "future commercial and social activity in the Far North."[63] Increased commercial and industrial activities will add additional stressors to marine systems and species already under considerable stress due to the pace and extent of climate change and ocean acidification.

C. IMPACTS ON FISH

1. Shifting Stocks: Changes in Distribution and Habitat Availability

There are multiple effects of climate change on fish, including impacts to prey availability, increasing low oxygen zones, and a host of others. This subsection will briefly outline two key impacts related closely to existing fishery management tools: shifting stocks, and impacts on fish productivity.

The warming of ocean waters is already having a profound effect on the distribution of marine organisms, especially fish. Marine species respond to changing temperatures by changing their geographic distribution and depth range. In response to warming, normally temperate species are moving to higher latitudes, either due to active migration or due to changes in productivity of local populations.[64] Recent studies have documented the worldwide shift of fish toward the poles and to deeper water as they seek cooler water.[65] A study published in the journal *Fish and Fisheries* found that climate change may lead to numerous local extinctions in sub-polar regions and simultaneous species invasions in the Arctic.[66] The study predicts dramatic species turnovers of more than 60 percent of the present biodiversity.[67]

In the North Pacific, sea surface temperatures are expected to increase by 1–1.5 °C (1.8–2.7 °F) by the middle of the century.[68] Studies investigating potential ecosystem

---

[62] Alex DeMarban, *Bering Strait Ship Traffic Grows, with Russia Leading Way and Alaska Lagging*, ALASKA DISPATCH, July 14, 2013, http://www.alaskadispatch.com/article/20130714/bering-strait-ship-traffic-grows-russia-leading-way-and-alaska-lagging.

[63] Lee Berthiaume, *Coast Guard to Scope Out Arctic Shipping Lanes*, CANADA.COM (Jan. 21, 2014), http://o.canada.com/news/coast-guard-to-scope-out-arctic-shipping-lanes/.

[64] Anne B. Hollowed et al., *Projected Impacts of Climate Change on Marine Fish and Fisheries*, 70 ICES J. MARINE SCI. 1023, 1027 tbl. 1 (2013) (citing Pierre Petitgas et al., *Anchovy Population Expansion in the North Sea*, 444 MARINE ECOLOGY PROGRESS SERIES 1 (2012)).

[65] *See, e.g.*, Richard D. Norris et al., *Marine Ecosystem Reponses to Cenozoic Global Change*, 2 SCI. 492 (2013); Malin L. Pinsky et al., *Marine Taxa Track Local Climate Velocities*, 13 SCI. 1239 (2013); Poloczanska et. al., *supra* note 33.

[66] Cheung et al., *supra* note 30, at 242.

[67] *Id.* at 235.

[68] James J. Anderson et al., *Modeling Climate Change Impacts on Phenology and Population Dynamics of Migratory Marine Species*, 264 ECOL. MODELLING 83, 84 (2013) (citing Michael T. Burrows et al., *The Pace*

changes in the North Pacific under climate change predict habitat shifts for fish species and overall reduction in fish catches for the North Pacific.[69] In 2013, scientists assessed the potential movement of fish and shellfish stocks from the sub-Arctic to the Arctic Ocean and found that six out of seventeen assessed species had high potential for establishing resident populations in the Arctic.[70]

2. Impacts on Fish Productivity

In addition to shifting stocks in response to temperature changes, one of the important ways in which fish population productivity is affected by climate change is through impacts on recruitment success. For example, recruitment for walleye pollock—the second most valuable fish in the North Pacific[71]—is predicted to decline by 32–58 percent.[72] One potential explanation for this predicted decline with increasing sea surface temperature is a change in the food web due to warming and cooling on the southeastern Bering Sea shelf. During cooler years, pollock under one year old have been found to prey on large copepods and euphausiids (two types of small crustaceans), whereas in warmer years, they consume smaller copepods.[73] Therefore, under warmer ocean temperatures, young pollock are smaller and are thus eaten by predators such as adult pollock and salmon, which would normally prey on large zooplankton under cooler temperatures.[74]

Overall, the productivity of fish populations is expected to decrease globally, but with large regional variation. The science has yet to be settled. A 2010 study estimated that fishery catch potential will increase by 30–70 percent in high-latitude regions and decrease by up to 40 percent in the tropics.[75] Fisheries productivity in the California Current Ecosystem might decline, while fisheries productivity in the North Pacific—particularly the Bering Sea—might increase.[76] A 2013 study, on the other hand, predicted

---

of Shifting Climate in Marine and Terrestrial Ecosystems, 4 Sci. 652 (2011)). *See also* INTERGOVERNMENTAL PANEL ON CLIMATE CHANGE, CONTRIBUTION OF WORKING GROUP I TO THE FOURTH ASSESSMENT REPORT OF THE IPCC: CLIMATE CHANGE 2007—THE PHYSICAL SCIENCE BASIS (2007), http://www.ipcc.ch/pdf/assessment-report/ar4/wg1/ar4_wg1_full_report.pdf).

[69] *See, e.g.*, Scott C. Doney et al., *Climate Change Impacts on Marine Ecosystems*, 4 ANN. REV. MARINE SCI. 11, 20 (2012); Jeffrey J. Polovina et al., *Projected Expansion of the Subtropical Biome and Contraction of the Temperate and Equatorial Upwelling Biomes in the North Pacific under Global Warming*, 68 ICES J. MAR. SCI. 986, 989–90 (2011).

[70] Anne Babcock Hollowed, Benjamin Planque & Harald Loeng, *Potential Movement of Fish and Shellfish Stocks from the Sub-Arctic to the Arctic Ocean*, 22 FISHERIES OCEANOGRAPHY 355, 355 (2013).

[71] NMFS, *supra* note 7, at 17.

[72] Franz J. Mueter et al., *Expected Declines in Recruitment of Walleye Pollock* (Theragra chalcogramma) *in the Eastern Bering Sea under Future Climate Change*, 68 ICES J. MARINE SCI. 1284, 1284 (2011).

[73] Ken O. Coyle et al., *Climate Change in the Southeastern Bering Sea: Impacts on Pollock Stocks and Implications for the Oscillating Control Hypothesis*, 20 FISHERIES OCEANOGRAPHY 139, 152 (2011).

[74] *Id.* at 152–53.

[75] William W.L. Cheung et al., *Large-Scale Redistribution of Maximum Fisheries Catch Potential in the Global Ocean under Climate Change*, 15 GLOBAL CHANGE BIOLOGY 24, 24 (2010).

[76] *Id.* at 28–29.

that fisheries productivity will increase in the California Current Ecosystem region and decrease in the central North Pacific.[77] Authors of the second study attribute this different result to their inclusion of food web processes in their simulation model.[78] These two studies illustrate the uncertainty that exists around predicting regional changes in fisheries productivity due to climate change, and the corresponding challenges posed for framing forward-looking management approaches.

IV. Adapting Fisheries Management for Climate Change

We are already, or soon will be facing, a new ocean reality. This new reality will demand that we push the tools we have as far as they can go to manage for resilience in rapidly changing systems, while developing new tools better suited to our future. As the impacts of global climate change and ocean acidification become more apparent, a broader approach to management is required to ensure ocean ecosystems can support healthy fish populations into the future. To ensure continued success in restoring marine ecosystems and maintaining healthy fish populations, lawmakers and managers in the Pacific and Arctic regions are recognizing that they must take the next logical step in fishery management: a shift toward ecosystem-based fishery management, placing a greater focus on the health and long-term resilience of the ecosystems that support productive fisheries.

Ecosystem-based management is achievable under existing law, and for more than a decade numerous experts have been recommending a shift to an ecosystem approach.[79] Congress has acknowledged the importance of an ecosystem-based fishery management approach, requiring the Secretary of Commerce in the last two Magnuson-Stevens Act reauthorizations to develop recommendations and identify needs for a successful transition.[80] A study authorized as part of the 2006 Magnuson-Stevens Act amendments

---

[77] Phoebe A. Woodworth-Jeffcoats et al., *Ecosystem Size Structure Response to 21st Century Climate Projection: Large Fish Abundance Decreases in the Central North Pacific and Increases in the California Climate*, 19 GLOBAL CHANGE BIOLOGY 724, *7–9 (2013), *available at* http://www.researchgate.net/publication/236057328_Ecosystem_size_structure_response_to_21st_century_climate_projection_large_fish_abundance_decreases_in_the_central_North_Pacific_and_increases_in_the_California_Current/file/e0b4951f7eaa6c75c7.pdf.

[78] *Id.*

[79] *See, e.g.,* JOINT OCEAN COMM'N INITIATIVE, FROM SEA TO SHINING SEA: PRIORITIES FOR OCEAN POLICY REFORM 6 (2006), http://jointoceancommission.org/resource-center/1-Reports/2006-06-13_Sea_to_Shining_Sea_Report_to_Senate.pdf; PEW OCEANS COMM'N, AMERICA'S LIVING OCEANS: CHARTING A COURSE FOR SEA CHANGE, at x (2003), http://www.pewtrusts.org/uploadedFiles/wwwpewtrustsorg/Reports/Protecting_ocean_life/env_pew_oceans_final_report.pdf; U.S. COMM'N ON OCEAN POLICY, AN OCEAN BLUEPRINT FOR THE 21ST CENTURY 63 (2004), http://govinfo.library.unt.edu/oceancommission/documents/full_color_rpt/000_ocean_full_report.pdf.

[80] 16 U.S.C. § 1882 (2012); Magnuson-Stevens Fishery Conservation and Management Reauthorization Act of 2006, Pub. L. No. 109-479, § 210, 101 Stat. 3575, 3617 (2007); Sustainable Fisheries Act, Pub. L. No. 104-297, § 207, 110 Stat. 3559, 3612 (1996) (prior to 2007 amendment).

found that tools already exist for transitioning to a system that better considers the complexities of the marine environment, but that Regional Fishery Management Councils need more definitive and detailed guidance on their role in implementing ecosystem-based fishery management.[81] As Congress prepares to reauthorize the Magnuson-Stevens Act for a third time, fishermen, conservationists, and scientists are focusing on the legislative and regulatory tools needed to make the transition from a focus on a single-species maximum sustainable yield paradigm to a broader ecosystem-based management paradigm that allows consideration of and adjustments to the emerging new ocean reality.

This section discusses progressive steps that the North Pacific and Pacific Fishery Management Councils are already taking using existing tools.

A. ARCTIC FISHERY MANAGEMENT PLAN

Of the eight regional fishery management councils in the United States, the North Pacific Fishery Management Council ("North Pacific Council") has taken the most concrete step to date to adapt management for current and future impacts of climate change. In 2009, the North Pacific Council approved a new FMP for fish resources in the Chukchi and Beaufort Seas north of the Bering Strait, known as the Fishery Management Plan for Fish Resources of the Arctic Management Area, or Arctic FMP.[82] The Arctic FMP prohibits commercial fishing for Arctic fish in the Arctic Management Area.[83] Please refer to Figure 6.3 which is located between pages 118 and 119.

The impetus for the Arctic FMP was the effects of climate change on the region. Both the North Pacific Council and the National Marine Fisheries Service (NMFS) recognized the profound and swift changes in the northern area occurring as a result of climate change, even in the absence of fishing pressure, and chose a forward-looking and precautionary approach to the resource for which they have tools to manage: commercial fisheries.

The Arctic FMP discusses many of the climate change impacts discussed above. The FMP notes that the "Council's policy is to proactively apply judicious and responsible fisheries management practices, based on sound scientific research and analysis, to ensure the sustainability of fishery resources, to prevent unregulated fishing, and to protect associated ecosystems for the benefit of current users and future generations."[84] The FMP

---

[81] Ecosystem Principles Advisory Panel, Ecosystem-Based Fishery Management: A Report to Congress by the Ecosystem Principles Advisory Panel as Mandated by the Sustainable Fisheries Act Amendments to the Magnuson-Stevens Fishery Conservation and Management Act 1996, at 37 (1998), http://www.nmfs.noaa.gov/sfa/EPAPrpt.pdf.

[82] N. Pac. Fishery Mgmt. Council, Fishery Management Plan for Fish Resources of the Arctic Management Area (2009), http://www.npfmc.org/wp-content/PDFdocuments/fmp/Arctic/ArcticFMP.pdf. The FMP went into effect on December 3, 2009. Final Rule to Implement the Arctic Fishery Management Plan, 74 Fed. Reg. 56,734 (Nov. 3, 2009) (to be codified at 50 C.F.R. pt. 679).

[83] Final Rule, *supra* note 82, at 56,735. The Final Rule excludes from the definition of "Arctic fish" Pacific salmon and Pacific halibut, which are managed pursuant to other authorities and for which fishing is otherwise prohibited in the Arctic Management Area.

[84] N. Pac. Fishery Mgmt. Council, *supra* note 82, at ES-2 tbl. ES-1.

discusses the current limited understanding of the ecological processes in the Arctic, and acknowledges that climate change will continue to change the Arctic in fundamental ways, from warming oceans, to loss of seasonal ice cover, to changes in the range of commercial fish species.[85] The Arctic FMP underscores the rapid changes, including changes to the Arctic's "physical attributes which drive much of the seasonal habitat availability and resultant primary production," and notes that sea ice cover is diminishing faster than models had predicted.[86] The FMP similarly notes a "complex whole ecosystem change which may be driven by climate warming [...] in the Northern Bering Sea," due in part to fish extending their ranges into northern waters.[87] In light of these changes, the Council and agency concluded the prohibition would "afford the greatest protection of the Arctic ecosystem in the face of a changing climate."[88] The Arctic FMP accordingly closed the Arctic Ocean under U.S. jurisdiction to all commercial fishing pending further research.

The recognition of the new ocean reality, and the corresponding Arctic FMP decision, was met with wide support from fishermen, conservationists, tribal representatives, members of the public, and others.[89] Alaska's senators, Mark Begich and Lisa Murkowski, wrote a joint letter in support of the Arctic FMP, citing climate change stressors:

> Climate change is having profound effects on the Beaufort and Chukchi Seas off the coast of Alaska. Season sea ice cover is diminishing and ocean temperatures are increasing. These rapid changes are causing enormous stress to Alaskans who live in the arctic, and to the animals and fish on which they depend. A prohibition on commercial fishing in the arctic is needed until stocks can be assessed and plans made that will safeguard the subsistence needs of people and protect the sustainability of the region's natural resources.[90]

It is difficult to overstate how forward-thinking the Arctic FMP is, particularly in light of the management regime that Congress established in the Magnuson-Stevens Act. The trigger for development of an FMP is the determination that a fishery is in need of conservation and management.[91] In other words, FMPs are developed to bring fisheries that are already operating without significant regulation into a regulatory regime. The Act includes discretionary provisions for closure of a fishery,[92] but due to

---

[85] *Id.* at 4.

[86] *Id.* at 60.

[87] *Id.*

[88] Availability of a Fishery Management Plan and Fishery Management Plan Amendment; Request for Comments, 74 Fed. Reg. 24,757, 24,760 (May 26, 2009) (to be codified at 50 C.F.R. pt. 679).

[89] Final Rule to Implement the Arctic Fishery Management Plan, 74 Fed. Reg. 56,734, 56,735 (Nov. 3, 2009) (to be codified at 50 C.F.R. pt. 679).

[90] Letter from Senator Lisa Murkowski and Senator Mark Begich to Department of Commerce Secretary Gary Locke (July 22, 2009) (on file with author).

[91] 16 U.S.C. § 1852(h)(1) (2012).

[92] 16 U.S.C. § 1853(b)(2) (2012).

scientific uncertainty or changing environmental conditions does not expressly contemplate proactive measures, and is largely designed to facilitate fisheries, subject to targeted limitations.[93] Particularly in regions other than the North Pacific, this has often resulted in a reactive governance system in which measures are implemented only after stocks are found to be depleted.[94] The North Pacific Council brilliantly used the FMP tool, which had been designed to regulate fisheries already in existence, to get in front of a potentially significant ecological problem and hold off fisheries in the Arctic before they got started. Never before has such a large area of the exclusive economic zone been explicitly placed off limits in the face of scientific uncertainty and in service to taking a precautionary approach, wisely flipping the traditional system of federal fisheries on its head in light of new and changing conditions.

B. FISHERY ECOSYSTEM PLANS

In addition to using the Arctic FMP as a precautionary fishery management tool in the face of climate change, the North Pacific and Pacific Regional Fishery Management Councils have also used Fishery Ecosystem Plans to catalog and assess ecosystem considerations, including increasing climate change impacts, alongside traditional FMPs.

The Fishery Ecosystem Plan (FEP) concept has existed for many years, but its use by Fishery Management Councils is recent. Section 406 of the Sustainable Fisheries Act of 1996 called for the establishment of an advisory panel to "develop recommendations to expand the application of ecosystem principles in fishery conservation and management activities,"[95] resulting in the Ecosystem Principles Advisory Panel, which submitted a report to Congress in 1999.[96] The report recommends that a fishery ecosystem plan be developed for each major ecosystem under Council jurisdiction and specifies the objectives that FEPs are to have.[97]

FEPs are management guidance tools rather than management tools themselves. FEPs allow fishery managers to consider the fisheries they manage at an ecosystem level and to consider and account for interactions between system-wide impacts such as climate change and ocean acidification, and managed fisheries or other resources. Management action taken in light of FEP analyses must still occur via FMPs. While Congress has yet

---

[93] *See* Sarah M. Kutil, *Scientific Certainty Thresholds in Fisheries Management: A Response to a Changing Climate*, 41 ENVTL. L. 233, 235–36 (2011).

[94] *See id.* at 235 ("NPFMC's decision to close the Arctic Management Area is unprecedented and unique because fisheries management is generally reactive, not proactive, and because this is the first closure of a fishery due to climate change.").

[95] 16 U.S.C. § 1882(a) (2012).

[96] ECOSYSTEM PRINCIPLES ADVISORY PANEL, *supra* note 81.

[97] *Id.* at 3–5.

to mandate the use of FEPs for fishery management, some Regional Fishery Management Councils, including the Pacific and North Pacific, have recognized the value of FEPs and adopted them as guidance.[98]

The Pacific and North Pacific Fishery Management Councils have both developed and adopted FEPs that are advisory in nature and do not authorize any management measures or changes to fishery regulations.[99] Despite their lack of regulatory power, the FEPs are an important step toward considering the impacts of climate change in fishery management in both regions. The FEPs analyze interactions among climate factors and ecosystem components and identify indicators for the Councils to monitor and consider for future management action.

1. Aleutian Islands Fishery Ecosystem Plan

The North Pacific Fishery Management Council's FEP for the Aleutian Islands, adopted in 2007, is the result of a pilot project to create "an overarching document, which provides an ecological context for fishery management decisions affecting the Aleutian Islands area."[100] The Council selected the Aleutian Islands ecosystem for the FEP pilot project because it is both complex and the least predictable ecosystem in which the Council manages commercial fisheries.[101] (See Figure 6.4.) The Council intended the FEP as an "early warning system" designed to "help the Council respond to changing conditions in a proactive rather than reactive mode."[102]

---

[98] N. Pac. Fishery Mgmt. Council, Aleutian Islands Fishery Ecosystem Plan 2 (2007), http://www.npfmc.org/wp-content/PDFdocuments/conservation_issues/AIFEP/AIFEP12_07.pdf; Pac. Fishery Mgmt. Council, Pacific Coast Fishery Ecosystem Plan for the U.S. Portion of the California Current Large Marine Ecosystem, Public Review Draft (2013), http://www.pcouncil.org/wp-content/uploads/FEP_February2013_Draft_for_web.pdf.

[99] The North Pacific Fishery Management Council explains the FEP's advisory nature as follows:

> The FEP is intended to be a guidance document for the Council. The FEP does not authorize management measures or changes to fishery regulations. Under the Magnuson-Stevens Act, only a FMP can authorize regulations to implement management measures. The role of the FEP is to provide an understanding of the ecosystem context in which the FMPs operate, thereby assisting the Council to better integrate ecosystem principles into fishery management. Because the FEP evaluates relationships among components of the ecosystem that are typically managed separately, this geographically-based ecosystem perspective may suggest areas for changes and improvements, which would be implemented through the normal fishery management plan amendment process.

N. Pac. Fishery Mgmt. Council, *supra* note 98, at 2.

[100] Brooke Glass-O'Shea, *Watery Grave: Why International and Domestic Lawmakers Need to Do More to Protect Oceanic Species from Extinction*, 17 Hastings W.-Nw. J. Envtl. L. & Pol'y 101, 140 (2011) (quoting Diana L. Stram & Diana C. K. Evans, *Fishery Management Responses to Climate Change in the North Pacific*, 66 ICES J. Marine Sci. 1633, 1637 (2009)).

[101] N. Pac. Fishery Mgmt. Council, *supra* note 98, at 2.

[102] *Id.* at 1.

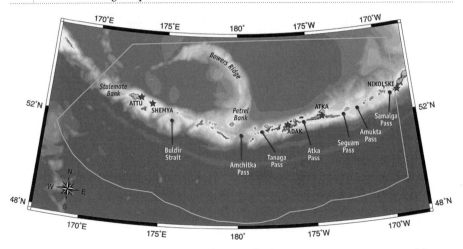

ALEUTIAN ISLANDS MAP, FIGURE 6.4 The Aleutian Islands FEP area encompasses most of the Aleutian Island archipelago.

Photo credit: North Pacific Fishery Management Council, Aleutian Islands Fishery Ecosystem Plan map.

The Aleutian Islands FEP has several purposes: (1) "to integrate information from across the FMPs with regard to the Aleutian Islands"; (2) "to identify a set of indicators for the Aleutian Islands to evaluate the status of the ecosystem over time"; (3) "to provide a focal point to develop and refine tools, such as ecosystem models to evaluate the indicators"; (4) "to identify sources of uncertainty and use them to determine research and data needs"; and (5) "to assist the Council in (1) setting management goals and objectives, and (2) understanding the cumulative effects of management actions."[103] The FEP is not a legally binding document; rather it is an educational tool to assist the Council and provide an ecosystem context for fishery management.[104] It is a "living document" designed to be reevaluated and updated periodically for ecosystem trends and key interactions.[105]

Fisheries management typically involves considering the direct and indirect effects of fishing on target species, other species, and marine habitat. Other aspects of the marine ecosystem are managed separately, if at all. The Aleutian Islands FEP seeks to understand and depict the ecosystem context in which the fisheries operate, and examine not only the effects of fishing on other marine resources, but also consider "the impacts of climate, and the cumulative impacts on ecosystems from all fisheries and non-fishing impacts."[106] The FEP takes a risk-assessment approach, and chief among the documented and discussed

---

[103] *Id.* at 2.

[104] N. Pac. Fishery Mgmt. Council, Overview of Aleutian Islands Fishery Ecosystem Plan 4 (2007), http://www.npfmc.org/wp-content/PDFdocuments/conservation_issues/AIFEP/ AIFEPbrochure1207.pdf. *See also* N. Pac. Fishery Mgmt. Council, *supra* note 98, at 5.

[105] *Id.* at 22.

[106] N. Pac Fishery Mgmt. Council, *supra* note 98, at 2.

risks is ocean acidification, and its potentially widespread impacts on the Aleutian Island ecosystem.[107] Indeed, the FEP concludes that coral dissolution in the Aleutian Islands as a result of ocean acidification "could impact primary production and the carrying capacity of the A[leutian] I[slands] ecosystem."[108] The risk assessment summary ratings for ocean acidification include high probability, high ecosystem impact, high economic impact, a multi-decadal timescale, and spatial scale covering the entire region.[109]

The implications for management of this risk are less clear. While one of the primary resources for which the Council and NMFS are responsible—fisheries—is likely to be significantly affected by ocean acidification, the tools fisheries managers have to address the primary cause of ocean acidification—greenhouse gas emissions—are limited and indirect at best. The FEP ultimately calls for increased monitoring of acidification as a next step to fully understand how and how quickly acidification will affect managed species.

2. Pacific Coast Fishery Ecosystem Plan

The Pacific Fishery Management Council adopted an FEP in 2013, using the North Pacific's Aleutian FEP as an example.[110] The stated purpose of the Pacific FEP is "to enhance the Council's species-specific management programs with more ecosystem science, broader ecosystem considerations and management policies that coordinate Council management across its [FMPs] and the California Current Ecosystem (CCE)."[111] The FEP is designed to "provide a framework for considering policy choices and trade-offs as they affect FMP species and the broader CCE."[112] In addition, the Pacific FEP includes a list of potential ecosystem initiatives that the Council plans to address as time permits.[113]

Initiative 8 is titled "Cross-FMP Effects of Climate Change Shift." Under this initiative, the Council plans to "assess and articulate its questions about the longer-term effects of climate change on its managed species, so as to better direct public and private efforts to provide management-relevant science."[114] This initiative will potentially

---

[107] *Id.* at 76–78.

[108] *Id.* at 77.

[109] *Id.*

[110] Pac. Fishery Mgmt. Council, Pacific Coast Fishery Ecosystem Plan for the U.S. Portion of the California Current Large Marine Ecosystem, Public Review Draft (2013), http://www.pcouncil.org/wp-content/uploads/FEP_February2013_Draft_for_web.pdf.

[111] *Id.* at 1.

[112] *Id.*

[113] Pac. Fishery Mgmt. Council, Ecosystem Initiatives Appendix to the Pacific Coast Fishery Ecosystem Plan for the U.S. Portion of the California Current Large Marine Ecosystem (2013), http://www.pcouncil.org/wp-content/uploads/FEP_Initiatives_Appendix_FINAL_July2013.pdf.

[114] *Id.* at A-22.

provide a valuable tool for prioritization of management resources and coordination of efforts to address climate change impacts to West Coast fisheries and the communities that depend on them. The first step for Initiative 8 is a literature review on the current state of knowledge, focusing on measures of exposure to climate change, sensitivity of fisheries-dependent communities, and adaptive capacity of fisheries and communities. The Council would begin implementation of this initiative by assembling an ad hoc advisory committee, which would "develop recommendations for forward-looking scientific investigations into the effects of climate change on West Coast fish and fisheries."[115]

This initiative is a laudable step in the right direction and could greatly advance the state of knowledge on, and the adaptability and resilience of, West Coast fisheries. However, the initiative is merely a blueprint for future potential action. Implementation of the ideas expressed in Initiative 8 is subject to the workload capacities of the Council; no action is planned for the near-term, and no concrete implementation schedule has been set. Moreover, much like in the North Pacific, the plan is focused on information gathering. The Pacific and North Pacific Councils should advance the FEPs beyond mere guidance tools. Instead, the information gained through the FEP processes should form the basis of mandatory actions to address impacts from climate change.

C. ALTERNATIVE MANAGEMENT TOOLS

The management goals and tools embodied in the Magnuson-Stevens Act were not designed to address the impacts of climate change on fisheries and fish habitats; however, an underused provision in the MSA—optimum yield—may provide managers with a useful and adaptable tool. The MSA's definition of overfishing is "a rate or level of fishing mortality that jeopardizes the capacity of a fishery to produce the maximum sustainable yield on a continuing basis."[116] Although maximum sustainable yield (MSY) is not defined in the Act, it refers to the highest possible annual catch that can be sustained over time.[117] The goal of an MSY-based management strategy is to maximize fish production;[118] it typically involves fishing a population down to 40 percent of its historic unfished biomass.[119]

---

[115] *Id.* at A-23.

[116] 16 U.S.C. § 1802(34) (2012).

[117] THEODORE PANAYOTOU, FOOD & AGRIC. ORG., FISHERIES TECH. PAPER No. 228, MANAGEMENT CONCEPTS FOR SMALL-SCALE FISHERIES: ECONOMIC AND SOCIAL ASPECTS (1982), http://www.fao.org/docrep/003/X6844E/X6844E02.HTM.

[118] *Id.*

[119] National Standard Guidelines, 74 Fed. Reg. 3,178, 3,187 (Jan. 16, 2009) (to be codified at 50 C.F.R. pt. 600). *See also* CHARLES J. KREBS, THE MESSAGE OF ECOLOGY 48 (2007).

However, MSY was not designed to incorporate ecological, economic, and social factors such as climate change and the cost of fishing.[120] MSY critics point out that MSY-based management does not promote economic or social values, and that MSY fails to account for dynamic ocean processes, the goals of recreational fishing, or the interactions between species.[121] In fact, Peter Larkin, famed fisheries biologist and professor, wrote an epitaph for MSY in 1977, calling for its abandonment merely one year after MSY was enshrined as the goal of the nation's federal fisheries law.[122]

In 1996, Congress recognized stock depletion and added conservation-minded provisions via the Sustainable Fisheries Act.[123] Among other things, the 1996 Act amended the definition of optimum yield (OY), which is designed to add ecological, social, and economic factors into the equation by making explicit trade-offs and considering risks and benefits. The MSA defines OY as "the amount of fish which ... will provide the greatest overall benefit to the Nation, particularly with respect to food production and recreational opportunities, and taking into account the protection of marine ecosystems."[124] OY is now "prescribed on the basis of maximum sustainable yield from the fishery, as reduced by any relevant social, economic, or ecological factor."[125] Yet, despite MSA's OY mandate,[126] most FMPs fail to consider the necessary OY factors in any meaningful or explicit way.[127] The latent OY mandate provides an opportunity to make the shift from

---

[120] PANAYOTOU, *supra* note 117, at *2 n.7. *See also* Catherine M. Dichmont et al., *On Implementing Maximum Economic Yield in Commercial Fisheries*, 107 PROCEEDINGS NAT'L ACADS. SCI. 16, 19 (2010); TOM KOMPAS & R. QUENTIN GRAFTON, AUSTL. BUREAU OF AGRIC. & RES. ECON. & SCIENCES, TECH. REPORT NO. 11.3, TARGET AND PATH: MAXIMUM ECONOMIC YIELD IN FISHERIES MANAGEMENT 5 (2011), http://data.daff.gov.au/brs/data/warehouse/pe_abares99010704/TR11.03MEYfish_hr.pdf ("[MSY] maximises the gross value of production for a fishery, it does not ensure that the fishery is maximising economic returns. Depending on the price of fish and the cost of fishing it is also possible that economic returns from fishing at MSY may be zero or negative.").

[121] *See, e.g.*, CARMEL FINLEY, ALL THE FISH IN THE SEA: MAXIMUM SUSTAINABLE YIELD AND THE FAILURE OF FISHERIES MANAGEMENT (2011); Ray W. Hilborn, *The Dark Side of Reference Points*, 70 BULL. MARINE SCI. 403 (2002); Peter A. Larkin, *An Epitaph for the Concept of Maximum Sustained Yield*, 106 TRANSACTIONS AM. FISHERIES SOC'Y 1 (1977); Hiroyuki Matsuda & Peter A. Abrams, *Can We Say Goodbye to the Maximum Sustainable Yield Theory? Reflections on Trophic Level Fishing in Reconciling Fisheries with Conservation*, AM. FISHERIES SOC'Y SYMPOSIUM 587 (2007), *available at* http://www.fisheriessociety.org/proofs/wfc/matsuda.pdf).

[122] Larkin, *supra* note 121, at 3.

[123] P. L. 104–297, 110 Stat. 3559 (Oct. 11, 1996).

[124] 16 U.S.C. § 1802(33)(A) (2012).

[125] 16 U.S.C. § 1802(33)(B) (2012).

[126] 16 U.S.C. § 1853(a)(3) (2012) (All FMPs are required to "assess and specify" OY and "include a summary of the information utilized in making such specification.").

[127] *See, e.g.*, MID-ATL. FISHERY MGMT. COUNCIL, OMNIBUS ANNUAL CATCH LIMIT AND ACCOUNTABILITY MEASURE AMENDMENT (2011) ("OY will be the long term average catch, which is designed not to exceed the ACL, and will fall between ACL and ACT."); PAC. FISHERY MGMT. COUNCIL, PACIFIC COAST GROUNDFISH FISHERY MANAGEMENT PLAN FOR THE CALIFORNIA, OREGON, AND WASHINGTON GROUNDFISH FISHERY 19–20 (2014) ("The OY for a stock or stock complex is the long-term average of the stock or stock complexes ACLs.").

reactionary defense against the threat of overfishing to forward-thinking management and consideration of climate change stressors.

Additionally, an alternative concept called maximum economic yield (MEY) is gaining popularity in other countries, and may provide a workable solution in the quest to adapt fisheries management to climate change. The MEY concept is not new: it has been discussed by fishery economists since the 1950s.[128] MEY "provides the maximum possible returns to fishers from their effort, given the biological characteristics of the stock/species the fishery targets and the requirement of biological sustainability."[129] MEY management typically results in stock biomass levels that are greater than those managed for MSY.[130] MEY proponents describe it as being more conservation-minded than MSY,[131] and it is touted as a "win-win" by simultaneously providing ecosystem benefits and higher profits.[132]

MEY is more than mere theory—Australia designated MEY as its fishery management goal in 2007, with implementation required by January 2008. A comprehensive review was completed by the Commonwealth of Australia's Department of Agriculture, Fisheries, and Forestry (DAFF) in 2013. The review was largely positive, and asserts that Australia's management regime "represent[s the] world's best practice in most respects."[133] Though MEY is not specifically designed with climate change in mind, fishery managers could use it as an adaptation tool to address impacts from climate change in fisheries of the Pacific and Arctic regions.

Conclusion

Federal fisheries management in the United States has evolved from an era of domesticating and fostering fisheries with a focus on maximum sustained yield of individual stocks to one with increased attention to the collateral impacts of that focus—ending overfishing, rebuilding stocks, and considering impacts on habitat and non-targeted species. The legal and regulatory system was not designed with ecosystem resilience and integrity as a primary purpose. It is still largely concerned with the effects of fishing on fish, and the effects of fishing on other aspects of the marine environment. Nor was it

---

[128] *See, e.g.*, RAYMOND J.H. BEVERTON & SIDNEY J. HOLT, ON THE DYNAMICS OF EXPLOITED FISH POPULATIONS (1957); H. Scott Gordon, *The Economic Theory of a Common-Property Resource: The Fishery*, 62 J. POLITICAL ECON. 124 (1954).

[129] KOMPAS & GRAFTON, *supra* note 120, at 3.

[130] Dichmont, *supra* note 120, at 16.

[131] KOMPAS & GRAFTON, *supra* note 120, at 5.

[132] R. Quentin Grafton, Tom Kompas & Ray W. Hilborn, *Economics of Overexploitation Revisited*, 318 SCI. 1601, 1601 (2007).

[133] AUSTL. DEP'T OF AGRIC., FISHERIES, & FORESTRY, FINAL REPORT ON THE REVIEW OF THE COMMONWEALTH FISHERIES HARVEST STRATEGY POLICY AND GUIDELINES 7 (2013), http://www.daff.gov.au/__data/assets/pdf_file/0011/2294705/report-harvest-strategy.pdf.

designed with climate change in mind. It was not built to consider the effects of changes to the marine environment on fish, on habitat, and ultimately on fishing.

Although the need to move toward an ecosystem-based management approach has been recognized by a number of high-level policy directives,[134] progress is still only halting. Tools (most notably, integrated ecosystem assessments and management strategy evaluations) to support ecosystem-based management are being developed, but funding for this development has been inconsistent and uneven across regions. Additionally, there are still vast data gaps in some regions that limit the potential to apply these tools.

Layered on top of these limits are climate change and ocean acidification, which pose great challenges to ocean habitats in the Pacific and Arctic regions, to the abundance and distribution of fish stocks, and to the effectiveness and utility of current fisheries management systems. In the face of changing marine environments caused by climate change and ocean acidification, the North Pacific and Pacific Fishery Management Councils and NMFS are using the available tools to at least consider current, foreseeable, and some as yet unknown impacts from carbon emissions. These tools are limited, and cannot address emissions themselves, but their use up and down the West Coast reflects some foresight and adaptability in management strategy that will be increasingly necessary.

Scientists predict far-reaching impacts in the Pacific, the North Pacific, and the Arctic, and many impacts are already taking place. In addition to impacts already being felt, climate change and ocean acidification will add to the variability of marine ecosystems, introducing new challenges for fisheries governance. As the North Pacific and Pacific Councils have demonstrated, there are some existing governance tools that can and must be used now to plan and prepare for the continuing impacts of climate change and ocean acidification on fisheries and habitats. At the same time, however, new tools and legal and regulatory regimes will be necessary.

If fisheries governance is to succeed under a new ocean reality, it must be able to function effectively even with increased uncertainty. This will require building adaptive capacity and preparing for increased variability. Increased uncertainty and variability will demand the development of new, faster, and probably simpler tools. Development of early warning systems, such as that contemplated in the Aleutian Islands FEP, will be important. A focus on the resilience of marine ecosystems as one of the key, if not *the*

---

[134] *See, e.g.*, Pew Oceans Comm'n, America's Living Oceans: Charting a Course for Sea Change (2003), http://www.pewtrusts.org/uploadedFiles/wwwpewtrustsorg/Reports/Protecting_ocean_life/env_pew_oceans_final_report.pdf; U.S. Comm'n on Ocean Policy, An Ocean Blueprint for the 21st Century (2004), http://govinfo.library.unt.edu/oceancommission/documents/full_color_rpt/000_ocean_full_report.pdf; White House Council on Envtl. Quality, Final Recommendations of the Interagency Ocean Policy Task Force (2010), http://www.whitehouse.gov/files/documents/OPTF_FinalRecs.pdf.

key, management priority will be needed, and mandates and resources must be brought to bear. We have accomplished much as a nation in the past several decades of fisheries management. We have evolved our approach in a stepwise fashion to consider the broader effects of fisheries on the marine environment. A slow evolution of our management will no longer be sufficient, however. We are facing a new ocean reality, and we must be ready for the change it will bring.

7 The Endangered Species Act and Marine Species Protection in the Climate Change Era

Alexis K. Segal*

* Much gratitude for the support and assistance of family, professors, and friends who encouraged the author through this project, especially: Antonio Crespo, Sara Aminzadeh, Adrian Albino, Sean Houton, Christine Klein, Mom, Dad, and Randy Abate for patience and the opportunity. May we continue to be inspired by our oceans. The content of this chapter is offered by the author alone and is not representative of any other person or entity.

Introduction

The oceans, at once especially vulnerable to climate change, and essential to mitigate climate change impacts, present unique and difficult challenges as protection of its species and ecosystems are so critical to our future. Although hardly a new phenomenon, the numerous impacts of heat-trapping greenhouse gases in our atmosphere are beginning to garner more attention in civic and social spheres.[1] In particular, extensive political and scholarly debate has focused on how the challenges posed by these impacts will fit into and influence our current environmental regulatory scheme. [2]

The Endangered Species Act (ESA) has emerged as a primary regulatory mechanism to protect marine species and habitat. Historically underutilized in the marine context relative to terrestrial species and habitat,[3] there is some concern as to whether the ESA is properly equipped to protect ocean resources in light of issues such as ocean acidification, warming temperature, current flow, pollution, and weather patterns. Due to their global scope, the origins of these issues are difficult to pinpoint and thus pose regulatory challenges. Historically, localized and specific ecosystem challenges qualified species listings under the ESA. Other characteristics, such as large area migration patterns; unique reproductive characteristics such as larval dispersal of marine species such as corals; sea-ice dependency; and habitat transitions between fresh and saline and land and sea; also present regulatory challenges under the ESA due to difficulties with data collection and monitoring of marine species.

Increased attention to how climate change impacts ecosystems and species has drawn a range of responses regarding how this multifaceted, global issue can be woven into the current U.S. environmental regulatory framework, the forefront of which is the Endangered Species Act.[4] Both internationally and in the United States, measures have been taken to increase scientific research and cooperative efforts in order to mitigate global and local impacts resulting from the increased levels of greenhouse gases in our atmosphere.[5] Yet, despite increasing levels of recognition and scientific data, arguably little has been done via regulatory mechanisms to mitigate climate change impacts to ecosystems and biodiversity, not to mention human health and safety.

---

[1] *See generally* Scott C. Doney et al., *Climate Change Impacts on Marine Ecosystems*, 4 ANN. REV. MARINE SCI. 11 (2012).

[2] For the purposes of this chapter, the climate change debate as to the existence of climactic shifts due to anthropogenic contributions of greenhouse gases and corresponding impacts is acknowledged, yet is not a part of the discussion.

[3] Robin Kundis Craig, *Coral Reefs, Fishing, and Tourism: Tension in U.S. Ocean Law and Policy Reform*, 27 STAN. ENVTL. L.J. 3, 26–27 (2008); *see also* Natalie Harrison, *Rent a Reef? How the Privatization of Florida Coral Reefs May Advance Local Conservation Efforts*, 68 U. MIAMI L. REV. 189 (2013).

[4] 16 U.S.C. §§ 1531–1544 (2012).

[5] The United Nations adopted the Kyoto Protocol in December 1997, and it entered into force in February 2005. *See* https://unfccc.int/kyoto_protocol/items/2830.php (assigning mandatory targets for industrialized nations to reduce greenhouse gas emissions). The United States declined to ratify the Kyoto Protocol; *see* S. Res. 98. 105th Cong. (1997). As early as 1978, Congress enacted the National Climate Program Act (92

As climate change impacts imperiling marine species and ecosystems are increasingly revealed by science, increasing numbers of marine species will qualify for and depend on ESA protections. As the gatekeeper to ESA protections, section 4 of the statute establishes factors that must be considered when an agency determines whether to list a species on the endangered or threatened species list. Section 4 also provides the opportunity to list critical habitat for a species, and offer a broader ecosystem-based level of protection, an example of which is coral reefs.

This chapter will discuss the advantages and disadvantages of protecting marine species and habitat under ESA section 4 listing and critical habitat designations, with a focus on coral. As an indicator species for ocean ecosystems and a barometer of ocean health in many areas, coral has suffered drastic declines in the past few decades. Coral became the first marine species to be listed under the Endangered Species Act due to climate change impacts. Corals are key to healthy fisheries, water quality, and coastal protection. As individual animals, and the foundation for complex marine reef ecosystems, corals highlight ESA implementation struggles with climate change impacts as a global and local issue.

Section I of this chapter describes climate change impacts on oceans and the increasing number of endangered marine species. It also discusses the history of the ESA legislation and the reaction in the political sphere to the consideration of climate change in the ESA framework. Section II reviews the mechanics of marine species listing and critical habitat designation under section 4 of the ESA and explores the challenges of ESA implementation in the marine context. Section III provides an account of the coral "listing story," which is an instructive example of the debut of climate change impacts into listing determinations. It then contrasts this story with other examples of decisions not to categorize marine species impacted by climate change as either threatened or endangered. The chapter concludes with some proposals for how the ESA framework can move forward in this Anthropocene era.

I. ESA Policy, Politics, and the Plight of the Oceans

A. CLIMATE CHANGE IMPACTS ON OCEAN ECOSYSTEMS

Our oceans are particularly vulnerable to climate change impacts, which exacerbate an already-fragile state for marine species and their ecosystems. Warming ocean temperatures, ocean acidification, and elevated sea levels compound concurrent man-induced threats such as marine pollution, coastal development, overfishing, and ocean dumping.[6]

Stat. 601), which required the president to establish a program to "assist the Nation and the world to understand and respond to natural and man-induced climate processes and their implications."

[6] IPCC, 2013: Summary for Policymakers, *in* Climate Change 2013: The Physical Science Basis. Contribution of Working Group I to the Fifth Assessment Report of the Intergovernmental Panel on Climate Change 16–17 (T.F. Stocker et al. eds., 2013).

Contemporaneous with their acute vulnerability, oceans are arguably one of the Earth's foremost assets in mitigating greenhouse gas impacts. Serving as a large carbon sink, the world's oceans have absorbed approximately one-third of the carbon dioxide emitted by anthropogenic activities.[7] As elevated atmospheric greenhouse gas concentrations increase global average temperatures, the oceans' absorption of carbon dioxide (among other greenhouse gases), affect oceans in two major ways: (1) warming ocean temperatures, and (2) ocean acidification.[8] Rising water temperatures cause a variety of changes, including rising sea levels, increased ocean stratification, and melting sea ice, as well as alterations in ocean circulation patterns and precipitation.[9] Intertwined with these changes is increased storm intensity, increased introduction of invasive species, and susceptibility, as well as increased spread of disease.[10]

Coupled with existing threats to the oceans, the cumulative impacts of climate change have been predicted to supersede the natural resilience of many marine ecosystems and the species they support.[11] In its report released March 31, 2014, the Intergovernmental Panel on Climate Change (IPCC) described significant near- and long-term impacts to ocean and coastal marine systems due to projected climate change by the mid-twenty-first century and beyond. The report noted that global marine-species redistribution and marine-biodiversity reduction in sensitive regions and ocean acidification will challenge the sustained provision of fisheries productivity and other ecosystem services and will pose substantial risks to marine ecosystems, especially polar ecosystems and coral reefs.[12] The ocean is made up of a range of diverse ecosystems, all of which will be impacted in some way by changing climate conditions. Warming temperatures causing drastic reduction of sea ice in the Arctic Ocean pose an immediate threat to the many species that depend on sea-ice habitat. These new threats have prompted several new ESA listings and proposed listings for those species.[13] Additionally, warming temperatures have

---

[7] *Ocean Acidification: Carbon Dioxide Is Putting Shelled Animals at Risk,* NAT'L GEOGRAPHIC, http://ocean.nationalgeographic.com/ocean/critical-issues-ocean-acidification/ (last visited Aug. 2, 2014).

[8] *Id.*

[9] Doney et al., *supra* note 1.

[10] *Id.*

[11] Intergovernmental Panel on Climate Change (IPCC), *Summary for Policymakers, in* CLIMATE CHANGE 2007: THE PHYSICAL SCIENCE BASIS. CONTRIBUTION OF WORKING GROUP I TO THE FOURTH ASSESSMENT REPORT OF THE INTERGOVERNMENTAL PANEL ON CLIMATE CHANGE, IPCC Doc. (Nov. 2007), *available at* http://www.ipcc.ch/pdf/assessment-report/ar4/wg1/ar4-wg1-spm.pdf. On March 31, 2014, the IPCC released its latest report, entitled CLIMATE CHANGE 2014: IMPACTS, ADAPTATION, AND VULNERABILITY, from Working Group II, which details the impacts of climate change to date, the future risks from a changing climate, and the opportunities for effective action to reduce risks, *available at* http://www.ipcc-wg2.gov/AR5/.

[12] IPCC, *supra* note 11.

[13] *See* "Determination of Threatened Status of the Polar Bear throughout Its Range, Final Rule." 50 C.F.R. § 17 (May 15, 2008) (explaining that Arctic sea ice would "continue to be affected by climate change" and that these changes in sea ice "negatively impact polar bears by increasing the energetic demands of movement in seeking prey…" among other impacts). Similarly, in September 2008, NMFS began a status review

decreased snow cover and in turn impacted flow levels and temperatures of coastal rivers and streams, which serve as home to numerous anadromous salmon species where they hatch, and then return to spawn after maturing in the oceans.[14] In coastal areas with shallow water habitat, rising sea levels will diminish beach habitat, heightening risks of salinity intrusion.[15] More frequent and more intense storm events are already occurring, impacting both terrestrial and near-shore habitats.[16] For example, warmer water temperatures intensify hurricane destruction to near-shore ecosystems such as coral reefs.[17]

Ocean acidification has particularly deleterious effects on species such as reef-building corals. For such species acutely sensitive to alkalinity and carbonate concentrations, acidification decreases calcification rates, impacting skeletal density and reproductive ability, which increases vulnerability to storms and other physical damage.[18] Ocean acidification directly impacts corals' ability to rebuild, which in turn jeopardizes the numerous species that rely on the coral reefs for food or protection.[19] Healthy coral ecosystems provide habitat, food, and shelter to millions of species of plants and animals, even though they occupy only 0.1 percent of the ocean environment.[20] Studies have estimated that one-quarter of marine species utilizes coral reef habitat at some stage of their life cycle.[21] Like marine species, humans, estimated at nearly half a billion worldwide, are greatly dependent on coral reefs for a variety of reasons such as subsistence, economies, cultural heritage, and coastal storm protection.[22]

As individual animals and essential marine ecosystems, coral are especially vulnerable to the myriad of challenges introduced or intensified by climate change. These threats are instructive as an example of the particular challenges an invertebrate marine species can pose to the provisions of the ESA with respect to climate change impacts.[23] Additionally, the ESA itself has faced a myriad of challenges in the oft-shifting political and regulatory landscape, as well as in keeping pace with advances in science and technology.

---

of three ice seal species pursuant to a listing petition based largely on climate change impacts similar to those outlined in the polar bear listing. *See* Fed. Reg. 51,615 (Sept. 4, 2008).

[14] Habiba Gitay et al, *Climate Change and Biodiversity,* IPCC Technical Paper V (Apr. 2002), *available at* https://www.ipcc.ch/pdf/technical-papers/climate-changes-biodiversity-en.pdf.

[15] *Id.*

[16] *Id.*

[17] IPCC, *supra* note 11; *see also* Donald Scavia et al., *Climate Change Impacts on U.S. Coastal and Marine Ecosystems,* 25 ESTUARIES 149 (2002).

[18] Scavia, *supra* note 17.

[19] Blake Armstrong, Note, *Maintaining the World's Marine Biodiversity: Using the Endangered Species Act to Stop the Climate Change Induced Loss of Coral Reefs,* 18 HASTINGS W.-Nw. J. ENVTL. L. & POL'Y 429, 432–33 (2012).

[20] Mary Gray Davidson, *Protecting Coral Reefs: The Principal National and International Legal Instruments,* 26 HARV. ENVTL. L. REV. 499, 501–02 (2002).

[21] *Id.* at 501–02.

[22] *Id.* at 503.

[23] Ryan P. Kelly, *Spineless Wonders: How Listing Marine Invertebrates and Their Larvae Challenges the U.S. Endangered Species Act,* 19 PENN ST. ENVTL. L. REV. 1, 2 (2011).

B. INCORPORATING CLIMATE CHANGE INTO THE ENDANGERED SPECIES ACT

Climate change issues have brought the ESA into the spotlight with a new wave of litigation addressing procedural and substantive implementation of the Act in light of climate change impacts. In addition, the ESA has been subject to the push and pull of the political arena. Both USFWS and NMFS have approached the role of climate change impacts in ESA protections with conservative caution.

Enacted in 1973 with overwhelming majorities in the House and Senate,[24] the purpose of the ESA is to ensure the conservation of "ecosystems upon which endangered and threatened species depend."[25] The ESA's primary purpose is not only to protect fish and wildlife from overexploitation and habitat destruction, but also to create a regulatory regime that could proactively manage and conserve species to avoid approaching the brink of extinction.[26] In the landmark Supreme Court case, *Tennessee Valley Authority v. Hill,*[27] the Court described the ESA as "the most comprehensive legislation for the preservation of endangered species ever enacted by any nation."[28] In further endorsement of its breadth and statutory strength, the Court stated that the "plain intent of Congress in enacting this statute…was to halt and reverse the trend toward species extinction, whatever the cost. This is reflected not only in the stated policies of the Act, but in literally every section of the statute."[29]

Perhaps due to its broad reach and strength, the ESA has been subject to challenges in the courts, halls of Congress, and within the executive agencies, most recently due to climate change and its potential role in species protection under the ESA. The issue of climate impacts, although a relatively recent phenomenon in the ESA implementation arena, is neither new to the science realm nor to U.S. legislative efforts to study or curb greenhouse gas emissions.[30]

Balancing policy interests and agency authority under the ESA is a precarious exercise, one where agencies must walk the fine line of honoring the Act's aggressively protective mandate while avoiding an ESA interpretation that paralyzes the system with exponentially increased listings and the ensuing protections the ESA requires. Impacts from climate change arguably fall within the ESA's statutory purview; however, despite the

---

[24] Michael J. Bean, *The Endangered Species Act: Science, Policy and Politics*, 1162 YEAR IN ECOLOGY & CONSERVATION BIOLOGY 369, 369 (2009).

[25] 16 U.S.C. § 1531(b) (2012).

[26] S. Rep. No. 93-307, at 2 (1973), *reprinted in* 1973 U.S.C.C.A.N. 2989. *See also* Takahashi, *supra* note 33.

[27] 437 U.S. 153 (1978).

[28] *Id.* at 180.

[29] Babbitt v. Sweet Home, 515 U.S. 687, 699 (quoting Tennessee Valley Auth. v. Hill, 437 U.S. at 184).

[30] *See, e.g.*, National Climate Program Act, 92 Stat. 601 (1978) (requiring the president to "assist the Nation and the world to understand and respond to natural and man-induced climate processes and their implications"); Global Climate Protection Act, § 1102(1), 101 Stat. 1408 (1987) (finding that man-made pollution "may be producing a long-term and substantial increase in the average temperature on Earth").

breadth and scope of the ESA's statutory language, impacts from climate change were not likely a factor contemplated as a threat in general nor to habitat or species at the time of its enactment.[31] Thus, due to the varying levels of available scientific data, political debate, and increasing strain on strapped agencies, incorporating climate change under the Act adds another layer of complexity and potential controversy to the scientific and legal analysis.

In May 2006, Caribbean Acropora corals (elkhorn and staghorn) were listed as threatened species based on climate impacts such as ocean acidification and warming temperatures.[32] However, it is the polar bear, listed as a threatened species almost exactly two years later on May 14, 2008, that seemed to capture more attention as to how and whether climate change impacts had a role in ESA application.

Upon announcing listing of the polar bear, then—Secretary of the Interior, Dirk Kempthorne, issued a statement of the administration at the time, reiterating a previous announcement by President George W. Bush, that addressed climate change's role in ESA implementation: "[W]hile the legal standards under the ESA compel me to list the polar bear as threatened, I want to make clear that this listing will not stop global climate change or prevent any sea ice from melting. Any real solution requires action by all major economies for it to be effective. That is why I am taking administrative and regulatory action to make certain the ESA isn't abused to make global warming policies."[33]

Two years later, in May 2010, under the Obama administration, then DOI Secretary Salazar stated that the Obama administration continued to hold the position that the ESA is not the proper regulatory mechanism for addressing climate change.[34] Nevertheless, Secretary Salazar simultaneously acknowledged the Obama administration's view that if the ESA was inappropriate to regulate greenhouse gas emissions degrading species survival rates, there needed to be further legislative action to do so, stating: "we need a comprehensive energy and climate strategy that curbs climate change and its impacts—including the loss of sea ice. Both President Obama and I are committed to achieving that goal."[35]

Although not legislative action, on October 5, 2009, President Obama signed Executive Order 13514 entitled "Federal Leadership in Environmental, Energy and Economic Performance," which sought to create a platform for "coordinated action on climate change preparedness and resilience across the Federal Government...."[36]

[31] Bean, *supra* note 24, at 389.

[32] *See* Elkhorn and Staghorn Corals Listed as Threatened, 71 Fed. Reg. 26,852 (May 9, 2006).

[33] *See* Press Release, Department of Interior, Secretary Kempthorne Announces Decision to Protect Polar Bear under Endangered Species Act, Rule Will Allow Continuation of Vital Energy Production in Alaska (May 14, 2008), *available at* http://www.doi.gov/news/archive/08_News_Releases/080514a.html.

[34] *See* Press Release, U.S. Department of the Interior, Salazar Retains Conservation Rule for Polar Bears (May 8, 2009), *available at* http://www.fws.gov/news/ShowNews.cfm?ID=20FB90B6-A188-D B01-04788E0892D91701.

[35] *Id.*

[36] Exec. Order No. 13514, 74 Fed. Reg. 194 (Oct. 5, 2009), *available at* http://www.gpo.gov/fdsys/pkg/ FR-2009-10-08/pdf/E9-24518.pdf.

Building on a variety of interagency initiatives, including the 2013 National Ocean Policy Implementation Plan, President Obama also issued Executive Order 13653 entitled "Preparing the United States for the Impacts of Climate Change."[37] The Order requires all federal agencies to assess and update their regulations to "make the Nation's watersheds, natural resources and ecosystems…where possible focus on…policy adjustment that promote…greater climate resilience and carbon sequestration or other reductions to the sources of climate change."[38] As of mid-2014, neither Congress nor the agencies has passed specific laws of clarifying guidance on the role of climate change impacts in ESA implementation. Thus, many of these questions are brought to the courts to make a determination of whether agency implementation of the ESA comports with the law.

II. Application of ESA Section 4 to Marine Species and Climate Change Era Challenges

As detailed below, climate change and its role in ESA implementation may play out to a large degree in section 4 listing decisions as the gateway to ESA protections. Section 4 of the ESA describes the criteria and process for listing of a species and critical habitat.

A. MARINE SPECIES LISTING UNDER SECTION 4

Congress' main goal in enacting the ESA was to "halt and reverse the trend toward species extinction."[39] In order to receive ESA protections that mandate federal agency action to "halt and reverse" extinction, a species must first be listed by either NMFS or USFWS as either threatened or endangered.[40] A listing petition may either be initiated by the corresponding agency[41] through the formal rulemaking process or by an interested member of the public.[42] Citizen petitions significantly outnumber those initiated by the agencies.[43] Citizen-listing (or delisting) petitions are considered petitions for formal

---

[37] Exec. Order No. 13653 (Nov. 1, 2013), *available at* http://www.whitehouse.gov/the-press-office/2013/11/01/executive-order-preparing-united-states-impacts-climate-change.

[38] *Id.*

[39] Tennessee Valley Auth. v. Hill, 437 U.S. 153, 184 (1978).

[40] 16 U.S.C. § 1533 (2012).

[41] *Id.* § 1533(b)(2) (2012). Congress granted two federal agencies, the Department of the Interior and Department of Commerce, the authority to implement the Endangered Species Act. In turn the Department of the Interior has delegated its authority to the Fish and Wildlife Service, and the Department of Commerce has delegated its authority to the National Marine Fisheries Service.

[42] 16 U.S.C. § 1533(b)(3) (2012).

[43] "The Service was petitioned to list an average of twenty species per year from 1994 to 2006. By contrast, since 2007, the Service has been petitioned to list more than 1,250 species, nearly as many species as the agency listed during the previous 30 years of administering the ESA. The Service was petitioned to list 695 species in 2007, 56 species in 2008, 63 species in 2009, and 451 species in 2010." *See* "U.S. Fish and

rulemakings and are subject to the applicable procedures and regulations pertinent to either the USFWS or NMFS under the Administrative Procedure Act.[44]

Upon receipt of a petition, the ESA requires the agency to make a finding within ninety days as to whether the listing petition presents "substantial scientific or commercial information" to indicate that a listing action may be warranted.[45] A finding of "may be warranted" then triggers the "12-month finding" process in which the agency must make the listing determination within twelve months of the date from which the original petition was received.[46] During this twelve-month period, the agency reviews the current status of the species[47] and decides on one of three outcomes: (1) the petitioned action is warranted, (2) the petitioned action is not warranted, or (3) the petitioned action is warranted but precluded.[48]

Section 4 describes the criteria and process for listing of a species. First, the agency must determine that the animal population concerned is a "species" or otherwise a "subspecies" or "distinct population segment."[49] USFWS and NMFS apply the term "species" "according to the best biological knowledge and understanding of evolution, specialization and genetics."[50] An "endangered" species is one that is in danger of extinction through all or a significant portion of its range.[51] An invertebrate species must be endangered or threatened across all or a significant portion of its range to be eligible for ESA listing; however, vertebrate species may be classified into "distinct population segments" and still become listed.[52] A threatened species, with slightly less protections afforded, is defined as "likely to become an endangered species within the foreseeable future through all or a portion of its range."[53]

The listing criteria are:

1) The present or threatened destruction, modification, or curtailment of the species' habitat or range;

Wildlife Service Listing Program Work Plan Questions and Answers," *available at* http://www.fws.gov/endangered/improving_esa/FWS%20Listing%20Program%20Work%20Plan%20FAQs%20FINAL.PDF (last visited Aug. 2, 2014).

[44] 5 U.S.C. § 553(e) (2012); *see* 50 C.F.R. § 424.14(a) (2014) (requiring the agency to acknowledge receipt of petitions in writing within thirty days).

[45] 16 U.S.C. § 1533(b)(3)(A) (2012).

[46] 16 U.S.C. § 1533(b)(3)(B) (2012).

[47] *Id.* § 1533(b)(3)(A) (2012).

[48] *Id.* § 1533(b)(3)(B)(i)–(iii) (2012). The Secretary must also demonstrate that "expeditious progress" is being made to add and remote species from ESA lists. *Id.*

[49] *Id.* § 1532 (16) (2012).

[50] 61 Fed. Reg. 4709, 4710 (Feb. 7, 1990). "Species" is defined broadly by the ESA and includes "any subspecies of fish or wildlife or plants, and any distinct population segment of any species of vertebrate fish or wildlife that interbreeds when mature." 16 U.S.C. § 1532 (16) (2012).

[51] 16 U.S.C. § 1532 (20) (2012).

[52] *Id.* §§ 1532(6), (20) (2012).

[53] *Id.*

2) Overutilization for commercial, recreational, scientific, or educational purposes;

3) Disease or predation;

4) The inadequacy of existing regulatory mechanisms; and

5) Other natural or man-made factors affecting the species' continued existence.[54]

Any one or combination of the five listing criteria can qualify as a basis for a threatened or endangered determination under the ESA.[55] Species listing assessments must be made "solely on the basis of the best scientific and commercial data available," after a comprehensive review process of the status of the species and in consideration of protection efforts by other governmental entities.[56] When the agency reviews a petition to decide on listing status, agencies may not consider economic criteria.[57]

B. CRITICAL HABITAT DESIGNATION

The ESA identifies the importance of protecting habitat to species survival.[58] Section 4 establishes procedures for designation of critical habitat. Congress itself highlighted the link between species and their habitats and hinged the success of the ESA on habitat designation, stating that the "ultimate effectiveness of ESA will depend on designation of critical habitat."[59]

As outlined in section 4, the listing agency is required to designate critical habitat for a species at the time of listing, or within one year of listing if critical habitat is not determinable at the time of listing.[60] "Critical habitat" is defined as a specific area that has the physical and biological features "essential to the conservation of the species and which may require special management considerations or protection."[61] Although the ESA directs the agencies to designate critical habitat, it adds "to the maximum extent prudent and determinable," which provides some flexibility for agency implementation.[62] Critical habitat must be determined based on the best scientific data available and after taking into consideration economic and other relevant factors, in contrast to listing determinations, which forbids any economic criteria to

---

[54] *Id.* § 1533(1)(A)–(E) (2012).

[55] *Id.* § 1533(b)(1)(A) (2012).

[56] *Id.*

[57] 50 C.F.R. § 424.11(b) (2014).

[58] *See* Emily Brand, *Considering Open Ocean Critical Habitat under the Endangered Species Act: Does Critical Habitat Actually Help Protect the Pacific Leatherback Sea Turtle?*, 1 SEA GRANT L. & POL'Y J. 40 (Dec. 2008) (citing 16 U.S.C. § 1531(b) (2005), "the purposes of this Act are to provide a means whereby the ecosystem upon which endangered species and threatened species depend may be conserved.").

[59] H.R. Rep. No. 887 at 3 (1976).

[60] 16 U.S.C. §§ 1533(a)(3)(A), § 1533(a)(6)(C)(ii) (2012).

[61] *Id.* § 1532 (5)(A) (2012).

[62] *Id.* § 1532 (5) (2012).

be considered.[63] Critical habitat determinations can be excluded if exclusion benefits outweigh the benefits of its designation, with the caveat that exclusion will not result in the extinction of the species.[64]

C. CHALLENGES TO MARINE SPECIES PROTECTION UNDER THE ESA IN THE CLIMATE CHANGE ERA

The full extent of climate change impacts to ocean ecosystems is still unknown. The National Oceanic and Atmospheric Administration (NOAA) reports that while oceans cover 71 percent of the Earth's surface and contain 97 percent of the planet's water, more than 95 percent of the underwater world remains unexplored.[65] The size and complexity of marine systems make it more difficult to evaluate and monitor the effects of climate impacts relative to their terrestrial counterparts.[66] Thus, regulatory decisions based on climate effects may be faced with the additional challenge of less-studied climate impacts and fewer historical monitoring programs for marine systems.[67]

The agencies tasked with ESA implementation are the United States Fish and Wildlife Service (USFWS) within the Department of the Interior (DOI) and the National Marine Fisheries Service (NMFS) within the Department of Commerce (DOC).[68] The NMFS is primarily responsible for administering the ESA for marine and anadromous species, while the USFWS has jurisdiction generally over terrestrial and freshwater fish species.[69] Of the approximately 2,140 species listed under the ESA,[70] ninety-four are marine or anadromous species under the purview of NMFS,[71] comprised of approximately twenty-eight marine mammals, sixteen marine turtles, forty-four marine and anadromous fish, four invertebrates, and one plant.[72] There are currently eighty marine

[63] *Id.* § 1533(b)(2) (2012).

[64] *Id.*

[65] Anthony J. Richardson & Elvira S. Ploczanska, *Under-Resourced, Under Threat.* 320 SCI. 1294, 1295 (2008); Michelle M. McClure et al., *Incorporating Climate Science in Applications of the U.S. Endangered Species Act for Aquatic Species,* 27 CONSERVATION BIOLOGY 1222, 1223 (2013).

[66] Ove Hoegh-Guldberg & John F. Bruno, *The Impact of Climate Change on the World's Marine Ecosystems,* 328 SCI. 1523, 1523 (2010).

[67] *See* McClure et al., *supra* note 65, at 1223.

[68] *See* 50 C.F.R. § 424.01 (2014).

[69] The ESA divides administration for terrestrial and marine species between the DOI, which houses the USFWS, and the DOC, which contains NOAA and NMFS. *See* 16 U.S.C. § 1532 (15) (2006); *see also* Erin Seney et al., *Climate Change, Marine Environments, and the U.S. Endangered Species Act,* 27 CONSERVATION BIOLOGY 1138 (2013).

[70] *See* NOAA Fisheries Species Information, http://www.nmfs.noaa.gov/pr/species/ (last updated Dec. 31, 2013).

[71] *Id.*

[72] Approximately eleven marine mammals, such as the polar bear, manatee, and sea otter are managed by the USFWS. Additionally, marine turtles are managed by the USFWS while on land and by NMFS when at sea. *See* http://www.nmfs.noaa.gov/pr/species/. *See also* Erin Seney et al., *supra* note 69.

species proposed by NMFS for ESA listing.[73] Distinct from USFWS, NMFS also maintains two additional lists aside from the Threatened and Endangered Species Lists, which are the Candidate Species List and the Species of Concern List.[74]

Arguably, the large discrepancy between ESA-listed marine and terrestrial species is due to the greater difficulty for marine species to fit within the ESA's regulatory scheme. The vastness of the ocean and lack of data may also make it difficult to apply ESA section 4 listing standards, discussed below, to highly migratory fish when it comes to defining the species and its range.[75] For example, with so much yet to understand regarding ocean ecosystems, it may not be possible to meet a "best available science" standard with respect to the accurate population size for a given species. ESA protections are also tested when it comes to some of the ESA's main provisions, such as critical habitat designation or required consultation among federal agencies, for listed marine invertebrates such as corals, with complex life cycles and often multiple larval stages.[76]

The debate regarding the scope of ESA protections and the adequacy of the ESA framework to address global climate change impacts to species and ecosystems is especially poignant with regard to marine species and ecosystems. As described above, the two main climate-change related, and arguably most detrimental, threats to oceans are: (1) warming ocean temperatures, and (2) ocean acidification, both of which are closely tied to greenhouse gas emissions that cannot be easily attributed to one specific source, and the effects of which are enhanced by multiple global and localized factors. On the one hand, the ESA can be considered effective only in circumstances where habitat loss or species decline is the result of easily identifiable causes that are able to be directly regulated by specific mechanisms.[77] On the other hand, NMFS and USFWS arguably possess the technical ability to address climate change impacts within the context of the ESA, and are legally bound to do so due to the strong and broad statutory directives. Nevertheless, the limitations—some practical (e.g., funding, staffing) and some political (e.g., limitations to regulatory reach)—make this difficult or implausible.[78]

---

[73] *See* http://www.nmfs.noaa.gov/pr/species/.

[74] *See* 16 U.S.C. § 1533(c)(1) (2012). The Candidate Species List contains species for which the public, NMFS, or both believe listing is appropriate, including those under consideration for ESA listing, but not yet in a formal proposed rule. The Species of Concern List may include species for which there are significant concerns or uncertainties, regardless of whether they have been denied ESA listing. NMFS maintains that neither the Species of Concern nor Candidate Species Lists confers any ESA protections, and the lists are uniquely NMFS. *See* Taiga Takahashi, *Left Out at Sea: Highly Migratory Fish and the Endangered Species Act*, 99 CAL. L. REV. 179 (2011).

[75] Takahashi, *supra* note 74, at 222–23.

[76] Kelly, *supra* note 23.

[77] J. B. Ruhl, *Keeping the Endangered Species Act Relevant*, 19 DUKE ENVTL. L. & POL'Y F. 275, 282 (2009) (stating that "three circumstances largely define this divide when the ESA is at its most and least effective: (1) the nature of the causal mechanism leading to species decline, (2) the degree of federal presence in that causal mechanism, and (3) the closeness of match between the ESA's species-specific focus and the ecosystem management policy objective.").

[78] A. Moritz et al., *Biodiversity Baking and Boiling: Endangered Species Act Turning Down the Heat*, 44 TULSA L. REV. 205, 234 (2008).

Without legislative directives, and with conflicting and shifting agency regulation implementation policies, the courts have become ensconced in the debate over climate change's role in ESA implementation vis-á-vis various legal challenges to agency action and whether to list certain species. It may be argued that ESA listing criteria under section 4 are facially broad enough to encompass climate change impacts in listing status reviews of marine species. For example, climate change impacts could fall under the fifth listing criteria factor: "Other natural or man-made factors affecting the species' continued existence."[79] However, the agencies charged with ESA implementation have the authority to apply the ESA's provisions within their discretion and may not conclude climate change impacts are relevant to a listing or not warranted determination.

III. Boundaries and Benefits of Section 4 in the Marine Context

As a pioneer in listing based on impacts of climate change effects, that is, ocean acidification and warming, corals are an instructive example. The preliminary listing decision, subsequent critical habitat designation, and pending listing decisions demonstrate NMFS's increased willingness to acknowledge and incorporate climate change impacts into the listing analyses. Yet, this is not always the case for other species impacted by climate change. Understandably, arguably already under-resourced and increasingly burdened agencies are still grappling with how and to what degree to fuse existing and emerging data regarding climate change into listing studies and listing determinations.

A. CLIMATE CHANGE PIONEER: THE CORAL LISTING STORY

Over the past few decades, coral has served as a forerunner in species listing under the ESA, with increased evidence showing direct threats to a species resulting from global climate change impacts on our oceans. Relative to other species, the climate change threats to coral are well supported by scientific data. As early as 1991, NMFS identified nine corals and listed them as candidates for the ESA.[80] Although they all had declined in population in some locations, they were removed from the candidate list because, at that time,

---

[79] 16 U.S.C. § 1533(1)(E) (2012). *See also* Bean, *supra* note 24, at 376. ("The fifth factor…is a catchall that makes clear that species may be listed based upon factors that are not anthropogenic in origin. The fact that a species is at risk of extinction as a result of entirely natural factors—assuming that could be shown as the case—does not matter; it qualifies for listing just as much as a species that is put at risk by human activity.")

[80] Andrew W. Bruckner, *Proceedings of the Caribbean Acropora Workshop: Potential Application of the U.S. Endangered Species Act as a Conservation Strategy*, NOAA Technical Memorandum NMFS-OPR-24 (2002).

NMFS was not able to obtain sufficient data on their status or threats to their survival to meet the scientific documentation required for inclusion on the 1997 candidates list.[81]

In 1999, NMFS began to consider two reef-building Caribbean corals, elkhorn and staghorn, for ESA listing, citing a nearly 96 percent disappearance of these two species in the preceding two decades due to hurricane damage, coral diseases, increased predation, boat groundings, and sedimentation, among other factors.[82] In April 2002, NOAA fisheries convened a workshop to discuss the potential application of the ESA to Caribbean corals as a protection measure for the declining populations. The resulting workshop report concluded that elkhorn and staghorn corals "could benefit from the protection the ESA affords and the listing will provide valuable added protection for many other reef species dependent on them."[83]

Citing climate change as the preeminent threat, the Center for Biological Diversity petitioned NMFS to list elkhorn, staghorn, and fused staghorn corals as endangered or threatened and to simultaneously list critical habitat for these species in March 2004.[84] The petition stated, "Global warming is a particularly insidious threat as increasing sea surface temperatures cause a higher incidence of disease, induce repeated severe bleaching episodes, and elevate the frequency and severity of storms."[85] Pursuant to this petition, NMFS deemed listing elkhorn and staghorn corals threatened as "warranted" on March 18, 2005.[86] However, NMFS concluded a finding of "not warranted" for fused staghorn, because as a hybrid, NMFS concluded it was not a species for purposes of the ESA.[87]

In its 2006 summary documenting the implementation of the "National Coral Reef Action Strategy," the United States Coral Reef Task Force (USCRTF)[88] reported to Congress that 70 percent of the world's coral reefs were in jeopardy, with 20 percent of

---

[81] *Id.* (citing Endangered and Threatened Species; Revision of Candidate Species List under the Endangered Species Act); 62 Fed. Reg. 37,560 (July 14, 1997), *available at* https://www.federalregister.gov/articles/1997/07/14/97-18326/endangered-and-threatened-species-revision-of-candidate-species-list-under-the-endangered-species.

[82] *See* Endangered and Threatened Species; Request for Information on Candidate Species List under the Endangered Species Act, 64 Fed. Reg. 2629, 2629–30 (Jan. 15, 1999).

[83] Bruckner, *supra* note 80.

[84] Center for Biological Diversity, Petition to List Acropora Palmate (Elkhorn Coral), Acropora Cervicornis (Staghorn Coral), and Acropora Prolifera (Fused-Staghorn Coral) as Endangered Species under the Endangered Species Act (Mar. 3, 2004), *available at* http://www.biologicaldiversity.org/species/invertebrates/staghorn_coral/pdfs/petition.pdf.

[85] *Id.*

[86] *See* http://www.nmfs.noaa.gov/pr/species/invertebrates/elkhorncoral.htm.

[87] *Id.*

[88] In 1998, the United States Coral Reef Task Force (USCRTF) was established by Executive Order 13089 to coordinate government efforts to protect, restore, and sustain coral reef ecosystems. *See* http://coralreef.noaa.gov/education/educators/resourcecd/background/resources/ncras_ex_sum_bm.pdf. Aside from creating the USCRTF, the Executive Order requires all federal agencies to identify actions that may affect U.S. coral reefs and to ensure, subject to certain exceptions, that their actions will not degrade those ecosystems. *See* Exec. Order No. 13,089, 63 Fed. Reg. 32,701 (June 16, 1998).

those reefs damaged beyond repair.[89] It further reported that the Caribbean suffered a widespread and severe bleaching event in 2005 that resulted in extensive coral death in much of the region, which caused significant impacts on people and communities in the United States and beyond.[90] In a paper concerning coral decline and coral bleaching events presented at the Coral Reef Task Force meeting in 1999, the Department of State reported: "Significant attention needs to be given to the monitoring of coral reef ecosystems, research on the projected and realized impacts of global climate change, and measures to curtail greenhouse gas emissions."[91] In the summer of 2005, the Caribbean region experienced the hottest water temperatures ever recorded, with large-scale bleaching followed by disease, as well as record hurricanes.[92]

In May 2006, NMFS issued the final rule listing elkhorn and staghorn corals as threatened under the ESA.[93] The listing stated that "the major threats to the species' persistence (*i.e.* disease, elevated sea surface temperature and hurricanes) are severe, unpredictable, likely to increase in the foreseeable future, and at current levels of knowledge, unmanageable."[94] Although disease was cited by the final listing rule as the largest threat to coral survival, other factors such as elevated sea surface temperature and increased atmospheric carbon dioxide levels were a direct link to considering climate change factors contributing to ESA listing status.[95]

Although Acropora listing based on climate change impacts was not as outwardly controversial as the potential listing other species grappling with climate-related challenges, it was not immune to conflict. Prompted by a lawsuit to list critical habitat for elkhorn and staghorn,[96] two years after listing elkhorn and staghorn as threatened, NMFS issued a final rule in November 2008 designating critical habitat for these two species.[97] However, NMFS did not include the same climate change impacts that informed the species listing in its critical habitat determination, stating that such habitat was not determinable at that time due to the extremely complex biological and physical

---

[89] NATIONAL OCEANIC AND ATMOSPHERIC ADMINISTRATION, IMPLEMENTATION OF THE NATIONAL CORAL REEF ACTION STRATEGY, REPORT TO CONGRESS: REPORT ON U.S CORAL REEF TASK FORCE AGENCY ACTIVITIES FROM 2004 TO 2006, http://coralreef.noaa.gov/education/educators/resourcecd/background/resources/ncras_ex_sum_bm.pdf. (last visited Aug. 2, 2014).

[90] *Id.*

[91] U.S. Department of State, *Coral Bleaching, Coral Mortality, and Global Climate Change* (Hawaii. 1999) (paper presented at the second meeting of the U.S. Coral Reef Task Force).

[92] Lara Hansen & Christopher R. Pyke, *Climate Change and Federal Environmental Law*, 7 SUSTAINABLE DEV. L. & POL'Y 26, 26 (2007) (citing Kevin E. Trenberth & Dennis J. Shea, *Atlantic Hurricanes & Natural Variability in 2005*, 33 GEOPHYSICAL RES. LETTERS, L12704, at 1 (June 27, 2006)).

[93] Final Listing Determinations for Elkhorn and Staghorn Coral, 71 Fed. Reg. 26,852 (May 9, 2006).

[94] *Id.* at 26,852.

[95] *Id.*

[96] *See* Press Release, Center for Biological Diversity (Feb. 6, 2008), *available at* http://www.biologicaldiversity.org/news/press_releases/2008/corals-02-06-2008.html.

[97] Endangered and Threatened Species; Critical Habitat for Threatened Elkhorn and Staghorn Corals, 73 Fed. Reg. 72,210 (Nov. 26, 2008).

requirements of the species.[98] In characterizing the physical or biological features essential for conservation of these coral species, NMFS determined habitat described as an available surface where coral larvae could settle, recruit, and reattach to rebuild itself and continue growth qualified as critical habitat.[99] It further stated that water temperature and "other aspects of water quality are more appropriately viewed as sources of impacts or stressors that can harm the corals, rather than habitat features" and these features "would therefore be analyzed as factors that may contribute to a jeopardy determination pursuant to section 7 of the ESA rather than to a determination whether the corals' critical habitat is likely to be destroyed or adversely modified."[100] In response, the Center for Biological Diversity filed a notice of intent to sue "for illegally excluding global warming and ocean acidification threats from a new rule protecting habitat for elkhorn and staghorn corals."[101]

In response to another coral listing petition proffered by the Center for Biological Diversity, this time proposing eighty-two coral species from various regions, NMFS issued a proposed rule on December 7, 2012, to list sixty-six of the eighty-two corals—twelve as endangered and fifty-four as threatened, with elkhorn and staghorn to be reclassified from threatened to endangered.[102] This time climate change impacts played a central role in the proposed rule: "Overall, there is ample evidence that climate change (including that which is already committed to occur from past GHG emissions and that which is reasonably certain to result from continuing and future emissions) will follow a trajectory that will have a major impact on corals."[103] The final rule is pending as of August 2014.

Subsequently, in 2013, WildEarth Guardians petitioned NMFS to list eighty-one marine species, including twenty-three corals, citing climate change and global warming effects as a main listing reason for its petition.[104] On October 25, 2013, NMFS published

---

[98] 73 Fed. Reg. 6895 (Feb. 6, 2008); *see also* M. Feldman & S. Snodgrass, *Consideration of Climate Change in NEPA and ESA Processes*, Rocky Mountain Mineral Law Foundation Resources Development and Climate Change, Apr. 10–11, 2008.

[99] Endangered and Threatened Species; Revision of Candidate Species List under the Endangered Species Act, 62 Fed. Reg. 37,560 (July 14, 1997), *available at* https://www.federalregister.gov/articles/1997/07/14/97-18326/endangered-and-threatened-species-revision-of-candidate-species-list-under-the-endangered-species.

[100] *Id.*

[101] *See* Press Release, Center for Biological Diversity (Nov. 25, 2008), *available at* http://www.biologicaldiversity.org/news/press_releases/2008/corals-11-25-2008.html. The author did not find evidence of a suit being filed after the expiration of the notice period.

[102] Endangered and Threatened Wildlife and Plants: Proposed Listing Determinations for 82 Reef-Building Coral Species; Proposed Reclassification of Acropora Palmate and Acropora Cervicornis from Threatened to Endangered, Proposed Rule, 77 Fed. Reg. 73,220 (Dec. 7, 2012), *available at* http://www.gpo.gov/fdsys/pkg/FR-2012-12-07/pdf/2012-29350.pdf.

[103] *Id.* at 73,229.

[104] WildEarth Guardians, Petition to List 81 Marine Species (July 15, 2013), *available at* http://www.wildearthguardians.org/site/DocServer/Multi_Species_Marine_Petition.pdf?docID=9702.

its ninety-day petition finding and request for information, indicating twenty of the twenty-three coral species as not warranted due to lack of "substantial scientific or commercial information indicating the petitioned action may be warranted..." after its review of the information contained in the petition "as well as information readily available in our files...."[105]

B. LIMITATIONS OF SECTION 4 LISTING: THE RIBBON SEAL

Following the coral "listing story," the role climate change has had in various listing petitions and decisions is increasing.[106] Not all predominantly climate-impacted species have been listed, however. As in all listing determinations, regardless of climate change effects, NMFS may determine a listing is not warranted, using the same statutorily prescribed criteria. Perhaps one element that keeps courts' dockets populated with challenges to listing determinations is the breadth and scope of the ESA language itself, which is on a collision course with deference afforded to agency decisions as mandated by the APA standard of review for listing determinations. With continual recognition of emerging challenges, such as climate change impacts, listing decisions may vary despite similar threats and application of the same listing criteria. Particular to climate change within the ESA framework, lack of available scientific data, vague terms of art within the statutory language (explored below), and the global nature and often tenuous nexus of climate impacts to marine environs may lead to often unpredictable and divergent listing determinations.

For example, both "best scientific and commercial data available" and "in danger of extinction throughout all of a significant portion of its range" are articulated in section 4, but neither is clearly defined by Congress. The agency's application of these criteria to consider climate change in deciding a species listing determination has been the subject of much controversy and increasing litigation. For example, new streams of scientific data are being constantly introduced as to the impacts of climate change, and species ranges may be steadily shifting in response to warming temperatures.

In instances where agency decisions based on these criteria are challenged, courts generally defer to the agencies' discretion in section 4 listing decisions. In one such case in 1988, *Conner v. Burford,* the Ninth Circuit Court of Appeals interpreted the provision "best scientific and commercial data available" as one in which an agency generally has

---

[105] Endangered and Threatened Wildlife; 90-Day Finding on a Petition to List 23 Species of Corals as Threatened or Endangered under the Endangered Species Act, 78 Fed. Reg. 63,941 (Oct. 25, 2013), *available at* https://www.federalregister.gov/articles/2013/10/25/2013-25095/endangered-and-threatened-wildlife-9 0-day-finding-on-a-petition-to-list-23-species-of-corals-as.

[106] *See, e.g.,* WildEarth Guardians, Petition to List 81 Marine Species (July 15, 2013), *available at* http:// www.wildearthguardians.org/site/DocServer/Multi_Species_Marine_Petition.pdf?docID=9702; *See also* 90-Day Finding on a Petition To List 23 Species of Corals as Threatened or Endangered Under the Endangered Species Act, 78 Fed. Reg. 63,941 (Oct. 25, 2013).

wide latitude, yet cannot ignore available biological information.[107] If those who challenge an agency action on the basis of failure to use best available science or data cannot identify relevant data not considered, agencies are granted deference and are presumed to have used best available data.[108]

Two decades later, in 2008, NMFS published its twelve-month finding that the listing of the ribbon seal was "not warranted." To complete its assessment and threat level for the species, NMFS configured a Biological Review Team (BRT), which conducted a Status Review of the ribbon seals.[109] The BRT's findings stated that the population was "likely to decline gradually for the foreseeable future [to 2050], primarily from slight but chronic impacts on reproduction and survival caused by reduced frequency of years with sea ice of suitable extent, quality and duration of persistence"[110] but that the ribbon seals were not in current danger of extinction throughout all or a significant portion of their range.[111] In a case challenging this "not warranted" finding as arbitrary and capricious,[112] plaintiffs argued that NMFS conducted a flawed analysis applying listing criteria regarding whether the ribbon seal is threatened or endangered in a "significant portion of its range," and did not utilize the best available science, among other issues.[113]

In contrasting the ribbon seal with the listed coral species, as well as the sea-ice-dependent and recently listed polar bear, NMFS addressed factors that played a role in the corals and polar bear[114] listings, such as loss of sea ice, ocean acidification due to increased carbon dioxide in the atmosphere, ocean warming, and disease, and found that these factors "have the potential for negative impacts, but these impacts are not well understood."[115] Similar to the *Conner v. Burford* ruling, the court also granted agency deference to NMFS on challenges to its status review and use of best available scientific data, stating that "NMFS considered the data cited by Plaintiffs... Plaintiffs have not pointed to any data or scientific evidence that NMFS failed to consider on this issue...."[116]

---

[107] Conner v. Burford, 848 F. 2d 1441, 1445 (9th Cir. 1988), *cert. denied* 489 U.S. 1012 (1989) ("[I]n light of the ESA requirement that the agencies use the best scientific and commercial data available to ensure that protected species are not jeopardized, the FWS cannot ignore available biological information").

[108] *Id; see also* Pacific Coast Fed'n of Fishermen's Ass'n v. Nat'l Marine Fisheries Serv., 71 F. Supp. 2d 1063, 1073 (W.D. Wash. 1999).

[109] Center for Biological Diversity v. Lubchenco, 758 F. Supp. 2d 945, 949 (N.D. Cal. 2010).

[110] *Id.*

[111] *See* Endangered and Threatened Wildlife; Notice of 12-Month Finding on a Petition to List the Ribbon Seal as a Threatened or Endangered Species, 73 Fed. Reg. 79,822 (Dec. 30, 2008).

[112] Courts review challenges under the the ESA to determine if in the course of a rulemaking, an agency has acted in a way that is "arbitrary, capricious, an abuse of discretion or otherwise not in accordance with law." 5 U.S.C. § 706 (2012).

[113] *Lubchenco*, 758 F. Supp. 2d at 949.

[114] As detailed above, USFWS, not NMFS, is the listing agency for the polar bear.

[115] 73 Fed. Reg. 79,822, 79,826 (Dec. 30, 2008).

[116] *Lubchenco*, 758 F. Supp. 2d at 974.

The "arbitrary and capricious" standard that governs judicial review of agency listing decisions is highly deferential.[117] If a statute is "silent or ambiguous with respect to the specific issue" at hand, for example the finding of "not warranted" of the ribbon seal, a court must defer to an agency's interpretation as long as it was "based on a permissible construction of the statute."[118]

Although not related to a marine fish, a 2012 decision from the D.C. Circuit specifically addresses considerations of climate change in a challenge to FWS's "not warranted" finding regarding listing of Colorado cutthroat trout.[119] Here, the plaintiffs argued that "FWS should have considered the impact of climate change in its assessment" of the status of the trout species as climate change will, per one example, cause "significant additional reductions in suitable habitat."[120] The court addresses this claim by recognizing that although the ESA "does not expressly require consideration of climate change effects, it does direct the agency to address 'natural or manmade factors affecting [a species'] continued existence.'"[121] In this way, the court has acknowledged the inclusive and broad scope of the language of the ESA selection criteria, as well as its own legal obligation to defer to an agency's (in this case FWS's) application of the statute. In addition, the court noted that in this circumstance, the plaintiff had not previously raised the issue of climate change in its public comments regarding the potential listing:

> As scientific assessments increasingly incorporate in-depth analyses of climate change effects, explicit consideration of climate change-related threats may become a necessary component of the status review. The record in this case, however, contains only occasional references to climate change-related threats. There is no statutory requirement that the FWS discuss climate change in its listing decisions and the Court is reluctant to impose a judicially-created requirement where, as here, climate change is not discussed at length in the record, where the issue was not raised by plaintiffs in their comments to the FWS and where the record is ambivalent as to its effects.[122]

The court determined that climate change fits within the rubric of ESA listing criteria; however, in the shifting landscape of scientific data, agency deference and public

---

[117] The ESA provides for judicial review of an agency's "not warranted" finding under 16 U.S.C. § 1533(b)(3)(C) (ii) (2012). The APA provides the standard for judicial review of agency listing decisions to set aside agency actions, findings or conclusions when they are "arbitrary, capricious, an abuse of discretion or otherwise not in accordance with the law." 5 U.S.C. § 706(2)(A) (2012). *See* American Wildlands v. Kempthorne, 530 F.3d 991, 997 (D.C. Cir. 2008) (describing the standard of review of agency action as a "highly deferential one.").

[118] Chevron U.S.A., Inc. v. Natural Res. Def. Council, Inc., 467 U.S. 837, 843 (1984).

[119] *Cf.* Colorado River Cutthroat Trout v. Salazar, Civ. Action No. 09–2233 (PLF), 2012 WL 4890100, *11 (D.D.C. Oct. 16, 2012).

[120] *Id.*

[121] *Id.* (quoting 16 U.S.C. § 1533(a)(1)(E) (2012)).

[122] *Id.* at 11.

pressure for listings, it is unclear to what degree climate change will play a role. It may be that the extent to which agencies must accommodate considerations for climate change in listing criteria will depend on how much data is available.

Conclusion

As climate change impacts continue and increasing numbers of species become more vulnerable, whether due to habitat changes from climate changes or exacerbating circumstances due to increased impacts from climate change, the regulatory framework must respond. In the case of marine species, numbers of imperiled flora and fauna will only increase in the years to come, as oceans and their ecosystems are especially vulnerable to impacts such as changes in ocean temperature, heightened acidification, increased storm intensity, and greater ocean stratification. Despite the debate concerning the scope and breadth of the ESA, ample scientific evidence points to climate change as a major factor in the severe decline of corals, which have served as trailblazers for other species to be listed with climate change as a main factor. Without additional legislative action targeting greenhouse gas emissions, the ESA will continue to be used as a major regulatory tool for ecosystem and species protection. As such it will continue to face challenges in confronting the increasing role of climate change in species and ecosystem protection within this rubric as more and more species impacted by the effects of climate change require the increased protections that the ESA provides.

As evidenced by the examples herein, climate change impacts have yet to be incorporated systematically or rigorously into ESA decision-making.[123] Based on review of the above-discussed cases, it appears that once an agency considers climate change to some degree, and articulates these considerations in its listing or "not warranted" decisions, the courts are hesitant to impose any requirements on how an agency incorporates or chooses not to incorporate climate change impacts into its decision-making.

Thus, once an agency shows it has considered climate change impacts, courts will apply great deference in reviewing such determinations. With many remaining gaps in scientific data, and limited agency resources, it will often be the case that agencies simply do not have the best available science, or the little information known would not support a climate-change-based listing; this determination is within the agency's discretion. By broadening ways in which supporting science is applied and used in listing determinations, climate change impacts, both direct and indirect, especially in the marine context, may assist agencies in keeping pace with new information and the increased numbers of marine species imperiled.

---

[123] See McClure et al., *supra* note 65, at 1223.

8 Offshore Wind and Wave Energy and Ocean Governance
Megan E. Higgins and Jason Busch*

---

* The authors would like to thank Cindi McGee for her research assistance, and Dale Bennett and Sarah
Hutchins for their technical assistance.

Introduction

Ocean renewable energy resources include winds, tides, waves, currents, and temperature gradient (ocean thermal energy conversion), all of which may be used for electricity generation.[1] Resources derived from the motions of the oceans, such as waves, tides, and currents, are referred to as marine hydrokinetic (MHK) resources.[2] Offshore wind has been successfully deployed throughout Northern Europe, and increasingly in Asia. The other forms of ocean renewable energy are largely pre-commercial, with only a few megawatts (MW) of installed capacity; these installations are generally engineering prototype test devices or small single-unit demonstration wave and tidal projects.[3] "According to Ocean Energy Systems (OES), the international technology collaboration initiative on ocean energy under the International Energy Agency (IEA), total worldwide installed MHK power was about 530 MW in 2012, of which 517 MW was from tidal range power plants."[4]

These resources represent substantial opportunities for new sources of reliable, clean, and carbon-free energy. According to the Electric Power Research Institute, for example, ocean wave and tidal power could be two of the most environmentally benign electricity generation technologies yet developed, with "proper care in design, [siting], deployment, operation, and maintenance...."[5] OES estimates a worldwide potential of up to 337 gigawatts (GW) (337,000 MW) of wave and tidal energy capacity by 2050, and possibly a similar contribution from ocean thermal energy conversion.[6]

In the United States, large-scale electricity production using terrestrial wind turbine generators is a reasonably mature industry, with a total installed wind capacity of 60,078 MW (as of October 31, 2013).[7] However, this number is reflective of land-based wind

---

[1] See generally OCEAN ENERGY SYSTEMS, ANNUAL REPORT 2012: IMPLEMENTING AGREEMENT ON OCEAN ENERGY SYSTEMS (2012), http://www.iea.org/media/openbulletin/OES2012.pdf.

[2] 42 U.S.C. § 17211 (2006) (defining the term "marine and hydrokinetic renewable energy").

[3] R. Thresher et al., Ocean Energy Technologies, in 2 NATIONAL RENEWABLE ENERGY LABORATORY, RENEWABLE ELECTRICITY FUTURES STUDY, P9-1 (2012).

[4] Ernst & Young, Rising Tide: Global Trends in the Emerging Ocean Energy Markets 4 (2013), http://www.ey.com/Publication/vwLUAssets/EY-Ocean-energy-Rising-tide-2013/$FILE/EY-Ocean-energy-Rising-tide-2013.pdf.

[5] ROGER BEDARD, ELECTRIC POWER RESEARCH INSTITUTE, POWER AND ENERGY FROM THE OCEAN ENERGY WAVES AND TIDES: A PRIMER 1 (May 14, 2007), http://www.oceanrenewable.com/wp-content/uploads/2008/03/power-and-energy-from-the-ocean-waves-and-tides.pdf.

[6] Ernst & Young, supra note 4, at 5.

[7] AMERICAN WIND ENERGY ASSOCIATION, AWEA U.S. WIND INDUSTRY THIRD QUARTER 2013 MARKET REPORT (2013), http://awea.files.cms-plus.com/AWEA%203Q%20Wind%20Energy%20Industry%20Market%20Report%20Executive%20Summary.pdf.

farms *only*; currently, there are no installed commercial-scale offshore wind farms.[8] The United States' Department of Energy (DOE), Office of Energy Efficiency & Renewable Energy's National Renewable Energy Lab has estimated the total technical potential for offshore wind power off the coast of the United States to be 4,223 GW (4,223,000 MW); that projection may be even higher today.[9] By comparison, according to the European Wind Energy Association, there are already over 6.6 GW (6,600 MW) of installed offshore wind capacity in Europe (as of October 31, 2013).[10]

By tapping into that wind energy potential, the United States has the ability to achieve significant reductions in greenhouse gas emissions. The United States must be proactive because the U.S. Energy Information Administration, in its Annual Energy Outlook 2014, estimates that "[t]otal primary energy consumption [will grow] by 12%[,]...[]...%[,]...from 95 quadrillion Btu in 2012 to 106 quadrillion Btu in 2040...."[11] At a time when emissions-free sources of energy should be encouraged, domestic production of natural gas and crude oil continues to grow and reshape the United States' energy economy, with crude oil production approaching the historical high achieved in 1970, of 9.6 million barrels per day.[12] Continual reliance on fossil fuels will only aggravate existing concerns about climate change, which have spurred many industries, policymakers, environmentalists, and utilities to call for reductions in greenhouse gas emissions. Conservation and efficiency, conversion to lower carbon fuels, and adoption of carbon-free energy sources such as wind power are the means by which greenhouse gas emissions can be controlled.

Although the cost of reducing emissions is uncertain, the most affordable near-term strategy likely involves wider deployment of currently available energy efficiency and investment in clean energy technologies. Regional and state initiatives have encouraged the growth of renewable energy development through CO_2 emission caps, renewable energy mandates, and energy efficiency. For example, the Regional Greenhouse Gas Initiative, the nation's first market-based regulatory program to reduce greenhouse gas pollution, includes renewables as part of a portfolio strategy to reduce overall emissions from energy production[13] and is investing more than 10 percent of total CO_2 allowance

---

[8] Navigant Consulting, Inc., *Offshore Wind Market and Economic Analysis: Annual Market Assessment* 5 (prepared for U.S. Department of Energy DE-EE0005360, Feb. 22, 2013).

[9] Anthony Lopez et al., *U.S. Renewable Energy Technical Potentials: A GIS-Based Analysis* 15 (U.S. Dep't of Energy, Technical Report NREL/TP-6A20-51946 (2012)) (noting that the offshore wind resource potential, as of 2010, does not factor in resources off the coasts of Alaska or Florida).

[10] European Wind Energy Association, Wind in Power: 2013 European Statistics 3 (2014), http://www.ewea.org/fileadmin/files/library/publications/statistics/EWEA_Annual_Statistics_2013.pdf.

[11] U.S. Department of Energy, U.S. Energy Information Administration, Annual Energy Outlook 2014 Early Release Overview 11 (2014), http://www.eia.gov/forecasts/aeo/er/pdf/0383er(2014).pdf.

[12] *Id.* at 12.

[13] Regional Greenhouse Gas Initiative (RGGI), *Memorandum of Understanding* (2005), http://www.rggi.org/docs/mou_final_12_20_05.pdf.

proceeds from auction in renewable energy programs.[14] More than thirty-five states have renewable energy targets in place, and more than twenty-five states have set energy efficiency targets.[15] On the international level, significant private investment in renewables continues across the world, such as investment bank Goldman Sachs Group Inc.'s $40 billion commitment to the renewable energy sector, declaring it to be one of the most compelling and attractive markets.[16] In January 2014, Goldman Sachs was approved for a $1.5 billion investment as an approximately 20 percent stakeholder in DONG Energy, a Danish offshore wind energy developer.[17]

Despite the potential for, and monetary support of, ocean-based renewable energy development, significant legal, technological, and economic challenges threaten to drown this new industry before it can prosper and provide enough carbon-free energy to help reduce global greenhouse gas emissions. In particular, negative experiences with conventional energy-related uses of the ocean, such as offshore oil and gas exploration, present serious challenges to the efficient and timely addition of offshore renewable resources into the U.S. energy portfolio.

To successfully address energy security and environmental issues, it is essential for the United States to pursue a diverse portfolio of energy options. Existing onshore wind power is a proven supply-side solution to the climate change problem,[18] and offshore wind offers an equally robust potential contribution. However, these new industries must overcome significant technological and systemic barriers before they will be able to secure a foothold in the energy sector.[19] If offshore wind and wave energy are to contribute substantially to a carbon-free energy future, the United States will need to profoundly shift its energy and environmental paradigm.

This chapter will address two ocean-based renewable energy technologies: (1) electricity generation through the power of offshore wind, and (2) ocean waves. Section I of this chapter examines the history and present status of the industry, Section II discusses the regulatory and practical obstacles confronting the industry, and Section III addresses

---

[14] RGGI, *Why Renewable Energy?* (2014), http://www.rggi.org/rggi_benefits/why_renewables.

[15] Executive Office of the President, *The President's Climate Action Plan* (2013), http://www.whitehouse.gov/sites/default/files/image/president27sclimateactionplan.pdf.

[16] Giles Parkinson, *Goldman Sachs Sees "Transformational Moment" in Renewables Investment*, RENEW ECON. (Jan. 31, 2014), http://reneweconomy.com.au/2014/goldman-sachs-sees-transformational-moment-in-renewables-investment-90317.

[17] Peter Levring & Christian Wienberg, *Goldman Deal on Danish Energy Splits Copenhagen Coalition*, BLOOMBERG.COM (Jan. 20, 2014), http://www.bloomberg.com/news/2014-01-29/goldman-1-5-billion-bid-imperils-danish-government-re-election.html.

[18] UNITED STATES DEPARTMENT OF ENERGY, 20% WIND ENERGY BY 2030: INCREASING WIND ENERGY'S CONTRIBUTION TO U.S. ELECTRICITY SUPPLY, 14 (2008) (citing R.H. Socolow & S.W. Pacala, *A Plan to Keep Carbon in Check*, SCI. AM. 28–35 (Sept. 2006)).

[19] *See generally* Megan Higgins, *Is Marine Renewable Energy a Viable Industry in the United States? Lessons Learned from the 7th Marine Law Symposium*, 14 ROGER WILLIAMS U.L. REV. 562 (2009).

recommendations to promote the use of offshore ocean renewable energy as a mitigation measure in the context of climate change.

I. Offshore Wind and Wave Energy: Background and Status of the Industry

The availability of inexpensive oil has encouraged the United States to adopt patterns of socioeconomic organization and investment premised on cheap and readily available oil resources. Although understandable when oil was inexpensive and access secure, this dependence has become less sustainable as economic, strategic, and environmental conditions have changed. Today, in the United States, a similar emphasis on natural gas development has resulted in extensive tax incentives and exemptions from environmental laws. Enthusiasm for renewables has not yet resulted in such supportive policies.

A. HISTORICAL ANALYSIS OF OFFSHORE RESOURCE EXPLORATION

1. Oil, Gas, and Methane Hydrates

> "[T]he Santa Barbara incident has frankly touched the conscience of the American people."[20]
> *President Richard Nixon, March 21, 1969, while visiting the Santa Barbara Oil Spill in the*
> *Santa Barbara Channel, the largest oil spill off of the California coast to date.*

The United States was the world's leading oil producer for the first three-quarters of the twentieth century, accounting for almost two-thirds of world oil production in 1920. Five of the seven great oil corporations that dominated the international oil industry from the 1920s to the 1970s were American companies. Control of oil bolstered United States' military and economic might and enabled the United States and its allies to win World War I, World War II, and the Cold War.[21] The control of oil resources is seen as a (if not *the*) major driver of U.S. policy. The increasing demand for oil in the twentieth century was due to a combination of ready availability and artificial demand created by state and federal policies promoting oil consumption.

The availability of inexpensive oil led the nation to reshape its society and economy in ways that guaranteed a large and growing demand for oil. For example, in the United States, "[T]he number of cars registered increased from 3.4 million in 1916 to 23.1 million by the end of the 1920s."[22] Furthermore, in the 1930s, the United States began moving away from public transit, thus furthering the reliance on high levels of oil use.[23] "[B]y

---

[20] Richard Nixon, *Remarks following Inspection of Oil Damage at Santa Barbara Beach* (Mar. 21, 1969), *available at* http://www.presidency.ucsb.edu/ws/?pid=1967.

[21] David Painter, *Oil and the American Century*, 99 J. AMER. HIST. 24, 25 (June 2012), *available at* http://jah.oxfordjournals.org/content/99/1/24.full.

[22] *Id.*

[23] *Id.*

1925[,]...oil accounted for almost one-fifth of [U.S.] energy consumption" and by World War II "that figure rose to one-third."[24]

Looking to expand the nation's oil production, President Harry S. Truman issued Proclamation 2667, less than a month after Japan formally surrendered on September 2, 1945, to end World War II, regarding "Policy of the United States with Respect to the Natural Resources of the Subsoil and Sea Bed of the Continental Shelf."[25] In Proclamation 2667, the government recognized "the long range world-wide need for new sources of petroleum and other minerals...and that efforts to discover and make available new supplies of these resources should be encouraged...."[26] The Proclamation further noted that "these resources underlie many parts of the continental shelf...and that with modern technological progress their utilization is already practicable or will become so at an early date...and...jurisdiction over these resources is required in the interest of their conservation and prudent utilization...."[27] The ensuing years saw a number of deepwater developments, including the Deep Water Royalty Relief Act,[28] key deepwater discoveries, the realization of high production rates, and the evolution of deepwater development technologies.

The Gulf Coast was the first area of the world to rigorously employ geophysical technology in a successful hunt for oil. In the 1940s and 1950s, the move from onshore leasing conducted by private and public landowners to offshore leasing conducted by state and federal governments by competitive bid placed an even greater premium on geological and geophysical capabilities, as incentives for speculative leasing were fewer for offshore ventures. Oil firms faced unprecedented challenges and made strides in learning how to drill and produce hydrocarbons from increasing water depths offshore, but not without steep rises in the costs of development, which mandated greater accuracy and effectiveness in exploration.

Although connected to the shore by a series of wooden piers, the first coastal "offshore" oil well was drilled in 1896 off the coast of Santa Barbara County, California, in a coastal area known as Summerland.[29] Subsequent offshore drilling followed this model until 1938 with the construction of the first truly offshore drilling platform located in unprotected waters of the Gulf of Mexico (GOM).[30] Offshore, the entity known as Standard

---

[24] *Id.*

[25] Exec. Order No. 9633, Reserving and Placing Certain Resources of the Continental Shelf under the Control and Jurisdiction of the Secretary of the Interior, 10 Fed. Reg. 12,305 (Oct. 2, 1945); Proclamation No. 2667: Policy of the United States with Respect to the Natural Resources of the Subsoil and Sea Bed of the Continental Shelf (Sept. 28, 1945).

[26] *Id.*

[27] *Id.*

[28] 43 U.S.C. § 1337 (2012).

[29] Dan Rothbach, *Rigs-to-Reefs: Refocusing the Debate in California*, 17 DUKE ENVTL. L. & POL'Y F. 283, 284 (2007).

[30] *Id.* at 284–85.

Oil Company of California (now Chevron) discovered a tract called the Summerland Offshore Oil Field that was productive through 1940. In 1947, after a period of significant technological improvement, Kerr-McGee Oil Industries, Inc. drilled the first productive well beyond the sight of land, about 10.5 miles off the Louisiana coast.

The Summerland Offshore Oil Field is still productive today. In 1969, however, the Santa Barbara Oil Spill—an oil blowout disaster of 80,000 barrels of crude oil—led to an intensive environmental focus on energy exploration.[31] The Santa Barbara Oil Spill, which killed thousands of birds and other marine life, prompted the creation of the National Environmental Policy Act of 1969 (NEPA), followed by the establishment of the Environmental Protection Agency in 1970 and federal regulation of the offshore oil industry. The California State Lands Commission, which was also created as a result of the catastrophe, is the state agency responsible for leasing submerged lands in state waters, and halted further leasing of state offshore tracts after the oil spill. Furthermore, in 1994, the California state legislature codified the ban on new leases by passing the California Coastal Sanctuary Act, which prohibited new leasing of state offshore tracts.

Environmental threats close to shore, coupled with technological developments of oil platforms, enabled deepwater production to begin in the GOM in 1979 with Shell Oil Company's Cognac Field. Five years later, the next deepwater field, ExxonMobil Corporation's Lena Field, began production.[32] Under section 18 of the Outer Continental Shelf Lands Act (OCSLA), it is the responsibility of the Secretary of the Department of the Interior ("Secretary") to take into account a range of important principles and considerations specified by the Act (e.g., potential for adverse environmental impacts) while preparing and maintaining a schedule of proposed Outer Continental Shelf (OCS) oil and gas lease sales determined to best meet national energy needs for the five-year period following its approval or re-approval.[33] Under the authority of the Department of Interior's Bureau of Ocean Energy Management (BOEM), the OCS oil and gas exploration and development program, a component of which is the lease sales, yields 24 percent of domestic oil production and 7 percent of domestic natural gas production.[34]

---

[31] Michael J. McHale, *An Introduction to Offshore Energy Exploration—A Florida Perspective*, 39 J. Mar. L. & Com. 571–72 (2008).

[32] U.S. Department of the Interior, Minerals Management Service, *Gulf of Mexico OCS Region. 2008. Deepwater Gulf of Mexico 2008: America's Offshore Energy Future* 4 (U.S. DOI, OCS Report MMS 2008-013 2008).

[33] U.S. Department of the Interior, Bureau of Ocean Energy Management, *2012–2017 OCS Oil and Gas Leasing Program Final Programmatic Environmental Impact Statement* (July 2012), (citing section 18 of the Outer Continental Shelf Lands Act, 43 U.S.C. §§ 1331–1353 (2012), http://www.boem.gov/uploadedFiles/BOEM/Oil_and_Gas_Energy_Program/Leasing/Five_Year_Program/2012-2017_Five_Year_Program/01_Introduction_Purpose_Need.pdf).

[34] U.S. Department of the Interior, Bureau of Ocean Energy Management, *OCS Lands Act History* (2014), http://www.boem.gov/Oil-and-Gas-Energy-Program/Leasing/Outer-Continental-Shelf/Lands-Act-History/OCSLA-HIstory.aspx.

OCSLA was amended in part by the Energy Policy Act of 2005 (EPAct), which expanded the Secretary's authority[35] to grant a lease, easement, or right of way on the OCS for energy development activities from sources *other than* oil and gas.[36] Concurrent with the amendments made for offshore renewable energy development, amendments to section 357 of EPAct required the Secretary to conduct an inventory and analysis of oil and natural gas resources beneath all the waters of the OCS, but prohibited drilling. The moratorium on drilling was relaxed due to the passage of the Gulf of Mexico Energy Security Act of 2006, which increased available area in the GOM by 8.3 million acres. However, a portion of the Central Gulf of Mexico Planning Area and most of the Eastern Gulf of Mexico Planning Area is under restriction until 2022, as part of the Gulf of Mexico Energy Security Act of 2006. In 2007, President George W. Bush lifted the moratorium on offshore drilling in Alaska's Bristol Bay and the Central Gulf of Mexico.

In June 2012, the Secretary published the Five Year OCS Oil and Gas Leasing Program for 2012–2017, as described in the Proposed Final OCS Oil and Gas Leasing Program. The Program scheduled fifteen potential lease sales in six offshore areas, with twelve of the lease sales in the GOM, which, in 2012, supplied more than a quarter of the U.S. domestic oil production.[37] The Program ended a long-standing moratorium on oil exploration along the East Coast, from the northern tip of Delaware to the central coast of Florida. The coastline from New Jersey northward and the entire Pacific Coast (from Mexico to the Canadian border) would remain closed to all oil and gas activity. The environmentally sensitive Bristol Bay in Southwestern Alaska would be protected, and no drilling would be allowed through June 30, 2017. However, large tracts in the Chukchi Sea and Beaufort Sea in the Arctic Ocean north of Alaska—nearly 130 million acres—would be eligible for exploration and drilling after extensive studies.[38]

Besides oil and gas, and ocean energy, there are additional offshore resources that may have the capacity to contribute to the energy needs of the United States. According to the Department of the Interior, methane gas hydrate-bearing sand resources "may be 30 to 300 times greater than conventional oil and gas reserves."[39] The volume of carbon

---

[35] In May 2010, the Secretary announced that MMS would be separated into three agencies: the Bureau of Safety and Environmental Enforcement (BSEE), BOEM, and the Office of Natural Resources Revenue (ONRR). In June 2010, MMS was renamed the Bureau of Ocean Energy Management, Regulation and Enforcement (BOEMRE). The revenue-collection functions of BOEMRE were transferred to ONRR in October 2010, and a year later BOEMRE was then divided into two new agencies, BSEE and BOEM.

[36] Section 8(p) of OCSLA was amended by EPAct section 388: Alternate Energy-Related Uses on the Outer Continental Shelf. Pub. L. 109-58 (2005).

[37] U.S. Department of the Interior, Bureau of Ocean Energy Management, *Proposed Final Outer Continental Shelf Oil & Gas Leasing Program 2012–2017*, at 5 (June 2012), http://www.boem.gov/uploadedFiles/BOEM/Oil_and_Gas_Energy_Program/Leasing/Five_Year_Program/2012-2017_Five_Year_Program/PFP%2012-17.pdf.

[38] John M. Broder, *Obama to Open Offshore Areas to Drilling for First Time*, N.Y. TIMES, Mar. 31, 2010, http://www.nytimes.com/2010/03/31/science/earth/31energy.html.

[39] U.S. DEPARTMENT OF THE INTERIOR, MINERALS MANAGEMENT SERVICE, GULF OF MEXICO OCS REGION, DEEPWATER GULF OF MEXICO 2008: AMERICA'S OFFSHORE ENERGY FUTURE 11 (2008).

contained in methane hydrates worldwide is estimated to be twice the amount contained in all fossil fuels on Earth, including coal.[40] A methane hydrate consists of methane (a gas at normal temperatures and pressures) trapped in a solid lattice of water molecules, somewhat like ice. "Hydrates are formed at and just below the seafloor under conditions of low temperature, high pressure, and in the presence of natural gas."[41] "In the GOM, hydrates occur in water depths greater than 1,450 feet (ft)...."[42]

According to the U.S. Geological Survey, "estimates of the global resources of natural gas hydrate range from 100,000 to almost 300,000,000 trillion cubic feet (TCF)...."[43] To put these quantities in context, estimates of the remaining global reserves and undiscovered resources of conventional natural gas total about 13,000 TCF. "The Methane Hydrate Research and Development Act of 2000 authorized the expenditure of $43 million over five years" and designated DOE as the lead U.S. agency for methane hydrate research and development as a source of energy.[44] The EPAct renewed the Methane Hydrate Research and Development Act and provided the Secretary with the authority to create incentives through royalty relief for gas hydrate production on the OCS.[45]

In order for methane hydrates to become a viable energy source, there will need to be technically feasible and clean ways of extracting methane from the hydrate in commercial quantities. However, the industry is still in the research phase; therefore, a regulatory framework for methane hydrates is premature. Given that methane is a powerful greenhouse gas, approximately twenty times more potent than carbon dioxide, there is growing concern about the release of large amounts of the gas from the ocean floor, as it would greatly accelerate global warming. As ocean temperatures increase, as a direct result of climate change, destabilization or dissociation of the gas hydrate deposits in marine sediments occurs, releasing the potent greenhouse gas into the atmosphere. Thus, the serious potential exists for methane, or its oxidative byproduct carbon dioxide, to reach the atmosphere.[46]

2. Offshore Wind Energy

The world's first offshore wind farm, Vindeby, was built off the north coast of Lolland Island, Denmark. Vindeby was the largest offshore wind farm, with a project capacity

---

[40] U.S. Department of the Interior, U.S. Geological Survey. *Natural Gas Hydrates—Vast Resource, Uncertain Future* (USGS Fact Sheet FS–021–01, 2001).

[41] *Supra* note 37, at 11.

[42] *Id.*

[43] *Id.* at 38.

[44] Natural Gas Intelligence, *BLM, MMS Request Comments on Enhanced Recovery, Gas Hydrate Royalty Relief Plans* (Mar. 13, 2006), http://www.naturalgasintel.com/articles/14316.

[45] *See* Energy Policy Act of 2005, 42 U.S.C. § 15909, § 353, Gas Hydrate Production Incentive (2012).

[46] *See* C.D. Ruppel, *Methane Hydrates and Contemporary Climate Change*, 3 NATURE EDUC. KNOWLEDGE 29 (2011), *available at* http://www.nature.com/scitable/knowledge/library/methane-hydrates-and-contemporary-climate-change-24314790.

of almost 5 MW, until the erection almost ten years later of the Middelgrunden Wind Farm, with a project capacity of 40 MW.[47] As of June 30, 2012, the Global Wind Energy Council estimated that there was 4,620 MW of offshore wind power installed globally, representing about 2 percent of total installed wind power capacity.[48] More than 90 percent of the wind farms are installed off of Northern Europe in the North, Baltic, and Irish Seas, and the English Channel.[49] Similarly, the European Wind Energy Association reported a total of 4,995 MW in fifty-five wind farms in ten European countries for the entire year of 2012.[50] Technologically speaking, this figure represents the following offshore wind turbine foundations: monopole substructures (73 percent), jacket technology (13 percent), tripods (6 percent), triples (5 percent), and gravity-based (3 percent).[51] In addition, there are two full-scale grid-connected floating wind turbines, and two downscaled (experimental) prototypes comprising the cumulative offshore wind power market overseas.[52] Companies such as DONG Energy continue to improve these technologies with the introduction of its Suction Bucket Jacket, in an effort to find solutions to the high cost of foundations, as well as perceived lower environmental impacts, and installation versatility.[53]

The United Kingdom is the leader of installed offshore wind capacity with 3.68 GW (3,681 MW) (as of July 2013),[54] and Denmark ranks second with 1.27 GW (1,270 MW). Since 2012, however, other countries have made significant contributions in planning for, siting, and constructing offshore wind development. China has made significant advances with its first offshore wind development east of Shanghai in the Shanghai Sea (e.g., 102 MW Shanghai Donghai Bridge Offshore Wind Farm (Phase I)). Phase II of the project began construction in 2012 and will support "China's goal of boosting offshore wind power capacity to 30 GW by 2020...."[55] There are also great expectations for

---

[47] 4C Offshore (2014), *available at* http://www.4coffshore.com/windfarms/vindeby-denmark-dk06.html and http://www.4coffshore.com/windfarms/middelgrunden-denmark-dk08.html.

[48] Global Wind Energy Council, *Global Offshore: Current Status and Future Prospects* (2014), http://www. gwec.net/global-offshore-current-status-future-prospects/.

[49] *Id.*

[50] European Wind Energy Association, *The European Offshore Wind Industry—Key Trends and Statistics 2012*, at 11 (Jan. 2013).

[51] *Id.* at 8.

[52] *Id.* at 15. *See also* 4C Offshore's Global Offshore Wind Farm Map and Database for maps and current statistics on global offshore wind farms, http://www.4coffshore.com/windfarms/. (last visited May 8, 2014).

[53] Carbon Trust, *DONG Energy and Carbon Trust Team Up to Cut the costs of Offshore Wind* (Jan. 28, 2014), http://www.carbontrust.com/about-us/press/2014/01/dong-energy-and-carbon-trust-team-up-to-cut-the-costs-of-offshore-wind.

[54] An additional 3.8 GW is either in construction or has planning approval, and a further 7.8 GW is in the planning stage. *See* renewableUK, http://www.renewableuk.com/en/renewable-energy/wind-energy/offshore-wind/#sthash.mFVWLT6B.dpuf (last visited May 8, 2014).

[55] Feifei Shen, *Shanghai Donghai to Start Work on Offshore Wind Farm at Year End*, BLOOMBERG NEWS: BLOOMBERG BUS. WEEK (June 20, 2013), http://www.businessweek.com/news/2013-06-20/shanghai-donghai-to-start-work-on-offshore-wind-farm-at-year-end.

major deployment elsewhere. Governments and companies in Japan, Korea, the United States, Canada, Taiwan, and India have expressed interest for developing offshore in their respective waters. "According to the more ambitious projections, a total of 80 GW [of] offshore wind could be installed by 2020 worldwide, with three quarters of the projects in Europe."[56]

The North Sea, with its optimal combination of shallow waters and strong winds, is dotted with the world's largest wind turbines. The size of offshore wind turbines is not restricted by terrestrial limitations, such as transporting equipment to inaccessible areas. As a result, offshore wind turbines dwarf their terrestrial counterparts, and continue to increase in size, power, and efficiency. In 2013, Hamburg-based Suzlon Group's REpower Systems SE (now Senvion SE), one the world's leading wind turbine manufacturers, unveiled the REpower 6.2M152, an offshore turbine with a rotor diameter of 499 feet (152 m) and a rated power of 6.15 MW, capable of supplying approximately 4,000 homes with electricity.[57] Compared to the previous generation, the REpower 6.2M126 (413 feet or 126 m), the new turbine will increase energy yield by up to 20 percent. In 2014, the V164-8.0 MW wind turbine, the world's largest wind turbine, was revealed by another leading wind turbine manufacturer, Vestas Wind Systems A/S, at the Danish National Test Centre for Large Wind Turbines. At "720 feet tall, with 260-foot blades, the prototype has the capacity to generate 8 MW of power...."[58]

In the United States, on the other hand, no offshore wind farms currently exist. However, several companies have proposed offshore wind farms and, particularly along the Atlantic Coast, a few have made progress with regard to obtaining local, state, and federal permits necessary to plan, construct, and operate projects.[59] In Nantucket Sound off of Cape Cod, Massachusetts, Cape Wind Associates, LLC is furthest along with its fully permitted Cape Wind project, a 468 MW (total nameplate capacity) project with 130 turbines that would supply 75 percent of the power for Cape Cod, Martha's Vineyard, and Nantucket.[60]

The procession of Cape Wind legal challenges filed by local opposition organizations and the NEPA review process has critically hampered the progression of the project, now in its thirteenth year. Aside from the multi-year process of completing an environmental

---

[56] *Supra* note 47.

[57] offshoreWIND.biz, *Suzlon to Expose Its New 6.15 MW Offshore Wind Turbine in Germany* (Nov. 18, 2013), http://www.offshorewind.biz/2013/11/18/suzlon-to-expose-its-new-6-15-mw-offshore-wind-turbine-in-germany/. http://mnre.gov.in/file-manager/UserFiles/draft-national-policy-for-offshore-wind.pdf.

[58] Ari Phillips, *World's Largest Wind Turbine Starts Generating Power for First Time*, CLIMATE PROGRESS (Jan. 28, 2014), http://thinkprogress.org/climate/2014/01/28/3212831/worlds-largest-wind-turbine/.

[59] *See generally* U.S. Offshore Wind Collaborative, *Offshore WindHub: States Overview* (2012), http://www.offshorewindhub.org/; *see also* U.S. Department of the Interior, Bureau of Ocean Energy Management, *Renewable Energy Program: State Activities* (2014), http://www.boem.gov/Renewable-Energy-State-Activities/.

[60] U.S. Department of the Interior, Bureau of Ocean Energy Management, *Cape Wind Fact Sheet* (Aug. 2013), http://www.boem.gov/Renewable-Energy-Program/Studies/CapeWindFactSheet.aspx.

assessment or the larger environmental impact statement, NEPA also is the most readily available legal mechanism to impede projects. The Cape Wind project, although the first commercial offshore wind project to receive a lease from BOEM (in 2011),[61] provides a ready example of how well-funded adversaries can delay a project and potentially kill the project through legal fees. The process that culminated ultimately in a positive Record of Decision from the lead federal permitting agency for the project took nine years, due in large part to multiple legal challenges pursuant to NEPA.[62]

Cape Wind's legal challenges are still ongoing as of this writing. Most recently, on March 14, 2014, a federal district court issued a weighty opinion regarding administrative decisions made by federal agencies approving the construction of Cape Wind. The Court upheld BOEM's approval of the project's Construction and Operations Plan (COP), thus rejecting the opponents' request to vacate the lease, but remanded the case to both the National Marine Fisheries Service and the U.S. Fish and Wildlife Service regarding the issuance of an Endangered Species Act "incidental take" permit for North Atlantic right whales and independent determination for operational restrictions related to migratory birds, respectively.[63] The pending administrative actions are perceived as minor by the developer and will not impact the financing schedule.[64]

Rhode Island, in competition with Massachusetts for the designation as the first state with an offshore wind farm to be built in its waters, has a five-turbine, 30 MW demonstration project off of Block Island, which is being developed by Deepwater Wind, LLC. The Block Island Wind Farm would be connected to mainland Rhode Island by a bidirectional submarine cable known as the Block Island Transmission System. After three years of intensive data gathering, Deepwater Wind, LLC submitted its applications in October 2012 to the local, state, and federal permitting authorities for both project components. In May 2014, the state's coastal zone management agency granted approval for the project.

Like Cape Wind, Fishermen's Energy has secured all of its federal and state permits for its 25 MW, five turbine demonstration-scale Atlantic City Windfarm, to be located in state waters off the coast of Atlantic City, New Jersey.[65] Approximately one year after

---

[61] U.S. Department of the Interior, Bureau of Ocean Energy Management, *Cape Wind* (2014), http://www.boem.gov/Renewable-Energy-Program/Studies/Cape-Wind.aspx.

[62] *See* Kevin Grandia, *History of the Cape Cod Offshore Wind Energy Project*, HUFFINGTON POST (Apr. 28, 2010), http://www.huffingtonpost.com/kevin-grandia/history-of-the-cape-cod-o_b_555725.html; *see also* Alliance to Protect Nantucket Sound, Inc. v. U.S. Dep't of the Army, 398 F.3d 105 (1st Cir. 2005).

[63] Pub. Emp. for Envtl. Responsibility v. Beaudreu, D.D.C., Civil Action No. 10-1067, Mar. 14, 2014 (noting that claims related to navigational safety, OCSLA, section 106 of the National Historic Preservation Act, NEPA, and biological opinions issued by the federal agencies, as well as other claims, were favorable to the federal agencies and project proponents).

[64] Environment News Service, *Court Upholds First U.S. Offshore Wind Farm Permit* (Mar. 14, 2014), http://ens-newswire.com/2014/03/14/americsan-mar-14-2014/.

[65] Permits secured in 2012. For project updates, see http://www.fishermensenergy.com/atlantic-city-windfarm.php (last visited May 8, 2014).

issuing the first noncompetitive lease, in November 2012, BOEM issued its second non-competitive lease to Bluewater Wind Delaware, LLC (NRG Bluewater Wind) for an area eleven nautical miles (nm) off the coast of Delaware.[66]

The first offshore renewable energy competitive lease sale occurred in July 2013, where BOEM auctioned approximately 165,000 acres on the OCS offshore of Rhode Island and Massachusetts (an area designated as one of mutual interest) for wind energy development. Deepwater Wind, LLC won the lease sale and has proposed a 1,000 MW offshore "regional offshore wind energy center" known as Deepwater ONE.[67] A few months after the first competitive lease sale, BOEM held an auction for a designated wind energy area 23.5 nm off Virginia Beach, Virginia. Virginia-based Dominion Resources, Inc., in addition to developing its 12 MW demonstration project, Virginia Offshore Wind Technology Advancement Project (VOWTAP), won the lease of approximately 113,000 acres with the potential to generate 2,000 MW, and the proposed project has even won the approval of climate change skeptics such as then Governor Bob McDonnell (R). The leased areas are expected to be able to support more than 4,000 MW of wind generation, enough electricity to power an estimated 1.4 million homes.[68] Auctions off the coasts of Maryland, New Jersey, and Massachusetts are expected in 2014.

On the Pacific Coast, where the OCS drops off dramatically into deep waters, developers are proposing offshore floating wind structures as a new form of energy generation in that the wind turbines can be floated in a variety of manners in deep offshore environments where water depths greatly exceed 164 feet. This technology differs from traditional fixed foundation, bottom-mounted wind turbines (e.g., monopile) secured directly to the seabed-in waters up to approximately 164 feet, a depth considered to be the limit for fixed foundations.

All forms of floating wind, including the tension-leg mooring, semi-submersible floating platform, and ballasted catenary mooring, are new and not proven to commercial-scale. However, in the United States, the DOE is providing funding for research and development of these floating technologies.[69] For example, Principle

---

[66] U.S. Department of the Interior, Bureau of Ocean Energy Management, *Delaware Activities* (2014), http://www.boem.gov/Renewable-Energy-Program/State-Activities/Delaware.aspx.

[67] *See* Deepwater ONE, http://dwwind.com/dww-deepwater-one/ (last visited May 8, 2014).

[68] Press Release, U.S. Department of Interior, Bureau of Ocean Energy Management, Interior Announces First-Ever Renewable Energy Lease Sales on the Outer Continental Shelf: BOEM Proposes Leasing Nearly 278,000 Acres Offshore Rhode Island, Massachusetts and Virginia for Wind Energy (Nov. 30, 2012), http://www.doi.gov/news/pressreleases/interior-announces-first-ever-renewable-energy-lease-sales-on-the-outer-continental-shelf.cfm.

[69] Press Release, U.S. Department of Energy, Office of Energy Efficiency & Renewable Energy, Offshore Wind Advanced Technology Demonstration Projects (May 7, 2014), http://energy.gov/eere/wind/offshore-wind-advanced-technology-demonstration-projects. (In May 2014, DOE selected three projects, Dominion Virginia Power's VOWTAP, Fishermen's Energy Atlantic City Windfarm, and Principle Power's WindFloat, to each receive $46.7 million in additional funding over four years, subject to congressional appropriations and annual progress reviews.)

Power, Inc. (Principle) received a $4 million grant (in December 2012) and an additional $47 million grant (in May 2014) from the DOE for its proposed 30 MW pilot project, known as the WindFloat Pacific Demonstration Project. The semi-submersible substructures and floating foundations would be nineteen miles (approximately 16 nm) from Coos Bay, Oregon, in about 1,400 feet of water. Principle was one of seven projects to receive funding and the only one on the West Coast.

Principle submitted an Unsolicited Application for an Outer Continental Shelf Renewable Energy Commercial Lease to BOEM on May 14, 2013.[70] BOEM issued its Decision of No Competitive Interest on February 5, 2014, allowing Principle to prepare a more detailed Construction and Operations Plan (COP) as part of its permit application. The developer hopes to submit the COP to BOEM by late 2014, in anticipation of deployment by 2017, at a cost of about $200 million. The recent $47 million DOE grant will help Principle move the project toward full financing. Principle has already demonstrated success with this technology with its first WindFloat unit, a 2 MW turbine located off the coast of Aguçadoura, Portugal, which was deployed in 2012 and continues to supply power to the grid.

Another example of floating wind technology is the 12 MW Maine Aqua Ventus I pilot project proposed by Maine Aqua Vetus GP LLC, comprised of Maine Prime Technologies, a spin-off company representing the University of Maine, and Cianbro Corp. and Emera, Inc. In January 2014, the Maine Public Utilities Commission approved a term sheet where the project will produce about 43,000 MWh/year of energy at $0.23/kWh, with an annual increase of 2.5 percent per year for twenty years. Long term, Maine Aqua Ventus GP LLC plans to construct a 500 MW offshore wind farm in the Gulf of Maine and to produce wind-generated electricity at $0.10/kWh within approximately the next ten years. Despite these developments and signals of progress, the United States still has zero MW of installed offshore wind capacity. That lack is all the more striking given the 6,562 GW of installed capacity in Europe.[71]

The technological improvement most vital to accelerate floating wind on the whole is the mechanism or method used to float the wind tower and turbine. Wind turbine manufacturing companies, such as Siemens AG, have already built marine turbines; furthermore, in the case of Siemens AG, it has invested roughly $264 million in production and installation facilities based on its recognition of the growing offshore wind energy potential.[72]

---

[70] Principle Power, Inc., *Unsolicited Application for an Outer Continental Shelf Renewable Energy Commercial Lease for the Principle Power WindFloat Pacific Pilot Project* (Lease Report, May 14, 2013), http://www.boem.gov/Wind-Float-Lease-Report/.

[71] European Wind Energy Association, *Offshore Statistics* (Jan. 2014), http://www.ewea.org/statistics/offshore-statistics/.

[72] Stanley Reed, *Siemens to Invest $264 Million in British Wind Turbine Project*, N.Y. TIMES, Mar. 25, 2014, http://www.nytimes.com/2014/03/26/business/international/siemens-to-invest-264-million-in-british-wind-turbine-project.html?_r=0.

3. Wave Energy

Waves are formed by wind blowing over the surface of the sea, and the amount of energy in the waves depends on the wind's speed, duration, and the distance of water over which it blows.[73] Therefore, the best wave resources occur where strong winds travel over long distances, such as along the coasts of Western Australia, Europe, North America, and South America. Wave energy devices capture the kinetic energy in waves in a variety of ways, but almost all types produce electricity by harnessing the motion of the ocean either to spin a generator or transfer hydraulic pressure to an onshore facility.

Current wave energy converter technologies include, but are not limited to, the point absorber, oscillating water column, subsurface pressure differential, attenuator, and rotating mass.[74] The point absorber is a floating structure, like a buoy, that usually absorbs energy from either the heave (vertical motion) or surge and pitch (horizontal motions) of the waves. Point absorbers may be designed for nearshore or deepwater deployments.

The oscillating water column (OWC) is a partially submerged, hollow structure open to the sea below the waterline, enclosing a column of air on top of a column of water. Waves cause the water column to rise and fall, which in turn compresses and decompresses the air column. This trapped air is allowed to flow to and from the atmosphere via a turbine, which has the ability to rotate in the same direction regardless of the direction of the airflow. The rotation of the turbine is used to spin a generator to create electricity. OWC technologies can be located at sea or onshore with a footprint in the sea. Other technologies are emerging as well, but all ultimately use the energy in the waves to spin generators.[75]

Wave energy is arguably three to five years away from the first full-scale commercial project. There are several ground-breaking companies endeavoring to be first to market with their respective technologies. As forerunners in this emerging field, each company has suffered the travails of uncharted technology development, securing project financing, and undertaking the required environmental surveys to advance in the state and federal permitting process. As a result, these developers bear such pioneering scars, but are hopeful they can launch their technologies while reaping the rewards of being first to market.

Scotland is the clear leader in ocean renewable energy development, as evidenced by its extensive testing and demonstration projects and centers (i.e., European Marine Energy Centre [EMEC]), supportive policies, and dedicated funds (i.e., Marine Renewables Commercialisation Fund). For example, full consent for the world's largest commercial

---

[73] Oregon Wave Energy Trust (OWET), *Utility Market Initiative, Integrating Oregon Wave Energy into the Northwest Power Grid, Resource Potential* (2009), sections 2, 3.

[74] A discussion of the individual technologies is beyond the scope of this chapter, but readers are encouraged to review online resources of the European Marine Energy Centre, http://www.emec.org.uk/marine-energy/wave-devices/ (last visited May 8, 2014).

[75] Some newer technologies are exploring alternative means of producing electricity, including piezoelectric and magnetostrictive power generators, but none of those technologies have been deployed at scale.

wave farm to be located off the northwest coast of Lewis, Scotland, has been given to Edinburgh developer Aquamarine Power, whose Oyster technology has been tested in the water and connected to the grid at EMEC for the past several years. Once operational testing has proven successful, numerous other commercial-scale wave projects are proposed.

The United States, Portugal, Australia, and others are actively supporting this industry with policies, incentives, and cash grants, but at a greatly reduced level. Due to the nascence of the technologies, it is premature to distinguish one technology as better than another. As the industry matures, certain types of technologies will likely emerge as the least expensive, most efficient, or most resilient, but that process is expected to take many years. Furthermore, local conditions will dictate what types of technology will be suitable. For example, a tropical Atlantic island community-based project will require a different size and type of technology than a full-scale utility-sized project in the open Pacific Ocean.

Globally, the vast majority of wave energy projects are located at temporary demonstration test sites. The only permanent wave energy facility is a breakwater wave power plant, consisting of sixteen Wells turbines, each with a rated performance of 18.5 kilowatts (kW). The Basque Energy Board (EVE) commissioned it in 2011 on the Spanish Atlantic coast at Mutriku.[76] That project, using the WaveGen OWC technology, has a nominal output of some 300 kW, and can power around 250 households.[77] Voith Hydro, Inc., which now owns WaveGen, claims that its Mutriku project is currently the only commercially operated wave power station in the world.[78] Voith Hydro WaveGen Limited continues to operate its Land Installed Marine Powered Energy Transformer, a fourteen-year-old 250 kW OWC demonstration project located on the Isle of Islay, off the west coast of Scotland.[79]

Floating wind and wave technologies are in the pre-commercial stage, though floating wind may be closer to commercialization than wave energy due to its evolution from the established terrestrial wind industry.

B. OFFSHORE ENERGY AS A VIABLE ALTERNATIVE TO TRADITIONAL ENERGY RESOURCES

The overall wind-based electricity generation capacity expansion required to meet projected demand growth in the United States through 2030 has been estimated by DOE's National Renewable Energy Laboratory's Wind Deployment System (WinDS) model, a

[76] See Voith, *Ocean Energies* (2014), http://voith.com/en/markets-industries/industries/hydro-power/ocean-energies-539.html.

[77] *Id.*

[78] See Voith, *Wave Power Plants* (2014), http://voith.com/en/products-services/hydro-power/ocean-energies/wave-power-plants-590.html.

[79] See Waveplam, *Voith Hydro Wavegen Passes 50,000 Generating Hours Milestone* (2014), http://www.waveplam.eu/page/default.asp?id=473.

model designed to address the principal market issues related to the penetration of wind energy technologies (both onshore and offshore) into the electric sector. WinDS estimates that there is a potential of 293 GW (293,000 MW) of wind resource to be added, including more than 50 GW (50,000 MW) of offshore wind energy potentially harnessed along the northeastern and southeastern seaboards.[80] Another WinDS estimate includes 4,000 GW (4,000,000 MW) of technical wind resource potential in state and federal waters off of the United States, as well as in the Great Lakes.[81]

Like offshore wind energy, wave energy is readily available to many population centers and has tremendous energy-generating potential. In fact, the Electric Power Research Institute has estimated the U.S. potential to be 2,640 terawatt hours per year (TWh/yr).[82] Off the coast of Oregon alone, the oceans have the potential to provide conservatively 322 TWh/yr.[83] With a technically recoverable rate of 25 percent, estimated on the low side by the Electric Power Research Institute, that is 80.5 TWh/yr, which is many times Oregon's current level of generation of 4.9 TWh/yr.[84] Of course, only a portion of the total energy available is actually recoverable. Future developments will determine the amount of recoverable energy, based on such factors as the efficiency of the technologies, the spatial relation and amount of collocated devices, and the extent to which the population will tolerate these devices in the ocean.

Wave energy is considered to be an inexhaustible resource that is highly predictable.[85] The intermittency of wind and solar energy creates problems for the electrical grid; the wind does not always blow, and the sun does not always shine. However, wave energy promises to mitigate the problem of intermittency. At any given moment, grid operators must balance the supply of electricity on the grid with the demand. When grid operators are working to balance the supply and demand on the grid, the wave energy available at a given facility can be predicted with great accuracy an hour or more in advance. Grid operators generally look "an hour out" to predict the generation supply necessary to meet the predicted load. Having wave energy measurement devices "an hour out" from a given

---

[80] Department of Energy, Energy Efficiency & Renewable Energy, *20% Wind Energy by 2030: Increasing Wind Energy's Contribution to U.S. Electricity Supply, Executive Summary* (DOE/GO-102008-2578, Dec. 2008).

[81] U.S. Department of Energy Wind and Water Power Technologies Office, *Offshore Wind Projects, 2006–2012*, at 2 (2012) (citing W. Musial & B. Ram, *Large-Scale Offshore Wind Power in the United States: Assessment of Opportunities and Barriers* (2010), http://www1.eere.energy.gov/wind/pdfs/offshore_energy_projects.pdf).

[82] Electric Power Research Institute, *Mapping and Assessment of the United States Ocean Wave Energy Resource*, at ix (Technical Report, 2011), http://www1.eere.energy.gov/water/pdfs/mappingandassessment.pdf.

[83] *Id.* at 4-2.

[84] Energy Information Administration, *Oregon: State Profile and Energy Estimates* (Mar. 27, 2014), http://www.eia.gov/state/?sid=OR#tabs-4.

[85] Oregon Wave Energy Trust, *Wave Energy Utility Integration: Advanced Resource Characterization and Integration Costs and Issues* 2 (forthcoming).

facility provides the grid operator adequate time to compute how much power will be needed to meet a predicted load.

Furthermore, to avoid the high costs associated with lengthy subsea transmission lines, significant waste, and inefficiency through line loss, offshore wind and wave energy projects can be sited close to shore (e.g., within 3 nm). A cost-effective offshore wind and wave industry has the capacity to supply the nation with a substantial amount of energy; this is encouraging news considering that approximately 55 percent of the American population lives within fifty miles of the coast[86] and worldwide, approximately 40 percent of the population lives within sixty miles of the coast,[87] two-thirds of which consist of all megacities, most of which are in the developing world.[88] In summary, the ocean energy resource is tremendous, the need is great,; and ocean energy is abundant, continuous, and inexhaustible.

II. Existing Legal Framework and Incompatibility with Offshore Renewable Energy

A. INTRODUCTION

While technological challenges and financial conditions represent significant barriers to the success of the ocean renewable energy industry, the regulatory environment has created its own set of challenges, which have the potential to delay the implementation of this relatively new source of emission-free electricity. For example, in the United States, ocean energy-generating technologies may be deployed in either state or federal waters, or straddle both. State waters, over which states have partial jurisdiction, extend out three nm from the mean low-water mark (or baseline) of the shoreline, and are also referred to as the state's territorial sea.[89]

In the 1940s, several states claimed jurisdiction over minerals and other resources off their coasts, but in 1947, the United States Supreme Court determined that states had neither title to nor property interest in these resources.[90] In response, Congress enacted the Submerged Lands Act in 1953 giving coastal states jurisdiction over certain aspects of their waters extending three nm seaward from the baseline.[91] For historical reasons

---

[86] U.S. Department of Commerce, National Oceanic and Atmospheric Administration, Ocean and Coastal Resource Management, *The Coastal Community Development Partnership* (2010), http://coastalmanagement.noaa.gov/partnership.html.

[87] Socioeconomic Data and Applications Center, *Percentage of Total Population Living in Coastal Areas* (n.d.), http://sedac.ciesin.columbia.edu/es/papers/Coastal_Zone_Pop_Method.pdf.

[88] Save the Sea, *Interesting Ocean Facts* (2014), http://www.savethesea.org/STS%20ocean_facts.htm.

[89] The Submerged Lands Act, 43 U.S.C. §§ 1301–1315 (2012) (vesting title and ownership in the states to three nautical miles from the mean low-water mark).

[90] United States v. California, 332 U.S. 19 (1947).

[91] 43 U.S.C. §§ 1301–1315 (2012).

relating to their previous sovereign status, Louisiana, Texas, and the Gulf Coast of Florida are an exception, with state jurisdiction extending as far out as nine nm offshore.

The development of ocean energy projects on the OCS, from three nm where state waters end and extend out two hundred miles,[92] is governed by the "Final Programmatic Environmental Impact Statement for Alternative Energy Development and Production and Alternate Use of Facilities on the Outer Continental Shelf" ("Final Renewable Energy Framework"), finalized by BOEM in 2009. BOEM shares jurisdictional responsibilities for MHK projects on the OCS with the Federal Energy Regulatory Commission (FERC),[93] with roles clarified in the agencies' memorandum of understanding,[94] while FERC alone has jurisdiction over MHK projects in state waters. The federal government has exclusive jurisdiction over projects on the OCS, while projects in the territorial seas are regulated by both state and federal agencies. The associated subsea transmission cables of OCS projects passing through the territorial sea and making landfall are regulated by the federal agencies and, in most cases, the respective state's coastal zone management agency.

While the framework reflects the current need for "alternative energy" and an assessment of the potential impacts of renewable projects in the offshore environment, a more comprehensive policy framework with a long-term strategy for a diversified alternative energy portfolio is necessary. A comprehensive review of the full array of permits and consultations applicable to ocean energy projects in the United States is beyond the scope of this chapter.[95] However, it is important to recognize the extraordinary amount of state and federal regulations that are required to license a modern ocean renewable energy project. For example, the following permits and statutory reviews apply to a wave energy project on the OCS:

- Lease from the Department of Interior's Bureau of Ocean Energy Management (BOEM);[96]
- Federal Hydroelectric License from the Federal Energy Regulatory Commission (FERC);[97]
- Clean Water Act § 404 dredge and fill permit from the United States Army Corps of Engineers (USACE);[98]

---

[92] Outer Continental Shelf Lands Act, 43 U.S.C. §§ 1331–1356 (2012).

[93] *See* Energy Policy Act of 2005 (Pub. L. 109-58).

[94] *BOEM/FERC Guidelines on Regulation of Marine and Hydrokinetic Energy Projects on the OCS* (Version 2, July 19, 2012), http://www.boem.gov/BOEM-Newsroom/Press-Releases/2012/BOEM-FERC-staff-guidelines-pdf.aspx.

[95] *See* Oregon Wave Energy Trust, *Wave Energy Development in Oregon, Licensing & Permitting Requirements* (2009), http://oregonwave.org/oceanic/wp-content/uploads/2013/05/OWET_Licensing_-Permitting_July2009.pdf.

[96] Outer Continental Shelf Lands Act, 43 U.S.C. § 1337(p)(1) (2012).

[97] Federal Power Act, 16 U.S.C. §§ 797 (e), (f) (2012).

[98] 33 U.S.C. § 1344(a) (2012).

- Rivers and Harbors Act § 10 permit from the USACE;[99]
- Private Aids to Navigation Act permit from the United States Coast Guard;[100] and
- Clean Water Act § 401 Water Quality permit administered by the State.[101]

In addition to the above-mentioned permits, there are several regulatory reviews with which a wave energy project must comply, including:

- NEPA;[102]
- Endangered Species Act (ESA);[103]
- Marine Mammal Protection Act (MMPA);[104]
- Magnuson-Stevens Conservation and Management Act;[105]
- Migratory Bird Treaty Act;[106]
- Bald and Golden Eagle Protection Act;[107]
- National Historic Preservation Act;[108] and
- Coastal Zone Management Act.[109]

If a wave energy project is sited in or crosses state waters, then several additional state-based permits or reviews will be required. For example, in Oregon, the following are required:

- Site lease,[110] Removal/Fill permit,[111] and easements for cables[112] from the Oregon Department of State Lands;
- Hydropower license[113] and Water Right permit[114] from the Oregon Water Resources Department;

---

[99] Rivers and Harbors Appropriation Act of 1899 § 10, 33 U.S.C. § 403 (2012).
[100] 33 C.F.R. § 66.01 (2014).
[101] 33 U.S.C. § 1341(a) (2012).
[102] 43 U.S.C. §§ 4321–4347 (2012).
[103] 16 U.S.C. §§ 1531–1544 (2012).
[104] 16 U.S.C. §§ 1361–1423 (2012).
[105] 16 U.S.C. §§ 1801-1884 (2012).
[106] 16 U.S.C. §§ 703–711 (2012).
[107] 16 U.S.C. § 668(a)–(d) (2012).
[108] 16 U.S.C. § 470 (2012).
[109] 16 U.S.C. § 1456 (2012).
[110] OR. REV. STAT. § 274.040 (2011).
[111] Id. § 196.810 (2011); see also OR. ADMIN. R. 340-048-0032 (2014).
[112] OR. ADMIN. R. 141-083-0800–0860 (2014).
[113] OR. REV. STAT. § 543.260 (2011).
[114] Id. § 537.110 (2011).

- Coastal Zone Management Act Consistency Determination from the Oregon Department of Land Conservation and Development;[115]
- Water Quality Certificate from the Oregon Department of Environmental Quality;[116] and
- Ocean Shores Alteration Permit from the Oregon Parks and Recreation Department.[117]

Local land use permits from municipal or county governments also would be required for the upland components of a wave energy project.

B. REGULATORY ROADBLOCKS TO OCEAN RENEWABLE ENERGY DEVELOPMENT IN THE UNITED STATES

The above-mentioned representative list, though not exhaustive, of applicable state and federal requirements demonstrates the fundamental problem that the industry faces: ocean renewable energy is scrutinized under an expensive and time-consuming framework of regulatory controls. One could justifiably conclude first, that an evolving nascent industry could not possibly meet these requirements without the financial wherewithal of established industries, such as oil and gas; and second, that this regulatory environment is likely to lock out competing ocean uses and lock in incumbent industries.

Existing federal statutes, most of which were enacted in the late 1960s and 1970s, that govern activities on the OCS and within territorial seas represent an example of a regulatory regime designed to regulate long-established industries such as commercial fishing, oil and gas exploration, and shipping. However, BOEM has stated publicly that concerns about climate change are considered throughout the NEPA process when addressing the potential outcomes of not issuing a lease for renewable energy development activities on the OCS.[118] This is considered to be encouraging news for the future of ocean renewable energy, given the recent findings by the National Science and Technology Council and the U.S. Global Change Research Program outlined in *Climate Change Impacts in the United States.*[119]

---

[115] 15 C.F.R. § 930.57 (2014); *see also* OR. REV. STAT. § 196.405–515 (2011); OR. ADMIN. R. 660-015-0010(4) (2014).

[116] OR. REV. STAT. §§ 468.065, 468B.035 (2011); OR. ADMIN. R. 340-048-0005-0020 (2014).

[117] OR. REV. STAT. § 390.124 (2011); OR. ADMIN. R. 736-020-001-0032 (2014).

[118] *See generally* C.G. Rein, et al., *Offshore Wind Energy Development Site Assessment and Characterization: Evaluation of the Current Status and European Experience* (prepared for U.S. Department of the Interior, Bureau of Ocean Energy Management, Office of Renewable Energy Programs) (OCS Study BOEM 2013-0010, 2013).

[119] "[E]vidence of human-induced climate change continues to strengthen and that impacts are increasing across the country." *See Climate Change Impacts in the United States: The Third National Climate Assessment* (Jerry M. Melillo, Terese (T.C.) Richmond, & Gary W. Yohe eds. 2014). U.S. Global Change Research Program, 1, doi:10.7930/J0Z31WJ2.

In the United States, the extensive regulatory structure is a function of our federalist divisions of power,[120] the piecemeal approach of additional regulatory protections, and our history of devastating human-induced marine disasters that have led to public calls for action and the resultant regulatory reactions. These factors create significant difficulties for ocean renewable energy development to meet current regulatory standards in the United States. If ocean renewable energy is to develop into a meaningful alternative energy source and supplement the United States' power needs, both domestic and international investment must be encouraged. Clarifying the interrelation between the existing environmental laws and potential offshore projects would be a large step toward convincing investors to devote the capital necessary to fund the development and deployment of ocean energy technologies in the United States.

A more simplified statutory scheme, particularly with regard to the jurisdictional authorities and permitting framework, would aid in the proliferation of entrepreneurs and expand the sector's domestic market. As discussed here within, current ocean energy developers face a labyrinth of laws and regulations that are each devoted to small and discrete pieces of the environmental puzzle. The environmental laws governing wind and wave power projects lack a cohesive voice, due to the piecemeal manner by which the statutes were promulgated.[121]

Several more specific regulatory roadblocks will also affect ocean energy's ability to develop expeditiously. Ocean renewable energy is not developing in a vacuum, but rather is being developed in the aftermath of fifty years or more of resource extraction from the oceans. That legacy of development, and the associated ecological disasters that accompanied that development, define the modern regulatory and public mindset around new deployments in the ocean. Even if ocean renewable energy represents a remarkable new source of carbon-free energy with low predicted ecological effects, our national experience with energy development on the oceans dictates our future and ensures that this new industry will be subject to the highest public scrutiny.

As current regulations are essentially a response to the development of incumbent energy sources, such as oil and gas, ocean renewable energy development must either occur within the existing legal framework or await new laws and regulations that are specific to renewable energy. No major legislative advances have occurred in the United States that would fundamentally alter the basic regulatory environment for renewable energy, despite the enactment of the EPAct. One recent and encouraging development has been the push to proactively plan for new uses of the ocean, under the heading of coastal and marine spatial planning (MSP), which will be discussed more fully in

---

[120] *See* Robert W. Eberhardt, *Federalism and the Siting of Offshore Wind Energy Facilities*, 14 N.Y.U. ENVTL. L. J. 374 (2006) (discussing the state and federal interactions around offshore energy regulation).

[121] For a more detailed discussion, see generally Adam M. Dinnell & Adam J. Russ, *Legal Hurdles to Developing Wind Power as an Alternative Energy Source in the United States: Creative and Comparative Solutions*, 27 Nw. J. INT'L L. & BUS. 535 (2007).

Section III of this chapter. The regulatory agencies, particularly at the federal level, have done an admirable job of using the existing regulatory frameworks to accommodate the development of renewable energy in the marine environment. However, the agencies are bound by the legal framework, including both the language of the laws and regulations, as well as by the lessons learned from countless lawsuits. Two notable exceptions include the BOEM's Smart from the Start initiative applicable to wind energy development and FERC's adoption of the Verdant exemption.[122]

FERC's preliminary permits for "water power projects"[123] are a good example of how existing laws and regulations do not satisfy the needs of the MHK industry. The first step in the FERC licensing process is receipt of a preliminary permit, which essentially allows a "first in time, first in right" to develop at a specific location. A prime spot to dam a river is a rare opportunity, and the FERC preliminary permit is the tool companies use to secure a site. The permit gives the holder three years to assemble its plan for development of that site, and prohibits other developers from usurping the site during the feasibility study period. Unfortunately, the preliminary permit process does not work well with ocean energy's phased development approach.

The initial phase of an MHK project may be only one or a few devices, even though the final project may be a hundred or more devices. Unless the FERC preliminary permit is for the full buildout site, another developer could undermine the viability of the project by locating nearby the project site. Once a developer files for a preliminary permit, it has essentially announced to the world that it has acquired enough information about a given site to justify a major investment in the next developmental steps. However, in order to acquire such a permit and license, the applicant must provide various elements of the project, including environmental impact studies, and demonstrate financial capability for the entire project. At the research and development phase of a technology, developers are simply unprepared to answer all of the questions related to the final phases of the project. Given the economic realities of the industry, developers may want to develop plans only for the first phase of the project and, furthermore, may only do so if they are guaranteed at least the "first in time, first in right" to build the subsequent phases.

Another major issue with the existing offshore renewable energy regulatory structure in the United States concerns the dual federal jurisdiction over MHK energy shared between BOEM and FERC. A wave energy project, for example, located on the OCS

---

[122] The "Verdant exemption," which draws its name from the Verdant Power tidal company, is a special condition that FERC created to accommodate this company's specific deployment. Verdant's project is in navigable waters (the East River of New York), but the company does not plan to connect the power to the grid, or sell the electricity into interstate commerce. As a result, FERC determined that Verdant did not need a license from FERC, even though the plain language of part 1 of the Federal Power Act states that FERC jurisdiction applies to any hydrokinetic projects in U.S. navigable waters. Legality aside, the Verdant exemption is the prime example of the agency's attempt to facilitate this new technology.

[123] 18 C.F.R. § 4.31 (2014).

requires a license from FERC and a lease from BOEM.[124] Aside from the obvious and unnecessary redundancy of having two lead agencies, each of those authorizations constitutes a "major federal action" with the potential to significantly affect the human environment, which triggers an analysis under NEPA.[125]

NEPA analysis is an expensive, time-consuming, and daunting task; such environmental analyses constitute a nonstarter for small companies, who lack the deep pockets and experience of large, established companies. Ironically, offshore oil drilling platforms, like the semisubmersible Deepwater Horizon whose explosion in the Gulf of Mexico in 2010 killed eleven people and resulted in the worst offshore environmental catastrophe in U.S. history, are routinely granted a Categorical Exclusion (CatEx) from the typical environmental effects analysis generally required under NEPA. The CatEx issued for Deepwater Horizon was based on findings that a major oil spill would be unlikely to happen.[126] Since the time of the explosion, the Council on Environmental Quality has issued *guidance* for federal agencies on how to "establish, apply, and revise [CatExes]" in accordance with NEPA.[127]

There is no shortage of historical warnings regarding the need to take significant precautionary measures to prevent environmental degradation to the marine environment from ocean renewable energy technologies.[128] This concern has dominated the discussion of wave and wind energy projects in the United States, despite the suite of environmental protections in place. Although both the public and private sectors continue to invest in an ongoing range of environmental studies, there are, as yet, no wave energy projects currently in development.

Furthermore, the litany of environmental tragedies confronting the world's oceans is a product of society's existing energy paradigms, not of ocean renewable energy. Crashing fisheries stocks, marine mammal fatalities, marine pollution (e.g., chemicals, garbage, and waste products), acidification, and warming are not probable, or even possible, results from ocean energy production. Other authors have asserted that if wave energy and other sources of ocean renewable energy are going to "green" the grid, then further research must prove such technologies are benign.[129] This mindset positions ocean energy at a disadvantage to existing energy sources and continues to maintain

---

[124] This dual jurisdiction does not apply to offshore wind because FERC has no jurisdiction over wind projects.

[125] 42 U.S.C. §§ 4321-4375 (2012).

[126] 40 C.F.R. § 1501.4 (2014). A CatEx is prepared when the reviewing agency determines that a proposed action does not individually or cumulatively have a significant effect on the human environment, and has been found to have no such effect in the procedures adopted by a federal agency in the implementation of NEPA, and for which neither an EA nor an EIS is required. *See also* 40 C.F.R. § 1508.4 (2014).

[127] *See* Council on Environmental Quality, *Final Council on Environmental Quality Guidance on Categorical Exclusions under the National Environmental Policy Act* (Nov. 23, 2010).

[128] *See* Rachael E. Salcido, *Rough Seas Ahead: Confronting Challenges to Jump-Start Wave Energy*, 39 ENVTL. L. 1073 (2009) (emphasizing need for extensive environmental protections beyond existing suite of environmental laws).

[129] *Id.* at 1099.

the status quo, which is extraordinarily destructive and dangerous to our long-term health.[130] Discounting the development of ocean energy as a viable source of power, until it proves itself benign, simply ensures continued degradation of the environment, and does so unnecessarily.

Another significant hindrance to the timely development of ocean renewable energy, and other renewables sources as well, has been a general lack of strong financial incentives. The piecemeal federal incentives such as the production tax credit, investment tax credit, and the Modified Accelerated Cost Recovery System that have been adopted to promote renewable energy have lacked long-term consistency. At a time when the industry could count on the availability of the benefits, the incentives were very effective. However, the inconsistent availability of these incentives has had a dramatic impact on their overall effectiveness. Development companies simply cannot reliably plan for large projects two or three years in advance if federal incentives come and go with the political winds. Even lower incentives would be advantageous over large incentives, if proven to be reliable over the years.

III. Recommendations for Promoting Offshore Energy Development

Problems cannot be solved with the same mindset that created them.
ALBERT EINSTEIN

If the goal is to avoid the worst effects of climate change by reducing greenhouse gas emissions, then the surest way to fail is to maintain the status quo. As this chapter has shown, if ocean renewable energy is treated as just another fossil fuel, this new energy resource will not develop with the expedience and sufficiency to make a serious difference in reducing energy-related greenhouse gas emissions. Ocean renewable energy has enormous potential to provide clean, reliable energy for this and future generations. In the United States, we have not taken the necessary steps to nurture this new industry.[131] The following recommendations are intended to spur the development of ocean energy resources and to strike at the heart of the comfortable but dangerous status quo.

---

[130] *See* Jeffrey Thaler, *Fiddling as the World Floods and Burns: How Climate Change Urgently Requires a Paradigm Shift in the Permitting of Renewable Energy Projects*, 42 ENVTL. L. 1101 (2012) (arguing that the existing regulatory structure is not adequate to address the imminent threats from anthropogenic climate change).

[131] *See* Navigant Consulting, Inc., *Offshore Wind Market and Economic Analysis: Annual Market Assessment* (prepared for U.S. Department of Energy DE-EE0005360, Feb. 22, 2013) (providing a more comprehensive assessment of the U.S. offshore wind market than is within the scope of this chapter).

A. PROMOTION OF NATIONAL RENEWABLE ENERGY TEST CENTERS

Test and demonstration sites are essential to support the commercialization and deployment of innovative technologies, anchoring and moorings, and related deployment procedures. These facilities also provide the industry with the ability to better understand the potential effects of these new technologies in a controlled environment. According to the United Nations Intergovernmental Panel on Climate Change (IPCC), the deployment of ocean energy could benefit from testing centers for demonstration projects, and from dedicated policies and regulations that encourage early deployment.[132] The United Kingdom has a large proportion of all European offshore demonstration sites under development, most significantly, the European Offshore Wind Deployment Centre (EOWDC) in Aberdeen Bay and the National Renewable Energy Centre (Narec) demonstration site at Blyth, which also has world-class facilities for testing components. EMEC is located in the Orkney Islands, in Northern Scotland, and has emerged as the leading test center for tidal and wave energy technologies.

In the United States, three ocean energy test centers exist: the Southeast National Marine Renewable Energy Center at Florida Atlantic University (Boca Raton, Florida), the Hawaii National Marine Renewable Energy Center (Honolulu, Hawaii), and the Northwest National Marine Renewable Energy Center, a partnership between Oregon State University (Corvallis, Oregon) and the University of Washington (Seattle, Washington). Each of these centers has received federal support from the U.S. DOE.[133] The Northwest National Marine Renewable Energy Center (NNMREC), located at Oregon State University, specializes in wave and offshore wind, while its sister school, the University of Washington, focuses primarily on tidal technologies. NNMREC has emerged as the flagship test center in North America, with its existing onshore facilities and offshore Pacific Marine Energy Center North Energy Test Site (PMEC NETS), and its planned grid-connected test site, the PMEC South Energy Test Site (PMEC SETS).

These types of facilities are a first step in facilitating the development of ocean renewable energy. In order to receive private financial support and obtain regulatory permits necessary to plan, site, construct, and decommission a project, developers must have access to significant amounts of data. That data can come only from at-sea deployments, which are expensive and time-consuming. Given that these centers are intended to test technologies and obtain data from temporary deployments, one might expect them to have a less burdensome permitting process; however, this is not the case.

Even for these federally supported research facilities, the regulatory process presents an obstacle and undermines the goal of the facilities: to provide a safe, expedient, and

[132] IPCC, 2011: Summary for Policymakers, *in* IPCC SPECIAL REPORT ON RENEWABLE ENERGY SOURCES AND CLIMATE CHANGE MITIGATION 13 (Ottmar Edenhofer et al. eds., 2012).

[133] United States Department of Energy, U.S. Department of Energy Wind and Water Power Technologies Office, *Funding in the United States: Marine and Hydrokinetic Energy Projects, Fiscal Years 2008–2012*, http://energy.gov/sites/prod/files/2013/12/f5/mhk_projects_2013.pdf.

inexpensive option to test technologies in the water. For example, the PMEC SETS project, which is currently at the beginning of its permitting phase for a research lease, faces, at best, a three-year permitting process, at a cost that will certainly exceed $1 million.[134] Regulators appear willing to advance this permitting process as quickly as possible, yet, even with that willingness, existing rules primarily related to NEPA and ESA require an extended three-year review process. Additionally, National Oceanic and Atmospheric Administration's Fisheries Service (NOAA Fisheries) and other resource agencies are treating this proposed grid-connected test site under the same guise as a permanent commercial project, and are requiring extensive and expensive environmental studies and ongoing monitoring even at this early stage of development.

Optimally, once PMEC SETS is operational, developers will have an easier and cheaper means of deploying their devices. However, given the experience with other temporary deployments to date, developers will likely be held to the highest standards, and permitting for individual deployments of specific technologies could easily take a full year or more. Every effort should be made to ensure that such testing facilities are expedited and facilitated by federal financial support and reduced regulatory requirements. The federal DOE should provide immediate and substantial assistance to these test facilities, and agencies such as FERC, BOEM, and DOE should provide a CatEx from NEPA for these federally funded sites. If the agencies are unable or unwilling to take those steps, then Congress should provide the appropriate direction.

B. REMOVAL OF FERC JURISDICTION OVER PILOT AND TESTING PROJECTS IS NOT ENOUGH

The United States Senate Committee on Energy and Natural Resources Subcommittee on Water and Power held a hearing in February 2014[135] regarding the Marine and Hydrokinetic Renewable Energy Act of 2013 (S. 1419), which seeks to improve the approval process for hydrokinetic projects using wave, tidal, and current energy. The legislation, introduced in August 2013, would seek to facilitate and expedite test centers and qualified demonstration programs, including the National Marine Renewable Energy Research, Development, and Demonstration Centers, that produce 10 MW or less of power. The bill also authorizes FERC to issue a pilot license for projects that produce 10 MW or less of power. FERC appears amenable to facilitating testing and demonstration projects, as demonstrated by its willingness to accommodate the industry through such efforts as the Verdant exemption.[136] If FERC's authority under the Federal Power Act

---

[134] Despite the research based purpose of PMEC SETS, the existing permitting time frame associated with a FERC license, BOEM lease, and associated environmental consultations, including NEPA and ESA, puts PMEC SETS on a three-year timeline, regardless of agency willingness to move this project forward expeditiously.

[135] *See* S. 1419, 113th Cong. (2013), *available at* http://beta.congress.gov/bill/113th-congress/senate-bill/1419.

[136] *See supra* note 122.

locks it into a three-year review process, then an exemption from FERC jurisdiction for these testing and demonstration projects could provide a reasonable first step to expedite these projects. However, simply removing FERC jurisdiction over test centers and demonstration projects does not necessarily provide the needed facilitation of these MHK projects. For a variety of reasons, additional regulatory reforms will be necessary.

First, FERC's organic statute, the Federal Power Act of 1935, establishes the primary focus of FERC as an energy agency,[137] albeit with significant cautionary limitations. If FERC jurisdiction were eliminated, some *other* agency would need to take over as the lead consulting agency. In the absence of FERC jurisdiction in federal waters, BOEM would retain primary jurisdiction and function as the lead agency for purposes of guiding review and consultation under NEPA.

However, if a project were to develop in state waters, BOEM would not have jurisdiction, and the USACE would likely play that role as an extension of the two federal permits for which it would be the lead agency: the Section 10 permit under the Rivers and Harbors Act and Section 404 permit under the Clean Water Act. In this situation, the lead federal agency, USACE, would not have energy development as its primary federal goal, and may not provide adequate leadership. Thus, eliminating FERC jurisdiction altogether may not be the most advantageous approach, especially in state waters. Rather, the applicant ought to retain discretion to choose to work with FERC as the lead agency. Three years with FERC may be preferable to an indeterminate number of years with no federal leadership.[138]

Additionally, in the absence of FERC and BOEM, NOAA Fisheries would likely play a more dominant role. NOAA Fisheries, as a resource agency, has even less incentive than USACE to facilitate ocean energy development, for that is not its mandate. This leads to the second, and perhaps most important observation about facilitating ocean renewable energy projects: regardless of which federal agency is the lead, the environmental rampart of existing laws remains fully applicable, and dictates the multi-year, multimillion dollar regulatory pathway for any ocean renewable energy project.

The federal environmental statutes governing ocean energy projects lack a cohesive voice, due to the piecemeal manner in which they were enacted. Flexibility in the regulatory system would promote the development of these projects (both at demonstration and commercial scales) and allow investors to perceive less risk in supporting

---

[137] 16 U.S.C. § 792 (2012).

[138] As Congress has never explicitly granted FERC authority over any type of ocean energy projects, other authors have argued that FERC authority should be eliminated entirely from the regulatory process and, instead, coastal states should be authorized as lead agencies for projects in state waters. For an in-depth analysis of the multi-year regulatory squabble between FERC and the Department of the Interior's Minerals Management Service (MMS [now BOEM]) over which agency has jurisdiction to license wave energy projects on the OCS, see generally Mark Sherman, *Wave New World: Promoting Ocean Wave Energy Development through Federal State Coordination and Streamlined Licensing*, 39 ENVTL. L. 1161 (2009).

these projects. In particular, NEPA, ESA, MMPA, and the Migratory Bird Treaty Act (MBTA) represent the most intractable obstacles to expedited projects. While each statute provides important protections, NEPA is perhaps the most problematic.

As discussed briefly in Section II, the only viable way to avoid the most stringent requirements of NEPA is to acquire a CatEx. Reflecting the national interest in cheap natural gas, terrestrial gas fracking under the EPAct has received exemptions from several major federal environmental statues, including the Safe Drinking Water Act; the Resource Conservation and Recovery Act; the Emergency Planning and Community Right-to-Know Act; the Clean Water Act; the Clean Air Act; the Comprehensive Environmental Response, Compensation, and Liability Act; and NEPA.[139] Although one may argue that natural gas fracking should never have received such exemptions from federal environmental law, the case demonstrates that the federal government can fast track development, if it so chooses, but has not done the same for ocean renewable energy, even though ocean renewable energy, with little potential for environmental damage and no greenhouse gas emissions, should be a viable candidate for similar regulatory easing. Furthermore, any federal funding for wind or wave energy development triggers NEPA review. That trigger imposes completely unnecessary regulatory burdens on small projects, including environmental tests and temporary deployments with little or no potential to impact the human environment.

Unfortunately, given the current state of congressional paralysis, no significant effort is expected to modify the existing gamut of environmental laws, which are intended to protect our environment. Nevertheless, fossil fuel projects are allowed to proceed via explicit exceptions, while new carbon-free energy sources, such as ocean renewable energy, remain handicapped by exorbitant initial permitting costs and requirements. A piecemeal revision of the existing laws seems unlikely. Perhaps a wholesale modification in the form of a single lead agency, or "one stop shop," as it is sometimes called, is the only possible solution. The United Kingdom presents an effective model for just such an approach.

C. LESSONS LEARNED FROM THE UNITED KINGDOM

The United Kingdom is a global leader in offshore wind and wave development, and is considered to be "the most attractive destination for [offshore] investment in the world."[140] The United Kingdom also has more wave and tidal-stream devices installed than the rest of the world combined, according to RenewableUK.[141] The United

---

[139] *See* Renee L. Kosnik, *The Oil and Gas Industry's Exemptions to Major Environmental Statutes* (2007), http://www.earthworksaction.org/files/publications/PetroleumExemptions1c.pdf (discussing oil and gas industry exemptions from major environmental statutes).

[140] Offshore Wind Programme Board, *Offshore Wind Programme Board 2014 Annual Report* (2014) (citing Ernst & Young Renewable Energy Country Attractiveness Index 5 (Nov. 2013)).

[141] *Supra* note 4, at 26.

Kingdom has done more than any other country to support the development of a sustainable and ambitious offshore wind and wave energy industry. Specifically, the government has stimulated investment in the market sector by offering industry guaranteed price support and has provided much-needed certainty to underpin long-term investment. The United Kingdom has ambitious plans to decarbonize the economy as part of the drive to tackle climate change,[142] which have involved a comprehensive approach to advancing the ocean renewable industries through financial investments aimed at reducing the costs of offshore energy and establishing a predictable fiscal environment for private investors, greater predictability in siting decisions through a one-stop permitting approach, and marine spatial planning.

1. Financial Investment in Offshore Energy

The United Kingdom has undertaken several efforts to advance the development of ocean renewable energy. Most important, it provides approximately £1.4 billion (about $2.3 billion) per year for wind, wave, and tidal energy.[143] In addition to significant governmental funding for the past several years, the United Kingdom has also implemented a "5 for 1" renewable obligation certificate for ocean energy projects under 30 MW, which provides five certificates for every one MW-hour of energy generated.[144] The United Kingdom also has begun a feed-in-tariff program that provides a guaranteed rate of return on electricity generated from renewable sources. For example, the United Kingdom currently has a 20.57 p/kWh for small hydrokinetic sources (under 15kWh).[145] Both of these incentives are significantly more effective than the existing tax incentives available in the United States, in large part because of the continuity of the incentives and their significantly larger value.

In addition, as part of a larger effort referred to as "electricity market reform," the United Kingdom is in the process of moving away from the use of Renewable Obligation Certificates as an incentive to the industry toward the use of a new form of feed-in tariff called Contract for Difference mechanism. Contract for Difference ensures that a project developer receives a set amount of money per megawatt hour of generation. For wave energy, the price is recommended to be £300–320 per megawatt hour ($500–532).[146]

---

[142] *UK Renewable Energy Roadmap Update 2013* 50 (Nov. 2013), https://www.gov.uk/government/uploads/system/uploads/attachment_data/file/255182/UK_Renewable_Energy_Roadmap_-_5_November_-_FINAL_DOCUMENT_FOR_PUBLICATIO___.pdf.

[143] Severin Carrell & Fiona Harvey, *Scotland Warned Independence Could Cost Billions in Renewables Subsidies*, GUARDIAN (May 22, 2013), http://www.theguardian.com/environment/2013/may/22/scotland-independence-cost-billions-renewables.

[144] *Supra* note 4, at 6.

[145] Feed-In Tariffs Ltd., *Feed-In Tariffs: The Information Site for the New Guaranteed Payments for Renewable Electricity in the UK* (Mar. 30, 2014), http://www.fitariffs.co.uk/eligible/levels/.

[146] Renewable UK, *Wave and Tidal Energy in the UK 2013: Conquering Challenges, Generating Growth* 2 (Feb. 27, 2013), http://www.renewableuk.com/en/publications/index.cfm/wave-and-tidal-energy-in-the-uk-2013.

This guaranteed price creates a tremendous market pull by ensuring a set level of return, reducing risk, and incentivizing private investment.

The United Kingdom has also provided policy and regulatory leadership. For example, the UK Renewable Energy Roadmap, published by the Department of Energy & Climate Change (DECC) in July 2011, established an industry-led task force, the Offshore Wind Cost Reduction Task Force (CRTF), consisting of experienced industry practitioners, to consider ways in which costs could be reduced, and to produce an action plan to get the cost of energy down to £100/MWh. The CRTF recommended the establishment of the Government Offshore Wind Programme Board (OWPB), a joint government and industry body responsible for driving cost reduction in offshore wind. OWPB's role is to identify and remove barriers to deployment of offshore wind generation, to share best practices across the industry, and to bring forward innovative and collaborative solutions to build a competitive United Kingdom–based supply chain that supports the delivery of a levelized cost of energy of £100/MWh for projects reaching final investment decision in 2020.

The UK Renewable Energy Roadmap Update 2013 reported that "[b]etween January 2010 and September [2013], DECC recorded…£31 billion [worth] of private sector investment in renewable electricity generation[,]" including both onshore and offshore projects.[147] The investments in offshore development are a direct result of the government's ability to work in partnership with private industry to implement the Offshore Wind Industrial Strategy and provide the tools necessary to support large-scale investment, raise awareness of the commercial opportunities, and deliver the innovation and competition needed to bring down costs for consumers.

2. "One Stop Shop" for Consents and Marine Spatial Planning

The United Kingdom has established a comprehensive approach to siting and consenting ocean energy projects through a combination of a simplified agency structure and marine spatial planning. The United Kingdom regulates offshore energy siting and installations pursuant to the Energy Act 2004, an act that established renewable energy zones adjacent to the United Kingdom's territorial waters, within which renewable energy can be installed,[148] and also enabled The Crown Estate to award licenses for offshore wind farm sites in the renewable energy zones on much the same basis as it currently leases sites within territorial waters. Furthermore, the Offshore Production of the Energy section of the Energy Act 2004 created a comprehensive streamlined permitting scheme for offshore renewable energy projects beyond the United Kingdom's territorial waters. For more than a decade, The Crown Estate has conducted leasing rounds in the

---

[147] *Supra* note 142, at 4.

[148] Energy Act 2004, *Part 2 Sustainability and Renewable Energy Sources, Chapter 2 Offshore Production of Energy, Renewable Energy Zones* ¶¶ 81–132 (2004), http://www.iea.org/media/pams/uk/PAMs_UK_EnergyAct2004.pdf.

United Kingdom for the siting and development of offshore energy projects using this streamlined framework.

The Crown Estate is the corporate body, reporting to Parliament, which manages the resources located within the United Kingdom's seabed out to the 12 nm territorial limit and grants leases for renewable energy, natural gas storage, and carbon dioxide storage sites outside territorial waters and within the declared exclusive economic zone around the United Kingdom.[149] The United Kingdom's framework approach for lease issuance includes a national Strategic Environmental Assessment (SEA) aimed at facilitating significant further expansion for offshore wind and an extensive marine spatial planning mapping process undertaken by The Crown Estate with consultation with stakeholders. Coastal and marine spatial planning (MSP), commonly referred to as ocean zoning, is a stakeholder engagement process using the best available science and understanding of current and future ocean uses to facilitate new economic development opportunities, while protecting existing users and the ocean environment.

In December 2007, the Department for Business, Enterprise and Regulatory Reform announced the commencement of an SEA. A target of 25 GW of additional capacity by 2020 was also announced. In January 2009, the UK Offshore Energy SEA Environmental Report was issued for public consultation. The SEA indicated that the preferred approach of DECC is to apply spatial and operational limitations to offshore wind development zones, where required, to mitigate unacceptable environmental impacts, while supporting the overall use of the United Kingdom's marine environment for achievement of the government's energy policy objectives. Suitable areas for offshore wind development have been identified through SEAs.

Furthermore, the Marine and Coastal Access Act 2009, together with the Marine (Scotland) Act 2010 and Northern Ireland Marine Bill,[150] have set up a maritime planning system for all UK waters. The Marine and Coastal Access Act 2009 established the Marine Management Organization (MMO), an agency designated as the "competent marine planning authority on behalf of the UK Government" and through its licensing authority "provide[s] a consistent and unified approach to the coordination and distribution of information and data, and improve[s] efficiency by replacing existing separate organisations."[151] The MMO has the responsibility of preparing marine spatial plans for the English territorial seas and offshore waters as well as implementing a streamlined marine licensing system under the Act. Primarily, the MMO is responsible for managing most aspects of the consenting process for offshore projects less than 100 MW (e.g., a consent under section 36 of the Electricity Act and a marine license). For offshore

---

[149] The Crown Estate, *Offshore Wind Energy* (2014), http://www.thecrownestate.co.uk/energy-infrastructure/offshore-wind-energy/.

[150] The Marine Act (Northern Ireland) 2013 gained Royal Assent on September 17, 2013 and became effective the following day.

[151] Joint Nature Conservation Committee, *Marine and Coastal Access Act 2009* (Mar. 2010), http://jncc.defra.gov.uk/page-5230.

renewable energy projects over 100 MW, a Development Consent Order pursuant to the Planning Act 2008 from the Infrastructure Planning Commission is required.

MSP processes have taken place in other areas, most notably in Germany, Belgium, and the Netherlands. The United States gleaned lessons learned from these examples. In the July 2010 Executive Order (E.O. 13547), National Policy for the Stewardship of the Ocean, Our Coasts and the Great Lakes ("National Ocean Policy"), President Obama named MSP as one key component of the National Ocean Policy.[152] Even prior to the executive order, MSP efforts were underway in the United States. Rhode Island is perhaps the best example of a comprehensive and transparent MSP process. Oregon, on the other hand, whose efforts commenced a few years later, provides a less comprehensive planning approach.

a. MSP in Rhode Island

The Rhode Island Ocean Special Area Management Plan ("Ocean SAMP") is an adaptive ecosystem-based management approach to guide the development and protection of ocean resources off the coast of Rhode Island. The planning effort began in 2008 under the directive of Rhode Island's Renewable Energy Standard, a standard that called for 16 percent of Rhode Island's energy needs to be supplied by renewable energy by 2019.[153] With extensive stakeholder involvement, state and federal financial support, and integration of the best available science in its decision-making processes, the Ocean SAMP is considered to be a living document to define how Rhode Island's waters and adjacent federal waters can be best utilized. The overall objectives of the Ocean SAMP are mitigation of and adaptation to global climate change with the development of offshore renewable energy. Throughout the planning process, however, those objectives expanded to zone management of the diverse activities occurring within both state and federal waters.[154]

In order to "build a framework for coordinated decision-making between state and federal management agencies," one of the goals of the Ocean SAMP, federal and state permitting agencies were involved in all planning phases to ensure that appropriate regulatory requirements were integrated into the process.[155] The premise for involving the agencies early in the process was to reduce the expected time frame for a NEPA-compliant permitting process by an estimated two years. The Ocean SAMP established a Joint Agency Working Group composed of applicable federal and state regulatory agencies and the Narragansett Indian Tribe to assure that permitting decisions are well informed and complementary to the regulatory requirements of relevant agencies.[156]

---

[152] Executive Order 13547: Stewardship of the Ocean, Our Coasts, and the Great Lakes, (July 19, 2010).

[153] R.I. Gen. Laws § 39-26-4 (2004).

[154] Kate Mulvaney, *First Biennial Assessment of the Rhode Island Ocean Special Area Management Plan Process* (Nov. 2013), http://seagrant.gso.uri.edu/oceansamp/pdf/documents/doc_osamp_evaluation.pdf.

[155] *Id.* at 12.

[156] Rhode Island Coastal Resources Management Council, *Rhode Island Ocean Special Management Plan, Volume I*, Chapter 11: The Policies of the Ocean SAMP (Oct. 19, 2010).

According to the conclusions of the Ocean SAMP assessment, the relationships formed among the regulators have already streamlined energy permitting requirements across jurisdictional boundaries.[157] Nevertheless, some stakeholders, such as developers, view the Ocean SAMP as one more bureaucratic layer of the permitting process. For example, the Ocean SAMP is recognized as a comprehensive plan by FERC; therefore, in addition to its own regulatory standards, FERC will consult the Ocean SAMP when the agency's jurisdiction applies to MHK projects within the Ocean SAMP boundary.

b. MSP in Oregon

In January 2013, Oregon completed and approved its revisions to the Territorial Sea Plan (TSP) Part Five: Use of the Territorial Sea for the Development of Renewable Energy Facilities or Other Related Structures, Equipment or Facilities.[158] The TSP includes a policy document providing the conditions for ocean energy development, as well as a geographical information system spatial analysis to map where development may occur within the state's territorial sea. Unlike efforts in Europe and Rhode Island, Oregon's MSP process was limited solely to the integration of wave energy, and, in that sense, it was not a true MSP process. A more thoughtful approach would have considered ocean uses comprehensively, rather than singling out a use such as ocean energy.

Although Oregon is well known for its leadership in promoting sustainable technologies and carbon-free energy production, Oregon's approach to MSP was not optimal. Rather than approaching the planning process as a means to maximize safe and beneficial use of the ocean, Oregon essentially accepted the status quo of uses, and attempted to add ocean energy as an additional use that was not allowed to encumber any existing uses or values. The process was driven by established social and economic stakeholders, lacked a clear vision for MSP, and did not consider the benefits of clean, emissions-free energy generation. As a result, the plan relegated wave energy to an area equal to approximately 1.5 percent of the entire state territorial waters, and established a precautionary approach to this new use that made no allowances for its potential to reduce greenhouse gases. Additionally, the prescriptive plan aggravated existing stakeholder divisions, and any proposed modifications of the plan will be extremely difficult.

MSP, when developed properly, is a valuable planning tool, if it leads to a coordinated and proactive approach to ocean energy development that facilitates siting and permitting of the projects within multi-use areas. Offshore energy development occurs in a very

---

[157] *Supra* note 154, at 35 (citing as examples: (1) the Area of Mutual Interest (AMI) Memorandum of Understanding signed by the governors of Rhode Island and Massachusetts to clarify the joint goals between the states to encourage offshore wind energy development and enhance coordination, and (2) the AMI being evaluated and designated by BOEM as an appropriate federal offshore WEA).

[158] Oregon Land Conservation and Development Commission, *Oregon Territorial Sea Plan, Part 5: Uses of the Territorial Sea* (Mar. 31, 2014), http://www.oregon.gov/LCD/OCMP/Pages/Ocean_TSP.aspx.

busy context: offshore energy resources tend to be located in areas where there are many other active uses of the ocean. The GOM is one of the nation's most valuable fisheries, for example, and oil and gas development takes place in the midst of active shipping lanes, vibrant recreational activities, priceless ecological systems, and many other human uses. A holistic, ecosystem-based analysis of ocean uses must recognize that there are better and worse uses of limited ocean space. Therefore, simply because a given industry has historically used the ocean does not necessarily mean it should remain a dominant user.

D. ADAPTIVE MANAGEMENT AND THE PRECAUTIONARY PRINCIPLE

As the MSP process reflects, when deciding where to site an offshore energy facility, objectives to maximize energy production are weighed against objectives to minimize impacts on biological and physical resources, maintain commercial uses (e.g., fish and shellfish harvests), and minimize impacts on marine transportation and recreation within the designated MSP boundaries. Another tool to achieve these concurrent objectives is adaptive management.

Adaptive management depends on a clear statement of project objectives, intended outcomes, or performance measures to guide decision-making and recognize success. Objectives represent benchmarks against which to compare the potential effects of different management actions such as the issuance of a license, lease, or both for an offshore energy project. Adaptive management is an effective way to make decisions in the face of uncertainties, particularly in its application to offshore ocean projects, because of the dynamic natural environment and changing environment in response to climate. In order for adaptive management to work, there must be the opportunity to engage in experimentation and then to incorporate what is learned. Relevant questions include whether management actions can be adjusted in response to what has been learned and whether an adaptive management process can be established within the appropriate legal framework.[159]

In the absence of perfect information, agency discretion tends to shrink behind what has been termed the precautionary principle. The precautionary principle states "[w]here there are threats of serious or irreversible damage, lack of full scientific certainty shall not be used as a reason for postponing cost-effective measures to prevent environmental degradation."[160] The burden of proof that it is *not* harmful falls on those proposing the action. This principle allows policymakers to make discretionary decisions in situations where there is the possibility of harm from taking a particular course or making a certain decision when extensive scientific knowledge on the matter is lacking. These protections

---

[159] B. K. Williams et al., *Adaptive Management: The U.S. Department of the Interior Technical Guide.* (Adaptive Management Working Group, U.S. Department of the Interior, Washington, DC, 2009).

[160] 1992 Rio Declaration on Environment and Development, Pr. 15, UN Doc. A/CONF.151/26 (vol. I), 31 I.L.M. 874 (1992).

can be relaxed only if further scientific findings emerge that provide sound evidence that no harm will result. Unfortunately, the precautionary principle hinders new uses such as renewable energy, while existing uses, which are well known via general scientific consensus to cause environmental damage, are allowed to proceed. Offshore renewable energy, including avoiding environmental impacts, would be better served by a policy of adaptive management and MSP than the current regulatory framework that relies on the precautionary principle.

Pilot projects and continued monitoring will be essential in shaping the future of co-location of activities. For example, pilot testing protocols must include environmental benchmarks and require adaptive management to meet those benchmarks. The U.S. Department of the Interior defines adaptive management as "learning-based management of natural resources."[161]

Permitting agencies have a difficult time accommodating unproven uses of the ocean, such as ocean renewable energy, because of the systemic tendency to be risk averse. The agencies' reliance on the precautionary principle is a reasonable response to scenarios when a proposed use has potentially catastrophic effects. The irony and downside of this approach is that the agencies, whose job it is to protect the environment and natural resources, are hampered in dealing with the most catastrophic man-made environmental threat ever created, climate change, because of their reliance on the precautionary principle. Ocean warming, rising sea levels, and ocean acidification will unquestionably continue if we do not change our routines. Agencies have demonstrated their willingness to accommodate ocean renewable energy, but NEPA, ESA, MMPA, and other environmental protection laws are having the unintended consequence of magnifying and aggravating the impacts of climate change. Furthermore, the principle is often not applied to existing technologies, such as oil and gas exploration, because of the agencies' historical familiarity with such uses, even when they have routine catastrophic impacts.

There are opportunities for adaptive management, and they continue to grow because systemic environmental change, primarily due to climate change, will continue into the future, producing highly unpredictable changes in natural resource systems. Natural resource managers and permitting agencies will need to learn about these systems as they are changing. An adaptive management objective for a climate change project would be the reduction or elimination of its causes (via reduction of greenhouse gas emissions). Throughout the construction, operation, and, ultimately, decommission of ocean energy projects, the objectives would be reducing impacts on resources (both biological and socioeconomic). Adaptive management as well as phased development of ocean energy technologies further ensures that there is a mechanism to handle unintended effects and a process to acquire data over both the short-term and long-term. Phased development puts a progressive number of devices in the water in a way that allows the developer

---

[161] B.K. Williams & E.D. Brown, *Adaptive Management: The U.S. Department of the Interior Applications Guide* (Adaptive Management Working Group, U.S. Department of the Interior, Washington, DC, 2012).

and regulators to monitor cumulative effects and make changes as necessary. Regulators and the public have an opportunity to grow accustomed to the project, while ensuring that the cumulative effects of the project do not exceed expectations. If the effects do exceed expectations, the developer makes the necessary adjustments to reduce the effects or no further development may occur. If serious unforeseen effects arise, the project is discontinued.

E. PROPER ALLOCATION OF ENVIRONMENTAL COSTS

There is no question that a great deal of environmental monitoring remains to be conducted to demonstrate the long-term potential effects of ocean renewable energy development. Some of those ongoing baseline environmental studies should be conducted and funded by the industry that is reaping financial benefits from use of the public commons. However, costs of the significant environmental studies that agencies require prior to permit approval for an early stage project should be shared by the public and private parties.

The primary environmental questions relating to ocean renewable energy include five major areas: benthic impacts, sediment transport, effects of electromechanical forces, marine mammal impacts, and acoustics. None of those issues can be addressed conclusively until projects are in the water. Many such studies have already been performed by private companies and by publicly financed organizations. Although these studies can begin to describe the potential effects, they are only the beginning. Many of those studies are simply baseline ones that seek to describe the current conditions of the ocean. Although that knowledge is absolutely crucial and valuable to our long-term understanding of the oceans, early-stage private companies cannot be expected to finance the public's improved ocean data. The benefit of that information extends well beyond the ocean renewable energy companies and their small projects. Efforts to develop wave energy in Oregon, for example, have led to a tremendous improvement in the state's knowledge of its waters. The Oregon Marine Map now has over 150 data layers describing the state's territorial sea. Much of that information was provided with the ocean renewable energy industry's support. More information is necessary, but public agencies ought to contribute to the collection of that data, especially if agencies continue to insist on having data before allowing the developers to proceed. Developers are currently caught in a circular pattern: agencies will not allow them to proceed until they provide the data, but the data is not available until they are allowed to proceed.

A second recommendation is to monetize carbon as either a tax or as part of a cap and trade program, which will level the playing field with fossil fuels. This approach has been demonstrated as the most direct and economically efficient means to incentivize renewable energy development. Fossil fuels dominate the energy sector because they have successfully managed to internalize profits and externalize costs, such as health and environmental harms. A price on carbon is the most direct way to internalize costs associated with climate change. Once renewables can compete on a level playing field with carbon-based fuels, the renewables industry and its investors need not speculate about the availability of an incentive. Nor will they need to engage in complex ownership models, such as the so-called "flip model" for large wind projects, which relied on large investment banks with large tax liabilities to be able to use the significant tax credits provided under the Investment Tax Credit. Pricing carbon (and other greenhouse gases relative to carbon) simply and directly internalizes the costs associated with greenhouse gas emissions, and provides a market mechanism that allows consumers to decide between options without ignoring significant costs not included in the price.[162]

Conclusion

The IPCC Fifth Assessment Report (AR5) has declared now until 2040 as the era of climate responsibility, a time during which we as policymakers, consumers, and technology developers have an obligation to take urgent action and reduce our emissions of greenhouse gases.[163] As this chapter has shown, ocean renewable energy from wind and waves has tremendous potential to reduce emissions by providing clean, reliable, and emissions-free electricity. Unfortunately, the potential benefits of these energy sources are not being realized, and are not likely to be realized, at least not in the United States, without significant policy changes. Factors hindering the development of this industry are largely controllable and even of our own making. Most insidious are those regulatory features that are rooted in our past experience with fossil fuels, which lock us into the existing fossil-fuel-based energy paradigm.

The existing order of environmental laws and the resulting agency modus operandi will not change without congressional action. This chapter's primary recommendation is to provide a more streamlined and manageable permitting structure, perhaps similar to the United Kingdom's approach. That structure should work in tandem with well-designed MSP. If MSP at the national level is implemented in a comprehensive, ecosystem-wide approach, it could be very helpful. However, if implemented incorrectly, MSP will only serve to benefit existing ocean users, to the exclusion of ocean energy development. At a minimum, agencies, or perhaps Congress, should provide for a CatEx from NEPA for testing and early-stage development.

---

[162] Consider, for example, the experience of British Columbia, which phased in a carbon tax in 2008, and has had great success with it. The benefits of that approach and some suggestions for improvements were presented by authors from the Northwest Economic Research Center at Portland State University. Jenny H. Liu & Jeff Renfro, *Carbon Tax and Shift: How to Make It Work for Oregon's Economy*, Northwest Economic Research Center Report (2013), *available at* http://www.pdx.edu/nerc/carbontax2013.pdf.

[163] IPCC Working Group II, Fifth Assessment Report, *Climate Change 2014: Impacts, Adaptation, and Vulnerability* (2014), http://www.ipcc.ch/.

Adequate federal financial and regulatory support for national renewable energy test centers will play an important role in expediting the development of the nascent technologies, and this effort can be beneficial regardless of the implementation or success of the other recommendations. Finally, the United States should implement a mechanism that prices carbon, which will force incumbent industries to internalize the true cost of their production, and consumers to pay for the full cost for their consumption.

Once these efforts are implemented, new clean, efficient, safe, and reliable energy technologies such as offshore wind and wave energy will move more quickly to market, and provide significant levels of reduction of greenhouse gas emissions. In the United States, the alternative is to maintain the status quo and continue on the path of reliance on fossil fuels. However, this scenario in the era of climate change has been deemed unacceptable by the most recent IPCC findings and is therefore not an option.

9 Marine Mammal Protection Act Implementation in an Era of Climate Change
Keith W. Rizzardi*

* The author is grateful to Edward (Trey) Nazzaro and Gamila Elmaadawy for their research and editorial assistance.

Introduction

Climate change and sea-level rise present immediate threats not only to coastal wildlife, but to marine mammals in the open oceans as well. Historically, the Marine Mammal Protection Act (MMPA)[1] sought to reduce threats by prohibiting the "take" of marine mammals in U.S. waters and by U.S. citizens on the high seas. But the implementation of the MMPA by the National Marine Fisheries Service (NMFS) and the U.S. Fish & Wildlife Service (FWS), with the assistance of their influential independent advisory board, the Marine Mammal Commission,[2] must adjust to a changing factual seascape afflicted by climate change impacts. As the planet changes, ocean currents, prey abundance, shipping routes, and habitats also will change. Marine mammals will be affected, and the MMPA objective of protecting marine mammals may become an impossible ideal.

This chapter explores the history of the MMPA, revealing an evolving, data-intensive and species-specific adaptive approach to marine mammal protection and regulation. The MMPA ultimately embraces the "precautionary principle," prohibiting human actions from taking marine mammals unless otherwise authorized by the federal agencies and supported by adequate information.[3] Consequently, this chapter also considers how climate change may affect the implementation of the MMPA. In the context of U.S. ocean management, and in the absence of statutory reform, the uncertainties of a changing climate will conflict with the MMPA's rigid prohibitions of harm or harassment to marine mammals. Difficult decisions lie ahead as to how our nation will reconcile marine mammal protection with other competing policy needs.

I. Essential Goals and Concepts in the MMPA

Originally passed in 1972, and modified thereafter, the MMPA provides special protection to marine mammals, and further ensures that the MMPA takes precedence over

---

[1] 16 U.S.C. §§ 1361–1423(h) (2012).

[2] 16 U.S.C. § 1401 (2012). The Marine Mammal Commission, an independent and scientific body with structural barriers to limit partisan bias, acts in a special advisory capacity over the agencies. *See, e.g.*, MMPA, 16 U.S.C. § 1402(d) (2012) (requiring the agencies to respond to Commission recommendations and provide a detailed explanation of why recommendations are not followed or adopted); Animal Welfare Inst. v. Kreps, 561 F.2d 1002, 1011 (D.C. Cir. 1977) (relying on Commission statements to reject agency regulation).

[3] *See, e.g.*, United Nations Conference on Environment and Development, Rio Declaration on Environment and Development (June 14, 1992), Principle 15 ("In order to protect the environment, the precautionary approach shall be widely applied by States according to their capabilities. Where there are threats of serious or irreversible damage, lack of full scientific certainty shall not be used as a reason for postponing cost-effective measures to prevent environmental degradation.").

all other less-restrictive state laws,[4] and even over the Endangered Species Act.[5] Seeking to reduce human harvest and "virtual genocide" of marine mammal species through intentional slaughter and bycatch, the MMPA created a comprehensive framework for protecting dolphins,[6] seals,[7] whales,[8] and other species.[9] The statute recognizes that certain species and population stocks face the danger of extinction or depletion, and its primary goal is to maintain the health and stability of the marine ecosystem.[10] To prevent continued depletion of marine mammal populations, the law also requires immediate measures to replenish species stocks and to protect essential habitats for populations suffering from the adverse effects of human actions.[11] The MMPA explicitly recognizes the constraints created by inadequate knowledge of population dynamics,[12] the need for international negotiations to coordinate marine mammal research and conservation,[13] and the effects of interstate commerce upon marine mammals and their ecosystems.[14]

The MMPA imposes an indefinite moratorium on taking and importation of marine mammals and marine mammal products,[15] and prohibits importation of marine mammals and marine mammal products.[16] To "take" a marine mammal means to harass,

---

[4] 16 U.S.C. § 1379(a) (2012); *see also* Fouke Co. v. Mandel, 386 F. Supp. 1341, 1360 (D. Md. 1974) (finding that Maryland law banning marine mammal importation was "by the very nature of the enactment of the MMPA, necessarily preempted for federal control."); Consolidated Appropriations Act, Pub. L. No. 108-447, 118 Stat. 2809 (2004) (clarifying state authority to be more protective of marine mammals in Hawaiian waters); UFO Chuting of Haw. v. Young, 327 F. Supp. 2d 1220 (D. Haw. 2004), *vacated*, 380 F. Supp. 2d 1166 (D. Haw. 2005).

[5] 16 U.S.C. § 1543 (2012) ("no provision of the [ESA] shall take precedence over any more restrictive provision of the [MMPA]").

[6] H.R. Rep. No. 92-707, at 4144 (1971). Congress referred to the "virtual genocide" of dolphins created when purse seine net fishing was used in the tuna fishery. *Id.*

[7] *See, e.g.,* Treaty for the Preservation and Protection of the Fur Seals, July 7, 1911, 37 Stat. 1542, 156 U.N.T.S. 363.

[8] *See, e.g.,* International Convention for the Regulation of Whaling, Dec. 2, 1946, 62 Stat. 1716, 10 U.S.T. 952.

[9] *Marine Mammals: Hearings Before the Subcomm. on Fisheries & Wildlife Conservation of the H. Comm. on Merchant Marine & Fisheries,* 92nd Cong. 2 (Sept. 9, 1971) (opening statement of Representative John Dingell, who discussed "whales, seals, walruses, sea otters, polar bears and the sea cows"); *see also* George Coggins, *Legal Protection for Marine Mammals: An Overview of Innovative Resource Conservation Legislation,* 6 ENVTL. L. 1 (1975) (reviewing species affected by MMPA).

[10] 16 U.S.C. §§ 1361(1), (6) (2012). Scholars have observed that the MMPA embodies all of the various ethical underpinnings for species conservation: an anthropomorphic approach that allows for sustainable harvest, a holistic approach that recognizes the value of marine mammals and ecosystems, and an animal rights approach that appreciates the value of each species. DALE D. GOBLE & ERIC T. FREYFOGLE, WILDLIFE LAW: CASES AND MATERIALS 834–35 (2d ed. 2010) (citing MICHAEL BEAN & MELANIE ROWLAND, THE EVOLUTION OF NATIONAL WILDLIFE LAW (3d ed. 1997)); Sanford Gaines & Dale Schmidt, *Wildlife Population Management under the Marine Mammal Protection Act of 1972,* 6 ENVTL. L. REP. 50,096 (1976); Alice Herrington & Lewis Regenstein, *The Plight of the Ocean Mammals,* 1 ENVTL. AFF. 792 (1972).

[11] 16 U.S.C. § 1361(2) (2012).

[12] *Id.* § 1361(3).

[13] *Id.* § 1361(4).

[14] *Id.* § 1361(5).

[15] *Id.* § 1371(a).

[16] *Id.* §§ 1362(8), 1372(c).

hunt, capture, or kill, or attempt to harass, hunt, capture, or kill any marine mammal.[17] To "harass" means to pursue, torment, or annoy with potential to injure a marine mammal or with potential to cause disruption of behavioral patterns, including migration, breathing, nursing, breeding, feeding, or sheltering.[18] Yet the MMPA also embraces the notion of sustainability, and seeks to achieve optimal sustainable populations (OSPs) of species, defined as "the number of animals which will result in the maximum productivity of the population or the species, keeping in mind the carrying capacity of the habitat and the health of the ecosystem."[19] Accordingly, notwithstanding the moratorium, the statutory scheme allows limited take of species, empowering NMFS and FWS[20]to assert regulatory authority and to authorize some "incidental" take of marine mammals.

Allowable take comes in many forms. For example, marine mammals may be incidentally harmed or even killed by commercial fishing operations,[21] including tuna fisheries and subsistence fishing by Alaskan natives.[22] In addition, non-lethal harassment of marine mammals resulting from military readiness activities, scientific research, or educational or commercial photography may also be authorized.[23] Takings that result from self-defense or defense of others, good Samaritan activities to rescue marine mammals, and national defense are also exempt from the prohibitions, as is an incidental taking by U.S. citizens employed on foreign vessels outside the United States Exclusive Economic Zone when operating in compliance with the International Dolphin Conservation Program.[24] History reveals controversy involving most of these circumstances.

Another core objective of the MMPA and its regulations is to achieve a "zero mortality rate goal" (ZMRG). The ZMRG requires a reduction of incidental mortality and serious injury of marine mammals to insignificant levels approaching a zero rate.[25] But the MMPA also acknowledges that species may have a potential biological removal level (PBR). The PBR is defined as the maximum number of animals, not including natural mortalities, which may be removed from a marine mammal stock while allowing that

---

[17] *Id.* § 1362(13).

[18] 16 U.S.C. § 1362(18)(A) (2012).

[19] *Id.* § 1362(9).

[20] FWS has authority under the MMPA for eight amphibious or nearshore species, including the Amazonian manatee (*Trichechus inunguis*), West Indian manatee (*Trichechus manatus*), dugong (*Dugong dugon*), marine otter (*Lutra felina*), sea otter (*Enhydra lutris*), polar bear (*Ursus martitimus*), and walrus (*Odobenus rosmarus*). 50 C.F.R. § 18.3 (2014).

[21] 16 U.S.C. §§ 1371(a)–(d); 1374(a); 1383(a); § 1387 (2012).

[22] *Id.* § 1371(b).

[23] *Id.* § 1362(18).

[24] *Id.* § 1371(c), (d), (f).

[25] *See, e.g.,* 16 U.S.C. § 1371(a)(2) (2012) ("In any event it shall be the immediate goal that the incidental kill or incidental serious injury of marine mammals permitted in the course of commercial fishing operations be reduced to insignificant levels approaching a zero mortality and serious injury rate."); 69 Fed. Reg. 43,338 (July 20, 2004) (rule implementing ZMRG); 16 U.S.C. § 1387(b)(2) (2012) ("Fisheries which maintain insignificant serious injury and mortality levels approaching a zero rate shall not be required to further reduce their mortality and serious injury rates.").

stock to reach or maintain its OSP.[26] The two concepts are linked. Generally, if incidental mortality of marine mammals is below 10 percent of the PBR, the take is deemed
insignificant for purposes of the ZMRG.[27] The ZMRG and PBR concepts require sufficient information, however. Regulators need to know, or at least estimate, the species
population size and the rate of take. In addition, the ZMRG and PBR concepts reflect
values. On the one hand, the ZMRG embraces an idealistic desire to allow zero take of
marine mammals. On the other hand, the PBR recognizes that some take of marine
mammals may be biologically sustainable.

As this chapter demonstrates, these various concepts, the prohibitions of take and
harassment, coupled with the goals of zero morality and simultaneous recognition of
sustainable rates of removal, have created a rich and interesting history of MMPA implementation. But in a world of climate change, past performance is not necessarily a predictor of future results.

II. Past: The Adaptive, Data-Driven, and Value-Laden Implementation of the MMPA

The MMPA's regulatory and management schemes have evolved, incrementally, adapting to new conditions just like the species the MMPA protects. History shows that disputes over data and values often lie at the center of the swirling controversies over the
MMPA. Regulators, already facing the challenges of uncertainty and inadequate information, must confront the challenges of litigation, too.

A. THE TUNA-DOLPHIN CONTROVERSIES

During the 1970s, 1980s, and 1990s, the interaction of dolphins with the tuna fishery generated significant MMPA-related controversy, undergoing three phases. In the first phase
during the early and mid-1970s, NMFS sought to implement a general permit process—
including formal adjudication procedures using an administrative law judge—to impose
fishery gear limits.[28] But when the NMFS permits finally faced a legal challenge, a court
invalidated NMFS action.[29] Citing criticisms from the Marine Mammal Commission,

---

[26] 16 U.S.C. § 1362(20) (2012) ("The potential biological removal level is the product of the following factors: (A) The minimum population estimate of the stock. (B) One-half the maximum theoretical or estimated net productivity rate of the stock at a small population size. (C) A recovery factor of between 0.1
and 1.0.").

[27] 50 C.F.R. § 229.2 (2014) ("An insignificance threshold is estimated as 10 percent of the Potential Biological
Removal level for a stock of marine mammals.").

[28] 16 U.S.C. §§ 1373–1376 (2012).

[29] 16 U.S.C. § 1371(a)(2) (2012). The MMPA set a *zero* mortality goal, but NMFS regulations required fishermen to use specified fishing gear for tuna purse seining to *reduce* incidental porpoise mortality. 39 Fed. Reg.
32,117 (1974), creating 50 C.F.R. § 216.24(d)(2) (2014).

the court held that the MMPA "was not intended as a balancing act" between the fishing industry and the animals, and ordered NMFS to make proper estimates of the existing and OSP levels of each species affected, to better understand the expected impacts.[30] In the second phase of the tuna-dolphin controversies, for the rest of the 1970s and early 1980s, NMFS began imposing quotas of dolphin catch on the U.S. fishing vessels. That process led to substantial reductions in marine mammal take,[31] but reduced the size of the MMPA-regulated U.S. fishing vessel fleet, and foreign fishing vessels filled the void.[32] As a result, the third phase of the tuna-dolphin controversy involved global diplomacy. Treaties, specific statutory amendments, and international trade litigation emerged,[33] supplemented by greener but still controversial business practices by seafood companies who refuse to process tuna products that are not deemed "dolphin safe."[34]

B. REFORMING COMMERCIAL FISHERY REGULATION

By 1988, the reach of the MMPA had expanded beyond the tuna-dolphin controversies, shaping other aspects of ocean and fishery management. In *Kokechik Fishermen's Ass'n v. Sec'y of Commerce*,[35] Alaskan subsistence fishermen proved that commercial salmon gill-net fishing by Japanese boats in the Pacific Northwest violated the MMPA. The court struck down the incidental take permits issued by NMFS, finding them contrary to the MMPA. NMFS and the fishermen knew that large numbers of Dall's porpoises, fur seals,

---

[30] Comm. for Humane Legislation, Inc. v. Richardson, 414 F. Supp. 297, 306–09 (D.D.C.), *aff'd* 540 F.2d 1141 (D.C. Cir. 1976).

[31] MARINE MAMMAL COMM'N, 1991 ANNUAL REPORT TO CONGRESS 94 (1992), *available at* http://www.mmc.gov/reports/annual/pdf/2010-2011/MMC_annual_report_2010-2011_low-resolution.pdf (noting that the MMPA generally permits reduced dolphin take from approximately 368,000 in 1972 to 15,000 in 1980).

[32] BEAN & ROWLAND, *supra* note 10, at 126.

[33] *See, e.g.*, MMPA, 16 U.S.C. § 1378 (2012) (requiring the Secretary of State to engage in negotiations to revise the Convention for the Establishment of an Inter-American Tropical Tuna Commission); Dolphin Protection Consumer Information Act, 16 U.S.C. § 1385 (2012) (setting standards for labeling of tuna as "dolphin safe"); GATT Dispute Panel Report on Mexican Complaint concerning United States Restrictions on Imports of Tuna (Aug. 16, 1991), 30 I.L.M. 1594 (1991); GATT Dispute Panel Report on European Economic Community Complaint concerning United States Restrictions on Imports of Tuna (June 1994), 33 I.L.M. 839 (1994); Defenders of Wildlife v. Hogarth, 330 F.3d 1358 (Fed. Cir. 2003).

[34] *See* United Press Int'l, *StarKist Adopts "Dolphin-Safe" Policy on Tuna*, L.A. TIMES (Apr. 12, 1990), http://articles.latimes.com/1990-04-12/business/fi-1772_1_starkist-tuna (last visited Jan. 3, 2014). Predictably, the reduction in purse-seining techniques for tuna fishing led to the development of new fishing techniques, and sometimes, dolphin-safe fishing techniques extracts even more bycatch of other species. *See, e.g.*, Elizabeth Eaves, *Dolphin Safe but Not Ocean Safe*, FORBES (July 24, 2008), http://www.forbes.com/2008/07/24/dolphin-safe-tuna-tech-paperplastic08-cx_ee_0724fishing.html (last visited Jan. 3, 2014); *Proliferating Use of Fish Aggregating Devices*, PEW CHARITABLE TRUSTS (June 11, 2013), http://www.pewenvironment.org/news-room/data-visualizations/proliferating-use-of-fish-aggregating-devices-85899482838 (last visited Jan. 3, 2014).

[35] Kokechik Fishermen's Ass'n v. Sec'y of Commerce, 839 F.2d 795 (D.C. Cir. 1988).

and other marine mammals would be taken. But the court held that NMFS could not issue general permits for commercial fishing unless it found, based upon adequate evaluation of sustainable population sizes for every species, that the take "will not disadvantage the species," will not take depleted species, and would be consistent with the MMPA.[36] With that decision, commercial fisheries faced increasing risks of MMPA violations—civil penalties of $10,000 for each violation,[37] criminal penalties of $20,000 or one year in prison for knowing violations,[38] civil penalties of up to $100,000 for knowing misrepresentations related to dolphin conservation in the tuna fishery,[39] and additional penalties, including forfeiture, related to the use of vessels resulting in illegal take of marine mammals.[40]

Congress initially responded to the *Kokechik* decision by establishing a five-year exemption for commercial fishery vessels and requiring onboard monitors to collect data from fisheries vessels.[41] Eventually, in 1994, Congress would substantially modify the MMPA, replacing the formally adjudicated incidental take permitting scheme with a new program. For all marine mammal species populations, NMFS now requires periodic stock assessment reports[42] and calculated estimates of the PBR.[43] For "strategic stocks" considered to be depleted under the MMPA or otherwise listed as threatened or endangered under the Endangered Species Act, Congress added another regulatory mechanism for NMFS to implement. The MMPA amendments required the development of "take reduction plans" designed to achieve the goal of "insignificant" incidental take that approached "zero mortality."[44]

---

[36] *Id.* at 802–803. *See also* Mary Sauer, *Balancing Marine Mammal Protection against Commercial Fishing: The Zero Mortality Rate Goal, Quotas, and the Gulf of Maine Harbor Porpoise*, 45 ME. L. REV. 419 (1993).

[37] 16 U.S.C. § 1375(a) (2012). *See also* Strong v. United States, 5 F.3d 905 (5th Cir. 1993) (reversing injunction of regulation defining the feeding of mammals in the wild as harassment in a challenge brought by commercial eco-tourboat business that fed porpoises).

[38] 16 U.S.C. § 1375(b) (2012) ("Any person who knowingly violates any provision of this title or of any permit or regulation issued thereunder (except as provided in section 118) [related to taking of marine mammals incidental to commercial fishing operations] shall, upon conviction, be fined not more than $20,000 for each such violation, or imprisoned for not more than one year, or both.").

[39] 16 U.S.C. § 1385(e) (2012) ("Any person who knowingly and willfully makes a statement or endorsement described in subsection (d)(2)(B) [related to the dolphin protection and consumer information labels] that is false is liable for a civil penalty of not to exceed $100,000 assessed in an action brought in any appropriate district court of the United States on behalf of the Secretary.").

[40] 16 U.S.C. § 1376 (2012).

[41] Pub. L. No. 100-711, 102 Stat. 4755 (providing the Marine Mammal Protection Act Amendments of 1988).

[42] Marine Mammal Stock Assessment Reports (SARs) by Species/Stock, NOAA FISHERIES, http://www. nmfs.noaa.gov/pr/sars/species.htm (last visited Dec. 19, 2013) (providing NMFS stock assessments for each MMPA-protected species).

[43] 16 U.S.C. § 1386 (2012).

[44] 16 U.S.C. § 1387 (2012). *See also* Earth Island Inst. v. Brown, 865 F. Supp 1364 (N.D. Cal. 1994) (holding that although Congress, through the MMPA, allowed some incidental take of dolphins due to the Pacific tuna fishery (*see, e.g.*, 16 U.S.C. §§ 1374(h) and 1416(a) (2012), it did not authorize NMFS to allow take of depleted populations); Am. Tunaboat Ass'n v. Baldrige, 738 F.2d 1013, 1015 (9th Cir. 1984) ("The basic approach of the statute and regulations has been to impose yearly quotas on the taking of abundant porpoise species by tuna fishermen, and to prohibit the taking of any species deemed depleted.").

C. TAKE REDUCTION TEAMS AND THE AUTHORIZATION OF
INCIDENTAL TAKE

The 1994 MMPA Amendments required NMFS to achieve the ZMRG by 2001. That date came and went without NMFS meeting the ZMRG objective. Environmental advocacy litigation eventually led to a settlement agreement requiring NMFS to adopt relevant regulations and submit required reports to Congress.[45] NMFS regulations now provide for fisheries to be categorized as frequently (Category I), occasionally (Category II), or rarely (Category III) killing or injuring marine mammals. The first two categories trigger additional requirements, including the development of a "take reduction plan" to reduce marine mammal mortality and serious injury. The MMPA established lofty ambitions for these plans—they should achieve the potential biological removal rate within six months, and approach the zero rate within five years.[46] Take reduction plans include "recommended regulatory or voluntary measures for the reduction of incidental mortality and serious injury."[47] In addition, if the agency finds that a fishery is likely to have immediate and significant adverse effects on marine mammal species or stocks, it can adopt emergency regulations.[48]

Typically, take reduction plans are developed by teams that can include an array of federal, regional, state, academic, commercial, nonprofit, and tribal representatives.[49] These teams of experts have been assembled by NMFS for multiple whale and dolphin species,[50] but the process has its weaknesses. In an audit of NMFS take reduction planning, the U.S. Government Accountability Office (GAO) concluded that improvements were needed, noting that NMFS faces significant data limitations, failed to establish teams for marine mammals that met the statutory requirements, often had only limited success meeting statutory deadlines, and lacked a comprehensive strategy for evaluating the effectiveness of take reduction regulations.[51] NMFS officials also told GAO

---

[45] Ctr. for Biological Diversity v. National Marine Fisheries Serv., No. C-02-3901-SC (N.D. Cal. Apr. 30, 2003) (including the Stipulated Settlement Agreement).

[46] 16 U.S.C. §§ 1387(c) (2012) (establishing categories I, II, and III) and 1387(f) (describing criteria for take reduction plans).

[47] 16 U.S.C. § 1387(f)(4)(C) (2012).

[48] 16 U.S.C. § 1387(g) (2012).

[49] 16 U.S.C. § 1387(f)(6)(C) (2012) (describing requirements for and categories of take reduction team membership).

[50] Take Reduction Teams, NOAA FISHERIES, *available at* http://www.nmfs.noaa.gov/pr/interactions/trt/teams.htm (last visited Jan. 3, 2014) (discussing Atlantic Large Whale Take Reduction Team, Atlantic Offshore Cetacean Team, Atlantic Trawl Gear Team, Bottlenose Dolphin Team, False Killer Whale Team, Gulf of Maine Harbor Porpoise Team, Mid-Atlantic Harbor Porpoise Team, Mid-Atlantic Team, Pacific Offshore Cetacean Team, Pelagic Longline Team).

[51] U.S. Government Accountability Office, Improvements Are Needed in the Federal Process Used to Protect Marine Mammals from Commercial Fishing, GAO-09-78 (Dec. 2008) *available at* http://www.nmfs. noaa.gov/pr/pdfs/gao-09-78.pdf; *see, e.g., id.* at 1 (emphasizing that "Significant limitations in available data make it difficult for NMFS to accurately determine which marine mammal stocks meet the statutory

they were aware of the data limitations but lacked funding to implement their plans to improve the data.[52]

Take reduction plans, despite their data and funding limitations, help reduce take of marine mammals, and provide a form of authorization for some vessels to engage in otherwise legal activities that incidentally take marine mammals.[53] The MMPA, however, established a moratorium on *all* unapproved marine mammal take. To authorize the unintentional taking of even small numbers of marine mammals, FWS and NMFS developed regulations governing "small take" of marine mammals.[54] NMFS also created special categories of small takes for certain native Americans[55] and for state or local officials,[56] as well as special exceptions involving scientific research and enhancement,[57] and export of living marine mammals.[58]

In general, taking of small numbers of marine mammals may be allowed only if the agency finds, based on the best scientific evidence available, that "the total taking by the specified activity during the specified time period will have a negligible impact on species or stock of marine mammals and will not have an unmitigable adverse impact on the availability of those species or stocks of marine mammals intended for subsistence uses."[59] If the agency finds that the application meets this standard, then U.S. citizens may receive a "letter of authorization" from NMFS, allowing the incidental take or harassment of marine mammals. NMFS may also specify a period of validity or impose other conditions.[60] These types of "small take" authorizations have often been applied to matters involving ocean noise,[61] as well as the regulation of ocean energy exploration

---

requirements for establishing take reduction teams. For most stocks, NMFS relies on incomplete, outdated, or imprecise data on stocks' population size or mortality to calculate the extent of incidental take.").

[52] *Id.*

[53] *See, e.g.,* 16 U.S.C. § 1371 (5)(E)(i)(III) (2012) (providing that incidental take of marine mammals by vessels engaged in commercial fishing is allowed if the vessels are monitored and registered, and if a take reduction plan has been or is being developed for the species).

[54] 50 C.F.R. § 18.27 (2014) (providing FWS regulations governing small takes of marine mammals incidental to specified activities); 50 C.F.R. § 216.1 (2014) (providing the NMFS approval process governing small takes of marine mammals incidental to specified activities).

[55] 50 C.F.R. § 216.23 (2014) (relating to take of marine mammals by Indian, Aleut, or Eskimo people who reside on the coast of the North Pacific Ocean or the Arctic Ocean).

[56] 50 C.F.R. § 216.22 (2014) (relating to taking by state or local government officials, such as actions taken in the context of enforcement or salvage).

[57] 50 C.F.R. § 216.41 (2014) (providing for permits for scientific research and enhancement); § 216.45 (providing for General Authorization for Level B harassment for scientific research).

[58] 50 C.F.R. § 216.33(b) (2014) (providing for applications to export living marine mammals).

[59] 50 C.F.R. § 216.102 (2014) (specifying scope); 50 C.F.R. § 18.27 (2014) (providing parallel provisions).

[60] 50 C.F.R. § 216.102 (2014); 50 C.F.R. § 18.27 (2014).

[61] *See generally* Elena McCarthy & Flora Lichtman, *The Origin and Evolution of Ocean Noise Regulation under the U.S. Marine Mammal Protection Act*, 13 OCEAN & COASTAL L.J. 1 (2007).

and extraction,[62] an industry for which additional MMPA rulemaking by the Bureau of Ocean Energy Management is likely.[63]

D. PROTECTING SPECIES HABITAT

The take prohibition, and the regulations related to authorizing incidental and small takes, represents the primary and most powerful aspect of the MMPA's protective reach. Nevertheless, even though the MMPA does not provide explicit mechanisms for protecting species habitat, the statutory findings do acknowledge the "need to protect those geographic areas of significance for each species."[64] Individual letters authorizing take might focus on quantification of precise numbers of marine mammals that may be taken by an activity, or use qualitative process improvements that focus on modification or improvement of fisheries gear. Sometimes, however, achieving the MMPA's ambitions also requires consideration of habitat-oriented solutions.

For example, gear modifications, coupled with closures of some open-ocean areas, were adopted as part of the bottlenose dolphin take reduction plan for many East Coast fisheries.[65] The Gulf of Maine harbor porpoise take reduction team used similar measures.[66] Yet measures to protect marine mammal habitat reach beyond fisheries management.

Boat strikes present significant threats to populations of some species. The MMPA, therefore, led to new regulatory approaches that restricted places in which boats could travel. In Florida waters, for example, the manatee tends to congregate near warm water outfalls from power plants and in spring-fed watersheds, especially in cooler winter months.[67] Eventually, the demands of the MMPA (and the Endangered Species Act) led FWS to implement a series of rules creating Manatee Protection Areas where boating was slowed or eliminated to avoid incidental take.[68] The rules reflect the result of years of litigation, a settlement agreement, a court-ordered deadline, and thousands of public comments.[69]

---

[62] *See, e.g., Shell 2012 Exploration Plan—Chukchi Sea*, BUREAU OF OCEAN ENERGY MGMT., http://www.boem.gov/ShellChukchi2012/ (last visited Dec. 12, 2013).

[63] *See generally* 78 Fed. Reg. 27, 427-27, 430 (May 10, 2013) (discussing Bureau of Ocean Energy Management plans for Outer Continental Shelf Geological and Geophysical Exploration Activities in the Gulf of Mexico).

[64] 16 U.S.C. § 1361 (2012).

[65] *See, e.g.,* 71 Fed. Reg. 24,776 (Apr. 26, 2006); 73 Fed. Reg. 77,531 (Dec. 19, 2008).

[66] *See, e.g.,* 78 Fed. Reg. 61,821 (Oct. 4, 2013).

[67] David Laist & John E. Reynolds, *Florida Manatees, Warm-Water Refuges, and an Uncertain Future*, 33 COASTAL MGMT. 279, 280 (2005), *available at* http://www.mmc.gov/reports/publications/pdf/floridamanatees.pdf.

[68] *See, e.g., Federal Manatee Protection Areas, North Florida Ecological Services Office*, U.S. FISH & WILDLIFE SERV., http://www.fws.gov/northflorida/Manatee/federal-manatee-protection-areas.htm (last updated May 1, 2013) (listing the locations of manatee sanctuaries in Florida).

[69] Save the Manatee Club v. Ballard, 215 F. Supp. 2d 88 (D.D.C. 2002) (ordering the agency to publish a final rule for manatee refuges and sanctuaries in Florida by November 1, 2002, and finding that FWS failed to

Cetaceans have also been the beneficiaries of habitat-oriented regulatory approaches. When the MMPA was first passed, it was especially focused on the killing of whales, inspired by the Stockholm Convention and the international call for a ten-year moratorium on commercial whaling[70] (which is also addressed at an international level by the International Whaling Commission).[71] Another accomplishment of the MMPA benefiting whales was to create the Marine Mammal Stranding Network, a group of organizations working with the government agencies to rescue or humanely euthanize non-endangered marine mammals in severe distress.[72]

Through the years, the risk of direct and intentional take of whales by harpoon has been replaced with the risk of indirect and unintended take by ship strikes or sonar. Recent regulatory actions by NMFS reflect that shift, including the adoption of rules creating shipping corridors and speed limits to protect the North Atlantic right whale[73] and a comprehensive effort to develop similar protective measures for large whales off the California coast near the Channel Islands.[74] The measures can be especially effective, too: in the five-year period since the boating channel rules were adopted for right whales in Florida and Georgia waters, zero fatal takes have occurred due to ship strikes.[75]

---

adhere to the terms of a magistrate-approved and court-ordered settlement agreement). Thereafter, FWS adopted dozens of manatee protection areas through notice-and-comment rulemaking proceedings. *See* U.S. FISH & WILDLIFE SERV., *supra* note 68.

[70] UNITED NATIONS, REPORT OF THE UNITED NATIONS CONFERENCE ON THE HUMAN ENV'T at 3 (1972), *available at* http://www.un-documents.net/aconf48-14r1.pdf; *see also* A. W. Harris, *The Best Scientific Evidence Available: The Whaling Moratorium and Divergent Interpretations of Science*, 29 WM. & MARY ENVTL. L. & POL'Y REV. 375 (2005), *available at* http://scholarship.law.wm.edu/wmelpr/vol29/iss2/4.

[71] *See generally* William C. G. Burns, *From the Harpoon to the Heat: Climate Change and the International Whaling Commission in the 21st Century*, PACIFIC INST. FOR STUDIES IN DEV., ENV'T & SEC. 4, 20 (2000), http://www.pacinst.org/press_center/IWCOP.pdf (emphasizing that even though the International Whaling Commission (IWC) recognized the threats of climate change for cetaceans, the research needs were significant, and the funding remained insufficient, well demonstrated by the fact that the parties to the IWC allocated less than $200,000 at the 50th IWC meeting to address the impact of eight major environmental threats to cetaceans, including climate change).

[72] 16 U.S.C. § 1421(a)–(h) (2012). *See also Office of Protected Resources*, NOAA FISHERIES, http://www.nmfs.noaa.gov/pr/health/networks.htm (last updated Feb. 12, 2014) (providing a listing of network members by NOAA Fisheries).

[73] Final Rule to Implement Speed Restrictions to Reduce the Threat of Ship Collisions with North Atlantic Right Whales, 73 Fed. Reg. 60173–60191 (Oct. 10, 2008), *available at* http://www.nmfs.noaa.gov/pr/pdfs/fr/fr73-60173.pdf; Final Rule to Remove the Sunset Provision of the Final Rule Implementing Vessel Speed Restrictions to Reduce the Threat of Ship Collisions with North Atlantic Right Whales, 78 Fed. Reg. 73,726 (Dec. 9, 2013), *available at* http://www.gpo.gov/fdsys/pkg/FR-2013-12-09/pdf/2013-29355.pdf.

[74] Letter from David M. Kennedy, Assistant Adm'r for Ocean Services & Coastal Zone Mgmt, to Linda Krop, Chief Counsel, Envtl Def. Ctr., NOAA FISHERIES (Mar. 30, 2012) *available at* http://cordellbank.noaa.gov/protect/petition_shipstrike_response_2012.pdf.

[75] Orlando Montoya, *Federal Officials Enforce Ship Speed Limits to Protect Endangered Whales*, GPB NEWS (Dec. 27, 2013, 11:00 AM), *available at* http://www.gpb.org/news/2013/12/27/federal-officials-enforce-ship-speed-limits-to-protect-endangered-whales.

E. NUISANCES AND INTERSPECIES DISPUTES

Demonstrating the law of unintended consequences, the MMPA's powerful take prohibition is sometimes perceived as offering *too much* protection for marine mammals. When a Pacific fishermen fired rifle shots into the waters, purportedly to scare off the dolphins trying to steal the tuna on his lines, it led to years of litigation. The result was an important U.S. Court of Appeals decision interpreting the meaning of MMPA harassment, holding that "reasonable actions...not resulting in severe disruptions of the mammal's normal routine...are not rendered criminal by the MMPA or its regulations."[76] Congress, responding to the matter, further redefined the term "harassment" to its current state.[77]

Elsewhere, at the Ballard Locks in Seattle, Washington, seals and sea lions have been known to congregate and engage in lazy predation of prized and sometimes endangered steelhead and salmon species as they try to swim by. Again, the MMPA's protections created troublesome policy dilemmas, and it took controversial regulatory action by the federal agencies to authorize take of these nuisance animals to stem the predation. Agency control efforts focused on non-lethal deterrence at first, and then translocation, but eventually resorted to lethal removal.[78] The controversy triggered years of litigation. Ultimately, the federal appellate court upheld the lethal takings policy. NMFS found that the marine mammals had "significant negative impact" on salmonid species, and the Court was further comforted by NMFS's commitment to reconsider the data after five years.[79]

F. SOUND AND SONAR CONFLICTS WITH MARINE MAMMALS

Sound can dramatically affect marine mammals, even causing mass strandings, because marine mammals use their sense of hearing to orient themselves in space and to navigate through their environment.[80] In a joint agency report, NMFS and the Marine Mammal Commission recognized that the effects of noise on marine mammals are uncertain, and that the "extent of research required to address the environmental consequences of

---

[76] United States. v. Hayashi, 22 F.3d 859, 866 (9th Cir. 1993) (reversing magistrate's MMPA-based conviction and finding insufficient evidence of "harassment" because the species were engaged in nonnatural behavior).

[77] After *Hayashi*, Congress amended the MMPA definition of "harassment" to the version codified in 16 U.S.C. § 1362(18)(A) (2012).

[78] *See generally* Nina M. Young, *At Point Blank Range: The Genesis and Implementation of Lethal Removal Provisions under the Marine Mammal Protection Act*, 5 OCEAN & COASTAL L.J. 1, 22 (2000).

[79] Humane Soc'y of United States v. Locke, 626 F.3d 1040, 1048 (9th Cir. 2010) (holding that the NMFS's decision to allow Oregon, Washington, and Idaho to kill certain California sea lions was arbitrary, capricious, and an abuse of discretion); Humane Soc'y of United States v. Pritzker, 2013 WL 5405317, *2 (9th Cir. 2013) (upholding NMFS's new explanation).

[80] NOAA Fisheries, *Blinded by the Noise—Whales and Dolphins in a Noisy Ocean* (Sept. 3, 2013), *available at* http://www.fisheries.noaa.gov/podcasts/2013/09/blinded_noise.html#.UsGlKNJDstE.

anthropogenic marine sound can seem overwhelming."[81] Nevertheless, to better understand the effects of noise, both acute and cumulative, the report made a series of recommendations to direct coordinated federal agency effort on the highest priorities.[82] Implementing one small component of the report's many recommendations, NMFS proposed guidance in 2013 to better evaluate the temporary and permanent effects of anthropogenic sound on marine mammal species.[83]

The reach of the MMPA to regulate sound has proven especially inconvenient for the U.S. military. While the MMPA contains an exemption from the takings prohibition for actions necessary for national defense,[84] the statute still creates limitations for military readiness activities, and the effect of Navy sonar on marine mammals has been controversial.[85] When multi-nation submarine and naval vessel training exercises were stopped because of disputes with the environmental community related to the harm caused by sonar to marine mammals, it led to actions by the White House,[86] U.S. Supreme Court,[87] and Congress.[88] NMFS eventually adopted regulations creating a letter authorization program.[89] Using a process similar to small takes, NMFS can authorize incidental take

---

[81] B. Southall et al., Addressing the Effects of Human-Generated Sound on Marine Life: An Integrated Research Plan for U.S. Federal Agencies, Interagency Task Force on Anthropogenic Sound and the Marine Environment of the Joint Subcommittee on Ocean Science and Technology 7 (2009), *available at* http://www.nmfs.noaa.gov/pr/pdfs/acoustics/jsost2009.pdf.

[82] *Id.* at 7–10.

[83] NOAA Fisheries, Draft Guidance for Assessing the Effects of Anthropogenic Sound on Marine Mammals— Acoustic Threshold Levels for Onset of Permanent and Temporary Threshold Shifts, 78 Fed. Reg. 78,822 (Dec. 27, 2013).

[84] 16 U.S.C. § 1371(f) (2012) (exempting of actions necessary for national defense).

[85] *See, e.g.,* KRISTINA ALEXANDER, CONG. RESEARCH SERV., RL34403, WHALES AND SONAR: ENVIRONMENTAL EXEMPTIONS FOR THE NAVY'S MID-FREQUENCY ACTIVE SONAR TRAINING (2009).

[86] *See* Winter v. Natural Resources Def. Council, 555 U.S. 7 (2008). The Council on Environmental Quality (CEQ), an advisory body within the Executive Office of the President charged with overseeing the National Environmental Policy Act (NEPA), concluded that the suspension of naval training constituted "emergency circumstances" under 40 C.F.R. § 1506.1133 (2012), and CEQ created "alternative arrangements" so that the Navy could comply with NEPA.

[87] *See id.* In *Winter*, a case involving the Coastal Zone Management Act, ESA, and NEPA, the Supreme Court reversed injunctions applied by the lower courts, stressing that preliminary injunctions are an extraordinary remedy rather than a right, emphasizing the need for deference to the professional judgment of military authorities, and applying a public interest test to find environmental interests "plainly outweighed" by the Navy's need for realistic training exercises. *Id.* at 367.

[88] *See, e.g., News Release: National Defense Exemption to MMPA Authorized for Navy,* U.S. DEP'T OF DEF., http://www.defense.gov/releases/release.aspx?releaseid=9706 (June 30, 2006) (discussing Department of Defense's six-month national defense exemption from the MMPA for naval training activity involving mid-frequency active sonar use as part of the National Defense Authorization Act of Fiscal Year 2004).

[89] *See* Taking Marine Mammals Incidental to U.S. Navy Operations of Surveillance Towed Array Sensor System Low Frequency Active Sonar, 77 Fed. Reg. 50,290 (Aug. 20, 2012); Takes of Marine Mammals Incidental to Specified Activities; U.S. Navy Training and Testing Activities in the Atlantic Fleet Training and Testing Study Area; Final Rule, 78 Fed. Reg. 73,010 (Dec. 4, 2013).

of marine mammals resulting from military naval exercises.[90] Litigation over the military taking of marine mammals and the use of the letter of authorization program continues.[91]

III. Future: How Climate Change Will Change the MMPA

The past is not necessarily a predictor of the future. Although management of environmental issues has long been based on data-intensive assessments of conditions within a range of possible outcomes, the upper and lower limits of the past might no longer apply in a future with rising, warmer, and more acidic oceans, and fundamentally altered estuarine environments. Even the fundamental assumptions of MMPA implementation—for example, the notion that modest rates of incidental mortality of marine mammals can be deemed insignificant for purposes of the ZMRG—might be called into question. Scholars studying water management have referred to this new reality as "the death of stationarity."[92] Climate change now presents the likelihood of substantial changes for marine ecosystems, marine mammal populations, and the MMPA, a point the Marine Mammal Commission made clear in its Climate Change Adaptation Policy:

> Climate disruption poses many challenges to marine mammals and their conservation. It is a driving force in the loss of polar bear sea ice that is now and will continue to have profound effects on the Arctic and Antarctic marine ecosystems. It is leading and will continue to lead to acidification of the world's oceans, a phenomenon that may fundamentally disrupt the base of oceanic food webs with severe ecological consequences. It is causing, and will continue to cause, the melting of land-bound glaciers, which is raising and will continue to raise sea levels with

---

[90] *See, e.g.,* 50 C.F.R. § 218.238 (2014). *See generally* 50 C.F.R. pt. N (2014) (Taking of Marine Mammals Incidental to Missile Launch Activities from San Nicolas Island, CA), pt. P (Taking of Marine Mammals Incidental to U.S. Navy Training in the Hawaii Range Complex), pt. Q (Taking of Marine Mammals Incidental to Navy Operations of Surveillance Towed Array Sensor System Low Frequency Active (SURTASS LFA sonar)) (creating process for military to implement mitigation, monitoring, and reporting requirements, and allowing agency to determine that the take will have no more than a negligible impact on the affected marine mammals).

[91] *See, e.g.,* NRDC v. Pritzker, 2014 WL 1211556 (N.D. Cal. Mar. 28, 2014)(generally upholding the Supplemental Overseas Environmental Impact Statement analyzing the potential impact of the U.S. Navy's Surveillance Towed Array Sensor System Low Frequency Active (SURTASS LFA) sonar, but requiring the Navy to use the best available data from the 2010 Pacific Stock Assessment Report to analyze the potential impact of SURTASS LFA sonar on the individual stocks within the Hawaiian Islands Stock Complex of common bottlenose dolphins); *see generally* Randall S. Abate, *NEPA, National Security, and Ocean Noise: The Past, Present, and Future of Regulating the Impact of Navy Sonar on Marine Mammals,* 13 J. INT'L WILDLIFE L. & POL'Y 326 (2010).

[92] *See, e.g.,* P. C. D. Milly et al., *Stationarity Is Dead: Whither Water Management?* 319 SCI. 573 (2008), *available at* http://www.sciencemag.org/content/319/5863/573.short; Robin K. Craig, *Stationarity Is Dead—Long Live Transformation: Five Principles for Climate Change Adaptation Law,* 34 HARV. ENVTL. L. REV. 9 (2010).

potentially severe effects on coastal ecosystems. And it is now altering and will continue to alter weather patterns, leading to increased variability and/or severity of weather events such as hurricanes, tornadoes, drought, floods and temperature anomalies. Some marine mammal species are expected to adapt successfully to climate disruption and, indeed, may benefit from it. However, many others may not be able to adapt.[93]

A. INSIGHTS FROM SEA-ICE-DEPENDENT SPECIES

The tension between climate change and the MMPA is not a new topic. In fact, when the western Alaskan population of Steller sea lions declined precipitously in the 1970s, causing fishery restrictions, it triggered substantial controversy.[94] But in 1998, NMFS issued a Biological Opinion (BiOp) finding that commercial fisheries were likely to jeopardize the Steller sea lion (listed by then as a threatened species) because the fishery depleted localized sea lion prey. Waves of litigation and research followed. Ted Stevens, the then—U.S. senator for Alaska, argued that changing environmental conditions, not the fishery, were the cause, and his "Stevens' Rider" in the 2001 appropriations made sea lion research a national priority.[95] NOAA still considers climate change to be one of many factors affecting the species, making the decision-making process highly data-dependent.[96]

The dispute over fishery management and sea lion protection followed a familiar pattern. Controversial agency decisions related to commercial fishery regulation[97] or the

---

[93] *Climate Change Adaption Policy*, MARINE MAMMAL COMM'N (Jun. 19, 2012), http://mmc.gov/reports/administrative/pdf/cca_policy.pdf; *see also* Jennifer A. Learmonth et al., *Potential Effects of Climate Change on Marine Mammals*, 44 OCEANOGRAPHY & MARINE BIOLOGY: AN ANNUAL REV. 431 (2006).

[94] *See generally* NOAA Technical Memorandum from R.C. Ferrero et al., Sea Lion Research and Coordination: A Brief History and Summary of Recent Progress, ALASKA FISHERIES SCIENCE CTR. (June 2002), *available at* http://www.afsc.noaa.gov/Publications/AFSC-TM/NOAA-TM-AFSC-129.pdf; *see also* Beth C. Bryant, *Adapting to Uncertainty: Law, Science, and Management in the Steller Sea Lion Controversy*, 28 STAN. ENVTL. L.J. 171, 205 (2009).

[95] *See Steller Sea Lion Coordinated Research Program*, ALASKA FISHERIES SCI. CTR., http://www.afsc.noaa.gov/archives/stellers/coordinatedresearch.htm (last visited Dec. 12, 2013) (providing that Fiscal Year 2001 appropriations legislation included conference report H.R.106-1033 (on H.R. 4577)). Sections 206 and 209 are specifically relevant to Steller sea lion research funding, requiring research on predator/prey relationships as they relate to the decline of the western population of Steller sea lions, and further requiring a "coordinated, comprehensive research and recovery program for the Steller sea lion" to study, among other topics, "regime shift, climate change, and other impacts associated with changing environmental conditions in the North Pacific and Bering Sea." *Id.*

[96] *See, e.g., Steller Sea Lions NMML Research—Population Decline*, National Marine Mammal Laboratory, NOAA FISHERIES, http://www.afsc.noaa.gov/nmml/alaska/sslhome/decline.php (last visited Dec. 12, 2013).

[97] *See, e.g.*, NMFS v. Greenpeace, No. C98-0492Z (W.D. Wash. 2003) (including the joint stipulation for entry of agreed order and judgment); *see also* Taking of Threatened or Endangered Marine Mammals Incidental to Commercial Fishing Operations, 75 Fed. Reg. 81,972 (Dec. 29, 2010).

authorization of incidental take for research[98] are routinely litigated and settled, or otherwise subjected to additional scientific scrutiny. But the era of climate change presents new challenges. An ocean full of species faces the threat from climate change, so funding may not be available to develop the type of robust data system that has helped NMFS in its efforts to protect sea lions. In fact, as the Marine Mammal Commission emphasized, climate change, and its impact on habitats, especially sea ice, presents a direct threat to the survival of many marine mammal species.

Polar bears represent the signature species affected by climate-change-related policy changes. FWS listed the species as threatened with extinction pursuant to the Endangered Species Act, finding that the changing climate caused extensive recession of sea ice habitat, reduced availability of ice seals and prey, and allowed for fewer denning and feeding opportunities.[99] That conclusion, in turn, means that polar bears are also considered a depleted stock for purposes of the MMPA.[100] In the coming years, this type of analysis projecting declining sea ice and foreseeable species decline will probably be applied to many other species—including beluga whales, whose uncertain status led NMFS to deny an importation and display permit to the Georgia Aquarium.[101]

In 2000, the Marine Mammal Commission issued a substantial report discussing the vast range of already-occurring effects of climate change on marine mammals in the

---

[98] *See, e.g.*, Memorandum Opinion, Humane Society of the United States v. Dep't of Commerce, Civil Action No. 05-1392 (Esh) (D.D.C. May 26, 2006), *available at* http://alaskafisheries.noaa.gov/protectedresources/stellers/litigation/researchopinion52506.pdf; *see also Environmental Impact Statement for Steller Sea Lion and Northern Fur Seal Research, NOAA Office of Protected Resources,* NOAA FISHERIES, http://www.nmfs.noaa.gov/pr/permits/eis/steller.htm (last visited Dec. 12, 2013) (including links to relevant agency documents authorizing take of sea lions).

[99] U.S. Fish & Wildlife Service, Determination of Threatened Status for the Polar Bear (*Ursus maritimus*) Throughout Its Range, 73 Fed. Reg. 28,212 (May 15, 2008); *In re* Polar Bear Endangered Species Act Listing & Section 4(d) Rule Litig., 709 F.3d 1, 8 (D.C. Cir. 2013) ("The Listing Rule rests on a three-part thesis: the polar bear is dependent on sea ice for its survival; sea ice is declining; and climate changes have and will continue to dramatically reduce the extent and quality of Arctic sea ice to a degree sufficiently grave to jeopardize polar bear populations....No part of this thesis is disputed and we find that FWS's conclusion—that the polar bear is threatened within the meaning of the ESA—is reasonable and adequately supported by the record.")

[100] *See generally In re Polar Bear Endangered Species Act Listing & Section 4(d) Rule Litig., supra* note 99, at 1 (upholding FWS conclusion that the MMPA absolutely prohibited the issuance of hunting trophy import permits for polar bears). FWS also issued a special rule concluding that the polar bear did *not* require protection under the taking prohibition of the ESA because the MMPA already applied. Special Rule for the Polar Bear under Section 4(d) of the Endangered Species Act, 78 Fed. Reg. 11,766 (Feb. 20, 2013).

[101] *See Georgia Aquarium Application to Import 18 Beluga Whales (File No. 17324),* NOAA FISHERIES, *available at* http://www.nmfs.noaa.gov/pr/permits/georgia_aquarium_belugas.htm (last updated Aug. 6, 2013); 16 U.S.C. § 1374(a) (2012); letter from Donna S. Wieting, Dir., Office of Protected Res., to Billy Hurley, Georgia Aquarium, National Marine Fisheries Serv. (Aug. 5, 2013). Although the MMPA includes an exception allowing for public display, 16 U.S.C. § 1374(a) (2012); 50 C.F.R. §§ 216.12, 216.33–35 (2014), NMFS concluded that the aquarium's permit application had not met standards, in part because climate change made the status of the species uncertain. *Georgia Aquarium Application, supra.*

Arctic.[102] Existing data suggested changes in species timing, health and abundance, an increase in unusual species sightings, and a decrease in fish and benthic organisms.[103] Observed ecosystem changes were documented, too, including changes in ice locations, movements, depths and patterns, beach erosion, a warmer tundra, and unpredictable weather changes.[104] The report predicted that these changes would affect the human community as well, causing changes in shipping routes; increased access to and decreased extraction costs for offshore and land-based mineral resources, including ores and fossil fuels; larger port facilities; and fundamental cultural changes for local and subsistence-based communities.[105]

B. THE LIMITATIONS OF DATA, FUNDING, AND RESEARCH IN TIMES OF UNCERTAINTY

As demonstrated by history, MMPA implementation often depends on the availability of adequate information to assess the trends of and effects on marine mammal stocks. In a 2003 report, the Marine Mammal Commission offered a vision of the future, emphasizing information needs associated with protecting marine mammals in a climate-changed world.[106] The report identified traditional data needs related to fisheries, acoustics, ship strikes, and other human interactions, but also described other areas affected by climate change, such as disease, contaminants, and harmful algal blooms, or habitat transformation and long-term environmental change.[107] Other Marine Mammal Commission reports have also called for improved climate change data to better understand resource management needs related to the Antarctic toothfish,[108] the BP oil spill in the Gulf of Mexico,[109] and the

---

[102] HENRY HUNTINGTON ET AL., IMPACTS OF CHANGES IN SEA ICE AND OTHER ENVIRONMENTAL PARAMETERS IN THE ARCTIC, FINAL REPORT OF THE MARINE MAMMAL COMM'N WORKSHOP GIRDWOOD, ALASKA (Aug. 2000), *available at* http://www.mmc.gov/reports/workshop/pdf/seaicefinal.pdf.

[103] *Id.* at 22–23.

[104] *Id.* at 18–24.

[105] *Id.* at 21.

[106] RANDALL R. REEVES & TIMOTHY J. RAGEN, FUTURE DIRECTIONS IN MARINE MAMMAL RESEARCH, MARINE MAMMAL COMM'N (Aug. 4–7, 2003), *available at* http://www.mmc.gov/reports/workshop/pdf/futuredirectionsreport.pdf.

[107] *See id.* at 8.

[108] *Workshop to Identify Significant Uncertainties concerning the Effects of Climate Change and the Antarctic Toothfish Fishery on the Ross Sea Marine Ecosystem*, HT HARVEY & ASSOC. (Mar. 2012), *available at* http://mmc.gov/reports/workshop/pdf/RossSea_workshop_rpt_091212.pdf.

[109] *Assessing the Long-Term Effects of the BP Deepwater Horizon Oil Spill on Marine Mammals in the Gulf of Mexico: A Statement of Research Needs*, MARINE MAMMAL COMM'N (Aug. 2011), *available at* http://www.mmc.gov/reports/workshop/pdf/longterm_effects_bp_oilspill.pdf ("spill effects may be confounded by the effects of other risk factors such as climate change, fisheries, commercial shipping, military activities, and coastal development").

assessments of marine mammal population viability.[110] Funding all of this research, however, may prove unlikely, because NOAA, like other federal agencies, faces tough choices of how best to balance science, service, and stewardship priorities entrusted to the agency, while at the same time living within its means.[111]

The history discussed above also shows that the combination of research and data has empowered NMFS to adhere to the MMPA by implementing species-specific management decisions based on scientifically supported estimates of the amount of sustainable take. In most of the examples discussed in this chapter—regulating fisheries by calculating PBR, authorizing incidental take through take reduction planning, protecting known corridors and habitats, minimizing and mitigating harms from nuisances or sonar—agency decisions were based on studies, monitoring, and a careful process. But it is no simple task to distinguish between natural and human-induced mortality, and climate change could make precise calculations increasingly uncertain.

Notably, NMFS scientists have already recognized the fundamental tension between data-based management and the uncertainties of climate change. Agency personnel need to conduct initial research to decide which species are vulnerable enough to require further research. In fisheries management, for example, the Fish Stock Climate Vulnerability Assessment methodology is designed to help identify vulnerable stocks, identify additional information needed for stock risk assessments, provide decision tools to consider potentially available actions, and identify other information needs that can be used to help prioritize research, monitoring, and modeling efforts.[112] Similar efforts to assess the effects of climate change on endangered and threatened species were previously undertaken by the U.S. Environmental Protection Agency.[113] To ensure that sufficient information exists to comply with the MMPA's take prohibitions and demands for precisely calculated incidental mortality, a parallel assessment of risks and information needs is needed for marine mammal stocks, too. Otherwise, in the absence of improved information and in the face of climate-based uncertainty, the MMPA's moratorium on take could, in theory, absolutely prohibit human actions that adversely affect marine mammals, even when other causes are contributing factors.

---

[110] REPORT OF THE WORKSHOP ON ASSESSING THE POPULATION VIABILITY OF ENDANGERED MARINE MAMMALS IN U.S. WATERS, MARINE MAMMAL COMM'N (Sept. 2005), *available at* http://www.mmc. gov/reports/workshop/pdf/pvareport.pdf (discussing data needs for right whales, killer whales, beluga whales, Florida manatees, Hawaiian monk seals, Steller sea lions, and California sea lions).

[111] Statement from Dr. Jane Lubchenco on NOAA's FY 2013 Budget Request (Feb. 13, 2012), *available at* http://www.noaanews.noaa.gov/stories2012/20120213_budget_statement.html (last visited Feb. 2, 2014).

[112] *Assessing the Vulnerability of Fish Stocks in a Changing Climate*, NOAA OFFICE OF SCIENCE AND TECHNOLOGY, *available at* http://www.st.nmfs.noaa.gov/ecosystems/climate/activities/assessing-vulnerability-of-fish-stocks (last visited Apr. 24, 2014).

[113] A Framework for Categorizing the Relative Vulnerability of Threatened and Endangered Species to Climate Change, 74 Fed. Reg. 61671–61673 (Nov. 25, 2009).

C. POLICY, DISCRETION, AND THE LACK OF THE CITIZEN ATTORNEY GENERAL

Idealistic theory, however, may quickly yield to policy pragmatism. Despite its rigorous and restrictive moratorium on take of marine mammals, the MMPA is just one of many laws guiding the decisions made by the agency's technical experts. Our nation cannot afford vast new research programs for each individual marine mammal species, so the unique lessons learned from past experiences, often involving management decisions based on improved data, may have only limited applicability.

Agencies will be forced to make decisions anyway. Despite uncertain information and unprecedented declines in marine mammal species or ecosystems, pressure for the regulators to act, or to authorize someone else to act, will remain. For example, in 2011, NMFS faced a decision as to whether to authorize harassment impacts on Cook Inlet beluga whales resulting from use of airguns and other seismic equipment to obtain bathymetry data for a 3D survey of Cook Inlet, Alaska. Reviewing existing data showing already-declining trends, the Marine Mammal Commission conservatively recommended that the decision be deferred until more information was available.[114] NMFS disagreed, authorizing the activity by concluding that any take that would occur would have negligible impact on the species.[115] The contrast in policy choices by NMFS is striking: an aquarium request for a permit to obtain beluga whales for public display was denied, but a request for seismic exploration harassing the species was granted.

The adoption of the National Ocean Policy makes it even more likely that human activities that impact marine mammals will be pursued, even when they adversely affect marine mammals. As made clear by Executive Order 13,547, the oceans serve multiple purposes, providing jobs, food, energy resources, ecological services, recreation, and tourism opportunities, and playing critical roles in transportation, the economy, and the global mobility of the U.S. armed forces.[116] Notably, in the National Ocean Policy Implementation Plan, the lone reference to marine mammals or the MMPA was one emphasizing the need to obtain better information so that "offshore development

---

[114] Letter from Timothy J. Ragen, Exec. Dir., Marine Mammal Comm'n, to P. Michael Payne, Chief, Permits Division, Nat'l Marine Fisheries Serv., Office of Protected Res. (Oct. 21, 2011) at 4, *available at* http://mmc.gov/letters/pdf/2011/nmfs_aci_survey_12111.pdf.

[115] 77 Fed. Reg. 27,720, 27,728 (May 11, 2012) ("To date, there is no evidence that serious injury, death, or stranding by marine mammals can occur from exposure to airgun pulses, even in the case of large airgun arrays."); 77 Fed. Reg. 27,734 (May 11, 2012) ("Given the required mitigation and related monitoring, no injuries or mortalities are anticipated to occur…and none are proposed to be authorized.").

[116] Exec. Order No. 13,547, Stewardship of the Ocean, Our Coasts, and the Great Lakes (July 19, 2010).

activities important to the region" could continue.[117] A focus on coastal and ocean energy decisions, however, may continue to put marine mammals at risk.[118]

Indeed, the example of the beluga whales shows that despite the strict language of the MMPA, and even though climate change presents unknown risks for ocean ecosystems and marine mammals, the extent to which the MMPA will restrict federal agency or individual actions still depends on executive branch discretion.

Federal agencies usually have discretion to decide whether to pursue enforcement actions. To implement the MMPA, NMFS relies on MMPA policies that distinguish between serious and non-serious injuries to marine mammals,[119] and can conclude that some actions, even if they take or harass marine mammals, do not rise to a level requiring civil actions or criminal punishment. The exercise of this type of prosecutorial discretion pursuant to the MMPA is generally unreviewable in the courts.[120] Moreover, unlike the Endangered Species Act, the MMPA does not contain a citizen suit provision entitling individuals to pursue private causes of action against others who allegedly violate the MMPA's prohibitions, a point that the U.S. Department of Justice has emphasized to the U.S. Supreme Court in related amici briefs.[121] In the context of the MMPA, therefore, agency discretion is especially high.

Some agency decisions may still be subject to judicial review based on the MMPA and the Federal Administrative Procedure Act through a claim that an agency decision is "arbitrary, capricious, an abuse of discretion, or otherwise not in accordance with law."[122] But the ultimate effects of climate change on MMPA implementation will depend on

---

[117] National Ocean Council, National Ocean Policy Implementation Plan 23 (July 2013) ("Examples of potential focus areas for marine planning could include...Identifying and developing information that better informs agency or government-to-government consultations under the Endangered Species Act, Marine Mammal Protection Act, and the National Environmental Policy Act that apply to offshore development activities important to the region"), *available at* http://www.whitehouse.gov/sites/default/files/national_ocean_policy_implementation_plan.pdf.

[118] For example, the Fukushima nuclear disaster in Japan may have unexpected radioactivity effects on tuna; *see* Marisa Corley, *Fukushima Radiation Hits US West Coast* (Dec. 28, 2013), *available at* http://guardianlv.com/2013/12/fukushima-radiation-hits-us-west-coast/; and the BP gulf oil spill has adversely affected dolphins; *see* VN Sreeja, *US Government-Backed Study Links Increased Dolphin Sickness in Gulf of Mexico to BP's Deepwater Horizon Accident; BP Disputes Findings* (Dec. 19, 2013), *available at* http://www.ibtimes.com/us-government-backed-study-links-increased-dolphin-sickness-gulf-mexico-bps-deepwater-horizon.

[119] *Process for Distinguishing Serious from Non-serious Injury of Marine Mammals*, NOAA FISHERIES (Jan. 13, 2012), http://www.nmfs.noaa.gov/pr/pdfs/serious_injury_policy.pdf.

[120] Heckler v. Chaney, 470 U.S. 821, 822 (1985) ("the presumption that agency decisions not to institute proceedings are unreviewable under 5 U.S.C. § 701(a)(2) [the Federal Administrative Procedure Act] is not overcome by the enforcement provisions of the [Food, Drug & Cosmetic Act]"), *cited in* Strahan v. Linnon, 967 F. Supp. 581 (1997). In *Heckler v. Chaney*, the Court held that plaintiff could not compel an enforcement action because the ESA and the MMPA "do not contain the detailed language necessary to remove the enforcement decision from absolute prosecutorial discretion."

[121] Brief for the United States as Amicus Curiae, Coates v. Strahan, 525 U.S. 978 (1998) (No. 97-1485), *available at* http://www.justice.gov/osg/briefs/1998/2pet/6invit/97-1485.ami.pet.inv.pdf.

[122] 5 U.S.C. § 706(2)(A) (2012); *see also* City of Sausalito v. O'Neill, 386 F.3d 1186, 1205 (9th Cir. 2004) ("Because the statutes...do not contain separate provisions for judicial review, our review is governed by the APA.").

the federal agency's exercise of policy discretion, and whether those decisions are properly challenged by interested persons,[123] whether the agency adequately explains its decision,[124] and the degree to which the courts afford special deference to the agency's expertise.[125]

Conclusion

The precautionary principle lies at the very heart of the MMPA, as the House Merchant Marine Committee made clear during the 1971 debate over the legislation:

> [I]t seems elementary common sense to the Committee that legislation should be adopted to require that we act conservatively—that no steps should be taken regarding these animals that might prove to be adverse or even irreversible in their effects until more is known.[126]

By creating a moratorium on take, and by prohibiting take of marine mammals unless otherwise expressly permitted, Congress manifested its bias in favor of species conservation and data-driven decision-making.[127]

---

[123] Animal Welfare Institute v. Kreps, 561 F.2d 1002 (D.C. Cir. 1977) (finding that environmental organization's claim of standing to challenge MMPA decision "has a firm statutory foundation"); *but see* Michelle A. Doyle, *CEASE vs. New England Aquarium: Standing to Challenge Marine Mammal Permits*, 2 OCEAN & COASTAL L.J. 189 (1996).

[124] *See* Lands Council v. McNair, 537 F.3d 981, 987 (9th Cir. 2008); Baltimore Gas & Elec. Co. v. Natural Resources Def. Council, Inc., 462 U.S. 87, 105 (1983). An agency's decision is arbitrary and capricious "only if the agency relied on factors Congress did not intend it to consider, entirely failed to consider an important aspect of the problem, or offered an explanation that runs counter to the evidence before the agency or is so implausible that it could not be ascribed to a difference in view or the product of agency expertise." *Lands Council*, 537 F.3d at 987 (*en banc*) (internal quotations omitted). *See also Baltimore Gas & Elec. Co.*, 462 U.S. at 105 (noting that if the agency "considered the relevant factors and articulated a rational connection between the facts found and the choice made," the court must uphold the agency action).

[125] *See Baltimore Gas & Elec. Co.*, 462 U.S. at 103 (noting that a court generally must be "at its most deferential" when reviewing scientific judgments and technical analyses within the agency's expertise.); Marsh v. Or. Natural Resources Council, 490 U.S. 360, 378 (1989) ("When specialists express conflicting views, an agency must have discretion to rely on the reasonable opinions of its own qualified experts even if, as an original matter, a court might find contrary views more persuasive."); *Lands Council*, 537 F.3d at 988, 993 (a court should not "act as a panel of scientists that...chooses among scientific studies..." and should "conduct a 'particularly deferential review' of an 'agency's predictive judgments...as long as they are reasonable.'") (quoting Earthlink, Inc. v. FCC, 462 F.3d 1, 12 (D.C. Cir. 2006)).

[126] H.R. REP. No. 92-707, at 15 (1971).

[127] Comm. for Humane Legislation v. Richardson, 414 F. Supp. 297, n.24, n.29 (D.D.C. 1976) (noting that the MMPA is "to proceed knowledgably and cautiously" for the benefit of protecting marine mammals "and not for the benefit of commercial exploitation"); Kokechik Fishermen's Assoc'n v. Sec'y of Commerce, 839 F.2d 795, 802 (D.C. Cir. 1988) ("the interest in maintaining health populations of marine mammals comes first.").

The MMPA had some success managing direct take or harassment of marine mammals, but has been less effective with indirect effects on marine mammals.[128] NMFS has been quite open in acknowledging that it lacks sufficient data and financial resources to comply with the statute.[129] With new unknowns, and new species facing problems in a climate-changed future, the inadequacies of data and funding to support MMPA implementation will be exacerbated. In response, agencies will be forced to establish priorities.[130] Inevitably, some marine mammals will receive more protection than others.

The continued existence of the MMPA and the marine mammals it protects, and any hope of the MMPA remaining relevant in a climate-changed future, depends on the political will of the nation to make compromises and sacrifices for the benefit of marine mammals. While environmental advocacy groups may find the MMPA a useful litigation tool in efforts to shape future ocean policy, it is also likely that future litigation, and budgetary realities, will lead to statutory reform of the MMPA.[131] To paraphrase Herman Melville, whether the herds of creatures in the oceans, as they flee from climate change, will suffer the same fate as the bison of the prairies, depends largely upon the madness of men.[132]

---

[128] Joe Roman et al., *The Marine Mammal Protection Act at 40: Status, Recovery, and Future of U.S. Marine Mammals*, ANN. N.Y. ACAD. SCI. 1 (2013), *available at* http://www.uvm.edu/giee/pubpdfs/Roman_2013_Annals_of_the_NYAS.pdf.

[129] U.S. Government Accountability Organization, Improvements Are Needed in the Federal Process Used to Protect Marine Mammals from Commercial Fishing, GAO-09-78 (Dec. 2008) at 1 ("Under 16 U.S.C. § 1387(f)(3), if there is insufficient funding available to develop and implement a take reduction plan for all stocks that meet the requirements, the Secretary of Commerce must establish teams according to the priorities listed in the statute."), *available at* http://www.nmfs.noaa.gov/pr/pdfs/gao-09-78.pdf.

[130] *Id.* at 1 ("Under 16 U.S.C. § 1387(f)(3), if there is insufficient funding available to develop and implement a take reduction plan for all stocks that meet the requirements, the Secretary of Commerce must establish teams according to the priorities listed in the statute."), *available at* http://www.nmfs.noaa.gov/pr/pdfs/gao-09-78.pdf (last visited July 22, 2014).

[131] *See generally* Keith Rizzardi, *The Duty to Advise the Lorax: Environmental Lawyering in an Era of Reform*, 37 WM. & MARY ENVTL. L. & POL'Y REV. 25 (2011).

[132] HERMAN MELVILLE, MOBY DICK 362 (1892) ("Though banding together in tens of thousands, the lion-maned buffaloes of the West have fled before a solitary horseman. Witness, too, all human beings, how when herded together in the sheepfold of a theatre's pit, they will, at the slightest alarm of fire, rush helter-skelter for the outlets, crowding, trampling, jamming, and remorselessly dashing each other to death. Best, therefore, withhold any amazement at the strangely gallied whales before us, for there is no folly of the beast of the earth which is not infinitely outdone by the madness of men…").

10 Confronting the Marine Invasive Species Threat:
PRACTICAL AND LEGAL CHALLENGES
Stephanie Showalter Otts*

* The author would like to thank the members of her faculty writing group at the University of Mississippi
  School of Law—Jack Nowlin, Desiree Hensley, William Berry, Christopher Green, and Antonia Eliason—
  for their insightful comments and feedback on chapter outlines and drafts.

Introduction

In October 2013, 20,000 salmon were killed when a swarm of Mauve stinger jellyfish, *Pelagia noctiluca*, drifted through an open-ocean aquaculture operation in Ireland.[1] On one summer day in July 2008, 300 swimmers at beaches in Barcelona were treated for *P. noctiluca* stings, with eleven requiring hospital treatment.[2] While Mauve stingers have plagued swimmers in the Mediterranean for at least 200 years, their presence in the Irish Sea is quite recent. Experts generally thought the waters around Ireland were too cold for the species until a massive bloom in 2007 swept through an organic salmon farm resulting in the loss of 120,000 fish and over $2 million in damages.[3]

In addition to altering environmental conditions that may favor a new range of species, such as Mauve stingers, climate change is opening up new invasion pathways for nonnative species as humans change their maritime activities. For instance, in September 2013, the *M/V Nordic Orion* became the first bulk carrier to traverse the fabled Northwest Passage departing from Canadian waters, a journey only made possible due to the melting of the Arctic sea ice.[4] The Northwest Passage route is approximately 1,000 miles and one week shorter than the traditional route between Europe and Asia through the Panama Canal, a significant shortcut that has the potential to save shipping companies millions.[5] An increase in shipping traffic in the Arctic has the potential to introduce nonnative species through both the discharge of ballast water and the transport of species on ships' hulls. The Arctic currently has a low risk of invasion due to the extremely cold temperatures. As the Arctic waters warm, however, more species will be able to survive, which will increase the risk of a successful introduction.[6]

Lawmakers have traditionally responded to concerns over the environmental and economic impact of invasive species by prohibiting the import, sale, transport, possession, and release of nonnative species designated as harmful.[7] Although these laws are

---

[1] Loran Siggins, *Jellyfish "Bloom" Kills Thousands of Farmed Salmon off Co Mayo*, IRISH TIMES (Oct. 21, 2013), http://www.irishtimes.com/news/ireland/irish-news/jellyfish-bloom-kills-thousands-of-farmed-salmon-off-co-mayo-1.1567468.

[2] Elisabeth Rosenthal, *Stinging Tentacles Offer Hints at Oceans' Decline*, N.Y. TIMES (Aug. 3, 2008), http://www.nytimes.com/2008/08/03/science/earth/03jellyfish.html?pagewanted=all&_r=0.

[3] *Jellied Salmon: Scientists Mystified by Jellyfish Attack on Salmon Farm*, SPIEGEL ONLINE (Nov. 26, 2007), http://www.spiegel.de/international/europe/jellied-salmon-scientists-mystified-by-jellyfish-attacks-on-fish-farm-a-519666.html.

[4] John McGarrity & Henning Gloystein, *Northwest Passage Crossed by First Cargo Ship, the Nordic Orion, Heralding New Era of Arctic Commercial Activity*, NAT'L POST (Sept. 27, 2013), http://news.nationalpost.com/2013/09/27/northwest-passage-crossed-by-first-cargo-ship-the-nordic-or ion-heralding-new-era-of-arctic-commercial-activity/.

[5] *Id.*

[6] Christopher Ware, *Arctic at Risk from Invasive Species*, ECOLOGIST (Nov. 25, 2013), http://www.theecologist.org/News/news_analysis/2173097/arctic_at_risk_from_invasive_species.html.

[7] *See, e.g.*, 16 U.S.C. § 3372(a) (2012); Ariz. Stat. § 17-255.02(1) (West 2014); WY Stat. § 34-2-202(a)(ii) (West 2014).

useful for controlling intentional introductions, they are generally ineffective at preventing unintentional or accidental introductions where individuals often do not know that they are moving species or what those species are. As a result, attention has shifted in recent years to directly regulating the human activities that lead to marine species introductions, such as ballast water discharge and the aquarium trade.[8] This is a positive development that should increase the legal framework's flexibility and ability to adapt as the climate changes.

However, due to its exclusive focus on nonnative species introductions, the foundation of the entire legal framework is unstable and open to criticism. The line between native and nonnative species is often unclear and will become even blurrier as a result of climate change. Consider what might happen if a scenario similar to the Mauve stinger blooms were to occur in the United States. Government agencies would spend significant sums to develop and implement rapid response plans to control or eradicate the blooms of the "invasive" jellyfish in the Irish Sea, even though the species' presence is due to natural migration. In the Mediterranean, agencies would have little authority to take action, despite the significant tourism and human health impacts, as the Mauve stingers would be considered "native" species whose preservation is desirable. Attention needs to shift away from preventing and controlling nonnative species introductions to preventing and controlling *any* ecosystem imbalance with the potential to cause significant environmental, economic, or public health harm.

Section I of this chapter provides an overview of marine invasions and the environmental concerns surrounding the introduction and spread of marine invasive species. Section II discusses the existing legal and policy framework for addressing marine invasions on both the international and U.S. domestic levels. Section III examines the challenges a changing climate poses to this regime. This chapter concludes in Section IV by recommending an increased focus on risk assessment to more effectively identify and respond to marine invasion threats.

I. Marine Invasions in a Changing Climate

Species have been traveling the globe since the beginning of time. Reference is often made to the five oceans of the world—Antarctic, Arctic, Atlantic, Indian, and Pacific. These oceans, however, are all connected to one another, and marine species are routinely transported outside their native ranges by wind, currents, debris, and other species. Humans are by far the dominant force by which species can be introduced to new

---

[8] *See generally* INVASIVE SPECIES: VECTOR AND MANAGEMENT STRATEGIES (Gregory M. Ruiz & James T. Carlton eds., 2003); Susan L. Williams et al., *Managing Multiple Vectors for Marine Invasions in an Increasingly Connected World*, 63 BIOSCI. 952 (2013); Aquatic Invasive Species Vector Risk Assessments, California Ocean Science Trust, http://calost.org/science-initiatives/?page=aquatic-invasive-species (last visited Mar. 27, 2014).

environments. Marine species are transported unintentionally as "stowaways" in the ballast tanks or on the hulls of ships. They are also introduced intentionally through the release of baitfish, aquarium species, and other live organisms. Lionfish, for example, most likely arrived in the Atlantic Ocean from their native range in the western Pacific through the aquarium trade.[9] Jellyfish were introduced into the Black Sea and numerous other waters through the discharge of ballast water.[10] Once established in a new area, the nonnative species can further spread through natural means, actively swimming or passively riding on currents, and additional human activities.

Invasive species are a subset of nonnative species that thrive in their new environment, causing environmental, economic, and other damage. An estimated 50,000 nonnative species have been introduced into the United States.[11] Invasive species are nonnative "species whose introduction does or is likely to cause economic or environmental harm or harm to human health."[12] Invasive species compete with native species for food and habitat, and can significantly impact ecosystems by altering food webs and habitats, reducing native biodiversity, and changing water chemistry.[13] In 2005, researchers estimated that the economic damages associated with invasive species and their control is approximately $120 billion per year.[14]

Eradication of a nonnative species, once established, is rare. One of the few successful cases of eradication involved a very rapid response to the discovery of the invasive tropical marine alga, *Caulerpa taxifolia*, in a small lagoon north of San Diego, California, in 2000.[15] The containment and treatment efforts, which included intensive surveillance by divers, lasted for two years and were followed by periodic surveys, with costs estimated in 2006 at over $7 million.[16]

Climate change is anticipated to alter the behavior of both humans and nonnative species, with five possible consequences for invasive species management.[17] First, as illustrated above by the recent voyage of the *Nordic Orion*, climate change will alter patterns

---

[9] *CORIS: NOAA's Coral Reef Information Service*, NAT'L OCEANIC & ATMOSPHERIC ADMIN., http://www.coris.noaa.gov/exchanges/lionfish/ (last visited Mar. 27, 2014).

[10] *Marine Bioinvasions Fact Sheet: Ballast Water*, MIT SEA GRANT COASTAL RESOURCES, http://massbay.mit.edu/exoticspecies/ballast/fact.html (last visited Mar. 27, 2014).

[11] David Pimentel et al., *Update on the Environmental and Economic Costs Associated with Alien-Invasive Species in the United States*, 52 ECOLOGICAL ECON. 273, 273 (2005).

[12] Exec. Order No. 13,112, 64 Fed. Reg. 6183, 6183 (Feb. 3, 1999).

[13] U.S. ENVIRONMENTAL PROTECTION AGENCY, EPA/600/R-08/014, EFFECTS OF CLIMATE CHANGE ON AQUATIC INVASIVE SPECIES AND IMPLICATIONS FOR RESEARCH AND MANAGEMENT (2008).

[14] Pimentel et al., *supra* note 11, at 282.

[15] *See* Lars W.J. Anderson, *California's Reaction to* Caulerpa taxifolia: *A Model for Invasive Species Rapid Response*, 7 BIOLOGICAL INVASIONS 1003 (2005) (discussing California's response to the discovery of *Caulerpa* in state waters).

[16] MERKEL & ASSOCIATES, FINAL REPORT ON ERADICATION OF THE INVASIVE SEAWEED CAULERPA TAXIFOLIA FROM AGUE HEDIONDA LAGOON AND HUNTINGTON HARBOUR, CALIFORNIA 1 (2006).

[17] J.J. Hellman et al., *Five Potential Consequences of Climate Change for Invasive Species*, 22 CONSERVATION BIOLOGY 534, 534–43 (2008).

of human transport. The actual mechanisms, or pathways, by which marine species invade new environments are unlikely to be affected by climate change. The primary human activities that result in the movement of species around the globe—shipping and trade—will remain predominant. However, the locations where those activities occur are expected to change, shifting and expanding the invasion risk to new marine environments.[18] As transportation routes shift, the "propagule pressure"[19] of nonnative species will change. Introductions may occur in areas previously unaffected by invasive species, or introductions may increase in a particular area if seasonal activities are lengthened or shorter shipping routes enable more individuals to survive the journey.

Climate change may alter the climatic constraints on invasive species.[20] Nonnative species currently unable to invade an area may be able to do so in the future under different environmental conditions, such as higher temperatures, decreased salinity, shifts in ocean circulation and currents, or changing ecosystem interactions. Warmer waters, for example, may enable nonnative species to survive currently fatal winter months. The population and distribution of established populations of invasive species may also change or expand.[21] Just as the ranges of native marine species are shifting as the environmental conditions change, climate change will alter the range limits of invasive species.[22] As temperatures increase or salinity decreases as the result of greater freshwater inputs, invasive species may be able to expand into new areas. A decline in native species, as the result of a range shift or extinction, may also open a niche for a nonnative to invade.

The lionfish (*Pterois volitans*), a tropical fish native to the Pacific and Indian Oceans and the Red Sea, was released into southern Florida waters in the mid-1980s as the result of the aquarium trade and quickly became invasive, expanding into the Caribbean Sea and northward along the Eastern Seaboard of the United States.[23] Lionfish have thrived in the Caribbean, with populations five times denser in the Bahamas than in their native range, resulting in reductions in the recruitment of native reef fish, which likely threatens the resiliency of the broader coral reef ecosystem.[24] For a time, it appeared that the lionfish were not able to survive the cold winter temperatures of the northern Atlantic Ocean. Warmer ocean temperatures, however, have allowed the lionfish to establish

---

[18] *Id.* at 537.

[19] Propagule pressure is a composite measure of the number of individual species introduced into an area. *See* Julie L. Lockwood, Phillip Cassey & Tim Blackburn, *The Role of Propagule Pressure in Explaining Species Invasions*, 20 TRENDS ECOLOGY & EVOLUTION 223, 223 (2005).

[20] Hellman et al., *supra* note 17, at 538.

[21] *Id.* at 539.

[22] *See generally* J.B. Cascade, et al., *Marine Range Shifts and Species Introductions: Comparative Spread Rates and Community Impacts*, 19 GLOBAL ECOLOGY & BIOGEOGRAPHY 303 (2010) (discussing the rates and consequences of shifts in marine species' ranges as a result of climate change).

[23] STANLEY W. BURGIEL & ADRIANNA A. MUIR, GLOBAL INVASIVE SPECIES PROGRAMME, INVASIVE SPECIES, CLIMATE CHANGE AND ECOSYSTEM-BASED ADAPTATION: ADDRESSING MULTIPLE DRIVERS OF GLOBAL CHANGE 16 (2010).

[24] *Id.*

populations in the southern Atlantic, and in some areas lionfish are now as abundant as native groupers.[25] Currently, the northward spread of the invasive Asian green mussel (*Perna viridis*) along the Florida coast appears to be limited by cold temperatures.[26] Increasing water temperatures may eliminate this environmental barrier and allow the mussel to expand its range.

Climate change may also alter the impact of existing invasive species.[27] If climatic changes are favorable to invasive species, populations may increase, which further stresses native species and ecosystems and leads to additional environmental or economic harm. Finally, changing climate conditions may alter the effectiveness of management strategies.[28] Control may become harder if populations increase, or if climate conditions reduce the effectiveness of chemical or biocontrol agents. Restoration of native ecosystems, which is often part of broader attempts to prevent and control invasive species, may become less feasible if climatic changes are unfavorable to native species.

II. Existing Legal Framework

International consensus has emerged that nations should take action to address invasive species threats. Article 8(h) of the Convention on Biological Diversity, the overarching international treaty pertaining to ecology and biodiversity, explicitly instructs Parties to "Prevent the introduction of, control or eradicate alien species which threaten ecosystems, habitats or species."[29] Article 196 of the United Nations Convention on the Law of the Sea requires that States "take all measures necessary to prevent, reduce and control…the intentional or accidental introduction of species, alien or new, to a particular part of the marine environment, which may cause significant and harmful changes thereto."[30]

Although the United States is a signatory to these treaties, there is no comprehensive legal regime in the United States. Numerous international, federal, and state laws, regulations, and policies govern aspects of the invasive species problem, and the resultant overlaps, conflicts, and gaps lead to confusion among individuals and entities subject to regulation and limit effectiveness.[31] This section will discuss the existing legal framework

---

[25] *Id.*

[26] Ocean and Marine Resources in a Changing Climate: A Technical Input to the 2013 National Climate Assessment 54 (Roger Griffis & Jennifer Howards eds., 2013).

[27] Hellman et al., *supra* note 17, at 539.

[28] *Id.* at 540.

[29] Convention on Biological Diversity, art. 8(h), June 5, 1992, 1760 U.N.T.S. 79; 31 I.L.M. 818 (entered into force Dec. 29, 1993).

[30] U.N. Convention on the Law of the Sea, art. 196, Dec. 10, 1982, 1833 U.N.T.S. 3; 21 I.L.M. 1261 (entered into force Nov. 16, 1994).

[31] *See generally* David A. Strifling, *An Ecosystem-Based Approach to Slowing the Synergistic Effects of Invasive Species and Climate Change*, 22 Duke Envtl. L. & Pol'y F. 145 (2011); James S. Neal McCubbins et al.,

in the United States, focusing on the primary approaches to invasive species prevention: species-based regulation and pathway-based regulation.

Traditionally, policymakers in the United States and other countries have focused on responding to individual species threats as they arise, enacting laws focused on preventing the introduction of and controlling the spread of a single species, such as zebra mussels and brown tree snakes, known to be harmful. Recently, attention has shifted to regulating the pathways by which species are transported, based on the risk of introduction. Pathway-based regulations, which do not require harmful species to be identified ahead of time, have the potential to be much more effective at preventing the introduction and establishment of invasive species.

A. SPECIES-BASED APPROACHES

One of the oldest wildlife protection statutes in the United States, the Lacey Act of 1900,[32] was enacted, in part, to address invasive species threats by prohibiting the importation of "injurious species." The statute, as amended, currently prohibits

[t]he importation into the United States…of the mongoose of the species Herpestes auropunctatus; of the species of so-called "flying foxes" or fruit bats of the genus Pteropus; of the zebra mussel of the species Dreissena polymorpha; of the bighead carp of the species Hypophthalmichthys nobilis; and such other species of wild mammals, wild birds, fish (including mollusks and crustacea), amphibians, reptiles, brown tree snakes, or the offspring or eggs of any of the foregoing which the Secretary of the Interior may prescribe by regulation to be injurious to human beings, to the interests of agriculture, horticulture, forestry, or to wildlife or the wildlife resources of the United States….[33]

This provision, often referred to as the "injurious species provision," is an example of a "dirty list" or "black list" approach to invasive species prevention, whereby imported species are presumed to pose no threat and species are regulated only once their capacity to cause harm has been established and they have been identified on the list.[34]

Under the Lacey Act's black list approach, imported species are presumed to pose little or no risk until deemed otherwise by the U.S. Fish and Wildlife Service (FWS), the federal agency responsible for implementing the Lacey Act. The FWS is unable to

---

Frayed Seams in the "Patchwork Quilt" of American Federalism: An Empirical Analysis of Invasive Plant Species Regulation, 43 ENVTL. L. 35 (2013); PETER T. JENKINS, DEFENDERS OF WILDLIFE, BROKEN SCREENS: THE REGULATION OF LIVE ANIMAL IMPORTS IN THE UNITED STATES (2007).

[32] 18 U.S.C. § 42 (2012).

[33] *Id.* § 42(a)(1).

[34] ENVIRONMENTAL LAW INSTITUTE, HALTING THE INVASION: STATE TOOLS FOR INVASIVE SPECIES MANAGEMENT 106, 111 (2002) [hereinafter HALTING THE INVASION].

act proactively to prevent the importation of a species, as before importation can be prohibited there must be a determination that the species is "injurious," after which regulations have to be developed and implemented.[35] By the time the Lacey Act listing process is complete, the species of concern has likely already become established. As a result, the Lacey Act is widely considered to be ineffective.[36]

Although the terminology and scope vary, most states prohibit the possession, sale, purchase, transport, and release of aquatic invasive species.[37] These laws, similar to the Lacey Act, regulate species only upon designation as "invasive" on a black list. A more proactive and effective species-based regulatory approach is the "white list" or "clean list," which presumes all nonnative species to be harmful until proven otherwise and permits the importation of only those species found to pose a minimal risk of harm.[38]

A few states have developed clean lists, often to facilitate a particular industry or common activity. Arkansas, for example, has an "Approved Aquaculture Species List," which identifies species that may be freely imported into the state for aquaculture purposes.[39] The state of Alaska maintains a "Clean List of Animals." Animals on the clean list, primarily common domestic pets and livestock, can be possessed, imported, bought, and sold without a permit, although they may not be released into the wild.[40] Although these lists are far from comprehensive, they are a step in the right direction. By adopting a default presumption of "harmful, unless proven otherwise," policymakers tighten the regulatory net and shift the burden of proof to establish that it poses minimal risk to those wishing to import a species.

Even through clean lists, species-based regulation is generally ineffective at preventing the indirect, unintentional, or accidental introductions of nonnative species. It is virtually impossible to identify every species that might possibly make its way into a particular geographic area and accurately assess its invasiveness to determine whether to permit or prohibit its importation. Furthermore, permit regimes are only effective if coupled with adequate enforcement. Importers are often unaware of or disregard permit requirements, and weak enforcement provides little incentive for parties to comply. Once an organism has been released into the environment, it is extremely difficult to identify the responsible party, further contributing to a lack of accountability and compliance.

---

[35] KRISTINA ALEXANDER, CONGRESSIONAL RESEARCH SERVICE, INJURIOUS SPECIES LISTINGS UNDER THE LACEY ACT: A LEGAL BRIEFING (2013).

[36] See generally Andrea J. Fowler et al., Failure of the Lacey Act to Protect U.S. Ecosystems against Animal Invasions, 5 FRONTIERS ECOLOGY & ENV'T 353 (2007).

[37] See, e.g., ARIZ. REV. STAT. § 17-255.02 (West 2014); COLO. REV. STAT. § 33-10.5-105 (West 2014).

[38] HALTING THE INVASION, supra note 34, at 32, 111.

[39] Approved Aquaculture Species List, Ark. Game & Fish Comm'n, Fisheries Div. Policy, (Oct. 1, 2002), available at www.agfc.com/resources/publications/aquaculturecleanlist.pdf.

[40] 5 ALASKA ADMIN. CODE § 92.029(b) (West 2014).

B. PATHWAY-BASED APPROACH

Due to the ineffectiveness of the current species-based regulatory regime, attention has shifted to vector, or pathway, management. Pathways are "the means and routes by which invasive species are imported and introduced into new environments."[41] In 1999, Executive Order 13,112 on Invasive Species called on the newly created National Invasive Species Council to develop a management plan that, among other things, was "to include a review of existing and prospective approaches and authorities for preventing the introduction and spread of invasive species, including those for identifying pathways by which invasive species are introduced and for minimizing the risk of introductions via those pathways."[42]

The primary pathways for marine invasions are maritime shipping and live trade in marine organisms.[43] With respect to maritime shipping, there are two major areas of concern or sub-pathways—ballast water discharge and hull fouling.[44] With respect to the live trade, the major subcategories are live bait, aquarium trade, aquaculture, live seafood, and aquatic plants.[45] In recent decades, significant progress has been made to reduce the risk of invasion from the release of ballast water. Many of the other pathways, however, remain under-regulated.

Ballast water often contains a diverse array of organisms, and the discharge of ballast water is the prime suspect for many marine invasions, including the zebra and quagga mussels' introduction into the Great Lakes and the European green crab into San Francisco Bay.[46] Ballast water, as the Smithsonian Environmental Research Center states, "is carried by ships to provide balance, stability, and trim during sailing and to keep them upright during loading and offloading operations."[47] The primary law in the United States addressing aquatic invasive species is the Nonindigenous Aquatic Nuisance Prevention and Control Act of 1990 (NANPCA).[48] Passed in the wake of the invasion of the zebra mussel and other aquatic species in the Great Lakes, NANPCA authorized pathway-based regulation, establishing a federal program "to prevent unintentional

---

[41] NAT'L INVASIVE SPECIES COUNCIL, MEETING THE INVASIVE SPECIES CHALLENGE: MANAGEMENT PLAN 2 (2001).

[42] Exec. Order No. 13112, *supra* note 12, at § 5(b).

[43] *Preventing Aquatic Species Invasions in the Mid-Atlantic: Outcome-Based Actions in Vector Management* 6 (Fedricka Moser & Merrill Leffler eds., 2010), *available at* http://www.mdsg.umd.edu/sites/default/files/files/AIS2009Report.pdf.

[44] *Id.*

[45] *Id.*

[46] *See* Felicity Barringer, *New Rules Seek to Prevent Invasive Stowaways*, N.Y. TIMES (Apr. 7, 2012), http://www.nytimes.com/2012/04/08/science/earth/invasive-species-target-of-new-ballast-water-rule.html?_r=0.

[47] *Ballast Water*, MARINE INVASIONS RESEARCH LAB, SMITHSONIAN ENVTL. RESEARCH CTR., http://www.serc.si.edu/labs/marine_invasions/vector_ecology/bw.aspx (last visited Feb. 11, 2014).

[48] NANPCA was reauthorized in 1996 and renamed the National Invasive Species Act. *See* 16 U.S.C. § 4701 (2012).

introduction and dispersal of nonindigenous species into waters of the United States through ballast water management and other requirements."[49]

Ballast water management has evolved significantly from the early 1990s. As an initial control measure, the Coast Guard required most vessels desiring to discharge ballast water in U.S. waters to conduct ballast water exchange (BWE) (i.e., exchange the coastal freshwater in their ballast tanks with ocean saltwater while far from shore) to minimize the risk of aquatic invasive species introductions.[50] Although BWE does reduce the risk that a viable nonnative species will be discharged into the environment, BWE is not always possible, due to vessel design, safety, or weather, nor is it completely effective at removing all organisms.[51] Ballast water treatment, designed to achieve stringent ballast water discharge standards, has emerged as the preferred risk reduction strategy.[52]

The International Convention for the Control and Management of Ships' Ballast Water and Sediment was adopted by the International Maritime Organization (IMO) in 2004.[53] The Ballast Water Convention is pathway-specific; as such, its sole objective is to prevent, minimize, and ideally eliminate the risk to human health and the environment from the transfer of aquatic organisms and pathogens via ships' ballast water.[54] The Convention seeks to reduce the risk that harmful aquatic organisms will be introduced into new environments; it does so through requirements that all ships of Convention parties develop ballast water management plans, carry out ballast water exchanges, and meet certain ballast water performance standards, which require that discharged ballast water has organism concentrations below specified limits.[55]

The Ballast Water Convention has not yet entered into force. It will do so twelve months after ratification by thirty States, representing 35 percent of world merchant shipping tonnage. As of January 9, 2013, thirty-eight States have ratified the Convention, representing approximately 30 percent of the world merchant shipping tonnage.[56] Although the necessary number of States have ratified, they do not represent a high enough percentage of the merchant shipping tonnage for the Convention to enter into force. The

---

[49] 16 U.S.C. § 4701(b)(1) (2012).

[50] Eugene Buck, Congressional Research Service, Ballast Water Management to Combat Invasive Species 4 (2010).

[51] *Mid Ocean Ballast Water Exchange*, SMITHSONIAN ENVTL. RESEARCH CTR., http://www.serc.si.edu/labs/marine_invasions/vector_ecology/bw_exchange.aspx (last visited Mar. 27, 2014).

[52] Buck, *supra* note 50, at 2–3, 6.

[53] *See Ballast Water Management*, IMO, http://www.imo.org/OurWork/Environment/BallastWaterManagement/Pages/Default.aspx (last visited Feb. 11, 2014).

[54] *See International Convention for the Control and Management of Ships' Ballast Water and Sediments (BWM)*, INT'L MARITIME ORGANIZATION, http://www.imo.org/About/Conventions/ListOfConventions/Pages/International-Convention-for-the-Control-and-Management-of-Ships%27-Ballast-Water-and-Sediments-%28BWM%29.aspx (last visited Mar. 27, 2014).

[55] *Id.*

[56] IMO, Summary of Status of Convention (2013), *available at* http://www.imo.org/About/Conventions/StatusOfConventions/Documents/Summary%20of%20Status%20of%20Conventions.xls.

United States has yet to ratify the Ballast Water Convention. Although U.S. ratification is highly desirable for a variety of legal and political reasons, it is not enough to bring the Convention immediately into force as the U.S. share of the world merchant shipping tonnage is only about 2 percent.[57] Because of the proliferation of open registries, most merchant vessels fly the flag of Panama or Liberia, also nonparties to the Convention.

In 2012, the U.S. Coast Guard issued new regulations to phase out ballast water exchange as an acceptable management strategy. Coast Guard regulations now require all non-recreational vessels equipped with ballast tanks that operate in U.S. waters, with some exceptions, to install and operate a U.S. Coast Guard–approved ballast water management system (BWMS), in addition to adhering to best management practices.[58] Vessels employing a Coast Guard–approved BWMS must meet stringent ballast water discharge standards on a phased-in schedule beginning in January 2014.[59] The Coast Guard discharge standards are identical to the international standards in the IMO Ballast Water Convention.

In addition, ballast water discharges are regulated by the U.S. Environmental Protection Agency (EPA) under the Clean Water Act (CWA). The CWA's main goal is "to restore and maintain the chemical, physical, and biological integrity of the Nation's waters."[60] In assuring compliance, the statute mandates that any discharge of a pollutant into navigable waters constitutes a violation. "Discharge of a pollutant" is defined by the CWA as "any addition of any pollutant to navigable waters from any point source."[61] A pollutant is defined as "dredged spoil, solid waste, incinerator residue, sewage, garbage, sewage sludge, munitions, chemical waste, biological materials, radioactive materials, heat, wrecked or discarded equipment, rock, sand, cellar dirt and industrial, municipal and agricultural waste discharged into water."[62] Invasive species are considered a pollutant as they are "biological materials."[63]

The EPA regulates discharges incidental to the normal operations of commercial vessels greater than seventy-nine feet in length, such as ballast water discharges, primarily through the Vessel General Permit (VGP). The current version of the VGP took effect on December 19, 2013. All discharges of ballast water by vessels subject to VGP coverage must comply with the ballast water requirements set forth in the permit and with applicable U.S. Coast Guard regulations. The ballast water discharge standards and implementation schedule are identical to those adopted by the Coast Guard in its regulations.[64]

---

[57] *See Modern Merchant Marine*, AMERICAN MARITIME CONGRESS, http://www.americanmaritime.org/merchant/ (last visited Feb. 11, 2014).

[58] *See* 33 C.F.R. § 151.2025 (2014).

[59] *See id.* § 151.2030.

[60] 33 U.S.C. § 1251(a) (2012).

[61] *See id.* § 1362(12)(A).

[62] *Id.* § 1362(6).

[63] Northwest. Envtl. Advocates v. EPA, 537 F.3d 1006, 1021 (9th Cir. 2008).

[64] *See* ENVIRONMENTAL PROTECTION AGENCY, VESSEL GENERAL PERMIT FOR DISCHARGES INCIDENTAL TO THE NORMAL OPERATION OF VESSELS (VGP), §§ 2.2.3.5, 2.2.3.5.2 (2013).

III. Policy Challenges

Pathway-based regulation is well suited to a changing climate, as it focuses on reducing the risk of introduction from particular human activities regardless of where they occur. If shipping routes or aquaculture operations shift to new areas, for instance, the invasive species risk management measures remain in effect. Policymakers simply need to ensure that the regulatory framework takes into account these climate-induced changes and is flexible enough to adapt to changing circumstances.

With respect to ballast water management, for example, the opening of the Northwest Passage is unlikely to change the ports at which the vessels are discharging ballast water. However, vessels may be arriving at port sooner, and more organisms may therefore be able to survive the journey. Ballast water discharge standards establish discharge thresholds, which vessels may not exceed, based on the number of viable organisms of various size classes contained in a certain volume of ballast water discharge. These standards may be sufficiently protective regardless of the length of the vessel's journey, but it is important that regulators review these standards to ensure they are still capable of achieving policy goals. For other, less regulated pathways, the impacts of climate change should be taken into account when developing laws and regulations.

A. WHAT IS NATIVE?

Climate change will pose a larger challenge to species-based regulation and the underlying assumptions of aquatic invasive species laws. The call to action to address invasive species threats arises from a desire to protect native biodiversity and ecosystems. As stated by the Ecological Society of America:

> Biotic invasions are altering the world's natural communities and their ecological character at an unprecedented rate. If we fail to implement effective strategies to curb the most damaging impacts of invaders, we risk impoverishing and homogenizing the very ecosystems on which we rely to sustain our agriculture, forestry, fisheries and other resources and to supply us with irreplaceable natural services.[65]

According to the dominant paradigm, nonnative species are a threat simply because they are foreign. They are brought by humans from some faraway place, and the few who survive wreak havoc on native ecosystems. This paradigm, however, implies that

---

[65] ECOLOGICAL SOC'Y OF AM., 5 BIOTIC INVASIONS: CAUSES, EPIDEMIOLOGY, GLOBAL CONSEQUENCES AND CONTROL, ISSUES IN ECOLOGY 18 (2000).

nature is static and that there is some timeless state of "nature" that can be preserved.[66] This assumption is incorrect, as natural systems are constantly in a state of flux as the plants, animals, and microbes respond to natural and human-induced changes in the environment.

In addition, the line between native and nonnative is not always clear. Rainbow trout, native to the Pacific Northwest, have been stocked in rivers around the country to improve sport fishing for so long that few anglers or management agencies recognize it as what it is—a nonnative species that threatens the existence of native species of frogs and fish.[67] Whether a species is considered native or nonnative often depends on the time frame considered.

The dominant paradigm is also based on the assumption that native species are good and nonnative species are bad. This assumption is also incorrect. Some nonnative species, such as soybeans, are extremely valuable agricultural crops viewed as beneficial to the economic and social well-being of the United States.

Native species can also reach levels of abundance that cause environmental and economic harm. So called "native invaders," such as white-tailed deer, raccoons, and Canadian geese have altered plant diversity, reduced the populations of native songbirds, and contributed to eutrophication of lakes and ponds, respectively.[68] Yet, because these species are considered "native" they receive protected status under the law and are generally managed for preservation even when causing harm. Canadian geese, for instance, are protected by the federal Migratory Bird Treaty Act of 1918, which makes it illegal for anyone to take, possess, import, export, transport, sell, purchase, barter, or offer for sale, purchase, or barter, any migratory bird, or the parts, nests, or eggs of such a bird.[69] Special permits are required by the FWS and state agencies to take action against flocks of Canadian geese causing damage to local environments.[70] Contrast this with the response to nonnative population explosions ("invasions") in which biological, chemical, mechanical, and other controls are deployed, often at great expense, to prevent the spread, mitigate the damage, and reduce, or ideally eliminate, the species.

---

[66] Brendon M.H. Larson, *Who's Invading What? Systems Thinking about Invasive Species*, 87 Can. J. Plant Sci. 993, 995 (2007).

[67] Columbia University, *Introduced Species Summary Project: Rainbow Trout* (Oncorhynchus mykiss), http://www.columbia.edu/itc/cerc/danoff-burg/invasion_bio/inv_spp_summ/Oncorhynchus_mykiss.html (last visited Feb. 12, 2014).

[68] Michael P. Carey et al., *Native Invaders—Challenges for Science, Management, Policy, and Society*, 10 Frontiers in Ecology & Env't 373, 375 (2012).

[69] 16 U.S.C. § 703 (2012).

[70] *See, e.g., Nuisance Canada Geese*, N.Y. Dep't of Envtl. Conservation, http://www.dec.ny.gov/animals/7003.html (last visited Feb. 12, 2014).

B. WHAT IS AN INTRODUCTION?

Invasive species regulation is often triggered by the "introduction" of a nonnative species into the environment as the result of a human act, either intentional or accidental. What if human activity is not the direct cause of the introduction? There are natural means by which species introductions can occur, as evidenced by Mauve stingers in the Irish Sea. Species have expanded their ranges across the oceans for millennia by hitching a ride on currents and floating debris. In 1995, a fisherman observed more than a dozen green iguanas swimming ashore from a floating mat of uprooted trees to the Caribbean island of Anguilla.[71] Researchers concluded that the iguanas became castaways from the island of Guadeloupe during a hurricane. Although Anguilla had previously been iguana-free, the castaways survived and reproductive male and female iguanas were found in 1998.[72] Should these iguanas be classified as invasive, as they are not native to Anguilla, even though they arrived via a natural pathway?

The Anguilla iguanas and Mauve stingers are illustrative of the far end of the direct-indirect human cause continuum. Although a human fingerprint is hard to detect in the iguana's journey, humans are arguably contributing to the range shifts of the Mauve stinger and other species by accelerating climate change, as well as by polluting waters and altering habitat. Humans also build structures in coastal environments that can break away during storms and other events, establishing a more direct link to species movement. As a result of the 9.0 magnitude earthquake that struck off the coast of Japan in March 2011 and the ensuing tsunami, an estimated 24.9 million tons of debris was washed into the Pacific Ocean.[73] Much of the debris sunk relatively close to shore, but millions of tons floated out of Japanese waters and drifted toward the North Pacific Current and the Washington, Oregon, and California coasts. On June 5, 2012, a dock the size of a train car washed ashore on Oregon's Agate Beach.[74] Hundreds of species, weighing more than two tons, survived the year-long ocean voyage, including a few high-risk invasive species such as the European blue mussel and Japanese sea star.[75] Federal and state natural resource managers acted quickly to remove the dock and other debris from the coastal waters, which was a prudent risk management response.

A lingering management question remains, however. If humans are not the primary cause of the introduction, is floating ocean debris a pathway that should be managed? Natural resource managers have limited resources, personnel, and enforcement capacity

---

[71] Mary Caperton Morton, *Setting Sail on Unknown Seas: The Past, Present, and Future of Species Rafting*, EARTH MAG. (Jan. 1, 2013), http://www.earthmagazine.org/article/setting-sail-unknown-seas-past-present-and-future-species-rafting.

[72] *Id.*

[73] Amal Bagulayan et al., *Journey to the Center of the Gyre: The Fate of the Tohoku Tsunami Debris Field*, 25 OCEANOGRAPHY 200, 200 (2012).

[74] *See* Morton, *supra* note 71.

[75] *Id.*

to address invasive species issues. How can U.S. marine invasive species law and policy help ensure that limited funds are used most effectively in a world of changing climate? Risk management involves identifying and "triaging" priority species and habitats. The legal framework needs to facilitate this prioritization, enabling managers in the field to make tough decisions about where to invest scarce resources.

IV. Minimizing Risk of Harm

Invasive species managers should "organize priorities around whether species are producing benefits or harm to biodiversity, human health, ecological services, and economies."[76] For marine invasive species that are already here and doing quite well, such as lionfish, complete eradication is likely not possible, at least not on a large scale. Policymakers should therefore focus on minimizing harm to ecosystem values of importance in particular geographic areas. Sport fishing and recreational diving is incredibly important in the Florida Keys. Spending time and money to control lionfish populations to minimize pressure on native reef fish might be a very wise investment of resources. In other locations where populations may be kept low because of colder temperatures or other environmental conditions, lionfish may have less of an impact on the ecosystem, and control efforts should be a lower priority.

For species that have not yet arrived, a focus on pathway management and risk assessment is crucial. Prevention is the key to avoiding environmental and economic harm from marine invasions. Because the primary pathways for marine invasions involve important economic sectors, it is impractical and undesirable to shut down trade routes and commercial activities. Completely eliminating the risk of introduction will therefore be impossible, as some species will inevitably get through. However, as illustrated by the ballast water case study, risk of introductions can be significantly reduced. Increased focus is needed on other high-risk pathways, especially the aquarium trade, to minimize the risk that species of concern are moved around and released into favorable environments.

In addition to continuing the trend toward pathway management, managers need to integrate climate change impacts into decision-making on all aspects of invasive species management. Unfortunately, no law currently explicitly requires the consideration of climate change in the management of aquatic invasive species. Managers, however, do have the flexibility to do so. With the passage of NANPCA, Congress encouraged states to develop and adopt aquatic invasive species management plans identifying actions needed "to eliminate or reduce the environmental, public health, and safety risks associated with aquatic nuisance species."[77] State plans are reviewed and approved by the Aquatic Nuisance Species Task Force. Upon approval, states are eligible for federal

---

[76] Mark A. Davis et al., *Don't Judge Species on Their Origins*, 474 NATURE 153, 154 (2011).

[77] 16 U.S.C. § 4724(a)(1) (2012).

grants to assist with the implementation of the plans.[78] Thirty-eight states currently have developed aquatic nuisance species management plans.[79] A 2007 review of the state invasive species management plans found that all state plans reviewed, including twenty-three aquatic species plans, "had the capacity to adapt some aspect of their programs or activities to changing conditions," although only a handful actually included a discussion of climate change.[80]

A. RISK ASSESSMENT

As climate change has the potential to alter the invasiveness of nonnative species in certain areas or enable the spread of established invasive species, consideration of climate impacts is important for both risk assessment and prioritization of management actions. Climate matching tools, for instance, can be used to identify areas at risk due to the expansion of the range of invasive species. "Climate matching" refers to the identification of geographic areas that are at risk of colonization "by a potential invasive species on the basis of similarity to climates found in the species' native range."[81] Simulation models such as CLIMEX, which "enables the user to estimate the potential geographical distribution and seasonal abundance of a species in relation to climate,"[82] have been used extensively for insects and plants. Climate matching can be useful both for predicting which areas might be at risk for new introductions of nonnative species and those areas that might be at risk due to the expansion or range shift of an established invader. The results of such simulations and studies can then be used to inform management plans and identify appropriate control and eradication measures.

The FWS has recently begun working to supplement the Lacey Act injurious species listing process by actively partnering with the live organisms trade industry to encourage voluntary commitments to refrain from engaging in the trade of invasive species.[83] The foundation of this approach is an ecological risk screening process that seeks to classify species as either potentially noninvasive (low risk), invasive (high risk), or of uncertain

---

[78] *Id.* § 4724(b).

[79] *State ANS Management Plans*, ANS TASK FORCE, http://anstaskforce.gov/stateplans.php (last visited Feb. 12, 2014).

[80] Britta G. Bierwagen, Roxanne Thomas & Austin Kane, *Capacity of Management Plans for Aquatic Invasive Species to Integrate Climate Change*, 22 CONSERVATION BIOLOGY 568, 571 (2008).

[81] Gordon H. Rodda et al., *Climate Matching as a Tool for Predicting Potential North American Spread of Brown Tree Snakes, in* MANAGING VERTEBRATE INVASIVE SPECIES: PROCEEDINGS OF AN INTERNATIONAL SYMPOSIUM (G.W. Witmer et al. eds., 2007), *available at* http://www.aphis.usda.gov/wildlife_damage/nwrc/symposia/invasive_symposium/nwrc_TOC_index.shtml.

[82] *CLIMEX 3.0.2*, HEARNE SOFTWARE, http://www.hearne.com.au/Software/CLIMEX/Editions (last visited Feb. 12, 2014).

[83] *Invasive Species Prevention: Keeping Risky Aquatic Species out of the United States—How We Are Working with Industry and State Partners*, U.S. FISH & WILDLIFE SERV. FISH & AQUATIC CONSERVATION, *available at* http://www.fws.gov/injuriouswildlife/Injurious_prevention.html (last visited July 16, 2014).

risk due to lack of information.[84] Ideally, partnering industry members would agree not to import high risk species, or trade such species only in geographic areas that present a low risk of establishment or in adherence to best management practices, such as limiting trade to reproductively sterile organisms.[85] The FWS is currently focusing its efforts on freshwater aquatic species that are not yet present in the United States, which have shown a history of invasiveness in other countries and could develop self-sustaining populations in U.S. climates.[86] The Service's risk-screening standard operating procedures utilizes CLIMATCH, a software program developed by the Bureau of Rural Sciences within the Australia Department of Agriculture, Fisheries, and Forestry.[87] The Ecological Risk Screening Summaries (ERSS) are publicly released by the FWS as they become available to guide industry and management decisions.

B. CALIFORNIA CASE STUDY

Considering the impact of climate change is also important when conducting pathway risk assessments. In 2008, the California Ocean Science Trust (OST), at the request of the California Ocean Protection Council, began coordinating risk assessments for the introduction of aquatic invasive species into California's marine waters.[88] In an effort to learn more about lesser-understood vectors, OST focused on the following pathways: commercial fishing, recreational boating, live bait, live imported seafood, aquariums and aquascaping, and aquaculture. The risk assessment of the live bait trade was released in 2012 and illustrates the value such assessments can provide to managers and policymakers.

The sale of live marine or estuarine organisms, such as fish, worms, and shrimp, as saltwater fishing bait is a pathway of concern because the organisms themselves may be released into the environment (*i.e.*, break free of the lure), and bait is sometimes shipped in seaweeds or saltwater that can harbor other species. To assess the risk of the trade in live saltwater bait to introduce or spread aquatic invasive species in California waters, OST compiled information on each saltwater species sold as live bait in California, identified hitchhiker species that have been detected in commercial bait shipments received in California, reviewed past invasions associated with live bait, and assessed the environmental suitability of nonnative bait species.[89]

---

[84] *Id.*

[85] *Id.*

[86] *Id.*

[87] *Source Map*, AUSTL. DEP'T OF AGRIC., FISHERIES, & FORESTRY, http://data.daff.gov.au:8080/Climatch/climatch.jsp (last visited Feb. 12, 2014).

[88] Cal. Ocean Sci. Trust, *Aquatic Invasive Species Vector Risk Assessment Project, available at* http://calost.org/pdf/science-initiatives/ais/AIS_Handout.pdf (last visited July 16, 2014).

[89] *See* ANDREW N. COHEN, AQUATIC INVASIVE SPECIES VECTOR RISK ASSESSMENTS: LIVE SALTWATER BAIT AND THE INTRODUCTION OF NON-NATIVE SPECIES INTO CAL., FINAL REPORT SUBMITTED TO THE CAL. OCEAN SCI. TRUST 47 (2012).

The risk assessment revealed that, in general, this pathway poses little risk of introducing nonnative species into new regions because "most of the live saltwater bait sold in California consists of native species, and that most of it is harvested and used locally within a region of the state."[90] Several species, however, did pose concerns: nonnative pileworms and bloodworms imported from Maine, lugworms from Korea, nuclear worms from Vietnam, ghost shrimp from Washington and Oregon, and mud shrimp from Oregon.[91] The nuclear worm was identified as offering the least risk, because it is not commonly sold and is considered unsuited to cold Californian waters. The report, however, makes an important note regarding the changing climate: "If anthropogenic climate change raises the temperature of California's coastal waters, they could become more hospitable to this worm."[92]

The report concluded that the greatest risk was not posed by a bait species directly, but rather by the Atlantic seaweed used to pack the two baitworm species imported from Maine.[93] The seaweed can transport a wide range of organisms, including known invasive species. The report identified several actions that could be taken to reduce the risk of introduction, including "requiring distributors or retailers to remove and dispose of the packing seaweed before sale to customers, banning the use of seaweed as packing for imported worms, or banning the import and sale of these worms."[94] These recommendations are valuable concrete, tangible, and focused next steps for policymakers to pursue.

The report also identified a crucial regulatory gap that if closed would provide improved data collection and pathway management. Although California law requires importers to obtain a permit from the California Department of Fish and Game before importing live bait species, the report authors discovered no evidence that these permitting requirements had ever been enforced.[95] The report stated that the law "provides a mechanism for monitoring and managing current and potential future imports of live saltwater bait species, if the state chooses to implement that law."[96] The report's inclusion of potential management responses is a valuable contribution to natural resource managers' decision-making that is often overlooked. Researchers have found that "most attempts to model pathways have focused on describing the likelihood of invader establishment and rather few have attempted to model explicit management strategies."[97] Management strategies need to be identified and evaluated as part of the pathway risk assessment to help managers identify and pursue the most effective strategies.

---

[90] *Id.* at 47.

[91] *Id.*

[92] *Id.* at 48.

[93] *Id.* at 50.

[94] *Id.*

[95] *Id.* at 49.

[96] *Id.* at 50.

[97] Philip E. Hulme, *Trade, Transport, and Trouble: Managing Invasive Species Pathways in an Era of Globalization*, 26 J. APPLIED ECOLOGY 10, 16 (2009).

Conclusion

Marine invasive species present a complex management challenge. The interconnectedness of the oceans facilitates the movement of both humans and other organisms. Many marine species migrate vast distances, and slight changes in environmental conditions can change the natural diversity of a coastal or marine ecosystem. Human activity has significantly altered marine ecosystems through pollution, habitat alteration, and species introductions. Given the wide-scale impact humans have had on the marine environment, it is not possible to restore ecosystems to some sort of prehuman contact, "native" state. Rather, marine ecosystems must be managed to protect and restore desired ecosystem functions. For many marine invasive species, eradication is not possible. That ship has sailed. In many cases, however, populations can be controlled to reduce, when possible, their negative impacts.

Overall, the legal framework for marine invasive species should be designed and implemented to minimize the risk that species are moved via human activities. Laws and policies should therefore require pathway risk assessments, and Congress and state legislatures should provide natural resources managers with adequate funding to complete such studies. These risk assessments will be essential tools in the prioritization of which pathways to regulate, which species to restrict, and which marine environments to protect.

11 The Impact of Marine Invasive Species on Endangered Species Protection Efforts in a Changing Ocean Environment
Eric V. Hull*

* The author would like to thank Courtney Gaver, a student at Florida Coastal School of Law, for her invaluable research assistance, and Professor Helia Hull for her editorial contributions.

Introduction

Worldwide, human activities continue to significantly impact species and the environments they inhabit.[1] Climate change poses an urgent threat to species conservation and threatens to fundamentally alter natural systems.[2] Under current projections, approximately 20–30 percent of all species on Earth may face increased risk of extinction by the end of this century as a result of habitat loss or destruction due to human encroachment and climate change.[3] The Endangered Species Act (ESA) was enacted to promote the conservation of threatened and endangered plants and animals and to preserve their critical habitats.[4] However, in a rapidly changing marine environment, absent change the Act may prove incapable of protecting vulnerable marine species.

Marine systems around the world continue to decline as a result of pollution, overfishing, habitat destruction, loss of biodiversity, and other stressors.[5] The presence of invasive species may exacerbate these stressors.[6] Once introduced into a marine system, invasive species may act to alter critical habitats and trophic dynamics, decrease juvenile recruitment through increased predation on native species, increase parasitism, alter genetic diversity, decrease species resilience, impair nutrient cycling, and alter water quality.[7] As a result of these and other impacts, marine invasive species compromise the effectiveness of the ESA. In fact, next to habitat loss, invasive species pose the greatest threat to listed species.[8]

---

[1] IUCN, World's oldest and largest species in decline—IUCN Red List, July 2, 2013, http://www.iucn.org/?13243%2FWorlds-oldest-and-largest-species-in-decline-IUCN-Red-List (noting that of the 70,294 species assessed, 20,934 are threatened with extinction).

[2] *See generally* John Kostyack & Dan Rohlf, *Conserving Endangered Species in an Era of Global Warming*, 38 ENVTL. L. REP. 10203 (2008), *available at* http://www.nwf.org/~/media/PDFs/Global-Warming/ConservingEndangeredSpeciesinanEraofGlobalWarming.ashx.

[3] *See generally* U.S. Envtl. Prot. Agency, EPA/600/R-08/014, Effects of Climate Change on Aquatic Invasive Species and Implications for Management and Research (2008), *available at* http://ofmpub.epa.gov/eims/eimscomm.getfile?p_download_id=472114 [hereinafter EPA Management].

[4] 16 U.S.C. § 1531(b) (2012).

[5] Benjamin Halpern et al., *A Global Map of Human Impact on Marine Ecosystems*, 319 SCI. 948, 949 (2008) (noting that of twenty marine ecosystems examined, each one was affected by human influence, and 41 percent were strongly affected by multiple anthropogenic drivers of ecological change).

[6] *See* U.S. Envtl. Prot. Agency, Invasive Species, http://www.epa.gov/glnpo/invasive/ (last visited Nov. 9, 2012) (noting how over the last two centuries invasive species have impacted ecosystems in the United States).

[7] *See* U.S. Federal Aquatic Nuisance Species Task Force, What Are ANS?, http://anstaskforce.gov/ans.php (last visited Nov. 9, 2012) [hereinafter ANSTF]; *see also* Alexandre Meinesz, *The Impact of Invasive Species*, NOVA, Apr. 1, 2003, http://www.pbs.org/wgbh/nova/nature/impact-invasive-species.html.

[8] *Invasive Species Mgmt. on Federal Lands: Oversight Hearing Before the H. Natural Res. Subcomm. on Pub. Lands and Envtl. Regulations*, 113th Cong. (2013) (statement for the record by U.S. Department of the

The synergistic effects of climate change and invasive species on marine species may intensify the overall impact of both.[9] Altered biogeochemical processes, increasing atmospheric CO_2, decreasing ocean pH, hydrological modification, altered food webs, and habitat fragmentation are all anticipated impacts of climate change.[10] These and other climate-induced changes may create conditions favorable to invasion by nonnative species, increase the capacity of native species to exploit resources in new ways, or result in species hybridization that further challenges protection efforts.[11] Although species will respond to these changes in different ways, climate change is likely to decrease overall system resilience and increase the probability that marine invasive species will become established in more areas.[12]

Despite considerable state and federal efforts to address the problem, invasive species continue to pose major challenges to protected species in the United States.[13] Collectively, the existing patchwork of state and federal regulations developed to address invasive species has had only limited success.[14] This is particularly true in marine environments.[15]

Interior), *available at* http://www.doi.gov/ocl/hearings/113/invasivespeciesmanagement_051613.cfm [hereinafter SOR].

[9] *See generally* EPA Management, *supra* note 3, at 1-3, 1-5.

[10] *See* Lewis H. Ziska, *Evaluation of the Growth Response of Six Invasive Species to Past, Present and Future Atmospheric Carbon Dioxide*, 54 J. EXPERIMENTAL BOTANY 395 (2003); John P. McCarty, *Ecological Consequences of Recent Climate Change*, 15 CONSERVATION BIOLOGY 320, 326 (2001).

[11] *See generally* J.P. Barry et al., *Climate-Related, Long-Term Faunal Changes in a California Rocky Intertidal Community*, 267 SCI. 672 (1995) (reporting that temperature increases caused certain southern invertebrate species to increase and expand their ranges while northern species that were not tolerant of warmer waters declined); *see also* John J. Stachowicz et al., *Linking Climate Change and Biological Invasions: Ocean Warming Facilitates Nonindigenous Species Invasions*, 99 PNAS 15497 (2002), *available at* http://woodshole.er.usgs.gov/project-pages/stellwagen/didemnum/images/pdf/stach_2002.pdf; Scott C. Doney et al., *Climate Change Impacts on Marine Ecosystems*, 4 ANN. REV. MARINE SCI. 12 (2012) (noting that climate change may cause marine species restricted in range by thermal strata to migrate and expand their range); Jennifer Viegas, *Arctic Animal Hybrids Threaten Biodiversity*, DISCOVERY NEWS, DEC. 15, 2010, http://news.discovery.com/animals/arctic-animal-hybrids-threaten-biodiversity.htm (discussing animal hybrids that have occurred or could occur among animals in and around the Arctic as a result of climate-change-induced alterations in the environment).

[12] *See supra* note 10.

[13] *See generally* NAT'L OCEAN COUNCIL, NATIONAL OCEAN POLICY IMPLEMENTATION PLAN, 5, 14 (2013), *available at* http://www.whitehouse.gov//sites/default/files/national_ocean_policy_implementation_plan.pdf [hereinafter National Ocean Policy Plan](recognizing that marine and aquatic invasive species cost the U.S. economy billions of dollars each year in damage to fisheries, tourism, and coastal infrastructure and that federal agencies need to take actions to improve the ability to detect and reduce invasive species); *see also* ANSTF, *supra* note 7 (noting that invasive species have been a major factor in the decline of protected species and a significant impediment to their recovery).

[14] National Ocean Policy Plan, *supra* note 13, at 14 (noting that invasive species alter habitats, threaten native aquatic life, and cause billions of dollars in natural and infrastructure damage each year).

[15] *See generally* Iméne Meliane & Chad Hewitt, *Gaps and Priorities in Addressing Marine Invasive Species* (2005), *available at* https://cmsdata.iucn.org/downloads/ais_gaps_priorities.pdf (noting that many eradication and control methods that have found success in terrestrial environments have proven to be ineffective for or inapplicable to marine systems); *see also* R.E. Thresher & A.M. Kuris, *Options for Managing Invasive Marine Species*, 6 BIOLOGICAL INVASIONS 295 (2004); A.A. Batabyal, *International Aspects of Invasive*

This chapter addresses the application of the ESA to a rapidly changing marine environment, with emphasis on how current responses to marine invasive species and climate change may affect application of the ESA to protect marine species.

I. The Endangered Species Act and Marine Invasive Species

As amended, the ESA provides a comprehensive legal regime to address the challenge of averting species extinction.[16] It provides a legal basis for protecting imperiled species and the ecosystems on which they depend, and seeks to return imperiled species to a point where protection under the Act is no longer required.[17] Today, numerous species of marine and anadromous fish, marine mammals, marine turtles, marine invertebrates, and a marine plant are afforded protection under the Act.[18] Yet these represent only a fraction of the species currently at risk.[19] The inadequacy of current efforts to address marine invasive species in U.S. waters undermines the ability to protect vulnerable marine species under the ESA.

A. INVASIVE SPECIES: BACKGROUND

Invasive species are broadly defined to include those nonnative or non-indigenous species "whose introduction does or is likely to cause economic or environmental harm or harm to human health."[20] The introduction and spread of invasive species into new ecosystems poses extraordinary environmental and economic challenges to the planet and has far-ranging impacts on human well-being.[21] Most species introduced into new

---

Species Management: A Research Agenda, 21 STOCHASTIC ENVTL. RES. & RISK ASSESSMENT 717 (2007) (noting that compared to terrestrial systems, considerably less is known about the biology of most marine species or about the intricate community dynamics in marine systems that may facilitate invasions).

[16] ALISON RIESER ET AL., OCEAN AND COASTAL LAW: CASES AND MATERIALS 749 (4th ed. 2013).

[17] *Id.*; 16 U.S.C. § 1531(b)(2012).

[18] Nat'l Oceanic and Atmospheric Admin., Endangered and Threatened Marine Species, http://www.nmfs.noaa.gov/pr/species/esa/ (last visited Nov. 18, 2013); *see also* Nat'l Oceanic and Atmospheric Admin., All Endangered and Threatened Marine Species, http://www.nmfs.noaa.gov/pr/pdfs/species/esa_table.pdf (last visited Jan. 17, 2014) (identifying marine species currently protected under the ESA).

[19] *See* Kostyack & Rohlf, *supra* note 2, at 10207 (asserting that climate change will result in the need to increase species listings under the ESA).

[20] Exec. Order No. 13112, 64 Fed. Reg. 6183 (Feb. 3, 1999).

[21] IUCN, Invasive Species, http://www.iucn.org/about/union/secretariat/offices/esaro/what_we_do/invasive_species/ (last visited Jan. 17, 2014) (noting that biological invasions are a serious threat to ecosystems and species across the world as well as to human development, human health, and human livelihoods); *see also* Int'l Maritime Org., Ballast Water Management, http://www.imo.org/OurWork/Environment/BallastWaterManagement/Pages/Default.aspx (last visited Nov. 7, 2012) (noting that "the spread of invasive species is now recognized as one of the greatest threats to the ecological and the economic well being of the planet"); David Pimentel et al., *Economic and Environmental Threats of Alien Plant, Animal, and*

environments do not survive long enough to become established, but those that do typically exhibit characteristics that make them more resilient to disturbances in the system, such as pollution, disease, and other stressors.[22] Many also benefit from the absence of natural predators or disease that would otherwise keep their populations in check.[23] As a result, some introduced species thrive and quickly dominate over native species that are less adaptable.[24] Once established, invasive species exhibit strong resilience to eradication efforts. The problem is particularly acute in marine systems.

B. THE IMPACTS OF MARINE INVASIVE SPECIES ON ESA LISTINGS

A prerequisite to protection under the ESA is the designation of a species as threatened or endangered.[25] A species may be listed if that species is threatened or endangered due to a number of factors, including: (1) the present or threatened destruction, modification, or curtailment of species habitat or range; (2) overutilization of the species for commercial, recreational, scientific, or educational purposes; (3) disease or predation; and (4) the inadequacy of existing regulatory mechanisms.[26] The presence of marine invasive species impacts each of these factors and must be considered when deciding whether to list a species.

Microbe Invasions, 84 AGRIC. ECOSYSTEMS & ENV'T 1, 14 (2001) (finding that globally, the costs of damage caused by invasive species is approximately US $1.4 trillion per year—close to 5 percent of global GDP).

[22] Univ. of Cal., Riverside: Ctr. for Invasive Species Res., Invasive Species FAQs, http://cisr.ucr.edu/invasive_species_faqs.html (last visited Jan. 17, 2014) [hereinafter UC Riverside] (noting that of all nonnative species that enter a new ecosystem, about 10 percent of these will survive, and of those survivors a further 10 percent—or just 1 percent of the original number—will become invasive pests).

[23] *See, e.g.*, Mark Hixon et al., *Lionfish Invasion: Super Predator Threatens Caribbean Coral Reefs*, NOAA (Feb. 8, 2009), http://www.nurp.noaa.gov/Spotlight/Lionfish_2009.html (noting that invasive lionfish, with few known natural predators, pose a major threat to coral reef ecosystems in the Caribbean region).

[24] Nat'l Ctr. for Coastal Ocean Sci., Lionfish, http://coastalscience.noaa.gov/research/pollution/invasive/lionfish (last visited Jan. 17, 2014) [hereinafter NCCOS] (reporting that lionfish have surpassed some native species with densities over 1,000 lionfish per acre); *see also* Hixon et al., *supra* note 23 (noting that "due to their population explosion and aggressive behavior, lionfish have the potential to become the most disastrous marine invasion in history by drastically reducing the abundance of coral reef fishes and leaving behind a devastated ecosystem").

[25] 16 U.S.C. § 1533(a)(1)(2012). A species is considered endangered when that species is in danger of extinction throughout all or a significant part of its range, and is threatened when it is likely to become an endangered species within the foreseeable future. The Act is administered jointly by the Secretary of Commerce and the Secretary of Interior. 50 C.F.R § 402.01(2012).

[26] 16 U.S.C. § 1533(a)(1) (2012). The species may also be listed if that species is threatened or endangered due to other natural or man-made factors affecting the species continued existence. *Id.*

1. Present or Threatened Destruction, Modification, or Curtailment of Species Habitat or Range

Healthy ecosystems are more resilient to change.[27] Unfortunately, as a result of human activities, most natural systems are already impaired to some degree.[28] The cumulative impact of human exploitation of marine resources is becoming clear, and the impact appears greater than previously understood.[29] One recent study suggests that the impact has been so significant that the Earth may be in the midst of a sixth mass extinction.[30]

Invasive species have already fundamentally altered complex ecosystems around the world.[31] More than 6,500 invasive species are now established in the United States alone.[32] Of these, approximately 500 exist within U.S. coastal waters.[33] These species alter habitats in a multitude of ways.[34] They often exploit impaired systems and take advantage of their unique ability to cope with environmental disturbances better than native species.[35] In some cases, the same factors that create a poor environment for native species may allow an introduced species to thrive.[36] In the absence of natural predators, their populations

---

[27] See IUCN, Why Do Ecosystems Matter for Disaster Risk Reduction?, http://iucn.org/about/work/programmes/ecosystem_management/disaster/ecosystems/index.cfm (last visited Jan. 21, 2014); see also IUCN, ECOSYSTEM-BASED ADAPTATION: A NATURAL RESPONSE TO CLIMATE CHANGE 1 (2009), available at http://cmsdata.iucn.org/downloads/iucn_eba_brochure.pdf, (noting that healthy ecosystems, such as forests, wetlands, mangroves, and coral reefs, have a greater potential to adapt to climate change themselves, and recover more easily from extreme weather events).

[28] Millennium Ecosystem Assessment, LIVING BEYOND OUR MEANS, NATURAL ASSETS AND HUMAN WELL-BEING 3 (2005), http://millenniumassessment.org/documents/document.429.aspx.pdf; see also ALEX ROGERS & DAN LAFFOLEY, INTERNATIONAL EARTH SYSTEM EXPERT WORKSHOP ON OCEAN STRESSES AND IMPACTS SUMMARY REPORT 6 (2011), http://www.stateoftheocean.org/pdfs/1906_IPSO-LONG.pdf (noting that marine ecosystem collapse is occurring as a result of both current and emerging stressors).

[29] Rogers & Laffoley, supra note 28, at 7. Id. (noting that the extinction threat to marine species is rapidly increasing).

[30] See generally Anthony Barnosky et al., Has the Earth's Sixth Mass Extinction Already Arrived?, 471 NATURE 51 (2011).

[31] See supra note 6.

[32] USGS, Invasive Species Program, http://www.usgs.gov/ecosystems/invasive_species/index.html (last visited Jan. 21, 2014).

[33] IUCN, MARINE MENACE ALIEN INVASIVE SPECIES IN THE MARINE ENVIRONMENT 5 (2009), http://data.iucn.org/dbtw-wpd/edocs/2009-011.pdf.

[34] GARY L. RAY, AQUATIC NUISANCE SPECIES RESEARCH PROGRAM INVASIVE ANIMAL SPECIES IN MARINE AND ESTUARINE ENVIRONMENTS: BIOLOGY AND ECOLOGY 1, 17–30 (2005), http://el.erdc.usace.army.mil/elpubs/pdf/trel05-2.pdf (discussing a variety of ways that invasive species alter habitats and increase the difficulty of restoring an impaired habitat).

[35] See D. Simberloff & M. Alexander, Biological Stressors, U.S. EPA ECOLOGICAL RISK ASSESSMENT ISSUE PAPERS, EPA/630/R-94/009 (1994).

[36] For example, in the 1970s, the Atlantic comb Jelly (Mnemiopsis leidyi) was introduced via ballast water discharge into the Black Sea ecosystem, which was already significantly impaired by elevated salinity, pollution, and overfishing. The organism had no natural predators in the new environment, and tolerated the pollution and elevated salinity better than native species. As a result of overfishing in the area, the invader encountered only minimal competition for the zooplankton that it fed on exclusively. Populations of the organism quickly grew to reach 10 billion tons, more than ten times the annual global fish catch. Soon it

may quickly expand and place increasing stress on the system.[37] Some introduced species may alter trophic dynamics by outcompeting native species for available resources while providing little to no food value to other species in the system.[38] These and other changes can result in decreased system biodiversity that renders the system less resilient to change.[39]

2. Overutilization of the Species for Commercial, Recreational, Scientific, or Educational Purposes

Systems that are more biologically diverse appear to be more resistant to invasive species.[40] Yet, throughout the world marine biodiversity continues to decline.[41] The exponential growth in human population has led to increased demand for marine living resources.[42] This, in turn, has led to the development of more sophisticated technologies capable of extracting marine resources at unsustainable rates.[43] These actions and others have contributed to a significant loss of biodiversity in marine systems.[44] This loss impairs system dynamics in ways that can limit the ability of affected species to respond to other environmental stressors that, in turn, contribute to further biodiversity loss.[45] The unsustainable use of marine living resources may facilitate invasions that place greater stress on native species and their ability to respond to changing conditions.

---

completely dominated the fishery, causing widespread species collapse that resulted in the loss of hundreds of millions of dollars to the area's fishing and tourism industries. *See* NSF, Jellyfish Gone Wild, http://www.nsf.gov/news/special_reports/jellyfish/textonly/locations_blacksea.jsp (last visited Dec. 9, 2013).

[37] Posting of Caitlin Leutwiler to Defenders of Wildlife Blog, http://www.defendersblog.org/2011/02/lionfish-on-the-loose/ (Feb. 24, 2011) (reporting that a single female lionfish can produce up to 2 million eggs).

[38] *Id.*

[39] Carl Folke, *Regime Shifts, Resilience, and Biodiversity in Ecosystem Management*, 35 Ann. Rev. Ecol. Evol. Syst. 557, 575 (2004) (concluding that human actions, including actions that reduce biodiversity, may cause loss of resilience that renders an ecosystem more vulnerable to changes that previously could have been absorbed).

[40] John J. Stachowicz, *Species Diversity and Invasion Resistance in a Marine Ecosystem*, 286 Sci. 1577 (1999) (showing that increased species richness significantly decreased invasion success); *see also* S.R. Palumbi et al., *Ecosystems in Action: Lessons from Marine Ecology about Recovery, Resistance, and Reversibility*, 58 Biosci. 33 (2008).

[41] NSF, Accelerating Loss of Ocean Species Threatens Human Well-Being (Nov. 2, 2006), http://www.nsf.gov/news/news_summ.jsp?cntn_id=108149 (discussing report indicating that "loss of biodiversity is profoundly reducing the ocean's ability to produce seafood, resist diseases, filter pollutants and rebound from stresses such as overfishing and climate change").

[42] *See* Environmental Literacy Council, Overexploitation, http://www.enviroliteracy.org/article.php/1514.html (last visited Nov. 13, 2013).

[43] FAO Fisheries and Aquaculture Department, The State of World Fisheries and Aquaculture 12 (2012), http://www.fao.org/docrep/016/i2727e/i2727e.pdf (discussing how the state of world marine fisheries is worsening and has had a negative impact on fishery production).

[44] NSF, *supra* note 41.

[45] *See supra* note 42.

3. Disease or Predation

The spread of disease and changes in predator-prey interactions can have profound impacts on marine biodiversity. Most marine species carry some form of parasite or other vector for transmitting disease.[46] Diseases and organisms capable of causing disease are often transmitted from prey to predator during predation events.[47] Some parasitize or transmit novel diseases to native species.[48] These host-vector and predator-prey relationships are often established along evolutionary timelines, so rapid changes in environments can have significant negative effects. Species whose populations are kept in check by disease may flourish when placed into environments absent of such disease.[49] Similarly, species whose populations are kept in check by existing predators may flourish in environments without such predators.[50] Some invasive species thrive when introduced into new environments due to the emergence of favorable predatory-prey relationships, or the absence of natural predators or disease.[51] Others prey on native species and drive down native populations by interfering with reproduction events, feeding on juveniles, or outcompeting native species for available resources.[52] These system dynamics often act synergistically to the benefit of the species introduced.[53]

4. Inadequate Existing Regulatory Mechanisms

A key impediment to addressing invasive species is the multitude of invasion pathways.[54] In most cases, however, invasive species arrive in new environments as a direct result of human activity uncontrolled by effective regulation.[55] Prior to 1990, the Lacey Act was the primary authority to prevent the introduction of invasive species into the United

---

[46] Marine Parasitology, http://www.marineparasitology.com/MarineParasitology.htm (last visited Nov. 15, 2013).

[47] Id.

[48] Id.

[49] See, e.g., NOAA, Lionfish Fact Sheet, http://www.habitat.noaa.gov/pdf/best_management_practices/fact_sheets/Lionfish%20Factsheet.pdf (last visited July 28, 2014). (noting that in their native range lionfish populations are kept in check by many factors, including disease, but since their introduction into the North Western Atlantic and Caribbean oceans their populations have rapidly expanded due, in part, to their resistance to disease in those regions).

[50] Id.

[51] Id.; see also R. Poulin et al., Biological Invasions and the Dynamics of Endemic Diseases in Freshwater Systems, 56 FRESHWATER BIOLOGY 678 (2011) (noting that biological invasions have resulted in the introduction of disease, and sudden increases in the incidence and severity of existing diseases).

[52] Nat'l Wildlife Federation, Invasive Species, http://www.nwf.org/Wildlife/Threats-to-Wildlife/Invasive-Species.aspx (last visited Jan. 13, 2014).

[53] Martin Enserink, Biological Invaders Sweep In, 285 SCI. 1834, 1835 (1999) (discussing how invasive species place increasing stress on existing species and add to biodiversity loss, which, in turn, can create conditions favorable for further invasions).

[54] See ANSTF, supra note 7 (discussing the multitude of ways species may be introduced into a new environment).

[55] See id.

States.[56] The Act makes it illegal to import into the United States any species that the Secretary of the Interior designates as "injurious to human beings...or to wildlife or the wildlife resources."[57] The reactive format of the Act has proven inadequate to address the problem of invasive species because the determination that a species is in fact injurious is made after the species has been introduced into the United States, and often after it has caused harm.[58] Past efforts to shift the burden of proof of harm to the party seeking to import a species have failed at the federal level.[59]

Regulatory efforts to address marine invasive species have focused primarily on ballast water discharge because that route of entry has historically represented the single largest invasion pathway for marine invasive species into new areas.[60] Those efforts have been largely ineffective at preventing the introduction of foreign organisms into marine environments.[61] Current ballast water management rules limit the number of living organisms that may be discharged into marine water, but they do not prevent future invasions.[62] This is because biological organisms may reproduce once introduced into the new environment. Indeed, the inability of existing approaches to address the complex problem of species invasions has led some legal scholars to call for the enactment of a comprehensive federal statute that directly addresses the problem.[63]

---

[56] Lacey Act, 16 U.S.C. §§ 3371–3378 (2012).

[57] 18 U.S.C.§ 42 (a)(1) (2012). Importation includes any place subject to U.S. jurisdiction. *See* 16 U.S.C. § 3371(b) (2012).

[58] *Hearing Before the H. Natural Res. Subcomm. on Fisheries, Wildlife and Oceans Regarding Aquatic Nuisance Species*, 110th Cong. (2007) (statement of Dr. Mamie Parker, Asst. Dir. for Fisheries and Habitat Conservation, U.S. Fish and Wildlife Serv.), *available at* http://www.doi.gov/ocl/hearings/110/aquaticnuisancespecies_072709.cfm.

[59] Julianne Kurdila, *The Introduction of Exotic Species into the United States: There Goes the Neighborhood*, 16 B.C. ENVTL. AFF. L. REV. 95, 103–04 (1988).

[60] Ballast water often contains a mixture of viable organisms from different coastal regions because ships travel among various ports. As the ballast water is pumped off the vessel, these foreign organisms are introduced into the new environment. *See* Corrina Chase et al., Marine Bioinvasions Fact Sheet: Ballast Water Treatment Options, http://massbay.mit.edu/resources/pdf/ballast-treat.pdf (last visited Jan. 21, 2014).

[61] *See generally* Nonindigenous Aquatic Nuisance Prevention and Control Act of 1990, Pub. L. No. 101-646, 104 Stat. 4761 (codified at 16 U.S.C. §§ 4701–4751) (mandating, inter alia, the prevention of unintentional introductions of foreign species via ballast water discharge into the Great Lakes); National Invasive Species Act of 1996, Pub. L. No. 104-332, 110 Stat. 4073 (expanding the scope of ballast water discharge to restrictions to apply to all vessels entering U.S. waters); Exec. Order No. 13,112, 64 Fed. Reg. 6,183 (Feb. 3, 1999) (creating the Invasive Species Council charged with creating a National Invasive Species Management Plan to coordinate federal and state programs to address pathways of introduction, prevention, eradication, control, restoration, early detection and response, education, and research directed to invasive species).

[62] EPA, VESSEL GENERAL PERMIT FOR DISCHARGES INCIDENTAL TO THE NORMAL OPERATION OF VESSELS (VGP) (2013), http://www.epa.gov/npdes/pubs/vgp_permit2013.pdf; *see also* USCG, STANDARDS FOR LIVING ORGANISMS IN SHIPS' BALLAST WATER DISCHARGED IN U.S. WATERS (2012), http://www.uscg.mil/hq/cg5/cg522/cg5224/docs/2012-06579_PI.pdf.

[63] *See generally* Jane Cynthia Graham, *Snakes on a Plane, or in a Wetland: Fighting Back Invasive Non-native Animals—Proposing a Federal Comprehensive Invasive Non-native Animal Species Statute*, 25 TUL. ENVTL. L.J. 19 (2011).

C. THE IMPACT OF MARINE INVASIVE SPECIES ON DESIGNATION OF CRITICAL HABITAT UNDER THE ESA

When a species is listed as endangered, the ESA requires that "to the maximum extent prudent and determinable" the Secretary concurrently designate areas as critical habitat for the species.[64] In determining what areas constitute critical habitat, the Secretary is required to consider those physical and biological features that are essential to the conservation of the species, including habitats that are protected from disturbance.[65] The area identified as critical habitat may be expanded to include areas outside the geographical area occupied by the species at the time it is listed if essential for the conservation of the species.[66] Once a critical habitat is established, unless otherwise exempted, each federal agency must ensure that its actions "will not jeopardize the continued existence of the listed species or otherwise result in the destruction or adverse modification of that habitat."[67] Unfortunately, many species afforded protection under the ESA do not have a critical habitat designated.[68]

For marine species, the designation of critical habitat is particularly difficult. This is because each species' bio-climate envelope is tied directly to ocean chemistry and temperature, two factors that continue to change in marine systems.[69] These physical changes add to existing marine stressors to undermine efforts to conserve species.[70] Although it is still unclear how particular species will adapt to physical changes in the

---

[64] 16 U.S.C. § 1533 (a)(3)(A)(i) (2012). Critical habitat is defined as the "specific areas within the geographical areas occupied by the species, at the time it is listed...on which are found those physical and biological features that are (I) essential to the conservation of the species and (II) which may require special management considerations or protections...". See 16 U.S.C. § 1532(5)(A)(i) (2012). See also 50 C.F.R. § 424.12(a)(2) (2014) ("Critical habitat is not determinable when one or both of the following situations exist: (i) Information sufficient to perform required analyses of the impacts of the designation is lacking, or (ii) The biological needs of the species are not sufficiently well known to permit identification of an area as critical habitat.").

[65] 50 C.F.R. § 424.12(b) (2014). The Secretary does not have to designate critical habitat where either: (i) "[t]he species is threatened by taking or other human activity, and identification of critical habitat could increase the degree of such threat to the species," or (ii) "[s]uch designation would not be benefit the species." See 50 C.F.R. §424.12(a)(1)(i-ii)(2014). That decision must be made "based on the best scientific data available, after taking into consideration the probable economic and other impacts of making such a designation." See 50 C.F.R. §424.12(a) (2014).

[66] 16 U.S.C. § 1533(5)(A)(ii)(2012).

[67] 16 U.S.C § 1536(a)(2)(2012).

[68] The designation of critical habitats is not required for species, including highly migratory marine species, that spend part of their life outside U.S. jurisdiction, or for species listed prior to the 1978 ESA amendments that added the critical habitat provisions. See NOAA, Endangered and Threatened Marine Species, http://www.nmfs.noaa.gov/pr/pdfs/species/esa_table.pdf (last updated Jan. 29, 2014).

[69] Carbon Mitigation Initiative, Annual Report 2011, at 4, http://cmi.princeton.edu/annual_reports/pdfs/2011.pdf (last visited July 28, 2014).

[70] See generally William W.L. Cheung et al., Projecting Global Marine Biodiversity Impacts under Climate Change Scenarios, 10 FISH & FISHERIES 235 (2009).

ocean, there is emerging evidence of significant phenologic response by some species.[71] As ocean temperature increases and ocean chemistry changes, marine species will likely shift their range and alter migration, feeding, and breeding patterns to match changes in the seasonal activity of plants and animals critical to their survival.[72] This movement will bring species into new environments, which may result in the same damaging interactions observed currently for invasive species.[73] Declines in biodiversity in some areas will likely augment the impact of invasive species in those areas because the response rate is likely to be different for different species.[74] These impacts, coupled with other changing marine conditions, will increase the difficulty of accurately identifying critical habitat essential to the conservation of many marine species.[75]

II. Legal and Policy Responses to Address Marine Invasive Species under the ESA

In enacting the ESA, Congress empowered federal agencies to "use…all methods and procedures which are necessary…" to ensure that the status of any listed species is restored to the point where the species no longer requires protection under the Act.[76] All federal agencies have an affirmative obligation to "utilize their authorities in furtherance of the purposes of [the ESA] by carrying out programs for the conservation of endangered species and threatened species listed under the Act."[77] These broad requirements appear to provide the tools necessary to protect vulnerable species from harm, including harm caused by invasive species and climate change. Yet, the impacts from invasive species continue and will likely become more severe as marine systems continue to change as climate change progresses. The ESA could provide the legal basis to effectively address invasive species in some areas, but its effectiveness will be as much dependent on the availability of meaningful scientific data as the sociopolitical will to make difficult choices.

---

[71] D.L. Mackas et al., *Changing Zooplankton Seasonality in a Changing Ocean: Comparing Time Series of Zooplankton Phenology*, 97–100 Progress Oceanography 31 (2012) (showing that changes in ocean temperature lead to changes in zooplankton population that can lead to mismatches in timing between plankton blooms and the presence of species that rely on the zooplankton).

[72] *See generally* Cheung et al., *supra* note 70.

[73] *Id.*

[74] *Id.* at 246 (noting that empirical evidence suggests that evolutionary processes and adaptations are not an alternative to range movements, but operate synergistically by modulating the magnitude and dynamics of range-shift).

[75] *Id.*

[76] 16 U.S.C. § 1532(3) (2012).

[77] *Id.* § 1536.

A. LEGAL RESPONSES

The primary tools available under the ESA to protect listed species from the impacts of invasive species include the Act's prohibition on taking and the requirement to avoid jeopardy. Unfortunately, as currently interpreted neither one is fully effective to address the problem of marine invasive species in an era of climate change.

1. The Takings Prohibition

Unless otherwise exempted, the ESA makes it unlawful for any person subject to the jurisdiction of the United States to take any endangered species.[78] For marine species, this prohibition extends throughout most of the ocean.[79] As currently defined, a "take" may occur when an action results in significant habitat modification or degradation that causes the death or injury of the listed species.[80] Habitat modification alone without proof of death or injury may constitute a take if such modification significantly impairs essential behavioral patterns of a listed species.[81] These behavioral patterns include, but are not limited to, breeding, feeding, or sheltering.[82] An imminent threat of future harm may also be sufficient to warrant the issuance of an injunction.[83] These provisions appear to provide a strong legal basis to succeed on a claim that the introduction of marine invasive species, or the failure to prevent such introduction, violates the take prohibition because invasive species cause harm to listed species and the ecosystems they inhabit.

Use of the take prohibition to protect species from such harm in this context may be limited, however.[84] Existing law requires a causal connection between the action and actual injury to a listed species.[85] Some courts have required strict proof of proximate causation for a particular injury, while other courts have taken a broader perspective and considered indirect impacts that harm species. In either case, proving that the introduction of a particular marine species has constituted a taking is problematic because the process of invasion and the ability to predict particular impacts is still poorly understood.[86]

---

[78] *Id.* § 1532(19) (defining a "take"); *see also* 50 C.F.R. § 17.21(c) (2014) (noting that it is unlawful to take endangered wildlife within the United States, within the territorial sea of the United States, or on the high seas).

[79] The prohibition applies to all waters "except waters officially recognized by the United States as the territorial sea of another country, under international law." 50 C.F.R. § 17.21(c) (2014).

[80] Endangered and Threatened Wildlife and Plants, 46 Fed. Reg. 54,748 (Nov. 4, 1981).

[81] *Id.*

[82] 50 C.F.R. § 17.3 (2014); *see also* Babbitt v. Sweet Home Chapter of Communities, 515 U.S. 687 (1995).

[83] 16 U.S.C.§ 1540(g)(1)(A) (2012); *see also* Marbled Murrelet v. Babbitt, 83 F.3d 1060 (9th Cir. 1996).

[84] Friends of the Earth, Inc. v. Laidlaw Envtl. Servs., 528 U.S. 167, 180–81 (1992) (noting that any person bringing such claim must meet the Article III standing requirements); *see also* 16 U.S.C. § 1540(g)(2)(A) (2012) (requiring plaintiffs to file a sixty-day notice prior to filing suit).

[85] *See Babbitt*, 83 F.3d at 708.

[86] ADRIANNA A. MUIR, MANAGING COASTAL AQUATIC INVASIVE SPECIES IN CALIFORNIA: EXISTING POLICIES AND POLICY GAPS (2011), http://www.library.ca.gov/crb/11/11-001.pdf. In most cases, even if the invasion pathway is known, the individual or entity causing the specific introduction may be unknown.

Moreover, in many cases, marine invasive species represent only one of multiple threats to a protected species. The application of proximate cause analysis to the take of a species is often inconsistent with traditional evaluations of risk to species that consider a multitude of factors, including direct injury, habitat loss, fragmentation, and other impacts.[87] Thus, use of the take provision to address the introduction of marine invasive species may be beneficial only where the individual or entity causing the introduction is known and where there is clear evidence linking the introduction to a specified harm. Moreover, it is unclear whether action taken to combat climate change that directly or indirectly facilitate species invasions would violate the takings prohibition.

2. Preventing Jeopardy

Once a species is listed under the ESA, each federal agency must ensure that any subsequent action authorized, funded, or carried out by such agency is not likely "to jeopardize the continued existence of" the listed species "or result in the destruction or adverse modification of" the species critical habitat, unless otherwise exempted.[88] Whenever an agency finds that a proposed action may adversely affect a species listed under the ESA, the agency must formally consult with the FWS or NMFS.[89] The FWS or NMFS is required to issue a biological opinion on whether the proposed action will jeopardize the species, destroy its critical habitat, or cause adverse modification to the species habitat.[90]

In developing the biological opinion, the service is required to consider the current state of the environment that may be impacted, the direct and indirect effects of a proposed action on the species or critical habitat, and any cumulative effects to the species that may result from the proposed action.[91] If any of these factors reveals that the action is likely to decrease "the likelihood of both the survival and recovery of a listed species in the wild," the action jeopardizes the species.[92] If jeopardy is found, the service must propose alternative actions if such exist.[93] If jeopardy is not found, the service may still find that the action will result in adverse modification or destruction of critical habitat if the action will likely cause "a direct or indirect alteration that appreciably diminishes the value of the critical habitat for both the survival and recovery of a listed species."[94]

In many instances, there is a time lag between the introduction of a nonnative species and the point at which that species begins to impact other marine species or habitats. *Id.* at 18.

[87] Dale D. Goble, *Recovery*, in ENDANGERED SPECIES ACT, LAW, POLICY, AND PERSPECTIVES 86 (2d ed. 2009).

[88] 16 U.S.C § 1536(a)(2) (2012).

[89] 50 C.F.R. § 402.14 (2014). A more limited consultation is required where such acts may impact a species proposed for listing. 50 C.F.R. § 402.10 (2014).

[90] 16 U.S.C. § 1536(b)(3)(a) (2012); 50 C.F.R. § 402.14(g)(4) (2014).

[91] 50 C.F.R. § 402.14(g) (2014).

[92] *Id.* § 402.02.

[93] *Id.* § 402.14(g)(5).

[94] *Id.* § 402.02.

As applied to invasive species, the benefit of these duties to consult and to avoid jeopardy remains unclear because these duties apply only to discretionary agency actions.[95] As climate change progresses and agencies are forced to take responsive actions that may directly or indirectly augment the impact of invasive species on listed species, such action is likely to go unchallenged if required under the agency's statutory mandate.[96] However, the possibilities of challenging discretionary agency action are much broader.[97] The need for consultations is likely to increase as climate change progresses and facilitates range expansion for many species. It remains unclear how either service, already burdened by thousands of consultations each year, will respond to this increased demand for review. Thus, changes in policy are needed to adequately address the impact of invasive species on listed species.

B. POLICY RESPONSES

Foreign species have invaded ecosystems throughout the United States, and each has occurred within distinct ecological, societal, and political contexts.[98] It is important to consider how these factors influence the effectiveness of efforts to protect listed species because efforts to address these invasions require public support and political will.[99] For some, a response must be tailored to address the specific invasion and be supported by policy directed toward that particular invasion.[100] Others support a broader policy where information and time are inadequate to develop species-specific policies, and immediate action is needed to address the impact of the invasion.[101] Fundamentally, these approaches seek to conserve what is deemed worthy of protection by addressing the impacts of invasive species.

---

[95] National Ass'n of Home Builders v. Defenders of Wildlife, 551 U.S. 644, 652 (2007) (noting that the duty applies only to discretionary agency activities).

[96] Id. (noting that the duty to consult does not apply to actions an agency is required by statute to undertake).

[97] Discretionary agency decisions may be challenged. However, review of agency action is subject to the deferential "arbitrary and capricious" standard. A court will not vacate an agency decision unless the agency "relied on factors which Congress had not intended it to consider, entirely failed to consider an important aspect of the problem, offered an explanation for its decision that runs counter to the evidence before the agency, or is so implausible that it could not be ascribed to a difference in view or the product of agency expertise." See Motor Vehicle Mfrs. Ass'n. of United States, Inc. v. State Farm Mut. Automobile Ins. Co., 463 U.S. 29, 43 (1983).

[98] A.E.S. Ford-Thompson et al., *Implications of Social and Political Context for Mechanisms in Invasive Species Management, in* CONSERVATION, SOCIETY AND ENDANGERED SPECIES 53–55 (2011).

[99] MUIR, *supra* note 86.

[100] Sabrina J. Lovell et al., *The Economic Impacts of Aquatic Invasive Species: A Review of the Literature*, 35 AGRIC. & RES. ECON. REV. 195 (2006); *see also* NATIONAL INVASIVE SPECIES COUNCIL, MEETING THE INVASIVE SPECIES CHALLENGE: NATIONAL INVASIVE SPECIES MANAGEMENT PLAN (2001), http://www.invasivespeciesinfo.gov/docs/council/mpfinal.pdf. (noting that certain invasive species vectors are driven by economic incentives and financial gains that can conflict with invasive species management).

[101] Id.

Yet, the ESA does not specifically identify what should be conserved. Perhaps the most ecologically sound approach is to require conservation of the species' functional role in the ecosystem it occupies.[102] As one scholar has noted, the value of this approach is the recognition that "species interact with the biotic and abiotic elements of the system and play a dynamic role in shaping the system."[103] Requiring protection of sufficient numbers to ensure that a species continues to be a functioning component of the ecosystem it occupies has important implications for combating invasive species and for responding to climate change. Increased biodiversity is known to increase species resilience to both, in part, by improving the overall health of the ecosystem.[104] Such a response will require changes in the way species are protected. This, in turn, will likely require more listings, more critical habitat designation, changes in the way invasive species are identified and addressed, and greatly increased funding.

1. Listing and Critical Habitat Challenges

In enacting the ESA, Congress included broad provisions to address all threats to wildlife, regardless of origin. The synergistic impacts of climate change and invasive species will likely cause the number of marine species in need of protection to increase, lead to increased demand for listing and critical habitat designation, cause delays in delisting decisions, and increase litigation related to these issues.[105] These changes will likely have negative impacts on conservation efforts.[106]

A fundamental shift in perspective is required to adequately protect species. Given the multitude of existing stressors, and those expected to emerge as climate change progresses, conservation efforts must focus on retaining and restoring ecosystem resilience. In the absence of meaningful action to address climate change, it is imperative that policymakers reassess the environmental and economic value of preserving marine ecosystems, particularly coastal marine systems, as a frontline defense to invasive species and climate change. Intact systems mitigate the impacts of climate change by acting as large carbon sinks.[107] Moreover, healthy systems are more resilient to change and to invasions. It is now widely recognized that maintaining and restoring marine biodiversity is

---

[102] Goble, *supra* note 87.

[103] *Id.*

[104] Folke, *supra* note 39.

[105] The ESA permits any person or organization to petition to add a species to the list. The decision to list or not list a species is subject to review under APA, but that review is limited. Any person may petition the Secretary to revise a critical habitat designation.

[106] *See, e.g.,* U.S. Fish and Wildlife Service, Flood of Court Orders Preclude New Listings of Threatened and Endangered Species in FY 2001 (2000), http://www.fws.gov/news/ShowNews.cfm?ID=F41A0A59-C 574-11D4-A17B009027B6B5D3 (noting that in 2000 the FWS, responding to court orders requiring it to designate critical habitats, announced that it was unable to add any new species to the endangered species lists the following year except on an emergency basis).

[107] *See* Daniel C. Donato et al., *Mangroves among the Most Carbon Rich Forests in the Tropics,* 4 NATURE GEOSCI. 293 (2011).

necessary to sustain ecosystem health and resilience to climate change.[108] Listing and designation of critical habitat should be guided primarily by considerations of the species' role in the ecosystem and those factors that promote a healthy ecosystem.[109]

2. Toward a More Comprehensive Invasive Species Policy

Despite the enormous impact invasive species have had on wildlife and the ecosystems they inhabit, the United States has failed to develop a comprehensive invasive species statute to address the problem. As a result, harmful species continue to enter the United States, and those species already established continue to cause measurable harm. The United States must become more proactive to adequately address the impacts of marine invasive species on listed species. New Zealand's Biosecurity Act provides a useful framework for developing policy changes in the United States.[110]

The Biosecurity Act was the first comprehensive law specifically designed to support the systematic protection of all biological systems from harmful pests and diseases within a country.[111] It acts as an enabling tool by providing broad powers that can be utilized by all levels of government to manage pests and unwanted organisms. Among its provisions, several could prove useful to address marine invasive species in the United States. First, the Act prevents "risk organisms" or new organisms from entering the country until the organism receives a biosecurity clearance.[112] Second, the Act eliminates reactionary, case-by-case funding and policy decision-making framework by providing a centralized national standard for action. Third, the Act provides a framework that enables the government and members of industry to work together to improve biosecurity by making joint decisions and by jointly funding the costs of activities in shares that take into account the public benefit and the benefit to industry that the activities deliver.[113] These provisions and others contained in the Act encourage collaboration among interests groups to develop meaningful strategies that protect native species and the environments on which they depend. Adoption of such a collaborative response framework will be essential to develop strategies that protect marine species listed under the ESA from the impacts of marine invasive species and climate change as climate change progresses.

---

[108] *See* John J. Stachowicz et al., *Understanding the Effects of Marine Biodiversity on Communities and Ecosystems*, 38 Ann. Rev. Ecology Evolution & Systematics 739 (2007).

[109] Goble, *supra* note 87. *See also* 41 Fed. Reg. 22073–22075 (June 1, 1976) (proposing to list seven species occupying the same ecosystem as endangered species).

[110] Biosecurity Act 1993, Public Act 1993 No. 95, *available at* http://www.legislation.govt.nz/act/public/1993/0095/latest/DLM314623.html (last visited July 28, 2014).

[111] *Id.*

[112] *Id.* at part 3 (27)(1)(a); (28); *see also* part 1(2) (defining "risk good" to include any organism that causes unwanted harm to natural or physical resources or human health).

[113] *Id.* at part 5(A) 100X.

Conclusion

As marine systems continue to decay, the impact of marine invasive species on listed species could be significant in an era of climate change. The ESA was created to address all threats to listed species without exception. However, its ability to protect listed species is limited by the fragmented, often reactionary responses taken to address invasive species and climate change in the United States. More species will face extinction and even more will require protection as climate change progresses and its impacts become increasingly severe. The presence of invasive species will likely exacerbate the problem. It is imperative that action be taken to increase the resiliency of marine systems to change in order to protect species in a changing environment. This will require more funding, more regulatory flexibility in protecting species and habitats, a renewed focus on the value of preserving marine ecosystems, and a fundamental shift in perception of the critical role species invasions play in conservation efforts under the ESA.

12 Climate Change and the International Law of the Sea:
MAPPING THE LEGAL ISSUES
Dr. Marcos A. Orellana

Introduction

The international law of the sea has been a dynamic field of international law through-out several centuries, and its flexibility to adapt to changes will once again be tested.

Environmental impacts on the oceans resulting from a changing climate, and the measures necessary to address these changes, are the new challenges that must be confronted.

The impacts of a changing climate on the marine environment are multifaceted and they carry serious political, economic, and security implications. On a number of issues, the challenges that climate change presents for law-of-the-sea governance are of a magnitude unforeseen in public international law. For example, sea-level rise resulting from climate change can cause the submersion of the land territory of an entire state, thereby raising complex issues of sovereignty, self-determination, migration, and access to natural resources.[1]

Climate change thus poses decisive challenges to the existing international legal structures governing the oceans, as established in the UN Convention on the Law of the Sea (UNCLOS)[2] and other international law sources.[3] Some issues may be approached within existing legal frameworks, while other issues may require new law. Whether the law of the sea will be able to respond to the climate change challenge will be a topical point of debate during the twenty-first century.

This chapter provides an overview of the salient issues involved in the interface between climate change and the law of the sea. These issues are elaborated in further detail in subsequent chapters in this unit on international ocean governance challenges. This overview is not meant to be comprehensive or detailed; rather, it intends to set the stage for the analysis that follows in this unit.

Section I of this chapter addresses sea-level rise and its impacts on two issues: statehood and baselines. The chapter then examines key provisions of part XII of UNCLOS pertaining to environmental protection,[4] focusing on the reduction of emissions of greenhouse gases and the dumping of iron in the seas as a means of sequestering carbon. Section III considers marine biodiversity issues. Section IV examines the implications of melting polar ice for navigation, focusing on the legal issues pertaining to the potential opening of the Northwest Passage in the Arctic. Finally, Section V identifies the contours and key elements of UNCLOS part XV on dispute settlement,[5] focusing on its potential application to potential climate change claims.

---

[1] *See generally* Rosemary Rayfuse, *International Law and Disappearing States: Utilising Maritime Entitlements to Overcome the Statehood Dilemma* (Univ. of New S. Wales Faculty of Law Research Series 2010, Working Paper No. 52, 2010), *available at* http://law.bepress.com/unswwps-flrpsio/art52; Maxine Burkett, *The Nation Ex-situ: On Climate Change, Deterritorialized Nationhood and the Post-Climate Era*, 2 CLIMATE L. 345 (2011) (addressing climate change and statelessness).

[2] United Nations Convention on the Law of the Sea, Dec. 10, 1982, 1833 U.N.T.S. 397 [hereinafter UNCLOS].

[3] For example, the law on self-determination may be relevant in examining issues of sea-level rise and sovereignty, migration, and access to natural resources.

[4] UNCLOS *supra* note 2, arts. 192–237.

[5] *Id.* arts. 279–99.

I. Sea-Level Rise

In May 2013, the concentration of carbon dioxide (CO_2) in the atmosphere exceeded the 400 parts per million mark, the highest level since 3 million years ago.[6] Then, sea levels may have been as much as twenty meters above today's levels.[7] Global warming and climate change cause sea-level rise in two principal ways, namely thermal expansion, which refers to increase in volume as water warms, and the melting of glaciers on land.[8]

The Intergovernmental Panel on Climate Change (IPCC) concluded in its Fifth Assessment Report that "[g]lobal mean sea-level will continue to rise during the 21st century. Under all []scenarios, the rate of sea-level rise will very likely exceed that observed during 1971 to 2010 due to increased ocean warming and increased loss of mass from glaciers and ice sheets."[9] The IPCC also estimated a maximum of 0.98m rise by 2100.[10] Given the rates of melting in ice sheets in Greenland and Antarctica, many scientists conclude that sea-level will rise about one meter by 2100.[11] An expert panel of NOAA adopted a two-meter rise as its highest of four scenarios by 2100.[12] And if the Thwaites Glacier in West Antarctica flows to the sea, the rise would be more than three meters.[13] Although uncertainty remains regarding the rate and extent of the rise, there is ample consensus that sea levels are rising as a result of climate change.

A. LOSS OF STATEHOOD

Rising sea levels may mean that low-lying islands will become either submerged under the waters or uninhabitable for lack of access to fresh water. The Maldives in the Indian Ocean, for example, is composed of numerous islands that lie between one and 1.5 meters above sea level.[14] The inhabitants of these islands depend on fresh water resources found within the atoll, which may become infiltrated by salt water due to sea-level rise.

---

[6] Robert Kunzig, *Climate Milestone: Earth's CO2 Level Passes 400 ppm*, NAT'L GEOGRAPHIC (May 9, 2013), http://news.nationalgeographic.com/news/energy/2013/05/130510-earth-co2-milestone-400-ppm/.

[7] Tim Folger, *Rising Seas*, 224 NAT'L GEOGRAPHIC 30 (Sept. 2013), *available at* http://ngm.nationalgeographic.com/2013/09/rising-seas/folger-text.

[8] John Theodore Houghton, GLOBAL WARMING: THE COMPLETE BRIEFING 146 (3d ed. 2004).

[9] INTERGOVERNMENTAL PANEL ON CLIMATE CHANGE 2013, SUMMARY FOR POLICYMAKERS: THE PHYSICAL SCIENCE BASIS WORKING GROUP I CONTRIBUTION TO THE FIFTH ASSESSMENT REPORT 23 (Thomas F. Stocker et al. eds., 2013).

[10] *Id.*

[11] Folger, *supra* note 7.

[12] *Id.*

[13] *Id.*

[14] Hunt Janin & Scott A. Mandia, RISING SEA LEVELS: AN INTRODUCTION TO CAUSE AND IMPACT 96 (2012).

International law will face several unique challenges in addressing the issue of submerging States.[15] First is the principle that sovereignty over the land territory gives rights over the appertaining seas and natural resources found therein, that is, the land dominates the sea.[16] This principle has found expression in the law of delimitation, the creation of maritime zones, and the drawing of straight baselines, among other concepts and norms in the law of the sea.

Climate change potentially disrupts this principle, however, posing the question whether a new law of the sea could be developed on the basis of entitlements to the sea based on marine occupation, rather than land occupation. Technology may enable human communities closely tied to the marine environment to continue to use the seas, including with respect to natural resources. In such a case, there may be claims to territorial seas and other maritime zones not on the basis of appurtenance to the land, but on the basis of historical occupation and equity.

B. SHIFTING BASELINES

Baselines perform a basic function in the law of the sea: they establish the points on the coasts from which the outer limits of the coastal State's maritime zones are to be measured.[17] Rising sea levels will impact the low-water lines along the coast that are used to define the normal baselines.[18] Similarly, a changing coastal landscape will also impact straight baselines, given the criterion established in UNCLOS, which closely follows the International Court of Justice's (ICJ) judgment in the *Anglo Norwegian Fisheries* case.[19]

---

[15] *See generally* Rosemary Rayfuse, *Sea Level Rise and Maritime Zones: Preserving the Maritime Entitlements of "Disappearing" States, in* THREATENED ISLAND NATIONS: LEGAL IMPLICATIONS OF RISING SEAS AND A CHANGING CLIMATE (Michael B. Gerrard & Gregory E. Wannier eds., 2012); Moritaka Hayashi, *Sea-Level Rise and the Law of the Sea: Future Options, in* THE WORLD OCEAN IN GLOBALISATION: CLIMATE CHANGE, SUSTAINABLE FISHERIES, BIODIVERSITY, SHIPPING, REGIONAL ISSUES 187 (Davor Vidas & Peter Johan Schei eds., 2011); Jenny Grote Stoutenburg, *Implementing a New Regime of Stable Maritime Zones to Ensure the (Economic) Survival of Small Island States Threatened by Sea-Level Rise*, 26 INT'L J. MARINE & COASTAL L. 263, 271–75 (2011); Clive Schofield & I Made Andi Arsana, *Imaginary Islands? Options to Preserve Maritime Jurisdictional Entitlements and Provide Stable Maritime Limits in the Face of Coastal Instability*, 6th IHO-IAG ABLOS Conference, 6 (Oct. 26, 2010), *available at* http://www.iho.int/mtg_docs/com_wg/ABLOS/ABLOS_Conf6/S2P1-P.pdf.

[16] North Sea Continental Shelf (Ger. v. Den. & Neth.), 1969 I.C.J. 3 (Feb. 20); *see generally* UNCLOS, *supra* note 2, arts. 2, 33, 55, 76 (establishing rights to the sea for coastal states).

[17] R.R. CHURCHILL & A.V. LOWE, THE LAW OF THE SEA 25 (1983).

[18] David D. Caron, *Climate Change, Sea Level Rise and the Coming Uncertainty in Oceanic Boundaries: A Proposal to Avoid Conflict, in* MARITIME BOUNDARY DISPUTES, SETTLEMENT PROCESSES, AND THE LAW OF THE SEA 1 (Seoung-Yong Hong & Jon M. Van Dyke eds., 2009); David D. Caron, *When Law Makes Climate Change Worse: Rethinking the Law of Baselines in Light of a Rising Sea Level*, 17 ECOLOGY L.Q. 621, 634 (1990). *See also* Charles Di Leva & Sachiko Morita, *Maritime Rights of Coastal States and Climate Change: Should States Adapt to Submerged Boundaries?* (Legal Vice Presidency The World Bank, L. & Dev., Working Paper No. 5), *available at* http://siteresources.worldbank.org/INTLAWJUSTICE/Resources/L&D_number5.pdf. (last visited July 16, 2014).

[19] Fisheries (U.K. v. Nor.), 1951 I.C.J. 116 (Dec. 18).

The Court in that case held that straight baselines should not depart to any appreciable extent from the general direction of the coast.[20]

Accordingly, shifting baselines resulting from sea-level rise will introduce changes in the maritime zones of the coastal State,[21] namely, (1) the territorial sea,[22] (2) the contiguous zone,[23] (3) the continental shelf,[24] and (4) the exclusive economic zone (EEZ).[25] For example, access to, and conservation of, valuable living and nonliving natural resources found in the continental shelf or EEZ may provide a fertile ground for conflict among States. Similarly, standards pertaining to navigation, such as innocent passage in the territorial sea or freedom of navigation in the EEZ, may introduce sources of tensions.

Baselines also play a key role in delimitation between opposing or neighboring States.[26] Thus, shifting baselines will destabilize existing boundaries between States, for example where they have been calculated on the basis of equidistance. More generally, shifting baselines will unsettle the stability, certainty, and predictability sought by maritime boundaries. In this regard, climate change and shifting baselines alter the notion that geography provides a stable basis for the determination of boundaries in the law of the sea.[27]

The shifting baselines problem is not simply one of topographic measurements in large-scale charts: it is also a political issue involving entitlement to territory and natural resources. Climate change therefore calls on the international community to revisit the basis upon which the maritime zones are calculated, in order to secure the rights of States that would otherwise suffer the loss of territory or access to natural resources.

II. Environmental Protection in UNCLOS

The Third UN Conference on the Law of the Sea was launched the year after the UN Conference on the Human Environment was held in Stockholm in 1972.[28] Environmental

---

[20] *See id.*

[21] José Luís Jesus, *Rocks, New-Born Islands, Sea Level Rise and Maritime Space, in* VERHANDELN FÜR DEN FRIEDEN NEGOTIATING FOR PEACE-LIBER AMICORUM TONO EITEL 599, 602 (Jochen Abr. Frowein et al. eds., 2003).

[22] *See* UNCLOS, *supra* note 2, at arts. 2–16.

[23] *See id.* art. 33.

[24] *See id.* arts. 76–85.

[25] *See id.* arts. 55–75.

[26] A.H.A. Soons, *The Effects of a Rising Sea Level on Maritime Limits and Boundaries,* 37 NETH. INT'L L. REV. 207, 216–18 (1990); Lewis M. Alexander, *Baseline Delimitations and Maritime Boundaries,* 23 VA. J. INT'L L. 503 (1982–1983).

[27] Davor Vidas, *International Law and Sea Level Rise: The Role of the International Law Association,* MEPIELAN EBULLETIN (Feb. 18, 2014), http://www.mepielan-ebulletin.gr/default.aspx?pid=18&CategoryId=4&ArticleId=174&Article=International-Law-and-Sea-Level-Rise-The-Role-of-the-International-Law-Association.

[28] John A. Duff, *The United States and the Law of the Sea Convention: Sliding Back from Accession and Ratification,* 11 OCEAN & COASTAL L.J. 1, 5 (2005–2006).

consciousness was capturing the imagination of the public and policymakers at a time when the deleterious impacts of transboundary air pollution such as acid rain were beginning to be felt. Thus, it is not surprising that UNCLOS addresses environmental protection in a comprehensive fashion. Although still lacking in a number of operative elements typical of a domestic environmental regime, part XII of UNCLOS reflects broad principles that enable international cooperation and progressive development of the law of the sea in addressing what was then a novel issue, environmental protection.[29] Climate change will test whether part XII of UNCLOS is capable of withstanding, and responding to, the challenges posed by climate change.

A. REDUCTION OF EMISSIONS OF GREENHOUSE GASES

Part XII of UNCLOS reversed the ancien régime wherein the seas could be used as a waste site, and affirmed in its stead the notion that the marine environment must be protected and preserved.[30] This change in paradigm is evident in the first provision of part XII entitled general obligation: "States have the obligation to protect and preserve the marine environment."[31] The question thus arises whether such a general provision would suffice to require States to reduce emissions of greenhouse gases (GHGs) into the atmosphere, given the increasing scientific knowledge regarding the causal connections between land-based atmospheric contamination and the harm inflicted on the marine environment. The specific context of the inquiry thus largely refers to non-accidental damage to the marine environment resulting from the emissions to the atmosphere of GHGs within a State's territory. In addition to this focus on land-based sources of GHGs, situations involving dumping and geoengineering call for inquiry,[32] as do emissions of GHGs from vessels.[33]

The general obligation to protect and preserve the marine environment is followed by other general provisions of part XII, including measures to prevent, reduce, and control pollution of the marine environment.[34] UNCLOS employs the following formulation: "States shall take all measures necessary to ensure that activities under their jurisdiction or control are so conducted as not to cause damage by pollution to other States and their environment [...]."[35] This construct benefits from an explicit definition

---

[29] See UNCLOS, supra note 2, arts. 197–201.

[30] Id.

[31] UNCLOS, supra note 2, art. 192.

[32] See infra Subsection B.

[33] For a discussion of the regulation of GHG emissions from vessels, see generally International Council on Clean Transportation, Reducing Greenhouse Gas Emissions from Ships: Cost Effectiveness of Available Options, White Paper No. 11 (July 2011), available at http://www.theicct.org/sites/default/files/publications/ICCT_GHGfromships_jun2011.pdf.

[34] See UNCLOS, supra note 2, arts. 192–237.

[35] Id. art. 194.

of "pollution of the marine environment" in UNCLOS article 1 as "the introduction by man, directly or indirectly, of substances or energy into the marine environment, including estuaries, which results or is likely to result in such deleterious effects as harm to living resources and marine life, hazards to human health, hindrance to marine activities, including fishing and other legitimate uses of the sea, impairment of quality for use of sea water and reduction of amenities."[36]

Whether climate change emissions satisfy the UNCLOS definition of pollution raises several issues. A first approach could distinguish between direct and indirect introduction of substances into the marine environment. For example, the precipitation of certain chemicals from the atmosphere into the seas resulting in ocean acidification could be regarded as a form of direct introduction of pollution, while the melting of inland glaciers resulting in accelerated sea-level rise could be addressed as a form of indirect introduction of pollution. Second, the UNCLOS definition also presents the questions of what "substances," such as CO_2 and other GHGs, have been introduced to the marine environment, in what quantity, and in what way. Yet another issue relating to the definition of pollution in the climate change context relates to the deleterious effects on the marine environment, including harm to coral reefs and migratory species, resulting from climate change.

The obligation to avoid causing damage by pollution is similar to the general obligation in international environmental law to avoid causing transboundary environmental harm, although it is focused on damage to other States and their environment.[37] Whether this general obligation is capable of effectively addressing climate change emissions remains an open question, however.[38] If the answer were to be affirmative, then claims of responsibility and liability under this head could be presented in the context of dispute settlement, addressed further below.

One of the elements of the controversy relating to the customary law obligation not to cause transboundary harm, including harm to the global commons, is its formulation as a due diligence standard.[39] By contrast to a strict liability standard, which would attach liability to a State where its activity is causally connected to environmental harm, a due diligence standard examines the conduct of the State in relation to the foreseeable risks involved.[40] In applying a due diligence standard, several issues must be examined,

---

[36] *Id.* art. 1(4).

[37] Legality of the Threat or Use of Nuclear Weapons, Advisory Opinion, 1996 I.C.J. 226 (July 8, 1996); *see* TRANSBOUNDARY HARM IN INTERNATIONAL LAW: LESSONS FROM THE TRAIL SMELTER ARBITRATION (Rebecca M. Bratspies & Russell A. Miller eds., 2010); *see generally* XUE HANQIN, TRANSBOUNDARY DAMAGE IN INTERNATIONAL LAW (2003).

[38] *Palau Seeks UN World Court Opinion on Damage Caused by Greenhouse Gases*, UN NEWS CENTRE (Sept. 22, 2011), http://www.un.org/apps/news/story.asp?NewsID=39710&Cr=pacific+island&Cr1#.U1hMgNz7GYQ.

[39] John H. Knox, *The Boundary Waters Treaty: Ahead of Its Time, and Ours*, 54 WAYNE L. REV. 1591, 1594 (2008).

[40] SS Lotus (France v Turkey) 1927 PCIJ (Ser. A) No 10; Alabama Claims Arbitration (United States/Great Britain) (1872) 29 RIAA 125, 129. *See also* Jan Arno Hessbruegge, *The Historical Development of the Doctrines*

including: the State's material capacity to control activities within its territory,[41] measures adopted to prevent foreseeable harm,[42] and precautionary measures in situations of insufficient evidence.[43]

The Seabed Disputes Chamber of the International Tribunal for the Law of the Sea, in its 2011 Advisory Opinion on *Responsibilities and Obligations of States Sponsoring Persons and Entities with respect to Activities in the Area*, noted that due diligence is a variable concept. Emphasis on variability in the conceptual construct of due diligence allows, indeed calls for, consideration of the particular issues and context of the problem under scrutiny; in this instance climate change. The Seabed Disputes Chamber further noted that due diligence may change over time in relation to the risks involved and in light of new scientific and technological knowledge.[44]

The application of a due diligence standard to the climate change problem raises several issues. First of all, in regards to State conduct, a key question is the extent to which the State has adopted effective measures of prevention based on the best scientific evidence available, including a legal framework governing GHG emissions. The existence of an international regulatory scheme setting clear limits on the emission of GHGs to the atmosphere would further aid in evaluating the adequacy of the internal legal framework of the State. Second of all, in regards to material capacity, one of the crucial questions pertains to the level of development and resources available to the State. The relevance of the level of development and material capacity is reinforced in the principle of common but differentiated responsibilities and respective capabilities established in the UN Framework Convention on Climate Change (UNFCCC).[45] The greater the availability of resources and concomitant capacity to effect climate change mitigation, the higher the diligence due. This notion of due diligence also finds strong support in considerations of equity on the basis of historical contributions to the concentration of GHGs in the atmosphere.

In addition to the difficulties of proving breach of due diligence in relation to conduct and capacity, the standard also requires evidence of environmental injury and causal

---

of Attribution and Due Diligence in International Law, 36 N.Y.U. J. Int'l L. & Pol. 265, 283 (2003–2004); Riccardo Pisillo-Mazzeschi, *The Due Diligence Rule and the Nature of the International Responsibility of States, in* State Responsibility in International Law (Rene Provost ed., 2002).

[41] International Law Commission, Draft Articles on Prevention of Transboundary Harm from Hazardous Activities, UN GAOR 56th Sess., Supp. No. 10, U.N. Doc. A/56/10 (2001), Commentary to Article 3.

[42] Pulp Mills on the River Uruguay (Argentina v Uruguay), [2010] ICJ Rep 14, ¶ 101.

[43] Responsibilities and Obligations of States Sponsoring Persons and Entities with Respect to Activities in the Area (Seabed Dispute Chamber of the International Tribunal of the Law of the Sea, Case No 17, 1 Feb. 2011), ¶ 131.

[44] *Id.* ¶ 117.

[45] *Id.* ¶ 161 ("Principle 15 provides that the precautionary approach shall be applied by States 'according to their capabilities'. It follows that the requirements for complying with the obligation to apply the precautionary approach may be stricter for the developed than for the developing sponsoring States."). *See also* Mary J. Bortscheller, *Equitable but Ineffective: How the Principle of Common but Differentiated Responsibilities Hobbles the Global Fight against Climate Change*, 10 Sustainable Dev. L. & Pol'y 49 (2010).

connection between the harm and State conduct. In regards to evidence of harm to the marine environment, negligible impact is not the type of environmental damage that would qualify as a viable international claim. At the same time, international customary law does not establish with precision the requisite threshold of harm. Therefore, evidence that shows appreciable or serious injury is central to a viable claim. Given the negative impacts of climate change on the marine environment highlighted elsewhere in this volume,[46] the application of the due diligence standard is less likely to present difficulties in the gathering of relevant evidence of harm; rather, it is likely to hinge on whether the harm is sufficiently serious as to present a cognizable claim.

Regarding the causal link required between the emissions arising in one country and environmental harm, the climate change context involves a situation where a number of States are contributing GHG emissions that result in harm to the marine environment. Would application of the *Monetary Gold* standard, subjecting the valid exercise of jurisdiction to the consent of each and every country whose conduct is relevant to the subject matter of the decision,[47] defeat a climate change claim? In other words, would jurisdiction pose an insurmountable bar to the viability of an international climate change claim, given that an international tribunal's exercise of jurisdiction would arguably determine the legality of conduct not only of the respondent, but would also affect the legal interests of States not parties to the dispute? Alternatively, would *Barcelona Traction*'s emphasis on *erga omnes*[48] obligations due to the international community as a whole[49] underscore the common interests at stake in climate change litigation? Would the *erga omnes* character of the obligation provide *jus standi*[50] to an injured State, or to a State other than the injured State?[51] The ability of international law to effectively answer these questions in the face of the serious climate change challenge appears to be a litmus test regarding the effectiveness of international law.

Given the difficulties involved in operationalizing the general obligation to protect and preserve the marine environment for specific environmental issues, such as operational pollution from vessels, dumping, and land-based sources of pollution, part XII of UNCLOS established a framework of authority that enables international

---

[46] For a discussion of the negative impacts of climate change on the marine environments, see *infra* Chapters 13–18.

[47] Monetary Gold Removed from Rome in 1943 (It. v. Fr., U.K., & U.S.), Preliminary Hearing, 1954 I.C.J. 19 (June 15); East Timor (Port. v. Austl.), 1995 I.C.J. 1 (June 30).

[48] *Erga omnes* refers to international obligations owed to the international community as a whole, and all States can be held to have a legal interest in their protection. *See* Commentary to Draft Articles on Responsibility of States for Internationally Wrongful Acts, ILC, art. 1 ¶ 4.

[49] Barcelona Traction, Light and Power Co., Ltd. (Belg. v. Spain), 1970 I.C.J. 3 (Feb. 5).

[50] *Jus standi* refers to the right of standing, that is, who has the right to appear before an international tribunal and present international claims.

[51] *See* Draft Articles on Responsibility of States for Internationally Wrongful Acts, *in* Report of the International Law Commission on the Work of Its Fifty-Third Session, UN GAOR, 56th Sess., Supp. No. 10, at 29, UN Doc. A/56/10 (2001), *available at* http://www.un.org/law/ilc.

cooperation.[52] This approach is characteristic of UNCLOS as a framework convention, a model that has been replicated in varying forms in several international environmental agreements.[53]

The specific context of land-based pollution from and through the atmosphere that results in harm to the marine environment contemplates a general formulation: "States shall adopt laws and regulations to prevent, reduce and control pollution of the marine environment from land-based sources."[54] The text makes it plain that the obligation is to adopt laws and regulations; thereby it signals a due diligence standard. A subsequent paragraph in that same provision states: "Laws, regulations, measures, rules, standards and recommended practices and procedures [...] shall include those designed to minimize, to the fullest extent possible, the release of toxic, harmful or noxious substances, especially those which are persistent, into the marine environment."[55] The use of the words "to the fullest extent possible" employed in this provision again highlights and qualifies the due diligence standard applicable in this area.

A similar legal construct emphasizing contextual elements[56] is apparent in the structure and text of the provision in part XII concerning measures to prevent, reduce, and control pollution of the marine environment.[57] This provision states: "The measures taken pursuant to this Part shall deal with all sources of pollution of the marine environment. These measures shall include, *inter alia*, those designed to minimize to the fullest possible extent: (a) the release of toxic, harmful or noxious substances, especially those which are persistent, from land-based sources, from or through the atmosphere or by dumping."[58] Here, the wording "designed to minimize to the fullest possible extent" again suggests a due diligence standard.

Although part XII is largely designed to offer a framework for cooperation for the elaboration of more detailed regimes for the protection of the marine environment, the obligations established in part XII would be deprived of much of their legal value if they were interpreted as mere programmatic aspirations. Still, the application of general obligations to the climate change mitigation context must overcome formidable obstacles, as examined above, evincing the weaknesses of the legal tools available in UNCLOS to address climate change. The law in this area thus needs to be strengthened, so that the commitment of the international community to the protection of the

---

[52] *See* UNCLOS, *supra* note 2, arts. 192–237.

[53] *See* Peter H. Sand, *UNCED and the Development of International Environmental Law*, 8 J. Nat. Resources & Envtl. L. 209 (1992–1993).

[54] UNCLOS, *supra* note 2, art. 207(1).

[55] *Id.* art. 207(5) (referring to paragraphs 1, 2, and 4 of article 207).

[56] *See* Daniel Barstow Magraw, *Legal Treatment of Developing Countries: Differential, Contextual, and Absolute Norms*, 1 Colo. J. Int'l Envtl. L. & Pol'y 69, 74–76 (1990).

[57] UNCLOS, *supra* note 2, art. 194(3).

[58] *Id.* art. 194(3)(a).

marine environment, expressed in UNCLOS and in the Rio+20 UN Conference on Sustainable Development, can transition from words to reality.

B. IRON DUMPING IN THE HIGH SEAS

Ocean iron fertilization (OIF) refers to a controversial form of geoengineering to reduce atmospheric carbon dioxide.[59] OIF would involve the spreading of iron dust into the ocean in order to promote the growth of phytoplankton that would draw CO_2 out of the atmosphere.[60] OIF has raised several concerns, including (1) whether it would actually work effectively, (2) whether manipulating large ecosystems could result in serious environmental harm, and (3) whether it would even be possible to measure and verify any carbon reductions.[61]

Field tests conducted since 1993, including in the eastern equatorial Pacific, have not delivered the results expected by the proponents of this technique.[62] Nevertheless, in 2007, the *Weatherbird II* departed from Fort Lauderdale, Florida, in the initial phase of a large-scale OIF expedition named "Voyage of Recovery."[63] The owner of the vessel, Planktos Corporation, planned to dump up to 600 tons of iron in a 10,000 km^2 portion of the eastern equatorial Pacific Ocean.[64]

The United States notified the Scientific Groups of the London Convention and Protocol[65] of Planktos' activities and invited them to take appropriate action.[66] Subsequently, the Meeting of the Contracting Parties to the London Convention considered the issue, agreed that the OIF is covered by the London Convention and Protocol, in particular, in relation to their objective to protect the marine environment from all sources, and concluded that large-scale OIF projects were not currently justified.[67]

Nevertheless, OIF as a potential mitigation technique presents several legal questions. For instance, the London Convention and its 1996 Protocol apply to the elimination of

---

[59] Raphael Sagarin et al., *Iron Fertilization in the Ocean for Climate Mitigation: Legal, Economic, and Environmental Challenges* 2 (Nicholas Inst. for Envtl. Pol'y Solutions, Duke University, Working Paper No. 07-07, 2007), *available at* http://nicholasinstitute.duke.edu/sites/default/files/publications/iron-fertilization-in-the-ocean-for-climate-mitigation-legal-economic-and-environmental-challenges-paper.pdf.

[60] *Id.*

[61] *Id.*

[62] James Peterson, *Can Algae Save Civilization? A Look at Technology, Law, and Policy regarding Iron Fertizilization of the Ocean to Counteract the Greenhouse Effect*, 6 COLO. J. INT'L ENVTL. L. & POL'Y 61, 74 (1995).

[63] Kalee Thompson, *Carbon Discredit*, POPULAR SCI. 55 (July 2008).

[64] *See* Catherine Brahic, *Company Plans "Eco" Iron Dump off Galapagos*, NEW SCIENTIST, June 25, 2007.

[65] Convention on the Prevention of Marine Pollution by Dumping of Wastes and Other Matter, Dec. 29, 1972, 26 U.S.T. 2403 [hereinafter London Convention].

[66] Sagarin et al., *supra* note 59, at 7.

[67] *Large-Scale Ocean Fertilization Not Currently Justified*, IMO NEWS, Nov. 1, 2008, at 13, *available at* http://www.imo.org/MediaCentre/NewsMagazine/Documents/2008/IMO_NEWS_1_2008_WEBweb.pdf.

pollution caused by dumping.[68] The definition of dumping in the London Convention and Protocol is virtually identical to UNCLOS. It defines dumping, in pertinent part, as "any deliberate disposal into the sea of wastes or other matter from vessels ...," but does not include "placement of matter for a purpose other than the mere disposal thereof, provided that such placement is not contrary to the aims of this Convention...."[69]

This definition of dumping calls for a fresh reading of the aims of the London Dumping Convention. The challenge of climate change would raise issues such as (1) the relevance of the precautionary principle, (2) the holistic approach to pollution control and prevention from all sources, (3) the obligation to avoid transferring damage from one part of the environment to another, and (4) the duties regarding environmental impact assessment.

C. CARBON CAPTURE AND STORAGE

These issues relevant to the analysis of OIF involve broader systemic implications pertaining to carbon capture and storage. This mitigation technique would sequester carbon in the deep sea or in geological formations beneath the seabed. Carbon sequestration has raised significant controversy,[70] mainly for two reasons: the potentially serious harmful effects of increased concentrations of CO_2 in the marine environment, and the eventual return of the CO_2 to the atmosphere through natural processes.

In 2007, the London Protocol asserted control over deep sea and sub-seabed carbon sequestration.[71] An amendment was added to Annex 1 stating that "carbon dioxide streams may be considered as dumping if ... disposal is into a sub-seabed geological formation...."[72] The amendment considers sub-seabed geological formations and excludes the deep sea bed.[73] Therefore, the absence of deep sea carbon capture and storage from Annex 1 means that that specific practice is banned.

The examples of OIF and carbon capture and storage show the extent to which international environmental instruments may interact to respond to climate change issues. As discussed in the next section, similar issues are evident in connection with marine biodiversity.

---

[68] London Convention, *supra* note 65.

[69] 1996 London Protocol to the Convention on the Prevention of Marine Pollution by Dumping of Wastes and Other Matter, Nov. 2, 1996, 36 I.L.M. 1, arts. 1(8), 2(9), 4(10) [hereinafter London Protocol].

[70] Nadine R. Hoffman, *The Emergence of Carbon Sequestration: An Introduction and Annotated Bibliography of Legal Aspects for CCS*, 29 PACE ENVTL. L. REV. 218, 220 (2011).

[71] Ann Brewster Weeks, *Subseabed Carbon Dioxide Sequestration as a Climate Mitigation Option for the Eastern United States: A Preliminary Assessment of Technology and Law*, 12 OCEAN & COASTAL L.J. 245, 261 (2007).

[72] Press Release, IMO, New International Rules to Allow Storage of CO_2 under the Seabed (Feb. 9, 2007) (on file with author).

[73] London Protocol, *supra* note 69.

III. Marine Biodiversity

The massive loss of biodiversity in the age of Anthropocene has been compounded by the challenges of climate change.[74] Ocean acidification threatens the productivity and even the survival of coral reef ecosystems.[75] Changing currents, water temperatures, and ice formations pose obstacles to the migration patterns of several species, including pelagic fish, marine mammals, and seabirds.[76] Effective responses in international law have yet to be developed, however.

In the face of biodiversity loss, several questions need to be answered, including the following. How do instruments governing the protection of migratory species account for the impacts of climate change? More specifically, would the protection of habitat require measures to address climate change impacts?

Instruments and institutions governing fisheries face similar challenges. How do regional fisheries management organizations (RFMOs) account for climate change impacts in their modeling and conservation measures? This question raises related issues of uncertainty and the need for precaution in the management of species. A related question pertains to the ability of an RFMO to designate an area of the high seas under its jurisdiction as a protected area.[77] Protected areas under the law of the sea raise issues of jurisdiction and maritime entitlement. In particular, the creation of protected areas in areas beyond national jurisdiction has been a hotly debated issue.[78] The Convention for the Conservation of Antarctic Marine Living Resources (CCAMLR) has made progress in this regard through the protection of the South Orkney Islands Southern Shelf,[79] but has not yet managed to set up a system of protected areas.

The 2012 UN Conference on Sustainable Development (Rio+20) reaffirmed the value of marine ecosystems and biodiversity for present and future generations and

---

[74] Alexandra Scuro, *Are GMOs Good or Bad Seeds in the Developing World?: A Discussion of the Growing Role of Developing Countries in the Debate over Climate Change and the Loss of Biodiversity*, 18 FORDHAM ENVTL. L. REV. 369, 378 (2007).

[75] C. Mark Eakin et al., *Global Climate Change and Coral Reefs: Rising Temperatures, Acidification, and the Need for Resilient Reefs, in* STATUS OF CORAL REEFS IN THE WORLD 2008, at 29 (Clive Wilkinson ed., 2008), *available at* http://www.reefbase.org/download/gcrmn_download.aspx?type=10&docid=13311.

[76] Lawrence R. Liebsman et al., *The Endangered Species Act and Climate Change— Current Issues*, SR021 ALI-ABA 227, 232 (2009).

[77] Erick J. Molenaar & Alex G. Oude Elferink, *Marine Protected Areas in Areas beyond National Jurisdiction: The Pioneering Efforts under the OSPAR Convention*, 5 UTRECHT L. REV. 5, 7 (June 2009).

[78] LEE KIMBALL, THE INTERNATIONAL LEGAL REGIME OF THE HIGH SEAS AND THE SEABED BEYOND THE LIMITS OF NATIONAL JURISDICTION AND OPTIONS FOR COOPERATION FOR THE ESTABLISHMENT OF MARINE PROTECTED AREAS (MPAs) IN MARINE AREAS BEYOND THE LIMITS OF NATIONAL JURISDICTION, SECRETARIAT OF THE CONVENTION ON BIOLOGICAL DIVERSITY, TECHNICAL SERIES NO. 19 v (2005).

[79] *See* Protection of the South Orkney Islands Southern Shelf, Conservation Measure 91-03 (2009), *available at* http://www.ccamlr.org/sites/drupal.ccamlr.org/files//91-03.pdf.

committed "to address, on an urgent basis, the issue of the conservation and sustainable use of marine biological diversity of areas beyond national jurisdiction, including by taking a decision on the development of an international instrument under the Convention on the Law of the Sea."[80] A new instrument in this area would provide an opportunity for the international community to establish new and necessary tools to address the challenges that climate change poses to marine biodiversity.

IV. Melting of Polar Ice and Arctic Navigation

One of the notorious impacts of climate change is the melting of the polar ice cap during the Northern summer.[81] The retreating ice poses an immediate threat to imperiled species, such as polar bears.[82] The melting ice also makes commercial navigation possible in areas formerly covered by ice. This is the situation affecting the Northwest Passage, a sea route along Canada's Northern islands that links the Atlantic and Pacific Oceans.[83] The melting ice also presents the question whether special protection for Arctic waters is necessary in the new environment posed by climate change.

A. IS THE NORTHWEST PASSAGE AN INTERNATIONAL STRAIT?

Canada maintains that some of the waters of the Northwest Passage are under its full sovereignty as part of Canadian internal waters.[84] Internal waters are those waters found inland from the relevant baselines; generally there is no right of innocent passage along those waters, unless straight baselines enclose waters that had been used for navigation.[85] The United States, by contrast, argues that the Northwest Passage is an international strait that is open to passage by vessels flying the flag of any State.[86]

There are a number of policy questions associated with this dispute, including commercial, environmental, and security considerations. From a commercial perspective, the reduction in about 1,000 nautical miles distance, and the concomitant days, required to complete the voyage between the Atlantic and Pacific Oceans, as compared with the use of the Panama Canal, significantly reduces the cost of transport of goods that enter international trade.[87] From an environmental perspective, the operational pollution as

---

[80] G.A. Res. 66/288, ¶ 162, U.N. Doc. A/RES/66.288 (July 27, 2012).

[81] John Kostyack & Dan Rohlf, *Conserving Endangered Species in an Era of Global Warming*, 38 ENVTL. L. REP. 10203, 10204 (2008).

[82] *Id.* at 10206.

[83] Christopher Mark Macneill, *Gaining Command & Control of the Northwest Passage: Strait Talk on Sovereignty*, 34 TRANSP. L.J. 355, 358 (2007).

[84] *Id.* at 365.

[85] *See* UNCLOS, *supra* note 2, art. 8.

[86] Macneill, *supra* note 83, at 364.

[87] *Id.* at 390.

well as the risk of accidents associated with navigation in a fragile ecosystem presents serious concerns.[88] From a security angle, the potential entry of terrorists, pirates, or other unlawful groups into Canadian territory, or their passage through the waters of the Northwest Passage, also raises serious concerns.[89]

The dispute also presents several interesting legal questions, perhaps the most critical of which pertains to the definition of a strait under customary international law and UNCLOS. Part III of UNCLOS addresses the regulation of straits used for international navigation.[90] A key threshold question is thus whether the Northwest Passage is a strait used for international navigation, and critically whether such use is actual or potential use. Potential use as the criterion to define an international strait would call for cartographic and commercial evidence relating to the feasibility of navigation through the sea route. An actual use criterion, by contrast, would require evidence of actual passage by vessels.

As the Northwest Passage has been covered by ice for most of recorded history, only icebreakers and submarines have completed the voyage.[91] Climate change, however, is presenting a new scenario. In September 2013, the *MS Nordic Orion*, a Danish bulk carrier flying the flag of Panama, became the first large sea freighter (carrying 73,500 tons of cooking coal) to complete the voyage through the Northwest Passage.[92]

B. SPECIAL PROTECTION FOR ARCTIC WATERS

In light of the fragility of ice-covered ecosystems, UNCLOS contemplates the possibility of coastal States adopting laws and regulations for the prevention, reduction, and control of pollution from vessels in ice-covered areas within the limits of the EEZ.[93] This provision raises several interpretative questions that are beyond the scope of this chapter. What is, however, relevant for this discussion is that the International Maritime Organization adopted non-binding Guidelines for Ships Operating in Arctic Ice-Covered Waters that set out construction, equipment, operational, and environmental provisions with special consideration for the risks of navigating in the ice-covered

---

[88] *Id.*

[89] *Id.*

[90] UNCLOS, *supra* note 2, arts. 34–45.

[91] *See generally* Rob Huebert, *Climate Change and Canadian Sovereignty in the Northwest Passage* in Canadian Arctic Sovereignty and Security: Historical Perspectives, Calgary Papers in Military and Strategic Studies, Occasional Paper No. 4, 383-99 (P. Whitney Lackenbauer, ed., 2011), *available at* http://cpmss.synergiesprairies.ca/cpmss/index.php/cpmss/article/view/18.

[92] John McGarrity & Henning Gloystein, *Northwest Passage Crossed by First Cargo Ship, the Nordic Orion, Heralding New Era of Arctic Commercial Activity*, NAT'L POST (Sept. 27, 2013), *available at* http://news.nationalpost.com/2013/09/27/northwest-passage-crossed-by-first-cargo-ship-the-nordic-orion-heralding-new-era-of-arctic-commercial-activity/.

[93] UNCLOS, *supra* note 2, art. 234.

waters of the Arctic.[94] In light of increased navigation expected in Arctic waters as a result of climate change, the question surfaces whether these guidelines should be transformed into a binding legal regime.[95]

V. Dispute Settlement in UNCLOS

Part XV is an integral element of UNCLOS that sets out a comprehensive framework for settlement of disputes relating to the law of the sea.[96] Part XV establishes compulsory jurisdiction whereby States consent to submitting UNCLOS-related disputes to international adjudication, albeit subject to certain exclusions.[97] Part XV thus serves basic functions in the legal regime governing the oceans. Part XV preserves the balance between rights and obligations established in the Convention. Part XV also establishes a governance arrangement that can contribute to the progressive development of the law.

An examination of climate change issues under part XV must consider two broad and intertwined issues: jurisdiction and substantive claims. On jurisdiction, a key question is whether part XV establishes compulsory jurisdiction with respect to claims pertaining to climate change and the law of the sea. On substantive claims, the relevant questions relate to the causes of action and theories that could be articulated in relation to climate change and the law of the sea. These issues are examined in turn.

A. JURISDICTION

The jurisdictional gateway of part XV is established in the interplay of several provisions, and their application to climate-change-related claims would need to positively overcome several hurdles. The first such hurdle is found in article 281(1) of the Convention. Article 281(1) provides that the compulsory dispute settlement mechanisms of part XV will operate only where disputing parties have not reached settlement of the dispute in accordance with any means they have agreed to, and the agreement of the parties does not exclude any further procedure.[98]

This provision thus calls for careful analysis of the essential character of a dispute involving both climate change and the law of the sea. In simplified terms: Is it a law-of-the-sea dispute, a climate change dispute, or both? A defendant seeking to exclude jurisdiction is likely to argue that the climate change dispute falls only marginally under

---

[94] INTERNATIONAL MARITIME ORGANIZATION, GUIDELINES FOR SHIPS OPERATING IN POLAR WATERS 5 (electronic ed., 2010).

[95] See ØYSTEIN JENSEN, THE IMO GUIDELINES FOR SHIPS OPERATING IN ARCTIC ICE-COVERED WATERS: FROM VOLUNTARY TO MANDATORY TOOL FOR NAVIGATION SAFETY AND ENVIRONMENTAL PROTECTION? 19 (2007), available at http://www.fni.no/doc&pdf/FNI-R0207.pdf.

[96] UNCLOS, supra note 2, arts. 279–299.

[97] Id.

[98] Id.

UNCLOS, if at all, and that the climate change dispute essentially pertains to the UNFCCC, which provides for a different dispute settlement mechanism that excludes recourse to compulsory adjudication under part XV.[99] This line of argumentation would be analogous to Japan's position in the *Southern Bluefin Tuna* arbitration conducted under Annex VII of part XV.[100] In that case, the Annex VII arbitral tribunal concluded that the disputing parties had agreed to seek settlement of the dispute under the terms of a regional fisheries convention that excluded any further procedure not accepted by all disputing parties, and accordingly dismissed the claims for want of jurisdiction.[101]

By contrast, the claimant would likely argue that the dispute concerns the protection of the marine environment and thus arises under UNCLOS. The claimant also would likely attempt to distinguish its case from the *Southern Bluefin Tuna* arbitration based on the subject matter of GHG emissions and marine pollution, the interplay of the various instruments involved, and the global dimension of the environmental threat. The claimant may also argue that the UNFCCC does not constitute a bar to part XV jurisdiction with respect to violations of UNCLOS.

The debate over the framing of the dispute in relation to article 281 would be influenced by another key jurisdictional provision: article 288. This provision establishes broad jurisdiction for the dispute settlement procedure with respect to two key sources. The procedure may exercise jurisdiction to address any dispute concerning: (1) the application or interpretation of UNCLOS (submitted consistently with part XV), and (2) the application or interpretation of an international agreement consistent with the purposes of UNCLOS (submitted consistently with that agreement).[102] This jurisdictional question is different from the question of applicable law addressed further below.

A key consideration to the questions raised by articles 281 and 288 pertains to the framing of the issues and the dispute. If the dispute is seen as essentially one over climate change and the UNFCCC, then part XV may be displaced by the dispute settlement mechanism of the UNFCCC. However if the essential character of the dispute is seen to involve marine protection issues governed by UNCLOS, then part XV may provide a jurisdictional basis.

If a UNCLOS/UNFCCC claim successfully overcomes the hurdle of article 281(1), part XV section 2, regarding compulsory procedures entailing binding decisions, enters into operation.[103] A pivotal provision here is article 287, which concerns the choice of procedure for settlement of the dispute, namely: the International Tribunal for the Law of the Sea (ITLOS), the International Court of Justice (ICJ), Annex VII Arbitral

---

[99] United Nations Framework Convention on Climate Change, May 9, 1992, 1771 U.N.T.S. 10.

[100] *See, e.g.,* Marcos Orellana, *The Law on Highly Migratory Fish Stocks: ITLOS Jurisprudence in Context,* 34 GOLDEN GATE U. L. REV. 459, 463 (2004).

[101] Southern Bluefin Tuna (N.Z. v. Japan; Austl. v. Japan), Jurisdiction and Admissibility, Award of the Arbitral Tribunal, 39 I.L.M. 1359 (2000).

[102] UNCLOS, *supra* note 2, art. 288.

[103] *See id.* arts. 286–296.

Tribunal, or Annex VIII Specialized Arbitral Tribunal.[104] Annex VII arbitration is the default procedure if the parties do not otherwise agree on any procedure.[105]

Once the procedure is established, another relevant question is what law shall be applied. UNCLOS article 293(1) directs a court or tribunal exercising jurisdiction under part XV to apply UNCLOS and other rules of international law not incompatible with UNCLOS.[106] It is likely that sources of international environmental law, including customary law and the UNFCCC, would be relevant applicable law, as part of this category of rules of international law not incompatible with UNCLOS.

B. CLAIMS AND REMEDIES

Does the law of the sea provide viable claims of State responsibility in the general context of climate change and the marine environment? In more specific terms, does the inadequate control of activities within a State's territory that produces GHG emissions that result in harm to the marine environment breach any international obligation established in UNCLOS? The various options available to formulate the relevant legal questions raise conceptual and linguistic nuances that go beyond this chapter. Still, it is worth recalling that the framing of the question is most likely to have a material influence on the answer provided by a dispute settlement mechanism.

The discussion above[107] regarding environmental protection and UNCLOS presents the key legal issues relevant to identifying a viable cause of action relating to climate change and the marine environment.

The discussion of remedies would center on cessation, restitution, and compensation, as these are the traditional tools established in general international law.[108] From the outset it could be asked whether these remedies are sufficient or even adequate to address harm to the marine environment resulting from GHG emissions. For example, compensation could provide monetary resources to a State that has suffered injury, but these may be meaningless to the inhabitants of a State that has lost its territory in whole or part. Similarly, physical restitution may be impossible in the presence of irreversible harm.

Cessation, on the other hand, may provide a strong legal, moral, and political argument for a change in conduct.[109] The strength of the argument, however, would hinge on the subject matter of the specific obligation found in breach. This discussion would involve the substantive analysis of part XII of UNCLOS discussed above. At the same

---

[104] *Id.* art. 287(1).

[105] *Id.* art. 287(1)(c).

[106] *Id.* art. 293(1).

[107] *See supra* Section II(A).

[108] *See* Draft Articles on Responsibility of States for Internationally Wrongful Acts, *supra* note 51. *See also* James Crawford, State Responsibility: The General Part (2013).

[109] Roda Verheyen, Climate Change Damage and International Law: Prevention Duties and State Responsibility 242–43 (2005).

time, cessation would be incapable of preventing the impacts on the marine environment resulting from the GHGs already emitted to the atmosphere. Given the limitations of the traditional remedies established in the law of State responsibility, new concepts, tools, and methods may be necessary to effectively protect the marine environment from climate change.

Conclusion

This chapter has provided an introductory overview of the salient issues that arise in the interface between climate change and the international law of the sea. Sea-level rise resulting from climate change can cause the submersion of existing land territories, thereby raising complex issues of sovereignty and access to natural resources. Sea-level rise is also expected to change the existing boundaries of maritime zones, with concomitant political, economic, and security implications.

The UN Convention on the Law of the Sea establishes a general obligation to protect the marine environment, as well as more specific obligations pertaining to pollution, and these obligations may carry potential implications for the emission of greenhouse gases to the atmosphere. The dumping of iron in the seas as a means of sequestering carbon similarly raises legal issues with respect to the application of specialized regimes dealing with dumping and the protection of the marine environment. The opening of navigation channels as a result of the melting of Arctic ice caps such as the Northwest Passage also poses legal questions.

Finally, the applicability of the dispute settlement mechanism established in UNCLOS could also eventually attract claims relating to climate change. The chapter has explored the basic boundaries of these issues, with a view to setting the stage for the more detailed examination and analysis that follows in this unit.

13 Governance of Arctic Ocean Marine Resources
Dr. Kamrul Hossain

Introduction

The Arctic region is roughly equal to the size of Africa.[1] One-third of the region is land-covered containing a portion of landmass from eight states—the so-called Arctic states—of which only five are Arctic Ocean coastal states. Another third of the region consists of continental shelves located in less than 500 meters of water, whereas the final third is the sea floor deeper than 500 meters.[2] Of the approximately 14 million square kilometers of the Arctic Ocean, a significant portion—especially along the coastlines—is

---

[1] Andreas Østhagen, *The Arctic and Need for Greater Differentiation in a Non-coherent Region*, THE ARCTIC INSTITUTE 1 n.2 (Feb. 23, 2012), http://www.thearcticinstitute.org/2012/02/arctic-and-need-for-greater.html.

[2] *See* Peter F. Johnston, *Arctic Energy Resources and Global Energy Security*, 12 J. MIL. & STRATEGIC STUD. 1, 15 (2010).

now ice-free for a substantial period of time each year because of the rapid and ongoing melting of Arctic sea ice resulting from climate change.

The prospect of a new era of resource exploitation in the Arctic has contributed to a broader range of economic and commercial activities,[3] further accelerating the impacts of climate change. Although most of the high sea space of the Arctic Ocean is still covered with thick ice sheets, some climate studies predict that an ice-free summer Arctic Ocean could occur as early as 2030.[4]

Experts believe that the high seas of the Arctic Ocean—a global commons area subject to multilateral governance—will probably remain inaccessible.[5] Nevertheless, increasing commercial activities along the coastlines, and within the exclusive economic zone and the seabed underneath the continental shelves, may have effects on the marine-based resources. The Arctic marine area is considered a resource-rich region not only for its huge reserves of nonliving resources, such as oil and gas, but also for living renewable resources, such as fisheries and other marine wildlife resources.[6] Therefore, the region is of tremendous significance, both in terms of resource exploitation and of the dynamics of the region's geopolitical interests.[7]

While the exploration and subsequent exploitation of some of the mineral resources are seen as contemporary activities, the exploitation of marine living resources has been traditionally conducted for centuries. The latter served as traditional subsistence for the region's coastal and indigenous communities throughout many generations, and continues to be the tradition-based livelihood for many of the remote communities in the Arctic. With melting sea ice and greater accessibility, the emerging trend of

---

[3] Peter Hough, *Worth the Energy? The Geopolitics of Arctic Oil and Gas*, 6 CENT. EUR. J. INT'L & SEC. STUD. 65, 67 (2012).

[4] *See* ACIA, ARCTIC CLIMATE IMPACT ASSESSMENT 8 (2005); *see also* Scott G. Borgerson, *The Coming Arctic Boom as the Ice Melts, the Region Heats Up*, 92 FOREIGN AFF. No. 4 (July–Aug.) (2013), http://www. foreignaffairs.com/articles/139456/scott-g-borgerson/the-coming-arctic-boom (stating that although in 2007, the Intergovernmental Panel on Climate Change estimated that Arctic summers would become ice free beginning in 2070, the more sophisticated simulations in 2012 moved the date up to 2020).

[5] Mia Bennett, *Canadian and Russian Claims to the Arctic: The Allure of the North Pole*, KAUPPAYHDISTYKSET (Dec. 31, 2013), *available at* http://kauppayhdistys.fi/2014/01/02/canadian-russian-claims-arctic-allure-no rth-pole/.

[6] The consequences of climate change have effects both on accessibility to the marine area as well as on northward migration of living resources because of warmer temperature. The water area of the Arctic Ocean is nearly five times the size of the Mediterranean. *See* Jennifer Jeffers, *Climate Change and the Arctic: Adapting to Changes in Fisheries Stocks and Governance Regimes*, 37 ECOLOGY L.Q. 917, 919 (2010).

[7] According to some analysts, the previously inaccessible oil and gas deposits may now be accessible permanently or periodically. *See* Scott G. Borgerson, *The Great Game Moves North: As the Arctic Melts, Countries Vie for Control*, FOREIGN AFF. (Mar. 25, 2009), *available at* http://www.foreignaffairs.com/articles/64905/ scott-g-borgerson/the-great-game-moves-north; *see also* George Kolisnek, *Canadian Arctic Energy Security*, J. ENERGY SEC. (Dec. 14, 2008), http://www.ensec.org/index.php?option=com_content&view=article& id=172:canadian-arcticenergy-security&catid=90:energysecuritydecember08&Itemid=334; *see also* Barry S. Zellen, *Viewpoint: Cold Front Rising, as Climate Change Thins Polar Ice, a New Race for Arctic Resources Begins*, STRATEGIC INSIGHTS (Feb. 2008).

commercial utilization of these resources presents conflicting interests between both national and international actors and between national authority and the traditional user communities.[8]

The Arctic is regarded as the world's next resource frontier. Both on-land and offshore resources make the region lucrative to the rest of the world. The availability of these resources, coupled with the continued demand for access, causes both international and regional tension regarding resource exploitation. The demand for nonliving resources—hydrocarbons—is becoming important to the rest of the world. Some scholars have suggested that the competition for these resources could precipitate territorial conflicts.[9]

Similarly, excessive exploitation of living resources, such as fish resources, consumption of which is increasing dramatically, will result in an imbalance in the functioning of Arctic marine ecosystems. Although terrestrial resources are composed of a number of valuable mineral substances, such as iron ore, nickel, gold, and diamonds, the region has recently attracted attention for its huge potential reserves of offshore hydrocarbon resources.

Resource exploitation in the Arctic will intensify in the coming years. The potential consequence of this trend will include not only the geopolitical tension arising out of competition over resource consumption, but also concerns over protection of the environment both for sustainable resource utilization and preservation and conservation of marine resources. Besides international and regional tension, conflict in the domestic realm will likely escalate because of the high number of local and indigenous communities inhabiting the region that depend on marine living resources in the area.

Based on this two-dimensional tension, this chapter reviews the existing legal frameworks governing Arctic marine resources. However, before examining the governance framework, it provides an overview of Arctic marine resources, focusing on fishery and offshore hydrocarbon resources. The chapter identifies governance gaps with a view to evaluating the effectiveness of a core concept of sustainable resource governance applicable to the Arctic marine area. Given that the Arctic marine area involves complex sociocultural and environmental characteristics, this chapter makes recommendations on how to deal effectively with governance of the marine resources, in particular fisheries and offshore hydrocarbons, so that the existing level of uncertainty can be mitigated.

---

[8] In the Arctic countries, indigenous peoples are becoming more recognized as legitimate actors in resource governance, at least to the extent decisions remain at the local and national level. Creation of the Nunavut Territory in Canada; Home Rule, and subsequently self-governance in Greenland; and the Home Rule in Sakha Republic in Russia are examples that illustrate how indigenous peoples have secured a stronger role in resource governance. *See* Richard A. Caulfield, *Resource Governance, in* Arctic Human Development Report 122 (Niels Einarssen et al. eds., 2004), *available at* http://www.svs.is/ahdr/AHDR%20chapters/English%20version/Chapters%20PDF.htm.

[9] *See, e.g.*, Scott G. Borgerson, *Arctic Meltdown: The Economic and Security Implications of Global Warming*, 87 Foreign Aff. 63, 63 (2008).

I. Arctic Marine Resources: Fisheries and Hydrocarbons

The availability of ample living and nonliving resources makes the Arctic special as climate change gradually creates opportunities for exploitation of these resources. This chapter focuses primarily on fisheries and offshore hydrocarbons, and this part of the chapter provides an overview of the availability of these two categories of resources.

Despite accessibility to most of the Arctic Ocean being limited due to the presence of sea ice, the coastal states as well as the communities inhabiting the coast have been exploiting the resources of the regional seas in the Arctic for many generations, particularly with respect to fisheries. These seas contained the world's oldest and richest commercial fishing grounds.[10] Commercial fisheries in the maritime area have occurred mainly in the more southerly waters of the Arctic marine area. In the Bering Sea and Aleutian Islands, Barents Sea, and Norwegian Sea, annual fish harvests in the past have exceeded 2 million tons. Important fisheries also exist around Iceland, Svalbard, Greenland, and Canada. Exploitation of fisheries in these seas played a significant role in supporting the food supply chain for Arctic countries and the rest of the world.[11]

In the Arctic Ocean itself, however, primarily small-scale subsistence fisheries now exist. No significant commercial fisheries exist here, and no commercial fisheries exist anywhere in the central Arctic Ocean.[12] Although some argue that it is unlikely that fish stocks in the high seas portion of the Arctic Ocean will allow commercial fisheries to remain viable in the short term,[13] other commercial activities, such as hydrocarbon exploitation or shipping, may compete with fishing in a spatial sense or otherwise affect them by pollution.[14] The Arctic Climate Impact Assessment (ACIA) report conducted an extensive survey of Arctic fisheries that examined the impact of climate change on the health, distribution, and migration patterns of fish stocks in different parts of the Arctic marine area.[15] The distribution of potentially significant commercial fish stocks in the marine Arctic is confined to the North Pacific or the North Atlantic, while some stocks have circumpolar distribution.[16]

---

[10] Jeffers, *supra* note 6, at 922.

[11] *Id.* at 932.

[12] Erik J. Molenaar, *Status and Reform of International Arctic Fisheries Law, in* ARCTIC MARINE GOVERNANCE OPPORTUNITIES FOR TRANSATLANTIC COOPERATION 103, 105 (Elizabeth Tedsen et al. eds., 2014).

[13] A.H. Hoel, Presentation at the Second Arctic Ocean Review Project Workshop in Reykjavik: Living Marine Resources in the Arctic, Trends and Opportunities (Sept. 20, 2011).

[14] Molenaar, *supra* note 12, at 106.

[15] *See* ACIA, *supra* note 4 at 400–03.

[16] Important North Pacific fish stocks include Alaska pollock, pacific cod, snow crab, and various Pacific salmon species. In the North Atlantic, important fish stocks include North-East Arctic cod, haddock, Norwegian spring-spawning, herring, Atlantic salmon, and red king crab. Significant circumpolar fish stocks include capelin, Greenland halibut, and northern shrimp. Polar cod and Arctic char also have

Exploitation of the nonliving offshore resources—the hydrocarbons—has started comparatively recently, and it is gradually extending. It is estimated that the Arctic holds approximately a quarter of the world's undiscovered hydrocarbon resources,[17] and is therefore regarded as the next reservoir of the globe's oil and gas reserves, although the exact quantity held in the region is unclear. The ACIA report estimated that there are significant oil and gas reserves in the Arctic marine area, and that most of these are located within the jurisdiction of Russia, with additional fields in Canada, Alaska (United States), Greenland (Denmark), and Norway.[18] The United States Geological Survey (USGS) found further evidence to support these findings, first in 2008 and again in 2010. These surveys concluded that the area north of the Arctic Circle holds approximately 30 percent of the world's undiscovered gas and 13 percent of its undiscovered oil, and that most of these resources are located under fewer than 500 meters of water depth.[19] It has been further estimated that approximately 84 percent of the undiscovered oil and gas is located in the offshore Arctic, representing around 90 billion barrels of technically recoverable oil.[20] Geographic areas with the highest potential are Arctic Alaska, eastern Greenland, the East and West Barents basins in Norway and Russia, and the South Kara/Yamal basins of Russia.[21]

Although the Eurasian side of the Arctic has greater reserves of natural gas, the North American side is more oil-rich; the latter is estimated to contain approximately 65 percent of the undiscovered Arctic oil, but only 26 percent of the undiscovered Arctic natural gas.[22] It is presumed that the remainder of the resources is in the Eurasian Arctic, and

---

circumpolar distribution, but the former is only marginally targeted by commercial fisheries and the latter is predominantly fished for subsistence purpose. *See id.; see also* Molenaar, *supra* note 12.

[17] Borgerson, *supra* note 9, at 63.

[18] *See* Susan Joy Hassel, Impacts of a Warming Arctic: Arctic climate Impact assessment 44 (2004); *see also* Bruce C. Forbes & Florian Stammler, *Arctic Climate Change Discourse: The Contrasting Politics of Research Agendas in the West and Russia,* 28 Polar Res. 31 (2009).

[19] Donald L. Gautier et al., *Assessment of Undiscovered Oil and Gas in the Arctic,* 324 Sci. 1175, 1175 (2009).

[20] K.J. Bird et al., U.S. Geological Survey Fact Sheet 2008-3049, Circum-Arctic Resource Appraisal: Estimates of Undiscovered Oil and Gas North of the Arctic Circle (2008), http://pubs.usgs.gov/fs/2008/3049/fs2008-3049.pdf.

[21] P.E. Long et al., U.S. Dep't of Energy, Preliminary Geospatial Analysis of Arctic Ocean Hydrocarbon Resources § 4.0 (2008), http://www.pnl.gov/main/publications/external/technical_reports/PNNL-17922.pdf.

[22] Nong Hong, *The Energy Factor in the Arctic Dispute: A Pathway to Conflict or Cooperation?* 5 J. World Energy L. & Bus. 1 (2012), *available at* http://www.nanhai.org.cn/include_lc/upload/UploadFiles/20121211219155332.4.pdf; *see also* Gautier, *supra* note 19, at 1178. It is estimated that 60 percent of oil resources is located in six locations: the Alaska Platform, the Canning-Mackenzie Basin, the North Barents Basin, the Northwest Greenland Rifted Margin, the South Danmarkshavn Basin, and the North Danmarkshavn Salt Basin. Of these, the Alaska Platform is the most significant in that it is estimated to contain approximately 31 percent of the undiscovered Arctic oil. Similarly, approximately 66 percent of undiscovered gas is believed to lie in just four areas: the South Kara Sea, the South Barents Basin, the North Barents Basin, and the Alaska Platform. Of these, the South Kara Sea, a Russian possession, is believed to contain nearly 39 percent of undiscovered gas. *See* Hong, *supra.*

these are believed to be located primarily in the Russian Arctic. Interestingly, 97 percent of these resources are thought to be within the exclusive jurisdictions of the Arctic coastal states; in other words, within 200 nautical miles of continental shelves, according to the USGS.[23] In addition to the resources available underneath the continental shelves of the Arctic coastal states, a relatively small amount of the whole reserves are projected to be located in the "Area"[24]—the legal regime that applies universally for all nations.[25]

Due to the harsh climate, inadequate technology, and presence of polar ice, none of these resources has been previously tapped. The accuracy of these figures is yet to be confirmed with further precision as they are currently only estimates. Extreme climatic conditions, the presence of a thick ice sheet, and remoteness hinder appropriate assessments. Moreover, the Russian Arctic shelves are poorly mapped, and research and exploration have been inadequately conducted. Consequently, the amount of resources currently believed to be available may have been either over- or underestimated. This reality notwithstanding, the likelihood of resource reserves in this region cannot be ignored.

II. Geopolitical Aspects of Arctic Resources

The world's natural resources are shrinking dramatically due to the growth in consumption, which has placed significant pressure on existing resources. It has been suggested that, with increasing demands, the reserves that are known to be available will run out by as early as 2050, or perhaps sooner, unless exploitation of new discoveries begins.[26] The search for new resources has been, and continues to be, a constant process to mitigate the increasing demands. Because of the estimated resource availability, the Arctic has been found to offer natural resources to exploit in the future. The region has therefore become an important area for nation-states both within and beyond the Arctic.

The potential for fisheries and offshore hydrocarbon has been extensively discussed in recent years. The complexity of the Arctic marine area, in terms of its natural resources management regime, lies in its absence of a comprehensive governance structure. There is an existing governance framework in place in the Arctic, but it is fragmented with

---

[23] See KINGDOM OF DENMARK STRATEGY FOR THE ARCTIC 2011–2020, available at http://ec.europa. eu/enterprise/policies/raw-materials/files/docs/mss-denmark_en.pdf (last visited July 20, 2014); see also Gautier et al., supra note 19, at 1175–76.

[24] BIRD ET AL., supra note 20.

[25] As a party to both UNCLOS and the 1994 Agreement related to the implementation of part XI (The European Community became a party to both agreements through a formal confirmation on April 1, 1998), the European Union is subject to the regime of the International Seabed Authority (ISA). Article 4(2) of the 1994 Continental Shelf Agreement requires a state first to ratify UNCLOS to become party to the agreement.

[26] A.R. Brandt, R.J. Plevin & A.E. Farrell, Dynamics of the Oil Transition: Modeling Capacity, Depletion, and Emissions, 35 ENERGY 2852, 2852 (2010).

respect to resource management. A lack of overarching or crosscutting structure for resource governance is likely to cause tension in response to emerging geopolitical interests prevailing in the Arctic in light of climate change impacts.

The jurisdictional basis within the Arctic marine area is determined by the established rules of the law of the sea, including the UN Convention on the Law of the Sea (UNCLOS).[27] In the Arctic, all but the United States are parties to the Convention. Surface and subsurface water resources within the 200 nautical miles exclusive economic zone (EEZ) are under the jurisdiction of coastal states. Jurisdiction of the coastal states over seabed resources, however, extends even beyond 200 nautical miles when natural prolongation of the landmass exists; in other words, to the outer edge of the continental margin.[28]

Although the demarcation limits for the exploitation of surface or subsurface water resources, such as fisheries, are clearly set by the Convention, the ownership rights over the fish stocks are complex. Because of the highly dynamic and variable characteristics of Arctic ecosystems, it is difficult to predict Arctic water temperature. Consequently, some existing stocks may collapse and never recover, whereas other new fish species migrating from the southern waters may become more dominant.[29] The patterns of fish migration, and alteration and distribution of species, become apparent, resulting in huge uncertainty over the ownership of the stocks.

The ownership rights of the seabed resources, such as offshore hydrocarbon, are clearly settled within the 200 nautical miles of the continental shelf. But beyond 200 nautical miles, the right depends on the establishment of final demarcation of the outer limits of the continental shelf. The issue of different types of ocean floor features makes the Arctic Ocean's continental shelves determination difficult.[30] Three of the five Arctic coastal states have already filed their submission to the Commission on the Limits of the Continental Shelf (CLCS). Russia was the first country to lodge its submission in 2001, claiming almost half of the Arctic Ocean seabed as its extended continental shelf[31]—a

---

[27] U.N. Convention on the Law of the Sea arts. 61–64, *opened for signature* Dec. 10, 1982, 1833 U.N.T.S. 397 [hereinafter UNCLOS]. As of October 2013, 166 states are parties to the Convention. *See* Division for Ocean Affairs and the Law of the Sea, http://www.un.org/Depts/los/reference_files/chronological_lists_of_ratifications.htm#The%20United%20Nations%20Convention%20on%20the%20Law%20of%20the%20Sea (last visited July 20, 2014).

[28] According to article 76 of UNCLOS, the continental shelf extends to a distance of 200 nautical miles regardless of the natural prolongation of the landmass of the coastal state. However, if natural prolongation continues beyond 200 nautical miles, a coastal state has the right to delineate an extended continental shelf, following certain procedures embodied in the Convention.

[29] *See* Molenaar, *supra* note 12.

[30] *See* Nele Matz-Lück, *Planting the Flag in Arctic Waters: Russia's Claim to the North Pole*, 1 GÖTTINGEN J. INT'L L. 235, 253 (2009).

[31] Russia's submission on the outer limits of the continental shelf included a sizeable area of the Arctic Ocean over the Lomonosov and Alpha-Mendeleev Ridges. Russia's delineation is thus based on the postulation that both of those ridges are "submarine elevations," not "submarine ridges," and thus are natural components

move that was widely criticized by the other coastal states immediately after the submission. Norway submitted its claim in 2006, and the CLCS gave its final recommendation in 2009. Canada just recently filed its submission, whereas Denmark is preparing to file its claim in 2014.[32] The other Arctic coastal state—the United States—is not yet a party to UNCLOS, and is thus not yet able to lodge any formal submission to the CLCS. However, the country has submitted its reactions to Russia's claims.[33] Establishing jurisdiction over the seabed extension will have consequences on oil and gas development in the Arctic.

The disputes concerning the demarcation lines in the Arctic Ocean floor will probably lie in determining the right over Lomonosov Ridge, which contains overlapping claims among three of the five Arctic coastal states—Canada, Denmark, and Russia.[34] Russia has already claimed the continental shelf over the Lomonosov Ridge. Canada has not yet completely finished gathering scientific data about its Arctic seabed claims. However, in its preliminary submission, Canada indicated its claims over the Arctic seabed extended to the North Pole. The claims upheld the previous assumption that the Lomonosov Ridge was a natural prolongation of its land territory north of Ellesmere Island.[35] It is likely that Denmark will also submit its claim over the Lomonosov Ridge based on the result of the joint study conducted with Canada on the ridge, called LORITA-1 (Lomonosov Ridge Test of Appurtenance-1). Denmark is expected to claim at least part of the Lomonosov Ridge as a natural prolongation of its territory, provided that it finds the ridge system meets the definition of a submarine ridge or submarine elevation.[36]

---

of its continental margin. For different modes of delineation for the Russian claims in the Arctic Ocean, see the charts and discussions in Alexander Proelss & Till Müller, *The Legal Regime of the Arctic Ocean*, 68 HEIDELBERG J. INT'L L. 651, 665–77 (2008). *See also* Matz-Lück, *supra* note 30, at 250–51.

[32] According to UNCLOS, each coastal state has ten years after it has ratified the Convention to submit its extended continental shelf claim. The ten-year time limits for Canada and Denmark expire in 2013 and 2014, respectively. Article 4 of Annex II to UNCLOS, http://www.un.org/depts/los/convention_agreements/texts/unclos/annex2.htm (last visited July 20, 2014).

[33] Practice shows that the CLCS accepts reaction notifications from third parties regardless of the existence of any overlapping claims. Third parties do not necessarily have to be neighboring states of the submitting state. For example, the United States is not a neighbor of Brazil, and India, Germany, the Netherlands, Japan, the United States, and the Russian Federation are not neighboring states of Australia. All of these states sent notifications seeking to preserve certain rights under international law. Michael Sheng-ti Gau, *Third Party Intervention in the Commission on the Limits of the Continental Shelf regarding a Submission Involving a Dispute*, 40 OCEAN DEV. & INT'L L. 61, 72 (2009).

[34] For a detailed discussion on this point, see MICHAEL BYERS, INTERNATIONAL LAW AND THE ARCTIC 107–09 (2013).

[35] *See generally* PARLIAMENTARY INFO. & RESEARCH SERV., LIBRARY OF PARLIAMENT, THE ARCTIC: CANADA'S LEGAL CLAIMS (2008), *available at* http://www.parl.gc.ca/content/lop/researchpublications/prb0805-e.pdf.

[36] *See* Lomonosov Ridge Test of Appurtenance Project (LORITA-1), Continental Shelf Project, Fieldwork during April/May 2006 North of Canada/Greenland, http://a76.dk/greenland_uk/north_uk/gr_n_expeditions_uk/lorita-1_uk/index.html. (last visited July 20, 2014).

The CLCS has not yet been in any position to make a determination on the possible overlapping claims with Russia over the ridge. Immediately after Russia's submission in 2001, the CLCS asked Russia to resubmit the claims with further supporting seabed information. Russia has since been working hard to collect undersea geomorphological and oceanic data to support its claims.[37] Although hydrocarbons reserves in the overlapping area seem to be smaller, the area is politically significant because it contains two huge regions spanning the North Pole: Lomonosov-Makarov and the Eurasia Basin.[38] Thus, the question of jurisdiction over the seabed extension will apparently continue, and some fear Russia may proceed to develop oil and gas, where feasible, in the disputed areas of the Arctic that it claimed, even before any final settlement over the continental shelf dispute has been accomplished.[39]

The likelihood of intensified tension will also occur not only from a jurisdictional perspective, but also from competition over resource usage. Concerning fisheries, for example, the northward movement of fish populations will lead fishing fleets to increasingly move to the north. Climate change results in an alteration of fish migration patterns. Some sea areas see significant expansion of fish stocks, while others see fish population straddling into the EEZs of a number of adjacent states. It is feared that the accessible marine area will be overfished both inside and outside of the EEZ, resulting in declining yields and increased pressure on the remaining resources.[40] On one hand, there is potential for unsustainable "race to bottom" fishing practices among the nations within their own EEZs. On the other hand, the overexploitation will cause potential tension over the resource ownership among these nations.[41]

Conflicts over fishing rights and resource ownership also may contribute to potential conflict in the Arctic,[42] when states' economic interests over the resources are jeopardized. For example, the European Union relies heavily on the Arctic fisheries. Although EU fishing fleets themselves are not greatly involved in Arctic fisheries, its citizens consume one-third of the fish caught in the Arctic marine area, especially from the European part of the Arctic.[43] A large part of EU consumption increasingly depends on the resources

---

[37] Matz-Lück, *supra* note 30, at 250.

[38] Hough, *supra* note 3, at 250.

[39] *See* Andrew Holland, Nick Cunningham & Xander Vagg, American Sec. Project, Critical Security Challenges in the Arctic 3 (2013), http://americansecurityproject.org/ASP%20Reports/Ref%200139%20-%20Critical%20Security%20Challenges%20in%20the%20Arctic.pdf.

[40] Caulfield, *supra* note 8, at 126.

[41] *See generally* James McGoodwin, *Effects of Climatic Variability on Three Fishing Economies in High-Latitude Regions: Implications for Fisheries Policies*, 31 Marine Pol'y 40, 40 (2007); Kathleen Miller & Gordon Munro, *Climate and Cooperation: A New Perspective on the Management of Shared Fish Stocks*, 19 Marine Resource Econ. 367, 367 (2004).

[42] Jeffers, *supra* note 6, at 920.

[43] High Representative of the European Union for Foreign Affairs & Security Policy, European Comm'n, Developing a European Union Policy towards the Arctic Region: Progress since 2008 and Next Steps 10 (2012), http://eeas.europa.eu/arctic_region/docs/join_2012_19.pdf.

occurring in the Barents Sea, where the production is constantly moving northward from the south and southeast North Sea. As the demand is expected to increase in the future, high seas fishing rights of all other nations, including those of the European Union, could clash with the interests of the Arctic coastal states.

In a similar vein, in light of increasing energy demands, the fossil fuel reserves that are known to be available could be depleted by 2050, if not sooner, unless exploitation of new reserves is undertaken.[44] In addition, increases in oil prices and ongoing conflicts in the oil-rich region of the Middle East reveal a troubling picture of energy supply security in the near future, which has prompted a heightened demand for Arctic hydrocarbon resources. Advances in ship design and drilling equipment have enhanced the feasibility of resource exploitation in the Arctic. Today the use of robotic and sophisticated communications systems makes resource extraction far beneath the sea ever more technically feasible. As the world is seeking alternative sources of energy, both in terms of its nature and of the region capable of supplying it securely, it is more frequently looking to the Arctic because of its huge hydrocarbon potential.

Due to an estimated increase in global oil,[45] and, even more so, natural gas demand,[46] it is believed that the expansion of hydrocarbon extraction in the Arctic is just a matter of time. In recent years, energy industries and the Arctic states have expressed increasing interest in exploiting oil and gas in the region. Indeed, in many areas within the circumpolar north, exploitation of oil and gas has already become the major economic driver.[47] However, Arctic offshore drilling is relatively more expensive, and the high cost of doing business in the area suggests that only the world's largest oil and gas companies will have the financial, technical, and managerial strength to accomplish the costly, long-lead-time projects dictated by Arctic conditions.[48] The extraction of resources will also likely be decided by the price of the resource weighed against the extraction, processing, and transportation costs of getting it to market.[49]

Despite these challenges, the energy supply from the Arctic has gained significant momentum in recent years. The European Union, for example, is one of the major importers of Arctic oil and gas. Currently 50 percent of total EU consumption is imported, with 53 percent coming from the Arctic (Russia and Norway),[50] and an additional 14 percent

---

[44] Brandt et al., *supra* note 26, at 2852.

[45] The International Energy Agency projects in a current policy scenario as well as in a new policy scenario (with more oil use efficiency and switching to other fuels) an absolute global primary oil uses increase, even if the share of oil in total primary energy demand is expected to decrease. *See* Int'l Energy Agency, World Energy Outlook 2010, at 102 (2010).

[46] *Id.* at 180.

[47] Arctic Monitoring & Assessment Programme, Arctic Oil and Gas 1 (2007), http://www. govmin.gl/images/stories/petroleum/Oil_Gas_Assessment_Overview_Report_2008.pdf.

[48] Hong, *supra* note 22, at 11–12.

[49] Johnston, *supra* note 2, at 3.

[50] Since 2004, more than half of the EU-27's gross inland energy consumption was supplied by net imports. Much of the energy for EU consumption comes from Russia. The European Union is especially dependent

from North America—a part of which is produced in the American Arctic. It has been estimated that the import will grow by approximately 65–70 percent over the next twenty years,[51] resulting in a further push for the exploitation of resources available underneath the Arctic continental shelves. In addition to the European Union, other non-Arctic actors, such as China and India, are increasingly showing interest in the Arctic due to the prospect of possible import of hydrocarbons from the region.

Geopolitical interests in the Arctic coincide with the question of the maintenance of the region's environmental integrity, which requires vigilant efforts to preserve the unique nature of the Arctic ecosystem. As environmental integrity runs counter to developmental activities, hydrocarbon activities, if allowed, will only accelerate the process of greater greenhouse gas emissions, thereby promoting more rapid climate change consequences unless a proper management regime is in place. Competition over resources would therefore shift the governance structure of the Arctic from an environmental-protection-focused regime to a political-economic approach, where the rising new powers from beyond the region, such as China, India, and others interested in the Arctic, exert tremendous pressure on the resources. As a result, a change in state actors' approach to the Arctic will occur. Their internal policy goals toward Arctic resource governance practices may be regarded as interference in Arctic matters jeopardizing the states' sovereign interests in energy development. Such an attitude may result in an international tension if resource governance is not clearly structured.

III. Existing Governance Framework for Arctic Marine Resources

The Arctic is often criticized for not having a comprehensive governance regime. The characteristics of the Arctic as a region are complex, which present an ocean in the center, surrounded by land and ice masses, making up the territories of sovereign states and the indigenous peoples inhabiting the region for thousands of years. The governance of the Arctic is widely recognized as a system of fragmented international, regional, and bilateral regulations, which are complemented by non-binding soft law mechanisms,

---

on the import of hard coal, lignite, and crude oil. In 2007, almost one-third (30.3 percent) of the EU-27's imports of crude oil were from Russia; this was higher than the rate seven years earlier. Russia also became the principal supplier of hard coal, its share of EU-27 imports rising from 7.9 percent in 2000 to 22.6 percent by 2007. Almost two-thirds (63.6 percent) of the EU imports of natural gas in 2007 came from Russia, Norway, or Algeria. A similar analysis shows that 64.5 percent of EU imports of hard coal were from Russia, South Africa, Australia, or Colombia, while 59.5 percent of crude oil imports came from Russia, Norway, Libya, or Saudi Arabia. The volume of imports from countries other than Russia and Norway remain relatively small. This was notably the case for crude oil imports from Libya and Kazakhstan, coal imports from Indonesia and Ukraine, or natural gas imports from Nigeria and Libya. *See* EUROSTAT, EUROPEAN COMM'N, ENERGY PRODUCTION AND IMPORTS (Aug. 2012), http://epp.eurostat.ec.europa.eu/statistics_explained/index.php/Energy_production_and_imports.

[51] Adele Airoldi, THE EUROPEAN UNION AND THE ARCTIC: POLICIES AND ACTIONS 76 (2008).

usually as a result of the initiatives undertaken by the Arctic Council.[52] The Arctic coastal states—the so-called Arctic 5, the states surrounding the Arctic Ocean—see no need for any overarching governance regime for the Arctic.[53] Instead, according to these states, UNCLOS and the Arctic Council initiatives effectively serve as the framework for Arctic governance.

As a purely legal framework, UNCLOS is the most appropriate instrument to provide a governance framework in the Arctic. Most of the challenges, requiring international and regional response, have emerged from the transformation of the Arctic Ocean, making it gradually accessible and facilitating subsequent human activities. The general provisions of UNCLOS applicable to the Arctic will be briefly discussed here. The Arctic coastal states, like any other state parties to the Convention with coastlines, have a legal right to exploit surface and subsurface economic interests within the 200- nautical-miles EEZ in the Arctic Ocean, albeit with contingent obligations,[54] pertaining to the protection and preservation of marine environment.[55] In particular with respect to ice-covered sea, the Arctic coastal states have a special privilege to adopt and enforce stricter laws and regulations within their EEZ to protect any irreversible disruption of the ecological balance of the marine area, such as from pollution from vessels.[56]

The coastal states also have sovereign rights over the continental shelf up to 200 nautical miles and even far beyond that where the continental margin forms a natural prolongation of the landmass of the coastal states—the so-called extended continental shelf (ECS). Establishing sovereignty claims over this marine area is most often connected to resource access, as the wording of article 77(1) of UNCLOS affirms.[57] Coastal states'

---

[52] The Arctic Council is a high-level intergovernmental initiative that addresses common issues and concerns faced by Arctic governments and indigenous peoples of the High North. It is the most active intergovernmental forum concerned with the Arctic, and the only one to be comprised of all eight Arctic nations: Canada, Denmark, Finland, Iceland, Norway, the Russian Federation, Sweden, and the United States. The Arctic Council is primarily concerned with the promotion of environmental protection and sustainable development of the region. *See* Arctic Council, http://www.arctic-council.org/index.php/en/ (last visited: July 20, 2014).

[53] Arctic Ocean Conference, May 27–29, 2008, *Ilulissat Declaration* (May 28, 2008), *available at* http://www.oceanlaw.org/downloads/arctic/Ilulissat_Declaration.pdf.

[54] Although the coastal states have a right to exploit living resources, such as fishing, in the EEZ, their duty lies also in the maintenance of proper conservation and management strategy, based on best available scientific assessments, to promote sustainable resource utilization. In regard to promoting conservation, where fish stocks, for example, occur within two or more coastal states' EEZs or beyond within the adjacent areas, UNCLOS requires the parties to cooperate either directly or through appropriate regional or subregional organizations. A similar approach is also endorsed in the context of highly migratory species both within and beyond the EEZ, such that states cooperate either directly or through appropriate organizations, and where no such organization exists, coastal states will cooperate to establish one. *See* UNCLOS, *supra* note 27, arts. 61–64.

[55] *Id.* art. 56(1)(b)(iii).

[56] *Id.* art. 234.

[57] According to article 77(1) of UNCLOS, coastal states exercise sovereign rights over the continental shelf "for the purpose of exploring it and exploiting its natural resources." *Id.* art. 77(1).

exercise of resource usage in the Arctic Ocean therefore lies both in the EEZ as well as in the established portion of the continental shelf, whereas the coastal states, as with all other states, enjoy a set of rights in the area beyond national jurisdiction both in the high sea (beyond the 200-nautical-miles EEZ) as well as in the "area" (the seabed beyond the determined portion of the continental shelf). Even though the central Arctic Ocean around the North Pole is characterized as polar-cap, consisting of thick ice sheets and not accessible, the surrounding areas not ice-capped must necessarily be treated as high sea, and be regarded as *res communis omnium*—the common heritage of mankind, where all the state parties to the Convention effectively enjoy basically all traditional freedoms,[58] albeit with certain legal obligations, such as peaceful and lawful use of the marine area,[59] and with commitment for the conservation of marine living resource,[60] in the high seas.[61]

Given the likelihood of its status as a semi-enclosed sea, the Arctic Ocean offers coastal states certain other privileges, such as to take measures to coordinate the management, conservation, exploration, and exploitation of the living resources at sea, and to set joint standards concerning rights and duties pertaining to protection and preservation of the marine environment.[62] Concerning the "area"—the seabed beyond the continental shelf—the responsibility is placed under the control of the International Seabed Authority (ISA), where activities must be conducted in accordance with the provisions of the Convention governing the protection and preservation of the marine environment.[63]

The exercise of resource usage both in surface and subsurface water as well as in the seabed of the continental shelf may have various consequences, the most alarming of which is the risk concerning the protection and preservation of the marine environment. Living resources can be overexploited, resulting in destruction of ecological balance. Extraction of nonliving resources, such as, hydrocarbons exercises, may cause extensive pollution to marine environment if, for example, an accident occurs in the process of extraction or transportation. In addition, other human activities, such as shipping, may also contribute to pollution affecting marine living resources.

A broader range of anthropogenic threats affect marine biodiversity, causing depopulation and migration of species. UNCLOS includes provisions for the protection and

---

[58] These traditional freedoms include: navigation, overflight, laying of submarine cables and pipelines, construction of artificial islands and other installations, fishing and scientific research—the so-called six freedoms of the high seas. *See id.* art. 87.

[59] *See, e.g., id.* art. 88.

[60] *Id.* art. 117.

[61] Non-ice-capped areas in the Arctic Ocean, include: the Banana Hole and Loophole in the Norwegian and Barents Seas, respectively; and the Donut Hole in Bering Sea.

[62] *See* UNCLOS, *supra* note 27, art. 123.

[63] *See id.*, Preamble, Agreement Relating to the Implementation of Part XI, *available at* http://www.un.org/depts/los/convention_agreements/texts/unclos/closindxAgree.htm (last visited: July 20, 2014).

preservation of marine environment in part XII. This part provides that sovereign rights to exploit natural resources in the marine area coexist with the duty to protect and preserve the marine environment,[64] while addressing an overall framework for marine environmental governance. On one hand, it sets out the "general" obligations of all states to safeguard the marine environment in its entirety, and, on the other hand, it offers a "comprehensive" structure for dealing with all sources of pollution at sea. Accordingly, part XII of the Convention is regarded as an international "constitution" on the protection and preservation of the marine environment,[65] which is applicable to resource governance in all marine areas, including the Arctic Ocean.

The Convention offers only the framework tools by which states are required to extend their national legislation to the EEZ and, where necessary, to conclude bilateral, multilateral, and regional agreements concerning, for example, environmental matters for marine governance connected to resources. To implement the provisions of the Convention, there are already two related but separate agreements in place addressing resource governance: the Agreement relating to International Seabed[66] and the UN Fish Stock Agreement.[67] UNCLOS also requires states to establish appropriate regional or international organizations and agreements to address these issues. Thus, the Convention sets forth only the general framework whereby the concrete actions to be undertaken are left to the states or the relevant regional and international organizations.

Consequently, other existing legal instruments complement the provisions of UNCLOS in the governance of marine resource. The Convention on Biological Diversity (CBD), for example, addresses the protection of marine biodiversity. In its preamble, the CBD directs the parties to adopt the precautionary approach,[68] which

---

[64] *Id.* art. 193.

[65] Julian Roberts, MARINE ENVIRONMENT PROTECTION AND BIODIVERSITY CONSERVATION: THE APPLICATION AND FUTURE DEVELOPMENT OF THE IMO's PARTICULARLY SENSITIVE SEA AREA CONCEPT 23 (2007).

[66] Agreement Relating to the Implementation of Part XI of the United Nations Convention on the Law of the Sea of 10 December 1982, U.N. Doc. A/RES/48/263 (Jul. 28, 1994).

[67] U.N. Conference on Straddling Fish Stocks and Highly Migratory Fish Stocks, July 24–Aug. 4, 1995, *Agreement for the Implementation of the United Nations Convention on the Law of the Sea of 10 December 1982 Relating to the Conservation and Management of Straddling Fish Stocks and Highly Migratory Fish Stocks,* U.N. Doc. A/Conf. 164/37 [hereinafter UNFSA], *available at* http://www.un.org/depts/los/convention_agreements/texts/fish_stocks_agreement/CONF164_37.htm.

[68] The precautionary approach has to be differentiated from the precautionary principle. While the latter refers to a "hard line" rule originally conceptualized as a means of managing highly polluting activities in the absence of scientific evidence, the former is created as a somewhat more flexible alternative that incorporates socioeconomic considerations along with the essential requirement of promoting the long-term sustainability of natural resources. *See* Pamela M. Mace & Wendy L. Gabriel, *Evolution, Scope, and Current Applications of the Precautionary Approach in Fisheries,* Proceedings, 5th NMFS NSAW. 1999. NOAA Tech. Memo. NMFS-F/SPO-40, at 65, http://www.st.nmfs.noaa.gov/StockAssessment/workshop_documents/nsaw5/mace_gab.pdf. (last visited July 20, 2014).

is then again reiterated by COP Decision II/10 concerning the marine environment.[69] Although the CBD does not provide additional guidance on the nature and scope of this mandate, the Arctic coastal states that are parties to the Convention, like all other state parties, are necessarily guided by the principle of the precautionary approach in marine resources governance.[70]

One other important feature that the CBD offers is the creation of Marine Protected Areas (MPAs).[71] MPAs may be established for a wide range of purposes, including the protection of marine species and habitats and the minimization of conflicts between diverse resource users.[72] UNCLOS provides a legal foundation for the creation of MPAs under the general obligation set forth in article 192 in combination with article 194(5) of the Convention.[73] However, it is not explicit whether MPAs can be established in areas beyond national jurisdiction (ABNJ). According to Erik J. Molenaar and Alex G. Oude Elferink, MPAs can be established in ABNJ within the framework of UNCLOS on the basis of article 194(5).[74] The other articles of UNCLOS also lend support to the creation of MPAs in ABNJ for the purpose of, for example, conservation and management of living resources in article 61, exploration of the continental shelf and management of its resources in article 77, the assessment and monitoring of environmental impacts in article 204, and the protection of archaeological and historical objects in article 303(1).

---

[69] Conference of the Parties to the Convention on Biological Diversity, Jakarta, Indonesia, Nov. 6–17, 1995, *Conservation and Sustainable Use of Marine and Coastal Biological Diversity*, Decision II/10, part XI, UNEP/CBD/COP/DEC/II/10, *available at* http://www.cbd.int/decision/cop/?id=7083. (last visited July 20, 2014).

[70] *See* UNFSA, *supra* note 67, arts. 5 & 6 (requiring state parties to adopt a precautionary approach in the exploitation of straddling and highly migratory fish stocks).

[71] Conference of the Parties to the Convention on Biological Diversity, Kuala Lumpur, Malaysia, Feb. 9–20, 2004, *Marine and Coastal Biological Diversity*, Decision VII/5, UNEP/CBD/COP/DEC/VII/5, *available at* http://www.cbd.int/decision/cop/default.shtml?id=7742 (last visited July 20, 2014). In the broadest sense, a marine protected area can be defined as any area of the coastal zone or open ocean with some level of protection conferred for the purpose of managing the use of resources and ocean space, or protecting vulnerable or threatened habitats and species. *See* TUNDI SPRING AGARDY, MARINE PROTECTED AREAS AND OCEAN CONSERVATION 99 (1997). The most frequently used definition, however, is that of the International Union for the Conservation of Nature (IUCN), which states: "Any area of intertidal or sub-tidal terrain, together with its overlying water and associated flora, fauna, historical and cultural features, which has been reserved by law or other effective means to protect part or all of the enclosed environment." *See* Timo Koivurova, *Governance of Protected Areas in the Arctic*, 5 UTRECHT L. REV. 44, 45 (2009).

[72] ROBERTS, *supra* note 65, at 30.

[73] By virtue of these articles, states are to take "all measures" necessary to protect and preserve rare or fragile ecosystems as well as the habitat of depleted, threatened, or endangered species and other forms of life. *Id.* at 32.

[74] UNCLOS, *supra* note 27, art. 194(5) ("The measures taken in accordance with this Part shall include those necessary to protect and preserve rare or fragile ecosystems as well as the habitat of depleted, threatened or endangered species and other forms of marine life.") *See* Erik J. Molenaar & Alex G. Oude Elferink, *Marine Protected Areas in Areas beyond National Jurisdiction—The Pioneering Efforts under the OSPAR Convention*, 5 UTRECHT L. REV. 5, 9 (2009).

The Conference of the Parties (COP) to the CBD has also addressed the issue of MPAs in ABNJ on a number of occasions.[75] MPAs in ABNJ have been established under the auspices of the regional sea organizations. The coverage of the MPAs in the high seas is, however, limited to only four sea areas at the moment: the Northern Ocean, the Northeast Atlantic, the Mediterranean, and the central Pacific.[76] In the Northeast Atlantic marine area, the Convention for the Protection of the Marine Environment of the North-East Atlantic (OSPAR) encompasses a sizeable ABNJ. Its Annex V,[77] in particular, provides a comprehensive legal framework for the implementation of part XII of UNCLOS consistent with the objective of the CBD concerning marine biodiversity.[78] A small part of the Arctic Ocean high sea (the Loop Hole) in the Barents Sea falls within the coverage of the OSPAR Convention for the purpose of the protection of marine and coastal biodiversity at the regional level.[79] Thus, the Barents Sea is an example of governance by the CBD within the framework of UNCLOS.[80]

There are several other regulatory arrangements in place to govern Arctic marine resources. Concerning fisheries, in addition to the general applicability of the UN Fish Stock Agreement, there are a few other bilateral or regional arrangements under the jurisdiction of a number of Regional Fisheries Management Organizations (RFMOs) that partly cover the Arctic Ocean.[81] The Banana Hole[82] and the Loophole are, for example, located in the regulatory area of the North East Atlantic Fisheries Commission (NEAFC).[83] However, the Loophole located in the Barents Sea is not fully covered by

---

[75] Molenaar & Elferink, *supra* note 74, at 11.

[76] J. Ardron, *Marine Spatial Planning in the High Seas*, 32 MARINE POL'Y 832, 833 (2008).

[77] By virtue of article 2 of Annex V, the Contracting Parties are obliged to "(a) take the necessary measures to protect and conserve the ecosystems and the biological diversity of the maritime area, and to restore, where practicable, marine areas which have been adversely affected." Annex—V, the OSPAR Convention, http://www.ospar.org/html_documents/ospar/html/ospar_convention_e_updated_text_2007_annex_v.pdf (last visited July 20, 2014).

[78] Molenaar & Elferink, *supra* note 74, at 14.

[79] *Id.*

[80] Peter Johan Schei & R. Douglas Brubaker, *Developments in Environmental Protection—The Barents Sea and European Union Waters, in* NEW ERA IN FAR EAST RUSSIA AND ASIA 243 (Kitagawa Hiromitsu ed., 2006), *available at* http://www.fni.no/doc&pdf/PJS-DB-2006-JANSROP1.PDF.

[81] The RFMOs include: North East Atlantic Fisheries Commission (NEAFC), the North Atlantic Fisheries Organization (NAFO), and the North Pacific Fisheries Management Council. Erik Molenaar, *Arctic Fisheries Conservation and Management: Initial Steps of Reform of the International Legal Framework*, 1 Y.B. POLAR L. 427, 439 (2009). In addition, there are also a number of regional agreements, including, for example, the North East Atlantic Fisheries Convention, *available at* http://ec.europa.eu/world/agreements/prepareCreateTreatiesWorkspace/treatiesGeneralData.do?step=0&redirect=true&treatyId=503 (last visited July 20, 2014); Convention for the Conservation of Salmon in the North Atlantic, *available at* http://www.nasco.int/convention.html (last visited July 20, 2014); and a Barents Sea tripartite agreement among Iceland, Russia, and Norway—Agreement concerning Certain Aspects of Co-operation in the Area of Fisheries, *available at* http://eelink.net/~asilwildlife/RussIceNorFish.html (last visited July 20, 2014).

[82] The Banana Hole is located in the Norwegian Sea, which is mapped within the Arctic in accordance with the AMAP definition of the Arctic area.

[83] *See generally* N.E. ATLANTIC FISHERIES, http://www.neafc.org/ (last visited Mar. 12, 2014).

NEAFC as the marine area is governed by the Norway-Russian Federation Fisheries Commission and the Loophole Agreement and Protocols.[84] The Donut Hole is regulated by the Convention on the Conservation and Management of the Pollock Resources in the Central Bering Sea.[85] The Banana Hole, Loophole, and Donut Hole are regarded as the high seas, thus located within the ABNJ.[86]

In regard to hydrocarbon activities, the most recent and relevant instrument covering the Arctic marine area is the Agreement on Cooperation on Marine Oil Pollution Preparedness and Response in the Arctic.[87] The agreement, which addresses the measures for preparedness and response for oil pollution in the Arctic marine area, has been concluded under the auspices of the Arctic Council. The International Maritime Organization (IMO) adopted a number of instruments, such as the London Convention 1972,[88] the International Convention for the Prevention of Pollution from Ships (MARPOL),[89] and the International Convention on Oil Pollution Preparedness, Response and Cooperation (OPRC),[90] which have particular relevance for hydrocarbon activities in addressing marine pollution from the discharge of oil. These instruments are applicable to the Arctic marine area.[91] At the regional level, the Espoo Convention on Environmental Impact Assessment in a Transboundary Context[92] and OSPAR Conventions[93] are repeatedly referred to in the regional regulation of hydrocarbon activities.[94] There are also several other regulations[95] providing mechanisms to prevent and control pollution from offshore activities, including hydrocarbon development.

---

[84] *See* Molenaar, *supra* note 81.

[85] *See generally* FISHERIES & OCEANS CAN., www.dfo-mpo.gc.ca/index-eng.htm (last visited Mar. 12, 2014).

[86] *See* Molenaar, *supra* note 81. The Arctic Ocean contains four high-sea pockets (enclaves) in the AMAP area, which include: the Banana Hole in the Norwegian Sea, the Loop Hole in the Barents Sea, the Donut Hole in the central Bering Sea, and the central Arctic Ocean. *Id.*

[87] Agreement on Cooperation on Marine Oil Pollution, Preparedness and Response in the Arctic (May 15, 2013) [hereinafter Oil Spill Agreement], *available at* http://www.arctic-council.org/eppr/agreement-on-cooperation-on-marine-oil-pollution-preparedness-and-response-in-the-arctic/.

[88] Convention on the Prevention of Marine Pollution by Dumping of Wastes and Other Matter, *adoption* Nov. 13, 1972, 138 U.N.T.S. 1977.

[89] International Convention for the Prevention of Pollution from Ships, Nov. 2, 1973, 1340 U.N.T.S. 184, modified by the Protocol of 1978 and by the Protocol of 1997.

[90] 1990 International Convention on Oil Pollution Preparedness, Response and Co-operation, Nov. 30, 1990, 1891 U.N.T.S. 51 (entered into force May 13, 1995). Further information is available at: www.imo.org.

[91] Most of the Arctic states are parties to all of these instruments.

[92] Convention on Environmental Impact Assessment in a Transboundary Context, Feb. 25, 1991, 1989 U.N.T.S. 309 (entered into force Sept. 10, 1997).

[93] Convention for the Protection of the Marine Environment of the North-East Atlantic, *opened for signature* Sept. 22, 1992, 2354 U.N.T.S. 67 (entered into force Mar. 25, 1998), *available at* www.ospar.org/eng/html/welcome.html.

[94] The applicability of these instruments to hydrocarbon activities offers room for adopting precautionary measures to minimize the adverse consequences detrimental to the marine environment.

[95] *See generally* The Agreement between Denmark, Finland, Iceland, Norway, and Sweden concerning Cooperation in Measures to Deal with Pollution of the Sea by Oil or Other Harmful Substances, *available at* http://untreaty.un.org/unts/144078_158780/10/5/3331.pdf (last visited July 20, 2014);

In addition to these legally binding agreements, the Arctic Council has produced a set of documents that also complement resource governance structure. These documents present "soft law" norms because of their character as not legally binding. Although the Council has not yet focused on the conservation and management of targeted species in terms of living resources, it has produced substantial documents concerning hydrocarbon governance. The Council does not have any working group with a mandate to deal with fishery issues, but the Conservation of Arctic Flora and Fauna (CAFF) and the Sustainable Development Working Group (SDWG) have produced the Arctic Biodiversity Assessment report[96] and the Best Practices in Ecosystems-Based Ocean Management report,[97] respectively, which are useful for fisheries conservation and management. Specific to offshore hydrocarbon issues, the combined efforts of its working groups—the Protection of Arctic Marine Environment (PAME), the Emergency Preparedness, Prevention and Response (EPPR), the Arctic Monitoring and Assessment Programme (AMAP), and the CAFF—have been involved in developing the regulatory framework.

The production of the Arctic Offshore Oil and Gas Guidelines (AOOGG) was a major achievement. The guidelines were adopted in 1997 and have since been revised twice, first in 2002 and then in 2009.[98] The Guidelines recognize a uniform understanding of the minimum actions needed to protect the Arctic marine environment from unwanted environmental effects caused by offshore oil and gas activities. The Guidelines also present a set of recommended practices for the regulation of offshore oil and gas

---

Agreement for Cooperation Relating to the Marine Environment, *available at* http://untreaty.un.org/unts/60001_120000/12/2/00022093.pdf (last visited July 20, 2014); the 1974 Agreement Relating to the Establishment of Joint Pollution Contingency Plans for Spills of Oil and Other Noxious Substances (Canada and the United States), *available at* http://www.cec.org/pubs_info_resources/law_treat_agree/transbound_agree/SourceFiles/F15-AGREEMENT.HTML; the 1989 Agreement between the United States and the Soviet Union concerning Cooperation in Combating Pollution in the Bering and Chukchi Seas in Emergency Situation, *available at* http://www.akrrt.org/mou/Kp-US_USSR_89.pdf; the 1994 Agreement between the Government of the Kingdom of Norway and the Government of Russian Federation on Cooperation and Response to Oil Pollution in the Barents Sea, *available at* http://www.crrc.unh.edu/workshops/arctic_spill_summit/oil_transport_ru_no_2007.pdf.

[96] CONSERVATION OF ARCTIC FAUNA & FLORA, ARCTIC COUNCIL, ARCTIC BIODIVERSITY ASSESSMENT: REPORT FOR POLICY MAKERS (2013), *available at* http://www.arcticbiodiversity.is/index.php/the-report.

[97] NORWEGIAN POLAR INST., BEST PRACTICES IN ECOSYSTEM-BASED OCEANS MANAGEMENT IN THE ARCTIC (Alf Håkon Hoel ed., 2009), *available at* http://www.sdwg.org/media.php?mid=1017.

[98] The Guidelines document, first adopted in 1997 and later revised—first in 2002 and then finally in 2009—is available at ARCTIC COUNCIL, ARCTIC OFFSHORE OIL AND GAS GUIDELINES (2009), http://www.pame.is/images/PAME_NEW/Oil%20and%20Gas/Arctic-Guidelines-2009-13th-Mar2009.pdf. Important work to make this instrument influence the offshore oil and gas laws and practices in the Arctic countries has been done by The Institute for Energy and the Environment of the Vermont Law School by producing five white papers on how to implement these in different regions. *Publications*, INST. FOR ENERGY & ENV'T, VERMONT LAW. SCHOOL, http://www.vermontlaw.edu/Academics/Environmental_Law_Center/Institutes_and_Initiatives/Institute_for_Energy_and_the_Environment/Publications.htm (last visited Mar. 12, 2014).

exploration and extraction, including transportation and onshore activities that are an integrated part of the offshore operations in the Arctic. The Guidelines highlight the requirement of having an environmental impact assessment (EIA) procedure and plans for emergencies and responses. Given that each oil spill is unique as to the local environmental conditions and the specific types of oil spilled,[99] the Guidelines provide prior risk assessments to identify accidental events that may occur. Overall, the AOOGG is a comprehensive document that specifically addresses the concerns relating to offshore hydrocarbon activities in the Arctic.

IV. Shortcomings in Existing Resource Governance

Given the region's unique environmental and climatic conditions, the Arctic marine area requires particular, and focused, attention. Compared to other marine areas, any pollution or unsustainable utilization of resources in the Arctic marine area may cause major harm to the ecosystem, which could result in irreversible damage to the ecological balance. In addition to the adoption by all states of precautionary measures, the Arctic marine area needs an effective governance structure with an immediate response mechanism against any potential damage to its ecosystem affecting sustainable resource management. However, the existing regime presents weak application of the precautionary principle; little progress in the creation of MPAs; inadequate protection of identified species at risk from, for example, oil pollution; and a regulatory model that favors economic development over environmental sustainability.[100] Thus, the existing governance regime demonstrates gaps in resource management precisely required in the Arctic condition.

With respect to fisheries, relying on UNCLOS is problematic because its gaps in authority and scope pose substantial obstacles to adequately managing fisheries impacts from climate change. With an ice-free Arctic Ocean in the future, high-sea fisheries are likely to be particularly problematic. Even though other legal mechanisms, such as the UN Fish Stocks Agreement, are applicable in the Arctic Ocean for straddling and highly migratory fish species,[101] they do not cover other fisheries regimes. Moreover, problems concerning illegal, unregulated, and unreported fishing would arguably undermine any sustainable management plans,[102] unless any focused, and Arctic-wide, regime with

---

[99] EDWARD H. OWENS ET AL., FIELD GUIDE FOR OIL SPILL RESPONSE IN ARCTIC WATERS (1998), *available at* http://arctic-council.org/eppr/wp-content/uploads/2010/04/fldguide.pdf.

[100] E.A. Barry-Pheby, *The Growth of Environmental Justice and Environmental Protection in International Law: In the Context of Regulation of the Arctic's Offshore Oil Industry*, 13 SUSTAINABLE DEV. L. & POL'Y 48, 48 (2012).

[101] The Agreement defined the "straddling" fish stocks as stocks of fish such as pollock, which migrate between, or occur in both, the economic exclusive zone (EEZ) of one or more States and the high seas." Thus, the definition also includes highly migratory fish stocks.

[102] *See, e.g.*, Rosemary Rayfuse, *Melting Moments: The Future of Polar Oceans Governance in a Warming World*, 16 REV. EUROPEAN, COMP. & INT'L ENVTL. L. 212–13 (2007).

explicit authority is introduced. Although the Northeast Atlantic region of the Arctic is governed by a number of regional fishery agreements, their mandates overlap and the implementation of the agreements is either delayed or lacking altogether.[103] Moreover, the geographic scope of the agreements covers only a very small part of the Arctic Ocean, with no agreed-upon regional fisheries management regime covering the whole of the Arctic Ocean.[104]

The OSPAR Convention calls for an ecosystem-based approach requiring parties to apply the precautionary principle, when there are "reasonable grounds for concern."[105] In effect, it provides a stronger governance mechanism driven by the OSPAR Commission to monitor the implementation. Although fishery issues are beyond the scope of the Convention,[106] the effects of hydrocarbon practices on biodiversity and ecosystem protection (within OSPAR's mandate under Annex V) have consequences on marine species, including fisheries. Yet, OSPAR does not cover the Arctic Ocean as a whole.[107] Moreover, only two Arctic states (Denmark and Norway) are parties to the Convention.

With regard to hydrocarbon exercises, the only Arctic-wide instrument—the 2013 Arctic Council Oil spill agreement[108]—adopted under the auspices of the Arctic Council, is also limited in scope. Its scope is restricted to maintaining cooperation among the parties in the event oil spills occur, by providing logistical and other support for the response efforts. It does not address all aspects of offshore oil and gas development. The other existing regulations, such as the Espoo Convention, are also limited. They are either limited in scope (sectorally or geographically) or not endorsed by all relevant Arctic states.

The Arctic Council's initiatives also have limitations. In fisheries management, for example, it does not have any fishery working group with a mandate to develop conservation, protection, and management strategies. Although the Arctic Council endorsed the Offshore Oil and Gas Guidelines document, which provides a comprehensive structure addressing the minimum actions needed in the practice of offshore development in the region, it lacks evaluation of its implementation, monitoring, and follow-up procedures, thereby limiting the capability to set and maintain higher standards. Moreover, the Arctic Council documents, by their nature, are only soft law documents with no legally binding force.

---

[103] See Rosemary Rayfuse, *Protecting Marine Biodiversity in Polar Areas beyond National Jurisdiction*, 17 REV. EUROPEAN, COMP. & INT'L ENVTL. L. 3, 7 (2008).

[104] Jeffers, *supra* note 6, at 960.

[105] Convention for the Protection of the Marine Environment of the North-East Atlantic, art. 2(2)(a)9, Sept. 22, 1992, 2354 U.N.T.S. 67, *available at* http://www.ospar.org/html_documents/ospar/html/ospar_convention_e_updated_text_2007.pdf.

[106] Jeffers, *supra* note 6, at 960.

[107] The OSPAR covers only 8 percent of the surface area of the Arctic Ocean. Barry-Pheby, *supra* note 100, at 49.

[108] *Id.*

The other governance shortcoming involves the traditional view of sovereignty that fails to maintain indigenous peoples' participation as an actor in multilateral engagement. Although UNCLOS has established rules and principles for the use and management of the natural resources in the ocean, it nevertheless fails to address the rights of indigenous peoples in resource management. Professor Rebecca M. Bratspies has seen this failure as "striking a jarring note of discord with recent developments in international law."[109] However, in the event of increasing threats to marine living resources, delegation of management has been referred to by transferring power to more local and regional jurisdiction.[110] The failure to adapt to the development at the intergovernmental level shows uncertainty regarding the role of various nonstate actors, including indigenous peoples. Although the Arctic Council recognizes the indigenous peoples' organizations as "permanent participants," they have nonetheless been largely ignored in the process of crafting the Ilulissat Declaration,[111] a relatively recent development in Arctic politics. Although their inclusion in the Arctic Council is an innovative development, the indigenous "permanent participants" do not have a right to vote in its decision-making.

The limitations of the governance regime thus include: (1) procedural failures and weaknesses, including inadequate implementation, evaluation, outcome targets, follow-up procedures, and integration of science into practice and policy; (2) a lack of integration of recognized and accepted environmental principles and approaches such as ecosystem-based management, biodiversity, creation of MPAs, sustainable development, precautionary principle, and the polluter-pays principle; and (3) a range of other faults, including lack of funding as well as an absence of a permanent secretariat in the functioning of the Arctic Council, geopolitical tensions over resource practices, and lack of real integration of indigenous and other local peoples' input.[112]

V. The Way Forward: An Effective Resource Governance Regime

Considering the governance shortcomings outlined above, the Arctic Ocean needs a rather robust approach, particularly in terms of its resource management regime, to promote both sustainability and protection of marine environment. Although various options for the governance of the Arctic are being considered,[113] it appears that no dramatic change will take place, at least in the near future. The political strategies of the

---

[109] Rebecca M. Bratspies, *Human Rights and Arctic Resources*, 15 Sw. J. Int'l Law 251, 269 (2009).

[110] Caulfield, *supra* note 8, at 131.

[111] Oran Young, *Arctic Governance—Pathways to the Future*, 1 Arctic Rev. on L. & Pol. 164, 171 (2010).

[112] Barry-Pheby, *supra* note 100, at 48–49.

[113] The options broadly included: Ilulissat approach, unilateral/bilateral approach, piecemeal approach, regional agreement approach, Arctic treaty approach, and ecosystem-based management approach. *See, e.g.*, Heather Exner-Pirot, *New Directions for Governance in the Arctic Region*, Arctic Resources & Transp. Info. Sys., http://www.arctis-search.com/New+Directions+for+Governance+in+the+Arctic+Region (last visited Mar. 12, 2014).

Arctic states, in particular of the coastal states, suggest sticking to the existing framework of governance under UNCLOS in combination with the Arctic Council's efforts to promote mitigating governance challenges.[114]

Considering the unique characteristics of the Arctic Ocean, which is similar to that of a semi-enclosed sea offering specific rights to the coastal states under part IX of UNCLOS to manage marine area even beyond the EEZ,[115] according to Oran Young—one of the most prominent Arctic governance scholars—it is unlikely that non–Arctic States will agree on considering the Arctic Ocean as a semi-enclosed sea.[116] On the other hand, adoption of article 234 authorizing stricter environmental protection regulations in the ice-covered sea remains limited to coastal states' EEZ, excluding the high seas. However as both the high seas and the seabed beyond the outer limits of the continental shelf are international commons, all other states, including the Arctic ones, have legitimate interests, as well as obligations, in that part of the marine area.

Resource governance in the commons would therefore need to reflect the interests of all other states, while at the same time remaining sensitive to the unique challenges of the sensitive Arctic ecosystem. Consequently, some have advocated for a regional seas agreement similar to the OSPAR model that exists in the Northeast Atlantic, which offers an ecosystem-based governance regime. Although OSPAR's mandate does not explicitly refer to fishery issues, conservation of ecosystem and biodiversity (under part V) implies that fishery issues are probably not excluded either. Thus, an Arctic-style OSPAR probably would provide a robust marine environmental governance regime. Some fear, however, whether such a regime would receive support even from all the Arctic states as countries such as the United States are sensitive to multilateral agreements,[117] and Russia's implementation of environmental regulations is already labeled as poor.

The so-called piecemeal[118] approach has received wider support for overall Arctic governance, including resource management. Prominent Arctic scholars have apparently been convinced of the advantages of such an approach. Supporting the approach, Young asserted that despite being "a messy process," the piecemeal approach "yields effective governance with respect to some important issues"; and according to him, the approach is better than having a more comprehensive and orderly process that actually fails to achieve success across the board.[119] He thus rejects the idea of any comprehensive and

---

[114] As discussed previously, the Ilulissat Declaration provides the clear and firm statement that there is no need to develop a new arrangement for Arctic governance. *Ilulissat Declaration, supra* note 53.

[115] UNCLOS, *supra* note 27, art. 123 (addressing "semi-enclosed" sea).

[116] Young, *supra* note 111, at 171.

[117] Rob Huebert & Brooks B. Yeager, WWF INT'L ARCTIC PROGRAMME, A NEW SEA: THE NEED FOR A REGIONAL AGREEMENT ON MANAGEMENT AND CONSERVATION OF THE ARCTIC MARINE ENVIRONMENT 40 (2006).

[118] Exner-Pirot, *supra* note 113.

[119] Oran Young, *The Arctic in Play: Governance in a Time of Rapid Change*, INT'L J. MARINE & COASTAL L. 423, 423 (2009).

unique governance structure for the Arctic in the form of, for example, an Arctic treaty similar to the regime that exists for Antarctic governance.[120] Young suggests that there is nothing to be gained from any new potential regime for the Arctic Ocean.[121] Moreover, any initiative for introducing a comprehensive regime would require not only huge efforts to gain support from the international community, which is time-consuming, but would be impractical as it may offer overlapping competence with the prevailing legal regime. Accordingly, it could create further confusion given that the law of the sea, including UNCLOS, is an overarching legal framework applicable to the Arctic Ocean as a whole,[122] to which all the Arctic states have expressed a firm commitment.

As a result, despite the dynamism of the complex socioecological system prevalent in the Arctic, current trends favor the "piecemeal" approach, and thus endorse a sectoral approach, such as separate governance regimes—one for fisheries, and another for oil and gas development. There is, however, no reason to believe that interrelated issues cannot be addressed in an integrated manner.[123] The problems for resource management can also be clustered into one broader institutional framework to make governance easer.[124] However, any efforts to develope such a robust mechanism concerning Arctic specific cross-sectoral resource governance are unlikely in the near future.

Nonetheless, the non-binding soft law initiatives of the Arctic Council effectively complement the governance structure by filling the gaps exposed by the hard legal regime. The Arctic Council has so far taken an innovative approach, considering the complex sociocultural and environmental characteristics of the Arctic. Its structure involves indigenous peoples of the region as "permanent participants" whose knowledge on the conservation of ecosystems is regarded as an important element in governing the region. Granting the "permanent participants" status to indigenous peoples in the governance structure of an international body is novel. The novelty set an example for an inclusive model of regional governance system that combines robust international engagement with active participation from local-level actors, the indigenous peoples. Although in terms of decision-making it still holds the traditional method of engaging states only, the permanent participants' right to make statements or to put forward proposals, as well as to participate in the meetings and the working groups of the Council, have influence on decision-making. The focus of the institutional setup provides knowledge generation, soft-norm promulgation, and, to some extent, capacity enhancement.

---

[120] *But see* Borgerson, *supra* note 4. According to Borgerson, new geopolitical developments in the Arctic present an extraordinary opportunity to rewrite the rules of the game for developing frontier economies. *See also* Bonnie A. Malloy, *On Thin Ice: How a Binding Treaty Regime Can Save the Arctic*, 16 W.-Nw. J. Envtl. L. & Pol'y 471 (2010).

[121] Young, *supra* note 111, at 177.

[122] Hans Corell, *The Arctic: An Opportunity to Cooperate and to Demonstrate Statesmanship*, 42 Vand. J. Transnat'l L. 1065, 1069 (2009).

[123] Young, *supra* note 111, at 174.

[124] Jeffers, *supra* note 6, at 966.

Even though the Arctic Council produces only soft-law documents, the knowledge generated from its initiatives contributes to a unique process of governance focusing on the region's specific characteristics. Thus, the Council is today regarded as a meta-institutional body operating in the new context of globalization and transnationalism. It offers a dynamic, rather than a static, model to successfully develop scientific knowledge to contribute to the negotiation in mitigating the uncertainties inherent, for example, in climate change predictions, and anticipating the effects of climatic changes on resource management. Given that ensuring sustainable development is the primary objective of the Arctic Council, "traditional knowledge" has been identified as essential to developing a fuller understanding of sustainable development.[125] Since 1998, under the auspices of the Sustainable Development Working Group, a number of reports have been produced, including the Best Practices in Ecosystems-Based Ocean Management, which has enhanced its influence in developing and disseminating a discourse of ecosystem-based management.[126]

Considering that resource governance in the Arctic requires a strengthened management regime with robust influence on human behavior,[127] concerned Arctic states as well as the other states and actors engaged in the region have a responsibility to fulfill with Arctic governance. Because the Arctic regime is managed by a myriad of powerful nation-states[128] with commitments to behave in compliance with international law, the strengthened Arctic Council complementing the previously mentioned "piecemeal" approach suggests an understanding of efficient resource governance. For fishery governance, a new Arctic-wide RFMO, whose basis is already in place within the framework of the U.N. Fish Stocks Agreement,[129] could be established. Despite the doubt concerning the cost-effectiveness of an Arctic-wide RFMO, as it is likely that no commercially viable fisheries will occur in the central Arctic Ocean in the near future,[130] establishing such a regime seems realistic and most appropriate for Arctic fishery management.[131] The Arctic Council's knowledge production on sustainable resource assessments may be utilized in offering the mandate to this RFMO. Creation of an additional Arctic Council working group to focus solely on fisheries issues would facilitate knowledge building on fishery issues in the Arctic, which will eventually also interact with other wildlife resource management-approach this will facilitate developing better frameworks for ecosystem- and precautionary-principle-based resource management practices.[132]

---

[125] See FINNISH MINISTRY OF THE ENV'T, ARCTIC ENVIRONMENT PROTECTION STRATEGY 1997: GUIDELINES FOR ENVIRONMENTAL IMPACT ASSESSMENT (EIA) IN THE ARCTIC 4 (1997), available at http://arcticcentre.ulapland.fi/aria/procedures/eiaguide.pdf.

[126] See Young, supra note 111, at 175.

[127] Caulfield, supra note 8, at 121.

[128] Jeffers, supra note 6, at 971.

[129] All eight Arctic nations have ratified the Agreement.

[130] Molenaar, supra note 12, at 118.

[131] Jeffers, supra note 6, at 922.

[132] Id. at 974.

Concerning offshore hydrocarbon, the AOOGG of the Arctic Council seems to be a living instrument, as the member states of the Council have already revised it twice. An Arctic-specific multilateral agreement based on AOOGG, and capturing all-encompassing aspects of offshore oil and gas exercise, with a monitoring and implementation mechanism, would be the best fit for hydrocarbon governance. It may be too ambitious at this stage, however. It may be more effective to at least establish a monitoring mechanism to supervise the activities regulated by various legal mechanisms, including the Arctic Council guidelines. The Arctic Council might think of also developing a "coordination mechanism" to oversee the implementation of various resource management regimes to establish an effective governance structure. Maintaining a coordination mechanism will ease identification of the overlapping aspects of resource management, which will then promote efficiency in governance.

Conclusion

The chapter presents complex aspects of Arctic Ocean resources governance, taking into consideration the specific characteristics the region possesses. Although the Arctic Ocean contains international space, that is, the high seas as well as the seabed beyond national jurisdiction—the "area"—where all the states have legitimate rights, the resource situations show that resources in international space are rather limited. Increasing demands from beyond the Arctic, of the resources available within the coastal states' national jurisdiction, potentially may result in geopolitical tension.

The other dimension of tension exists in the historic and traditional usage rights of the resources, in particular the living resources, by the significant number of indigenous peoples inhabiting the region. This chapter, addressing this twofold tension, has argued that Arctic Ocean resource governance has to be adapted to the overarching existing framework by endorsing specific sector-based regulations. Thus, a piecemeal approach is found to offer a viable tool to adapt to the existing regime. However, the chapter further argues for development of a mechanism, possibly by the Arctic Council, to maintain coordination of various fragmented regimes to help identify the overlapping aspects so that better implementation of cross-sectoral resource management can be achieved.

14 Climate Change and the Shifting International Law and Policy Seascape for Arctic Shipping
Dr. David L. VanderZwaag*

* This chapter attempts to be accurate as of April 15, 2014. This chapter was facilitated by the research projects, "Tracking and Envisioning the Future of Arctic Ocean Governance", funded by the Social Sciences and Humanities Research Council of Canada, and "Arctic Shipping through Challenging Waters", financed by the Norwegian Research Council.

Introduction

Decreasing sea ice in the Arctic has spawned high expectations for the growth of polar shipping.[1] The region is known to contain vast mineral and hydrocarbon resource potentials.[2] Marine tourism interest remains high.[3] The prospect of time and cost savings through shortened shipping routes across Arctic waters has already spurred increased transits of the Northern Sea Route off the Russian Federation and through the Northwest Passage in the Canadian archipelago. In September 2013, the *Nordic Orion*, carrying a load of coking coal from Vancouver to Pori, Finland, became the first commercial bulk carrier to transit the Northwest Passage,[4] and further commercial transits are expected.[5] Transits of the Northern Sea Route have risen from forty-one and forty-six in 2011 and 2012, respectively, to seventy-one in 2013.[6]

The pace of future Arctic shipping increases continues to be subject to varying opinions[7] and is difficult to predict because of the numerous factors entering the equation.[8] It remains uncertain how fast the remaining ice may melt and the extent to which reduced sea ice may still cause major threats to shipping.[9] Other complicating factors include the rate of infrastructure improvements, pace of resource discoveries and developments, costs of insurance, and global trade dynamics.[10]

---

[1] The volume of sea ice in the Arctic Ocean is estimated to have decreased by some 70 percent during the past three decades. *See* Int'l Mar. Org. [IMO], *Workshop on Safe Ship Operations in the Arctic Ocean, IMO, Headquarters, London, 28 February 2014*, MSC 93/INF.12, 2 (Mar. 11, 2014). *See also* Peter Wadhams, *Diminishing Sea-Ice Extent and Thickness in the Arctic Ocean, in* ENVIRONMENTAL SECURITY IN THE ARCTIC OCEAN 15–30 (P.A. Berkman & A.N. Vylegzhanin eds., 2013).

[2] For example, the region is expected to contain about one-fourth of the world's undiscovered oil and gas deposits. *See* TIMO KOIVUROVA & KAMRUL HOSSAIN, ARCTIC TRANSFORM: OFFSHORE HYDROCARBON, *available at* http://www.arctic-transform.org/download/OffHydSum.pdf (last visited Apr. 15, 2014).

[3] For the view that cruise ship tourism may be modest rather than explosive, see Frédéric Lasserre & Pierre-Louis Têtu, *The Cruise Ship Tourism Industry in the Canadian Arctic: Analysis of Activities and Perceptions of the Cruise Ship Operators*, POLAR REC., doi: 10.1017/S0032247413000508 (2013).

[4] *See* Wendy Stueck, *Ship Crosses Northwest Passage, Sails into History*, GLOBE AND MAIL, Sept. 25, 2013.

[5] Bob Weber, *More Northwest Passage Travel Planned by Danish Shipper*, CBC NEWS, Jan. 3, 2014.

[6] NORTHERN SEA ROUTE INFORMATION OFFICE, TRANSIT STATISTICS, http://www.arctic-lio.com/nsr_transits (last visited Apr. 19, 2014). Some listed transits are partial.

[7] *See, e.g.,* Laurence C. Smith & Scott R. Stephenson, *New Trans-Arctic Shipping Routes Navigable by Midcentury*, 110 PROC. NAT'L ACAD. SCI. (PNAS) U.S. E1191 (2013); Frédéric Lasserre, *Simulations of Shipping along Arctic Routes: Comparison, Analysis and Economic Perspectives*, POLAR RECORD, doi: 10.1017/S0032247413000958 (2014).

[8] *See* Lawson W. Brigham, *The Challenges and Security Issues of Arctic Marine Transport, in* ARCTIC SECURITY IN AN AGE OF CLIMATE CHANGE 26–27 (James Kraska ed., 2011).

[9] Predictions as to when the Arctic Ocean may become ice-free in summer vary from within the next ten years to as late as 2100. *See* U.S. NATIONAL SNOW AND ICE DATA CENTER, FREQUENTLY ASKED QUESTIONS ON ARCTIC SEA ICE, http://nsidc.org/arcticseaicenews/faq/#north_pole (last visited Apr. 19, 2014).

[10] More than 120 factors that could shape the future of Arctic marine navigation have been identified. *See* Lawson W. Brigham, *The Arctic Council's Arctic Marine Shipping Assessment, in* CHANGES IN THE ARCTIC ENVIRONMENT AND LAW OF THE SEA 163–65 (Myron H. Nordquist, John N. Moore & Thomas H. Heidar eds., 2010).

Regardless of pace, the present international governance framework for Arctic shipping stands out for its substantial limitations. The regulatory regime, consisting of more than fifty conventions and protocols and numerous guidelines negotiated under the auspices of the International Maritime Organization (IMO),[11] has by and large not been tailored to address the special shipping conditions of the Arctic.[12] Guidelines for Ships Operating in Polar Waters[13] are only aspirational, suggesting construction and design standards for new Polar Class ships and various equipment, personal survival, and crewing measures applicable to ships engaged in international voyages in Arctic waters.[14] Only one chapter of the Guidelines is devoted to environmental protection where the emphasis is on ensuring damage control in case of accidents.[15] While the Antarctic has been designated as a special area under the International Convention for the Prevention of Pollution from Ships (MARPOL) where stricter than normal standards apply for discharges of oil, noxious liquid substances, and garbage,[16] no such designations have occurred for the Arctic. The present system might be described as "fragmented" with Canada and the Russian Federation in particular imposing their own pollution discharge standards in their Arctic waters[17] and both countries relying on the special legislative and enforcement powers bestowed on coastal states by article 234 of the 1982 UN Law of the Sea Convention[18] to control marine pollution in ice-covered waters.[19]

This chapter highlights how the international community has become aware of the need to strengthen Arctic shipping governance in this era of climate change and globalization[20] and reviews the shifting law and policy seascape through a three-part analysis. Section I discusses regional efforts to move the shipping governance agenda

---

[11] Edward Kleverlaan, *IMO and Measures for the Protection of the Marine Environment*, PAME WORKSHOP, REYKJAVIK, ICELAND 11 (June 13, 2013). For further reviews of the complex regulatory regime, see Aldo Chircop, *The Growth of International Shipping in the Arctic: Is a Regulatory Review Timely?*, 24 INT'L J. MARINE & COASTAL L. 355 (2009); J. Ashley Roach, *International Law and the Arctic: A Guide to Understanding the Issues*, 15 Sw. J. INT'L L. 301 (2009); Heike Deggim, *Ensuring Safe, Secure and Reliable Shipping in the Arctic Ocean*, in ENVIRONMENTAL SECURITY IN THE ARCTIC, *supra* note 1, at 241–54.

[12] Special risks include remoteness, cold temperatures, presence of ice, and the relative lack of good charts, communication systems, and navigational aids. *See* Loji Sekimizu, *Opening Remarks*, in IMO, *supra* note 1, at Annex III, 1.

[13] Int'l Mar. Org. [IMO], *Guidelines for Ships Operating in Polar Waters*, Res A. 1024(26) (Dec. 2, 2009).

[14] *Id.* at chapter 1, para. 1.1.1.

[15] *Id.* at chapter 16.

[16] INT'L MAR. ORG., MARPOL CONSOLIDATED EDITION 2011, Annexes I, II, and V (2011).

[17] For example, Canada has established "zero discharge" standards for vessel-source oil pollution and other wastes, including garbage. *See* David L. VanderZwaag, *Canada and the Governance of the Northwest Passage: Rough Waters, Cooperative Currents, Sea of Challenges*, in NAVIGATING STRAITS: CHALLENGES FOR INTERNATIONAL LAW 87, 94 (David D. Caron & Nilufer Oral eds., 2013).

[18] United Nations Convention on the Law of the Sea, art. 234, Dec. 10, 1982, 1833 U.N.T.S. 397.

[19] For a review of various questions of interpretation surrounding article 234, see Kristen Bartenstein, *The "Arctic" Exception in the Law of the Sea Convention: A Contribution to Safer Navigation in the Northwest Passage?*, 42 OCEAN DEV. & INT'L L. 22 (2011).

[20] For an overview of the many environmental shifts occurring in both the Arctic and Antarctic, see Tim Stephens & David L. VanderZwaag, *Polar Oceans Governance: Shifting Seascapes, Hazy Horizons*, in POLAR OCEANS GOVERNANCE IN AN ERA OF ENVIRONMENTAL CHANGE 1 (Tim Stephens & David L. VanderZwaag eds., 2014).

forward, including the role of the Arctic Council, the main forum for facilitating regional cooperation.[21] Section II describes efforts within the International Maritime Organization to negotiate a legally binding Polar Shipping Code and the numerous regulatory shifts looming on the horizon in the wake of a new global code. Section III summarizes some of the major governance challenges in relation to Arctic shipping still remaining, such as deciding whether to ban heavy fuel oil use and carriage in the region and effectively addressing black carbon emissions from ships. A review of national shipping law and policy shifts in light of climate change is beyond the scope of this chapter.[22]

I. The Regional Seascape

Regional initiatives relevant to the control of Arctic shipping[23] might be described as involving a "mainstream" and two "side streams." The main regional forum for addressing Arctic shipping issues has been the Arctic Council, established pursuant to a 1996 declaration,[24] where eight member states[25] and six indigenous organizations as Permanent Observers[26] have edged the shipping agenda forward on multiple fronts. Two more tangential initiatives are the establishment of an Arctic Regional Hydrographic Commission to encourage cooperation in nautical charting, and the efforts by the five Arctic coastal states (Arctic 5) to forge interim measures to prohibit commercial fishing activities in the high seas of the central Arctic Ocean until appropriate management arrangements are in place.

---

[21] *See* Timo Koivurova & David L. VanderZwaag, *The Arctic Council at 10 Years: Retrospect and Prospects*, 40 U. B.C. L. Rev. 121 (2007); Klaus J. Dodds, *Anticipating the Arctic and the Arctic Council: Pre-emption, Precaution and Preparedness*, 49 Polar Rec. 193 (2013).

[22] For reviews of national regulatory approaches and developments, see R. Douglas Brubaker, *The Arctic-Navigational Issues under International Law of the Sea*, 2 Y.B. Polar L. 7 (2010); Erik Molenaar et al., Legal Aspects of Arctic Shipping Summary Report (2010), *available at* http://ec.europa. eu/maritimeaffairs/documentation/studies/documents/legal_aspects_arctic_shipping_summary_en.pdf; VanderZwaag, *supra* note 17; and Ivan N. Bunik & Vladimer V. Mikhaylichenko, *Legal Aspects of Navigation through the Northern Sea Route*, *in* Environmental Security in the Arctic Ocean, *supra* note 1, at 231–39.

[23] For a further regional review, see Olav Schram Stokke, *Regime Interplay in Arctic Shipping Governance: Explaining Regional Niche Selection*, 13 Int'l Envtl. Agreements 65 (2013).

[24] Joint Communiqué and Declaration on the Establishment of the Arctic Council, Sept. 19, 1996, 35 I.L.M. 1382 (1996).

[25] *See id.* (citing member states as Canada, Denmark/Greenland, Finland, Iceland, Norway, Sweden, Russian Federation, and the United States).

[26] Aleut International Association, Arctic Athabaskan Council, Gwich'in Council International, Inuit Circumpolar Council, Russian Association of Indigenous Peoples of the North (RAIPON), and the Saami Council.

A. THE ARCTIC COUNCIL

The Council's initiative having the greatest impact on Arctic shipping governance has been the 2009 Arctic Marine Shipping Assessment (AMSA).[27] Besides documenting present shipping uses in the Arctic,[28] predicting regional shipping futures to 2020,[29] and highlighting the many possible social and environmental impacts of increased polar shipping,[30] the report included a chapter on the governance of Arctic shipping,[31] and most important, seventeen recommendations for follow-up actions. Recommendations were grouped under three headings. Key recommendations under the theme of "Enhancing Arctic Marine Safety" included admonitions for Arctic states to support the updating and mandatory application of relevant parts of the *Guidelines for Ships Operating in Arctic Ice-Covered Waters*;[32] to augment global IMO ship safety and pollution prevention conventions with specific mandatory requirements or other provisions for ship construction, design, equipment, crewing, training and operations in the Arctic context;[33] and to develop and implement a comprehensive, multinational Arctic Search and Rescue (SAR) instrument.[34] Under the second theme, "Protecting Arctic People and the Environment," Arctic states were encouraged to, among other things, identify and protect areas of heightened ecological and cultural significance in light of changing climate conditions and increasing multiple marine uses;[35] to explore the need for designating areas of the Arctic Ocean for special environmental protection, for example as Special Areas or Particularly Sensitive Sea Areas (PSSAs) through the IMO;[36] and to work at reducing air emissions.[37]

Four recommendations were made under the third theme, "Building the Arctic Marine Infrastructure." The need to address the infrastructure deficit was emphasized with many improvements needed in such areas as navigational charts, communications systems, port services including reception facilities for ship-generated wastes, accurate

---

[27] ARCTIC COUNCIL, ARCTIC MARINE SHIPPING ASSESSMENT 2009 REPORT (2009). For a more detailed discussion, see Timo Koivurova, *Governing Arctic Shipping: Finding a Role for the Arctic Council*, 2 Y.B. POLAR L. 115, 127–32 (2010).

[28] In 2004, approximately 6,000 individual vessels were reported operating in the Arctic with slightly less than 50 percent being fishing boats. *Id.* at 72–73.

[29] *Id.* at 92–121.

[30] *Id.* at 122–33 and 134–53.

[31] *Id.* at 50–69.

[32] *Id.* at 6, Recom. I(B). The Guidelines, adopted in 2002, were subsequently revised and expanded to include Antarctic waters in 2009 with a new title of *Guidelines for Ships Operating in Polar Waters*. For reviews of the negotiation histories, see Øystein Jensen, *Arctic Shipping Guidelines: Towards a Legal Regime for Navigation Safety and Environmental Protection?*, 44 POLAR REC. 107 (2008); Peter K. Kikkert, *Promoting National Interests and Fostering Cooperation: Canada and the Development of a Polar Code*, 43 J. MAR. L. & COM. 319 (2012).

[33] ARCTIC COUNCIL, *supra* note 27, at 6, Recom. I(B).

[34] *Id.* at 6, Recom. I(E).

[35] *Id.* at 7, Recom. II(C).

[36] *Id.* at 7, Recom. II(D).

[37] *Id.* at 7, Recom. II(H).

and timely ice information, places of refuge, and ice-breaker assistance.[38] Arctic states were encouraged to support development of a comprehensive Arctic marine traffic awareness system to improve monitoring and tracking of Arctic marine activities.[39] Arctic states were urged to continue developing circumpolar environmental pollution response capabilities, for example, through circumpolar cooperation and agreements.[40] Further investing in hydrographic, meteorological, and oceanographic data collection and dissemination was also advocated.[41]

Two of the most obvious and concrete impacts of the AMSA report was the follow-up by Arctic states with the establishment of Arctic Council task forces to negotiate regional shipping-related agreements. First, the Agreement on Cooperation on Aeronautical and Maritime Search and Rescue in the Arctic[42] was signed by ministers from the eight Arctic states on May 12, 2011. The Agreement delimits search and rescue regions where each Party is given primary responsibility to ensure maintenance of adequate and effective SAR capabilities.[43] The Agreement seeks to facilitate cooperative and expeditious responses to search and rescue emergencies[44] and pledges future collaborations, such as carrying out joint SAR exercises and sharing information on SAR techniques and facilities.[45] Second, the Agreement on Cooperation on Marine Oil Pollution Preparedness and Response in the Arctic[46] was signed on May 15, 2013, in association with the Council's eighth ministerial meeting in Kiruna, Sweden. The Agreement requires Parties to maintain a system of responding promptly and effectively to oil pollution incidents and to establish a minimum level of pre-positioned oil spill combating equipment.[47] The Agreement sets out notification[48] and mutual assistance responsibilities[49] in case of an oil pollution incident and encourages future cooperation in undertaking joint exercises and training.[50]

---

[38] *Id.* at 7, Recom. III(A).

[39] *Id.* at 7, Recom. III(B).

[40] *Id.* at 7, Recom. III(C).

[41] *Id.* at 7, Recom. III(D).

[42] Agreement on Cooperation on Aeronautical and Maritime Search and Rescue in the Arctic, May 12, 2011, *available at* http://www.arctic-council.org/index.php/en/document-archive/category/20-main-documents-from-nuuk?download=73:arctic-search-and-rescue-agreement-english [hereinafter SAR Agreement]. *See generally* Corine Wood-Donnelly, *The Arctic Search and Rescue Agreement: Text, Framing and Logics*, 5 Y.B. POLAR L. 299 (2013).

[43] SAR Agreement, *supra* note 42, at art. 3.

[44] *Id.* at arts. 7,8.

[45] *Id.* at art. 9.

[46] Agreement on Cooperation on Marine Oil Pollution Preparedness and Response in the Arctic, May 15, 2013, *available at* http://www.arctic-council.org/index.php/en/document-archive/category/425-main-documents-from-Kiruna-ministerial-meeting [hereinafter Marine Oil Response Agreement].

[47] *Id.* at art. 4.

[48] *Id.* at art. 6.

[49] *Id.* at arts. 8, 9, and 10.

[50] *Id.* at art. 13.

The AMSA report might be described as a "living document" as the PAME Working Group has continued to monitor and advance implementation of the various recommendations. Progress reports on AMSA implementation were delivered to ministerial meetings in 2011 and 2013,[51] and a further report is expected for the ministerial meeting in 2015.[52] Some key follow-up initiatives include publication of a Phase 2 report on heavy fuel oil use in the Arctic;[53] a study on specially designated marine areas of the high seas, which has raised the possibility of establishing a PSSA for a "core sea ice area" as a sanctuary for unique and vulnerable species and ecosystems;[54] and a decision to prepare a work or project plan for drafting a regional waste reception facilities plan specific to one or more regions of the Arctic.[55] Canada is leading an initiative to develop sustainable tourism guidelines for the Arctic.[56]

Three of the Council's working groups collaborated in issuing a report identifying Arctic marine areas of heightened ecological and cultural significance.[57] About ninety-seven areas of heightened ecological significance have been identified covering more than half of the total area of the ice-covered part of the marine Arctic.[58] However, because of limited data, the report was not able to provide a detailed description of the three types of culturally significant areas; namely, communities, archeological and historical sites, and traditional use areas.[59]

Other initiatives relevant to shipping have also occurred under the auspices of the Arctic Council. The Emergency Prevention, Preparedness and Response (EPPR) Working Group has published various reports and guidelines having shipping relevance[60] and a series of maps picturing sensitive environments that could be at risk of an oil spill.[61] The Council's Arctic Ocean Review (AOR) Report,[62] published in 2013, with an overall

---

[51] Arctic Council, Status on Implementation of the AMSA 2009 Report Recommendations (May 2011); Arctic Council, Status on Implementation of the AMSA 2009 Report Recommendations (May 2013).

[52] *See* Protection of the Arctic Marine Environment [PAME], Record of Decisions and Follow-up Actions PAME I—2014, 3 (Feb. 11–13, 2014).

[53] Actually a two-part report with one covering the broader region and the other the Bering Sea area. Det Norske Veritas, Report on HFO in the Arctic—Phase 2 (2013); Report on HFO in the Arctic—Phase 2B (2013).

[54] Det Norske Veritas, Report on Specially Designated Marine Areas in the Arctic High Seas 56 (2014).

[55] PAME, *supra* note 52, at 2.

[56] *Id.*

[57] AMAP/CAFF/SDWG, Identification of Arctic Marine Areas of Heightened Ecological and Cultural Significance: Arctic Marine Shipping Assessment [AMSA] IIc (2013).

[58] *Id.* at 1.

[59] *Id.* at 101–03.

[60] For example, a report on *Behaviour of Oil and Other Hazardous Substances in Arctic Waters* was published in 2011 and *Guidelines and Strategies for Oily Waste Management in the Arctic Region* were completed in 2009. *See generally* Emergency Prevention Preparedness and Response [EPPR], http://www.arctic-council.org/eppr/completed-work/ (last visited Apr. 20, 2014).

[61] *Id.*

[62] Protection of the Arctic Marine Environment [PAME], The Arctic Ocean Review Project, Final Report (Phase II 2011–2013) (2013).

purpose of suggesting ways forward in strengthening regional and global arrangements for the protection of the Arctic marine environment, includes a chapter on shipping[63] and five related recommendations. For example, Arctic states are encouraged to undertake research into ballast water management systems that are effective in cold polar regions;[64] to consider possible development at the IMO of port state control guidelines and/or initiatives within existing port state arrangements;[65] and to consider the need to address safety and environmental concerns respecting vessels that will not be subject to the Polar Code.[66]

The Council has established a Task Force on Arctic Marine Oil Pollution Prevention to recommend a plan of action for preventing marine oil pollution in the Arctic, with a final report to be delivered to the ministerial meeting in 2015.[67] However, the extent to which the Task Force will address shipping-related aspects is still unclear.[68]

The prospects of new shipping corridors and access to vast mineral resources in the wake of decreasing ice in the Arctic have also contributed to the expansion of observer states in the Arctic Council. At the May 2013 ministerial meeting, six new states were added as observers (China, India, Italy, Japan, Republic of Korea, and Singapore).

B. ARCTIC REGIONAL HYDROGRAPHIC COMMISSION

The Arctic Regional Hydrographic Commission (ARHC) was established in October 2010 to assist in addressing one of the major shipping support limitations in the Arctic. A large proportion of the Arctic Ocean has not been surveyed to modern standards. For example, according to the Canadian Hydrographic Service, only some 10 percent of the Canadian Arctic has been adequately charted.[69]

The ARHC, consisting of five member states (Canada, Denmark, Norway, Russian Federation, and the United States) and two observers (Finland and Iceland), has met on an annual basis.[70] The Commission has facilitated the sharing of national approaches and advances in nautical charting and worked at coordinating the production of paper and electronic charts to support ships engaged in international voyages.[71]

---

[63] *Id.* at 32-42.

[64] *Id.* at 95, Recom. 3.

[65] *Id.* at 96, Recom. 5.

[66] *Id.* at 96, Recom. 7.

[67] TASK FORCE ON ARCTIC MARINE OIL POLLUTION PREVENTION (TFOPP), http://www.arctic-council.org/index/php/en/about-us/working-groups/task-forces (last visited Apr. 20, 2014).

[68] The PAME Working Group has itself been seeking information on the shipping aspects to be considered. PAME, *supra* note 52, at 2.

[69] ARCTIC COUNCIL, *supra* note 27, at 158.

[70] The 4th meeting was held in Portsmouth, New Hampshire (USA), Jan. 29–30, 2014. *See generally* 4TH ARHC MEETING LIST OF DOCUMENTS, http://iho.int/srv1/index.php?option=com_content&view=article&id=435&Itemid=690 (last visited Apr. 20, 2014).

[71] An Arctic International Charting Coordination Working Group (AICCWG) has been established to coordinate charting in the region. *See generally* TERMS OF REFERENCE FOR THE ARCTIC INTERNATIONAL CHARTING COORDINATION WORKING GROUP (AICCWG), http://iho.int/srv1/index.php?option=com_content&view=article&id=435&Itemid=690 (last visited Apr. 20, 2014).

C. THE ARCTIC 5

Representatives from the five littoral states to the Arctic Ocean have met independently of the Arctic Council on occasion to discuss matters of common concern.[72] At a meeting in Ilulissat, Greenland in May 2008, representatives issued a declaration emphasizing that the law of the sea provides a solid foundation for managing uses of the Arctic Ocean, including navigation and marine scientific research.[73] The declaration also indicated the lack of need to develop a new comprehensive legal regime to govern the Arctic marine environment and pledged future cooperation in working together through the IMO to improve the safety of maritime navigation and to reduce the risk of ship-based pollution in the Arctic.[74]

The Arctic 5 process has not been active specifically on the shipping front, but since 2010 representatives have met on a number of occasions to discuss possible future commercial fisheries in the high seas portion of central Arctic Ocean.[75] At a meeting in Nuuk, Greenland, February 24–26, 2014, government officials agreed on the desirability of developing interim measures where participating states would authorize their vessels only to conduct commercial fishing in the high seas area pursuant to one or more regional or subregional fisheries management organizations or arrangements that are or may be established to manage such fishing in accord with modern international standards.[76] The meeting agreed to develop a Ministerial Declaration relating to interim measures for signature or adoption by the five states.[77] The meeting also reaffirmed the interest of other states on the topic and proposed a broader process involving additional states be initiated before the end of 2014 where the final outcome could be a binding international agreement.[78]

II. IMO and the Polar Code

In light of expected increases in polar shipping in the wake of climate change, the drafting of a mandatory Polar Shipping Code has been on the IMO agenda since 2009, but

---

[72] Regarding the tensions between the Arctic 5 and the broader Arctic Council membership, see Heather N. Nicol & Lassi Heininen, *Human Security, the Arctic Council and Climate Change: Competition or Co-existence?*, 50 POLAR REC. 80 (2014); Tobjørn Pedersen, *Debates over the Role of the Arctic Council*, 43 OCEAN DEV. & INT'L L. 146 (2012).

[73] Ilulissat Declaration, May 28, 2008, *available at* http://www.oceanlaw.org/downloads/arctic/Ilulissat_Declaration.pdf (last visited Apr. 15, 2014).

[74] *Id.* at 2.

[75] For a brief history, see Alf Håkon Hoel, *Fish, Fisheries and Fisheries Management in the Arctic Ocean*, BARENTS OBSERVER, Mar. 11, 2014, http://barentsobserver.com/en/opinion/2014/03/fish-fisheries-and-fisheries-management-arctic-ocean-11-03.

[76] CHAIRMAN'S STATEMENT, MEETING ON ARCTIC FISHERIES, Nuuk, Greenland 1–2 (Feb. 24–26, 2014) (copy on file with the author).

[77] *Id.* at 2.

[78] *Id.*

negotiations became protracted.[79] The original target date of 2012 for completing negotiations had to be extended to 2014. Key issues in controversy included: the geographical scope of application and whether the scope should be broadened to cover more southerly waters; types of ships to be covered beyond cargo and passenger ships; training standards for ice navigators and crews; phase-in requirements, if any, for existing ships; provisions to be mandatory versus aspirational; pollution prevention measures; and the question whether some differential standards would be appropriate for the Arctic and Antarctic.[80]

A controversy over how the Polar Code should be made mandatory, whether as a stand-alone agreement or developing amendments to relevant conventions, particularly the MARPOL and Safety of Life at Sea (SOLAS) Conventions, was resolved in 2012. Agreement was reached to follow the path of amending all relevant existing instruments to give force to provisions of the future Code.[81]

Especially controversial were the environmental standards that should be included for oil pollution. At the 65th session of the MEPC, agreement in principle was reached to prohibit any discharge into the sea of oil or oily mixtures from any ships.[82] However, a number of states subsequently questioned the commitment. The United States suggested the possibility of exempting ships less than 400GT operating in Arctic waters from complying with "zero discharge" requirement in relation to oil and oily mixtures from machinery spaces.[83] The Russian Federation questioned a total ban on oil discharges on various grounds including the limited port reception facilities in the Arctic and the fact that some ships, such as hydrographic survey ships and research vessels, may navigate in Arctic waters for months without calling at ports.[84] At the 66th session of MEPC, in April 2014, the Russian proposal was rejected,[85] but the issue of possible exemptions was left for further consideration.[86]

---

[79] *See* Laura Boone, *International Regulation of Polar Shipping, in* THE LAW OF THE SEA AND THE POLAR REGIONS: INTERACTIONS BETWEEN GLOBAL AND REGIONAL REGIMES 198–200 (Erik J. Molenaar, Alex G. Oude Elferink & Donald R. Rothwell eds., 2013); H. Edwin Anderson III, *Polar Shipping, the Forthcoming Polar Code and Implications for the Polar Environments*, 43 J. MAR. L. & COM. 59 (2012).

[80] *See* David L. VanderZwaag, *The IMO and Arctic Marine Environmental Protection: Tangled Currents, Sea of Challenges, in* THE ARCTIC IN WORLD AFFAIRS: A NORTH PACIFIC DIALOGUE ON ARCTIC MARINE ISSUES 111 (Oran R. Young, Jong Deog Kim & Yoon Hyung Kim eds., 2012).

[81] *Id.* at 119.

[82] Marine Environment Protection Committee [MEPC], *Report of the Marine Environment Protection Committee on Its Sixty-Fifth Session*, MEPC 65/22, para. 11.49 (May, 24 2013).

[83] Marine Environment Protection Committee [MEPC], *General Applicability of Part II–A of the Polar Code, Submitted by the United States*, MEPC 66/11/12 (Feb., 21 2014).

[84] Marine Environment Protection Committee [MEPC], *Environmental Issues Related to the Draft Code for Ships Operating in Polar Waters (Polar Code), Submitted by the Russian Federation*, MEPC 66/11/3 (Jan. 24, 2014).

[85] Marine Environment Protection Committee [MEPC], *Report of the Marine Environment Protection Committee on Its Sixty-Sixth Session*, MEPC 66/21, para. 11.29 (Apr. 25, 2014).

[86] *Id.* at para. 11.22.

Whether to ban the use of heavy fuel oil on ships operating in Arctic waters was another point of contention. At the MEPC's 65th session, the Committee endorsed the view of the majority of delegations who spoke that it was premature to regulate HFO use on ships operating in the Arctic.[87] However, the Committee further noted the view of some delegations that it might be desirable and possible to develop such regulations in the future.[88]

Although the January 2014 version of the Polar Code still contained a substantial number of instances of unresolved language,[89] the basic parameters have become clear. Part I-A will include various mandatory ship safety measures, such as: ice-strengthened construction standards, stability to withstand flooding due to hull penetration from ice impact; machinery and equipment capabilities to withstand polar environmental conditions, life-saving appliances and arrangements, navigational and communication equipment, voyage planning requirements, and personnel qualifications and training in polar shipping operations. Part II-A will include mandatory pollution prevention standards. Parts I-B and II-B will include aspirational provisions regarding ship safety and environmental pollution prevention, respectively.[90] Ships subject to the Code would be required to have a valid Polar Ship Certificate attesting to design for operation in ice conditions.[91] Carrying of a Polar Water Operations Manual, including instructions on ship-specific capabilities and limitations and emergency procedures, would also be mandatory.[92]

Agreement in principle has also been reached on a number of pollution standards. Prohibitions on the discharge of noxious liquid substances and garbage except for food wastes have been agreed to.[93] Sewage discharge and treatment provisions have also been generally resolved.[94]

The MEPC at its April 2014 session decided to establish a further Polar Code Correspondence Group to finalize parts II-A and II-B of the Code along with draft amendments to MARPOL. The Correspondence Group is to submit a report to MEPC's 67th session in October 2014.[95]

A further looming issue is the extent to which coastal states that rely on article 234 for taking special protective measures for Arctic shipping will be willing to harmonize

---

[87] MEPC, *supra* note 82, para. 11.53.

[88] *Id.*

[89] *See* Sub-Committee on Ship Design and Construction [SDC], *Report to the Maritime Safety Committee*, SDC 1/26, Annex 3 (Feb. 11, 2014).

[90] *Id.*

[91] *See* INT'L MAR. ORG. [IMO], *Shipping in Polar Waters: Development of an International Code of Safety for Ships Operating in Polar Waters (Polar Code)*, http://www.imo.org/MediaCentre/HotTopics/polar/Pages/default.aspx (last visited Apr. 20, 2014).

[92] *Id.*

[93] SDC, *supra* note 89, at 38.

[94] *Id.* at 41.

[95] MEPC, *supra* note 85, para. 11.53.

their standards with the Polar Code.[96] At the MEPC's 66th session, Canada made its view clear; namely that the new MARPOL amendments stemming from the Polar Code will not prejudice states' rights under the UN Convention on the Law of the Sea.[97] An example of an environmental standard that Canada seems likely to maintain is the zero discharge approach to garbage disposals form ships in the Arctic,[98] even though the Polar Code promises to allow some food waste discharges under limited conditions.

III. Sea of Challenges

Future international challenges for Arctic shipping governance fall into three categories— global, regional, and bilateral.

A. GLOBAL

Three major challenges at the global level stand out as especially important for the Arctic. First is the ongoing challenge of regulating gray water discharges from passenger ships. Waste water from sinks, showers, and laundries is presently not regulated under Annex IV of MARPOL, which sets standards for sewage discharges.[99] The average cruise ship can generate 3.8 million liters of waste water each week.[100] A proposal to include regulation of gray water discharge in the Polar Code did not receive support at the May 2013 meeting of the MEPC.[101] If and when the IMO might further address gray water discharges remains to be seen.

A second governance challenge is further addressing greenhouse gas emissions from ships. The IMO has taken some initial steps by amending Annex VI of MARPOL in July 2011 to add a new chapter 4, which sets out regulations on energy efficiency from ships of 400 gross tonnage and above.[102] Taking additional measures to control GHG emissions has been controversial, with tensions over whether a common but differentiated principle should apply in the shipping context and debates over whether market-based measures (MBM), such as applying a levy on fossil fuel use, should be adopted.[103] The

---

[96] For a further review of the tensions, see Andrea Scassola, *An International Polar Code of Navigation: Consequences and Opportunities for the Arctic*, 5 Y.B. POLAR L. 271, 274–80 (2013).

[97] *See Statement by the delegation of Canada relating to Agenda Item 11*, MEPC, *supra* note 85, Annex 20, at 12.

[98] Arctic Waters Pollution Prevention Act, R.S.C. 1985, c. A-12, s. 4 (Can.).

[99] For a description of the sewage discharge standards, see VanderZwaag, *supra* note 80, at 103–04.

[100] ARCTIC COUNCIL, *supra* note 27, at 137.

[101] MEPC, *supra* note 82, at para. 11.55.

[102] Marine Environment Protection Committee [MEPC], *Inclusion of Regulations on Energy Efficiency for Ships in MARPOL Annex VI*, MEPC Res. 203(62) (July 15, 2011). New ships will be required to meet Energy Efficiency Design Index (EEDI) requirements while each ship, including existing ships, will be required to keep on board a Ship Energy Efficiency Management Plan (SEEMP).

[103] *See* VanderZwaag, *supra* note 80, at 113–14; Bernd Hackmann, *Analysis of the Governance Architecture to Regulate GHG Emissions from International Shipping*, 12 INT'L ENVTL. AGREEMENTS 85 (2012); James

MEPC at its May 2013 meeting decided to postpone discussions of MBM issues to a future session.[104]

Getting a firm grip on ballast water discharges represents a third challenge with two issues being paramount. One is reaching full ratification of the 2004 Ballast Water Convention.[105] As of April 1, 2014, the Convention had received just thirty-eight ratifications representing slightly more than 30 percent of the world shipping tonnage[106] While the Convention requires thirty ratifications representing 35 percent of world tonnage for entry into force, only five of the eight Arctic states have ratified the Convention (Canada, Denmark, Norway, the Russian Federation, and Sweden).[107]

A second issue is ensuring timely implementation of the phase-in of ballast water management systems (BWMS) required for various ships by 2016.[108] Countries have been moving very slowly in ordering and installing ballast water management systems because of various factors, including costs, and limited shipyard capacity and manufacturing capabilities.[109] In light of the implementation difficulties, the IMO's Assembly passed a resolution at its 28th session, November 25—December 4, 2013, easing the required application date for BWMS according to a rather complicated schedule largely based on when first renewal surveys are due under MARPOL Annex I.[110]

B. REGIONAL

Four regional challenges in the governance of Arctic shipping stand out.[111] First is the further regulation of air emissions from ships. Black carbon, emitted from ships through incomplete combustion of fuels, is a growing concern because of its climate-warming potential and capacity to accelerate snow and ice melts.[112] Since 2011, the IMO's Bulk

---

Harrison, *Recent Developments and Continuing Challenges in the Regulation of Greenhouse Gas Emissions from International Shipping*, 27 OCEAN Y.B. 359 (2013).

[104] MEPC, *supra* note 82, para. 5.1.

[105] International Convention for the Control and Management of Ships' Ballast Water and Sediments, Feb. 23, 2004, IMO Doc. BWM/CONF/36, Annex [hereinafter Ballast Water Convention].

[106] IMO, *Summary Status of Convention, available at* http://imo.org/About/Conventions/Statusof conventions/Pages/Default.aspx (last visited Apr. 15, 2014).

[107] IMO, *Status of Conventions, available at* http://www.imo.org/About/Conventions/StatusOfConventions/ Pages/Default.aspx (last visited Apr. 15, 2014).

[108] Ballast Water Convention, *supra* note 105, at Reg. B-3.

[109] *See* VanderZwaag, *supra* note 80, at 107.

[110] Int'l Mar. Org. [IMO], *Application of the International Convention for the Control and Management of Ships' Ballast Water and Sediments 2004*, Res. A. 1088(28) (Jan. 28, 2014).

[111] For a review of other regional challenges, such as further developing regional approaches to port state inspections, sharing of Arctic marine traffic data, and implementation of IMO's Guidelines on Places of Refuge, see Erik J. Molenaar, *Status and Reform of International Arctic Shipping Law, in* ARCTIC MARINE GOVERNANCE 127–57 (E. Tedsen et al. eds., 2014).

[112] *See* Sub-Committee on Bulk Liquids and Gases, *Investigation of Appropriate Control Measures (Abatement Technologies) to Reduce Black Carbon Emissions from International Shipping, Note by the Secretariat,*

Liquids and Gases Sub-Committee (now Pollution Prevention and Response (PPR)) has been considering black carbon management issues and options through a correspondence group process, but consensus has been difficult to reach on a definition of black carbon, measurement methods, and appropriate control measures.[113] The PPR Sub-Committee is scheduled to report to the MEPC's 67th session in October 2014, where decisions on a definition and appropriate measurement methods are expected.[114] The target date to complete the overall black carbon review has been extended to 2015.[115] The need to consider working through the IMO to designate one or more areas of the Arctic as special emission control areas (ECAs) where the maximum sulphur content of fuel would be set lower than the general standard is a further air pollution challenge.[116]

A second regional challenge is meeting the shipping infrastructure deficits. This is a challenge to be met primarily at national levels, and infrastructure varies considerably across the region being much further advanced in northern Norway and in the Russian Federation.[117] A practical constraint has been the limited financial and human resources needed to improve bathymetric charts, with a 30 percent decline in funding for hydrographic services reported across the Arctic.[118] Even where there are regional agreements relating to infrastructure enhancements, it remains to be seen how Arctic states will follow through with their commitments. Both the regional SAR agreement and Marine Oil Response Agreement contain a similar provision making implementation subject to the availability of relevant resources.[119]

Deciding whether to ban the use of heavy fuel oil in the Arctic is a third challenge. Although the MEPC at its May 2013 meeting decided against such regulation,[120] the door is not completely closed. Some delegations were of the opinion that such regulations might be desirable in the future.[121] Ships sailing in the three largest national parks of Svalbard are already not allowed to use or carry HFO.[122] The PAME Working Group has invited member governments to identify and inform PAME of any discrete marine

---

BLG 17/INF.7, 8 (Nov. 21, 2012); Laura Boone, *Development of an Environmental Chapter in the Polar Code: Introducing a New Player—Black Carbon*, 4 Y.B. POLAR L. 541 (2012).

[113] *See* Sub-Committee on Pollution Prevention and Response, *Consideration of the Impact on the Arctic of Emissions of Black Carbon from International Shipping: Report of the Correspondence Group*, PPR 1/8 (Nov. 1, 2013).

[114] Sub-Committee on Pollution Prevention and Response, *Report to the Marine Environment Protection Committee*, PPR 1/16, para. 8.28 (Feb. 12, 2014).

[115] MEPC, *supra* note 85, para. 18.22.

[116] *See* VanderZwaag, *supra* note 17, at 105 and 113; and James Kraska & Betsy Baker, *Emerging Arctic Security Challenges*: Policy Brief, CENTER FOR A NEW AMERICAN SECURITY 9 (Mar. 25, 2014).

[117] *See* ARCTIC COUNCIL, *supra* note 27, at 154, 187.

[118] IMO, *supra* note 1.

[119] SAR Agreement, *supra* note 42, art. 12; and Marine Oil Response Agreement, *supra* note 46, art. 15.

[120] MEPC, *supra* note 82.

[121] *Id.*

[122] DET NORSKE VERITAS, REPORT ON HFO IN THE ARCTIC–PHASE 2, *supra* note 53, at 69.

areas that would benefit from a more detailed risk analysis of heavy fuel oil use.[123] The ban on the use or carriage of HFO on ships operating in the Antarctic Treaty Area is likely to keep the Arctic debate alive.[124]

A fourth challenge is identifying and protecting areas of heightened ecological and cultural importance. Although identification of ecologically important areas has progressed quite well, the identification of culturally significant areas has lagged.[125] Protective shipping measures to date might be described as sparse.[126] No PSSAs have been established in Arctic waters.[127] Vessel routing measures remain very limited[128] with the exception of traffic separation schemes and recommended routes off Northern Norway.[129]

C. BILATERAL

Bilateral challenges related to Arctic shipping also exist, with two of the most prominent issues being between Canada and the United States. One issue is the legal status of the Northwest Passage.[130] Canada maintains that the waters are internal, and Canada substantiated that claim by drawing straight baselines around the Canadian archipelago effective on January 1, 1986.[131] The United States continues to argue that the Northwest Passage is a strait used for international navigation subject to the right of transit passage.[132]

Canada and the United States have been able to quell the dispute through an Agreement on Arctic Cooperation, adopted in 1988.[133] Through the Agreement the United States pledged that future navigation by U.S. icebreakers within waters claimed

---

[123] PAME, *supra* note 52, at 2.

[124] MARPOL CONSOLIDATED EDITION 2011, *supra* note 16, at Annex I, Reg. 43.

[125] *See* AMAP/CAFF/SDWG, *supra* note 57.

[126] *See* VanderZwaag, *supra* note 80, at 114.

[127] For a listing of the existing fourteen PSSAs, see IMO, *Particularly Sensitive Sea Areas*, http://www.imo. org/OurWork/Environment/PollutionPrevention/PSSAs/Pages/Default.aspx (last visited Apr. 20, 2014). *See also* Suzanne Lalonde, *The Arctic Exception and the IMO's PSSA Mechanism: Assessing Their Value as Sources of Protection for the Northwest Passage*, 28 INT'L J. MARINE & COASTAL L. 401 (2013).

[128] *See* ALDO CHIRCOP, *International Arctic Shipping: Towards Strategic Scaling-Up of Marine Environment Protection, in* CHANGES IN THE ARCTIC ENVIRONMENT AND LAW OF THE SEA, *supra* note 10, at 197.

[129] Tankers of all sizes and other cargo ships of 5,000 gross tonnage and above engaged in international voyages are encouraged to navigate about thirty nautical miles from land. *See* Int'l Mar. Org. [IMO], *New Traffic Separation Schemes and Recommended Routes off the Coast of Norway from Vardø to Røst*, COLREG.2/Cir. 58, Annex 1 (Dec. 11, 2006).

[130] *See generally* Mahealani Kraft, *The Northwest Passage: Analysis of the Legal Status and Implication of Its Potential Use*, 40 J. MAR. L. & COM. 537 (2009); Donat Pharand, *The Arctic Waters and the Northwest Passage: A Final Revisit*, 38 OCEAN DEV. & INT'L L. 3 (2007).

[131] *See* VanderZwaag, *supra* note 80, at 98–99.

[132] *See id.* at 100–01; MICHAEL BYERS, INTERNATIONAL LAW AND THE ARCTIC 131–43 (2013); Suzanne Lalonde & Frédéric Lasserre, *The Position of the United States on the Northwest Passage: Is the Fear of Creating a Precedent Warranted?*, 44 OCEAN DEV. & INT'L L. 28 (2013).

[133] Agreement on Arctic Cooperation (1989), Jan. 11, 1988, 28 I.L.M. 141.

by Canada to be internal would be undertaken with the consent of Canada.[134] The Parties further agreed to disagree over their legal positions in relation to the Northwest Passage.[135]

A second issue is the ocean boundary in the Beaufort Sea, with some 6,250 square nautical miles in dispute.[136] Canada claims the 141st west meridian is the boundary line based on the wording of an 1825 Treaty between Russia and Britain, which set the land boundary at that meridian and provided its prolongation as far as the frozen ocean.[137] The United States argues for an equidistant line.[138] Although the dispute is considered well managed,[139] legal jurisdiction over shipping in such a disputed zone remains uncertain.[140]

Conclusion

While the pace of shipping expansion in the Arctic remains subject to considerable speculation and differing opinions, one thing is certain. The law and policy seascape of Arctic shipping is shifting on multiple fronts. At the regional level, two new regional agreements related to shipping have already been concluded under Arctic Council auspices, and recommendations of the 2009 Arctic Marine Shipping Assessment continue to be monitored and advanced. At the global level, a new Polar Shipping Code is in the process of being finalized, which will provide a wide array of new standards for ship safety and marine environmental protection in the Arctic.

Although there has been substantial progress in addressing the special circumstances of Arctic shipping, the regulatory voyaging is far from over. Numerous challenges loom on the horizon, including the need to tighten air emission standards for ships, bolster infrastructure improvements from port and waste reception facilities to nautical charting, and advance identification and protection of areas of heightened ecological and cultural significance. Exactly where the ice-covered waters provision, article 234, of the Law of the Sea Convention applies will likely become an increasing issue as ice cover decreases.

Whether the many governance shifts will be able to effectively counter the looming shipping pressures on Arctic communities and ecosystems remains to be seen. The adequacy of new Polar Shipping Code standards will likely be a continuing topic of debate in the coming decades.

---

[134] *Id.* para. 3.

[135] *Id.* para. 4.

[136] *See* TED L. MCDORMAN, SALT WATER NEIGHBORS: INTERNATIONAL OCEAN LAW RELATIONS BETWEEN THE UNITED STATES AND CANADA 181–90 (2009); James S. Baker & Michael Byers, *Crossed Lines: The Curious Case of the Beaufort Sea Maritime Boundary Dispute*, 43 OCEAN DEV. & INT'L L. 70 (2012).

[137] BYERS, *supra* note 132, at 58–59.

[138] *Id.* at 60–62.

[139] MCDORMAN, *supra* note 136, at 187–90.

[140] ARCTIC COUNCIL, *supra* note 27, at 54.

15 Governance of Climate Change Impacts on the Antarctic Marine Environment
Elizabeth Burleson and Jennifer Huang

Introduction

Antarctica has been described as a continent on the brink.[1] While remote from humanity, the planet's coldest regions are an early warning system.[2] They provide a network of natural indicators of climate change in a warming world.[3] The international community has offered limited recognition of the Antarctic continent's significance by focusing on climate-change-related scientific research—arguably at the expense of a coordinated response to climate change.[4] Global climate change is an appropriate backdrop—an expedient framework—within which to assess the current health of the polar and related environmental legal regimes.[5]

This chapter seeks to locate the Antarctic Treaty System within the world of environmental regimes. Polar regions are growing in importance, increasingly impacting various areas of global, regional, and national development. Calling for a closer look at the role of law in addressing current and emerging environmental issues relevant to the Antarctic, Section I describes climate change impacts on Antarctica, with a focus on the marine environment.

Section II identifies challenges to an aging Antarctic Treaty System that must cope with climate change, tourism, overfishing and ecosystem management, and coordinated scientific research. It then briefly introduces existing legal regimes governing the Antarctic marine environment: the Stockholm Convention on Persistent Organic Pollutants, the International Maritime Organization, the United Nations Convention on the Law of the Sea, and the United Nations Framework Convention on Climate Change.

Section III introduces relevant law from the Arctic region, highlighting strengths and weaknesses in both regimes and potential remedies. Section IV recommends that the legal regimes governing the Antarctic and the Arctic should be more closely integrated with one another, but especially with other multilateral environmental agreements, particularly the United Nations Convention on the Law of the Sea and the United Nations Framework Convention on Climate Change process, to better coordinate efforts and to systematize standards and practices to better protect the marine environment against the impacts of climate change.

---

[1] Kevin Tray, *Fear and Loathing in the South Pole: The Need to Resolve the Antarctic Sovereignty Issue and a Framework for Doing It*, 22 TEMP. INT'L & COMP. L.J. 213, 213 (2008).

[2] Alex Morales, *Ice Melting Faster in Greenland and Antarctica in UN Leak*, BLOOMBERG (Sept. 6, 2013, 6:49 AM), http://www.bloomberg.com/news/2013-09-05/ice-melting-faster-in-greenland-and-antarctica-in-un-leak.html.

[3] *Id.*

[4] Duncan French & Karen Scott, *International Legal Implications of Climate Change for the Polar Regions: Too Much, Too Little, Too Late?*, 10 MELB. J. INT'L L. 631, 633 (2009).

[5] *Id.* at 654.

The chapter concludes by stressing Antarctica's paramount importance to effectively address the climate challenge. It argues that its marine ecosystems deserve far greater attention and responsible action than the international community has afforded it to date. Strengthening a system of Arctic coordination based on Antarctic lessons learned and incorporating both polar approaches into the most comprehensive and effective of environmental conventions will build relationships that will not only provide more crucial and technical scientific data but fortify the necessary polar and global environmental governance that can protect the world's most vulnerable marine environments.

I. Climate Change Impacts on Antarctica's Marine Environment

The Antarctic polar region represents a barometer for global climate change, warming as a whole more rapidly than the global average.[6] It has been increasingly recognized as being geopolitically and economically important, significantly affected by both current and projected climate change, and a region with great potential to affect global climate.[7]

An appreciation of Antarctica's climate and geography is essential to understanding how it can be affected by global climate change, and how changes in Antarctica can modulate aspects of the planet's response to greenhouse gas-induced warming. Antarctica is the coldest, highest, driest, iciest, most remote area on Earth. Antarctica receives the least solar radiation of any other continent. Eighty percent of the sunlight that reaches it is reflected by its icy surface.[8] The water and sea ice of the Southern Ocean encircles the continent,[9] acting as an important transmitter of energy and mass among all the global oceans.[10]

Antarctica can roughly be divided into East Antarctica, covered by the East Antarctic Ice Sheet (EAIS); West Antarctica, covered by the West Antarctic Ice Sheet (WAIS); and the Antarctic Peninsula, with a milder climate strongly influenced by the ocean surrounding it on three sides.[11] The instability of the WAIS presents a significant threat to humankind and the global environment, the collapse of which may occur as early as this century.[12] A marine-based ice sheet, the WAIS is subject to increased melting

---

[6] Intergovernmental Panel on Climate Change, Climate Change 2007: Impacts, Adaptation and Vulnerability: Contribution of Working Group II to the Fourth Assessment Report of the Intergovernmental Panel on Climate Change 656–58 (M.L. Parry et al. eds., 2007) [hereinafter IPCC AR4 WGII]; Intergovernmental Panel on Climate Change, Climate Change 2013: The Physical Science Basis, Working Group I Contribution to the Fifth Assessment Report of the Intergovernmental Panel on Climate Change 368 (Thomas F. Stocker et al. eds., 2013) [hereinafter IPCC AR5 WGI].

[7] IPCC AR4 WGII, *supra* note 6, at 655.

[8] Andrew Monaghan, *Antarctica and Climate Change*, 22 WORLD WATCH MAG. 1 (Jan./Feb. 2009), *available at* http://www.worldwatch.org/node/5958.

[9] *Id.*

[10] *Id.*

[11] *Id.*

[12] *Antarctica*, INTERNATIONAL CRYOSPHERE CLIMATE INITIATIVE, http://iccinet.org/antarctica (last visited Mar. 30, 2014).

at the ocean-ice interface. Ocean warming is accelerating the ice sheet's shrinkage and contributing to sea-level rise.[13] Melting ice sheets will exacerbate the planetary radiation imbalance, and additional global warming will likely result in ice sheet disintegration in a few centuries.[14]

The UN Intergovernmental Panel on Climate Change (IPCC) reports are widely used as accepted accounts of the state of the global environment. However, these reports and their current generation of global climate models to project future climate have been criticized for not including the effects of climate change on accelerating the flow of polar ice sheets, causing considerable debate about whether the IPCC sea-level projection for the end of the twenty-first century—18 to 50 centimeters—is too low.[15] This omission is significant, considering that the IPCC has stated that the "rate of warming on the Antarctic Peninsula is among the highest seen anywhere on Earth in recent times, and is a dramatic reminder of how subtle climate-dynamic processes can drive regional climate change, and the complexity of its impacts in an environment where human influence is at a minimum."[16]

As of the IPCC AR4 report, approximately 14,000 km^2 of ice has been lost from ten floating ice shelves, a minimum not reached for at least 10,000 years, suggesting a unique warming not due to cyclic variations in local climate.[17] Eighty-seven percent of glacier termini have retreated, and seasonal snow cover has decreased significantly, resulting in newly exposed rock and permafrost, which provides new habitats for invading flora and fauna.[18]

Scientific data gleaned from ice cores extracted across the WAIS show that the region has probably warmed by two degrees since 1950, with large temperature fluctuations tied to ocean temperatures in the tropics.[19] Antarctic ecosystems face the most serious potential threats from rapid warming.[20] Ecosystem impacts include decreases in the populations of Adélie and emperor penguins, Weddell seals,[21] and krill,[22] with concurrent increases in other species such as shallow water sponges,[23] some native flowering plants,[24] and a number of nonnative species,[25] one of the most significant short- to medium-term

---

[13] Monaghan, *supra* note 8.

[14] Michael Oppenheimer & R.B. Alley, *Ice Sheets, Global Warming, and Article 2 of the UNFCCC: An Editorial Essay*, 68 CLIMATIC CHANGE 259 (2005).

[15] Monaghan, *supra* note 8.

[16] IPCC AR4 WGII, *supra* note 6, at 675.

[17] *Id.* at 674–75.

[18] *Id.*

[19] Monaghan, *supra* note 8.

[20] *Antarctica*, http://iccinet.org/antarctica (last visited Mar. 30, 2014).

[21] IPCC AR4 WGII, *supra* note 6, at 666.

[22] *Id.* at 658.

[23] *Id.*

[24] SCIENTIFIC COMM. ON ANTARCTIC RESEARCH, ANTARCTIC CLIMATE CHANGE AND THE ENVIRONMENT xvii (John Turner et al. eds., Nov. 25, 2009) [hereinafter SCAR ACCE Review Report].

[25] IPCC AR4 WGII, *supra* note 6, at 658.

consequences of climate change for Antarctic wildlife.[26] Increased acidification threatens cold-water corals. In addition, marine pelagic mollusks in the Antarctic Southern Ocean are predicted to be unable to survive after 2100, a loss with significant consequences for the marine food web.[27]

The AR5 report has significantly increased the projected sea-level rise over the next century due to new projections that reflect improved understanding of ice sheet movement and melting.[28] These models show an increase of 0.26 to 0.55 meters (10–22 inches) by 2100 under a low emissions scenario, and 0.52 to.98 meters (20–39 inches) under a high emissions scenario.[29] The AR5 report states that ice in Antarctica is actually disappearing faster than previously predicted, adding close to five times more ice to sea levels in the decade through 2011 than in the previous ten years.[30]

Glaciers worldwide have continued to shrink, and more than 600 have disappeared, although the report recognizes that "the real number is certainly higher."[31] Of significant concern is Antarctica's Pine Island Glacier, an enormous feature covering more than 160,000 square kilometers, which is currently and very probably in "headlong, self-sustaining retreat," regardless of whether the region maintains its current conditions or becomes colder.[32] The glacier drains approximately 20 percent of all the ice flowing off the continent. Its retreat means the glacier will be an even more significant contributor to global sea-level rise, on the order of 3.5–10 mm in the next twenty years.[33] Although computer model simulations carry uncertainties, all model runs predicted that the glacier's marine ice sheet instability has been triggered into an irreversible decline due to warm ocean bottom-waters underneath that erode the floating ice shelf at its head.[34]

The complex interrelationships of the Antarctic region present a particular positive twist to the warming of the region, however. A new study suggests that climate change can accelerate the processes of rock weathering and bacterial activity, which would increase iron leaching into the sea, leading to larger blooms of phytoplankton and more carbon dioxide uptake by the ocean.[35] Photosynthetic algae in the Southern Ocean take up roughly 40 percent of all the carbon dioxide that the planet's seas absorb. This process

---

[26] Scientific Comm. on Antarctic Research, Antarctic Climate Change and the Environment 359 (John Turner et al. eds., Nov. 25, 2009) [hereinafter SCAR ACCE Review Report].

[27] IPCC AR4 WGII, *supra* note 6, at 658.

[28] *Id.* at 23–24.

[29] *Id.* at 21.

[30] Morales, *supra* note 2; IPCC AR5 WGI, *supra* note 6, at 320.

[31] Morales, *supra* note 2.

[32] Jonathan Amos, *Pine Island Glacier's Retreat "Irreversible,"* BBC News (Jan. 14, 2014, 7:23 AM), http://www.bbc.com/news/science-environment-25729750.

[33] *Id.*

[34] *Id.*

[35] Mark Schrope, *Iron from Antarctic Rocks Fuels Algae Growth,* Chemical & Engineering News (May 28, 2013), http://cen.acs.org/articles/91/web/2013/05/Iron-Antarctic-Rocks-Fuels-Algae.html.

is fueled by iron, a mineral in short supply in Antarctic waters.[36] As global temperatures rise and Antarctic ice melts, the magnitude of these iron releases will likely grow as weather and rock drainage expand due to increased rock exposure, resulting in a small but welcome mitigating effect: the acceleration of phytoplankton growth and carbon dioxide uptake in the Southern Ocean.[37]

II. The Limitations of the Antarctic Treaty System

A. THE ANTARCTIC TREATY SYSTEM

The Antarctic Treaty System (ATS) is a unique international management system that has evolved from its original purpose of settling sovereignty claims in the Antarctic to one that provides for the governance of Antarctica. In the first half of the twentieth century, seven states (Argentina, Australia, Chile, France, New Zealand, Norway, and the United Kingdom) staked claims on land in Antarctica based on discovery.[38] The United States and the Soviet Union, in particular, refused to recognize any claims.[39] Against the background of the Cold War, the possibility of discovering natural resources on the continent and the potential for the movement of nuclear weapons to the southern polar region created an unstable and tense state of affairs.[40] The desire to keep the continent demilitarized prompted the United States to invite twelve nations[41] that had engaged in scientific investigation in and around Antarctica during the International Geophysical Year (IGY) of 1957–1958 to participate in a conference that would preserve the legal status quo of Antarctica, allow scientific cooperation to continue, and reserve the continent for peaceful purposes.[42]

The ATS was signed on December 1, 1959, and entered into force on June 23, 1961.[43] The new treaty addressed the legitimacy of sovereignty claims by declaring that no acts or activities could support a claim for sovereignty nor could a new or enlarged claim be asserted while the treaty was in force.[44] The treaty further promoted scientific investigation and cooperation[45] and declared that "Antarctica shall be used for peaceful purposes

---

[36] *Id.*

[37] *Id.*

[38] *The Antarctic Treaty*, SECRETARIAT OF THE ANTARCTIC TREATY, http://www.ats.aq/e/ats.htm (last visited Mar. 27, 2014).

[39] *The Antarctic Treaty*, STATE.GOV, http://www.state.gov/www/global/arms/treaties/arctic1.html (last visited Mar. 27, 2014).

[40] *Id.*

[41] These nations were the seven claimant states plus five other states that conducted research in the Antarctic region during the IGY 1957–1958. *The Antarctic Treaty*, SECRETARIAT OF THE ANTARCTIC TREATY, http://www.ats.aq/e/ats.htm (last visited Mar. 27, 2014).

[42] *Id.*

[43] The Antarctic Treaty, Dec. 1959, 402 U.N.T.S. 71.

[44] *Id.* art. IV(2).

[45] *Id.* arts. II–III.

only."[46] Antarctic governance would be implemented via Antarctic Treaty Consultative Meetings (ATCMs) by Antarctic Treaty Consultative Parties (ATCPs), initially the original twelve signatories.[47]

Currently, fifty states are parties to the Treaty: twenty-eight are ATCPs involved in the Antarctic consensus-based decision-making process, and twenty-two are contracting, or non-consultative, parties.[48] ATCMs serve as the primary discussion and decision-making forum for the ATS and are now held annually.[49] The ACTPs conduct Antarctic policy through internationally legally binding "recommendations," decisions that are incorporated into the ATS.[50] A permanent secretariat was established in Buenos Aires, Argentina, in September 2004.[51] The Convention on the Conservation of Antarctic Marine Living Resources (CCAMLR) Secretariat,[52] the Council of the Managers of the National Antarctic Programs (COMNAP),[53] and the Scientific Committee on Antarctic Research (SCAR)[54] have been granted Delegate Observer status. Other select nongovernmental and international organizations have been assigned Delegate Expert Status.

A series of international treaties were concluded to address the legal gap posed by the frozen sovereignty claims: without continental sovereignty, no coastal states in the Antarctic could establish maritime sovereignty, potentially opening the Southern Ocean to economic exploitation by parties outside the ATS.[55] These agreements are linked to but are otherwise independent of the Antarctic Treaty.[56] The first of these treaties is the

---

[46] *Id.* art. I(1).

[47] *Id.* art. IX; Antarctic Treaty Consultative Meeting Revised Rules of Procedure ¶ 1, http://www.ats.aq/ documents/recatt/Att468_e.pdf (2011).

[48] *Parties*, SECRETARIAT OF THE ANTARCTIC TREATY, http://www.ats.aq/devAS/ats_parties.aspx?lang=e (last visited Mar. 28, 2014).

[49] *The Antarctic Treaty Consultative Meeting (ATCM)*, SECRETARIAT OF THE ANTARCTIC TREATY, http:// www.ats.aq/e/ats_meetings_atcm.htm (last visited Mar. 28, 2014).

[50] Antarctic Treaty Consultative Meeting Revised Rules of Procedure ¶ 1, http://www.ats.aq/documents/ recatt/Att468_e.pdf (2011).

[51] *About Us*, SECRETARIAT OF THE ANTARCTIC TREATY, http://www.ats.aq/e/about.htm (last visited Mar. 28, 2014).

[52] *See* COMMISSION FOR THE CONSERVATION OF ANTARCTIC MARINE LIVING RESOURCES, http:// www.ccamlr.org/en (last visited Mar. 28, 2014).

[53] *See* COUNCIL OF MANAGERS OF NATIONAL ANTARCTIC PROGRAMS, https://www.comnap.aq/ SitePages/Home.aspx (last visited Mar. 28, 2014).

[54] *See* SCIENTIFIC COMM. ON ANTARCTIC RESEARCH, http://www.scar.org (last visited Mar. 28, 2014).

[55] Timo Koivurova, *Environmental Protection in the Arctic and Antarctic: Can the Polar Regimes Learn from Each Other?*, 33 INT'L J. LEGAL INFO. 204, 205–06 (2005).

[56] The 1988 Convention on the Regulation of Antarctic Mineral Resource Activities (CRAMRA) was concluded in order to govern mining activity in the southern polar region with the aim of prohibiting those activities that would damage the Antarctic environment or ecosystems or affect global or regional climate patterns. It was signed by nineteen states; however, no state ratified the Convention. As the need to develop more extensive Antarctic conservation measures became evident, the Convention was abandoned in 1991 and never entered into force. *See* Convention on the Regulation of Antarctic Mineral Resource Activities,

1972 Convention for the Conservation of Antarctic Seals (CCAS), as seal hunting in the nineteenth century had seriously depleted Antarctic seal populations.[57] CCAS aimed to protect, rationally use, and scientifically study Antarctic seals, and to maintain a balanced ecological system.[58]

The conclusion of the CCAS paved the way for consideration of the potential large-scale exploitation of krill, a keystone organism in the Antarctic ecosystem. The 1980 Convention on the Conservation of Antarctic Marine Living Resources provided for the conservation and rational use of krill, fin fish, and other marine living resources.[59] CCAMLR provides an ecosystem approach to conservation; the effects on the marine environment must be taken into account in managing the harvesting of marine resources.[60]

The 1998 Madrid Protocol on Environmental Protection to the Antarctic Treaty ("Madrid Protocol") recognized Antarctica's unique and fragile environment in claiming protection of the region's ecosystem as a "natural reserve, devoted to peace and science" in service of all mankind's interests and prohibiting mineral mining indefinitely.[61] The Madrid Protocol, open only to the contracting parties of the Antarctic Treaty, supplements the treaty and established its administrative organ, the Committee on Environmental Protection (CEP), which reports annually to the ATCM.[62] Six annexes currently supplement the Protocol and address environmental impact assessment (Annex I),[63] conservation of Antarctic fauna and flora (Annex II),[64] waste disposal and waste management (Annex III),[65] prevention of marine pollution (Annex IV),[66] area protection and management (Annex V),[67] and liability for environmental emergencies (Annex VI).[68] Collectively, the Protocol and its annexes suggest a comprehensive environmental protection regime.

adopted June 2, 1998 (not in force); *Convention on the Regulation of Antarctic Mineral Resource Activities*, N.Z. MINISTRY OF FOREIGN AFFAIRS & TRADE, http://www.mfat.govt.nz/Treaties-and-International-Law /o1-Treaties-for-which-NZ-is-Depositary/0-Antarctic-Mineral-Resource.php (last visited Mar. 28, 2014).

[57] *Related Agreements*, SECRETARIAT OF THE ANTARCTIC TREATY, http://www.ats.aq/e/ats_related.htm (last visited Mar. 28, 2014).

[58] *History of the Convention*, COMMISSION FOR THE CONSERVATION OF ANTARCTIC MARINE LIVING RESOURCES, http://www.ccamlr.org/en/organisation/history-convention (last visited Mar. 28, 2014).

[59] *Related Agreements*, SECRETARIAT OF THE ANTARCTIC TREATY, http://www.ats.aq/e/ats_related.htm (last visited Mar. 28, 2014).

[60] *Id.*

[61] Protocol on Environmental Protection to the Antarctic Treaty pmbl., art. 2, Oct. 4, 1991, 30 I.L.M. 1455 (entered into force Jan. 14, 1998) [hereinafter Madrid Protocol].

[62] *Id.* arts. 1, 4, 11.

[63] *Id.* Annex I.

[64] *Id.* Annex II.

[65] *Id.* Annex III.

[66] *Id.* Annex IV.

[67] *Id.* Annex V.

[68] *Id.* Annex VI.

B. CHALLENGES FOR THE ANTARCTIC TREATY SYSTEM

Ultimately, the ATS provides for a collective legal regime with binding, "hard law," but also remains flexible enough to adapt to changing circumstances. The regime has been considered a success for its ability to, over the course of half a century, largely preserve the Antarctic continent, ensure freedom of scientific research, and circumvent territorial claim issues. However, the aging legal structure of the ATS may not be well suited to address the challenges of the twenty-first century. The southern polar region faces a number of significant developments in established areas of concern, and the ATS has only recently begun to address previously unanticipated environmental stressors. These challenges include climate change, tourism, overfishing and ecosystem preservation, and scientific research.

1. Climate Change

Until relatively recently, the ATS discussed climate change only within the context of scientific research or invasive species. Despite the Intergovernmental Panel on Climate Change's (IPCC's) recognition of Antarctica as an area of special concern as early as 2001, the ATS reluctantly moved climate change onto its agenda in the mid- to late-2000s. In 2007, the Madrid Protocol's CEP added climate change onto its environmental monitoring and reporting agenda[69] and identified climate change as a high priority issue within its Work Programme.[70] The XXX ATCM then adopted *Resolution G* (2007), which encouraged greater scientific monitoring of environmental change in the region in order to better understand and forecast environmental and climate impacts.[71]

In 2009, the Scientific Committee on Antarctic Research (SCAR) presented its *Antarctic Climate Change and the Environment (ACCE) Review Report*, which built on a previous report to synthesize available information about current and future impacts of climate change in Antarctica, and recommended that all treaty parties assess their Antarctic operations with an eye toward mitigating emissions.[72] The report was instrumental in raising the profile of climate change in the ATS: the ATCM endorsed the report and forwarded it to the United Nations Framework Convention on Climate Change (UNFCCC) for consideration at the Copenhagen climate conference later that

---

[69] Antarctic Treaty Consultative Mtg., Final Rep. of the XXX Antarctic Treaty Consultative Meeting ¶ 100 (Apr. 30–May 11, 2007).

[70] *Id.* app. 1.

[71] Scientific Comm. on Antarctic Research Res. G, Long-Term Scientific Monitoring and Sustained Environmental Observation in Antarctica, Antarctic Treaty Consultative Meeting, XXX mtg. (Apr. 30–May 11, 2007).

[72] Scientific Comm. on Antarctic Research, Antarctic Climate Change and the Environment (ACCE) Review Rep., Antarctic Treaty Consultative Meeting, XXXII mtg. (Apr. 6–17, 2009); *see also* Commission for the Conservation of Antarctic Marine Living Resources Res. 30/XXVII, Climate Change, XXIII mtg. (Oct. 26–Nov. 6, 2009).

year.[73] In 2010, an Antarctic Treaty Meeting of Experts was held on the impacts of climate change for the management and governance of the Antarctic region; it produced thirty recommendations for the upcoming XXXIII ATCM.[74]

In 2011, the ACCE report was updated.[75] Climate change received greater attention in the 2012 XXXV ATCM in the context of "Climate Change Implications for the Environment: Strategic Approach."[76] The ATS continued its relationship with the UNFCCC, most recently through SCAR's participation in a number of events at the UNFCCC COP 19 climate change conference in Warsaw, Poland in November 2013.[77] Much within the ATS legal framework lends itself to a more proactive approach to climate change and Antarctic impacts;[78] however, it remains to be seen whether the ATS would benefit from a more integrated approach with other environmental regimes.

2. Tourism

Fishing and tourism are the only significant economic activities in the Antarctic.[79] Yet the multiple stresses of climate change and increased human activity in the region present a clear vulnerability.[80] Antarctic tourism has grown rapidly, from about 16,000 tourists in the 1991–1992 season[81] to an all time high of 46,000 in the 2007–2008 season.[82] Although the economic crisis has caused numbers to drop significantly, last season saw a 29.4 percent increase over the prior year at 34,316 tourists[83] and the 2013–2014 season is

---

[73] Antarctic Treaty Consultative Mtg. Dec. 8, Letter to UNFCCC, XXXII mtg. (Apr. 6–17, 2009). *See also* Commission for the Conservation of Antarctic Marine Living Resources Res. 30/XXVII, Climate Change, XXVIII mtg. (Oct. 26–Nov. 6, 2009).

[74] Antarctic Treaty Consultative Mtg. Dec. 1, Meeting of Experts on Climate Change, XXXII mtg. (Apr. 6–17, 2009).

[75] Antarctic Climate Change and the Environment—2011 Update, Scientific Comm. on Antarctic Research, Commission for the Conservation of Antarctic Marine Living Resources, 30th mtg., CCAMLR-XXX/BG/14 (2011).

[76] Antarctic Treaty Consultative Mtg., Final Rep. of the XXXV Antarctic Treaty Consultative Meeting, Agenda Item 5, (June 11–20, 2012).

[77] *SCAR Participation at UN Climate Change Meeting in Warsaw, SCAR Science and Business News,* SCIENTIFIC COMM. ON ANTARCTIC RESEARCH (Nov. 14, 2013), http://www.scar.org/news/scarbusiness.

[78] Madrid Protocol, *supra* note 61, art. 3 (*e.g.*, minimization of negative impacts, EIS).

[79] IPCC AR4 WGII, *supra* note 6, at 676.

[80] *Id.*

[81] Overview of Tourism 2001-02, *2001–2002 Statistics,* INT'L ASS'N OF ANTARCTICA TOUR OPERATORS, http://iaato.org/c/document_library/get_file?uuid=7a61aae1-542e-47b1-b4b6-a5c5afcd9fd2&groupId=10157.

[82] 2007–2008 Tourism Summary, 2007–2008 Statistics, INT'L ASS'N OF ANTARCTICA TOUR OPERATORS, http://iaato.org/c/document_library/get_file?uuid=bcd40dfe-3145-4951-88e4-915b59448b03&groupId=10157.

[83] Int'l Ass'n of Antarctica Tour Operators, Rep. of the Int'l Ass'n of Antarctica Tour Operators 2012-13, XXXVI Antarctic Treaty Consultative Meeting (May 14, 2013).

expected to increase slightly to 35,354 tourists.[84] As the world economic slump improves and global warming makes visiting one of the last true remaining wildernesses more attractive, further sustained growth in the Antarctic tourism sector can be expected.[85]

From the inception of the Madrid Protocol, parties expressed concerns over the development of tourism activities in Antarctica. Yet despite receiving substantial attention for the first few years,[86] the issue of tourism was only addressed at the XVIIIth ATCM (1994) via the adoption of Recommendation XVIII-1,[87] a set of non-binding guidelines for visitors and organizers of nongovernmental expeditions, despite proposals for an additional annex to the Protocol on tourism and nongovernmental expeditions.[88] In 2001, the XXIVth ATCM recognized the "increase in the diversity of tourism activities, which may present new management challenges."[89] Again, there was a general reluctance to adopt an additional legal instrument, particularly in light of the growing and substantive system of self-regulation of the International Association of Antarctica Tour Operators (IAATO), which promotes "safe and environmentally responsible travel to Antarctica" and routinely reports to the ATCM on trends in Antarctic tourism.[90]

Despite highlighting the issue of tourism in several key meetings and papers over the course of the next decade, only a limited number of additional measures were passed, most of which had "resolution status" and were, therefore, not legally binding,[91] or expressed general principles on managing Antarctic tourism activities.[92] Resolution 4 (2007), prohibiting ships carrying 500 or more passengers from landing in Antarctica, was an exception, as it was "upgraded" to a measure that, once officially approved by all ATCPs, will become legally binding.[93] Discussions on tourism continue through the present, essentially centering on how Antarctica ought to look in a decade or two under international management; it remains to be seen whether the ATCM will move beyond talk and soon enough.[94] Greater international regulation of heightened tourism, with its

---

[84] Int'l Ass'n of Antarctica Tour Operators, IAATO Overview of Antarctic Tourism: 2012–13 Season and Preliminary Estimates for 2013–14 Season, XXXVI Antarctic Treaty Consultative Meeting (May 14, 2013).

[85] POLAR LAW TEXTBOOK II 131 (Natalia Loukacheva ed., 2013).

[86] *Id.* at 136.

[87] Antarctic Treaty Consultative Mtg., Final Rep. of the XVIII Antarctic Treaty Consultative Meeting ¶¶ 34–45 (1994).

[88] Antarctic Treaty Consultative Mtg., Final Rep. of the XI Antarctic Treaty Consultative Meeting ¶¶ 29–30 (1991).

[89] Antarctic Treaty Consultative Mtg., Final Rep. of the XXIV Antarctic Treaty Consultative Meeting ¶ 106 (2001).

[90] *What Is IAATO?*, INT'L ASS'N OF ANTARCTICA TOUR OPERATORS, http://iaato.org/what-is-iaato (last visited Aug. 2, 2014).

[91] POLAR LAW TEXTBOOK II, *supra* note 85, at 140–42.

[92] Res. 7, Final Rep. of the XXXII Antarctic Treaty Consultative Meeting ¶ 185 (2009).

[93] Res. 4, XXX Antarctic Treaty Consultative Meeting (Nov. 5, 2007); Measure 15, XXXII Antarctic Treaty Consultative Meeting—CEP XII (2009).

[94] POLAR LAW TEXTBOOK II, *supra* note 85, at 151–52.

attendant greenhouse gas emissions and potential for environmental damage, in the face of rising temperatures remains a pressing concern.

3. Overfishing and Ecosystem Management under CCAMLR

CCAMLR's General Framework for the Establishment of CCAMLR has as an objective the establishment of scientific reference areas in order to monitor the natural variability and long-term change or to monitor the effects of harvesting on Antarctic marine living resources and their ecosystems.[95] It also aims to protect areas in order to maintain resilience or adaptability to the effects of climate change.[96]

CCAMLR evolved into a comprehensive regime to address the unsustainable approach of Southern Ocean fisheries. It is unique among other multilateral, single species-based fisheries agreements, both for being the first regional fishery management organization to implement an ecosystem approach and for doing so under a "long term" ecosystem management mandate.[97] Article II seeks to minimize risk that the target stock will be overfished and recruitment impaired and to maintain a stable ecological relationship between predators and prey.[98] CCAMLR has been facing three key issues: (1) management of illegal, unregulated, and unreported fishing (IUU), particularly of toothfish; (2) intensification of industrial fishing for krill; and (3) a stalemate over a proposal to create the world's largest marine reserve.

The popularity of the slow-growing Patagonian and Antarctic toothfish, commonly marketed as Chilean sea bass, soared in the 1980s and 1990s, causing considerable management problems when IUU decimated sustainable fisheries, challenging CCAMLR's effectiveness.[99] Third-party states often escaped CCAMLR enforcement. For instance, Belize, Indonesia, Panama, St. Vincent, and the Grenadines were all identified as states whose vessels had been involved in the harvesting, landing, or importing of toothfish in 2001.[100] The CCAMLR Commission could only provide information about the CCAMLR approach and invite them to participate, as none were CCAMLR Contracting Parties.[101] CCAMLR Contracting Parties have been caught fishing illegally, too.[102] Further complicating matters, a Contracting Party can skirt its obligations

---

[95] Conservation Measure 91-04, General Framework for the Establishment of CCAMLR Protected Areas, Convention on the Conservation of Antarctic Marine Living Resources XXX (2011).

[96] Id.

[97] POLAR LAW TEXTBOOK 67–68 (Natalia Loukacheva ed., 2010).

[98] Convention on the Conservation of Antarctic Marine Living Resources art. II, May 20, 1980, 33 U.S.T. 3476; 1329 U.N.T.S. 48; 19 I.L.M. 841.

[99] POLAR LAW TEXTBOOK, *supra* note 97, at 66.

[100] Commission, Rep. of the Twentieth Meeting of the Commission, art. 5.25, Convention on the Conservation of Antarctic Marine Living Resources (2001).

[101] Id.

[102] Gail L. Lugten, *A Review of Measures Taken by Regional Marine Fishery Bodies to Address Contemporary Fishery Issues*, FAO FISHERIES CIRCULAR (Food & Agriculture Org. of the United Nations, Rome, Italy), Apr. 1999, at 35.

by "reflagging" its vessels, or changing the state registration and the flag under which they sail, to avoid the international obligations imposed on their home state.[103]

Krill, a small, protein-rich shrimp, is a keystone prey species in the Southern Ocean ecosystem for several bird, whale, seal, and squid stocks.[104] An increase in demand for krill products such as omega-3 supplements and high protein feed for aquaculture, combined with technology allowing for rapid processing at sea, has led to increasingly high krill catches.[105]

Recently, CCAMLR has been fielding a proposal from the United States and New Zealand to create an 875,000-square-mile marine protected area in the Ross Sea.[106] Commercial fishing, especially of Patagonian toothfish; oil drilling; and other development would be limited or excluded in the relatively pristine ecosystem, home to thousands of whales, seals, penguins, and the small fish and crustaceans upon which they depend.[107] CCAMLR will also consider a concurrent proposal from Australia, France, and the European Union for a network of protected areas totaling 994,000 square miles in the East Antarctic region.[108] However, concessions on the size of the Ross Sea reserve were already being made before the October 2013 CCAMLR meeting in Hobart, Australia, with New Zealand reducing the overall size of the proposed Ross Sea reserve by 40 percent.[109] Russia and Ukraine questioned the proposal's legality, Norway expressed concerns about how the zones would affect its fishing fleet, and New Zealand further conceded environmental protections by offering a "sunset clause" that would limit the area's no-take zone timeline.[110] Although plans were successfully blocked, the issue may be revisited at the October 2014 meeting.[111]

4. Scientific Research

Scientific research and international cooperation has long held an honored position in the ATS. However, the development of the ATS has further emphasized the freedom of scientific research, and the increasing effects of climate change have led to the data from the Antarctic region being received by the international community with an understanding of its deepening significance. The Antarctic region acts as a repository of

---

[103] *Id.*

[104] Polar Law Textbook, *supra* note 97, at 67.

[105] *Id.* at 70.

[106] David Jolly, *Proposal to Protect Antarctic Waters Is Scaled Back*, N.Y. Times, Sept. 10, 2003, http://www.nytimes.com/2013/09/11/world/proposal-to-protect-antarctic-waters-is-scaled-back.html?_r=0.

[107] *Id.*

[108] *Id.*; Oliver Milman, *Antarctic Marine Reserve Threatened by Sunset Clause, Conservationists Warn*, Guardian, Oct. 24, 2013, http://www.theguardian.com/world/2013/oct/24/antarctic-marine-reserve-threat-sunset-clause.

[109] Jolly, *supra* note 107.

[110] Milman, *supra* note 109.

[111] Pauline Askin, *Russia, Ukraine Halt Giant Antarctic Marine Sanctuary Plan*, Reuters, Nov. 1, 2013, http://uk.reuters.com/article/2013/11/01/us-antarctic-environment-idUKBRE9A00DX20131101.

valuable scientific information on past climates while also serving as an early indicator for global warming impacts. The retreat of sea ice, glaciers, snow, and the collapse of ice shelves due to warming temperatures are highly likely to have significant global impacts, such as sea-level rise.[112] Substantial resources are being expended to maintain a robust scientific presence in the Antarctic.

Despite funding struggles and the recent government shutdown, which impacted Antarctic programs,[113] the United States National Science Foundation requested $465 million for the Division of Polar Programs, with the intention of kick-starting a long-term plan to modernize its U.S. Antarctic Program facilities.[114] The plan is to improve docking access to the Palmer Station pier by large vessels, purchasing rigid-hull inflatable boats to improve access to areas of scientific interest, and "robotizing" the South Pole Traverse, a tractor train that moves fuel and cargo between research stations.[115] Aside from the increase in tourism, long-term scientific presence in the region poses its own dangers to the environment; such research "will inevitably result in some harm to the Antarctic environment."[116] Scientific programs and research stations continue to produce such polluting waste as laboratory chemicals, acids, alkalis, ash, and batteries.[117]

The recent Australasian Antarctic Expedition, which made headlines in 2013 after being trapped in pack ice, is a prime example of the risks faced not just by scientists,[118] but by the region itself. Although the crewmembers were safely rescued and the ship itself was later freed by a shift in weather conditions,[119] the ship could have faced the same fate as the Brazilian "Endless Sea," which in 2012 became trapped in ice and began leaking oil, presumably when the ice crushed the ship's hull.[120] The ship was carrying nearly 2,100 gallons of oil.[121] Expedition ships trapped in Antarctic ice not only risk oil

---

[112] French & Scott, *supra* note 4, at 634–35.

[113] *See, e.g.*, Becky Oskin, *Ax Falls for Antarctic Research Projects after Shutdown*, NBC NEWS, Oct. 21, 2013, http://www.nbcnews.com/science/science-news/ax-falls-antarctic-research-projects-after-shutdown-f8C11435682.

[114] Peter Rejcek, *NSF FY 2014 Budget: Polar Programs Would Get Funds to Begin McMurdo, Palmer Facility Upgrades*, ANTARCTIC SUN, Apr. 26, 2013, http://antarcticsun.usap.gov/features/contenthandler.cfm?id=2842.

[115] *Id.*

[116] Paul Lincoln Stoller, *Protecting the White Continent: Is the Antarctic Protocol Mere Words or Real Action?*, 12 ARIZ. J. INT'L & COMP. L. 335, 361 (1995).

[117] *See, e.g.*, Anna Mason, A Review of Waste Management in the Antarctic (unpublished graduate project, University of Canterbury), http://www.anta.canterbury.ac.nz/documents/GCAS%20electronic%20projects/Anna%20Mason%20Review.pdf (last visited Mar. 30, 2014).

[118] Alok Jha, *Antarctic Rescue: Passengers of Research Ship Back on Dry Land after Two Months*, GUARDIAN, Jan. 22, 2014, http://www.theguardian.com/world/2014/jan/22/antarctic-rescue-passengers-akademik-shokalskiy-dry-land.

[119] *Id.*

[120] *Brazilian Yacht Sinks Crushed by Antarctic Ice Close to Chilean Base*, MERCOPRESS, Apr. 9, 2012, http://en.mercopress.com/2012/04/09/brazilian-yacht-sinks-crushed-by-antarctic-ice-close-to-chilean-base.

[121] *Oil Spills in Antarctic Waters? The Growing Threat*, MARITIME PASSIVE SAFETY, May 21, 2012, http://www.maritimepassivesafety.com/2012/05/21/oil-spills-in-antarctic-waters-the-growing-threat.

spills but force international efforts to rescue trapped crew members, endangering other vessels such as icebreaker ships that carry their own risks. For instance, the antifouling paints used to coat the ships' hulls contain toxic chemicals that continue to pollute the Antarctic seas.[122]

The ATS is a remarkable treaty system, expanding both its purpose and scope beyond territorial disputes and scientific research to a reasonably comprehensive environmental regulatory and protective legal regime. Any party can call for a review conference after the expiration of thirty years. As a testament to the Treaty's continued strength relevance, no party has called for a review.[123]

III. Legal Regimes Governing the Antarctic Marine Environment

A. POPS

The 2004 Stockholm Convention on Persistent Organic Pollutants (POPs) is an international environmental treaty that was established to eliminate or restrict the production, use, and disposal of POPs,[124] which the Governing Council of the United Nations Environment Programme (UNEP) has defined as "chemical substances that persist in the environment, bio-accumulate through the food web, and pose a risk of causing adverse effects to human health and the environment."[125] Global warming multiplies the harmful effects of POPs by mobilizing otherwise stable environments and by their being absorbed into the organisms at all food-chain levels.

In the Arctic, POPs accumulate through a combination of processes: via prevailing ocean and wind currents that bring contaminants up to the northern latitudes, where they are subsequently trapped by the cold climate; migratory animal waste and decomposition; and tributary bodies that empty into Arctic waters.[126] As the Arctic has a greater capacity for storage of POPs than other regions, these chemicals are readily absorbed into biological systems and bioaccumulate to a toxic level in the tissues of Arctic organisms, including humans.[127] Concentrations in humans present a significant health hazard.[128]

---

[122] *Toxic Chemicals from Icebreaking Ships Are Polluting Antarctic Seas*, NEW SCIENTIST, May 22, 2004, at 18.

[123] *Frequently Asked Questions*, BRITISH ANTARCTIC SURVEY, http://www.antarctica.ac.uk/about_antarctica/geopolitical/treaty/faq.php (last visited Mar. 30, 2014).

[124] Stockholm Convention on Persistent Organic Pollutants, May 22, 2001, 40 I.L.M. 532 [hereinafter Stockholm Convention].

[125] *Persistent Organic Pollutants*, UNITED NATIONS ENVIRONMENT PROGRAMME, http://www.chem.unep.ch/pops (last visited Mar. 30, 2014).

[126] Samuel C. Byrne, Alaska Community Action on Toxics, Persistent Organic Pollutants in the Arctic 3, 4th Conf. of the Parties Stockholm Convention on Persistent Organic Pollutants (May 2009).

[127] *Id.*

[128] *Id.*

A recent SCAR report reveals that the data on POPs concentrations in the Antarctic lags far behind that of the Arctic.[129] However, new data still indicates that long-range atmospheric transport is the primary mechanism by which POPs are brought into the region, and that local species and the Antarctic food web are impacted by temporal trends in contaminant levels.[130] Although more and comprehensive data is needed, the information obtained indicates that increased warming may provide further threats as POPs buried or immobilized in soils by permafrost could remobilize if released, impacting Antarctic ecosystems.[131]

The Stockholm Convention was influenced in large part by the Arctic Council, and the region's vulnerability received acknowledgment in the Convention text itself: "Acknowledging that the Arctic ecosystems and indigenous communities are particularly at risk because of the biomagnification of persistent organic pollutants and that contamination of their traditional foods is a public health issue."[132] The Convention remains a priority in the Arctic region, with the Arctic Council's various working groups managing projects that provide capacity building to assist countries in implementing the Convention and continuing to demonstrate practical solutions to reduce POPs.[133]

B. IMO AND MARPOL

The International Maritime Organization (IMO) is the UN specialized agency responsible for the safety and security of shipping and the prevention of marine pollution by ships.[134] It currently boasts 170 member states.[135] The International Convention for the Prevention of Pollution from Ships (MARPOL) is one of the most important IMO conventions for the polar regions. The IMO's efforts to draft a mandatory Polar Code is also a critical and timely endeavor.

MARPOL is the main international convention addressing the prevention of pollution of the marine environment from operational or accidental shipping incidents.[136] The convention establishes detailed marine pollution and protection standards through six annexes, addressing vessel-source pollution in both polar regions. Annex VI seeks to control air emissions, such as ozone-depleting substances, nitrogen oxides, and sulfur

---

[129] Scientific Comm. on Antarctic Research, Persistent Organic Pollutants in the Antarctic: An Update, XXXII Antarctic Treaty Consultative Meeting (Apr. 6–17, 2009).

[130] *Id.*

[131] *Id.*

[132] Stockholm Convention, *supra* note 125.

[133] Arctic Council Working Groups: Rep. on Their Achievements in 2011–2013 and Work Plans for 2013–2015 1, 7, Arctic Council, Kiruna Ministerial Mtg. (May 31, 2013).

[134] *Introduction to IMO*, INT'L MARITIME ORG., http://www.imo.org/About (last visited Mar. 30, 2014).

[135] *Member States, IGOs and NGOs*, INT'L MARITIME ORG., http://www.imo.org/About/Membership/Pages/Default.aspx (Mar. 30, 2014).

[136] International Convention for the Prevention of Pollution from Ships, Nov. 2, 1973, 12 I.L.M. 1319, 34 U.S.T. 3407, 1340 U.N.T.S. 184 [hereinafter MARPOL].

oxides, and applies uniformly to ships operating in both the Arctic and Antarctic.[137] Both regions are also subject to similar sewage discharge standards; Regulation 11 of Annex IV sets a global standard for sewage discharges.[138] The Regulation is applicable to the Arctic so long as coastal states do not adopt stricter standards pursuant to the special legislative and enforcement powers granted by article 234 of UNCLOS, and is implemented by Annex IV to the Madrid Protocol of the ATS.[139]

However, the polar regions are not equally enforced. The Antarctic is listed as a special area under Annexes I (oil),[140] II (noxious liquid substances),[141] and V (garbage).[142] This special status is not extended to any area in the Arctic Ocean, where pollutant discharge standards for some areas are less stringent than for the Antarctic.[143] ATS Resolution 5 (2010) further aims to improve the "co-ordination among Antarctic Treaty Parties on Antarctic proposals under consideration in the IMO," with Resolution 7 (2010) requesting that "Parties proactively apply, through their national maritime authorities, the existing regime of port State control to passenger vessels bound for the [ATS] area," but the adoption of a mandatory code for polar shipping within the IMO promises not only more comprehensive regulation of ship safety in the Antarctic, but in the Arctic as well.[144]

C. UNCLOS

The United Nations Convention on the Law of the Sea (UNCLOS) is a comprehensive legal framework that establishes rules governing the world's oceans and seas and their resources, recognizing that ocean space issues are interrelated and need to be addressed holistically.[145] In force since 1994, the Convention is comprised of 320 articles and nine annexes governing, inter alia, delimitation, environmental control, marine scientific research, economic and commercial activities, transfer of technology, and the settlement of disputes relating to ocean matters.[146] It has been ratified by 166 countries.[147] The

---

[137] *Id.*

[138] *Id.* annex IV, reg. 11.

[139] French & Scott, *supra* note 4, at 639.

[140] Stockholm Convention, *supra* note 125, annex I.

[141] *Id.* annex II.

[142] *Id.* annex V.

[143] Polar Law Textbook, *supra* note 97, at 67–68.

[144] Polar Law Textbook II, *supra* note 85, at 145.

[145] United Nations Convention on the Law of the Sea, Dec. 10, 1982, 21 I.L.M. 1245, 1833 U.N.T.S. 3 [hereinafter UNCLOS].

[146] *Id.*

[147] Status of the United Nations Convention on the Law of the Sea, of the Agreement relating to the implementation of Part XI of the Convention and of the Agreement for the implementation of the provisions of the Convention relating to the conservation and management of straddling fish stocks and highly migratory fish stocks: Table recapitulating the status of the Convention and of the related Agreements, as at 10 January 2014, *Division for Oceans and Law of the Sea,* UN.ORG, http://www.un.org/depts/los/reference_files/status2010.pdf (last visited Mar. 30, 2014).

Convention addresses six main sources of ocean pollution: (1) land-based and coastal activities, (2) continental-shelf drilling, (3) potential seabed mining, (4) ocean dumping, (5) vessel-source pollution, and (6) pollution from or through the atmosphere.[148]

However, it is the Convention's framework for delimiting exclusive economic zones (EEZs), the surveying of those areas, their monitoring, the utilization of those resources, and their management and development that has a vital but contrasting effect on the polar regions.[149] UNCLOS allows coastal states the right to exercise sovereignty over their territorial sea, which can be established up to a limit of twelve nautical miles from the coastline.[150] Coastal states may further claim sovereign rights with respect to natural resources and certain economic activities, and exercise jurisdiction over marine science research and environmental protection in an area extending 200 nautical miles from the coast.[151] Landlocked and geographically disadvantaged states have a right to participate on an equitable basis in also exploiting a portion of the surplus of living resources of the EEZs of coastal states in the same region.[152] These rights are incredibly significant: almost 99 percent of the world's fisheries fall under some nation's jurisdiction.[153] Furthermore, a similarly large percentage of the world's oil and gas production is offshore.[154] Careful management of states' rights to these coveted marine resources is of critical importance for both the economic and national security of states as much as it is for the protection of the marine environment in which they are found.

The Arctic region, unlike the Antarctic region, is surrounded by countries that have claimed their sovereign rights under UNCLOS to their respective marine areas. They are subject to division through the operation of article 234, which authorizes coastal states to develop and administer special regulations for human activities in ice-covered waters:

> Coastal States have the right to adopt and enforce non-discriminatory laws and regulations for the prevention, reduction and control of marine pollution from vessels in ice-covered areas within the limits of the exclusive economic zone, where particularly severe climatic conditions and the presence of ice covering such areas for most of the year create obstructions or exceptional hazards to navigation, and

---

[148] *United Nations Convention on the Law of the Sea of 10 December 1982 Overview and Full Text*, UN.ORG, http://www.un.org/depts/los/convention_agreements/convention_overview_convention.htm (last visited May 1, 2014) [hereinafter *UNCLOS Overview*].

[149] *Id.*

[150] *Id.*

[151] UNCLOS, *supra* note 145, arts. 55, 57.

[152] *UNCLOS Overview, supra* note 148.

[153] *Exclusive Economic Zone*, The United Nations Convention on the Law of the Sea (A Historical Perspective), UN.ORG, http://www.un.org/depts/los/convention_agreements/convention_historical_perspective. htm#Exclusive Economic Zone (last visited May 1, 2014).

[154] *Id.*

pollution of the marine environment could cause major harm to or irreversible disturbance of the ecological balance. Such laws and regulations shall have due regard to navigation and the protection and preservation of the marine environment based on the best available scientific evidence."[155]

As warming in the Arctic continues to significantly reduce sea ice, open up sea lanes, and lengthen the navigational season, increased accessibility to the region—and its valuable marine resources—implicates heightened challenges to UNCLOS's governance regime, as well as calling into play the reach and strength of other regimes' capacities to protect the region, such as MARPOL. The limits of UNCLOS, in the absence of a binding Arctic treaty, will be aggressively tested by the impacts of climate change.

The ATS, by contrast, excludes the high seas[156] and prevents nations from making sovereign claims over the region.[157] Even if that were not the case, the geographic characteristics of Antarctica would make it difficult to apply UNCLOS to the continent given that the territorial sea and EEZs are measured from baselines usually taken from the low-tide limit of the land. The land continent, covered in moving ice, makes identifying the low-tide limit very difficult.[158] To date, the ATS has largely provided comprehensive, rational management of the area's marine environment. Climate change, however, may still threaten the ATS's legal primacy in the region and bring it into legal conflict with UNCLOS if the ice sheets melt enough to reveal the continent's land mass. Renewed interest in claims to sovereignty in Antarctica could threaten to revive the very conflicts the ATS was created to mute.

D. UNFCCC

The United Nations Framework Convention on Climate Change (UNFCCC) ultimately aims to prevent "dangerous" human interference with the climate system.[159] The Convention, which entered into force in 1994, currently has 195 parties.[160] Many of these countries have formed coalitions around special interests that take on particular import in the climate negotiations. For instance, the Alliance of Small Island States (AOSIS)

---

[155] UNCLOS, *supra* note 145, art. 234.

[156] The Antarctic Treaty, *supra* note 44, art. VI (specifying "the area south of 60° South Latitude" as the area to which this treaty applies).

[157] The Antarctic Treaty, *supra* note 43.

[158] Erika Lennon, *A Tale of Two Poles: A Comparative Look at the Legal Regimes in the Arctic and the Antarctic,* 8 Sustainable Dev. L. & Pol'y 32, 35 (2008); Polar Law Textbook II, *supra* note 85, at 81.

[159] United Nations Framework Convention on Climate Change, May 9, 1992, 1771 U.N.T.S. 107; 31 I.L.M. 849 [hereinafter UNFCCC].

[160] *Status of the Ratification of the Convention,* United Nations Framework Convention on Climate Change, http://unfccc.int/essential_background/convention/items/6036.php (last visited Mar. 30, 2014).

consists of small island and low-lying coastal countries that are especially vulnerable to sea-level rise.[161] However, as Duncan French and Karen Scott note:

> [t]hough the spectre of the impact of climate change on the polar regions has played an important scientific and rhetorical function in the global debates, political and normative discussion on the effect of climate change in the polar regions at the global level has generally been notable by its absence.[162]

This omission is striking considering how crucial the polar regions are to achieving the objective of the Convention.[163] Preservation of the Arctic and Antarctic regions is critical to the achievement of the requisite decrease in greenhouse gases to stabilize the global climate. Disintegration of the West Antarctic ice sheet, which would cause sea-level rise of 4–6 meters, is considered by some to be an example of "dangerous anthropogenic interference with the climate system."[164] The ATS established a link with the UNFCCC in 2009 when the Chair of the ATCM forwarded SCAR's *Antarctic Climate Change and the Environment (ACCE) Review Report* to the Executive Secretary of the UNFCCC "in light of the relevance of the ACCE report to the work of the UNFCCC."[165] In 2010, the Antarctic Treaty Meeting of Experts on Implications of Climate Change for Antarctic Management and Governance recommended that the ATCM consider developing an Antarctic climate change communication plan to bring the findings of the report to other decision-makers, the general public, and the media.[166] The plan, which was presented in 2011, noted that events scheduled and organized by non-Antarctic organizations, such as the Conference of the Parties of the UNFCCC, could serve as prime opportunities to disseminate SCAR's work.[167] In 2012, Executive Secretary of the UNFCCC Christiana Figueres brought attention to both the importance and vulnerability of the Antarctic region when she was invited to join Al Gore's Climate Reality Project expedition.[168]

---

[161] *See* ALLIANCE OF SMALL ISLAND STATES, http://aosis.org (last visited Mar. 30, 2014).

[162] French & Scott, *supra* note 4, at 639.

[163] Copenhagen Accord, U.N. Doc. FCCC/CP/2009/L.7 (Dec. 18, 2009).

[164] Oppenheimer & Alley, *supra* note 14, at 257.

[165] Dec. 8 Letter to UNFCCC, Final Rep. of the XXXII Antarctic Treaty Consultative Meeting 261 (Apr. 6–17, 2009).

[166] Recommendation 2, Co-Chairs' Rep. from Antarctic Treaty Meeting of Experts on Implications of Climate Change for Antarctic Management and Governance 4, Meeting of Experts on Climate Change (Apr. 6–9, 2010); Antarctic and Southern Ocean Coalition, An Antarctic Climate Change Plan, XXXIV Antarctic Treaty Consultative Meeting (June 20–July 1, 2011).

[167] Antarctic and Southern Ocean Coalition, An Antarctic Climate Change Plan 6, XXXIV Antarctic Treaty Consultative Meeting (June 20–July 1, 2011).

[168] *See* Christiana Figueres, *A Message from Christiana Figueres*, CLIMATE REALITY PROJECT BLOG (Feb. 16, 2012, 2:33 PM), http://climaterealityproject.org/climate-science/a-message-from-christiana-figueres.

Engagement with the UNFCCC now forms an integral part of SCAR activities in highlighting the key role of Antarctic science in understanding climate change.[169] At the June 2013 Climate Change Meeting in Bonn, SCAR presented and hosted a press briefing on its updated ACCE report, gave short reviews on ice mass balance and marine ecosystem response, and made a presentation on Antarctica and global climate change.[170] The ACCE Executive Summary update is the "most significant SCAR publication in the area of Climate Change since 2009."[171] SCAR was further represented at the COP 19 Climate Change Meeting in Warsaw, Poland, in November 2013,[172] hosting a press briefing on "Cryosphere Day," a day devoted to the regions of snow and ice on Earth and "their importance to the global climate system, the changes they are exhibiting and implications for ecosystems and human communities."[173] Cryosphere Day served as an important opportunity to highlight the importance of the cryosphere within the recently released IPCC Physical Science Case Assessment Report 5.[174] SCAR also noted the new report on climate change and the cryosphere recently released by the World Bank and the International Cryosphere Climate Initiative (ICCI), "On Thin Ice."[175] In 2014, the ACCE group will launch a regularly updated "wiki" version of their report, which is intended to serve as a living document and focal point of future SCAR climate change communications.[176]

Attention will increasingly be focused on the scope and form of a new climate agreement. Under the Ad hoc Working Group on the Durban Platform for Enhanced Action ("ADP"), parties are preparing an agreement "applicable to all," due to be adopted at the twenty-first Conference of the Parties to the UNFCCC ("COP 21") in 2015. The goal is to meet the objective of the Convention while enabling communities to adapt to the inevitable climatic changes that will occur. The importance of the Antarctic region will remain critical. Current climatic impacts and new scientific data will provide necessary

---

[169] Scientific Comm. on Antarctic Research, *SCAR Focus On…Advice to Policymakers: The UNFCCC*, SCAR NEWSL. (Cambridge, UK), Dec. 2013, at 2, *available at* http://www.scar.org/news/newsletters/issues2013/SCARnewsletter35_Dec2013.pdf.

[170] *SCAR Participation at UN Climate Change Meeting in Warsaw*, Scientific Comm. on Antarctic Research (Nov. 14, 2013), http://www.scar.org/news/scarbusiness.

[171] *Id.*

[172] *Id.*

[173] "Cryosphere" refers to the regions of the globe that are covered in ice and snow, either seasonally or year-round. *What Is the Cryosphere?*, INTERNATIONAL CRYOSPHERE CLIMATE INITIATIVE, http://iccinet.org/the-cryosphere (last visited Apr. 29, 2014). *The ICCI at COP19*, INT'L CRYOSPHERE CLIMATE INITIATIVE, http://iccinet.org/cryosphere-day-at-cop19 (last visited Mar. 30, 2014).

[174] *SCAR Participation at UN Climate Change Meeting in Warsaw*, *supra* note 165; IPCC AR5 WGI, *supra* note 6.

[175] WORLD BANK & INTERNATIONAL CRYOSPHERE INITIATIVE, ON THIN ICE: HOW CUTTING POLLUTION CAN SLOW GLOBAL WARMING AND SAVE LIVES (2013), *available at* http://www.worldbank.org/content/dam/Worldbank/document/SDN/Full_Report_On_Thin_Ice_How_Cutting_Pollution_Can_Slow_Warming_and_Save_Lives.pdf.

[176] *SCAR Participation at UN Climate Change Meeting in Warsaw*, *supra* note 165.

input to the climate negotiations, and the region itself will be impacted by future decisions on the new agreement.

IV. The Arctic Council

The Antarctic Treaty System today is itself a reflection of the increasing sophistication and globalization of regional and global environmental treaties. Its legacy, as well as the advancement of the Arctic Council, has contributed to a nascent body of legal knowledge. Polar Law is a growing field of law encompassing the international and domestic legal regimes that govern the Arctic, Antarctic, and/or both Polar Regions.[177] As testament to unique polar characteristics and history, Polar Law covers international law treaties that address specific regional issues related to each polar region as well as those that apply to both regions, includes the domestic law of the Arctic states and certain Antarctic Treaty Consultative Meeting regulations that have been incorporated into the national legal systems of Consultative parties, and embraces both legally binding "hard law" and non-legally binding "soft law" instruments.[178] An overview of the legal regimes of both polar regions demonstrates that despite significant differences, both systems share the need to address issues of common concern: climate change, environmental integrity, biodiversity, and questions of sovereignty.[179]

The Arctic is the sister polar region to the Antarctic, rife with its own legal and ecological challenges, risks, and shortcomings. Significantly, the Arctic is an important source of fossil fuels, with a third of the remaining global hydrocarbon reserves located north of the Arctic Circle within clear national jurisdictions and others in disputed territorial areas.[180] Circum-Arctic nations are responsible for a significant percentage of global CO_2 emissions.[181] Furthermore, the Arctic environment has become an urgent focus of concern as climate change and the rapid rate at which the ice cap is melting opens up sea lanes to additional shipping traffic and accessibility to those fossil fuel reserves. However, the Arctic regime differs considerably from its polar counterpart, the ATS.

The Arctic lacks the comprehensive legal framework that protects the Antarctic environment, operating in reverse of the ATS in that national environmental laws apply to the region except for international areas, with various bilateral and multilateral agreements governing other specific aspects of activity in the Arctic, such as the United Nations

---

[177] POLAR LAW TEXTBOOK II, *supra* note 85, at 17.

[178] *Id.* at 17–18.

[179] *Id.* at 19.

[180] Betsy Baker, *Law, Science, and the Continental Shelf: The Russian Federation and the Promise of Arctic Cooperation*, 25 AM. U. INT'L. REV. 251, 257 (2010); Rebecca.M. Bratspies, *Human Rights and Arctic Resources*, 15 SW. J. INT'L. L. 265 (2009).

[181] IPCC AR4 WGII, *supra* note 6, at 672.

Convention on the Law of the Sea,[182] the International Convention for the Prevention of Pollution from Ships,[183] and the Polar Bear Treaty.[184] Eight Arctic states—Canada, Denmark, Finland, Iceland, Norway, Sweden, the Russian Federation, and the United States—signed the Rovaniemi Declaration in 1991, adopting the Arctic Environmental Protection Strategy (AEPS), which identified six priority environmental problems facing the region: persistent organic pollutants, radioactivity, heavy metals, noise, acidification, and oil pollution.[185] The AEPS outlined remedies to counter these threats, identified international environmental protection treaties that would apply in the region, and established four environmental protection working groups: Conservation of Flora and Fauna (CAFF), Protection of the Arctic Marine Environment (PAME), Emergency Prevention, Preparedness and Response (EPPR), and the Arctic Monitoring and Assessment Programme (AMAP).[186]

In 1996, the Arctic Council was established, providing for three categories of AEPS participants: members, permanent participants, and observers.[187] Permanent participants significantly include six indigenous peoples groups, which have banded together to form the Indigenous Peoples' Secretariat to support those groups and their role in the Arctic Council.[188] The Arctic Council chair state has a great deal of freedom in choosing its priorities for its tenure, but the rotating position hinders long-term policy planning.[189] In recent years, the Council has focused much of its energy on scientific research, particularly given the projected intense climate change in the Arctic.[190]

The polar regimes, despite their similarities, differ significantly. First, the importance of territorial sovereignty has enormous implications for the functioning of either regime. In the Antarctic, the sovereignty question has been "frozen," while in the Arctic, all land area is managed under the sovereignty of the respective Arctic states, Arctic waters fall under their exclusive maritime jurisdiction, and the core of the Arctic Ocean is considered high seas. Warming in the Arctic has caused significant reductions in sea ice, improving access to the region and potentially lengthening the navigational season. It has been predicted that the Northwest Passage may be open for commercial shipping

---

[182] UNCLOS, *supra* note 145.

[183] International Convention for the Prevention of Pollution from Ships, 17 I.L.M. 546, 1340 U.N.T.S. 61 (1983) [hereinafter MARPOL 73/78].

[184] Agreement on the Conservation of Polar Bears, Nov. 15, 1973, 13 I.L.M 13, pmbl. (1974).

[185] POLAR LAW TEXTBOOK, *supra* note 97, at 30.

[186] *Id.* at 30–31.

[187] *Id.* at 31.

[188] *About*, ARCTIC COUNCIL INDIGENOUS PEOPLES' SECRETARIAT, http://www.arcticpeoples.org/about (last visited Aug. 2, 2014).

[189] *Id.* at 32.

[190] *See, e.g.*, Arctic Climate Impact Assessment (policy document), Arctic Council Ministerial Meeting, 4th mtg. (Nov. 24, 2004) (establishing the Arctic as a barometer of climate change).

by 2020.[191] Increased accessibility increases the politicization and number of legal issues in the region—exacerbating a bilateral dispute between the United States and Canada over the legal status of the Passage (international strait or internal waters)[192] and inviting the adoption of the Arctic Offshore Oil and Gas Guidelines. The Guidelines attempt to address the trifecta of the oil and gas industry, climate change, and environmental protection in the region.[193]

Second, Arctic-wide cooperation is relatively recent in comparison to the ATS's fifty-five-year history. Third, Arctic human habitation in addition to high tourist traffic means that the governance regime must balance human needs and indigenous rights with environmental protection, a consideration largely absent in an Antarctic region with no permanent human communities.[194]

Fourth, as compared to the ATS, the Arctic Council is a "soft law" regime with no ability to make binding law; it serves only as an advisory body. The Council has attempted, like its polar counterpart, to emphasize that the Arctic polar region is unique, and requires different threshold levels and sensitivity criteria, by establishing Arctic Environmental Impacts Assessments (EIA) Guidelines to promote sustainable development.[195] While the EIA Guidelines improve policy uniformity and promote cooperation, flexibility, and inclusiveness among countries, they do not replace any national or international EIA guidelines, and are purely voluntary.[196] Unlike the ATS, the Arctic Council has lacked a permanent secretariat for years, with each working group having its own secretariat with its own home city, a disjointed arrangement with no enforcement mechanism. The 2009 Tromsø Declaration introduced several important reforms in this regard, notably the 2011 decision to establish an Arctic Council permanent secretariat and to launch it in 2013.[197]

---

[191] Arctic Council, Arctic Marine Shipping Assessment 2009 Report 5 (2009), *available at* http://www.arctic. noaa.gov/detect/documents/AMSA_2009_Report_2nd_print.pdf.

[192] Nathan VanderKlippe, *Northwest Passage Gets Political Name Change: "Internal Waters" Hoped to Bolster Canada's Case*, EDMONTON J., Apr. 9, 2006, http://www2.canada.com/reginaleaderpost/news/story.htm l?id=6d4815ac-4fdb-4cf3-a8a6-4225a8bd08df&k=73925&p=2. *See also* Elizabeth Elliot-Meisel, *Politics, Pride and Precedent: The United States and Canada in the Northwest Passage*, 40 OCEAN DEV. & INT'L L. 204, 215 (2009); Agreement on Arctic Cooperation, Canada–US, 1852 U.N.T.S. 59 (1988); Gillian MacNeil, *The Northwest Passage: Sovereign Seaway or International Strait? A Reassessment of the Legal Status*, 15 DALHOUSIE J. LEGAL STUD. 204, 238 (2006); Donat Pharand, *The Arctic Waters and the Northwest Passage: A Final Revisit*, 38 OCEAN DEV. & INT'L L. 3 (2007).

[193] Protection of the Arctic Marine Environment Working Group, Arctic Council, Arctic Offshore Oil and Gas Guidelines 35 (Apr. 29, 2009).

[194] Arctic Human Development Report, Arctic Council (2004).

[195] Paula Kankaanpää, Finnish Ministry for the Environment, Guidelines for Environmental Impact Assessment (EIA) in the Arctic: Arctic Environmental Protection Strategy 4 (1997), *available at* http:// arcticcentre.ulaland.fi/aria/procedures/eiasguide.pdf.

[196] *Id.* at 9–11, 45.

[197] POLAR LAW TEXTBOOK II, *supra* note 85, at 28.

Even where international treaties are binding, not all Arctic states have ratified the relevant instruments: for instance, Russia has not ratified the Convention for the Protection of the Marine Environment for the North East Atlantic,[198] and the United States failed to ratify either the Kyoto Protocol or the Convention on Biological Diversity.[199] Therefore, despite growing and successful collaboration, increasing innovation in governance arrangements, and strengthening of various regional networks, the Arctic institutional and governance complex is still relatively nascent and fragmented.[200]

Fifth, while the ATS ATCPs have not been particularly involved in the negotiation processes combating global environmental problems, the Artic Council has been active in this regard, increasing its participation in international environmental protection processes, such as the negotiations on the Stockholm Convention on Persistent Organic Pollutants and the Johannesburg World Summit on Sustainable Development.[201] Despite its soft law collaborative decision-making structure, the Arctic Council has moved in the direction of using binding legal instruments.

Such a comparison between the Arctic and the Antarctic not only encourages a discussion of what the polar regimes can learn from one another, but further invites a broader look at how the polar regimes are situated within the network of multilateral environmental agreements and other international environmental treaties, and whether these relationships serve to address the impacts and effects of climate change in the polar regions, particularly the Antarctic. The Stockholm Convention on Persistent Organic Pollutants, International Maritime Organization, the UN Convention on the Law of the Sea, and the UN Framework Convention on Climate Change all address specific issues and provide sets of legal protections and regulations for a number of relevant climate issues.

V. The Need for Integrated Polar Governance

Both Antarctic and Arctic polar regions have similar climatic stressors but with vastly different geopolitical issues that affect approaches to these areas that are critical to the welfare of the planet. Recommendations on improving polar governance and protection include building the Arctic legal system into one more closely mirroring that of the Antarctic Treaty System, and the unlikely but comprehensive proposition of a global government that would remedy existing failings. A closer look at these proposals reveals

---

[198] Convention for the Protection of the Marine Environment for the North East Atlantic ("OSPAR"), Mar. 25, 1998, 32 I.L.M. 1072 (opened for signature Sept. 22, 1992).

[199] Kyoto Protocol to the United Nations Framework Convention on Climate Change, Dec. 10, 1997, U.N. Doc FCCC/CP/1997/7/Add.1, 37 I.L.M. 22 (1998); Convention on Biological Diversity, June 5, 1992, 1760 U.N.T.S. 79; 31 ILM 818.

[200] Polar Law Textbook, *supra* note 97, at 128.

[201] *Id.* at 32.

that a middle solution of more muscular integration of one or both polar regimes into existing environmental agreements holds the greatest political promise of reaching agreement.

The international community has yet to push a regionally binding Arctic regime into either a broader framework treaty model or a more narrow regional seas convention.[202] A number of authors have suggested that climate change would serve as a "tipping point," resulting in the adoption of a legally binding regime for the Arctic, considering the increasing interlinkages between Arctic and Antarctic issues.[203] Linda Nowlan has suggested formalizing Arctic cooperation through an international treaty that would contain principles, substantive legal obligations, and other innovative features such as having the five annexes of the Madrid Protocol transposed to become the main or substantive obligations of, in essence, an Arctic Treaty System.[204] However, this approach faces significant hurdles,[205] particularly when the structural governance, sovereignty issues, and Arctic human population are acknowledged.[206] For instance, while the Antarctic has been declared a "nature reserve," the Arctic is unlikely to be so similarly deemed in light of the large Russian cities established in the region and the need for indigenous communities to survive and function economically.[207]

While opportunities to draw directly from the Antarctic model may appear limited, a convergence in regime governance already seems to be developing. The new Arctic Council secretariat is expected to bring (1) more continuity and efficiency to its operational capacity, (2) elaboration on agreed criteria for Council observers, (3) a collective financial foundation via a Project Support Instrument, and (4) a binding legal agreement.[208] Accordingly, an emerging Arctic framework can build on the strong species and habitat treaties comprising the ATS, such as the Madrid Protocol's restriction on mineral extraction and environmental impact assessments for all activities.[209] The Arctic Council might also consider ATCMs of the ATS as a model for regional marine environmental protection, to enhance procedural governance and flesh out substantive regulatory provisions.[210] The listing of "special areas" in the Arctic may be one of the best

---

[202] French & Scott, *supra* note 4, at 644–45.

[203] *E.g., id.*

[204] Linda Nowlan, *Arctic Legal Regime for Environmental Protection* (IUCN Environmental Policy and Law Paper No. 44, 2001), *available at* http://weavingaweb.org/pdfdocuments/EPLP44EN.pdf. *See also* Bonnie A. Malloy, *On Thin Ice: How a Binding Treaty Regime Can Save the Arctic*, 16 HASTINGS W. -Nw. J. ENVTL. L. & POL'Y 471 (2010).

[205] *Id.*

[206] Koivurova, *supra* note 55, at 218.

[207] Lennon, *supra* note 158.

[208] POLAR LAW TEXTBOOK II, *supra* note 85, at 28.

[209] Elizabeth Burleson, *Polar Law and Good Governance, in* ROUTLEDGE HANDBOOK OF INTERNATIONAL ENVIRONMENTAL LAW 11 (Shawkat Alam, Jahid Hossain Bhuiyan, Tariq M.R. Chowdhury, Erika J. Techera eds., 2012).

[210] *Id.* at 15.

practices of the Antarctic regime that could be implemented. A similarly fragile area, the Arctic could benefit from comprehensive designation as a special area where certain activities are prohibited, with the exception of minor and well-defined instances.[211] In turn, the Arctic Council's work highlighting the profound and pervasive impact of polar chemical pollution provides a model for the ATS to support global sustainable development decision-making.[212]

One of the more bold suggestions to gaps, failings, and weak enforcement measures in the polar regimes is the establishment of a world government.[213] Martin Lishexian Lee has rather quixotically argued that the remedy for the ATS's "incurable" weak enforcement mechanisms and self-policing policy, ambiguity, and loopholes present in the regime's instruments and hortatory recommendations is a vertical world government.[214] Lee recognizes, however, that a more "realistic" solution is the evolution of the United Nations into a more centralized administrative institution.[215] Yet, there is reason to believe that even United Nations' coordination of Antarctic decision-making would be unwieldy given the vast number of parties needed to be persuaded before any action could occur.[216] The current regime in the Antarctic may have evolved into the most politically acceptable Antarctic decision-making approach. Nevertheless, much more can and ought to be done both to ameliorate the gaps and weaknesses in the ATS and bring the southern polar region into the greater international dialogue on environmental protection and climate change.

What is needed is greater political and legal integration of the various regimes, particularly of the polar systems. French and Scott explain that "[a]s trustees (in effect) for the polar regions, Arctic states and parties to the [ATS] have a special responsibility to support and advocate polar interests within international fora."[217] Polar states need to move beyond merely presenting scientific findings and "engaging in hortatory hand-wringing"[218] to collaborate effectively within the international community to

---

[211] Arctic Ocean Conference, Ilussiat Declaration of May 28, 2008 Annex I, V, 48 I.L.M. 382 (2009) (as amended Mar. 17, 1992); E.A. Norse & J. Amos, *Impacts, Perception, and Policy Implications of the BP/Deepwater Horizon Oil and Gas Disaster*, 40 ENVTL. L. REP. 11058 (2010). *See also* INT'L MARITIME ORG. RES. A.982(24), Revised Guidelines for the Identification and Designation of Particularly Sensitive Sea Areas, Assembly, 24th Sess., Feb. 6, 2006, A 24/Res.982 (adopted Dec. 1, 2005).

[212] *See Arctic Contaminants Action Program*, ARCTIC COUNCIL, http://www.arctic-council.org/index.php/en/arctic-contaminants-action-program-acap (last visited Mar. 31, 2014). *Cf. Prevention of Marine Pollution*, SECRETARIAT OF THE ANTARCTIC TREATY, http://www.ats.aq/e/ep_marine.htm (last visited Mar. 31, 2014).

[213] *See* Martin Lishexian Lee, *A Case for World Government of the Antarctic*, 9 GONZ. J. INT'L L. 73 (2005).

[214] *Id.*

[215] *Id.*

[216] Tray, *supra* note 1, at 222.

[217] French & Scott, *supra* note 4, at 653.

[218] *Id.* at 654.

implement greenhouse gas emissions reductions that genuinely protect Polar regions and stabilize global climate.[219]

The international community has a profound stake in greater polar convergence in terms of stringency of policies and comprehensiveness of protections. Yet, global coordination may not be politically feasible, particularly as climate stressors invite further political stressors. For instance, the increased melting of Arctic ice will invite Arctic nations to vie for shipping lanes and rights and potentially militarize the region. A true convergence or world of mirror polar regimes may not ever come to pass, but both regimes can continue to learn from one another while more closely aligning their mutual concerns and aims in other multilateral forums. Coordination efforts should recognize and account for the unique environments, interests, and issues in the polar regions that have global impacts.

The ATS should continue to develop its relationship with the Stockholm Convention on POPs, perhaps with the assistance or guidance of the Artic Council. Although less is known about the Antarctic's capacity as a POPs sink, there are enough similarities between the regions to be deeply concerned about the ongoing and future impacts of POPs on the southern polar ecosystem. As atmospheric transport of POPs continues, likely aggravated by increased shipping and tourism and compounded by melting ice and permafrost, the Antarctic marine ecosystems will face dangerous levels of contamination as the climate warms.

The establishment of a Polar Code under MARPOL will be a tremendous legal and institutional advancement for the Antarctic and the Arctic, finally harmonizing dissimilar shipping and environmental protection policies in both regions. A final text should not be unduly rushed, but pressure to finalize the Code as expeditiously as possible should be applied, considering the implications of global warming and accelerated ice melt in the polar areas. One of these implications would invite increased resort to provisions under UNCLOS, particularly on designations of EEZs. Here, a close dialogue between the two polar regimes may be necessary to address sensitive questions of sovereignty and militarization.

UNCLOS may be an important legal vehicle for better legal and administrative coordination among the various environmental agreements that impact the polar regions, as well as those polar regimes themselves. UNCLOS's comprehensive legal framework adopts a holistic approach to ocean management, one that is sorely needed as climate and polar impacts increase in tandem and stress the limits of applicable MEAs, the ATS, and the Arctic Council. Increased attention to form a convention with such active global participation will also legitimize polar issues as those relevant to all.

As two of the most vulnerable areas on the planet, the polar regions are notably absent as a presence in the UNFCCC negotiations. Although the current efforts at

---

[219] *Id.*

engagement, through communications to the UNFCCC secretariat and side events, have been a welcome start, they are not nearly enough to apply adequate pressure to bear on the process. One entry point would be for either the ATS or Arctic system, or both together, to register with the UNFCCC as an observer organization. Under article 7, paragraph 7 of the UNFCCC, observer organizations, which include representatives of UN secretariat units and bodies and its specialized agencies and related organizations, intergovernmental organizations (IGOs), and nongovernmental organizations (NGOs), can attend sessions of the COP and its subsidiary bodies.[220] However, the main focus of attention and action at these meetings is largely on parties and their positions, with observer organizations generally being allowed to give interventions only at the discretion of the chairs where time allows and at special events that take place on the margins of the meetings.[221]

A better entrée into the negotiation forum would be for the Antarctic and Arctic regimes to develop into one or more negotiating groups. The Convention recognizes that certain groups of developing countries are especially vulnerable to the adverse impacts of climate change, particularly countries with low-lying coastal areas and those prone to desertification and drought.[222] Although those countries that compose the ATS and the Arctic system are not, in large part, developing countries, the Convention ought to recognize a bloc that advocates in the interests of and for the protection of the polar regions, which are sensitive and vulnerable to the adverse impacts of global warming and climate change. The development of such a group would remedy the lack of a voice for the polar regions in the clamor of coalitions that represent, inter alia, small-island developing states, least-developing countries, rainforest nations, mountainous regions, and the African continent. By advocating with, ideally, one voice, the polar bloc could have an active and potentially influential voice in the Convention process.

Few international regimes are ever as complete or effective as observers wish them to be. The Antarctic regime has done an admirable job of overcoming divisive issues that has plagued its sister Arctic regime to develop an adaptable system of protection. The Arctic regime itself has gradually been flexing its political and legal muscles to improve its resiliency and provide further protections. Enhanced communication and collaboration can

---

[220] UNFCCC, *supra* note 159, art. 7, ¶ 6. *See also Parties & Observers*, UNITED NATIONS FRAMEWORK CONVENTION ON CLIMATE CHANGE, http://unfccc.int/parties_and_observers/items/2704.php (last visited Mar. 30, 2014).

[221] Indigenous Arctic groups have long been frustrated by their inability to gain more impactful roles on the UNFCCC decision-making process, particularly since Copenhagen. *See, e.g., Inuit Call to Global Leaders: Act Now on Climate Change in the Arctic*, INUIT CIRCUMPOLAR COUNCIL (Nov. 13, 2009), http://inuit.org/fileadmin/user_upload/File/2009/PR-2009-11-13-call-to-action.pdf; Inuit Circumpolar Council (Canada), Annual Report 2008–2009, at 7 (2009), http://inuitcircumpolar.com/files/uploads/icc-files/0809annualreport_english.pdf.

[222] UNFCCC, *supra* note 159, arts. 4.1(b), 4.1(e), 4.1(f), 4.4, 4.8, 4.9.

only improve matters further. Global cooperation in the face of unprecedented environmental and security challenges remains a sensible path forward.[223]

Conclusion

This chapter advocates an integrated and measured development of the Antarctic ATS during a critical moment in the history of polar regions and international environmental law. The onslaught of climate change impacts globally has highlighted the importance of the adoption, in 2015, of a "protocol, another legal instrument, or an agreed outcome with legal force under the [UNFCCC] applicable to all Parties."[224] While this chapter calls for greater Antarctic, as well as Arctic, participation under the Convention, it does not recommend specific provisions of the new agreement. As high as hopes are for the future climate regime, trade-offs exist in extensive binding details versus a vague but flexible arrangement.

The urgency of climate change and the fragility of the Antarctic continent call for greater integration of these otherwise piecemeal regimes to provide the action and protection necessary to ensure the region's environmental integrity. Polar participation in the UNFCCC can come in the form of greater observer organization engagement, or preferably regional coalition building. Yet, any climate agreement still needs a strong support network of multilateral environmental agreements to cover, supplement, or enhance a core framework convention. Issues such as the determination of EEZs, the designation of polar marine reserves, shipping compliance regimes, and enforcement of the reduction or elimination of the production and use of POPs are likely to be more effectively implemented through specialized instruments that have language linking back to framework instruments.

Antarctica is a critical piece of the climate change puzzle. Impacts to Antarctica will be life-threatening and global, the full extent of which is currently unknown. Improved institutional coherency, enhanced cooperative governance, beginning at least between the two polar regimes, and stronger environmental protections are prudent and far-sighted measures. Preservation of the polar regions, particularly Antarctica, can safeguard the global environment against increasingly destabilizing climate change.

---

[223] Burleson, *supra* note 209, at 22.

[224] Dec. 1/CP.17, Establishment of an Ad Hoc Working Group on the Durban Platform for Enhanced Action, UNFCCC, 10th plenary mtg., FCCC/CP/2011/9.Add.1, ¶ 2 (Dec. 11, 2011).

16 Climate Geoengineering and Dispute Settlement under UNCLOS and the UNFCCC: Stormy Seas Ahead?
Dr. Meinhard Doelle

Introduction

Over the course of the past two decades, our collective understanding of the interactions between climate change and oceans has evolved significantly. There has been a growing understanding that unmitigated climate change results in significant changes to ocean

345

ecosystems. Among the most direct impacts are changes in ocean temperature, ocean currents, and ocean acidification. These changes, in turn, are having a range of secondary impacts on marine ecosystems, including sea-level rise, changes in species populations, ecosystem health, and overall resilience.[1] Our understanding of these impacts has and will continue to evolve as science matures and as our understanding of the scale of these changes improves.

Impacts of climate change on oceans are not limited to the impacts of unmitigated climate change. Efforts to mitigate and adapt to climate change also affect ocean ecosystems. Efforts to produce renewable energy in the marine environment, for example, through offshore wind, wave, and tidal energy projects, all will have some impact on marine ecosystems. More recently, geoengineering has emerged as a possible tool to respond to climate change, but with potentially significant implications for ocean systems.

As concern over our ability to avoid the worst impacts of climate change through traditional mitigation efforts has risen in the past decade, geoengineering has moved rapidly from the periphery into the mainstream. With the ongoing impasse in efforts under the United Nations Framework Convention on Climate Change (UNFCCC)[2] to ensure an adequate global mitigation effort to avoid a runaway climate scenario, some scientists and policymakers are turning to geoengineering as an alternative tool.[3]

For purposes of this chapter, geoengineering is defined as the "intentional large-scale manipulation of the environment."[4] The key aspects of the definition are the intent and the effect of the action: environmental change must be the primary intent of the action, and its effects must be at a continental or global scale.[5] Geoengineering can affect a range of environmental systems for various purposes. The focus in this chapter is on marine-based efforts to alter the climate system to mitigate climate change impacts.

A number of the options currently considered either propose making direct use of oceans to engineer the climate, or are expected to have significant impacts on oceans. Given the current absence of a global consensus on how to best tackle climate change—and the uneven distribution of emissions, mitigation efforts, adaptation capacity, and vulnerability—it is not difficult to anticipate a future where countries faced with the impacts of unmitigated climate change will have divergent views on whether and how to use geoengineering technologies to avoid the worst impacts.

---

[1] IPCC, *2013: Summary for Policymakers, in* CLIMATE CHANGE 2013: THE PHYSICAL SCIENCE BASIS. CONTRIBUTION OF WORKING GROUP I TO THE FIFTH ASSESSMENT REPORT OF THE INTERGOVERNMENTAL PANEL ON CLIMATE CHANGE 6, 9, 22 (Thomas F. Stocker et al. eds., 2013).

[2] United Nations Framework Convention on Climate Change, May 9, 1992, 1771 U.N.T.S. 107 (entered into force Mar. 21, 1994).

[3] *See, e.g.*, IPCC, *supra* note 1, at 27 (referencing geoengineering).

[4] David W. Keith, *Geoengineering the Climate: History and Prospect*, 25 ANN. REV. ENERGY & ENV'T 245, 247 (2000). This is also the definition adopted by the IPCC Expert Meeting on Geoengineering. *See* IPCC, *IPCC Expert Meeting on Geoengineering: Meeting Report* 6 (Ottmar Edenhofer et al. eds., 2011).

[5] Keith, *supra* note 4, at 247.

Geoengineering options, however, come with their own impacts, risks, and uncertainties. These impacts, risks, and uncertainties will likely be viewed differently in different parts of the world. Countries at risk from the impacts of sea-level rise or extreme weather events, for example, after decades of failed attempts to push for adequate mitigation, may at some point feel justified to implement geoengineering options unilaterally, especially if they offer cost-effective ways to prevent impacts that can no longer be avoided through global emission reduction efforts. More generally, some regions will be more vulnerable to climate change, some regions will be more dependent on ocean resources, and some regions will have higher capacity to adapt to climate change. Consequently, the uneven distribution of potential benefits, impacts, risks, and uncertainties can reasonably be expected to lead to disputes over the deployment of geoengineering.

This chapter explores how the dispute settlement procedures under the 1982 Convention on the Law of the Sea (UNCLOS)[6] and the UNFCCC are likely to respond to disputes over ocean-based geoengineering initiatives designed to counter the effects of climate change. This focus is chosen to illustrate the challenge of resolving such disputes, recognizing that there are many other forums that may be utilized to resolve geoengineering disputes. Among these are other multilateral environmental agreements (MEAs), such as the Convention on Biological Diversity,[7] human rights tribunals, and domestic courts.[8]

This chapter addresses the issues surrounding dispute resolution over geoengineering in five steps. First, the promise, impacts, risks, and uncertainties surrounding geoengineering in the oceans are briefly explored. Second, possible violations of substantive provisions of UNCLOS or UNFCCC as a result of unilateral ocean iron fertilization (OIF) effort by member states are identified. Third, an overview of the various dispute settlement procedures under UNCLOS and the UNFCCC is provided. An assessment of key issues, such as the choice of procedure, triggering, and mechanism for resolving disputes over geoengineering, is offered. The chapter concludes with some final thoughts on dispute settlement at the intersection of ocean governance and climate change.

I. Ocean-Based Geoengineering Methods

In a post-Kyoto world of stalled climate negotiations and continuously rising greenhouse gas emissions, geoengineering has attracted the interest of those looking beyond

---

[6] United Nations Convention on the Law of the Sea, Dec. 10, 1982, 1833 U.N.T.S. 3 [hereinafter UNCLOS].

[7] Convention on Biological Diversity, June 5, 1992, 1760 U.N.T.S. 79.

[8] *See* Climate Change Liability: Transnational Law and Practice (Richard Lord et al. eds., 2012) (providing an overview of a range of possible climate-related disputes). Unless otherwise specified, it is assumed for purposes of this chapter that the proponents and opponents of geoengineering projects are states rather than private actors, as the dispute resolution mechanisms considered in this chapter are designed for state actors.

conventional mitigation solutions. Geoengineering can be classified into two basic methods: direct carbon dioxide removal (CDR), and solar radiation management (SRM).[9] CDR refers to mechanisms that remove atmospheric CO_2, and thus address one of the causes of anthropogenic climate change by reducing the greenhouse effect.[10] CDR methods include large-scale enhancements of land-based sinks, weather modification, and biochemical and mechanical schemes intended to increase the oceanic uptake of CO_2.[11] SRM methods aim to mitigate climate change by reducing the amount of solar radiation that the Earth absorbs, by changing the planetary albedo, or reflectivity.[12] One notable advantage of SRM over CDR is that the climate change mitigation effects can be observed much faster for SRM methods.[13] Geoengineering activities can take place on land, in the ocean, in the atmosphere, or in space, though land- and ocean-based methods have been the subject of the most experiments to date. In the following section, SRM and CDR methods of geoengineering that utilize the oceans are briefly described.

A. SRM METHODS

1. Aerosol Marine Cloud Brightening

Injection of aerosols into clouds is an SRM strategy that can be deployed from the oceans. It would involve a fleet of remote-controlled vessels that would spray water droplets into marine clouds with the aim of increasing cloud condensation, and thus raising cloud albedo.[14] Models show that impacts are unlikely to be homogeneous,[15] so it is difficult to predict the efficacy of this strategy. Cost estimates of marine cloud modification by aerosol injection from ships are generally significantly lower than conventional mitigation measures, though estimates are subject to considerable uncertainties.[16] Aerosol marine cloud brightening can cause changes in precipitation and weather patterns, and can have potentially adverse effects on the ozone layer and high-altitude clouds.[17]

---

[9] Catherine Redgwell, *Geoengineering the Climate: Technological Solutions to Mitigation—Failure or Continuing Carbon Addiction*, 2 CARBON & CLIMATE L. REV. 178, 179 (2011).

[10] THE ROYAL SOCIETY, GEOENGINEERING THE CLIMATE; SCIENCE, GOVERNANCE AND UNCERTAINTY 1 (2009).

[11] The IPCC Expert Meeting on Geoengineering notes that not all CDR activities fall within the definition of geoengineering, but they take the view that any could given a large enough scale and intent. *See* Edenhofer, *supra* note 4, at 6.

[12] THE ROYAL SOCIETY, *supra* note 10.

[13] Ken Caldeira et al., *The Science of Geoengineering*, 41 ANN. REV. EARTH & PLANETARY SCI. 231, 250 (2013).

[14] H. Korhonen et al., *Enhancement of Marine Cloud Albedo via Controlled Sea Spray Injections: A Global Model Study of the Influence of Emission Rates, Microphysics and Transport*, 10 ATMOSPHERIC CHEMISTRY & PHYSICS 4133, 4134 (2010) "Albedo" refers to the reflectivity of a surface, measured as a function of the amount of solar irradiation to the amount that is reflected. *See* Gernot Klepper & Wilfried Rickels, *The Real Economics of Climate Engineering*, 2012 ECON. RES. INT'L Article ID 316564 at 3 (2012).

[15] Korhonen et al., *supra* note 14, at 4141.

[16] Klepper & Rickels, *supra* note 14, at 7.

[17] THE ROYAL SOCIETY, *supra* note 10, at 31.

2. Ocean Surface Albedo Modification

This SRM method involves altering the reflectivity of the surface of the ocean. Russel Seitz, for example, describes a technology where instead of injecting aerosols into clouds, tiny bubbles of air, or hydrosols, are injected into the surface of the water.[18] The brightened surface has higher albedo, which results in lower heat absorption. Hydrosols may be preferable to aerosols, because they have a shorter life cycle, and their effect can be more tailored if negative ecological impacts are observed.[19] Ships equipped with the technology to disperse hydrosols already exist, and the application of hydrosols can be more localized compared to cloud-brightening aerosols.[20] Although this method does not pose as much risk to the global weather patterns, it could alter ocean convection patterns, increase ocean acidification, and affect marine life through pollution and changing light conditions.[21]

B. CDR METHODS

1. Ocean-Based Weathering

This CDR method works by increasing the ocean's alkalinity, either by adding strong bases into the water, or through an electrochemical reaction.[22] As higher uptake of atmospheric CO_2 by the oceans can lead to ocean acidification, this method would counter that process, and encourage further absorption of CO_2. Some of the drawbacks include the safety concerns with transporting the chemicals necessary for dissolution, or the energy necessary to complete the electrochemical reaction.[23] In addition, large areas of ocean would be involved in deploying this technology, and substantial land areas affected by the mining of the resources needed.[24] As an alternative, the chemical reaction can take place at a power plant where CO_2 is being released, and the solution that would be created by that process would then be released to the oceans.[25]

---

[18] Russel Seitz, *Bright Water: Hydrosols, Water Conservation and Climate Change*, 105 CLIMATIC CHANGE 365, 366 (2011).

[19] *Id.* at 376.

[20] *Id.* at 375–76.

[21] Alan Roboc, *Bubble, Bubble, Toil and Trouble: An Editorial Comment*, 105 CLIMATIC CHANGE 383, 383–84 (2011).

[22] Kurt Zenz House et al., *Electrochemical Acceleration of Chemical Weathering for Carbon Capture and Sequestration*, 1 ENERGY PROCEDIA 4953, 4954, 4958 (2009).

[23] *Id.*

[24] Caldeira et al., *supra* note 13, at 249.

[25] *Id.* at 247.

2. Physical Pump

Another CDR technology that can use the oceans is a physical pump, consisting of large vertical pipes that will enhance the downwelling and upwelling effects within the ocean. The idea is that increasing the circulation of the water will increase CO_2 sequestration rates.[26] Despite the natural solubility pump contributing more to the deep ocean CO_2 deposits than the biological pump, current estimates of the efficacy of this CDR method show that a displacement of 1 million m^3/s would result in only a sequestration of 0.01 to 0.02 GtC/year.[27] Solubility pump projects carry the risk of transporting dissolved CO_2 from the deep ocean to the surface, and releasing it into the atmosphere.[28]

3. Biological Pump: Ocean Iron Fertilization (OIF)

Phytoplankton close to the ocean surface draws CO_2 from the atmosphere by performing photosynthesis and turning CO_2 into organic carbon.[29] OIF works as a CDR mechanism by increasing the productivity of the plankton, and thus drawing down CO_2 from the atmosphere.[30] The most efficient location for OIF is in the Southern Ocean, an area with high-nutrient low-chlorophyll (HNLC) waters, where the main factor limiting CO_2 absorption is iron.[31] Once iron is added, plankton growth is encouraged, and more photosynthesis occurs. The definition of OIF under the London Convention and the London Protocol is "any activity undertaken by humans with the intention of stimulating primary productivity in the oceans."[32] The economic appeal of OIF is potentially strong: the estimated cost, again subject to high uncertainties, is significantly lower than conventional mitigation options.[33]

OIF is perhaps the most piloted and researched ocean-based method. Between 1993 and 2009, thirteen in situ ocean fertilization experiments were conducted. A number of factors that may limit OIF's efficacy were discovered.[34] Despite the extensive research that has been conducted, the potential environmental effects of OIF are not well known. Some of the possible negative effects include increased ocean acidification and algal

---

[26] THE ROYAL SOCIETY, *supra* note 10, at 19.

[27] *Id.*

[28] Rosemary Rayfuse & Robin Warner, *Climate Change Mitigation Activities in the Ocean: Turning up the Regulatory Heat, in* CLIMATE CHANGE AND THE OCEANS: GAUGING THE LEGAL AND POLICY CURRENTS IN THE ASIA PACIFIC AND BEYOND 234, 239 (Robin Warner & Clive Shofield et al. eds., 2012).

[29] Caldeira et al., *supra* note 13, at 247.

[30] THE ROYAL SOCIETY, *supra* note 10, at 17.

[31] Randall S. Abate & Andrew B. Greenlee, *Sowing Seeds Uncertain: Ocean Iron Fertilization, Climate Change, and the International Environmental Law Framework*, 27 PACE ENVTL. L. REV. 555, 564 (2010).

[32] Int'l Mar. Org., *Resolution on the Regulation of Ocean Fertilization*, Res. LC-LP.1 (Oct. 31, 2008).

[33] Klepper & Rickels, *supra* note 14, at 6.

[34] Till Markus & Harald Ginzky, *Regulating Climate Engineering: Paradigmatic Aspects of the Regulation of Ocean Fertilization*, CARBON & CLIMATE L. REV. 477, 478 (2011).

blooms, leading to eutrophication and anoxia.[35] Algal blooms can travel, and thus cause an impact on a much larger area of the ocean than what was originally fertilized. The increase in phytoplankton resulting from OIF comes at the base of the food chain.[36] There is a potential positive aspect associated with the growth of algae: an OIF technique was actually patented as a way of increasing fish stocks.[37] It is unclear, however, how the increase in productivity will affect individual species and ecosystems.

C. CONCERNS REGARDING GEOENGINEERING METHODS

In addition to specific concerns associated with each of the individual SRM and CDR methods described above, there are general concerns with the use of geoengineering to mitigate climate change. First, given the current state of knowledge, which is largely theoretical, it is difficult to determine whether the negative impacts of some geoengineering projects would outweigh the promised results, and whether it would lead to yet unknown environmental and social damage.[38]

Second, successfully deploying geoengineering strategies risks reducing the incentive to lower greenhouse gas emissions, and thus cause a moral hazard by becoming a substitute to more direct action on climate change.[39] Even the serious consideration of geoengineering may result in a reduction of effort to pursue more traditional climate mitigation solutions by governments and private investors alike. This moral hazard is exacerbated by the fact that some geoengineering proposals do not mitigate all negative impacts of climate change; for example, albedo modification still leaves the oceans open to acidification from atmospheric CO_2. Geoengineering could leave important effects of the increase in greenhouse gas concentrations unmitigated, but could nevertheless gain traction with those reluctant to change because it does not challenge the status quo of high carbon consumption.[40]

Finally, and perhaps most pertinent to this chapter, the explicit purpose of geoengineering is to cause global effects on the climate system, whereas most ocean-based SRM and CDR

---

[35] Karen N. Scott, *International Law in the Anthropocene: Responding to the Geoengineering Challenge*, 34 MICH. J. INT'L L. 309, 324 (2013).

[36] Terry Barker et al., *Mitigation from a Cross-Sectoral Perspective, in* CLIMATE CHANGE 2007: MITIGATION. CONTRIBUTION OF WORKING GROUP III TO THE FOURTH ASSESSMENT REPORT OF THE INTER-GOVERNMENTAL PANEL ON CLIMATE CHANGE 619, 625 (B. Metz et al. eds., 2007).

[37] Method of Increasing Seafood Production in the Barren Ocean with Fertilizer Comprising Chelated Iron, U.S. Patent No. 6,408,792 (filed Oct. 19, 2001). In 2012, a Canadian First Nation carried out an OIF experiment in the Pacific Ocean for the expressed purpose of capturing carbon and restoring salmon populations. *See* Jim Lee, *The Haida Salmon Restoration Project: Dumping Iron in the Ocean to Save Fish, Capture Carbon,* CV NEWS (Oct. 10, 2013), http://climateviewer.com.

[38] Scott, *supra* note 35, at 321.

[39] Jesse Reynolds, *The Regulation of Climate Engineering*, 3 LAW, INNOVATION & TECH. 113, 123 (2011).

[40] John Virgoe, *International Governance of a Possible Geoengineering Intervention to Combat Climate Change*, 95 CLIMATIC CHANGE 103, 105 (2009).

methods can be carried out unilaterally. This means proponents may be faced with international conflict and questions about the legitimacy of their efforts.[41] In the final analysis, it is the cost and the ability to act unilaterally that has the greatest potential to make geoengineering attractive to states most vulnerable to unmitigated climate change who may grow increasingly frustrated by the global stalemate on conventional mitigation, adaptation, and loss and damage, and the increasing evidence of dramatic impacts.

II. Possible Geoengineering Disputes under the UNFCCC

Identifying specific substantive disputes related to geoengineering under the UNFCCC regime is a particular challenge given the state of the UNFCCC regime. Some of the key elements of the current regime, particularly those contained in the Kyoto Protocol,[42] are not likely to survive past 2020. Many new elements are currently under active negotiation. Elements of the framework convention itself could be amended as a result of the negotiations currently underway. It is far from clear whether the issue of geoengineering will be specifically addressed as part of the 2015 agreement, or whether agreement will be reached at all.[43] As a result of these uncertainties, possible disputes under the UNFCCC related to geoengineering are considered at a fairly high level.

Disputes under the UNFCCC with respect to geoengineering would likely fall into two broad categories. One would explore whether geoengineering generally or a specific method is prohibited under the UNFCCC. There is little basis for such positions under the UNFCCC as it stands as of this writing, but it is conceivable that the 2015 agreement could address the appropriateness of geoengineering as a way to achieve the objectives of the UNFCCC.

The second category would consider whether geoengineering generally or specific methods are recognized, endorsed, or otherwise sanctioned under the UNFCCC in some form. Framed most broadly, disputes could focus on whether geoengineering efforts are considered to be efforts consistent with the ultimate objective of the UNFCCC in article 2. More specifically, they could entail questions about whether efforts to pursue geoengineering would count toward a party's mitigation or adaptation efforts, finance obligations, or commitments regarding the development and dissemination of climate technologies. An emerging issue might include whether impacts from geoengineering could be the basis for assistance under the emerging loss and damage mechanism.[44]

---

[41] Markus & Ginzky, *supra* note 34, at 483.

[42] Kyoto Protocol to the United Nations Framework Convention on Climate Change, Dec. 11, 1997, 2303 U.N.T.S. 148 (entered into force Feb. 16, 2005).

[43] For an overview of the state of the negotiations, see "Warsaw Highlights: Monday 11 November 2013," *Earth Negotiation Bulletin* (12 November 2013) 12(584), International Institute for Sustainable Development online: IISD http://www.iisd.ca/climate/cop19/enb/.

[44] The current state of the mechanism is reflected in decisions made in Warsaw in November 2013. *See* Decision 2/CP.19, Warsaw International Mechanism for Loss and Damage Associated with Climate Change

In the absence of more specific agreement on the role of geoengineering, there are some general provisions in the UNFCCC that may offer some basis for resolving these disputes. The UNFCCC preamble, for example, draws on a number of principles from the 1972 Stockholm Declaration.[45] Some of the provisions that may be relevant to a dispute include Principles 2, 3, 6, 7, and 21. Of these, Principle 21, a codification of the customary international law principle against transboundary harm, is the one specifically referenced in the preamble, so it is most likely to be given weight in case of a dispute under the UNFCCC.

Article 2 also has the potential to be relevant in disputes over geoengineering: the ultimate objective of the convention is to "achieve, in accordance with the relevant provisions of the Convention, the stabilization of greenhouse gas concentrations in the atmosphere at a level that would prevent dangerous anthropogenic interference with the climate system."[46] With regard to SRM methods, this provision makes it clear that the UNFCCC priorities lie in addressing the root causes of climate change, namely concentrations of atmospheric CO_2, so it seems unlikely that proponents of SRM geoengineering will be able to argue that their purpose is to fulfil the ultimate objective of the Convention.

Article 3.3 potentially raises complex questions about the application of precaution to geoengineering.[47] Assuming that uncertainty over the impacts of geoengineering continues, it seems clear that as long as conventional mitigation measures still have a reasonable chance to succeed, precaution would weigh against implementing geoengineering methods. However, if geoengineering methods are pursued at a time when conventional mitigation is unlikely to prevent runaway climate change, it will be much more debatable whether a precautionary approach would advocate for or against the use of geoengineering. Furthermore, differences between SRM and CDR methods would suggest some significant differences in the application of precaution, most notably the fact that CDR methods may address ocean acidification and other effects of greenhouse gas emissions while SRM methods do not.

Finally, article 4.1(b) and (d) are likely to be relevant to disputes over the use of geoengineering as mitigation measures. Subsection (b) provides a general mandate that "[p]arties shall formulate and implement programmes containing measures to mitigate climate change by addressing anthropogenic emissions by sources and removals by sinks of all greenhouse gases."[48] Subsection (d) more specifically commits parties to "promote sustainable management, and promote and cooperate in the conservation and

---

Impacts, Jan. 31, 2014, *Report of the Conference of the Parties on Its Nineteenth Session, Held in Warsaw from 11 to 23 November 2013*, U.N. Doc. FCCC/CP/2013/10/Add.1 (2014).

[45] United Nations Conference on the Human Environment, Stockholm, Sweden, June 16, 1972, *Declaration of the United Nations Conference on the Human Environment*, U.N. Doc. A/CONF.48/14/Rev.1 (1973).

[46] United Nations Framework Convention on Climate Change, art. 2.

[47] *Id.* art. 3.

[48] *Id.* art. 4.1(b).

enhancement, as appropriate, of sinks and reservoirs…including…oceans as well as other terrestrial, coastal and marine ecosystems."[49]

Oceans are specifically identified as a significant sink for greenhouse gases. These provisions could therefore be used by a party to seek to justify geoengineering projects as fulfilling these commitments under the Convention. For developed country parties, this commitment is further reiterated in article 4.2(a), which states that they shall develop national measures to mitigate climate change by protecting and enhancing greenhouse gas sinks and reservoirs. Similarly to article 4.1(b), the provision does not mandate a specific activity.

On balance, it would seem difficult to use UNFCCC articles 3.3, 4.1(b), and 4.1(d) as persuasive justifications for deploying geoengineering projects, because the UNFCCC does not mandate the impugned action specifically. According to article 33.3(b) of the Vienna Convention on the Law of Treaties, in interpreting a treaty, "any subsequent practice in the application of the treaty which establishes the agreement of the parties regarding its interpretation" shall be taken into account.[50] This would imply that if parties have not generally accepted the meaning of the UNFCCC to be that of *compelling* specific action, they cannot use it as a defense. To date, the more reasonable interpretation of the UNFCCC would seem to be that it is not compelling specific actions. Furthermore, paragraph (c) states that one must also consider "any relevant rules of international law applicable in the relations between the parties," meaning the position could not be supported without discharging the state's responsibility pursuant to general principles of international environmental law, notably the prevention of transboundary harm.[51]

The role of geoengineering as an appropriate mitigation strategy under the UNFCCC has been brought to the attention of UNFCCC negotiators as a result of the release of the IPCC Fifth Assessment report.[52] To date, however, there has been no official endorsement by the IPCC, which defines mitigation as "actions that reduce net carbon emission and limit long-term climate change."[53] In its Fourth Assessment Report in 2007, geoengineering is referred to as "speculative."[54] It is not examined thoroughly, due to a lack of studies showing reliable results.[55]

In 2011, the Intergovernmental Panel on Climate Change (IPCC) Expert Meeting on geoengineering concluded that there could be some overlap between geoengineering and

---

[49] *Id.* art. 4.1(d).

[50] Vienna Convention on the Law of Treaties, art. 31.3(b), May 23, 1969, 1155 U.N.T.S. 331.

[51] *Id.*

[52] IPCC, *supra* note 1. *See also* Catherine Redgwell, *Geoengineering the Climate: Technological Solutions to Mitigation—Failure or Continuing Carbon Addiction*, 2 CARBON & CLIMATE L. REV. 178, 180 (2011).

[53] Brian Fisher et al., *Issues Related to Mitigation in the Long-Term Context, in* CLIMATE CHANGE 2007: MITIGATION. CONTRIBUTION OF WORKING GROUP III TO THE FOURTH ASSESSMENT REPORT OF THE INTER-GOVERNMENTAL PANEL ON CLIMATE CHANGE 169, 225 (B. Metz et al. eds., 2007).

[54] Barker et al., *supra* note 36, at 624.

[55] This is consistent with the IPCC's overall mandate, which is to assess the existing research literature, not to carry out its own research. *Id.*

mitigation, but did not discuss the possibility of updating the definition of mitigation to include geoengineering.[56] The report does, however, refer to CDR geoengineering methods as addressing the same point of the carbon cycle as some accepted mitigation techniques.[57]

The Summary for Policy Makers released as part of the Fifth Assessment Report of the IPCC only briefly mentions geoengineering. It points out, for example, that many impacts of climate change are already irreversible unless greenhouse gases are actively removed from the atmosphere. The IPCC refrains from making a comprehensive quantitative assessment of geoengineering, pointing again to the lack of sufficient evidence. It does, however, highlight some of the limitations of CDR methods, and states that SRM methods "have the potential to substantially offset a global temperature rise," but could give rise to further environmental concerns.[58]

III. Dispute Settlement under the UNFCCC

MEAs have generally distinguished between noncompliance procedures (NCP) and dispute settlement procedures (DSP). NCPs focus on questions of a party's compliance with its treaty commitments and obligations, whereas DSPs are designed more broadly to deal with disputes related to or arising out of a treaty. The UNFCCC makes provision for both, though the NCP has to date not been set up, and neither process has been used.

The NCP in the form of a multilateral consultative process, contemplated under article 13 of the Convention, is not required. The Conference of the Parties (COP) is required to consider establishing such a process to be available for parties to resolve questions regarding the implementation of the Convention.[59] After some effort to develop this multilateral consultative process during the early COPs, this effort has been abandoned for the time being.

Article 14 of the UNFCCC establishes the more traditional DSP.[60] Although it has not been used to date, its essential elements are set out in article 14 of the Convention with the following three defining features. First, the process contemplates only disputes among parties.[61] Second, parties have some choice over the process, with compulsory conciliation serving as the default if parties have not either selected the same compulsory process or otherwise agreed on a process for resolving their dispute.[62] Third, the outcome of the compulsory conciliation process is non-binding.[63]

---

[56] Edenhofer et al., *supra* note 4, at 2.

[57] *Id.* at 3.

[58] IPCC, *supra* note 1, at 27.

[59] United Nations Framework Convention on Climate Change, art. 13.

[60] *Id.* art. 14.

[61] *Id.* art. 14.1.

[62] *Id.* art. 14.5.

[63] *Id.* art. 14.6.

Process options other than the default conciliation process include the International Court of Justice (ICJ) and arbitration.[64] Declarations regarding choice of forum can be made under article 14.[65] The Netherlands have accepted both the ICJ and arbitration as compulsory with regards to countries that have accepted one or both of these forums, and the Solomon Islands have accepted arbitration as compulsory.[66] As a result, a dispute under the UNFCCC DSP is most likely to proceed through conciliation, assuming disputing parties do not otherwise agree after the dispute has been formally registered.

The dispute settlement mechanism under article 14 of the UNFCCC is open to parties to the Convention, which include states and regional economic integration organizations (the European Union). Private actors are not parties to the Convention, and would therefore not be able to initiate a DSP. If a state party wanted to pursue the settlement of a dispute relating to a geoengineering project, the dispute would have to be brought against a state party with some responsibility for the project, even if a privately owned corporation executed it.

UNFCCC does not exclude other avenues for settling disputes; it actually provides for this possibility under article 14.1.[67] If, however, the dispute is not settled twelve months after the notification of the existence of a dispute, it shall be submitted to conciliation.[68] An exception arises where both parties have made [the same] default selection under article 14.2.[69] It is unlikely that this would arise under current conditions, given the small number of parties who have made a selection, so an unresolved dispute is most likely to go to conciliation after twelve months.

Article 14 does contemplate guidance from the COP on the design of arbitration and conciliation procedures,[70] though no such procedures have been finalized to date. The focus of the COP instead has shifted to the Kyoto Protocol. The Protocol adopted the DSP of the UNFCCC, but also developed a detailed NCP in the form of a compliance system to deal with the full range of commitments and obligations parties accepted under the Protocol, ranging from accounting and reporting on emissions and credits to meeting specific emission reduction targets.

The Kyoto compliance system consists of a facilitative branch responsible for a broad range of party commitments, and an enforcement branch with a mandate to impose prescribed consequences for breaches of obligations dealing with emission reduction targets and accounting of emissions and credits. Although the DSP and the facilitative branch of the Kyoto compliance system have been essentially inactive, the enforcement branch

---

[64] *Id.* art. 14.2.

[65] *Id.*

[66] United Nations Framework Convention on Climate Change, *Declarations by Parties*, Online: UNFCCC, https://unfccc.int (last visited July 16, 2014).

[67] United Nations Framework Convention on Climate Change, art. 14.1.

[68] *Id.* art. 14.5.

[69] *Id.*

[70] *Id.* art. 14.6.

of the Kyoto compliance system has rendered a number of decisions, and is likely to continue to be active for a few more years. The rulings of the enforcement branch could potentially serve as a resource to other dispute settlement processes.[71] Although an assessment of the Kyoto compliance mechanism is beyond the scope of this chapter, its future is currently very much in doubt as the current negotiations are based on an expectation that the Kyoto Protocol itself will not continue past its second commitment period.[72]

Beyond these noncompliance and dispute settlement procedures under the UNFCCC and the Kyoto Protocol, the COP itself has played a significant role in dealing with disputes that have arisen under the UNFCCC. Among such disputes that have come before the COP have been appeals of decisions of the Kyoto compliance committee[73] and complaints about decisions of other institutions created within the UNFCCC, such as the Clean Development Mechanism.[74] As the number of institutions under the UNFCCC grows, so will the pressure to develop formal dispute resolution mechanisms to respond to complaints from parties and private actors about the manner in which these institutions are carrying out their mandates.

There is only limited guidance on how disagreements over the appropriate forum for resolving disputes might be resolved. The Kyoto compliance system is clear on the limits of its mandate, as is the appeal procedure from the Kyoto compliance system to the COP. This still leaves ample room for disagreements among parties as to which forum would be most appropriate to resolve a given dispute. Furthermore, none of the current mechanisms is accessible to nonparties, though negotiations are underway on a possible appeal mechanism for decisions of the CDM executive board by nonparties affected by a decision.[75]

It is conceivable that a dispute over geoengineering under the UNFCCC would turn into a debate over the seriousness of environmental impacts, risks, and uncertainties of the geoengineering technology as compared to the impacts, risks, and uncertainties of unmitigated climate change, with the precautionary principle at the center of the debate. At the heart of such a dispute would be the magnitude of the harm. Which set of negative effects will be more serious: the loss of fish stocks and damage to the marine

---

[71] *See* Ruth MacKenzie, *The Role of Dispute Settlement in the Climate Regime, in* Promoting Compliance in an Evolving Climate Change Regime 403 (Jutta Brunnee et al. eds., 2012).

[72] *See* Meinhard Doelle, *Experience with the Kyoto Compliance System, in* Promoting Compliance in an Evolving Climate Change Regime (Jutta Brunnee et al. eds., 2012) (providing an overview of the Kyoto compliance system).

[73] *Id.*; see discussion of the case against Croatia at 115.

[74] International Institute for Sustainable Development, *Warsaw Highlights: Monday 11 November 2013*, Earth Negotiation Bulletin (12 November 2013) 12(584), *available at* http://www.iisd.ca/climate/cop19/enb/.

[75] International Institute for Sustainable Development, *Summary of the Warsaw Climate Change Conference: 11–23 November 2013*, Earth Negotiation Bulletin (26 November 2013) 12(594), *available at* http://www.iisd.ca/climate/cop19/enb/.

ecosystem due to anoxia, for example, or the increase in the effects of climate change as a result of a decision not to deploy geoengineering?

In addition to comparing the magnitude of harm, the resolution of a dispute over geoengineering under the UNFCCC would likely also turn on the nature of the harm. For example, article 3.3 of the UNFCCC seems to place climate change "above" other environmental impacts in terms of the application of the precautionary principle.[76] The argument could be centered on the effectiveness of the geoengineering technology, the question of how much CO_2 it could sequester, and what climate impacts these efforts could avoid. Underlying all these issues would be the risk and uncertainties, which are considerable both with respect to the impacts of geoengineering, and the impacts of unmitigated climate change. As discussed in the following sections, a dispute under UNCLOS may have a different focus, as it may be more squarely focused on the impacts on marine ecosystems.

IV. Possible Geoengineering Disputes under UNCLOS

Compared to the UNFCCC, relevant provisions under UNCLOS are easily identified, have been in place for decades, and are not subject to active negotiations. This allows for a more concrete assessment of how the provisions of UNCLOS may respond to geoengineering disputes. The most relevant group of obligations under UNCLOS that are likely to be relevant are provisions in part XII dealing with the protection of the marine environment, particularly articles 192, 194, 195, and 210.[77]

UNCLOS part XII deals generally with state obligations with respect to the marine environment. As early as 1991, academics characterized part XII as constitutional in character, reflecting in part existing custom, but at the same time providing the first comprehensive statement on the protection of the marine environment in international law.[78]

The starting point for part XII is a general obligation under article 192 to "protect and preserve the marine environment,"[79] balanced with a reaffirmation of the right of states to exploit their natural resources "in accordance with their duty to protect and preserve the marine environment."[80] Under this part of the Convention, states are obligated to take all measures consistent with the Convention necessary "to prevent,

---

[76] United Nations Framework Convention on Climate Change, art. 3.3.

[77] UNCLOS, *supra* note 6, arts. 192, 194, 195, 210.

[78] *See* Moira L. McConnell et al., *The Modern Law of the Sea: Framework for the Protection and Preservation of the Marine Environment?*, 23 CASE W. RES. J. INT'L L. 83, 84 (1991). *See also* Jonathan L. Hafetz, *Fostering Protection of the Marine Environment and Economic Development: Article 121(3) of the Third Law of the Sea Convention*, 15 AM. U. INT'L L. REV. 583, 597 (2000).

[79] *See* UNCLOS, art. 192. This article is considered to reflect customary international law, and as such is binding on all states, not only member states. *See* Hafetz, *supra* note 78, at 598.

[80] UNCLOS, art. 193. This article is also considered to reflect customary international law. *See* Hafetz, *supra* note 78, at 598.

reduce and control pollution of the marine environment *from any source*, using the best practical means."[81] Article 194 is central to any analysis of state obligations regarding geoengineering. It provides the foundation for the following specific obligations that provide further guidance on what a state may be expected to do to protect and preserve the marine environment:

- an obligation for States to act individually or jointly as appropriate;[82]
- an obligation to take all measures necessary to prevent, reduce, and control pollution of the marine environment;[83]
- an obligation for States to use best practical means at their disposal;[84]
- an obligation for States to act in accordance with their capabilities;[85]
- an obligation to endeavour to harmonize policies with other States;[86]
- an obligation for States to control activities under their control or jurisdiction so as to not cause damage by pollution to other States and their environment;[87]
- an obligation to prevent pollution from spreading to areas outside of a State's jurisdiction of control;[88] and
- a specific obligation for the preservation and projection or rare or fragile ecosystems, and the habitat of species at risk.[89]

Article 195 directs states on measures to prevent, reduce, and control pollution of the marine environment.[90] It does so by obliging states to prevent the transfer of harm from one type or area to another. Although the exact scope of this provision is not clear, it does, at a minimum, introduce the concept that measures must be designed so as to not result in other environmental damage, an issue that has been the subject of considerable controversy in the context of geoengineering. In so doing, UNCLOS may have been ahead of its time, providing a simple, yet potentially very effective tool to require states to take a holistic and integrated approach to addressing environmental issues.[91]

---

[81] UNCLOS, art. 194.

[82] *Id.* arts. 197, 207(4), and 212(3).

[83] The definition of "pollution" includes the addition of energy to the marine environment; *see id.* art. 1.

[84] *Id.* art. 194.

[85] *Id.*

[86] *Id.*

[87] *Id.* art. 194(2).

[88] *Id.*

[89] *Id.* art. 194(1), (2), and (5).

[90] *Id.* art 195.

[91] *See* Jonathan I. Charney, *Implementing the United Nations Convention on the Law of the Sea: Impact of the Law of the Sea Convention on the Marine Environment*, 7 GEO. INT'L ENVTL. L. REV. 731, 732 (1995). *See also* Jonathan I. Charney, *The Marine Environment and the 1982 United Nations Convention on the Law of the Sea*, 28 INT'L LAW. 879 (1994).

Article 210 calls on states to adopt regulations "to prevent, reduce and control pollution of the marine environment by dumping."[92] This provision is generally interpreted as giving power to the 1972 London Convention, which provides for detailed international rules regulating dumping.[93] Breaching the general prohibition on OIF under the London Convention could be argued as a breach of UNCLOS pursuant to article 210.[94] This could apply to other geoengineering methods that include actions that constitute "dumping." The importance of this link is accentuated by the recent negotiation of an amendment to the 1996 Protocol to the London Convention.[95] The exact relationship between the London ocean dumping regime and UNCLOS is far from clear. Uncertainties include whether the placement of iron constitutes dumping for purposes of article 210, and whether the reference to the London Convention includes the 1996 Protocol and its 2013 amendments, which provide for a permitting process for the placement of iron for scientific purposes.[96]

Under certain circumstances, UNCLOS could be used as a possible justification for geoengineering. A party might make the case that the threat of climate change to ocean pH in the form of ocean acidification is more severe than the environmental harm of the geoengineering project. As there is a strong link between atmospheric CO_2 and ocean acidification, sequestering CO_2 might be argued to fulfill a state's responsibility under UNCLOS article 192 or 194(1).[97] This justification would, however, not be available for SRM methods. It is also less likely to be successful for OIF given the breadth of evidence regarding its potential negative environmental impacts.

V. Dispute Settlement under UNCLOS

The UNCLOS dispute settlement procedures set out in part XV of UNCLOS have been described as rivaling the process set up under the World Trade Organization in terms of potential for resolving party-to-party disputes and the power conferred on dispute resolution tribunals,[98] although they are limited in scope to defined subject matters set out in

---

[92] UNCLOS, art. 210.

[93] Scott, *supra* note 35, at 339.

[94] Abate & Greenlee, *supra* note 31 (providing an overview of ocean iron fertilization under UNCLOS).

[95] As of this writing, the text of the amendments to the 1996 Protocol was not available. For the announcement of the amendment, see http://www.imo.org/MediaCentre/PressBriefings/Pages/45-marine-geoengieneering.aspx (last visited July 16, 2014).

[96] *Id.*

[97] UNCLOS, art. 192, 192(1).

[98] *See* Hafetz, *supra* note 78, at 597, 632. *See also* DUNCAN BRACK, INTERNATIONAL ENVIRONMENTAL DISPUTES 11 (Royal Institute of Int'l Affairs 2001); Brian K. Myers, *Trade Measures and the Environment: Can the WTO and UNCLOS Be Reconciled*, 23 UCLA J. ENVT'L. L. & POL'Y 37 (2005).

UNCLOS.[99] The process is set out in three sections of part XV. The first section establishes the rules under which the parties to a dispute are to agree on a dispute settlement tool.[100] The second section sets rules for initiating a dispute settlement process in the absence of agreement.[101] The third section provides some limited exceptions to the binding dispute settlement process.[102] Two features of the UNCLOS process that have been particularly noted by commentators are the ability to initiate the process without having to agree on a procedure, on a case-by-case basis, and the binding nature of the outcomes.[103]

This section of the chapter considers how the dispute settlement process under UNCLOS would respond to a claim related to a state's use of marine-based geoengineering to reduce the impacts of climate change. It focuses on aspects of the UNCLOS dispute settlement process that are likely to be relevant to geoengineering.

As with many international dispute settlement procedures, the overriding obligation on parties is to resolve disputes through peaceful means.[104] Parties are encouraged to seek agreement on how to resolve disputes. The binding settlement process set out in part XV of UNCLOS is intended as a safeguard for cases where disputes cannot be resolved by parties on their own, and where they are unable to agree on a process for resolving the dispute peacefully.[105] Consensus on how to resolve a dispute will often take the form of a specific agreement reached at some point after the dispute arises. Agreement can also arise from state obligations enshrined in another treaty to which the disputing countries are parties, if that treaty sets out a process for resolving disputes under UNCLOS.[106] Whether the UNCLOS dispute settlement process can be initiated, therefore, depends in general terms on whether a settlement is reached through an alternate process agreed to by the parties, and whether the alternate process excludes the application of the UNCLOS dispute settlement process.[107]

Subject to these conditions, any party to UNCLOS can initiate a binding dispute settlement process against another party to the Convention.[108] The choice of procedure

---

[99] *See* Yuval Shany, The Competing Jurisdiction of International Courts and Tribunals 5 (2003). *See also* Natalie Klein, The Role of Dispute Settlement in the UN Convention on the Law of the Sea 29–124 (2005).

[100] *See* UNCLOS, arts. 279–285.

[101] *Id.* arts. 286–296.

[102] *Id.* arts. 297–299.

[103] *See, e.g.*, Barbara Kwiatkowska, *The Australia and New Zealand v. Japan Southern Bluefin Tuna (Jurisdiction and Admissibility) Award of the First Law of the Sea Convention Annex VII Arbitral Tribunal*, 16 Int'l J. Mar. & Coastal L. 239 (2001).

[104] *See* UNCLOS, art. 280.

[105] *Id.* arts. 279–281.

[106] *Id.* art. 288(2). For a treaty that specifically relies on the UNCLOS binding dispute resolution process, see 1995 U.N. Fish Stock Agreement, art. 30, Aug. 4, 1995, 34 I.L.M. 1542.

[107] UNCLOS, art. 281(1). This provision was at the heart of the recent Bluefin Tuna Arbitral Tribunal ruling discussed *infra*.

[108] *Id.* art. 286.

is determined based on a number of factors, including any declarations filed by the parties under article 287(1) on which of the following procedures are acceptable to it:

- the International Tribunal for the Law of the Sea (ITLOS) process under Annex VI;[109]
- the International Court of Justice (ICJ);[110]
- an arbitral tribunal established under UNCLOS, Annex VII;[111] or
- a special arbitral tribunal established under UNCLOS Annex VIII.[112]

In the absence of a declaration, a party is deemed to have selected the arbitral tribunal procedure under Annex VII.[113] In cases where two parties to a dispute have not selected a common procedure in their respective declarations, the arbitral tribunal procedure under Annex VII will likewise be the applicable procedure. Regardless of the choice of procedure, the tribunal chosen has general jurisdiction concerning the interpretation and application of UNCLOS, and has the authority to determine its own jurisdiction to hear a particular dispute.[114] In addition to UNCLOS, a tribunal selected to resolve a dispute under these provisions is authorized to consider other rules of international law to the extent that they are not incompatible with the rules set out in UNCLOS.[115] A tribunal's findings are final and binding on the parties to the dispute, but not binding on other parties to UNCLOS, and, therefore, at least in theory, are not precedent-setting for purposes of interpreting the provisions of UNCLOS.[116]

While there are a number of differences among the four procedures set out in article 287, the most important factor for parties is likely to be the level of control over the selection of members of a tribunal on the one hand, and the level of expertise of those members on the other hand. ITLOS and the ICJ have the advantage of being permanent tribunals and as such are more likely to make predictable rulings, and rulings that take into account the implications of specific rulings for the future of dispute settlement

---

[109] For an overview of the ITLOS process and its rulings to date, see Alfred Rest, *Enhanced Implementation of International Environmental Treaties by Judiciary—Access to Justice in International Environmental Law for Individuals and NGOs: Efficacious Enforcement by the Permanent Court of Arbitration*, 1 MACQUARIE J. INT'L & COMP. ENVTL. L. 1, 13 (2004). For a survey of recent rulings, *see also* Robin Churchill, *The International Tribunal for the Law of the Sea: Survey for 2002*, 18 INT'L J. MAR. & COASTAL L. 447(2003).

[110] For a discussion of the potential for conflict between the UNCLOS dispute settlement process and the ICJ, see SHANY, *supra* note 99, at 32–33.

[111] *See* UNCLOS, art. 287(1)(c).

[112] *Id.* art. 287(1)(d).

[113] *Id.* Articles 297 to 299 provide opportunities to further limit the options parties have with respect to binding dispute settlement procedures. These provisions include a number of limitations that are fairly specific and restricted in scope. They do not appear to apply to obligations and responsibilities in UNCLOS that could be relevant to a dispute over climate change mitigation, and are therefore not considered further here.

[114] *Id.* art. 288.

[115] *Id.* art. 293(1).

[116] *Id.* art. 296.

under UNCLOS. The arbitration process under Annex VII has the advantage of providing a party with more control over the membership of the specific tribunal hearing a particular dispute. In addition, the Annex VIII special arbitration tribunal process has the advantage of the flexibility to be able to ensure special expertise in the subject matter under dispute.[117]

Given the consistency in terms of jurisdiction, scope, and outcome of these four processes, a detailed comparison of the four options is not necessary for purposes of determining whether a dispute over the deployment of geoengineering could be brought under UNCLOS. More important for purposes of this analysis of whether a party can bring a successful claim under UNCLOS is the question of jurisdiction with respect to a claim, as well as substantive issues related to such a claim. On the issue of jurisdiction to force a tribunal ruling under UNCLOS, the most important rulings to date under UNCLOS have been two rulings related to a dispute over Southern bluefin tuna.[118] In addition, the ruling of the ITLOS in the dispute between Ireland and the United Kingdom (The MOX Plant Case)[119] offers some indication that the ITLOS will be reluctant to accept claims for which the UNCLOS process is available where the issue under dispute is also relevant under another international agreement binding with a binding dispute settlement process.[120]

There is a reasonable basis for concluding that the environmental degradation caused by a geoengineering project could be covered by the UNCLOS articles pertaining to protection of the marine environment, namely articles 192, 194, and 195. Furthermore, the London Convention and its 1996 Protocol can be viewed as implementing UNCLOS article 210, and could constitute an appropriate international standard for purposes of

---

[117] One example is expertise on climate change impacts and mitigation, which is expertise a standing tribunal such as the ITLOS or the ICJ may not always possess to the same extent.

[118] *See* Southern Bluefin Tuna cases (New Zealand v. Japan; Australia v. Japan), Request for the Prescription of Provisional Measures under Article 290, Paragraph 5, of the UN Convention on the Law of the Sea (1999), 38 ILM 1624 (International Tribunal for the Law of the Sea). For the final ruling, see *Southern Bluefin Tuna Case* (2000), 39 ILM 1359 (UNCLOS Arbitral Tribunal). The case arose out of a long-standing dispute among the parties over the conservation of Southern bluefin tuna. An initial ruling determined that the dispute was properly brought under UNCLOS. The ITLOS then proceeded to award provisions measures for the protection of bluefin tuna pending the resolution of the dispute. The final ruling concluded that provisions of the Convention for the Conservation of Southern Bluefin Tuna (CCSBT) amounted to an agreement by the parties not to be bound by the UNCLOS dispute settlement procedure for purposes of disputes related to the conservation of bluefin tuna. For a more detailed assessment of these rulings, see MEINHARD DOELLE, FROM HOT AIR TO ACTION? CLIMATE CHANGE, COMPLIANCE AND THE FUTURE OF INTERNATIONAL ENVIRONMENTAL LAW 205 (2005).

[119] The MOX Plant Case (Ir. v. U.K.), Case No. 10, Order of Dec. 3, 2001, 5 ITLOS Rep. 95. The case arose out of a dispute between Ireland and the United Kingdom over radioactive waste pollution in the Irish Sea originating from a UK nuclear facility. *Id.* For more details, see Michael Bruce Volbeda, *The MOX Plant Case: The Question of "Supplemental Jurisdiction" for International Environmental Claims under UNCLOS*, 42 TEX. INT'L L.J. 211 (2006).

[120] *Id. See also* Victoria Hallum, *International Tribunal for the Law of the Sea: The Mox Nuclear Plant Case*, 11 R.E.C.I.E.L. 372, 373 (2002).

article 297(1) to extend the application of the compulsory dispute settlement process to geoengineering projects in coastal waters. Even disputes pertaining to OIF undertaken within a coastal country's territory could, therefore, potentially be subject to compulsory dispute settlement under UNCLOS.

Another important feature of the UNCLOS DSP is the availability of provisional measures for the purpose of prevention of serious environmental harm, pursuant to article 290.[121] This may be helpful when dealing with environmental problems associated with geoengineering. Provisional measures are available only when specified conditions are met. For example, in *The MOX Plant* case, the applicant did not meet the bar of sufficient urgency to warrant the enactment of provisional measures.[122] In the *Southern Bluefin Tuna* dispute, the declining of fish stocks fulfilled the urgency requirement, and ITLOS set fish catch totals as a provisional measure.

Conclusion

The relationship between the UNCLOS DSP and those of other international regimes has attracted the attention of academics in a variety of contexts, from trade to whaling.[123] There is potential for either or both DSPs as well as the NCPs under the UNFCCC to be invoked in case of a dispute over geoengineering affecting the marine environment. As a general rule, parties concerned about the environmental impact of geoengineering projects are more likely to pursue resolution under the DSP under UNCLOS. One caution with regard to UNCLOS in this regard is that it does not explicitly endorse the precautionary principle, largely a product of the time it was negotiated.

Questions about the contribution of geoengineering toward the commitments regarding mitigation, finance, technology, and loss and damage under the UNFCCC regime are most likely to come before either the NCPs or DSPs under the UNFCCC regime. The regime is in such a state of flux, however, that it is difficult to make any firm predictions about the substance of such a dispute. Much will depend on whether and how the new regime under negotiation will formally address the role of geoengineering in managing climate change.

It is uncertain at this early stage whether a dispute under either regime would be resolved through a careful balancing of benefits, impacts, risks, and uncertainties of a given geoengineering proposal, or whether each regime will focus on its perceived areas of priority. Would a DSP under UNCLOS give adequate weight to the potential role of

---

[121] UNCLOS, art. 290.

[122] KLEIN, *supra* note 99.

[123] *See, e.g.*, Jared Zemantauski, *Has the Law of the Sea Convention Strengthened the Conservation Ability of the International Whaling Commission?*, 43 U. MIAMI INTER-AM. L. REV. 325 (2011); Myers, *supra* note 98, at 37; and Patrizia Vigini, *The Overlapping of Dispute Settlement Regimes; An Emerging Issue in International Law*, 11 ITALIAN Y.B. INT'L L. 139 (2001).

geoengineering in mitigating climate change? Would a DSP under the UNFCCC give adequate weight to the risks to marine ecosystems?

From a process perspective, the UNCLOS DSP is currently more robust, tried, and tested than the DSP under the UNFCCC. Most important, perhaps, the UNCLOS DSP is compulsory, whereas the UNFCC's DSP is not. The NCP under the Kyoto Protocol is also quite robust, and compulsory, and has been used regularly since its inception in 2006. However, its role in resolving disputes over geoengineering is unsettled, as its future is very much uncertain, and its mandate is currently quite limited.

It is unlikely that the DSP under the UNFCCC would eliminate the UNCLOS DSP as an available process for a party concerned about the impact of geoengineering projects on marine ecosystems. Alternative procedures under any other relevant agreements to which the parties may belong will supersede the UNCLOS mechanisms, but only if they provide for a binding decision. The parties to the dispute can also agree to address the dispute under UNCLOS, which means they may have a choice between multiple regimes with binding dispute settlement procedures.[124] UNFCCC conciliation would not satisfy this requirement because it does not result in a binding decision, but rather a recommendatory award, which the parties are required to consider in good faith.[125] In the final analysis, a dispute over geoengineering could be brought before multiple dispute settlement and noncompliance bodies because the claims could be structured so differently that each would amount to a different dispute.[126]

---

[124] UNCLOS, art. 282.
[125] United Nations Framework Convention on Climate Change, arts. 1, 31.
[126] KLEIN, *supra* note 99.

17 The Regulation of Ocean Fertilization and Marine Geoengineering under the London Protocol
Bettina Boschen

Introduction

On October 18, 2013, the Contracting Parties to the London Convention and Protocol on the Prevention of Marine Pollution by Dumping of Wastes and Other Matter[1] adopted a resolution to amend the Protocol so as to provide a global regulatory mechanism for ocean iron fertilization (OIF) and other marine geoengineering activities. In doing so, the Contracting Parties submit to an international legal framework their right to sponsor activities that were previously unregulated and within the scope of the "freedom of the high seas" principle.

As global awareness of global climate change impacts has increased in the past decade, the ocean's natural function as a carbon sink has received increasing attention. Scientific research experiments over the last twenty years have demonstrated the potential of OIF as a technique to sequester CO_2 from the atmosphere, and sparked interest in the technique as a geoengineering option. Proposals to apply unconventional methods based on geoengineering science, which involve the large-scale manipulation of the climate system in order to combat the effects of anthropogenic climate change, are mired in controversy. Apart from the ethical issues surrounding the development of alternatives to conventional emission reduction schemes to mitigate global warming, uncertainties regarding impacts on the environment and human health are of particular concern in the context of geoengineering techniques involving the marine environment.

Since 2007, OIF has been the subject of discussions in international forums such as the Conference of Parties to the Convention on Biological Diversity and the Consultative Meetings of the Parties to the London Convention and Protocol, with a view to establish a regulatory framework for OIF and other marine geoengineering activities. Section I of this chapter provides a brief background on marine geoengineering as an activity that takes place in the high seas and affects the global commons. Section II provides a detailed account of the international institutional reactions and legal responses to OIF that eventually led to the development of a legally binding mechanism to effectively regulate ocean fertilization. Section III provides an assessment of the effectiveness of the new regulatory regime, its implications for the extended scope of the London Protocol, and its impact on the freedom of marine scientific research on the high seas.

---

[1] Convention on the Prevention of Marine Pollution by Dumping of Wastes and Other Matter, London, Dec. 29, 1972, 1046 U.N.T.S. 120 [hereinafter London Convention]; Protocol to the Convention on the Prevention of Marine Pollution by Dumping of Wastes and Other Matter, Nov. 7, 1996, 36 I.L.M. 1 [hereinafter London Protocol].

I. Background

A. GEOENGINEERING ACTIVITIES IN THE MARINE ENVIRONMENT

Grouped under the term "geoengineering," a number of methods to cool our planet's temperature may provide alternative responses to mitigate the effects of climate change.[2] The term "geoengineering" literally means "engineering the earth" and can be used in relation to a wide array of activities, which involve the intentional large-scale manipulation of the environment.[3] However, the general meaning of the term has increasingly become associated with activities that seek to reduce the effects of climate change.[4] Geoengineering strategies may include a wide variety of techniques, some of which are purely theoretical and others are more developed.[5] Among these different techniques, OIF has been the subject of numerous small-scale experiments, and its deployment on a large scale showed the most potential to be carried out in reality.

OIF is classified as a carbon dioxide removal technique (CDR) because it seeks to increase the ocean's natural function as a carbon sink, enhancing the uptake and storage of CO_2 through the natural mechanisms that control the distribution of carbon in the oceans.[6] OIF involves the introduction of iron particles into the ocean in order to stimulate the growth of phytoplankton to increase the uptake of carbon by the ocean, which would eventually be transported into the deep ocean and remain sequestered for 100–1000 years.[7] Despite its promise as a CDR technique, OIF remains highly controversial due to significant scientific uncertainties regarding the effectiveness of the technique and the potential risks of widespread harmful effects on the environment.[8]

---

[2] John Shepherd et al., Geoengineering the Climate: Science, Governance and Uncertainty (The Royal Society, 2009), *available at* https://royalsociety.org/~/media/Royal_Society_Content/policy/publications/2009/8693.pdf.

[3] Int'l Mar. Org. [IMO], *Marine Geo-engineering—Types of Schemes Proposed to Date,* submitted *by the Chairman of the Scientific Groups*, IMO Doc. LC 32/4 (July 28, 2010).

[4] For a useful chronological sketch of different geoengineering activities and the corresponding development in the use of the term, see Karen N. Scott, Conference Contribution, *Marine Geo-engineering: A New Challenge for the Law of the Sea, in* Australia New Zealand Society of International Law (ANZSIL) 18th Annual Conference: International Law in the Second Decade of the 21st Century—Back to the Future or Business as Usual? (June 24–26, 2010).

[5] Shepherd et al., *supra* note 2; IMO Doc. LC 32/4, *supra* note 3.

[6] Shepherd et al., *supra* note 2, at 16.

[7] Doug W.R. Wallace et al., Ocean Fertilization: A Scientific Summary for Policy Makers IOC/UNESCO, Paris, 12 (2010).

[8] *Id.*; Sallie W. Chisholm, Paul G. Falkowski & John J. Cullen, *Dis-crediting Ocean Fertilization*, 294 Sci. 309–10 (2010). *See also* Randall S. Abate, *Ocean Iron Fertilization: Science, Law, and Uncertainty, in* Climate Change Geoengineering: Philosophical Perspectives, Legal Issues & Governance Frameworks (Wil C.G. Burns & Andrew L. Strauss eds., 2013); Karen N. Scott, *International Law in the Anthropocene: Responding to the Geoengineering Challenge*, 34 Mich. J. Int'l L. 309 (2013).

Between 1993 and 2005, twelve OIF experiments were conducted by noncommercial marine scientific research collaborations.[9] The majority of these experiments took place in the high seas, also known as marine areas beyond national jurisdiction. These areas are desirable for OIF experiments not only because of the regulatory freedom available in these areas[10] but also because these areas are the most suitable for such experiments.[11] Although these experiments were initially not intended to examine the potential to sequester CO_2, and the results of first experiments did not document a net transfer of CO_2 from the atmosphere to the deep sea,[12] media coverage of the experiments encouraged the idea that the stimulation of algae blooms in order to take up CO_2 from the atmosphere could hold the cure for global warming.[13]

Increased media attention and scientific study of OIF sparked commercial interest in fertilizing the ocean in anticipation of the development of a global market in which credits for carbon sequestered through fertilization might be traded.[14] Such ventures proposed to carry out significantly scaled-up fertilization projects as compared to the relatively small-scale experiments carried out by the scientific community.[15] The prospect of large-scale ocean fertilization activities conducted by private companies,[16] the potential environmental risk associated with such activities, and the absence of an international regulatory framework that could adequately address ocean fertilization have highlighted the challenges to regulate OIF projects.

B. HIGH SEAS GOVERNANCE

The United Nations Convention on the Law of the Sea (UNCLOS)[17] sets out the jurisdictional and substantive framework for the oceans. It contains far-reaching environmental

---

[9] Phillip W. Boyd et al., *Mesoscale Iron Enrichment Experiments 1993–2005: Synthesis and Future Directions*, 315 SCI. 612–17 (2007).

[10] On the issue of high seas governance and implications of the freedom of scientific research on the high seas, see *infra* Section II. B.

[11] Boyd et al., *supra* note 9, at 3.

[12] Chisholm, Falkowski & Cullen, *supra* note 8, at 309.

[13] Scott, *supra* note 8, at 311; Chisholm, Falkowski & Cullen, *supra* note 8, at 309; *see also* Randall S. Abate & Andrew B. Greenlee, *Sowing Seeds Uncertain: Ocean Iron Fertilization, Climate Change, and the International Environmental Law Framework*, 27 PACE ENVTL. L. REV. 555 (2010).

[14] Chisholm, Falkowski & Cullen, *supra* note 8, at 309.

[15] *Id;* Rosemary Rayfuse, Mark G. Lawrence & Kristina M Gjerde, *Ocean Fertilisation and Climate Change: The Need to Regulate Emerging High Seas Uses*, 23 INT'L J. MARINE & COASTAL L. 297, 299 (2008).

[16] In May 2007, a group of international NGOs, including ETC Group and Greenpeace, blew the whistle on Planktos Inc., a U.S.-based for-profit company that had planned to introduce 100 tons of iron particles in a 100 km by 100 km area in the high seas approximately 350 miles west of the Galapagos Islands, and brought the matter to the attention of the parties to the London Convention and Protocol. *See infra* notes 34–36 and accompanying text.

[17] United Nations Convention on the Law of the Sea, Dec. 10, 1982, 21 I.L.M. 1261 (entered into force Nov. 16, 1994).

obligations[18] and requires states to cooperate through competent international organizations, as necessary, to develop specific regulation of substantive areas such as navigation, fisheries, and the protection and conservation of the marine environment.[19]

Beyond the limits of coastal state jurisdiction, where OIF activities generally take place, the principle of the freedom of the high seas and the corresponding principle of exclusive flag state jurisdiction apply.[20] While the exercise of high seas freedoms is subject to the conditions of UNCLOS and rules derived from other sources of international law, the regulatory framework for activities on the high seas is comprised of a myriad of legal instruments, and global or regional sectoral and environmental management regimes, complemented by international legal principles such as those on the environment.[21]

This patchwork of international law governing the high seas results in a number of regulatory gaps. OIF conducted for commercial or scientific research purposes is affected by this high seas governance problem as it falls within such a regulatory gap, and because the nature of climate engineering affects the global environment more broadly, making international cooperation on the matter indispensable. Another aspect of the high seas governance problem lies in the fact that the international community finds it difficult to deal with the management of the marine commons.[22] This is due to the general reluctance of states to restrict their exercise of high seas freedoms, the global participation ideally required to regulate activities in the marine commons, and the potential problem posed by states that choose not to subscribe to such regulatory restrictions.[23]

---

[18] *See* UNCLOS Part XII on the Protection and Preservation of the Marine Environment.

[19] As clarified in Law of the Sea Bulletin No. 31, *Competent or Relevant International Organizations under the United Nations Convention on the Law of the Sea*, United Nations Division of Ocean Affairs and the Law of the Sea (1996). For further discussion of the dynamics of the elaboration of the law of the sea following the adoption of UNCLOS, see JAMES HARRISON, MAKING THE LAW OF THE SEA: A STUDY IN THE DEVELOPMENT OF INTERNATIONAL LAW, CAMBRIDGE STUDIES IN INTERNATIONAL AND COMPARATIVE LAW (2011).

[20] *See* UNCLOS, art. 87 on Freedom of the High Seas.

[21] For a discussion of the high seas governance issue, see generally KRISTINA M. GJERDE ET AL., REGULATORY AND GOVERNANCE GAPS IN THE INTERNATIONAL REGIME FOR THE CONSERVATION AND SUSTAINABLE USE OF MARINE BIODIVERSITY IN AREAS BEYOND NATIONAL JURISDICTION, IUCN MARINE SERIES (2008); David Freestone, *Problems of High Seas Governance, in* WORLD OCEAN IN GLOBALISATION: CLIMATE CHANGE, SUSTAINABLE FISHERIES, BIODIVERSITY, SHIPPING, REGIONAL ISSUES (Davor Vidas & Peter Johan Schei eds., 2010); ROBIN WARNER, PROTECTING THE OCEANS BEYOND NATIONAL JURISDICTION: STRENGTHENING THE INTERNATIONAL LAW FRAMEWORK LEGAL ASPECTS OF SUSTAINABLE DEVELOPMENT (2009).

[22] Philomène Verlaan, *Marine Scientific Research: Its Potential Contribution to Achieving Responsible High Seas Governance*, 27 INT'L J. MARINE & COASTAL L. 805, 805 (2012).

[23] Freestone, *supra* note 21, at 122.

C. INTERNATIONAL LAW AND INSTITUTIONAL REACTIONS

Apart from UNCLOS, the most relevant global treaty regimes applicable to OIF are the Convention on Biological Diversity,[24] the United Nations Framework Convention on Climate Change,[25] and the London Convention and Protocol. In addition to these instruments, the international environmental legal principles that form part of the corpus of international customary law also provide a frame of reference for the conduct of marine geoengineering activities.[26]

As OIF, and climate geoengineering more generally, became a subject of concern in international forums, it became clear that the issue touched the mandates of a number of treaty regimes and international institutions.[27] Scientific and technical reports on the issue emanated from the work of the UNESCO/IOC ad hoc Consultative Group on Ocean Fertilization,[28] the CBD Subsidiary Body on Scientific Technical and Technological Advice in collaboration with UNEP's World Conservation Monitoring Centre,[29] and the Intergovernmental Panel on Climate Change.[30] However, the political and policy responses emerged primarily from the biannual Conference of Parties to the CBD ("CBD COP") and the annual Consultative Meetings of Parties to the London Convention and Protocol ("LC/LP Meetings"). The interaction between the CBD and the LC/LP, and a detailed account of the developments leading to the establishment of "a global, transparent, and effective control and regulatory mechanism for ocean fertilization and other marine geoengineering activities" will be discussed in the following section.

---

[24] Convention on Biological Diversity, June 5, 1992, 1760 U.N.T.S. 79 [hereinafter CBD].

[25] United Nations Framework Convention on Climate Change, May 9, 1992. 31 I.L.M. 851.

[26] Daniel Bodansky, *May We Engineer the Climate?*, 33 CLIMATE CHANGE 309, 313 (1996); Scott, *supra* note 8, at 350.

[27] For discussions of international law and governance of OIF, see generally Robin Warner, *Marine Protected Areas beyond National Jurisdiction—Existing Legal Principles and Future Legal Frameworks, in* MANAGING RISKS TO BIODIVERSITY AND THE ENVIRONMENT ON THE HIGH SEA, INCLUDING TOOLS SUCH AS MARINE PROTECTED AREAS—SCIENTIFIC REQUIREMENTS AND LEGAL ASPECTS—PROCEEDINGS OF THE EXPERT WORKSHOP HELD AT THE INTERNATIONAL ACADEMY FOR NATURE CONSERV (Hjalmar Thiel & Anthony Koslov eds., 2001); Philomène Verlaan, *Geo-engineering, the Law of the Sea, and Climate Change*, 4 CARBON CLIMATE L. REV. 446 (2009); Scott, *supra* note 8; Abate, *supra* note 8.

[28] WALLACE ET AL., *supra* note 7.

[29] Secretariat of the Convention on Biological Diversity (2009), Scientific Synthesis of the Impacts of Ocean Fertilization on Marine Biodiversity. Montreal, Technical Series No. 45; Secretariat of the Convention on Biological Diversity (2012), *Geoengineering in Relation to the Convention on Biological Diversity: Technical and Regulatory Matters*, Montreal, Technical Series No. 66.

[30] IPCC, 2012: Meeting Report of the Intergovernmental Panel on Climate Change Expert Meeting on Geoengineering (O. Edenhofer, R. Pichs-Madruga, Y. Sokona, C. Field, V. Barros, T.F. Stocker, Q. Dahe, J. Minx, K. Mach, G.-K. Plattner, S. Schlömer, G. Hansen, M. Mastrandrea, eds.). IPCC Working Group III Technical Support Unit, Potsdam Institute for Climate Impact Research, Potsdam, Germany.

II. Developing a Regulatory Regime within the London Convention and Protocol Framework

A. MANDATE OF THE LC/LP AND THE REGULATION OF OCEAN FERTILIZATION

The 1972 London Convention and its 1996 Protocol comprise the global legal framework for protection of the marine environment from deliberate pollution at sea.[31] The Protocol embodies a complete revision of the London Convention. Until the Protocol eventually replaces the Convention as Contracting Parties ratify the Protocol, the two instruments exist in parallel.[32] In addition to including earlier amendments to the Convention, the Protocol incorporates modern developments in international law such as prevention and precaution as expressed in the 1992 Rio Declaration, and responds to the recommendations contained in Agenda 21, chapter 17 § 30(b)(i). The London Convention and the Protocol are each implemented through Consultative Meetings of Contracting Parties, which are held annually. Both the LC and LP Meetings have established a Scientific Group, which is a subsidiary body comprised of government experts that advise the respective Consultative Meeting on scientific and technical matters.[33]

OIF was first discussed within an intergovernmental framework at the 2007 meeting of the LC/LP Scientific Groups when Greenpeace, IUCN, and the United States invited the members of the groups to consider the matter in response to imminent plans to conduct large-scale OIF by the U.S.-based for-profit company, Planktos Inc.[34]

As the jurisdictional reach of the United States over OIF activities does not extend beyond U.S. ports and U.S. flagged vessels, and given Planktos' intention to avoid U.S. jurisdiction, the matter was brought to the attention of Parties to the LC and LP because the United States felt that any state with jurisdiction over such activities should carefully evaluate OIF projects and their potential environmental impact.[35] Concerning the applicability

---

[31] In addition to the accession of ten new Contracting Parties, thirty-three of the eighty-seven Contracting Parties to the Convention have ratified the Protocol. Status of the Convention and Its Protocol, Apr. 1, 2014.

[32] To avoid the more onerous entry into force requirements that an amendment to the London Convention entails (London Convention, art. 15), the Contracting Parties chose to adopt the Protocol, which supersedes the Convention (London Protocol, art. 23). For a more detailed analysis, see Eric J. Molenaar, *The 1996 Protocol to the 1972 London Convention*, 12 INT'L J. MARINE & COASTAL L. 396 (1997); Louise A. De la Fayette, *The London Convention 1972 : Preparing for the Future*, 13 INT'L J. MARINE & COASTAL L. 515 (1998).

[33] As per the revised Rules of Procedure, meetings held under both the Convention and the Protocol are held concurrently through an arrangement whereby the Chairman, or Vice-Chairman, represent Parties to both instruments, though formal decision-making under each instrument remains separate. *See* IMO Doc. LC 23/16, Revised Rules of Procedure.

[34] *See* Report of the 30th Meeting of the Scientific Group of the London Convention and the first meeting of the Scientific Group of the London Protocol, IMO Doc. LC/SG 30/14, July 25, 2007.

[35] *See* IMO Doc. LC/SG 30/INF.28, "Planktos, Inc., Large-Scale Ocean Iron Addition Projects," submitted by the United States.

of the LC/LP to OIF, the United States highlighted that under the London Convention "dumping" does not include "placement of matter into the ocean for purposes other than the mere disposal thereof, provided it is not contrary to the aims of the Convention."[36]

The Scientific Groups noted the potential for large-scale OIF projects to have negative impacts on the marine environment and human health, and issued a Statement of Concern, in which the groups concluded that "current knowledge about the effectiveness and potential environmental impacts of ocean iron fertilization was insufficient to justify large-scale operations" and recommended that such projects be "evaluated carefully to ensure they were not contrary to the aims of the London Convention and Protocol."[37] This statement was endorsed by the subsequent Consultative Meetings of Contracting Parties to the LC/LP, which further agreed that the scope of the LC/LP extends to OIF due to the general objective to "protect and preserve the environment from all sources of pollution" contained in article I of the Convention and article 2 of the Protocol. On the other hand, the Meetings recognized that it was within the purview of each state to consider OIF proposals on a case-by-case basis.[38]

The reaction to OIF during the Ninth Conference of Parties to the CBD in 2008 was much less reserved. CBD Decision IX/16 is sometimes referred to as a moratorium on ocean fertilization, though the non-binding status of CBD Decisions and the hortatory wording in this case does not support such a claim.[39] The Decision requests Parties and urges other governments to ensure that OIF activities do not take place until they can be justified on the basis of adequate scientific knowledge and a "global, transparent and effective regulatory and control mechanism" is in place.[40] This measure leaves room for small-scale ocean fertilization activities conducted for the purposes of scientific research studies if they take place in coastal waters and are subject to strict control and prior environmental impact assessment.[41]

The discussion of OIF at the Ninth COP to the CBD appears to have provided additional impetus to the work on this matter undertaken under the framework of the London Convention and Protocol. Although the CBD Decision does not confirm the LC/LP as the competent international organization to deal with the regulation of OIF, it does urge Parties and other governments to act in accordance with the LC/LP Statement of Concern. The influence of the CBD discussions and Decision IX/16 C is apparent in the measures subsequently adopted within the framework of the LC/LP.

---

[36] *Id.*

[37] "Statement of Concern," Report of the 30th Meeting of the Scientific Group of the London Convention and the first meeting of the Scientific Group of the London Protocol, IMO Doc. LC/SG 30/14, 25 July 2007, ¶¶ 2.23–2.25 [hereinafter "Statement of Concern"].

[38] Report of the 29th Consultative Meeting and the Second Meeting of Contracting Parties, IMO Doc. LC 29/17, ¶ 4.23.

[39] *See also* Scott, *supra* note 8, at 332–33.

[40] Conference of the Parties to the CBD at Its Ninth Meeting, *Decision IX/16 on Biodiversity and Climate Change*, C. Ocean Fertilization, UNEP/CBD/COP/IX/16 (Oct. 9, 2008).

[41] *Id.*

B. LC/LP NON-BINDING MEASURES

The subsequent measure adopted under the framework of the LC/LP is a case in point. The formula employed in Resolution LC-LP.1 (2008) on the Regulation of Ocean Fertilization no longer focuses on the spatial scale of the activity in order to distinguish activities that are deemed acceptable from those that are subject to regulation.[42] Instead, it follows the approach reflected in the CBD Decision and seeks to prohibit OIF activities generally, allowing for "legitimate scientific research" as an exception. Resolution 1 defines OIF as "any activity undertaken by humans with the principle intention of stimulating primary productivity in the oceans." By adopting the resolution, the Contracting Parties reaffirm that the scope of the LC/LP includes OIF, and that such activities are considered to be "placement of matter for a purpose other than the mere disposal thereof, which are contrary to the aims of the Convention and Protocol" and therefore do not qualify for an exemption from the definition of dumping under the Convention and the Protocol.[43] OIF operations constituting legitimate scientific research, however, do qualify for this exemption and are permitted if such operations are assessed and found acceptable under an assessment framework to be developed by the LC/LP Scientific Groups.

OIF was the most controversial and time-consuming topic at the 2008 LC/LP Consultative Meetings. Despite the non-binding status, Resolution 1 was regarded by some delegations as a sufficiently strong measure allowing for scientific research while restricting other OIF activities, and setting out the basis for regulation through a specific assessment framework that ensures the development of international standards to be applied by Contracting Parties when considering OIF for research studies. Other Parties, led by Australia, advocated for more aggressive regulation in the form of an amendment to the London Protocol to provide a "global, transparent and effective regulatory and control mechanism" for OIF as called for by CBD Decision IX/16 C.[44] In addition to adopting Resolution 1, the 2008 Consultative Meeting of Contracting Parties agreed to further consider a potentially legally binding measure to be adopted under the LC/LP framework.[45]

The Assessment Framework for Scientific Research Involving Ocean Fertilization was adopted by the LC/LP Consultative Meeting with Resolution LC-LP.2 (2010).[46] As

---

[42] Resolution LC-LP.1 on the Regulation of Ocean Fertilization (adopted on Oct. 31, 2008), IMO Doc. LC 30/16, Annex 6 [hereinafter "Resolution 1"].

[43] London Convention art. III.1(b); London Protocol art. 1.4.2.

[44] "Report of the 30th Consultative Meeting, 3rd Meeting of Contracting Parties," IMO Doc. LC 30/16, Dec. 9, 2008, ¶ 4.7.

[45] *Id.* ¶ 4.14.

[46] Resolution LC-LP.2 (2010) on the Assessment Framework for Scientific Research Involving Ocean Fertilization (adopted on Oct. 14, 2010), IMO Doc. LC 32/15, Annex 5 [hereinafter "Resolution 2"]; Assessment Framework for Scientific Research Involving Ocean Fertilization (adopted on Oct. 14, 2010), IMO Doc. LC 32/15 Annex 6 [hereinafter "OF Assessment Framework"].

with the preceding measure, Resolution 2 was adopted by consensus and is not legally binding. The Resolution affirms that Contracting Parties to the LC/LP should use the OF Assessment Framework to determine whether the activity constitutes legitimate scientific research that is not contrary to the aims of the Convention and Protocol.

The requirements to seek prior consultation and notification from all parties with jurisdiction in the region of potential impact was a point of contention during the development of the OF Assessment Framework.[47] This is reflected in the wording of Resolution 2, which emphasizes that the consultation, notification, and reporting provisions of the Assessment Framework are integral to the assessment of a proposed OIF research activity. The OF Assessment Framework has been adopted as a "living document," which may be subject to amendment in light of new and relevant scientific information and experience gained in applying it.[48]

C. TOWARDS BINDING REGULATION

The need for a legally binding solution to establish an effective regulatory and control mechanism was underscored by the controversy that ensued when the German-Indian OIF experiment, "Lohafex," was about to take place in January 2009.[49] The experiment attracted considerable opposition as NGOs claimed the experiment would contravene the CDB and LC/LP decisions issued in 2008, and criticized the experiment as breaking a taboo, referring to the relatively large scale of this experiment compared to previous OIF research experiments conducted.[50] Moreover, the German Federal Ministry of Education and Research, and the German Federal Ministry for the Environment, Nature Conservation and Nuclear Safety, could not reach an agreement concerning the authorization of the project, despite the presentation of a number of peer-reviewed environmental assessments and legal opinions by the research institute.[51] Although the Research Ministry authorized the Lohafex experiment on the basis of these assessments, the Ministry for the Environment issued a statement expressing regret about the authorization of the project and referred to the need to clarify uncertainties as to the legality of such experiments.[52]

---

[47] "Report of the 32nd Consultative Meeting 5th Meeting of Contracting Parties," IMO Doc, LC 32/15, 9 Nov. 2010, ¶ 4.2.

[48] Id. ¶ 4.10.

[49] For background on the research collaboration between the Alfred-Wegener-Institut of Germany and India's National Institute of Oceanography (NIO), see http://www.awi.de/de/aktuelles_und_presse/selected_news/2009/lohafex/experiment/ (last visted on July 23, 2014).

[50] For well-informed comments, see Ginzky, infra note 57, 57–59; Abate & Greenlee, supra note 13, at 556–58.

[51] Reports on the Environmental Impact Assessments of the Lohafex experiment conducted by NOAA and the AWI, as well as additional scientific reviews and legal assessments provided by Prof. Alexander Proelß (Univ. Kiel) and Prof. Rüdiger Wolfrum (Univ. Heidelberg) are available on the website of the AWI, supra note 49.

[52] See the press releases referred to in Ginzky, infra note 57, at 59; Abate & Greenlee, supra note 13, at 557.

Following this controversy and in accordance with Resolution 1, work on the possible development of a legally binding measure addressing OIF continued within the framework of the LC/LP. A review of the reports on the LC/LP Consultative Meetings held between 2009 and 2013 reveals that the overarching issues in this regard focus on: (1) the type of measure to be developed, and (2) on the scope of such a measure.[53]

The issue relating to the extent of the scope of the regulatory framework arose when concern was raised during the discussions held in 2009 regarding emerging marine geoengineering technologies that had effects similar to OIF. Although most Contracting Parties were in agreement that the primary focus should remain on OIF, the possibility of including other marine geoengineering activities remained a subject under discussion. In anticipation of another regulatory gap, considerations by some Parties to the LC/LP to broaden the scope of the regulatory framework that they envisaged were in line with developments in other forums, particularly the CBD.[54] Increasing interest in the regulation of other forms of geoengineering is further reflected in Resolution 2, which extends the commitment of Contracting Parties "to work towards providing a global, transparent, and effective control and regulatory mechanism for ocean fertilization activities" to include "other activities that fall within the scope of the London Convention and Protocol."[55] Similarly, CBD Decision X/33 reaffirms Decision IX/16 C and extends its advice to geoengineering in general.[56]

Proposals to further develop the regulatory framework varied greatly, reflecting different positions on the regulation of OIF and other marine geoengineering activities. Following the adoption of the OF Assessment Framework, discussions centered on three main strategies: (1) an amendment to the London Protocol, (2) an interpretative resolution, and (3) a gathering of experience from the implementation of Resolution 1 and the OF Assessment Framework without the adoption of further measures.[57]

Options for the amendment to the London Protocol included an amendment to Annex 1 of the Protocol, effectively adding OIF as an additional waste stream and subjecting the activity to the existing permitting regime.[58] However, this proposal would not just involve an amendment to the Annex, but also an amendment to the definition of dumping contained in the Protocol itself. Questions as to whether OIF should be treated as dumping, the procedural complexity involved in amending the definition of

---

[53] IMO Docs. LC 31/15 (2009), LC 32/15 (2010), LC 33/15 (2011), LC 34/15 (2012), LC 35/15 (2013).

[54] IMO Doc. LC 31/15 (2009), ¶¶ 4.17–4.23.

[55] Resolution LC-LP.2(2010), ¶ 5.

[56] Conference of the Parties to the CBD at Its Tenth Meeting, Nagoya, Japan, Oct. 18–29, 2010, X/33 Biodiversity and Climate Change, 8(w), UNEP/CBD/COP/DEC/X/33 (Oct. 29, 2010).

[57] *See also* Harald Ginzky, *Ocean Fertilization as Climate Change Mitigation Measure—Consideration under International Law*, 7 J. EUROPEAN ENVTL. & PLANNING L. 57, 71–73 (2010); Rosemary Rayfuse, *Climate Change and the Law of the Sea*, *in* INTERNATIONAL LAW IN THE ERA OF CLIMATE CHANGE 171–72 (Rosemary Rayfuse & Shirley V. Scott eds., 2012).

[58] IMO Doc. 32/4/1 (2010), "Discussion of an Additional Option to Achieve the Regulation of Legitimate Scientific Research Involving Ocean Fertilization under the London Protocol," submitted by Canada.

dumping, and questions as to the compatibility of the London Protocol and UNCLOS provisions concerning pollution at sea following an amendment to the definition, prompted further discussion and the exploration of other proposals.[59] Subsequent amendment options envisaged the inclusion of one new article on "Placement of Matter into the Sea" in the Protocol, and additional provisions creating a permitting regime set out in one or two additional annexes.[60] The latter variant separates generic criteria regarding the validity of the placement activity under the Protocol from the more specific OF Assessment Framework. Such an approach would correspond to the existing structure of the permitting regime under the London Protocol dealing with dumping of wastes, which contains a list of waste streams that may be considered for dumping and a generic assessment framework in separate Annexes.[61] Moreover, a two-annex amendment would also leave room for the possible inclusion of other marine geoengineering activities in the future.

A different regulatory option was offered in the proposal to adopt an interpretative resolution on OIF, which would constitute a subsequent agreement between the Contracting Parties regarding the interpretation and application of the London Convention and Protocol pursuant to article 31(3)(a) of the Vienna Convention on the Law of Treaties.[62] The effect of such a resolution would be that OIF activities conducted for purposes other than scientific studies would be considered dumping and thus prohibited under the Convention and Protocol. On the other hand, this option would not entail the regulation of scientific research involving OIF under the LC/LP, and once the activity meets the requirements for legitimate scientific research, it is not covered by the Convention or the Protocol.[63] In contrast to the amendment proposals, this option would address both the London Convention and the Protocol and an interpretative resolution would be effective immediately upon adoption.[64]

There are, however, some uncertainties with respect to the procedural implications for achieving binding effect of an interpretative resolution. In the view of the IMO Secretariat legal office, such a resolution should be based on consensus rather than a

---

[59] IMO Doc. 32/15 (2010), ¶ 4.18.

[60] IMO Doc. 33/4 (2011), Report of the 3rd Meeting of the Intersessional Working Group on Ocean Fertilization.

[61] Annex 1 of the London Convention lists different waste streams for which a dumping permit may be granted in accordance with the assessment framework contained in Annex 2. In addition to this generic assessment framework, the Scientific Groups develop specific guidelines to be applied to the disposal of the type of waste in question.

[62] Vienna Convention on the Law of Treaties, May 23, 1969, 1155 U.N.T.S. 331.

[63] For a draft interpretative resolution on OIF including commentary, see IMO Doc. LP/CO2 2/5 "Report of the 1st Meeting of the LP Intersessional Legal and Related Issues Working Group on Ocean Fertilization," Feb. 20, 2009, Annex 5; a further developed draft interpretative resolution can be found in IMO Doc. LC 34/15, "Report of the 34th Consultative Meeting of Contracting Parties to the [LC] and the 6th Meeting of Contracting Parties to the [LP]," Nov. 23, 2012, Annex 6.

[64] Rayfuse, *supra* note 57, at 171.

vote because the outvoted parties would not be bound by the subsequent agreement.[65] In addition, the Secretariat indicated that other cases of interpretative resolutions have shown that, although Parties have the competence to interpret a treaty, this is still subject to the rule of law as determined by provisions dealing with interpretation of the treaty concerned, the International Court of Justice, or national courts. Thus, while an interpretative resolution would apply to the parties of the London Convention and not just those of the London Protocol, this option may not be fully effective in further developing the regulatory framework for OIF, and if pursued, this option should be accompanied by an amendment to the Convention and Protocol.[66]

The third strategy supports the position that "a global, transparent, and effective control and regulatory mechanism" for OIF activities has already been achieved by the adoption of Resolution 1 and Resolution 2, including the OF Assessment Framework. This option for further development of the regulatory framework for OIF therefore involves the implementation of these measures and gaining experience from the application of the OF Assessment Framework, which is intended to evolve over time.[67] This option reflected the position of a number of Contracting Parties, particularly that of the United States.

At the 2011 Consultative Meeting, the United States argued that questioning the adequacy of the OF Assessment Framework would be premature given the work that had gone into the development of the OF Assessment Framework and the fact that it had not yet been necessary to apply it.[68] This option offers the advantages of (1) procedural and substantive flexibility, as additional resolutions and assessment frameworks for other marine geoengineering activities requiring regulation in the future can enter into effect immediately upon adoption; (2) consistency between the London Convention and the Protocol; and (3) adoption of existing and future measures on the basis of consensus of Parties to both the London Convention and the Protocol. On the other hand, this option has been subject to strong criticism as to its effectiveness due to its non-binding nature. For example, critics have questioned whether this option will provide effective control over OIF activities in the absence of binding reporting requirements ensuring consistency in the application of the OF Assessment Framework.[69]

These criticisms were given further strength, and support for an amendment of the London Protocol grew stronger, following another OIF project. This nonscientific

---

[65] *See* IMO Doc. LC 33/15, "Report of the 33rd Consultative Meeting and the 6th Meeting of Contracting Parties," Nov. 8, 2011, ¶ 4.10.

[66] *Id.*

[67] The reader is referred to references of Option 3 in the Reports of LC/LP Meetings held between 2010 and 2012. This option is further elaborated on in a document submitted by the United States, IMO Doc. LC CO2 4/2, "Proposal to Continue the Work of Resolution LC-LP.2(2010)," Jan. 31, 2011.

[68] IMO Doc. LC 33/15, "Report of the 33rd Consultative Meeting and the 6th Meeting of Contracting Parties," Nov. 8, 2011, Annex 2 "Statement by the Delegation of the United States on Ocean Fertilization."

[69] For a detailed report of the different positions on this option, see IMO Doc. LC 33/4/3, "Report of the Correspondence Group on Ocean Fertilization—Part 3," Aug. 9, 2011.

project took place in the summer of 2012 in the high seas near the islands of Haida Gwaii, an archipelago off the west coast of Canada. The Haida Salmon Restoration Corporation, a venture involving the local village community and a private company, whose CEO, Russ George, also headed Planktos Inc., intended to stimulate salmon runs by creating plankton blooms through the release of 120 tons of iron sulphate into the ocean.[70] Because the project was conducted in collaboration with the local authority but absent any authorization by Environment Canada, it illustrates the regulatory problems that can occur in the absence of a binding international mechanism requiring implementation in national legal systems. Canada is a strong supporter of the amendment to the London Protocol to regulate OIF and formally stated that it would investigate the matter.[71]

D. LP AMENDMENT

During the 2013 LC/LP Consultative Meetings, consensus developed on an option to further regulate OIF, based on an amendment proposal submitted by Australia, Nigeria, and the Republic of Korea.[72] This amendment addresses marine geoengineering activities that fall within the scope of the LC/LP and includes a definition of marine geoengineering. The amendment follows the format of the existing permission regime under the Protocol, adding a new article to the Protocol as well as two new annexes: new Annex 4 sets out a positive list of marine geoengineering activities to be regulated, and new Annex 5 contains a generic assessment framework for matters that may be considered for placement in connection with such activities. The procedural route chosen for the adoption of the amendment was a Resolution under the London Protocol, to which the amendments are annexed.[73] In accordance with Articles 21(3) and 22(6) of the Protocol, the amendments will enter into force for those Parties that have accepted it sixty days after two-thirds of the Contracting Parties have deposited instruments of ratification at the International Maritime Organization.[74]

---

[70] The story was made public by *The Guardian* on October 15, 2012; *see* http://www.guardian.co.uk/environment/2012/oct/15/pacific-iron-fertilisation-geoengineering. For further reporting, see http://www.theglobeandmail.com/news/british-columbia/experiment-to-seed-pacific-defended/article4622528/ (last visited July 23, 2014); H.J. Buck, "Village Science Meets Global Discourse: The Haida Salmon Restoration Corporation's Ocean Iron Fertilization Experiment," Case Study, Geoengineering Our Climate Working Paper and Opinion Article Series, *available at* http://wp.me/p2zsRk-9M.

[71] *See* IMO Doc. LC 35/15 (2012) Annex 3, "Statement by the Delegation of Canada on the Issue of the Ocean Fertilization Incident off the West Coast of Canada in July 2012."

[72] IMO Doc. LC 35/15 "Report of the 35th Consultative Meeting and the 8th Meeting of Contracting Parties," Oct. 21, 2013, ¶¶ 4.2–4.8.

[73] Resolution LP.4(8) on the Amendment to the London Protocol to Regulate the Placement of Matter for Ocean Fertilization and Other Marine Geoengineering Activities (adopted on Oct. 18, 2013), IMO Doc. LC 35/15 Annex 4 [hereinafter "2013 LP Amendment"].

[74] For a summary and comment on the amendment, see Philomène Verlaan, *New Regulation of Marine Geo-engineering and Ocean Fertilization*, 28 INT'L J. MARINE & COASTAL L. 729 (2013).

1. Basic Structure of the Regulatory Mechanism

New article 6bis sets out the basic structure of the new regulatory mechanism for marine geoengineering under the LP. Accordingly, marine geoengineering activities that involve the placement of matter into the sea from vessels, aircraft, platforms, or other man-made structures fall within the scope of the LP and may be considered for inclusion in new Annex 4. Once listed, such activities are prima facie prohibited unless the listing in Annex 4 provides that the activity, or the subcategory of an activity, may be considered for a permit. Such permits are issued by the Contracting Party with jurisdiction to regulate the activity; article 6bis(2) therefore requires Contracting Parties to adopt administrative or legislative measures so as to ensure that permits comply with the provisions of Annex 5, and take into account the requirements of the specific assessment framework developed for the relevant activity under the LP.

The basic requirement for the issuance of a permit is that the assessment of the proposed activity must determine that: (1) the activity is not contrary to the aims of the Protocol, and (2) that pollution of the marine environment is, as far as practicable, prevented or reduced to a minimum. This wording is in line with article 2 of the Protocol, which means that, as in the case of dumping of wastes, the phrase "contrary to the aims of the convention" does not prohibit pollution from marine geoengineering activities per se.[75] The final paragraph of the new provision ensures that there is no overlap between the marine geoengineering permitting regime and the core provision of the dumping regime contained in article 4 of the LP. To that effect, article 6bis(3) states that article 4 does not apply to activities listed in Annex 4.

2. Scope of the Amendment and Integration into the LP

The fact that the new LP article is no longer entitled "Placement of Matter into the Sea" as suggested under previous proposals, but emerged as addressing "Marine Geoengineering," is indicative of the developments regarding the scope of the regulatory mechanism as well as the type of regulatory regime developed under the LP. While the previous non-binding measures adopted under the LC/LP solely address OIF, and treat the activity as a subset of dumping in order to integrate it within the LC/LP, this amendment will create a new regime under the LP dealing with "marine geoengineering," separating it from "dumping." Indeed, the definition of marine geoengineering will be integrated into article 1 containing definitions for the purposes of the Protocol, as a separate entry rather than as part of the definition of dumping. Article 1(5bis) defines marine geoengineering as "a deliberate intervention in the marine environment to manipulate natural processes, including to counteract anthropogenic climate

---

[75] This distinction was highlighted during the discussions of the wording of paragraphs (2) and (3) of the new article 6bis; *see* IMO Doc. LC 34/4, "Report of the 4th Meeting of the Intersessional Working Group on Ocean Fertilization," July 27, 2012, ¶ 2.18.

change and/or its impacts, and that has the potential to result in deleterious effects, especially where those effects may be widespread, long lasting or severe."[76] The definition draws on the text of a definition developed under the CBD,[77] and incorporates terminology found in the ENMOD Convention.[78] The text taken from the CBD example has been adjusted for the purposes of the Protocol, limiting its scope to the marine environment. Another significant adjustment results in a definition that is much broader than the CBD example. As such, the LP definition is not limited to climate-related geoengineering but extends to marine geoengineering activities conducted for other purposes, leaving room for future regulation of yet unknown activities that fall within the scope of the LP and that may pose an unacceptable threat to the marine environment.[79] On the other hand, activities that fall within the LP definition are limited to those that have the potential to result in deleterious effects that are "widespread, long lasting or severe." These terms were adopted from the ENMOD Convention and are intended to include only activities with a high risk of potential harm.[80]

Although the LP definition of marine geoengineering is very broad, it must be read together with article 6bis(1), which limits the scope of the regulatory mechanism on marine geoengineering to those activities that fall within the scope of the Protocol. Therefore, the crucial criterion determining whether an activity may be covered by the new regulatory regime is that the activity entails "placement of matter into the sea from vessels, aircraft, platforms or other man-made structures at sea."[81]

3. New Annex 4

Annex 4 lists the activities that are subject to control under the new regulatory mechanism established under the Protocol. It follows the positive list approach; consequently, only marine geoengineering activities that are listed are subject to the prohibition contained in article 6bis(1) and may only be authorized in accordance with the relevant assessment procedures should the listing in Annex 4 provide for consideration of a permit. The only activity currently listed in Annex 4 is OIF. Paragraph 1 of this listing defines OIF, which remains unchanged from the definition already developed for Resolution LC-LP.1(2008) and which has been applied consistently in subsequent

---

[76] Resolution LP 4(8), Annex, art. 1, ¶ 5*bis*

[77] Secretariat of the Convention of Biological Diversity, "Geoengineering in Relation to the Convention on Biological Diversity: Technical and Regulatory Matters," 23 (2012).

[78] Convention on the Prohibition of Military or Any Other Hostile Use of Environmental Modification Techniques, Dec. 10, 1976, 1108 U.N.T.S. 151.

[79] For an explanatory note on the definition of LP article 1(5*bis*) on the definition of marine geoengineering, see IMO Doc. LC 34/4, "Report of the 4th Meeting of the Intersessional Working Group on Ocean Fertilization," July 27, 2012, ¶ 2.15.

[80] *Id.*

[81] Resolution LP 4(8), Annex, art. 6*bis*.

instruments and reports issued by the LC/LP.[82] The next paragraph stipulates that OIF activities may not be permitted unless they constitute legitimate scientific research, which is to be assessed as such in accordance with the specific assessment framework developed for this activity, as required by paragraph 3. In the case of OIF, this refers to the OF Assessment Framework adopted in 2010.

As this particular amendment package began to crystallize during the LC/LP meetings, the need for a procedure for the inclusion of additional activities in Annex 4 was noted. In 2012, the Consultative Meetings decided to develop a potential text for guidance of such a procedure, which is expected to be completed and considered for adoption at the Consultative Meeting of the LP in 2014.[83] Although some delegates have questioned the need for such a procedure, arguing that the procedural requirements contained in articles 21 and 22 of the Protocol provide for sufficient clarity, the current draft text of the "guidance for a procedure" suggests such a procedure is warranted due to the complex nature of marine geoengineering activities and the range of technical issues that require consideration.[84] The draft guidance advises that following the introduction of a proposal to include a new activity to Annex 4, the Scientific Groups of the LC/LP are to review such proposals involving external experts as appropriate. Following the review, the Scientific Groups are to provide recommendations to aid the Parties to the LP in their consideration of the proposal. The draft guidance also includes specific points for consideration by the Parties at this stage of the process.

4. New Annex 5

Another component of the amendment package is Annex 5, which sets out a "General assessment framework for matter that may be considered for placement under Annex 4" ("GAF"). The purpose of the GAF is to provide a legally binding minimum standard of assessment requirements for all marine geoengineering activities listed in Annex 4.[85] Thus, in accordance with article 6bis(2), a permit shall only be issued for an activity if all the conditions in Annex 5 are met. The text of paragraph 1 of the GAF expounds two aspects of its purpose, as providing the basic framework for the evaluation of newly listed activities, and serving as the basis of the development of any specific assessment frameworks addressing new marine geoengineering activities. The fact that the GAF sets out the minimum requirements of any specific assessment framework can also be

---

[82] Under the LC/LP, OIF has been defined as "any activity undertaken by humans with the principal intention of stimulating primary productivity in the oceans. Ocean fertilization does not include conventional aquaculture, or mariculture, or the creation of artificial reefs."

[83] *See* IMO Doc. 34/15, ¶ 4.23(2); IMO Doc. 35/15, ¶ 4.24.

[84] IMO Doc. 35/15, Annex 5 "Draft Guidance on a Procedure for Considering the Inclusion of New Activities in Annex 4 to the London Protocol."

[85] For a summary of considerations regarding the need, feasibility, and content for the GAF, see IMO Doc. LC 34/4, "Report of the 4th Meeting of the Intersessional Working Group on Ocean Fertilization," July 27, 2012, ¶¶ 3.4–3.6.

inferred from paragraph 3 of the GAF, which provides that Parties meeting the terms of any specific assessment framework shall be deemed to be in compliance with Annex 5.

As a result of this rule of reference, the non-binding specific assessment framework that is likely to have much more stringent requirements has been integrated into the regulatory mechanism. However, it would be incorrect to conclude that the OF Assessment Framework will be legally binding once the amendment enters into force; rather, an assessment under the specific assessment framework is considered as fulfilling the legally binding conditions contained in Annex 5 necessary to issue a permit for an activity listed in Annex 4. A comprehensive analysis of the provisions contained in the GAF is outside the scope of this chapter; however, the following details its basic elements and notable provisions.

As a first step, the GAF requires a description of the activity so as to establish that the activity is indeed subject to authorization under Annex 4.[86] In this regard, this section contains provisions on "marine scientific research related to marine geoengineering." Paragraph 7 lists specific purposes for which such scientific research activities are recognized, which include the better understanding of natural processes generally, as well as the better understanding of the potential environmental impact and efficacy of geoengineering techniques themselves. This list is not exhaustive, and it provides an indicator of legitimate marine scientific research purposes in the context of the regulatory regime established by the London Protocol. Paragraph 8 of the GAF sets out the attributes of marine scientific research recognized under this regulatory regime, mostly reproducing the list of criteria found in the specific assessment framework developed for OIF.[87] In accordance with these criteria, research activities must: (1) be designed to answer questions that will add to the body of scientific knowledge; (2) apply appropriate methodologies based on the best available knowledge and technology; (3) be subject to scientific peer review at appropriate stages in the assessment process; (4) ensure that economic interests do not influence the design, conduct, and/or outcomes of the proposed activity; and, (5) ensure that the proponents of the proposed activity make a commitment to publish the results in peer-reviewed scientific publications.

The bulk of the GAF provisions comprise the environmental impact assessment and monitoring requirements, which will not be analyzed in this chapter. However, the provisions addressing consultation merit some attention. Paragraphs 10–12 of the GAF set out a consultation procedure where the activity may affect maritime areas under the jurisdiction of another state, or where the activity affects areas beyond national jurisdiction. The language of these provisions is predominantly hortatory. Only two obligations are found in these paragraphs. The first requires Parties to establish a consultation process with all stakeholders nationally or internationally at the point where a proposal is submitted, as well as during the assessment process. The second requires a peer review of

---

[86] The OF Assessment Framework refers to this stage as the "initial assessment."
[87] OF Assessment Framework, para. 2.2.

the information and data provided by the proponent with regard to its scientific and techni-cal quality. Finally, the issue of prior consent that surfaced during the development of the OF Assessment Framework is not treated differently under the GAF. Accordingly, prior consent is not required, but Parties proposing marine geoengineering activities should seek the consent of all countries with jurisdiction or interests in the region of potential impact.

III. Assessment of the LC/LP Regulatory Mechanism for Marine Geoengineering

Since the threat of the deployment of large-scale ocean fertilization activities for com-mercial purposes was brought to the attention of the LC/LP Scientific Groups in 2007, a "global, transparent and effective regulatory and control mechanism" for marine geo-engineering has been developed under the framework of the LC/LP. Although the ini-tial non-binding measures dealt only with ocean fertilization and addressed Parties to both instruments, further development of a global, transparent, and effective regulatory and control mechanism led to the amendment of the London Protocol so as to create a regulatory regime for marine geoengineering. The following discusses the ramifica-tions of this regulatory regime in the context of the development of the law of the sea and governance of the marine commons. In doing so, the LC/LP Resolutions on OIF and the LP amendment will be evaluated focusing on three issues: (1) the scope of the LC/LP, (2) the effectiveness of the regulatory regime for marine geoengineering, and (3) the implications of the LP amendment on the high seas freedom of marine scientific research.

A. SCOPE

In the Resolution to which the amendments are attached,[88] the Parties to the LP recall that the objectives of the LP include the protection and preservation of the environ-ment from all sources of pollution,[89] and that, in implementing the London Protocol, Contracting Parties are obliged to apply a precautionary approach to environmen-tal protection.[90] Nevertheless, the amendment results in a significant evolution of the Protocol, particularly as it develops rules dealing with "placement of matter" other than placement activities that are exempt from the definition of dumping. The interpretation of the placement exemption has been noted as being part of an unfinished voyage in the evolution of the dumping regime as no consensus could be achieved on the matter when

---

[88] Resolution LP.4(8).
[89] London Protocol, art. 2.
[90] London Protocol, art. 3(1).

it was discussed during the 24th to 27th Consultative Meetings.[91] The development of the non-binding measures dealing with OIF, and the amendment to the London Protocol in particular, is therefore indicative of the Parties' willingness to broadly interpret "placement," and consequently the breadth of the scope of the London Convention and Protocol, if this is necessary to attain the LC/LP objective to protect and preserve the environment from all sources of pollution.

Linking OIF and other marine geoengineering activities to placement of matter under the LC/LP also weighs against the argument that the development of the regulatory regime for marine geoengineering effectively extends the scope of the LC/LP. This argument supports the view that the primary mandate of the LC/LP concerns the regulation of dumping, the objective of which is the deliberate disposal of waste, whereas OIF seeks to manipulate the marine environment.[92] The application of the LC/LP framework for the regulation of OIF is thus seen as a "creative solution" to the lack of a regulatory framework that could adequately address geoengineering.[93] However, the link between OIF and other marine geoengineering activities with the introduction of substances into the marine environment ensures that the regulatory regime can only address activities that fall within the scope of the LC/LP.

Perhaps it is more useful to regard this latest development as an *elaboration* of the scope of the London Protocol, rather than an extension. In fact, this is not the first time that the Parties to the LC/LP have interpreted the scope of the Convention to include activities that do not fall within the definition of dumping.[94] Also in the case of incineration of industrial wastes at sea, the Parties' approach was to elaborate on the scope of the London Convention so as to include incineration of wastes in the regulatory framework of the LC/LP.[95] The dumping of industrial wastes was subject to the permitting regime established under the London Convention; however, the incineration of industrial wastes onboard a vessel fell outside the scope of the definition of dumping. The Parties to the Convention amended Annex 1 so as to include the incineration of industrial wastes under the existing permitting regime,[96] because incineration involved the

---

[91] David VanderZwaag & Anne Daniel, *International Law and Ocean Dumping: Steering a Precautionary Course aboard the 1996 London Protocol, but Still an Unfinished Voyage, in* THE FUTURE OF OCEAN REGIME-BUILDING : ESSAYS IN TRIBUTE TO DOUGLAS M. JOHNSTON 515, 522 (2009).

[92] This view is expounded in the statement submitted by the U.S. delegation to the 2011 LC/LP Meetings; *see* IMO Doc. LC 33/15, Annex 2.

[93] Karen Scott, for example, argues that the development of a new protocol on geoengineering to the UNFCCC would be more adequate; Scott, *supra* note 8, at 355.

[94] The author is grateful to have benefitted from Prof. A.H.A. Soons's experience and comments on the subject, which have highlighted the similarities of the approaches to incorporate incineration and OIF into the LC/LP framework.

[95] On the development of the London Convention, including details in regard to incineration at sea, see Olav Schram Stokke, *Beyond Dumping ? The Effectiveness of the London Convention*, 8 YB. INT'L CO-OPERATION ENVTL. DEV. 39 (1998).

[96] Resolution LC.50(16), "Amendment to Annex 1 to the [LC] concerning Incineration at Sea;" IMO Doc. 16/14, "Report of the 16th Consultative Meeting of Contracting Parties to the [LC]," Nov. 12, 1993, Annex 4.

deliberate disposal of waste and posed threats to the marine environment due to the risk of spills or, more importantly, due to the transfer of the resulting atmospheric pollution into the marine environment.[97] Under the London Protocol, the treatment of incineration of waste is similar to that which would later be applied to marine geoengineering.[98] Accordingly, incineration is integrated into the Protocol where it is defined in article 1(5) as an activity separate from dumping, and the general prohibition on incineration is found in article 5 of the Protocol.

The development of the regulatory mechanism for OIF and other marine geoengineering activities reflects the Parties' continued willingness to interpret the scope of the London Convention and Protocol. The LP amendment has also shown that its scope may be continuously elaborated so as include activities that are not related to dumping but require a risk assessment so as to prevent pollution of the marine environment. While the LP regulatory mechanism ensures that the scope of LP will not extend beyond activities that involve the placement of matter into the sea, the mechanism is limited in its ability to address the issue of geoengineering in its broader context. However, future consideration concerning the listing of marine geoengineering activities in Annex 4 of the LP and the development of specific assessment frameworks is likely to prompt their discussion in other relevant international forums as in the case of OIF.

B. EFFECTIVENESS

Regarding the effectiveness of the regulatory regime developed for marine geoengineering, the global scope of the LC/LP framework offers a clear advantage so that, at least from a geographical perspective, the LC/LP marine geoengineering provisions will apply to all marine areas once they enter into force, including areas beyond national jurisdiction. Furthermore, the legal framework established by the London Convention and Protocol has a very broad membership, with ninety-seven Parties, which includes most coastal states with developed or emerging economies. Although the membership to the Protocol comprises just forty-three Parties, the Protocol is intended to eventually supersede the Convention, and Parties to the Convention are continuously encouraged to ratify the Protocol, while the meetings of the administrative bodies to both instruments are held concurrently and follow joint work programs.[99] Many major coastal states are already a Party to the Protocol, and a number of important Parties to the London

---

[97] Similar to the case of OIF, the positions of the Contracting Parties to the London Convention on whether its scope could be interpreted to include waste incineration were divided. *See* George C. Kassoulides, *Ban on Marine Incineration*, 19 MARINE POLLUTION BULL. 648 (1988); Scott Davison, *Atmospheric Depositions*, *in* THE NORTH SEA: PERSPECTIVES ON REGIONAL ENVIRONMENTAL CO-OPERATION (SPECIAL ISSUE OF THE INTERNATIONAL JOURNAL OF ESTUARINE AND COASTAL LAW) (David Freestone & Ton Ijlstra eds., 1990).

[98] *See supra* Section II.

[99] *See supra* notes 32–33 and accompanying text.

Convention are actively working toward ratification of the Protocol, including Brazil, Argentina, and importantly, the United States.[100]

The current state of the LC/LP framework, which is made up of two separate instruments that exist in parallel until the reforming London Protocol replaces the London Convention, also affects the new regulatory regime dealing with marine geoengineering. This new regime should be understood as encompassing two elements: a non-binding element focused on OIF that addresses all LC/LP Parties, and a binding element that primarily reinforces the non-binding measures once the LP amendment enters into force. Although the scope of the binding element is more extensive, as it provides the Parties to the LP with the option to apply a basic assessment framework to other marine geoengineering activities, the binding element does not currently extend to activities other than OIF. Moreover, the full implementation of the OF Assessment Framework, arguably the most crucial component of the regulatory regime, continues to be dependent on the position of the Parties to the LC and the LP concerning the permissibility of OIF experiments. Even when the amendment enters into force, LP Parties must apply the standards contained in the generic assessment framework, which are less extensive than those under the OF Assessment Framework.

Given that the Protocol is to eventually replace the Convention, the binding element of the marine geoengineering regime should attract broader membership. On the other hand, the adoption of a binding measure that effectively extends the scope of the Protocol may hinder this process as it may discourage additional ratifications of the Protocol.[101] A considerable advantage of the amendment to the Protocol is that it creates a legally binding permitting regime making the regulation of OIF and other marine geoengineering activities more effective.[102] Indeed, the requirement to adopt national legislation regulating marine geoengineering activities in accordance with the amendment will prevent controversy regarding the legality of projects such as that of the 2009 German-Indian LOHAFEX ocean fertilization experiment[103] and that of the 2012 Haida Salmon Restoration Corporation.[104]

In addition, the legal effect of rules and standards developed under the LC/LP may extend beyond the membership of the LC/LP and affect nonmember States that are bound by UNCLOS.[105] Under UNCLOS, parties must cooperate through competent international organizations to implement the provisions of UNCLOS and develop specific rules for the regulation of activities governed by the law of the

---

[100] *See* summary concerning the status of the London Convention and the Protocol contained in the annual reports of the LC/LP Consultative Meetings.

[101] *See* IMO Doc. LC33/15, ¶ 4.21.

[102] *See* IMO Doc. LC 33/4 Report of the 3rd Meeting of the Intersessional Working Group on Ocean Fertilization (June 20, 2011); *see also* Rayfuse, *supra* note 57.

[103] *See supra* notes 49–52 and accompanying text.

[104] *See supra* notes 70–72 and accompanying text.

[105] De la Fayette, *supra* note 32, at 516.

sea.[106] In the context of pollution from dumping, UNCLOS article 210 requires parties to adopt national laws, regulations, and other measures to prevent, reduce, and control marine pollution by dumping, which are no less effective than the global rules and standards established by competent international organizations. Thus, it may be argued that the international rules, standards, and recommended practices and procedures developed under the London Convention and Protocol may be applicable to states as a result of their obligations under UNCLOS even if they are not a party to the LC/LP.[107] However, it is unclear whether this requirement under UNCLOS will apply to the LC/LP measures taken in regard to OIF or marine geoengineering, particularly as these activities do not involve "dumping" as defined in UNCLOS or the London Convention and Protocol.[108] Given the different positions on the further development of a binding regulatory framework on marine geoengineering among LC/LP Parties, and the more limited membership of the London Protocol, the LP amendment and its provisions on marine geoengineering will certainly have to be widely ratified before they may be considered as "generally accepted international rules and standards" that will bind third states as a result of the obligations contained in UNCLOS.

C. HIGH SEAS FREEDOM OF SCIENTIFIC RESEARCH

The development of a regulatory regime for marine geoengineering shows that the freedom of scientific research on the high seas is no longer seen as providing a carte blanche to explore potential uses of the oceans where such research activities may pose a significant threat to the marine environment. While this freedom is qualified by other rules of international law, including broad international legal principles on the environment,[109] these norms do not impose specific constraints on conducting marine scientific research, and their implementation by individual states depends on the position they may take toward the need and risks associated with such research activities.[110]

---

[106] For a list of UNCLOS provisions and relevant competent international organizations, see DOALOS, "Competent or Relevant International Organizations under the United Nations Convention on the Law of the Sea," No. 31 LAW OF THE SEA BULL. 79 (1996).

[107] *See* Tullio Treves, *The Law of the Sea "System" of Institutions*, MAX PLANCK YB. UNITED NATIONS LAW 325 (1998); Budislav Vukas, *Generally Accepted International Rules and Standards*, *in* IMPLEMENTATION OF THE LAW OF THE SEA CONVENTION THROUGH INTERNATIONAL INSTITUTIONS (Alfred H.A. Soons ed., 1990); Bernard H. Oxman, *The Duty to Respect Generally Accepted International Standards*, 24 N.Y.U. J. INT'L L.& POL. 109 (1991); De la Fayette, *supra* note 32, at 516.

[108] Verlaan, *supra* note 22, at 810–11.

[109] UNCLOS article 87 provides that high seas freedoms are subject to the provisions found elsewhere in UNCLOS as well as in other rules of international law. This includes international environmental legal principles, many of which are reflected in the environmental obligations found in part XII of UNCLOS. For marine scientific research specifically, UNCLOS article 240(d) requires that marine scientific research be conducted "in compliance with regulations... for the protection and preservation of the environment." *See also supra* notes 20–27 and accompanying text.

[110] For a discussion of the limits of international environmental law in relation to marine geoengineering, see Bodansky, *supra* note 26, at 312–13; Scott, *supra* note 8, at 333–50.

Reconciling these different positions has necessitated that a balance be struck between the protection of the environment and the pursuit of marine geoengineering for scientific research purposes. This balance is reflected in the LP Resolution adopting the amendment under discussion here, which recognizes the importance of the conservation and sustainable use of the oceans. The Resolution also references UN General Assembly resolutions recalling the "importance of marine scientific research for understanding and conserving the world's marine environment and its resources,"[111] as well as the need to support the further study of OIF.[112]

In developing a specific regulatory framework for OIF and other marine geoengineering activities through the multilateral framework provided by the LC/LP, its parties have agreed on the specific implementation of the precautionary approach in relation to marine geoengineering activities conducted for scientific research purposes. To this end, and in the absence of an internationally agreed definition of marine scientific research,[113] the LC/LP process has articulated a number of criteria to apply in assessing whether activities constitute scientific research as part of the OF Assessment Framework and the General Assessment Framework.[114]

The approach taken toward the regulation of marine geoengineering and the concomitant formulation of scientific attributes represent an important development both in relation to addressing an issue of high seas governance and the development of a definition of scientific research in international law. Indeed, the recent judgment of the ICJ concerning whaling in the Antarctic illustrates that it has become increasingly necessary to scrutinize under international law activities that are conducted under the chapeau of scientific research.[115] While a moratorium on marine geoengineering activities generally would have prevented further consideration of marine geoengineering as an option to address climate change, the approach taken under the LC/LP leaves room for scientific investigation of geoengineering and its impact on the marine environment.[116]

However, particularly where such activities may affect the interests of other states and the international community as a whole, as in the case of scientific research relating to global commons such as the climate and the marine environment, it is necessary to establish clear international legal standards so as to distinguish activities conducted

---

[111] The relevant preambular paragraph of Resolution LP 4(8) quotes UNGA resolution 67/78 (adopted Dec. 11, 2012).

[112] LP 4(8) refers to UNGA resolution 62/215, ¶ 98(adopted Dec. 22, 2007).

[113] Verlaan, *supra* note 22, at 1.

[114] For further detail on these criteria, see *supra* notes 46–71 and accompanying text.

[115] Whaling in the Antarctic (Australia v. Japan: New Zealand intervening), Judgement of the International Court of Justice of Mar. 31, 2014, *available at* http://www.icj-cij.org/docket/files/148/18136.pdf (last visited Apr. 10, 2014).

[116] For a detailed analysis on the need for international law to allow scientific research exploring the geoengineering option, see Kerstin Güssow et al., *Ocean Iron Fertilization: Time to Lift the Research Taboo*, *in* CLIMATE CHANGE GEO-ENGINEERING: PHILOSPHICAL PERSPECTIVES, LEGAL ISSUES, AND GOVERNANCE FRAMEWORKS (Wil C.G. Burns & Andrew L. Strauss eds., 2013).

for the purpose of scientific research from those that are not, and to ensure that such activities are conducted in accordance with the international legal obligation to protect and preserve the environment. The parties to the LC/LP have applied the precautionary approach to marine geoengineering for scientific purposes, and, through the development of specific assessment frameworks, they have set international standards for acceptable environmental risks associated with such marine scientific research activities. An international permitting regime for marine geoengineering therefore ensures that such activities are conducted with due regard for the interests of other states and in accordance with the conditions that are placed on the exercise of the high seas freedom of scientific research.

Conclusion

The amendment to the London Protocol to regulate placement of matter for ocean fertilization and other marine geoengineering activities is an important development in the context of high seas governance. While the principle of freedom of the high seas is an essential element of the legal order of the oceans, the exercise of high seas freedoms is subject to the conditions set out in other rules of international law, as well as the frame of reference for regulation provided by principles of international environmental law.

As an existing international legal framework, the London Protocol has been elaborated so as to establish a regulatory regime for emerging ocean uses such as marine geoengineering, ensuring the application of a precautionary approach to OIF, and other marine geoengineering activities as they may emerge in the future. In addition, by adopting the amendment to the London Protocol, its Parties have struck a balance between two competing values; namely, the protection of the marine environment from activities that can potentially cause it severe harm, and the necessity to further study the effect of geoengineering on the marine environment.

However, the international community's effort to regulate OIF is incomplete. While the amendment to the London Protocol sets an important precedent for the international regulation of geoengineering, its applicability is limited to marine geoengineering techniques that fall within the scope of the London Protocol, which has left other geoengineering techniques unregulated at the international level. The international community is yet to assign a forum in which to discuss the broader policy questions arising from geoengineering and encourage broad membership to regulatory mechanisms such as that established for OIF.

18 Law, Climate Change, and the Marine Environment in the Indian Ocean Region
Dr. Erika J. Techera

Introduction

The Indian Ocean region stretches from South Africa north to the Arab Sea, east across South and Southeast Asia, and south again to Australia. The countries of the region include about 30 percent of the world's population and 25 percent of the global landmass. It is an area that is rich in natural resources. This region provides approximately 40 percent of the world's energy sources, and a significant proportion of international trade passes through it.[1]

The Indian Ocean rim countries are diverse in almost every way—geographically, environmentally, politico-legally, economically, and socioculturally. Yet many of them have historically been linked in some way, most commonly by their connection with the sea.[2] The Arabs and Persians were great seafarers, and their legacy is evident in the

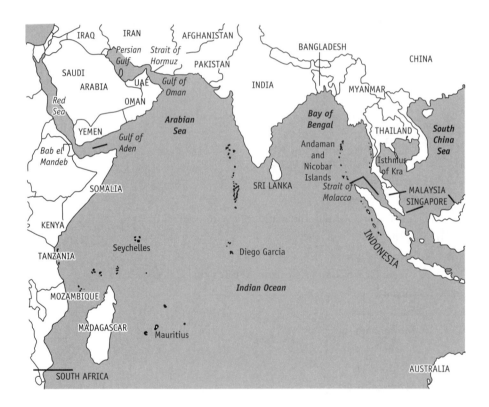

[1] See Brahma Chellaney, *Indian Ocean Maritime Security: Energy, Environmental and Climate Challenges*, 6 J. INDIAN OCEAN REGION 155 (2010) (quoting Manmohan Singh, Prime Minister of India, PM Inaugurates Indian Ocean Naval Symposium Seminar (Feb. 14, 2008) (transcript available at http://pmindia.nic.in/speech-details.php?nodeid=633)).

[2] Regarding South Africa, see Thean Potgieter, *South Africa and Maritime Power in the Indian Ocean*, 7 J. INDIAN OCEAN REGION 52 (2011).

widespread adherence to the Islamic faith from the Middle East to Southeast Asia.[3] The African states were well connected with the Indian subcontinent through trade still evidenced today, for example, by the rupee, which remains the currency in the Seychelles.[4] The legacy of European exploration and colonization is also apparent. Despite these historical linkages, the great differences among the countries around the Indian Ocean rim have contributed to the lack of regional cohesion.

As will be explored in this chapter, there has tended to be a lack of focus on the Indian Ocean as a region. The area spans three continents, and many of the Indian Ocean rim countries participate in other multilateral institutions. This may explain the lack of regionally based initiatives; it is, however, unhelpful in addressing climate change for the following reasons. The Indian Ocean is one marine area and includes many species that migrate in and out of the inshore waters of multiple countries. In addition, across the region, coastal communities face similar challenges in adapting to climate change. The marine environment is of commercial value too, both in terms of fishing and shipping. For example, most of India's trade still comes by sea. It is therefore timely and appropriate to explore the Indian Ocean rim countries as one region, particularly in the context of marine and coastal issues. This chapter addresses the underlying legal frameworks that have shaped the responses to environmental issues in general, and climate change in particular, in the Indian Ocean region.

I. Background

The Indian Ocean region is facing serious consequences as a result of environmental degradation due to both natural and anthropogenic causes. The environmental impacts are perhaps unsurprising given that this rapidly developing region contains the largest concentration of population in the world, which places substantial pressures on the environment and resources in the region.[5]

Climate change and its consequences are some of the most recent, and potentially most severe, impacts. The causes of anthropogenic climate change are clear: burning of fossil fuels and production of methane through agriculture, which produce greenhouse gases (GHGs), together with degradation of GHG sinks through processes such as deforestation. Responsibility for anthropogenic climate change rests largely with the industrialized nations of the global North. Nevertheless, nations in the global South with rapidly growing populations and rising economic development are likely to continue to contribute significantly to GHG emissions as energy security and economic development remain national priorities. In this region, India is a notable example. Eight of the

---

[3] *See* Chellaney, *supra* note 1.
[4] *See* Alex Vines & Bereni Oruitemeka, *Engagement with the African Indian Ocean Rim States*, 14 S. Afr. J. Int'l Affairs 111 (2007).
[5] *See* Chellaney, *supra* note 1, at 165–66.

world's top twenty GHG emitters are located in the Indian Ocean region: Australia, India, Indonesia, Iran, Malaysia, Saudi Arabia, South Africa, and Thailand.[6] In addition, the region includes some of the world's highest per capita emitters of CO_2: Qatar, Kuwait, United Arab Emirates, Bahrain, Australia, Oman, Saudi Arabia, and Brunei.

Despite being a global issue, climate change is likely to have a greater impact on the Indian Ocean region than in other areas because of its geography, population density, large low-lying areas, and many coastal cities.[7] Impacts include sea-level rise, ocean acidification, changing meteorological patterns (*i.e.*, increase in severity and frequency of extreme weather events leading to freshwater concerns and resulting in human migration), and changes in land use practices.[8] The developing countries in the region are particularly vulnerable to climate change as they rely heavily on natural systems.[9] Although the issues have been well recognized, and the likely impacts and necessary policy responses have been explored for some time,[10] beneficial outcomes cannot be assured, and results to date have not been positive.

The impacts of climate change extend beyond environmental issues to socioeconomic concerns as coastal retreat affects land use and coastal communities, and oceanic changes impact food and livelihoods. For example, India may well face inward migration from Bangladesh as saltwater inundates land areas, whereas the Maldivian population may have to relocate away from its islands as sea level continues to rise in the future.[11] Low-lying islands such as the Maldives, with 80 percent of its landmass just one meter or less above sea level, are highly susceptible to the threat of sea-level rise from the erosion it has already caused and the destruction it is likely to cause in the future. Other countries, such as India, have a high population and face food security issues as coastal communities can no longer rely on marine resources for food and livelihoods.

In responding to this challenge, nations in the region face varying difficulties, depending on their geography, population density, capacity (or lack of it) to respond, proximity to the sea, and respective levels of existing and predicted environmental degradation.[12] For example, by far the most wealthy and developed country on the Indian Ocean rim is Australia. It has a relatively low population and large land area, and can therefore afford to respond to climate change in a variety of ways. Nations such as the

---

[6] Dennis Rumley, *Ideology, Carbon Emissions and Climate Change Discourses in the Indian Ocean Region*, 6 J. INDIAN OCEAN REGION 147, 150 (2010).

[7] *See* Chellaney, *supra* note 1.

[8] *See* Weiqing Han et al., *Patterns of Indian Ocean Sea-Level Change in a Warming Climate*, 3 NATURE GEOSCI. 546 (2010) (discussing sea-level rise); *see also* Igor M. Belkin, *Rapid Warming of Large Marine Ecosystems*, 81 PROGRESS OCEANOGRAPHY 207 (2009).

[9] *See* Lydia Powell, *Climate and the Clash between the Diversely Developed*, 6 J. INDIAN OCEAN REGION 169 (2010).

[10] For an early analysis, see F.J. Gable, D.G. Aubrey & J.H. Gentile, *Global Environmental Change Issues in the Western Indian Ocean Region*, 22 GEOFORUM 401 (1991).

[11] *See* Chellaney, *supra* note 1, at 162.

[12] *Id.* at 165.

Maldives are developing countries and, in some cases, are also small-island developing states or least-developed countries, or both. Others have historically been less politically stable and only recently have begun to address socioeconomic issues, and have yet to tackle complex environmental ones. The Arab states, also on the Indian Ocean rim, have economic interests associated with oil production that, when combined with less serious impacts such as sea-level rise, make them less inclined to take aggressive regulatory measures.

Therefore, although the Indian Ocean region contains significant GHG emitters—most notably India and South Africa[13]—the small-island developing states in the region are among the least responsible for climate change. The developing nature of many Indian Ocean rim countries makes it likely that this reality will increase over the next century.[14]

This chapter first outlines the responses that Indian Ocean rim countries have taken to address climate change impacts. The status of regional law and policy is then examined, followed by an analysis of four case study countries: South Africa, Mozambique, the Seychelles, and the Maldives. These nations each illustrate a different context in which environmental challenges are faced, and have prompted a variety of legal responses. The Maldives is an Asian state, whereas the other nations are African. The Seychelles and the Maldives are island nations. South Africa and Mozambique are continental countries with some shared history but different contemporary context. Significantly, they each have a different legal history and system in place. Therefore, the legal foundations for environmental law in each country are explored with a focus on laws relating to coastal climate change adaptation.

II. The Law and Policy Response

A. INTERNATIONAL

1. Overview

There has been a rapid expansion in international environmental law in the past three decades. Simultaneously, there has been an emergence of international environmental principles, many of which are associated with sustainable development. These include the precautionary principle, polluter pays, conservation of biodiversity, and common but differentiated responsibilities.[15] It is this last principle that has allowed for different obligations and time frames to be applied to developing and developed countries. The flexibility of the common but differentiated responsibility principle was a factor in

---

[13] *See* Rumley, *supra* note 6, at 150.

[14] Ross Garnaut, Climate Change Review, Commonwealth of Australia, 88 (2008).

[15] For a detailed examination of such environmental principles, see Nicolas de Sadeleer, Environmental Principles: From Political Slogans to Legal Rules (2002).

the success of the Montreal Protocol treaty regime on stratospheric ozone depletion.[16] Despite these developments, some areas of international environmental law remain contested. This tension is perhaps best illustrated by the UN Framework Convention on Climate Change (UNFCCC) and the accompanying Kyoto Protocol, including the ongoing international negotiations for a future agreement as of this writing. Despite broad acceptance of anthropogenic climate change and a legal framework that follows a similar approach to that used in addressing ozone depletion, the international community has struggled to meet obligations, and remains divided over future regimes.

Each of the four case study countries considered in this chapter have ratified the key international environmental treaties: the Convention on Biological Diversity (CBD),[17] Convention on Migratory Species (CMS),[18] Convention on International Trade in Endangered Species (CITES),[19] UN Convention on the Law of the Sea (UNCLOS),[20] the Montreal Protocol,[21] and the International Convention for the Prevention of Pollution from Ships (1973), as modified by the 1978 Protocol to the International Convention for the Prevention of Pollution from Ships (MARPOL 1973/78).[22] All but the Maldives are also parties to the Convention on Wetlands of International Importance especially as Waterfowl Habitat (1971).[23] Although endorsement of the Kyoto Protocol resulted only in emission reductions for developed countries, less than 50 percent of Indian Ocean states have supported the more recent Copenhagen Accord, including only three of the largest emitters: India, South Africa, and Australia.[24]

This support for international environmental law demonstrates a commitment to working within the international framework to address these environmental issues, and it is important for Indian Ocean countries to do so.[25] Identifying common international commitments among Indian Ocean countries is important as it demonstrates "convergent and mutual expectations on the accepted international

---

[16] ERICH VRANES, TRADE AND THE ENVIRONMENT: FUNDAMENTAL ISSUES IN INTERNATIONAL LAW, WTO LAW, AND LEGAL THEORY 353 (2009).

[17] Convention on Biological Diversity, opened for signature June 5, 1992, 1760 U.N.T.S. 79 (entered into force Dec. 29, 1993) [hereinafter CBD].

[18] Convention on the Conservation of Migratory Species of Wild Animals, opened for signature June 23, 1979, 19 I.L.M. 15 (entered into force Nov. 1, 1983) [hereinafter CMS].

[19] Convention on International Trade in Endangered Species of Wild Fauna and Flora, opened for signature Mar. 3, 1973, 993 U.N.T.S. 243 (entered into force July 1, 1975) [hereinafter CITES].

[20] United Nations Convention on the Law of the Sea, opened for signature Dec. 10, 1982, 1833 U.N.T.S. 3 (entered into force Nov. 16, 1994) [hereinafter UNCLOS].

[21] Protocol on Substances That Deplete the Ozone Layer, opened for signature Sept. 16, 1987, 26 I.L.M. 154 (entered into force Jan. 1, 1989) [hereinafter Montreal Protocol].

[22] International Convention for the Prevention of Pollution by Ships, opened for signature Nov. 2, 1973, 1340 U.N.T.S. 61 (entered into force Oct. 2, 1983) [hereinafter MARPOL].

[23] Convention on Wetlands of International Importance especially as Waterfowl Habitat, opened for signature Feb. 2, 1971 996 U.N.T.S. 245 (entered into force Dec. 21, 1975) [hereinafter Ramsar Convention].

[24] See Rumley, supra note 6.

[25] See Gable, Aubrey & Gentile, supra note 10.

principles, norms, rules, and procedures of the international regimes" and provides a common platform for law and policy developments.[26] International environmental law can form a foundation for national, subregional, and regional initiatives.[27] For example, the UNFCCC, CBD, and UNCLOS provide a basis for protected area management, and MARPOL governs marine pollution protection and allows for the designation of special management areas. Broad endorsement also shows that each country is prepared to make commitments; however, there is little evidence of regional collaboration or coalitions that might identify and enhance opportunities to meet these obligations.

2. The Indian Ocean in International Environmental Law

Under the UNFCCC, parties are organized into five regional groups,[28] but in practice other groupings are of far more significance. These groupings, however, are not regionally based. One example is the Alliance of Small Island States (AOSIS), which is a coalition of forty-three low-lying and small island countries, including the Seychelles, Mauritius, and Comoros. The Umbrella Group of non-EU developed countries is another example, as is the Least Developed Countries grouping.[29] The only relevant regional alliances are the European Union (EU), which meets privately to formulate common negotiating positions and periodic African regional workshops.[30]

There is more evidence of regional initiatives under the CBD, including some Regional Biodiversity Strategies and Action Plans formulated through preexisting regional organizations.[31] These are based on continental groupings, and none cross these boundaries. Nonetheless, the CBD has catalyzed a great deal of relevant work through its programs. Examples of these programs include the *Southern Indian Ocean Regional Workshop to*

---

[26] Aldo Chircop et al., *Governance of Marine Protected Areas in East Africa: A Comparative Study of Mozambique, South Africa, and Tanzania*, 41 OCEAN DEV. & INT'L L. 1, 3 (2010).

[27] *See* José Guerreiro et al., *Establishing a Transboundary Network of Marine Protected Areas: Diplomatic and Management Options for the East African Context*, 34 MARINE POL'Y 896 (2010).

[28] African States, Asian States, Eastern European States, Latin American and the Caribbean States, and the Western European and Other States (the "Other States" include Australia, Canada, Iceland, New Zealand, Norway, Switzerland, and the United States, but not Japan, which is in the Asian Group): *see Party Groupings*, UNITED NATIONS FRAMEWORK CONVENTION ON CLIMATE CHANGE, http://unfccc.int/parties_and_observers/parties/negotiating_groups/items/2714.php (last visited Jan. 5, 2014).

[29] Mozambique is listed as a Least Developed Country. *See UN List of Least Developed Countries*, UNITED NATIONS CONFERENCE ON TRADE AND DEVELOPMENT, http://unctad.org/en/pages/aldc/Least%20 Developed%20Countries/UN-list-of-Least-Developed-Countries.aspx (last visited Jan. 5, 2014).

[30] UNITED NATIONS FRAMEWORK CONVENTION ON CLIMATE CHANGE, AFRICAN REGIONAL WORKSHOP ON ADAPTATION, http://unfccc.int/adaptation/adverse_effects_and_response_measures_ art_48/items/3743.php (last visited Jan. 5, 2014).

[31] *Regional Biodiversity Strategies and Action Plans*, CONVENTION ON BIOLOGICAL DIVERSITY, http://www.cbd.int/nbsap/related-info/region-bsap/ (last visited Mar. 10, 2014).

Facilitate the Description of Ecologically or Biologically Significant Marine Areas, the *West Indian Ocean Partnership*, and the program on Climate Change and Biodiversity.[32]

UNCLOS encourages regional cooperation, but there are no regional initiatives within the treaty framework itself. Much more has been accomplished under the auspices of the UNEP Regional Seas Programme.[33] This program covers eighteen regions of the world, but not the Indian Ocean region as a whole. The East African Region adopted the *Nairobi Convention for the Protection, Management and Development of the Marine and Coastal Environment of the Eastern African Region* in 1985, which was amended in 2010. Both Mozambique and the Seychelles are parties to that Convention and the *Protocol Concerning Protected Areas and Wild Fauna and Flora in the Eastern African Region*, which does not refer to climate change. The only other relevant regional program is the South Asian Seas, of which India and the Maldives are members. The 1995 South Asian Seas Action Plan "focuses on Integrated Coastal Zone Management, oil-spill contingency planning, human resource development and the environmental effects of land-based activities."[34] Although climate change issues are acknowledged, there are no legal instruments or programs that focus on it.[35]

With respect to fisheries, the Food and Agriculture Organization (FAO) lists five regional fishery bodies: South Indian Ocean Fisheries Agreement (SIOFA),[36] the Indian Ocean Tuna Commission (IOTC),[37] Bay of Bengal Programme Inter-Governmental Organization (BOBP-IGO),[38] Regional Commission for Fisheries (RECOFI),[39] and Regional Organization for the Conservation of the Environment of the Red Sea and Gulf of Aden (PERSGA).[40] The focus of most of these bodies is conservation and

---

[32] West Indian Ocean Partnership, *available at* http://www.cbd.int/islands/doc/wiop/wiop-factsheet-en.pdf (last visited June 18, 2014).

[33] *UNEP Administered Programmes*, United Nations Environment Programme, http://www.unep.org/regionalseas/programmes/unpro/default.asp (last visited July 28, 2014).

[34] *South Asian Seas*, United Nations Environment Programme, http://www.unep.org/regionalseas/programmes/nonunep/southasian/default.asp (last visited July 28, 2014).

[35] *See, e.g.*, Malé Declaration on Control and Prevention of Air Pollution and Its Likely Transboundary Effects for South Asia, *available at* http://www.sacep.org/html/docs_mos_maledec.htm (last visited July 28, 2014), which makes no mention of climate change.

[36] Parties to SIOFA are Australia, Cook Islands, the European Union, Mauritius, and the Seychelles. *See Southern Indian Ocean Fisheries Agreement*, Department of Agriculture, Fisheries and Forestry (DAFF), http://www.daff.gov.au/fisheries/international/siofa (last visited July 28, 2014).

[37] Membership includes the Maldives, Mozambique, and the Seychelles, as well as South Africa as a cooperating non-contracting party. *See Structure of the Commission*, Indian Ocean Tuna Commission, http://www.iotc.org/about-iotc/structure-commission (last visited July 28, 2014).

[38] India and the Maldives are parties. *See Regional Fishery Bodies*, FAO Fisheries and Aquaculture Department, http://www.fao.org/fishery/rfb/bobp_igo/en (last visited July 28, 2014).

[39] *Regional Commission for Fisheries*, FAO Fisheries and Aquaculture Department, http://www.fao.org/fishery/rfb/recofi/en (last visited July 28, 2014).

[40] *Regional Organization for the Conservation of the Environment of the Red Sea and Gulf of Aden*, FAO Fisheries and Aquaculture Department, *available at* http://www.fao.org/fishery/rfb/persga/en (last visited July 28, 2014).

management of fisheries for the purposes of economic development and food security. For example, the IOTC includes within its objectives the promotion of cooperation among members to ensure management, conservation, and optimum utilization of stocks and encouragement of sustainable development of such fisheries.[41] The SIOFA has the objective of ensuring the long-term conservation and sustainable use of non-highly migratory fish stocks in the high seas of the southern Indian Ocean.[42]

The above analysis shows that there are a number of initiatives and projects in the Indian Ocean region, but they rarely involve all relevant countries or address climate change on a regional basis. As will be discussed below, the lack of relevant regional initiatives flowing directly from international agreements has been compounded by the relative dearth of agreements and organizations emerging from within the region.

B. REGIONAL

1. Overview

Although other regions of the world have developed significant joint responses to environmental issues, including climate change, such as the Asia Pacific Economic Cooperation (APEC) Action Plan regarding low carbon energy uses and energy security,[43] initiatives in the Indian Ocean region have been disjointed and lack a unified environmental law framework. The first relevant regional organization to be established was the Indian Ocean Commission (IOC), formed by Mauritius in 1984. Despite focusing principally on regional economic development, it has done relatively little.

There are, however, some early regional agreements. The most notable of these are the African Convention on the Conservation of Nature and Natural Resources (ACCNNR)[44] and the Nairobi Convention for the Protection, Management and Development of the Marine and Coastal Environment of the Eastern African Region.[45] The ACCNNR focuses on "individual and joint action for the conservation, utilization and development of soil, water, flora and fauna."[46] The Nairobi Convention coordinates member states' efforts to plan and develop programs that strengthen their capacity to protect, manage, and develop their coastal and marine environment sustainably. It also

---

[41] IOTC, MISSION, *available at* http://www.iotc.org/English/info/mission.php (last visited May 1, 2014).

[42] *See* DAFF, *supra* note 36.

[43] *See* Rumley, *supra* note 6, at 150.

[44] Not signed by South Africa, India, or the Maldives. *See* African Convention on the Conservation of Nature and Natural Resources, Sept. 15, 1968, 1001 U.N.T.S. 3, *available at* http://www.au.int/en/treaties.

[45] Originally formulated in 1968, it was signed by the Seychelles in 1977 and Mozambique in 1981, then revised in Maputo in 2003. It has not been signed by India or Maldives, whereas South Africa is not a signatory to the amended 2010 Convention. *See* NAIROBI CONVENTION CONTRACTING PARTIES, UNITED NATIONS ENVIRONMENT PROGRAMME (last visited Mar. 10, 2014), http://www.unep.org/NairobiConvention/ The_Convention/Contracting_Parties/index.asp.

[46] African Convention, *supra* note 44, art. II.

provides a forum for intergovernmental discussions and promotes sharing of information and experiences. A number of relevant conferences have been held, and publications prepared, that build capacity in the region. Examples of these developments are the Regional Conference on Climate Change Impacts, Adaptation and Mitigation in the WIO Region: Solutions to the Crisis, and final report, *Climate Change Impacts in Coastal and Marine Areas of the Western Indian Ocean Region: An Assessment of Problems, Solutions, and Strategic Options for Promoting Climate Resilient Development in the WIO Region*. It has also facilitated the establishment of the Consortium for Conservation of Coastal and Marine Ecosystems in the Western Indian Ocean (WIO-C) between major NGOs in the Western Indian Ocean that have marine programs.

Without the support of strong regional organizations, such efforts are unlikely to succeed. The Indian Ocean Marine Affairs Cooperation Conference (IOMAC) established by the *Colombo Declaration* in 1987 was intended to be at the center of a network of organizations.[47] Its mandate includes building a cooperative framework, strategy for enhancing national development, and consultative forum for reviewing economic uses and protection of the Indian Ocean and its resources.[48] Nevertheless, this five-nation study of the Indian Ocean region underscores the difficulty in designing and implementing a unified approach to environmental law in such a culturally, politico-legally diverse, and economically developing region. Rather than a region-wide approach, what has emerged are some bi- and multilateral, subregional initiatives. For example, conservation agreements in Africa have emerged, such as the General Trans-Frontier Conservation and Resource Area Protocol among South Africa, Mozambique, and Swaziland, amd the recent decision to create transboundary marine protected areas by Tanzania, Mozambique, and South Africa.[49] Other examples are the trade agreements between Mauritius-Seychelles and the Mauritius-Madagascar arrangement on fisheries, tourism, and textiles.[50]

One commitment that is evident across the region relates to integrated coastal management, critical to climate change adaptation, evidenced through initiatives such as the Arusha Resolution in 1993,[51] the 1996 Seychelles Second Policy Conference on

---

[47] Barbara Kwiatkowska, *Institutional Marine Affairs Cooperation in Developing State Regions: Part 2: The Indian Ocean and IOMAC*, 14 MARINE POL'Y 399, 400 (1990).

[48] *Id.*

[49] *See* United Nations Conference on Trade and Development, *supra* note 29; United Nations Framework Convention on Climate Change, *supra* note 30.

[50] MAURITIUS EMBASSY, ANTANANARIVO, MAURITIUS-ANTANANARIVO MISSION, *available at* http://www.gov.mu/portal/sites/mfamission/antananarivo/mission.htm (last visited May 1, 2014). Mauritius Government, AGREEMENT SIGNED TO BOOST COOPERATION WITH SEYCHELLES (Sept. 5, 2013), *available at* http://www.gov.mu/English/News/Pages/Agreement-Signed-to-Boost-Cooperation-with -Seychelles.aspx (last visited July 28, 2014).

[51] Mauritius, Mozambique, Madagascar, the Seychelles, Tanzania, and later Kenya were signatories of the Arusha Resolution. *See* L. Celliers et al., *Pathways of Integrated Coastal Management from National Policy to Local Implementation: Enabling Climate Change Adaption*, 39 MARINE POL'Y 72, 73 (2013).

Integrated Coastal Zone Management in Eastern African and Island States, and the 1998 Maputo Declaration from the Pan-African Conference on Sustainable Integrated Coastal Management.[52] The Resolution "set the stage for increased national support for, and efforts in, coastal management and successfully began a dialogue between the scientific community and high-level policy makers;" however, there is no explicit focus on climate change.[53] Indeed, none of these developments makes any significant advances in the area of climate change adaptation.

Subregional initiatives may be an appropriate approach where small groups of countries have preexisting ties, similar historical and cultural foundations, and contemporary incentives to work together. They are less than ideal, however, when attempting to address a broad concern such as climate change. A region-wide approach can have many benefits, including establishing a common framework for cooperation and action as well as facilitating regional knowledge sharing.

Common security threats and economic opportunities, rather than environmental concerns, have led to some regional cooperative organizations such as the South African Development Community (SADC) and South Asian Association for Regional Cooperation (SAARC), the African Union (AU), the Gulf Coordination Council (GCC), the Association of Southeast Asian Nations (ASEAN), and the Asia Pacific Economic Community (APEC).[54] Some of these organizations address environmental issues, such as SADC and its Protocol on Wildlife Conservation and Law Enforcement and the Protocol on Fisheries. Nevertheless, there is relatively little tangible regional cooperation among the Indian Ocean Rim States.

2. Indian Ocean Rim—Association for Regional Co-operation

The most promising avenue for a region-wide approach is the Indian Ocean Rim—Association for Regional Co-operation (IOR-ARC). This organization was established in 1997 in response to the creation of other major regional trading organizations.[55] It has twenty member states[56] and is based on the principle of "open regionalism." Its goals include "sustained growth and balanced development of the region and of the member states, and to create common ground for regional co-operation," including stimulating

[52] *Id.*

[53] Elin Torell, *Adaption and Learning in Coastal Management: The Experience of Five East African Initiatives*, 28 COASTAL MGMT. 353, 353 (2000).

[54] Christian Wagner, *The Indian Ocean Rim—Association for Regional Co-operation (IOR-ARC): The Futile Question for Regionalism?*, 9 J. INDIAN OCEAN 6, 6 (2013).

[55] Saman Kelegama, *Can Open Regionalism Work in the Indian Ocean Rim Association for Regional Co-operation?*, 15 ASEAN ECON. BULL. 153, 155 (1998). It was formed with fourteen member states: Australia, India, Indonesia, Kenya, Madagascar, Mauritius, Malaysia, Mozambique, Oman, Singapore, South Africa, Sri Lanka, Tanzania, and Yemen. *Id.* As of this writing, it has expanded to twenty states.

[56] Bangladesh, Comoros, the Seychelles, Iran, Thailand, and the United Arab Emirates are the additional members, of fifty-one littoral states, with China, Egypt, France, Japan, and the United Kingdom as dialogue partners. Interestingly, the IO Tourism Organization is an observer.

regional trade and investment, synergizing competitive advantage, building networks, information sharing, and promoting standardization and harmonization.[57] The organization is supported by the Working Group of Trade and Investment (WGTI), the Indian Ocean Rim Business Forum (IORBF), and the Indian Ocean Rim Academic Group (IORAG). Specifically, the IORAG "promotes dialogue on the peaceful uses and ecologically sustainable development of maritime resources and initiates informed debate on issues of concern within the region."[58] The group has published several books but these are focused on issues of security rather than climate change.

The cultural, economic, and political divergences among the IOR-ARC's twenty members are significant,[59] which has limited the organization's impact to date. It has produced "few tangible results" despite its impressive appearance and regular meetings.[60] Many authors have expressed doubts about its potential to respond effectively to regional issues, noting that economic and political divergences hamper efforts[61] and that simply sharing an ocean space will not ensure successful regional cooperation.[62] In particular, it has not resulted in a common agenda or effective coordination on global environmental law, including climate change. Nevertheless, the IOR-ARC could respond to maritime and environmental concerns such as climate change, albeit fifteen years after its inception.[63] One of the more recent developments is the 2013 Perth Communique, which endorses work undertaken in IORA to strengthen ocean monitoring, seasonal climate forecasting capacities, and knowledge of climate change adaption practices.[64] In addition, the 2013 Perth Principles recognize the importance of building the capacity of countries to understand, forecast, and address marine, ocean, and climate science issues in the region.[65] In addition, there is a commitment "to understand and address the main threats to the Indian Ocean and its resources, including…ocean acidification."

Although there are some relevant initiatives in the region, the lack of a strong regional framework focused on climate issues highlights the critical nature of national initiatives to both implement international law and provide an effective domestic response to local climate change concerns.

---

[57] See Kelegama, *supra* note 55.

[58] *UWA Academic Appointed to Indian Ocean Rim Academic Group*, RESEARCH CAREER (Apr. 20, 2011), http://www.researchcareer.com.au/archived-news/uwa-academic-appointed-to-indian-ocean-rim-academic-group.

[59] See Wagner, *supra* note 54, at 11.

[60] Alex Vines & Bereni Oruitemeka, *Engagement with the African Indian Ocean Rim States*, 14 S. AFR. J. INT'L AFF. 111, 113 (2007).

[61] See Wagner, *supra* note 54.

[62] See, e.g., Kelegama, *supra* note 55. This article focuses primarily on regional economic development. *Id.*

[63] See Wagner, *supra* note 54, at 6.

[64] *Perth Communiqué*, AUSTRALIAN GOVERNMENT: DEPARTMENT OF FOREIGN AFFAIRS AND TRADE (Nov. 1, 2013), https://www.dfat.gov.au/geo/indian-ocean/perth-communique-2013.html.

[65] *Perth Principles*, AUSTRALIAN GOVERNMENT: DEPARTMENT OF FOREIGN AFFAIRS AND TRADE (Nov. 1, 2013), https://www.dfat.gov.au/geo/indian-ocean/perth-principles-2013.html.

C. NATIONAL

Most of the Indian Ocean region countries, and certainly South Africa, Mozambique, the Seychelles, and the Maldives, have national environmental policies in place to combat the effects of climate change and foster protection and conservation of the marine and coastal environment. In addition, there are a myriad of laws that could be used to address climate change impacts and adaptation challenges.

1. South Africa

The Republic of South Africa is located at the southern tip of the continent of Africa, bordering both the Atlantic and Indian oceans.[66] It has a subtropical climate, with warm, dry, and temperate conditions. The terrain consists of a vast interior plateau rimmed by rugged hills and a narrow coastal plain. The ocean surrounds South Africa on three sides with two major ocean currents—the warm south-flowing Mozambique-Agulhas and the cold Benguela.[67] The contrast in temperature partly accounts for significant differences in climate and vegetation between the east and west coasts of South Africa.[68] This contrast also explains the differences in marine life.[69]

South Africa's legal system is an amalgamation of Roman-Dutch civil law, English common law, and customary law.[70] Since 1994 when apartheid ended and democracy was established, South African governance has changed significantly.[71] The Preamble of the Constitution reiterates the focus on South Africa recognizing and healing the injustices and divisions of its apartheid past, and establishing a new united sovereign state founded on democratic values, social justice, and fundamental human rights for all.[72] The Constitution incorporates rights to an environment not harmful to human health, and also addresses conservation, sustainable development, ecological integrity, and a right of access to natural resources. The approach was not surprising given that the Constitution was drafted at a time when environmental issues had obtained global attention in the wake of the UN Conference on Environment and Development in Rio de Janeiro in 1992.

Environmental policy in South Africa is set at the national level, but the provinces are largely responsible for implementation.[73] Centralization allows for a common strategic

---

[66] *About SA—Geography and Climate*, SOUTH AFRICAN GOVERNMENT ONLINE, http://www.gov.za/aboutsa/geography.htm (last visited July 28, 2014).

[67] *Id.*

[68] *Id.*

[69] *Country Profile—South Africa*, CONVENTION ON BIOLOGICAL DIVERSITY, http://www.cbd.int/countries/profile/default.shtml?country=za#status (last visited Mar. 28, 2014).

[70] CIA, THE WORLD FACTBOOK: SOUTH AFRICA, *available at* https://www.cia.gov/library/publications/the-world-factbook/geos/sf.html (last visited July 28, 2014).

[71] *See* United Nations Framework Convention on Climate Change, *supra* note 30, at 24.

[72] S. AFR. CONST. pmbl. 1996, *available at* http://www.gov.za/documents/constitution/1996/96preamble.htm (last visited July 28, 2014).

[73] *See* United Nations Framework Convention on Climate Change, *supra* note 30.

approach, as well as consideration of international obligations and regional concerns. Local implementation has the benefit of engaging with those being governed and carries the opportunity to address environmental concerns where they are experienced. It has been recognized that South Africa has "the political will to address the difficult balance they need to strike between poverty and conservation at the domestic level;" yet the country still faces challenges in responding effectively at a regional level.[74]

South Africa faces many significant environmental issues: pollution of rivers from agricultural runoff and urban discharge,[75] soil erosion, desertification, and air pollution that results in acid rain.[76] Moreover, a lack of important arterial rivers or lakes requires extensive water conservation and control measures in South Africa, with the growth in water usage far outpacing supply.[77] Drafted in response to these challenges, the Strategic Plan for the Environmental Sector (2009–2014)[78] recognizes the importance of developing responses to climate change. The Strategic Plan adopts an outcome-based approach. Outcome 10 seeks to "reduce greenhouse gas emissions, prepare strategies to cope with projected climate change impacts and reverse the rising trend in relation to the release of pollutants into the atmosphere."[79] The Sector Plan further emphasizes the need for effective management of issues such as sea-level rise and natural disasters on livelihoods and marine and coastal systems through controlling unsustainable coastal developments, implementing sustainable livelihoods programs, and increasing research to understand the vulnerability of marine and coastal systems. Similarly, Outcome 10 addresses the reduction of GHG emissions and the preparation of strategies to cope with projected climate change impacts.[80]

In addition, South Africa has developed a specific climate change policy, the National Climate Change Response White Paper (2011). It addresses mitigation and adaptation across a range of sectors such as water, agriculture, health, and biodiversity. The White Paper notes the need to "review legislation to determine the legal requirements to support the institutional and regulatory arrangements proposed ... and to ensure policy and legislative alignment."[81]

Despite ample environmental legislation in South Africa, there are relatively few initiatives that respond directly to climate change and that promote preparedness for climate change at the local level. As in Mozambique, there are a number of laws that

---

[74] *Id.*

[75] *See* Wagner, *supra* note 54.

[76] *Id.*

[77] *Id.*

[78] South African Department of Environmental Affairs, Strategic Plan for the Environmental Sector 2009–2014, *available at* https://www.environment.gov.za/sites/default/files/strategic_plans/2009_2014.pdf (last visited July 28, 2014).

[79] *Id.* at 6.

[80] *See* Torell, *supra* note 53.

[81] South African Government, National Climate Change Response White Paper, 37 (2011), *available at* https://www.info.gov.za/view/DownloadFileAction?id=152834.

can be used by local governments, including the National Environmental Management Act 2004 (NEMA); Integrated Coastal Management Act 2008 (ICMA); Disaster Management Act; Local Government Systems Act together with Municipal Town Planning Schemes; National Parks Act 1976; Biodiversity Act 2004; World Heritage Convention Act 1999; and Environment Conservation Act 1989.[82] The NEMA implements some of the constitutional obligations and takes a principled approach. It covers issues such as sustainable development, a human right to a decent environment, standing to challenge environmental issues, intergenerational equity, integration, precaution, pollution prevention, the polluter pays principle, local-level governance, ecosystem-based management, and common but differentiated responsibilities.[83] The most recent statute is the ICMA 2008, which provides for coastal protection zones and coastal protected areas. The Act addresses erosion and accretion, both of which can be the result of climate change impacts.

South Africa has taken steps to adopt law and policy to protect coastal areas and address climate change. As will be further discussed below, this is not uncommon in the region, but translating these initiatives into positive outcomes has yet to be achieved.

2. Mozambique

The Republic of Mozambique is located on the east coast of southern Africa, bordering the Mozambique Channel and situated between South Africa and Tanzania. The climate of Mozambique is tropical to subtropical, with significant hurricanes and cyclones on the coast during the wet season.[84] Its terrain is mostly coastal lowlands, though it also contains uplands in the center, high plateaus in the northwest, and mountains in the west. Mozambique's Indian Ocean coastline is rich in biodiversity. Mozambique is comprised nearly entirely of native Africans.

In Mozambique, there has been a period of reconstruction in the wake of the civil war that started in the 1980s and continued until 1992. The war caused considerable damage to the social and economic well-being of Mozambique, but also negatively impacted the environment as a whole and harmed many species.[85] Under the 2004 Mozambique Constitution, the national government and local authorities, in cooperation with other environmental associations, are required to adopt policies for environmental protection and to promote rational utilization of resources.[86] There is, however, no specific legislation related to climate change and practically no provision or recognition of

---

[82] *See* Torell, *supra* note 53.

[83] *See* United Nations Framework Convention on Climate Change, *supra* note 30, at 8.

[84] C. MCSWEENEY, M. NEW & G. LIZCANO, UNDP Climate Change Country Profiles: Mozambique, *available at* http://www.geog.ox.ac.uk/research/climate/projects/undp-cp/UNDP_reports/Mozambique/ Mozambique.hires.report.pdf (last visited July 28, 2014).

[85] *See* United Nations Framework Convention on Climate Change, *supra* note 30, at 24.

[86] 1990 CONST. art. 90 (Mozambique), *available at* http://www1.chr.up.ac.za/undp/domestic/docs/c_ Mozambique.pdf (last visited July 28, 2014).

climate change in Mozambican legislation.[87] Mozambique's Constitution and environmental law incorporate rights and duties in relation to the environment. Nevertheless, implementation of these objectives has been hampered by a range of factors, including a lack of capacity and resources, insufficient inter-institutional coordination, and lack of awareness and education leading to insufficient public understanding and support. These factors have delayed the national implementation of Mozambique's international commitments.[88]

There are, however, various laws that could be used to address climate change adaptation such as the legal obligation of local governments to prepare development and land-use plans, and take measures to protect the environment.[89] For example, the Environment Law 1997 provides for environmental protection zones over terrestrial and marine areas to facilitate protection of ecosystems that have ecological, socioeconomic, aesthetic, cultural, scientific, and other values. Other relevant laws include the Land Law and the Forestry and Wildlife Law, Fisheries Law, and Local Organs Law.

With respect to climate change, Mozambique has developed a National Adaption Programme of Action (2007), which has four key goals: strengthening of early warning systems, strengthening of the agricultural sector to withstand the impacts of climate change, reduction of climate change impacts in coastal zones, and management of water resources under climate change.[90] Goals include climate change adaptation measures to be adopted in strategic plans and local development.[91] Although reference is made to gaps and evaluations of current legal and institutional frameworks, there is no comprehensive plan for law reform. The Environmental Strategy for Sustainable Development (2007) calls for the integrated and sustainable management of the marine environment and of climate change. In addition, the Programme of the Government (2010–2014) includes the objective of promoting environmental quality as well as policies and strategies for adaptation and mitigation to climate change. Furthermore, the *National Forest Policy* expressly notes that it is guided by the principles of the UNFCCC.

Despite a number of sound environmental policies in place in the low-lying nation of Mozambique, there is little internal understanding of the consequences of environmental degradation and loss of access to natural resources in rural and poor Mozambican communities.[92] Reflected in the lack of implemented environmental legislation, there is "deliberate and careless exploitation of the natural environment" due to continuing

---

[87] *See* Torell, *supra* note 53.

[88] *See* United Nations Framework Convention on Climate Change, *supra* note 30, at 9.

[89] *See* Torell, *supra* note 53.

[90] Mozambique Ministry for the Co-ordination of Environmental Affairs, Mozambique National Adaptation Programme of Action (2007), *available at* http://unfccc.int/resource/docs/napa/moz01.pdf.

[91] *See* Torell, *supra* note 53.

[92] Simon Norfolk & Michaela Cosijn, The Balancing of Interests in Environmental Law in Africa 296 (Michael Faure & Willemien du Plessis eds., 2011).

institutional weaknesses after decades of conflict and also deliberate acts of governing elites to promote private interests.[93] Existing environmental regulations are often eased in the case of large development projects.[94] There appear to be "systemic failures to apply the law in natural resource concession allocation, in the EIA process, in the territorial planning arena, and in the general provision of environmental services and support."[95] A weak governance framework and fragile oversight mechanisms have resulted in "many unresolved tensions between economic development objectives and environmental sustainability" in Mozambique.[96]

3. Seychelles

The Republic of Seychelles is an archipelago of 115 islands scattered across the western Indian Ocean, to the northeast of Madagascar.[97] The islands are separated into two broad groups: thirty-two islands of the Mahé group in the north, including all of the principal islands; and eighty-three coral islands in the south, which are largely uninhabited.[98] The Mahé group islands comprise a narrow coastal strip of rocky and hilly terrain, while the other coral islands are flat, elevated reefs.[99] Interestingly, the Seychelles are the only mid-oceanic islands of granite in the world.[100]

The Seychelles has a hot, moist, tropical oceanic climate with a monsoon season.[101] The islands of the Seychelles are estimated to comprise eighty species of endemic flowering plants, out of 900 in total, with approximately 1,000 marine fish species; thirteen species and seventeen subspecies of endemic birds; and twenty-one species of marine mammals.[102] Significantly, 47 percent of the total surface area of the Seychelles is protected as conservation areas, including 23,000 hectares of protected reef and marine areas.[103]

In terms of climate change impacts, these are of less concern than to other states in the area because Seychelles is located outside the cyclone belt, so severe storms are rare. However, there are occasional short droughts, and water supply is heavily dependent on

---

[93] *Id.* at 337.

[94] *Id.* at 338–39.

[95] *Id.* at 339.

[96] *Id.* at 296.

[97] *Geography—Seychelles*, FOOD AND AGRICULTURE ORGANIZATION OF THE UNITED NATIONS (last updated May 28, 2012), http://www.fao.org/forestry/country/18310/en/syc/.

[98] *Id.*

[99] CIA, THE WORLD FACTBOOK: SEYCHELLES, *available at* https://www.cia.gov/library/publications/the-world-factbook/geos/se.html (last visited July 28, 2014).

[100] Deryck Scarr, *Seychelles since 1770: History of a Slave and Post-slavery Society*, HURST & COMPANY 2 (2000).

[101] *Id.*

[102] *Country Profile—Seychelles*, CONVENTION ON BIOLOGICAL DIVERSITY, http://www.cbd.int/countries/profile/default.shtml?country=sc#status (last visited Jan. 5, 2014).

[103] *Id.*

rainwater. The most critical issue is reef management. Conservation is essential as the competing concerns of fishing and tourism need to be reconciled.[104] The Seychelles is almost exclusively reliant on fish exports and tourism for foreign revenue[105] and both are at risk from warming oceans and acidification. There has been a significant study of the 1998 bleaching event, being the most severe recorded in the western Indian Ocean, with the authors suggesting that "climate-mediated disturbances, such as coral bleaching, be at the fore of conservation planning for coral reefs."[106]

The Seychelles legal system is based on the Westminster model, with two fundamental tenets: the rule of law and the separation of powers.[107] Nonetheless, English common law, French civil law, and customary law coexist and interact in the Seychelles. Although English common law regulates daily administration in the Seychelles, French civil law continues to "form the bedrock of Seychelles law."[108] The legislature, however, remains "in practice governed by the ruling party and … as a result, the Assembly does not have the most conducive environment and the means to effectively perform its role of independent control over the executive."[109]

Despite numerous laws to protect the environment, the most significant problem in the Seychelles is implementation. There are very limited national resources[110] resulting in poor monitoring and enforcement combined with a lack of public awareness.[111] Significant urbanization is exerting immense pressure on the Seychelles' limited land resources and coastal environment, and climate change will only exacerbate this developing crisis.[112]

The Seychelles is a party to the key international environmental law treaties and the limited regional initiatives. At the national level, the Constitution includes the right of every person "to enjoy a clean, healthy and ecologically balanced environment."[113] This is balanced by the duty of every Seychelles citizen to protect, preserve, and improve the environment.[114] In addition, the state implements measures to promote the protection,

---

[104] Simone Jennings, Suzanne Marshall & Nicholas Polunin, *Seychelles' Marine Protected Areas: Comparative Structure and Status of Reef Fish Communities*, 75 BIOLOGICAL CONSERVATION 201, 201 (1995).

[105] SEYCHELLES DEPARTMENT OF ENVIRONMENT, ENVIRONMENTAL MANAGEMENT PLAN OF THE SEYCHELLES 1990–2000 (1990).

[106] Nicholas Graham et al., *Lag Effects in the Impacts of Mass Coral Bleaching on Coral Reef Fish, Fisheries, and Ecosystems*, 21 CONSERVATION BIOLOGY 1291, 1296–98 (2007).

[107] REPUBLIC OF SEYCHELLES—EUROPEAN COMMUNITY, COUNTRY STRATEGY PAPER AND NATIONAL INDICATIVE PROGRAMME FOR THE PERIOD 2008–2013, at 7 (2007), *available at* http://ec.europa.eu/development/icenter/repository/scanned_sc_csp10_en.pdf.

[108] *Id.*

[109] *Id.*

[110] *Id.* at 16.

[111] *Id.* at 7.

[112] *Id.* at 16. The Seychelles is one of the most urbanized countries in the Indian Ocean region.

[113] CONST. art. 38 (Seychelles), *available at* http://www.ilo.org/wcmsp5/groups/public/—ed_protect/—protrav/—ilo_aids/documents/legaldocument/wcms_127610.pdf (last visited July 28, 2014).

[114] *Id.* art. 40.

preservation, and improvement of the environment, which is primarily advanced through the Environmental Protection Act 1994.

Most of the Seychelles' national response to environmental concerns has been through legislative regulations or orders; however, such legislative responses require significant updating.[115] For example, the National Parks and Nature Conservancy Ordinance 1969 and numerous regulations prohibiting fishing and damage to reefs are old pieces of legislation.[116] One of the more modern statutes is the Environmental Protection Act 1994, which was enacted to implement the African Convention on Conservation of Nature and Natural Resources.[117] Furthermore, the Fisheries Act 1987 was amended in 1997 and 2001. Enforcement remains the main challenge.

In response to the issues of climate change, the Seychelles has adopted a National Climate Change Strategy (2009). This initiative seeks to minimize the impacts of climate change through concerted and proactive action at all levels of society.

The Seychelles possesses above-average wealth per capita and thus the theoretical capacity to expand its environmental law framework. However, the overall economic strength of such nations remains in the lower echelons of global state actors. The Seychelles is a positive example of a developing nation that is able to legislate for the protection of marine life, yet lacks the capacity to ensure these laws are upheld.

4. Maldives

The Republic of the Maldives is located in Southern Asia, southwest of India. It is a small-island developing state and one of the least-developed countries.[118] It is comprised of twenty-six low-lying atolls comprising 1190 islands. Significantly, 80 percent of the Maldives is less than one-and-a-half meters above sea level and is therefore extremely susceptible to global warming and beach erosion. It has a hot and humid climate and a monsoon season.

The most prevalent diversity occurs in the coral reefs of the Maldives, with at least 1090 species of fish and 187 coral species recorded with relatively little land-based biodiversity. Habitat destruction and overexploitation are significant threats to the Maldives's biodiversity. Coastal development activities are adversely affecting the reefs.

The Maldives was a sultanate from the twelfth to the nineteenth century. It became a British protectorate in 1887. The Maldives gained independence in 1965 and became

---

[115] *See* Republic of Seychelles—European Community, *supra* note 107, at 17.

[116] *See* Jennings et al., *supra* note 104, at 201.

[117] ROSE MWEBAZA ET AL., A SITUATION REPORT: THE NATURE AND EXTENT OF ENVIRONMENTAL CRIMES IN SEYCHELLES (2009), *available at* http://dspace.cigilibrary.org/jspui/bitstream/123456789/31096/1/SitRepSeychellesNov09.pdf?1.

[118] MALDIVES GOVERNMENT, MALDIVES STRATEGIC NATIONAL ACTION PLAN FOR DISASTER RISK REDUCTION AND CLIMATE CHANGE ADAPTATION IN 2010–2020 (2009), *available at* http://ndmc.gov.mv/wordpress/wp-content/uploads/2012/10/Strategic-National-Action-Plan-for-Disaster-Risk-Reduction-and-Climate-Change-Adaptation-2010-2020-Provisional-Draft.pdf.

a republic in 1968. Today, the legal system is based on the Islamic religious legal system (sharia law) with English common law influences, primarily in commercial law.

The Maldives faces numerous challenges, including strengthening a fractured democracy, combating widespread poverty and drug abuse, and responding to significant public protests. Tourism is the most significant economic activity in the Maldives, followed by fisheries, both of which are impacted by climate change. It is not a large emitter of GHGs but is likely to suffer the earliest effects of climate change. Due to these factors, combined with the Maldives' low elevation and resulting threat from sea-level rise, the government has played a significant role in international climate change discussions.

Mohamed Nasheed, former president of the Maldives, has been very vocal in outlining the risks that climate change poses, particularly to small-island states. He has given speeches at various climate change negotiations and at many other fora, and has become something of a climate hero.[119] The former president has been a leader in calling for carbon neutrality. He has committed his own country to this goal, encouraged developing countries to form a bloc of carbon-neutral nations, and called for the United States to further engage with climate change science and issues.[120] Dr. Nasheed has also created the first UNESCO Biosphere reserve in the Maldives' Baa Atoll, and announced plans to make the entire country a marine protected area by 2017, which will make it the world's largest marine reserve.[121]

In the domestic context, the Maldivian government has also committed to a number of other measures and policies to address climate change. The third Constitution of 2008 includes the fundamental duty of the state to protect and preserve the natural environment, biodiversity, and resources, and to uphold people's rights and freedoms to such protection for the benefit of present and future generations.[122] The state must balance environmental, economic, and social goals through ecologically sustainable development. Article 23 sets out the rights of citizens and the duty of the state to achieve the realization of such rights. The Constitution also supports decentralized administration.

The National Sustainable Development Strategy includes seven goals, including adaptation to climate change, protection of coral reefs, the achievement of carbon

---

[119] Gloria Ramos, *Maldives President Nasheed—A Climate Hero*, GLOBAL NATION INQUIRER, Nov. 16, 2009, *available at* http://globalnation.inquirer.net/cebudailynews/opinion/view/20091116-236579/ Maldives-President-Nasheed—A-Climate-Hero. Indeed, he is now the subject of a documentary by John Shenck, THE ISLAND PRESIDENT (Metro Goldwyn Films 2012).

[120] James Gerken, *Mohamed Nasheed, Former Maldives President, Calls for U.S. to Embrace Climate Change Reality*, HUFFINGTON POST, July, 6, 2012, *available at* http://www.huffingtonpost.com/2012/07/06/ mohamed-nasheed-maldives-climate-change-united-states_n_1652409.html.

[121] Timon Singh, *The Maldives to Become the World's Largest Marine Reserve by 2017*, INHABIT.COM, June 24, 2012, *available at* http://inhabitat.com/the-maldives-to-become-the-worlds-largest-marine-reserve-by-2017/.

[122] 2008 CONST. art. 22 (Maldives), *available at* http://www.maldivesinfo.gov.mv/home/upload/downloads/ Compilation.pdf (last visited July 28, 2014).

neutrality, and the establishment of a carbon-neutral transport system. In addition, the Maldives has adopted a Third National Environment Action Plan (2009–2013) and National Adaptation Programme of Action, which describes the National Adaptation Policy Framework, identifies the adaptation needs, and prioritizes activities and projects.

In the context of climate change specific measures, the Maldives has taken a combined approach to risk reduction and climate change.[123] The Action Plan includes both mitigation and adaptation actions. The Action Plan recognizes the importance of legal preparedness and outlines the Disaster Management Bill and National Building Bill. The former creates a framework for disaster management and the latter a regulatory framework for building works, in the absence of a building code.

As with many nation-states in the Indian Ocean region, the Maldives does not possess the resources to adequately and effectively respond to any such environmental concerns with appropriate legislation or implementation. Despite the significant threat the Maldives faces from climate change, it is unable to effectively guard against future sea-level rises and the destruction that would ensue.

III. Future Directions

A significant barrier to effective Indian Ocean regionalism to respond to climate change is the varying causes of GHG emissions across its vast array of nations.[124] This could further explain the scarce quantity of research conducted on effective Indian Ocean region environmental law frameworks. The case studies presented here display the common recognition of the realities of climate change in the Indian Ocean region; however, mere recognition is an insufficient response. A collective will to discuss, present, and implement complex solutions to the realities of climate change must also be present.[125]

Future responses in the Indian Ocean region can be adopted from the experiences and successes of their Pacific counterparts where countries are supported by many strong regional organizations, such as the Secretariat of the Pacific Community, the Pacific Islands Forum Secretariat, and the Secretariat of the Pacific Environment Programme (SPREP). Regional compliance treaties that have developed in areas such as fisheries could provide useful examples for governments in advancing responses to climate change.[126] Legislative models developed to assist Pacific Island countries in preparing domestic legislation could also be extended to climate action. The Indian Ocean region should look to such approaches to ensure a foundation of strong regionalism upon which

---

[123] *See* Maldives Government, *supra* note 118.

[124] *See* Chellaney, *supra* note 1, at 149.

[125] *Id.* at 153.

[126] *See, e.g., Niue Treaty on Cooperation in Fisheries Surveillance and Law Enforcement in the South Pacific Region* (1992), opened for signature, July 9, 1992, 32 I.L.M. 136 (entered into force May 20, 1993).

to develop fresh and unified approaches to combating climate change. As in the legally pluralist Pacific Ocean region, differences in each nation's state-based and customary law must be acknowledged if governments are to deal effectively with both the causes and consequences of climate change in the Indian Ocean region.[127]

Collaborative approaches to environmental law can only be fostered by a region that promotes cooperation, which has been lacking to date in Indian Ocean regional organizations. The IOR-ARC could provide the impetus for such future directions. It could, for example, catalyze action by holding regional workshops on key issues and acting as a valuable forum for discussion. Furthermore, it could assist with building regional capacity by providing a clearinghouse of successful programs, policies, and regulations.

Alternatives to broad regional cooperation could also prove successful. Options that facilitate site-specific environmental concerns and innovative national approaches to bilateral and regional issues in marine protected area management could extend more broadly to a general environmental law framework in the Indian Ocean region.[128] Such responses will depend significantly on the political will and legal and economic capacity of each Indian Ocean state.

Many of the laws and policies relating to climate change assessed above are contemporary, having been developed since 1992, and therefore include modern concepts. They have, however, largely been untested.[129] Therefore, these measures are nascent, and it will take some time before they can be fully implemented and their success or failure tested.

Conclusion

Responding to environmental concerns must play a central role in Indian Ocean regional cooperation in the future.[130] A regional approach to climate change adaptation law and policy is justified on a number of bases. First, it is sensible to cooperatively design laws and policies for the coastal zone, including development, land use, and physical construction. Second, a cooperative approach would allow for the sharing of limited legal and technical resources and expertise on shared impacts and adaptation responses. From a scientific perspective, it would be beneficial to have data collected across the region. Regional frameworks can also provide developing countries, which form the majority of the Indian Ocean rim countries, a stronger voice globally.[131] Although the need for

---

[127] *Id.*

[128] *See* United Nations Conference on Trade and Development, *supra* note 29, at 908.

[129] *See* United Nations Framework Convention on Climate Change, *supra* note 30, at 24.

[130] *See* Chellaney, *supra* note 1, at 166.

[131] Ian H. Rowlands, *Mapping the Prospects for Regional Co-operation in Southern Africa*, 19(5) THIRD WORLD Q. 917, 917 (1998).

regional approaches and responses to climate change was recognized at an early date[132] it has not come to fruition.

Perhaps the most activity to date has been seen in the context of MPAs where the East African states are working closely together. These areas will become increasingly important as ocean temperatures rise, and more mobile species' ranges are likely to be altered. Much may be learned from the East African states in this regard and transposed elsewhere.

For the SIDS, transboundary land issues are often not a problem, but in some cases states share maritime borders. However, the main issue is technical and financial capacity to develop law and policy and thereafter ensure compliance and enforcement. This is likely to remain a challenge in the future. Because of the particular context of Indian Ocean region, much is to be achieved from regional discussion and cooperation. It is to be hoped that such collaboration emerges in the future to ensure the biological and cultural diversity of the Indian Ocean has a future.

---

[132] *See, e.g.*, Chellaney, *supra* note 1.

II Coasts

19 Climate Change and the Coastal Zone Management Act:
THE ROLE OF FEDERALISM IN ADAPTATION STRATEGIES
Chad J. McGuire

Introduction

Coastal areas are dynamic places lying at the intersection between land and water, a boundary that is never static.[1] For example, gravity constantly pushes

---

[1] *See generally* CHAD J. MCGUIRE, ADAPTING TO SEA LEVEL RISE IN THE COASTAL ZONE: LAW AND POLICY CONSIDERATIONS 1–3 (2013).

and pulls at the water, exerting its influence and, in the process, altering coastal boundaries.[2] Nevertheless, the changes observed at the coastline are relatively consistent, sitting within our expectations based on past and current observations. Gravity will pull the sea away from the coastline to an average low-tide mark, and it will also push the sea landward to an average high-tide mark.[3] Full and new moons can further influence high and low tides, creating larger tidal ranges beyond the averages normally observed.[4] Storms can do the same.[5] But collectively these historically observed phenomena are part of the observed experiences of humans, and as such, they have been internalized into the decision-making frameworks that coincide with the development and regulation of coastal areas.[6]

Climate change brings a new variable—uncertainty—into our expectations about coastal dynamics. Rising sea levels result in water moving inland, altering the observed average high and low tidelines.[7] Coastal storms derived from ocean-based cyclones are occurring with greater intensity, and there is evidence suggesting conditions are ripe for a greater frequency of such storms in the future.[8] These observations increase the uncertainty associated with coastal area dynamics by challenging previous assumptions about coastal system equilibrium, thereby questioning the validity of legal and policy frameworks developed under previous assumptions. For example, is it wise to develop along coastal areas where uncertainty from climate change makes it difficult, if not impossible, to discern future coastal impacts? Or do preexisting legal and policy frameworks need to be examined, and potentially changed, to accommodate the realities of coastal areas in an era of climate change? These are but a few of the inquiries that highlight difficulties presented when planning for coastal management under conditions of increasing uncertainty.[9]

---

[2] RICHARD A. DAVIS JR. & DUNCAN M. FITZGERALD, BEACHES AND COASTS 189–95 (2004).

[3] Id.

[4] Id.

[5] Id. at 76–77.

[6] McGUIRE, supra note 1, 76–80.

[7] Id. at 15–16.

[8] INTERGOVERNMENTAL PANEL ON CLIMATE CHANGE, CLIMATE CHANGE 2007: SYNTHESIS REPORT 30, 147 (Abdelkader Allali et al. eds., 2007), available at http://www.ipcc.ch/pdf/assessment-report/ar4/syr/ar4_syr.pdf (noting observational evidence of an increase in intense tropical cyclone activity in the North Atlantic since about 1970, and also suggestions of increased cyclone activity in other regions); GLOBAL CLIMATE CHANGE IMPACTS IN THE UNITED STATES 24–25 (Thomas R. Karl et al. eds., 2009), available at http://downloads.globalchange.gov/usimpacts/pdfs/climate-impacts-report.pdf (noting models project a tendency for more extreme wind events and higher ocean waves in a number of regions, and also noting more rain-producing tropical storms and hurricanes are generally more likely due to increased precipitation and surface water temperatures).

[9] There is always uncertainty at the coastline; however, the degree of uncertainty is increasing, making previous observations inadequate as the basis of evidence for planning that includes assumptions about future events. See CLIMATE CHANGE 2007: SYNTHESIS REPORT 30 (discussing observations of climate change and concluding that warming of the climate system is unequivocal).

This chapter discusses the role of coastal zone management under conditions of climate change in the United States. More specifically, this chapter explores coastal zone management by examining the relationship between coastal states and the federal government, political entities that share interests and rights in coastal areas under constitutional federalism.[10] To help place this review of federalism into a coastal management context, a particular federal law, the Coastal Zone Management Act (CZMA),[11] will provide the context to highlight federal and coastal state interactions when managing coastal resources in an era of climate change. The CZMA will also provide a legal foundation from which coastal states and federal government interactions will be analyzed to see the influence of federalism when responding to threats in coastal areas caused by climate change.

This chapter will focus on adaptation policies to respond to climate change impacts in the coastal zone. The chapter begins with an exploration of the impacts of climate change on coastal areas. It then addresses the legal context of federalism by identifying how climate change adaptation strategies under the CZMA are impacted when coastal state and federal government interests diverge. The chapter concludes with suggestions to overcome or otherwise mitigate conflicts that arise between federal and state activities in coastal regions related to climate change adaptation, identifying pathways for cooperative federalism to help achieve meaningful and proactive adaptation strategies along the coast.

I. The Impacts of Climate Change on Coastal Areas

Climate change is having numerous impacts on coastal areas, with the degree of impact influenced by morphological and spatial considerations. For example, a low-lying coastal area will experience greater impacts from sea-level rise than a coastal region dominated by high bluffs.[12] Also, coastal areas that exist in storm-prevalent regions may experience increased intensity and frequency of storm events due to climate change, while coastal regions existing outside of storm-prevalent areas may continue to experience reduced storm-related impacts.[13] For the most at-risk areas (low lying and geographically situated

---

[10] The term "federalism" in this context refers to the relationship between state governments and the federal government of the United States. State governments adjacent to coastlines enjoy sovereignty both in principle and practice. However, the extent of state sovereignty is limited when applied to matters of federal (national) concern. For example, while the state government owns the water adjacent to the coastline, the federal government has supremacy in controlling navigation routes along the coastline. Or, in the case of climate change, state government goals regarding climate change may be impacted by conflicting federal goals under principles of federalism.

[11] Coastal Zone Management Act of 1972, 16 U.S.C. §§ 1451–1466 (2012).

[12] *See generally* INTERGOVERNMENTAL PANEL ON CLIMATE CHANGE, MANAGING THE RISKS OF EXTREME EVENTS AND DISASTERS TO ADVANCE CLIMATE CHANGE 76–89 (Christopher B. Field et al. eds., 2012), *available at* http://ipcc-wg2.gov/SREX/images/uploads/SREX-All_FINAL.pdf.

[13] *Id.*

in storm-prone areas), there are various threats based on changes in localized conditions experienced compared to historical conditions.[14] These changes can lead to biogeochemical alterations that have significant consequences for the management of coastal areas. Current and future impacts to coastal regions from climate change may be divided into three categories: *physical* impacts focusing on the features of the coast and the processes that both drive and are impacted by climate change, *ecosystem* impacts that consider the effect of climate change on vulnerable coastal species and associated habitat, and *societal* impacts that consider the effect climate change has on the human-built environment.

A. PHYSICAL IMPACTS

Physical impacts to the coast vary depending on several factors, including elevation and proximity to storm centers.[15] In general, lower lying coastal regions with a gradual slope are at greater risk than higher coastal elevations or coastlines with a more dramatic slope. In addition, the proximity of the coastal area to epicenters of strong storm activity (e.g., hurricanes, tsunamis, earthquakes, etc.) can increase physical impacts associated with climate change as the increased proximity of human habitation to the shoreline can intensify the effects of the seismic event. Nearshore water depth impacts the ability of ocean-borne storm surges to reach closer to the shoreline before releasing their energy. Greater ocean depths brought on by sea-level rise associated with climate change can increase a storm's proximity to coastal land before releasing the brunt of its force. Warming ambient surface temperatures increase the temperature of surface waters, which in turn increases the intensity of storms such as ocean-borne hurricanes. Warmer surface waters moved inland through sea-level rise also increase the probability and reach of coastal storms, intensifying their potential impact.[16]

Expected climate-change-induced physical changes associated with coastlines include the flooding of low-lying areas. Flooding, or inundation, generally occurs in sheltered, low-energy areas where physical processes such as sediment accumulation are minimal.[17] The levees of New Orleans, Louisiana, are an example of human-built protection against flooding in a low-lying area; the levees create an artificial environment where the water's edge buttresses up against human development. When Hurricane Katrina struck in 2005, the sea was pushed inland—albeit by a storm surge—unabated by natural

---

[14] *Id.* The newest observations indicate a changing climate leads to changes in the frequency, intensity, spatial extent, duration, and timing of extreme weather and climate events, and can result in unprecedented extreme weather and climate events. *See generally id.* at 115–202.

[15] *See generally* Nick Brooks et al., *The Determinants of Vulnerability and Adaptive Capacity at the National Level and the Implications for Adaptation*, 15 GLOBAL ENVTL. CHANGE 151 (2005).

[16] MANAGING THE RISKS OF EXTREME EVENTS AND DISASTERS TO ADVANCE CLIMATE CHANGE ADAPTATION, *supra* note 12, at 76.

[17] *See* SAMUEL D. BRODY, WESLEY H. HIGHFIELD & JUNG EUN KANG, RISING WATERS: THE CAUSES AND CONSEQUENCES OF FLOODING IN THE UNITED STATES 71–80 (2011).

sediment buildup or wetlands. The result was the immediate inundation (submergence) of low-lying portions of the city nearest to the levees.[18] The extent of inundation is physically based on the relative slope of the land; coastal areas with minimal slopes have the greatest potential to be impacted by sea-level rise. Seas moving landward create shifting coastal boundaries. Some of the upland connected to the ocean is more susceptible to erosion, depending on the makeup of the soil and the dynamics associated with the new land-sea boundary. A strong surging tide can also impact the shape of the shoreline, creating shifting land that is relatively unstable. In addition, the rate of sea-level rise in a given coastal area can impact existing wetlands and the development of new wetlands or intertidal areas, depending on local conditions.[19] Approaching seawater can also mix with existing underground aquifers, impacting freshwater resources.[20]

Many of the physical impacts of climate change are already being felt along coastal regions. For example, global sea levels have been observed to be rising recently in the late nineteenth and early twentieth centuries.[21] Recent analysis has shown that global averages of sea-level rise have been approximately 7.5 inches during the twentieth century, and the rate of sea-level rise has been increasing over the past fifteen years.[22] Finally, there is strong evidence that the rate of sea-level rise in the twenty-first century will exceed that of the twentieth century.[23] Areas of the coast exhibiting combinations of at-risk characteristics identified above that are located in dynamic areas will be prime targets for continued and sustained physical impacts for the foreseeable future.

There are economic consequences to the physical impacts described above. Impacts on tourism, for example, can provide some measure of the direct economic costs associated with climate-induced physical changes. Tourism activity in the United States contributed approximately 2 trillion dollars of economic output in 2012.[24] While the percentage of this total tourism attributable to coastal activities is hard to quantify, eight of the top ten U.S. states visited in 2011–2012 by overseas tourists were coastal states, suggesting a

---

[18] *See* John W. Day Jr. et al., *Restoration of the Mississippi Delta: Lessons from Hurricanes Katrina and Rita*, 315 Sci. 1679, 1680 (2007).

[19] *See generally* Brooks et al., *supra* note 15.

[20] *See* Adrian D. Werner & Craig T. Simmons, *Impact of Sea-Level Rise on Sea Water Intrusion in Coastal Aquifers*, 47(2) Groundwater 197 (2009).

[21] *See generally* Kirk Lambeck et al., *Sea Level in Roman Time in the Central Mediterranean and Implications for Recent Change*, 224 Earth & Planetary Sci. Letters 563 (2004); W. Roland Gehrels et al., *A 20th Century Acceleration of Sea-Level Rise in New Zealand*, 35 Geophysical Res. Letters L02717 (2008).

[22] *See* Lisa Alexander et al., Intergovernmental Panel on Climate Change, Twelfth Session of Working Group I Approved Summary for Policymakers 20 (2013), http://www. climatechange2013.org/images/uploads/WGI_AR5_SPM_brochure.pdf. *See generally* Svetlana Jerejeva et al., *Nonlinear Trends and Multiyear Cycles in Sea Level Records*, 13 J. Geophysical Res. C09012 (2006), *available at* ftp://soest.hawaii.edu/coastal/Climate%20Articles/Jevrejeva_2005%20Nonlinear%20sea%20 level%20trends.pdf.

[23] *See* Alexander et al., *supra* note 22, at 21.

[24] U.S. Travel Ass'n, *2012 Travel Economic Impact Overview* (2013), *available at* http://www.ustravel.org/sites/ default/files/page/2009/09/EconomicImpactTravelandTourism2013update.pdf.

substantial portion of total tourist economic activity is tied to coastal attributes.[25] One recent case study suggests complete coastal erosion along Waikiki Beach in Hawaii will result in a revenue loss of $2 billion out of total revenue of $5.2 billion, representing a loss of approximately 39 percent in tourism for Waikiki Beach alone.[26] If we conservatively assume half of the total 2012 tourism ($2.0 trillion) is related to coastal tourism, and the percentage of revenue loss in the Waikiki Beach case study is roughly representative of expected tourism revenue losses along coastal areas (39 percent), then we are left with a potential tourism revenue loss associated with sea-level rise of roughly $390 billion based on 2012 total tourism revenue. Even if these rough estimates are only half true, the direct economic impacts of climate change to coastal areas are substantial.

B. ECOSYSTEM IMPACTS

Ecosystem impacts consider the effect of climate change on vulnerable coastal species and associated habitat. A "coastal zone" often contains a variety of characteristics that are consistent among such areas across the globe. These features include a waterline that distinguishes between land and sea, an intertidal zone that represents the fluctuation of the land-sea interface based on tidal range, an area above the influence of the tide (sometimes a sandy beach), and a vegetation line that represents the landward extent of the coastal area.[27]

Many coastal zones contain wetland areas that are either always partially wet or intermittently wet, and usually subject to tidal influences.[28] Wetlands often contain unique plant species that, collectively, form important habitat for a variety of marine and terrestrial animals. Many coastal wetlands are often considered ecologically important zones because of the richness and diversity of species present.[29] As sea-level rise associated with climate change inundates inland areas, the existing ecological footprint of wetlands changes. Areas that were partially submerged become completely submerged underwater. Plants not adapted to full submergence underwater die off as the water overtakes

---

[25] Office of Travel and Tourism Industries, *Overseas Visitation Estimates for U.S. States, Cities, and Census Regions: 2012* (2012), *available at* http://travel.trade.gov/outreachpages/download_data_table/2012_ States_and_Cities.pdf

[26] Amber Himes-Cornell et al., *Impacts of Climate Change on Human Uses of the Ocean, in* OCEAN AND MARINE RESOURCES IN A CHANGING CLIMATE: TECHNICAL INPUT TO THE 2013 NATIONAL CLIMATE ASSESSMENT 64, 100–01 (Roger Griffis & Jennifer Howard eds., 2013) (projected revenues are based on 2007 tourist revenue for Waikiki Beach, and the estimated losses are based on the presumption of a totally eroded beach due to sea-level rise).

[27] DAVIS & FITZGERALD, *supra* note 2, 115–28.

[28] *Id.* at 263–77.

[29] *See generally* Robert Costanza et al., *The Value of the World's Ecosystem Services and Natural Capital*, 387 NATURE 253 (1997), *available at* http://www.esd.ornl.gov/benefits_conference/nature_paper.pdf (ecosystem services are often given little weight in policy decisions but they are important to human sustainability).

them. Sea-level rise changes the balance of wetland ecosystems, which disrupts the functions and processes of these systems.[30]

Current sea-level rise is already causing significant impacts in coastal ecosystems. For example, in low-lying regions of the United States, ocean storm surges and particularly high spring tides are increasingly causing flooding of coastal areas. These events are causing the loss of wetlands and the conversion of coastal forest and developed lands (farmlands, residential properties) to wetlands.[31] Freshwater areas (lakes, ponds, aquifers) that are found near the land-sea boundary are also increasingly becoming flooded with salt water from sea-level rise, which is changing the salinity of the freshwater bodies, leading to significant impacts on those localized ecosystems.[32]

Climate change impacts to coastal ecosystems and the services they provide can be substantial in both direct and indirect economic terms. Coastal wetland resources provide valuable nursery habitat for commercial and recreational fisheries.[33] In addition, coastal wetlands buffer the impacts of ocean-derived storms on inland resources.[34] There are other valuable provisioning, regulating, and aesthetic services provided by coastal wetlands. The value of these services has been estimated to range from billions to trillions of dollars.[35]

Climate change impacts on these coastal ecological values are substantial and will likely increase over time.[36] Choices about development in undisturbed coastal areas today can have a substantial impact on the extent of ecological impacts in the future. For example, the choice to armor against the rising sea by building walls prevents the opportunity for coastal features, such as coastal wetlands, to migrate inland. Coastal management planning needs to incorporate the ecological values at stake in the coastal zone from climate change risks, particularly values that are not directly associated with direct human consumption of coastal resources.

C. SOCIETAL IMPACTS

Societal impacts observed from climate change in the coastal zone vary depending on a variety of factors. "Vulnerability" is a term often used as a multiple variable factor to describe and analyze these impacts to society.[37] Vulnerability suggests a mix of actual

---

[30] *See generally* James T. Morris et al., *Responses of Coastal Wetlands to Rising Sea Level*, 83 ECOLOGY 2869 (2002).

[31] *Id.*

[32] GLOBAL CLIMATE CHANGE IMPACTS IN THE UNITED STATES 31 (Thomas R. Karl et al. eds., 2009), *available at* http://downloads.globalchange.gov/usimpacts/pdfs/climate-impacts-report.pdf.

[33] Costanza et al., *supra* note 29, at 256.

[34] DAVIS & FITZGERALD, *supra* note 2, at 371–79.

[35] Costanza et al., *supra* note 29, at 256.

[36] Degradation of existing coastal assets will lead to scarcity of those assets. Assuming demand either remains constant or increases for those assets, the value of a depleted remaining supply will increase over time.

[37] W. Neil Adger & Katherine Vincent, *Uncertainty in Adaptive Capacity*, 337 GEOSCI. 399, 400–04 (2005).

environmental risk (e.g., the geographic characteristics of the coastline) and human decisions related to those risks. How humans decide to plan and respond to risk—including assessing the capacity to plan and respond to risks—is an important consideration when determining the vulnerability of a region.[38] Human-based factors impacting this kind of risk assessment of vulnerability include: awareness of the hazard, intensity and sophistication of development along coastal regions, and the kinds of public policy institutions established to deal with the risk.[39] As Anthony Oliver-Smith points out, "[v]ulnerability...explicitly links environmental issues, such as hazards, with the structure and organization of society, and the rights associated with membership."[40]

Vulnerability thus links environmental hazards to the capacity of institutions to provide for the needs of its society. Where institutions are weak, allowing for inequitable distribution of the risks from these hazards across society, vulnerability will generally be high. Conversely, a society with stronger institutions and more equitable distribution of rights and benefits between citizens will tend to have lower vulnerability. This is true even where the environmental factors are similar between governments, such as where two coastal states share similar exposure to climate change hazards and similar population densities near coastal areas. The extent of vulnerability between these two governments with similar environmental factors will be determined by their respective sociopolitical structures. Institutions with sociopolitical structures capable of dealing with climate risks will generally have less societal vulnerability toward climate change than those with weaker sociopolitical structures.[41]

Coastal states currently exercising their planning capacities are finding ways to mitigate and adapt to the current impacts of climate change. In general, the coastal regions where purposeful management and planning are occurring are developing more resilient policy plans than similar coastal areas where management and planning are not occurring to the same extent.[42] Even so, climate change impacts are occurring in many areas where institutional capacity exists and planning is ongoing, suggesting that even early adaptive planning cannot completely negate the impacts of climate change. On the Atlantic Seaboard of the United States, for example, "ghost forests" of standing dead

---

[38] For example, a community located on a large continental coastline with a diverse economic base and strong distributed political system is generally more capable of limiting the societal impacts of climate change than a small, geographically and economically isolated coastal state; the continental coastal community can simply move inland, and the socioeconomic system in place can more easily absorb this migration. The same cannot be said of the small coastal state; it does not have the same "capacity" as the continental coastal community in terms of geographic options and economic tools, which limits its ability to mitigate the impacts of climate change.

[39] Brooks et al., *supra* note 15, at 157–58.

[40] Anthony Oliver Smith, *Sea Level Rise and the Vulnerability of Coastal Peoples*, 7 INTERSECTIONS. 8, 15 (2009).

[41] ROBERT NICHOLS & FRANK M.J. HOOZEMANS, *Global Vulnerability Analysis*, in ENCYCLOPEDIA OF COASTAL SCIENCE 486–91 (Maurice Schwartz ed., 2005).

[42] *See generally* GLOBAL CLIMATE CHANGE IMPACTS IN THE UNITED STATES, *supra* note 32, at 61–70.

trees killed by saltwater intrusion are becoming increasingly common in southern New Jersey, Maryland, Virginia, Louisiana, and North Carolina.[43] In addition, many coastal regions are experiencing moderate-to-severe erosion along coastal areas due to a mix of natural processes (storms and sea-level rise) and human activities (development, dredging, and armoring) as population densities increase in coastal regions of the United States. These realities suggest institutional capacity can only go so far in stemming coastal vulnerability from the effects of climate change.

Climate change is impacting coastal areas physically, degrading ecosystem services provided by coastal systems, and influencing the capacity of society to address dynamic changes to coastal systems. These categorical impacts help define the context through which existing legal frameworks are examined in light of climate-induced changes. For example, a coastal state with an active beach tourism industry likely places a high value on its coastline because of the physical attributes of the coast. As such, coastline protection is prioritized to ensure the underlying "asset base" (the coast itself) is preserved to ensure future economic opportunity from tourism.

Climate change can alter this asset base. Sea-level rise, coupled with increased storm intensity and duration, can erode tourism demand. Coastal states are empowered under the law to adapt to climate change impacts, but their strategies can be limited by federal government priorities and actions. An exploration of state and federal law interactions, commonly referred to as federalism, can highlight how coastal state powers to adapt to climate change can be limited. Through this highlighting of coastal state limitations through a lens of state and federal interactions, the importance of federal cooperation in coastal state adaptation strategies becomes apparent.

II. The Coastal Zone Management Act and Climate Change

The Coastal Zone Management Act (CZMA) is a federal statute passed in 1972.[44] The coastal management program of the CZMA established a uniform set of standards for the creation and implementation of coastal management plans to promote sustainable coastal development and protection.[45] By providing financial assistance and helping to frame the priorities for coastal development and planning, the CZMA initially acted as a mechanism to create consistency among coastal states in how they planned for coastal development and protection. As of 2013, all eligible coastal states in the United States,

---

[43] *See* U.S. Climate Change Sci. Program Synthesis and Assessment Product 4.1, Coastal Sensitivity to Sea-Level Rise: A Focus on the Mid-Atlantic Region 22 (2009), *available at* http://downloads.globalchange.gov/sap/sap4-1/sap4-1-final-report-all.pdf.

[44] Coastal Zone Management Act of 1972, 16 U.S.C. §§ 1451–1466 (2012).

[45] 16 U.S.C. § 1451 (2012) (noting the purpose of national coastal management planning is to preserve, protect, develop, and where possible, restore or enhance the resources of the nation's coastal zone for this and succeeding generations).

with the exception of Alaska, which allowed its participation to lapse in 2011, have accepted the terms of the CZMA and have developed coastal management plans within the framework of the federal law.[46]

A. FEDERAL CONSISTENCY UNDER THE CZMA

Beyond the financial incentives offered by the federal government to develop and implement coastal management planning, the CZMA also provides for "federal consistency" under the Act, a condition sometimes referred to as "reverse supremacy" whereby the federal government assures the state that federal activities with the potential to affect identified coastal resources—to the extent practicable—are consistent with the coastal state's management plan.[47] Precisely what kinds of federal actions have the potential to affect identified coastal resources in such a way that trigger federal consistency requirements under the CZMA have been the subject of both legislative and judicial inquiry.

In supporting the importance of federal consistency under the CZMA, has noted the review process is "the single greatest incentive for State participation in the coastal zone management program."[48] Indeed, Congress has gone to great lengths to ensure coastal state rights remain paramount when federal actions come into conflict with state coastal management planning. In one historical example, a judicial interpretation that limited the application of federal consistency was legislatively overruled by Congress. This occurred in the U.S. Supreme Court case of *Secretary of the Interior v. California.*[49] The original language under the CZMA dealing with federal consistency required a review only when federal actions had a *direct effect* on the coasts.[50] The Supreme Court interpreted this language conservatively, limiting the scope of federal actions that must comply with a state-approved coastal management plan.[51] Following this decision, Congress passed the Coastal Zone Management Reauthorization Amendments of 1990, changing the language triggering a federal consistency review to any federal "activity within

---

[46] *See* NOAA, *Coastal Programs: Partnering with States to Manage Our Coastline*, last updated Jan. 30, 2013, http://coastalmanagement.noaa.gov/programs/czm.html (last visited Nov. 29, 2013); *see also* NOAA Action Notice, Alaska Coastal Management Program Withdrawal from the National Coastal Management Program under the Coastal Management Zone Act (CZMA), 76 Fed. Reg. 39857–39858 (July 7, 2011), *available at* http://www.gpo.gov/fdsys/pkg/FR-2011-07-07/html/2011-16987.htm (noting that the Alaska Coastal Management Plan expired on June 30, 2011).

[47] 16 U.S.C. §1456(c) (2012); *see also* Chad J. McGuire, *Coastal Planning, Federal Consistency, and Climate Change: A Recent Divergence of Federal and State Interests*, 27 NAT. RESOURCES & ENV'T 41 (2012).

[48] S. REP. No.94-277, at 8 (1975), *reprinted in* 1976 U.S.C.C.A.N. 1768, 1776; *see also* Martin J. LaLonde, *Allocating the Burden of Proof to Effectuate the Preservation and Federalism Goals of the Coastal Zone Management Act*, 92 MICH. L. REV. 438, 442–44 (1993).

[49] Sec'y of the Interior v. California, 464 U.S. 312 (1984).

[50] 16 U.S.C. § 1456(c)(1) (1990).

[51] *See supra* note 48, at 342–43.

or outside the coastal zone that affects any land or water use or natural resource."[52] Congress noted in its record that its primary objective in amending the federal consistency requirement of the CZMA was to overturn the Supreme Court's decision in *Secretary of the Interior v. California.*[53]

What this example shows is a strong legislative preference favoring coastal state rights under federal consistency when federal actions have the potential, whether directly or indirectly, to impact coastal state resources. With our knowledge of this preference for advancing coastal state rights under federal consistency requirements of the CZMA, what remains to be understood is the impact this preference has on federal and state interactions that influence coastal assets when compared against traditional interpretations of federalism.

Traditionally, the federal government need not *legally* concern itself with state priorities when acting wholly within federal legal jurisdiction. And even when there may be a conflict between federal actions and state goals, the federal actions take precedence.[54] In coastal areas, states have ownership rights over the submerged lands and resources within the ocean up to three miles out to sea from an established baseline.[55] The federal government has ownership rights past this three-mile limit to the extent of its exclusive economic zone (at least 200 miles from the established baseline).[56] In addition, the federal government maintains management rights and responsibilities within the three-mile state jurisdiction of waters for a host of purposes that are in the national interest.[57] Thus, federal activities that occur within federal jurisdiction, even if they impact state marine or coastal resources, traditionally cannot be *legally* challenged by coastal states.

The federal consistency requirement under the CZMA changes this traditional legal hierarchy between federal and state government. When federal actions have the potential to impact identified state priorities, the federal government must ensure, to the extent practicable, that its actions conform to documented state priorities. Without a federal consistency requirement, there is little in the law mandating that the federal government consider the potential impact of its proposed actions on coastal state resources, and this is particularly true when proposed federal actions contemplate the use of federally owned marine resources—resources existing beyond the three-mile state jurisdiction to the extent of the federal government's exclusive economic zone.

---

[52] 16 U.S.C. § 1456(c)(1)(A) (2012).

[53] 136 CONG. REC. H8075 (daily ed. Sept. 26, 1990); *see also* LaLonde, *supra* note 48, at 443–44.

[54] U.S. CONST., art. VI, cl. 2.

[55] Submerged Lands Act, 43 U.S.C. §§ 1301–1315 (2012).

[56] Proclamation No. 5030, 60 Fed. Reg. 43, 825 (Aug. 25, 1995).

[57] These include responsibilities for securing the shoreline from threats, ensuring navigability, protecting interstate commerce, and other similar obligations that are in the nation's collective interest.

B. THE CONTEXT OF CLIMATE CHANGE

In the context of climate change, the relationship between federal actions and coastal state impacts is optimally presented through the example of offshore oil and gas development. Historically, the federal assertion of jurisdiction to submerged lands after World War II for resource development (and leasing royalties) led to battles between coastal states and the federal government over ownership rights of marine resources. In *United States v. California*, the U.S. Supreme Court held that ownership rights accrued to the federal government.[58] Congress overturned this ruling by legislating ownership rights between coastal states and the federal government with the passage of the Submerged Lands Act of 1953,[59] effectively creating a "buffer" of coastal state ownership and rights up to three miles seaward of an agreed baseline. Congress further established rules regarding the development of offshore resources in federal jurisdiction with the passage of the Outer Continental Shelf Lands Act.[60]

Collectively these laws helped to provide a framework for offshore oil and gas development at the federal level (ownership and process), but the coastal states relied on the CZMA to protect their interests from federal activities that the states thought would have the potential to harm coastal assets. As offshore oil spills had historically been seen as a major threat to coastal assets such as tourism (e.g., as the Santa Barbara Oil Spill of 1969), many early coastal management plans highlighted the pristine nature of coastal areas as a resource priority under approved plans, and then sought to enforce protection of these resources from federal government actions. These historical antecedents provide the conditions upon which a coastal state may proactively seek to protect its coastline from the harms of climate change by acting to limit both continuation and expansion of federal offshore oil and gas development.

A coastal state might identify its natural shoreline attributes as a major priority of its coastal plan because of the importance the coastline plays in tourism, recreation, and supporting services. Meanwhile, the federal government may propose additional offshore oil and gas development that adds to carbon redistribution from the lithosphere to the atmosphere. If this proposed oil and gas development conceivably threatens shoreline attributes, then the validity of that federal action may be challenged by coastal states under the consistency requirements of the CZMA.[61]

---

[58] United States. v. California, 332 U.S. 19, 38–39 (1947).

[59] 43 U.S.C. §§ 1301–1315 (2012).

[60] 43 U.S.C. §§ 1331–1356(a) (2012).

[61] States can object to proposed federal actions that may affect the coastal zone. 16 U.S.C. § 1456 (c)(3)(A) (2012); 15 C.F.R § 930.34(b) (2014). Federal and state governments may request mediation to resolve the objection. 16 U.S.C. § 1456(h) (2012). In the alternative, the state also has the right to bring suit in federal court. 15 C.F.R. § 930.116 (2014) (state is not required to mediate prior to brining suit). There is also an option for the president of the United States, responding to a request from the Secretary of the Interior, to exempt the federal activity from federal consistency requirements under the CZMA if the president deems the federal activity is in the paramount interests of the United States. 16 U.S.C. § 1456(c)(1)(B) (2012).

The coastal state will identify the coastal resource at-risk from the federal activity and challenge the federal action as inconsistent with its obligations to ensure, to the extent practicable, that federal activities do not interfere with coastal priorities. The coastal state challenge identifies the connection between federal activity and state impact, creating an avenue for state-federal negotiations in a way that may not be apparent under traditional roles of federalism. In order to understand how this can occur, a more detailed explanation of this example follows.

Domestic offshore energy production contributes to the entire portfolio of energy production within the United States, although its relative importance has been impacted by several factors over the last decade. In 1954, offshore oil production represented 0.10 percent of the entire U.S. oil production, and offshore gas production represented 0.69 percent of the entire U.S. domestic gas production.[62] In 2011, offshore oil production accounted for approximately 25 percent of total U.S. production, while offshore gas accounted for approximately 8 percent of total U.S. production.[63] Based on historical trends while accounting for political and technological factors, it is very likely that offshore oil and gas development will continue into the foreseeable future.

Assuming federal offshore oil and gas development continues into the future, one important issue is whether the federal government is obliged to alter its offshore oil and gas production when such actions threaten coastal resources by reinforcing climate change. Under traditional concepts of federalism, the federal government likely has no *legal* obligation to coastal states under such circumstances. However, assuming these federal activities can be causally linked to climate change impacts on coastal state resources, the CZMA's federal consistency requirement may provide leverage to examine the causal relationships between federal actions and coastal state impacts.

III. Utilizing Federal Consistency to Respond to Climate Change Impacts

A. TWO LEGAL ARGUMENTS FOR STATES

Coastal states have, at minimum, two legal arguments when utilizing the federal consistency requirements of the CZMA in response to planned federal activities that may intensify the impacts of climate change. The first argument is not marine dependent, but

---

[62] Bureau of Safety & Envtl. Enforcement, Federal OCS Oil and Gas Production as a Percentage of Total U.S. Production: 1954–2010 (2010), *available at* http://www.bsee.gov/uploadedFiles/BSEE/Newsroom/Offshore_Stats_and_Facts/ANNUAL%20PERCENTAGE.pdf.

[63] *Id.* Both oil and gas production offshore has reduced in recent years in terms of both total output and as a percentage of total U.S. production. Events such as the 2010 Deep Water Horizon oil spill in the Gulf of Mexico have influenced federal proposals to increase offshore oil and gas leases to include the Mid-Atlantic region. *See* Juliet Eilperin & Steve Mufson, *Offshore Drilling Policy Reversed*, Wash. Post, Dec. 2, 2010, http://www.washingtonpost.com/wp-dyn/content/article/2010/12/01/AR2010120107185.html. In addition, technological advancements such as "fracking" and favorable price points have increased the onshore domestic production of natural gas, thereby further reducing offshore natural gas production as a percentage of total domestic natural gas production.

rather focuses on the relationship between federal actions connected to climate change and the impacts those actions, in the aggregate, can have on priority coastal resources. The second argument is focused on a subset of federal actions occurring in marine waters that have the potential, as both singular and aggregated events, to harm coastal assets. What follows is a summary discussion of each legal argument highlighting the role the CZMA plays in helping to bring coastal state concerns into the discussion of federal activities that arguably contribute to climate change.

1. Carbon Intensity of Federal Activities

The first argument utilizing the federal consistency requirements of the CZMA focuses on the carbon intensity of federal activities and their connection to climate change. This argument borrows from the causality discussions described in parts of the *Massachusetts v. EPA* decision.[64] In that case, coastal states argued the Environmental Protection Agency (EPA) of the federal government was obliged under a federal statute (the Clean Air Act) to make a determination as to whether carbon qualified as a "pollutant" under the Act because of the association between human-induced atmospheric carbon emissions and climate change. Coastal states argued harm that included the loss of coastal uplands due to sea-level rise, and claimed the federal government had an obligation to control that harm under the Clean Air Act (or at least decide whether or not to attempt to control the harm) because the federal government had authority over the issue under principles of federalism.[65]

The standing argument, in part, focused on whether coastal states could connect the harm claimed—loss of landmass due to sea-level rise—to the inaction of the EPA when deciding whether to control carbon as a pollutant under the Clean Air Act. The federal government argued that even if it regulated carbon in the United States, the actions of other countries in expanding their utilization of greenhouse gases would render the regulation useless *as it pertained* to stopping sea-level rise because other countries would continue to mine and burn carbon, and sea-level rise would continue to harm coastal states regardless of the federal government's actions.[66] The U.S. Supreme Court dismissed the federal government's claim that its actions alone cannot redress the harm of sea-level rise suffered by coastal states. Accepting the causal connection between carbon emissions and sea-level rise, the Court concluded that *any* action undertaken by

---

[64] Massachusetts. v. EPA, 549 U.S. 497 (2007).

[65] *Id.* at 518–19. The argument stems from the fact that Congress created a federal statute, the Clean Air Act, which covers the field of emissions from automobiles that harm air quality. By creating this law, the federal government becomes responsible for protecting coastal states against the harms caused by pollution of the atmosphere.

[66] *Id.* at 523–25. "EPA does not believe that any realistic possibility exists that the relief petitioners seek would mitigate global climate change and remedy their injuries. That is especially so because predicted increases in greenhouse gas emissions from developing nations, particularly China and India, are likely to offset any marginal domestic decrease." *Id.* at 523–24.

the federal government, even if not definitive, would be a positive factor in reducing the impacts of climate-induced sea-level rise and associated coastal hazards.[67]

Under the CZMA's federal consistency requirement, coastal states can draw on the logic from the *Massachusetts v. EPA* decision to assert that any federal activity allowing an increase in greenhouse gas emissions is inconsistent with existing priorities contained in approved coastal management plans. Thus, when the federal government engages in actions, terrestrial or ocean bound, that increase the *likelihood* of priority coastal assets being harmed, the federal consistency requirement of the CZMA requires the federal government to consider these impacts, and to the extent practicable, alter its actions to mitigate such impacts. Coastal states can argue the question of causation, at least for legal standing purposes, is somewhat settled based on the logic announced in *Massachusetts v. EPA* by noting that any activity that adds to carbon concentrations in the atmosphere is a contributing factor to coastal zone degradation. Thus, continued development of domestic carbon-based energy production triggers federal consistency review under the CZMA because, whether viewed individually or in the aggregate, these actions conflict with federally accepted coastal state priorities.

2. Federal Offshore Activities

The second legal argument under the CZMA's federal consistency requirements emphasizes federal *offshore* oil and gas development, highlighting the additional risks based on the proximity of the development to coastal resources. Borrowing from the greenhouse gas emissions argument above (any addition of carbon into the atmosphere from human activities harms coastal resources), the focus is on the dangers associated with offshore oil and gas development as an *activity* rather than, as in the first argument, focusing on the *effects* of the federal activity.[68] This second legal argument identifies the direct dangers associated with drilling, such as oil spills through malfunctioning drilling platforms. These kinds of dangers, because they are directly connected to the offshore activity, pose far less of a proximate cause hurdle than the more attenuated first argument. The additional benefit of this second legal argument is that it contains precedent in terms of linking these direct dangers of federal offshore activities to federal consistency obligations under the CZMA. Through the analysis of the precedent of federal consistency for these

---

[67] In supporting its contention that incremental steps can justify agency actions, the Court noted the following: "EPA overstates its case. Its argument rests on the erroneous assumption that a small incremental step, because it is incremental, can never be attacked in a federal judicial forum. Yet accepting that premise would doom most challenges to regulatory action. Agencies, like legislatures, do not generally resolve massive problems in one fell regulatory swoop." *Id.* at 524–25.

[68] The first legal argument above focuses mainly on the *indirect* danger accompanying offshore oil and gas exploration. The future use of the oil and gas removed from the ocean's depth will result in greenhouse gas emissions that will help to cause climate change, and then the effects of climate change will be the cause of coastal resource degradation, through sea-level rise and increased storm impacts as described above.

more direct dangers associated with federal actions, the groundwork is established to revisit the more indirect argument of how the CZMA can aid in helping to align federal and state actions relative to climate change adaptation strategies.

Historically there have been instances where the federal government has altered its actions to meet federal consistency requirements under the CZMA, and there have also been instances where the federal government has sought to move ahead with its actions even where there is clear evidence the federal action will impact coastal interests explicitly identified under approved coastal management plans. There is probably no greater example of the potential conflict between federal desires and coastal state priorities than the energy crisis of the 1970s associated with the Arab oil embargo. Early adopters of coastal management planning under the CZMA sought to limit the impact of expanded federal offshore oil and gas development plans to counter the reduced global supply of oil. The federal government responded to protective coastal state management planning legislatively, amending the CZMA in 1976 to include a Coastal Energy Impact Program.[69] This program acknowledged the potential impact that increased oil and gas exploration could have on coastal resources by including additional federal funding to coastal states to help mitigate these impacts.[70] However, the program also included a key change in applying federal consistency requirements—the so-called "national interest" provision—that allowed the federal government to essentially bypass federal consistency considerations when the federal activity was deemed by the Secretary of Commerce to be in the "national interest" of the country.[71]

Today the "national interest" exception is one of the main mechanisms by which the federal government can avoid its consistency obligation under the CZMA.[72] Because

---

[69] Biliana Cicin-Sain & Robert W. Knecht, The Future of U.S. Ocean Policy: Choices for the New Century 118–20 (2000).

[70] Id.

[71] 15 C.F.R. § 930.122 (2014). "A federal license or permit activity, or a federal assistance activity, is 'necessary in the interest of national security' if a national defense or other national security interest would be significantly impaired were the activity not permitted to go forward as proposed. Secretarial review of national security issues shall be aided by information submitted by the Department of Defense or other interested Federal agencies. The views of such agencies, while not binding, shall be given considerable weight by the Secretary. The Secretary will seek information to determine whether the objected-to activity directly supports national defense or other essential national security objectives." Id.

[72] 15 C.F.R. § 930.121 (2014). "A federal license or permit activity, or a federal assistance activity, is 'consistent with the objectives or purposes of the Act' if it satisfies each of the following three requirements:

(a) The activity furthers the national interest as articulated in § 302 or § 303 of the Act, in a significant or substantial manner,

(b) The national interest furthered by the activity outweighs the activity's adverse coastal effects, when those effects are considered separately or cumulatively.

(c) There is no reasonable alternative available which would permit the activity to be conducted in a manner consistent with the enforceable policies of the management program. The Secretary may consider but is not limited to considering previous appeal decisions, alternatives described in state objection letters and alternatives and other information submitted during the appeal. The Secretary shall not

the concept of national interest implicitly weighs the state interest against the federal interest, coastal states must be careful in how they employ the CZMA as a means of negotiating federal actions, particularly federal actions that deal with "core" national interests such as energy security.[73]

When the focus is moved back to climate change, coastal states find themselves in an awkward position: they are the owners of the coastline, but their ability to ensure the security of that coastline is limited. Federal activities beyond three miles have the capacity to intensify coastal insecurity. The question is really: What can coastal states do to engender federal actions that aid in increasing coastal security in the face of climate change? Although federalism places limitations on coastal states in forcing the federal government's hand from a legal standpoint, the CZMA's existing legal structure helps coastal states position themselves into a cooperative position with federal planning.[74]

B. SUGGESTIONS FOR IMPLEMENTATION

This section offers recommendations for how coastal states can facilitate federal cooperation in adapting to the challenges of climate change along the coastline of the United States. First, coastal states can lead by example. Alternative, non-carbon offshore energy projects can help to establish a carbon-neutral path to energy security. Such alternatives can mitigate the "national interest" exception and thus bolster federal consistency claims by showing the promise of carbon-free offshore energy development. Massachusetts, Rhode Island, and other coastal states are leading the charge in supporting offshore wind energy development, and this includes fostering federal offshore wind energy projects that have been sited just outside the coastal state jurisdictional limit.

---

consider an alternative unless the State agency submits a statement, in a brief or other supporting material, to the Secretary that the alternative would permit the activity to be conducted in a manner consistent with the enforceable policies of the management program." *Id.*

[73] Coastal states have previously attempted to use the federal consistency provision of the CZMA as a means to intervene in federal offshore activities wholly within federal jurisdiction. These attempts aimed at oil and gas activities were thwarted when the U.S. Supreme Court held that federal offshore oil and gas leasing activities do not "directly affect" coastal states as contemplated under the federal consistency provision of the CZMA. *See* Sec'y of Interior v. California., 464 U.S. 312 (1984). Later amendments to the CZMA replaced the "directly affecting" language with a more generalized "effects test" providing latitude for coastal states to apply federal consistency to federal offshore activities. *See* 15 C.F.R. § 930.11(g) (2014).

[74] *Discretionary* offshore federal activities provide the clearest avenue for coastal state interdiction and cooperation opportunities because federal consistency compliance is not required when the federal government is acting pursuant to a *mandatory* obligation under a different statute, such as the leasing provisions of the Outer Continental Shelf Lands Act (OCSLA). *See* 16 U.S.C. § 1456(c)(1) (2012). For example, if the federal government acts pursuant to a mandatory leasing requirement under OCSLA, then the federal government is not required to alter its actions under a federal consistency determination, even if the action can result in harm to documented coastal priorities.

Second, coastal states can strategically employ the CZMA's federal consistency provision by highlighting the correlation between federal expansion of offshore oil and gas projects and the effects of climate change, in particular sea-level rise and increased storm impacts. Indeed, the congressional findings contained in the CZMA identify the threat of global-warming-induced sea-level rise, noting that coastal states must anticipate and plan for such occurrences.[75] Coastal states can directly engage the federal government through a public awareness campaign on the issue, drawing on arguments similar to those that the coastal states made in *Massachusetts v. EPA*.[76] This combination of legal maneuvering and political pressure can help to align state and federal interests in a manner that overcomes the challenges of federalism, particularly when that challenge is defined in the context of protecting coastal resources at the expense of national energy security.[77]

These recommendations demonstrate how an existing legal framework such as the federal consistency requirement of the CZMA can be strategically employed to help protect coastlines from the impacts of climate change. The fact that the federal government has the power and authority to act unilaterally under the guise of the nation's interest does not mean a forward-looking coastal state cannot help to move the conversation of coastal impacts from climate change onto the federal agenda. Strategic use of laws, including the CZMA's federal consistency requirement, can help to overcome traditional federalism barriers and help in the development and implementation of rational strategies to address the threat of climate change, both today and tomorrow.

Conclusion

Climate change has the potential to significantly impact coastal systems, particularly through the phenomenon of sea-level rise. Coastal nations must be responsive to changing conditions, for example, by developing meaningful adaptation strategies that incorporate planning and accommodation of coastal climate change phenomena. But this does not mean coastal nations will always prioritize climate change and its impacts at the coastline. In nations structured under cooperative federalism principles such as the United States, situations can arise where coastal state and federal government priorities

---

[75] 16 U.S.C. §1451(l) (2012) ("Because global warming may result in a substantial sea level rise with serious adverse effects in the coastal zone, coastal states must anticipate and plan for such an occurrence").

[76] *Massachusetts. v. EPA*, 549 U.S. at 521–26. The CZMA contains mediation provisions to help resolve state-federal conflicts over federal actions claimed to be inconsistent with state coastal priorities. 16 U.S.C. § 1456(h) (2012). The mediation process includes public hearings in the affected coastal state. *Id.* This public mediation process can provide coastal states with a platform to advocate for federal policies that reduce carbon intensity both within and outside the coastal zone.

[77] By utilizing the consultative processes of the CZMA's federal consistency requirements, coastal states can highlight current federal practices that reinforce climate change, including federal activities emanating from other statutory mandates where coastal states might lack a legal basis for intervention.

diverge: coastal states wish to advance climate adaptation policies, but federal activities might frustrate coastal state goals.

The question examined in this chapter focused on the federal consistency requirement of the CZMA as a legal mechanism that can offer coastal states an advantage when attempting to implement climate change adaptation policies that run counter to federal activities. For example, as was discussed, federal offshore oil and gas leasing can bolster carbon emissions, thus leading to increases in climate change. Coastal states can challenge these federal actions on the grounds that they conflict with the protection of coastal resources, and thus are inconsistent with approved coastal management plans under the CZMA. Although this may not guarantee the federal government alters its offshore oil and gas leasing activities, it does provide a legal mechanism for consultation between the federal government and coastal states. Consultation, including the potential for mediation, creates a dialogue that can help identify interests at stake, potentially leading to better outcomes for coastal climate adaptation.

There is little argument that adapting to the impacts of climate change is a daunting task, particularly for low-lying coastal areas. Ultimately government, at all levels, has a vested interest in helping to mitigate the potential impacts of climate change while planning proactively to adapt to impacts that are inevitable. The use of existing legal instruments such as the CZMA can help create important pathways in moving toward more immediate mitigation and adaptation planning at the coastline.

20 Coastal Construction and Beach Nourishment in the New Climate
Patrick W. Krechowski*

---

* The author thanks Randy Abate for his invitation, Phil Flood for his instruction, R. David Jackson for his contribution, and Jennifer M. Krechowski for her support and partnership.

Introduction

"N.J. Shore Faces Sea-Level Rise Not Seen for 6,000 Years."[1] "In Florida, Always on the Edge of Disaster."[2] "After 33 Years, Time to Update Jersey Shore Master Plan, Officials Say."[3] "South Florida Delegations Urged to Recognize Reality of Sea-Level Rise."[4] "Kennedy Space Center Seeks Sandy Money as Ocean Chews Toward Launch Pads."[5] "How Long until Florida Becomes Uninsurable?"[6] "Where Sand Is Gold, the Reserves are Running Dry."[7]

These are just a few of the headlines seen over the past few years in newspapers and on websites in New Jersey, Florida, Maryland, the Carolinas, and other states similarly situated on the coast and similarly impacted by severe storms, storm surge, and rising sea levels. Though headlines are written to catch the reader's eye, the actual impacts from Hurricanes Ivan, Dennis, Katrina, Wilma, Ike, Charley, and tropical storms such as Sandy and her cousins, have been much more than visually stunning. These storms have wreaked havoc on private property owners, local governments, interstate commerce, and untold animal species. They have also shown us that the myriad of regulations the coastal community has counted on for protection from storms are not as dependable as we had expected.

Severe impacts from major storms and their surges have produced unanticipated results. For example, in the months following the landfall of Hurricane Dennis in 2005, over four miles of Florida's coastal shoreline in Walton County became reinforced with rigid coastal armoring, more commonly known as sea walls. Millions of dollars were invested in wood, steel, fabric, and PVC materials to construct walls and tubes for the sole purpose of protecting private homes and some public infrastructure. Millions of dollars were spent on armoring structures that, due to the emergency nature and timing

---

[1] Christa Marshall, *N.J. Shore Faces Sea-Level Rise Not Seen for 6,000 Years*, CLIMATEWIRE (May 30, 2013), http://m.accuweather.com/en/outdoor-articles/beach-marine/nj-shore-faces-sealevel-rise-n/13591584.

[2] Craig Pittman, *In Florida, Always on the Edge of Disaster*, ST. PETE TIMES (July 5, 2013), http://www.tampabay.com/features/humaninterest/in-florida-always-on-the-edge-of-disaster/2130094.

[3] Phil Gregory, *After 33 Years, Time to Update Jersey Shore Master Plan, Officials Say*, NEWSWORKS (Mar. 4, 2013), http://www.newsworks.org/index.php/local/new-jersey-feature/51823-after-33-years-time-to-update-jersey-shore-master-plan-officials-say.

[4] Bruce Ritchie, *South Florida Delegations Urged to Recognize Reality of Sea Level Rise*, FLA. CURRENT (Feb. 24, 2013), http://www.thefloridacurrent.com/article.cfm?id=31555726.

[5] Jim Waymer, *KSC Seeks Sandy Money as Ocean Chews toward Launch Pads*, FLA. TODAY (Feb. 8, 2013), http://www.floridatoday.com/article/20130208/SPACE/302080026/KSC-seeks-Sandy-money-ocean-chews-toward-launch-pads.

[6] Terrell Johnson, *How Long until Florida Becomes Uninsurable?*, WUNDERGROUND.COM (June 27, 2013), http://www.wunderground.com/news/will-florida-be-uninsurable-one-day-20130627.

[7] Lizette Alvarez, *Where Sand Is Gold, the Reserves Are Running Dry*, N.Y. TIMES (Aug. 24, 2013), http://www.nytimes.com/2013/08/25/us/where-sand-is-gold-the-coffers-are-running-dry-in-florida.html?_r=0.

of their construction, had little or no coastal engineering, environmental, or regulatory oversight despite the litany of specific permitting criteria on the books in Florida.

In the year after "Superstorm" Sandy made landfall in New Jersey, a deluge of federal and state legislative initiatives were passed to address relief, recovery, and potential private property buyouts. But an interesting trend may be developing in these areas. Instead of racing to rebuild or demanding that the shoreline be more heavily fortified, some citizens and government agencies seem to be recognizing the flaw in those concepts.[8] Section I of this chapter will look back at post-storm reactions in an effort to give context to the coastal regulations examined in Section II and the questions posed in Section III.

Hurricanes and other storms are not a recent phenomenon, nor are the inevitable impacts of "normal" coastal erosion. Consequently, there are regulatory programs and acts such as Florida's Coastal Construction Control Line program[9] and North Carolina's Coastal Area Management Act.[10] These programs, and other similar regulatory schemes, require construction and engineering designs and standards that take into account the inevitability of coastal fluctuations caused by storms and other coastal forces. Structures must be built in certain ways with certain materials, especially in vulnerable areas on the shore. But what happens when those regulations are no match for the strength and frequency of the storms in the past decade? Perhaps the time has come for coastal construction regulations to focus less on storm models and predictors, and less on structural engineering of homes and high rises, and instead acknowledge that retreat, while difficult and costly, may be the only option that offers actual solutions. States and their citizenry may benefit more in the long term from land acquisition for conservation, recreation, and flood protection. In places such as Florida, however, beachfront property, both for private use and public tourism, is so valuable that the never-ending battle with Mother Nature, no matter how severe her storms can be, may be worth millions, if not billions, to sustain.

"Beach building" or nourishment is a popular answer to the constant battle against erosion in coastal areas. Local communities, states, and the country as a whole have an endless list of reasons for having their coasts bordered by wide, deep, sandy beaches. Tourism and recreation, marine habitat, public access, and storm protection or buffering are just some of the benefits these beaches offer. But man-made forces, in addition to the constant battering of Mother Nature, make it virtually impossible for a sandy beach to remain healthy and undisturbed without some serious and costly intervention. Florida's Shore and Beach Preservation Act[11] provides for millions of dollars in

---

[8] Barbara Goldberg, *First Superstorm Sandy Home Buyout Set to Close in New York*, REUTERS (Oct. 3, 2013), http://www.reuters.com/article/2013/10/03/us-storm-sandy-buyouts-idUSBRE9920QZ20131003.

[9] FLA. ADMIN. CODE ANN. r. 62B-33.005 (2013).

[10] N.C. GEN. STAT. §§ 113A-100-134 (2013).

[11] FLA. STAT. § 161 (2013).

dedicated funding to replenish or "re-nourish" beaches that are designated by the state as "critically eroded."[12]

But can Florida and states like it find enough money and sand to continue rebuilding beaches every year? And are the existing construction and planning regulations in coastal states designed to account for the severity and frequency of the storms recently seen, compounded by the inevitability of persistent sea-level rise?

Section I of this chapter examines recent activities in a few states that have been forced to deal with significant storms and surges on their developed beaches. It will address what has happened to these areas when storms that were thought to occur only once every 100 years instead make landfall nearly seasonally. Section II addresses the existing regulatory scheme in Florida and compares Florida's regulations to other states that frequently deal with the same coastal construction problems. This examination will include the construction or development regulations as well as Florida's beach nourishment program and the problems it faces going forward. Section III will pose some important and difficult questions that all coastal communities are facing. While recognizing the long-standing concepts of private property rights and the inevitability of coastal activities, coastal regulations must take into account the new climate era.

I. The Walton County Experience

A. HURRICANE DENNIS

On September 9, 2004, Hurricane Ivan became a Category 5 storm with sustained winds of 160 m.p.h as it passed to the south of the Dominican Republic.[13] With sustained winds of 120 m.p.h, Ivan made landfall just west of Gulf Shores, Alabama, on September 16, 2004.[14] Just short of a year later, on July 10, 2005, Hurricane Dennis weakened from a Category 4 storm with winds of 145 mph to a category 3 storm, making landfall on the western panhandle of Florida near Navarre Beach.[15] Ivan caused twenty-five deaths in the United States and an estimated $14.2 billion in damage.[16] Dennis is responsible for over $2 billion in damage along with three deaths in the United States.[17]

---

[12] *Id.* § 161.088 (2013).

[13] National Weather Service, National Hurricane Center, http://www.nhc.noaa.gov/outreach/history/#ivan (last visited July 16, 2014); Willie Drye, *Hurricane Ivan Slams U.S. Gulf Coast*, NAT'L GEOGRAPHIC NEWS (Sept. 16, 2004), http://news.nationalgeographic.com/news/2004/09/0916_040916_hurricaneivan.html (last visited July 16, 2014); Manuel Roig-Franzia and Catharine Skipp, *Hurricane Ivan Tears into U.S. Gulf Coast*, WASH. POST (Sept. 16, 2004), http://www.washingtonpost.com/wp-dyn/articles/A23454-2004Sep15.html.

[14] National Weather Service, National Hurricane Center, http://www.nhc.noaa.gov/outreach/history/ (last visited July 16, 2014).

[15] *Id.*

[16] *Id.*

[17] *Id.*

Situated just east of where both Ivan and Dennis made landfall is a stretch of coast in Walton County, Florida, that is known for its wide beaches, high dune bluffs, and quiet Florida beach lifestyle. This is not a part of Florida dominated by high-rise condos or hotel resorts. Instead, on the tops of the historic dune bluffs are one- and two-story homes, mostly constructed in the 1950s, 1960s, and 1970s. Picture a two-lane road winding down the coast with ice-cream and T-shirt shops on one side and quaint family-owned homes for seasonal rent on the other, dotted with areas of Florida scrub and public access points. Most of these homes were built by vacationing residents of Alabama, Mississippi, Tennessee, and Georgia. Some were built after World War II, and some families built together—three or four houses in a row so that brothers, sisters, aunts, uncles, and cousins have all known this beach as their favorite vacation spot for six decades. Given that the porches and decks of these homes are perched on a dune bluff that can reach as high as forty feet, the view of the sugary beach and the sprawling Gulf of Mexico can be breathtaking.

On July 11, 2005, those views were markedly different. The beach was gone. The beautiful, sea-oats-covered bluff was a jagged cliff; portions of dune walk-overs were left dangling with stairs to nowhere. Gone too were some of these homes, the sand that held them up swept away by Dennis' winds and seven-foot surge.[18] Those homes that remained were perched atop a cliff of sand or teetering on piles almost completely exposed. A beach that had been designated by the State of Florida as critically eroded,[19] but had not seen any new sand in years because of the lengthy litigation that was the subject of *Stop the Beach Renourishment v. Florida*,[20] was now severely eroded and offered no protection, habitat, access, or recreation.

The reaction, while confused and desperate, was swift. Within four days of Dennis' landfall, the Walton County Commission exercised its authority under Florida law and began permitting the installation of "rigid coastal armoring," (sea walls).[21] By the time the 2006 hurricane season approached the following year, nearly the entire Gulf front of Walton County was armored. Owners were frightened that in the ten months between Ivan and Dennis they had been impacted by two storms that forecasters and bureaucrats alike told them they would see only once every 100 years. So they acted by installing structures intended for the sole purpose of protecting their Gulf-front homes. Steel sheet pile, vinyl sheet pile, wood, creosote-treated telephone poles, and giant, sediment-filled geo-tubes were constructed up and down the beach. Some owners pooled their resources and built one long wall across their collective properties. Others dug down into the sand until it turned black with peat. Still others built their walls with little regard for where their property boundary may be, thinking of only one thing: protecting their homes from the next certain and impending storm.

---

[18] Jack Bevan, *Tropical Cyclone Report, Hurricane Dennis, 4–13 July 2005*, at 3, NAT'L HURRICANE CTR. (Nov. 22, 2005), *available at* http://www.nhc.noaa.gov/pdf/TCR-AL042005_Dennis.pdf.

[19] FLA. STAT. §§ 161.101, 161.161 (2013).

[20] Stop the Beach Renourishment, Inc., v. Fla. Dep't of Envtl. Prot., 560 U.S. 502 (2010).

[21] FLA. STAT. § 161.085(3) (2013).

B. RIGID COASTAL ARMORING

All of these structures in and on the beach in Walton County were constructed under the authority of a Florida statute that allows local governments to authorize the installation of "rigid coastal armoring structures" as the result of a "storm event which threatens private structures or public infrastructure."[22] This delegation of state authority to local governments requires that the same criteria the state would examine in otherwise permitting an armoring structure must also be "considered and incorporated" into the authorized emergency measure.[23] Those considerations are:

1. Protection of the beach dune system;
2. Siting and design criteria for the protective structure;
3. Impacts on adjacent properties;
4. Preservation of public beach access; and,
5. Protection of native coastal vegetation, nesting state or federally threatened or endangered species, and nesting marine turtles and their hatchlings.[24]

In addition, should the local government exercise its authority as outlined above and more particularly described in section 161.085(6), Florida Statutes, any structure constructed in compliance with the law is considered temporary and shall either be removed within sixty days after completed installation,[25] or, in the alternative to removal, the party that has constructed the sea wall can submit an application to the state agency for a permanent structure.[26]

Examinination of the practical implications of Florida's law reveals a myriad of pitfalls that in the case of post-Hurricane Dennis Walton County resulted in more than five years of contentious, controversial, and costly review, debate, litigation, and politics. First, section 161.085(3), Florida Statutes, essentially hands over all engineering, design, siting, and species impact review to a local government that has just been severely impacted by a major storm.[27] While some local governments may have the knowledge, resources, and sophistication to handle such a responsibility during such desperate times, most do not. This is especially true given that the statute also requires that the local governments take into account the impacts of the sea wall installation to the beach dune system, public access, neighboring properties, and species, and where the structure is installed and with what materials, keeping in mind the statute's purpose is that these structures be temporary.[28]

---

[22] FLA. STAT. §161.085(3) (2013).
[23] Id.
[24] Id. §§ 161.085(3)(a)–(e) (2013).
[25] Id. § 161.085(6) (2103).
[26] Id.
[27] Id. § 161.085(3) (2013).
[28] Id. §§ 161.085(3)(a)–(e) (2013).

In post-Hurricane Dennis Walton County, the debate among private property owners, the county government, concerned citizens, watch-dog groups, and the state regulators waged on with such little progress that a law was enacted to address the problem. In 2011, almost exactly six years after Hurricane Dennis made landfall, Florida Law 2011-261 was passed.[29] Pursuant to this sweeping law, the sea walls installed in Walton County after Hurricane Dennis made landfall are deemed permanent and do not require any formal review or approval from either the local government or the Department of Environmental Protection.[30] No evaluation of the eligibility or vulnerability of a structure as required by Florida statutes and regulations is required under this new law.[31] The only criteria that an owner of a sea wall needs to address are the potential impacts to any endangered or threatened species;[32] otherwise, the walls remain, as they do today.

As discussed in Section III of this chapter, the reactions in New York and New Jersey to "Superstorm" Sandy were also less focused on coastal engineering criteria and, rightly so, more focused on relief and recovery to the devastated neighborhoods. Nevertheless, recent legislation and budgeting in those states has revealed that rebuilding, replacing, and shoring up might not be the answer.

II. Coastal Construction Regulations

A. OVERVIEW OF FLORIDA'S COASTAL CONSTRUCTION CONTROL LINE PROGRAM

Although this chapter focuses on what happens when severe storms make landfall and what changes may need to be implemented to coastal development in the age of climate change, it would be incomplete without an examination, albeit brief, of existing coastal regulations. Florida's Coastal Construction Control Line Program ("CCCL Program") is the most comprehensive coastal development program in the nation. Administered by the State of Florida Department of Environmental Protection's Division of Water Resource Management ("FDEP"), the CCCL Program "is an essential element of Florida's coastal management program."[33] The CCCL Program administers all permits for activities that take place seaward of the coastal construction control line. The CCCL Program's mission includes the following:

> Recognizing the value of the state's beaches, the Florida legislature initiated the Coastal Construction Control Line Program to protect the coastal system from

---

[29] 2011 Fla. Laws 2011-261.

[30] *Id.* § 1.

[31] FLA. STAT. § 161.085(2)(a) (2013); FLA. ADMIN. CODE ANN. r. 62B-33.0051(1)(a)1 (2013).

[32] 2011 Fla. Laws 2011-261(6).

[33] The Coastal Construction Control Line Permitting (CCL), FLORIDA DEPARTMENT OF ENVIRONMENTAL PROTECTION, http://www.dep.state.fl.us/beaches/programs/ccclprog.htm (last visited Dec. 14, 2013).

improperly sited and designed structures which can destabilize or destroy the beach and dune system. Once destabilized, the valuable natural resources are lost, as are its important values for recreation, upland property protection and environmental habitat. Adoption of a coastal construction control line establishes an area of jurisdiction in which special siting and design criteria are applied for construction and related activities. These standards may be more stringent than those already applied in the rest of the coastal building zone because of the greater forces expected to occur in the more seaward zone of the beach during a storm event.[34]

In this short paragraph published on its website, the CCCL Program recognizes the various factors and influences on coastal construction from private and public property interests to environmental resources. Chapter 161, Florida Statutes, known as the Beach and Shore Preservation Act, has four parts that deal with coastal construction: (1) the regulation of coastal construction, (2) preservation districts, (3) coastal zone protection, and (4) ocean and coastal resources.[35] Enacted by FDEP to administer chapter 161's coastal construction mandates is chapter 62B-33, Florida Administrative Code.[36] The mandates of chapters 161, Florida Statutes; and 62B-33, Florida Administrative Code; are regulatory lines in the sand for which certain types of activities either may not cross at all or must otherwise be permitted based on FDEP's specific engineering, siting, and design criteria.

The most important and influential of those lines is the coastal construction control line (CCCL).[37] Established in each county that contains a shoreline of sandy beach,[38] the CCCL gives FDEP jurisdiction over all construction-related activities that take place seaward of the CCCL. The CCCL defines that portion of the beach and dune system that is subject to severe fluctuations caused by a 100-year storm[39] or similar forces such as wind and surge.[40] Although construction seaward of the CCCL is not prohibited outright, applicants seeking to build in this area must provide FDEP with "sufficient information" about the proposed construction to demonstrate that adverse impacts

---

[34] *Id.*; FLA. ADMIN. CODE ANN. r. 62B-33.005 (2013).

[35] FLA. STAT. § 161 (2013).

[36] FLA. STAT. § 161.0415 (2013); FLA. ADMIN. CODE ANN. r. 62B-33 (2013).

[37] The mean high-water line is defined as the average height of the waters over a nineteen-year period, or for shorter periods of time, it is the average height of the high waters after corrections for known variations are made to reach the equivalent of a nineteen-year period. FLA. STAT. §177.27(14) (2013). This line is recognized as the boundary between the submerged or "foreshore" land owned by the state in its sovereign capacity and the upland that may be subject to private ownership. FLA. STAT. § 177.28 (2013).

[38] Not all coastal counties in Florida are bordered by "sandy" beaches. Some, such as those in the "Big Bend" area of the state, are bordered by tidally influenced marshes and river deltas.

[39] As defined by Section 62B-33.002(45), Florida Administrative Code, the "100-year Storm" is "a shore-incident hurricane or any other storm with accompanying wind, wave, and storm surge intensity having a one percent chance of being equaled or exceeded in any given year."

[40] FLA. ADMIN. CODE ANN. r. 62B-33.005(1) (2013).

associated with the project have been minimized and that no significant adverse impact will result.[41] Among many other considerations, FDEP focuses on the protection of the beach dune system, other structures on the beach, and public access. The Fifty-Foot Setback Line, which is the "line of jurisdiction established pursuant to the provisions of section 161.052, Florida Statutes, in which construction is prohibited within fifty feet of the line of mean high water at any riparian coastal location fronting the Gulf of Mexico or the Atlantic coast shoreline,"[42] works in conjunction with the CCCL to protect against adverse impacts.

1. Thirty-Year Erosion Zone

While the CCCL is a line that establishes FDEP's jurisdiction, a thirty-year erosion zone was created as part of the 1985 growth management legislation in Florida within which no structures are permitted unless specifically excepted.[43] The zone is defined as the area of coastal property seaward of the location of the seasonal high-water line (shoreline) as projected thirty years from the date of the filing of a permit application.[44] The seasonal high-water line is defined in section 161.053(5)(a)2, Florida Statutes, as "the line formed by the intersection of the rising shore and the elevation of 150 percent of the local mean tidal range above local mean high water."[45] The zone is site-specific and calculated pursuant to an FDEP rule based on historical measurements in the vicinity of the project under consideration.[46]

By statute and rule, the zone may not extend landward of the established coastal construction control line.[47] By FDEP rule, the zone's landward extent may be limited under two additional circumstances: (1) if there is an armoring structure demonstrated as able to survive and provide protection from the effects of a thirty-year storm, or (2) at sites where beach restoration projects are fully permitted and funded.[48]

The practical effect of establishing the zone is to create a zone of prohibition seaward of the thirty-year erosion line. The rationale for the zone is to avoid imprudent construction. The thirty-year erosion line prevents construction of structures that could be severely threatened by erosion within thirty years of the date of application.

In 2006, the First District Court of Appeal held that the FDEP "misconstrued" the word "rebuilding" and that the FDEP failed to take into account the "reasonably continuous and uniform line of construction" in its permit application review.[49] In so

---

[41] *Id.* r. 62B-33.005(2) (2013).

[42] *Id.* r. 62B-33.002(23) (2013); FLA. STAT. § 161.052 (2013).

[43] FLA. STAT. § 161.053(5)(b) (2013).

[44] *Id.*; FLA. ADMIN. CODE ANN. r. 62B-33.002(60) (2013).

[45] FLA. STAT. § 177.27(14) (2013).

[46] FLA. ADMIN. CODE ANN. r. 62B-33.024(1) (2013).

[47] FLA. STAT. § 161.053(5)(b) (2013); FLA. ADMIN. CODE ANN. r. 62B-33.024(2)(e) (2013).

[48] FLA. ADMIN. CODE ANN. r. 62B-33.024(2) (2013).

[49] Atlantis at Perdido Assoc., Inc. v. Warner, 932 So. 2d 1206, 1211, 1212 (Fla. 1st Dist. Ct. App. 2006).

doing, the FDEP acted outside the scope of its discretion and acted inconsistently with its own rules.[50]

Implementation of the thirty-year erosion zone can result in a taking of property. In one case, applications for the construction of habitable structures on two different sites were denied because they were seaward of the thirty-year erosion line and did not qualify for any exception.[51] One of the applicants was successful in a Circuit Court proceeding in which a regulatory taking was found. That decision was affirmed *per curiam* on appeal by the Fifth District Court of Appeal, and the Department of Natural Resources[52] subsequently purchased the property.[53]

In another case, the Fourth District Court of Appeal upheld the trial court's decision, which ruled that the appellants failed to establish they were denied "all economically viable" uses of their property as a result of the FDEP denying their application to construct a duplex seaward of the seasonal high-water line.[54] The court held that the appellants' application was defective for failure to comply with section 161.053, Florida Statutes, but that the appellants "could possibly build otherwise appropriate (e.g., with a more structurally sound foundation) 'single family dwellings' on their lots."[55]

Section 161.053(5)(b), Florida Statutes, provides that the prohibition on construction within the thirty-year erosion zone is subject to the following exceptions: coastal or shore protection structures, minor structures, piers, or power plant intake or discharge structures.[56] A further exception applies to single-family homes as long as the following conditions are met: (1) the parcel for the single family home must have been platted or subdivided by metes and bounds before October 1, 1985, (2) the owner of the parcel for the proposed dwelling does not own another immediately adjacent and landward parcel, (3) the proposed dwelling is located landward of the frontal dune structure, and (4) the proposed dwelling will be as far landward on its parcel as is practical without being located seaward of or on the frontal dune system.[57]

Finally, section 161.053(12)(a), Florida Statutes, allows the FDEP to issue a permit for repair or rebuilding of a major structure seaward of a thirty-year erosion protection line if it is within the confines of an existing foundation.[58] Nevertheless, FDEP will apply all of the requirements of section 161.053(4), Florida Statutes (ordinarily seaward of the coastal

[50] *Id.* at 1214.

[51] Doran v. Florida Dep't of Natural Resources, 550 So. 2d 479 (Fla. 5th Dist. Ct. App. 1989).

[52] In 1993, the Department of Natural Resources and the Department of Environmental Regulation were merged to create the Department of Environmental Protection. *See* FLA. DEP'T OF ENVTL. PROT., ADMIN. DIRECTIVE DEP 100, DELEGATIONS OF AUTHORITY (Mar. 23, 2011), *available at* http://www.dep.state.fl.us/admin/depdirs/pdf/100.pdf.

[53] *See Doran*, 550 So. 2d. at 479.

[54] Leto v. Florida Dep't of Envtl. Prot., 824 So. 2d 283, 283, 285 (Fla. 4th Dist. Ct. App. 2002).

[55] *Id.* at 285.

[56] FLA. STAT. § 161.053(12)(a) (2013).

[57] *Id.* § 161.053(5)(c) (2013).

[58] *Id.* § 161.053(12)(a) (2013).

construction control line requirements).[59] Alternatively, FDEP may require a more landward relocation or rebuilding of a damaged or existing structure. Repair or rebuilding that expands the capacity of the structure beyond the thirty-year erosion protection line is strictly prohibited.[60] FDEP must specifically consider changes in shoreline conditions and the availability of other locations for the structure and design adequacy when reviewing the application to rebuild or relocate a major structure.[61]

2. The Mean High-Water Line and Joint Coastal Permit

Regardless of the ownership interests at stake, FDEP determines the allowable uses of lands below the mean high-water line. FDEP regulates all construction and other activities that occur below the mean high-water line as part of its authority to protect the beach dune system.[62] Prior to 1994, whenever these activities involved dredging and filling, permission to use the land, generally in the form of a submerged lands lease, would have to be obtained from the Trustees of the State of Florida's Internal Improvement Trust Fund pursuant to chapter 253, Florida Statutes, as well as a permit under section 161.041, Florida Statutes, and a dredge and fill permit (now Environmental Resource Permit) under part IV of chapter 373, Florida Statutes.[63] The Governor and Cabinet sit collectively as the Trustees and constitute the agency head for the Division of State Lands of the FDEP. Under this authority, the state determines the allowable uses of state lands in its capacity as landowner.[64] At times, the Trustees' staff recommendations ran counter to those of FDEP's regulatory permitting staff, and both the applicant and the Governor and Cabinet were conflicted as to whose recommendation to follow.

To address this problem, the Florida Legislature adopted section 161.055, Florida Statutes, in 1994, which authorizes a joint coastal permit. When an activity is subject to a section 161.041 permit, it also requires authorization from the Trustees to use land below the mean high-water line; the applicant must request a "joint coastal permit" and submit all the information necessary to satisfy the requirements for any proprietary authorization under chapters 253, 258, and section 161.055, Florida Statutes, and chapter 62B-49, Florida Administrative Code (FAC). The Trustees have, by rule, delegated authority to the Secretary of FDEP to approve certain activities below the mean high-water line.[65]

---

[59] *Id.* § 161.053(4) (2013).

[60] FLA. ADMIN. CODE ANN. r. 62B-33.024 (2013).

[61] *Id.*

[62] FLA. STAT. § 161.041(1) (2013.

[63] *Id.* §§ 253; 161.041; 373.413.

[64] *See generally* R. David Jackson & Patrick Krechowski, *Coastal Construction Regulation and Beach Nourishment, in* TREATISE ON FLORIDA ENVIRONMENTAL & LAND USE LAW (2013).

[65] FLA. ADMIN. CODE ANN. r. 62B-49.001 (2013).

Typically, the types of construction attempted in areas below the mean high-water line are groins, breakwaters, revetments,[66] hardbottom restoration,[67] and beach nourishment projects. Chapter 62B-41, Florida Administrative Code, includes a comprehensive set of rules that addresses coastal construction permits on sovereignty lands in Florida below the mean high-water line of any tidal water of the state. Chapter 62B-41, Florida Administrative Code, became effective in August 1992, and reflects the policies pertaining to coastal armoring and construction below the mean high-water line that the Cabinet has long favored. The primary departure in these rules from historical permitting of coastal armoring (including sea walls and revetments) is the threshold requirements that will entitle a property owner to armoring protection for a vulnerable shoreline. This type of construction generally occurs landward of the mean high-water line but seaward of FDEP's established coastal construction control line.

3. Vulnerable and Eligible

Section 161.085(1), Florida Statutes, contains specific language recognizing the need to "protect private structures and public infrastructure from damage or destruction caused by coastal erosion." Absent a regional approach to erosion reduction, such as beach nourishment, the state provides for the protection of property and infrastructure by way of "rigid coastal armoring structures."[68] This statute requires that FDEP make a determination that the upland private structure or public infrastructure is "vulnerable to damage from frequent coastal storms."[69] FDEP regulations also require that the upland private structure be "eligible."[70] In addition, a rigid coastal armoring structure may be installed provided it is between and adjoining both ends of an existing coastal armoring structure, follows a continuous and uniform line of armoring construction, and is no more than 250 feet in length.[71] This is known as the "closing the gap" exception.

Like the Walton County and Hurricane Dennis scenario discussed above, local governments having jurisdiction over an impacted area are also empowered to either install rigid coastal armoring structures or authorize their installation in response to an emergency storm event that threatens private structures or public infrastructure.[72] A local

---

[66] These are known as "Rigid Coastal Structures" and are usually characterized by their solid or impermeable design; they are most often used to protect shorelines from wave and/or current action. *See* Fla. Admin. Code Ann. r. 62B-33.002(59)(a) (2013).

[67] Hardbottom restoration involves the placement or restoration of materials in the near shore hardbottom habitat of beaches. *See* Kenyon C. Lindeman et al., Fla. Dep't of Envtl. Prot., Ecological Functions of Nearshore Hardbottom Habitats in East Florida: A Literature Synthesis, ES-4, 1–1, 1–7, 1–8 (2009).

[68] Fla. Stat. § 181.085(2) (2013).

[69] *Id.* § 161.085(2)(a) (2013); Fla. Admin. Code Ann. r. 62B-33.0051(1)(a)(2) (2013).

[70] Fla. Admin. Code Ann. r. 62B-33.002(18); 62B-33.0051(1)(a)(1) (2013).

[71] Fla. Stat. § 161.085(2)(c) (2013).

[72] *Id.* § 161.085(3).

government must notify FDEP of its intent to act according to the statute and address the following factors: (1) protection of the beach dune system; (2) siting and design criteria for the coastal armoring structure; (3) impacts on adjacent properties; (4) preservation of public beach access; and (5) protection of native coastal vegetation, nesting state or federally threatened or endangered species, and nesting marine turtles and their hatchlings.[73] In practice, this local government authority can lead to complicated and inconsistent long-term results. There is no greater testament to this reality than what occurred in Walton County.

Any rigid coastal armoring structure installed under the authority of section 161.085(3), Florida Statutes, shall be deemed "temporary" and the owner (whether private or public) shall either remove the structure or submit a permit application to FDEP for a permanent rigid coastal armoring structure within sixty days after the completed installation of the structure.[74] FDEP will apply all statutory and regulatory criteria in evaluating such a permanent permit application, unless, of course, a law is passed stating otherwise.[75]

The threshold step in determining whether a structure may be protected by armoring is whether the structure is "eligible." An "eligible structure" is defined to include "nonconforming habitable structures, public roads or safety facilities, bridges, water or wastewater treatment facilities, hospitals, or structures of local governmental, state, or national significance that are also vulnerable."[76] The term "nonconforming" indicates that the structure was not built pursuant to the coastal construction permitting program authorized pursuant to section 161.053, Florida Statutes, or that it cannot be demonstrated to meet "current structural requirements" for coastal construction.[77] An eligible structure is only eligible for coastal armoring protection if the structure to be protected is vulnerable to erosion from a fifteen-year return interval storm event as determined by FDEP.[78] From an engineering standpoint, this is a low impact storm event, which means that the upland structure must be extremely vulnerable before FDEP will consider it eligible for coastal armoring protection. There are other less quantifiable measures that must be met before a permit may be issued, including whether the applicant considered other alternatives and whether the construction reduces public access along the beach.[79]

Once a structure has been deemed eligible for coastal armoring protection, DEP rules provide design and siting criteria that limit (with some exceptions) the protection to that level necessary to protect against the impacts of a ten-year return interval storm event.[80] This is a radical departure from previous design requirements for coastal armoring, when

---

[73] *Id.* §§ 161.085(3), (4).

[74] *Id.* § 161.085(6).

[75] *See* discussion in Section I regarding: Florida Law 2011–261.

[76] Fla. Admin. Code Ann. r. 62B-33.002(18) (2013); 62B-33.0051(1) (2013).

[77] *Id.* r. 62B-33.002(43) (2013).

[78] *Id.* r. 62B33.0051(1)(a)(2) (2013).

[79] *Id.* r. 62B-33.0051(2) (2013).

[80] Fla. Admin. Code Ann. r. 62B-41.007 (2013).

FDEP had preferred that such structures be designed for a minimum of a thirty-year return interval storm event. These design regulations reflect FDEP's understanding that coastal armoring generally accelerates erosion along Florida's shorelines in storm events, and should thus be designed to fail in a major storm. This philosophy has prompted debate in engineering circles and remains a controversial topic.

4. Species Protection

In addition to the design and siting criteria, FDEP rules also include protections for marine turtles.[81] FDEP rules further provide guidelines for experimental coastal construction permits that also include provisions to protect marine turtles, nests, and their habitat, including lighting plans.[82] Also, the rule's limiting thresholds and conditions for rigid coastal protection structures have encouraged engineering innovation in the area of flexible coastal protection structures that may be considered, under certain circumstances, as experimental. Most of Florida's sandy beach coastline is eroding, some of it critically. Contributing causes include sea-level rise, past imprudent construction, inlet construction and maintenance, and construction attempts to alter the shoreline through a variety of coastal structures such as groin fields, jetties, and breakwaters. The maintenance and deepening of ports is also a contributing factor.

5. Beach Nourishment

Over time, beach nourishment became a preferred method for addressing erosion and maintaining beaches for recreational and residential use throughout the country. Beach nourishment is the relocation of sand, typically from an offshore submerged borrow site, to an eroding beach. State and federal permits are required to authorize such a project. In some states, such as Florida, there is a joint coastal permitting program that deals with both the environmental aspects of the project and the sovereign submerged lands authorization(s) that are required.[83] In addition, the U.S. Environmental Protection Agency may also become involved through the Corps' permitting process. Before the issuance of these permits, extensive studies are required to analyze the impacts of the proposed project on both the fill area and the borrow site, as well as potential impacts to endangered or threatened species.

Beach nourishment studies often involve the review of a number of factors, including: (1) benthic and hardbottom communities in the fill and borrow areas, and the likelihood of such communities reestablishing themselves after construction; (2) compatibility of the borrow material with the existing beach sediments; (3) the silt-clay ratios in the proposed borrow material, which is related directly to turbidity problems during

---

[81] *Id.* r. 62B-41.0055 (2013).

[82] *Id.* r. 62B-41.0075(3)(c) (2013).

[83] *See* Fla. Stat. § 161.055 (2013).

and after construction; (4) the proposed frequency for future renourishment to maintain the nourished beach; (5) the effect of borrow site dredging on nearby shorelines; and (6) effects on sea turtle and shorebird nesting periods.[84]

The issuance of an Environmental Resource Permit from FDEP constitutes the agency certification that is required for the Corps' permit pursuant to sections 401 and 404 of the Federal Clean Water Act.[85] The FDEP's permitting jurisdiction is derived from section 373.414, Florida Statutes. This statute requires that dredge and fill projects in waters of the state must not be contrary to the public interest and, in areas designated as Outstanding Florida Waters, these projects must be "clearly in the public interest."[86] The statute lists seven factors that the FDEP must consider to arrive at a determination as to whether the project is not contrary to, or is clearly in, the public interest. For example, a project may involve long-term impacts on marine life or fishing values, but may provide extensive recreational benefits or increased storm protection to upland areas on a critically eroded shoreline. The FDEP examines and weighs all factors in making its public interest determination.

As with other state permitting, FDEP's permitting decision for beach nourishment or other projects along the coastline is subject to the licensing and hearing provisions of chapter 120, Florida Statutes, otherwise known as Florida's Administrative Procedures Act. Intervention is available to interested third parties who may join an administrative proceeding concerning a permit application under section 403.412(5), Florida Statutes.[87] The intervention provisions of this statute have been held to apply only to permitting and licensing proceedings; therefore, the right to intervene may not be applicable to authorizations from the Trustees.[88]

FDEP has several functions regarding beach nourishment projects. In addition to the need for a coastal construction permit pursuant to chapter 161, Florida Statutes, the Trustees also must give their permission for the use of state lands. In addition, if an applicant is seeking state funding, this is also reviewed pursuant to chapter 161, Florida Statutes. However, these various FDEP programs are subject to concurrent processing under joint coastal permitting.[89]

Sections 161.141-161.211, Florida Statutes, detail the involvement of the Trustees in the beach nourishment process. Their primary function is to establish an erosion control line that delineates state ownership from private ownership after project completion. Before beginning the project, the mean high-water line is surveyed and legally described

---

[84] *See* Jackson & Krechowski, *supra* note 64, at 15.

[85] 33 U.S.C. §§ 1341, 1344 (2012).

[86] FLA. STAT. § 373.414(1) (2013).

[87] Greene v. Fla. Dep't of Natural Resources., 414, So. 2d 251, 253 (Fla. 1st Dist. Ct. App. 1982); Environmental Confederation of S.W. Fla., Inc. v. Florida Dep't of Envtl. Prot., 886 So. 2d 1013, 1015–16 (Fla. 1st Dist. Ct. App. 2004).

[88] *Greene*, 414 So. 2d at 253.

[89] FLA. STAT. § 161.055 (2013); FLA. ADMIN. CODE ANN. r. 62B-49 (2013).

by a metes and bounds description, and must be approved by the Governor and Cabinet. This is the erosion control line recorded in the records of the county where the project is located and serves as the state's ownership boundary. Thus, even though a new high-water line will exist when the new beach is created, the state retains ownership of the new beach based on the originally surveyed line.

Furthermore, section 161.201, Florida Statutes, provides that once the line has been established, the state will not allow any structure to be constructed on lands created through a beach nourishment project except structures required for the prevention of erosion. The underlying theory for this procedure is that the property owner should not gain any ownership to state land by the filling necessary in a beach nourishment project. If the beach face erodes in future years and the high-water line comes back to the location of the erosion control line, the high-water line again becomes the property boundary, and the doctrines of erosion and accretion[90] come into play. FDEP has allowed dune crossover structures because these structures protect the dunes from pedestrian traffic; they are in effect designed to prevent erosion.[91]

In *Board of Trustees v. Sand Key,* the Florida Supreme Court addressed ownership of accreted land in which the accretion was caused by artificial means but not by the action of the upland property owner.[92] The court held that these accretions inured to the upland owner if that owner did not participate in or contribute to the improvement.[93] The court upheld the portion of section 161.051, Florida Statutes, that prevents upland owners causing or contributing to accretion from acquiring title to accreted lands.[94]

The 1986 Florida Legislature passed comprehensive legislation dealing with beach nourishment. The legislation amended chapter 161, Florida Statutes, and established sources of funding for beach nourishment projects throughout the state, contained strong expressions of the public interest in maintaining Florida's beaches as a treasured national resource, and set a favorable tone for future beach nourishment projects.[95] A problem that has come to light, however, is the lack of beach-compatible quality sand that will be available in the future for large-scale beach nourishment projects.

More recently, the constitutionality of the Florida Beach and Shore Preservation Act was challenged in *Stop the Beach Renourishment v. Florida Department of Environmental Protection.*[96] This case began in 2003 as the city of Destin and Walton County obtained the necessary permits to construct 6.9 miles of additional beach on its critically eroded

---

[90] Erosion is the gradual and imperceptible wearing away of land bordering water by natural elements. Accretion is the additions to land by gradual deposits of material. Reliction is often used interchangeably with accretion as it is the recession of water, thus exposing land.

[91] *See* Fla. Dep't of Envtl. Prot., *available at* http://www.dep.state.fl.us/beaches/publications/pdf/wlkovrglo6.pdf (last visited July 16, 2014).

[92] Bd. of Trs. of the Internal Improvement Trust Fund v. Sand Key Assoc., 512 So. 2d 934, 938 (Fla. 1987).

[93] *Id.*

[94] *Id.* at 938–39.

[95] Fla. Stat. §§ 161.26, 161.33, 161.37 (2013).

[96] Stop the Beach Renourishment, Inc. v. Florida Dep't of Envtl. Prot., 560 U.S. 702 (2010).

shoreline.[97] A group of beachfront property owners incorporated themselves and challenged the permit issuance before the Division of Administrative Hearings.[98] That challenge was lost and appealed to the First District Court of Appeals, which found that ownership of beachfront property included the right of the property owner to "touch" the water.[99] The First District Court of Appeals then certified the following question to the Florida Supreme Court:

> Has Part I of Chapter 161, Florida Statutes (2005), referred to as the Beach and Shore Preservation Act, been unconstitutionally applied so as to deprive the members of Stop the Beach Renourishment, Inc. of their riparian rights without just compensation for the property taken, so that the exception provided in Florida Administrative Code Rule 18-21.004(3), exempting satisfactory evidence of sufficient upland interest if the activities do not unreasonably infringe on riparian rights, does not apply?[100]

The Florida Supreme Court ruled that the statute was constitutionally applied and additionally quashed the First District Court of Appeal's order finding that there was no right of a beachfront property owner to forever touch the water.[101]

Stop the Beach Renourishment, Inc. then petitioned to the U.S. Supreme Court, this time arguing that the opinion of the Florida Supreme Court amounted to a judicial taking of property in violation of the Fifth and Fourteenth Amendments.[102] The U.S. Supreme Court unanimously affirmed, finding that the Florida Supreme Court had properly interpreted Florida law, and that the Florida doctrine of avulsion applies to beach restoration.[103] The theory of avulsion provides that land created by a sudden event or series of events belongs to the entity or party that owns the submerged lands thereafter covered by the avulsive event.[104] In other words, in the context of beach renourishment, that land once submerged (located below the mean high-water line) and held by the state of Florida, which is subsequently covered by sand, remains held by the state.

The true confusion of the U.S. Supreme Court's ruling, however, lies in the dueling concurrences. Justice Scalia wrote for four justices and concluded that there is such a thing as judicial taking, and that such a taking arises when a party can show that it was deprived of a property right that it previously possessed.[105] The problem in the Florida

---

[97] *Id.*

[98] Walton Cty. v. Stop the Beach Renourishment, Inc., 998 So. 2d 1102 (Fla. 2008).

[99] *Id.* at 1119.

[100] *Id.* at 1105.

[101] *Id.* at 1119.

[102] Stop the Beach Renourishment, Inc. v. Florida Dep't of Envtl. Prot., 560 U.S. 702 (2010).

[103] *Id.*

[104] *See* Oregon State Land Bd. v. Corvallis Sand & Gravel Co., 429 U.S. 363, 370 (1977).

[105] *Stop the Beach Renourishment*, 560 U.S. at 723.

case, according to Scalia, is that Stop the Beach Renourishment, Inc. failed to make that showing.[106] Two separate partial concurrences (by Justices Kennedy and Breyer) express significant reservations about recognizing a cause of action for a judicial taking as a general matter.[107] As an owner of beachfront property in Florida, Justice Stevens recused himself, but in total, the remaining eight justices agreed that the Florida Supreme Court's decision did not amount to a judicial taking.[108] Given the 4-4 split as to the possibility of judicial taking, the matter remains open.

B. OTHER JURISDICTIONS

Florida's system, while comprehensive and complex, is not the only elaborate coastal development regulation program in the nation. In Texas, the General Land Office administers the Texas Open Beaches Act, the Dune Protection Act (DPA), and the Coastal Erosion Planning and Response Act (CEPRA).[109] The CEPRA provides funding to coastal communities for projects that "slow the effects of coastal and shoreline erosion."[110] The DPA requires "local governments" to administer a permitting program that allows for construction seaward of "their dune protection line."[111] The main difference between Texas and Florida is that a permit for construction on or near the beach is not a state-issued permit, but rather one issued by the local government's building department.[112]

In North Carolina, the Division of Coastal Management administers the Coastal Area Management Act (CAMA), which divides coastal permits into three categories (Major, General, and Minor) and requires that any "development" in an "Area of Environmental Concern" be authorized by one of these permits.[113] Like Texas, most of these permits are administered by local governments, but the permitting stage is set by the state's program.

New Jersey, like Florida, has post-storm emergency standards for beach restoration.[114] These include bulldozing; placement of "clean" fill material; placement of concrete,

---

[106] *Id.* at 727–28.

[107] *Id.* at 724–26.

[108] *Id.* at 733.

[109] Tx. Gen. Land Office, Texas Coastal Construction Handbook 6 (2001), *available at* http://www.texasgulfcoastonline.com/portals/o/TexasCoastconstructionhandbook.pdf (last visited Dec. 27, 2013).

[110] *Id.* at 6.

[111] *Id.*

[112] *Id.* at 7.

[113] N.C. Gen. Stat. §§ 113A-118, 118.1 (2013); Div. of Coastal Mgmt., N.C. Dep't of Env't & Nat. Resources, CAMA Permits: Will My Project Require a Permit?, http://dcm2.enr.state.nc.us/Permits/aecs.htm (last visited Dec. 27, 2013).

[114] N.J. Admin. Code § 7:7E-3A.3 (2013).

rubble, or rock; and placement of sand-filled geotextile bags or tubes.[115] In New Jersey's current Water-Front and Harbor Facilities regulations, the "repair, replacement or renovation of a permanent dock, wharf, pier, bulkhead or building" that was in existence prior to January 1, 1981, is exempt.[116]

Although some of these states have more regulations than others, varying degrees of detail, and different regulatory roles for their local governments, one thing that they all have in common is that not only do they allow for a myriad of construction activities on or near the beach, they also allow for significant rebuilding following frequent storm events. The general theme of them all is that if an applicant designs a coastal development project to meet certain engineering and siting criteria, the applicant can build or rebuild. This reality begs the somewhat oversimplified question: Are the current regulations doing enough?

III. Regulatory Questions and Solutions

A. REACTING OR PLANNING?

Florida's coastal development program above, coupled with similar programs in other states such as Texas, North Carolina, and New Jersey, indicate that the overall focus of these regulatory programs is to *allow* certain types of construction on the coast. For instance, Florida's Coastal Construction Control Line is characterized as a "regulatory line," not a setback line or a line of prohibition, often regardless of what the actual history of storm impacts may be for that area. In other words, if you, as a permit applicant, can show that your proposed activity meets the written criteria of a given regulation, you can build your structure, or rebuild your structure that was recently destroyed by a storm. There are several complicated factors that help explain why the regulations are written this way.

The first, and most obvious, is twofold: money and private property rights. This country has a long-standing and well-established recognition of private property rights. Many would contend that private property rights take a second seat only to freedom itself. Thus, it is very expensive for governments to compensate its citizenry for infringing on those rights by taking property. And nowhere is it more expensive than on or near the beach. So that, in and of itself, is one of the main reasons the regulations essentially allow construction activities on privately held beach front property. To simply prohibit construction would cost governments untold sums in staff resources, legal fees, and compensatory damages.

The second reason is related to the first. People love the beach. And businesses love people who frequent the beaches. Beach use in the state generates enormous sums of

[115] *Id.* § 7:7E-3A.3(b).
[116] N.J. STAT. ANN. § 12:5–3 (2013).

revenue for private commerce and public finance. Prohibiting construction on or near the beach would be the death knell for thousands of local governments and hundreds of thousands of businesses.

Another important reason underlying the intent of coastal regulations that has not been addressed in this chapter is the public's right to access the beach. A right arguably stronger and more legally recognized than private property rights is the public's right to access the water for purposes of commerce, recreation, and navigation.[117] What follows from that right is the ability to construct the method and means for such access.

B. THE PRACTICALITY OF CONTINUING TO BUILD BEACHES

Related to commerce, the beaches of this country are constantly being impacted, both negatively and favorably, by interstate commerce and navigation. While countering erosion from storms is one of the purposes of beach nourishment projects, the genesis of every state's beach-building program stems from the need to maintain open coastal navigable ports. These ports require regular dredging and (re)deepening and require protection from the constant distribution of down drift sand by way of jetties and other types of breakwaters. As sand flows through the nearshore system (on the east coast of the United States this flow is north to south) and encounters the various inlets, the natural effect is for that sand to fill in or deposit itself in that inlet. The U.S. Army Corps of Engineers is responsible for keeping those inlets navigable and operational, and the agency does this most often by way of the aforementioned dredging and structure placement. The impact of these activities on the natural system is that beaches down drift of maintained inlets or ports become "sand starved." The sand is either doing its best to fill in the deep inlet channel, or it is being held back by a permanent jetty. Not only are these down drift beaches being constantly impacted by the inevitable forces of normal erosion and irregular storm surge impacts, they are also being starved of the natural distribution of sand down the coast.

In an attempt to counter both the man-made and nature-made forces of coastal erosion, the U.S. Army Corps of Engineers partners with states and local governments to build beaches. These are usually large and expensive projects that deposit huge amounts of sand in the nearshore and on the beach in regular intervals. For these large projects, "borrow sites" of sand are identified and surveyed, huge dredges are used to bring the sand to the surface, and earth-moving equipment is used on the beach to reshape and rebuild miles of eroded coast. This is an expensive process that involves years of consultation and permitting review. There are impacts to protected species, private property rights, and public access. Occasionally, litigation over these issues can further interrupt an already bureaucratic and sometimes arduous process. More recently, with the country mired in a recession and a coast battered year after year by powerful, sand-eating storms,

---

[117] Such rights stem from the common law.

this process has hardly been able to keep pace. Even more troubling is the fact that some coastal areas are running out of sources of beach-compatible sand. Where will Dade and Broward County, Florida, look to in a few years when the sand they need to rebuild their beaches is simply gone?

C. QUESTIONS TO BE ANSWERED

There are a myriad of questions facing everyone that has a vested interest in coastal property. Regulators, developers, residents, tourists, legislators, and business people must determine if they can work together to identify the answers to the fundamental question: Do our notions of allowable and prudent coastal development need to change in light of the increasing impacts associated with climate change and the storms and tides associated therewith?

While our coasts generate untold sums of revenue for local and state governments and private businesses, they are also clearly subject to the undeniable impacts from severe storms and rising tides. It has been made clear over the past decade that regulations based on estimating and modeling the frequency, duration, and intensity of coastal storms and the associated changes in tides have been woefully inadequate. And our continued reliance on these regulations should be considered nothing short of ignorant and shortsighted.

So other than continuing to shove their collective heads farther in the sand, are the key players in this arena willing to acknowledge what is happening, and strong enough to take the responsibility for effecting change? Do more states need to take what some are calling drastic "coastal retreat" steps such as the California Coastal Commission is suggesting in its Draft Sea-Level-Rise Policy Guidance document?[118] Should Florida's dedicated funding source for the renourishment of critically eroded beaches include funds to acquire storm-damaged or otherwise vulnerable private beachfront property? Will New Jersey's efforts to purchase private property devastated by Super Storm Sandy be sufficiently funded and administratively and legally practical to be a model for coastal areas throughout the nation?[119] Will Florida's counties be able to agree on a sand-sharing

---

[118] CAL. COASTAL COMM'N, CAL. NATURAL RES. AGENCY, DRAFT SEA-LEVEL RISE POLICY GUIDANCE (Oct. 14, 2013), *available at* http://www.coastal.ca.gov/climate/slr/guidance/CCC_Draft_SLR_Guidance_PR_10142013.pdf.

[119] In cooperation with the U.S. Department of Agriculture (USDA) and its Natural Resources Conservation Service (NRCS), New Jersey is making financial assistance available to owners of New Jersey property impacted by Hurricane Sandy. Although the details are scarce, the funding comes from the "Emergency Watershed Protection—Flood Plain Easement Program" for the purpose of purchasing easements on public and private properties that were damaged by Hurricane Sandy. Applicants may be eligible to receive the fair market value of their land, and the NRCS will be responsible for restoring the land, including the demolition or removal of damaged structures. The eligibility requirements are that: (1) the property damage must have been the result of Hurricane Sandy; (2) owners of residentially zoned properties must secure a public sponsor who will assume the ultimate ownership of the property; and (3) the property must be outside of the Federal Emergency Management Agency "Coastal" Flood Zones. Currently there is very little, if

cooperative that enables them to continue to build long, wide, deep, and protective sandy beaches? Will people who want to live and do business near the coast be able to insure their properties, and will state-created property insurance companies[120] have the financial security to survive the next catastrophic storm event?

Conclusion

Severe coastal storms will continue to batter our shores in the years to come. The regulators know, the builders know, the insurance companies know, and the residents are aware of this reality. And the storms are getting bigger and stronger. More important, the storms are coming more frequently—at least more frequently than storm models that are the basis for many coastal regulations would take into account. While complicated and based on engineering and science, these regulations contemplate that they may not actually provide adequate protection because they allow for rebuilding, repairing, shoring up, armoring, and nourishing eroded beaches. Finally, the questions that come from storm impacts, extreme tides, and coastal construction are very hard to answer.

This chapter has provided an example of the reaction to severe storm impacts. It is a common example that is authorized, if not encouraged, by the existing regulations. Regulations that have proven in the past to be reliable and sufficient now may be bending under the pressure of climate change. The cost of insuring coastal development and feeding the appetite of constant and inevitable erosion appears to be applying further pressure to those regulations. However, there is no one true solution. Coastal regulations are based on scientific models, common law principles, balancing of rights, environmental concerns, and, to a certain degree, hope and faith. To ignore the recent changes in storm activity and sea-level rise would be beyond ignorant and a disservice to all involved. From the local level to areas beyond our national geopolitical boundaries, the impacts of coastal activity and the inadequacies of the existing regulations must be examined. These challenges must be addressed and reconciled in the new climate change era.

---

any, data on exactly how many property owners have applied for relief, satisfied the eligibility requirements, or obtained funding for the purchase of their property. *See* Nat. Resources Conservation Serv., U.S. Dep't of Agric., Hurricane Sandy Watershed Protection Flood Plain Easement Program (2013), http://www.nrcs.usda.gov/Internet/FSE_DOCUMENTS/stelprdb1167117.pdf.

[120] *See, e.g.*, Citizens Property Insurance Corporation, www.citizensfla.com (last visited July 16, 2014).

21 Temporary Takings, More or Less
Timothy M. Mulvaney*

---

* The author would like to acknowledge Professors Daniel Farber, Eric Freyfogle, Jerrold Long, Stephen Miller, Sarah Schindler, and Kenneth Stahl, as well as Matthew McGowan and Daniel Siegel.

Introduction

As noted by a leading property scholar in a recent article, "In an era of climate change...new forms of regulation are needed."[1] It is unsurprising, then, that many of the chapters in this book call for innovative government action to manage and protect land and other environmental resources in the face of today's unprecedented anthropogenic global warming.[2] However, the Fifth Amendment's Takings Clause—which has been interpreted to prohibit government acts, including regulations, from taking private property for public use without the payment of just compensation[3]—can pose significant obstacles to such innovation.[4] While several scholars recently have explored the interplay between takings law and specific impacts associated with climate change (most prominently sea-level rise),[5] this chapter approaches the topic from a different and broader perspective by focusing on the disjunction between a progressive conception of ownership that is open to evolutionary property rules and modern jurisprudence relating to a particular species of what have been labeled "temporary takings."

While many of the U.S. Supreme Court's takings decisions have served to depress regulatory experimentation, the Court's 1987 decision in *First English Evangelical Lutheran Church of Glendale v. County of Los Angeles*,[6] establishing the principle of retroactive temporary takings compensation, seemingly remains the most chilling for government officials seeking to employ new regulatory tools.[7] To illustrate, imagine that a governmental entity promulgates a regulation that significantly limits development possibilities in an erosion-prone coastal area. Given the ad hoc nature of regulatory takings

---

[1] Daniel A. Farber, Property Rights and Climate Change 15 (Mar. 31, 2014) (unpublished manuscript, *available at* http://papers.ssrn.com/sol3/papers.cfm?abstract_id=2418756).

[2] *See, e.g., infra* Chapters 23–29.

[3] *See* Lingle v. Chevron U.S.A. Inc., 544 U.S. 528 (2005).

[4] U.S. Const. amend. V ("nor shall private property be taken for public use, without just compensation").

[5] *See, e.g.,* John R. Nolon, *Regulatory Takings and Property Rights Confront Sea Level Rise: How Do They Roll?,* 21 Widener L.J. 735 (2012); J. Peter Byrne, *The Cathedral Engulfed: Sea-Level Rise, Property Rights, and Time,* 73 La. L. Rev. 69 (2012); Michael Allan Wolf, *Strategies for Making Sea-Level Rise Adaptation Tools "Takings Proof,"* 28 J. Land Use & Envtl. L. 157 (2013); Robin K. Craig, *Of Sea-Level Rise and Superstorms: The Public Health Police Power as a Means of Defending against "Takings" Challenges to Coastal Regulation,* N.Y.U. Envtl. L.J. (forthcoming 2014); Farber, *supra* note 1. Noted earlier works in this area include Joseph L. Sax, *The Fate of Wetlands in the Face of Rising Sea Levels: A Strategic Proposal,* 9 UCLA J. Envtl. L. & Pol'y 143 (1991); James G. Titus, *Rising Seas, Coastal Erosion, and the Takings Clause: How to Save Wetlands and Beaches without Hurting Property Owners,* 57 Md. L. Rev. 1279 (1998); Marc R. Poirier, *A Very Clear Blue Line: Behavioral Economics, Public Choice, Public Art and Sea Level Rise,* 16 Southeastern Envtl. L.J. 83 (2007).

[6] First English Evangelical Lutheran Church of Glendale v. Los Angeles Cnty., 482 U.S. 304 (1987) [hereinafter *First English*].

[7] The *First English* Court was not ignorant of the decision's impact, noting that the ruling "will undoubtedly lessen to some extent the freedom and flexibility of land-use planners and governing bodies." *Id.* at 321 (quoting Pennsylvania Coal Co. v. Mahon, 260 U.S. 393, 416 (1922)).

analysis, it is often difficult to predict upon adoption whether a regulation will be considered a taking. Assume that, here, a landowner successfully challenges that regulation as a taking several years after its passage.

Prior to *First English*, government defendants in this position routinely responded to such a verdict by either (1) repealing the offending regulation or (2) continuing to enforce the regulation upon the payment to the claimant property owner of compensation equivalent to the reduction in the property's fair market value resulting from that regulation.[8] After *First English,* however, government entities that immediately repeal a regulation found to be a taking must pay compensation for losses incurred during the period for which that offending regulation was in effect—that is, they are forced to purchase retroactively a property interest that already has been terminated and that they did not plan or budget for, even if the regulation at issue was enacted (and later repealed) in good faith.

Section I of this chapter recounts *First English's* explication of the retroactive temporary takings compensation principle, and explains how the U.S. Supreme Court extended the reach of this principle in two takings decisions handed down in its 2012–2013 term. Section II introduces a conception of ownership grounded in humility, that is, a conception of ownership that recognizes the limited reach of human knowledge and the variability of normative positions. It suggests that a conception of ownership grounded in humility calls for a more contextual analysis in temporary takings cases than *First English* allows, and raises for discussion the possibility that such an analysis might appropriately turn in part on whether the governmental entity acted in good faith when attempting to update property rules via regulation.

I. The Retroactive Temporary Takings Compensation Principle

Until the 1980s, many state courts, lawmakers, planning officials, and scholars understood that the state need not pay compensation for property later found to be taken by a regulatory action if the state repealed that regulatory action immediately upon the takings finding.[9] However, in a dissenting opinion in *San Diego Gas & Electric Co. v. San Diego* in 1981, Justice Brennan—in a case where the majority dismissed a takings suit on procedural grounds—suggested that injunctive relief would "hardly compensate the landowner for any economic loss suffered during the time his property was taken."[10]

---

[8] *First English*, 482 U.S. at 318.

[9] *See, e.g.,* Agins v. City of Tiburon, 598 P.2d 25, 32 (Cal. 1979), *aff'd on other grounds,* 447 U.S. 255 (1980); Fred F. French Investing Co. v. City of New York, 350 N.E.2d 381, 384–85 (N.Y. 1976), *appeal dismissed and cert. denied,* 429 U.S. 990 (1976); De Botton v. Marple Twp., 689 F. Supp. 477, 480 n.1 (E.D. Pa. 1988). *See also* Daniel R. Mandelker, *Land Use Takings: The Compensation Issue,* 8 HASTINGS CONST. L.Q. 491, 515 (1981); Donald W. Large, *The Supreme Court and the Takings Clause: The Search for a Better Rule,* 18 ENVTL. L. 3, 38 (1987).

[10] San Diego Gas & Elec. Co. v. City of San Diego, 450 U.S. 621, 655–60 (1981) (Brennan, J., dissenting).

Justice Brennan apparently found persuasive landowners' allegation that, under the prevailing sentiment of the day, a win was a loss because even when they successfully proved that regulations restricting almost all productive uses of land should be enjoined, landowners contended that they faced years of continuing litigation over revised, only slightly narrower restrictions.[11] As one group of commentators described it, Brennan assumed that, given the way the "land-use-control system [then] work[ed], landowners and developers [were] most in need of help from the protective arm of the courts."[12]

This Section explains that, in the Court's 6-3 decision six years later in *First English*, Justice Brennan's position on a compensatory remedy for "temporary" regulatory takings prevailed, and that in its 2012–2013 term, the Court extended the retroactive temporary takings compensation principle into two new areas of takings law.

A. *FIRST ENGLISH* AND THE RETROACTIVE TEMPORARY TAKINGS COMPENSATION PRINCIPLE

First English Evangelical Lutheran Church owned land along the banks of a creek. The Church used the living quarters, dining hall, and chapel on the property to operate a recreational program for handicapped children.[13] A fire destroyed the surrounding forest, creating a significant flood hazard; soon after, a flood destroyed all of the Church's buildings.[14] The County of Los Angeles adopted an interim ordinance precluding construction "within the boundary lines of the interim flood protection area" located along the creek.[15] The Church alleged that this ordinance amounted to a regulatory taking of its creek-front property for which it should be compensated.[16]

Procedurally, the Supreme Court presumed that a taking occurred, which allowed it to determine whether injunctive relief is sufficient in such an instance, or, instead, whether compensation is due.[17] In an opinion authored by Chief Justice Rehnquist, the

---

[11] For literature supporting the view that government entities are regularly inclined to exercise their powers in this manner, *see, e.g.*, Douglas Kmiec, *The Supreme Court Runs Out of Gas in* San Diego, 57 IND. L.J. 45 (1982); Richard Epstein, *Takings: Descent and Resurrection*, 1987 SUP. CT. REV. 1. For critical looks at this vision of government, *see, e.g.*, Joan Williams, *The Constitutional Vulnerability of American Local Government: The Politics of City Status in American Law*, 1986 WIS. L. REV. 83, 121–37; Gregory Alexander, *Takings, Narratives, and Power*, 88 COLUM. L. REV. 1752 (1988).

[12] Norman Williams Jr., et al., *The White River Junction Manifesto*, 9 VT. L. REV. 193, 197 (1984). For an article responding to these scholars that offers strong support for Justice Brennan's position, see Michael Berger & Gideon Kanner, *Thoughts on* The White River Junction Manifesto: *A Reply to the "Gang of Five's" Views on Just Compensation for Regulatory Taking of Property*, 19 LOY. L. REV. 685 (1986).

[13] First English Evangelical Lutheran Church of Glendale v. Los Angeles Cnty., 482 U.S. 304, 307 (1987).

[14] *Id.*

[15] *Id.* Though classified by the County as an "interim" ordinance, it seems evident to some commentators that the County did not intend to allow construction in the floodplain at any point in the future. *See, e.g.*, Frank Michelman, *Takings, 1987*, 88 COLUM. L. REV. 1600 (1988).

[16] *First English*, 428 U.S. at 308.

[17] *Id.* at 311.

Court concluded that "where the government's activities have already worked a taking of all use of property, no subsequent action by the government can relieve it of the duty to provide compensation for the period during which the taking was effective."[18]

There is broad agreement that *First English's* holding requiring compensation in these instances has a chilling effect on government regulation.[19] Determining whether a regulation amounts to a compensable taking is dependent on a fact-sensitive analysis that, according to the Supreme Court's 1978 decision in *Penn Central Transportation Co. v. New York City*,[20] requires inquiries about the economic impact of the regulation, the claimant's investment-backed expectations, and the character of the government action at issue.[21] After *First English*, legislators and administrators alike are hesitant to adopt new regulatory programs in light of the possibility that, given the nature of a *Penn Central* analysis, they might inadvertently step over the indistinct *Penn Central* line[22] and possibly be forced to pay a considerable amount of money for the period during which the now-deemed-unconstitutional measure was in place.[23]

B. EXTENDING THE REACH OF *FIRST ENGLISH*'S RETROACTIVE TEMPORARY TAKINGS COMPENSATION PRINCIPLE

Two decisions from the Court's 2012–2013 term, *Arkansas Game and Fish Commission v. United States*[24] and *Koontz v. St. John's River Water Management District*,[25] extend *First English's* retroactive liability logic to the arenas of dam management and land use permit conditions, respectively.

---

[18] *Id.* at 321.

[19] *See, e.g.,* Daniel L. Siegel, *The Impact of* Tahoe-Sierra *on Temporary Takings Law*, 23 J. ENVTL. L. 273, 274 (2005); Large, *supra* note 9, at 42. This chapter addresses the chilling effect that *First English* imposes on the states' efforts to adopt land use and environmental restrictions designed to be permanent. *First English* is perhaps less chilling on the state's implementation of development moratoria designed to allow time for the development of a comprehensive plan to address, say, the preservation of an environmentally sensitive resource. *See* Tahoe-Sierra Preservation Council v. Tahoe Regional Planning Agency, 535 U.S. 302 (2002). The *Tahoe-Sierra* court noted, however, that moratoria lasting for more than one year may "be viewed with special skepticism." *Id.* at 304.

[20] Penn Cent. Transp. Co. v. City of New York, 438 U.S. 104, 109 (1978).

[21] *Id.* at 134.

[22] The decision in *First English* technically does not increase the likelihood that a court will find a taking; indeed, on remand, a California appellate court held that First English Evangelical Church did not meet its burden under *Penn Central*. *See* First English Evangelical Lutheran Church of Glendale v. County of Los Angeles, 258 Cal. Rptr. 893, 904 (Ct. App. 1989) (concluding that "agricultural and recreational uses" were reasonable remaining uses). Nonetheless, "[e]ven spurious challenges raise the cost of environmental regulation." *See* Lynda L. Butler, *State Environmental Programs: A Study in Political Influence and Regulatory Failure*, 31 WM. & MARY L. REV. 823, 834 (1990).

[23] *Id.* at 830; Corwin W. Johnson, *Compensation for Invalid Land-Use Regulations*, 15 GA. L. REV. 569, 594 (1981); Williams et al., *supra* note 12, at 219–25.

[24] Arkansas Game & Fish Comm'n v. United States, 133 S. Ct. 511 (2012).

[25] Koontz v. St. John's River Water Mgmt. Dist., 133 S. Ct. 2586 (2013).

1. Dam Management

A series of cases in the mid-twentieth century determined that the government must retroactively compensate owners for affirmatively taking outright physical possession of private property on a temporary basis.[26] In the context of flooding, however, lower federal courts prior to the Supreme Court's 2012–2013 term generally understood takings liability to extend only to those permanent or regularly recurring government-induced flood events.[27] Yet in *Arkansas Game*, a unanimous Supreme Court (with Justice Kagan recused) agreed that recurrent flooding over a temporary period resulting from the government's operation of a dam is not categorically immune from takings liability.[28] The Court noted that its earlier decisions that included language regarding floods resulting in a "permanent invasion of land" had been "superseded by subsequent developments in our jurisprudence," including *First English*.[29]

The *Arkansas Game* holding raises the specter of retroactive temporary takings compensation for every decision made by a governmental entity with respect to dam releases that, as is often the case, involves a choice between two or more inevitable harms.[30] As explained in the next section, a similar extension of *First English* is evident in *Koontz*.

2. Land Use Permit Conditions

By way of background, state and local governments routinely attach certain conditions, or "exactions," to development permits in an effort to alleviate the environmental and infrastructural burdens posed by individual projects. However, presumably to protect landowners from exactions that are either unrelated or disproportionate to the problems

---

[26] *See* United States v. Gen. Motors Corp., 323 U.S. 373 (1945) (occupying a portion of a leased building); Kimball Laundry Co. v. United States, 338 U.S. 1 (1949) (taking physical possession of a laundry company's facilities); United States v. Pewee Coal Co., 341 U.S. 114 (1951) (taking physical possession of a coal mine).

[27] *See, e.g.,* Goodman v. United States, 113 F.2d 914, 917 (8th Cir. 1940); Fromme v. U. S. & Victoria County Navigation Dist., 412 F.2d 1192, 1197 (Ct. Cl. 1969); Barnes v. United States, 538 F.2d 865, 872 (Ct. Cl. 1976). These decisions understandably stemmed from the Supreme Court's 1924 decision in *Sanguinetti v. United States,* where the Court insinuated that the Takings Clause did not require compensation for a government-induced flood event unless the flood event constituted a "permanent invasion of land." Sanguinetti v. United States, 264 U.S. 146, 149 (1924).

[28] *Arkansas Game & Fish Comm'n,* 133 S. Ct. at 519 (holding that such claims are to be reviewed under the *Penn Central* framework).

[29] *Id.* at 520 (noting that the primary case cited for the "permanent invasion of land" language "was decided in 1924, well before the World War II-era cases and *First English,* in which the Court first homed in on the matter of compensation for temporary takings"). David Baake explains that the Court's "reliance on *First English* [in *Arkansas Game*] was necessary to support its conclusion," for "no other precedent directly supports the proposition that a temporary incidental taking can be compensable." Comment, *Arkansas Game and Fish Commission v. United States,* 37 HARV. ENVTL. L. REV. 577, 580 n.38 (2013).

[30] Brief for the Internat'l Mun. Lawyers Ass'n. et al. as Amici Curiae Supporting Appellee at 15, Arkansas Game & Fish Comm'n v. United States, 133 S. Ct. 511 (2012). *But see Arkansas Game & Fish Comm'n,* 133 S. Ct. at 521 (asserting, without explanation, that "today's modest decision augurs no deluge of takings liability").

caused by their proposed developments, the U.S. Supreme Court curtailed the exercise of this power in its conveniently rhyming *Nollan v. California Coastal Commission*[31] and *Dolan v. City of Tigard*[32] decisions by establishing a constitutional takings framework unique to exaction disputes.[33] Under this peculiar framework, it is the government—as the defendant—who has the burden of proving that a challenged exaction bears both an "essential nexus" to and "rough proportionality" with the development's impacts.[34]

In *Koontz*, the government originally posed conditions allegedly aimed at mitigating wetland impacts.[35] It later withdrew those conditions and denied the requested permit, before reconsidering and unconditionally granting that permit.[36] A five-justice majority concluded that, where a governmental entity (1) proposes permit conditions but (2) later withdraws those proposed conditions, and (3) makes a decision to approve or deny the requested permit, those temporarily proposed conditions are subject to the heightened scrutiny of *Nollan* and *Dolan*.[37] The existence of a temporary exaction takings doctrine could prove even more chilling for conditional permitting regimes than the extension of *First English* in *Arkansas Game* will be for dam management, for, according to one scholar's exhaustive empirical research, appellate decisions applying *Dolan's* "rough proportionality" standard reveal that the "government flunks the test about half the time."[38]

---

[31] Nollan v. Cal. Coastal Comm'n, 483 U.S. 825 (1987).

[32] Dolan v. City of Tigard, 512 U.S. 374 (1994).

[33] The predicate for *Nollan/Dolan* application—only those instances where the government bargains with a landowner over a discretionary permit—thoughtfully has been described as dependent on a "doubtful proposition: that land use 'bargains'…can be readily picked out from land use controls more generally…. [M]ost if not all land use law can be framed as deal making given that laws are conditional in nature and subject to frequent and fine-grained revision." Lee Ann Fennell & Eduardo Penalver, *Exactions Creep*, SUP. CT. REV. (forthcoming 2014) (manuscript at 12, *available at* http://ssrn.com/abstract=2345028).

[34] *See Nollan*, 483 U.S. at 837; *Dolan*, 512 U.S. at 391.

[35] *See* Koontz v. St. Johns River Water Mgmt. Dist., 133 S. Ct. 2586, 2593 (2013).

[36] *See* St. Johns River Water Mgmt. Dist. v. Koontz, 77 So. 3d 1220, 1224–25 (Fla. 2011) ("St. Johns chose to issue the permits to Mr. Koontz after it received additional evidence which demonstrated that the amount of wetlands on Mr. Koontz's property was significantly less than originally believed.").

[37] *Id.* at 2596. The state appellate court determined that Koontz was entitled to approximately $400,000 in takings compensation for lost rents over the period of time between the denial of his original development application and the issuance of the permit. *See* St. Johns River Water Mgmt. Dist. v. Koontz, 5 So. 3d 8, 17 (Fla. Dist. Ct. App. 2009), *decision quashed*, 77 So. 3d 1220 (Fla. 2011), *rev'd*, 133 S. Ct. 2586 (U.S. 2013). A unanimous U.S. Supreme Court, however, conceded that no property actually was taken from Koontz and that he therefore is not entitled to just compensation under the U.S. Constitution's Takings Clause. Yet the majority confusingly offered that the potentially unconstitutional act is the government's "impermissibly burden[ing] the right not to have property taken without just compensation." *See* Koontz v. St. Johns River Water Mgmt. Dist., 133 S. Ct. 2586, 2590 (2013). The Court did not discuss what remedy, if any, might be available to a claimant who successfully argues that a proposed exaction does not pass *Nollan* and *Dolan* muster. For a thorough, critical review of *Koontz*, see Sean F. Nolon, *Bargaining for Development Post-*Koontz: *How the Supreme Court Invaded Local Government*, 66 FLA. L. REV. (forthcoming 2014).

[38] John Echeverria, Koontz: *The Very Worst Takings Decision Ever?*, N.Y.U. ENVTL. L.J. (forthcoming 2014) (manuscript at 7 n.38, *available at* http://ssrn.com/abstract=2316406). Additional empirical work probing the specific reasons behind the government's propensity to lose in *Dolan* cases—behind the obvious and highly significant point that the government bears the burden of proof in such cases—is fodder for future research.

II. Humility and Retroactive Temporary Takings Compensation

Section I discussed the scope and growing breadth of the retroactive temporary takings compensation principle. This principle places a premium on the stability of ownership interests, which can serve the important social aims of stimulating economic enterprise, promoting self-expression, and securing private space to engage in voluntary relationships. Yet for such an emphasis on stability, society is paying a high social and ecological price.[39] The very existence of retroactively compensable temporary takings seems sufficient to discourage lawmakers from regulatory innovation in the land use and environmental realm.

Section II introduces a conception of ownership grounded in humility that is distinct from the conception centered on stability that underlies *First English* and its progeny. It raises the possibility that such a conception may call for limiting the application of the retroactive temporary takings compensation principle to those instances where the regulating entity acts in bad faith when updating property rules.[40]

A. HUMILITY AND OWNERSHIP

A progressive conception of property should be grounded in, among other themes, humility.[41] Humility in this context refers to recognition of the limited reach of human knowledge and the variability of our normative positions. Such recognition necessitates allowing space for creative reflection on and the reconfiguration of property rules as the extent of knowledge and the values attendant to it change.[42] Even if it were possible to determine society's core values at this moment, doing so could not explain under what

---

[39] For a particularly thoughtful summary of the ways in which a system of private ownership can both contribute to and detract from human flourishing, see Eric Freyfogle, *Private Ownership and Human Flourishing: An Exploratory Overview*, 24 STELLENBOSCH L. REV. 430 (2013).

[40] An openness to good faith innovation and experimentation on the part of governmental entities is certainly not the only feature—or even a core feature—of a conception of property that reflects the theme of humility outlined here. Rather, this chapter simply suggests that it may be *a* feature worthy of further consideration when parsing out humility's place within our property system.

[41] *See* Timothy M. Mulvaney, *Progressive Property Moving Forward*, 5 CAL. L. REV. CIR. (forthcoming 2014). This section of the text draws heavily on that prior work. Given the subject's breadth and in light of space constraints, the discussion in this chapter proceeds in the form of an overview.

[42] *See, e.g.*, Eric Freyfogle, *Taking Property Seriously, in* PROPERTY RIGHTS AND SUSTAINABILITY: THE EVOLUTION OF PROPERTY RIGHTS TO MEET ECOLOGICAL CHALLENGES 43, 55 (D. Grinlinton & P. Taylor eds., 2011) ("If property has a foundational background principle, it is that lawmakers are free to redefine harm, generation upon generation."); Francis S. Philbrick, *Changing Conceptions of Property in Law*, 86 U. PA. L. REV. 691, 691 (1938) ("It is self-evident that neither the things recognized as objects of property rights nor the nature of these rights themselves could possibly be the same under a land economy of 1700 and our industrial economy of today.").

circumstances that reference point must or should give way to the reality that such values change over time.[43]

Consider the well-known matter of *Lucas v. South Carolina Coastal Council* involving a prohibition on development in coastal areas particularly prone to erosion.[44] It seems that the *Lucas* Court feared that if transformation of nature to a human use were considered harmful, then many land uses previously considered lawful could be declared illegitimate. For this reason, according to Professor Joseph Sax, the Court turned the discussion from (1) landowners' obligation to do no harm to (2) landowners' "irreducible right" to development.[45] On the view set out in *Lucas*, vacant land merely is in waiting to be transformed.

But an evolving society very well may take a different attitude with respect to owning nature—it is an attitude that appreciates "sentient landscapes"[46] and understands land as part of a far larger and significantly more complex ecological fabric than the lines of subdivision maps suggest.[47] Property is a socially constructed institution, and today's lawmakers are morally responsible for this institution because they have the power to update it. Thus, according to the conception of property outlined here, property rules previously justified—based on what society, in a given moment, agreed upon—regularly *must* be reconsidered in light of changing conditions and changing human values, and they should be revised accordingly to avoid the perpetuation of injustices in the existing distribution of entitlements.[48] This is not to suggest that such reconsideration is an easy task; rather, in the words of one scholar, it calls for "honest grappling with hard truth."[49]

---

[43] *See, e.g., id.* at 696 ("[T]he concept of property never has been, is not, and never can be of definite content.... Changing culture causes the law to speak with new imperatives, invigorates some concepts, devitalizes and brings to obsolescence others."); T. Nicolaus Tideman, *Takings, Moral Evolution, and Justice*, 88 COLUM. L. REV. 1714, 1715–22 (1988); LAURA S. UNDERKUFFLER, THE IDEA OF PROPERTY: ITS MEANING AND POWER 80–81 (2003); Timothy M. Mulvaney, *Foreground Principles*, 20 GEO. MASON L. REV. 837, 866–67 (2013).

[44] Lucas v. South Carolina Coastal Council, 112 S. Ct. 2886 (1992).

[45] *See* Joseph L. Sax, *Property Rights and the Economy of Nature: Understanding* Lucas v. South Carolina Coastal Council, 45 STAN. L. REV. 1433, 1441 (1992).

[46] *See* THOMAS HEYD & NICK BROOKS, *Exploring Cultural Dimensions of Adaptation, in* ADAPTING TO CLIMATE CHANGE 271 (2009).

[47] *See* Joseph Singer & Jack M. Beerman, *The Social Origins of Property*, 6 CAN. J.L. & JURIS. 217, 238 (1993).

[48] UNDERKUFFLER, *supra* note 43, at 45; Tideman, *supra* note 43, at 1714; Eric Freyfogle, *Property and Liberty*, 34 HARV. ENVTL. L. REV. 75, 115 (2010); Lynda Butler, *The Pathology of Property Norms: Living within Nature's Boundaries*, 73 S. CAL. L. REV. 927, 932 (2000); Singer & Beerman, *supra* note 47, at 243–44; Mulvaney, *supra* note 43, at 848 n.43.

[49] Laura Underkuffler, *Property and Change: The Constitutional Conundrum*, 91 TEX. L. REV. (forthcoming 2014) (manuscript at 19–20, on file with author).

B. GOOD FAITH AS A FEATURE OF HUMILITY

What might incorporating a sense of humility into our understanding of ownership mean for takings doctrine? First, most dramatically, it could challenge the very idea of applying the Takings Clause to regulatory acts that do not result in outright appropriations.[50] Second and less dramatic (though quite significant in its own right), it could call into question the prospect of all temporary regulatory takings claims; indeed, there is some force to Justice Stevens's assertion, in a dissent two years prior to *First English*, that temporary harms resulting from regulatory decisions may be best understood as "an unfortunate but necessary byproduct of disputes over the extent of the government's power to inflict permanent harms without paying for them."[51] However, this chapter does not pursue those two ambitious challenges here—that is, for purposes of this chapter, the following two general points are conceded: (1) some regulations can amount to takings, and (2) some regulations can command retroactive temporary takings compensation. The focus of the analysis that follows is confined to offering one possible, though hardly uncontroverted, justification for narrowing the class of regulations for which retroactive temporary takings compensation is due.

In its present form, retroactive temporary takings compensation presumably is available to *all* developers in *all* instances where a regulation is repealed after a takings verdict.[52] Perhaps, however, such compensation should be limited to those instances where, in addition to the traditionally applicable takings test (*Penn Central* or *Nollan/Dolan*) weighing in favor of the takings claimant, there is a considerable indicium of bad faith on the government's part.[53] After all, the "*honest* grappling" described above at least implicitly demands that those lawmakers in positions to engage in reconsideration of property rules in light of changing conditions and changing human values act in good faith. Therefore, perhaps the focus of temporary takings law should be on pressing claimants to identify those instances where government action does not reflect a sincere effort to engage in "the ongoing updating of ownership norms."[54]

---

[50] For historical analyses suggesting that the original meaning of the Takings Clause was so confined, see William M. Treanor, *The Origins and Original Significance of the Just Compensation Clause of the Fifth Amendment*, 94 YALE L.J. 694 (1985); William M. Treanor, *The Original Understanding of the Takings Clause and the Political Process*, 95 COLUM. L. REV. 782 (1995); John F. Hart, *Colonial Land Use Law and Its Significance for Modern Takings Doctrine*, 109 HARV. L. REV. 1252 (1996).

[51] Williamson County Reg'l Planning Comm'n v. Hamilton Bank of Johnson City, 473 U.S. 172, 204 (1985) (Stevens, J., dissenting).

[52] *See* Williams et al., *supra* note 12, at 243.

[53] This chapter is not suggesting that bad faith should serve as an independent basis for the finding of a taking.

[54] *See* Eric Freyfogle, *Regulatory Takings, Methodically*, 31 ENVTL. L. REP. 10313, 10321 (2001). After Justice Brennan's dissent in *San Diego Gas & Electric*, but before *First English*, a group of scholars posed the idea of legislation requiring that, once a land use restriction is declared an unconstitutional taking and a slightly modified version of the same restriction thereafter is declared an unconstitutional taking, courts "direct a remedy giving the developer what he asked for, whatever its impact." Williams et al., *supra* note 12, at 241. The relief posed by these scholars seems excessive, compared at least to, for instance, the court's retaining continuing jurisdiction to review the subsequent government agency proceedings or shifting the burden of proof to the government after the first (or some subsequent) takings finding.

This proposal admittedly begs an important question: What constitutes "bad faith?" A Pennsylvania court's admonition that "bad faith is generally the opposite of good faith" is obviously of limited use,[55] though it is illustrative of the great difficulty in specifically defining the phrase. On the conception of property advocated here, it seems appropriate to extend a strong presumption in favor of the state's acting in good faith, a presumption that the claimant might rebut by proving that the stated purpose for the government action at issue was dishonestly and furtively designed with (and perhaps even plainly contradicted by) a conscious, actual alternative purpose.[56]

C. OBJECTIONS TO LIMITING RETROACTIVE TAKINGS COMPENSATION TO BAD FAITH ACTS

Under the simple if controversial proposal outlined above, government acts undertaken in bad faith that are later deemed takings and repealed are retroactively compensable, while government acts taken in good faith that are later deemed takings require compensation only if the state chooses to continue enforcing the offending act. There are several potential objections to implementation of this proposal, including the common perspective that (1) the government's intent is irrelevant in takings cases, and (2) bad faith government conduct is more appropriately addressed under the Due Process Clause than under the Takings Clause. These potential objections are discussed here in turn.

1. Governmental Intent in Takings Cases

Concurring in *Hughes v. Washington,* Justice Potter Stewart stated that "the Constitution measures a taking of property not by what a State says, or by what it intends, but by what it does."[57] Although the face of takings law has changed markedly since that decision in 1967, respected commentators on takings doctrine recently have expressed continued agreement with Justice Stewart's premise.[58] However, the unanimous *Arkansas Game*

---

[55] *See* Redev. Auth. of Erie v. Owens, 274 A.2d 244, 247 (Pa. Commw. Ct. 1971).

[56] For potentially instructive case law, *see, e.g.,* Pheasant Ridge Assocs. v. Town of Burlington, 506 N.E.2d 1152, 1156 (Mass. 1987); Earth Mgmt., Inc. v. Heard County, 283 S.E.2d 455, 460 (Ga. 1981). Although the conceivable class of "bad faith" government actions envisioned here admittedly is not specifically delineated, it should be evident that this class is nowhere near as expansive as that offered by Steven Eagle, who has suggested that "bad faith typically manifests itself through actions that make land-use decisions unreasonable." *See* Steven J. Eagle, *Planning Moratoria and Regulatory Takings: The Supreme Court's Fairness Mandate Benefits Landowners,* 31 FLA. ST. U. L. REV. 429, 483 (2004). There is, however, some apparent common ground between Eagle's position and the position set out in this chapter, for Eagle questioned a takings jurisprudence that "require[s] government agencies to pay when they are forthright and not to pay when they tell the truth slowly (or, more accurately, permit the truth to dawn slowly among the regulated)." *Id.*

[57] Hughes v. Washington, 389 U.S. 290, 298 (1967) (Stewart, J., concurring).

[58] *See, e.g.,* Robert Meltz, Substantive Takings Law: A Primer 11 (Nov. 18, 2011) (unpublished manuscript, *available at* http://www.vermontlaw.edu/Documents/2011TakingsConference/3%20Meltz-%20 Substantive%20Takings%20Law%20Primer.pdf) ("A showing of governmental intent to take is not required.").

Court in several instances spoke as if the government's motivations always have played an obvious and primary role in adjudicating regulatory takings disputes.[59] And there is some, albeit largely implicit, support in the lower courts for the position that bad faith, if not a stated prerequisite of takings liability, at least serves as strong support for the claimant's case.

Loveladies Harbor, Inc. v. United States[60] provides a useful illustration. In this case, the state of New Jersey negotiated with a developer to reduce the footprint of his development proposal from 51 to 11.5 acres, for which it issued the necessary state wetlands fill permit as part of the settlement. Thereafter, though, when the landowner sought a necessary federal wetlands permit to fill those 11.5 acres, New Jersey opposed the issuance of that federal permit on the same environmental grounds on which it originally had resisted any development of the tract before the settlement. Some property scholars have suggested that New Jersey's seemingly inconsistent positions may have swayed the court to side with the landowner on the takings issue.[61]

Other matters discussing governmental motivations have arisen specifically in the temporary takings context, though admittedly in situations distinct from those on which this chapter is focused in that they involve governmental delay in deciding whether to grant or deny land use permit applications. For instance, in *Landgate, Inc., v. California Coastal Commission*,[62] the California Supreme Court noted in dicta that a taking might occur where the state's position is "so unreasonable from a legal standpoint as to lead to the conclusion that it was taken for no purpose other than to delay the development project before it."[63] Indeed, *First English* itself sought to distinguish normal delays in the

---

[59] *See, e.g.*, Arkansas Game & Fish Comm'n v. United States, 133 S. Ct. 511, 520 (2012) (distinguishing an earlier case by noting that the Court's decision in that case "emphasized that the Government did not intend to flood the land or have 'any reason to expect that such [a] result would follow from [its action]'"); *id.* at 522 ("relevant to the takings inquiry is the degree to which the invasion is intended or is the foreseeable result of authorized government action"); *id.* at 523 (finding it important that the Court of Federal Claims "found that the flooding the Commission assails was foreseeable").

[60] Loveladies Harbor, Inc. v. United States, 28 F.3d 1171 (Fed. Cir. 1994). The case is regularly cited as an outlier in the literature discussing the common view that the extent of deprivation effected by a regulatory action is measured against the value of the parcel as a whole. *Loveladies* held that the relevant parcel for takings purposes did not include portions of the parcel sold before promulgation of the regulation at issue. *Id.* at 1181.

[61] *See, e.g.*, Marc R. Poirier, *Property, Environment, Community*, 12 J. ENVTL L. & LITIG. 43, 77–79 (1997); Marc R. Poirier, *The Virtue of Vagueness in Takings Doctrine*, 24 CARDOZO L. REV. 93, 173–74 (2002). Of course, there are a number of conceivable rationales for New Jersey's position on the federal permit that are not grounded in bad faith.

[62] Landgate, Inc., v. Cal. Coastal Comm'n, 17 Cal. 4th 1006 (1998). The hypothetical situation set out in *Landgate's* dicta can be distinguished from those instances in which the government acted based on a reasonable misreading of a regulation. *See, e.g.*, Bio Energy, L.L.C. v. Town of Hopkinton, 891 A.2d 509 (N.H. 2005) (finding no taking where a town's cease-and-desist order was based on a misreading of variance terms).

[63] *Landgate, Inc.*, 17 Cal. 4th at 1024. *See also* Loewenstein v. City of Lafayette, 103 Cal. App. 4th 718, 728 (Cal. Ct. App. 2002) (explaining the relevance of the fact that the city's action was not taken "solely to delay the proposed project"); Cooley v. United States, 324 F.3d 1297, 1307 (Fed. Cir. 2003) (stating that, in the temporary takings context, "[a] combination of extraordinary delay and intimated bad faith, under the third prong of the *Penn Central* analysis, influence the character of the governmental action").

land use permitting process from extraordinary delays,[64] and the Federal Circuit Court of Appeals has noted that "extraordinary delay rarely travels without bad faith."[65]

These select examples certainly do not make a dispositive case for considering the government's motivations in takings cases. However, they suggest that it at least seems worthwhile to consider the possibility that governmental intentions should be a relevant component, at the very least as a background matter, of some takings analyses.

2. Takings and Due Process

Since the cases referenced in the preceding section were decided, the U.S. Supreme Court concluded in *Lingle v. Chevron, Inc.*[66] that "if a government action is found to be impermissible—for instance because it fails to meet the 'public use' requirement or is so arbitrary as to violate due process—that is the end of the inquiry. No amount of compensation can authorize such action."[67] One could interpret *Lingle* as suggesting that acts undertaken in bad faith are not considered within the actor's scope of authority and thus cannot be for a public use, whereby such acts cannot violate the Takings Clause but rather only the Due Process Clause.[68] Such an interpretation may foreclose consideration of the proposal offered for discussion in this chapter.[69]

---

[64] First English Evangelical Lutheran Church of Glendale v. Los Angeles Cnty., 482 U.S. 304, 321 (1987).

[65] Boise Cascade Corp. v. United States, 296 F.3d 1339, 1347 n.6 (Fed. Cir. 2002). *See also* Wyatt v. United States, 271 F.3d 1090, 1098 (Fed. Cir. 2001); Cooley, 324 F.3d at 1307.

[66] Lingle v. Chevron U.S.A. Inc., 544 U.S. 528 (2005).

[67] *Id.* at 543. Indeed, the *First English* Court noted that the Takings Clause "is designed not to limit governmental interference with property rights *per se,* but rather to secure *compensation* in the event of otherwise proper interference amounting to a taking." *First English,* 482 U.S. at 315 (emphasis in original). *See also* PI Elec. Corp. v. United States, 55 Fed. Cl. 279, 288 (2003) ("An unauthorized action cannot predicate liability for a compensable taking, given that it does not vest some kind of title in the government and entitlement to just compensation in the owner or former owner.... Therefore, a claimant must concede the [authorization] of the government action which is the basis of the taking[s] claim to bring [a federal takings] suit[.]") (internal quotations omitted).

[68] *See, e.g.,* John D. Echeverria, *Making Sense of* Penn Central, 23 UCLA J. ENVTL. L. & POL'Y 171, 202 (2005) ("*Lingle* appears to preclude the notion that allegations of bad faith can support a taking claim. Allegations of bad faith ... sound in due process rather than in takings."). Among other scholars, John Echeverria regularly pressed this claim long before *Lingle. See* John D. Echeverria & Sharon Dennis, *The Takings Issue and the Due Process Clause: A Way out of a Doctrinal Confusion,* 17 VT. L. REV. 695 (1993); John D. Echeverria, *Does a Regulation That Fails to Advance a Legitimate Governmental Interest Result in a Regulatory Taking?,* 29 ENVTL. L. 853, 879 (1999); John D. Echeverria, *Takings and Errors,* 51 ALA. L. REV. 1047 (2000) [hereinafter Echeverria, *Takings and Errors*]. Similarly, Lee Fennell and Eduardo Penalver recently argued that "favoritism and corruption ... are much closer in their nature and seriousness to the harms encompassed by the due process clause than they are to those that form the subject of protection against uncompensated takings." Fennell & Penalver, *supra* note 33, at 58. Others have noted that bad faith government actions in the land use realm may implicate the Equal Protection Clause. *See, e.g.,* Robert H. Freilich, *Time, Space, and Value in Inverse Condemnation: A Unified Theory for Partial Takings Analysis,* 24 HAW. L. REV. 589, 601–02 (2002); John C. Cooke & Christine Carlisle Odom, *Judicial Deference to Local Land Use Decisions and the Emergence of Single-Class Equal Protection Claims,* 30 ENVTL. L. REP. 11049 (2000). The leading, if controversial, case in this area is *Village of Willowbrook v. Olech,* 528 U.S. 562 (2000).

[69] In an article published pre-*Lingle,* John Echeverria concluded that "[a]n erroneous government action is not a compensable taking because it is not a taking for 'public use' within the meaning of the Fifth Amendment."

However, *Lingle* has not necessarily been reconciled with several of the Court's prior assertions in takings cases.[70] For example, when affirming a takings award in *Del Monte Dunes at Monterey Ltd. v. City of Monterey* in 1999, the Court quoted with approval the lower court's characterization of the takings claim: "Del Monte argued that the City's reasons for denying their application were invalid and that it unfairly intended to forestall any reasonable development of the [property]."[71] For another example, a majority of the Supreme Court remarked in the well-known takings case of *Tahoe-Sierra Preservation Council, Inc. v. Tahoe Regional Planning Agency* that "were it not for the findings of the District Court that [the Tahoe-Sierra Preservation Council] acted diligently and in good faith, we might have concluded that the agency was stalling in order to avoid promulgating the environmental threshold carrying capacities and regional plan mandated by [a pre-existing multi-state compact]."[72] In this light, the *Lingle* language quoted above conceivably could be interpreted to apply only to (1) those actions that were made in good faith but nonetheless later deemed "impermissible" because they

---

Echeverria, *Takings and Errors, supra* note 68, at 1093. This chapter's message may conflict with Echeverria's thesis, for Echeverria equated erroneous government action with "essentially any type of illegality." *Id.* at 1048. *See also id.* at 1080 ("Because the validity of the action is a *precondition* for a taking for a 'public use,' the invalidity of the action cannot be treated as beside the point. Just as the public use requirement precludes the idea that a government error provides an affirmative basis for finding a taking, it also precludes the idea that government error can be ignored in takings analysis."). However, few if any of Echeverria's many examples of erroneous government action involved bad faith, such that there may be room to reconcile Echeverria's position and the one presented for consideration in this chapter. Indeed, Echeverria expressed some sympathy for the types of situations to which this chapter refers. *See* Echeverria, *id.* at 1090–91 ("It needs to be acknowledged that enforcing the 'public use' requirement as proposed [in Echeverria's article] creates the possibility of some intuitively 'hard' cases. One such scenario…involves a case in which the claimant would have a perfectly viable takings claim but for the fact that the government erred.").

[70] For a small sampling of the many post-*Lingle* works tackling the distinction between the Takings Clause and the Due Process Clause, see, e.g., David Spohr, *"What Shall We Do with the Drunken Sailor?": The Intersection of the Takings Clause and the Character, Merit, or Impropriety of the Regulatory Action*, 17 SOUTHEASTERN ENVTL. L.J 1 (2008); Mark Fenster, *The Stubborn Incoherence of Regulatory Takings*, 28 STAN. ENVTL. L.J. 525 (2009); Alan Romero, *Ends and Means in Takings Law after* Lingle v. Chevron, 23 J. LAND USE & ENVTL. L. 333 (2008); Steven J. Eagle, *Property Tests, Due Process Tests and Regulatory Takings Jurisprudence*, 2007 B.Y.U. L. REV. 899 (2007).

[71] Del Monte Dunes at Monterey Ltd. v. City of Monterey, 526 U.S. 687, 698 (1999) (quoting Del Monte Dunes at Monterey Ltd. v. City of Monterey, 95 F.3d 1422, 1431 (9th Cir. 1996)). *See also* Steven J. Eagle, Del Monte Dunes, *Good Faith, and Land Use Regulation*, 30 ENVTL. L. REP. 10100, 10100 (2000) (suggesting that *Del Monte Dunes* "evince(s) the Court's growing concern that government officials deal with property owners with good faith"); Steven J. Eagle, *Some Permanent Problems with the Supreme Court's Temporary Regulatory Takings Jurisprudence*, 25 HAW. L. REV. 325, 351 (2003) (describing the *Del Monte Dunes* opinion as upholding "the award of regulatory takings damages based on a pretextual refusal to accept one development plan after another, when each plan complied with the city's previous demands").

[72] Tahoe-Sierra Preservation Council, Inc. v. Tahoe Reg'l Planning Agency, 535 U.S. 302, 333–34 (2005). Steven Eagle has asserted: "In *Tahoe-Sierra*, a lack of good faith may be evidenced by the fact that TRPA's 1981 plan marked not an interim regulation or a temporary freeze on development of lands belonging to [owners of land surrounding Lake Tahoe], but rather the beginning of a ban on development that has continued through this day. The need for a permanent ban seems to have been obvious from the outset." Eagle, *supra* note 56, at 483. Contrary to Eagle's position, if the need for a permanent ban was indeed obvious

were not for a public use or otherwise were arbitrary, and not to (2) those non-arbitrary actions that served a public use but were undertaken in bad faith from the outset.[73]

For instance, consider a regulatory restriction on private land uses (say, zoning a certain part of town for open space) enacted solely to allow future condemnation at a lower price than the government otherwise would obtain.[74] It is not that the regulation did not serve a public use (it did—open space preservation) or that the regulation was arbitrary (it was not—a zoning restriction is a very rational way to preserve open space). Rather, the problem here is that the government did something that was permissible, but did it in bad faith.[75] This distinction seemingly could allow sincere efforts to alter the meaning of property ownership in accord with evolving community values to continue—and thereby avoid the perpetuation of injustices and ecological degradation furthered by the status quo—while simultaneously protecting, through the Takings Clause's compensation remedy, against the rare instance of targeted bad faith abuses of power.[76]

---

from the outset, enacting such a permanent ban seems to reflect just the type of ongoing, non-compensable updating of ownership norms for which a conception of property grounded in humility calls.

[73] *See* Timothy M. Mulvaney, *Exactions for the Future*, 64 BAYLOR L. REV. 511, 548 (2012) ("[*Lingle's*] elimination of 'substantial advancement' takings claims relegates *most* challenges to the merits of governmental action to the judiciary's substantive due process jurisprudence and the attendant deferential rational basis review.") (emphasis added).

[74] *See, e.g.*, Robertson v. City of Salem, 191 F. Supp. 604, 611 (D. Or. 1961) (concluding that pre-condemnation downzoning to lower cost of acquisition is an "unlawful device to take property for public use without the present payment of just compensation"); Wital Corp. v. Township of Denville, 225 A.2d 139 (1966); Carl M. Freeman Assocs., Inc. v. State Roads Comm'n, 250 A.2d 250 (1969); City of Miami v. Silver, 257 So. 2d 563 (Fla. 1972); Klopping v. City of Whittier, 8 Cal.3d 39 (1972); Dep't of Public Works v. So. Pacific Transp. Co., 33 Cal. App. 3d 960 (1973); Washington Metro. Area Transit Auth. v. One Parcel of Land, 413 F. Supp. 102 (D. Md. 1976); Oceanic Cal., Inc. v. City of San Jose, 497 F. Supp. 962 (N.D. Cal. 1980); Joint Venture, Inc., v. Dep't of Transp., 563 So. 2d 622 (Fla. 1990). For a different though closely related case, consider *Osborn v. City of Cedar Rapids*, in which an Iowa court, prior to *First English*, awarded compensation for a temporary taking after the city had initiated and dropped four condemnation suits to acquire land, then offered to consider rezoning the land in return for a dedication. *See* Osborn v. City of Cedar Rapids, 324 N.W.2d 471 (Iowa 1982).

[75] Determining appropriate evidentiary standards or proxies for divining when indeed the government is acting in bad faith (a burden that this chapter sees as appropriately resting with the person or entity alleging bad faith) is an admittedly difficult challenge that is fodder for future work. (On the difficulties of this challenge, see generally Alan E. Brownstein, *Illicit Legislative Motive in the Municipal Land Use Regulation Process*, 57 U. CINN. L. REV. 1 (1988)). However, suffice it to say here that there are a variety of areas of law in which governmental bad faith seemingly serves as a threshold requirement from which such future work might draw. *See, e.g.*, City of Cleburne v. Cleburne Living Ctr., 473 U.S. 432, 450 (1985) (striking down a permitting scheme found to be based on "an irrational prejudice against the mentally retarded"); Romer v. Evans, 517 U.S. 620, 635 (1996) (striking down a state law that "classifies homosexuals not to further a proper legislative end but to make them unequal to everyone else [because] [a] State cannot so deem a class of persons a stranger to its laws"); United States v. Loud Hawk, 474 U.S. 302, 316 (1986) (asserting that, in speedy trial disputes, the government is responsible for delays attributable to its filing interlocutory appeals in bad faith or with a dilatory motive).

[76] The perspective offered in this chapter aligns to some extent with that offered by Justice Stevens in his *First English* dissent, though Justice Stevens saw the Due Process Clause, not the Takings Clause, as the filter of bad faith action. First English Evangelical Lutheran Church of Glendale v. Los Angeles Cnty., 482 U.S. 304 (1987) (Stevens, J., dissenting). Dissenting in another matter two years prior to *First English*, however,

It admittedly is quite possible, though, that the Takings Clause is not designed to address the narrow class of government actions that, under the proposal herein, would be construed as having been promulgated in bad faith. After all, retroactive compensation for government acts undertaken in bad faith that are later deemed takings and repealed might seem punitive in nature, when the Constitution's "just compensation" requirement is more commonly understood as remedial. And yet, the very idea of retroactive temporary takings compensation as set out in *First English* "punish[es] the well-intentioned…legislature as well as the odious one."[77] To declare all government acts taken in bad faith as immune from takings liability, as some scholars have suggested, sets up the peculiar scenario in which a claimant could have a perfectly viable temporary takings claim under *First English* but for the fact that the government had a nefarious motive from the start. This chapter poses for discussion the possibility of transposing that scenario by insulating from retroactive temporary takings liability those good faith efforts to update property rules in accord with changing times and conditions, while leaving those rare bad faith efforts exposed.

Conclusion

In accord with modern constitutional takings jurisprudence, when a property owner successfully challenges a regulation as a taking and the government chooses to repeal that offending regulation, the government must pay compensation for losses sustained during the period for which the regulation was in effect, regardless of whether that regulation originally was enacted in good faith. This principle places a premium on the stability of ownership interests, which can serve important social aims. However, such a concentration on stability produces social ills, as well, for the very existence of retroactively compensable temporary takings seems sufficient to discourage lawmakers from regulatory innovation not only in the context of climate change—this book's central focus—but in many other contexts as well.

This chapter offers an alternative viewpoint from the one centered on stability. It conceives of property as a social institution of rules that regularly need to be openly and honestly reconsidered in light of changing conditions and changing human values. From

---

Justice Stevens took what might be considered a different approach. He wrote: "We must presume that regulatory bodies…generally make a good faith effort to advance the public interest…but we must also recognize that they will often become involved in controversies that they will ultimately lose. Even though these controversies are costly and temporarily harmful to the private citizen, *as long as* fair procedures are followed, I do not believe there is any basis in the Constitution for characterizing the inevitable byproduct of every such dispute as a 'taking' of private property." Williamson County Reg'l Planning Comm'n v. Hamilton Bank of Johnson City, 473 U.S. 172, 205 (Stevens, J., dissenting) (emphasis added). These words could be interpreted as suggesting that if fair procedures are *not* followed, there *is* a basis in the Constitution for characterizing the byproduct as a taking.

[77] Williams et al., *supra* note 12, at 243.

this viewpoint, it raises the possibility that retroactive temporary takings compensation should be available only in those infrequent cases where a governmental entity enacts the offending regulation in bad faith. In doing so, the chapter acknowledges several potentially significant theoretical, practical, and doctrinal objections to implementation, including (1) the common perspective that the government's intent is irrelevant in takings cases, and (2) the ordinary course of addressing bad faith government conduct under the rubric of the Due Process Clause, not the Takings Clause. The chapter offers preliminary impressions on and possible responses to these objections in the hopes of furthering academic discussion on the matter moving forward.

As addressed in other chapters in this book, the community's understanding of ownership very well may be in—or at least on the precipice of—a transition phase in light of the impacts associated with a changing climate.[78] Given property's social nature, pursuing regulatory innovations in good faith to reflect this transition would seem to be an essential task for lawmakers. To the extent that *First English's* support for the idea of retroactive temporary takings compensation impedes such innovation, the issue deserves a fresh look.

---

[78] *See, e.g.*, Farber, *supra* note 1, at 11–14 ("Climate change will surely affect public attitudes toward land development and property rights."); Eric Freyfogle & Bradley C. Karkkainen, PROPERTY LAW: POWER, GOVERNANCE, AND THE COMMON GOOD 232 (2013) ("each generation can, and probably should, make its own decisions about good land use").

22 Climate Change Adaptation Strategies in New England
Julia B. Wyman

Introduction

The shattered water made a misty din.
Great waves looked over others coming in,
And thought of doing something to the shore
That water never did to land before.
The clouds were low and hairy in the skies,
Like locks blown forward in the gleam of eyes.
You could not tell, and yet it looked as if
The shore was lucky in being backed by cliff,
The cliff in being backed by continent;
It looked as if a night of dark intent
Was coming, and not only a night, an age.
Someone had better be prepared for rage.
There would be more than ocean-water broken
Before God's last Put out the light was spoken.[1]

New England is a densely populated area dependent on the coast and rich in maritime history. The impacts of climate change, such as sea-level rise, increased storm intensity and frequency, and erosion are causing New England municipalities and states to creatively adapt their laws and policies within complex environmental, economic, and political systems. This chapter will explore some of the innovative ways coastal communities and states in New England have adapted, and plan to adapt, to climate change. Many of the climate change impacts that New England is experiencing are similar to the impacts in other parts of the United States and around the world. The pioneering ways that New England has begun to adapt to these changes can provide other states, municipalities, and communities with lessons learned, both successful and not successful, for climate change adaptation.

Section I of this chapter describes some of the historical background on how climate change is impacting coastal New England states. Section II uses case studies as a way to understand the different approaches that communities in coastal New England have recently used for adapting to those climate change impacts. It will do that by breaking down into subsections for the five coastal New England states: Maine, New Hampshire, Massachusetts, Connecticut, and Rhode Island. Each subsection will provide case studies of specific strategies municipalities or states have employed to address climate change impacts.[2] In many cases, these strategies incorporate strategic partnerships

---

[1] ROBERT FROST, ONCE BY THE PACIFIC (1928).

[2] These case studies were documented as part of the Northeast Climate Change Adaptation project, with support from National Oceanic and Atmospheric Administration's (NOAA's) Climate and Societal Interactions Program. The project, led by the Northeast Regional Ocean Council and the Gulf of Maine Council in 2011-2013, supported efforts to: 1) help communities in the Gulf of Maine reduce the vulnerability of their built and natural environment to the effects of sea level rise and/or climate change; and 2) document

among federal, state, municipal, academic, and nongovernmental agency actors, which enable resource sharing to accomplish goals that no one actor could accomplish alone. These strategies often incorporate "working around" existing policies and regulations to accomplish a goal. As discussed at length in other chapters of this book, climate change adaptation law and policy is a fairly new and growing area of law and policy. Many successfully implemented climate change plans and policies have occurred on the municipal and state levels because they were politically possible under existing policies and regulations related to, but not so named, climate change, such as hazard mitigation plans, or coastal zone management plans. Section III of this chapter will provide some recommendations on how other communities can use the lessons learned from these New England communities to better prepare for climate change.

I. Historical Importance of Coastal Communities in New England: How Climate Change Threatens Their Livelihoods

The United States is "a nation intrinsically connected to and immensely reliant on the ocean[,]"[3] and in no place is that more true than New England. New England has a long history of basing its communities on the coasts. Some of the first communities settled in the United States were in New England, and growth there has not slowed. In fact, the Northeast has experienced tremendous growth in housing and resort development and escalated coastal property values in the last century.[4] In addition to population growth, New England has dramatically developed its coastline through the filling of marshes, dredging of channels and harbors, beach renourishment, and construction of jetties, sea walls, and other man-made structures.[5] The increased level of infrastructure on vulnerable land poses a great risk for infrastructure loss, as well as loss of life in New England.

Coastal flooding poses a great threat to coastal communities in New England. Due to its geography, New England is vulnerable to a variety of storms, ranging from frequent "nor'reasters" to less common tropical storms and hurricanes.[6] When storms approach shallow nearshore waters, a storm surge can be generated, causing flooding in low-lying

---

and better understand steps communities are already taking in this direction. All of the work from the project can be found at: http://necca.stormsmart.org/. The author wishes to thank the following partners from the project: Julia Knisel, Massachusetts Office of Coastal Zone Management; Wesley Shaw, Blue Urchin; Roger Stephenson, Stephenson Strategic Communication; Adrianne Harrison, NOAA; Cynthia Krum, Krum Steele Consulting; and David Keeley, The Keeley Group. Research and initial documenting of the case studies was done by the following Rhode Island Sea Grant Law Fellows: Kate Kramer, Kaitlin Sweeney, and Kristen Bonjour.

[3] U.S. COMM'N ON OCEAN POLICY, AN OCEAN BLUEPRINT FOR THE 21ST CENTURY, FINAL REPORT 1 (2004), *available at* http://www.oceancommission.gov.

[4] Peter Frumhoff et al., *Confronting Climate Change in the U.S. Northeast: Science, Impacts, and Solutions* 17 (Union of Concerned Scientists 2007) (synthesis report of the Northeast Climate Impacts Assessment).

[5] *Id.* at 17.

[6] *Id.*

areas.[7] If surges occur during a high tide, or over several tidal cycles, damages can be substantial.[8] In New England, some of the largest cities, such as Boston, are in low-lying coastal areas extremely vulnerable to storm surge and flooding.[9]

To plan for potential damage from storms and flooding, researchers typically have used a benchmark called the "100-year flood" that predicts a frequency and magnitude of potential storms.[10] The 100-year flood represents a historical average and may no longer be an accurate way to predict storm surges. In New England, storm surges have occurred in intervals much shorter than 100 years.[11] Substantial changes in coastal flooding in New England are already documented.[12] Furthermore, as discussed earlier in this book, a warming climate also impacts storm activity. The warmer sea surface temperatures that brew "fiercer storms" and hurricane intensity have already been observed in the North Atlantic Ocean.[13]

Chapter nineteen discusses the role of federalism and the importance of the Coastal Zone Management Act (CZMA) in the management of the nation's coastal areas. The nation's coastal zone management has a long history rooted in the public trust doctrine.[14] The incorporation of the public trust doctrine within the states of the nation recognizes the importance of states in managing the precious resources of the coasts. The Supreme Court has recognized the need for this delegation to the states, noting, "[g]reat caution…is necessary in applying precedents in one State to cases arising in another."[15] Each state within New England has evolved its interpretation of the public trust doctrine over time to best serve the needs of its jurisdiction. The CZMA provides the authority for the states to manage the coastal zone, and the federal government, "recognizing that most adaptation occurs at the local level,"[16] provides several financial incentives to state and local governments that are taking affirmative measures to adapt to the reality of climate change.

Because municipalities are also playing a critical role in climate change policy, this chapter focuses on the legal relationship between state and municipal government and the unique measures that local governments are employing to adapt to climate change. "Not only are municipal governments the first responders when disasters strike but their state legislatures have delegated to them the principal legal authority to determine how much and what type of development may be built in disaster-prone areas."[17] The selected

---

[7] *Id.*

[8] *Id.*

[9] *Id.*

[10] *Id.* at 18.

[11] *Id.*

[12] *Id.*

[13] David Archer, The Long Thaw: How Humans Are Changing the Next 100,000 Years of Earth's Climate, 31, 34 (2010).

[14] *See* Julia B. Wyman, *In States we Trust: The Importance of the Preservation of the Public Trust Doctrine in the Wake of Climate Change*, 35 Vt. L. Rev. 507 (2010).

[15] Shively v. Bowlby, 152 U.S. 1, 26 (1894).

[16] Climate Change Adaptation Task Force, Federal Actions For A Climate Resilient Nation 2 (2011), *available at* http://www.whitehouse.gov/sites/default/files/microsites/ceq/2011_adaptation_progress_report.pdf.

[17] John R. Nolon, *Disaster Mitigation through Land Use Strategies*, 23 Pace Envtl. L. Rev. 959, 963 (2006).

municipal strategies examined in this chapter provide useful examples to inform the discussion of local adaptation. These examples demonstrate the importance of collaboration among municipal, state, and federal actors, as well as the importance of academic and nongovernmental agency partners.

II. Case Studies of Innovative Approaches to Climate Change Adaptation in Coastal New England

The following case studies represent some of the innovative ways coastal communities in New England are adapting to climate change. The case studies will explore how individual municipalities are adapting to climate change, how some municipalities are partnering with other municipalities to address climate change impacts, and even how municipalities across state lines are leveraging funds and resources to creatively approach climate change impacts.

A. MAINE

Maine has 3,478 miles of tidal shoreline.[18] Studies have shown that components of Maine's coastal sand dunes systems, coastal wetlands, and coastal eroding bluffs may see significant coastal erosion and inundation based on historic rates of sea-level change, irrespective of accelerated rates due to climate change.[19] Maine has taken a proactive approach to examining the impacts climate change is having, and will continue to have, on its state, and the legal and policy approaches that can best assist the state in diminishing impacts. In 2009, the state of Maine conducted a study on the impacts of climate change on its transportation system.[20] Also in a statewide effort, in 2010 the Department of Environmental Protection conducted a stakeholder-based process to evaluate and prepare communities for likely climate change impacts.[21] A report, *People and Nature Adapting to Climate Change: Charting Maine's Course*, was released as a result of the study.[22] Changes in administration and the state's climate policy have curtailed many statewide efforts.[23] The following case studies will explore some of the statewide efforts and local efforts that have led to the current state of adaptation in Maine today.

---

[18] United States Census Bureau, *Statistical Abstract of the United States* (2010), *available at* http://www.census.gov/compendia/statab/2012/tables/12s0364.pdf.

[19] *See generally* JOSEPH KELLEY, ET AL., LIVING WITH THE COAST OF MAINE (1989).

[20] Me. Dep't of Transp. Envtl. Office, Climate Change and Transportation in Maine, Oct. 14, 2009, *available at* http://www.maine.gov/mdot/env/documents/pdf/ClimateChangeandTransportationinMaine-Final.pdf; *see also* http://www.georgetownclimate.org/resources/climate-change-and-transportation-in-maine.

[21] Me. Dep't of Envtl. Prot., People and Nature Adapting to a Changing Climate, Charting Maine's Course (2010) (124th Me. Legislature), *available at* http://umaine.edu/maineclimatenews/files/2011/06/NAT_003_Booklet_6_forWeb_Single.pdf.

[22] *Id.*

[23] *Id.*

1. Anticipatory Planning for Sea-Level Rise along the Coast of Maine

This case study examines a report of Maine's first systematic assessment of its vulnerability to a change in shoreline position as a result of accelerated sea-level rise associated with global climate change, which was published in 1995.[24] The study assesses the state's vulnerability and identifies options for the state to consider as an anticipatory response strategy for climate change in Maine.

The study was prepared as a state-university cooperative project and was funded by a grant from the United States Environmental Protection Agency's Climate Change Division to the Maine State Planning Office.[25] A common theme throughout state vulnerability assessments is partnerships: federal, state, municipal, academia, and nongovernmental organizations. The partnerships allow for shared resources, maximizing the use of limited funding, staffing, and expertise within each sector.

The study examines projected rates of sea-level rise and current planning underway for it in the state of Maine, specific scenarios for vulnerability assessment, policy response options for sea-level rise, and associated legal considerations.[26] Geologists and climate modelers have been able to verify the sea-level has continued to gradually rise in all of Maine's major coastal municipalities during the past fifty years.[27] A continuation of sea-level rise places many shoreline properties in jeopardy from coastal erosion and inundation.[28]

Using a range of sea-level rise scenarios derived from national studies to assess vulnerability to projected changes in shoreline position, the study focuses on study sites within Casco Bay and Saco Bay, with three different environmental settings: salt marshes, bluffs, and sand beaches.[29] The study analyzes possible adaptive response strategies the state might adopt to mitigate the negative impacts of a change in shoreline position and associated impacts of global climate change.[30] The study analyzes possible adaptive response strategies from several different angles:

- The relative costs and benefits of selected preliminary response strategies for one specific case study area;
- The responsiveness of existing state and federal laws and policies to address the most significant negative impacts on coastal resources identified by the vulnerability assessment;

---

[24] Envtl. Prot. Agency, *Anticipatory Planning for Sea Level Rise Along the Coast of Maine* (1995), *available at* http://papers.risingsea.net/federal_reports/maine_0.pdf. The report was a joint effort in cooperation with State of Maine's State Planning Office. It was one of the first studies of its kind in New England.

[25] *Id.*

[26] *Id.*

[27] *Id.* at Summary-1.

[28] *Id.*

[29] *Id.* at Summary-3.

[30] *Id.*

- The legal considerations for Maine's policy response, including potential legal challenges to regulatory tools; and
- Approaches already adopted or evaluated by other states for coastal erosion or coastal hazard mitigation.[31]

The report of the study makes two major recommendations: (1) the state should protect and strengthen the ability of natural systems to adjust to changes in shoreline position; and (2) the state should prevent new development that is likely to interfere with the ability of natural systems to adjust to changes in shoreline position.[32] The report also recommends that the state: (1) make concrete anticipatory policies and design standards to guide public investment, (2) create specific planning and regulatory policies, and (3) explore longer-range strategic assessment, research, and educational actions.[33]

2. York, Maine: Climate Change Impacts on Economic Activity

Communities throughout New England are seeing economic impacts due to climate change. The nation relies on coastal counties for more than 40 percent of the nation's economic output.[34] Maine is no exception in its economic reliance on the coasts: an estimated 60 percent of Maine's GDP can be linked to marine-related businesses, including tourism, fisheries, and shipbuilding.[35] When coastal communities are impacted by climate change, their economies suffer.

To examine the possible consequences of sea-level rise and coastal storm damage on the economies of communities in Maine most likely to be vulnerable, a study looked to the county of York, Maine.[36] York County Coast is one of the coastal areas most vulnerable to impacts of climate change; it is comprised of nine towns: Kittery, York, Ogunquit, Wells, Kennebunk, Kennebunkport, Biddeford, Saco, and Old Orchard Beach.[37] In 2006, the communities generated $1.5 billion in wages.[38]

In order to understand the potential economic changes in Maine from climate change, this study explored four different effects: changed outputs (referring to change in what is produced in Maine), changed opportunities (reflecting that efforts to adapt to and mitigate climate change will create new opportunities for economic activities in Maine),

---

[31] *Id.* at Summary-7.

[32] *Id.* at Summary-11-13.

[33] *Id.*

[34] Judith Kildow Et Al., National Ocean Economics Program, State of the U.S. Ocean and Coastal Economies 15 (2009).

[35] NOAA Coastal Services Center, *NOAA Report on Ocean and Great Lakes Economy of the United States* 42 (2012), *available at* http://www.csc.noaa.gov/digitalcoast/_/pdf/econreport.pdf.

[36] Charles S. Colgan & Samuel B. Merrill, *The Effects of Climate Change on Economic Activity in Maine: Coastal York County Case Study*, 17 Me. Pol'y Rev. 2, 66, 67 2008), *available at* http://efc.muskie.usm.maine.edu/docs/effects_of_clim_change_on_eco_activity.pdf.

[37] *Id.* at 71.

[38] *Id.* at 72.

changed costs, and changed perceptions of time and risk (referring to the fundamental economic problem of how to assess the costs and benefits of different actions to mitigate climate change and to adapt to it).[39]

The hazards to Maine's economy from climate change are real, but are still largely unknown. A better understanding of the risks of climate change to peoples' livelihoods and property is a vital part of preparing the way for effective action. A better understanding of the risks, probabilities, and vulnerabilities of climate change on the economy in Maine will be important as the state moves forward with adaptation efforts.[40]

3. Sea-Level Rise Adaptation Working Group Action Plan

In 2009, the Saco Bay Sea Level Adaptation Working Group (SLAWG) was created to develop and implement regional climate change adaptation strategies to respond to rising sea levels and to become more resilient to coastal storms.[41] The purpose of the SLAWG is to review information from the Coastal Hazard Resiliency Tools Project that has analyzed the problem of sea-level rise, to create a Vulnerability Assessment for Saco Bay, and to develop and implement an Action Plan of implementation strategies for regional solutions.[42] Currently, the SLAWG has completed its initial versions of a Vulnerability Assessment and Action Plan.[43]

The Action Plan lists several implementation strategies and objectives, including but not limited to:

1. Use regional approaches to plan for improvements;
2. Create a ranking process and prioritize a list of potential sea-level adaptation, construction, and conservation projects;
3. Comment on dune restoration;
4. Recommend the standardizing of floodplain management standards and building code interpretations;
5. Recommend standardizing ordinance review standards;
6. Complement the efforts of the Towns and Cities that participate in the FEMA Risk Map program by sharing relevant information already generated by SLAWG projects;

---

[39] *Id.*

[40] *Id.*

[41] Sea Level Adaptation Working Group, *Sea Level Rise and Potential Impacts by the Year 2100: A Vulnerability Assessment for the Saco Bay Communities of Biddeford, Saco, Old Orchard Beach, and Scarborough* (2001), *available at* http://www.sacomaine.org/departments/boards/slawg-vulnerability.pdf.

[42] *Id.* at 2.

[43] *Id.*

7. Coordinate stormwater planning programs with EPA and DEP requirements; and

8. Monitor changes to statutes, regulations, and ordinances affecting permitting of improvements.[44]

Many adaptation efforts in New England involve more than one state. The next case study is an example of how some tools for climate change adaptation are best examined across more than one state.

4. Sea-Level Rise and Storm Surge Adaptation Analysis via COAST (Coastal Adaptation to Sea Level Rise Tool)

An example of successful collaboration by numerous partners and states for climate change adaptation is *Coast in Action: 2012 Projects from Maine and New Hampshire*.[45] The comprehensive report was prepared for EPA's Climate Ready Estuaries Program in collaboration with Casco Bay Estuary Partnership and Piscataqua Region Estuaries Partnership.[46] The report focuses on Hampton and Seabrook, New Hampshire, and Portland, Maine, where climate change adaptation processes are underway, but stand to be greatly enhanced by their use of the Coastal Adaptation to Sea Level Rise Tool (COAST).[47] The primary objective of the COAST project is to furnish support for climate change adaptation planning processes in the cities by providing visual, numeric, narrative, and presentation-based products based on the COAST decision-support tool.[48] It is anticipated these products will increase support for processes underway and represent specific actions to be evaluated.[49]

COAST was developed to enable local governments to address the rising threat of sea-level rise and storm surge.[50] The technique projects polygons representing hypothesized extreme weather events on top of vulnerable economic assets.[51] Using economic data, climate projections, and depth-damage functions developed by the U.S. Army Corps of Engineers, COAST can present the total economic loss for specific severe weather event scenarios.[52] The program gives a "birds-eye" view in a three-dimensional perspective of both lost structural value and lost content value.[53] The tool does not advocate for one adaptation method over another but rather serves as a mechanism

---

[44] *Id.*

[45] Samuel Merrill et al., *Coast in Action: 2012 Projects from Maine and New Hampshire*, New England Envtl. Fin. Ctr. Series Rep. No. 12-05, (2012), *available at* http://www.cascobay.usm.maine.edu/pdfs/cre_coast_final_report.pdf.

[46] *Id.*

[47] *Coast in Action, supra* note 45, at 4.

[48] *Id.*

[49] *Id.*

[50] *Id.*

[51] *Id.*

[52] *Id.*

[53] *Coast in Action, supra* note 45, at 4.

to spur conversations and enable public process to decide which adaptation, if any, is appropriate.[54] For successful climate change adaptation methods, providing numerous science-based options is a strong strategy to address the numerous policies and regulations that may be in effect in a municipality or a state. A state or municipality can then choose what method of adaptation works best in its community, weighing practical, economic, and political factors.

Public stakeholder meetings are an important part of educating stakeholders in the process of climate change adaptation. To this end, in May 2011, a conference on sea-level rise was held in Portland, Maine, along with several meetings of the city council's Energy, Environment, and Sustainability Committee.[55] The conference allowed stakeholder groups to examine potential impacts of sea-level rise and storm surge on the coastal city of Portland, Maine, if no climate change adaptation action is taken, and to identify possible stimulations on sea-level rise thresholds and storm surge frequencies.[56] This dramatically increased public support for a city-wide sea-level rise planning process through the use of visualizations and stimulations of sea-level rise possibilities.[57]

Similarly, in New Hampshire, an adaptation workgroup (NH CAW) has conducted pilot adaptation planning and training efforts since 2009.[58] The NH CAW group consists of stakeholders preparing for climate change impacts on the seacoast of New Hampshire.

Both communities and stakeholders are examining potential impacts of sea-level rise and storm surge if no action is taken, specifically the costs and benefits of specific actions they might take to protect vulnerable assets they have prioritized.[59] Demonstrating a distinct positive economic relationship to proactive climate change adaptation can be an extremely useful tool for communities and stakeholders seeking to promote adaptation and climate change education.

The communities are also identifying appropriate time horizons, sea-level rise thresholds, and storm surge frequencies' and intensities to simulate.[60] The identification is being done by securing data, conducting cost-benefit analyses, and providing interpretation of avoided costs associated with adaptation action being considered.[61] Through 3D visualizations of avoided costs and multi-decade tallies of expected damage, practical steps in planning processes are being discussed.[62]

---

[54] Id.

[55] Id.

[56] Id.

[57] Id.

[58] Id.

[59] Coast in Action, supra note 45, at 4.

[60] Id.

[61] Id.

[62] Id.

Through the examination and visualizations conducted under this project, including cost-benefit analysis, the stakeholder groups can identify possible practical steps to be taken to forward their adaptation planning processes.[63]

B. NEW HAMPSHIRE

New Hampshire has the smallest amount of coastline of any state in the nation (131 tidal shoreline miles[64]), yet it has been proactive in protecting those areas. In 2009, The New Hampshire Climate Change Policy Task Force released a Climate Action Plan that addressed both mitigation and adaptation.[65] The following are examples of planning and action currently underway in New Hampshire for climate change adaptation.

1. Adaptation Strategies to Protect Areas of Increased Risk from Coastal Flooding due to Climate Change: Seabrook, New Hampshire

New Hampshire is facing many of the same threats other coastal states in New England are facing from climate change: increased sea-level rise, increased storm intensity and frequency, and erosion.[66] The 2005 Natural Hazard Mitigation Plan for the Town of Seabrook identified flooding as the primary hazard threat in the town.[67] Seabrook is a relatively flat town: 95 percent of its land is less than sixty feet above sea level.[68] Additionally, tidal wetlands constitute 30 percent of the land, approximately 1,734 acres, the largest wetlands area in New Hampshire.[69]

In 2009, The Rockingham Planning Commission, one of nine regional planning commissions in New Hampshire, received funds from the town of Seabrook and the New Hampshire Coastal Program to develop adaptation strategies to examine flooding threats and protect areas of town at risk.[70] The project sought to: (1) research the estimates of sea-level rise affecting the New England coast, (2) look to the approaches taken by other states and communities to respond to climate change threats, (3) create maps

---

[63] *Id.*

[64] *United States Census, supra* note 18.

[65] N.H. Climate Change Policy Task Force, The N.H. Climate Change Action Plan, a Plan for N.H.'s Energy, Envtl. and Econ. Dev. Future (2009), *available at* http://www.georgetownclimate.org/resources/new-hampshire-climate-action-plan-a-plan-for-new-hampshires-energy-environmental-and-econo; *see also* http://des.nh.gov/organization/divisions/air/tsb/tps/climate/action_plan/nh_climate_action_plan.htm.

[66] *N.H. Climate Change Action Plan, supra* note 65.

[67] Rockingham Planning Commission, *Adaptation Strategies to Protect Areas of Increased Risk From Coastal Flooding Due to Climate Change: Seabrook, NH* (2009), *available at* http://des.nh.gov/organization/divisions/water/wmb/coastal/documents/seabrook_adaptation.pdf.

[68] *Id.* at 4.

[69] *Id.*

[70] *Adaptation Strategies, supra* note 67, at 1.

identifying areas of increased flood risk to Seabrook based on the information gathered, and (4) identify regulatory and non-regulatory options for the town to consider for adaptation.[71]

To create flood risk maps and land use recommendations for Seabrook, the Commission looked to Miami-Dade County, Florida, and the state of Rhode Island, two locations that had already adopted similar maps and land use recommendations for their coastal areas.[72] The Commission also collected elevation data from the U.S. Army Corps of Engineers and LiDAR (Light Detection and Ranging, imaging used to generate high resolution vertical terrain data) to create an accurate and detailed digital elevation map of Seabrook. Five maps of this data were included in the final report.[73]

The Commission also considered policy options, including regulatory recommendations, non-regulatory recommendations, and emergency management and hazard mitigation recommendations.[74]

2. Examining Floodplain Maps in Coastal New Hampshire

A study conducted by The National Sea Grant Law Center Grants Program at the University of Mississippi (NSGLC) and the Vermont Law School Land Use Clinic (VLS) examined the use of new floodplain maps in coastal communities in New Hampshire by exploring legal authority, measures, and possible consequences associated with their use based on current and projected land use patterns and precipitation amounts.[75] To respond to rising costs related to flooding in New Hampshire, the National Oceanic and Atmospheric Administration (NOAA) funded a team led by the University of New Hampshire (UNH) to develop new floodplain maps for the Lamprey River watershed in southeastern New Hampshire.[76] The primary objective of the study by NSGLC and VLS was to provide legal research and analysis to address legal issues relating to whether local governments can and should apply UNH's new flood mapping information to plan for projected environmental conditions.[77] To accomplish that objective, the study examined four potential legal challenges related to: (1) municipal liability, (2) enabling authority, (3) the use of climate maps as evidence, and (4) takings.[78] The study provided recommendations based on these four areas.

Legal and policy research such as the NSGLC and VLS study can be vital in assisting municipalities assess their options for climate change adaptation. Having information

---

[71] *Id.*

[72] *Id.* at 3.

[73] *Id.*

[74] *Id.*

[75] Vermont Law School Land Use Clinic, *New Floodplain Maps for a Coastal New Hampshire Watershed and Questions of Legal Authority, Measures and Consequences* (2012), *available at* http://100yearfloods.org/resources/pdf/2012_VermontLawSchool_LampreyRiverReport.pdf.

[76] *Id.* at 6.

[77] *Id.*

[78] *Id.* at 8. The study examined five primary questions: (1) What is the potential liability of government, particularly of the municipalities within the Lamprey River watershed, if it fails to take steps to reduce the vulnerability of its landowners and other citizens to the risk of flood and storm damage as revealed by

on applicable laws, policies, and regulations, laid out in a clear, concise manner, can assist municipalities in determining what their best options are for action, and increase community comfort with those actions.

3. Portsmouth Coastal Resilience Initiative

The Gulf of Maine Council on the Marine Environment (GOMC) and the Northeast Regional Ocean Council (NROC) funded a project that allows the City of Portsmouth, New Hampshire, to advance local efforts to adapt land use, infrastructure, policies, and programs to reduce the vulnerability of the built and natural environment to changing environmental conditions.[79] The project report, released in 2013, suggests how to integrate these adaptation strategies into city-wide plans, regulations, and policies.[80] Specifically, the report details how the city can update its Master Plan, building codes, and capital improvement plan.[81] The report allows decision-makers, planners, and the public to have access to new information on adapting to changing environmental conditions due to climate change.

GOMC and NROC funded the study because Portsmouth's location makes the city particularly vulnerable to certain weather events. The city has a high likelihood of experiencing hurricanes and other high-wind events as well as severe winter weather.[82] As a coastal community on an estuary, Portsmouth is highly vulnerable to storm surges and high tides.[83] Increased intensity and frequency of coastal storms and sea-level rise has the potential to result in extensive property damage and costly repairs for the city, as well as residents and businesses. Of particular concern is the potential for irreplaceable historic property loss in the city's Historic District, portions of which are located in high hazard areas.[84]

UNH's research efforts and mapping information?; (2) What legal and policy approaches may communities in the Lamprey River basin adopt to reduce the risks to property owners and other citizens in the expanded flood hazard area as revealed by the new floodplain maps?; (3) Do New Hampshire communities have the legal authority under the state planning and zoning enabling legislation, or other state legislation, to design and implement regulatory controls based on current and predicted environmental conditions, specifically projected flooding levels?; (4) What legal standard of scientific and technical reliability must planners and other local officials meet in order to support regulatory measures that are based on current and future—as opposed to past—environmental conditions?; (5) What is the potential regulatory takings exposure of New Hampshire communities if they impose regulatory controls that are designed at least in part to address anticipated future environmental conditions?

[79] Rockingham Planning Commission, *Climate Change Vulnerability Assessment and Adaptation Plan* (2013), *available at* http://www.planportsmouth.com/cri/CRI-Report.pdf.

[80] *Id.*

[81] *Id.*

[82] *Id.*

[83] *Id.*

[84] *Id.*

C. MASSACHUSETTS SOUTH SHORE

Massachusetts has 1,519 miles of tidal shoreline.[85] Massachusetts has been one of the most proactive states in the nation regarding coastal climate change planning. The Massachusetts Office of Coastal Zone Management (CZM), part of the Executive Office of Energy and Environmental Affairs (EEA), is responsible for managing the Massachusetts coastline.[86] CZM developed the Massachusetts Ocean Plan, released on December 31, 2009, in response to a requirement by the 2008 Oceans Act for EEA to develop a comprehensive ocean management plan.[87] The Plan "provides protections for critical marine habitat and natural resources in the Commonwealth's waters and sets standards for the development of offshore renewable energy, as well as for other infra-structure, to foster sustainable uses in the state's ocean waters."[88] Every five years, EEA must review and update the plan; in January 2013, CZM began the review and update process.[89] CZM also developed the StormSmart Coasts program, a national model to help communities and homeowners address climate change issues such as coastal erosion, flooding, and storm damage.[90] Statewide, Massachusetts has also released several reports related to climate change: in 2007, *Preparing for the Storm: Recommendations for Management of Risk from Coastal Hazards in Massachusetts*;[91] in 2010, *Climate Change and Massachusetts Fish and Wildlife Reports*; and in 2011, the *Massachusetts Climate Change Adaptation Report*.[92] Most recently, in December 2013, Massachusetts released a report, *Sea-Level Rise: Understanding and Applying Trends and Future Scenarios for Analysis and Planning*.[93] In addition to many statewide efforts, Massachusetts is approaching climate change on the municipal level as well. The following case study explores some of those efforts.

The towns of Marshfield, Duxbury, and Scituate are located south of Boston along Massachusetts Bay.[94] In the aggregate, they span across twenty-five miles of the

---

[85] *United States Census Bureau, supra* note 18.

[86] Mass. Office of Coastal Zone Mgmt., *available at* http://www.mass.gov/eea/agencies/czm/.

[87] *See* M.G.L.A. 10, § 35HH; *see also* Mass. Exec. Office of Energy and Envtl. Affairs, *Mass. Ocean Plan, avail-able at* http://www.mass.gov/eea/waste-mgmt-recycling/coasts-and-oceans/mass-ocean-plan/.

[88] *Mass. Ocean Plan, supra* note 87.

[89] *See generally* Mass. Office of Coastal Zone Mgmt., *available at* http://www.mass.gov/eea/agencies/czm/.

[90] *Id. See also* Storm Smart Coasts, *available at* http://stormsmartcoasts.org/.

[91] Georgetown Climate Center, *available at* http://www.georgetownclimate.org/node/3324?page=1.

[92] *Id.*

[93] *Id. See also* Mass. Office of Coastal Zone Mgmt., *Sea Level Rise: Understanding and Applying Trends and Future Scenarios for Analysis and Planning* (2013), *available at* http://www.mass.gov/eea/docs/czm/stormsmart/slr-guidance-2013.pdf.

[94] Metropolitan Area Planning Council, *South Shore Coastal Hazards Adaptation Study* (2001), *available at* http://www.mapc.org/sites/default/files/FINAL_South_Shore_Coastal_Adaptation_Planning_Report_12-31-11_sm.pdf, 5. This case study appears as part of the Northeast Climate Change Adaptation project, *available at* http://necca.stormsmart.org/. It was researched and drafted by Rhode Island Sea Grant Law Fellow, Kate Kramer, under the supervision of Rhode Island Sea Grant Legal Program staff attorney, Julia Wyman.

shoreline.[95] At present, each of the towns has some form of coastal protection structures along its shoreline, such as bulkheads, sea walls, revetments, or jetties.[96] The purpose of the structures is to protect public and private property along, and in the vicinity of, the coastline.[97] However, due to weather impacts and natural processes, the structures are in varying states of decline.[98] In 2006, it was estimated that to bring the structures up to "excellent condition" from "fair/poor condition," it would cost 57.8 million dollars.[99] Climate change is predicted to not only have an impact on sea-level rise, but also on stronger and more frequent storms, such as hurricanes and nor'easters. As a result, sea-level rise in the towns of Duxbury, Marshfield, and Scituate is estimated to increase by one to three feet by the end of this century.[100]

In 2011, the towns of Marshfield, Duxbury, and Scituate, along with the Metropolitan Area Planning Council and CZM, completed a climate change adaptation study to examine coastal hazard impacts that could occur as a result of climate change.[101] Importantly, the study fostered partnership among the three towns, the Council, and the state, allowing for regional perspectives to be incorporated into local planning for these impacts.[102] The four main goals for the study were:

- Identify current and potential future coastal hazards;
- Identify adaptation strategies;
- Identify funding options to support adaptation; and
- Hold a public workshop to report the findings and receive public feedback.[103]

In examining coastal hazards, the study identified those that could occur as a result of climate change.[104] One of the coastal hazards identified as highly likely to occur was coastal flooding and storm surges.[105] The study found that changes in the shoreline width and erosion are more likely to occur.[106] Additionally, the study found rising sea level will lead to the potential loss of critical habitat coastal marsh because adjacent human land uses and coastal structures may prevent the coastal marsh from naturally moving inland.[107]

---

[95] *Id.*

[96] *Id.*

[97] *Id.*

[98] *Id.*

[99] *Id* .

[100] *South Shore Coastal Hazards, supra* note 94.

[101] *Id.* at 4.

[102] *Id.*

[103] *Id.*

[104] *Id.*

[105] *Id.*

[106] *South Shore Coastal Hazards, supra* note 94, at 4.

[107] *Id.*

In identifying adaptation strategies, the strategies were classified into three major categories: protect, accommodate, or retreat.[108] Adaptation strategies were further evaluated for the built environment, infrastructure protection, natural resources, and outreach and education.[109]

Concerning the built environment, the towns focused on protecting existing development and infrastructure, enabling safe access for homeowners and emergency response, and minimizing the loss of life, destruction of property, and environmental damage.[110] The towns further broke the adaptation strategies into four options: land acquisition, regulation, building guidelines, and flood proofing.[111]

First, the towns could acquire land that is vulnerable to sea-level rise by purchasing it from private property owners. Once purchased, the land would be cleared and development on the property would no longer be allowed. However, the land could be used for a public park or wildlife refuge.

Second, regulations were identified as a good means to impose more stringent setback requirements, designed to allow natural erosion and accretion of beaches to occur, and to protect the built environment. Setbacks assist in protecting the built environment because they allow sediments and nutrients to be effectively removed and for waterbodies to adjust and maintain equilibrium.

Third, development and building guidelines in the towns could be amended to require redevelopment proposals that consider possible climate change impacts. Additionally, changes to zoning maps and existing floodplain zones were also identified as a means to protect the built environment.

Fourth, establishing minimum building design standards for development in floodplain zones that are consistent with Federal Emergency Management Agency (FEMA) guidelines is an accommodation method that may be adopted. Examples of standards include: (1) raising the elevation of the lowest floor by two feet above the base flood elevation, (2) using walls that are impermeable to flood waters, and (3) ensuring that all utilities and sanitary facilities are located above the base flood elevation and are enclosed by watertight walls.

Adaptation strategies to protect infrastructure such as septic systems, sewer lines, waste water treatment facilities, and transportation systems were also identified. Concerns were discussed regarding allowing new coastal engineered structures that armor shorelines because the structures, such as sea walls, restrict the movement of sand and cause beach erosion. However, the study pointed out that there is a need to repair

---

[108] *Id.* For more information on these adaptation strategies, see James Titus, *EPA Climate Ready Estuaries, Rolling Easements* (2011), *available at* http://water.epa.gov/type/oceb/cre/upload/rollingeasementsprimer.pdf.

[109] *Id.*

[110] *Id.*

[111] *Id.*

existing structures to protect existing buildings and public infrastructures such as roads, water mains, and sewer lines.

To protect sewer and septic systems, planning and monitoring of the systems should occur. To protect drinking water, the adoption of a long-term integrated water management plan that entails additional filtering and treatment systems and building protection walls around treatment facilities was identified as critical. Additionally, protection of low-lying transportation facilities was also identified as an important aspect of adaptation planning. Adapting these facilities will likely include changes that maintain their function as access points while reducing their impacts on nearby water resources, such as marshes, that are assets during storm events.

The study recommended preserving green space and protecting water resources such as wetlands and the shoreline. Some ways to achieve this preservation and protection is for towns to amend their wetland bylaws to take into account rising sea level and climate change, and restore wetlands by removing structures and redesigning impediments to tidal flow.

Furthermore, shoreline management strategies should be implemented to accept an increase in sea-level elevation and storm surges, including beach nourishment, planting of dune grasses, marsh creation, and planting of submerged aquatic vegetation. Last, town regulations can also be changed to create a conservancy district, rolling easements, and land acquisition opportunities.

Education and outreach is important. One implementation strategy for this goal is organizing stakeholder meetings. Groups that should be invited to the meetings include municipal groups, residents, local businesses, real estate agents, developers/engineers, and neighboring cities and towns.

Several sources of funding for the town projects were identified, including FEMA and state grants, and other state funding. Additionally, by reviewing and improving their floodplain management program activities, towns will help lower flood insurance premium rates for both public and private property.

In October 2011, a public workshop about climate change adaptation was held for town officials and residents of the Massachusetts' towns of Marshfield, Duxbury, and Scituate. It provided the opportunity for the study to be shared with stakeholders, to increase public awareness about climate change, and to receive community feedback on the planning process.

The study helped to trigger further efforts to adapt to climate change in coastal locations. For example, each of the three towns has taken steps to amend regulations to reflect climate change adaptation. For example, Scituate has included a 100-year flood elevation plus an additional one-foot of free board in its wetlands regulations.[112] Duxbury's wetlands regulations now include performance standards for Land Subject

---

[112] Town of Scituate, Code of Bylaws, Section 30770, S.W.R. 10.02(1)(g), *available at* http://www.maccweb. org/bylaws/scituate_regs.pdf.

to Coastal Storm Flowage (LSCSF).[113] The performance standards include preventing adverse or cumulative effects, protecting wildlife habitat, and preventing pollution. The regulations prohibit new construction or placement of new structures and septic systems within defined "Resource Areas," including any freshwater or coastal wetland areas. Additionally, the public workshop that was held not only further informed the public about climate change adaptation, but it also educated the towns about the level of public knowledge about the issue.

D. NEW HAVEN, CONNECTICUT

Connecticut has 618 miles of tidal shoreline.[114] Connecticut has several statewide climate change mitigation and adaptation efforts. Notably, the 2007 *State of Connecticut Natural Hazards Mitigation Plan 2007–2010*, the 2007 *The Green Plan—Guiding Land Acquisition and Protection in Connecticut 2007–2012*, the 2009 *Facing Our Future—Adapting to Connecticut's Changing Climate*, the 2010 *Natural Hazard Mitigation Plan Update*, and the 2011 *Connecticut Climate Change Preparedness Plan* all address aspects of climate change adaptation.[115] The following case study is an example of how Connecticut is also addressing climate change adaptation on a local level.

In 2011, New Haven revised its Natural Hazard Mitigation Plan, reassessing the vulnerabilities of the municipality and naming recommendations for changes for the town to make.[116] The Plan will be updated every five years in accordance with the federal regulations in order to gain access to grant money.[117] The Plan has implemented regulations and ordinances to protect most vulnerable areas in the city.[118] The city has also increased its drainage system maintenance to decrease inland flooding.[119]

New Haven has recognized that the Plan is a great tool to connect town departments, nongovernmental actors, and constituents for planning and issue spotting related to hazards.[120] The Plan is also essential to qualify for funding from any federal grants.[121] City planners in New Haven also recognize that zoning can be a useful tool for hazard

---

[113] Duxbury Wetland Regulations, 19.0, *available at* http://www.town.duxbury.ma.us/public_documents/DuxburyMA_Conservation/BylawsRegulations/r&rfinaldraft2006.pdf.

[114] *United States Census Bureau, supra* note 18.

[115] *Georgetown Climate Center, supra* note 91.

[116] City of New Haven, *Natural Hazard Mitigation Plan Update* (2011), *available at* http://www.cityofnewhaven.com/cityplan/pdfs/HazardMitigation/Final%20Draft.pdf. This case study appears as part of the *Northeast Climate Climate Change Adaptation Project, available at* http://necca.stormsmart.org/. It was researched and drafted by Rhode Island Sea Grant Law Fellow, Kaitlyn Sweeney, under the supervision of Rhode Island Sea Grant Legal Program staff attorney, Julia Wyman.

[117] *Id.* at 1-1.

[118] *Id.*

[119] *Id.*

[120] *Id.*

[121] *Id.*

planning; however, it is a long-term instrument, and there are other immediate actions that need to be taken for New Haven to adapt to the current climate changes.[122] Recently, New Haven was impacted by Hurricane Irene, which demonstrated that sea walls and other naturalized measures that were implemented in the town could not withstand the force of a severe storm.[123] Alternative measures are being examined to deal with the extensive rivers and estuaries the city has, which contribute to coastal and inland flooding.[124]

New Haven's governmental structure is a mayor-council form of government.[125] The city departments play a role in implementing the Hazard Mitigation plan, including the New Haven office of Energy Management; Chief Administrator's office; City Plan Department; Engineering Department/Public Works; and Department of Parks, Recreation, and Trees.[126] The Chief Administrator's Office coordinates the interdepartmental activities of the City's agencies.[127] The City Plan department facilitates the physical development of the city, and is directly involved in the hazard mitigation through implementation of appropriate zoning and planning.[128] By coordinating numerous city departments, the Plan has been an effective tool for sharing information and lessons learned, and unifying city-wide systems.

E. NEW SHOREHAM, RHODE ISLAND

Rhode Island, the Ocean State, has 384 miles of tidally influenced shoreline.[129] In 2010, Rhode Island established a Climate Change Commission to study the projected impacts of climate change on Rhode Island.[130] Additionally, in 2011, Rhode Island amended its Comprehensive Planning and Land Use Regulation Act to include new requirements for community comprehensive plans, including natural hazards identification.[131] Furthermore, Rhode Island is currently engaged in a Shoreline Change Special Area Management Plan under the CZMA, or "Beach SAMP," to prepare a state management plan incorporating policies and regulations addressing sea-level rise.[132]

---

[122] *Natural Hazard Mitigation Plan, supra* note 116.

[123] *Id.*

[124] *Id.*

[125] *Id.*

[126] *Id.*

[127] *Natural Hazard Mitigation Plan, supra* note 116.

[128] *Id.*

[129] *United States Census Bureau, supra* note 18.

[130] New England Municipal Coastal Resilience Initiative Grant Program, *Block Island Harbors Sea Level Rise Adaptation Study* 27 (2013), *available at* http://stormsmart.org/uploads/csi/final-products/harborssea-levelrisestudyfinalreport.pdf.

[131] *Id.*

[132] *Id.*

New Shoreham, also known as Block Island, is twelve miles south of mainland Rhode Island. The Island has over thirty miles of walking trails, seventeen miles of coastal beach, and a small population with just over 1,000 residents.[133] With ten square miles of land, Block Island is known for tourism during the summer months and has a strong fishing community.[134] Aside from a small airport, the ferry is the main transportation for the residents and tourists to the Island.[135] The infrastructure for the ferry is imperative for the citizens of New Shoreham to transport the goods needed to live and remove waste from the island.[136]

In 2011, New Shoreham was the recipient of grant funding from the GOMC and NROC to examine the impact of various sea-level rise and storm surge scenarios on the town.[137] The overall focus of the study was to examine transportation structures utilized by New Shoreham, and to develop structural concepts and a contingency plan to respond to the potential inundation of the ferry terminals that connect the Island to the mainland.[138]

The two harbor sections of New Shoreham, Old and New Harbor, are both vulnerable to flooding, specifically the land around New Harbor with lower-lying roads.[139] In 2011, the town conducted a public climate change session in October 2011 sponsored by the town planner, Block Island Office of The Nature Conservancy, Scenic Block Island, and the committee for the Great Salt Pond.[140] At that time, the community learned that although most of the town would not be affected by sea-level rise, the town's infrastructure in the village and harbor was extremely vulnerable to it.[141] The low-lying harbors are the main focus of adaptation plans on New Shoreham because impairment of their uses would cut off the residents from deliveries to the island and transportation to the mainland.[142]

The funding allowed the town to map the town at various sea-level rise scenarios: one, three, and five feet.[143] Using those maps, the town was able to show what areas of the town, and critical infrastructure, would be impacted by sea-level rise.[144] The maps showed that the ferry terminals, as well as many roads vital for connecting the island to the mainland, would be unusable under even a three-foot sea-level rise.[145] The report

---

[133] *Id.*
[134] *Id.*
[135] *Block Island Harbors, supra* note 130.
[136] *Id.*
[137] *Id.*
[138] *Id.*
[139] *Id.*
[140] *Id.*
[141] *Block Island Harbors, supra* note 130.
[142] *Id.*
[143] *Id.*
[144] *Id.*
[145] *Id.* at 16.

then suggested some adaptation strategies, including retrofitting marine facilities, to cope with rising sea levels.[146]

III. Recommendations for Moving Forward: Lessons Learned from New England

Although climate change will impact every community and state differently, there are important lessons that communities can learn from how other communities have approached adaptation. Proactive planning can result in better adaptation strategies and community support. In Maine, a report in 1995 assessing accelerated sea-level rise due to climate change allowed the state to examine possible adaptive strategies from different angles, providing a strong foundation for future vulnerability assessments and adaptation plans. A state report acknowledging potential climate change impacts and assessing benefits of different adaptation strategies can provide a framework for municipalities within the state to develop an adaptation plan that best fits their community. If a state report evaluates different approaches to adaptation, a municipality can use the state report as a guideline document to help determine what approaches will be most successful based on the on-the-ground information available to municipal planners.

Stressing the economic benefits of proactive climate change adaptation is another tool municipalities, states, regions, and the nation should use in climate change adaptation planning. The nation is extremely reliant on its coastal communities. Demonstrating that climate change will have a negative impact on the economic output of a community can assist municipalities and states with attaining funding for climate change adaptation. Similarly, demonstrating that an investment in adaptation efforts will ultimately cost a community less than no action, such as in the case study in York, Maine, provides a strong incentive for communities to undertake proactive adaptation measures. Economic incentive can also be a powerful political tool for achieving more support for climate change adaptation efforts.

A theme throughout the case studies examined in this chapter is the importance of collaboration and partnerships. By bringing together various stakeholders, climate change vulnerability assessments and adaptation plans become much stronger. Different stakeholders bring unique perspectives to many of the issues faced with climate change. A homeowner may be most impacted by potential changes in floodplain management in her neighborhood, a seaside restaurant owner may notice a sharp decline in business when coastal flooding forces him to close his restaurant more frequently, and a firefighter may be concerned by the increased inability to access a road where there is a nursing home. Each of these stakeholder voices brings a different perspective to the conversation

---

[146] *Id.* at 17.

of climate change adaptation. Fostering an environment where each voice can be heard, as seen in the case studies through public workshops and meetings, allows the conversation to be multifaceted and ultimately results in a stronger adaptation plan. Similarly, partnerships among businesses, nonprofits, academia, and government agencies allows for leveraging of funds and representation of different stakeholders.

Another theme throughout the case studies is the use of the best available science and tools for vulnerability assessments and adaptation planning. Often, this is where federal government and private industry can assist state and local governments most meaningfully with adaptation planning. If the federal government provides data based on the best available science, for example through the National Oceanic and Atmospheric (NOAA)-funded Sea Grant programs, states and municipalities can use that federally supported information to better inform decisions on the state and local level.

While many climate change adaptation efforts are succeeding on a municipality and state level, regional efforts as demonstrated in the COAST project are becoming more common throughout the nation. Climate change impacts do not know state boundaries. Sharing of information and tools, and leveraging funding and partnerships, will allow for more robust regional climate change adaptation.

Lastly, adaptation planning needs to be an adaptive process. Even using the best available science and tools for vulnerability assessments and adaptation plans, the changing climate is creating unknown territory for coastal managers and municipal planners. It is important for adaptation plans to allow for periodic evaluations and alterations. Municipalities and states should consider appropriate time frames for reevaluation, such as every five years.

Conclusion

The impacts of climate change will continue to affect New England and the nation. Collaboration—within municipalities, across multiple communities, among states, and regionally—can be an extremely effective tool for maximizing resources and exchanging useful information for climate change adaptation. Federal-state partnerships can also provide federal agencies with crucial information from coastal managers on-the-ground, while helping states with funding and national data. Furthermore, academic and non-governmental agencies can be extremely effective partners for communities adapting to climate change, often providing reliable research and resources. Lastly, the sharing of information through larger online networks, such as the StormSmart Coasts Network, can provide communities with a way to directly connect with one another, sharing up-to-date information.

To successfully adapt to climate change, communities need to assess their risks, determine their potential impacts, evaluate different options for adaptation, and determine what adaptation options are feasible within their environmental, economic, and political systems. Next, the communities need to create a plan for implementing the best strategies. Finally, communities need to determine how to regularly evaluate and amend those plans. Climate change adaptation will require multiple efforts: municipal, state, regional, and national. Success will only be achieved through collaboration and partnerships.

23 The Role of Alaska Natives in Climate Change Decision-Making in the Alaskan Arctic

David Roche, Ramona Sladic, Jordan Diamond, and
Dr. Kathryn Mengerink*

* The authors express their gratitude to their colleagues at the Environmental Law Institute, specifically Graham May, Intern (Spring 2014), Elizabeth Lewis, Law Clerk (Fall 2013), Zachary Jylkka, Research Associate (2010–2012), Carolyn Clarkin, Law Clerk (Spring 2012), and Greta Swanson, Visiting Attorney, for their assistance with the research summarized within this chapter. The authors also appreciate the assistance from Karina Valencia, J.D. Candidate at Roger Williams University School of Law. In addition, none of this work could have occurred without the invaluable guidance, advice, and input received from individuals and organizations involved with marine resources and management in Alaska, including members and staff of the Alaska Eskimo Whaling Commission, Inuit Circumpolar Council, Indigenous People's Council for Marine Mammals, and Kawerak, Inc., along with numerous others from Alaska Native communities, federal agencies, and nongovernmental and academic entities. This work was made possible by the support of the Coastal and Ocean Climate Applications Program of the National Oceanic and Atmospheric Administration (NOAA) Climate Program Office, the Wilburforce Foundation, and the Oak Foundation. All views presented in the chapter are those of the authors.

Introduction

The Arctic region is a unique and varied environment that poses a wide array of management challenges and opportunities. Extreme environmental conditions, geography on a vast scale, limited infrastructure, remote indigenous communities, and an evolving legal framework combine to create a complex natural resource management matrix. At the same time, climate change is rapidly and dramatically altering the known environment. The management community is working to adapt to changing conditions and support sustainability over the long term. Indigenous communities of the Arctic have a pivotal role to play in these processes, as they hold traditional knowledge that can inform management practices, have established creative approaches to address resource management and conflict among user groups, and face enormous threats to their traditional way of life.

This chapter explores the framework that exists for engaging Alaska Natives in off-shore resources management of the Alaskan Arctic. It focuses on the way in which subsistence communities are uniquely poised to inform and improve decision-making in the region, and how engagement with subsistence communities is occurring in practice.

Section I of the chapter describes the impacts of climate change on coastal communities in Alaska and the federal government's unique trust relationship with Alaska Native communities. Section II outlines the formal and informal mechanisms that form the framework for engagement between the Alaska Native communities and the federal government. Next is an in-depth analysis of the specific pathways of engagement between Alaska Native communities, U.S. federal government entities, and researchers regarding government-to-government consultation (Section III) and research (Section IV). These two sections review the current state of policies and practice in the U.S. Arctic, drawing additional insight from a comparison to Canadian practice, and offer a structure for strengthening the relevant legal and policy frameworks.[1]

---

[1] This chapter draws from the Environmental Law Institute's body of work on Alaska Native involvement and leadership in Arctic offshore natural resources management. For more information, see ELI, Ocean Program: Arctic, www.eli-ocean.org/arctic (last visited July 23, 2014).

I. Climate Change and Federal-Tribal Relations

A. CLIMATE CHANGE AND ALASKA NATIVES

The rate and magnitude of climate change in the Arctic is greater than anywhere else on Earth, taking place at a rate approximately twice the world average.[2] Climate change has had and is projected to continue to have enormous ecological ramifications throughout the region. In the U.S. portion of the Arctic, parts of Alaska are more than 4°F warmer today than thirty years ago, glaciers are retreating at up to 15 percent per decade, permafrost is thawing, erosion is causing the loss of coastal land, and sea ice is retreating rapidly.[3] Some models predict an Arctic that is sea-ice free by 2037,[4] with temperature increases up to 8°C by 2100.[5] These changes already impact Arctic communities, with more dire impacts expected in the future.

Indigenous people in the Arctic are particularly susceptible to the effects of climate change on marine environments.[6] Subsistence communities rely on marine resources for their sustenance, economy, and culture.[7] Alaska Native communities have hunted local marine fauna for millennia, including expeditions at sea to hunt polar bear, seal, walrus, and whale, using animal products for food, clothing, tools, and building material.[8] Although subsistence communities have adapted to environmental fluctuations throughout their history, the pace of climate change in the Arctic is threatening their ability to adapt.[9]

Rapid changes in the Arctic create substantial challenges for subsistence communities and threaten their way of life.[10] Hunters depend on knowledge of season-to-season and year-to-year patterns of weather, hunting conditions, ice flow, and animal behavior, among other things, for successful hunts and for safety. In some locations, sea ice retreat and other climate-related factors influencing access to subsistence resources are

---

[2] ARCTIC COUNCIL, ARCTIC CLIMATE IMPACT ASSESSMENT: IMPACTS OF A WARMING ARCTIC 8–9 (2004).

[3] Alaska Native Science Commission, *Impact on Climate Change on Alaska Native Communities*, NATIVE SCI. 4, http://www.nativescience.org/pubs/Impact%20of%20Climate%20Change%20on%20Alaska%20Native%20Communities.pdf (last visited Apr. 23, 2014) [hereinafter *Alaska Native Science Commission*].

[4] Muyin Wang & James E. Overland, *A Sea-Ice Free Summer Arctic within 30 Years: An Update from CMIP5 Models*, 39 GEOPHYSICAL RES. LETTERS L18501, at 1 (2009), *available at* http://projects.iq.harvard.edu/files/climate/files/wangoverland2012.pdf.

[5] *See id.*

[6] Daniel R. Wildcat, *Introduction: Climate Change and Indigenous Peoples of the USA*, 120 CLIMATIC CHANGE 509, 509 (2013).

[7] *See id.* at 509–11.

[8] *Id.*

[9] Patricia Cochran et al., *Indigenous Frameworks for Observing and Responding to Climate Change in Alaska*, 120 CLIMATIC CHANGE 557, 557–60 (2013).

[10] Kathy Lynn et al., *The Impacts of Climate Change on Tribal Traditional Foods*, 120 CLIMATIC CHANGE 545, 545–46 (2013).

thwarting hunting efforts, or making them prohibitively dangerous.[11] In other locations, wind shifts are preventing use of traditional harbors during hunting season.[12] In addition, changing habitat, food supplies, predator-prey relationships, and migration cycles are shifting animal ranges outside of the reach of subsistence hunting communities.[13] Short-term animal behavior is changing as well—there have been recent beachings, die-offs, stampedes, and haul-outs that are difficult to attribute to specific causal agents, but could be related to climate change.[14] These hunting impacts are layered on top of rising seas and coastal erosion—issues that threaten the continued geographic existence of some Alaska Native communities.[15]

Changing environmental conditions have enabled increased development, which could affect marine resource access and availability for subsistence communities. Loss of sea ice is enabling expansion of Arctic oil and gas development, tourism, and shipping, with the possibility of associated infrastructure development.[16] Populations of bowhead whales, seals, and other subsistence resources all intersect with existing or proposed development areas.[17]

Moreover, with expanding concern about climate change impacts to the Arctic comes expanding research. The research community provides an opportunity to shed light on climate change impacts that will support Arctic communities as they adapt to foreseeable change. At the same time, researchers may put additional strain on Arctic communities.[18] In 2008, scientific research in Alaska was a $300 million endeavor, which the state characterized as a "growth sector."[19] Given the remote and unforgiving nature of the Arctic region, many projects involve the interaction of communities, researchers, and subsistence resources. However, the needs of relatively abundant researchers can overwhelm small Arctic communities.[20]

Like the coastal communities, the framework for managing these resources must be adaptable in the face of changing information and responsive to shifting risks and

---

[11] *Alaska Native Science Commission, supra* note 3, at 16.

[12] *Id.* at 7. This sentiment was also expressed in a meeting that the authors attended in December 2013.

[13] Kathy Lynn et al., *supra* note 10, at 550–52.

[14] These observations were described in many interviews the authors conducted and meetings related to marine mammal subsistence resources. Meeting and interview summaries are on file with the authors.

[15] *See Alaska Native Science Commission, supra* note 3, at 6.

[16] *See* Alaska State Legislature, Final Commission Report: Alaska Climate Impact Assessment Commission 9–11 (2008), *available at* http://www.housemajority.org/coms/cli/cli_final-report_20080301.pdf [hereinafter *Alaska Climate Impact Assessment*].

[17] Jeff Goodyear et al., Environmental Risks with Proposed Offshore Oil and Gas Development off Alaska's North Slope 9–11 (Nat'l Resources Defense Council 2012), *available at* http://www.nrdc.org/land/alaska/files/drilling-off-north-slope-IP.pdf.

[18] *See Alaska Climate Impact Assessment, supra* note 16, at 10–11, 14–15.

[19] *Id.* at 10.

[20] *See generally* Henry P. Huntington et al., *Less Ice, More Talk: The Benefits and Burdens for Arctic Communities of Consultations concerning Development Activities*, 1 Carbon Climate L. Rev. 33 (2012).

priorities. Simply put, the dynamic Arctic environment necessitates dynamic systems of management and engagement.

B. FEDERAL-TRIBAL GOVERNMENT-TO-GOVERNMENT RELATIONS

In addition to the benefits of engaging with and learning from indigenous communities in the Alaskan Arctic, the U.S. federal government also bears a trust responsibility to Native American tribes, which includes 229 tribes in Alaska. The Bureau of Indian Affairs has indicated that "[t]he federal Indian trust responsibility is...a legally enforceable fiduciary obligation on the part of the United States to protect tribal treaty rights, lands, assets, and resources, as well as a duty to carry out the mandates of federal law with respect to American Indian and Alaska Native tribes and villages."[21]

The federal government's trust responsibilities developed out of the history of the federal government's treaty-making with tribes.[22] In part because tribes were often at a disadvantage when making treaties with the federal government, the Supreme Court and lower courts have interpreted treaties by resolving unclear language in favor of tribes, as they have done with federal statutes.[23] Federal agencies must balance their tribal trust responsibilities with other federal obligations, including protection of the environment and federal lands and waters.[24]

To navigate climate change management and adaptation in subsistence communities, there is a pressing need for engagement among tribes, the federal government, and researchers, among others, both to inform communities of activities that relate to their region and resources and to optimize resource management design and implementation. The following section provides an overview of the current engagement framework, setting the stage for an analysis of how to best confront the dynamic challenges of climate change management and adaptation in the Arctic.

II. Framework for Engagement

Many challenges exist to effective engagement of Alaska Native communities in the numerous governmental and scientific efforts related to Arctic climate change, including the sheer number of relevant activities that require engagement; variability in

---

[21] Frequently Asked Questions, U.S. DEPARTMENT OF THE INTERIOR, BUREAU OF INDIAN AFFAIRS, http://www.bia.gov/FAQs/index.htm (last visited Mar. 10, 2014).

[22] Rebecca Tsosie, *The Conflict between the "Public Trust" and the "Indian Trust" Doctrines: Federal Public Land Policy and Native Nations*, 39 TULSA L. REV. 271, 272–74 (2003) (describing the origins of the Indian trust doctrine); *see also* Seminole Nation v. United States, 316 U.S. 286, 296–97 (1942).

[23] *See, e.g.*, Winters v. United States, 207 U.S. 564 (1908); *see also* Minnesota v. Mille Lacs Band of Chippewa Indians, 526 U.S. 172 (1999); Alaska Pacific Fisheries Co. v. United States, 248 U.S. 78, 79 (1918).

[24] *See* Tsosie, *supra* note 22, at 308–11; Mary Turnipseed, Larry B. Crowder, Raphael D. Sagarin & Stephen E. Roady, *Legal Bedrock for Rebuilding America's Ocean Ecosystems*, 324 SCI. 183, 183–84 (2009) (discussing federal public trust obligations).

approaches to communication by location, subject matter, and parties involved; lack of clarity about issues; and lack of understanding about who should be involved in specific discussions. All of these challenges can lead to frustration and inefficiency, such as overlap and/or gaps in the information shared. These challenges must be addressed and solutions developed to facilitate meaningful, robust, and continuing engagement among the parties involved. The framework for engagement with Alaska Native communities can be divided into four types of interrelated processes: (1) management, (2) emergency response, (3) research, and (4) informal engagement.

Management consists of three types of processes in accordance with the existing legal system: (1) co-management, (2) consultation, and (3) public participation. Co-management is a decentralized cooperative management approach that typically involves local resource users, governments, and potentially others.[25] Section 119 of the Marine Mammal Protection Act allows the Secretaries of the Interior and Commerce to enter into cooperative agreements with Alaska Native organizations for the purpose of co-managing subsistence use by Alaska Natives.[26] In practice, the National Oceanic and Atmospheric Administration and the Fish and Wildlife Service enter into cooperative agreements with Alaska Native organizations, which vary in terms of agreed-upon approaches, resources at issue, and the capacity of the Alaska Native organization.

Consultation is an "accountable process to ensure meaningful and timely input by tribal officials in the development of regulatory policies that have tribal implications."[27] Executive Order 13175 requires all agencies to engage in consultation with tribes when making decisions that affect them. Each agency has policies and procedures to implement the Order, and they face a variety of implementation challenges.[28]

Public participation involves the public in decision-making through sharing information, soliciting public input, and enabling some members of the public to participate in decision-making.[29] Many laws, including overarching procedural requirements (e.g., under the National Environmental Policy Act and the Administrative Procedure Act) as well as substantive laws (e.g., the Endangered Species Act and the Marine Mammal Protection Act), provide a legal basis for public participation through information sharing, notice and comment requirements, and other tools.[30]

---

[25] See, e.g., ASSEMBLY OF FIRST NATIONS, CO-MANAGEMENT DISCUSSION PAPER 6 (2012), available at http://www.afn.ca/uploads/files/env/comanagement_paper.pdf; ASSEMBLY OF FIRST NATIONS, CO-MANAGEMENT DEFINITIONS GUIDE 3–9 (2012), available at http://www.afn.ca/uploads/files/env/comanagement_definitions_guide.pdf.

[26] 16 U.S.C. § 1388 (2012).

[27] Exec. Order No. 13175, 65 Fed. Reg. 67,249, 67,250 (2000), available at http://www.gpo.gov/fdsys/pkg/FR-2000-11-09/pdf/00-29003.pdf.

[28] See infra Section III for a more detailed discussion of consultation policies and practice.

[29] See, e.g., Gene Rowe & Lynn J. Frewer, Public Participation Methods: A Framework for Evaluation, 25 SCI., TECH. & HUMAN VALUES 3, 6–7 (2000).

[30] See Administrative Procedure Act, 5 U.S.C. § 552 (2012); National Environmental Policy Act, 42 U.S.C. § 4332 (2012); Endangered Species Act, 16 U.S.C. §§ 1531–1544 (2012), including §§ 4(f)(1)(4), 4(h)(4), 10(a)

The second engagement process is emergency planning, response, and restoration, which includes actions before, during, and after a human-caused or natural disaster. Of particular relevance to Alaska Native subsistence users are hazardous material spill prevention, containment, and response systems, as oil and gas development and shipping expansion raise concerns of potential hazardous waste and oil-related disasters. In addition to human-caused emergencies, climate change may also lead to natural disasters. For example, lack of sea ice combined with strong winds and cold temperatures to cause a multi-day power outage in the remote community of Savoonga in the middle of the Bering Sea in December 2010.[31] The Clean Water Act, Oil Pollution Act, and Comprehensive Environmental Response, Compensation, and Liability Act establish requirements for emergency planning, response, and restoration. The role of federally recognized tribes in these processes includes that of natural resource trustees in assessment, planning, and restoration of injured natural resources under their trusteeship.[32]

Research projects and programs in the Arctic make up a third type of engagement. Research in the Alaskan Arctic often relates to and intersects with Alaska Native communities in one way or another, whether by virtue of project design (e.g., taking place within or near a community) or subject matter (e.g., focused on or potentially affecting tribal resources). Few specific legal requirements address the relationship between researchers and communities; however, a variety of policies from Alaska Native organizations and political subdivisions as well as federal agencies exist addressing how researchers should engage with communities before, during, and after projects.[33]

The fourth engagement approach is informal engagement. Agencies use a variety of informal mechanisms to improve linkages with communities. These include, for example, attending state, regional, or local meetings; presenting information about agency activities; being responsive to communities; and participating in informal phone calls and meetings. Such approaches can help build relationships and trust, which are necessary elements to achieve success in formal engagement processes.[34]

In the remainder of this chapter, we focus on two of these components. First, within the management processes, we explore the policies and practice of consultation. Second, within the research processes, we review federal and Alaska Native policies and practice related to the conduct of research in the Alaskan Arctic. For each, we review the status of the processes and identify ways to strengthen them.

---

(2)(B); and Marine Mammal Protection Act, 16 U.S.C. § 1361 (2012), each of which provides considerable opportunity for public comment.

[31] Amy Murphy, *Savoonga's Power Outage*, Alaska Village Electric Newsletter (ALASKA VILLAGE ELECTRIC COOP., Anchorage, AK), Feb. 2011, at 4, *available at* http://www.avec.org/newsletter/Savoonga%20Power%20Outage%20Dec-2010.pdf.

[32] Oil Pollution Act of 1990, 33 U.S.C. § 2706(c)(4) (2012).

[33] *See infra* Section IV for a more detailed discussion of research policies and practice.

[34] For a discussion of this issue, see ENVIRONMENTAL LAW INSTITUTE, STRENGTHENING GOVERNMENT-TO-GOVERNMENT CONSULTATION RELATED TO MARINE SUBSISTENCE RESOURCES IN ALASKA (forthcoming 2014).

III. Consultation Policies and Practices

As climate change continues to alter Arctic conditions, it is critical for Alaska Natives to be integrated into the U.S. regional offshore resources management structure. This engagement helps develop the strongest management systems possible, and helps fulfill the U.S. federal trust responsibility. Incorporating Alaska Native experience, expertise, and traditional knowledge will help ensure that management is based on the best available information. Integrating Alaska Native priorities, concerns, and approaches will help ensure the framework supports communities as they adapt to changing conditions.

Section III of the chapter explores the exchange of information and engagement as it occurs through government-to-government consultation. In the United States, the federal government is required to consult with tribal governments when making decisions that may affect tribal interests, which has proven to be a challenging mandate to implement.[35] Federal agencies are required to engage in consultation but have not received additional resources to support these efforts. Similarly, Alaska Native communities that wish to engage in consultation must find the personnel, time, and funding to effectively participate in myriad processes. These difficulties are exacerbated in Alaska, in the face of the state's tremendous size, remote populations, extreme weather, and complex social and community structures.

A. CONSULTATION LAWS AND POLICIES

1. U.S. Consultation Policy

As an overarching matter, the processes that have developed for U.S. federal government consultation with tribal governments stem from the fundamental trust responsibilities that the U.S. government bears to protect the rights and resources of Native Americans. Native American tribes are considered domestic dependent nations with inherent sovereign powers that are recognized by the Constitution, treaties, statutes, executive orders, court decisions, and policies.[36]

In 2000, President Clinton issued Executive Order 13175, *Consultation and Coordination with Indian Tribal Governments* (EO 13175),[37] establishing consultation requirements for all federal agencies as a mechanism to satisfy their trust obligations. First, when developing

---

[35] The information contained herein about U.S. consultation policies draws from the authors' previously published work on the subject, including Greta Swanson, Kathryn Mengerink & Jordan Diamond, *Understanding the Government-to-Government Consultation Framework for Agency Activities That Affect Marine Natural Resources in the U.S. Arctic*, 43 ENVTL. L. REP. 10872 (2013) and Jordan Diamond, Greta Swanson & Kathryn Mengerink, *Rights and Roles: Alaska Natives and Marine Subsistence Resources*, 8 FLA. A&M L. REV. 219 (2013).

[36] E.O. 13175, *supra* note 27.

[37] *Id.*

policies that have tribal implications, EO 13175 requires federal agencies[38] to recognize the unique legal relationship between the federal government and Indian tribes as domestic dependent nations, to work with Indian tribes on a government-to-government basis, and to acknowledge the right of Indian tribes to self-government and tribal self-determination. The Executive Order (EO) recognizes that statutes and regulations "establish and define a trust relationship," and it is a fundamental principle that the federal government "work with Indian tribes on a government-to-government basis."[39] The federal government must encourage tribes to develop their own policies, defer to tribal standards when possible, and consult with tribal officials when determining whether to establish federal standards.[40]

Second, EO 13175 identifies specific consultation requirements for when agencies are developing regulatory policies that have tribal implications. Each agency must have "an *accountable* process to ensure *meaningful* and *timely* input by tribal officials in the development of [such] policies."[41] Agencies must also designate an official tasked with implementing the EO, and must submit a description of the agency's consultation process to the Office of Management and Budget (OMB).

If an agency promulgates a regulation that has tribal implications and either (1) imposes unfunded costs on tribal governments not required by statute, or (2) preempts tribal law, then the agency must consult with tribal officials early in the process of developing the proposed regulation.[42] The agency must document this consultation through a "tribal summary impact statement" in the Federal Register and show the extent to which the agency has met the concerns of tribal officials.[43] The agency also must provide OMB with copies of written communication between tribes and agencies.[44]

Almost a decade after it was established, President Obama revived EO 13175 when he issued a memorandum that required agencies to develop detailed plans of action to implement the Order.[45] According to the memorandum, agencies were to draft plans within ninety days of the memorandum and submit final plans to OMB by August 2,

---

[38] "Agencies" are defined as "any authority of the United States that is an 'agency' under 44 U.S.C. § 3502(1), other than those considered to be independent regulatory agencies, as defined in 44 U.S.C. § 3502(5)." *Id.* § 1(c).

[39] *Id.* § 2.

[40] *Id.* § 3.

[41] *Id.* § 5(a) (emphasis added). "Policies that have tribal implications" "refers to regulations, legislative comments or proposed legislation, and other policy statements or actions that have substantial direct effects on one or more Indian tribes, on the relationship between the Federal Government and Indian tribes, or on the distribution of power and responsibilities between the Federal Government and Indian tribes." *Id.* § 1(b).

[42] This specific process applies only when developing "regulations." *Id.* § 5(b). However, the requirement to consult, guided by the agency's plan or policy for consultation, applies to all "regulatory policies" that have tribal implications. *Id.* § 5(a).

[43] *Id.* § 5(b).

[44] *Id.* § 5(b)–(c).

[45] Presidential Memorandum for the Heads of Executive Departments and Agencies on Tribal Consultation (Nov. 5, 2009), *available at* http://www.whitehouse.gov/the-press-office/memorandum-tribal-consultation-signed-president.

2010, followed by annual progress reports. Departments and agencies were directed to consult with Indian tribes and tribal officials to develop the action plans[46] and to designate an agency official to coordinate implementation plans and progress reports.

In addition, through a provision in a 2010 omnibus bill, the requirement for OMB to consult with tribes under EO 13175 was explicitly extended to include Alaska Native corporations "on the same basis as Indian tribes."[47] One of the issues that the OMB Guidance addresses is the role of the tribal consultation official, who has the "principal responsibility for the agency's implementation" of the order. It requires agency tribal consultation officials to "assure that the agency program personnel have considered the fundamental principles and policymaking criteria stated in [the EO] in formulating or implementing policies, and in the development of legislative proposals, that have tribal implications."[48] Although EO 13175 "is not intended to create any right, benefit, or trust responsibility, substantive or procedural, enforceable at law,"[49] OMB Guidance states that the tribal consultation official must certify that EO requirements are met "in a meaningful and timely manner" when submitting draft regulations to OMB.[50]

Although tribal beneficiaries do not have the right to enforce the consultation policies of the EO in court, the Order is a mandate to agencies to fulfill trust obligations in part through consultation. As a result of these policies and statutory requirements, all federal agencies are to consult with tribal officials on issues that affect tribal trust resources.

In the not-too-distant past, relatively few federal agency actions affected Arctic communities. With climate change, however, federal agencies are making myriad decisions that may affect tribal trust resources, including those related to oil and gas development, shipping, safety of life at sea, and protection of species threatened by climate change. In the face of such climate-related federal action, consultation is gaining prominence as an important component of federal agency decision-making processes.[51]

---

[46] *Id.* at 1.

[47] Peter Orszag, Memorandum for the Heads of Executive Departments and Agencies, and Independent Regulatory Agencies on Guidance for Implementing E.O. 13175, Consultation and Coordination with Indian Tribal Governments, 2–3 (July 30, 2010) [hereinafter *OMB Guidance*] (stating that, "pursuant to Pub. L. 108-199, 118 Stat. 452, as amended by Pub. L. 108-447, 118 Stat. 3267, OMB and all Federal agencies are required to 'consult with Alaska Native corporations on the same basis as Indian tribes under Executive order No. 13175'"). *Id.* § 161. The Consolidated Appropriations Act requires that "[t]he Director of the Office of Management and Budget shall hereafter consult with Alaska Native corporations on the same basis as Indian tribes under Executive Order No. 13175." Consolidated Appropriations Act, 2004, Pub. L. 108–99, Div. H., Sec. 161, 118 Stat. 3, 452 (2004), as amended by Consolidated Appropriations Act, 2005, Pub. L. 108–447, Div. H., Title V., Sec. 518, 118 Stat. 2809, 3267 (2004).

[48] *OMB Guidance, supra* note 47.

[49] E.O. 13,175, *supra* note 27, § 10 (Judicial Review).

[50] OMB Guidance, *supra* note 47, at 4.

[51] The issue of meaningful and timely consultation is gaining prominence in light of expanding human activity and therefore expanding federal agency decision-making in the Arctic. This focus is reflected in the Marine Mammal Commission's 2014 Strategic Plan in which it noted, "[c]ommercial development, which promises greater economic opportunities for many Alaskans, requires careful management, in *consultation with Alaska Natives*, so as not to compromise the subsistence and cultural value of marine mammals to

2. Examples from Canada

When considering the overarching framework for consultation, it may be useful to look at examples from the Canadian approach. The Canadian government holds significant consultation obligations with respect to Aboriginal persons. The consultation obligation, also referred to as the Crown's constitutional duty to consult and, if appropriate, accommodate Aboriginal persons, is based on the honor of the Crown.[52] The honor of the Crown affirms that the Crown must act honorably in any and all dealings with Aboriginal persons.[53] It has at its source the historic assertion by the Crown of sovereignty over Aboriginal persons, an assertion made despite prior Aboriginal occupation.[54] The Supreme Court of Canada's seminal explanation of the honor of the Crown is the following:

> Put simply, Canada's Aboriginal peoples were here when Europeans came, and were never conquered. Many bands reconciled their claims with the sovereignty of the Crown through negotiated treaties. Others [...] have yet to do so. The potential rights embedded in these claims are protected by s. 35 of the *Constitution Act, 1982*. The honor of the Crown requires that these rights be determined, recognized and respected. This, in turn, requires the Crown, acting honorably, to participate in processes of negotiation. While this process continues, the honor of the Crown may require it to consult and, where indicated, accommodate Aboriginal interests.[55]

The honor of the Crown is to be interpreted expansively, not narrowly, at all times.[56] The honor of the Crown has been "enshrined" in section 35(1) of the *Constitution Act, 1982*, which both recognizes and affirms existing Aboriginal rights and titles.[57]

The Crown's duty to consult arises when the Crown has knowledge (actual or constructive) of Aboriginal or treaty rights (potential or established) that may be adversely affected by contemplated Crown conduct.[58] This bears similarities to the United States' formulation of "policies that have tribal implications" as described in EO 13175.

---

these communities." MARINE MAMMAL COMMISSION, STRATEGIC PLAN 2015–2019 6 (2014), *available at* http://www.mmc.gov/reports/administrative/pdf/StrategicPlan_02192014.pdf (emphasis added).

[52] Taku River Tlingit First Nation v. British Columbia, [2004] SCC 74, ¶ 24 (Can.).

[53] *Id.*

[54] *Id.*

[55] *Id.* ¶ 25.

[56] *Id.* ¶ 24.

[57] *Id.*

[58] *Id. See generally* Mikisew Cree First Nation v. Canada (Minister of Canadian Heritage), [2005] SCC 69 (Can.), which amended the test for whether the Crown has a duty to consult to reflect that the duty to consult is also engaged when established aboriginal or treaty rights are at issue. This differed from earlier iterations of the test, which set out that the duty to consult was engaged only when potential (rather than established) aboriginal or treaty rights were at issue.

The test for whether the Crown has a duty to consult contains three key elements. First, the Crown must have real or constructive knowledge of a potential or established Aboriginal or treaty right.[59] Second, the Crown must be contemplating conduct or making a decision.[60] Third, there must be a possibility that the Crown's contemplated conduct or the decision being made may affect the potential or established Aboriginal or treaty right.[61] The heart of the test for whether the Crown has a duty to consult is the claimant having to show that, if the Crown action were to proceed, there would be a causal relationship between the contemplated Crown conduct or decision and possible adverse impacts on potential or established Aboriginal claims or rights.[62] United States' consultation under EO 13175 significantly differs in that the Order "is not intended to create any right, benefit, or trust responsibility, substantive or procedural, enforceable at law."[63]

Because Canada's Crown as a whole is responsible for meeting the Crown's duty to consult and accommodate, all federal government departments and agencies are responsible for supporting the Canadian Crown's efforts in fulfilling this requirement.[64] The Crown's duty to consult is not limited to the federal government—the duty applies to Canada's provincial and territorial governments as well, for activities falling into each province's and territory's jurisdiction.[65] This is a marked difference from the U.S. framework, which is limited to federal government responsibilities.

B. CONSULTATION IN PRACTICE

Having reviewed the policy basis for consultation in the United States and how it compares to the framework in Canada, we will next consider U.S. consultation in practice. Federal agencies and tribes must translate guidance from consultation policy into practices that ensure a meaningful, timely, and accountable process, which is necessary not only to comply with legal requirements but also to ensure an effective and sustainable response to the challenges of climate change. Consultation in Alaska poses additional challenges related to, among other things, the fact that the processes often involve communication across vast distances and across varying cultural and resource management perspectives. By identifying key challenges that federal and tribal participants face while preparing for, engaging in, and following up on consultation, it may be possible to

---

[59] Rio Tinto Alcan Inc. v. Carrier Sekani Tribal Council, [2010] SCC 43, ¶ 31 (Can.).

[60] *Id.* ¶ 42.

[61] *Id.* ¶ 45.

[62] *Id.*

[63] E.O. 13175, *supra* note 27, at § 10.

[64] Minister of the Department of Aboriginal Affairs and Northern Development Canada, Aboriginal Consultation and Accommodation—Updated Guidelines for Federal Officials to Fulfill the Duty to Consult 6, 10 (2011), *available at* http://www.aadnc-aandc.gc.ca/DAM/DAM-INTER-HQ/STAGING/texte-text/intgui_1100100014665_eng.pdf.

[65] *Id.*

discern opportunities for strengthening the process and its outcomes, reinforcing sustainable management and adaptation practices in the face of climate change.[66]

The consultation process includes activities that occur before formal leadership meetings, during such meetings, and after such meetings occur. The following discussion reviews some of the most significant considerations during three stages: (1) before, (2) during, and (3) after. It also considers some crosscutting challenges in promoting effective consultation.

Prior to consultation meetings come the steps that enable meaningful consultation to occur. Setting the stage for consultation meetings can be complex. For example, it is essential to determine what federal actions trigger consultation. The scope of "policies that have tribal implications" is uncertain—generally, policies that directly or indirectly affect marine subsistence resources should require consultation. In the context of climate change and development activities, policies that have tribal implications include decisions to designate species as threatened due to climate change, establishment of shipping lanes in light of sea ice retreat, and other decisions that enable development in a changing Arctic.

When considering wide-ranging activities or decisions such as threatened species listings, it can be difficult to identify potentially affected tribes from those that will not be affected, leading to a practice of over-inclusivity when announcing consultation opportunities. Such over-inclusivity may be better than risking excluding an important tribe. However, frequent notices of consultation opportunities may create a substantial burden on tribes, especially if development activities continue to increase as a result of growing accessibility to the Arctic due to diminishing sea ice, and in light of growing pressure for environmental and species protection as a result of climate change.

Next, adequate notice must be given to the necessary parties. Notice has two components—first, agencies need to know the right tribal authorities to contact for consultation; second, agencies need to know who the actual people are within those tribal authorities who hold the relevant positions, and how to contact them. Agency approaches to providing consultation notice vary, as do the processes for tribes to initiate consultation. For example, some agencies use e-mail, telephone, and radio announcements, while others primarily rely on mail. A related issue is whether agencies have a positive duty to consult, not just a duty to offer consultation opportunities. Currently, most federal agencies send notices about opportunities to consult, but leave it to the tribal authorities to respond; communities can also request consultation without prior agency notice.

It is important to include appropriate participants in the consultation process. However, it can be challenging to have consistent participation and to know precisely who to contact to initiate consultation on either side. Some agencies, such as the EPA and Coast Guard, have tribal liaisons that build and maintain connections with

---

[66] The information contained herein about U.S. consultation in practice in Alaska draws from the authors' previously completed work on the subject, including ENVIRONMENTAL LAW INSTITUTE, *supra* note 34.

communities. Even with dedicated liaisons, staff and community member turnover can add uncertainty to consultation outreach and conduct. On the tribal side, there is no "one-size-fits-all" approach to determining who participates in consultation on behalf of a tribe—generally, it is the tribal council speaking on behalf of the tribe, though this may vary significantly depending on the matter at issue, the nature of the contemplated decision, and timing and location. There are varying views of the roles that Alaska Native organizations (ANOs) play in consultation; in some instances, tribes have explicitly delegated consultation authority to ANOs for particular matters, whereas the tribes retain all consultation authority in other contexts.

The next stage of consultation is for the federal agency and tribe to engage in consultation meetings, which may occur in person or remotely. Given the vast, sometimes unforgiving landscape of the U.S. Arctic, organizing meetings is often not simple. Alaska is an enormous state with extreme weather, and is home to 229 federally recognized tribes with both overlapping and distinct interests. In addition to the logistical difficulties with communication in Alaska, mismatches between subsistence calendars and agency action calendars can lead to situations where agencies initiate consultation when potentially affected Alaska Native communities are not available to participate. It is important to consult at the right time to allow the right participants to engage.

Furthermore, expanding federal action due to climate change decision-making and development activities means that without effective agency coordination, numerous consultation meetings can overwhelm communities that have low capacity and few resources. Therefore, federal coordination of consultation activities is another need. For a variety of reasons, the federal government rarely engages with Alaska Native communities on an interagency basis, which can create inefficiency, confusion, and repetitive information sharing. Such single-agency approaches are both a strain on the federal agencies and make it difficult for tribes to engage, as both parties typically have limited capacity, resources, and training.

Additional uncertainty surrounds whether certain communication constitutes consultation—it is important to know and clarify whether particular exchanges count as consultation. Because the consultation process may vary among agencies, communities, and issues, participants may have differing understandings of a series of interactions. On the one hand, it is critical that the process be flexible. On the other, the lack of a consistent approach to consultation creates uncertainty about process and procedure that can make it difficult for parties to meaningfully engage.

After consultation, the federal agency as ultimate decision-maker should follow up with the process participants with the results and outcomes of the consultation to ensure accountability and transparency. Agencies often fail to inform tribes about how consultation informs decision-making, informally or formally. Lack of communication can lead to diminished confidence in the consultation process as a meaningful system of engagement.

Crosscutting challenges facing consultation may pose the most substantial obstacles to timely and meaningful engagement. Establishing trust and demonstrating respect are overarching concerns that cut across other challenges, from communicating effectively to ensuring accountability.

Effective consultation should include mechanisms to incorporate traditional knowledge into the decision-making process. Alaska Native traditional knowledge should be accorded respect, and concerns about the potential sensitivity and confidential nature of information considered.

In addition, it is important to frame consultation as collaborative decision-making rather than just an information-sharing exercise. Establishing a flexible and collaborative process requires increasing predictability, preserving flexibility, and maintaining a two-way dialogue. Community priorities, needs, structures, and circumstances vary throughout Alaska, as do environmental and resources conditions. For communities to be able to meaningfully and appropriately engage in consultation, the process has to be able to adapt to these variations while also being consistent locally or regionally to limit confusion.

Flexible collaboration is challenged by the difficulty of operating effectively in a complex system of engagement. Other processes, such as co-management and public participation, can create confusion among the various engagement processes. It is important to view consultation as one element of a broader engagement framework, which includes everything from formal consultation to more informal researcher-community interactions.

While the challenges with consultation are broader than the activities that relate to climate change, the increased public attention and federal decision-making in the Arctic in light of climate change is an underlying factor driving increased consultation between federal agencies and communities. Therefore, addressing climate change through meaningful engagement with Alaska Native communities requires improvement to the consultation process. Opportunities for such improvement are discussed in the following subsection.

C. CONSULTATION OPPORTUNITIES

In the Alaskan Arctic, broad consultation policy is implemented by federal agency and Alaska Native tribal representatives. Ideally, these representatives meet to discuss an issue long before a decision is made, with an ongoing dialogue that informs federal agency management alternatives, which consider everything from the impacts of climate change to the importance of a sustainable subsistence lifestyle. However, consultation can be difficult to achieve in the face of the challenges discussed above, leading instead to ineffective engagement that raises questions about the utility of the consultation process.

Considering the challenges facing consultation and the increased federal decision-making that is occurring in light of climate change, it is important to identify opportunities for improved approaches to consultation related to marine subsistence resources in Alaska. Beginning the process as early as possible at the equivalent of a "scoping" stage is one way to improve consultation. To ensure the right participants are engaged, it may be helpful to clarify contact pathways and share government and community calendars to facilitate more efficient communication at all stages. It may also be beneficial to establish greater clarity about which federal actions may trigger consultation requirements; Canada's developed jurisprudence may be a useful example.

During consultation, procedures can guide the process to clarify how consultation will occur in practice. To achieve accountability and transparency, the consultation meeting outcomes and decisions should be recorded and tracked. Greater transparency may increase trust that information provided in one meeting will be carried over to another, reducing the need to expend resources sharing it again. In-person engagement can help build relationships among the participants. Coordination between agencies can help reduce the burden on tribal and federal participants.

Most important, a dialogue is needed regarding not only the challenges of consultation, but also the opportunities it affords. Both Alaska Native communities and federal agencies are substantially constrained by budgets and capacity to meaningfully engage in consultation in many instances. These constraints are exacerbated in Alaska where the large number of tribes, extremely remote nature of communities, and harsh conditions make engagement costly and challenging. At the same time, climate change and development are driving the need for more robust consultation. Coordination mechanisms may strengthen the ability of Alaska Natives to speak together on key issues—in essence, to speak with a louder voice. The first step to coordination and collaboration is conversation—a discussion regarding the best way to translate consultation policy into meaningful practices, with the ultimate goal of achieving more efficient and effective management of marine subsistence resources in the Alaskan Arctic.

Consultation is one of the tools that agencies are using to engage with Alaska Native communities when making decisions that affect resources in the Arctic—a region undergoing rapid alteration as a result of climate change. Improving the effectiveness and efficiency of these tools, including consultation, will help federal agencies make stronger decisions related to the marine environment and to satisfy their tribal trust obligations. Alaska Native community members may share traditional knowledge gleaned from generations of experience with the ecosystem and firsthand understanding and observation of the impacts of climate change. The outcomes may be collaborative decisions and solutions that protect both the marine environment and the coastal communities faced with adapting to the changing conditions.

IV. Research in a Changing Arctic

In adapting to the ecological and environmental changes of the twenty-first century, communities in the U.S. Arctic will be operating at the intersection of traditional ecological knowledge and climate change research. Simultaneously, the most effective resource management processes, including but not limited to consultation, will integrate community knowledge and outside expertise. Meaningful and ongoing communication between researchers and communities is critical to the success of marine resource management objectives and the fulfillment of U.S. trust responsibilities to Alaska Native tribes.

Recognizing that expanding human use and federal regulation in the Arctic is accompanied by expanding research efforts, Section IV of this chapter focuses on the policy framework related to Alaska Native community and science linkages in the Alaskan Arctic, with a particular emphasis on policies produced by Alaska Natives. Following review of the pieces of the policy framework is a summary of overarching themes that could help shape best practices for researchers in the climate change context going forward.[67]

A. RESEARCH POLICIES

1. Research Needs in a Changing Arctic

Studies have explored and are exploring Arctic communities' climate change concerns and research needs,[68] and agencies are developing research programs based on these and other climate change research needs. These studies provide guidance to researchers about which climate change questions may be particularly relevant for communities. However, the climate change research process deserves additional attention. Research needs vary from community to community and change as conditions change. Communities may lend valuable expertise and experience to the research methodology. Furthermore, communities' needs may include the need for research results to be shared with communities in appropriate ways. Therefore, this subsection explores policies and approaches that relate to research in the U.S. Arctic, recognizing that climate change research programs should not only focus on the right issues, but also linkages to affected communities.

2. Alaska Native Organizations and Local/Regional Bodies

The Alaska Federation of Natives (AFN), the Alaska Native Science Commission (ANSC), and the Alaska Native Knowledge Network (ANKN) each have produced research policies targeting, respectively, general guidelines for research, research ethics, and cultural knowledge. A brief summary of these approaches follows.

More than twenty years ago, AFN established "Guidelines for Research" in response to research-related abuses of Alaska Natives.[69] The Guidelines for Research recognize that the "best scientific and ethical standards are obtained when Alaska Natives are

---

[67] The policies information contained in this section draws from the authors' previously completed work on research conduct in the Alaskan Arctic. For more information, see ENVIRONMENTAL LAW INSTITUTE, CLIMATE & COMMUNITIES: CONDUCTING MARINE RESEARCH IN A CHANGING ARCTIC (2014). This report was made possible by support from the Coastal and Ocean Climate Applications Program of the National Oceanic and Atmospheric Administration.

[68] *Id.* at 15–23.

[69] ALASKA NATIVE KNOWLEDGE NETWORK, ALASKA FEDERATION OF NATIVES GUIDELINES FOR RESEARCH (1993), *available at* http://ankn.uaf.edu/IKS/AFNguide.html.

directly involved in research conducted in our communities and in studies where the findings have a direct impact on Native populations."[70]

To this end, AFN recommends to researchers working among Alaska Natives and funders that funding for research projects include a category aimed at ensuring Alaska Native participation.[71] According to AFN, Alaska Natives who will be affected by research should be informed of the research methodology, including the purpose, time frame to achieve goals, data gathering techniques, and positive and negative implications of the research. Furthermore, the appropriate Alaska Native governing body should give informed consent.[72] Throughout the process, Alaska Natives languages should be used when English is the second language.[73]

The Guidelines for Research address the integration of Alaska Natives into the oversight and carrying out of research, for example, through the hiring and training of locals to assist in substantive research.[74] The Guidelines for Research further state that on a per-project basis, funding should be made available to support a Native Research Committee, whose role would be to assess and monitor the particular research project. In addition, research projects should comply with the wishes of Alaska Natives.[75] The Research Guidelines indicate that final research results should include Native viewpoints and acknowledge Native peoples' contributions, with a nontechnical summary of major findings being communicated directly to the associated Native Research Committee, and copies of the study made available to local Alaska Natives.[76]

The ANSC produced a "Sample Code of Research Ethics" ("Code") in 1997, which sets out a model partnership agreement to be implemented when an Alaska Native community and researchers form a research relationship.[77] The Code identifies specific obligations summarized in Table 23.1 for the key players in the research process, namely researchers, community researchers, and community partners.

The underlying premises in the Code are that obligations flow between the partners to the agreement; each partner has relevant experience, knowledge, and capabilities that will strengthen the project and associated outcomes; and community-based research is a significant method by which information can be both learned about a community, and contributed back to a community.[78] Partners make the commitment to cooperate and

---

[70] Id.

[71] Id.

[72] Id.

[73] Id.

[74] Id.

[75] Id.

[76] Id.

[77] ALASKA NATIVE SCIENCE COMMISSION, CODE OF RESEARCH ETHICS (1997), *available at* http://www.nativescience.org/html/Code%20of%20Research%20Ethics.html.

[78] Id.

TABLE 23.1.

ANSC SAMPLE CODE OF RESEARCH ETHICS—ROLES AND OBLIGATIONS

Role in the Research Process	Research Obligations
Researchers—project researchers external to the communities	Researchers have obligations vis-á vis the community to do no harm, encourage active community participation, ensure research methodologies and projects chosen are culturally relevant and contribute value to communities, answer resultant issues raised by communities, and remain involved in subsequent data analysis once researchers have provided data back to communities.
Community researchers—project researchers employed from within the community	Community researchers are to assume caregiver and educator roles in addition to duties as community researchers, and are to essentially act as a liaison and reviewer as between outside researchers and communities.
Community partners—representatives from community organizations	Community partners review and agree or disagree with data analysis, act as a repository for the research data, and interface with future researchers wishing to use the data generated.

Source: ALASKA NATIVE SCIENCE COMMISSION, CODE OF RESEARCH ETHICS (1997), *available at* http://www. nativescience.org/html/Code%20of%20Research%20Ethics.html. (Table 23.1 compiled per the referenced *Code of Research Ethics.*)

collaborate with respect to research design, implementation, analysis, interpretation, conclusion, reporting, and publication.[79]

The policy underlying the Code is based in community sovereignty—a community's capacity to make decisions with respect to research in the community must be both recognized and respected.[80] The Code contains explicit guidelines on communicating applications to conduct research to communities, data collection processes, and the communication of research results to others outside of the community targeted by the research, recognizing that the experience of the project should be shared widely with the largest possible audience that may potentially benefit from the experience.[81]

---

[79] *Id.*
[80] *Id.*
[81] *Id.*

In addition, the Code's principles applicable to all in the research process focus on the robust role of the community, through language on continuous community consultation and collaboration, informed consent, confidentiality, propriety of data and return of data to the community, and the requirement for community agreement with respect to release of information.[82]

In 2000, the ANKN developed "Guidelines for Respecting Cultural Knowledge" to address issues of concern to Alaska Natives with respect to the use, documentation, and representation of traditional cultural knowledge; it sets out specific guidelines for various groups with roles in the transmission of traditional cultural knowledge.[83] Specific guidelines are identified for Native Elders, Native community organizations, and researchers, among others, in the knowledge transmission process, and are summarized in Table 23.2.[84]

Various state of Alaska and Alaska Native local and regional institutions also have implemented research policies. The Northwest Arctic Borough (NAB), Bristol Bay Native Association (BBNA), and the Tanacross Tribal Council (TTC) have produced research policies applicable to their respective areas.

The NAB passed the February 2013 Northwest Arctic Borough Ordinance 02-03 on Research Principles, which requires, among other matters, that potential project participants are provided with written details prior to participating in research, participants are guaranteed anonymity in the research process, research results are reported in nontechnical terminology, and that intellectual property rights are respected, with the recommendation that fair compensation is made available to participants who disseminate traditional knowledge.[85]

Furthermore, recognizing how climate change has increased researcher presence, a NAB workgroup at the *2013 Workshop on Improving Local Participation in Research in Northwest Alaska* has recommended that a permanent Northwest Arctic Research Panel be formed to develop final research principles for Northwest Alaska. It also has developed *Draft Principles for Conducting Research in the Northwest Arctic Borough*.[86] The Draft Principles address pre-research coordination, research methodology, and reporting of research results. They are built on the premise that local people should play a role in research design, information collection, and report preparation. Specific emphasis is placed on communication between researchers and communities.[87]

---

[82] *Id.*

[83] Alaska Native Knowledge Network, Guidelines for Respecting Cultural Knowledge (2000), *available at* http://ankn.uaf.edu/Publications/Knowledge.pdf.

[84] *See id.* at 4–21.

[85] *See* Northwest Arctic Borough, Draft Principles for Conducting Research in the Northwest Arctic Borough 8 (2013), *available at* http://www.nwabor.org/style/forms/ NorthwestAlaskaResearchWorkshopSummary.pdf (referencing the NAB document—the primary source has not been found in preliminary searches).

[86] *Id.* Attachment E, at 4.

[87] *Id.*

TABLE 23.2.

ANKN GUIDELINES FOR RESPECTING CULTURAL KNOWLEDGE

Role in the Research Process	Research Obligations
Native elders	Native elders are responsible for transmitting knowledge in a way that is compatible with traditional teachings and practices; have a duty to protect intellectual property and copyright authority over knowledge being shared; are to review contracts and release forms to understand who has control over future distribution of publications; and are to review transcripts of communicated cultural information to determine accuracy.
Native community organizations	Native community organizations should (1) establish a process by which activities that involve gathering, documenting, and using traditional cultural knowledge are reviewed; (2) establish a process for the review and approval of research proposals that may have an impact on Alaska Natives' areas; and (3) provide support to help elders to understand the giving of informed consent and filing of copyright protections.
Researchers	Researchers are ethically responsible in three main areas: (1) obtaining informed consent, (2) giving an accurate representation of the cultural perspective, and (3) protecting the rights and cultural integrity of research participants.
	Researchers should: use expertise housed in communities to enhance data; ensure access to sensitive cultural information is appropriately controlled; ensure research plans and results are submitted to those with local knowledge and abide by recommendations made; provide full disclosure with respect to funding sources, sponsors, institutions affiliated with research, and reviewers of research; explicitly recognize all research contributors; and abide by all research-applicable principles and guidelines established by organizations representing indigenous persons, including AFN, state, national, and international organizations.

Source: NORTHWEST ARCTIC BOROUGH, DRAFT PRINCIPLES FOR CONDUCTING RESEARCH IN THE NORTHWEST ARCTIC BOROUGH 8 (2013), *available at* http://www.nwabor.org/style/forms/NorthwestAlaskaResearchWorkshopSummary.pdf. (Table 23.2 compiled per details from Attachment E, at 4.)

The BBNA has produced Policy Guidelines for Research in Bristol Bay, which require, among other things, training for and employment of members of the Native community, a guarantee of confidentiality for culturally sensitive information, fair compensation for participants, the appropriate use of translators throughout the research process, and the opportunity for community members to comment on researchers' draft reports.[88]

The TTC has developed a Code titled Natural and Cultural Resources—Tanacross Tribal Government, which has the general purpose of providing guidelines for the "wise and continued use of the natural and cultural resources within the jurisdiction of the Tanacross Tribe, to reduce conflicts over natural resource use, and to preserve the cultural heritage of our Tribe."[89] It contains provisions specific to research, set out to protect the Tanacross Tribe's sacred knowledge, intellectual property, and cultural property.[90]

Pursuant to chapter 6 of the Code, research activities conducted on Tanacross Tribe members and Tanacross Land require the express permission of the Tanacross Tribal Council. In addition, data-gathering practices and positive and negative effects of participating must be communicated, participants must be compensated, and Tanacross Tribe members must be involved in research projects as employees or trainees "to the maximum extent feasible."[91] Further, the Tanacross Tribe members are to be involved in final research products by approving any research that is intended to be representative of Tribe members, in addition to having their perspectives included in final research outcomes.[92]

In sum, the research policies developed by Alaska Natives organizations and regional and local institutions focus on how, from the perspective of Alaska Natives, researchers undertaking research projects that involve Alaska Natives should interact with Alaska Natives, from the earliest moments of conceptualizing anticipated research to dissemination of results. The above policies share four common themes, which are outlined in Table 23.3 in the next page.

Therefore, to best adhere to the above Alaska Natives policies, researchers studying the impacts of climate change and other changes in the Arctic should integrate these four themes and associated considerations into research project design.

3. Federal Organizations and Agencies

Many federal organizations and agencies have formalized research engagement policies with respect to rapidly expanding research activities undertaken in Arctic and northern regions, which are applicable to research that is relevant to Alaska Native communities.

---

[88] *Id.* at 3.

[89] Natural and Cultural Resources—Tanacross Tribal Government (adopted Sept. 3, 2013) (on file with authors).

[90] *Id.* at 6 (discussing "Research on the Tanacross Tribe and Land").

[91] *Id.*

[92] *Id.*

TABLE 23.3.

FOUR COMMON THEMES OF ALASKA NATIVE RESEARCH POLICIES

Theme	Summary
Alaska Native Involvement and Funding	The policies emphasize that Alaska Natives should have direct involvement in research projects, early and often, for example in research design, data collection, and the compilation and communication of results. Funding should be made available for Alaska Natives to participate in these respects.
Informed Consent	The policies highlight that informed consent must be obtained from Alaska Natives at every step in the research process. This entails full disclosure by researchers of, for example, research methodologies, potential positive and negative implications of participating in the research, project funders, and institutions associated with the research.
Communication of Research	The policies identify the need to provide the research back to the Alaska Natives, whether ongoing throughout the research process, in draft and prior to finalization, or in final form. Communication of results should be done in a manner mindful of what tools can accompany research results to make the research useful and accessible to Alaska Natives.
Traditional Ecological Knowledge	The policies address the appropriate treatment of traditional cultural knowledge, which belongs to the Alaska Natives and is subject to intellectual property rights.

For example, the U.S. Interagency Social Science Task Force, at the direction of the U.S. Interagency Arctic Research Policy Committee and funded by the National Science Foundation, has developed "Principles for the Conduct of Research in the Arctic."[93] The principles provide guidance for researchers completing (or sponsors supporting) research in Arctic and northern regions. The Principles are intended for wide application—to all scientific investigations in the Arctic—and include a primary focus on the need for each research project to consider its potential human impact.[94]

---

[93] NAT'L SCI. FOUND., PRINCIPLES FOR THE CONDUCT OF RESEARCH IN THE ARCTIC (2006), *available at* http://www.doi.gov/subsistence/monitor/fisheries/upload/Principles-for-the-Conduct-of-Researd-in-the-Arctic.pdf.

[94] *Id.* at 1.

The Principles specifically emphasize the responsibilities of project leaders. For example, project leaders are to ensure community authorities are aware of all research anticipated to take place in their territories, authorities' informed consent is obtained (which entails communication of sources of funding), research results are communicated back to communities (in a format such as study materials appropriate for future use by local teachers, or suitable for display in the community), and traditional knowledge, languages, and meaningful experiences and training for younger persons are incorporated into research design.[95]

Federal agencies possess a variety of research policies, from general to region- or topic-specific, which may address community engagement explicitly, implicitly, or not at all. The U.S. Fish and Wildlife Service, via its Landscape Conservation Cooperatives, partners with outside agencies (federal and state), tribes, nongovernmental organizations, and others to support applied conservation science.[96] U.S. Geological Survey researchers are directed to work with Alaska Native governments to assure that rights are protected and concerns are addressed in projects that may produce results on or adjacent to Alaska Native lands,[97] and during projects an intern program exists that is aimed at encouraging tribal youth participation in research projects.[98] The Bureau of Ocean Energy Management directs researchers to coordinate with local communities with respect to research plans,[99] and the agency's program documents identify its commitment to open and transparent communication with tribal leaders.[100] Generally, when federal entities do have communication policies in place, they stress similar themes as Alaska Native policies, including open and transparent communication from project design through project completion. Given expanding research efforts related to climate change, communication and engagement with subsistence communities throughout the research process is necessary to optimize projects and avoid conflicts.

4. Examples from Canada

Additional examples can be gleaned from Northern Canadian approaches. In Canada's Arctic region, researchers intending to undertake research projects in the Northwest

---

[95] *Id.*

[96] Landscape Conservation Cooperatives for Alaska, U.S. Fish & Wildlife Serv., http://www.fws.gov/alaska/lcc/index.htm (last visited Feb. 10, 2014).

[97] U.S. Geological Survey, U.S. Geological Survey Manual § 500.4 (1995), *available at* http://www.usgs.gov/usgs-manual/500/500-4.html.

[98] SISNAR Internship Program, U.S. Geological Survey, http://www.usgs.gov/tribal/activities/index.html (last visited Feb. 10, 2014).

[99] Bureau of Ocean Energy Management, Environmental Studies Program, Studies Development Plan FY 2014–2016: Alaska OCS Region 5–6 (2013).

[100] Reaching Out to Alaska Communities, Bureau of Ocean Energy Management, http://www.boem.gov/About-BOEM/BOEM-Regions/Alaska-Region/Community-Liaison/Index.aspx (last visited Feb. 10, 2014).

Territories[101] must adhere to a robust regulatory scheme, supported by well-developed associated policies and guidelines, to be granted the necessary approvals to be able to proceed. All research projects taking place in the Northwest Territories must be licensed.[102] This requirement applies to all researchers, whether governmental or nongovernmental, and applies widely to research conducted in the physical, social, and biological sciences, in addition to research focusing on traditional knowledge and health matters.[103] The objective of the research licensing and permitting scheme is to ensure the Northwest Territories' natural, social, and cultural environments are not harmed through the implementation of research projects.[104]

Depending on the nature and scope of the research, permitting and licensing may be required from all three levels of regulators present in the Northwest Territories, namely federal, territorial, and local officials.[105] With respect to the local level, the Northwest Territories is divided into six Land Claim Regions, with multiple communities making up each Land Claim Region.[106]

Among the regulatory bodies associated with the three levels of regulatory review, focal areas vary, from reviewing aspects of research projects on more technical and/or environmental assessment bases, to facilitating robust communication between researchers and associated community groups, to ensuring, among other things, that community concerns are represented and addressed.[107]

While the permits and licenses required on a federal level are generally applicable to research conducted anywhere in Canada, key distinguishing features of the regulatory processes on the territorial and local levels are requirements grounded in community consultation, and the return of knowledge to communities.[108] The research and consultation requirements on the local level vary, as the Northwest Territories' six Land Claim Regions maintain distinct sociopolitical structures,[109] and the communities within each hold varying geopolitical influences.[110]

---

[101] Canada is divided into ten provinces making up southern Canada, and three territories filling Canada's north, with the Northwest Territories located in the central arctic region. The population of the Northwest Territories is approximately 43,000, about half of which is Aboriginal, and the territory is home to eleven official languages.

[102] *See* AURORA RESEARCH INST., DOING RESEARCH IN THE NORTHWEST TERRITORIES: A GUIDE FOR RESEARCHERS APPLYING FOR A SCIENTIFIC RESEARCH LICENSE 4 (2011), *available at* http://www.accessnwt.ca/docs/default-document-library/doing-research-in-the-northwest-territories.pdf.

[103] *Id.*

[104] Obtaining Your Research Licenses and Permits, ACCESS RESEARCH NORTHWEST, http://www.access-nwt.ca/licensing (last visited Apr. 23, 2014).

[105] DOING RESEARCH IN THE NORTHWEST TERRITORIES, *supra* note 102.

[106] *Id.* The six Land Claim Regions in the Northwest Territories are Inuvialuit, Gwich'in, Sahtu, North Slave, Dehcho, and South Slave. *Id.*

[107] Obtaining Your Research Licenses and Permits, *supra* note 104.

[108] *Id.*

[109] DOING RESEARCH IN THE NORTHWEST TERRITORIES, *supra* note 102.

[110] Obtaining Your Research Licenses and Permits, *supra* note 104.

B. RESEARCH IN PRACTICE

The purpose of research policies when working on projects that relate to Arctic communities focuses on the need to share information and appropriately engage key community leaders, knowledge holders, and participants, while at the same time enabling research projects to move forward. Fair dealing and open communication is at the heart of Arctic research policies—in order to make the policies meaningful, they must then be translated into practice from the inception of research ideas through the completion of projects and dissemination of results. At the same time, the existing limits of research funding may constrain the ways that researchers are able to effectively engage with communities. This section briefly considers ways climate change and other researchers engage with communities before, during, and after projects, based on interviews with researchers and community members.[111]

Before projects, examples of engagement identified include researchers attending local meetings, developing collaborations with tribal councils or regional bodies, and conducting local reviews of project proposals, among other strategies.

During projects, there is a need for ongoing engagement at the research site and in the community. Practical strategies that have been used in the Arctic include using local guides, involving community members in research projects, holding public lectures, using radio advertisements and commercials to describe research plans, and utilizing social media and electronic outreach to engage community members in ongoing research projects.

After projects, efforts to disseminate results are essential to ensure information flow. A primary climate change research need described by Alaska Native communities is for research results to make their way back to involved and/or affected communities. Effectively sharing information can lead to informed communities, which is important for climate change adaptation and for building relationships for future research efforts. Strategies include outreach methods such as flyers, posters, and summaries, presenting at local, regional, or state-wide meetings, lecturing at local schools, and conducting electronic outreach through newsletters or social media.

Across all stages of the research process, funding, capacity, and resource-allocation can present obstacles to effective engagement. Communication efforts require adequate resources, both financial investment and personnel time. At any time, but especially in light of today's tightly constrained budgets, resources for outreach and communication must be specifically built into the funding process if researchers and communities are going to have the capacity to engage.

There are special considerations when conducting research in the U.S. Arctic given the cultural differences between Alaska Native communities and many researchers coming

---

[111] The information contained herein regarding research in practice and in Section C, *infra*, regarding Research Opportunities draws from the authors' previously completed work on the subject, including ENVIRONMENTAL LAW INSTITUTE, *supra* note 67.

from either other parts of the region or outside the region entirely. As with consultation, trust, respect, and relationships are essential, too often neglected, aspects of community engagement.

Communication methods that are understandable and establish the relevance of research are also important. Different types of communication methods may be appropriate in different circumstances. In some situations, lectures and audiovisual presentations may be best. In others, websites and social media posts may provide the optimal opportunity for outreach. The best approach may vary depending on the issue and the attributes of the audience generally. For example, elders may have different needs than younger members of the community. Generally, it is important that subsistence communities have a point of reference that makes the issues being researched relevant to their experience. From these challenges also come opportunities to optimize the research process and to address Alaska Native communities' climate change research needs, which is the subject of the next subsection.

C. RESEARCH OPPORTUNITIES

Overall, Alaska Native policies and federal policies share approaches with respect to research activities undertaken in Arctic and northern regions. Considering the above review of the existing legal and policy framework governing how Alaska Native communities are involved in research projects, along with a brief introduction to research in practice, certain themes are evident that could be used as an opportunity to shape best practices for researchers in the climate change context going forward. The hope is for climate change research to be informed by communities' traditional knowledge, and to inform community subsistence activities and adaptation.

Before projects, Alaska Native and federal policies highlight the need for early engagement, information sharing, and informed consent with respect to research projects (and specifically for research methodologies). One possibility for improved communication would be for funding entities to demonstrate engagement before, during, and after projects in requests for proposals (RFPs), with an additional requirement that appropriately tailored outreach reports are shared with communities after projects are completed. In addition, researchers could include community partners on RFPs and project plans. Canadian research regulatory processes may provide additional examples of how community engagement can be incorporated.

During projects, it is important to provide information back to respective communities, and demonstrate respect for local knowledge contributed by community members. While federal policies identify multiple entry points for community members, it is the Alaska Native policies that directly raise the importance of fair compensation for participant community members. There are references in federal policies, however, to ensuring research project design incorporates training for younger community members, and more broadly, that projects integrate meaningful experiences for participants.

To continue the trend toward stressing engagement, researchers could contact tribal councils or other community contacts to make local hires, along with providing compensation for community involvement.

After projects, Alaska Native and federal policies emphasize a need for continued engagement and two-way dialogue. To facilitate meaningful dialogue, researchers could provide summary documents, visual presentations and posters, and publish online materials that are relevant to communities, in addition to giving communities an opportunity to review and comment on draft research reports.

Most of all, throughout the research process, the policies reviewed prioritize open and transparent communication between researchers and communities. All of these points speak to the importance of researchers and communities taking active steps to engage with one another from project inception to results dissemination, in a manner that demonstrates respect and builds trust. The existence of shared, rather than disparate, perspectives should therefore be considered encouraging by both Alaska Natives and federal research project participants. Given the pressing threats posed by climate change, it is important that researchers and communities engage effectively to best inform climate change knowledge and management.

Conclusion

Climate change is causing the Arctic to change at rates unprecedented in recent memory. Alaska Native communities that engage in subsistence hunting of marine resources face the challenge of adapting to these changing conditions. These communities have also protected the Arctic marine environment for countless generations, watching over not only the animals that are integral to their lifestyles and traditions but also the species' habitats and ecosystems. From both needs and knowledge perspectives, Alaska Native tribes and authorized bodies have a strong role to play in the governance of the region.

To support effective management of natural resources and the local populations' ability to adapt to changing conditions, U.S. resource managers and Alaska Native communities must share information and experience. There must be a continuing cycle of engagement between the parties, to ensure community information, priorities, and needs are integrated into existing ocean and coastal governance systems, and that U.S. managers and outside researchers benefit from community knowledge and understanding.

This chapter explored two pathways for strengthening Alaska Native engagement in Alaskan Arctic marine management activities and decision-making: government-to-government consultation, resulting from the communities' status as domestic dependent nations, and climate change research, which is growing rapidly in the region. The analysis of existing policies and practices and the recommendations offered focus on extracting key principles to guide engagement with Alaska Natives throughout the processes.

Alaska Native communities have been stewards of the Arctic for generations. Incorporating their knowledge and expertise into marine management and research is mandatory for the United States to fulfill its trust responsibilities and to ensure that the processes are effective, sustainable, and successful in a rapidly changing Arctic.

24 Rising to the Challenge:
CALIFORNIA COASTAL CLIMATE CHANGE ADAPTATION
Sara C. Aminzadeh*

---

* I dedicate this chapter to my husband, Maxwell Vaughn Pritt (MVP), who has poured over nearly everything I have written, offering meticulous edits and unreasonably enthusiastic support in equal measure.

Introduction

The desire to be close to the coast and ocean in California, as in many places around the world, puts an enormous number of people and a staggering amount of property at risk to sea-level rise. Eighty-five percent of California's population lives or works along coastal or bay areas experiencing sea-level rise.[1] In many areas of California, the shoreline is heavily developed with structures ranging from power plants to private estates. Those who have built right up to the edge will need to come to terms with an increasingly unrelenting and unforgiving sea.

The latest projections forecast an average rise in sea level of more than one foot over the next forty years, and four to five feet by the turn of the century, along the California coast.[2] Rising sea levels and natural land subsidence will "gradually drown the coastal zone"[3] over the next fifty years. Scientists warn that tides will not solely rise gently and gradually. Sea-level rise will be punctuated by episodic flood events as high tides and stronger and more frequent storm surges coincide, putting shoreline property and ecosystems at risk long before the oft-used 2050 and 2100 timelines.

California has a long history of confronting coastal planning and protection challenges, and a vested interest in protecting the quality of life and economy attached to the California coast. However, more than five years after the state's first official recognition of the need for coastal climate adaptation, ambiguity and uncertainty persist as to the application of California's fundamental laws. The degree to which resource management agencies have the authority, appetite, and capacity to address the complex legal, environmental, and societal issues triggered by sea-level rise also is unknown.

This chapter examines existing and potential legal and policy responses to sea-level rise and other climate change impacts to the California coast.[4] Section I of this chapter summarizes projected sea-level rise impacts to California's economy, environment, and

---

[1] California Natural Resources Agency, *2009 California Climate Adaptation Strategy: A Report to the Governor of the State of California in Response to Executive Order S-13-2006*, 1, 68 (2009), *available at* http://resources.ca.gov/climate_adaptation/docs/Statewide_Adaptation_Strategy.pdf (hereinafter Cal. Natural Res. Agency); Leslie Ewing, "Considering Sea Level Rise as a Coastal Hazard," Proceedings of Coastal Zone' 07, Portland, OR, July 22–26, 2007.

[2] Sea-Level Rise Projections Use 2000 as the Baseline and Differ North and South of Cape Mendocino. California Climate Action Team, Coastal and Ocean Working Group, *State of California Sea-Level Rise Guidance Document* (Ocean Protection Council, Mar. 2013); National Research Council, *Sea-Level Rise for the Coasts of California, Oregon, and Washington: Past, Present, and Future* 117, table 5.3 (2012).

[3] Margaret Peloso & Margaret Caldwell, *Dynamic Property Rights: The Public Trust Doctrine and Takings in a Changing Climate*, 30 STAN. ENVTL. L.J. 51, 53 (2011).

[4] Although this chapter refers to the "California coast" broadly, sea-level rise impacts and governing regulations and agencies vary between coastal and bay areas. For example, the coastal zone established by the California Coastal Act does not include San Francisco Bay, where development is regulated by the Bay Conservation and Development Commission.

people, and provides an overview of the state's sea-level rise response to date. Section II briefly describes two of California's key land use laws, the California Coastal Act and the California Environmental Quality Act, and briefly analyzes how these laws may be applied in light of sea-level rise. Section III provides case studies of the unique sea-level rise adaptation challenges facing communities in the Humboldt Bay Area in Northern California, the San Francisco Bay Area, and Southern California.

I. California's Initial Response to Sea-Level Rise

A. IMPACTS TO THE CALIFORNIA COAST

Challenges to living in, planning, and protecting California's coastal zone and bay shorelines predate climate change. The question of how to manage and regulate erosion, coastal flooding, storm surges, and other aspects of the dynamic shoreline environment has long been the subject of vigorous public debate, litigation, and policymaking. Sea-level rise and other climate change-driven impacts exacerbate and hasten existing coastal hazards, and create new issues.

California's coastal and bay areas will experience a variety of impacts stemming from sea-level rise, precipitation changes, and other climate change impacts. Scientists estimate that sea level has risen seven inches since 1900, and is projected to rise 12–18 inches by 2050 and 21–55 inches by 2100.[5] Projected sea-level rise, compounded by shifting precipitation and extreme weather events, will impact an estimated 480,000 residents and at least $100 billion in property throughout California.[6] If California does not take action to mitigate sea-level rise impacts and other projected climate impacts, the costs will be crippling. A 2008 report estimates that if no adaptation measures are taken in California, damages across sectors could result in "tens of billions of dollars per year in direct costs and expose trillions of dollars of assets to collateral risks."[7]

Large numbers of people and extensive infrastructure will be at risk from inundation during coastal storms as higher sea levels, high tides, storm surges, and inland flooding coincide.[8] Projected inundation will impact water supply canals, waste-water treatment plants, and power plants throughout California.[9] There are twenty-one waste-water treatment plants lining the San Francisco Bay, ten of which are vulnerable to inundation

---

[5] Dan Cayan et al., *Climate Change Scenarios and Sea Level Rise Estimates for the California 2008 Climate Change Scenarios Assessment* (2009), www.energy.ca.gov/2009publications/CEC-500-2009-014/CEC-500-2009-014-D.PDF.

[6] *See* Cal. Natural Res. Agency, *supra* note 1, at 85.

[7] *Id.* at 3 (quoting D. Roland-Holst & Fredrich Kahrl, *California Climate Risk and Response* (2008), *available at* http://www.next10.org/research/research_ccrr.html).

[8] *See* Matthew Heberger et al., *The Impacts of Sea-Level Rise on the California Coast*, 2–3 (2009), *available at* http://pacinst.org/wp-content/uploads/sites/21/2014/04/sea-level-rise.pdf; Cal. Natural Res. Agency, *supra* note 1, at 68.

[9] *See* Cal. Natural Res. Agency, *supra* note 1, at 65.

from sea-level rise by 2100.[10] The release of untreated sewage from even a fraction of California's waste-water treatment plants—which collectively treat 530 million gallons every day—would cause a serious public health and environmental disaster.[11]

As the ocean moves inland, California coastal and estuarine ecosystems will undergo changes of enormous magnitude. Sea-level rise will increase saltwater intrusion in coastal aquifers, impacting communities and farmers who rely on groundwater supplies.[12] Moreover, 350,000 acres of California's critically important coastal wetlands face flooding from sea-level rise.[13]

B. EARLY ACTION IS NON-BINDING, COLLABORATIVE

In 2008, former California governor Arnold Schwarzenegger issued the state's first official directive on sea-level rise. Executive Order S-13-08 recognized that "California must begin now to adapt and build our resiliency to coming climate changes through a thoughtful and sensible approach with local, regional, state and federal government using the best available science."[14] The Order called for the development of a state-wide Climate Adaptation Strategy and ordered state agencies to plan for sea-level rise impacts.[15]

There are three federally designated coastal management agencies charged with administering the federal Coastal Zone Management Act (CZMA).[16] The California Coastal Commission administers the coastal program for California's open coast. The San Francisco Bay Conservation and Development Commission (BCDC) is the designated coastal management agency for the San Francisco Bay segment of the California coastal zone. The California Coastal Conservancy serves as a "repository for lands whose reservation is required to meet the policies and objectives" of the Coastal Act.[17] The California Ocean Protection Council, formed by the California Ocean Protection Act of 2004, is charged with coordinating all state coastal and ocean management agencies.[18]

These agencies work together to coordinate policy and regulatory development, and issue sea-level rise projections through the Coastal and Ocean Working Group of the

---

[10] Matthew Heberger et al., *The Impacts of Sea Level Rise on the San Francisco Bay*, 14–16 (Pacific Institute 2012), *available at* http://www.energy.ca.gov/2012publications/CEC-500-2012-014/CEC-500-2012-014. pdf.

[11] Heberger, *supra* note 8, at 63.

[12] *Id.* at 81.

[13] *Id.* at 3.

[14] Office of Governor Arnold Schwarzenegger, Exec. Order No. S-13-08 (Cal. 2008), *available at* http://gov. ca.gov/news.php?id=11036.

[15] *Id.*

[16] 16 U.S.C. §§ 1451–1465 (2012).

[17] Cal. Pub. Res. Code § 31104.1 (West, WestlawNext current with urgency legislation through Ch. 185 of 2014 Reg. Sess., Res. Ch. 1 of 2013–2014 2nd Ex. Sess., and all propositions on the June 3, 2014 ballot).

[18] *Id.* § 35615.

California Climate Action Team (CO-CAT), which is led by the Ocean Protection Council.[19] The CO-CAT developed the 2009 California Climate Adaptation Strategy (CAS),[20] one of the earliest sources of guidance for both state and local agencies developing sea-level rise strategies. The California Attorney General's Office instructed local governments to refer to the California Climate Adaptation Strategy to develop "reasonable and rational risk reduction strategies."[21] Much of the CAS reiterates long-understood coastal planning best practices that have become strictly necessary in light of projected sea-level rise. The CAS articulates six key principles to guide coastal adaptation decision-making:

1. California must begin now to adapt to the current and future impacts of climate change.
2. California must protect public health and safety and critical infrastructure.
3. California must protect, restore, and enhance ocean and coastal ecosystems, on which our economy and well-being depend.
4. California must ensure public access to coastal areas and protect beaches, natural shoreline, and park and recreational resources.
5. New development and communities must be planned and designed for long-term sustainability in the face of climate change.
6. California must look for ways to facilitate adaptation of existing development and communities to reduce their vulnerability to climate change impacts over time.[22]

Instead of focusing solely on reducing the vulnerability of existing shoreline developments, the CAS specifies that activities to enhance "resilience"[23] should be pursued. A resilient ecosystem is measured by "the capacity of a system to absorb and utilize or even benefit from perturbations and changes that attain it, and so persist without a qualitative change in the system's structure."[24] The CAS states that California "should pursue activities that can increase natural resiliency, such as restoring tidal wetlands,

---

[19] State of California Ocean Protection Council, *The Coastal and Ocean Resources Working Group for the Climate Action Team* (2010), *available at* http://www.opc.ca.gov/2010/07/coastal-and-oc ean-climate-action-team-co-cat/.

[20] *See* Cal. Natural Res. Agency, *supra* note 1.

[21] California Attorney General's Office, *Straightforward Answers to Some Frequently Asked Questions. See also* Sarah Polgar, *Update on Guidance for Addressing Climate Change Impacts in California Environmental Quality Act Review* (2009), *available at* http://www.bcdc.ca.gov/planning/climate_change/adaptation/ CEQA_climate_impacts.pdf.

[22] *See* Cal. Natural Res. Agency, *supra* note 1, at 72.

[23] *See generally* Timothy Beatley, *Planning for Coastal Resilience: Best Practices for Calamitous Times* (2009).

[24] *See generally* Crawford Stanley Holling, *Resilience and Stability of Ecological Systems*, 4 ANN. REV. ECOLOGY & SYSTEMATICS 1 (1973).

living shoreline, and related habitats; managing sediment for marsh accretion and natural flood protection; and maintaining upland buffer areas around tidal wetlands."[25]

The CO-CAT continually updates sea-level rise projections based on the latest science, and provides guidance to inform agency planning and decision-making. In March 2011, the Ocean Protection Council adopted a non-binding resolution *encouraging*—but not requiring—all state agencies to adhere to the Sea-Level Rise Interim Guidance Document and to incorporate sea-level rise considerations into decision-making. California also participates in efforts of the West Coast Governors' Alliance for Ocean Health, partnering with Oregon, Washington, and federal agencies to study sea-level rise along the Pacific Coast.[26]

C. FUNDING FOR LOCAL COASTAL CLIMATE ADAPTATION

California's shoreline communities—like those around the world—need significant resources to conduct vulnerability assessments of projected impacts, and to develop and implement plans to deal with impacts. Some state funding has already been made available to support local adaptation work.

In 2013, the Coastal Conservancy awarded more than $3 million[27] for twenty Climate Ready projects to help California's coastal communities prepare for the effects of a changing climate. The projects are located from San Diego to Humboldt counties and will help communities adapt to rising seas, more severe storms, increased risk of fires, and changing rainfall levels and water availability. For example, the San Francisco International Airport was awarded $200,000 to study the vulnerability of a shoreline area northwest of the airport to sea-level rise and to prepare adaptation strategies.[28] Also in 2013, the California Governor's Budget authorized $2.5 million in funding to encourage local governments and other entities responsible for coastal planning to develop and adopt updated plans that protect coastal resources from future impacts from sea-level rise and related climate change impacts such as extreme weather events.

These two state programs provided a modest infusion of funding for local coastal climate adaptation planning to date, but are dependent on the governor's budget allocations. Long-term and comprehensive adaptation efforts will require a significant investment of targeted and accountable state funding. In 2013, promising legislation was introduced to create a Coastal Adaptation Fund with a permanent allocation

---

[25] *See* Cal. Natural Res. Agency, *supra* note 1, at 74 (recommendations include preservation of natural areas that contain critical habitat for tidal wetland restoration, habitat migration, or buffer zones).

[26] National Research Council Commission on Sea Level Rise in California, Oregon & Washington, *Sea-Level Rise for the Coasts of California, Oregon, and Washington: Past, Present, and Future* 108 (2012), *available at* http://www.nap.edu/catalog.php?record_id=13389.

[27] Funding is dependent on the California governor's budget.

[28] The study will complement the airport's SFO Shoreline Protection Feasibility Study, the purpose of which is to develop a shoreline protection system that will protect the airport from flooding and rising seas.

of funding from tideland oil revenue fees.[29] The bill would have required that the Governor's Annual Budget appropriate at least $6 million into a Coastal Adaptation Fund for climate change adaptation initiatives consistent with state guidance, but failed to pass the Assembly.[30] California state legislators subsequently convened a Committee on Sea Level Rise and the California Economy.[31]

Irrespective of the state funding program or programs that are established for adaptation, local governments in California are likely to need federal funding as well. In 2010–2011, the National Oceanic and Atmospheric Administration (NOAA) created the Coastal Resilience Networks (CRest) to fund projects that help communities become more resilient to the threats posed by coastal hazards. Grants were awarded between $100,000 and $350,000, based on annual congressional appropriations. Funding for CRest in California was last made available in 2011.

It may also be possible to leverage federal disaster funding to fund habitat conservation projects to mitigate coastal flooding associated with sea-level rise.[32] Wetland and habitat restoration is a proven and cost-effective multi-benefit flood mitigation tool.[33] The Federal Emergency Management Agency (FEMA) funds projects to mitigate flooding and other types of disasters. California recognizes ecosystem restoration as a disaster management tool in its State Hazard Mitigation Plan, which lays the groundwork for access to FEMA resources for habitat restoration and conservation.[34] Grant programs under FEMA's Hazard Mitigation Assistance (HMA) program could be used for flood risk mitigation.

These projects could take shape through the purchase of acreage in flood-prone and environmentally significant locations, with the purpose of mitigating flood risk and restoring natural ecosystems. In an initial study of California, areas concentrated along the Russian River in Sonoma County were identified as especially appropriate for federally funded multi-benefit habitat restoration and flood mitigation projects. NOAA is also working to incorporate sea-level rise into Monterey County's hazard mitigation

---

[29] Senate Bill 461 was introduced by State Senator Mark Leno of Marin County (2013). Bill text *available at* http://leginfo.legislature.ca.gov/faces/billNavClient.xhtml?bill_id=201320140SB461.

[30] *Id.*

[31] *See* California State Assembly, Select Committee on Sea Level Rise and the California Economy Homepage, *available at* http://sealevelrise.assembly.ca.gov (last visited Aug. 4, 2014).

[32] This discussion highlights work as presented by Juliano Calil et al. in a forthcoming article, *Aligning Natural Resource Conservation and Flood Hazard Mitigation in California* (2014) (unpublished manuscript on file with author).

[33] *See* Adam Z. Rose et al., *Estimating the Value of Foresight: Aggregate Analysis of Natural Hazard Mitigation Benefits and Costs* (2009), Non-published Research Reports, Paper 90, *available at* http://research.create. usc.edu/nonpublished_reports/90.

[34] Edmund Brown Jr. & Mark Ghilarducci, Governor's Office of Emergency Services, *California Multi-Hazard Mitigation Plan* (2013), *available at* http://hazardmitigation.calema.ca.gov/docs/SHMP_Final_2013.pdf. Specifically, the California Emergency Management Agency, 2013 State Hazard Mitigation Plan (SHMP) encourages hazard mitigation measures that result in the least adverse effect on the natural environment and natural processes. *Id.* at 27.

plan, which could make the county eligible for FEMA mitigation funding. Typically, disaster management agencies and habitat conservation agencies work independently to acquire land, but state and local governments, tribal entities, and nonprofit organizations are all eligible to receive HMA funds.[35] Seeking FEMA mitigation money to acquire land could provide an opportunity for cooperation between different entities, and create a source of funding for needed adaptation measures in California.

II. California Legal Framework

A. CALIFORNIA COASTAL ACT AND THE CALIFORNIA COASTAL COMMISSION

California provides more protections than most other states for the public's right to access and enjoy the public/private beach zone.[36] The California constitution guarantees the public's right of access to tidelands, subject to reasonable regulation, and directs the legislature to "enact such laws…so that access to the navigable waters of this State shall be always attainable for the people thereof."[37] The California Coastal Act formally recognizes these state constitutional rights and articulates a state directive to "maximize public access to and along the coast and maximize public recreational opportunities in the coastal zone consistent with sound resources conservation principles and constitutionally protected rights of property owners."[38] The California Coastal Act shapes coastal development, with specific policies to address shoreline public access and recreation, habitat protection, agricultural lands, industrial uses, and development design and siting, among many other issues.

The California Coastal Commission was established by voter initiative in 1972 (Proposition 20) and later made permanent by the state legislature through adoption of the California Coastal Act of 1976.[39] The Commission is charged with implementing coastal development plans and approving plans developed by local authorities under delegated authority. The public trust doctrine informs and bolsters the Coastal Commission's mandate to preserve and protect public trust rights, including the protection of the environment, natural resources, and open space.

The California Coastal Commission plans and regulates land use in the coastal zone along the state's 1,100-mile shoreline, as defined by the state legislature. On land, the coastal zone varies in width from several hundred feet in highly urbanized areas and up to five miles in rural areas, whereas the coastal zone offshore is a uniform three-mile-wide

---

[35] Federal Emergency Management Agency, Hazard Mitigation Grant Program (2013), *available at* http://www.fema.gov/hazard-mitigation-grant-program.

[36] Melissa K. Scanlan, *Shifting Sands: A Meta-Theory for Public Access and Private Property Along the Coast*, 65 S. C. L. Rev. 295, 362 (2013).

[37] Cal. Const. art. 10, § 4.

[38] *See* Cal. Pub. Res. Code § 30001.5(c) (West 2007).

[39] *See generally* California Coastal Commission, Program Overview (2012), *available at* http://www.coastal.ca.gov/whoweare.html.

band of ocean and submerged lands. California's coastal management program is carried out through a partnership between state and local governments. Coastal Act policies are implemented primarily through the preparation of local coastal programs (LCPs). Each of the fifteen counties and sixty-one cities located in whole or in part in the coastal zone has LCPs, which must be reviewed and approved by the Coastal Commission for compliance with the Coastal Act. Development within the coastal zone may not commence until either the Commission, or a local government that has a Commission-certified local coastal program, has issued a coastal development permit.[40]

In late 2013, the Coastal Commission released its Draft Sea Level Rise Policy Guidance.[41] The Guidance, still in draft form as of this writing, provides a comprehensive overview of best available science on sea-level rise for California and recommended steps for addressing sea-level rise through LCPs and coastal development permits. The Commission's efficacy in mitigating coastal climate change impacts depends in part on the final form that the Sea Level Rise Guidance takes, and in part on the vigor with which it is implemented at the state and local level.

B. HOW STRONG ARE CALIFORNIA'S PUBLIC TRUST ROOTS?

How regrettable it would be if, looking back a decade or two from now, the legal landscape were littered with takings lawsuits threatened and brought against state and local governments who chose to act while politicians continued to engage in demagoguery, and the waters continued to rise.[42]

The public trust doctrine is an ancient legal principle that creates a duty for states to protect coastal lands and waters for preservation and public use. The geographic scope of the public trust, and the specific public trust rights recognized, varies considerably from state to state.[43] Like the majority of states, ownership rights in California are based on the mean high tideline, meaning that the private title ends and state title begins at the mean high-water mark.[44] The California constitution and the Coastal Act supplement

---

[40] *See* California Coastal Commission Program Overview Website, *available at* http://www.coastal.ca.gov/whoweare.html (last visited Apr. 22, 2014).

[41] Edmund Brown Jr., Cal. Natural Res. Agency, *California Coastal Commission Draft Sea-Level Rise Policy Guidance* (2013), *available at* http://www.coastal.ca.gov/climate/slr/guidance/CCC_Draft_SLR_Guidance_PR_10142013.pdf.

[42] Michael Allan Wolf, *Strategies for Making Sea-Level Rise Adaptation Tools "Takings-Proof,"* 28 J. LAND USE & ENVTL. L. 157, 196 (2013).

[43] *See* Peloso & Caldwell, *supra* note 3, appendix A at 109.

[44] State ownership of tidelands and submerged lands is consistent with common law principles that "[t]he state owns all tidelands below the ordinary high water mark and holds such lands in trust for the public... [and] as the land along a body of water gradually builds up or erodes, the ordinary high water mark necessarily moves and thus the mark or line of mean high tide, i.e., the legal boundary, also moves." Lechuza Villas West v. Cal. Coastal Comm'n, 70 Cal. Rptr. 2d 399, 418 (Ct. App. 1997). There is one exception to this rule in California, where the upland private property owner does not gain from gradual artificial accretion.

and reinforce the public trust doctrine.[45] The Commission exercises its trust responsibilities when it acts on a permit, adopts a Local Coastal Plan, changes a regulation, or adopts a guidance document. The public trust doctrine and other common law principles provide a basis for a wide range of agency actions to limit risky coastal development, preserve open space, protect habitat, and provide buffers to accommodate rising sea levels or storm surge.[46] However, some government actions, such as the employment of a rolling easement or removal of shoreline armoring structures, test the limits of government authority and will likely trigger legal challenge by property owners and others.

1. Rolling Easements and Takings[47]

If property owners are not permitted to build coastal defense structures, then rising sea levels will advance the mean high tideline landward.[48] On a relatively flat beach, each centimeter of sea-level rise will result in the mean high tideline migrating forty centimeters inland.[49] Arguably, as shorelines erode, the public trust doctrine follows the eroding shoreline.[50] Legal scholars assert that the public trust doctrine should be applied to recognize the public's interest in privately owned land that becomes inundated as sea levels rise.[51] James G. Titus dubbed this concept a "rolling easement,"[52] borrowing the term from the Texas Open Beaches Act, which authorizes Texas to enforce a public easement over the dry sandy beach from the mean high tideline to the first line of natural vegetation, and to file petitions to remove encroachments on public beaches.[53] A rolling

---

California *ex rel.* State Lands Comm'n v. Superior Court, 11 Cal. 4th 50, 71–72 (1995); California *ex rel.* State Lands Comm'n v. United States, 457 U.S. 273, 277 (1982).

[45] *See* Megan M. Herzog & Sean Hecht, *Combatting Sea-Level Rise in Southern California: How Local Governments Can Seize Adaptation Opportunities while Minimizing Legal Risk*, 19 HASTINGS W.-Nw. J. ENVTL. L. & POL'Y 463 (2013) (citing CAL. PUB. RES. CODE §§ 30000–30900 (West 2012)).

[46] *See* Michael Allan Wolf, *supra* note 42, table 2 at 173.

[47] The application of coastal takings to sea-level rise and other climate change adaptation impacts is discussed in detail in Chapter 21. The purpose of this subsection is to discuss constitutional takings issues specific to California, under which certain adaptation strategies that impair private property rights may be vulnerable.

[48] *See also* Littoral Dev. Co. v. San Francisco Bay Conservation & Dev. Comm'n, 24 Cal. App. 4th 1050, 1057 (1994). The court held that BCDC's Bay jurisdiction extends to the mean high-tide line, but not to the line of highest tidal action.

[49] Edmund Brown Jr., Cal. Coastal Comm'n, Staff Rpt.: Regular Calendar (2014), *available at* http://documents.coastal.ca.gov/reports/2012/5/W23b-5-2012.pdf.

[50] James G. Titus, *Rising Seas, Coastal Erosion and the Takings Clause: How to Save Wetlands and Beaches without Hurting Property Owners*, 57 MD. L. REV. 1279, 1368 (1998).

[51] Meg Caldwell & Craig Holt Segall, *No Day at the Beach: Sea Level Rise, Ecosystem Loss, and Public Access along the California Coast*, 34 ECOLOGY L.Q. 533, 552–55 (2007). *Accord* Will Travis & Tim Eichenberg, *Using the Public Trust Doctrine to Adapt to Climate Change in San Francisco Bay* 13 (S.F. Bay Conservation & Development Comm'n 2009) (declaring that "[s]ea level rise will increase state ownership rights"); *A Report on Sea Level Rise Preparedness* 25 (Cal. State Lands Comm'n 2009) ("[C]oastal boundaries and the State's sovereign ownership should continue to move with ever shifting sands and seas.").

[52] *See* Titus, *supra* note 50.

[53] TEX. NAT. RES. CODE ANN. § 61.018 (West, WestlawNext current through the end of the 2013 Third Called Session of the 83rd Legislature).

easement could be used to prevent activities that interfere with public trust uses, such as blocking public access, constructing seawalls, or damaging public trust resources such as wetlands.[54]

Together, common law, case law, the California constitution, and the Coastal Act have created a robust public trust doctrine in California.[55] The use of rolling easement policies will depend on California's willingness "to reach beyond the present-day geographic contours of the public trust to prevent risky coastal development in the future."[56]

Application of the public trust doctrine to limit coastal development on private lands that will be inundated by sea-level rise is limited by regulatory takings liability.[57] The Takings Clause constrains government regulations and permit actions on private property. As discussed in Chapter 21, takings liability is determined by the application of the holding in *Lucas v. South Carolina Coastal Council*[58] for per se takings, and the multi-factor test set out in *Penn Central*.[59] One authoritative scholar concludes that "the true obstacle to implementing rolling easements and limiting wasteful coastal development [in California] is not legal, but rather, political … the real challenge … is to align public expectations with the state's understanding of coastal hazards."[60] Irrespective of the fate of rolling easements in California, various responses are available to address sea-level rise, such as enhanced floodplain restrictions, that pose either no takings risk or minimal takings risk.[61]

2. Nuisance and Coastal Armoring

The general public's perception is that seawalls, revetments, and other shoreline barriers protect the coast. However, seawalls and other structures frequently fail and can destroy the beaches, wetlands, and natural areas that drew people to build on the shoreline in the first place.[62] Coastal ecosystems can survive erosion, storm surges, and rising sea levels by migrating inland, or growing vertically or laterally, but seawalls prevent this natural migration.[63] Instead of moving inland as the rising sea erodes the shoreline, coastal barriers cause wetlands and beaches to become trapped between the seawalls and the rising water until eventually the ecosystems are destroyed.[64] Seawalls, levees, and

---

[54] Titus, *supra* note 50, at 1313.

[55] Herzog & Hecht, *supra* note 45, at 478.

[56] Peloso & Caldwell, *supra* note 3, at 106.

[57] *Id.* at 61.

[58] Lucas v. South Carolina Coastal Council, 505 U.S. 1003 (1992).

[59] Penn Cent. Transp. Co. v. City of New York, 438 U.S. 104 (1978).

[60] Peloso & Caldwell, *supra* note 3, at 107.

[61] *See* Michael Allan Wolf, *supra* note 42, at 173–78.

[62] California Department of Boating and Waterways, *The Economic Costs of Sea-Level Rise to California Beach Communities* (2011) at 72, *available at* http://www.dbw.ca.gov/PDF/Reports/CalifSeaLevelRise.pdf.

[63] Sorell E. Negro, *Built Seawalls: A Protected Investment or Subordinate to the Public Trust?* 18 OCEAN & COASTAL L.J. 89, 93 (2012).

[64] *Id.* at 94 (citing James G. Titus et al., *State and Local Governments Plan for Development of Most Land Vulnerable to Rising Sea Level Along the US Atlantic Coast*, 4 ENVTL. RES. LETTERS 44008 (2009)).

other structures also interrupt the sediment transport process that occurs from eroding bluffs and cliffs. With upstream dams capturing river sediment, and seawalls and other coastal armoring structures preventing natural erosion processes, sediment supply to beaches is significantly reduced.[65] Coastal armoring has resulted in the disappearance of many beaches along California's coastline, which impacts shorebirds and a wide array of coastal flora and fauna.[66]

Additionally, seawalls and revetments are very costly to build and maintain.[67] The costs of coastal armoring range from $7,500 to $10,000 per foot, with significant annual maintenance costs.[68] For example, the estimated cost of armoring San Francisco's Ocean Beach alone is approximately $55 million dollars, and would require $2.8 million dollars in annual maintenance spending.[69] The estimated cost of armoring Malibu's Zuma Beach is $92 million dollars.[70]

Over the next fifty years, as sea levels rise and extreme weather and coastal erosion accelerates, the pressure on coastal agencies to approve permits for seawalls and levees will increase exponentially.[71] The California Coastal Act generally limits the use of structural measures where a less environmentally damaging alternative is available and requires that "conflicts be resolved in a manner which on balance is the most protective of significant coastal resources."[72] The common law remedy of nuisance can be used to prevent inappropriate coastal armoring to hold back sea levels.

A public nuisance can be found for activities that endanger public life or health, obstruct the free use of property, interfere with the enjoyment of life or property, or unlawfully obstruct the free passage or use of navigable waters.[73] Coastal armoring, through the construction of seawalls, revetments, and other concrete barriers, can have significant public impacts, including reduced public access, destruction of sandy

---

[65] Michael Slagel & Gary Griggs, *Cumulative Loss of Sand to the California Coast by Dam Impoundment* (2006), *available at* http://www.dbw.ca.gov/csmw/PDF/Slagel&Griggs CA Dam Manuscript.pdf. ("As much as 50 percent of the sand originally delivered to the coast in Southern California, 31 percent in Central and 5 percent in Northern California has been lost, the great majority of this impounded behind dams in reservoirs.")

[66] Jennifer E. Dugan et al., *Ecological Effects of Coastal Armoring on Sandy Beaches*, 29 MARINE ECOLOGY 160–70 (2008) (noting that armored beaches had significantly fewer and smaller intertidal macro-invertebrates, three times fewer shorebirds, and four to seven times fewer gulls and other birds than unarmored beaches).

[67] In 1998, California residents were paying more than $75 million per year to armor the shoreline. Gary B. Griggs et al., *California Needs a Coastal Hazard Policy*, 13(3) COAST & OCEAN MAG. (1998), *available at* http://www.coastalconservancy.ca.gov/coast&ocean/autumn98/a04.htm.

[68] Cal. Dep't of Boating and Waterways, *supra* note 62, at 47.

[69] *Id.* at 59.

[70] *Id.*

[71] *See* Caldwell & Segall, *supra* note 51, at 534 ("As sea level rises, pressure to armor the coast will grow").

[72] CAL. PUB. RES. CODE § 30007.5 (West, WestlawNext current with urgency legislation through Ch. 185 of 2014 Reg.Sess., Res. Ch. 1 of 2013–2014 2nd Ex.Sess., and all propositions on the 6/3/2014 ballot).

[73] *See* CAL. CIV. CODE § 3479 (West, WestlawNext current with urgency legislation through Ch. 185 of 2014 Reg.Sess., Res. Ch. 1 of 2013–2014 2nd Ex. Sess., and all propositions on the 6/3/2014 ballot); People *ex rel.* Baker v. Mack, 19 Cal. App. 3d 1040, 1050 (1971).

beaches, and increased flooding. A seawall that encroaches on public land has been held in California to constitute a public nuisance justifying removal without the payment of compensation.[74] In *Scott v. City of Del Mar*, the court upheld the city's legislative right to declare that shoreline armoring encroaching upon the public's land was a nuisance per se.[75] The question of whether nuisance can be applied to shoreline armoring on private land in California is unresolved.

Some California coastal homeowners often believe that they have a constitutional property right to build a seawall to protect their property from erosion.[76] Coastal Act section 30235 provides that "existing structures" should be granted the privilege of armoring if specified conditions are met.[77] It is an ongoing debate as to whether "existing" means in place as of 1976, when the Act was passed, or at the time of the application to build a seawall.[78] The first interpretation would essentially bar seawalls for all structures built after 1976; the second interpretation would bar applications for seawalls for unbuilt structures, but leave all built structures with a possibility of obtaining a permit to armor.[79] The Commission's new Draft Sea Level Rise Guidance requires property owners to waive the right to shoreline protection for development in potentially hazardous locations, and restricts property development that "cannot be sited and designed to be safe for a 50- or 75-year proposed life, without reliance upon protection efforts or impacts to the coastal resources.[80]

C. THE UNCERTAIN FUTURE OF CEQA AND SEA-LEVEL RISE

The California Environmental Quality Act (CEQA)[81]—the state's counterpart to the National Environmental Policy Act—requires public agencies to conduct environmental reviews of projects affecting changes in the environment before they can be approved. CEQA requires agencies to determine whether projects have a "significant" effect on the environment, defined as any "substantial, or potentially substantial, adverse change"[82] in the area affected by the project.[83] Projects with a significant effect on the environment

---

[74] Scott v. City of Del Mar, 58 Cal. App. 4th 1296, 1306 (1997) (holdind that city's removal of seawall did not constitute inverse condemnation because the "legislature has the power to declare certain uses of property a nuisance and such use thereupon becomes a nuisance *per se*.") In this case, the city declared that the obstruction of a public right of way is an abatable nuisance.

[75] *Scott*, 58 Cal. App. 4th 1296.

[76] Todd T. Cardiff, *Conflict in the California Coastal Act: Sand and Seawalls*, 38 CAL. W. L. REV. 255, 256 (2001).

[77] CAL. PUB. RES. CODE § 30235 (West 2006).

[78] Herzog and Hecht, *supra* note 45, 558–59.

[79] *Id.*

[80] Rose, *supra* note 33, at 54, 67.

[81] CAL. PUB. RES. CODE § 21050 (West, WestlawNext current with urgency legislation through Ch. 185 of 2014 Reg. Sess., Res. Ch. 1 of 2013–2014 2nd Ex. Sess., and all propositions on the 6/3/2014 ballot).

[82] *Id.* § 21068; CAL. CODE REGS., tit. 14, § 15002(g) (West, WestlawNext current through 7/18/14 Register 2014, No. 29).

[83] CAL. PUB. RES. CODE § 21060.5 (West, WestlawNext current with urgency legislation through Ch. 185 of 2014 Reg. Sess., Res. Ch. 1 of 2013–2014 2nd Ex. Sess., and all propositions on the 6/3/2014 ballot).

trigger the preparation of an environmental impact report (EIR), which must analyze those effects and how they can be mitigated or avoided by project modifications or alternatives.[84]

In light of projected sea-level rise, public agencies can use CEQA to determine the extent to which future projects impact coastal ecosystems or put residents in harm's way.[85] For example, armoring projects or developments in coastal areas may significantly impede the ability of wetlands or other coastal ecosystems to migrate inland as the sea encroaches. If such environmental impacts are likely to occur, then CEQA requires the lead government agency to propose and implement feasible mitigation measures. CEQA also requires the lead agency to consider alternatives to the proposed project that may reduce or eliminate those impacts.[86] It follows then, that these features of CEQA would require agencies to propose—and to demand of their permit applicants—project modifications such as alternative site configurations to reduce projected sea-level rise impacts to local residents or ecosystems.[87]

In 2011, a California appellate court called into question the application of CEQA to sea-level rise-related impacts. In *Ballona Wetlands Land Trust v. City of Los Angeles*,[88] the Ballona Wetlands Land Trust and Ballona Ecosystem Education Project challenged an environmental impact report for a mixed-use real estate development in Southern California that was located approximately two miles from the coast, because the report failed to analyze projections that climate-change-driven sea-level rise could inundate the development. The court rejected the challenge and held that environmental effects on projects, such as the effects of locating projects in particular areas, do not have to be analyzed under CEQA.[89]

The *Ballona Wetlands* decision addressed the scope of the impacts that must be analyzed during CEQA review, including "converse-CEQA" analysis. Converse-CEQA analysis is used to evaluate and address problems caused by bringing people and new development to areas with poor air quality or hazardous conditions such as heightened seismic activity.[90] Section 15126(a) of the CEQA Guidelines provides that "[t]he EIR shall also analyze any significant environmental effects the project might cause by bringing development and people into the area affected."[91] As California continues to grapple with the effects of climate change, section 15126(a) could arguably be used to analyze

---

[84] *Id.*, §§ 21100(b), 21151; Cal. Code Regs., tit. 14, §§ 15124, 15125, 15126.6, 15362 (West, WestlawNext current through 7/18/14 Register 2014, No. 29).

[85] Herzog & Hecht, *supra* note 45, 485–90 (citing CAL. PUB. RES. CODE § 21151; CAL. CODE REGS., tit. 14, § 15002(f)(1)).

[86] *Id.*

[87] *Id.*

[88] Ballona Wetlands Land Trust v. City of Los Angeles, 201 Cal. App. 4th 455 (2011).

[89] Jennifer Hernandez & Chelsea Maclean, Comment, *Recommendations for Complying with Ballona Wetlands' Definitive Rejection of "Converse-CEQA" Analysis*, 42 ENVTL. L. REP. 11037, 11037 (2012).

[90] *Id.*

[91] CAL. CODE REGS., tit. 14, § 15126.2(a) (West, WestlawNext current through 7/18/14 Register 2014, No. 29).

the effect of climate impacts, such as increased risk of flooding from rising seas. But the *Ballona Wetlands* court narrowly interpreted Guidelines section 15126(a), holding that it "is consistent with CEQA only to the extent that such impacts constitute impacts on the environment caused by the development rather than impacts on the project caused by the environment."[92] The court held that whether a project put people in harm's way is not a consideration under CEQA; rather, "[t]he purpose of an EIR is to identify the significant effects of a project on the environment, not the significant effects of the environment on the project."[93] Many CEQA practitioners consider this statement an express rejection of "converse-CEQA" analysis.[94]

The case was appealed to the California Supreme Court, but the court denied review, making the *Ballona Wetlands* decision controlling law in all California trial courts. In 2012, the Office of the Attorney General of the California Department of Justice released a report on environmental justice and CEQA that seemed to controvert the *Ballona Wetlands* decision. The report stated that both section 15126(a) and appendix G of the CEQA Guidelines require a lead agency to examine existing environmental conditions in the CEQA review process, and that the section and appendix G are a critical component of legally required environmental justice evaluations.[95] One CEQA practitioner echoes this observation, pointing out that "the *Ballona Wetlands* decision could be seen as limiting certain environmental justice considerations under CEQA to the extent that challenges are made to zoning, programs, or projects that seek to channel minorities into communities exposed to disproportionate risks, thus perpetuating or exacerbating segregation and environmental racism."[96]

In 2013, state legislation (Assembly Bill 953) was introduced to overturn the *Ballona Wetlands* decision and to clarify that EIRs should include an assessment of the "effects of locating a proposed project near, or attracting people to, existing or reasonably foreseeable natural hazards or adverse environmental conditions such as sea-level rise...."[97] The legislation was stymied by opposition from the Chamber of Commerce and the building industry lobby. Nonetheless, the issue of converse-CEQA analysis may soon be settled by the California Supreme Court, which granted review in *California Building Industry Ass'n v. Bay Area Quality Management District*[98] to decide whether the *Ballona Wetlands* holding will endure. The fate of how CEQA can be utilized to require sea-level

---

[92] *Ballona Wetlands*, 201 Cal. App. 4th at 473 n.9.

[93] *Id.* at 473.

[94] *See* Hernandez & Maclean, *supra* note 85, at 11037.

[95] Office of the Attorney General, Cal. Dept. of Justice, *Environmental Justice at the Local and Regional Level–Legal Background* (2012).

[96] See Alan Ramo, *Environmental Justice as an Essential Tool in Environmental Review Statutes: A New Look at Federal Policies and Civil Rights Protections and California's Recent Initiatives*, 19 Hastings W.-Nw. J. Envtl. L. & Pol'y 41, 67 (2013).

[97] Melissa Sayoc, *California Environmental Quality Act* (2013), *available at* http://www.leginfo.ca.gov/pub/13-14/bill/asm/ab_0951-1000/ab_953_cfa_20130412_134944_asm_comm.html.

[98] California Bldg. Indus. Ass'n v. Bay Area Quality Mgmt. Dist., 312 P.3d 1070 (Cal. 2013).

rise vulnerability assessments in coastal development and planning remains unknown, although it will almost certainly be heavily litigated over the next decade.[99]

III. Local Adaptation to Climate Change

The vast majority of decisions about how to address sea-level rise and other climate-driven changes in the coastal corridor will happen at the local level. Every community will need to resolve often-conflicting priorities from an array of affected stakeholders: property owners, developers, businesses, municipal service providers, environmentalists, recreational users, and others. Local governments will also face legal limitations on tools for building adaptive capacity, as well as potential liability to private parties for harms related to the adverse effects both of adaptation actions and sea-level rise itself.[100]

Vastly differing natural landscapes, development patterns, and political dynamics in California's coastal and bay areas create unique climate adaptation challenges in different regions. This section presents three case studies that provide a window into how communities are grappling with California's legal, policy, and planning frameworks as they confront sea-level rise in their backyards. Humboldt Bay in Northern California must overcome vulnerabilities associated with the natural "sinking" phenomena of the shoreline area, which was exacerbated by the construction of an artificial shoreline. A controversial regional planning and policymaking process posed significant challenges to the San Francisco Bay Area. Finally, Southern California's coast has already been significantly armored, narrowing the nature and scope of available adaptation options as the region confronts sea-level rise.

A. CASE STUDIES

1. Rising Seas, Sinking Humboldt Bay

Humboldt Bay is an important harbor along the north coast of California and is home to residents from the cities of Eureka, Arcata, and Manila. It is the largest bay on the Pacific Ocean between San Francisco Bay and Washington's Puget Sound, an expanse of some eight hundred miles along the West Coast.

A combination of geology and shoreline infrastructure dating back to the 1800s makes Humboldt Bay one of the areas most vulnerable to sea-level rise in California. Tectonic faults that cause uplift along much of the coast actually work in reverse along the Bay, creating inter-seismic ground subsidence at levels faster than anywhere else along the California coast.[101] Combined with the subsidence of former marshes and

---

[99] Hernandez & Maclean, *supra* note 89, at 11041.

[100] *See* Maxine Burkett, *Litigating Climate Change Adaptation: Theory, Practice, and Corrective (Climate) Justice*, 42 ENVTL. L. REP. 11144 (2012).

[101] *Cal. Coastal Comm'n Draft Sea-Level Rise Policy Guidance*, *supra* note 41, at 4–5.

tidelands, sea levels have risen more than eighteen inches in the Bay in the past century alone.[102] Worse still, current forecasts predict another three to six *feet* of sea-level rise by this century's end.[103]

The early development of Humboldt Bay exacerbated geological conditions. Nearly 90 percent or 9,000 acres of Bay salt marsh is diked off from daily inundation by the tides. Many of these dikes were built between 1880 and 1910 and are quickly approaching the end of their design life. As organic material in the former salt marsh soils have oxidized, former tidelands have compacted by as much as three feet in many areas, making them much lower than the intertidal wetlands on the Bay-side of the dikes. Today, seventy-seven miles of Humboldt Bay's 102-mile shoreline is artificial.[104] In addition, more than half of the shoreline is rated highly vulnerable to flooding and failure in the face of rising seas.[105] Even if all forty-one miles of dikes were fortified, rising waters would make these compacted former tidelands useless for agriculture[106] and threaten the infrastructure built on these lands.

Of particular concern for Humboldt Bay is the presence of legacy contaminated sites at risk of inundation. More than three hundred contaminated sites are within ten meters of the current sea level, and more than forty are within just two meters—the amount that sea level is projected to rise by the year 2100. Many of these contaminated sites, including leaky underground storage tank sites, are in various stages of remediation. But many of the sites will become submerged if they remain in place when sea-levels surge upward, and will also mix with Bay waters as sea-levels rise, causing the release of petroleum, dioxins, and other hazardous substances into the Bay. The release of contaminants will jeopardize not only the health of the community but the fishing industry and much of the local economy, which depends on a healthy Bay. Local environmental groups[107] are urging prioritization of remediation for low-lying contaminated sites, which is no small feat given the thousands of underground storage tanks and other sites needing cleanup in California.[108] Such efforts will require substantial funding from U.S. EPA's Brownfields grants program or other sources.

A variety of land uses adjacent to Humboldt Bay—housing, agriculture, commercial, industrial, transportation, vital municipal services, and wildlife habitat—will be

---

[102] Aldaron Laird & Trinity Associates, *Humboldt Bay Shoreline Inventory, Mapping and Sea Level Rise Vulnerability Assessment*, State Coastal Conservancy 4 (2013), *available at* http://scc.ca.gov/webmaster/ftp/pdf/humboldt-bay-shoreline.pdf.

[103] *See Cal. Coastal Comm'n Draft Sea-Level Rise Policy Guidance, supra* note 41, at 5.

[104] Laird & Trinity Associates, *supra* note 102, at 44.

[105] *Id.* at 48.

[106] These former tidelands are susceptible to rising groundwater elevations in response to sea-level rise.

[107] Humboldt Baykeeper works to safeguard coastal resources for the health, enjoyment, and economic strength of the Humboldt Bay community. The organization has been working to identify and remediate legacy contaminant sites at risk from rising bay waters.

[108] *See* U.S. Envtl. Prot. Agency, *Underground Storage Tanks Program Status in California* (2013), *available at* http://www.epa.gov/oust/states/ca.htm.

impacted by rising sea levels, and decision-makers will need to confront a host of legal and planning questions about how to manage impacts to water quality, public health, the local economy, and Bay ecosystems: Can (and should) local governments exercise eminent domain powers to remove housing developed in high flood risk areas? What shoreline fortification measures can be undertaken to protect key transportation corridors, including Highway 101, trails, coastal airports, and other critical infrastructure, including three waste-water treatment facilities? Can tidal influence be restored to unproductive pastures to serve as habitat for King and Coho salmon?[109]

Local entities have tackled these challenges proactively and are leveraging state funding to develop and implement adaptation strategies. Three examples illustrate this new development. First, the California Coastal Conservancy funded a multi-agency effort to address sea-level rise around Humboldt Bay through a comprehensive effort to map and inventory existing shoreline conditions, conduct a vulnerability and risk assessment, and develop unified adaptation strategies to deal with flooding.[110] Second, the Ocean Protection Council awarded the City of Eureka $250,000 to update the Coastal Land Use Policy in its General Plan.[111] Third, the City of Arcata received a "Climate Ready Grant" to develop tools and programs to protect against rising sea levels that threaten shoreline lands and facilities, including the design of a twenty-two-acre "living shorelines" area of Humboldt Bay to serve as a buffer against rising seas.[112]

2. Politicized Bay Area Planning[113]

Even compared to the rest of California's coast, the San Francisco Bay Area is highly vulnerable to sea-level rise. Two-thirds of the property in California at risk of flooding from projected sea-level rise is concentrated on the San Francisco Bay. One meter of sea-level rise in the Bay Area could inundate two hundred square miles of low-lying shoreline areas, including Silicon Valley and other critical economic hubs.[114] Much of

---

[109] Low-gradient brackish slough channels are critical for overwintering juvenile Coho salmon.

[110] *Humboldt Bay Sea Level Rise Adaptation Planning Project*, HUMBOLDT BAY HARBOR, RECREATION & CONSERVATION DISTRICT (Apr. 25, 2014), *available at* http://humboldtbay.org/humboldt-bay-sea-le vel-rise-adaptation-planning-project.

[111] *See Staff Recommendation to Ocean Protection Council re: Project Selection for First Round of Local Coastal Program Sea-Level Rise Grant Program*, at 4 (Nov. 21, 2013), *available at* http://www.opc.ca.gov/webmaster/ftp/pdf/agenda_items/20131121/Item6-OPC-Nov2013-Staff-Rec-LCP-grant.pdf.

[112] Press Release, City of Arcata, Arcata Awarded $86,000 Grant for Sea Level Rise Preparations (Jan. 24, 2014), *available at* http://www.cityofarcata.org/node/1846.

[113] For a comprehensive discussion on this topic, see generally Tim Eichenberg, *The Challenges of Adapting to Climate Change in San Francisco Bay*, 19 HASTINGS W.-NW. J. ENVTL. L. & POL'Y 393 (2013); *accord* Tim Eichenberg et al., *Climate Change and the Public Trust Doctrine: Using an Ancient Doctrine to Adapt to Rising Sea Levels in San Francisco Bay*, 3 GOLDEN GATE U. ENVTL. L.J. 243 (2010).

[114] Eichenberg, *The Challenges of Adapting to Climate Change in San Francisco Bay, supra* note 113, at 395 (citing San Francisco Bay Conservation and Dev. Comm'n, *Living with a Rising Bay: Vulnerability and Adaptation in San Francisco Bay and on Its Shoreline* (2009), *available at* http://www.bcdc.ca.gov/BPA/LivingWithRisingBay.pdf).

the Bay Area's critical infrastructure lies close to the shoreline, at or near sea level: two international airports, multiple emergency and healthcare facilities, myriad industrial facilities, and twenty-one waste-water treatment plants. Estimates indicate that over $62 billion worth of property could be at risk in the Bay Area.[115] As seawater creeps inland, salt water will intrude into the Bay-Delta Estuary and groundwater basins, and put large swaths of Bay wetland areas at risk of inundation.[116] The magnitude of projected sea-level rise impacts to the Bay Area's economy and environment set the stage for a contentious planning process.

In 2009, the San Francisco Bay Conservation and Development Commission (BCDC) released a report titled *Living with a Rising Bay: Vulnerability and Adaptation in San Francisco Bay and on Its Shoreline*,[117] which provided the basis for a proposed amendment to the Bay Plan[118] and delineated guidance and sea-level rise adaptation strategies for areas in BCDC's jurisdiction.[119] BCDC's 2009 report served as a wake-up call for the Bay Area,[120] but also sparked intense lobbying efforts from a variety of stakeholders, some of whom challenged BCDC's regulatory authority to develop climate policies. Some developers and local governments, including entities with interests in a controversial multibillion dollar development in a low-lying area of the South San Francisco Bay, alleged that BCDC was using sea-level rise to mount a "power grab."[121] This allegation challenged BCDC's mandate to "protect and enhance the San Francisco Bay and encourage its responsible use"[122] dating back to 1965, when it became it the first coastal management agency in the United States.

BCDC's authority extends only to activities in the San Francisco Bay below the mean high tide and in the shoreline band one hundred feet above mean high tide, whereas most development occurs well beyond one hundred feet, within the jurisdiction of local governments. In California, public ownership extends to the high tide line and, pursuant to the McAtter-Petris Act, BCDC has regulatory jurisdiction over "all areas [in the San Francisco Bay] that are subject to tidal action to mean high tide and areas within the

---

[115] *See* Cal. Natural Res. Agency, *supra* note 1, at 68.

[116] *See* Heberger, *supra* note 8, at 29 (citing Hutzel 2008) ("Numerous wetland restoration projects have been initiated in the San Francisco Bay, with the cost of restoring these tidal marshes ranging from $5,000 to $200,000 per acre.").

[117] San Francisco Bay Conservation and Dev. Comm'n, *supra* note 114, at 103–13.

[118] *Id.* at 8.

[119] *Id.* at 119–41.

[120] *Id.* at 25–26.

[121] Eichenberg, *The Challenges of Adapting to Climate Change in San Francisco Bay*, *supra* note 113, at 399.

[122] "[BCDC] is dedicated to the protection and enhancement of San Francisco Bay and to the encouragement of the Bay's responsible use." *See* San Francisco Bay Conservation and Development Commission, BCDC's Mission Statement (2007), *available at* http://www.bcdc.ca.gov/mission.shtml.

100-foot shoreline band."[123] BCDC's jurisdiction, therefore, is "ambulatory" and moves landward as sea level rises.[124]

California courts have recognized this authority, holding that "if the sea-level does rise [due to global warming], so will the level or mean high tide. BCDC's jurisdictional limit might in the future move marginally landward."[125] In order to effectively address the impacts of sea-level rise, an agency with limited shoreline authority such as BCDC would need either to expand its jurisdiction landward or increase its land-use authority, or both.[126] Instead of pursuing either option through new legislation, BCDC sought to develop a set of climate change amendments to the San Francisco Bay Plan to provide additional clarification and guidance on existing policies in the San Francisco Bay Plan, which date back to July 2001.[127]

It took more than three years to develop the amendment to the Bay Plan amid a host of conflicting concerns raised by environmental organizations, businesses, local governments, environmental justice advocates, and labor organizations. During this time, BCDC significantly weakened the Bay Plan amendments, which were initially much more prescriptive. In October 2011, BCDC's new climate policies were adopted unanimously. The policies establish a range of sea-level rise projections for the Bay Area and require risk assessments to ensure large projects are resilient to those projections to the year 2100. The policies also establish requirements to protect new projects from flooding, protect public access from sea-level rise for the life of the project, and encourage ecosystem-based adaptation strategies such as allowing for wetlands migration and precluding development in vulnerable habitat areas.

But there were some important omissions in the climate policy, which was progressively weakened over the course of the three-year, heavily lobbied planning process. Language to "prohibit" new projects that require shoreline protection in vulnerable areas and "limit or discourage" development in low-lying areas was softened or removed altogether. BCDC also explicitly waived the application of the climate policies to CEQA

---

[123] Eichenberg, *Climate Change and the Public Trust Doctrine, supra* note 113, at 263 (citing Littoral Dev. Co. v. San Francisco Bay Conservation & Dev. Comm'n, 24 Cal. App. 4th 1050, 1057 (1994) and Cal. Gov't Code § 66610(a), (b) (Westlaw 2010)). BCDC also has jurisdiction over certain specified waterways and marshlands lying up to five feet above mean sea level. Cal. Gov't Code § 66610(a) (West, WestlawNext current with urgency legislation through Ch. 185 of 2014 Reg. Sess., Res. Ch. 1 of 2013–2014 2nd Ex. Sess., and all propositions on the 6/3/2014 ballot).

[124] Eichenberg, *Climate Change and the Public Trust Doctrine, supra* note 113 (citing *Littoral Dev. Co.,* 24 Cal. App. 4th at 1066 n.5). The court held that BCDC's Bay jurisdiction extends to the mean high-tide line, but not to the line of highest tidal action.

[125] *See Littoral Dev. Co.,* 24 Cal. App. 4th at 1050.

[126] Eichenberg, *The Challenges of Adapting to Climate Change in San Francisco Bay, supra* note 113, at 397.

[127] Sea-level rise is also referenced in the San Francisco Bay Plan in Finding k, at 28; Policy 5, at 29, in the section concerning Tidal Marshes and Tidal Flats around the Bay; and Policy 4, at 34, in the section concerning Subtidal Areas in the Bay.

and to federal or federally permitted activities under the Coastal Zone Management Act landward of the one-hundred-foot shoreline band.

3. Fortified Southern California: A Window into the Future?[128]

Local strategies to address sea-level rise generally fall into three categories: accommodation, retreat, and protection. Accomodation strategies such as rebuilding restrictions with minimum floor elevations aim to minimize damage to structures. Retreat policies such as rolling easements aim to minimize the hazards of sea-level rise and protect coastal resources by restricting, prohibiting, or removing development from vulnerable areas.[129] Protection measures defend a property or natural area from sea-level rise by constructing either "hard" or "soft" shoreline stabilization structures. Most often in California, protection measures such as seawalls and beach nourishment have become the de facto solution.[130] This is especially true in Southern California.

When faced with erosion, storm surges, and other coastal impacts that predated climate-change-driven sea-level rise, Southern California defaulted to protection measures, both "hard armoring" such as seawalls and "soft armoring" techniques such as beach nourishment (or beach replenishment).[131] Beach nourishment involves the addition of new sediment to an eroded area and can restore coastal access, although it can be costly and difficult to maintain. About one-third of California's most southerly county coastal areas are hardened or armored.[132] Moreover, beach nourishment has been employed for so long and in so many areas in Southern California that some scientists estimate that there is little "native" sand left on many Southern California beaches.[133]

When local governments are faced with an imminent threat that must be addressed, armoring may be, or may be perceived to be, the only option. With adequate time, data, and resources, coastal managers can pursue a wider range and combination of protection measures. For example, California recently began testing the use of "living shorelines" to stabilize and buffer coastal ecosystems,[134] a technique used by U.S. National Oceanic

---

[128] For an extensive analysis of adaptation issues in Southern California, see generally Herzog & Hecht, *supra* note 45.

[129] *See generally* J. Peter Byrne, *The Cathedral Engulfed: Sea-Level Rise, Property Rights, and Time*, 73 La. L. Rev. 69, 85 (2012); Jessica Grannis et al., *Coastal Management in the Face of Rising Seas: Legal Strategies for Connecticut*, 5 Sea Grant L. & Pol'y J. 59, 61 (2012).

[130] Todd T. Cardiff, *Comment, Conflict in the California Coastal Act: Sand and Seawalls*, 38 Cal. W. L. Rev. 255 (2001).

[131] *See* Herzog & Hecht, *supra* note 45, at 473–75.

[132] Cal. Natural Res. Agency, *supra* note 1, at 70.

[133] Cal. Coastal Sediment Mgmt.Workgroup, Beach Nourishment Project Peformance & Sediment Characteristics, Results from CSMW Task 3, at 2, *available at* http://dbw.ca.gov/csmw/beach_nourishment.aspx.

[134] In 2012, the San Francisco Bay Living Shorelines Project began testing oyster and restoration projects and assessing impacts on wildlife, wave action, and shoreline erosion at two sites in San Francisco Bay. *See* State Coastal Conservancy, *San Francisco Bay Living Shorelines Project, available at* http://www.sfbayliving-shorelines.org/sf_shorelines_about.html (last visited July 31, 2014).

and Atmospheric Administration (NOAA) for more than two decades on the East Coast and in areas of the Gulf Coast.[135] Managed retreat options such as rolling easements or conservation credits take time to develop and often must anticipate legal challenge. These options, to be effective, involve long-term planning and the requisite political consensus that such planning entails.

Many of the quintessential contrasts that characterize California coastal planning and land use are dramatically depicted in Southern California. The region has a highly urbanized and armored coastline, but depends heavily on coastal tourism and recreation. Southern California has also been the scene of countless battles over public access and open space preservation among wealthy private landowners, public access advocates, and environmentalists. Thus, Southern California's response to coastal change thus far provides a window into the possible future of California coastal climate adaptation, and is considered by some as a cautionary tale who fear that: *"where there used to be beaches, the water will meet a wall."*[136]

Based on an in-depth analysis of Southern California's coastal armoring to date, Megan Herzog and Sean Hecht offer the following recommendations to mitigate coastal armoring:[137]

1. Conduct an assessment of legal vulnerability to sea-level rise impacts.
2. Initiate a participatory adaptation planning process as soon as practicable.
3. Utilize local coastal programs as a vehicle for sea-level rise adaptation strategies.
4. Address sea-level rise impacts in environmental impact reports for appropriate projects.
5. Explore alternatives to hard armoring as a long-term adaptation strategy.

These recommendations are instructive to local governments in California and in coastal cities throughout the world.

Conclusion

California has the eighth largest economy in the world,[138] and the biggest coastal economy in the United States.[139] The manner in which the state develops and implements

---

[135] *See* National Oceanic and Atmospheric Administration (NOAA), *Habitat Conservation and Restoration Center, Living Shorelines, available at* http://www.habitat.noaa.gov/restoration/techniques/livingshorelines.html (last visited July 31, 2014).

[136] Todd T. Cardiff, *supra* note 130, at 278.

[137] Herzog & Hecht, *supra* note 45, at 543–45.

[138] Comparison between U.S. states and countries by Gross Domestic Product as based on International Monetary Fund and Bureau of Economic Analysis data.

[139] NOAA State of the Coast 2011 estimates California coastal shoreline counties' contribution to GDP at $1,525,527,173,627. Nat'l Oceanic and Atmospheric Admin., *available at* http://stateofthecoast.noaa.gov/coastal_economy/welcome.html (last visited July 31, 2014).

coastal climate adaptation strategies will profoundly influence coastal regions around the world. California's landmark greenhouse gas emissions reductions legislation[140] positioned the state as an international leader on climate change mitigation. However, it remains to be seen whether California will lead climate change adaptation efforts as well.

Some local governments have been proactive about assessing local vulnerability and convening multi-stakeholder efforts to develop well-suited adaptation plans.[141] However, many of California's forty-four coastal county and municipal governments do not have a framework in place to assess vulnerability and implement adaptation strategies in a coordinated and strategic manner. If coastal armoring intensifies and seawalls become the default approach to address sea-level rise, it would alter the appearance of the California coast and irrevocably alter the state's economic and cultural landscape as well. The portfolio of strategies that California pursues to address rising sea levels, coastal inundation, storm surges, and their associated impacts will profoundly influence the future of the California coast, and perhaps coastal areas around the world.

---

[140] In 2006, the legislature passed and Governor Schwarzenegger signed the California Global Warming Solutions Act. Also known as AB 32, this law established a state goal of reducing GHG emissions to 2000 levels by 2010. CAL. HEALTH & SAFETY CODE § 38500 (West, WestlawNext current with urgency legislation through Ch. 185 of 2014 Reg. Sess., Res. Ch. 1 of 2013–2014 2nd Ex. Sess., and all propositions on the 6/3/2014 ballot).

[141] For example, Los Angeles is coordinating a science-based process to respond to climate change called "Adapt LA: Climate Change Adaptation Planning for a Coastal, Urban Metropolis." San Diego has partnered with staff from surrounding local governments, public entities, academia, and nongovernmental organizations to develop a regional "San Diego Bay Sea Level Rise Strategy."

25 Sea-Level Rise and Species Survival along the Florida Coast

Jaclyn Lopez*

---

* The author would like to thank Catherine Kilduff for bringing the lawsuit that resulted in the critical habitat proposal for loggerhead sea turtles, and Shaye Wolf for her review of the climate change science presented in this chapter.

Introduction

This chapter describes how the Endangered Species Act[1] can help wildlife managers and communities plan for and adapt to sea-level rise while conserving species' habitats. This chapter does not address the most important aspect of adaptation, which is mitigation through reduction of greenhouse gas emissions. Instead, it focuses on how sections 4 and 7 of the Endangered Species Act can help identify and protect the habitat of imperiled species, specifically, nesting habitat for loggerhead sea turtles in Florida. Section 4 of the Act authorizes the designation of suitable, unoccupied upland habitat, and can help wildlife managers proactively identify and manage upland habitat for species retreat as rising seas and increasing storms threaten coastal species' habitats.[2] Section 7 ensures that federal agency actions do not jeopardize species or adversely modify their habitats.[3] The chapter addresses critical habitat for loggerhead sea turtles and how the National Flood Insurance Program can be helpful in preventing construction in flood plains and species' coastal habitats.

I. Sea-Level Rise and the Loggerhead Sea Turtle

A. STORMS, STORM SURGE, AND FLOODING

Global average sea levels rose by about eight inches over the past century, and sea-level rise continues to accelerate in pace.[4] Mean global sea level is predicted to rise by one to two meters by the end of this century, while intensifying storms and storm surge will worsen the effects of sea-level rise.[5] As sea level rises, storm surges will be riding on a higher sea surface that will push water farther inland and upland.[6] Extreme rainfall events leading to flooding may also occur with increasing frequency.[7]

Sea-level rise projections for the southeastern United States are 0.2 m to 0.5 m relative to 2008 levels by 2050.[8] Many areas of the Southeast coast, particularly south Florida,

---

[1] 16 U.S.C. §§ 1531–1544 (2012).

[2] *Id.* § 1533.

[3] *Id.* § 1536.

[4] THOMAS R. KARL ET AL., GLOBAL CLIMATE CHANGE IMPACTS IN THE UNITED STATES 18 (2009).

[5] *See generally* J.B. Elsner et al., *The Increasing Intensity of the Strongest Tropical Cyclones.* 455 NATURE 92–95 (2008); M.A. Bender et al., *Modeled Impact of Anthropogenic Warming on the Frequency of Intense Atlantic Hurricanes*, 327 SCI. 454–58 (2010).

[6] *See generally* Claudia Tebaldi et al., *Modeling Sea Level Rise Impacts on Storm Surges along US Coasts*, 7 ENVTL. RES. LETTERS 1 (2011).

[7] SIMON K. ALLEN ET AL., MANAGING THE RISKS OF EXTREME EVENTS AND DISASTERS TO ADVANCE CLIMATE CHANGE ADAPTATION. A SPECIAL REPORT OF WORKING GROUPS I AND II OF THE INTERGOVERNMENTAL PANEL ON CLIMATE CHANGE, A DECADE OF WEATHER EXTREMES, *available at* http://ipcc-wg2.gov.

[8] Tebaldi et al., *supra* note 6, figure 2.

have elevations at or below one to two meters, making these areas particularly vulnerable to sea-level rise.[9] Large parts of the Atlantic coast and Gulf of Mexico coast have already experienced significantly higher rates of relative sea-level rise than the global average, in part due to land subsidence.[10]

Sea-level rise, storms and storm surge, and flooding will significantly impact U.S. coastal communities where nearly 40 percent of U.S. residents live.[11] A nation-wide study estimated that approximately 3.7 million Americans live within one meter of high tide and are at extreme risk of flooding from sea-level rise in the next few decades, with Florida as the most vulnerable state, followed by Louisiana, California, New York, and New Jersey.[12] Rates of sea-level rise along portions of the U.S. Atlantic Coast are increasing three-to-four times faster than globally.[13] Meanwhile an estimated 40 percent of U.S. endangered species inhabit coastal ecosystems.[14] Significant risks of habitat loss and of entrapment between rising sea-levels and human developments that prevent land-ward movement, leading to "coastal squeeze," have been predicted.[15] Moreover, human responses to sea-level rise, including coastal armoring and inland development, pose significant risks to the ability of species and ecosystems to move inland. Florida's population density along the coast is already three times greater than in inland counties.[16]

---

[9] J.L.Weiss et al., *Implications of Recent Sea Level Rise Science for Low-Elevation Areas in Coastal Cities of the Coterminous*, 105 U.S.A. CLIMATIC CHANGE 635 (2011).

[10] KARL ET AL., *supra* note 4, at 37. *See also* V.R. Burkett et al., *Sea-Level Rise and Subsidence: Implications for Flooding in New Orleans, Louisiana, in U.S. Geological Survey Subsidence Interest Group Conference, Proceedings of the Technical Meeting, Galveston, Texas, Nov. 27–29, 2001* (2003), *available at* http://pubs. usgs.gov/of/2003/ofr03-308/pdf/OFR03-308.pdf (noting that land subsidence occurs when land sinks relative to surrounding lands; it can be caused by sediment compaction, oil and gas extraction, water pumping, drainage projects, and tectonic activity).

[11] *The U.S. Population Living at the Coast: State of the Coast*, NOAA.GOV, http://stateofthecoast.noaa.gov/ population/welcome.html (last visited July 16, 2014).

[12] Benjamin Strauss et al., *Tidally Adjusted Estimates of Topographic Vulnerability to Sea Level Rise and Flooding for the Contiguous United States*, 7 ENVTL. RES. LETTERS 014033 (2012).

[13] *See generally* Asbury Sallenger et al., *Hotspot of Accelerated Sea-Level Rise on the Atlantic Coast of North America*, 2 NATURE CLIMATE CHANGE 884 (2012).

[14] Olivia E. LeDee et al., *The Challenge of Threatened and Endangered Species Management in Coastal Areas*, 38 COASTAL MGMT. 4 (2010).

[15] D. Scavia et al., *Climate Change Impacts on US Coastal and Marine Ecosystems*, 25 ESTUARIES 149 (2002); D.M. FitzGerald et al., *Coastal Impacts due to Sea-Level Rise*, 36 ANN. REV. EARTH & PLANETARY SCI. 601 (2008); O. Defeo et al., *Threats to Sandy Beach Ecosystems: A Review.* 81 ESTUARINE, COASTAL AND SHELF SCI. 1–12 (2009); C. Craft et al., *Forecasting the Effects of Accelerated Sea-Level Rise on Tidal Marsh Ecosystem Services*, 7 FRONTIERS ECOLOGY & ENV'T 73 (2009); LeDee et al. 2010, *supra* note 14; S. Menon et al., *Preliminary Global Assessment of Terrestrial Biodiversity Consequences of Sea-Level Rise Mediated by Climate Change*, 19 BIODIVERSITY & CONSERVATION 1599 (2010); R.F. Noss, *Between the Devil and the Deep Blue Sea: Florida's Unenviable Position with Respect to Sea Level Rise*, 107 CLIMATIC CHANGE 1 (2011).

[16] JUDITH KILDOW, PHASE I FACTS AND FIGURES FLORIDA'S OCEAN AND COASTAL ECONOMIES (2006), *available at* http://www.floridaoceanscouncil.org/reports/Florida_Facts_&_Figures.pdf.

Therefore, coastal species are at risk of being trapped between rising sea levels and human developments.[17]

B. FUTURE SUITABLE UPLAND HABITAT FOR THE LOGGERHEAD SEA TURTLE

The loggerhead sea turtle nests on beaches from Texas to Virginia, and faces significant loss of nesting habitat due to sea-level rise.[18] About 90 percent of U.S. loggerhead sea turtle nesting occurs in Florida, and most of that occurs in Brevard, Indian River, St. Lucie, Martin, Palm Beach, Broward, and Sarasota counties.[19] According to the U.S. Army Corps of Engineers, sea-level rise projections for Broward and Palm Beach counties are estimated at 8 to 18 cm (3 to 7 inches) by 2030, 23 to 61 cm (9 to 24 inches) by 2060, and 48 cm to 1.45 m (19.5 to 57 inches) by 2100, relative to 2010 levels.[20]

Areas of the Florida coast at or below one to three meters elevation significantly overlap with mean annual loggerhead sea turtle nest density.[21] The predicted sea-level rise this century will significantly diminish available sea turtle nesting habitat. Tropical Storm Debby may be a preview of what is to come for this region. The July 2012 storm brought high winds and several feet of storm surge on the southwest coast of Florida along loggerhead nesting beaches. In what would have been a banner year for loggerhead nesting on the west coast of Florida, Debby swept thousands of eggs into the Gulf of Mexico before wildlife managers and volunteers were able to rescue some of them. In Collier County, 78 percent of loggerhead nests were lost; 71 percent of nests on Captiva Island were lost; Fort Myers Beach lost 52 percent of its nests; and Naples beaches lost 90 percent of their nests.[22]

---

[17] Defeo et al., *supra* note 15.

[18] NATIONAL MARINE FISHERIES SERVICE & U.S. FISH AND WILDLIFE SERVICE, RECOVERY PLAN FOR THE NORTHWEST ATLANTIC POPULATION OF THE LOGGERHEAD SEA TURTLE: CARETTA CARETTA, II-53 (2d rev. 2008), *available at* http://www.nmfs.noaa.gov/pr/pdfs/recovery/turtle_loggerhead_atlantic. pdf; *see generally* Mariana Fuentes et al., *Potential Impacts of Projected Sea Level Rise on Sea Turtle Rookeries*, 30 AQUATIC CONSERV.: MARINE AND FRESHWATER ECOSYSTEMS 132 (2009).

[19] *See* FWC Fish and Wildlife Conservation Commission, *Loggerhead Nesting in Florida*, http://myfwc. com/research/wildlife/sea-turtles/nesting/loggerhead/ (last visited Feb. 14, 2014); FWC Fish and Wildlife Research Institute Statewide Nesting Beach Survey Program Loggerhead Nesting Data, 2008–2012, *available at* http://myfwc.com/media/2078432/LoggerheadNestingData.pdf.

[20] SOUTHEAST FLORIDA REGIONAL CLIMATE CHANGE COMPACT TECHNICAL, UNIFIED SEA LEVEL RISE PROJECTION FOR SOUTHEAST FLORIDA 27 (2011), *available at* http://southeastfloridaclimatecompact.org.

[21] Weiss et al. 2011 at figure 1, *supra* note 9; *Statewide Nesting Beach Survey Program, Loggerhead Nesting Data*, FED. FISH WILDLIFE CONSERV. COMM'N., http://myfwc.com/research/wildlife/sea-turtles/nesting/loggerhead/ (last visited July 16, 2014).

[22] Andrea Stetson, *Loggerhead Turtle Eggs Rescued after Debby Hatch on Fort Myers Beach*, TORTOISE BLOGS (July 10, 2012, 10:23 PM), http://tortoise2013.wordpress.com/2012/07/11/loggerhead-turtle-eggs-rescued-after-debby-hatch-on-fort-myers-beach/; J. McCarthy, *Debby Damages Turtle Nests*, NEWSHERALD.COM (June 27, 2012), http://www.newsherald.com/articles/nests-103739-panama-beach.html#ixzz1zm4FwHfT,

It is no surprise that sea-level rise is a primary threat to sea turtle nesting beaches and nesting success.[23] It is predicted that up to one-third to three-quarters of the current available sea turtle nesting areas could be lost with projected sea-level rise.[24] In addition to the threats from rising seas, increased storms and storm surge, and flooding, rising water tables due to sea-level rise can flood turtle nests from below and reduce reproductive output.[25]

It is likely that the effects of sea-level rise will be exacerbated by coastal armoring efforts to protect human development, which will restrict landward beach recession as sea levels rise and prevent turtles from nesting farther up the beach away from flooded areas.[26] Coastal armoring, beach renourishment,[27] and beachfront development can also render sand inappropriate for nesting, disorient turtles, and block beach access.[28] In Florida, passive erosion at seawalls appears to inhibit turtle nesting inland on the armored beaches, and nests in front of sea walls are more likely to be washed away in storms.[29] As pressure to armor coasts mounts with rising sea levels and storm activity, loggerhead nesting beaches will be increasingly at risk from coastal squeeze.[30]

Loggerhead nesting beaches are also warming as temperatures rise. In the southeastern United States, annual average temperature has risen about 2°F since 1970, with a temperature rise of 1.2°F in spring and 1.6°F in summer during sea turtle nesting season.[31]

C. Waterfield, *Southwest Florida's Sea Turtles and Tropical Storm Debby*, TWENTYFIFTY (June 29, 2012), http://www.twenty-fifty.com/southwest-floridas-sea-turtles-after-tropical-storm-debby.

[23] Fuentes et al. 2009, *supra* note 18; L.A. Hawkes et al., *Climate Change and Marine Turtles*, 7 ENDANGERED SPECIES RES. 137 (2009); M.J. Witt et al., *Predicting the Impacts of Climate Change on a Globally Distributed Species: The Case of the Loggerhead Turtle*, 213 J. EXPERIMENTAL BIOLOGY 901 (2010); Mariana Fuentes et al., *Vulnerability of Sea Turtle Nesting Grounds to Climate Change*, 17 GLOBAL CHANGE BIOLOGY 140 (2010); M. Chaloupka et al., *Is Climate Change Affecting the Population Dynamics of the Endangered Pacific Loggerhead Sea Turtle?*, 356 J. EXPERIMENTAL MARINE BIOLOGY & ECOLOGY 136 (2008).

[24] R.C. Daniels, T.W. White & K.K. Chapman, *Sea-Level Rise: Destruction of Threatened and Endangered Species Habitat in South Carolina*, 17 ENVTL. MGMT. 373–85 (1993); M.R. Fish et al., *Predicting the Impacts of Sea-Level Rise on Caribbean Sea Turtle Nesting Habitat*, CONSERVATION BIOLOGY 482–91 (2005); J.D. Baker et al., *Potential Effects of Sea Level Rise on the Terrestrial Habitats of Endangered and Endemic Megafauna in the Northwestern Hawaiian Islands*, 4 ENDANGERED SPECIES RES. 1 (2006); A.D. Mazaris et al., *Evaluating the Impacts of Coastal Squeeze on Sea Turtle Nesting*, 52 OCEAN & COASTAL MGMT. 139 (2009).

[25] Fuentes et al., *supra* note 18; Witt et al., *supra* note 23.

[26] Carol E. Rizkalla & Anne Savage. *Impact of Seawalls on Loggerhead Sea Turtle* (Caretta caretta) *Nesting and Hatching Success*, 27 J. COASTAL RES. 166, 166 (2010); B.A. Shroeder & A.E. Mosier, *Between a Rock and a Hard Place: Coastal Armoring and Marine Turtle Nesting Habitat in Florida*, in PROCEEDINGS OF THE 18TH INTERNATIONAL SEA TURTLE SYMPOSIUM (MAZATLAN, MEXICO) 290–92. (F.A. Abreu-Grobois et al. eds., 1998).

[27] Hawkes et al., *supra* note 23; Kelly A. Brock et al., *The Effects of Artificial Beach Nourishment on Marine Turtles: Differences between Loggerhead and Green Turtles*, 17 RESTORATION ECOLOGY 297–307 (2007).

[28] Hawkes et al., *supra* note 23.

[29] *See* Rizkalla & Savage, *supra* note 26.

[30] Witt et al., *supra* note 23.

[31] Karl et al., *supra* note 4, at 111.

Under a lower emissions scenario, average temperatures in the region are projected to rise by about 4.5°F by the 2080s.[32] Rising temperatures may skew sex ratios toward more female-dominated clutches and may result in the northward shift of loggerhead nesting aggregations to cooler climates.[33]

II. The Endangered Species Act and Habitat Protection

The Endangered Species Act (ESA) is "the most comprehensive legislation for the preservation of endangered species ever enacted by any nation."[34] "The plain intent of Congress in enacting this statute was to halt and reverse the trend toward species extinction, whatever the cost."[35] The ESA reflects "an explicit congressional decision to require agencies to afford first priority to the declared national policy of saving endangered species" and "a conscious decision by Congress to give endangered species priority over the 'primary missions' of federal agencies."[36]

A. SECTION 4: AUTHORITY TO DESIGNATE SUITABLE UNOCCUPIED UPLAND HABITAT

The ESA requires the designation of critical habitat for listed species, encompassing all areas "essential to the conservation of the species."[37] Critical habitat designation is intended to promote conservation of listed species by protecting both occupied and unoccupied essential habitat needed for recovery of the species.[38] "[T]he designation of critical habitat serves as 'the principal means for conserving an endangered species, by protecting not simply the species, but also the ecosystem upon which the species depends.'"[39]

The ESA explicitly allows federal wildlife management agencies, U.S. Fish and Wildlife Service (FWS), and National Marine Fisheries Service (NMFS) to designate critical habitat "outside the geographical area occupied by a species at the time it was listed, upon a determination that such areas are essential for the conservation of the species."[40] As species and habitats shift in response to climate change, protecting habitat

---

[32] *Id.* at 111.

[33] Hawkes et al. 2009, *supra* note 23; J.S. Reece et al., *Sea Level Rise, Land Use, and Climate Change Influence the Distribution of Loggerhead Turtle Nests at the Largest USA Rookery (Melbourne Beach, Florida)*, 493 MARINE ECOLOGY PROGRESS SERIES 259 (2013).

[34] Tennessee Valley Auth. v. Hill, 437 U.S. 153, 180 (1978).

[35] *Id.* at 184.

[36] *Id.* at 185.

[37] 16 U.S.C. § 1532(5)(A)(i) (2012).

[38] 16 U.S.C. § 1532(5)(A) (2012).

[39] Ctr. for Biological Diversity v. Norton, 240 F. Supp. 2d 1090, 1101 (D. Ariz. 2003).

[40] 16 U.S.C. § 1532(5) (2012).

areas outside of the current range, including areas that facilitate species movements, is critical to allowing species to persist in a changing climate.

Indeed, FWS has already designated unoccupied habitat as critical habitat for at least seven species to help protect them from climate change impacts. FWS designated unoccupied inland coastal habitat for the western snowy plover to facilitate inland movement in response to sea-level rise.[41] It also designated unoccupied habitat for the Quino checkerspot butterfly in northern, higher-elevation habitat to facilitate movement in response to hotter, more arid conditions due to climate change.[42] FWS similarly designated unoccupied critical habitat for the dusky gopher frog for the purposes of reestablishing a population to help buffer it from the effects of climate change.[43] FWS also designated unoccupied critical habitat for three montane plant species to facilitate upslope and downslope movement in response to climate change.[44] FWS designated more than 10,000 acres of critical habitat for the Cape Sable thoroughwort, a rare South Florida coastal species threatened with sea-level rise.[45]

B. SECTION 7: DUTY TO ENSURE AGAINST JEOPARDY AND ADVERSE MODIFICATION

Section 7(a)(1) requires that all federal agencies utilize their authorities in furtherance of the purposes of the ESA by carrying out programs for the conservation of endangered species and threatened species. Section 7(a)(2) requires that each federal agency "insure that any action authorized, funded, or carried out" is not likely to jeopardize the continued existence of listed species or result in the destruction or adverse modification of their habitat. If, after consultation, the wildlife management agency determines that the project will result in jeopardy or adverse modification, it shall suggest reasonable and prudent alternatives (RPAs) to help avoid the violation. The agency must then adopt the qualifying RPAs, abandon the project, or seek an exemption from the Endangered Species Committee.[46]

This duty to consult and protect against jeopardy is triggered whenever a federal agency proposes to take discretionary action that "may affect" threatened or endangered

---

[41] Endangered and Threatened Wildlife and Plants; Revised Designation of Critical Habitat for the Pacific Coast Population of the Western Snowy Plover, 77 Fed. Reg. 36,728 (June 19, 2012).

[42] Endangered and Threatened Wildlife and Plants; Revised Designation of Critical Habitat for the Quino Checkerspot Butterfly (*Euphydryas editha quino*), 74 Fed. Reg. 28,776 (June 17, 2009).

[43] Endangered and Threatened Wildlife and Plants; Designation of Critical Habitat for Dusky Gopher Frog (Previously Mississippi Gopher Frog), 77 Fed. Reg. 35,118 (June 12, 2012).

[44] Endangered and Threatened Wildlife and Plants; Designation of Critical Habitat for *Ipomopsis polyantha* (Pagosa skyrocket), *Penstemon debilis* (Parachute beardtongue), and *Phacelia submutica* (DeBeque phacelia), 77 Fed. Reg. 48,368 (Aug. 13, 2012).

[45] Endangered and Threatened Wildlife and Plants; Designation of Critical Habitat for *Chromolaena frustrate* (Cape Sable thoroughwort), 79 Fed. Reg. 1,552 (Jan. 8, 2014).

[46] 16 U.S.C. § 1536 (2012).

species.[47] Agency action includes those "actions directly or indirectly causing modifications to the land, water, or air" where federal agencies exercise control.[48] The Federal Emergency Management Agency (FEMA) exercises discretionary control over parts of the National Flood Insurance Program (NFIP); therefore, the implementation of the NFIP is an agency action subject to ESA consultation.[49]

Under the current NFIP, the federal government underwrites flood insurance in participating communities to cover flood-related losses and damages sustained by residential and commercial structures.[50] FEMA dictates minimum floodplain management standards and identifies flood hazards by providing Flood Insurance Rate Maps (FIRMs). By statute, FEMA is charged with developing comprehensive criteria for land use and management that constricts development of land exposed to flood risk, guides development away from lands threatened by flood hazards, assists in reducing damage caused by floods, and otherwise improves the long-range land management and use of flood-prone areas.[51] Communities can then volunteer to participate in the NFIP, and in doing so, adopt land use and control measures in order to obtain lower-cost flood insurance.[52] As of 2012, 21,000 communities throughout the United States participate in this program, allowing property owners to purchase flood insurance as a condition of receiving federally related financial assistance to acquire or improve land.[53]

Congress recently authorized a NFIP extension that would keep the program operational through September 30, 2017.[54] The extension included a number of reforms that will likely help FEMA accomplish some of its goals with the NFIP. For example, FEMA can now phase in actuarial rates over a five-year period for nonresidential properties, non-primary residences, homes substantially damaged or improved, homes with multiple claims, and properties purchased after enactment, and is prohibited from extending

---

[47] *Id.*

[48] 50 C.F.R. § 402.02(d) (2014).

[49] Florida Key Deer v. Paulison, 522 F.3d 1133 (11th Cir. 2008); Nat'l Wildlife Fed'n v. FEMA, 345 F. Supp. 2d 1151 (W.D. Wash. 2004); Florida Key Deer v. Stickney, 864 F. Supp. 1222 (S.D. Fla. 1994).

[50] The purpose of the National Flood Insurance Act of 1968 was to provide affordable flood insurance and encourage sensible land use that minimizes the exposure of built structures to flood damage. The 1973 Flood Disaster Protection Act made flood insurance mandatory for property owners with property in vulnerable areas with mortgages from federally regulated lenders. The 1994 National Flood Insurance Reform Act sought to strengthen mandatory purchase requirements in Special Flood Hazard Areas (SFHAs). The 2004 Bunning-Bereuter-Blumenauer Flood Insurance Program attempted to require mitigation for properties that suffer repetitive flood loss by requiring higher premiums for those who opt to not mitigate. *See* AMERICAN INSTITUTE FOR RESEARCH, A CHRONOLOGY OF MAJOR EVENTS AFFECTING THE NATIONAL FLOOD INSURANCE PROGRAM (2005).

[51] 42 U.S.C. § 4011(a) (2012).

[52] 42 U.S.C. § 4012 (2012).

[53] FEMA, ADOPTION OF FLOOD INSURANCE RATE MAPS BY PARTICIPATING COMMUNITIES (2012), *available at* http://www.fema.gov/media-library-data/20130726-1903-25045-4716/fema_495.pdf.

[54] H.R. 4348, 112th Cong. § 100203 (2012).

discounted rates to new or lapsed policies.[55] The reforms require FEMA to better communicate with homeowners about flood risks, geographical boundaries of flood zones, and the requirement to purchase flood insurance, and to provide a general estimate of the cost.[56] Congress also authorized communities to use Community Development Block Grants to fund outreach regarding flood insurance rates and mapping, and to supplement existing state and local funding for building code enforcement.[57]

Despite these recent positive developments, significant problems with NFIP remain. Although NFIP was intended to discourage development in flood-prone areas, Congress and the Department of the Interior have found that the availability of federal flood insurance is often a significant factor in development of these areas.[58] Recognizing that flooding continues to be a primary source of damage from natural hazards in the United States,[59] and that NFIP has not achieved its primary goals of keeping development out of flood areas and providing affordable flood insurance, FEMA is undertaking a review of the NFIP.

FEMA has not historically engaged in broad, nationwide ESA consultation with FWS in implementing the NFIP. This is in spite of FWS's "numerous factual and policy determinations...that implementation of the NFIP by FEMA facilitates and encourages new development in undeveloped areas."[60] Indeed, a series of lawsuits brought against FEMA have alleged that the NFIP has had a detrimental effect on the habitat of endangered and threatened species.[61] FEMA must ensure that future implementation of NFIP does not jeopardize the survival or recovery of imperiled species, particularly in light of the predicted impacts of climate change on low-lying areas.

In *Florida Key Deer v. Stickney*, the U.S. District Court for the Southern District of Florida held that FEMA has broad discretion in issuing regulations implementing NFIP

---

[55] *What the Biggert-Waters Flood Insurance Reform Act Means for Communities*, (Jan. 7, 2013), http://us.stormsmart.org/2013/01/07/what-flood-insurance-reform-means/.

[56] H.R. 4348, 112th Cong. § 100216(d)(1)(C) (2012).

[57] H.R. 4348, 112th Cong. § 100243 (2012).

[58] *See* Coastal Barriers Study Group, Report to Congress: Coastal Barrier Resources System Report (1988), *available at* http://catalog.hathitrust.org/Record/002498823; *see also* U.S. Department of the Interior, Final Supplemental Legislative Environmental Impact Statement on the Proposed Changes to the Coastal Barrier Resources System (1988), *available at* http://catalog.hathitrust.org/Record/002473407.

[59] USGS, Flood Hazards—A National Threat (2006), *available at* http://pubs.usgs.gov/fs/2006/3026/2006-3026.pdf; National Weather Service, *NWS Weather Fatality, Injury and Damage Statistics*, http://www.nws.noaa.gov/om/hazstats.shtml (last visited Feb. 19, 2014).

[60] Florida Key Deer v. Stickney, 864 F. Supp. 1222, 1231 (S.D. Fla. 1994).

[61] Nat'l Wildlife Fed'n v. FEMA, 345 F. Supp. 2d 1151 (W.D. Wash. 2004) (holding FEMA's implementation of NFIP constitutes a discretionary and continuing action subject to the Endangered Species Act and FEMA's passage of minimum eligibility criteria, floodplain mapping, and implementation of the community rating system have ongoing effects on Chinook salmon habitat); Audubon Society of Portland v. FEMA, Case no. 3:09-cv-729-HA (D. Or. 2010); Wildearth Guardians v. FEMA, 1:09-cv-00882-RB-WDS (D.N.M. Feb. 11, 2011).

and is therefore subject to ESA consultation requirements.[62] The court also found that NFIP encouraged development of species' habitat and ordered FEMA to initiate consultation. As a result of the court order and subsequent consultation, FWS determined that FEMA's administration of the NFIP was jeopardizing the Key deer, Key Largo cotton mouse, Key Largo woodrat, Key tree-cactus, Lower Keys marsh rabbit, Schaus' swallowtail butterfly, silver rice rat, Garber's sponge, and Stock Island tree snail, and proposed RPAs, which FEMA adopted. Environmental groups then filed an amended complaint in 1997 claiming that the biological opinion and RPAs violated the ESA.

In 2003, FWS and FEMA reinitiated consultation and FWS issued an amended biological opinion, again finding the NFIP jeopardized listed species. Plaintiffs again filed suit challenging the sufficiency of the 2003 biological opinion. The court agreed that it was arbitrary and capricious and that FEMA had failed to implement any conservation plan with respect to listed species as required by ESA section 7(a)(1).[63] The court also enjoined FEMA from providing any flood insurance for new developments in the suitable habitat of listed species in Monroe County pending consultation.[64] The Eleventh Circuit Court of Appeals affirmed both of the district court orders.[65]

FEMA recently agreed to settle another lawsuit in Florida between it and the National Wildlife Federation and Florida Wildlife Federation over its implementation of NFIP.[66] In that settlement agreement, the parties stipulated that FEMA violated section 7 of the ESA by not consulting with FWS and NMFS on the impacts of five species of sea turtles in Florida. Pursuant to the agreement, FEMA will initiate consultation and produce a biological assessment.[67]

III. Protection of Loggerhead Nesting Habitat under the Endangered Species Act

Loggerhead sea turtle nesting sites will experience rapid change in the coming decades due to climate change and human response to it. If loggerhead sea turtles are to survive into the next century, FWS will need to protect important U.S. nesting habitat. The Endangered Species Act provides FWS with several tools to help ensure that loggerheads continue to enjoy viable nesting habitat. The Endangered Species Act authorizes FWS to designate unoccupied habitat, which will allow loggerhead sea turtles to naturally migrate to new suitable beaches, and requires that federal agency actions do not destroy or adversely modify critical habitat.[68]

---

[62] *Florida Key Deer*, 864 F. Supp. at 1231.
[63] Florida Key Deer v. Brown, 364 F. Supp. 2d 1345, 1361 (S.D. Fla. 2005).
[64] Florida Key Deer v. Brown, 386 F. Supp. 2d 1281, 1294 (S.D. Fla. 2005).
[65] Florida Key Deer v. Paulson, 522 F.3d 1133 (11th Cir. 2008).
[66] Nat'l Wildlife Fed'n v. Fugate, Case 1:10-cv-22300-KMM (S.D. Fla. July 13, 2010).
[67] *Id.*
[68] 16 U.S.C. § 1532(5)(A)(ii) (2012).

A. SECTION 4: DESIGNATE SUITABLE UNOCCUPIED UPLAND HABITAT

FWS and NMFS have designated critical habitat for the loggerhead sea turtle.[69] Although the agencies recognized that climate change, and specifically sea-level rise, threaten nesting loggerheads, they did not take measures to identify the upland or more northerly areas that will become important habitat for the landward migration of these imperiled species as the coasts are inundated by projected sea-level rise and intensified storm surge in this century.[70] Because other federal agencies have an obligation to refrain from taking or funding actions that are likely to "destroy or adversely modify" species habitat, identification and protection of this upland habitat will be vital to the continued existence of these species.

Climate change poses serious and increasing threats to loggerhead sea turtles and their nesting beaches, where rising sea levels, increasing hurricane intensity and storm surge, and warming temperatures are primary threats.[71] While the agencies considered the projected and reasonably likely impacts of climate change on terrestrial critical habitat, they failed to designate unoccupied areas at the time of listing, instead deferring to a later date when more specific forecasting becomes available.[72]

Designation of critical habitat in inland areas would have buffered loggerhead sea turtles from sea-level rise. Currently suitable nesting beaches will experience increasing inundation and erosion from sea-level rise, stronger storms, and increasing storm surge and flooding. At many current nesting sites, upslope retreat is blocked by development and coastal armoring. FWS must proactively identify, designate, and restore potential inland habitat in undeveloped areas to facilitate inland movement and compensate for increasing habitat loss and degradation due to climate change. Sea turtle experts have explicitly recognized the importance of "protecting beaches through changes to policy and legislation to ensure that sufficient nesting habitat is available in the future" to mitigate climate change threats.[73]

---

[69] Endangered and Threatened Wildlife and Plants; Designation of Critical Habitat for the Northwest Atlantic Ocean Distinct Population Segment of the Loggerhead Sea Turtle, 79 Fed. Reg. 39,756 (July 10, 2014); Endangered and Threatened Species: Critical Habitat for the Northwest Atlantic Ocean Loggerhead Sea Turtle Distinct Population Segment (DPS) and Determination Regarding Critical Habitat for the North Pacific Ocean Loggerhead DPS, 79 Fed. Reg. 39,856 (July 10, 2014).

[70] 79 Fed. Reg. 39,756, 39,764. FWS states "[a]s more specific forecasts become available in the future, a revision of critical habitat may be required to more effectively provide for the conservation of the species. At this time, however, such forecasts are unavailable."

[71] Fuentes et al., *supra* note 23, at 132–39; Hawkes et al., *supra* note 23; Witt et al., *supra* note 23.

[72] FWS did note however, that "[a]reas that are important to the conservation of the species, both inside and outside the critical habitat designation, may continue to be the subject of conservation actions, regulatory protections, and prohibitions on taking of the species, including taking caused by actions that affect habitat." 79 Fed. Red. 39,756, 39,763.

[73] M.M.P.B. Fuentes et al., *Management Strategies to Mitigate the Impacts of Climate Change on Sea Turtle's Terrestrial Reproductive Phase*, 17 MITIGATION ADAPTATION STRATEGIES GLOBAL CHANGE 51 (2012).

A recovery goal in the Loggerhead Sea Turtle Recovery Plan is the development of a model to identify climate change impacts on nesting habitat.[74] FWS has already employed this type of modeling to identify unoccupied upland habitat areas for critical habitat designation for the western snowy plover. In applying this modeling to this species, FWS: (1) used high-resolution Light Detection and Ranging (LiDAR) data to determine how unit boundaries should be extended to compensate for habitat loss due to sea-level rise,[75] (2) designated critical habitat outside of the snowy plover's occupied range to ensure the conservation of the plover under threats from sea-level rise,[76] and (3) proposed to restore habitat to increase the amount of suitable habitat for plovers to offset losses from sea-level rise and other threats.[77] FWS should use a similar approach for the loggerhead sea turtle.

B. SECTION 7: ENSURE FEDERAL AGENCY ACTIONS DO NOT ADVERSELY MODIFY CRITICAL HABITAT

The NFIP covers over 21,000 communities from all fifty states, plus a few territories. FEMA must assess the nationwide impact of NFIP on coastal species in light of climate change, and Florida nesting loggerhead sea turtles can provide a valuable, illustrative starting point for FEMA's analysis. During the coming decades, these beach nesting areas are expected to be impacted by sea-level rise, likely moving landward. Likewise, FEMA's future mapping, taking into account impacts of climate change, will likely expand the special flood hazard areas inland to reflect predicted impacts of climate change. It is evident that loggerhead sea turtles, and other coastal species, will not be able to survive increased development along the coastline compounded by sea-level rise and armoring in response to it. FEMA must exercise its authority and ensure that it is not subsidizing development in these areas.

In 2012, Congress ordered FEMA to overhaul its program.[78] FEMA should take this opportunity to update its mapping to reflect the best available science on the effects of climate change, identify suitable upland habitat for imperiled species, and eliminate federally subsidized destruction or adverse modification of species' habitat.

---

[74] NATIONAL MARINE FISHERIES SERVICE & U.S. FISH AND WILDLIFE SERVICE, *supra* note 18.

[75] Endangered and Threatened Wildlife and Plants; Revised Critical Habitat for the Pacific Coast Population of the Western Snowy Plover, 76 Fed. Reg. 16046, 16050 (Mar. 22, 2011).

[76] *Id.* at 16051.

[77] *Id.* at 16048, 16053.

[78] Two proposed bills, Homeowner Flood Insurance Affordability Act of 2014 (S. 1926) and Homeowner Flood Insurance Affordability Act of 2013 (H.R. 3370), threaten to delay the implementation of aspects of the Biggert-Waters Flood Insurance Reform Act of 2012.

1. Update Maps Using the Best Available Science

FEMA dictates minimum floodplain management standards and identifies flood hazards by providing FIRMs. FEMA must update these maps to reflect the growing scientific consensus regarding the impacts of climate change. The effects of climate change, including sea-level rise, increased storms, storm surge, and flooding activity threaten coastal ecosystems. In the coming decades, our shorelines will continue to change—through these natural systems and through human-made response to these changes—and these changes will impact coastal species. FEMA must use the best available science in anticipating these changes and mapping areas that will be increasingly vulnerable to flood damage. FEMA must use its authority to strengthen restrictions on floodway development, discourage fill in floodplains, and account for the impacts of floodplain development on the natural and beneficial functions of floodplains to include endangered and threatened species. FEMA's implementation of NFIP must take into account the certainty that coastal species' habitat will be lost to climate change impacts and new development in response to it.

2. No Flood Insurance for Post-NFIP Structures Built in Species' Habitat

FEMA identifies and maps flood hazards. It provides flood insurance for structures built in Special Flood Hazard Areas (SFHAs), areas that are subject to 1 percent chance of annual flood. Construction in these areas can impact imperiled species by altering species' habitat. FEMA also provides a loophole that allows landowners to remove their flood-prone lands from regulated special flood hazard areas by filling the floodplain above the base flood elevation.

This loophole incentivizes filling in floodplains so as to avoid more restrictive development regulations. Combined, these practices reduce and degrade species' habitat. Federal funds must not be used to drive species toward extinction. FEMA must strengthen restrictions in floodways to inhibit development, prohibit deposit of fill material in floodplains, remove subsidies for nonresidential structures and non-primary residences, phase out subsidies for remaining structures, and account for the impacts of floodplain development on the natural and beneficial functions of floodplains to include endangered and threatened species.

3. Adjust Premiums to Reflect Risks

NFIP insures 5.6 million homeowners, renters, and business owners and $1.2 trillion in assets. It generates about $2.3 billion in annual premiums and offers coverage of up to $250,000 for residential buildings and $500,000 for commercial buildings.[79]

---

[79] Dan Huber, Fixing a Broken National Flood Insurance Program: Risks and Potential Reforms, Center for Climate and Energy Solutions (2012), *available at* http://www.eenews.net/assets/2012/06/25/document_pm_02.pdf.

Between 1980 and 2005, insurers paid out $320 billion in weather-related insurance claims;[80] however, because collected premiums have not been sufficient to cover losses, the U.S. Treasury is in growing debt of approximately $20 billion. As a result, the U.S. Government Accountability Office rates the NFIP as high risk.[81] A recent report concluded that flooding due to climate change is likely to widen the gap, and recommends that reforms be instituted to fully account for the increased risk posed by climate change.[82] The study found that premiums are priced below private sector rates, "thereby offering below-market coverage to development in areas that are both environmentally sensitive and have high disaster risk...."[83] FEMA should adjust premiums to reflect risk, remove subsidies for nonresidential structures and non-primary residences, and phase out subsidies for remaining structures.

The current NFIP $18 billion debt is due to high interest rates and premium rates that do not reflect actual experiences or future risk. From 1978 to 2004, NFIP claims and expenses have exceeded income from flood insurance premiums by 5 percent. Since Hurricane Katrina, and the other named storms from 2005 to date, the program has continued to suffer even more significant financial shortfalls.[84] The projected increased storm activity and sea-level rise will only make risk of flooding and property damage worse.

NFIP offers subsidized and full risk premiums. In the past, FEMA has grandfathered properties that are identified as at risk, for the sake of equity, and to encourage participation in the NFIP. Homeowners in homes that were built before the NFIP was implemented, which accounts for 22 percent of NFIP-covered properties, pay only 35–40 percent of what FEMA considers actuarial risk.[85] This policy has resulted in continued lowered premium rates: mapping expands areas prone to flooding, yet structures are entitled to lower rates. Recognizing that newer mapping will reflect greater likelihood of flooding due to climate change, FEMA must eliminate or minimize the grandfathering of properties that are identified as within a flood zone. A separate program should be established to provide needs-based subsidies to homeowners in flood-prone areas.

---

80 JOHN B. STEPHENSON, U.S. GOV'T ACCOUNTABILITY OFFICE, GAO-07-820T, FINANCIAL RISKS TO FEDERAL AND PRIVATE INSURERS IN THE COMING DECADES POTENTIALLY SIGNIFICANT (2007), *available at* http://www.gao.gov/assets/120/116474.pdf.

81 U.S. GOV'T ACCOUNTABILITY OFFICE, HIGH RISK SERIES, GAO-13-283, HIGH-RISK SERIES, AN UPDATE (2013), *available at* http://www.gao.gov/assets/660/652133.pdf.

82 HUBER, *supra* note 79.

83 *Id.* at 3.

84 CONG. BUDGET OFFICE., THE NATIONAL FLOOD INSURANCE PROGRAM: FACTORS AFFECTING ACTUARIAL SOUNDNESS (2009), *available at* http://www.cbo.gov/sites/default/files/cbofiles/ftpdocs/106xx/doc10620/11-04-floodinsurance.pdf.

85 ORICE W. BROWN, U.S. GOV'T ACCOUNTABILITY OFFICE, GAO-10-631T, NATIONAL FLOOD INSURANCE PROGRAM CONTINUED ACTIONS NEEDED TO ADDRESS FINANCIAL AND OPERATIONAL ISSUES (2010), *available at* http://www.gao.gov/new.items/d10631t.pdf.

Furthermore, sea-level rise, erosion, land subsidence, and increased storm intensity, storm surge, and heavy rainfall threaten to inflict more damage than previously experienced.[86] One study found that sea-level rise could double the average annual loss from storm surge by 2030.[87] Therefore, FEMA is under even more pressure to promptly adjust premiums to reflect risk. Moving forward, FEMA must take the best available science into account in updating its maps and setting premium levels. In determining rates, FEMA should identify how many major storms are expected over a variety of time frames in various regions, ascertain how much natural buffer is predicted to be lost in critical areas, and consider creating separate risk levels for flooding, including flood probability of greater to and lesser than 100 years or 1 percent probability.

4. Enforce Existing Flood Insurance Requirements

Structures that occur within SFHAs that are financed by federally backed mortgages must be covered by flood insurance. Communities that participate in NFIP enable property owners to purchase subsidized flood insurance. A condition of participation in NFIP is that the community must require that properties located in SFHAs receive permits for new development, and mandate that the first floor must be above the base 100-year flood elevation.[88] However, actual flood insurance coverage in these SFHAs falls well below 100 percent.[89]

One study found that only about 75–80 percent of homes in SFHAs actually have flood insurance coverage,[90] while other studies indicate coverage is far less. A review of homeowners in northern Vermont after storms in 1998 found that 84 percent of homeowners in SFHAs did not have flood insurance, even though 45 percent were required to have it.[91] Another study concluded that only about 50 percent of property owners with property in SFHAs in the Northeast and Midwest that were required to have flood insurance actually had it.[92] In yet another study, four flood determination companies

[86] Evan Lehmann, *Flood-Prone Land Likely to Increase by 45 Percent—A Major Challenge to Federal Flood Insurance Program*, N.Y. TIMES, July 22, 2011, http://www.nytimes.com/cwire/2011/07/22/22climatewire-flood-prone-land-likely-to-increase-by-45-a-19117.html.

[87] LLOYD'S OF LONDON, COASTAL COMMUNITIES AND CLIMATE CHANGE: MAINTAINING FUTURE INSURABILITY (2008), *available at* http://www.lloyds.com/~/media/lloyds/reports/360/360%20climate%20reports/360_coastalcommunitiesandclimatechange.pdf#search=%27360%20Risk%20Project%20Maintaining%20Future%20Insurability%27.

[88] JACQUELYN MONDAY ET AL., AN EVALUATION OF COMPLIANCE WITH THE NATIONAL FLOOD INSURANCE PROGRAM PART A: ACHIEVING COMMUNITY COMPLIANCE (2006).

[89] *Id.*

[90] Lloyd Dixon et al., *The National Flood Insurance Program's Market Penetration Rate*, FEMA.GOV (Feb. 2006), http://www.fema.gov/media-library-data/20130726-1602-20490-6272/nfip_eval_market_penetration_rate.txt.

[91] Howard Kunreuther & Erwann Michel-Kerjan, *Encouraging Adaptation to Climate Change: Long-Term Flood Insurance*, U. PA. WHARTON SCL., 09-13 (2009), *available at* http://opim.wharton.upenn.edu/risk/library/RFF-IB-09-13.pdf.

[92] Dixon et al., *supra* note 90.

were asked to determine whether buildings covered by 9,500 loans were inside or out-side SFHAs. One or more companies disagreed on the placement of 68 percent of the buildings,[93] indicating that homeowners, mortgage lenders, and insurers may not even be certain of whether flood insurance is required.

Compounding the compliance issues is the fact that FEMA's enforcement of flood insurance requirements is lacking. Currently, mortgage holders are typically left to enforce the flood insurance requirement. However, they are only required to verify coverage when a loan is made or modified, not when maps are updated. Lenders who do not comply with flood insurance regulations may be subject to fines; however, these are only levied where there is a pattern or practice of violations.[94] FEMA should explore other avenues to ensure that property owners are purchasing and maintaining flood insurance by enforcing existing requirements, including maintaining flood insurance and development consistent with building codes and floodway restrictions.

One possible reform is to mandate longer-term policies. Studies suggest that many property owners allow their one-year policies to lapse soon after purchase. One study indicates that from 2001 to 2009 the average tenure of new policies was 2–4 years, indicating that many policyholders allowed coverage to lapse soon after initial purchase.[95] Another study of Florida residents found that one-third cancel their policies after two years, and two-thirds cancel after five years.[96] Requiring longer-term policies would likely result in better coverage.

FEMA could also review whether it can require participating communities to better enforce local building codes. One study found that if current building codes were applied to all residential properties in coastal Florida and New York, there would be a 61 percent and 39 percent reduction, respectively, in loss for a 100-year return period, or a savings of $51 billion.[97]

5. Make Risk Mitigation Mandatory or Increase Incentives

Communities are required to adopt minimum floodplain management regulations that specify when building permits are required, that ensure development does not increase

---

[93] Richard J. Tobin & Corinne Calfee, The National Flood Insurance Program's Mandatory Purchase Requirement: Policies, Process, and Stakeholders (2005).

[94] Id.

[95] Erwann Michel-Kerjan et al., Policy Tenure under the U.S. National Flood Insurance Program (NFIP), 32 Risk Analysis 4, 644 (2012).

[96] Erwann Michel-Kerjan & Carolyn Kousky, Come Rain or Shine: Evidence on Flood Insurance Purchases in Florida, J. Risk Ins. (2009), available at http://opim.wharton.upenn.edu/risk/partners/7_Come-Rain-or-Shine.pdf.

[97] Howard C. Kunreuther & Erwann Michel-Kerjan, At War with the Weather: Managing Large-Scale Risks in a New Era of Catastrophe (2009), available at http://opim.wharton.upenn.edu/risk/library/WHARTON-Managing_Large-Scale_Risks_%28Exec_Summary%29.pdf.

flooding, and that require mitigation standards for new construction.[98] Despite the ever-present threats and risks of flooding and other natural disasters, there is little evidence that communities or property owners proactively take steps to mitigate risks. One survey of Atlantic and Gulf Coast residents found that 83 percent had not taken any flood mitigation measures.[99] Additionally, the community rating system (CRS) is a voluntary incentive program that awards discounts in premium rates of up to 45 percent. The goal of the program is to reduce flood loss, facilitate accurate insurance ratings, and promote awareness of flood insurance. However, only 5 percent of communities participate in the CRS.[100]

The purpose of risk mitigation should be to minimize flood damage and prepare existing structures for future sea-level rise and the effects of climate change. Risk mitigation should include a variety of tactics, including wetlands restoration and prohibitions on construction within the floodplain. For repetitive loss properties, risk mitigation should be mandatory and should include non-repair or abandonment. Repetitive loss is defined as $1,000 of flood damage claims made more than two times in less than ten years. Repetitive loss properties comprise only 1 percent of properties but represent 25–30 percent of claims,[101] and the number of repetitive loss properties has increased more than 70 percent from 1997 to 2007.[102] With the anticipated effects of climate change, the number of repetitive loss properties will likely grow. Therefore, FEMA should analyze the alternative of not funding flood insurance for repetitive loss properties or, at least require mitigation that accounts for impacts to the floodplain's natural and beneficial functions and to imperiled species' habitats.

Conclusion

The Endangered Species Act requires that wildlife managers and communities plan for and adapt to sea-level rise without jeopardizing endangered species.[103] Sections 4 and

---

[98] FEMA, *Floodplain Management*, http://www.fema.gov/floodplain-management (last visited Feb. 19, 2014).

[99] Abby Goodnough, *As Hurricane Season Looms, State Aim to Scare*, N.Y. TIMES, May 31, 2006, http://www.nytimes.com/2006/05/31/us/31prepare.html.

[100] Federal Emergency Management Agency Office of Inspector General, Community Rating System: Effectiveness and Other Issues (2002).

[101] *Legislative Proposals to Reform the National Flood Insurance Program: Hearing on H.R. Before the Subcomm. on Insurance, Housing, & Community Opportunity of the H. Fin. Serv. Comm.*, 122nd Cong. (2011) (statement of Franklin W. Nutter, President, Reinsurance Association of America), *available at* http://financialservices.house.gov/uploadedfiles/112-16.pdf.

[102] ORICE W. BROWN, U.S. GOV'T ACCOUNTABILITY OFFICE, GAO 11-670T, FLOOD INSURANCE PUBLIC POLICY GOALS PROVIDE A FRAMEWORK FOR REFORM, TESTIMONY BEFORE THE COMMITTEE ON BANKING, HOUSING, AND URBAN AFFAIRS (2011), *available at* http://www.gao.gov/assets/130/126501.html.

[103] 16 U.S.C. §§ 1531–1544 (2012).

7 of the Endangered Species Act mandate that FWS identify and protect loggerhead sea turtle nesting habitat. Section 4 of the Act authorizes FWS to designate suitable, unoccupied upland habitat, which allows the proactive identification and management of upland habitat. Section 7 ensures that federal agency actions in response to climate change and sea-level rise do not jeopardize species or adversely modify their habitats.

FWS should proactively identify, designate, and restore potential inland and more northerly habitat in undeveloped areas to facilitate loggerhead movement and compensate for increasing habitat loss and degradation due to climate change. The prompt designation of unoccupied upland and northerly critical habitat will help buffer loggerhead sea turtles from sea-level rise. The designation will also require FEMA to assess the impact of NFIP on loggerhead nesting habitat. FEMA's flood zone mapping must take the impacts of climate change into account and ensure the agency does not subsidize development in loggerhead nesting habitat.

26 Sea-Level Rise and a Sinking Coast:
HOW LOUISIANA COASTAL COMMUNITIES ARE ADDRESSING CLIMATE CHANGE
Melissa Trosclair Daigle*

* Research for this publication was funded under award number NA10OAR4170077 from the National Oceanic and Atmospheric Administration, U.S. Department of Commerce, and by the Louisiana Sea Grant College Program, a part of the National Sea Grant College Program, maintained by NOAA, United States Department of Commerce. The statements, findings, conclusions, and recommendations are those of the author and do not necessarily reflect the views of NOAA or the U.S. Department of Commerce.

Introduction

> *As the Natural Research Council suggests in its 2006 report* Drawing Louisiana's New Map, *the region will need to find a balance between what is considered desirable and what is attainable. Indeed, the "new map" for Louisiana's coastline will forever be a moving target, and our vision for the future will need to be less of a snapshot and more of a motion picture.*[1]

While Louisiana will likely see impacts from climate change in many respects—including changes in weather patterns, emerging health issues, and agriculture and fisheries—the greatest impact will be from increased flooding and land loss due to relative sea-level rise. Coastal Louisiana is largely flat, low, and heavily populated. Land loss is not a new concern for the state. It is estimated that Louisiana has lost approximately 4877 km^2 since 1930.[2] The vast majority of the coast is below four feet in elevation, and approximately 60 percent of the state's population lives within fifty miles of the coast.[3]

Alarmingly, this flat, heavily populated area is experiencing some of the highest sea-level rise rates in the world. Between 1947 and 2006, NOAA tide gauges show a sea-level trend of 9.24 +/- 0.59 mm/year at Grand Isle, and between 1939 and 2006, NOAA tide gauges show a sea-level trend of 9.65 +/- 1.24 mm/year at Eugene Island.[4] These rates are much higher than the worldwide average of 1.7 +/- 0.05 mm/year documented in the 2007 IPCC report.[5] New data on relative sea-level rise rates along the coast show that the southeast portion of the state may face a 4.3-foot increase in water levels by the end of the century.[6] This, combined with the existing land elevation, could lead to increased daily flood risks from high tides, and, over time, complete loss of large portions of land to the Gulf of Mexico. Additionally, as the Gulf moves inland and sea level rises, areas that have historically not experienced flooding from storm surge may see water pushed farther inland than ever before.

In a study published in the summer of 2013, the economic vulnerability to sea-level rise of communities along the Gulf Coast was examined. One community in Louisiana—Lafourche

---

[1] Patty Glick et al., *Potential Effects of Sea-Level Rise on Coastal Wetlands in Southeastern Louisiana*, 63 J. COASTAL RES. 211, 213 (2013) (discussing the importance of models and how they will be necessary for decision-makers to understand the complexity of stressors on coastal environments facing sea-level rise).

[2] BRADY R. COUVILLION ET AL., U.S. DEP'T OF INTERIOR, LAND AREA CHANGE IN COASTAL LOUISIANA FROM 1932 TO 2010: U.S. GEOLOGICAL SURVEY SCIENTIFIC INVESTIGATIONS MAP 3164 (2011), *available at* http://pubs.usgs.gov/sim/3164/downloads/SIM3164_Pamphlet.pdf.

[3] *Coastal Erosion: Facts and Figures*, RESTORE OR RETREAT, http://www.restoreorretreat.org/la_erosion_facts.php (last visited Mar. 1, 2014).

[4] Andrew Morang et al., *Regional Sediment Processes, Sediment Supply, and Their Impact on the Louisiana Coast*, 63 J. COASTAL RES. 141, 148 (2013).

[5] INTERGOVERNMENTAL PANEL ON CLIMATE CHANGE, CLIMATE CHANGE 2007: THE PHYSICAL SCIENCE BASIS 409, http://www.ipcc.ch/publications_and_data/publications_ipcc_fourth_assessment_report_wg1_report_the_physical_science_basis.htm (S. Solomon et al. eds., 2012).

[6] Bob Marshall, *New Research: Louisiana Coast Faces Highest Rate of Sea-Level Rise Worldwide*, LENS (Feb. 21, 2013, 10:54 AM), http://thelensnola.org/2013/02/21/new-research-louisiana-coast-faces-highest-rate-of-sea-level-rise-on-the-planet/.

Parish—received the highest coastal vulnerability index score under the parameters set in the study, due to the "large amount of energy infrastructure located there, combined with high local shoreline erosion rates and high RSLR rates."[7] For similar reasons, Terrebonne Parish also received a high vulnerability ranking.[8] Other Louisiana communities, such as St. Bernard Parish, were shown to be highly vulnerable in terms of physical vulnerability but, due to lower levels of populations and infrastructure, received a lower index score.

Regardless of index score, all communities along the coast seek protection from increased flooding and restoration of the surrounding marshes and wetlands. While many scientists see these efforts as a way to delay the inevitable, residents without detailed knowledge of the complex delta system insist that the state and local governments hold the line—keeping the coastline (and their property) fixed in place. The state has the potential to receive large amounts of funding in the future for protection and restoration projects, but even if unlimited funds were available, it is unlikely that all areas could be saved. Thus, the state has to decide how to prioritize large-scale projects, local governments have to make decisions based on the impacts of limited funding, and individual property owners have to determine what level of risk is acceptable for investments in their own property.

This chapter will examine the impacts of, and potential legal concerns and responses to, sea-level rise along the Louisiana coast. Section I will examine background information on why the Louisiana coast is facing such high rates of relative sea-level rise, including how the delta was formed and what human activity has slowed or halted the natural land-building process. Section II will discuss the existing state-level legal framework that is already being impacted, or will likely be impacted, by sea-level rise in the future. Primarily, this section will focus on the 2012 Master Plan for Coastal Restoration. Section III proposes recommendations for the state, state agencies, and local communities on preparing for increased flooding due to relative sea-level rise.

I. Background on the Physical Threats to Louisiana's Coasts

Before examining the legal impacts of sea-level rise on the Louisiana coast, it is important to understand how the coast developed and what happened to stop the process of land building. By shifting course over thousands of years, the Mississippi River built the Louisiana coast that exists today. Over the past approximately 8,000 years, this process led to the creation, and eventual abandonment, of four major delta complexes, plus the current delta complex, known as the Balize.[9]

---

[7] Cindy A. Thatcher et al., *Economic Vulnerability to Sea-Level Rise along the Northern U.S. Gulf Coast*, 63 J. Coastal Res. 234, 241 (2013); *see also* Morang et al., *supra* note 4, at 159. Lafourche Parish is the home to Port Fourchon, "the most active oil field service port on the Gulf Coast and…the land base for the Louisiana Offshore Oil Port (LOOP)."

[8] Thatcher et al., *supra* note 7.

[9] Morang et al., *supra* note 4, at 143.

Until the 1927 flood, after which much of the lower Mississippi River was leveed, the overtopping of the banks of the river and its tributaries deposited sediment, fresh water, and nutrients that over time built up land at a rate that was greater than the rate of subsidence.[10] However, with the leveeing of the southern part of the river in response to economic, political, and social needs, the Balize delta complex could no longer deposit new sediment or maintain the health of the existing lands, swamps, and marshes. Instead, the freshwater, sediment, and nutrients that the river carries are currently deposited into deep water off the continental shelf.[11]

Even as the lower river was cut off from the surrounding lands, other changes impact the ability of the river to keep up with subsidence and rising seas. Upstream dikes and dams have reduced the amount of sediment that is able to make it downstream to the Louisiana coast, and bank stabilization projects have reduced the amount of sediment that is entering the system.[12] Some studies show that these types of projects have resulted in a reduction from 400 million metric tons per year of suspended sediment to approximately 150 million metric tons per year.[13] Some scientists determined that with such a reduced sediment load, the Mississippi River would not be able to provide enough sediment for the coast, even if levees were not hampering sediment distribution.[14]

Other local projects have also had an impact. In some sub-basins, canals dug for natural resource extraction have allowed salt water to infiltrate interior marshes, causing a change in marsh vegetation, and in some cases, marsh collapse, which directly leads to faster erosion rates.[15] Oil and gas extraction has also been shown to increase rates of land loss due to other impacts, such as disruption of normal plant growth and increased subsidence due to fault activation.[16] All of these issues have contributed to a coast that is losing land at a significantly higher rate than what it can create, or even could create under ideal circumstances.

---

[10] Subsidence along the Mississippi Delta is the process by which compacted soil and organic matter slowly sink over time. In a naturally functioning delta system subject to riverine overflow, newly deposited sediment would offset subsidence, as well as maintain the health of the plant life that holds the sediment together. The subsidence of the Mississippi Delta is well documented prior to the leveeing of the Mississippi River, as can be seen in an 1897 *National Geographic Magazine* article. *See* E.L. Corthell, *The Delta of the Mississippi River*, 8 NAT'L GEOGRAPHIC MAG. 351 (1897), http://www.lacoastpost.com/National_Geographic_Dec_1897.pdf.

[11] Morang et al., *supra* note 4, at 143.

[12] *Id.* at 147.

[13] *Id.*

[14] Michael D. Blum & Harry H. Roberts, *Drowning of the Mississippi Delta due to Insufficient Sediment Supply and Global Sea-Level Rise*, 2 NATURE GEOSCI. 488, 488 (2009).

[15] *See* John W. Day, Jr. et al., *Pattern and Process of Land Loss in the Mississippi Delta: A Spatial and Temporal Analysis of Wetland Habitat Change*, 23 ESTUARIES 425, 432–34 (2000).

[16] *See* Jae-Young Ko & John W. Day, *A Review of Ecological Impacts of Oil and Gas Development on Coastal Ecosystems in the Mississippi Delta*, 47 OCEAN & COASTAL MGMT. 597, 617–18 (2004).

II. Louisiana's Comprehensive Master Plan for a Sustainable Coast

Although the state does not have a plan that addresses climate change directly, it has slowly taken steps to address the issue of sea-level rise. The most recent example of this effort is *Louisiana's Comprehensive Master Plan for a Sustainable Coast*.[17] Until Hurricanes Katrina and Rita in 2005, truly integrated planning efforts between coastal protection and coastal restoration did not exist. The Louisiana legislature sought to address this shortcoming with a directive that the state develop one plan that coordinated efforts between protection and restoration and to update this plan every five years.[18] The first plan—*Integrated Ecosystem Restoration and Hurricane Protection: Louisiana's Comprehensive Master Plan for a Sustainable Coast*—was led by the state's Coastal Protection and Restoration Authority (CPRA) and was released in 2007.[19]

The goal of the 2012 update, *Louisiana's Comprehensive Master Plan for a Sustainable Coast (Coastal Master Plan)*, was to expand "the technical analysis and outreach and engagement (O&E) efforts to best identify specific projects that represent sound, efficient investments for Louisiana, considering resource and funding constraints, as well as future uncertainties."[20] In order to reach this goal, CPRA first created a planning tool[21] that was able to process massive amounts of data to "filter data, prioritize projects, and formulate groups of projects based on select specifications."[22] CPRA also held several community and public meetings to gather local knowledge about coastal conditions and concerns. When work on the revision began, there were over 1500 potential coastal protection and restoration projects. At the end of the revision process, 109 projects were selected for inclusion in the master plan.

Part of the process of selecting projects for inclusion was evaluating how the projects would function under differing future scenarios with "specific environmental

---

[17] Coastal Prot. & Restoration Auth. of La., Louisiana's Comprehensive Master Plan for a Sustainable Coast (2012) [hereinafter Comprehensive Plan 2012].

[18] 2005 La. Acts No. 8.

[19] Coastal Prot. & Restoration Auth. of La., Integrated Ecosystem Restoration and Hurricane Protection: Louisiana's Comprehensive Master Plan for a Sustainable Coast (2007), *available at* http://coastal.la.gov/resources/library/reports/.

[20] Natalie Peyronnin et al., *Louisiana's 2012 Coastal Master Plan: Overview of a Science-Based and Publicly Informed Decision-Making Process*, 67 J. Coastal Res. 1, 2 (2013).

[21] David G. Groves & Christopher Sharon, *Planning Tool to Support the Future of Coastal Louisiana*, 67 J. Coastal Res. 147, 148 (2013). There were five key objectives to the planning process: "(1) Reduce economic losses from storm-surge-based flooding to residential, public, industrial, and commercial infrastructure. (2) Promote a sustainable coastal ecosystem by harnessing the natural processes of the system. (3) Provide habitats suitable to support an array of commercial and recreational activities coast-wide. (4) Sustain the unique heritage of coastal Louisiana by protecting historic properties and traditional living cultures and their ties and relationships to the natural environment. (5) Promote a viable working coast to support regionally and nationally important businesses and industries." *Id.*

[22] Peyronnin et al., *supra* note 20, at 5.

uncertainties," such as "sea-level rise, subsidence, storm frequency, storm intensity, Mississippi River discharge, rainfall, evapotranspiration, Mississippi River nutrient concentration, and marsh collapse threshold."[23] These environmental uncertainties were then given values that were plugged into three models, referred to as "moderate, moderate with high sea-level rise, and less optimistic."[24] However, the study of the impacts of sea-level rise on project selection should not end with the publication of the *Coastal Master Plan*: "if the rate of sea-level rise follows a sharper increasing trend than is captured by the less optimistic scenario, the Master Plan may need to reassess the projects included to stabilize the coastal landscape."[25] Over the fifty-year time frame, and if all the selected projects are implemented and work in a way that reflects model output, the *Coastal Master Plan* could have a significant impact in reducing the cost of coastal hazards and increasing coastal land:

> The restoration projects in the master plan can substantially reduce expected annual flood damages predicted at year 50 under future without action strategies ($7.7 billion and $23.4 billion under the moderate and the less optimistic scenarios, respectively) compared to future with the master plan strategies ($2.4 billion and $5.5 billion under the moderate and the less optimistic scenarios, respectively). [...] The restoration projects in the master plan have the potential to build or maintain between 1500 and 2100 km² of land over the next 50 years, depending on future coastal conditions.[26]

The Louisiana Legislature passed the Coastal Master Plan unanimously, without amendment, on May 23, 2012.[27]

Although there is potential for benefit from implementing the projects outlined in the plan, there also are a number of concerns with it. Some of these concerns have been addressed in research articles, whereas others have not yet been considered in the scholarly literature. First, models have shown that the projects dealing with coastal restoration will not be able to keep up with some of the higher rates of sea-level rise. As Brady R. Couvillion et al. stated with respect to wetland morphology,

> Model results suggest that uncertainties in the rates of subsidence and ESLR [eustatic sea level rise] contribute significantly to the variability in wetland change projections.

---

[23] *Id.* at 7.

[24] *Id.*

[25] Groves & Sharon, *supra* note 21, at 160.

[26] Peyronnin et al., *supra* note 20, at 13.

[27] Work has already begun on the next-five year update to the plan, set to be released in 2017. According to the CPRA website (http://coastal.la.gov/2017-coastal-master-plan/), the 2017 plan will focus on strengthening the models used for the *2012 Coastal Master Plan*.

...

Our model simulations of elevation dynamics also suggest that even with protection and restoration efforts in place, coastal Louisiana as a whole will most likely experience a net elevation loss (or deficit) in the next 50 years if predicted ESLR rates become reality.[28] And while wetlands can attempt to mitigate the impacts of sea-level rise by migrating inland,[29] this process will only be successful if there are no hard structures, such as levees, impeding the migration.

Impacts to fisheries and other wildlife are also a concern for the projects proposed under the Coastal Master Plan, even though the drafters of the plan considered fisheries, wildlife habitat, and ecosystem services valuation as part of the decision metrics.[30] Researchers conducted studies on the impact of the recommended protection and restoration projects on fish and wildlife populations, focusing on fourteen species.[31] The study examined the ability of coastal areas to serve as suitable habitats for the species under project implementation.[32] The study revealed that if the master plan was not implemented, habitat quality will decline over the next fifty years for nine of the species studied.[33] However, even if the master plan is implemented, six of the habitats would still face decline, only at a slower rate.[34] The authors concluded that "all of the modeled species for which habitat is predicted to decline belong to the public, *i.e.* to the people of the state of Louisiana in the case of resident animals, to people living in countries bordering the Gulf of Mexico in the case of the estuarine-dependent fish, and to the people of the Americas in the case of migratory birds."[35]

---

[28] Brady R. Couvillion et al., *Forecasting the Effects of Coastal Protection and Restoration Projects on Wetland Morphology in Coastal Louisiana under Multiple Environmental Uncertainty Scenarios*, 67 J. COASTAL RES. 29, 37, 39 (2013).

[29] Glick et al., *supra* note 1, at 212.

[30] Peyronnin et al., *supra* note 20, at 10. "The ecosystem service models predict changes in characteristics of the coast that can be more readily predicted (e.g., habitat), recognizing that service provision is ultimately limited by those characteristics (e.g., oyster harvest cannot flourish unless there is a sufficient quantity of high-quality habitat for oysters). Scores for ecosystem service metrics were calculated as the change in a given suitability index attributable to a project or alternative." *Id.*

[31] J. A. Nyman et al., *Likely Changes in Habitat Quality for Fish and Wildlife in Coastal Louisiana during the Next Fifty Years*, 67 J. COASTAL RES. 60, 62 (2013). Species include American alligator, muskrat, river otter, juvenile spotted seatrout, juvenile brown shrimp, juvenile white shrimp, largemouth bass, eastern oyster, gadwall, green-winged teal, mottled duck, roseate spoonbill, neotrophic migrants, and red swamp crawfish. *Id.*

[32] *Id.* Specifically, the model broke the coast down into 500 m by 500 m cells (342,233 cells total). The models "were not population models; i.e. they did not estimate population size in each cell. Instead, each model estimated the capacity of each cell to support each species and thus may be classified as habitat suitability index models." *Id.*

[33] *Id.* at 63.

[34] *Id.*

[35] *Id.* at 66.

This view of ownership of the species is not in line with Louisiana law, as the state owns all wild animals, birds, fish, and shellfish.[36] Although no suits have yet been filed, there have been discussions among certain groups that they will use the courts to halt, or at least delay, the diversion projects presented in the Coastal Master Plan due to the impact on fisheries. Potential ways to avoid such delays are discussed below.

Finally, one of the main concerns for communities is that not all areas will be able to be protected or restored, and some communities will face the possibility of relocation. The Coastal Master Plan allows that voluntary relocation may be necessary, but does not directly address the issue:

> In addition to floodproofing and elevation, voluntary relocation and acquisition measures may be made available to residents as options in areas that will continue to have high flood risk levels even after actions recommended in the master plan are implemented. These options will be voluntary; the master plan makes no recommendations for relocation of specific communities. The plan acknowledges the need to support citizens facing change and to handle disruptions with sensitivity and fairness.[37]

Within some coastal communities, and even entire parishes, relocation to a safer area within the town or parish is not possible due to low elevation and flood risk. Entire communities may need to be relocated to another area of the state if the community wishes to remain intact.[38]

An example of this reality is the Isle de Jean Charles.[39] The Isle de Jean Charles is home to the Native American Community of the Isle de Jean Charles Band of Biloxi-Chitimacha-Choctaw Indians, which is quickly washing away due to subsidence and sea-level rise. The first road to the island was built in 1953 though marshland. The current road, which cuts through open water, is submerged during high tide and is subject to many washouts. The most recent repair, in June 2011, cost the parish $6.24 million.[40] It is becoming increasingly clear that such repairs, which will without question be needed in the future, may not receive funding. The tribe has tried to relocate together, but has faced several setbacks in this process. The tribe's website conveys these challenges effectively:

> A levee system is being built to protect communities along Coastal Louisiana, but will bypass Isle de Jean Charles because the Army Corps of Engineers, as well

---

[36] La. Civ. Code Ann. art. 3413 (2012). "Wild animals, birds, fish, and shellfish in a state of natural liberty either belong to the state in its capacity as a public person or are things without an owner. The taking of possession of such things is governed by particular laws and regulations. The owners of a tract of land may forbid entry to anyone for purposes of hunting or fishing, and the like. Nevertheless, despite a prohibition of entry, captured wildlife belongs to the captor."

[37] COMPREHENSIVE PLAN 2012, *supra* note 17, at 159. This is the only mention of "relocation" in the *Coastal Master Plan.*

[38] *See* ISLE DE JEAN CHARLES, LOUISIANA, http://www.isledejeancharles.com (last visited Apr. 19, 2014).

[39] *Id.*

[40] *Id.*

as the State Restoration Plan, has determined it is not cost-effective to extend it to include the island. This leaves our Tribal community even more vulnerable to the encroaching Gulf waters. We, as a barrier island, are first to face these issues, which will surely become commonplace for many areas now well inland. Leaving our people, our traditions, and, our ethnicity in jeopardy. In essence, we are fast becoming climate refugees.[41]

The problem with leaving local governments and coastal property owners unsure of how issues such as relocation and buyouts will be handled is that communities and property owners have to make decisions—some of them with long-term impact— that could have financial and legal repercussions as sea levels rise. One commentator, James Wilkins, examined Gulf Coast statutory and case law linked to flood events and the liability of local governments.[42] After examining a number of Louisiana cases,[43] Wilkins noted,

> Louisiana courts have held that governments can be liable for negligence in approving development that causes or exacerbates flooding.…… Governments have been found liable for flooding damages based on causes of action other than negligence, namely, unconstitutional takings for a public purpose, strict liability for damage to neighboring property, and interference with the natural servitude of drainage.[44]

Wilkins then goes on to question if technology—such as the projections used to develop the *Coastal Master Plan*—shows that areas may be subject to extreme flooding events, can the local government be held liable for permitting development in that area?[45] While local governments have the responsibility to promote development, they also are in charge of maintaining safety; this becomes difficult when areas left for development are also those that are subject to higher flood risks.[46]

---

[41] *Id.*

[42] *See generally* James Wilkins, *Is Sea Level Rise "Foreseeable"? Does It Matter?*, 26 J. LAND USE & ENVTL. L. 437 (2011).

[43] Some of the cases include, but are not limited to, Eschete v. City of New Orleans, 245 So. 2d 383 (La. 1971); McCloud v. Parish of Jefferson, 383 So. 2d 477 (La. Ct. App. 1980); Keich v. Barkley Place, Inc., 424 So. 2d 1194 (La. Ct. App. 1982).

[44] Wilkins, *supra* note 42, at 471–72.

[45] *See id.* at 483–84. "There were no instances found in the five states where local governments were held liable for permitting development in a flood hazard area that resulted in flooding of the permitted property as opposed to neighboring property, and it would apparently take extraordinary facts and circumstances for that to occur. Such extraordinary facts and circumstances may be upon us, however, and quite possibly sooner than we would like to believe." *Id.*

[46] *Id.* at 485.

As the risk of flooding increases, so do the costs to repair or protect communities that bear the brunt of that risk. For example, consider the cost to Terrebonne Parish to repair one road that services the singular community of Isle de Jean Charles, or on a larger scale, the price tag associated with the *Coastal Master Plan*. To extend Wilkins's argument, as changes in climate result in stronger, larger storms, higher sea levels, and increased flooding, combined with predicted decreases in federal disaster assistance, some communities will not be able to afford to return after a storm event. Can the residents then hold the local government liable for personal damages for their investment to live and build in that community?

III. Recommendations for Preparing for Sea-Level Rise Impacts

While the *Coastal Master Plan* provides an outline of what projects should be considered for implementation should funds become available, there is no guarantee that these projects will be funded, or if they are, that the funding is available with enough time to make a difference: "Securing funding will depend, in part, on making the case to decision makers at the federal level that investment in Louisiana's Master Plan will yield important national benefits."[47] Additionally, as pointed out above, it is possible that even if all projects are implemented, environmental conditions could offset benefits to the point that restoration projects cannot build land fast enough to prevent future losses. This is why it is so important for state and local governments to take other steps to prepare communities for the changes that are coming and to create the most resilient communities possible now in order to make communities as sustainable as possible in the face of higher sea levels. Below are some of the steps local communities and the state should consider and examples of where similar actions have been successful in Louisiana communities.

A. PROTECTION OF BENEFICIAL NATURAL FEATURES

There are several natural features that can protect coastal communities against some of the impacts of increased flooding risks, and communities should take every step possible to protect those features. For example, wetlands have been shown to reduce storm surge.[48] Some natural levees on the banks of rivers and bayous, formed from years of sediment buildup during flood events, can protect developments from riverine and surge flooding.

---

[47] Groves & Sharon, *supra* note 21, at 160.

[48] *See* Ty V. Wamsley et al., *The Potential of Wetlands in Reducing Storm Surge*, 37 Ocean Engineering 59, 67 (2010). According to this study, the level of reduction is dependent on the surrounding landscape and the characteristics (strength, duration, speed) of each specific storm. *Id.*

Cheniers are an example of a natural feature that has received protection from local government action. Cheniers are ridges composed of sand and shell that can develop downdrift of river mouths if conditions support development.[49] The cheniers range between three and nineteen feet, and they provide some protection from storm surges to the land behind them and a reduction in storm surge energy as the surge moves forward.[50] Cheniers also provide a first line of defense against increased tidal flooding due to relative sea-level rise. They are found in the southwest portion of the state, and in the past have been mined, reducing their height and the level of protection they are able to provide.

In 2012, Cameron Parish decided to take steps to protect the cheniers through adoption of a local Coastal Zone Management Ordinance.[51] The ordinance begins by stating that cheniers are "critical landforms" that "are unique geological features that are critical components of the ecology of coastal Louisiana[, and] they serve as critical wildlife habitat and offer substantial protection against coastal storm surge and flooding."[52] The ordinance then protects the ridges by prohibiting to the maximum extent possible any "surface alterations which have high adverse impacts."[53] Such alterations will only be allowed in situations where there is an "overriding reason" for the activity, and the person seeking the permit may have to submit engineering reports detailing impact to the structures, alternative site options, and any mitigation measures that will be used.[54] The ordinance also provides a list of activities that "require a strict local coastal program review" and states that the cheniers do not qualify for exemption even if the land in question is above the 5-foot contour.[55]

Cameron Parish's protection of the cheniers is a progressive step forward in reducing development impact to natural features that provide protection to the coast.[56] Other parishes should look to this response as an example of how to provide protection to similar natural features, whether they be marshes, wetlands, tree-lined ridges, or undeveloped land suitable for holding large amounts of floodwater.

---

[49] Morang et al., *supra* note 4, at 142.

[50] *See generally* D.E. Owen, *Geology of the Chenier Plain of Cameron Parish, Southwestern Louisiana*, 14 GEOLOGICAL SOC'Y AM. FIELD GUIDE 27 (2008) (providing a detailed description of cheniers).

[51] Cameron Parish Coastal Zone Management Ordinance, Sec. 5 ½–4, Sec. 5 ½–11 (Sept. 10, 2012).

[52] *Id.*

[53] *Id.*

[54] *Id.*

[55] *Id.* Activities that require strict review include "1. Open pit mining commercial or otherwise. 2. Large scale excavations that are not incidental to environmental remediation plans which include restoring property to its original condition. 3. Timber harvesting. 4. Any other uses that would severely degrade the structural integrity of these valuable coastal landforms." *Id.*

[56] Passing the ordinance in Cameron Parish was a significant achievement. A neighboring parish that also contains cheniers considered the idea of passing a similar ordinance, but was ultimately unable to secure approval for similar language.

B. PROTECTION OF FISHERIES CAPACITY

There is concern about the *Coastal Master Plan* impacts to fisheries, both due to loss of habitat and changes in salinity. The oyster is one species that will be impacted by both the *Coastal Master Plan* and sea-level rise. The successful growth of oysters along the Louisiana coast is dependent on salinity. Although pulses of higher- or lower-than-average salinity can be beneficial, if the salinity is too low for too long, the oyster will not be able to survive, whereas if it is too high for too long, predators are much more likely to reduce the population.[57] Until very recently in Louisiana, the only way to grow and harvest oysters was through the traditional waterbottom lease. This process requires an individual to secure an oyster lease from the state, if leases were being issued at the time. The individual then must place cultch and spat[58] along the sea floor and wait the appropriate length of time to harvest. The method cultivates oysters that were, essentially, permanently attached to the waterbottom. Problems arise when salinity levels in a given area shift. If the area becomes too salty (due to sea-level rise) or too fresh (due to diversions such as those presented in the *Coastal Master Plan*), it may cause what at one point were viable oyster grounds to become less productive. In those cases, the investment in preparing and seeding the lease may result in large losses for the oyster farmer.

The Louisiana Supreme Court had to confront the issue of oyster leases and freshwater diversions in *Avenal v. Louisiana*.[59] After extensive study, Congress authorized the construction of the Caernarvon freshwater diversion project in October 1986. Because the implications to the oyster industry were well known, the Louisiana Department of Wildlife and Fisheries (LDWF) "inserted a clause into its lease form, requiring the State to be indemnified and held harmless for any claims related to coastal restoration."[60] At the same time, LDWF began allowing private leaseholders in the impacted area to move oysters to another location outside of the area of impact. Construction of the diversion began in 1988, and it became operational in 1991.[61]

---

[57] *See* Megan K. LaPeyre, Bryan Gossman & Jerome F. LaPeyre, *Defining Optimal Freshwater Flow for Oyster Production: Effects of Freshet Rate and Magnitude of Change and Duration on Eastern Oysters and Perkinsus Marinus Infection*, 32 ESTUARIES & COASTS 522, 523 (2009).

[58] Spat are oyster larvae. Cultch is the substrate, often made of crushed oyster shell, to which spat can adhere in the formation of an oyster bed.

[59] Avenal v. Louisiana, 886 So. 2d. 1085 (La. 2004).

[60] *Id*. at 1090. The basic "hold harmless clause" found in most of the leases stated: "This lessee hereby agrees to hold and save the State of Louisiana, its agents or employees, free and harmless from any claims for loss or damages to rights arising under this lease, from diversions of fresh water or sediment, depositing of dredged or other materials or any other actions, taken for the purpose of management, preservation, enhancement, creation or restoration of coastal wetlands, water bottoms, or related renewable resources; said damages to include, but not limited to, oyster mortality, oyster disease, damage to oyster beds or decreased oyster production, due to siltation, pollution or other causes." Some leases, however, contained an even more detailed clause concerning coastal restoration activities. *Id*.

[61] *Id*. at 1091–91.

The plaintiffs filed suit in 1994, claiming that their oyster leases were destroyed due to the input of freshwater. "Plaintiffs asserted that the State's action of lowering salinity levels of the water in Breton Sound below that necessary to support oyster cultivation 'has resulted in a permanent and substantial interference with plaintiff's use and enjoyment of their land amounting to a taking of an interest in [their] property rights without compensation in violation of Article I, § 4 of the Louisiana Constitution.'"[62] The trial court awarded a judgment of more than $1 billion to the plaintiffs.

The Louisiana Supreme Court reversed the decision and dismissed the plaintiffs' claims. For the leases that contained the hold harmless clause, the Court held that the leases were valid and enforceable, leaving these plaintiffs without a valid takings claim.[63] For the twelve remaining leases that did not contain the hold harmless clause, the Court conducted a takings analysis.[64] However, the Court determined that the issue of impact to the oyster leases was not a taking, but was instead a damaging, which has a prescription period of two years. The Court based this conclusion on the fact that the state owned the sea floors and oysters, and thus could not take its own property. Additionally, the plaintiffs still had the ability, through their leases, to use the bottoms to collect oysters and to prevent other private persons from entering the leases and removing oysters: "the changes in salinity of the water resulting from Caernarvon affected neither of these rights."[65] The lease did not guarantee the leaseholder a certain salinity range, and although the leases were unproductive to oysters, there were still other uses that could result in value to the plaintiffs.[66] The Court concluded by returning to the prescription issue and noted that due to the timeline of the case, the claims would have prescribed prior to filing.[67]

Before concluding the discussion of this case, one point merits attention. The Court stated:

> First, the right of the state to disperse fresh water from the Mississippi River over saltwater marshes in order to prevent coastal erosion is derived from a background principle of Louisiana law.... Secondly, the freshening of these waters in

---

[62] *Id.* at 1092. Article I, § 4 of the Louisiana Constitution states: "Every person has the right to acquire, own, control, use, enjoy, protect, and dispose of private property. This right is subject to reasonable statutory restrictions and the reasonable exercise of the police power. Property shall not be taken or damaged by the state or its political subdivisions except for public purposes and with just compensation paid to the owner or into court for his benefit..." *Id.*

[63] *Id.* at 1102–03.

[64] *Id.* at 1104. The three-part test requires that a court must "(1) determine if a recognized species of property right has been affected; (2) if it is determined that property is involved, decide whether the property has been taken or damaged in a constitutional sense; and (3) determine whether the taking or damaging is for a public purpose under Article I, § 4 [of the Louisiana Constitution]." *Id.*

[65] *Avenal*, 886 So. 2d. at 1106.

[66] *Id.* at 1107. This includes the "right to claim damages from oil and gas interests for drilling, surveying, dredging, and other exploration activities conducted on their leases following the diversion..." *Id.*

[67] *Id.* at 1109.

order to prevent further coastal erosion and save Louisiana's coast is a matter of "actual necessity" as it will "forstall [*sic*] [a] grave threat to the lives and property of others."[68]

Therefore, the *Avenal* case demonstrates that oyster fishermen would have a hard time proving damages or takings to oyster leases due to restoration projects.

LDWF has recently made changes to oyster farming regulations that could be used to prevent these types of disturbances to the industry in the future. LDWF now allows for "alternative oyster aquaculture," which includes oysters grown in cages, either placed directly on the bottom or suspended in the water column, or grown on a long-line system. The benefit of these systems is that oysters tend to grow larger faster than conventional cultch on the bottom.[69] Although there are some limitations on how much of a given oyster lease can be converted into alternative oyster culture sites, and where these sites can be located,[70] it opens up a new earning potential for oyster farmers.

Although alternative oyster aquaculture will not immediately be able to replace the production capacity of traditional oyster culture, it is possible that such technology could be very useful in the event of salinity changes. Currently, there are no provisions for the relocation of alternative oyster sites. Oysters grown on long lines could be relocated relatively easily, especially when compared to traditional oyster culture techniques. The regulations could be expanded to provide options for relocation in the event of changes in salinity, whether due to sea-level rise or diversion projects. Although other fisheries in the state, such as shrimp and fish, are not tied to a specific geographic location the same way that oysters are, changes in salinity and habitat will certainly impact these fisheries, too. LDWF and other industry leaders should begin to think about how to use existing regulations, or develop new regulations, that improve the chances of survival for these fisheries. Progressive thinking may also help avoid potential delays to restoration and protection projects due to lawsuits filed by fishermen for impacts to their livelihood.

C. REGULATIONS FOR MORE RESILIENT DEVELOPMENT

One of the most important ways coastal Louisiana can prepare for coming climate changes, especially sea-level rise, is through advance planning. Local communities, whether on the parish or municipality level, have the ability to engage in land use

---

[68] *Id.* at n.28.

[69] For a description of the process and benefits of alternative oyster culture, see WILLIAM C. WALTON ET AL., ALA. COOP. EXTENSION SYSTEM FISHERIES & AQUACULTURE SERIES: OFF-BOTTOM OYSTER FARMING (2012), *available at* http://www.auburn.edu/~wcw0003/files/offbottomoysterfarmingexten.pdf.

[70] Prior to formulations of the regulations, a suitability mapping process was required. The goal of this process was to avoid conflict with other fisheries, navigation, other coastal use permits, coastal protection and restoration projects, private property, and oil and gas interests. *See* LA. REV. STAT. ANN. § 56:431.2 (2012).

planning. Louisiana communities have been very slow to engage in this process; however, more communities are starting to respond by creating their own land use or master plans.

One example of this trend is the comprehensive resiliency plan created by the town of Jean Lafitte, which was formally adopted in April 2013.[71] The plan was created from extensive community input, which drew on surveys, charrettes, and other public meetings.[72] The plan is divided into six chapters, each focused on one principle of resilience: assessing opportunities and threats, enhancing local assets, focusing on the heart of town, diversifying mobility options, building stronger and safer, and living with water. At the end of each section, the town identifies goals and policies needed to achieve the desired results, some of which are directly connected to providing the community with a plan to achieve long-term sustainability in the face of coastal hazards.

For example, in the section relating to building requirements, one goal states: "the Town should protect key assets from disturbance," and the policies used to support that goal include, "the Town should elevate critical infrastructure including electrical sub-stations, pump stations, and other vital infrastructure hubs above BFE [base flood elevation]," and "living spaces should continue to be elevated above BFE with state and federal assistance."[73] This section also calls on the town to provide education and assistance in utilizing dry flood-proofing techniques. Although these goals do not directly deal with climate changes, building improvements that provide protection from storm surge flooding also provide protection from sea-level rise impacts. The section on living with water expressly references sea-level rise in its first goal: "Jean Lafitte shall manage water more effectively given sea-level rise, hurricanes, and other foreseeable natural and anthropogenic events that lead to flood damage."[74] Overall, although the plan does not address climate change directly, it provides the town with a valuable vision of where it would like to be in twenty years and the steps it needs to take to get there. Other coastal communities would greatly benefit from a similar plan.

Some communities are choosing to address flooding hazards due to increased storm surge and sea-level rise through development requirements. St. Tammany Parish, which borders the northern shore of Lake Pontchartrain, is one of the most progressive communities in using development requirements that increase community resiliency. The most recent example of this practice is its drafting of a new requirement that developers build roads in new developments to a minimum elevation of 6.0' NAVD '88

---

[71] Jean Lafitte, La., Jean Lafitte Tomorrow: Town Resiliency Plan, adopted April 2013, *available at* http://www.townofjeanlafitte.com/town-plan/ (last visited July 25, 2014).

[72] A charrette is a planning session that is open to the public. The planners or designers are present and work with the citizens and other interested parties on developing a plan for whatever project they are working on. The benefit to the community is that it provides an open procedure for discourse and feedback on ideas for the project.

[73] Lafitte, *supra* note 71, at 79.

[74] *Id.* at 89.

GEOID 03.[75] This requirement was developed to improve evacuation routes and reduce spending due to washouts caused by flooding.

St. Tammany Parish also requires stricter drainage requirements for new development than other areas and requires buildings to be built above base flood elevation.[76] One of the most advanced plans that the parish may eventually implement is the acquisition of repetitive loss properties, areas likely to flood, and critical habitat areas next to waterbodies in an effort to create a linked green space for floodwater storage and habitat protection, as well as limiting structures in high hazard flood areas. This plan, however, has not yet moved forward. However, other communities can look to this approach, as well as the other building regulations implemented by St. Tammany Parish, as guidance on how to implement development requirements that lead to a more sustainable community.

One of the main reasons community planning is important, especially along the Louisiana coast, is because of concerns regarding possible escalating rates for flood insurance. In 2012, amendments were made to the National Flood Insurance Program (NFIP) through the Flood Insurance Reform Act of 2012, also known as the Biggert-Waters Act.[77] Prior to Biggert-Waters, certain categories of properties received subsidies or reduced rates, depending on when the structure was built and pursuant to what standards it was constructed. With these amendments, flood insurance for many properties, especially some of those along coastal Louisiana, had increased to actuarial rates. Some of the subsidized and reduced rates were reinstalled with the Homeowner Flood Insurance Affordability Act of 2014.[78] However, there is still the concern that eventually all rates will be raised to reflect the true risk of flooding.

In response, communities along the Louisiana coast have become increasingly interested in participating in the Community Rating System (CRS). CRS is a way that communities can reduce their residents' flood insurance costs by taking steps to improve hazard resilience above and beyond the base requirements of the NFIP. Different activities are given different point values, and the more points a community accumulates, the larger the discount on flood insurance the policyholders may realize.[79] The examples of enhanced building requirements discussed above—elevating above base flood elevation, acquiring green space, and even providing information on flood hazards to residents—not only make for more resilient communities, but can be used by a CRS community to save residents substantial amounts of money each year. This can make the passage of

---

[75] In laymen's terms, six feet above sea level.

[76] St. Tammany Parish Ordinance Sec. 7-050.00, St. Tammany Parish Ordinance Sec. 7-002.00(13)(a), St. Tammany Parish Ordinance Sec. 7-022.00.

[77] Public Law 112–141 (126 Stat. 405, July 6, 2012) (Division F of the conference report includes Flood Insurance Reform and Modernization).

[78] Homeowner Flood Insurance Affordability Act of 2014, Pub. L. No. 113–89, 128 Stat. 1020 (Mar. 21, 2014).

[79] For more information on the CRS program, see generally http://www.fema.gov/national-flood-insurance-program-community-rating-system (last visited Apr. 19, 2014).

tighter requirements easier for a community if the community understands the financial benefit of the regulations.

Conclusion

Almost all coastal citizens in Louisiana would agree that Louisiana's coast will be severely impacted by sea-level rise in the decades ahead, but not all would connect that impact to climate change. These climate change impacts, when combined with the implementation of projects in the *Coastal Master Plan*, will in some cases increase stressors to coastal communities, and in others will provide only limited risk reduction. While all of the above recommendations would lead to a more sustainable coastline, one of the most important responses a community can take is be informed about what the future may look like and base decisions made today on how the landscape will look ten, twenty, or even fifty years from now.

Louisiana Sea Grant has worked hard over the past three years to provide unbiased information to communities about the coming changes. An example of this work can be seen on our project page for the climate workshop held in Lafourche Parish.[80] In January 2013, the Louisiana Sea Grant held an all-day workshop devoted to climate change impacts in the parish. First, we provided attendees with information on the science behind climate change, including but not limited to historic air and water temperatures, sea level, vegetation, and precipitation, and how these historic numbers can be used to show what impact we might expect by the end of the century. Louisiana Sea Grant's GIS specialist provided information on how rising sea-levels will impact levee overtopping in the parish, including what levee segments and sections of the community are most vulnerable. The Law and Policy component of Louisiana Sea Grant provided information on local government liability in the face of rising seas and increased flooding due to climate change, as well as how the National Flood Insurance Program may impact the decision-making process. Finally, Louisiana Sea Grant's sustainability lead provided information on how land use planning and zoning could be used to address climate impacts and lead to a more sustainable community.

The feedback on the workshop was extremely positive, and this model is being used currently by Louisiana Sea Grant in other communities. Hopefully, over time, the information provided to communities on sea-level rise and climate change, whether from Sea Grant or another source, will lead to better long-term decisions and informed constituents on the true nature of the risks they face and the steps they can take to reduce those risks.

---

[80] *Lafourche Parish Coastal Hazards Workshop*, La. Sea Grant Law & Policy Program (Jan. 10, 2013), http://www.lsu.edu/sglegal/projects/LafourcheParish.htm.

27 Coastal Climate Change Adaptation and International Human Rights

Megan M. Herzog*

Introduction

The world's coastlines and the people who populate them are exceptionally vulnerable to climate change. Over the next century, coastal communities increasingly will experience rising sea levels, warmer ocean temperatures, shrinking sea ice, loss of arable land,

---

* The author would like to acknowledge Tendayi Achiume (UCLA School of Law).

stronger storms, and degradation of vitally important marine resources such as fisheries and coral reefs.[1] Adaptation measures—human adjustments to reduce the harm of present or anticipated climate change impacts[2]—are essential in small-island states, deltas, the Arctic, large port cities, and other vulnerable coastal areas to mitigate human suffering.[3] Coastal climate change adaptation measures range from minor projects and programs, such as replanting mangroves or improving regulatory oversight of fisheries, to the potential resettlement of entire states.[4] Massive humanitarian crises are a prospect for vulnerable coastal states that fail to adequately adapt to climate-change-related floods, storms, and inundation.[5]

The significant human impacts associated with adaptation actions, or the failure to adapt, raise the specter of international human rights law violations. Legal experts have concluded that climate change adaptation implicates fundamental freedoms and entitlements such as the rights to life, self-determination, health, and housing, although the exact scope of the relationship between adaptation and human rights obligations is unclear.[6] Analyses of the extent to which climate change adaptation interacts with human rights are nascent, but advancing in concert with the growing international attention to adaptation.[7]

Legal claims related to coastal adaptation may play an important role in shaping international human rights law in the coming decades.[8] While adaptation has the potential to impact human rights in all environments, adaptation poses an especially acute risk of human rights violations in coastal areas. First and foremost, coastal environments

---

[1] INTERGOVERNMENTAL PANEL ON CLIMATE CHANGE [IPCC], CLIMATE CHANGE 2013: THE PHYSICAL SCIENCE BASIS. CONTRIBUTION OF WORKING GROUP I TO THE FIFTH ASSESSMENT REPORT OF THE INTERGOVERNMENTAL PANEL ON CLIMATE CHANGE 24–27, 40 (T.F. Stocker et al. eds., 2013), *available at* http://www.ipcc.ch/report/ar5/wg1/ [hereinafter IPCC, WORKING GROUP I].

[2] IPCC, CLIMATE CHANGE 2007: IMPACTS, ADAPTATION AND VULNERABILITY. CONTRIBUTION OF WORKING GROUP II TO THE FOURTH ASSESSMENT REPORT OF THE INTERGOVERNMENTAL PANEL ON CLIMATE CHANGE 6 (M.L. Parry et al. eds., 2007), *available at* http://www.ipcc.ch/publications_ and_data/ar4/wg2/en/contents.html [hereinafter IPCC, WORKING GROUP II] (defining "adaptation" as "[a]djustment in natural or human systems in response to actual or expected climatic stimuli or their effects, which moderates harm or exploits beneficial opportunities."). *See also* Margaux J. Hall & David C. Weiss, *Avoiding Adaptation Apartheid*, 37 YALE J. INT'L L. 309, 321, 326 (2012) [hereinafter *Avoiding Adaptation Apartheid*]; Alejandro E. Camacho, *Adapting Governance to Climate Change: Managing Uncertainty through a Learning Structure*, 59 EMORY L.J. 1, 18–19 (2009).

[3] *See* IPCC, WORKING GROUP II, *supra* note 2, at 40.

[4] *See, e.g.*, U.S. AGENCY FOR INT'L DEVELOPMENT, ADAPTING TO COASTAL CLIMATE CHANGE 41, tbl.3.2 (2009), *available at* http://www.crc.uri.edu/download/CoastalAdaptationGuide.pdf; TERRY JOHNSON, CLIMATE CHANGE ADAPTATION PLANNING MANUAL FOR COASTAL ALASKANS AND MARINE-DEPENDENT COMMUNITIES 38–39 (2011), *available at* http://seagrant.uaf.edu/map/climate/ docs/climate-change-adaptation-manual.pdf.

[5] *See infra* Section I.

[6] *See generally Avoiding Adaptation Apartheid, supra* note 2.

[7] *Id.* at 312 n.14.

[8] *Cf. id.* at 347 ("[H]uman rights law itself will have to adapt to adaptation (and climate change more broadly), as lawyers and policymakers reevaluate a number of doctrines to account for the reality of climate change.").

are particularly vulnerable to climate-change-related storm events and sea-level rise, and therefore have specialized adaptation needs.[9] Retreat from hazardous coastlines and resettlement are likely adaptation measures in many coastal areas, with manifest human rights implications.[10] Small-island states and Arctic indigenous villages distinctively face complete inundation as a possible consequence of climate change.[11] The impacts of extreme storms and sea-level rise are compounded by the fact that a considerable portion of the world's population—roughly 10 percent—lives in low-lying coastal areas.[12] Overall, coastal populations could continue to grow up to 5.2 billion people by 2080.[13] Coastal communities also have strong economic and cultural ties to marine resources that may experience particularly severe impacts as a result of ocean warming and acidification.[14] Put simply, the necessity of significant adaptation measures to protect the large number of people vulnerable to injury in coastal areas warrants global attention to potential human rights impacts and violations.

Human rights present not just a potential liability risk, however, but also a potential opportunity. At both the state and global level, there are numerous advantages to using human rights law as a tool to promote effective coastal climate change adaptation. For instance, invoking human rights law could strengthen developing countries' calls for technical and financial assistance from wealthy countries, and foster international cooperation.[15] Additionally, the risk of legal action or public criticism associated with human rights infringements could encourage governments to engage proactively in adaptation planning, and to include socially vulnerable communities meaningfully in planning processes.[16] Human rights law also may help focus choices about adaptation strategies

---

[9] *See infra* Section I.

[10] *See infra* Section III.B.2.

[11] *See* U.N. Off. of the High Comm'r for Human Rights [OHCHR], *Report of the Office of the United Nations High Commissioner for Human Rights on the Relationship Between Climate Change and Human Rights*, ¶¶ 40, 51, U.N. Doc. A/HRC/10/61 (Jan. 15, 2009), *available at* http://www.ohchr.org/EN/Issues/ HRAndClimateChange/Pages/Study.aspx [hereinafter OHCHR Report]; ANTHONY OLIVER-SMITH, SEA LEVEL RISE AND THE VULNERABILITY OF COASTAL PEOPLES: RESPONDING TO THE LOCAL CHALLENGES OF GLOBAL CLIMATE CHANGE IN THE 21ST CENTURY, InterSecTions Pub. No. 7/2009 35 (U.N. Univ. Inst. for Env't & Human Sec. 2009); Submission of the Maldives to the Office of the U.N. High Commissioner for Human Rights under Human Rights Council Res. 7/23 (2008).

[12] OLIVER-SMITH, *supra* note 11, at 9 (reporting that roughly 10 percent of the world's population resides within ten meters of sea level).

[13] IPCC, WORKING GROUP II, *supra* note 2, at 40.

[14] *Id.* (reporting that climate change is associated with more frequent coral bleaching and ocean acidification).

[15] *See* SIOBHAN MCINERNEY-LANKFORD, MAC DARROW & LAVANYA RAJAMANI, HUMAN RIGHTS AND CLIMATE CHANGE, WORLD BANK STUDY 2, 30 (2011) [hereinafter WORLD BANK STUDY]; Marc Limon, *Human Rights and Climate Change: Constructing a Case for Political Action*, 33 HARV. ENVTL. L. REV. 439, 450–52 (2009); David B. Hunter, *Human Rights Implications for Climate Change Negotiations*, 11 OR. REV. INT'L L. 331, 360 (2009).

[16] *See* WORLD BANK STUDY, *supra* note 15, at 30; Limon, *supra* note 15, at 450; *Avoiding Adaptation Apartheid, supra* note 2, at 356; OHCHR Report, *supra* note 11, at ¶ 81.

and decisions regarding allocation of limited public resources.[17] Overall, articulating stronger linkages between human rights law and coastal climate change adaptation may help ensure that essential adaptation actions incorporate human rights considerations, thereby forestalling potential violations.[18] For these reasons, human rights advocates have called for increased linkages between climate change adaptation and human rights legal regimes.[19]

This chapter discusses the relationship between coastal climate change adaptation and international human rights legal protections. Section I begins with a brief overview of coastal climate change vulnerability, impacts, and adaptation. Section II then outlines the international human rights and climate change legal regimes and their linkages. Section III evaluates the utility of existing and emerging legal tools in preventing and responding to some of the potential human rights impacts of coastal climate change adaptation, and proposes strategies that governments could employ to reduce the risk of human rights violations.

I. Coastal Climate Change Vulnerability and Adaptation

Climate-change-related impacts to coastal regions include sea-level rise, ocean warming, changes in ocean chemistry, changes in weather patterns, and increased surface temperature. The most recent report from the Intergovernmental Panel on Climate Change (IPCC) finds that coastal areas are already experiencing climate change.[20] Over the course of the twenty-first century, ocean temperature will continue to increase, leading to changes in ocean circulation;[21] Arctic sea ice will continue to shrink and thin;[22] ocean acidification will accelerate;[23] and the rate of sea-level rise will increase.[24] By 2100, the

---

[17] WORLD BANK STUDY, *supra* note 15, at 29; Limon, *supra* note 15, at 450; *Avoiding Adaptation Apartheid, supra* note 2, at 356; Hunter, *supra* note 15, at 360.

[18] *But see* Observations by the United States of America on the Relationship between Climate Change and Human Rights, ¶¶ 4, 17, 26 (2008), *available at* http://www.ohchr.org/Documents/Issues/ClimateChange/Submissions/USA.pdf [hereinafter U.S. Submission] (arguing that "a human rights based approach to climate change would be impractical and unwise" and "unlikely to be effective" as states "would almost certainly not enforce human rights-based determinations against them[selves]," thus undermining the legitimacy of human rights law as a whole).

[19] *See infra* Section II.C.

[20] IPCC, WORKING GROUP I, *supra* note 1, at 8–9,11 (reporting that over the past several decades, salinity has changed in certain ocean regions, the Arctic has warmed substantially, and global mean sea level has risen markedly, mostly due to ocean thermal expansion and land ice melt).

[21] *Id.* at 24 (reporting that the top 100 meters of ocean will warm approximately 0.6 to 2.0 degrees Celsius by the end of the twenty-first century).

[22] *Id.*

[23] *Id.* at 27 (projecting a 0.06 to 0.32 global decrease in surface ocean pH by the end of the twenty-first century).

[24] *Id.* at 25.

IPCC estimates that global mean sea level will rise an additional twenty-six to eighty-two centimeters.[25]

Hundreds of millions of coastal residents and coastal infrastructure are vulnerable to climate change.[26] Coastal communities are particularly sensitive to storm events, which are expected to increase in frequency and intensity.[27] Low-lying urban areas, small islands, and the 200 million residents of the seven Asian megadeltas are at critical risk.[28] Saltwater intrusion, increased soil salinity, and loss of arable coastal land will significantly impact coastal livelihoods.[29] Additionally, climate change will negatively impact mangroves, coastal wetlands, and coral reefs,[30] with "serious implications for the well-being of societies dependent on coastal ecosystems for goods and services."[31] Ocean acidification and warming also are expected to cause fish range shifts and extinctions.[32] Impacts to fisheries will be especially devastating for the approximately 1 billion people who rely on fish as their primary animal protein source.[33]

Given the inertia of the climate system, most climate change impacts will persist for centuries into the future even if anthropogenic greenhouse gas emissions are stabilized.[34] Thus, adaptation is critical for coastal populations. Coastal adaptation strategies are generally divisible into three categories: (1) *protecting* assets with coastal armoring structures, (2) *accommodating* impacts by enhancing the resilience of vulnerable populations and development, and (3) facilitating human *retreat* from vulnerable areas.[35] Protection tools include hard-engineered flood- and erosion-control structures such as sea walls as well

---

[25] *Id.* (sea-level rise estimates are relative to 1986 to 2005 levels). *See also id.* at 26 (projecting that most coastlines will experience significant sea-level rise by the end of this century, although sea levels will not rise uniformly around the world).

[26] IPCC, WORKING GROUP II, *supra* note 2, at 40.

[27] *Id.*

[28] *Id.*

[29] OLIVER-SMITH, *supra* note 11, at 30 (describing how increasing soil salinity threatens cultivation of the main crop in Tuvalu, taro).

[30] IPCC, WORKING GROUP II, *supra* note 2, at 13 (describing threats to Africa's coral reefs, mangroves, and fisheries); *id.* at 14 (stating that increases in ocean temperature may harm Mesoamerican coral reefs); *id.* at 59 (projecting that sea-level rise will destroy almost half of the Mekong River Delta's mangroves and nearly one-third of Asian coral reefs by the end of the century).

[31] *Id.* at 40. *See generally* Edward B. Barbier et al., *The Value of Estuarine and Coastal Ecosystem Services*, 81 ECOLOGICAL MONOGRAPHS 169 (2011).

[32] NICHOLAS STERN, HER MAJESTY'S TREASURY, STERN REVIEW ON THE ECONOMICS OF CLIMATE CHANGE 72 (2006); IPCC, WORKING GROUP II, *supra* note 2, at 14, 39.

[33] STERN, *supra* note 32, at 72.

[34] IPCC, WORKING GROUP I, *supra* note 1, at 27. *See also* OHCHR Report, *supra* note 11, at ¶ 15 ("Irrespective of the scale of mitigation measures taken today and over the next decades…adaptation measures are required to enable societies to cope with the effects of now unavoidable global warming.").

[35] *See generally* MATTHEW M. LINHAM & ROBERT J. NICHOLLS, TECHNOLOGIES FOR CLIMATE CHANGE ADAPTATION (U.N. Env't Prog. 2010), *available at* http://www.unep.org/pdf/TNAhandbook_CoastalErosionFlooding.pdf; Megan M. Herzog & Sean B. Hecht, *Combatting Sea-Level Rise in Southern California: How Local Governments Can Seize Adaptation Opportunities while Minimizing Legal Risk*, 19 HASTINGS W.-Nw. J. ENVTL. L. & POL'Y 463 (2013); J. Peter Byrne, *The Cathedral Engulfed: Sea-Level*

as natural shoreline stabilization methods such as sand replenishment, revegetation, and wetland restoration.[36]

Importantly, climate change will not impact coastal populations uniformly. The degree to which climate change will impact an individual or community depends on the entity's adaptive capacity,[37] local geography and development patterns, and any preexisting environmental, social, and economic stressors.[38] The world's least-developed countries, small-island states, and Arctic indigenous groups are likely to experience the most severe impacts and adaptation challenges, although notably, they are least responsible for the historical greenhouse gas emissions that contribute to global climate change.[39]

Developing countries have especially low adaptive capacities and significant existing economic, social, and environmental stressors.[40] They generally also have the weakest human rights protection and only limited resources to devote to adaptation. Strikingly, the cost of adapting to projected sea-level rise in Africa by the end of this century could amount to 5 to 10 percent of gross domestic product.[41] Many densely populated coastal cities in African, Asian, and Latin American developing countries could suffer severe damage.[42] In Bangladesh—one of the poorest, most densely populated, and lowest-lying countries in the world—more than two-thirds of the population of 150 million people are likely to be impacted by sea-level rise, and 10 percent of fertile land could be ruined.[43] Adaptation is also a major challenge for small-island states, which are especially vulnerable to sea-level rise, storm events, beach erosion, and coral bleaching, all of which are projected to reduce fisheries and tourism revenues.[44] Options to respond to climate

---

Rise, Property Rights, and Time, 73 LA. L. REV. 69, 85 (2012); Jessica Grannis et al., *Coastal Management in the Face of Rising Seas: Legal Strategies for Connecticut*, 5 SEA GRANT L. & POL'Y J. 59, 61 (2012).

[36] Robert R.M. Verchick & Joel D. Scheraga, *Protecting the Coast*, in THE LAW OF ADAPTATION TO CLIMATE CHANGE 235, 250 (Michael B. Gerrard & Katrina Fischer Kuh eds., 2012).

[37] IPCC, WORKING GROUP II, *supra* note 2, at 727 (defining "adaptive capacity" as "the ability or potential of a system to respond successfully to climate variability and change, and includes adjustments in both behaviour and in resources and technologies").

[38] *See* Siobhan McInerney-Lankford, *Climate Change and Human Rights: An Introduction to Legal Issues*, 33 HARV. ENVTL. L. REV. 431, 436 (2009); *Avoiding Adaptation Apartheid*, *supra* note 2, at 336.

[39] INT'L COUNCIL ON HUMAN RTS. POL'Y, CLIMATE CHANGE AND HUMAN RIGHTS: A ROUGH GUIDE 1 (2008); OHCHR Report, *supra* note 11, at ¶ 10.

[40] *See* IPCC, WORKING GROUP II, *supra* note 2, at 13.

[41] *Id.*

[42] *See, e.g.*, *id.* at 14 (citing an increased risk of flooding in low-lying Latin American coastal areas); *id.* at 59 (reporting that sea-level rise could affect 7.5 to 9 million people residing in Asia's densely populated Red River and Mekong Delta regions over the next century); OLIVER-SMITH, *supra* note 11, at 36 (noting that Vietnam's Mekong Delta is one of the most densely populated areas in the world); STERN, *supra* note 32, at 105 (stating that, by the end of the century, projected sea-level rise could completely inundate Gambia's capital city and cause more than $470 million in mango, cashew nut, and coconut crop damage).

[43] OLIVER-SMITH, *supra* note 11, at 32.

[44] IPCC, WORKING GROUP II, *supra* note 2, at 15.

change on small islands are limited and expensive.[45] Coastal climate change also severely impacts Arctic coastal villages, where temperature increases and sea-ice melt threaten traditional ways of life for indigenous populations.[46] The severe and manifest human impacts of climate change in coastal states with limited adaptive capacity underscore the risk of potential human rights law violations.

II. The Human Rights Legal Regime

Coastal climate change adaptation action, or the failure to adapt, implicates international human rights law.[47] International human rights law requires states "to act in certain ways or to refrain from certain acts, in order to promote and protect human rights and fundamental freedoms of individuals or groups."[48] Human rights generally fall into two categories: *liberty rights*, including civil and political rights that prevent state interference with enjoyments of certain freedoms, and *socioeconomic and cultural rights*, including entitlements to goods, services, or resources.[49]

Human rights can find expression in binding international law or non-binding ("soft") international legal instruments, as well as domestic law.[50] A state is legally bound by both the treaties it ratifies and customary international law.[51] The nine core

---

[45] *Id.* at 63 (finding, *e.g.*, that coastal protection strategies could cost Singapore up to $16.8 million by the end of the century).

[46] *Id.* at 15; OLIVER-SMITH, *supra* note 11, at 34.

[47] *See generally Avoiding Adaptation Apartheid, supra* note 2.

[48] *What Are Human Rights*, U.N. OFF. OF THE HIGH COMM'R FOR HUMAN RIGHTS (2012), http://www. ohchr.org/en/issues/pages/whatarehumanrights.aspx [hereinafter *Human Rights*]. *See also* CTR. FOR INT'L ENVTL. LAW, CLIMATE CHANGE & HUMAN RIGHTS: A PRIMER 3 (2011), http://www.ciel.org/ Publications/CC_HRE_23May11.pdf [hereinafter CLIMATE CHANGE & HUMAN RIGHTS: A PRIMER]. Private parties may also, to some extent, have international human rights legal obligations, but such obligations are outside the scope of this chapter.

[49] Amy Hardberger, *Life, Liberty, and the Pursuit of Water: Evaluating Water as a Human Right and the Duties and Obligations It Creates*, 4 NW. J. INT'L HUM. RTS. 331, 331, 334 (2005).

[50] For example, most written national constitutions contain human rights protections. WORLD BANK STUDY, *supra* note 15, at 4. Additionally, more than ninety national constitutions explicitly protect the right to a healthy, clean, safe, favorable, or wholesome environment. Human Rights Council, *Report of the Independent Expert on the Issue of Human Rights Obligations Relating to the Enjoyment of a Safe, Clean, Healthy and Sustainable Environment*, ¶ 12, U.N. Doc. A/HRC/22/43 (Dec. 24, 2012); *see, e.g.*, CONST. S. AFR. § 24; CONST. FR., Charter for the Environment, art. 1. In only a small number of nations, however, have courts held that constitutional environmental rights protections are judicially enforceable. Randall S. Abate, *Climate Change, the United States, and the Impacts of Arctic Melting: A Case Study in the Need for Enforceable International Environmental Human Rights*, 26A STAN. ENVTL. L.J. 3, 8, 26 (2007) (stating that courts have enforced constitutional provisions protecting environmental rights in Portugal, Argentina, Costa Rica, and India).

[51] Statute of the International Court of Justice, 39 AJIL Supp. 215, art. 38(1) (1945). *See also* Hardberger, *supra* note 49, at 334 (describing that ratification of an international treaty typically requires an affirmative step in addition to a mere signature on the treaty).

international human rights treaties require ratifying states to *respect* (i.e., refrain from violating), *protect* (i.e., prevent public actors and private parties from violating), and *fulfill* (i.e., take appropriate positive measures toward full realization of) enumerated rights without discrimination.[52] All UN member states have ratified at least one of the core human rights treaties, and the majority of member states have ratified at least four of them.[53] Importantly, a customary legal principle can bind a government even if it is not a party to, does not sign, or does not ratify any convention enumerating the right. The obligation to uphold a human right is recognized as customary law if widespread practice among states is consistent with the protection of the right out of a sense of legal obligation.[54] There are certain customary principles—termed *jus cogens*—that international law recognizes as fundamental and non-derogable,[55] such as the prohibition on genocide.

Non-binding human rights instruments, such as UN resolutions and declarations that are not customary law, nonetheless carry political and moral authority. Soft law principles can have significant normative influence on international decision-making and discourse.[56] In particular, non-binding resolutions are "considered to be persuasive views on international law and often…articulate emerging principles of international law."[57] And beyond soft law instruments, invocations of general human-rights-related principles—which often underlie calls for a "human-rights-based approach" to international problem-solving—can effectively promote humanitarian goals outside of formal legal strictures.[58]

---

[52] WORLD BANK STUDY, *supra* note 15, at 4–5; *Human Rights, supra* note 48. The nine core international human rights treaties include: the International Convention on the Elimination of All Forms of Racial Discrimination, International Covenant on Civil and Political Rights, International Covenant on Economic, Social and Cultural Rights, Convention on the Elimination of All Forms of Discrimination against Women, Convention against Torture and Other Cruel, Inhuman or Degrading Treatment or Punishment, Convention on the Rights of the Child, International Convention on the Protection of the Rights of All Migrant Workers and Members of Their Families, International Convention for the Protection of All Persons from Enforced Disappearance, and Convention on the Rights of Persons with Disabilities. *Core International Instruments,* U.N. OFF. OF THE HIGH COMM'R FOR HUMAN RIGHTS (2012), http://www.ohchr.org/EN/ProfessionalInterest/Pages/CoreInstruments.aspx.

[53] *Human Rights Bodies,* U.N. OFF. OF THE HIGH COMM'R FOR HUMAN RIGHTS (2012), http://www.ohchr.org/EN/HRBodies/Pages/HumanRightsBodies.aspx.

[54] *See* Statute of the International Court of Justice, *supra* note 51, art. 38(1); RESTATEMENT (THIRD) FOREIGN RELATIONS LAW OF THE UNITED STATES § 102(2) (1987).

[55] *See* Vienna Convention on the Law of Treaties, May 23, 1969, 8 I.L.M. 679, art. 53.

[56] WORLD BANK STUDY, *supra* note 15, at 26–27; Belinda U. Calaguas, *The Right to Water, Sanitation and Hygiene and the Human Rights-Based Approach to Development* 4 (WaterAid Briefing Paper, July 1999) (stating that human rights advocates have harnessed non-binding authorities to pressure states into ratifying binding human rights treaties, lobby for the enactment of national human rights protections, and highlight inconsistent state practices).

[57] RIGHT TO WATER PROGRAMME, CENTRE ON HOUSING RIGHTS & EVICTIONS, SOURCE NO. 8: LEGAL RESOURCES FOR THE RIGHT TO WATER 15 (2004).

[58] *See* OFF. U.N. HIGH COMM'R FOR HUMAN RIGHTS, APPLYING A HUMAN RIGHTS-BASED APPROACH TO CLIMATE CHANGE NEGOTIATIONS, POLICIES AND MEASURES, *available at* http://www.ohchr.org/Documents/Issues/ClimateChange/InfoNoteHRBA.pdf (last visited Mar. 29, 2014) (defining a "human rights-based approach" as "a conceptual framework that is normatively based on international human rights

Mechanisms to protect and enforce international human rights are fairly elaborate, including complaint procedures and periodic reviews and investigations by the UN Human Rights Council and the expert "treaty bodies" overseeing implementation of each of the core human rights treaties.[59] Treaty bodies also publish authoritative interpretations of the covenants, often in the form of General Comments.[60] Additionally, regional and national tribunals may provide a forum for victims seeking redress for certain human rights violations.[61]

A. INTERNATIONAL HUMAN RIGHTS INSTRUMENTS

In 1948, the UN General Assembly adopted its historic Universal Declaration of Human Rights (UDHR),[62] the first international legal instrument to elaborate basic civil, political, economic, social, and cultural rights.[63] The UDHR contains thirty articles enumerating inter alia the rights to life,[64] equality before the law,[65] property,[66] and an adequate standard of living.[67] Although the UDHR is a non-binding declaration, many legal experts argue that some of the enumerated rights have risen to the level of customary law.[68] In 1966, the UN General Assembly built upon the UDHR with two binding human rights treaties: the International Covenant on Civil and Political Rights (ICCPR)[69] and the International Covenant on Economic, Social and Cultural Rights (ICESCR).[70] Together, the UDHR, ICCPR, and ICESCR have served as a basis for corresponding regional and national human rights protections.[71] The Convention

---

standards and operationally directed to promoting and protecting human rights. …plans, policies and programmes are anchored in a system of rights and corresponding obligations established by international law"); WORLD BANK STUDY, *supra* note 15, at 27–28 (discussing "human rights approaches" and "human rights-based approaches").

[59] WORLD BANK STUDY, *supra* note 15, at 4, 27. For a list of the treaty bodies, see *Human Rights Bodies*, U.N. OFF. OF THE HIGH COMM'R FOR HUMAN RIGHTS (2012), http://www.ohchr.org/EN/HRBodies/Pages/HumanRightsBodies.aspx.

[60] WORLD BANK STUDY, *supra* note 15, at 4.

[61] *Id. See also infra* Section II.B (discussing regional human rights mechanisms).

[62] G.A. Res. 217 A (III), U.N. Doc A/RES/217(III) (Dec. 10, 1948) [hereinafter UDHR].

[63] *Id.* pmbl.

[64] *Id.* art. 3.

[65] *Id.* art. 7.

[66] *Id.* art. 17.

[67] *Id.* art. 25.

[68] WORLD BANK STUDY, *supra* note 15, at 22.

[69] International Covenant on Civil and Political Rights, Dec. 16, 1966, 999 U.N.T.S. 171, 6 I.L.M. 368 [hereinafter ICCPR].

[70] International Covenant on Economic, Social and Cultural Rights, Dec. 16, 1966, 6 I.L.M. 360 [hereinafter ICESCR].

[71] U.N. OFF. OF THE HIGH COMM'R FOR HUMAN RIGHTS, FACT SHEET NO. 2 (REV. 1), THE INTERNATIONAL BILL OF HUMAN RIGHTS (1996), *available at* http://www.ohchr.org/Documents/Publications/FactSheet2Rev.1en.pdf.

on the Elimination of All Forms of Discrimination against Women (CEDAW)[72] and Convention on the Rights of the Child (CRC)[73] supplement these instruments with protections specific to women and children.

The ICCPR guarantees a variety of basic rights, including an individual's right to life[74] and a people's collective right to self-determination,[75] "to all individuals within [a state party's] territory and subject to its jurisdiction."[76] Significantly, the ICCPR both prohibits state parties from violating enumerated rights and imposes a positive obligation on parties to protect rights from violation by private entities.[77] The ICESCR protects, among other socioeconomic and cultural rights, the rights to an adequate standard of living,[78] health,[79] education,[80] and participation in cultural life.[81] The General Comments of the Committee on Economic, Social and Cultural Rights (CESCR) confirm that state parties have responsibilities to respect rights, to protect rights from violation by private entities, to provide and facilitate access to entitlements, and to promote rights.[82]

Notably, the ICESCR incorporates the concept of "progressive realization": each party is required "to take steps, individually and thorough international assistance and co-operation . . . to the maximum of its available resources, . . . to achiev[e] progressively the full realization of the [treaty's] rights."[83] Thus, the treaty contemplates that developing countries with limited capacity and resources may not immediately be capable of securing all socioeconomic rights protected under the treaty, but such states nonetheless must demonstrate that they are taking concrete steps to advance enumerated rights.[84] Additionally, all states, regardless of capacity, must protect basic survival needs, which constitute the "minimum cores" of the fundamental rights enumerated in the ICESCR.[85] Although there is some degree of debate, some legal

---

[72] Convention on the Elimination of All Forms of Discrimination against Women, Dec. 18, 1979, 19 I.L.M. 33 [hereinafter CEDAW].

[73] Convention on the Rights of the Child art. 24, Nov. 20, 1989, 1577 U.N.T.S. 3 [hereinafter CRC].

[74] ICCPR, *supra* note 69, art. 6.

[75] *Id.* art. 1(1).

[76] *Id.* art. 2(1). *See also* Human Rights Comm., General Comment 31, Nature of the General Legal Obligation on States Parties to the Covenant, ¶ 10, U.N. Doc. CCPR/C/21/Rev.1/Add.13 (2004) (interpreting ICCPR, *supra* note 69, art. 2(1) to extend state parties' obligations to "anyone within the power or effective control of that State Party, even if not situated within the territory of the State Party").

[77] WORLD BANK STUDY, *supra* note 15, at 5 (interpreting ICCPR, *supra* note 69, art. 2(1)).

[78] ICESCR, *supra* note 70, art. 12.

[79] *Id.* arts. 7(b), 10, 12.

[80] *Id.* art. 13.

[81] *Id.* art. 15.

[82] WORLD BANK STUDY, *supra* note 15, at 6.

[83] ICESCR, *supra* note 70, art. 2(1).

[84] WORLD BANK STUDY, *supra* note 15, at 5.

[85] *See* U.N. Econ. & Soc. Council, Comm. on Econ., Soc., & Cultural Rights [CESCR], General Comment 3, The Nature of States Parties' Obligations, U.N. Doc. E/1991/23 (1990). *See generally* Margaux J. Hall & David C. Weiss, *Human Rights and Remedial Equilibration: Equilibrating Socio-Economic Rights*, 36

scholars support the conclusion that the "minimum core" rights have reached the level of customary law.[86]

Although not one of the core human rights treaties, the Convention Relating to the Status of Refugees ("Refugee Convention")[87] contains important protections particularly relevant to coastal climate change impacts and adaptation. Under the Refugee Convention, state parties have legal obligations to anyone who has a

> well-founded fear of being persecuted for reasons of race, religion, nationality, membership of a particular social group or political opinion, is outside the country of his nationality and is unable, or owing to such fear, is unwilling to avail himself of the protection of that country; or who, not having a nationality and being outside the country of his former habitual residence as a result of such events, is unable, or owing to such fear, is unwilling to return to it.[88]

The principle of *non-refoulement*, which prevents a host country from returning a refugee to a state where she faces a serious threat to her life or freedom, serves as the backbone for other rights enumerated in the Refugee Convention, including the rights to work,[89] housing,[90] and education[91].[92]

Soft law instruments also may be relevant to coastal climate change adaptation, such as the numerous non-binding resolutions and declarations linking human rights, development, and the environment.[93] These instruments reinforce environmental rights

---

BROOK. J. INT'L L. 453 (2011) (describing the origins of "minimum core" theory, its advantages in human rights advocacy as an immediate and enforceable standard, and its disadvantages in potentially forestalling government action to fully satisfy rights beyond the minimum core).

[86] CTR. FOR HUMAN RIGHTS & GLOBAL JUSTICE ET AL., WOCH NAN SOLEY: THE DENIAL OF THE RIGHT TO WATER IN HAITI 45 (2008). Some experts further argue that certain socioeconomic rights have risen to the level of customary law, as evidenced by *inter alia* numerous national constitutions containing socioeconomic rights protections and universal acceptance of the Millennium Development Goals. WORLD BANK STUDY, *supra* note 15, at 22.

[87] Convention Relating to the Status of Refugees, July 28, 1951, 189 U.N.T.S. 150, *as amended by* Protocol Relating to the Status of Refugees, Jan. 31, 1967, 19 U.S.T. 6223, 606 U.N.T.S. 267.

[88] Convention Relating to the Status of Refugees, *supra* note 87, art. 1(A)(2); Protocol Relating to the Status of Refugees, *supra* note 87, art. 1.

[89] Convention Relating to the Status of Refugees, *supra* note 87, arts. 17–19.

[90] *Id.* art. 21.

[91] *Id.* art. 22.

[92] *Id.* art. 33.

[93] *See, e.g.*, Problems of the Human Environment, G.A. Res. 2398 (XXIII), U.N. Doc. A/Res/2398/23 (Dec. 3, 1968); Stockholm Declaration on the Human Environment of the United Nations Conference on the Human Environment, June 16, 1972, 11 I.L.M. 1416 (1972); Hague Declaration on the Environment, Mar. 11, 1989, 28 I.L.M. 1308; Need to Ensure a Healthy Environment for the Well-Being of Individuals, G.A. Res. 45/94, U.N. Doc. A/RES/45/94 (Dec. 14, 1990); The Future We Want, Final Rep. of the U.N. Conf. on Sustainable Development, Rio de Janeiro, Brazil, June 20–22, 2012; U.N. Conf. on Sustainable Development, Rio de Janeiro, Braz., June 3–14, 1992, *Report of the U.N. Conference on Environment*

advocates' continuing efforts to derive a human right to a healthy environment from existing instruments and principles.[94] The UN General Assembly also has specifically recognized the individual and collective rights of indigenous peoples in the non-binding Declaration on the Rights of Indigenous Peoples.[95]

B. REGIONAL HUMAN RIGHTS LAW

Regional mechanisms play a significant role in human rights protection. The three most established regional mechanisms are the American Convention on Human Rights,[96] the European Convention on Human Rights,[97] and the African Charter on Human and Peoples' Rights.[98] These three treaties and related agreements recognize a range of civil and political rights, including rights to life, liberty, religion, freedom from discrimination, movement, residence, family, and property, as well as socioeconomic rights such as the rights to education, food, housing, health, and an adequate standard of living.[99] Notably, the African Charter on Human and Peoples' Rights guarantees all people "the right to a general satisfactory environment favourable to their

---

and Development Volume I: Resolutions Adopted by the Conference, U.N. Doc. A/CONF.151/26 (Jan. 1, 1993) [hereinafter Rio Declaration].

[94] See McInerney-Lankford, supra note 38, at 431–32 (discussing ongoing international efforts to establish a right to a clean and healthy environment under, e.g., article 24 of the CRC, article 24 of the African Charter on Human and Peoples' Rights, and article 11 of the "Protocol of San Salvador" to the American Convention on Human Rights in the Area of Economic, Social and Cultural Rights); WORLD BANK STUDY, supra note 15, at 36–39 (providing an overview of international efforts to establish a human right to the environment); John Lee, The Underlying Legal Theory to Support a Well-Defined Human Right to a Healthy Environment as a Principle of Customary International Law, 25 COLUM. J. ENVTL. L. 283 (2000); Human Rights Council, Report of the Independent Expert on the Issue of Human Rights Obligations Relating to the Enjoyment of a Safe, Clean, Healthy and Sustainable Environment, John H. Knox, U.N. Doc. A/HRC/22/43 (Dec. 24, 2012), available at http://www.ohchr.org/Documents/HRBodies/HRCouncil/RegularSession/Session22/A-HRC-22-43_en.pdf.

[95] Declaration on the Rights of Indigenous Peoples, G.A. Res. 61/295, Annex, U.N. Doc. A/RES/61/295 (Oct 2, 2007). See also Convention Concerning Indigenous and Tribal Peoples in Independent Countries, adopted June 27, 1989, 28 I.L.M. 1382.

[96] American Convention on Human Rights, Nov. 22, 1969, 1144 U.N.T.S. 143, 9 I.L.M. 673. The Inter-American regional human rights regime is reinforced by the American Declaration on the Rights and Duties of Man, Apr. 1948, OAS Resolution XXX, OEA/Ser.L.V/II.82 doc.6 rev.1, which includes rights to life, liberty, property, security of person, inviolability of the home, and preservation of health and well-being.

[97] European Convention on Human Rights, Nov. 4, 1950, 213 U.N.T.S. 221. See also E.U. Charter on Fundamental Rights, Dec. 7, 2000, OJ 2000 C 364.

[98] African Charter on Human and Peoples' Rights, June 27, 1981, 1520 U.N.T.S. 217, 21 I.L.M. 58.

[99] WORLD BANK STUDY, supra note 15, at 5. The European and Inter-American regimes have separate agreements regarding socioeconomic and cultural rights (European Social Charter, Oct. 18, 1961, 529 U.N.T.S. 89; Additional Protocol to the American Convention on Human Rights in the Area of Economic, Social and Cultural Rights: Protocol of San Salvador, Nov. 17, 1988, 28 I.L.M. 161), while the African Charter directly incorporates socioeconomic rights. Id.

development."[100] Each of the three major regional human rights treaties is associated with a compliance entity or entities responsible for publishing legal interpretations and reviewing state actions.[101]

C. LINKING INTERNATIONAL HUMAN RIGHTS AND CLIMATE CHANGE LAW

There are growing linkages between international human rights law and the international climate change legal regime under the UN Framework Convention on Climate Change (UNFCCC).[102] The UNFCCC's broad goal is to "achieve…stabilization of greenhouse gas concentrations in the atmosphere at a level that would prevent dangerous anthropogenic interference with the climate system"[103] through coordinated international action to "anticipate, prevent, or minimize the causes of climate change and mitigate its adverse effects."[104] Article 4 of the UNFCCC requires parties to engage in international cooperation regarding adaptation measures.[105] Central to the UNFCCC framework is acknowledgment of the parties' "common but differentiated responsibility" to respond to climate change.[106] The UNFCCC distinguishes developed, industrialized countries, which are responsible for most historical greenhouse gas emissions, from developing countries, which are most vulnerable to climate change impacts.[107]

All of the state parties to the core international human rights treaties have also ratified the UNFCCC.[108] Yet, the UNFCCC does not explicitly address human rights. Indeed, parties to the UNFCCC historically have been reluctant to incorporate human rights considerations into related agreements and plans.[109] Some legal experts and advocates have proposed the development of new protocols, management systems, or

---

[100] African Charter on Human and Peoples' Rights, *supra* note 98, art. 24.

[101] Regional compliance entities include the Inter-American Commission and Court of Human Rights, European Court of Human Rights, and the African Commission and Court on Human and Peoples' Rights. WORLD BANK STUDY, *supra* note 15, at 4.

[102] U.N. Framework Convention on Climate Change, May 9, 1992, 1771 U.N.T.S. 107 [hereinafter UNFCCC]. *See also* Kyoto Protocol to the United Nations Framework Convention on Climate Change, Dec. 11, 1997, 37 I.L.M. 22, *as amended by* Doha Amendment to the Kyoto Protocol, UNFCCC Conf. of the Parties [UNFCCC COP] Dec. 1/CMP.8, U.N. Doc. C.N.718.2012 (Dec. 8, 2012) (requiring certain industrialized states, listed as "Annex-I" parties to the UNFCCC, to reduce greenhouse gas emissions within certain compliance periods).

[103] UNFCCC, *supra* note 102, art. 2.

[104] *Id.* art. 3(3).

[105] *Id.* art. 4(1)(b), (e).

[106] *Id.* art. 3. *See also* Rio Declaration, *supra* note 93, at 4 (formulating the principle of "common but differentiated responsibilities" to respond to global environmental degradation).

[107] WORLD BANK STUDY, *supra* note 15, at 3. *See also* UNFCCC, *supra* note 102, art. 3 (stating that "full consideration should be given to the needs of developing countries, especially those that are particularly vulnerable to the adverse effects of climate change").

[108] WORLD BANK STUDY, *supra* note 15, at 45, app. B.

[109] *Id.* at 9 (describing how "explicit human rights arguments have yet to gain traction to any appreciable extent within the climate change negotiations under the UNFCCC framework"); Bonnie Docherty &

expert working groups under the UNFCCC framework to address human rights issues directly.[110] Others have argued that the UNFCCC legal framework is not well suited to deal with human rights issues, for instance, because the UNFCCC's mandate does not address remedies, and the UNFCCC framework has a poor track record of achievement on climate change mitigation.[111]

Over the past decade, modest linkages have developed between the international climate change and human rights frameworks, mostly as a result of the concerted efforts of small-island states, indigenous groups, and human rights advocates.[112] In 2007, a group of small-island developing states executed the Malé Declaration on the Human Dimension of Global Climate Change,[113] which calls for enhanced cooperation among the UNFCCC, Human Rights Council, and the UN Office of the High Commissioner for Human Rights (OHCHR).[114] In 2008, the Human Rights Council adopted Resolution 7/23, which states that "climate change...has implications for the full enjoyment of human rights."[115] A resultant OHCHR study emphasizes states' legal obligations to protect human rights, including through international cooperation.[116] Significantly, however, the study finds that "[w]hile climate change has obvious implications for the enjoyment of human rights, it is less obvious whether, and to what extent, such effects can be qualified as human rights violations in a strict legal sense."[117]

In 2009, Human Rights Council Resolution 10/4 confirmed that climate change has implications for the enjoyment of human rights, and called for greater involvement of human rights officials in the UNFCCC process.[118] In 2010, the Conference of the Parties to the UNFCCC adopted a set of decisions known as the Cancun Agreements, which include multiple references to human rights.[119] The most significant recent development in climate change and human rights is the Warsaw International Mechanism, which the Conference of the Parties established in 2013 under the framework of the Cancun Agreements to provide technical support and address climate-change-related damage

---

Tyler Giannini, *Confronting a Rising Tide: A Proposal for a Convention on Climate Change Refugees*, 33 HARV. ENVTL. L. REV. 349 (2009); INT'L COUNCIL ON HUMAN RTS. POL'Y, *supra* note 39, at 2.

[110] CLIMATE CHANGE & HUMAN RIGHTS: A PRIMER, *supra* note 48, at 12–13.

[111] *See, e.g.*, WORLD BANK STUDY, *supra* note 15, at 8; Docherty & Giannini, *supra* note 109, at 394; McInerney-Lankford, *supra* note 38, at 434–35.

[112] Limon, *supra* note 15, at 440.

[113] Small Island States Conf., Malé, Maldives, Nov. 13–14, 2007, Malé Declaration on the Human Dimension of Global Climate Change, *adopted* Nov. 14, 2007, *available at* http://www.ciel.org/Publications/Male_Declaration_Novo7.pdf.

[114] *Id.* ¶ 3.

[115] Human Rights Council Res. 7/23, Rep. of the Human Rights Council, 7th Sess., March 3–28, 2008, A/HRC/7/78 (Mar. 28, 2008).

[116] OHCHR Report, *supra* note 11.

[117] *Id.* ¶ 70.

[118] Human Rights Council Res. 10/4, U.N. Doc. A/HRC/10/29 (Mar. 20, 2009).

[119] *See* CTR. FOR INT'L ENVTL. LAW, ANALYSIS OF HUMAN RIGHTS LANGUAGE IN THE CANCUN AGREEMENTS (2011), *available at* http://www.ciel.org/Publications/HR_Language_COP16_Mar11.pdf.

and losses in developing countries.[120] Overall, however, human rights advocates thus far have not succeeded in affecting the UNFCCC agenda significantly.[121] As discussed further below, the precise contours of the relationship between climate change and human rights law remain undefined.

III. Coastal Climate Change Adaptation and Human Rights

Human rights impacts associated with climate change are broadly divisible into *primary* and *secondary impacts*. Primary impacts include the various ways that sea-level rise, ocean acidification, and rising surface temperatures directly threaten or hinder enjoyment of basic human freedoms and entitlements. Secondary impacts include the various ways that actions or omissions in response to or in anticipation of climate change threaten or hinder human rights.[122] Legally protected human rights that may be impacted by coastal climate change adaptation include inter alia the rights to life,[123] self-determination,[124] property,[125] an adequate standard of living,[126] an adequate standard of health,[127] education,[128] participation in cultural life,[129] adequate and secure housing,[130] means of subsistence,[131] water,[132] and food,[133] as well as refugee rights under the Refugee Convention.[134] Importantly, not all human rights impacts are legal violations.[135]

---

[120] Warsaw International Mechanism for Loss and Damage Associated with Climate Change Impacts, UNFCCC COP Dec. 2/CP.19, ¶¶ 1, 5, 7, U.N. Doc. FCCC/CP/2013/10/Add.1 (Nov. 23, 2013).

[121] *See generally* WORLD BANK STUDY, *supra* note 15, at 9–10 (offering various possible explanations for the lack of international momentum to link the international human rights and climate change frameworks).

[122] *See* CLIMATE CHANGE & HUMAN RIGHTS: A PRIMER, *supra* note 48, at 9; McInerney-Lankford, *supra* note 38, at 436.

[123] ICCPR, *supra* note 69, art. 5; CRC, *supra* note 73, art. 6; UDHR, *supra* note 62, art. 3.

[124] ICCPR, *supra* note 69, art. 1(1); ICESCR, *supra* note 70, art. 1(1); U.N. Charter arts. 1, 55. *See also* Susannah Wilcox, *A Rising Tide: The Implications of Climate Change Inundation for Human Rights and State Sovereignty*, 9 ESSEX HUM. RTS. REV. 2, 6 (2012) (stating that the jus cogens right to self-determination is "both indivisible from and a prerequisite for the realisation of all other human rights").

[125] UDHR, *supra* note 62, art. 17.

[126] *Id.* art. 25; ICESCR, *supra* note 70, art. 12

[127] ICESCR, *supra* note 70, arts. 7(b), 10, 12; CEDAW, *supra* note 72, arts. 12, 14, ¶ 2(b); UDHR, *supra* note 62, art. 25; CRC, *supra* note 73, art. 24. *See also* CESCR, General Comment 14, The Right to the Highest Attainable Standard of Health (Art. 12 of the Covenant), ¶ 40, U.N. Doc. E/C.12/2000/4 (2000).

[128] ICESCR, *supra* note 70, art. 13

[129] *Id.* art. 15.

[130] *Id.* art. 11; CEDAW, *supra* note 72, art. 14, ¶ 2; CRC, *supra* note 73, art. 27, ¶ 3; UDHR, *supra* note 62, art. 25, ¶ 1. *See also* Human Rights Council Res. 6/27, U.N. Doc. A/HRC/6/27 (Dec. 14, 2007).

[131] ICESCR, *supra* note 70, art. 12

[132] *Id.* arts. 11, 12; CEDAW, *supra* note 72, art. 14, ¶ 2(h); CRC, *supra* note 73, art. 24, ¶ 2(c).

[133] ICESCR, *supra* note 70, art. 11; CEDAW, *supra* note 72, art. 14, ¶ 2(h); CRC, *supra* note 73, art. 24(c); UDHR, *supra* note 62, art. 25.

[134] Convention Relating to the Status of Refugees, *supra* note 87.

[135] WORLD BANK STUDY, *supra* note 15, at 11 ("[C]limate change may threaten or interfere with the enjoyment of a particular human right without necessarily implying that those bearing responsibilities under

Establishing a violation requires identification of a binding source of public international law that articulates a right-holder and a duty-bearer, plus causation: evidentiary proof that the duty-bearer's failure to fulfill its legal responsibility threatened or impeded the right-holder's enjoyment of her legally protected right or entitlement.[136] There is ongoing international debate over whether the primary impacts of climate change legally constitute human rights violations.[137] Some legal experts have suggested that governments could be legally responsible for primary human rights impacts by contributing to or failing to mitigate anthropogenic climate change, but no petitioner has yet succeeded with such a legal claim.[138]

Although it is likely easier to establish that secondary climate change impacts constitute legal violations, there may still be difficulties in the context of coastal adaptation.[139] For instance, although vulnerable states may require international adaptation assistance, human rights law does not clearly define extraterritorial legal obligations.[140]

---

international law for the realisation of that right have violated their obligations under human rights law."); John H. Knox, *Linking Human Rights and Climate Change at the United Nations*, 33 HARV. ENVTL. L. REV. 477, 478 (2009).

[136] WORLD BANK STUDY, *supra* note 15, at 11; Knox, *supra* note 135, at 478; McInerney-Lankford, *supra* note 38, at 433–34.

[137] *See* Wilcox, *supra* note 124, at 12 (citing, *e.g.*, U.S. Submission, *supra* note 18, ¶ 25).

[138] In 2005, the Inuit petitioned the Inter-American Commission on Human Rights with a claim that the United States' acts and omissions directly contributed to climate change, and therefore violated numerous human rights. Petition to the Inter-American Commission on Human Rights Seeking Relief from Violations Resulting from Global Warming Caused by Acts and Omissions of the United States (Dec. 7, 2005), *available at* http://www.inuitcircumpolar.com/files/uploads/icc-files/FINALPetitionICC.pdf. The Inter-American Commission on Human Rights declined to review the petition, claiming insufficient information upon which to determine that there has been a violation of protected rights. The viability of a similar future claim is uncertain. *See* WORLD BANK STUDY, *supra* note 15, at 12 (discussing the challenges of establishing a causal link between one country's emissions and the particular harm suffered in another country); Wilcox, *supra* note 124, at 13 ("There are no binding international human rights instruments that explicitly refer to climate change and thus, far, no legal cases relating to climate change have successfully invoked human rights law."); Limon, *supra* note 15, at 439, 458 (discussing the difficulties of using human rights law as a tool to address the primary impacts of climate change). *See generally* Hari M. Osofsky, *Complexities of Addressing the Impacts of Climate Change on Indigenous Peoples through International Law Petitions: A Case Study of the Inuit Petition to the Inter-American Commission on Human Rights*, *in* CLIMATE CHANGE AND INDIGENOUS PEOPLES: THE SEARCH FOR LEGAL REMEDIES 313 (Randall S. Abate & Elizabeth Ann Kronk eds., 2013).

[139] *See Avoiding Adaptation Apartheid*, *supra* note 2, at 343–44; Knox, *supra* note 135, at 167–68; Wilcox, *supra* note 124, at 10; McInerney-Lankford, *supra* note 38, at 433. *But see Avoiding Adaptation Apartheid*, *supra* note 2, at 346 (stating that "adaptation-related claims can meet the state actor and causation requirements of human rights law—the two hurdles that often prevent successful litigation or advocacy around mitigation-centered human rights campaigns"); OHCHR Report, *supra* note 11, at ¶ 72 (recognizing that, in comparison to climate change mitigation, "[h]uman rights law provides more effective protection with regard to measures taken by States to address climate change and their impact on human rights").

[140] INT'L COUNCIL ON HUMAN RTS. POL'Y, *supra* note 39, at 4. *See* I.C.J., Legal Consequences of the Construction of a Wall in the Occupied Palestinian Territory, Advisory Opinion, 2004 ICJ REP. 136 (July

Also, human rights may conflict with one another. In the context of coastal climate change adaptation, hard armoring may protect vulnerable communities' life and property at the expense of coastal environments essential to subsistence resources or culture.[141] Furthermore, on-the-ground circumstances can influence the scope of rights or duties. For instance, states may suspend certain human rights obligations in emergency situations, such as may arise as a result of sea-level-rise-related floods or storm events.[142] Additionally, the principle of progressive realization may moderate a developing country's socioeconomic rights obligations.[143] In some cases, states also are permitted to limit their legal obligations through formal treaty reservations.[144]

Even if an injured party can establish a human rights violation, weak or overburdened enforcement mechanisms may further complicate efforts to redress the violation.[145] And even if a tribunal hearing the claim renders a decision in favor of the injured party, achieving a remedy can be difficult in practice—particularly in the context of socioeconomic rights.[146] Nonetheless, "unsuccessful" lawsuits can draw attention to harms, motivate political action, serve as a foundation for continuing international dialogue, and refocus the international community on the human aspects of climate change.[147] Additionally, as mentioned above, soft law instruments and human-rights-based approaches that invoke normative ethics can be effective tools to advance social development.[148]

Building on the general principles outlined above, below is an overview of some of the ways in which particular coastal climate change adaptation actions or a government's failure to engage or cooperate in coastal adaptation ("adaptation omissions") might intersect with international human rights law.

A. ADAPTATION OMISSIONS

A state may violate its legal obligations where it fails to take reasonable steps to reduce through coastal climate change adaptation known risks to human rights. Although the full extent of a state's obligation to adapt is unclear, it is a well-established principle of

---

9, 2004) (finding that all states have certain extraterritorial obligations in response to Israel's illegal construction of a wall in and around East Jerusalem in the Occupied Palestinian Territory).

[141] *See infra* Section III.B.1.

[142] Int'l Council on Human Rts. Pol'y, *supra* note 39, at 5.

[143] *Id.* at 4–5.

[144] *Avoiding Adaptation Apartheid, supra* note 2, at 342.

[145] *Id.*; Int'l Council on Human Rts. Pol'y, *supra* note 39, at 4.

[146] *Avoiding Adaptation Apartheid, supra* note 2, at 353–54 (discussing *Gov't of the Rep. of South Africa v. Grootboom,* 2001 (1) SA 46 (CC) (S. Afr.)).

[147] *See* Int'l Council on Human Rts. Pol'y, *supra* note 39, at 41; Hari Osofsky, *The Inuit Petition as a Bridge? Beyond Dialectics of Climate Change and Indigenous Peoples' Rights,* 31 Am. Indian L. Rev. 675 (2007).

[148] *Accord* Limon, *supra* note 15, at 458 (acknowledging that human rights can be used not only as a tool to remedy particular violations but also "as a forward-looking means of encouraging the evolution of, and

human rights law that states have certain positive obligations to fulfill the human rights guaranteed by international and regional human rights treaties. For instance, CESCR has clarified that a state violates its ICESCR obligations by failing to provide minimum core entitlements where the state has sufficient resources to do so,[149] or failing to adopt national policies and programs to advance socioeconomic rights.[150] The Human Rights Committee has confirmed that a state's failure to act to prevent or mitigate life-threatening harms could violate the right to life protected by the ICCPR.[151] The UNFCCC framework reinforces ICCPR and ICESCR obligations by requiring state parties to take "precautionary measures to anticipate, prevent or minimize the causes of climate change and mitigate its adverse effects."[152]

At the regional level, the Inter-American Commission on Human Rights has confirmed that the rights to life and health could "give rise to an obligation on the part of a State to take reasonable measures" to mitigate threats to those rights.[153] The European Court of Human Rights has developed the most relevant jurisprudence regarding states' positive obligation to respond to environmental risks. In *Budayeva v. Russia*, the court held that Russia violated the European Convention on Human Rights by failing to take reasonable measures to prevent a mudslide that breached a dam, destroyed multiple homes, and killed eight people. In reaching its holding, the court was persuaded by findings that Russia ignored warnings, declined to allocate funds to repair the dam, and failed to warn residents of known risks.[154] Similarly, the European Court of Human Rights held in *Oneryildiz v. Turkey* that Turkey violated the rights of people killed in a methane gas explosion by declining to act on an expert report outlining potential dangers and by failing to inform vulnerable communities of risks.[155]

---

providing a qualitative contribution to, robust, effective, and sustainable policy responses at both the national and international level").

[149] CESCR, General Comment 15, ¶ 40, U.N. Doc. E/C.12/2002/11 (2003). *See also* ICESCR, *supra* note 70, art. 2(1).

[150] CESCR, General Comment 15, *supra* note 149, ¶¶ 28, 36 (stating that states' duty to fulfill the rights to water and health includes the positive obligation to adopt national policies to ensure access to water and reduce pollution).

[151] WORLD BANK STUDY, *supra* note 15, at 12–13 (citing H.R.C., General Comment 31, *supra* note 76, ¶ 6). *Accord* INTER-AGENCY STANDING COMM., IASC OPERATIONAL GUIDELINES ON THE PROTECTION OF PERSONS IN SITUATIONS OF NATURAL DISASTERS 15 (2011), *available at* https://docs.unocha.org/sites/dms/Documents/Operational%20Guidelines.pdf (confirming that states have a duty to protect vulnerable people's rights to life and health from "imminent risks created by natural disasters…to the maximum extent possible").

[152] UNFCCC, *supra* note 102, art. 3.

[153] Org. of American States, Inter-Am. C.H.R., Report on the Situation of Human Rights in Ecuador, at 88, OEA/Ser.L./V/II.96 doc. 10 rev. 1 (Apr. 24, 1997).

[154] Budayeva v. Russia, App. No 15339/00 (Eur. Ct. H.R. 2008).

[155] Oneryildiz v. Turkey, App. No. 48939/99 (Eur. Ct. H.R. 2004). *See also* Hatton v. United Kingdom, 34 Eur. Ct. H.R. 1 (2002) (finding that states have a positive obligation under the European Convention on

A state's positive obligation to fulfill human rights, as defined by the treaty bodies and regional tribunals, can be interpreted to impose adaptation obligations in the context of coastal climate change. For instance, climate-change-related coastal storm events directly threaten the rights to life, adequate standard of living, health, education, participation in cultural life, housing, and water.[156] As in *Oneryildiz* and *Budayeva*, states are on notice through the IPCC assessment reports and other sources that climate change is likely to increase the frequency and intensity of coastal storm events, which can result in the loss of life, as well as damage vital public infrastructure such as roads, transportation services, medical services, schools, places of worship, power plants, and public housing. Where a state fails to take reasonable steps to reduce through coastal climate change adaptation measures these known risks to human rights, the state may be in violation of its legal duties. Notably, the environmental jurisprudence and treaty body comments cited above suggest that states may have a heightened duty to take adaptation action where an individual's right to life is at risk. Although the question of what exactly constitutes a reasonable response measure remains, it seems a state's minimum obligation to act is defined relative to available public resources and the magnitude of the risk. For instance, per the ICESCR's progressive realization principle, a government could be liable for unreasonable adaptation omissions if the government failed to use its maximum available resources to respond to threats to socioeconomic rights.[157]

In the context of coastal climate change, it may be challenging for a vulnerable party to prove to a legal tribunal that a threat to human rights is sufficiently concrete to warrant implementation of any particular adaptation action. Even the most expert climate scientists do not fully understand various aspects of the climate system. Additionally, the future impacts of climate change are dependent on future global greenhouse gas emission levels, which are impossible to predict accurately. Also, climate change impacts are locally specific, necessitating locally specific impact assessments, which developing countries may lack.[158] Moreover, tribunals grant governments broad leeway to assess and interpret risks.[159] Consequently, it likely will be easier for injured parties to establish a human rights violation after the injury has occurred, or where a state has committed a

---

Human Rights to take steps to protect people against environmental harm that adversely affects health and well-being).

[156] *See* OHCHR Report, *supra* note 11, at ¶ 23. *See also* IPCC, Working Group II, *supra* note 2, at 40 (reporting that tropical cyclones alone already affect 120 million people per year and have resulted in hundreds of thousands of deaths over the past several decades).

[157] *Avoiding Adaptation Apartheid*, *supra* note 2, at 348–49.

[158] *See id.* at 321; Camacho, *supra* note 2, at 14–15; Robin Kundis Craig, *"Stationarity Is Dead"—Long Live Transformation: Five Principles for Climate Change Adaptation Law*, 34 Harv. Envtl. L. Rev. 9, 29 (2010).

[159] *See* John H. Knox, *Climate Change and Human Rights Law*, 50 Va. J. Int'l L. 163, 173–74, 196 (2009) ("[S]tates have discretion within wide limits to determine how to strike the balance between environmental harm and the benefits of the activities causing it, and, thus, to decide where to set levels of environmental

clear procedural failure such as failing to spend earmarked adaptation funds or failing to abide by public notice requirements.[160]

One strategy coastal states can employ to reduce the risk of adaptation-omission-related legal claims is to engage proactively in climate change adaptation and disaster planning processes. Proactive planning also will help states respect, protect, and fulfill human rights such as the rights to food, health, education, and housing in the case of a climate-change-related disaster.[161] According to the Inter-Agency Standing Committee, the primary coordinator of international emergency response, it is often the case that disaster-related human rights impacts "do not arise from purposeful policies but are the result of inadequate planning and disaster preparedness, inappropriate policies and measures to respond to the disasters, or simple neglect."[162] Planning processes can help states satisfy their human rights duties by providing an opportunity for states to inform vulnerable coastal communities about risks, plan for expected and worst-case climate change impacts, and consider adaptation measures to mitigate risks.[163] Significantly, the UNFCCC already provides a framework and technical resources for developing countries to identify priority adaptation projects in National Adaptation Programmes of Action (NAPAs).[164] The Cancun Adaptation Framework, established by the Conference of the Parties to the UNFCCC in 2010, initiated a national adaptation planning process building on the NAPAs.[165] States also could update any existing disaster plans to incorporate information about climate-change-related impacts. Additionally, states could improve the resilience of vulnerable coastal communities by requiring or encouraging local coastal communities to develop and implement adaptation plans.

Adequate resources are critical to both coastal climate change adaptation and human rights protections.[166] Consequently, a developed country may have an obligation under international human rights law to assist with climate change adaptation vulnerable coastal populations outside its territory or jurisdiction. The World Bank estimates, for instance, that developing countries will need to spend $70–$100 billion per year on adaptation over

---

protection."); OHCHR Report, *supra* note 11, at ¶ 91 (noting that "human rights litigation is not well-suited to promote precautionary measures based on risk assessments").

[160] *See infra* Section III.B.3.

[161] *See* OHCHR Report, *supra* note 11, at ¶ 24. *See generally* Inter-Agency Standing Comm., *supra* note 151.

[162] Inter-Agency Standing Comm., *supra* note 151, at 2.

[163] *Id.* at 15. *Cf.* Climate Change & Human Rights: A Primer, *supra* note 48, at 9 ("[D]isaster risk management could address the particular situation of the most vulnerable and marginalized.").

[164] UNFCCC COP Dec. 5/CP.7, U.N. Doc. FCCC/CP/2001/13/Add.1 (Nov. 10, 2001); UNFCCC COP Dec. 28/CP.7, U.N. Doc. FCCC/CP/2001/13/Add.4 (Nov. 10, 2001). For a database of all NAPAs submitted to date, see *Submitted NAPAs,* UNFCCC, https://unfccc.int/adaptation/workstreams/national_adaptation_programmes_of_action/items/4585.php (last visited Mar. 29, 2014). *See also Avoiding Adaptation Apartheid, supra* note 2, at 361 (noting that the fifty NAPAs submitted to date generally do not include human rights considerations).

[165] Cancun Agreements, UNFCCC COP Dec. 1/CP.16, ¶¶ 11–35, U.N. Doc. FCCC/CP/2010/7/Add.1 (Dec. 11, 2010).

[166] *See* OHCHR Report, *supra* note 11, at ¶ 15.

the next several decades.[167] Altogether, the resources of existing international adaptation funding mechanisms are inadequate to cover estimated costs.[168] The international community has engaged in extensive discussions about the responsibilities of wealthy countries to developing countries, small-island states, and indigenous groups.[169] Normative claims aside, whether human rights duties include positive extraterritorial legal obligations in the context of coastal climate change adaptation is an unsettled question.[170]

Some countries and legal experts argue that extraterritorial human rights obligations are limited to negative or procedural responsibilities, while others argue that international human rights law has evolved to require governments to provide financial or technical assistance under certain circumstances.[171] Proponents of resource transfers from developed countries to developing countries point to the numerous references to international cooperation in human rights instruments as a source for positive extraterritorial obligations. For instance, the ICESCR requires parties "to take steps, individually and through international assistance and co-operation, especially economic and technical, to the maximum of its available resources, with a view to achieving progressively the full realization of the rights recognized [in the ICESCR]… ."[172] Historically, developed-country parties have argued that this provision does not impose any extraterritorial duties on parties to assist developing countries,[173] while the CESCR has cited this provision as the basis for references to parties' "joint and individual responsibility… to cooperate in providing disaster relief and humanitarian assistance in times of emergency."[174] While

---

[167] World Bank, Economics of Adaptation to Climate Change 19, 89 (2009), *available at* http://documents.worldbank.org/curated/en/2010/01/16436675/economics-adaptation-climate-change-synthesis-report (estimating the cost, at 2005 prices, of adapting to an approximately two-degree Celsius warmer world between 2010 and 2050).

[168] Adaptation funding mechanisms and institutions include, for example, the Adaptation Fund, Global Environment Facility, Special Climate Change Fund, and World Bank. Climate Change & Human Rights: A Primer, *supra* note 48, at 11; Int'l Council on Human Rts. Pol'y, *supra* note 39, at 21–23; Hunter, *supra* note 15, at 360.

[169] *See* J.B. Ruhl, *Climate Change Adaptation and the Structural Transformation of Environmental Law*, 40 Envtl. L. 363, 404 (2010) (cataloging legal scholarship regarding the responsibilities of developed countries to assist other countries and communities in climate change adaptation).

[170] *See* World Bank Study, *supra* note 15, at 42 (quoting Philip Alston, *Ships Passing in the Night: The Current State of the Human Rights and Development Debate as Seen through the Lens of the Millennium Development Goals*, 27 Hum. Rts. Q. 755, 777 (2005) ("No UN body, nor any group of governments, has accepted the proposition that any given country is obligated to provide specific assistance to any other country.")). It also remains an open question whether countries that have contributed to anthropogenic climate change have legal obligations to assist people in other countries who are threatened by climate change impacts. *Id.* at 41 ("No authoritative body has addressed whether transboundary environmental harm may bring its victims within the effective control of the State where the harm originates.").

[171] World Bank Study, *supra* note 15, at 8. *See also* Wilcox, *supra* note 124, at 10; McInerney-Lankford, *supra* note 38, at 433.

[172] ICESCR, *supra* note 70, art. 2(1).

[173] World Bank Study, *supra* note 15, at 41–42; Knox, *supra* note 159, at 208.

[174] CESCR, General Comment 12, The Rights to Adequate Food, ¶ 12, U.N. Doc. E/C.12/1995/5 (1999); CESCR, General Comment 14, *supra* note 127, ¶ 40. *See also* Knox, *supra* note 159, at 207.

climate change could potentially be understood as a chronic emergency—particularly given the high costs of adaptation and the present struggles of developing countries to spare resources for adaptation—the ICESCR may be more useful as a tool to promote climate-change-related disaster assistance rather than a tool to facilitate resource transfers to vulnerable communities engaging in coastal adaptation.

Similar to the ICESCR, the UN Charter requires states to cooperate in the promotion of international human rights and prevention of human rights violations.[175] The UN Charter provisions could imply, in the context of climate change, a global duty to help vulnerable states meet their human rights obligations by way of providing climate change adaptation assistance.[176] Notably, this interpretation relies on the assumption that a state's failure to engage in domestic climate change adaptation can violate human rights law.[177] The fact that regional tribunals have shown an increasing willingness to enforce positive human rights obligations may bolster claims that human rights duties, in general, have evolved to include extraterritorial obligations.[178]

The OHCHR declares that states have extraterritorial obligations in the context of climate change, but it does not define those obligations.[179] Siobhan McInerney-Lankford et al. suggest, based on review of relevant international instruments and jurisprudence, that even if human rights duties do extend extraterritorially, a state could likely comply with such duties in the context of climate change adaptation through the extraterritorial extension of domestically applicable procedural safeguards rather than resource transfer.[180] Overall, the extent and scope of any extraterritorial human rights duties remains unclear.

Regardless, the UNFCCC obliges developed countries to assist developing countries to some extent in funding adaptation measures and protecting vulnerable populations. Article 4 of the UNFCCC emphasizes the urgency of international cooperation, financing, and technology transfer to promote effective adaptation in developing countries.[181] The Bali

---

[175] U.N. Charter art. 55 ("[T]he United Nations shall promote…universal respect for, and observance of, human rights and fundamental freedoms for all… ."); *id.* art 56 ("All Members pledge themselves to take joint and separate action…for the achievement of the purposes set forth in Article 55.").

[176] *See* CLIMATE CHANGE & HUMAN RIGHTS: A PRIMER, *supra* note 48, at 1; Wilcox, *supra* note 124, at 5. *See also* Trail Smelter Case (United States v. Canada), 3. R.I.A.A. 1905 (1938 & 1941) (recognizing states' obligation to refrain from causing significant harm through transboundary pollution); I.C.J., The Legality of the Threat or Use of Nuclear Weapons, Advisory Opinion, 1996 ICJ REP. 241, ¶ 29 (July 8, 1996) (recognizing states' obligation to "ensure that activities within their jurisdiction and control respect the environment of other states or of areas beyond national control"); Statute of the International Court of Justice, *supra* note 51, art. 38(1)(c) (promoting the "duty of due diligence").

[177] *See supra* Section III.A.

[178] WORLD BANK STUDY, *supra* note 15, at 6. *See also* Human Rights Comm., Concluding Observations on the Fourth Rep. of the United States of America, ¶ 22, 110th Sess. Mar. 10–28, 2014 (confirming that the ICCPR applies to U.S. surveillance activities outside U.S. borders).

[179] Knox, *supra* note 135, at 492–93.

[180] WORLD BANK STUDY, *supra* note 15, at 43.

[181] UNFCCC, *supra* note 102, art. 4(1)(e) ("All Parties…shall. …[c]ooperate in preparing for adaptation.…"); *id.* art. 4(8) ("Parties shall give full consideration to…funding, insurance and the transfer of technology, to meet the specific needs and concerns of developing country Parties arising from the adverse

Action Plan, a process adopted at the Conference of the Parties to the UNFCCC meeting in Bali in 2007 to frame future negotiations, explicitly emphasizes the need for international cooperation on finance and technology transfer to support adaptation.[182] Additionally, in 2010, the Conference of the Parties established the Green Climate Fund, a multilateral funding mechanism to facilitate the transfer of resources from developed countries to developing countries for mitigation and adaptation.[183] Notably, the decision establishing the Green Climate Fund explicitly acknowledges that climate change impacts human rights.[184] Future UNFCCC agreements may elucidate with greater specificity the duties of developed countries to contribute to climate change adaptation in developing countries.

Nonetheless, even if a state does not have a legal duty under international human rights law or climate change law to provide extraterritorial assistance, a state is legally permitted to take reasonable extraterritorial measures to protect and fulfill human rights.[185] Given the connection of adequate adaptation to human rights protection, this legal protection likely extends to extraterritorial coastal adaptation assistance. Consideration of human rights can help developed countries ensure that their resource transfers are both reasonable and effective.[186] To that end, states engaging in extraterritorial adaptation projects or providing adaptation assistance to other countries should incorporate proper procedural protections, as described further below.

B. ADAPTATION ACTIONS

Although it is not wholly apparent whether a state's failure to engage in coastal adaptation could constitute a human rights violation, it is much clearer that human rights law applies to the impacts of a state's adaptation projects or policies. A state may also be liable for failing to protect residents' human rights from the impacts of private party adaptation measures.[187]

---

effects of climate change and/or the impact of the implementation of response measures . . . ."); *id.* art. 4(9) ("The Parties shall take full account of the specific needs and special situations of the least developed countries in their actions with regard to funding and transfer of technology."). *See also id.* pmbl. ("[T]he global nature of climate change calls for the widest possible cooperation by all countries.").

[182] Bali Action Plan, UNFCCC COP Dec. 1/CP.13, ¶ 1(c)(i), U.N. Doc. FCCC/CP/2007/6/Add.1 (Mar. 14, 2008). *See also id.* ¶ 1(e) (calling for all countries to cooperate on climate adaptation, "taking into account the urgent and immediate needs of developing countries that are particularly vulnerable").

[183] The Cancun Agreements: Outcome of the Work of the Ad Hoc Working Group on Long-Term Cooperative Action under the Convention, UNFCCC COP Dec. 1/CP.16, ¶ 102, U.N. Doc. FCCC/CP/2010/7/Add.1 (Dec. 10-11, 2010) (establishing the Green Climate Fund); Launching the Green Climate Fund, UNFCCC COP Dec. 3/CP.17, U.N. Doc. FCCC/CP/2011/9/Add.1 (Dec. 11, 2011) (detailing the objectives and operations of the Green Climate Fund).

[184] The Cancun Agreements: Outcome of the Work of the Ad Hoc Working Group on Long-Term Cooperative Action under the Convention, *supra* note 183, pmbl.

[185] WORLD BANK STUDY, *supra* note 15, at 8.

[186] *See* CLIMATE CHANGE & HUMAN RIGHTS: A PRIMER, *supra* note 48, at 12.

[187] *See* Decision Regarding Communication 155/96 (Soc. & Econ. Rights Action Ctr./Ctr. for Econ. & Soc. Rights v. Nigeria) (African Comm'n on Human & Peoples' Rights, Oct. 2001), 96 AJIL 937, ¶ 57 (2002) [hereinafter SERAC v. Nigeria] (finding that Nigeria violated the African Charter on Human and Peoples'

The impacts of coastal armoring structures and resettlement are highlighted below, followed by a more general discussion of coastal adaptation planning, funding, decision-making, and implementation.

1. Hard Armoring

The decision to install a coastal hard armoring structure and the selection of its location implicate human rights. Coastal hard armoring structures have the potential to negatively impact subsistence or cultural resources such as shellfish, marine fish, marine mammals, and beaches. For example, sea walls could reduce access to coastal areas utilized for spiritual ceremonies or adversely affect subsistence fisheries through habitat destruction.[188] Any interference with subsistence resources could violate the right to means of subsistence, as well as a variety of related rights such as the rights to life, an adequate standard of living, food, health, and participation in cultural life. Interference with cultural resources, traditional ways of life, or traditional lands implicates numerous human rights, including the rights to property and participation in cultural life. The Inter-American Commission and Inter-American Court of Human Rights have emphasized the importance of protecting indigenous and tribal lands and resources, and have recognized that an indigenous community's collective right to property includes both traditionally occupied lands and traditionally used natural resources.[189] Similarly, the Human Rights Committee's General Comment 23 recognizes that minority groups' right to culture "may consist in a way of life which is closely associated with territory and use of [traditional] resources."[190] As discussed further below, states considering hard armoring as an adaptation strategy can reduce the risk of human rights violations by

Rights by failing in its duty to protect citizens' rights from the injurious acts of its partner in oil extraction, Shell Oil).

[188] Charles H. Fletcher, Robert A. Mullane & Bruce M. Richmond, *Beach Loss along Armored Shorelines on Oahu, Hawaiian Islands*, 13 J. COASTAL RES. 209 (1997) (finding that shoreline armoring leads to long-term narrowing and loss of culturally valuable beaches, and reduces public access for beach-dependent subsistence and religious ceremonies). *See also* Tundi Agardy et al., *Coastal Systems, in* ECOSYSTEMS AND HUMAN WELL-BEING: CURRENT STATE AND TRENDS 513, 515, 519 (Rashin Hassan, Roberts Scholes & Neville Ash eds., 2005) (finding that hard-engineered coastal structures such as armoring "account for widespread, usually irreversible, destruction of coastal habitats"); Letter from Mike Grayum, Exec. Dir., Nw. Indian Fisheries Comm'n, to Randi Thurston, Prot. Div. Mgr., Wash. Dept. of Fish & Wildlife & Bob Zeigler, Habitat Prog., Wash. Dept. of Fish & Wildlife 5–7 (Dec. 13, 2013), *available at* http://www.soundaction.org/nwifchpa.pdf (discussing the adverse impacts of hard armoring on subsistence salmonid fisheries); JIM JOHANNESSEN & ANDREA MACLENNAN, COASTAL GEOLOGIC SVS., INC., FINAL LUMMI RESERVATION COASTAL PROTECTION GUIDELINES 2–5 (2007), *available at* http://www.lummi-nsn.gov/nr/Water/WaterResourcesWeb/documents/CoastalZoneManagement/Lummi_Reservation_Coastal_Protection_Guidelines.pdf (describing the negative impacts of shoreline armoring on subsistence and ceremonial fisheries and coastal ecosystems).

[189] Saramaka People v. Surin, 2007 Inter-Am. Ct. H.R. (ser. C) No. 172, ¶ 121 (Nov. 28, 2007).

[190] Human Rights Comm., General Comment 23, Article 27 (Rights of Minorities), ¶ 3.2, U.N. Doc. CCPR/C/21/Rev.1/Add.5 (1994).

following robust decision-making procedures, meaningfully engaging affected communities in the decision-making process, and ensuring that the project is nondiscriminatory (e.g., does not disproportionately burden a socially vulnerable group or benefit a socially privileged group).[191]

Once installed, hard armoring structures could experience a breach or failure that directly threatens rights to life and property. Governments have a duty to take reasonable steps to mitigate significant risks to those rights.[192] For example, *Budayeva* emphasizes the importance of ensuring that armoring structures are in good repair, allocating necessary funds to structural inspection and maintenance, instituting early-warning systems, and educating vulnerable communities about risks.[193] Likewise, governments have a duty to enact policies and procedures to ensure that privately constructed armoring structures do not unduly threaten human rights.

2. Resettlement

Managed retreat and relocation programs also implicate human rights. Over the next century, climate-change-related sea-level rise, storm surges, melting sea ice, and other impacts will displace millions of people, with the most significant displacement occurring in developing countries.[194] Arctic indigenous communities, small-island states, and low-lying coastal deltas are especially at risk.[195] The OHCHR outlines four primary displacement scenarios: (1) acute disasters, such as hurricanes; (2) gradual deterioration of low-lying coastal areas; (3) increased risk, leading to proactive relocation programs; and (4) climate-change-related social disorder.[196] Displacement and relocation could impact a range of human rights, including the rights to housing, property, self-determination, and participation in cultural life.[197]

Full enjoyment of the right to adequate housing includes protection from weather hazards, access to housing outside of hazard zones, disaster planning, and adequate

---

[191] Knox, *supra* note 159, at 198–99.

[192] *Id.* at 195.

[193] Budayeva v. Russia, App. No 15339/00 (Eur. Ct. H.R. 2008).

[194] OLIVER-SMITH, *supra* note 11, at 9; Docherty & Giannini, *supra* note 109, at 349. *See also* Address by Kyung-wha Kang, OHCHR, *Climate Change, Migration and Human Rights*, at the Conference on Climate Change and Migration: Addressing Vulnerabilities and Harnessing Opportunities, Geneva, Feb. 19, 2008, *available at* http://www.ohchr.org/EN/NewsEvents/Pages/DisplayNews.aspx?NewsID=9162&LangID=E ("By 2050, hundreds of millions more people may become permanently displaced due to rising sea levels, floods, droughts, famine, and hurricanes.").

[195] OHCHR Report, *supra* note 11, ¶ 36.

[196] *Id.* ¶ 56.

[197] INT'L COUNCIL ON HUMAN RTS. POL'Y, *supra* note 39, at 2. *See also* OHCHR Report, *supra* note 11, ¶¶ 36, 57 (stating that people who relocate within a state remain entitled to all human rights protections); 1998 Guiding Principles on Internal Displacement, U.N. Comm'n on Human Rights, Report of the Representative of the Secretary General, Mr. Frances Deng, submitted pursuant to Commission on Human Rights Res. 1997/39, U.N. Doc. E/CN.4/1998/53/Add.1 (Feb. 11, 1998).

consultation regarding resettlement programs.[198] Accordingly, states may have an obligation under certain circumstances to prepare and implement plans for evacuation of vulnerable coastal areas.[199] Importantly, human rights law prevents arbitrary forced displacement; governments must adequately consult affected communities, and resettlement policies must be nondiscriminatory.[200] Policies of managed retreat from sea-level rise that disproportionately target low-income or minority communities for relocation programs could violate human rights.

Relocation of indigenous communities raises particular human rights concerns. Some Inuit communities in the Arctic region have already relocated due to climate change impacts, and erosion and storm-related flooding continue to threaten coastal Inuit villages.[201] Relocation of an indigenous community away from traditional lands implicates rights to property and participation in cultural life.[202] Again, adequate consultation with affected communities and protections against arbitrary resettlement are key to respecting human rights in the context of coastal retreat.[203]

On a larger scale, the resettlement of entire states implicates a state's *jus cogens* right to self-determination.[204] Small-island states such as Tuvalu, Kiribati, the Marshall Islands, and the Carteret Islands in the Pacific, and Mauritius and the Maldives in the Indian Ocean, may disappear as a result of sea-level rise, storm surges, and erosion. The potential disappearance of small-island states presents a legal puzzle, as states are by law the primary guarantors of human rights.[205] As Wilcox has noted, "Without territory—and, potentially, statehood—the individual and collective rights of a people are no longer adequately protected by their state, and are thus increasingly vulnerable to potential violations."[206]

The OHCHR recognizes that "[h]uman rights law does not provide clear answers as to the status of populations who have been displaced from sinking island States,"[207] and acknowledges that "long-term political solutions" likely will play the most important

---

[198] OHCHR Report, *supra* note 11, ¶ 38.

[199] *See* INTER-AGENCY STANDING COMM., *supra* note 151, at 15 (stating that states should facilitate evacuations of hazards areas where protection and accommodation strategies are insufficient to shield vulnerable communities from natural-disaster-related injuries).

[200] OHCHR Report, *supra* note 11, ¶ 57.

[201] *Id.* ¶ 51; OLIVER-SMITH, *supra* note 11, at 34–35.

[202] *See* Saramaka People v. Surin, *supra* note 189, at ¶ 121; H.R.C., General Comment 23, *supra* note 190, ¶ 3.2; OHCHR Report, *supra* note 11, at ¶ 51 (stating that relocation of indigenous communities "threatens their cultural identity, which is closely linked to their traditional lands and livelihoods").

[203] OHCHR Report, *supra* note 11, ¶ 79.

[204] *Id.* ¶ 40.

[205] Wilcox, *supra* note 124, at 6; OHCHR Report, *supra* note 11, ¶ 41 ("The disappearance of a State for climate change-related reasons would give rise to a range of legal questions, including concerning the status of people inhabiting such disappearing territories and the protection afforded to them under international law... .").

[206] Wilcox, *supra* note 124, at 7.

[207] OHCHR Report, *supra* note 11, ¶ 60.

role in human rights protection in this context.[208] Nevertheless, OHCHR affirms that the international community has an obligation "to take positive action, individually and jointly, to address and avert" the threat to small-island states' right to self-determination.[209] The Human Rights Council has recognized similar positive obligations in the context of the right to self-determination.[210] Overall, however, the scope of any positive obligation of states to assist sinking island states in relocation or other adaptation measures remains unclear. The OHCHR's reference to political solutions is illustrative of the limits of the international human rights legal framework to hold states accountable for relocating small-island states' populations.

In the context of sinking island states and other vulnerable coastal communities, people who attempt to migrate across international borders as a result of climate change, whether voluntarily or forcibly, likely do not have a legal right of entry into another state.[211] Most legal experts believe that the Refugee Convention's narrow definition of "refugee" fails to encompass climate change migrants.[212] In any case, the volume of climate change migrants could dwarf the number of traditional refugees, overwhelming UNHCR's current institutional capacity.[213]

The limits of existing refugee law have motivated calls for states to develop a new legal instrument guaranteeing rights to people who are forced to migrate across international borders as a consequence of climate change,[214] potentially as a protocol to either the UNFCCC or the Refugee Convention.[215] In the meantime, existing international law

---

[208] *Id.*

[209] *Id.* ¶ 41. *See also* Knox, *supra* note 159, at 205–06 (arguing that states have extraterritorial duties to respect, protect, and fulfill the right to self-determination in the context of sinking island states); East Timor (Portugal v. Australia), 1995 I.C.J. 90, ¶ 29 (1995) (recognizing the right to self-determination as an *erga omnes* principle of international law).

[210] Wilcox, *supra* note 124, at 7 (quoting Human Rights Comm., General Comment 12, ¶ 6, UN Doc. HR1/GEN/1/Rev.6 (1984) (states have duties "not only in relation to their own people, but vis-à-vis all peoples which have not been able to exercise or have been deprived of the possibility of exercising their right to self-determination")).

[211] OHCHR Report, *supra* note 11, ¶ 58.

[212] Docherty & Giannini, *supra* note 109, at 358, 362. *See supra* text accompanying note 88. *But see* Convention Governing the Specific Aspects of Refugee Problems in Africa art. 1(2), Sept. 10, 1969, 1001 U.N.T.S. 45 (defining "refugee" to include "every person who, owing to…events seriously disturbing public order in either part or the whole of his country of origin or nationality, is compelled to leave his place of habitual residence in order to seek refuge in another place outside his country of origin or nationality.")

[213] Docherty & Giannini, *supra* note 109, at 359. *See also Refugee Figures*, U.N. HIGH COMM'R FOR REFUGEES, http://www.unhcr.org/pages/49c3646c1d.html (last visited Mar. 29, 2014) (reporting that, as of 2013, there are 10.4 million refugees as defined by the Refugee Convention).

[214] *See* Docherty & Giannini, *supra* note 109, at 361 (proposing the definition of climate change refugee as "an individual who is forced to flee his or her home and to relocate temporarily or permanently across a national boundary as the result of sudden or gradual environmental disruption that is consistent with climate change").

[215] *See, e.g.*, Docherty & Giannini, *supra* note 109; Angela Williams, *Turning the Tide: Recognizing Climate Change Refugees in International Law*, 30 L. & POL'Y 502 (2008); Frank Biermann & Ingrid Boas, *Preparing for a Warmer World: Towards a Global Governance System to Protect Climate Refugees* 8 (Global

offers little protection for cross-border climate change migrants. As Bonnie Docherty and Tyler Giannini describe,

> While broad principles of international law may have some normative value and provide arguments for assisting these [migrants], there is a clear lacuna in the existing international legal system. No legal instrument specifically speaks to the issue of climate change refugees, and no international institution has the clear mandate to serve this population, which needs human rights protection and humanitarian aid.[216]

A critical qualification applies to situations where climate-change-related disasters or pressures create or contribute to the type of "persecution" that falls under the Refugee Convention.[217] History shows that natural resource conflicts can serve as predecessors to the conflicts that are at the root of the Refugee Convention.[218] Indeed, a recent report from International Alert and the Swedish International Development Cooperation Agency finds that climate change creates a high risk of armed conflict in forty-six countries, and a high risk of political instability in an additional fifty-six countries.[219] Importantly, where climate change migrants also have a "well-founded fear of being persecuted for reasons of race, religion, nationality, membership of a particular social group or political opinion,"[220] a receiving state may have legal obligations under the Refugee Convention.[221]

3. Adaptation Planning, Decision-Making, Funding, and Implementation

In recognition of the fact that coastal adaptation actions such as hard armoring and managed retreat have the potential to impact human rights, states can mitigate legal risk by explicitly integrating human rights considerations into coastal adaptation planning,

---

Governance Working Paper No. 33, 2007), *available at* http://www.sarpn.org/documents/d0002952/Climate_refugees_global_governance_Nov2007.pdf.

[216] Docherty & Giannini, *supra* note 109, at 357.

[217] *See* Convention Relating to the Status of Refugees, *supra* note 87, art. 1(A)(2); Protocol Relating to the Status of Refugees, *supra* note 87, art. 1.

[218] *See* U.N. ENV'T PROG., FROM CONFLICT TO PEACEBUILDING: THE ROLE OF NATURAL RESOURCES AND THE ENVIRONMENT 5 (2009), *available at* http://www.unep.org/pdf/pcdmb_policy_01.pdf ("Since 1990 at least eighteen violent conflicts have been fuelled by the exploitation of natural resources. ...[And] over the last sixty years at least forty percent of all intrastate conflicts have a link to natural resources.").

[219] DAN SMITH & JANANI VIVEKANANIDA, INT'L ALERT & SIDA, A CLIMATE OF CONFLICT 26 (2008), *available at* http://www.sida.se/Publications/Import/pdf/sv/A-climate-of-conflict.pdf. *See also* U.N. ENV'T PROG., *supra* note 218, at 5 (noting that "climate change ... may aggravate existing tensions and generate new conflicts.").

[220] Convention Relating to the Status of Refugees, *supra* note 87, art. 1(A)(2); Protocol Relating to the Status of Refugees, *supra* note 87, art. 1.

[221] *See* Docherty & Giannini, *supra* note 109, at 358 (discussing the customary norm of *non-refoulement*). *See also* Convention Relating to the Status of Refugees, *supra* note 87, art. 33.

decision-making, funding, and implementation.[222] Helpful tools to accomplish this include social vulnerability assessments, prioritization of minimum core resources, and procedural protections.

Vulnerability assessment is the first step in the climate change adaptation planning process. Such assessments help an entity understand the exposure of an area to climate change impacts by examining historical data and modeling projected impacts.[223] Following vulnerability assessment, the entity can engage in risk assessment to evaluate the sensitivity of resources within the area to projected impacts.[224] Based upon the vulnerability and risk assessments, the entity can then develop an adaptation plan that articulates objectives for the area and evaluates the suitability of various adaptation strategies to achieving those objectives.[225] Although vulnerability assessments commonly focus on physical resources such as development and infrastructure, socioeconomic assessments are equally important for effective adaptation planning—as well as valuable tools to help states meet their human rights obligations.[226]

Social and economic vulnerability assessments analyze "the effects of a change (e.g., a project or event) on communities and the services that they rely on and value, with specific attention to effects that are borne disproportionately due to existing inequalities."[227] Vulnerability to coastal climate change is defined by three factors: (1) *exposure*: the magnitude and likelihood of an impact; (2) *sensitivity*: the degree of damage caused by the impact; and (3) *adaptive capacity*: the ability of the affected entity to adjust to the impact.[228] Communities that lack equitable access to resources and political

---

[222] McInerney-Lankford, *supra* note 38, at 436.

[223] Nicole Russell & Gary Griggs, Adapting to Sea Level Rise: A Guide for California's Coastal Communities 10–11 (2012), *available at* http://www.opc.ca.gov/2012/06/new-sea-level-r ise-adaptation-guide-available/.

[224] *Id.* at 29

[225] *Id.* at 32.

[226] *See* Heidi Nutters, Addressing Social Vulnerability and Equity in Climate Change Adaptation Planning 5 (Adapting to Rising Tides White Paper, June 2012) (stating that "[p]hysical, social and economic vulnerability greatly influence each other. For example, the loss of the functionality of physical infrastructure, such as a hospital, can have major social and economic implications such as loss of employment, loss of services and loss of an emergency evacuation center."); Hunter, *supra* note 15, at 361 ("For adaptation policies to be effective, they must not reinforce differential levels of vulnerabilities between gender, race, or class.").

[227] Nutters, *supra* note 226, at 1. *See also* Susan L. Cutter et al., Social Vulnerability to Climate Variability Hazards: A Review of the Literature 2–3 (2009), *available at* http:// adapt.oxfamamerica.org/resources/Literature_Review.pdf (Social vulnerability assessment "explicitly focuses on those demographic and socioeconomic factors that increase or attenuate the impacts of hazard events on local populations…in other words who is at risk and the degree to which they can be harmed.").

[228] Nutters, *supra* note 226, at 3. *See also* IPCC, Working Group II, *supra* note 2, at 883 (defining the term "vulnerability" in the context of climate change adaptation as "the degree to which a system is susceptible to, and unable to cope with, adverse effects of climate change, including climate variability and extremes. Vulnerability is a function of the character, magnitude, and rate of climate change and variation to which a system is exposed, its sensitivity, and its adaptive capacity.").

participation, or experience other social inequalities (e.g., related to gender, age, disability, language, ethnicity, or race) are more vulnerable to adverse climate change impacts across all three factors.[229]

In comparison to the general population, socially vulnerable populations are more likely to live in areas of greater exposure to climate change impacts. In general, socially vulnerable populations also are more sensitive to adverse impacts because they are already stressed by inequality and oppression, and lack resources to improve their resiliency.[230] As a result of their lack of wealth, political power, social relationships, information, and agency, socially vulnerable populations also have lower capacity to withstand and recover from adverse climate change impacts.[231] As an illustration, women are more likely to live in poverty in communities without resources to invest in flood control, hold low-income jobs that disappear after a storm event, serve as caregivers for children or elders with limited mobility to flee from a hazard, wear clothing that inhibits movement, have difficulties accessing information about climate-change-related risks, and suffer gender-based violence in the aftermath of a disaster.[232]

Human rights law suggests that states should be particularly aware of the effects of adaptation policies and measures on socially vulnerable populations, including women, children, and ethnic minorities.[233] Indeed, the African Commission on Human and Peoples' Rights has highlighted that article 24 of the African Charter on Human and Peoples' Rights—the right to "a general satisfactory environment"—requires social impact studies prior to any major projects.[234] Many coastal adaptation measures likely constitute "major projects." The European Court of Human Rights has similarly opined that,

> Where a State must determine complex issues of environmental and economic policy, the decision-making process must first involve appropriate investigations and studies in order to allow them [sic] to predict and evaluate in advance the effects of those activities which might...infringe individuals' rights....[235]

In the context of coastal climate change adaptation, social vulnerability assessments can help states meet these obligations. Numerous technical resources regarding human rights impact assessment and social vulnerability assessment are available to help

---

[229] NUTTERS, *supra* note 226, at 1; CARE INT'L, CLIMATE VULNERABILITY AND CAPACITY ANALYSIS HANDBOOK 6 (2009), *available at* http://www.careclimatechange.org/cvca/CARE_CVCAHandbook.pdf.
[230] NUTTERS, *supra* note 226, at 9.
[231] *See id.* at 3.
[232] *See* CUTTER ET AL., *supra* note 227, at 21; OHCHR Report, *supra* note 11, ¶ 45.
[233] *See Avoiding Adaptation Apartheid, supra* note 2, at 349.
[234] SERAC v. Nigeria, *supra* note 187, ¶ 53.
[235] Taskin v. Turkey, App. No. 46117/99, ¶ 119 (Eur. Ct. H.R. 2004).

states fully investigate the impacts of coastal adaptation actions on socially vulnerable communities.[236]

As states progress in the adaptation planning process to the selection of adaptation objectives and strategies, their decisions should be guided by their duties to respect, protect, and fulfill minimum core entitlements. As the CESCR has clarified that a state can violate the ICESCR by failing to provide minimum core resources, adaptation plans can help states meet human rights obligations by prioritizing protection of minimum core entitlements.[237] For example, relocation strategies could incorporate consideration of the right to water by ensuring inter alia that every affected individual has continuous access to the minimum core amount of water, taking into consideration costs, physical barriers to access, and potential threats of violence.[238] Additionally, governments should consider that there may be synergies between certain coastal climate change adaptation projects and development goals.[239] When choosing between multiple coastal adaptation strategies, states may wish to identify strategies with co-benefits relevant to the fulfillment of human rights obligations.

Furthermore, "decision-makers should be guided by the core minimum human rights standards when weighing competing demands on limited resources."[240] The OHCHR has emphasized that developing countries must fulfill their minimum core obligations under the ICESCR indiscriminately, irrespective of the fact that climate change places additional burdens on already limited public resources.[241] Consideration of minimum core human rights obligations can help states make difficult choices regarding how to allocate limited available adaptation funds or prioritize adaptation projects.[242] For example, David B. Hunter proposes that consideration of the right to housing would position actions to provide shelter for hurricane victims "higher in the queue for adaptation funds" than, for instance, protecting vacation homes threatened by sea-level rise.[243] In accordance with the principle of "progressive realization," which requires governments to use maximum available resources to protect and fulfill socioeconomic rights,

---

[236] *See, e.g.,* Int'l Finance Corp., Guide to Human Rights Impact Assessment and Management (2014), http://www.ifc.org/wps/wcm/connect/topics_ext_content/ifc_external_corporate_site/ifc+sustainability/publications/publications_handbook_hria__wci__1319577931868; UNFCCC Secretariat, Compendium on Methods and Tools to Evaluate Impacts of, and Vulnerability and Adaptation to, Climate Change (2008), *available at* http://unfccc.int/files/adaptation/nairobi_workprogramme/compendium_on_methods_tools/application/pdf/20080307_compendium_m_t_complete.pdf.

[237] CESCR, General Comment 15, *supra* note 149, ¶ 40; McInerney-Lankford, *supra* note 38, at 436.

[238] Austl. Human Rights & Equal Opportunity Comm'n, Human Rights and Climate Change 14 (2008).

[239] *Avoiding Adaptation Apartheid, supra* note 2, at 323–24; Camacho, *supra* note 2, at 20; Hunter, *supra* note 15, at 359. *See generally* U.S. Agency for Int'l Development, *supra* note 4.

[240] Austl. Human Rights & Equal Opportunity Comm'n, *supra* note 238, at 14.

[241] OHCHR Report, *supra* note 11, ¶ 76.

[242] *See* Hunter, *supra* note 15, at 361.

[243] *Id.*

governments should also ensure that public and private actors properly utilize any funding earmarked for adaptation.[244]

As a legal matter, it is unclear whether a government with limited resources could be legally liable for choosing one adaptation measure over another, or choosing between climate change adaptation and fulfilling other human rights obligations.[245] In such cases, procedural protections are likely important.[246] Indeed, a recent World Bank review of international human rights jurisprudence identified as a common theme "that States may undertake or allow environmental degradation that interferes with the enjoyment of human rights, as long as they follow the procedural requirements and protect against environmental harm that goes too far."[247] Importantly, even the most proper and thorough procedures cannot shield a government from liability for violations of minimum core freedoms and entitlements, as described above.

The OHCHR confirms that coastal adaptation strategies can lead to rights violations where states fail to incorporate adequate procedural protections into design and implementation.[248] Overall, the human rights legal framework emphasizes "procedural safeguards like accountability, transparency, participation, and consultation."[249] States are advised to pay particular attention to the administrative procedures outlined in the Aarhus Convention,[250] as some legal experts have suggested that these procedures are emerging principles of customary law.[251] Environmental human rights jurisprudence emphasizes environmental impact assessment, public disclosure of information, timely notice of decision-making, informed stakeholder participation, and judicial review of state noncompliance as essential procedural protections.[252]

---

[244] *Avoiding Adaptation Apartheid, supra* note 2, at 348–49.

[245] *Id.* at 350. *But see* INT'L COUNCIL ON HUMAN RTS. POL'Y, *supra* note 39, at 1 (suggesting that "where governments are poorly resourced, climate change harms will tend to impact populations unevenly and unequally, in ways that are *de facto* discriminatory").

[246] *Avoiding Adaptation Apartheid, supra* note 2, at 349.

[247] WORLD BANK STUDY, *supra* note 15, at 32.

[248] OHCHR, APPLYING A HUMAN RIGHTS-BASED APPROACH TO CLIMATE CHANGE NEGOTIATIONS, POLICIES AND MEASURES, *available at* http://www.ohchr.org/Documents/Issues/ClimateChange/InfoNoteHRBA.pdf (last visited Mar. 29, 2014).

[249] Wilcox, *supra* note 124, at 15. *Accord* Knox, *supra* note 159, at 189. *See, e.g.*, Rio Declaration, *supra* note 93, at Principle 10 ("[E]ach individual shall have appropriate access to information concerning the environment that is held by public authorities, including information on hazardous materials and activities in their communities… ."); OHCHR, APPLYING A HUMAN RIGHTS-BASED APPROACH TO CLIMATE CHANGE NEGOTIATIONS, POLICIES AND MEASURES, *available at* http://www.ohchr.org/Documents/Issues/ClimateChange/InfoNoteHRBA.pdf (last visited Mar. 29, 2014).

[250] Convention on Access to Information, Public Participation in Decision-Making and Access to Justice in Environmental Matters, June 25, 1998, 38 I.L.M. 517 [hereinafter Aarhus Convention].

[251] *See* WORLD BANK STUDY, *supra* note 15, at 36. *See, e.g.*, Aarhus Convention, *supra* note 250, art. 7 ("Each party shall make appropriate practical and/or other provisions for the public to participate during the preparation of plans and programmes relating to the environment, within a transparent and fair framework, having provided the necessary information to the public.").

[252] WORLD BANK STUDY, *supra* note 15, at 32; Org. of Am. States, *supra* note 153, ch. VIII; SERAC v. Nigeria, *supra* note 187, ¶ 53; CESCR, General Comment 15, *supra* note 149. *See also* Case Concerning Pulp Mills

Lack of information and technical expertise presents a potential barrier to fulfilling procedural duties, particularly for developing countries.[253] For instance, the African Commission on Human and Peoples' Rights has interpreted the right to a general satisfactory environment to require states to disclose information about environmental risks to vulnerable communities.[254] Yet, developing useful local projections of climate change impacts requires a high level of scientific expertise and capacity, as well as long-term data sets, which are often lacking.[255] It may be challenging for governments to fulfill their duties to inform coastal communities about climate-change-related risks when governments themselves lack information about impacts and vulnerability.[256]

Information-poor states may find it helpful to draw on the knowledge of local human rights workers and engage in regional and international information sharing programs.[257] Traditional knowledge also could inform coastal adaptation planning processes.[258] The Stern Review further recommends that developing countries seek international assistance to improve national mechanisms to forecast, measure, and monitor climate-change-related impacts.[259] The Green Climate Fund could serve as a valuable source of financial and technical adaptation support for vulnerable communities seeking to improve their understanding of likely impacts.[260]

Conclusion

From the perspective of coastal states vulnerable to climate change, human rights present both risks and opportunities. Although the exact scope of the relationship between adaptation and human rights obligations is unsettled, the above discussion addressed various ways coastal climate change adaptation omissions or actions could intersect with international human rights law to create liability for states. For instance, coastal states may violate international human rights law by failing to take reasonable steps to reduce known climate-change-related risks. Additionally, although the extent

---

on the River Uruguay (Argentina v. Uruguay), 2010 I.C.J. 14 (2010) (recognizing environmental impact assessment as a requirement of customary law).

[253] STERN, *supra* note 32, at 563; *Avoiding Adaptation Apartheid, supra* note 2, at 357.

[254] SERAC v. Nigeria, *supra* note 187, ¶ 53.

[255] *See Avoiding Adaptation Apartheid, supra* note 2, at 321; Camacho, *supra* note 2, at 14–15; Craig, *supra* note 158, at 29.

[256] STERN, *supra* note 32, at 563.

[257] *Avoiding Adaptation Apartheid, supra* note 2, at 357.

[258] *See* OLIVER-SMITH, *supra* note 11, at 31.

[259] STERN, *supra* note 32, at 563.

[260] *See supra* text accompanying notes 183–84. *See also* Bali Action Plan, *supra* note 182, ¶ 1(c)(i)–(e) (urging developed countries to support a variety of developing country adaptation planning and implementation needs, including "vulnerability assessments, prioritization of actions, financial needs assessments, capacity-building and response strategies, integration of adaptation actions into sectoral and national planning, [and] specific projects").

and scope of any extraterritorial human rights duties remains unclear, the UNFCCC obliges developed countries to assist developing countries with coastal adaptation measures. Human rights law also applies to the impacts of a state's adaptation projects or policies. In particular, hard armoring structures may negatively impact subsistence or cultural resources, and threaten rights to life and property. Relocation, especially of indigenous communities or small-island states, also implicates a range of human rights, including the right to self-determination and protections against discriminatory or arbitrary displacement.

Recognizing that adaptation omissions and actions have the potential to impact human rights, states should mitigate legal risk by integrating human rights considerations into coastal adaptation planning, funding, decision-making, and implementation. As described above, developing information about climate-change-related risks, engaging proactively in adaptation and disaster planning processes, conducting social vulnerability assessments, prioritizing minimum core resources, and abiding by essential procedural protections are among the ways vulnerable states can forestall potential human rights violations. Overall, as discussed above, a human-rights-based approach to coastal climate change adaptation would not only reduce the risk of infringements but also contribute to improved adaptation planning and broader development goals. Thus, integrating human rights into climate change adaptation contributes to social development as well as coastal resilience.

28 The Ebb and Flow of Coastal Adaptation in Australia
Jan McDonald

Introduction

Australia depends on its coasts for a wide range of economic, ecosystem, recreational, and cultural uses and values. The Australian population and associated infrastructure are concentrated heavily along the coast,[1] creating tensions between competing land uses and placing considerable pressure on coastal resources. These demographic trends are projected to continue for the foreseeable future, highlighting the need for strong

---

[1] *See generally* AUST. DEP'T OF CLIMATE CHANGE, CLIMATE CHANGE RISKS TO AUSTRALIA'S COAST: A FIRST PASS NATIONAL ASSESSMENT (2009), *available at* http://www.climatechange.gov.au/sites/climatechange/files/documents/03_2013/cc-risks-full-report.pdf.

long-term coastal planning and management for the health, productivity, and amenity of the coasts.[2] The impacts of sea-level rise and the increased intensity of storms will exacerbate coastal hazards,[3] and planning is needed to ensure coastal communities, property, and ecosystems are protected, conserved, or able to adapt in response to climate change.[4]

Adapting to coastal climate change impacts will involve a mix of technological, management, behavioral, and attitudinal shifts.[5] There is broad endorsement in Australia for adaptation to be left primarily to the individual beneficiary, with the State having a role in protecting public assets, where the goods and services required for adaptation are underprovided by the market, and addressing externalities, such as the protection of vulnerable groups and public goods.[6] Legal and institutional arrangements and economic incentives may be necessary where adaptation decisions affect the wider community, and to promote private adaptation.[7] The legal regime for coastal land use planning and management is a critical element of these arrangements.

This chapter examines the current approaches of Australia's coastal planning regimes to climate change adaptation. Section I provides an overview of coastal zone governance in Australia. Section II examines in more detail the key instruments by which coastal adaptation is being delivered and discusses two recent cases to expose the challenges that these new techniques have encountered to date. Section III highlights the governance arrangements requiring ongoing attention and reform. It argues that coastal

---

[2] STATE OF THE ENV'T 2011 COMM., AUSTL. DEP'T OF SUSTAINABILITY, ENV'T, WATER, POPULATION & COMMUNITIES, AUSTRALIA STATE OF THE ENVIRONMENT 2011 849–58 (2011), *available at* http://www.environment.gov.au/system/files/pages/743e805c-4a49-42a0-88c1-0b6f06eaecoe/files/soe2011-report-complete.pdf [hereinafter STATE OF THE ENV'T 2011].

[3] VICT. COASTAL COUNCIL, VICT.DEP'T OF ENV'T & PRIMARY INDUST., DRAFT VICTORIAN COASTAL STRATEGY 2013 at 46 (2013), *available at* http://vcc.leadingedgehosting.com.au/assets/media/ckfinder_files/files/Draft%20VCS-2013.pdf [hereinafter DRAFT VICTORIAN COASTAL STRATEGY 2013].

[4] STATE OF THE ENV'T 2011, *supra* note 2, at 852, 863, 878–81; VICT. DEP'T OF ENV'T & PRIMARY INDUS., IMPROVING OUR WATERWAYS: VICTORIAN WATERWAY MANAGEMENT STRATEGY 168–69 (2013), *available at* http://www.depi.vic.gov.au/water/rivers-estuaries-and-wetlands/strategy-and-planning. *See also* ROBERT J. NICHOLLS ET AL., INTERGOVERNMENTAL PANEL ON CLIMATE CHANGE, *Coastal Systems and Low-Lying Areas, in* CLIMATE CHANGE 2007: WORKING GROUP II: IMPACTS, ADAPTATION AND VULNERABILITY (Martin Parry et al. eds., 2007), *available at* http://www.ipcc.ch/publications_and_data/ar4/wg2/en/frontmatter.html.

[5] Jan McDonald, *Mapping the Legal Landscape of Climate Change Adaptation, in* ADAPTATION TO CLIMATE CHANGE: LAW AND POLICY 1, 2 (T. Bonyhady, Andrew Macintosh & Jan McDonald eds., 2010); Jan McDonald, *The Role of Law in Climate Change Adaptation*, 2 WILEY INTERDISCIPLINARY REVIEWS: CLIMATE CHANGE 283, 283 (2011).

[6] AUSTL. DEP'T OF THE ENV'T, CLIMATE CHANGE COMMUNITY DISCUSSION: ROLES AND RESPONSIBILITIES FOR CLIMATE CHANGE ADAPTATION IN AUSTRALIA, http://www.climatechange.gov.au/community-discussion (last visited Mar. 17, 2014) [hereinafter CLIMATE CHANGE COMMUNITY DISCUSSION]; AUSTL. PRODUCTIVITY COMM'N, BARRIERS TO EFFECTIVE CLIMATE CHANGE ADAPTATION: PRODUCTIVITY COMMISSION INQUIRY REPORT NO. 59, 57 (2012), *available at* http://www.pc.gov.au/__data/assets/pdf_file/0008/119663/climate-change-adaptation.pdf (last visited Mar. 17, 2014).

[7] *Id.*

adaptation planning requires renewed attention to integrated and coordinated coastal decision-making both within and across states and territories. It further recommends that, to be durable in the face of long-term climate change impacts, adaptation planning must use instruments and processes that strike an appropriate balance between short-term and long-term, and public and private values.

I. Governance of Adaptation in the Coastal Zone

The governance of Australia's coastal zone is highly complex, in part by virtue of Australia's federal system of government, and in part because of the large number of "sectors" whose activities occur in, or affect, the coastal zone.[8] Coastal management involves multiple public and private sectoral actors across local, regional, state, and national scales. The result is both horizontal and vertical fragmentation, which can be overcome only through integrated approaches to governance and management. National, state, and territory governments have all embraced the principles and aspirations of Integrated Coastal Zone Management (ICZM) as the best model for recognizing these diverse actors and drivers,[9] but implementation has been poor.[10] The Australian House of Representatives Joint Standing Committee on Environment recently concluded that the challenges of climate change adaptation necessitated renewed attention to ICZM in Australia.[11]

Land use planning is the principal vehicle for delivering coastal adaptation within an integrated coastal management framework, with connections to coastal management, biodiversity conservation, fisheries, and water management. The legal framework for land use and spatial planning can influence the nature and location of development, thereby reducing exposure to new or increased coastal hazards.[12] In Australia's federal

---

[8] *See generally* AUSTL. HOUSE OF REPRESENTATIVES STANDING COMM. ON ENV'T & CONSERVATION, MANAGEMENT OF THE AUSTRALIAN COASTAL ZONE (1980); AUSTRL. HOUSE OF REPRESENTATIVES STANDING COMM. ON ENV'T, RECREATION & ARTS, THE INJURED COASTLINE: PROTECTION OF THE COASTAL ENVIRONMENT (1991); RESOURCE ASSESSMENT COMM'N, AUSTL. DEP'T OF THE ENV'T, COASTAL ZONE INQUIRY: FINAL REPORT (1993); AUSTL. HOUSE OF REPRESENTATIVES STANDING COMM. ON CLIMATE CHANGE, WATER, ENV'T & THE ARTS, MANAGING OUR COASTAL ZONE IN A CHANGING CLIMATE: THE TIME TO ACT IS NOW (2009) [hereinafter MANAGING OUR COASTAL ZONE].

[9] *See* NATURAL RES. MGMT. MINISTERIAL COUNCIL, AUSTL. DEP'T OF ENV'T, NATIONAL COOPERATIVE APPROACH TO INTEGRATED COASTAL ZONE MANAGEMENT: FRAMEWORK AND IMPLEMENTATION PLAN (2006), *available at* http://www.environment.gov.au/system/files/resource s/5ce3ba77-4b62-43f0-a1e0-4a1a2266500e/files/framework.pdf.

[10] *See generally* Nick Harvey, *Strategic Assessment and Integrated Coastal Management: Implications for Coastal Capacity Building in Australia, in* COASTAL MANAGEMENT IN AUSTRALIA: KEY INSTITUTIONAL AND GOVERNANCE ISSUES FOR COASTAL NATURAL RESOURCE MANAGEMENT AND PLANNING 89–101 (Neil Lazarow et al. eds., 2006), *available at* http://www.ozcoasts.gov.au/pdf/CRC/Coastal_ Management_in_Australia.pdf.

[11] MANAGING OUR COASTAL ZONE, *supra* note 8, at 286.

[12] Anita Foerster, Andrew Macintosh & Jan McDonald, *Transferable Lessons for Climate Change Adaptation Planning? Managing Bushfire and Coastal Climate Hazards in Australia*, 30 ENVT'L & PLANNING L.J. 469, 469 (2013) [hereinafter *Transferable Lessons for Climate Change Adaptation Planning*].

structure, land use planning is primarily a state responsibility. Commonwealth involvement is limited to approval/veto powers in cases involving "matters of national environmental significance," and to funding priority initiatives. Each state has its own statutory planning regime, with many functions delegated to local councils, including the preparation of strategic planning schemes (or equivalent), which are guided by state planning policies or strategies, for each local government area. State governments retain ultimate oversight in that local schemes must have state approval. State agencies may have concurrent approval powers, and controversial plans and proposals may be "called in" by the State Planning Minister to be decided at the state level.

There is no single approach to planning for coastal hazards or coastal climate adaptation across all Australian states.[13] State governments set overarching legislative objectives and processes and specify more detailed requirements in planning policies, most of which are statutory instruments. State planning policies provide guidance to local governments about how to account for erosion, shoreline recession, inundation, and storm surge in strategic coastal planning instruments and individual developments assessment decisions. They set out general principles to guide local decisions, and may also stipulate specific requirements such as planning benchmarks for sea-level rise, but in both cases, the precise interpretation and application of these measures is left to local planning authorities. Local governments are responsible for implementing these legislative and planning policy frameworks at the local level through the development of strategic planning documents, such as planning schemes and in the determination of development assessment decisions.[14]

The states of New South Wales, Queensland, South Australia, and Victoria complement their land-use planning regimes with specific coastal management frameworks. Typically, these provide for the development of statewide coastal strategies and local and/or regional coastal management plans setting out adaptation priorities and strategies for hazard-prone parts of the coast.[15] These strategies operate in conjunction with the broader planning framework, providing the criteria by which site-specific development proposals are assessed. Some schemes also contain prohibitions or restrictions on the erection of coastal protective structures, including the requirement for approval from coastal management agencies.[16]

Most state-level documents endorse the protection of coastal processes and promote urban infill and the containment of new development to existing urban areas.[17] Most refer to the need to protect coastal assets from climate-related hazards,[18] although some

---

[13] *See generally id.*

[14] ANDREW MACINTOSH, ANITA FOERSTER & JAN MCDONALD, NAT'L CLIMATE CHANGE RESEARCH FACILITY, LIMP, LEAP OR LEARN? DEVELOPING LEGAL FRAMEWORKS FOR CLIMATE CHANGE ADAPTATION PLANNING IN AUSTRALIA 36–38 (2013), *available at* http://apo.org.au/files/docs/McDonald-Limp-leap-learn-report-WEB.pdf [hereinafter LIMP, LEAP OR LEARN].

[15] *Id.*

[16] *See* discussion *infra* Section II.C.

[17] *See State Planning Policy 2014* (Queensl.) 28, 47, *available at* http://www.dsdip.qld.gov.au/resources/policy/state-planning/state-planning-policy-jul-2014.pdf ((last visited July 21, 2014).

[18] LIMP, LEAP OR LEARN, *supra* note 14, at 182, 193, 198, 212–14, 223–24, 235, 251.

refer to this only as "climate variability," having eliminated the term "climate change" from state policy generally.[19] Avoidance of development in hazard-prone areas is typically the preferred option, and the standard for overcoming the presumption of no new development or intensification of development is especially high in erosion-prone areas.[20] Planned retreat is preferred for areas of existing development facing unacceptably high risk, although there is limited guidance at the State level about when and how this strategy will be implemented.[21] In many states, accommodation through site design and construction standards, and defense strategies, are considered suitable only in cases where avoidance and planned retreat are not feasible options.[22]

The evolution of local adaptation planning has been impaired by fears of short- and long-term liability. Local authorities see themselves as caught between "the devil and the deep blue sea." On the one hand, planning restrictions that potentially diminish property rights have been met with strong opposition, including legal challenges.[23] On the other hand, local councils have been reluctant to approve new developments that may suffer from climate impacts in the future and expose them to legal actions.[24] Recent adaptation planning reforms in the states of Australia's heavily developed eastern seaboard, Queensland, and New South Wales, have been diluted or revoked soon after their introduction, but these changes have served to complicate the regulatory landscape for local planning agencies.

II. Features of Coastal Planning for Adaptation

A range of planning tools is available to state and local governments to promote adaptation to coastal climate risks.[25] While there are broad similarities in the general approach to adaptation planning, there is wide variation in the choice of instrument by which to deliver policy outcomes.

---

[19] *State Planning Policy 2014* (Queensl.), *supra* note 17, at 28.

[20] *Id.* at 51.

[21] *State Planning Policy No. 2.6 State Coastal Planning Policy 2013*, (W. Austl.) pt 5, s 5.5, *available at http://www. planning.wa.gov.au/publications/1168.asp, last visited 21 July 2014* http://www.slp.wa.gov.au/gazette/gazette. nsf/searchgazette/4306BA11984D436648257BB70023B9F8/$file/gg136.pdf.(last visited July 21, 2014).

[22] *Id.*

[23] *Taip v E. Gippsland Shire Council* (2010) 177 LGERA 236; *Gippsland Coastal Bd. v S. Gippsland Shire Council* [2008] VCAT 1545; *Northcape Properties v Dist. Council of York Peninsula* [2008] SASR 57; *Minister for Planning v Walker* (2008) 161 LGERA 423; *Myers v S. Gippsland Shire Council* (No 2) [2009] VCAT 2414; *Aldous v Greater Taree City Council* [2009] NSWLEC 17; *Ronchi v Wellington Shire Council* [2009] VCAT 1206.

[24] *See generally* Jan McDonald, *A Risky Climate for Decision-Making: The Liability of Development Authorities for Climate Change Impacts*, 24 ENVT'L & PLANNING L.J. 405 (2007); BAKER & MCKENZIE, LOCAL COUNCILS' RISK OF LIABILITY IN THE FACE OF CLIMATE CHANGE—RESOLVING UNCERTAINTIES: A REPORT FOR THE AUSTRALIAN LOCAL GOVERNMENT ASSOCIATION 41 (2011); Philippa England, *Heating Up: Climate Change Law and the Evolving Responsibilities of Local Government*, 13 LOCAL GOV'T L.J. 209 (2008).

[25] LIMP, LEAP OR LEARN, *supra* note 14, at 41–68 (discussing these tools in detail). *See also* Andrew Macintosh, Anita Foerster & Jan McDonald, *Policy design, spatial planning and climate change adaptation: a case study*

Section II of this chapter explores four interrelated elements of land-use planning for coastal adaptation in Australia that are growing in importance: hazard mapping, information instruments, the use of time-bound or event-bound development approvals, and restrictions on private landowners erecting hard coastal protection structures. It seeks to highlight the inconsistency in approaches across states, but also the variation within states due to differing approaches to implementation at the local government level and rapid changes in state government policy.[26]

A. HAZARD MAPPING AND SEA-LEVEL RISE PLANNING BENCHMARKS

Decisions about the future location of development, retreat strategies, the size of development-free coastal buffers, setbacks, and building standards must be informed by some understanding of future climate change impacts. No state requires local authorities to undertake hazard mapping or prescribe the manner in which it should be done. While most local governments attempt to identify coastal (and other) hazards in the preparation of strategic planning documents, such as planning schemes, this is not done consistently or comprehensively. Nor is there consistent practice around how mapping is undertaken when it is done, with much resting on the resources available to the planning authority. The hazard zones that were mapped for Queensland's 2011 Coastal Plan (now repealed) are the best example of standardized state-wide mapping, but were met with widespread criticism from the property industry for including 10 percent of all Queensland properties in the medium- or high-hazard zones.[27] A similar mapping exercise is underway for Tasmania. Unlike Queensland, the inundation component of that process in Tasmania faced little adverse reaction from the public or property industry.[28]

The mapping of current and future coastal hazards is used in the determination of mandatory coastal foreshore reserves in Western Australia and South Australia,[29] and in setting zones, building setbacks, and other requirements. Over the past ten years, all states have introduced sea-level rise planning benchmarks (Table 28.1), but they vary in relation to the baseline date for comparison (ranging from 1990 to 2010), the size of the

---

from Australia, 57 J. ENVTL. PLANNING & MGMT. 1 (2014), http://dx.doi.org/10.1080/09640568.2014.93 0706 (last visited July 21, 2014).

[26] Both Queensland and New South Wales have already significantly modified much of the trailblazing coastal planning instruments that they introduced only one or two years earlier, creating further uncertainty for landowners and local government alike. In December 2013, the new State Planning Policy was introduced in Queensland, replacing the QCP and a range of other instruments, and setting out "state interests" that must be reflected in new planning schemes and prescribed in development assessment decisions. *State Planning Policy 2014* (Queensl.), *supra* note 17, at 10.

[27] *Property Council Concerned About New Queensland Coastal Plan*, PROPERTY COUNCIL OF AUSTL. (Apr. 8, 2011), http://www.propertyoz.com.au/Article/Resource.aspx?media=1817.

[28] *New Tools to Improve Planning for Sea Level Rise and Coastal Hazards*, TAS. DEP'T OF PREMIER & CABINET, http://www.dpac.tas.gov.au/divisions/climatechange/what_the_government_is_doing/new_tools_to_improve_planning_for_sea_level_rise_and_coastal_hazards (last visited Jan. 31, 2014).

[29] *See State Planning Policy No. 2.6 State Coastal Planning Policy 2013*, (W. Austl.) 2013 sch 1.

TABLE 28.1

SEA-LEVEL RISE PLANNING BENCHMARKS FOR AUSTRALIAN STATES AND
TERRITORIES

Jurisdiction	2040/2050	2100/100 year mark
Queensland	None	None (0.8 meter above 1990 by 2100, repealed 2013)
New South Wales	None (0.4 meter above 1990 by 2050, repealed September 2012)	None (0.9 meter above 1990 by 2100, repealed September 2012)
South Australia	0.2 meter by 2050	1.0 meter by 2100
Tasmania	0.2 meter by 2050 above 2010	0.8 meter above 2010 by 2100
Victoria	0.2 meter above 2010 by 2040	0.8 meter above 2010 by 2100
Western Australia	None	0.9 meter above 2010 by 2110
Northern Territory	None	0.8 meter above 2010 by 2100

projected sea-level rise (ranging from 0.8 to 1.0 meter), and whether sea-level rise allowances can be "pro-rated" for developments with shorter life spans.[30]

The most precautionary of these benchmarks is also the oldest: South Australia has
a benchmark of 0.3 meter sea-level rise by 2050 and 1 meter by 2100.[31] The most recent
benchmark, Western Australia's *State Coastal Planning Policy* 2013, was informed by
projections from both the Intergovernmental Panel on Climate Change (IPCC) and
Australia's lead science agency, the Commonwealth Scientific and Industrial Research
Organization (CSIRO).[32] It prescribes a setback allowance of 0.9 meters by 2110, which
it equates to 90 meters of shoreward recession. It provides further that this allowance
may have to be increased where the impact of obstacles might reduce sediment transport
and thereby influence trends,[33] and sets an additional allowance of 0.2 meters per year of
horizontal erosion to allow for uncertainty.[34]

Victoria's *Draft Coastal Strategy* 2013 re-endorses the State's staged benchmarks: 0.2
meter on 2010 levels by 2040 for infill development; and 0.8 meter on 2010 levels by
2100. Like the WA coastal planning policy, there is an expectation in Victoria's strategy

---

[30] LIMP, LEAP OR LEARN, *supra* note 14, at 182, 193, 198, 212–14, 223–24, 235, 251.

[31] *Coast Protection Board Policy Document 1991: Revised May 22, 2012* (S. Austl.) (2012) app. 1(47).

[32] *State Planning Policy No. 2.6 State Coastal Planning Policy 2013*, (W. Austl.) (2013); CHARLIE BICKNELL,
W. AUSTL. DEP'T OF TRANSPORT, SEA LEVEL CHANGE IN WESTERN AUSTRALIA: APPLICATION TO
COASTAL PLANNING (2010), *available at* http://www.planning.wa.gov.au/dop_pub_pdf/Sea_Level_
Change_in_WA_Revo_FINAL.pdf.

[33] *State Planning Policy No. 2.6 State Coastal Planning Policy 2013* (W. Austl.) (2013) sch 1 s 4.4.3.

[34] *Id.* at s 4.4.

that additional allowance will be made for tides, storm surges, coastal processes, and local conditions.[35] The effect of benchmarks also differs. The WA setback of 90 meters is one factor to consider in setting the width of the mandatory coastal foreshore reserve, but the policy makes clear that current erosion trends and historical patterns are also relevant in setting this reserve, as are the other environmental variables that are likely to be affected by climate change such as wind and wave climate.[36] In other places, the benchmark was intended to guide planning authorities in all its planning decisions.

The NSW state government introduced a sea-level rise planning benchmark in 2009, requiring local authorities to base coastal and flood hazard assessments, development assessments, and the siting of public infrastructure on a 0.4 meter rise by 2050 and 0.9 meter by 2100.[37] This benchmark did not seek to prohibit development potentially affected by sea-level rise, but required planning authorities to factor it into planning, siting, and design of new development.[38] Since a change of state government in 2011, the 2009 Sea Level Rise Policy Statement has been abandoned and the planning benchmark revoked, reinstating the previous position that gave local authorities the discretion to adopt their own sea-level rise projections to suit local circumstances.[39] Queensland has also repealed its 2011 Coastal Plan, which set a sea-level rise benchmark of 0.8 meter by 2100.[40] These state government decisions to return decision-making power over such matters to local government may allow for consideration of local needs and circumstances. However, it is more likely to enable the interests of powerful property lobbies to prevail over public interest values, place an added burden on local planning authorities, and create unjustifiable differences in adaptation planning along hydrologically and geologically connected coastlines. These policy reversals also leave planning authorities more vulnerable to future liability should they approve development in hazard-prone areas.[41]

B. INFORMATION INSTRUMENTS

Over the past decade, time and resources have been focused on enhancing our understanding of hazard exposure for Australian coastal settlements. Adequate information

---

[35] DRAFT VICTORIAN COASTAL STRATEGY 2013, *supra* note 3, at 16.

[36] *State Planning Policy No. 2.6, State Coastal Planning Policy 2013* (W. Austl.) (2013) sch 1 s 4.

[37] N.S.W. DEP'T OF PLANNING, N.S.W. COASTAL PLANNING GUIDELINE: ADAPTING TO SEA LEVEL RISE 4 (2010), *available at* http://www.planning.nsw.gov.au/Portals/0/PlansForAction/pdf/SeaLevelRise_ Policy_web%5B1%5D.pdf [hereinafter N.S.W. COASTAL PLANNING GUIDELINE] (last visited July 21, 2014).

[38] *Id.* at 4.

[39] N.S.W. DEP'T OF ENV'T & HERITAGE, SEA LEVEL RISE: N.S.W. GOVERNMENT POLICY, http://www. environment.nsw.gov.au/climatechange/sealevel.htm (last visited Feb. 2, 2014).

[40] *State Planning Policy 3/11: Coastal Protection 2012* (Queensl.) (2012) s 2.1.1, Annex 2, 44 (repealed).

[41] Tina Perinotto, *NSW Coastal Planning in Storm of Confusion*, FIFTH ESTATE (Sept. 19, 2012), http://www. thefifthestate.com.au/archives/38793/. *See also* McDonald, *supra* note 24.

is essential for risk allocation to be effective in practice.[42] Information instruments are widely seen as a powerful tool by which to promote private adaptation for a wide range of climate risks and avoid the need for prohibitive regulation or restrictions on land use.[43] In recent times, local authorities have also embraced wider use of such instruments as a means of minimizing their exposure to potential legal liability.[44] Such instruments range in specificity and legal authority—from web-based maps showing broad hazard lines, to zones and overlays that form part of a planning scheme, to site-specific planning certificates and notations on title warning of the hazard itself or the implications of planning controls for the future use and development of the site.[45]

Until recently, New South Wales had a system of hazard mapping that provided for high levels of risk disclosure. Until 2012, the NSW *Coastal Protection Act 1979* allowed for the designation of land in a Coastal Zone Management Plan into one of three categories: (1) an immediate risk from coastal hazard, (2) likely to be at risk by 2050, and (3) likely to be at risk by 2100. This classification was noted on s149 certificates.[46] A s149(2) certificate details current restrictions on development or use of the land, and is a mandatory accompaniment to contracts for the sale of land. Section 149(5) certificates are additional optional documents that set out general information about past, current, or future matters that may potentially affect the land. The inclusion of general information about future exposure was intended to enable purchasers to make more informed decisions based on their own risk tolerance.

The new NSW state government revoked the coastal risk categories for CZMPs in 2012,[47] following pressure from property owners who claimed dramatic drops in property values.[48] A draft planning circular released for comment in 2014 proposes to circumscribe the hazard information that can be provided on s149 certificates, in order to "avoid adverse property market and other impacts by the disclosure of information prematurely, or by disclosing information that lacks necessary rigour and certainty."[49]

---

[42] Climate Change Community Discussion, *supra* note 6; Austl. Productivity Comm'n, *supra* note 6, at 7; Tas. Climate Change Office, Tas. Dep't of Premier & Cabinet, Adapting to Climate Change in Tasmania—Issues Paper 2012, at 6 (last visited Mar. 18, 2014).

[43] Climate Change Community Discussion, *supra* note 6.

[44] Limp, Leap or Learn, *supra* note 14, at 43.

[45] *Id.*

[46] *Coastal Protection Act 1979* (N.S.W.), ss 55C, 56B; *Coastal Protection Regulation 2011* (N.S.W.) pt 4; N.S.W. Coastal Planning Guideline, *supra* note 37, at 7.

[47] N.S.W. Dep't of Env't & Heritage, Stage One Coastal Reforms: Questions and Answers http://www.environment.nsw.gov.au/coasts/stage1CoastRefQaA.htm (last visited Feb. 27, 2014).

[48] Paul Govind, *Managing the Relationship between Adaptation and Coastal Land Use Development through the Use of Section 149 Certificates*, 7 Macquarie J. Int'l & Comp. Envtl. L. 94, 96 (2011). There is, in fact, very little evidence of long-term impacts on property values following the release of hazard information affecting a site. *See generally* Stephen Yeo, *Effects of Disclosure of Flood-Liability in Residential Property Values*, 18 Austl. J. Emergency Mgmt. 35 (2003).

[49] N.S.W. Dep't of Planning & Infrastructure, Draft Planning Circular, Coastal Hazard Notations on Section 149 Planning Certificates 2 (last visited Jan. 30, 2014) [hereinafter Draft Planning Circular].

Planning authorities will be required to distinguish between current and future exposure to coastal hazards. Information about future hazards may be included on a s149(5) certificate only if: (1) it is accurate, complete, and reliable; (2) it alerts the reader to the known information; and (3) council is in the process of adopting a policy or planning instrument to manage development on the land, which would then be disclosed in a s149(2) certificate. The implication of this is that once a planning authority has information about a future hazard, it is required either to act on it by preparing a policy or instrument, or make the decision not to disclose the information on the s149(5) certificate. If it chooses the first path, it may include the information on the certificate while the policy is being prepared. With the second option, it may disseminate such information via its website, but not use it in any site-specific way.[50]

The position in Western Australia contrasts sharply with NSW's recent changes. Western Australia's *State Coastal Policy* (2013) requires local authorities to undertake coastal hazard risk identification and management for existing or new development in areas at risk of being affected by coastal hazards within the relevant planning time frame.[51] Where a coastal hazard risk is identified, the Policy requires that it be disclosed to current and future lot owners, as "those likely to be affected." The method for doing this for existing development is not specified, but for sites that are the subject of subdivision or development applications, the following notation is required on the certificate of title:

VULNERABLE COASTAL AREA—This lot is located in an area likely to be subject to coastal erosion and/or inundation over the next 100 years.

Unlike the new guidance for planning certificates in NSW, the framing of this notation is very broad, and does not distinguish between present and future hazards.

To ensure that they operate fairly and avoid market distortions, information instruments require consistency in content, format, and the circumstances in which they are imposed.[52] This is particularly true between areas attracting similar pools of prospective purchasers. As noted in the discussion of planning benchmarks, no state currently has a general requirement for coastal hazard mapping and not all local governments have undertaken extensive hazard mapping to provide such information to property owners or the public. The absence of information on title or in a planning certificate may convey a false sense of safety about one site, while the provision of information about other sites may suggest that they are comparatively riskier.

---

[50] *Id.* at 3.

[51] *State Planning Policy No. 2.6 State Coastal Planning Policy 2013* (W. Austl.) (2013) s 5.5(i).

[52] A proposal to include climate change hazard information on land titles in Victoria was rejected because of risk of inconsistent notices, and problems in obtaining finance and insurance for properties subject to such notations.

C. CONDITIONAL DEVELOPMENT APPROVALS

Most jurisdictions have some capacity for local governments to impose conditions on development approval. The Australian Productivity Commission has recognized the potential value of time-limited or event-bound development approvals to manage climate risks in matching "the time frame of the relevant land use and its associated potential risks."[53] Time-bound development approvals contemplate the revocation of approval on a predetermined future date, with or without the right to seek an extension or re-validation of the approval. Contingent approvals specify a triggering event that may occur at some unascertained future date, for example the landward movement of an erosion line, or the increase of an annual event probability for a certain level of inundation or storm surge.[54] To be effective, event triggers often operate in conjunction with restrictions on the construction of protective structures, such as sea walls.

The former NSW *Sea-Level Rise Planning Guidelines* specifically contemplated the use of such measures,[55] but there have been limited examples of their use in practice. A well-publicized example of event triggers in Australia is the requirement of Byron Shire Council that new development is prohibited within 20 meters of the erosion escarpment and that structures that come within 20 meters of the erosion escarpment be removed at the cost of the landowner.[56] Prohibitions on the rebuilding of houses lost to erosion have been upheld by the Land and Environment Court,[57] but the requirement to remove at-risk structures has yet to be formally invoked, and there is some uncertainty about the precise manner in which it would be operationalized.[58]

The advantages of such measures are obvious in enabling development to take place while risks remain acceptable. Yet the uncertainty surrounding the life of a development will certainly make it hard to obtain financing and insurance for such developments. Thus, it is not surprising that they would be greeted with some opposition from landowners.[59] It is likely to be some time yet before Australia sees the widespread uptake of conditional approvals. Yet where the choice is between denial of development approval and the grant of a contingent approval, the latter should be considered preferable in most cases. For example, Western Australia's *State Coastal Planning Policy 2013* reflects a preference for avoidance of new development in areas of unacceptable risk, and planned

---

[53] AUSTL. PRODUCTIVITY COMM'N, *supra* note 6, at 178; *see also* LIMP, LEAP OR LEARN, *supra* note 14, at 55–58.

[54] LIMP, LEAP OR LEARN, *supra* note 14, at 55–58.

[55] N.S.W. COASTAL PLANNING GUIDELINE, *supra* note 37, at 17.

[56] *Development Control Plan 2010* (Byron Shire Council) pt J2.1 (New South Wales) (2010).

[57] BYRON SHIRE COUNCIL, PLANNED RETREAT IN BYRON SHIRE FACT SHEET 4, http://www.byron.nsw. gov.au/environmental-resources (last visited Mar. 17, 2014).

[58] LIMP, LEAP OR LEARN, *supra* note 14, at 85.

[59] Philippa England, *Too Much Too Soon? On the Rise and Fall of Australia's Coastal Climate Change Law*, 30 ENVT'L & PLANNING L.J. 390, 391 (2013).

or managed retreat of existing development.[60] If there is sufficient justification for not avoiding development, it contemplates the use of both design *and management* strategies to render risks from coastal hazards acceptable.[61] The use of event-trigger conditions attaching to approvals would be one such management strategy.

D. RESTRICTIONS ON COASTAL PROTECTION

Coastal protection works are expensive and likely to have only limited effectiveness over time, and can adversely affect neighboring properties. Restricting the construction of coastal defenses may be necessary to protect other public or private values, but is also a key mechanism by which to implement a form of staged retreat without requiring landowners to abandon their property before time or requiring planning agencies to pay compensation. Policy statements in most jurisdictions identify coastal protection as a measure of last resort.

For example, a key desired outcome of Victoria's draft coastal strategy 2013 is that "[n]atural coastal processes are adopted as the preferred form of defense against possible impacts of a changing climate."[62] Victoria requires that coastal protection avoid detrimental impacts on coastal processes and neighboring properties, and makes clear that the Crown has no obligation to minimize the impacts of coastal hazards and sea-level rise on private property.[63] In Queensland, coastal protection work must be a last resort where erosion poses an imminent threat to public safety or existing structures, the property cannot reasonably be relocated or abandoned, and the proposed works ensure that private property is located as far landward as practicable and that any increase in risks for adjacent areas is mitigated.[64] The position is similar in Western Australia. New coastal protection works are only permitted after all other options for avoiding and adapting to coastal hazards have been fully explored, where primarily proposed in the public interest, where there will be no off-site impacts, and where funding for construction and maintenance is provided from the outset.[65] This principle also applies to the repair and upgrade of existing works.[66]

By contrast, New South Wales has recently relaxed its tough restrictions on beach protection works on private property, which focused on the impacts of such structures on access to the beach, adjoining properties, and public safety.[67] Before 2010, all coastal defenses required development approval from the relevant planning authority. Following

---

[60] *State Planning Policy No. 2.6 State Coastal Planning Policy 2013* (W. Austl.) (2013) s 5.5(iii)(1)(2).

[61] *Id.* at s 5.5(iii)(3).

[62] DRAFT VICTORIAN COASTAL STRATEGY 2013, *supra* note 3, at 45.

[63] *Id.* at 47.

[64] *See State Planning Policy 2014* (Queensl.) 51, *available at* http://www.dsdip.qld.gov.au/resources/policy/state-planning/state-planning-policy-jul-2014.pdf (last visited July 21, 2014).

[65] *State Planning Policy No. 2.6 State Coastal Planning Policy 2013*, (W. Austl.) (2013) s 5.7(i).

[66] *Id.* at s 5.7(ii).

[67] *Coastal Protection Act* 1979 (N.S.W.) s 55M(1)(a),(b).

an amendment to the *Coastal Protection Act* 1979 (NSW) in 2010, temporary works could be installed for a maximum of twelve months to protect against imminent or foreseeable damage if they complied with an applicable Coastal Zone Management Plan. Works of more permanent duration required development approval.[68] The factors that consent authorities were required to consider in deciding whether to approve such measures included impacts on public safety or access to a beach or headland, and the ongoing costs of maintaining the structure.[69] Changes to the NSW regime in 2012 exempted "temporary" coastal protection works on private land from the need to obtain development approval, with unrestricted time frames for what constitutes "temporary."[70]

E. ADAPTATION PLANNING LITIGATION

Numerous planning appeals across the country have considered the operation of the applicable state planning schemes to climate change impacts on coastal hazards.[71] Two recent cases illustrate issues arising from the use of these planning measures for coastal adaptation and the difficulties of articulating a coherent legal framework for coastal adaptation in Australia. Both involved merits appeals against local government decisions on development applications. As merits appeals, the Court in each case was evaluating the correctness of actual decisions, rather than their legality. In this respect, the cases do not have significant precedential value, but they do highlight the importance of clear local planning policies and timely communication of such measures, and the relevance of existing development in areas that are the subject of adaptation planning measures.

Rainbow Shores P/L v Gympie Regional Council[72] was a merits appeal against the refusal of a large integrated resort and residential development at Rainbow Beach on Queensland's Sunshine Coast. The Queensland Planning and Environment Court concluded that the plan of development was inadequate due to erosion and storm surge issues, among other factors. Despite the development proposal having originated under earlier coastal planning measures, the Court considered the assumption underpinning the then-*Queensland Coastal Plan 2011*—that erosion-prone areas should not be developed[73] unless there is an overriding need in the public interest or a preexisting

---

[68] *Coastal Protection and Other Legislation Amendment Act 2010* (N.S.W.) ss55M(1), *available at* http://www.legislation.nsw.gov.au/sessionalview/sessional/act/2010-78.pdf (last visited July 21, 2014).

[69] *Coastal Protection Act* 1979 (N.S.W.) s 55M(1)(a),(b).

[70] *Coastal Protection Amendment Bill 2012* (N.S.W.) sch. 1, s 6 (amending the *Coastal Protection Act 1979*, (N.S.W.) ss 55O-S), *available at* http://www.parliament.nsw.gov.au/prod/parlment/nswbills.nsf/0/84469f e47600ba1eca257a760020e7fb/$FILE/05346535.pdf/b2012-101-d16-House.pdf (last visited July 21, 2014).

[71] Phillipa England & Jan McDonald, *Local Government and Climate Change*, in GLOBAL CLIMATE CHANGE: AUSTRALIAN LAW & POLICY (David Hodgkinson & Renee Garner eds., 2008) (looseleaf, ¶¶ 7.005–7.265).

[72] *Rainbow Shores Pty Ltd. v Gympie Reg'l Council* [2013] Planning and Environment Court of Queensland 26 (Austl.).

[73] *State Planning Policy 3/11: Coastal Protection 2012* (Queensl.) (repealed) Glossary. *See also Draft Coastal Protection State Planning Regulatory Provision 2012* (Queensl.); *State Planning Policy 2014* (Queensl.).

development commitment, or the proposal is a public benefit asset.[74] The proposed site was bounded to its seaward side by a coastal reserve, but was subject to an erosion-prone area setback of 175 meters, which placed the erosion line inside the site. Modification of the proposal to relocate buildings would require a major alteration and was therefore too significant to justify granting a conditional approval, especially because of the impacts on vegetation buffers and other environmental considerations.

Part of the site was fronted by a dune of only 3.5-4 meters in height, which would render it subject to overtopping during a one-in-100 year storm surge of 5.05 meters. This storm surge inundation risk would be higher on the applicable sea-level rise planning benchmark of 0.8 meters by 2100, such that the site would require dune enhancement or a sea wall to protect it. Given that the proponent had already accepted the need to consider a 100-year ocean surge level, the Court concluded that it was "difficult to justify ignoring the current predictions of sea-level rise" that influence which areas are identified as susceptible.[75] In rejecting the proposal on these grounds, the Court held that the cost of imposing the implications of future sea-level rise on the applicant had to be balanced against broader considerations relating to the long lifespan of the development.[76]

The second case is *Newton v Great Lakes Council*,[77] a merits appeal by property owners against the imposition of conditions on the development approval for a property in a highly erosion prone area, the Winda Woppa peninsula on NSW's midcoast. The property in question fronted Jimmy's Beach, separated only by a road running along the frontal dunes. Jimmy's Beach had experienced severe erosion in the past, the road itself having been undermined on past occasions.[78] Indeed, the Great Lakes Council had a moratorium on new development in place from 1984 to 1989, until it resolved to undertake and maintain beach replenishment works.[79] Since then, the beach had received extensive sand replenishment.[80]

Both a Local Environment Plan and a Development Control Plan (DCP)—statutory planning instruments made by the Council but approved by the NSW state government—were in place for the site.[81] A commentary about Jimmy's Beach in the DCP made clear that lifting the moratorium on new development was contingent on the beach replenishment continuing, and that special local contributions may be

---

[74] *State Planning Policy 3/11: Coastal Protection 2012* (Queensl.) pt. D, replaced by *Draft Coastal Protection State Planning Regulatory Provision 2012* in October 2012 (both repealed and replaced by *State Planning Policy 2014*).

[75] *Rainbow Shores* [2013] QPEC ¶ 360.

[76] Id. ¶¶ 359–360.

[77] *Newton v Great Lakes Council* [2013] New South Wales Land and Environment Court 1248 (Austl.).

[78] Id. ¶ 4.

[79] *Great Lakes Local Environment Plan 1996* (N.S.W.); *Hawks Nest Low Density Residential Development Control Plan No 48 2009* (Great Lakes Council) pt 3.

[80] *Newton* [2013] NSWLEC ¶ 4.

[81] *Great Lakes Local Environment Plan 1996* (N.S.W.); *Hawks Nest Low Density Residential Development Control Plan No 48 2009* (Great Lakes Council).

required in the future to cover the costs of these works.[82] The DCP required that a linear sea-level rise of 0.91 meter by 2100 was to be taken into account in development approval decisions, and that applicants on the Winda Woppa peninsula required specialist engineers' reports to inform the choice of building standards to protect against coastal erosion and storm surge.[83] The Council's 2033 erosion hazard line ran across the applicant's site.[84]

The Great Lakes Council commissioned coastal hazard studies for two areas, including Jimmy's Beach. The Council received the Jimmy's Beach report a month before the applicants purchased the development site, but the report was not yet made publicly available. Indeed, the Council had yet to consider the report at the time of the appeal in 2013.[85] The s149(2) certificate noted the application of SEPP 71—Coastal Protection, but only in general terms. The certificate did not foreshadow the possibility of additional controls in the future. By contrast, the Council's response to the first report, which related to the other area, was to include notations on the s149(2) certificates advising purchasers of minimum setback requirements and the possibility of future development restrictions being imposed because the land had reduced foundation capacity under Council's 2060 sea-level rise projections.[86]

Great Lakes Council granted development consent subject to several conditions, one of which had the effect of creating a "time-bound" approval that was limited to twenty years. The reason for the condition was said to be "[T]o allow reasonable expectation of development under current uncertainties in relation to beach renourishment and resulting effective hazard lines."[87] The condition required the 2033 property owner to vacate the dwelling at the expiration of the period, but granted an option of seeking continuation of the consent for an additional period upon completion of a coastal hazard study. This condition (condition 7) also noted that a severe storm could cause structural damage necessitating demolition of the building at any time in the future. Another condition required footings and foundations to be designed and constructed to ensure continued support of the building consistent with the hazard line and reduced foundation capacity relating to 2033 sea-level rise conditions, which was needed to ensure structural stability and avoid increased erosion of adjacent properties.[88]

Commissioner Moore of the Land and Environment Court struck down the time-limiting condition based on four factors. The major factor was that none of the existing dwellings in the area was subject to the same time limit. In his view, the condition

---

[82] *Newton* [2013] NSWLEC ¶ 17 (discussing *Hawks Nest Low Density Residential Development Control Plan No 48 2009* (Great Lakes Council) pt 3.

[83] *Newton* [2013] NSWLEC ¶ 16.

[84] *Id.* ¶ 51.

[85] *Id.* ¶ 25.

[86] *Id* ¶ 21.

[87] *Id.*

[88] *Id.*

was "so out of context" as to make it unreasonable.[89] If the application had concerned a greenfield site, different public policy considerations would have arisen.[90] The inclusion of the option to apply for an extension was also unreasonable for "holding out an illusion of hope…in circumstances where the outcome is highly speculative."[91] The second ground for striking down the time-limit condition was that all existing dwellings along Jimmy's Beach had a consistent setback from the road, so that this development would be no more vulnerable than any of the other existing dwellings. Third, compliance with the construction standards stipulated in condition 8 would make the property better protected than any of its neighbors, and this additional form of protection would be unjustifiably burdensome.[92] Finally, there had been no information available to the public generally, or to the Newtons as prospective purchasers, about the possible consequences of future coastal hazard management on development proposals, so the purchasers had not been adequately warned of the possibility of development restrictions.[93]

The Commissioner's rejection of this provision does not suggest that he was unconvinced of the impact of future conditions on the property. Indeed, an "inevitable corollary" of rejecting clause 7 was the need to uphold the validity of clause 8 relating to building standards:[94]

by 2033…there is a real and not insignificant risk that storm events could impact on the structural stability of this dwelling if conventional foundations construction standards…were to be adopted.[95]

Given that the deletion of clause 7 meant that the dwelling was likely to be occupied in 2033, it would be "completely irresponsible not to incorporate reasonable precautionary measures."[96] Indeed, Commissioner Moore made clear that it was only because of the requirement of better footings that he considered it appropriate to invalidate the time restriction on approval.

The different outcomes in the *Newton* and *Rainbow Shores* cases show that each new coastal development will be assessed on its merits and in its specific state legislative context, but some important themes emerge from the cases. The first is the importance of clear standards and benchmarks, clearly communicated to the public. In the case of *Rainbow Shores,* despite backtracking on aspects of their coastal hazards policy, the Queensland government had a consistent preference for avoiding new development

---

[89] *Newton* [2013] NSWLEC ¶ 41.
[90] *Id.* ¶ 34.
[91] *Id.* ¶ 40.
[92] *Id.* ¶¶ 31–33.
[93] *Id* ¶ 39.
[94] *Id.*
[95] *Id.* ¶ 53.
[96] *Id.* ¶ 55.

in erosion-prone areas. The exceptions to this general principle were clearly stipulated and were irrelevant to the proposed development. In *Newton*, Great Lakes Council had no development controls for Jimmy's Beach that restricted the construction of the proposed dwelling on coastal hazards grounds. The absence of any notation or warning on the planning certificate that accompanied the purchaser's contract of sale meant that the Newtons had no reason to suspect that their right to develop the land might be restricted as a consequence of climate change. This is especially noteworthy because, while the Land and Environment Court confirmed the importance of such measures, local governments' efforts to introduce information on planning certificates are being disciplined by proposed changes at the state government level.[97]

The second theme is the exposure of the property to *existing risk* and the current protection of the site. In the *Rainbow Shores* case, the development would have faced an inundation risk on basic storm surge probabilities, even without considering the exacerbating effects of sea-level rise. By contrast, the sand replenishment program undertaken for Jimmy's Beach managed the exposure of the property to immediate erosion risks.

The third theme relates to the importance of long-term adaptation planning for areas of existing development. The *Rainbow Shores* Court highlighted the implications of this being a major greenfield development and intensification of use in an area that otherwise faced fairly low exposure to coastal climate risks.[98] By contrast, *Newton* involved the development of a site that was surrounded by other houses, and the Commissioner specifically noted that his views may have differed had the application related to a greenfield coastal site.[99]

III. The Future of Coastal Climate Law in Australia

Coastal management in Australia has a long history of complexity, fragmentation, and failed attempts at integration. The addition of climate-related risks is exacerbating these weaknesses. In practice, the potential for planning regimes to drive coastal adaptation is constrained by the inherent trade-offs between short- and long-term values under uncertainty,[100] fragmented governance structures and resource allocation models, and a general tendency to protect private property rights over environmental or public interest values.[101] In particular, decision-makers are grappling with the tension between a precautionary approach to risk management, including a fear of legal liability if they get

---

[97] Draft Planning Circular, *supra* note 49.
[98] *Rainbow Shores, supra* note 75, ¶ 352 and ¶ 360.
[99] *Newton* [2013] NSWLEC ¶ 34.
[100] Nick Abel et al., *Sea Level Rise, Coastal Development and Planned Retreat: Analytical Framework, Governance Principles and an Australian Case Study*, 14 Envtl. Sci. & Pol'y 279, 285 (2011).
[101] Limp, Leap or Learn, *supra* note 14, at 33–34.

it wrong, and the risk of "over-adaptation"[102] in the face of uncertainty and discounting of future costs.

Like the coast itself, Australian coastal climate law is highly dynamic. But its shifts are driven as much by changes of government and the influence of landowner lobbying against new controls, as they are by being a response to the manifestation of erosion and inundation hazards or the scientific projections of future sea-level rise. The inconsistency in state approaches makes it hard for landowners or the wider community to understand or accept the need for strong measures.

These issues suggest that despite broad agreement about roles and responsibilities for adaptation in Australia, the question of who is best positioned to achieve particular adaptation objectives remains contentious. Many argue for stronger national leadership on many adaptation issues, either in setting national standards or coordinating a consistent position on matters, such as planning benchmarks and liability issues.[103] When the House of Representatives Standing Committee on Environment concluded in 2009 that reform was needed to adopt a nationally consistent planning benchmark, the Commonwealth government indicated its broad intention to develop a national coastal adaptation strategy. Nearly five years later, such a strategy is no closer to fruition, and indeed, the body most likely to develop such a framework—the Council of Australian Government's Standing Committee on Environment and Water—has been disbanded.[104] The need for a national framework remains.

The balance between state and local government roles and responsibilities, and the role of community stakeholders and private actors in adaptation planning, demands ongoing attention. Although the delegation of functions to local governments should, in theory, allow planning to reflect local needs and priorities, local government in Australia has very limited revenue-raising powers and, hence, limited resources.[105] Many smaller coastal councils have only limited resources with which to implement their planning responsibilities.[106] The high cost of mapping coastal hazards under climate change, and a lack of clear guidance on how to prioritize competing private and public values, has led to considerable variation in the quality of coastal management plans and adaptation strategies. A clear need is emerging for clarification in state statutory regimes to ensure that public goods and long-term interests are adequately protected in the face of strong pressure from the owners of at-risk properties.[107]

---

[102] AUST. DEP'T OF CLIMATE CHANGE, *supra* note 1, at 6.

[103] *See* MANAGING OUR COASTAL ZONE, *supra* note 8, at 253 (discussing submissions).

[104] COUNCIL OF AUSTL. GOV'TS, COAG COMMUNIQUE (2013), *available at* http://www.coag.gov.au/node/516 (last visited Feb. 20, 2014).

[105] LIMP, LEAP OR LEARN, *supra* note 14, at 39.

[106] *Id.*

[107] *See generally* Bruce Thom, *Climate Change, Coastal Hazards and the Public Trust Doctrine*, 8 MACQUARIE J. INT'L & COMP. ENVTL. L. 21 (2012).

State governments must play the lead role in setting basic planning benchmarks and assisting local governments with a consistent methodology to ensure that these benchmarks are operationalized in strategic planning and development approvals. In addition to mapping the coastal hazards likely to affect urban areas, effective long-term adaptation planning must also understand climate risks and exposure or adaptation options for coastal ecosystems and other environmental values. Clearer guidance is needed regarding the prioritization of public values, such as beach access and amenity and coastal ecosystem conservation, relative to private property protection, over a range of time frames.[108]

Recent experience in Australia suggests that coastal adaptation planning and decision-making has not yet succeeded in accommodating the differing values and risk tolerances of different actors.[109] If future reforms are to endure, decision-making processes will need to be adjusted to reflect the values and interests of a wide range of constituents, many of whom (like future generations and environmental objects) have no representation in current processes.[110] There are already isolated examples of more collaborative community engagement processes for coastal adaptation; project-specific processes have been trialed in a number of local and regional areas around the country, funded by the Commonwealth. Tasmania's Coastal Adaptation Pathways project, for example, transcended the boundaries of formal land use planning and involved deep stakeholder engagement in an effort to improve community buy-in on difficult decisions.[111] So far, these innovative processes are yet to result in equally innovative outcomes, and the case studies emphasize the need for mechanisms by which to ensure the representation and consideration of public interest values, especially environmental values, in coastal adaptation planning.[112]

Conclusion

Climate change poses significant threats to Australia's coastal identity. Important steps have been taken toward better adaptation planning to address these threats, but some

---

[108] *Id.; see also* John Corkill, Low Tide for Non-Governmental Interests in NSW Coastal Management, and L. Scarlett & P. Gangaiya, Local Government at the Interface between Federal and State Policy and Community Expectations for Coastal Hazard Management, papers presented to the 21st N.S.W. Coastal Mgmt. Conference, Kiama N.S.W. Austl. (Nov. 6–9, 2012).

[109] England, *supra* note 59, at 392.

[110] Donald R. Nelson, W. Neil Adger & Katrina Brown, *Adaptation to Environmental Change: Contributions of a Resilience Framework*, 32 ANN. REV. ENV'T & RESOURCES 395, 411 (2007), *available at* http://eprints. icrisat.ac.in/4245/1/AnnualReviewofEnvResources_32_395-419_2007.pdf.

[111] *See Transferable Lessons for Climate Change Adaptation Planning, supra* note 12.

[112] Western Australia's 2013 *State Coastal Planning Policy No. 2.6*, s 5.8 contains strong commitments to the public interest. It requires that local authorities make adequate provision for community participation in coastal planning and management, and that consultation strategies should promote informed community input. Public access to the coast, consistent with the interests of safety, security, and protection of coastal resources, is clearly prioritized.

of this progress has been undone before its positive effects could be realized. Australia's recent experience with coastal adaptation planning offers some valuable lessons for other countries. It illustrates the potential value of a range of planning instruments, both new and old, and the difficulty of introducing new restrictions on development rights, particularly in existing urban areas. It highlights the value of clearly defined roles and responsibilities, and statutory guidance on how to prioritize public and private interests. More than anything, however, it demonstrates the importance of strong commitment at all levels of government to long-term strategic adaptation planning that can safeguard the social, cultural, spiritual, ecological, and economic values of the Australian coast.

29 Legal and Policy Responses to Climate Change in the Philippines
Dr. Lowell Bautista*

* The author would like to thank Dean Antonio La Viña and Cecilia Therese Guiao of the Ateneo de Manila School of Government, and Professor Rommel Casis and Ms. Jennifer Castro of the University of the Philippines College of Law, for their invaluable research assistance. The author is also grateful to Dr. Lyra Reyes for her endless patience and support.

Introduction

The Philippines is among the most vulnerable countries in the world to climate change.[1] The 2014 Climate Change Vulnerability Index (CCVI) placed the Philippines, of 193 countries rated, as the ninth most at risk to the physical and economic impacts of climate change.[2] The country's capital, Manila, is considered the second most vulnerable of the world's megacities to the effects of climate change.[3]

The location, geography, and topography of the Philippines expose it to natural disasters, which are further exacerbated by the effects of climate change. In the 2012 World Risk Report, the Philippines was ranked third of 173 countries in terms of disaster risk.[4] The Philippines is highly vulnerable to climate change because of its large and growing population, long coastlines, abundant low-lying areas, reliance on the agricultural sector, and dependence on natural resources.

The Philippine archipelago is prone to natural hazards due to its location along the western North Pacific Basin typhoon belt, where one-third of all tropical cyclones originate, with approximately five to seven destructive tropical cycles per year. It is also located in the Pacific Ring of Fire where the Philippine Sea and Eurasian plates converge, causing a large number of earthquakes and volcanic eruptions to occur.[5]

Among the many threats posed by climate change, rising sea level poses both immediate and lasting impacts on the Philippines.[6] The impact of sea-level rise will have serious implications for the country's low-lying coastal areas. Although the actual land loss resulting from sea-level rise due to coastal erosion and coastal plain flooding is only a small fraction of the national territory, the impacts will nevertheless be substantial. Philippine coastal zones are not just densely populated; they are also areas of high

---

[1] ARIEF ANSHORY YUSUF & HERMINIA FRANCISCO, HOTSPOTS! MAPPING CLIMATE CHANGE VULNERABILITY IN SOUTHEAST ASIA 12 (2010). In this 2010 mapping assessment study, sixteen of the seventy-four Philippine provinces surveyed were ranked in the top fifty most vulnerable in Southeast Asia, with Manila as the most vulnerable in the country and the seventh in Southeast Asia. *Id.* at 25.

[2] *Climate Change and Environmental Risk Atlas 2014*, MAPLECROFT, http://maplecroft.com/portfolio/new-analysis/2013/10/30/31-global-economic-output-forecast-face-high-or-extreme-climate-change-risks-2025-maplecroft-risk-atlas/ (last visited Mar. 17, 2014).

[3] *Maplecroft: Climate Change Vulnerability Index 2013—Most at Risk Cities*, PREVENTIONWEB, http://www.preventionweb.net/english/professional/maps/v.php?id=29649 (last visited Mar. 17, 2014).

[4] WORLD RISK REPORT 2012 9 (2012), *available at* http://www.worldriskreport.com/uploads/media/WRR_2012_en_online.pdf.

[5] ROBERT GABLER, JAMES PETERSEN & L. MICHAEL TRAPASSO, ESSENTIALS OF PHYSICAL GEOGRAPHY 406 (2006). *See also* WORLD RISK REPORT 2012, *supra* note 4, at 19 (ranking the Philippines third in the world in terms of exposure to natural hazards).

[6] *See* BEN BOER, ROSS RAMSAY & DONALD R. ROTHWELL, INTERNATIONAL ENVIRONMENTAL LAW IN THE ASIA PACIFIC 152 (1998); *see* ALEX RENTON, SUFFERING THE SCIENCE: CLIMATE CHANGE, PEOPLE, AND POVERTY 35 (2009), *available at* http://www.oxfam.org/sites/www.oxfam.org/files/bp130-suffering-the-science.pdf (positing that a thirty-centimeter sea-level rise would affect 500,000 in the Philippines, and a one-meter rise would affect 2.5 million people).

economic activity such as tourism. Tourism is an important source of income, and the country is likely to suffer huge losses in revenue. In addition, nearshore or estuarine habitats for fish, and other wildlife and plants, are also at risk due to sea-level rise. Sea-level rise threatens the fresh water supply for drinking and irrigation because of saltwater intrusion into coastal and groundwater resources.

The potential impacts of climate change on the Philippines could be catastrophic. The economic exposure of the Philippines to the impacts of extreme climate-related events was recently highlighted by Typhoon Haiyan in 2013.[7] Haiyan caused an estimated $700 million in damage to agriculture and infrastructure, completely destroyed more than half a million homes, and caused a projected 0.3 to 0.8 percent decline in the country's economic growth.[8] Thus, it is clear that the economic damage caused by natural disasters is significant. In addition, extreme weather events caused by climatic variations also claim people's lives. In 2009, for instance, Typhoon Ketsana caused at least 295 deaths in the Philippines and $110 million in damages to crops and infrastructure.[9]

The climate vulnerability of the Philippines is further aggravated by non-climate-related factors such as environmental degradation and weak governance characterized by institutions that lack the necessary capacity, capital, and infrastructure to address these issues.[10] The unequivocal effects of climate change will certainly impinge on the country's decades of serious effort to address poverty and promote economic growth and sustainable development. Thus, climate change is an intergenerational equity issue.[11] Indeed, given the above realities, it is imperative for the Philippines to have a coordinated legal and policy framework, strategy, and mechanism to address climate change and its impacts.

This chapter will examine the legal and policy responses to climate change in the Philippines. Section I will discuss the Philippine legal framework on climate change. This section will cover the relevant constitutional provisions, national policies, and international law foundation of Philippine climate change law and policy. Section I also

---

[7] Haiyan is the deadliest Philippine typhoon on record, the strongest storm recorded at landfall, and unofficially the strongest typhoon ever recorded in terms of wind speed. The typhoon affected 16 million people, displaced 4 million people, with casualties of at least 6,000 people and damages in the amount of PhP40 billion. *See* National Disaster Risk Reduction and Management Council, NDRRMC Update, SitRep No. 107, Effects of Typhoon "Yolanda" (Haiyan) (Mar. 14, 2014) at 1–2, *available at* http://www.ndrrmc.gov.ph/attachments/article/1125/Update%20Yolanda%20Sitrep%20107.pdf.

[8] Cris Larano, *Typhoon's Economic Impact on Philippines Likely to Be Minimal*, WALL ST. J. (Nov. 30, 2013), http://blogs.wsj.com/searealtime/2013/11/30/typhoons-economic-impact-on-philippines-likely-to-be-minimal/.

[9] UNITED NATIONS, STATISTICAL YEARBOOK FOR THE ASIA AND THE PACIFIC 2009, at 219 (2010).

[10] *See, e.g.,* Paul D. Hutchcroft, *The Philippines, in* CLIMATE CHANGE & NATIONAL SECURITY: A COUNTRY-LEVEL ANALYSIS, 43, 47–48 (Daniel Moran ed., 2011).

[11] *Preface to* NATIONAL FRAMEWORK STRATEGY ON CLIMATE CHANGE, 2010–2022, at 3, *available at* http://www.neda.gov.ph/wp-content/uploads/2013/10/nfscc_sgd.pdf; Oposa v. Factoran, G.R. No. 101083, 224 S.C.R.A. 792, 808 (July 30, 1993) (Phil.), *reprinted in* 33 I.L.M. 173 (1994); CONST. (1987), art. II, sec. 16. (Phil.).

will address the primary pieces of domestic legislation relevant to climate change—the Philippine Climate Change Act[12] and the Philippine Disaster Risk Reduction and Management Act[13]—and will also discuss other domestic environment-related laws relevant to climate change regulation. Section II will address challenges, constraints, and opportunities that have positively impacted or hindered climate change efforts in the Philippines. Specifically, this section will focus on three interrelated factors: the relationship between climate change and economic growth, macroeconomic and sectoral vulnerabilities, and security and jurisdictional issues.

I. Philippine Legal Framework on Climate Change

The Philippines is regarded as a global and regional leader in climate change law.[14] In 2009, it enacted the first stand-alone climate change law in Southeast Asia, the Climate Change Act.[15] In 2012, United Nations Special Envoy Margareta Wahlström called it the "best in the world."[16] The Philippine Climate Change Commission, created under the Climate Change Act, formulated the National Strategic Framework on Climate Change (NSFCC), and the National Climate Change Action Plan (NCCAP), and has developed guidelines for the Local Climate Change Action Plan (LCCAP). In 2010, the Philippine Disaster Risk Reduction and Management Act was enacted.[17] In 2012, the Philippine Survival Fund was established to finance climate adaptation programs and projects based on the National Strategic Framework.[18] There is a plethora of other environment and climate-change-related domestic legislation. Indeed, the country has

---

[12] An Act Mainstreaming Climate Change into Government Policy Formulations Establishing the Framework Strategy and Program on Climate Change, Creating for This Purpose the Climate Change Commission and for Other Purposes, Rep. Act No. 9729 (Oct. 23, 2009) (Phil.), *available at* http://www.gov.ph/2009/10/23/republic-act-no/ [hereinafter Climate Change Act].

[13] An Act Strengthening The Philippine Disaster Risk Reduction and Management System, Providing for the National Disaster Risk Reduction and Management Framework and Institutionalizing the National Disaster Risk Reduction and Management Plan, Rep. Act No. 10121 (May 27, 2010) (Phil.), *available at* http://www.gov.ph/2010/05/27/republic-act-no-10121/ [hereinafter Philippine Disaster Risk Reduction and Management Act of 2010].

[14] Antonio G.M. La Viña & Cecilia T. Guiao, *Climate Change and the Law: Issues and Challenges in the Philippines*, 58 ATENEO L.J. 1, 23 (2013); Isabelle Whitehead, *Climate Change Law in Southeast Asia: Risk, Regulation and Regional Innovation*, 16 ASIA PAC. J. ENVTL. L. 141, 158 (2013).

[15] Climate Change Act, *supra* note 12.

[16] Michael Lim Ubac, *UN Lauds Philippines' Climate Change Laws "World's Best,"* PHIL. DAILY INQUIRER (May 4, 2012), http://globalnation.inquirer.net/35695/un-lauds-philippines'-climate-change-laws-'world's-best.'

[17] Philippine Disaster Risk Reduction and Management Act of 2010, *supra* note 13.

[18] An Act Establishing the People's Survival Fund to Provide Long-Term Finance Streams to Enable the Government to Effectively Address the Problem of Climate Change, Amending for the Purpose, Republic Act No. 9729, Otherwise Known as the "Climate Change Act of 2009", and for Other Purposes, Rep. Act No. 10174 (Aug. 16, 2012) (Phil.), *available at* http://www.gov.ph/2012/08/16/republic-act-no-10174/ [hereinafter Rep. Act No. 10174].

come a long way since the creation of the Inter-Agency Committee on Climate Change (IACCC) in the 1990s, which was among the earliest efforts undertaken to draft policies and prepare strategies for climate change negotiations.[19]

The Philippines is a state party to almost all of the major global agreements on climate change. The Philippines ratified the United Nations Framework Convention on Climate Change (UNFCCC) on August 2, 1994 and the Kyoto Protocol on November 20, 2003. The Philippines is a state party to the Vienna Convention for the Protection of the Ozone Layer and related protocols, having acceded on July 17, 1991.[20] In January 2005, the Philippines also adopted the Hyogo Framework for Action 2005–2015 (HFA): Building the Resilience of Nations and Communities to Disasters, the blueprint to guide efforts on disaster risk reduction and vulnerability to natural hazards.[21]

The Philippines is a good example of climate change adaptation integration and disaster risk reduction.[22] This discussion that follows will address the Philippine legal framework on climate change. The first and second subsections will explain the constitutional mandate and national policies, and international legal commitments with respect to climate change, respectively. The succeeding subsections will discuss the principal domestic legislation related to climate change: the Climate Change Act and the Philippine Disaster Risk Reduction and Management Act, as well as other domestic laws with a climate change implication.

A. CONSTITUTIONAL MANDATE AND NATIONAL POLICIES

Climate change is not directly mentioned in the 1987 Philippine Constitution, as the concept had not gained enough currency at the time it was drafted. However, the 1987 Philippine Constitution declares that the State shall protect and advance the right of the people to a balanced and healthful ecology in accord with the rhythm and harmony of nature.[23] The 1987 Philippine Constitution places a high regard on the environment

---

[19] Rodel D. Lasco et al., *The Role of Local Government Units in Mainstreaming Climate Change Adaptation: The Case of Albay, Philippines, in* LOCAL CLIMATE CHANGE AND SOCIETY 54, 61 (M.A. Mohamed Salih ed., 2013).

[20] Montreal Protocol on Substances That Deplete the Ozone Layer, Sept. 16, 1987, 1522 U.N.T.S. 3, 26 I.L.M. 1541, *as amended.*

[21] PHILIPPINES COUNTRY REPORT ON DISASTER RESPONSE MANAGEMENT 1 (2011), *available at* http://www.aipasecretariat.org/wp-content/uploads/2011/07/3.Disaster-Response-Management.pdf (last visited Mar. 30, 2014).

[22] Dewald van Niekerk, *Climate Change Adaptation and Disaster Law, in* RESEARCH HANDBOOK ON CLIMATE CHANGE ADAPTATION LAW 142, 161 (Jonathan Verschuuren ed., 2013). Tolentino opines that "[o]n a policy level alone, the Philippines is said to have one of the world's most developed approaches to environmental protection and preservation." Francis N. Tolentino, *An Environmental Writ: The Philippines' Avatar*, 35 IBP J. 117, 119 (2010).

[23] CONST. (1987), art. II, sec. 16 (Phil.).

and natural resources, and views them from a balanced perspective as a human rights concern, a matter of social justice, and a resource allocation issue. [24]

The imperative to take a balanced and integrated approach to environment and development issues by incorporating sustainable development principles and concepts in the national priorities of government has long been recognized in Philippine national policies. In 1991, the Philippine Strategy for Sustainable Development (PSSD) recognized the compelling need to integrate environmental considerations into decision-making.[25] The PSSD stressed the mutual compatibility of environmental protection and economic growth, with growth objectives allowing for not only the needs of society but also the natural dynamics and carrying capacities of ecosystems. The goal of the PSSD is to achieve economic growth that adequately protects the country's biological resources and its diversity, vital ecosystem functions, and overall environmental quality.[26]

The Philippines adheres to the sustainable development principles embodied in the Rio Declaration adopted by the United Nations Conference on Environment and Development (UNCED) in Rio de Janeiro, Brazil in 1992, to which the Philippines is a signatory.[27] The Philippine Agenda 21, adopted in 1996, is the nation's blueprint for sustainable development, which contained cross-sectoral strategies to attain an ecologically and socially rational economic growth path for the country.[28] Another major milestone that came out of national initiatives in response to UNCED was the creation of an Inter-Agency Committee on Climate Change (IACCC) in 1991.[29] The functions of IACCC, among others, include the formulation of policies and response strategies related to climate change, and to establish working groups to monitor and assess local climate change and its environmental and socioeconomic impact in coordination with international agencies.[30] The current 2011–2016 Philippine Development Plan (PDP), the country's economic blueprint, has identified disaster risk reduction and management (DRRM) and climate change adaptation (CCA) as principal cross-cutting priorities.[31]

---

[24] Myrna S. Feliciano, *Global Climate Change and Recent Developments in Philippine Environmental Law*, 35 IBP J. 93, 95 (2010).

[25] Creating a Philippine Council for Sustainable Development, Exec. Ord. No.15 (Sept. 1, 1992), *available at* http://www.gov.ph/1992/09/01/executive-order-no-15-s-1992/; Strengthening the Philippine Council for Sustainable Development, Exec. Ord. No. 370 (Sept. 26, 1996), *available at* http://www.gov.ph/1996/09/26/executive-order-no-370-s-1996/.

[26] *Philippine Strategy for Sustainable Development*, NAT'L ECON. & DEV. AUTH., http://www.psdn.org.ph/agenda21/pssd.htm (last visited Mar. 17, 2014).

[27] Feliciano, *supra* note 24, at 95.

[28] *Executive Summary*, PHIL. AGENDA 21, http://www.psdn.org.ph/agenda21/execsum.htm (last visited Mar. 30, 2014).

[29] Creating an Inter-Agency Committee on Climate Change, Admin. Ord. No. 220 (May 8, 1991) (Phil.), *available at* http://www.gov.ph/1991/05/08/administrative-order-no-220-s-1991/.

[30] *Id.* § 3.

[31] *Philippine Development Plan 2011–2016*, NAT'L ECON. & DEV. AUTH., http://www.neda.gov.ph/?p=1128 (last visited Mar. 30, 2014).

B. INTERNATIONAL LEGAL COMMITMENTS

Even though it is considered legally non-binding, the United Nations Framework Convention on Climate Change (UNFCCC) is regarded as the primary international agreement addressing anthropogenic climate change. The UNFCCC entered into force on March 21, 1994, and has almost universal membership with 196 states parties in 2014. The UNFCCC does not contain any enforcement mechanisms, nor does it set any binding limits on greenhouse gas emissions for individual countries. The Kyoto Protocol, however, established binding limits on greenhouse gas emissions.

The Philippines is a party to the UNFCCC having signed it on June 12, 1992, and ratified it on August 2, 1994. As such, the Philippines has committed itself to act to protect the climate system on the basis of "common but differentiated responsibilities," and to make general commitments to address climate change through, inter alia, climate change mitigation and adaptation.[32] As a developing country, the Philippines is classified as a Non-Annex I party. In fulfilment of its UNFCCC commitments, the Philippines submitted its First National Communication in May 2000.[33]

The Philippines ratified the Kyoto Protocol on November 20, 2003.[34] The Philippines adopted the Hyogo Framework for Action 2005–2015 in January 2005.[35] It is also a party to the UN Convention to Combat Desertification (UNCCD).[36] The Philippines is also a state party to other global conventions that address issues related to the environment with implications for climate change policies, such as the Convention on Biological Diversity,[37] the Convention on the Control of Transboundary Movement of Hazardous Wastes,[38] and the UN Convention on the Law of the Sea,[39] among others.

At the regional level, and within the Association of Southeast Asian Nations (ASEAN) framework, there have been numerous initiatives, declarations, and statements that address

---

[32] United Nations Framework Convention on Climate Change, art. 3(1), 4, *available at* https://unfccc.int/essential_background/convention/background/items/1349.php [hereinafter UNFCCC].

[33] *See generally* THE PHILIPPINES' INITIAL NATIONAL COMMUNICATION ON CLIMATE CHANGE (1999), *available at* http://climatedigitallibrary.org/sites/default/files/Philippines%201st.pdf.

[34] Montreal Protocol on Substances That Deplete the Ozone Layer, *supra* note 20.

[35] PHILIPPINES COUNTRY REPORT ON DISASTER RESPONSE MANAGEMENT 1 (2011), *available at* http://www.aipasecretariat.org/wp-content/uploads/2011/07/3.Disaster-Response-Management.pdf (last visited Mar. 30, 2014).

[36] *Secretariat of the United Nations Convention to Combat Desertification, Update on Ratification of the UNCCD, as of 28 March 2014*, UNCCD, http://www.unccd.int/Lists/SiteDocumentLibrary/convention/ratification-eng.pdf (last visited Mar. 30, 2014).

[37] Convention on Biological Diversity, June 5, 1992, 1760 U.N.T.S. 79, 31 I.L.M. 818, *available at* http://www.cbd.int/doc/legal/cbd-en.pdf [hereinafter CBD]. The Philippines ratified the Convention on October 8, 1993.

[38] Basel Convention on the Control of Transboundary Movements of Hazardous Waste and Their Disposal, Mar. 22, 1989, 1673 U.N.T.S. 126. The Philippines ratified the Convention on October 21, 1993.

[39] United Nations Convention on the Law of the Sea, Dec. 10, 1982, 1833 U.N.T.S. 3, 21 I.L.M. 1261 (entered into force Nov. 16, 1996). The Philippines ratified the Convention on May 8, 1984.

climate change.[40] Climate change constitutes one of the ten priority areas of regional importance as reflected in the Blueprint for the ASEAN Socio-cultural Community (ASCC Blueprint) 2009–2015.[41] In 2009, the ASEAN Working Group on Climate Change (AWGCC) was created to oversee the implementation of the relevant action lines in the ASCC Blueprint. In 2012, the Action Plan on Joint Response to Climate Change was developed to provide a more detailed reference in implementing the Blueprint.[42]

Another important related regional initiative is the ASEAN Agreement on Disaster Management and Emergency Response (AADMER), which the Philippines ratified on September 14, 2009. AADMER is a regional agreement binding on ASEAN Member States to promote regional cooperation and collaboration in reducing disaster losses and intensifying joint emergency response to disasters in the ASEAN region and as part of the region's commitment to the Hyogo Framework for Action (HFA).[43]

C. CLIMATE CHANGE ACT

1. Overview

The principal domestic legislation that addresses climate change in the Philippines is Republic Act No. 9729 or the Philippine Climate Change Act, enacted in 2009.[44] The Climate Change Act provides the legal framework to systematically integrate climate change and disaster risk reduction in national and sub-national government policies, plans, programs, and projects.[45] The law addresses climate change in the context of

---

[40] Some of these declarations and statements supporting climate change since 2007 include: ASEAN Declaration on Environmental Sustainability (13th ASEAN Summit in 2007); ASEAN Declaration on COP-13 to the UNFCCC and CMP-3 to the Kyoto Protocol (13th ASEAN Summit in 2007); Singapore Declaration on Climate Change, Energy and the Environment (3rd EAS Summit in 2007); Joint Ministerial Statement of the 1st EAS Energy Ministers Meeting (2007); Ministerial Statement of the Inaugural EAS Environment Ministers Meeting (2008); ASEAN Joint Statement on Climate Change to COP-15 to the UNFCCC and CMP-5 to the Kyoto Protocol (15th ASEAN Summit in 2009); Singapore Resolution on Environmental Sustainability and Climate Change (11th AMME in 2009). *See* Dr. Raman Letchumanan, *Is There an ASEAN Policy on Climate Change?, in* LSE IDEAS, CLIMATE CHANGE: IS SOUTHEAST ASIA UP TO THE CHALLENGE? 52 (2010), *available at* http://www.lse.ac.uk/IDEAS/publications/reports/pdf/SR004/ASEC.pdf.

[41] ASEAN SOCIO-CULTURAL COMMUNITY BLUEPRINT 19 (2009), *available at* http://www.asean.org/archive/5187-19.pdf.

[42] ASEAN Action Plan on Joint Response to Climate Change (2012), adopted 12th ASEAN Ministerial Meeting on Environment, Sept. 26, 2012, http://environment.asean.org/wp-content/uploads/2014/02/ANNEX-8-Lead-Countries-for-ASEAN-Action-Plan-on-Joint-Response-to-Climate-Change-27-March-2013.pdf (last visited Mar. 30, 2014).

[43] PHILIPPINES COUNTRY REPORT ON DISASTER RESPONSE MANAGEMENT, *supra* note 21, at 4; ASEAN Agreement on Disaster Management and Emergency Response, July 26, 2005, *available at* http://agreement.asean.org/media/download/20140119170000.pdf.

[44] Climate Change Act, *supra* note 12.

[45] *Id.* § 2.

sustainable development by adopting policies that are gender-sensitive, pro-children, and pro-poor. It incorporates disaster risk into climate change programs and initiatives. The law further integrates the concept of climate change in various phases of policy formulation, development plans, poverty reduction strategies, and other development tools and techniques by all agencies and instrumentalities of the government.[46]

2. Key Provisions

The Climate Change Act mandated the formulation of a National Strategic Framework and Program on Climate Change,[47] and a National Climate Change Action Plan.[48] The law recognized the front-line role of local government units (LGUs) and mandated the formulation of Local Climate Change Action Plans in their respective areas, consistent with the provisions of the Local Government Code, the Framework, and the National Climate Change Action Plan.[49]

The National Framework Strategy on Climate Change (NFSCC) 2010–2022, formulated through a broad-based consultation process, was signed and approved in April 2010. It was followed by the formulation and adoption of the Philippine Strategy on Climate Change Adaptation (PSCCA) 2010–2022, the National Climate Change Action Plan (NCCAP) 2011–2028, and the Philippine National REDD+ Strategy 2010–2020.[50]

In 2012, the Climate Change Act was amended by Republic Act No. 10174.[51] Among its amendments included the creation of the Peoples' Survival Fund, a special fund in the National Treasury for the financing of adaptation programs and projects based on the National Strategic Framework.[52] The fund is for adaptation activities of local governments and communities, including improvement of the monitoring of vector-borne diseases triggered by climate change; forecasting and early warning systems as part of preparedness for climate-related hazards; preventive measures, planning, preparedness, and management of impacts relating to climate change, including contingency planning, in particular, for droughts and floods in areas prone to extreme climate events; and community adaptation support programs by local organizations accredited by the Commission, among others.[53]

---

[46] *Id.*

[47] This initiative was originally named "Framework Strategy and Program on Climate Change." *See* Climate Change Act, *supra* note 12, § 11; *see also* Rep. Act No. 10174, *supra* note 18, § 7.

[48] Climate Change Act, *supra* note 12, § 13.

[49] *Id.* §14.

[50] *National Action Plans*, Phil. MEA Portal, http://mea.denr.gov.ph/index.php?option=com_content&view=article&id=121&Itemid=193&current=102 (last visited Mar. 30, 2014).

[51] Rep. Act No. 10174, *supra* note 18.

[52] *Id.* § 13.

[53] Climate Change Act, *supra* note 12, § 20, *as amended*.

3. Institutional Mechanisms

The Climate Change Commission is the principal agency created by the Climate Change Act. The Commission is an independent and autonomous body with the status of a national government agency attached to the Office of the President.[54] It is the sole policymaking body of the government, tasked to coordinate, monitor, and evaluate the programs and action plans of the government relating to climate change.[55] The Commission is composed of the President of the Republic of the Philippines, who serves as the Chairperson, and three Commissioners to be appointed by the President, one of whom serves as the Vice Chairperson of the Commission.[56]

The Commissioners, who must be experts in climate change by virtue of their educational background, training, and experience, hold office for a period of six years, and may be subject to reappointment.[57] The functions of the Climate Change Commission include (1) formulating a Framework Strategy on Climate Change to serve as the basis for a program for climate change planning, research and development, extension, and monitoring of activities on climate change;[58] (2) recommending key development investments in climate-sensitive sectors such as water resources, agriculture, forestry, coastal and marine resources, health, and infrastructure to ensure the achievement of national sustainable development goals;[59] (3) formulating strategies on mitigating greenhouse gases and other anthropogenic causes of climate change;[60] and (4) in coordination with the Department of Foreign Affairs, representing the Philippines in climate change negotiations.[61]

There are a number of other offices created under the Climate Change Act. The Climate Change Office is headed by a Vice Chairperson of the Commission as its Executive Director, who assists the Commission.[62] A national Panel of Technical Experts also needs to be constituted by the Commission, consisting of practitioners in disciplines that are related to climate change, including disaster risk reduction; the Panel shall provide technical advice to the Commission in climate science, technologies, and best practices for risk assessment and enhancement of adaptive capacity of vulnerable human settlements to potential impacts of climate change.[63] The Climate Change Act also created the Joint Congressional Oversight Committee to monitor the implementation of the Act, which is composed of five Senators and five Representatives to be appointed by the Senate President and the Speaker of the House of Representatives, respectively.[64]

---

[54] Climate Change Act, *supra* note 12, § 4; *see also* Rep. Act No. 10174, *supra* note 18, § 3.

[55] *Id.*

[56] Climate Change Act, *supra* note 12, § 5; *see also* Rep. Act No. 10174, *supra* note 18, § 4.

[57] Climate Change Act, *supra* note 12, § 7; *see also* Rep. Act No. 10174, *supra* note 18, § 6.

[58] Climate Change Act, *supra* note 12, § 9(c); *see also* Rep. Act No. 10174, *supra* note 18, §7.

[59] Climate Change Act, *supra* note 12, § 9(f); *see also* Rep. Act No. 10174, *supra* note 18, § 7.

[60] Climate Change Act, *supra* note 12, § 9(i); *see also* Rep. Act No. 10174, *supra* note 18, § 7.

[61] Climate Change Act, *supra* note 12, § 9(k); *see also* Rep. Act No. 10174, *supra* note 18, § 7.

[62] Climate Change Act, *supra* note 12, § 8.

[63] *Id.* § 10.

[64] *Id.* § 19.

In 2011, through Executive Order No. 43, the Cabinet Cluster on Climate Change Adaptation and Mitigation was created to take the lead in pursuing measures to adapt to and mitigate the effects of climate change on the Philippine archipelago and undertake all the necessary preparation for both natural and man-made disasters. Through Republic Act No. 10174, which amended the Climate Change Act in 2012, the People's Survival Fund Board was created to provide overall strategic guidance in the management and use of the Peoples' Survival Fund.[65]

D. PHILIPPINE DISASTER RISK REDUCTION AND MANAGEMENT ACT

1. Overview

The primary domestic legislation on disaster risk reduction is Republic Act No. 10121, otherwise known as the "Philippine Disaster Risk Reduction and Management Act of 2010," signed into law in 2010.[66] The law provides for the development of policies and plans and the implementation of actions and measures pertaining to all aspects of disaster risk reduction and management, including good governance, risk assessment and early warning, knowledge building and awareness raising, reduction of underlying risk factors, and preparedness for effective response and early recovery.[67]

The law adopts a holistic, comprehensive, integrated, and proactive disaster risk reduction and management approach in lessening the socioeconomic and environmental impacts of disasters, including climate change, and promoting the involvement and participation of all sectors and all stakeholders concerned, at all levels, especially the local community.[68] The law also aims to mainstream disaster risk reduction and climate change in development processes as well as into the peace process and conflict resolution approaches, while ensuring that such measures are gender-responsive, sensitive to indigenous knowledge systems, and respectful of human rights.[69]

2. Key Provisions

The law adopts Community-Based Disaster Risk Reduction and Management (CBDRRM), whereby communities and people at risk are at the heart of decision-making and implementation of disaster risk reduction and management activities to reduce their vulnerabilities and enhance their capacities[70]

An important feature of RA 101211 is the decentralization to local government units (LGUs) of responsibilities and authority for implementing disaster risk reduction

---

[65] *Id.* §§ 21, 22, *as amended.*

[66] Philippine Disaster Risk Reduction and Management Act of 2010, *supra* note 13.

[67] Rep. Act No. 10174, *supra* note 18, § 4.

[68] Philippine Disaster Risk Reduction and Management Act of 2010, *supra* note 13, § 2(d).

[69] *Id.* § 2(g)(i)(j).

[70] *Id.* § 3(e).

measures,[71] and the Civil Society Organizations (CSO), which include nongovernmental organizations (NGOs), professional associations, and community-based organizations (CBOs); faith-based organizations; peoples' organizations; social movements; and labor unions.[72] The law mandates that four members of the National Disaster Risk Reduction and Management Council come from the CSOs. Furthermore, the Office of Civil Defense is mandated to create an enabling environment for substantial and sustainable participation of CSOs, private groups, volunteers, and communities, and to recognize their contributions to the government's disaster risk reduction efforts.[73]

The law further mandates the formulation of a National Disaster Risk Reduction and Management Framework (NDRRMF) providing for a comprehensive, all hazards, multi-sectoral, interagency and community-based approach to disaster risk reduction and management,[74] and a National Disaster Risk Reduction and Management Plan (NDRRMP), to be formulated and implemented by the Office of Civil Defense (OCD) that sets out goals and specific objectives for reducing disaster risks, together with related actions to accomplish these objectives.[75]

3. Institutional Mechanisms

The Philippine Disaster Risk Reduction and Management Act of 2010 created the National Disaster Risk Reduction and Management Council (NDRMC), an agency tasked with crafting and implementing disaster risk reduction policies.[76] Among the functions of the NDRMC include formulation of the National Disaster Risk Reduction and Management Framework (NDRRMF), which is reviewable every five years or as necessary; it is the principal guide to disaster risk reduction and management efforts in the country.[77] The NDRMC's other duties include advising the President on the status of disaster preparedness, prevention, mitigation, response, and rehabilitation operations being undertaken by the government and other sectors;[78] and in coordination with the Climate Change Commission, formulating and implementing a framework for climate change adaptation and disaster risk reduction and management from which all policies, programs, and projects shall be based,[79] among others.

Other offices created under the law include the Office of Civil Defense, whose primary mission is to administer a comprehensive national civil defense and disaster risk reduction and management program.[80] Among its other functions include reviewing and evaluating

---

[71] *Id.* § 11.

[72] *Id.* § 3(c).

[73] RA 101211, §§ 5(hh), 9(l).

[74] Philippine Disaster Risk Reduction and Management Act of 2010, *supra* note 13, § 3(y).

[75] *Id.* § 3(z).

[76] *Id.* § 5 (listing the composition of the NDRMC).

[77] *Id.* § 6(a).

[78] *Id.* § 6(c).

[79] Philippine Disaster Risk Reduction and Management Act of 2010, *supra* note 13, § 6(n).

[80] *Id.* §§ 8, 9 (specifying the powers and functions of the OCD).

the Local Disaster Risk Reduction and Management Plans (LDRRMPs) to facilitate the integration of disaster risk reduction measures into the local Comprehensive Development Plan (CDP) and Comprehensive Land Use Plan (CLUP).[81]

The law further creates relevant organizational structures at the regional and local levels through the Regional Disaster Risk Reduction and Management Councils (RDRRMCs)[82] and the Provincial, City, and Municipal Disaster Risk Reduction and Management Councils.[83] The law further established a Local Disaster Risk Reduction and Management Office (LDRRMO) in every province, city, and municipality, and a Barangay Disaster Risk Reduction and Management Committee (BDRRMC) in every barangay responsible for setting the direction, development, implementation, and coordination of disaster risk management programs within their territorial jurisdiction.[84] The law also provides that two funds be established to support disaster risk management activities: the National Disaster Risk Reduction and Management Fund[85] and the Local Disaster Risk Reduction and Management Fund (LDRRMF).[86]

E. OTHER ENVIRONMENT-RELATED LAWS

There are other Philippine laws that address climate change and related environmental concerns. Before the passage of the above major laws that address climate change in a systematic and integrated fashion, there were already many laws that addressed issues related to climate change, and even disaster reduction, in a segmented and disparate way.[87] These include the following:

(1) Republic Act No. 8749 (1999), Philippine Clean Air Act of 1999;[88]
(2) Republic Act No. 8435 (1997), Agriculture and Fisheries Modernization Act of 1997;[89]

---

[81] *Id.* § 9(e).

[82] *Id.* § 10.

[83] *Id.* § 11.

[84] Philippine Disaster Risk Reduction and Management Act of 2010, *supra* note 13, § 12. Section 12(c) enumerates their functions. *Id.* § 12(c). The barangay, which traces its origins to the Spanish colonial era, is the smallest administrative unit in the Philippines. The Philippine Local Government Code defines the barangay as the "basic political unit," which serves as the "primary planning and implementing unit of government policies, plans, programs, projects, and activities in the community, and as a forum wherein the collective views of the people may be expressed, crystallized and considered, and where disputes may be amicably settled." Republic Act No. 7160, § 384 (1991).

[85] *Id.* § 22.

[86] *Id.* § 21.

[87] *See* Feliciano, *supra* note 24, at 96–110; Rommel Casis, *Constructing the Philippine Climate Change Legal Framework*, 83 PHIL. L.J. 1011, 1027–54 (2009).

[88] An Act Providing for a Comprehensive Air Pollution Control Policy and for Other Purposes, Rep. Act No. 8749, June 23, 1999 (Phil.), *available* at http://www.emb.gov.ph/mmairshed/Policies/ra8749-clean%20 air%20act.pdf.

[89] An Act Prescribing Urgent Related Measures to Modernize the Agriculture and Fisheries Sectors of the Country in Order to Enhance Their Profitability, and Prepare Said Sectors for the Challenges of

(3) Republic Act No. 9003 (2001), Ecological Solid Waste Management Act;[90]

(4) Republic Act No. 9275 (2004), Philippine Clean Water Act of 2004;[91]

(5) Republic Act No. 9483 (2007), Oil Pollution Compensation Act of 2007;[92]

(6) Republic Act No. 9367 (2007), Biofuels Act of 2006;[93]

(7) Republic Act No. 9513 (2008), Renewable Energy Act of 2008;[94]

(8) Republic Act No. 9512 (2008), National Environmental Awareness and Education Act of 2008.[95]

In addition to the above laws, there are also executive branch regulations that address climate change.[96] Some of these include: Administrative Order No. 220 (1991);[97] Executive Order No. 320 (2004);[98] Department of Environment and Natural Resources (DENR) Administrative Order No. 2005-17;[99] Administrative Order No. 171, as

Globalization through an Adequate, Focused and Rational Delivery of Necessary Support Services, Appropriating Funds Therefor and for Other Purposes, Rep. Act No. 8435, Dec. 22, 1997 (Phil.), *available at* http://www.prc.gov.ph/uploaded/documents/PRBagrifish.pdf.

[90] An Act Providing for an Ecological Solid Waste Management Program, Creating the Necessary Institutional Mechanisms and Incentives, Declaring Certain Acts Prohibited and Providing Penalties, Appropriating Funds Therefor, and for Other Purposes, Rep. Act No. 9003, Jan. 26, 2001 (Phil.), *available at* http://www.lawphil.net/statutes/repacts/ra2001/ra_9003_2001.html.

[91] An Act Providing for a Comprehensive Water Quality Management and for Other Purposes, Rep. Act No. 9275, Mar. 22, 2004 (Phil.), *available at* http://www.lawphil.net/statutes/repacts/ra2004/ra_9275_2004.html.

[92] An Act Providing for the Implementation of the Provisions of the 1992 International Convention on Civil Liability for Oil Pollution Damage and the 1992 International Convention on the Establishment of an International Fund for Compensation for Oil Pollution Damage, Providing Penalties for Violations Thereof, and for Other Purposes, Rep. Act No. 9483, June 2, 2007 (Phil.), *available at* http://www.senate.gov.ph/republic_acts/ra%209483.pdf.

[93] An Act to Direct the Use of Biofuels, Establishing for This Purpose the Biofuel Program, Appropriating Funds Therefor, and for Other Purposes, Rep. Act No. 9367, Jan. 12, 2007 (Phil), *available at* https://www.doe.gov.ph/issuances/republic-act/614-ra-9367.

[94] An Act Promoting the Development, Utilization and Commercialization of Renewable Energy Resources and for Other Purposes, Rep. Act No. 9513, Dec. 16, 2008 (Phil.), *available at* https://www.doe.gov.ph/issuances/republic-act/627-ra-9513.

[95] An Act to Promote Environmental Awareness through Environmental Education and for Other Purposes, Rep. Act No. 9512, Dec. 12, 2008 (Phil.), *available at* http://www.senate.gov.ph/republic_acts/ra%209512.pdf.

[96] Casis, *supra* note 87, at 1027–50.

[97] Creating an Inter-Agency Committee on Climate Change, *supra* note 29.

[98] Designating the Department of Environment and Natural Resources as the National Authority for Clean Development Mechanism, Exec. Ord. No. 320, (June 19, 2004) (Phil.), *available at* http://www.gov.ph/2004/06/25/executive-order-no-320-s-2004/.

[99] Rules and Regulations Governing the Implementation of Executive Order No. 320 Series of 2004, Designating the DENR as the National Authority for the Clean Development Mechanism, Dep't of Env't & Natural Res. (DENR) Admin. Ord. No. 2005–17, (Aug. 31, 2005) (Phil.), *available at* http://denr.gov.ph/policy/2005/dao/dao2005-17.pdf.

amended;[100] Department of Interior and Local Government (DILG) Memorandum Circular No. 69-08;[101] and Executive Order No. 774 (2008).[102]

The above list of laws and regulations is not exhaustive. In sum, the Philippine legal framework on climate change mitigation and adaptation including those laws addressing disaster reduction and management appears to be progressive, comprehensive, and responsive. However, it remains to be seen whether these laws and policies are indeed effective. There are no current studies that have evaluated the effectiveness of these laws in meeting their goals in the context of global and national efforts to mitigate and adapt, or even respond and build resilience against, the impacts of climate change. Moreover, many of these legal responses have not been in effect long enough to afford any meaningful evaluation of their effectiveness. Nonetheless, in terms of substance and content alone, if not on account of sheer number, the Philippines has made tremendous progress with domestic laws and policies on climate change.

II. Opportunities, Challenges, and Constraints

The Philippines is widely regarded as a global leader in climate change laws and policies. It is also an influential and strong voice in global climate change negotiations. The laws of the country that address climate change are said to be "well-designed, inclusive and progressive."[103] Not many states in the world could claim as comprehensive climate change legal and policy framework as that in place in the Philippines. Moreover, the passage of these laws should be regarded as a significant achievement in itself, especially in the unique context of the Philippine legislative processes, often characterized by fractious political divisions and ideological or patronage loyalties. The evolution in terms of increasing sophistication in both language and content, as well as in breadth of scope of these laws, over the years is also impressive. The well-defined mandates, clearly delineated composition of institutions, the provisions that allow genuine and meaningful participation of local government units and civil society in all aspects of the planning and implementation stages, are core strengths of these laws. Furthermore, the swiftness in the record of ratification of relevant international instruments as well as the incorporation into domestic legislation of commitments contained in these instruments reflect their importance and the urgent need for effective implementation. Indeed, all of these are positive indicators.

---

[100] Creating the Presidential Task Force on Climate Change, Admin. Ord. No. 171, (Feb. 20, 2007) (Phil.), *available* at http://www.abernales.com/ao171.htm.

[101] Department of Interior and Local Government (DILG) Memorandum Circular No. 69-08, (Apr. 28, 2008) (Phil.), *available at* http://www.dilg.gov.ph/PDF_File/issuances/memo_circulars/MC2008-069.pdf.

[102] Reorganizing the Presidential Task Force on Climate Change, Exec. Ord. No. 774, (Dec. 26, 2008) (Phil.), *available at* http://www.gov.ph/2008/12/26/executive-order-no-774-s-2008/.

[103] La Viña & Guiao, *supra* note 14, at 23.

However, their effective implementation is a separate, if not more important, aspect that would confirm a genuine success story.

The status of the Philippines as a developing economy, saddled with the burden of competing diverse national priorities alongside paramount goals of poverty reduction and alleviation while sustaining viable levels of economic growth without compromising environmental concerns, limits the nation's ability to effectively implement its domestic laws and policies on climate change.[104] The issue of implementation is not particularly complex. At a fundamental level, it is merely a fiscal, institutional, and human resources gap issue.[105] The best crafted laws with the noblest of intentions will not be implemented without the necessary and needed budget allocation from the government. Addressing the impacts of climate change on the Philippines requires full commitment from the whole apparatus of the State, including the mobilization of both public and private sector fiscal and human resources.

At a practical level, among the most significant and potentially the most devastating impacts of climate change on the Philippines will be on the country's coasts and the accompanying effects on coastal fisheries yield and the general welfare of coastal communities.[106] There is genuine need for concrete adaptation strategies to mitigate the effects of climate change on coastal communities, as well as coastal infrastructure and habitats. The government should intervene at the local government level to help communities assess their vulnerability to climate change and provide financial assistance to improve community resilience to climate change. This assistance should include measures to alleviate the effects of coastal flooding and erosion and the displacement of coastal communities. It could employ ecosystem-based approaches, such as using mangroves as natural barriers;[107] as well as building on existing institutional processes among agencies at all levels of government and involving academia and civil society.[108] It should also include the provision of alternative livelihood options to augment lost income from communities dependent on coastal and marine-based industries.

The Philippines, along with other developing countries who have contributed minimally in total global emissions, also face the practical and moral dilemma of whether to give more primacy to mitigation or adaptation measures and strategies. The immediacy of focusing limited resources on adaptation measures is tempered by global considerations

---

[104] See Moazzem Hossain & Eliyathamby Selvanathan, *Population, Poverty and CO2 Emissions in Asia: An Overview, in* CLIMATE CHANGE AND GROWTH IN ASIA 17 (Moazzem Hossain & Eliyathamby Selvanathan eds., 2011) (investigating the correlation between climate change and growth issues in Asia).

[105] La Viña & Guiao, *supra* note 14, at 23.

[106] See generally E.B. Capili, A.C.S. Ibay & J.R.T. Villarin, *Climate Change Impacts and Adaptation on Philippine Coasts, in* PROCEEDINGS OF OCEANS 2005 MTS/IEEE 1 (2005).

[107] M.L. PEREZ ET AL., ECONOMIC ANALYSIS OF CLIMATE CHANGE ADAPTATION STRATEGIES IN SELECTED COASTAL AREAS IN INDONESIA, PHILIPPINES AND VIETNAM 2 (2013).

[108] DEPARTMENT OF ENVIRONMENT AND NATURAL RESOURCES, AN INSTITUTIONAL COLLABORATION FOR THE FORMULATION OF THE PHILIPPINE STRATEGY ON CLIMATE CHANGE ADAPTATION 3 (2009).

addressed by mitigation efforts. However, developed countries should also offer financial assistance in keeping with the principles of common but differentiated responsibility and historical responsibility.[109]

Conclusion

Responding to climate change presents a formidable challenge for the Philippines. The impacts of climate change are already occurring in the Philippines and will last for generations to come. On balance, the Philippine legal and policy framework on climate change appears to be sound. The effectiveness of its implementation remains to be seen, but it is hindered by limited fiscal and human resources. In the long run, the vulnerability of the country to the impacts of climate change will be determined by its adaptive capacity.

Climate change regulation is essentially intergenerational in nature, with the present generation responsible for the right of future generations to a healthy environment. [110] The Philippine Supreme Court in the internationally celebrated case of *Oposa v. Factoran* recognized the intergenerational responsibility of the present generation to preserve the environment for future generations.[111] The concept of intergenerational rights initially was at the core of international climate change negotiations. Unfortunately, the current international legal regime has largely sidestepped the issue in view of the scientific complexities and political difficulties involved in controlling emissions and equitably sharing costs.[112]

The following points are raised as recommendations for future revisions of the current Philippine legal and policy framework on climate change. First, the laws need to be periodically assessed, evaluated, and revised. The above-mentioned laws provide for this process to a certain extent.[113] The dynamic and still largely scientifically unexplained nature of climate change requires the same adaptive perspective in legal drafting to

---

[109] La Viña & Guiao, *supra* note 14, at 25.

[110] E.B. Weiss, *In Fairness to Our Children: International Law and Intergenerational Equity*, 2 CHILDHOOD 22, 24 (1994).

[111] *Oposa v Factoran*, 224 SCRA 192 (1993); *reprinted in* 33 I.L.M. 173 (1994); *but see* Dante B. Gatmaytan, *The Illusion of Intergenerational Equity:* Oposa v. Factoran *as Pyrrhic Victory*, 15 GEO. INT'L ENVTL. L. REV. 457, 459 (2003) (arguing that "Oposa adds barely anything new either to Philippine jurisprudence or to the cause of environmental protection, and that it has faded from the practice of law because it does not strengthen the legal arsenal for environmental protection.").

[112] James C. Wood, *Intergenerational Equity and Climate Change*, 8 GEO. INT'L ENVTL. L. REV. 293, 304 (1996).

[113] Philippine Disaster Risk Reduction and Management Act of 2010, *supra* note 13, § 27 provides a "sunset review," mandating a systematic evaluation by the Congressional Oversight Committee of the accomplishments and impact of the Act, as well as the performance and organizational structure of its implementing agencies, for purposes of determining remedial legislation. Climate Change Act, *supra* note 12, § 19 provides for the creation of a Joint Congressional Oversight Committee to monitor the implementation of the Act.

address these issues. The imperative to revisit and assess the composition of the institutions created under the above-mentioned climate change laws should be a priority. For instance, the Chairmanship of the President of the Philippines of the Climate Change Commission may not be ideal as he may lack the expertise as well as the time to devote to this role with his many other important functions as head of state.[114] Furthermore, the expansive membership of almost all cabinet portfolios in the institutions created under the climate change laws presents a potential efficiency concern.[115]

Second, the climate change research agenda needs to be broadened and continued to be financed and supported. The impacts of climate change will continue to accelerate due to global anthropogenic climate change. The physical, social, and security implications of climate change on vulnerable sectors of Philippine society, as well as on critical infrastructures and industries, have yet to be fully assessed.

Third, the climate change targets and commitments to be adopted must be meaningful, realistic, and achievable. The Philippines is a developing economy. The government should carefully balance the country's global and moral commitment to reduce greenhouse emissions with the demands of a growing economy. The government also should support initiatives and industries that promote renewable energy technologies, energy-efficient production processes, disaster preparedness, and other environmentally sound solutions.

Fourth, the implementation strategy for any climate change law or policy should be people-centered, involving significant political decentralization and empowerment of local communities to enable their meaningful inclusion in all planning processes and decisions. The laws should not create unnecessary institutions or mechanisms but rather capitalize on and maximize existing institutional processes and emphasize collaboration among national and local agencies, academia, business, and civil society. The government should ensure education, training, and public awareness regarding climate change and disaster risk reduction is integrated in the relevant laws, safeguarding the right of the public to have access to information that will enable them to make adequate responses to the impacts of climate change.

---

[114] Climate Change Act, *supra* note 12, § 5.

[115] Philippine Disaster Risk Reduction and Management Act of 2010, *supra* note 13, § 5; Climate Change Act *supra* note 12, § 5.

Table of Cases

Index